AMERICAN SONG

The Complete
Musical Theatre Companion

AMERICAN SONG

The Complete
Musical Theatre Companion

SECOND EDITION, 1877–1995

VOLUME 2: T-Z AND INDEXES

KEN BLOOM

SCHIRMER BOOKS
An Imprint of Simon & Schuster Macmillan
New York

PRENTICE HALL INTERNATIONAL
London Mexico City New Delhi Singapore Sydney Toronto

Copyright © 1996 by Ken Bloom

Schirmer Books
An Imprint of Simon & Schuster Macmillan
1633 Broadway
New York, NY 10019

Library of Congress Catalog Card Number: 95–49840

Set ISBN: 0–02–870484–3
Volume 1: 0–02–864573–1
Volume 2: 0–02–864572–3

Printed in the United States of America

Printing Number
1   2   3   4   5   6   7   8   9   10

Library of Congress Cataloging-in-Publication Data

Bloom, Ken, 1949–
     American song : the complete musical theatre companion / Ken
Bloom. —2nd ed.
        p.   cm.
     ISBN 0–02–864573–1 (v. 1). — ISBN 0–02–864572–3 (v. 2)
     1. Musicals—United States—Bibliography. 2. Songs, English–
–United States—Indexes.   I. Title.
ML128.M78B6   1996
782.1'4'0973—dc20   95–49840
                                                                          CIP
                                                                          MN

This paper meets the requirements of ANSI/NISO Z39.48–1992
(Permanence of Paper).

Introduction

Volume 2 includes three indexes to *American Song*. The first is a list of the people, both performers and technical personnel, involved. The second is a complete list of the songs of the American musical. The third index lists all shows' titles by year.

Please note that references are to record numbers, not page numbers. Whole words are alphabetized before combinations of words; punctuation is generally ignored. The abbreviation "inst." or "Dance" indicates an instrumental number and is not part of the song's name. Alternate titles or expanded titles are included in parentheses.

Because there are more than 70,000 songs in the song index, size limitations prohibited including the names of composers and lyricists with the song titles. While numerous songs appeared in more than one show, bear in mind that several different songs may share the same song title. When I could identify distinct songs with the same title in the same show, I have noted them as (1) or (2), but please understand that song titles with multiple record numbers may refer either to the same song in different shows or different songs sharing the same title. I tried to cross-reference songs as much as possible, but I may well have missed some songs that appeared in more than one show. Note, too, that programs may have referred to the same song with slightly different titles, so if you cannot find a song under a title you know, consult different variations.

The name index includes more than 27,000 people. However, each participant's function is listed separately; for example, there are separate index entries for George Abbott (Director), George Abbott (Librettist), and George Abbott (Producer). Companies and groups are listed where appropriate. All the personnel whose names appear in Volume 1 are listed. To make the index more user friendly, I listed entries like "Benny Goodman and His Orchestra" under "Goodman and His Orchestra, Benny."

I have tried as much as possible to refrain from tampering with the credited spelling of names. At different points in their careers actors, directors, writers, producers, and others use variants of their names. Each variation must be looked up to get a complete list of credits. For example, although "Al Goodman" and "Alfred Goodman" are the same person, entries appear under both forms depending on his program billing. Listings will be found for "Sam H. Harris" and also for "Sam Harris." Sometimes two people share the same name, for example, Ronald Graham and Ronny Graham. And take the example of company member Elizabeth Taylor, not the movie star! For people who have changed their names during their careers or used pseudonyms, I have cross-references in the index. For example "June Carroll" and "June Sillman" are cross-referenced.

Correct spelling of names is problematic because of the wide diversity in printed records and early programs. Lyricists' and composers' names were all checked, when possible, with ASCAP or BMI records. Other names were checked through a variety of sources. I feel secure that all spellings are correct ... with three possible exceptions: "Frank Saddler" appears an equal number of times as "Frank Sadler." "Jack Squire" also appears as "Jack Squires." And "Caroline Siedel" also appears as "Carol Siedle" and "Caroline Seidle." For these three names, I haven't been able to determine the correct spelling.

The chronological list of titles offers the reader the opportunity to gain a sense of the development of American musical theatre year by year. As noted in the Introduction to Volume 1, all Broadway, off-Broadway, and off-off-Broadway productions from 1877 to fall 1995 are included, together with all resident theatre productions of shows by major artists, shows that toured the country, shows that closed out-of-town, English and French productions of shows by major American songwriters, important revues, nightclub and vaudeville shows, touring shows, and straight plays with single songs. When looking through the dates in this index you will notice dates like "00/00/1934." The zeros indicate that the exact opening date is not known; available records indicate only the year a particular show opened. Sometimes little is known except a year or maybe a month and a year. These shows turn up prior to the listings for January of each year.

KEN BLOOM
New York City
October 1995

Contents

T

4261 • T*TS D*AMOND
OPENED: 01/1977
Musical

Composer: Lee Pockriss
Lyricist: Steve Brown
Librettist: Mark Bramble

Notes: Produced at The Loft.

4262 • TABLE NUMBER SEVEN
Musical   Unproduced

Composer: Charles Burr
Lyricist: Charles Burr

Source: SEPARATE TABLES (Play Terrance Rattigan)

Songs: Hum Along; I Could Still Try; I Met My Love; Not a Thing in the Papers Anymore!; Not of This World; Other People's Waltzes; Separate Tables; Small Talk; Up in My Room

4263 • TABOO REVUE
Notes: *See TIMOTHY GRAY'S TABOO REVUE.*

4264 • TAFFETAS, THE
OPENED: 04/09/1989   Theatre: Cherry Lane
Musical   Off-Broadway: 165

Producer: James Shellenberger; Arthur Whitelaw
Director: Steve Harris

Choreographer: Tina Paul; **Costumes:** David Graden; **Lighting Designer:** Ken Billington; **Musical Director:** Rick Lewis; **Set Design:** Evelyn Sakash; **Vocal Arranger:** Rick Lewis

Songs: Achoo Cha-Cha (Gesundheit) (C/L: Michael Merlo; Patrick Welch); Allegheny Moon (C/L: Al Hoffman; Dick Manning); Around the World (C: Victor Young; L: Harold Adamson); Arriverderci Roma (C: R. Rascel; L: Giovanni; Carl Sigman); C-o-n-s- t-a-n-t-i-n-o-p-l-e (C/L: Harry Carlton); C'Est Si Bon (C: Henri Betti; L: Honeg; Jerry Seelen); Cry (C/L: Churchill Kohlman); Dedicated to the One I Love (C/L: Ralph Bass; Lowman Pauling); Happy Wanderer, The (Val-De Ri, Val-De Ra) (C: Friedrich Wilhelm Moeller; L: Antonia Ridge); Hot Canary, The (C: Peter Nero; L: Ray Gilbert); How Much Is That Doggy in the Window (C/L: Bob Merrill); I Cried (C/L: Unknown); I-M-4-U (C: Jose Melis; L: F. Marino); I'll Think of You (C/L: Clint Ballard Jr.; Noel Sherman); I'm Sorry (C/L: Dub Albritton; Bonnie Self); Johnny Angel (C/L: Lyn Duddy; Lee Pockriss); L-O-V-E (C/L: Milt Gabler; Bert Kaempfert); Little Darlin' (C/L: Maurice Williams); Lollipop (C/L: Julius Dixon; Beverly Ross); Love Is a Two-Way Street (C/L: J. Keller; Noel Sherman); Love Letters in the Sand (C: J. Fred Coots; L: Charles Kenny; Nick Kenny); Mockin' Bird Hill (C/L: Vaughn Horton); Mr. Lee (C/L: Heather Dixon; Helen Gathers; Emma Ruth Pought; Jannie Pought; Laura Webb); Mr. Sandman (C/L: Pat Ballard); Music! Music! Music! (C/L: Bernie Baum; Stephen Weiss); My Little Grass Shack (C/L: Bill Cogswell; Tommy Harrison; Johnny Noble); Nel Blue di Pinto di Blue (Volare) (C/L: Dominic Modugno; L: Migliani; Mitchell Parish); Old Cape Cod (C/L: Claire Rathrock; Milt Yakus; C: Allan Jeffrey; L: Alan Jeffrey); Oop Shoop (C/L: Joe Josea); Puppy Love (C/L: Paul Anka); Rag Mop (C/L: Deacon Anderson; Lee Wills); Ricochet (C: Larry Coleman; L: Joe Darion; Norman Gimbel); See the U.S.A. in Your Chevrolet (C/L: Leon Carr; Leo Corday); Sh-Boom (C/L: James Edwards; Carl Feaster; Claude Feaster; James Keyes; Floyd F. McRae); Sincerely (C/L: Alan Freed; Harvey Fuqua); Smile (C/L: Charlie Chaplin; Geoffrey Parsons; John Turner); Sweet Song of India (C/L: Clayton; Kaye); Tennessee Waltz (C/L: Pee Wee King; Red Stewart); Three Bells, The (C/L: Bert Reisfeld; Jean Villard); Tonight You Belong to Me (C: Lee David; L: Billy Rose); Tweedle Dee (C/L: Winfield Scott); Where the Boys Are (C/L: Howard Greenfield; Neil Sedaka); You Belong to Me (C/L: Pee Wee King; Chilton Price; Red Stewart); You, You, You (C: Lotar Olias; L: Robert Mellin; R. Olias); You're Just in Love (C/L: Irving Berlin)

Cast: Jody Abrahams; Karen Curlee; Melanie Mitchell; Tia Speros

Notes: No original songs in this show.

4265 • TAKE A BOW

OPENED: 06/15/1944   Theatre: Broadhurst
Revue   Broadway: 12

Producer: Lou Walters
Director: Wally Wenger

Choreographer: Marjery Fielding; **Costumes:** Ben Wallace; **Musical Director:** Ray Kavanaugh; **Set Design:** Kaj Velden

Songs: Take a Bow (C: Ted Murry; L: Benny Davis)

Cast: Jay C. Flippen; Chico Marx; Pat Rooney; Gene Sheldon

4266 • TAKE A CHANCE (1923)

Notes: *See GINGER.*

4267 • TAKE A CHANCE (1932)

OPENED: 11/26/1932   Theatre: Apollo
Musical   Broadway: 243

Composer: Nacio Herb Brown; Richard A. Whiting
Lyricist: B.G. DeSylva
Librettist: B.G. DeSylva; Laurence Schwab
Producer: B.G. DeSylva; Laurence Schwab
Director: Edgar MacGregor

Choreographer: Bobby Connolly; **Costumes:** Kiviette; Charles LeMaire; **Musical Director:** Max Meth; **Orchestrations:** Robert Russell Bennett; William Daly; Stephen Jones; Edward Powell; **Set Design:** Cleon Throckmorton; **Vocal Arranger:** Roger Edens

Songs: Charity; Eadie Was a Lady; Humpty-Dumpty [1]; I Got Religion (C: Vincent Youmans); I Want to Be with You [1] (C: Vincent Youmans); I'm Way Ahead of the Game [1]; Life of the Party, The; My Lover [2] (C: Vincent Youmans); Night, Hold Back the Dawn [1]; Oh How I Long to Belong to You (C: Vincent Youmans); Rise 'N' Shine [4] (C: Vincent Youmans); She's Nuts About Me; Should I Be Sweet (C: Vincent Youmans); So Do I (C: Vincent Youmans); Tickled Pink; Tonight Is Opening Night; Turn Out the Light; You're an Old Smoothie [3]

Cast: Josephine Dunn; Jack Haley; June Knight; Mitzi Mayfair; Ethel Merman; Oscar "Rags" Ragland; Sid Silvers; Jack Whiting; Douglas Wood

Notes: Titled HUMPTY DUMPTY during tryout. [1] Cut. [2] Cut. Music same as "Blue Bowery" from SMILES. [3] Also in London show NICE GOINGS ON. [4] Later interpolated into RISE AND SHINE (London).

4268 • TAKE FIVE

OPENED: 10/10/1957   Theatre: Upstairs at the Downstairs
Revue   Nightclub

Librettist: Don Adams; Dee Caruso; Bill Levine; Steven Vinaver
Producer: Julius Monk
Director: Max Adrian; John Heawood

Vocal Arranger: Stan Keen

Songs: Cast Call (C/L: Stan Keen); Doing the Psycho-Neurotique (C/L: Ronny Graham); Gossiping Grapevine (C/L: Edward C. Redding); Gristedes (C: Jonathan Tunick; L: Steven Vinaver); Perfect Stranger (C/L: Bart Howard); Portofino [2] (C/L: Michael Brown); Pour Le Sport [1] (C/L: Stephen Sondheim); Pro Musica Antiqua, The (C: Jonathan Tunick; L: Steven Vinaver); Upstairs at the Downstairs Waltz (C/L: Bart Howard); Westport! (C: Philip Springer; L: Carolyn Leigh); Witchcraft (C/L: Michael Brown)

Cast: Jean Arnold; Ceil Cabot; Ronny Graham; Ellen Hanley; Gerry Matthews; **Pianist:** Gordon Connell; Stan Keen

Notes: [1] Written for unproduced show THE LAST RESORTS. [2] Also in DEMI-DOZEN.

4269 • TAKE IT FROM ME

OPENED: 03/31/1919   Theatre: 44th Street
Musical   Broadway: 96

Composer: Will R. Anderson
Lyricist: Will B. Johnstone

Librettist: Will B. Johnstone
Producer: Joseph M. Gaites
Director: Fred A. Bishop; Joseph Gaites; Joseph C. Smith

Costumes: S. Zalud; **Musical Director:** George Trinkaus

Songs: Call of the Cozy Little Home, The; Camouflage; Explanations; From Then and Now [1]; Good, Bad, Beautiful Broadway; I Like to Linger in the Lingerie; It's Different Now [1]; Kiss, The; Movie Music; Opening Act I; Penny for Your Thoughts, A; Take It from Me; Tanglefoot, The; Tip Toe [1]; To Have and to Hold; Tomorrow; Vampire Dance (inst.); What Makes the Tired Businessman So Tired

Cast: Dorothy Betts; Fred Hillebrand; Ed Leech; Jack McGowan; Vera Michelena

Notes: [1] Out Washington, D.C. 12/22/18.

4270 • TAKE ME ALONG

OPENED: 10/22/1959   Theatre: Shubert
Musical   Broadway: 448

Composer: Bob Merrill
Lyricist: Bob Merrill
Librettist: Robert Russell; Joseph Stein
Producer: David Merrick
Director: Peter Glenville

Source: AH, WILDERNESS! (Play: Eugene O'Neill); **Choreographer:** Onna White; **Costumes:** Miles White; **Dance Arranger:** Laurence Rosenthal; **Lighting Designer:** Jean Rosenthal; **Musical Director:** Lehman Engel; **Orchestrations:** Philip J. Lang; **Set Design:** Oliver Smith; **Vocal Arranger:** Lehman Engel

Songs: Beardsley Ballet (dance); But Yours; Company of Men, The [6]; Hurt They Write About, The [2]; I Get Embarrassed; I Would Die; If Jesus Don't Love You [3]; Knights on White Horses [3]; Little Green Snake; Marvelous Fire Machine [5]; Nine O'Clock; Oh Please; Parade, The [4]; Patience of a Saint [2]; Promise Me a Rose (A Slight Detail); Sid, Ol' Kid; Staying Young; Take Me Along; That Man's Wife [7]; That's How It Starts; Thinkin' Things [1]; Volunteer Fireman Picnic (For Sweet Charity) (The Only Pair I've Got); We're Home; Wint's Song (Pleasant Beach House)

Cast: Peter Conlow; James Cresson; Arlene Galonka; Jackie Gleason; Luke Halpin; Valerie Harper; Eileen Herlie; Susan Luckey; Una Merkel; Robert Morse; Zeme North; Walter Pidgeon; Gene Varrone

Notes: *See also AH! WILDERNESS.* [1] Not used. [2] Added to 1984 Off-Off-Broadway revival. [3] Added to 9/15/84 Goodspeed revival. [4] Same song as "Marvelous Fire Machine." [5] Added to 9/15/84 Goodspeed revival. Same song as "The Parade." [6] Added to Off-Off-Broadway and Goodspeed revivals. [7] Out Boston 9/7/59.

4271 • TAKE THE AIR

OPENED: 11/22/1927   Theatre: Waldorf
Musical   Broadway: 208

Composer: Dave Stamper
Lyricist: Gene Buck
Librettist: Anne Caldwell
Producer: Gene Buck
Director: Alexander Leftwich

Choreographer: Ralph Reader; **Costumes:** Charles LeMaire; Cora MacGeachy; Lucille McCorder; **Lighting Designer:** Frank Detering; **Musical Director:** Charles Drury; **Set Design:** William Oden-Waller

Songs: All Aboard for Times Square; All I Want Is a Lullaby; Aviation Ballet; Carmela; Carmen Has Nothing on Me [1]; Ham and Eggs in the Morning (C: Con Conrad; Abner Silver; L: Al Dubin); Japanese Moon; Just Like a Wild, Wild, Rose; Maybe I'll Baby You; On a Pony for Two (C: James F. Hanley); Silver Wings; Take the Air; Tango Espagnol; We'd Rather Dance than Eat; We'll Have a New Home in the Morning (C/L: Gene Buck; J. Russel Robinson; Willard Robison); Wild and Wooly West, The

Cast: Greek Evans; Will Mahoney; Trini

Notes: [1] Also in ZIEGFELD MIDNIGHT FROLIC (6th Edition).

4272 • TAKING MY TURN

OPENED: 06/09/1983   Theatre: Entermedia
Revue   Off-Broadway: 345

Composer: Gary William Friedman
Lyricist: Will Holt

Producer: Joanne Cummings; Sonny Fox; Anthony Kane; Arleen Kane; Maurice Levine; Richard Seader; Sally Sears
Director: Robert H. Livingston

Choreographer: Douglas Norwick; **Costumes:** Judith Dolan; **Lighting Designer:** David F. Segal; **Musical Director:** Barry Levitt; **Orchestrations:** Gary William Friedman; **Set Design:** Clarke Dunham; **Vocal Arranger:** Gary William Friedman

Songs: Do You Remember?; Fine for the Shape I'm In; Good Luck to You; I Am Not Old; I Like It; I Never Made Money from Music; In April; In the House; It Still Isn't Over; Janet Get Up; Kite, The; Pick More Daisies; Somebody Else; Sweet Longings; Taking Our Turn; This Is My Song; Two of Me; Vivaldi

Cast: Mace Barrett; Victor Griffin; Tiger Haynes; Cissy Houston; Marni Nixon; Sheila Smith; Ted Thurston; Margaret Whiting

4273 • TALENT 50
OPENED: 04/28/1950   Theatre: Guild
Revue   Broadway: 1

Producer: Monroe B. Hack; Stage Managers Club
Director: Michael Ellis; Monroe Hack; George Hunter; David Jones; Ben Krany; Samuel Liff

Choreographer: Ted Cappy; Betty Lind; Patricia Newman; Vivian Smith; **Musical Director:** Herbert Kingsley

Songs: Big Top Parade (C: Jerry Bock; L: Larry Holofcener); Dear Old College Days (C: Jerry Bock; L: Fred Tobias); I Laughed at Spring (C: Don Gohman; L: Brown Furlow); Lil Ole Letter (C: Herbert Kingsley; L: Langston Hughes); New York Is Not a Town (C: Earl Cobb; L: John Morris); Outside Looking In (C/L: William Hunt); This Is Finale (C: Phil Kadison; L: Thomas B. Howell); Visions on Your Television Screen (C: Jerry Bock; L: Fred Tobias); We've Got a Date with Spring (C: Phil Kadison; L: Alice Hammerstein); We've Got Talent (C/L: William Hunt); When I Bounce Off to Bed (C: George Engles; L: Lowell Saloway); When We're Dancing (C/L: Elise Bretton; Sherman Edwards; Don Meyer)

Cast: Raimonda Arselli; Pat Carroll; Gene Kelley; Jay Lloyd; Janice Rule; Hiram Sherman; Swen Swenson

4274 • TALES OF PERICHOLE
Musical   Unproduced

Composer: Jacques Offenbach
Lyricist: Ray Evans; Jay Livingston

Notes: No other information available.

4275 • TALES OF RIGO
OPENED: 05/30/1927   Theatre: Lyric
Play   Broadway: 8

Composer: Ben Schwartz
Lyricist: Ben Schwartz
Author: Maurice V. Samuels
Producer: J. Oppenheimer
Director: Clarence Derwent

Source: UNKNOWN (Story: Hyman Adler); **Costumes:** Mahieu; **Set Design:** August Vimnera

Songs: I'll Tell You All Someday; In Romany; Little Princess; Rigo's Last Lullaby (C/L: Evelyn Adler); What Care We? (Song of Destiny); Zita

Cast: Hyman Adler; Madeline Grey; Mira Nirska; Warren Sterling

4276 • TALK ABOUT GIRLS
OPENED: 06/14/1927   Theatre: Waldorf
Musical   Broadway: 15

Composer: Harold Orlob
Lyricist: Irving Caesar
Librettist: William Cary Duncan; Daniel Kussell
Producer: Sam H. Grisman; Harry Oshrin
Director: Daniel Kussell

Source: LIKE A KING (Play: John Hunter Booth); **Choreographer:** Sammy Lee

Songs: All the Time Is Loving Time; Come to Lower Falls; Home Town; In Central Park; In Twos; Lonely Girl, A; Love Birds [1]; Maybe I Will; Nineteen Twenty-Seven; One Boy's Enough for Me; Only Boy, The; Oo, How I Love You; Sex Appeal; Talk About Girls (C: Stephen Jones); That's My Man

Cast: William Frawley; Marilyn Killeen; Russell Mack; Jane Taylor; Andrew Tombes; Frances Upton

Notes: No program available. A reworking of
SUZANNE. See that entry. [1] ASCAP only.

4277 • TALK OF NEW YORK, THE
OPENED: 12/03/1907   Theatre: Knickerbocker
Musical   Broadway: 157

Composer: George M. Cohan
Lyricist: George M. Cohan
Librettist: George M. Cohan
Producer: George M. Cohan; Sam H. Harris
Director: George M. Cohan

Costumes: F. Richard Anderson; **Musical Director:**
August Kleinecke; **Orchestrations:** Charles J.
Gebest

Songs: Burning Up the Boulevard; Busy Little
Broadway; Claremont; Drink with Me; Follow
Your Uncle Dudley; Gee, Ain't I Glad I'm Home!;
I Have a Longing for Long Acre Square [2];
I Want the World to Know I Love You;
I Want You; Mr. Burns of New Rochelle; Put a
Little Bet Down for Me; That's Some Love [1];
Under Any Old Flag at All; When a Fellow's on
the Level with a Girl That's on the Square; When
We Are M-A-Double-R-I-E-D

Cast: Jack Gardner; Emma Littlefield; Victor
Moore; Gertrude Vanderbilt

Notes: [1] Out of town. Also in THE AMERICAN
IDEA. [2] Sheet music only.

4278 • TALL STORY
OPENED: 01/29/1959   Theatre: Belasco
Play   Broadway: 108

Composer: Ben G. Allen; Joe Hornsby; Jerry
Teifer
Lyricist: Ben G. Allen; Joe Hornsby; Jerry Teifer
Author: Russel Crouse; Howard Lindsay
Producer: Emmett Rogers; Robert Weiner
Director: Herman Shumlin

Source: HOMECOMING GAME, THE (Novel:
Howard Nemerov); **Arrangements:** Edward
Thomas; **Costumes:** Noel Taylor; **Lighting
Designer:** George Jenkins; **Set Design:** George
Jenkins

Songs: That's My Daisy (C/L: Ben G. Allen; Mike
Hansen; Joe Hornsby)

Cast: Mason Adams; John Astin; Marc Connelly;
Hans Conreid; Robert Elston; Rex Everhart; Nina
Wilson; Marian Winters; Robert Wright

Notes: No songs listed in program.

4279 • TALLULAH
OPENED: 10/30/1983   Theatre: West Side Arts
                              Center
Musical   Off-Broadway: 42

Composer: Arthur Siegel
Lyricist: Mae Richard
Librettist: Tony Lang
Producer: John Van Ness Philip; Mark deSolla
Price; Leonard Soloway; David Susskind
Director: David Holdgrive

Choreographer: David Holdgrive; **Costumes:**
John Falabella; **Lighting Designer:** Ken
Billington; **Musical Director:** Bruce W. Coyle;
Set Design: John Falabella; **Vocal Arranger:**
Bruce W. Coyle

Songs: Darling; Don't Ever Book a Trip on the IRT;
Home Sweet Home; I Can See Him Clearly; If
Only He Were a Woman; I'm the Woman You
Wanted; It's a Hit; It's in the Cards [1]; I've Got
to Try Everything Once; Love Is on Its Knees;
Party Is Where I Am, The; Stay Awhile; Tallulah;
Talullahbaloo; When I Do a Dance for You; You
Need a Lift!; You're You

Cast: Joel Craig; Helen Gallagher; Russell Nype

Notes: [1] Not used.

4280 • TAMBOURITA
OPENED: 1949
Musical   Unproduced

Composer: Ernesto Lecuona
Lyricist: John Latouche
Librettist: Milton Herbert Gropper
Producer: Reginald Hammerstein

Notes: Apparently no score exists since Latouche's
family destoryed his papers at his death.

4281 • TAN MANHATTAN
OPENED: 1941
Revue   Closed out of town

Composer: Eubie Blake
Lyricist: Andy Razaf
Producer: Irvin C. Miller
Director: Irvin C. Miller

Choreographer: Addison Carey; Henry LeTang

Songs: Dixie Ann in Afghanistan; Dollar for a Dime; Down By the Railroad Track; Great Big Baby; Hep Cat, The; I'm Toein' the Line; Nickel for a Dime, A; Say Hello to the Folks Back Home; Shakin' Up the Folks Below; Sweet Magnolia Rose; Tan Manhattan; We Are Americans Too (C/L: Eubie Blake; Charles L. Cooke; Andy Razaf); With a Dream; Worry

Cast: Avon Long; Nina Mae McKinney; Flournoy Miller

Notes: Closed in Washington, D.C. No program available.

4282 • TAN TOWN TOPICS REVUE

OPENED: 1926
Revue

Producer: Cooper & Rector

Songs: Charleston Hound; I've Found a New Baby; Senorita Mine (C: Thomas "Fats" Waller; Clarence Williams; L: Eddie Rector; Spencer Williams)

Notes: No other information available.

4283 • TANGERINE

OPENED: 08/09/1921   Theatre: Casino
Revue   Broadway: 337

Composer: Monte Carlo; Alma Sanders
Lyricist: Howard E. Johnson
Librettist: Guy Bolton
Producer: Carle Carlton
Director: Bert French; George Marion

Source: UNKNOWN (Play: Philip Bartholomae; Lawrence Langner); **Costumes:** Dorothy Armstrong; Mme. Francis; Pieter Meyer; **Musical Director:** Max Steiner; **Set Design:** P. Dodd Ackerman; Lee Simonson

Songs: Asbury Park (L: Monte Carlo); Baccanale Dance; Civilization; Dance Tangerine; Give Me Your Love [2] (L: Monte Carlo); Hallucination of Love [1] (L: Monte Carlo); Idle House [1] (L: Monte Carlo); In Our Mountain Bower; Isle of Tangerine; It's a Sunbeam [1] (L: Monte Carlo); It's Great to Be Married (and Lead a Single Life); It's Only Your Carriage That Counts; Knit, Knit, Knit [2] (L: Monte Carlo); Listen to Me [2]; Listen to the Raindrops (L: Monte Carlo); Lords of Creation [1] (C: Jean Schwartz); Love Is a Business; Man Is the Lord of It All (C: Jean Schwartz); Multiplied by Eight; Multiplied by Six [2] (L: Monte Carlo); Old Melodies; Point to Bear in Mind, The [2] (L: Monte Carlo); Sea of the Tropics Dance; She Was Very Dear to Me (C/L: Benjamin Hapgood Burt); South Sea Island Blues; Stolen Sweets [2] (C: Carle Carleton; Monte Carlo; Alma Sanders); Sweet Lady (C: Dave Zoob; L: Frank Crumit); There's a Sunbeam for Every Drop of Rain; Tropic Love [1] (L: Monte Carlo); Tropic Vamps; Variety Is the Spice of Life [2] (L: Monte Carlo); Voice at the End of the Line, The [1] (L: Monte Carlo); We'll Never Grow Old; You and I Atta Baby [3]

Cast: Joseph Cawthorn; Frank Crumit; John E. Hazzard; Allen Kearns; Jeanette MacDonald; Harry Puck; Julia Sanderson

Notes: [1] Out Asbury Park 8/1/21. [2] Out Atlantic City 2/21/21. [3] Johnson wrote a song of the same name for ATTA BABY the next year.

4284 • TANGLETOES

OPENED: 02/17/1925   Theatre: 39th St.
Play   Broadway: 23

Author: Gertrude Purcell
Producer: Edmund Plohn
Director: Hubert Druce; Edwin Maxwell

Songs: Tangletoes (C: Vincent Rose; L: Gertrude Purcell)

Cast: Walker Ellis; Morgan Farley; Mildred MacLeod; Beatrice Nichols

4285 • TANTALIZING TOMMY

OPENED: 10/01/1912   Theatre: Criterion
Musical   Broadway: 31

Composer: Hugo Felix
Lyricist: Adrian Ross

Librettist: Paul Gavault; Michael Morton
Producer: A.H. Woods
Director: George Marion

Source: LA PETITE CHOCOLATIERE (Play : Paul Gavault); **Musical Director:** Hans S. Linne; **Set Design:** Percy Anderson

Songs: Ballad of the Seigneur; Cupid's Car; Fairy Bells; I Am a Tom-Boy; Irish Stew; Just Like You; Oh, Go Away; Opening Chorus Act I; Opening Chorus Act II; Opening Chorus Act III; Song, The; Tandem, A; This and That and the Other; You Don't Know; Zizi

Cast: George Anderson; Elizabeth Brice; Harry Clarke; Peggy Forsyth; Madeline Harrison; John Park

4286 • TAP DANCE KID, THE

OPENED: 12/21/1983   Theatre: Broadhurst
Musical   Broadway: 669

Composer: Henry Krieger
Lyricist: Robert Lorick
Librettist: Charles Blackwell
Producer: Evelyn Barron; Harvey J. Klaris; Michel Stuart; Stanley White
Director: Vivian Matalon

Source: NOBODY'S FAMILY IS GOING TO CHANGE (Novel: Louise Fitzhugh); **Choreographer:** Danny Daniels; **Musical Director:** Don Jones; **Orchestrations:** Harold Wheeler; **Set Design:** Michael Hotopp; Paul dePass; **Vocal Arranger:** Harold Wheeler

Songs: Another Day; Class Act; Crosstown; Daddy Says, Mama Says [1]; Dance If It Makes You Happy; Dancing Is Everything; Dipsey's Coming Over [1]; Dipsey's Vaudeville (inst.) [1]; Fabulous Feet; Four Strikes Against Me; I Could Get Used to Him; I Remember How It Was; Like Him; Lullabye; Man in the Moon; My Luck Is Changing; Someday; Something Better, Something More [1]; Tap Tap; They Never Hear What I Say; William's Song

Cast: Martine Allard; Hinton Battle; Barbara Montgomery; Alfonso Ribeiro; Alan Weeks; Hattie Winston; Samuel E. Wright

Notes: [1] Added for post-Broadway tour.

4287 • TARS AND SPARS

OPENED: 05/05/1944
Revue

Composer: Vernon Duke
Lyricist: Howard Dietz
Librettist: Howard Dietz
Producer: Max Liebman; U.S. Coast Guard
Director: Max Liebman

Choreographer: Gower Champion; Ted Gary

Songs: Apprentice Seaman; Arm in Arm; Civilian; Farewell for a While; Palm Beach; Silver Shield

Cast: Sid Caesar; Gower Champion; Victor Mature

Notes: This was the Coast Guard's equivilent to THIS IS THE ARMY, AT EASE, etc. The show played the Strand Theatre and then toured the country. No program available.

4288 • TATTERDEMALION

OPENED: 10/27/1985   Theatre: Douglas Fairbanks
Musical   Off-Broadway: 25

Composer: Judd Woldin
Lyricist: Judd Woldin
Librettist: Judd Woldin
Producer: Eric Krebs
Director: Eric Krebs

Source: KING OF SCHNORRERS, THE (Novel: Israel Zangwill); **Choreographer:** Mary Jane Houdina; **Costumes:** Patricia Adshead; **Dance Arranger:** Peter Howard; **Lighting Designer:** Whitney Quesenbery; **Musical Director:** Edward G. Robinson; **Orchestrations:** Robert M. Freedman; Judd Woldin; **Set Design:** Ed Wittstein; **Vocal Arranger:** Peter Howard

Songs: Blood Lines; Chutzpah; Dead; Each of Us; I Have Not Lived in Vain; I'm Only a Woman (L: Susan Birkenhead); It's Over (L: Herb Martin); Leave the Thinking to Me (L: Susan Birkenhead); Murder; Ordinary Man, An (L: Susan Birkenhead); Ours; Petticoat Lane; Tell Me (L: Susan Birkenhead; Judd Woldin); Well Done, Da Costa (L: Susan Birkenhead)

Cast: Robert Blumenfeld; Suzanne Briar; Annie McGreevey; Jack Sevier; Tia Speros; K.C. Wilson; Ron Wisinski; Stuart Zagnit

Notes: *See also KING OF SCHNORRERS, an earlier version of this show.*

4289 • TATTERED TOM

OPENED: 1968
Musical   Unproduced

Composer: Ralph Blane; Hugh Martin
Lyricist: Ralph Blane; Hugh Martin

Source: TATTERED TOM (Novel: Horatio Alger)

Songs: Don't Trust Anyone; Flame Water; He's a Fallen Angel; Heigh Ho for Mother (Heigh Ho for a Husband); How Do I Feel; I Love Your Vibrato; Kind of Girl I'd Like to Be, The; Melting Pot, The; New York; New York's Good Morning Song; One Good Friend's Enough; Tattered Tom; Tony Pastor's; 2 Is Company; Two's Company; Up to My Elbows; What's His Name; When I Join the Circus; Whenever I'm with You; Women Are Here to Stay

4290 • TATTLE TALES (1920)

OPENED: 1920
Musical   Closed out of town

Composer: Archie Gottler
Lyricist: Howard Johnson
Librettist: Jimmy Hussey
Producer: Jimmy Hussey

Songs: I'm an Indian Assassin [1]; I'm Out on Strike for a Beautiful Girl [1]; In Watermelon Time; Lead Me to Laughter [1]; Life Without a Cigarette [1]; Rose of the Rotisserie [1] (C: James F. Hanley; L: Joe Goodwin; Jimmy Hussey); Star Eyes; Taps [1]; Tattle Tales; Those Mason-Dixon Blues [1]; Tip-Tip Tippy Canoe [1]; When the Statues Come to Life [1]; You've Got to Keep on Moving [1]

Cast: Joe Browning; Cliff Edwards; Jimmy Hussey; Rae Samuels; Jean Tennyson

Notes: Program from Detroit. Later revised as THE WHIRL OF THE TOWN and THE MIMIC WORLD OF 1921. [1] Sheet music only.

4291 • TATTLE TALES (1933)

OPENED: 06/01/1933   Theatre: Broadhurst
Revue   Broadway: 28

Librettist: Nick Copeland; Frank Fay
Producer: Frank Fay
Director: Frank Fay; John Lonergan

Choreographer: Danny Dare; John Lonergan; LeRoy Prinz; **Costumes:** Elizabeth Zook; **Musical Director:** Arnold Johnson; **Orchestrations:** Howard Jackson; Edward Ward; **Set Design:** Martin

Songs: Another Case of the Blues (C: Richard Myers; L: Johnny Mercer); Breaking Up a Rhythm (C: Edward Ward; L: George Waggoner); Counting Sheep, Counting the Hours [2] (C: Louis Alter; L: Max Lief; Nathaniel Lief); Court of Louis XIV, The (C: Howard Jackson); First Spring Day, The (C: Howard Jackson; L: Edward Eliscu); Hang Up Your Hat on Broadway (C: Edward Ward; L: Grossman; Silverstein; George Waggoner); Harlem Lullaby (C/L: Margot Milhelm; Willard Robison); Hasta Manana (So This Is Havana) (C: Howard Jackson); Here We Are Together (C: Edward Ward; L: Frank Fay; William Walsh); I'll Take an Option on You (C: Ralph Rainger; L: Leo Robin); Jig Saw Jamboree (C: Eddie Bienbryer; L: William Walsh); Just a Sentimental Tune (C: Louis Alter; L: Max Lief; Nathaniel Lief); Percy with Perseverance (C: Edward Ward; L: George Waggoner); Sing American Tunes (1) (C: Harry Akst; L: Edward Eliscu); Sing American Tunes (2) [1] (C: Edward Ward; L: Frank Fay; William Walsh); You Got to Do Better Than That (C/L: Unknown)

Cast: Mary Barnett; Nick Copeland; Les Crane; Don Cumming; Dorothy Dell; Edith Evans; Frank Fay; William Hargrave; Ray Mayer; Lillian Reynolds; Barbara Stanwyck

Notes: [1] Out Wilkes-Barre 1933. [2] Not used.

4292 • TATTOOED COUNTESS, THE

OPENED: 04/03/1961   Theatre: Barbizon-Plaza
Musical   Off-Broadway: 4

Composer: Coleman Dowell
Lyricist: Coleman Dowell
Librettist: Coleman Dowell
Producer: Robert D. Feldstein; Dick Randall
Director: Robert K. Adams

Source: TATTOOED COUNTESS, THE (Novel: Carl Van Vechten); **Choreographer:** Alex

Palermo; **Costumes:** Bill Hargate; **Dance Arranger:** David Hollister; **Musical Director:** Phil Fradkin; **Orchestrations:** David Hollister; **Set Design:** Robert Soule

Songs: Advice; Autumn; Brushing Stone, The; Dusters, Goggles and Hats; Fin de Sickle; Gossip; Got to Find My Way; High Up; Home Town Girl; How She Glows; I Can Take It; Je M'em Fiche; Opening, The; Rolling Stone; Tattooed Woman; That's Her Life; These Acres; Too Old for Love; Too Young; Waterworks Madrigal, The; Woman's Much Better Off Alone, A; You Take Paris

Cast: Travis Hudson; Irene Manning; Coe Norton; John Stewart

4293 • TATTOOED MAN, THE

OPENED: 02/18/1907   Theatre: Criterion
Musical   Broadway: 59

Composer: Victor Herbert
Lyricist: Harry B. Smith
Librettist: A.N.C. Fowler; Harry B. Smith
Producer: Charles Dillingham
Director: Julian Mitchell

Costumes: Caroline Siedle; **Musical Director:** Arthur Weld; **Orchestrations:** Victor Herbert

Songs: Awfully Nice to Love One Girl [1]; Bedouin Chief; Boys Will Be Boys (and Girls Will Be Girls); Entrance of Arabs; Entrance of Shah; Floral Wedding, The; Hear My Song of Love (Serenade); I Say What I Mean and I Mean What I Say [1]; I'm Not So Particular Now [1]; It's Awfully Nice to Love One Girl; Kitten That Couldn't Be Good [1]; Land of Dreams, The; Legend of the Djin, The; Muezzins and Bayaderres; Never, Never Land [1]; Nobody Loves Me; Omar Khayyam; Opening Chorus; Oriental March (Entrance of Omar); Sleep Sublime and Perfect Poet [1]; Snake Charmer's Dance; Take Things Easy; There's Just One Girl I'd Like to Marry; Things We Are Not Supposed to Know; Watch the Professor; Wedding of the Lily and the Rose [1]

Cast: William P. Carleton; Gertie Carlisle; Harry Clarke; Frank Daniels; Sallie Fisher; Bessie Holbrook; May Vokes; Herbert Waterous

Notes: Complete song list not in program. Songs from vocal score. [1] ASCAP/Library of Congress only.

4294 • TAXI TALES

OPENED: 12/28/1978   Theatre: Century
Play   Off-Broadway: 6

Author: Leonard Melfi
Producer: Joe Regan
Director: Edward Berkeley

Costumes: Hilary Rosenfeld; **Lighting Designer:** Arden Fingerhut; **Set Design:** Hugh Landwehr

Songs: Taxi (C/L: Jonathan Hogan)

Cast: Paula Christopher; Al Corley; Julie DeLaurier; Dolly Jonah; Ken Olin; Michael Strong

4295 • TEANECK TANZI: THE VENUS FLYTRAP

OPENED: 04/20/1983   Theatre: Nederlander
Musical   Broadway: 2

Composer: Chris Monks
Lyricist: Claire Luckham
Librettist: Claire Luckham
Producer: Kenneth-Mark Productions; Stewart F. Lane; Charlene Nederlander; James M. Nederlander; Richard Vos
Director: Chris Bond

Cast: Caitlin Clarke; Clarence Felder; Deborah Harry; Andy Kaufman; Zora Rasmussen; Scott Renderer; Dana Vance; Thomas G. Waites

Notes: This show had two parts double cast, so there were two opening nights. Although the show closed opening night, there were two performances. No songs listed in program.

4296 • TED LEWIS FROLIC

OPENED: 1923
Revue   Closed out of town

Composer: Milton Ager
Lyricist: Jack Yellen
Librettist: Bugs Baer; William K. Wells
Producer: Ted Lewis; Arthur Pearson
Director: Walter Wilson

Choreographer: Allan K. Foster; **Costumes:** Harry Collins; Mme. Francis; Hugh Willoughby; **Lighting Designer:** Fred Murray; **Musical Director:** Louis Gress; **Set Design:** Hugh Willoughby

Songs: Back Home; Beautiful Girls You Have the World at Your Feet; Beyond the Moonbeam Trail; Change Your Step; Oui, Oui, Monsieur; Paisley Shawl; See-No-Evil Eye; Struttin' School; They Weren't Any Better in the Good Old Days; Tick Tock (The Dresden Clock); Twinkle, Twinkle Little Star; We're Not as Bad as We're Painted

Cast: Ted Lewis

4297 TEDDY & ALICE
OPENED: 11/12/1987   Theatre: Minskoff
Musical   Broadway: 77

Music Based On: John Philip Sousa
Composer: Richard Kapp
Lyricist: Hal Hackady
Librettist: Jerome Alden
Producer: Hinks Shimberg
Director: John Driver

Choreographer: Donald Saddler; **Costumes:** Theoni V. Aldredge; **Dance Arranger:** Gordon Lowry Harrell; **Lighting Designer:** Tharon Musser; **Musical Director:** Larry Blank; **Orchestrations:** Jim Tyler; **Set Design:** Robin Wagner; **Vocal Arranger:** Don Pippin

Songs: Battlelines; But Not Right Now; Can I Let Her Go?; Charge; Coming-Out Party, The; Election Eve; Fourth of July, The; He's Got to Go; Her Father's Daughter; House, The; Leg o' Mutton; Not Love; Nothing to Lose; Perfect for Each Other; Private Thoughts; She's Got to Go; Thunderer, The (inst.) (C: John Philip Sousa); Wave the Flag

Cast: Len Cariou; Beth Fowler; Nancy Hume; Nancy Opel; Gordon Stanley; Raymond Thorne; Christopher Wells; Karen Ziemba

Notes: Artistic consultant: Alan Jay Lerner.

4298 • TELEPHONE GIRL, THE
OPENED: 12/27/1897   Theatre: Casino
Musical   Broadway: 104

Composer: Gustave Kerker
Librettist: Hugh Morton
Producer: George W. Lederer; George B. McLellan

Source: LA DEMOISELLE DU TELEPHONE (Musical: Maurice Desvallieres; Anthony Mass; Gaston Serpette)

Songs: Estelle; Keep Your Eye on Pretty Sarah; Telephone Girl, The

Cast: Charles Dickson; Clara Lipman; James F. MacDonald; Louis Mann; Sarah McVicker; Millicent Willson; Bessie Wynn

Notes: No program available.

4299 • TELL HER THE TRUTH
OPENED: 10/28/1932   Theatre: Cort
Musical   Broadway: 11

Composer: Joseph Tunbridge; Jack Waller
Lyricist: Bert Lee; R.P. Weston
Librettist: Bert Lee; R.P. Weston
Producer: Tillie Leblang
Director: Morris Green; Henry Thomas

Source: NOTHING BUT THE TRUTH (Play: James Montgomery); **Source:** NOTHING BUT THE TRUTH (Novel: Frederic Isham); **Costumes:** Jay-Thorpe; **Musical Director:** Gene Salzer; **Set Design:** Teichner Studios

Songs: Happy the Day; Hoch, Caroline!; Horrortorio; Sing, Brothers!; Tell Her the Truth; That's Fine; Won't You Tell Me Why?

Cast: Hobart Cavanaugh; Edith Davis; Margaret Dumont; Lillian Emerson; William Frawley; Louise Kirtland; Lew Parker; John Sheehan Jr.; Andrew Tombes; Raymond Walburn; Thelma White

Notes: The source was used previously as the basis for the musical YES YES YVETTE.

4300 • TELL ME MORE
OPENED: 04/13/1925   Theatre: Winter Garden
Musical   Broadway: 100

Composer: George Gershwin
Lyricist: B.G. DeSylva; Ira Gershwin
Librettist: Fred Thompson; William K. Wells
Producer: Alex A. Aarons
Director: John Harwood; Sammy Lee

Musical Director: Max Steiner

Songs: Baby! [1] [5]; Baby! [2] [6]; Finaletto, Act II Scene 1 (Kenneth Won the Yachting Race); Gushing (Gush, Gush, Gushing) [7] (L: Ira

Gershwin; Brian Hooker); Have You Heard [2] (L: Claude Hulburt); He-Man, The [1]; How Can I Win You Now? [4]; I'm Somethin' on Avenue A [1]; In Sardinia (Where the Delicatessen Flows) [4]; Kickin' the Clouds Away; Love, I Never Knew [2] (L: Desmond Carter); Love Is in the Air; Mr. and Mrs. Sipkin (Monty! Their Only Child); Murderous Monty (And Light-Fingered Jane) [3] (L: Desmond Carter); My Fair Lady (Lady Fair); Oh So La Me (C/L: Unknown); Once [1] (C: William Daly; L: Ira Gershwin); Poetry of Motion, The; Shop Girls and Mannikins; Tell Me More!; Three Times a Day; Ukulele Lorelei; When the Debbies Go By; Why Do I Love You?

Cast: Phyllis Cleveland; Alexander Gray; Emma Haig; Portland Hoffa; Lou Holtz; Esther Howard; Andrew Tombes

Notes: Out of town the show was titled MY FAIR LADY. [1] Cut prior to opening. [2] Added to London production 5/26/25. [3] Written for London production but not used. [4] Cut after opening. [5] Music originally used (with a Clifford Grey lyric) for "Sweetheart" written for the unproduced musical FLYING ISLAND and later in THE RAINBOW. [6] Added to London production 5/26/25. New music for this song (same lyric) written for London. [7] Hooker's participation uncertain. Not used. Also not used in ROSALIE.

4301 • TELL ME ON A SUNDAY

OPENED: 01/1980   Theatre: BBC
TV Musical

Composer: Andrew Lloyd Webber
Lyricist: Don Black

Musical Director: Harry Rabinowitz

Songs: Capped Teeth and Caesar Salad; Come Back with the Same Look in Your Eyes; I'm Very You, You're Very Me; It's Not the End of the World (If He's Younger); It's Not the End of the World (If He's Married); It's Not the End of the World (If I Lose Him); Let Me Finish; Let's Talk About You; Letter Home to England; Nothing Like You've Ever Known; Second Letter Home; Sheldon Bloom; Take That Look Off Your Face; Tell Me on a Sunday; You Made Me Think You Were in Love

Cast: Marti Webb

Notes: *See also SONG & DANCE.* This became the first act of that show.

4302 • TELLING THE TALE

OPENED: 08/31/1918   Theatre: Ambassadors'
Musical   London: 90

Composer: Philip Braham
Lyricist: Douglas Hoare
Librettist: Sidney Blow; Douglas Hoare
Producer: Gerald Kirby; John Wyndham
Director: Sidney Blow

Source: OH, I SAY! (Play: Sidney Blow; Douglas Hoare); **Choreographer:** George Shurley; **Musical Director:** W. Vere Harker; **Set Design:** F. Bull; J. Hicks

Songs: Altogether Too Fond of You (C: Cole Porter; L: Melville Gideon; James Heard); Cocktail Time; Cook House Door, The; Queen of the South Sea Isles, The; Rin-tin-tin and Ninette

Cast: Marie Blanche; Douglas Blore; Edmee Dormeuil; Nancy Gibbs; Gerald Kirby; C. Dernier Warren

Notes: No program available.

4303 • TEMPEST IN A TEAPOT

OPENED: 11/17/1954
Musical   25

Composer: Ronald Lowden
Librettist: Richard Levinson; William Link
Producer: Robert Wickersham
Director: Chester R. Cooper

Choreographer: Walter F. Keenan; **Costumes:** Helen Stevenson West; **Incidental Music:** Al Boss; **Orchestrations:** Al Boss; **Set Design:** Robert Patterson

Songs: Boston Tea Party (inst.) (C: Allison Fleitas); Brazilian Interlude (C: Henning Ludlow; L: James McHugh); Coffee and Tea (C/L: Allison Fleitas); Gossip; If You'd Only Let Me (C/L: Allison Fleitas); I'm Through with You (C/L: Henning Ludlow); I've Changed My Mind; Loyalty (L: James McHugh); Meeting; Morality (C: Doun Bruce; L: James McHugh); Take a Look (C/L: Allison Fleitas); Toast, A; We've Got a Great Feeling (C: Henning Ludlow;

L: James McHugh); Where There's a Will
(L: Thomas Scotes; Philip Struthers); Who's Boss
in Boston (L: James McHugh); Wonderful You
(C: Sydney Fisher; L: James McHugh)

Notes: Amateur show. Mask & Wig Club,
University of Pennstylvania.

4304 • TEMPLE BELLES

OPENED: 03/20/1924
Musical

Composer: Richard Rodgers
Lyricist: Lorenz Hart
Librettist: Richard Rodgers
Producer: Park Avenue Synogogue
Director: Herbert Fields

Musical Director: Richard Rodgers

Songs: Bob-o-link (L: Dorothy Crowthers);
Hermits, The [1]; Just a Little Lie [3]; Penny for
Your Thoughts, A [2]

Notes: Amateur show. [1] Also in WINKLE
TOWN, A DANISH YANKEE IN KING TUT'S
COURT and DEAREST ENEMY. [2] Also in FLY
WITH ME. [3] Also in YOU'LL NEVER KNOW
and SAY IT WITH JAZZ.

4305 • TEMPORARY MRS. SMITH, THE

Notes: See LOVELY ME.

4306 • TEMPTATIONS

Notes: See FOLIES BERGERE COMPANY.

4307 • 10 DAYS TO BROADWAY

Notes: See 13 DAYS TO BROADWAY.

4308 • TEN FOR FIVE

OPENED: 1918
Musical

Composer: Henry Hanemann; Robert K.
Lippmann
Lyricist: Oscar Hammerstein II; Henry Hanemann
Librettist: Oscar Hammerstein II
Producer: Columbia University War Show
Committee
Director: Oscar Hammerstein II

Musical Director: Roy S. Webb

Notes: Amateur show.

4309 • TEN PERCENT REVUE

OPENED: 04/13/1988   Theatre: Susan Bloch
Revue   Off-Broadway: 239

Composer: Tom Wilson Weinberg
Lyricist: Tom Wilson Weinberg
Producer: Laura Green
Director: Scott Green

Choreographer: Tee Scatuorchio; Costumes:
Kevin-Robert; Set Design: Edwin Perez-Carrion

Songs: And the Supremes; Before Stonewall; Best
Years of My Life; Flaunting It; Gay Name Game;
High Risk for Afraids; Home; Homo Haven
Fight Song; I'd Like to Be; If I Were; Not
Allowed; Obituary; Personals; Safe Sex Slut;
Threesome; Turkey Baster Baby; We're
Everywhere; Wedding Song; Write a Letter

Cast: Lisa Bernstein; Valerie Hill; Trish Kane;
Robert Tate; Timothy Williams

4310 • TEN-ISH, ANYONE?

                            Theatre: Downstairs at the
                                        Upstairs
Revue   Nightclub

Songs: Daisy (C/L: G. Wood); Thor (C/L: Jack
Holmes)

Cast: Jane Connell; Jack Fletcher

4311 • TENDERFOOT, THE

OPENED: 02/22/1904   Theatre: New York
Musical   Broadway: 81

Composer: H.L. Heartz
Lyricist: Richard Carle
Librettist: Richard Carle
Producer: Dearborn Theatre Company
Director: Richard Carle

Songs: Adios; Dancing; Don't Forget You're
Talking to a Lady (C: William Spink; L: Henry
Blossom); Don't Mind Me; Fascinating Venus;
Gay Lothario, A; I'm a Peaceable Party;
Interrogative Child, The; Love Is Elusive [1];

Marriage Is a Lottery; Only a Kiss; Soldier of Fortune, A; Soldiery, The; Texas Rangers; Tortured Thomas Cat; Washing Song

Cast: Richard Carle; Helena Frederick; William Rock

Notes: [1] Also in MARY'S LAMB.

4312 • TENDERLOIN
OPENED: 10/17/1960   Theatre: 46th Street
Musical   Broadway: 216

Composer: Jerry Bock
Lyricist: Sheldon Harnick
Librettist: George Abbott; Jerome Weidman
Producer: Robert E. Griffith; Harold Prince
Director: George Abbott

Source: TENDERLOIN (Novel: Samuel Hopkins Adams); **Choreographer:** Joe Layton; **Costumes:** Cecil Beaton; **Dance Arranger:** Jack Elliott; **Musical Director:** Harold Hastings; **Orchestrations:** Irwin Kostal; **Set Design:** Cecil Beaton

Songs: Army of the Just, The; Artificial Flowers; Bless This Land; Dear Friend; Dr. Brock; Finally [3]; First Things First [3]; Good Clean Fun; How the Money Changes Hands; I Wonder What It's Like [2]; Little Old New York; Lord of All Creation [3]; Lovely Laurie [1]; My Gentle Young Johnny; My Miss Mary; Nobody Cares [3]; Not Peace but a Sword [1]; Orgy Burlesque, The [1]; Picture of Happiness, The; Reform; Sea Shell [1]; Tenderloin Celebration, The; Tis Thy Beauty [1]; Tommy, Tommy; Trial, The; What's in It for You?

Cast: Ralph Dunn; Maurice Evans; Rex Everhart; Margery Gray; Ron Husmann; Eddie Phillips; Eileen Rodgers; Lee Theodore

Notes: [1] Not used. [2] Cut prior to opening. [3] Not in programs.

4313 • TERENCE
OPENED: 01/05/1904   Theatre: New York
Play   Broadway: 56

Composer: Chauncey Olcott
Lyricist: Chauncey Olcott
Author: Mrs. Edmund Nash Morgan

Producer: Augustus Pitou
Director: Augustus Pitou

Source: UNKNOWN (Novel: Mrs. B.M. Croker); **Costumes:** H.A. Ogden; **Incidental Music:** Gustave Salzer; **Musical Director:** Clarence Rogerson

Songs: Girl I Used to Know, The; My Own Dear Irish Queen; My Sonny Boy; Terence; Tick, Tack, Toe

Cast: Harry Hanscombe; Adelaide Keim; Chauncey Olcott; Elizabeth Washburne; Amanda Wellington

4314 • TEXAS, LI'L DARLIN'
OPENED: 11/25/1949   Theatre: Mark Hellinger
Musical   Broadway: 293

Composer: Robert Emmett Dolan
Lyricist: Johnny Mercer
Librettist: Sam Moore; John Whedon
Producer: Anthony Brady Farrell; Studio Productions
Director: Paul Crabtree

Choreographer: Al White Jr.; **Costumes:** Eleanor Goldsmith; **Lighting Designer:** Theodore Cooper; **Musical Director:** Will Irwin; **Orchestrations:** Robert Russell Bennett; **Set Design:** Theodore Cooper

Songs: Affable Balding Me; Big Movie Show in the Sky, The; Down in the Valley; Hootin' Owl Trail; Horseshoes Are Lucky; It's Great to Be Alive; Little Bit o' Country [1]; Love Me, Love My Dog; Month of Sundays, A; Our Family Tree [1]; Politics; Ride 'Em Cowboy; Square Dance (dance); Take a Crank Letter; Texas Li'l Darlin'; They Talk a Different Language (The Yodel Blues); Whichaway'd They Go; Whoopin' and a-Hollerin'

Cast: Kenny Delmar; Mary Hatcher; Danny Scholl; Loring Smith

Notes: [1] Out Westport 8/29/49.

4315 • THANK HEAVEN FOR THE HEATHEN
Notes: *See HEATHEN!*

4316 • THANK YOU, COLUMBUS!

OPENED: 11/15/1940   Theatre: Hollywood
                                      Playhouse
Musical   Los Angeles

Composer: George Forrest; Robert Wright
Lyricist: George Forrest; Robert Wright
Librettist: Ben Barzman; Sol Barzman
Producer: Curt Bois; G.V. Gontard
Director: Curt Bois

Choreographer: Eddie Larkin; **Costumes:** Gerda
Vanderneers; **Musical Director:** Leo Arnaud;
Orchestrations: Leo Arnaud; **Set Design:**
Gabriel Scognamillo; **Vocal Arranger:** Leo
Arnaud

Songs: All's Well; Can You Can-Can; Dr.
Clambake's Ballet; Dream for Sale; Empty
Wigwam Blues; Genealogy of Daisy Belle, The;
I Discover New Worlds; I Hear America Singing;
I Never Had a Date Before; Make Way for
Tomorrow; Manhattan's Automatons; Pilgrim's
Chorus; Spinning Song; These Three; Thou Shalt
Not Dance; Voice of Tomorrow, The; We Were
Here First

Cast: Kenneth Stevens; Philip Van Zandt; Dave
Willcock; Vivian Yarbo

4317 THAT CASEY GIRL

OPENED: 10/22/1923
Musical   Closed out of town

Composer: Jean Schwartz
Lyricist: William Jerome
Librettist: George V. Hobart; Willard Mack

Songs: Casey Is a Wonderful Name; Ev'ry Day Is
Mother's Day; I Love Rosie Casey; Please Come
Again; Summer Days; When I Get in the Movies

Notes: Lyceum Theatre, Paterson, New Jersey.

4318 • THAT 5 A.M. JAZZ

OPENED: 10/19/1964   Theatre: Astor Place
Musical   Off-Broadway: 94

Composer: Will Holt
Lyricist: Will Holt
Librettist: Will Holt
Producer: Muriel Morse; Jay Stanwyck
Director: Michael Kahn

Choreographer: Sandra Devlin; **Dance Arranger:**
Ted Simons; **Lighting Designer:** Milton Drake;
Set Design: Lloyd Burlingame; **Vocal Arranger:**
Ted Simons

Songs: All-American Two-Step, The; Campaign
Song; Gonna Get a Woman; Happy Daze Saloon,
The; Nuevo Laredo; Some Sunday; Sweet Time;
Those Were the Days

Cast: James Coco; Lester James; Ruth Jaroslow;
Dolly Jonah

Notes: This was a bill of two one-act shows: THE
FIRST and THAT 5 A.M. JAZZ. All songs were
in part two.

4319 • THAT HAT!

OPENED: 09/23/1964   Theatre: Theatre Four
Musical   Off-Broadway: 1

Composer: Cy Young
Lyricist: Cy Young
Librettist: Cy Young
Producer: Bonard Productions; Justin Sturn;
Katherine Sturn
Director: Dania Krupska

Source: ITALIAN STRAW HAT, THE (Play:
Eugene Labiche; Marc- Michel); **Choreographer:**
Dania Krupska; **Costumes:** Bill Hargate; **Dance
Arranger:** Gerald Alters; **Lighting Designer:**
Patricia Collins; **Musical Director:** Gerald Alters;
Set Design: Bill Hargate; **Vocal Arranger:** Gerald
Alters

Songs: Apology, The; Do a Little Exercise; Draw
Me a Circle; Exposition; Give Me a Pinch; I Love
a Man; Interlude; Italian Straw Hat; It's All Off;
Mad Ballet, The; My, It's Been Grand; My
Husband; Pot of Myrtle, A; Sound of the Night;
Sounds of the Day; Tete-a-tete, A; This World of
Confusion; We Have Never Met

Cast: Carmen Alvarez; Merle Louise; Pierre Olaf;
Joe Ross; Barbara Sharma; Elmarie Wendel

4320 • THAT'S A GOOD GIRL

OPENED: 06/05/1928   Theatre: London
                                      Hippodrome
Musical   London: 363

Composer: Philip Charig; Joseph Meyer

Lyricist: Desmond Carter; Douglas Furber; Ira Gershwin
Librettist: Douglas Furber
Producer: Jack Buchanan; Moss Empires Ltd.; United Producing Corp.
Director: Jack Buchanan

Choreographer: Jack Buchanan; **Musical Director:** Leonard Hornsey; **Set Design:** F.L. Lyndhurst; Marc-Henri

Songs: Before We Were Married [1] (L: Ira Gershwin); Chirp- Chirp [2] (L: Ira Gershwin); Day After Day [1] (L: Ira Gershwin); Fancy Our Meeting (L: Douglas Furber); Finale Act I (L: Ira Gershwin); Hullo Hullo; Let Yourself Go! [3] (L: Ira Gershwin); Marching Song, A (L: Douglas Furber); One I'm Looking For, The (L: Douglas Furber; Ira Gershwin); Opening (What to Do) (L: Ira Gershwin); Parting Time (L: Douglas Furber); Sweet So-and-So [4] (L: Douglas Furber; Ira Gershwin); Tell Me Why (L: Desmond Carter); There I'd Settle Down [1] (L: Ira Gershwin); We've Got to Find William (L: Douglas Furber); Week End (L: Ira Gershwin); Whoopee (L: Ira Gershwin); Why Be Good? [1] (L: Ira Gershwin)

Cast: Jack Buchanan; Eight Tiller Girls, The; Dave Fitzgibbon; William Kendall; Elsie Randolph

Notes: [1] Not used. [2] Also in SHOOT THE WORKS. [3] Published music credits lyrics to Douglas Furber and Gershwin. [4] Gershwin's original lyric (written alone) was used in SWEET AND LOW.

4321 • THAT'S LIFE
OPENED: 1954

Composer: Ray Evans; Jay Livingston
Lyricist: Ray Evans; Jay Livingston

Songs: Chihuahua Choo-Choo [1]; Clink Clank Clunk; Livin' Lovin' Doll; That's Life; Why Am I in Love; You're So Right

Notes: No other information available. [1] Also in TV musical SATINS AND SPURS.

4322 • THAT'S MY BOY
OPENED: 11/1924
Play   Closed out of town

Composer: Robert Simonds
Lyricist: Billy DuVal
Author: Karyl Norman; Edward A. Paulton
Producer: Joseph M. Gaites
Director: Lawrence Marston

Choreographer: Vaughn Godfrey; **Costumes:** Kiviette; **Musical Director:** Karyl Norman

Songs: In a World of Our Own; Me and the Boy Friend; Paris Rose; Play That Melody of Love; Somebody Like You (C: Walter Donaldson; L: Cliff Friend); Spain; Wonderful Mother

Cast: Betty Byron; Dan Marble; Karyl Norman; Helen Weir; Isabelle Winlocke

Notes: Program from Wilmington 11/3/24. Karyl Norman played both male and female rolse in this show.

4323 • THAT'S THE TICKET
OPENED: 09/27/1948
Musical   Closed out of town

Composer: Harold Rome
Lyricist: Harold Rome
Librettist: Julius J. Epstein; Philip G. Epstein
Producer: Al Beckman; Joseph Kipness; John Pransky
Director: Jerome Robbins

Choreographer: Paul Godkin; **Costumes:** Miles White; **Lighting Designer:** Peggy Clark; **Musical Director:** Lehman Engel; **Orchestrations:** Robert Russell Bennett; **Set Design:** Oliver Smith; **Vocal Arranger:** Lehman Engel

Songs: Ballad of Marcia LaRue, The; Chivalry Reel; Cry, Baby [1]; Determined Woman, A; Dost Thou; Fair Sex, The; Gin Rummy Rhapsody; How Peaceful Is the Evening; I Shouldn't Love You; Looking for a Candidate; Money Song, The; Newsreel, The; Political Lady; Read All About It; Take Off the Coat [2]; We're Going Back; You Never Know What Hit You-When It's Love [2]

Cast: Rod Alexander; Kaye Ballard; Leif Erickson; Ralph Herz; George S. Irving; Edna Skinner; Loring Smith

Notes: [1] Later in ALIVE AND KICKING. [2] Later in BLESS YOU ALL.

4324 • THEBE

OPENED: 1906
Musical

Composer: Ben M. Jerome
Lyricist: I.L. Blumenstock
Librettist: I.L. Blumenstock

Songs: My Lotus Lady; My Sawdust Queen

Notes: No other information available.

4325 • THEDA BARA AND THE FRONTIER RABBI

OPENED: 01/09/1993
Musical   Off-Off-Broadway

Composer: Bob Johnston
Lyricist: Jeff Hochhauser; Bob Johnston
Librettist: Jeff Hochhauser
Director: Lynne Taylor-Corbett

Songs: Arab Death; Bish Ne Ara; Bolt of Love; Faster and Faster; Frontier Rabbi; G.O.T.O.; It's Like a Movie; Ladies and Mateys of Hades, The; Lulu; Meddler, The; Only Dreamin'; Scene with the Grapes, The; Sermon, The; Thump Thump; Velcome to Shul

Cast: Jonathan Hadley; Robin Irwin; Jeanine LaManna; Ellen Margulies; Allen Lewis Rickman

4326 • THEIR WEDDING NIGHT

Notes: *See OH, I SAY.*

4327 • THEODORE AND CO.

OPENED: 09/19/1916   Theatre: Gaiety
Musical   London: 503

Composer: Ivor Novello
Lyricist: Clifford Grey
Librettist: George Grossmith; H.M. Harwood
Producer: George Grossmith; Edward Laurillard
Director: Austen Hurgon

Source: THEODORE ET CIE (Play: Paul Gavault); **Choreographer:** Gwladys Dillon; **Costumes:** Lucille; Elspeth Phelps; Jules Poiret; **Musical Director:** Willie Redstone; **Set Design:** Alfred E. Craven; Joseph Harker; Phil Harker

Songs: All That I Want Is Somebody to Love Me [1] (C: Jerome Kern); Any Old Where; Candy Girls, The (L: Adrian Ross); Casino Music Hall, The (C: Jerome Kern); Ev'ry Little Girl Can Teach Me Something New (L: Adrian Ross); He's Going to Call on Baby Grand (L: Adrian Ross); I'll Make Myself at Home (L: Adrian Ross); I'm Getting Such a Big Girl Now (C: Philip Braham); Isn't There a Crowd Everywhere?; My Friend John; My Second Childhood (C: Philip Braham; L: Eric Blore; David Burnaby); That Come "Hither" Look [2] (C: Jerome Kern); 365 Days (C: Jerome Kern); Valse Saracenne (inst.); We Are Theodore & Company (L: Adrian Ross); We Can Jolly Along (C: Philip Braham; L: Eric Blore); What a Duke Should Be; You'd Better Not Wait for Him

Cast: Joyce Barbour; George Grossmith; Leslie Henson; Julia James; Madge Saunders

Notes: [1] Same music as "Can't You See I Mean You?" from 90 IN THE SHADE and as "Isn't It Great to Be Married" from VERY GOOD EDDIE. Grey revised M.E. Rourke's original lyric. [2] New lyric for "Those 'Come Hither' Eyes" from COUSIN LUCY.

4328 • THERE YOU ARE

OPENED: 05/16/1932   Theatre: George M.
                                    Cohan
Musical   Broadway: 8

Composer: William Heagney
Lyricist: Tom Connell; William Heagney
Librettist: Carl Bartfeld
Producer: Hyman Adler
Director: Horace Sinclair

Choreographer: Vaughn Godfrey; **Costumes:** Bertha Beres; Eaves; **Musical Director:** Fred Hoff; **Orchestrations:** Irving Schloss; Roy Webb; **Set Design:** Carlo Studios

Songs: Aces Up; Carolina; Haunting Refrain; Just a Little Penthouse and You; Legend of the Mission Bells; Love Lives On; Love Potion, The; Lover's Holiday; More and More; Safe in Your Arms; Sounds of the Drum, The; There You Are; They All Love Me; Wings in the Morning

Cast: Hyman Adler; Robert Capron; Roy Cropper; Berta Donn; Joseph Lertora; Ilse Marvenga; O'Connor; Adrian Rosley

4329 • THERE'S A GIRL IN MY SOUP

OPENED: 10/18/1967   Theatre: Music Box
Play   Broadway: 321

Author: Terence Frisby
Producer: Michael Codron; Saint-Subber
Director: Robert Chetwyn

Costumes: Stanley Simmons; **Lighting Designer:** Lloyd Burlingame; **Set Design:** Hutchinson Scott

Songs: Girl in My Soup (C/L: Norman Percival)

Cast: Erica Fitz; Rita Gam; George Hall; Jon Pertwee; Gig Young

4330 • THERE'S A HOLE IN MY SIDEWALK

Revue   Closed out of town

Composer: Portia Nelson
Lyricist: Portia Nelson
Librettist: Portia Nelson
Director: David Rounds

Source: THERE'S A HOLE IN MY SIDEWALK (Book: Portia Nelson); **Lighting Designer:** Dan Boylan; **Musical Director:** Manford Abrahamson; **Set Design:** David Rounds

Songs: All the Ifs and Maybes; Decisions; Hole in My Sidewalk; How Wise of You to Wait; I Crowed What I Knowed; I Don't Smoke; In the Beginning; Into the Bright of Loving; It's a Dreary Day; Love Theme; Pieces; Try to Be My Age; What Foolish Creatures We Are; You Have Made a Fool of Me; You Say You Love Me

Cast: Carol Morley; David Rounds; John Seidman

4331 • THEY CAN'T GET YOU DOWN

OPENED: 12/1941
Musical   Los Angeles

Composer: Jay Gorney
Lyricist: Edward Eliscu; Henry Myers
Librettist: Edward Eliscu; Henry Myers
Producer: Edward Eliscu; Jay Gorney; Jack Kirkland; Henry Myers; Dwight Deere Wiman

Choreographer: Danny Dare; **Costumes:** Georgia Anderson; **Set Design:** Frederick Stover; **Vocal Arranger:** Mort Werner; Leo Wolf

Songs: Ad Ripae Mildewensis Fluminis; Finaletto; It's No Fun Eating Alone; Love Can Settle Everything; Love in a Changing World; Mittel-Europa [1]; More Mittel-Europa; Musical Chairs; On the Banks of the Mildrew River; River to Dora Flora; Sir Pumphrey Mildew; Take Her My Boy [2]; They Can't Get You Down; Twenty-Five Bucks a Week; Twenty-One Bucks a Week; Unzer Amerika [2]; You're Only a Barefoot Boy

Cast: Gene Barry; Jan Clayton; Edward Emerson; Berni Gould; Jimmy Griffith; Eddie Johnson; Peggy Ryan; Julie Sherwin; Douglas Wood

Notes: [1] Also in LET FREEDOM SING. [2] ASCAP/Library of Congress only.

4332 • THEY DON'T MAKE 'EM LIKE THAT ANYMORE

OPENED: 06/06/1972   Theatre: Plaza 9 Music
                            Hall
Revue   Off-Broadway: 24

Composer: Hugh Martin
Lyricist: Timothy Gray; Hugh Martin
Producer: Timothy Gray; William Justus; Costas Omer
Director: Timothy Gray

Costumes: Stephen Chandler; E. Huntington Parker; **Lighting Designer:** Beverly Emmons; **Set Design:** Don Gordon

Songs: Architect, The; Buckle Down Winsocki [2] (C/L: Ralph Blane); Disraeli; Drama Quartet; Frank and Johnnies [3]; Get Me Out of Here [3]; Harvey; I Lost You; Invisible Man; Judy [3]; Once in Love with Amy [1] (C/L: Frank Loesser); Oscar; Paradise Lost [3]; Party's Over Now, The; Show Girl; Silence Is Golden; Something Tells Me; Sorry Wrong Valley; Sunset Boulevard; Swanislavsky; They Don't Make 'Em Like That Anymore; Victoria; What's His Name

Cast: Arthur Blake; Kevin Christopher; Dell Hanley; Clay Johns; Luba Lisa; Gene McCann; Phoebe Otis; Paris Todd

Notes: There may be some sketch titles in the song list as they weren't differentiated in the program. [1] From WHERE'S CHARLEY. [2] From BEST FOOT FORWARD. Though Ralph Blane wrote this song, he and Hugh Martin polished his version. [3] ASCAP/Library of Congress only.

4333 THEY LOVED A LASSIE

OPENED: 10/31/1909   Theatre: Whitney Opera House
Musical   Chicago

Composer: Lyle Bloodgood
Librettist: George Arliss; Benjamin Hapgood Burt
Producer: B.C. Whitney
Director: Gus Sohlke

Cast: Charles E. Evans; Forrest Huff; Eugene Moulan; Alice Yorke

Notes: No songs listed in program.

4334 • THEY'RE PLAYING OUR SONG

OPENED: 02/11/1979   Theatre: Imperial
Musical   Broadway: 1082

Composer: Marvin Hamlisch
Lyricist: Carole Bayer Sager
Librettist: Neil Simon
Producer: Emanuel Azenberg
Director: Robert Moore

Choreographer: Patricia Birch; **Costumes:** Ann Roth; **Lighting Designer:** Tharon Musser; **Musical Director:** Larry Blank; **Orchestrations:** Ralph Burns; Richard Hazard; Gene Page; **Set Design:** Douglas W. Schmidt

Songs: Fallin'; Fill in the Words; I Still Believe in Love; If He Really Knew Me; If We Give It Time [1]; I've Got Those One Foot Blues [1]; Just for Tonight; Right; They're Playing Our Song; When You're in My Arms; Workin' It Out

Cast: Lucie Arnaz; Robert Klein

Notes: [1] Cut prior to opening.

4335 • THIRD LITTLE SHOW, THE

OPENED: 06/01/1931   Theatre: Music Box
Revue   Broadway: 136

Librettist: Marc Connelly; Noel Coward; Edward Eliscu; S.J. Perelman; Peter Spencer; Harry Wall
Producer: Tom Weatherly; Dwight Deere Wiman
Director: Alexander Leftwich

Choreographer: Dave Gould; **Costumes:** Raymond Sovey; **Musical Director:** Max Meth; **Orchestrations:** Howard Jackson; **Set Design:** Jo Mielziner

Songs: Africa Shrieks (C: Ned Lehac; L: Edward Eliscu); Any Little Fish [2] (C/L: Noel Coward); Cinema Lorelei (C: Ned Lehac; L: Edward Eliscu); Falling in Love (C: Henry Sullivan; L: Earle Crooker); Going, Going, Gone! (C: Henry Sullivan; L: Edward Eliscu); I'll Putcha Pitcha in the Papers (C: Michael Cleary; L: Max Lief; Nathaniel Lief); I've Lost My Heart (C: Morris Hamilton; L: Grace Henry); Le Five O'Clock (C: Will Irwin; L: Carl Randall); Little Geezer (C: Michael H. Cleary; L: Max Lief; Nathaniel Lief; Dave Oppenheim); Mad Dogs and Englishmen [1] (C/L: Noel Coward); Say the Word (C: Burton Lane; L: Harold Adamson); Sevilla (C: Ned Lehac; L: Edward Eliscu); There Are Fairies at the Bottom of My Garden (C: Liza Lehmann; L: Rose Fyleman); When Yuba Plays the Rumba on His Tuba (C/L: Herman Hupfeld); You Forgot Your Gloves (C: Ned Lehac; L: Edward Eliscu); You Might As Well Pretend (C: Morgan Lewis; L: Edward Eliscu; Ted Fetter)

Cast: Edward Arnold; Constance Carpenter; Dorothy Fitzgibbon; Sandra Gale; William Griffith; Beatrice Lillie; Gertrude McDonald; Jerry Norris; Walter O'Keefe; Carl Randall; Ernest Truex

Notes: [1] Originally in WORDS AND MUSIC. [2] Cut during tryout of this show. Originally in COCHRAN'S 1931 REVUE.

4336 • THIRTEEN CLOCKS

OPENED: 08/17/1953
Musical   Closed out of town

Composer: Robert Gallico
Librettist: Frank Lowe

Source: THIRTEEN CLOCKS, THE (Story: James Thurber)

Notes: No program available.

4337 • 13 DAUGHTERS

OPENED: 03/02/1961 Theatre: 54th St.
Musical Broadway: 28

Composer: Eaton Magoon Jr.
Lyricist: Eaton Magoon Jr.
Librettist: Eaton Magoon Jr.; Leon Tolsatyan
Producer: Jack H. Silverman
Director: Billy Matthews

Choreographer: Rod Alexander; **Costumes:** Alvin Colt; **Dance Arranger:** Bob Atwood; **Lighting Designer:** George Jenkins; **Musical Director:** Pembroke Davenport; **Orchestrations:** Robert Russell Bennett; Joe Glover; **Set Design:** George Jenkins; **Vocal Arranger:** Pembroke Davenport

Songs: Alphabet Song; Calabash Cousins [1]; Cotillion, The; Daughter or Dowry [1]; Father and Son [2]; Goodbye Is Hard to Say [1]; Hiaka; Hoomalimali; House on the Hill; Ka Wahine Akamai; Kuli Kuli; Lei of Memories [1]; Let-a-Go Your Heart; Listen for the Rooster [2]; Long and Beautiful Life, A [1]; My Hawaii; My Pleasure; Never Without Your Love [2]; Nothing Man Cannot Do; Oriental Plan (C: Sherman Edwards; L: Sid Wayne); Paper of Gold; Puka Puka Pants; 13 Daughters; 13 Old Maids; Throw a Petal; Violets and Violins [2]; Wedding Processional [1]; When You Hear the Wind; You Fascinate Me So [2] (C: Cy Coleman; L: Carolyn Leigh); You Set My Heart to Music

Cast: Don Ameche; John Battles; Monica Boyar; Isabelle Farrell; Ed Kenney; Sylvia Syms; Richard Tone

Notes: [1] Written for Hawaiian production but dropped before Broadway. [2] Cut from score.

4338 • 13 DAYS TO BROADWAY

OPENED: 1985
Musical Unproduced

Composer: Cy Coleman
Lyricist: Barbara Fried
Librettist: Russell Baker
Director: Joe Layton

Costumes: Patricia Zipprodt; **Set Design:** Robin Wagner

Songs: You There in the Back Row

Notes: Workshopped but never produced. This show was known by many titles at one time or another. They include: 10 DAYS TO BROADWAY; BAKER'S BROADWAY; and SETS AND COSTUMES. This was a show based on the experiences of trying to bring HOME AGAIN, HOME AGAIN to the stage. The two shows shared some of the same songs.

4339 • THIS AND THAT

OPENED: 1919
Musical

Composer: C. Luckeyth Roberts
Lyricist: Alex Rogers
Librettist: Alex Rogers
Producer: C. Luckeyth Roberts; Alex Rogers
Director: Alex Rogers

Choreographer: Hazel Thompson Davis

Cast: Edna Brown; Lottie Harris; Ellis Stevens; Dink Stewart; Charley Woody

Notes: No other information available.

4340 • THIS IS THE ARMY

OPENED: 07/04/1942 Theatre: Broadway
Revue Broadway: 113

Composer: Irving Berlin
Lyricist: Irving Berlin
Producer: Uncle Sam
Director: Ezra Stone

Choreographer: Nelson Barclift; Robert Sydney; **Costumes:** John Koenig; **Musical Director:** Milton Rosenstock; **Set Design:** John Koenig

Songs: American Eagles; Army and the Shuberts Depend on You, The (Opening) [5]; Army's Made a Man Out of Me, The; Aryans Under the Skin; Fifth Army's Where My Heart Is, The [2]; How About a Cheer for the Navy?; I Get Along with the Aussies [6]; I Left My Heart at the Stage Door Canteen; I'm Getting Tired So I Can Sleep; Jap-German Sextette; Kick in the Pants, The [3]; Ladies of the Chorus; Mandy [1]; My British Buddy [3]; My Sergeant and I Are Buddies; Oh! How I Hate to Get Up in the Morning [7]; Oh to Be Home Again; Opening of Second Act [5]; Poor Little Me-I'm on KP [4]; Soldier's Dream, A; Some Dough for the Army Relief (Opening) [5];

That Russian Winter; That's What the Well Dressed Man in Harlem Will Wear; There Are No Wings on a Foxhole; This Is the Army, Mr. Jones; This Time (Is the Last Time); Ve Don't Like It [3]; What Are We Going to Do with All the Jeeps? [2]; What Does He Look Like?; With My Head in the Clouds

Cast: Irving Berlin; Stuart Churchill; Joe Cook Jr.; Burl Ives; Gary Merrill; Jules Oshins; Earl Oxford; Robert Shanley; Ezra Stone; Philip Truex

Notes: [1] Originally in YIP! YIP! YAPHANK! Also in ZIEGFELD FOLLIES OF 1919. [2] 1944 version-toured combat zones of Europe, Near East and Pacific. Added for that tour. [3] Overseas version of show toured England, Ireland and Scotland in 1943. Added for that tour. [4] Added for tour after Broadway. [5] Sheet music only. [6] 1945 tour. [7] Originally in YIP! YIP! YAPHANK!

4341 • THIS YEAR OF GRACE!

OPENED: 11/07/1928   Theatre: Selwyn
Musical   Broadway: 158

Composer: Noel Coward
Lyricist: Noel Coward
Librettist: Noel Coward
Producer: Charles B. Cochran
Director: Frank Collins

Choreographer: Tilly Losch; Max Rivers; **Costumes:** G.E. Calthrop; Norman H. Hartnell; Idare; Christabel Russell; Doris Zinkeisen; **Musical Director:** Frank Tours; **Set Design:** G.E. Calthrop; Laverdet; Oliver Messel

Songs: Britannia Rules the Waves; Caballero; Chauve Souris; Dance Little Lady; English Lido; I Can't Think; I'm Mad About You; Lido Beach, The; Lilac Time; Little Women; Lorelei; Mary Make Believe; Mother's Complaint; Room with a View, A; Teach Me to Dance Like Grandma; Try to Learn to Love; Velasquez; Waiting in a Queue; World Weary

Cast: Noel Coward; Florence Desmond; Dick Francis; Madeline Gibson; Mimi Hayes; Queenie Leonard; Beatrice Lillie; Marc-Henri; Oliver Messel; Billy Milton; Muriel Montrose; Sonnie Ray

4342 • THOSE WERE THE DAYS

OPENED: 11/07/1990   Theatre: Edison
Revue   Broadway: 130

Librettist: Zalmen Mlotek; Moishe Rosenfeld
Producer: Emanuel Azenberg; Moe Septee
Director: Eleanor Reissa

Choreographer: Eleanor Reissa; **Costumes:** Gail Cooper-Hecht; **Lighting Designer:** Tom Sturge; **Musical Director:** Zalmen Mlotek

Songs: Bei Mir Bist Du Schoen (To Me, You're Beautiful) (C: Sholom Secunda; L: Sammy Cahn; Saul Chaplin; Jacob Jacobs); Der Ayznban (The Train) (C/L: Traditional); Di Dinst (The Maid) (C/L: Traditional); Di Rod (The Circle) (C/L: M. Warshavsky); Figaro's Aria (C: Giochino Rossini; L: Robert Abelson; Moishe Rosenfeld); Halevay Volt Ikh Singl Geven (I Wish I Were Single Again) (C/L: Traditional; M. Younin); Hootsatsa (C/L: Finshl Kanapoff); Hudl Mitn Shtrudl (Hudl with the Shtrudl) (C/L: Aaron Lebedeff); In an Orem Shtibele (In a Poor Little House) (C/L: Traditional); Khazndl Oyf Shabes (A Cantor for the Sabbath), A (C/L: Traditional); Khosn — Kale Mazl Tov (Congratulations to the Bride and Groom) (C/L: Traditional); Litvak/ Galitsyaner (C/L: Hymie Jacobson); Lomir Loybn (Let Us Praise) (C/L: Traditional); Mamenyu Tayere (Dear Mama) (C: Traditional; L: Mani Leib); Mayn Alte Heym (C/L: Traditional); Motele (C/L: M. Gebirtig); My Yiddishe Mame (C: Lew Pollack; L: Jack Yellen); Oyfa Pripetshik (At the Fireplace) (C/L: M. Warshavsky); Palace of the Czar, The (C/L: Mel Tolkin); Papirosn (Cigarettes) (C/L: Bella Meisel; Herman Yablokoff); Rumania, Rumania (C/L: Aaron Lebedeff; Sholom Secunda); Saposhkelekh (The Boots) (C/L: Traditional); Sha Shtil (The Rabbi's Coming) (C/L: Traditional); Shabes, Shabes, Shabes (Welcome to the Sabbath) (C: Ben Yomen; L: Ben Bonus); Shloymele-Malkele (C: Joseph Rumshinsky); Shpil Gitar (Play Guitar) (C/L: Traditional); Those Were the Days (C/L: Gene Raskin); Ver Der Ershter Vet Lakhn (Who Will Laugh First?) (C/L: M. Gebirtig); Yiddish International Radio Hour (C: Traditional; L: Chana Mlotek); Yoshke Fort Avek (Yoshke's Going Away) (C/L: Traditional); Yosl Ber (C: Traditional; L: Itsik Manger); Yosl, Yosl (C: Samuel Steinberg; L: Nellie Casman)

Cast: Robert Abelson; Bruce Adler; Mina Bern; Eleanor Reissa; Lori Wilner

Notes: No original songs in this production.

4343 • THOUGHTS
OPENED: 03/19/1973   Theatre: Theatre de Lys
Revue   Off-Broadway: 24

Composer: Lamar Alford
Lyricist: Lamar Alford; Jose Tapla; Megan Terry
Producer: Dallas Alinder; Seth Harrison; Arthur Whitelaw
Director: Michael Schultz

Costumes: Joseph Thomas; **Lighting Designer:** Ken Billington; **Set Design:** Stuart Wurtzel; **Vocal Arranger:** David Horowitz

Songs: Accepting the Tolls; Ain't That Something; At the Bottom of Your Heart; Bad Whitey; Blues Was a Pastime; Day Oh Day; Gone; I Can Do It to Myself; Jesus Is My Main Man; Many Men Like You [1]; Music in the Air; One of the Boys; Opening; Roofs [1]; Separate but Equal; Strange Fruit; Sunshine; Thoughts; Trying Hard; Walking in Strange New Places

Cast: Barbara Montgomery; Jeffrey Mylett; Howard Porter; Sarallen; E.H. Wright

Notes: [1] Cut after opening.

4344 • THREE AFTER THREE
Notes: *See WALK WITH MUSIC.*

4345 • THREE CHEERS
OPENED: 10/15/1928   Theatre: Globe
Musical   Broadway: 210

Composer: Ray Henderson
Lyricist: B.G. DeSylva
Librettist: R.H. Burnside; Anne Caldwell
Producer: R.H. Burnside
Director: R.H. Burnside

Choreographer: David Bennett; Mary Read; **Set Design:** Raymond Sovey; Sheldon K. Viele

Songs: Americans Are Here, The; Because You're Beautiful; Bobby and Me; Bride Bells; Gee, It's Great to Be Alive; Happy Hoboes; It's an Old

Spanish Custom (L: Lew Brown; B.G. DeSylva); Lady Luck (Smile on Me); Let's All Sing the Lard Song (C: Leslie Sarony; L: Anne Caldwell); Look Pleasant; Maybe This Is Love (L: Lew Brown; B.G. DeSylva); My Silver Tree (C: Raymond Hubbell; L: Anne Caldwell); Orange Blossom Home (C: Raymond Hubbell; L: Anne Caldwell); Pompanola (L: Lew Brown; B.G. DeSylva); Putting on the Ritz; Two Boys

Cast: Alan Edwards; Patsy Kelly; Will Rogers; Dorothy Stone

4346 • 3 FOR TONIGHT
OPENED: 04/06/1955   Theatre: Plymouth
Revue   Broadway: 85

Composer: Walter Schumann
Lyricist: Robert Wells
Director: Gower Champion

Choreographer: Gower Champion; **Dance Arranger:** Nathan Scott; **Musical Director:** Richard Pribor; **Vocal Arranger:** Nathan Scott

Songs: All You Need Is a Song; Fly Bird

Cast: Harry Belafonte; Gower Champion; Marge Champion; Hiram Sherman

4347 • 3 FROM BROOKLYN
OPENED: 11/19/1992   Theatre: Helen Hayes
Revue   Broadway: 9

Composer: Sandi Merle; Steve Michaels
Lyricist: Sandi Merle; Steve Michaels
Producer: Michael Frazier; Don Ravella; Larry Spellman
Director: Sal Richards

Lighting Designer: Phil Monat; **Musical Director:** Steve Michaels; **Set Design:** Charles E. McCarry

Cast: Bobby Alto; BQE Dancers; Roslyn Kind; Buddy Mantia; Sal Richards; Raymond Serra; Adrianne Tolsch

Notes: No songs listed in program.

4348 • THREE GRACES, THE
OPENED: 04/02/1906   Theatre: Chicago Opera
                                              House
Musical   Chicago

Composer: Safford Watters
Lyricist: Harry B. Smith
Librettist: Harry B. Smith

Notes: No other information available.

4349 • 3 GUYS NAKED FROM THE WAIST DOWN

OPENED: 02/05/1985   Theatre: Minetta Lane
Musical   Off-Broadway: 160

Composer: Michael Rupert
Lyricist: Jerry Colker
Librettist: Jerry Colker
Producer: James B. Freydberg; Max Weitzenhoffer;
Stephen Wells
Director: Andrew Cadiff

Choreographer: Don Bondi; **Costumes:** Tom
McKinley; **Lighting Designer:** Ken Billington; .
Musical Director: Henry Aronson; **Orchestrations:**
Michael Starobin; **Set Design:** Clarke Dunham

Songs: Angry Guy; Don't Wanna Be No Superstar;
Dreams of Heaven; Father Now, A; Hello Fellas;
History of Stand-Up Comedy, The; I Don't Believe
in Heroes Anymore; Kamikaze Kabaret; Lovely
Day; Operator; Promise of Greatness; Screaming
Clocks (The Dummies Song); Three Guys Naked
from the Waist Down; What a Ride

Cast: Scott Bakula; Jerry Colker; John Kassir

4350 • THREE KISSES, THE

OPENED: 01/1921
Musical

Composer: Sigmund Romberg
Director: Hassard Short

Cast: Vivienne Segal

Notes: Closed in rehearsal before opening in
Springfield, Mass.

4351 • THREE LIGHTS, THE

OPENED: 10/31/1911   Theatre: Bijou
Play   Broadway: 7

Author: Charles T. Dazey; May Robson
Producer: L.S. Sire
Director: W.H. Post

Songs: Island of Roses and Love, The (C: Neil
Moret; L: Earle C. Jones)

Cast: Edith Conrad; Paul Decker; May Robson; Jack
Storey

4352 • THREE LITTLE GIRLS

OPENED: 04/14/1930   Theatre: Shubert
Musical   Broadway: 104

Composer: Walter Kollo
Lyricist: Harry B. Smith
Librettist: Gertrude Purcell
Producer: Messrs. Shubert
Director: J.J. Shubert

Source: DREI ARME KLEINE MADELS (Musical:
Herman Feiner; Bruno Hardt-Warden; Walter
Kollo); **Costumes:** Ernest Schrapps; **Lighting
Designer:** Marie Armstrong Hecht; **Musical
Director:** Louis Kroll; **Set Design:** Watson Barratt

Songs: Annette; Cottage in the Country; Doll Song;
Dream On; I'll Tell You; Letter Song; Love
Comes Once in a Lifetime (C: Harry Perella;
Harold Stern; L: Stella Unger); Love's Happy
Dream; Prince Charming; Waltz with Me;
Whistle While You Work, Boys

Cast: Margaret Adams; George Dobbs; Thelma
Goodwin; Bettina Hall; Natalie Hall; Charles
Hedley; Martha Lorber; Stephan Mills; Harry
Puck; Raymond Walburn; Lorraine Weismar

4353 • THREE LITTLE LAMBS

OPENED: 12/25/1899   Theatre: Fifth Avenue
Musical   Broadway: 49

Composer: E.W. Corliss
Librettist: R.A. Barnet
Producer: Edwin Knowles

Set Design: Ernest Gros; Henry E. Hoyt

Cast: Marie Cahill; William T. Carleton; Lillian
Collins; Raymond Hitchcock; Clara Palmer;
William E. Philp; Adele Ritchie

4354 • THREE LITTLE MAIDS (1903)

OPENED: 09/01/1903   Theatre: Daly's
Musical   Broadway: 130

Composer: Paul Rubens
Lyricist: Paul Rubens
Librettist: Paul Rubens
Producer: George Edwardes; Charles Frohman

Musical Director: Frank E. Tours; **Set Design:** Hawes Craven; Joseph Harker

Songs: Algy's Simply Awfully Good at Algebra; Do I Like Love!; Do You Think That You Have Known Me Long Enought? (C: Walter Rubens; L: Percy Greenbank); Finale Act I (C: Howard Talbot; L: Percy Greenbank); Fishes in the Sea, The; Girl You Love, The; Girls, Girls, Girls; Golf; I'll Dream of You; I'm Only the Caddie (C: Walter Rubens; L: Percy Greenbank); Je Vous Adore; Love, You're a Wonderful Game; Me and the Post; Men; Miller's Daughter, The; My Little Girlie; Opening Chorus (C: Howard Talbot; L: Percy Greenbank); Opening Chorus Act II (C: Howard Talbot; L: Percy Greenbank); Opening Chorus Act III (C: Howard Talbot; L: Percy Greenbank); Real Town Lady, A; Sal; Something Sweet About Me; Suppose We Have a Breakdown (C: Howard Talbot; L: Percy Greenbank); That's a Very Different Thing; There Really Must Be Something Nice About Me; Three Little Maids; Town and Country Mouse, The; Wedding March; What Is a Maid to Do?

Cast: Madge Crichton; Maurice Farkoa; G.P. Huntley; Maggie May

Notes: No songs listed in program. Songs in vocal selection.

4355 • THREE LITTLE MAIDS (1930)

OPENED: 1930
Musical   Unproduced

Composer: James P. Johnson
Producer: Shubert Brothers

Notes: No other information available.

4356 • THREE MILLION DOLLARS

Notes: *See THE WIFE HUNTERS.*

4357 • THREE MUSKETEERS, THE

OPENED: 03/13/1928   Theatre: Lyric
Musical   Broadway: 319

Composer: Rudolf Friml
Lyricist: Clifford Grey; P.G. Wodehouse
Librettist: William Anthony McGuire
Producer: Florenz Ziegfeld
Director: William Anthony McGuire

Source: THREE MUSKETEERS, THE (Novel: Alexandre Dumas); **Choreographer:** Richard Boleslavsky; Albertina Rasch; **Costumes:** John W. Harkrider; **Musical Director:** Gus Salzer; **Orchestrations:** Hans Spialek; **Set Design:** Joseph Urban

Songs: Ahoy for a Sailor [1]; All for One and One for All; Ballet Romantique (inst.); Colonel and the Major, The; Danse Bohemienne (inst.); Day of the Fair [1]; Every Little While (L: Clifford Grey); Finalette; Gascony (L: Clifford Grey); Gossips; 'He' for Me, The (L: Clifford Grey); Heart of Mine (L: Clifford Grey); Kiss Before I Go, A (One Kiss) (L: Clifford Grey); Love Is the Sun (L: Clifford Grey); Low Moon [1]; Ma Belle (L: Clifford Grey); March of the Musketeers (L: P.G. Wodehouse); My Dreams (L: Clifford Grey); My Sword and I (L: Clifford Grey); Opening Chorus (L: Clifford Grey); Pages; Queen of My Heart (L: Clifford Grey); Queen's Aria [2]; Sabot Dance (inst.); Summertime; Vesper Bell; Welcome to the Queen; With Red Wine; You Walked By [1]; Your Eyes (L: P.G. Wodehouse)

Cast: Lester Allen; Clarence Derwent; Douglas Dumbrille; Harriet Hoctor; Dennis King; Reginald Owen; The Albertina Rasch Girls; Vivienne Segal; Tiller Girls, The

Notes: [1] Composed by Friml for the 1947 San Francisco revival. [2] ASCAP/Library of Congress only.

4358 • THREE POSTCARDS

OPENED: 05/14/1987   Theatre: Playwrights
                                     Horizons
Musical   Off-Broadway: 22

Composer: Craig Carnelia
Lyricist: Craig Carnelia
Librettist: Craig Lucas
Producer: Playwrights Horizons
Director: Norman Rene

Choreographer: Linda Kostalik-Boussom; **Costumes:** Walter Hicklin; **Lighting Designer:** Debra Kletter; **Set Design:** Loy Arcenas

Songs: Cast of Thousands; I'm Standing in This Room; I've Been Watching You; Minute, A [1]; Opening; Picture in the Hall, The; See How the Sun Shines; She Was K.C.; Three Postcards; What the Song Should Say

Cast: Craig Carnelia; Jane Galloway; Brad O'Hare; Maureen Silliman; Karen Trott

Notes: [1] Added to 1994 revival.

4359 • THREE ROMEOS, THE
OPENED: 11/13/1911   Theatre: Globe
Musical   Broadway: 56

Composer: Raymond Hubbell
Lyricist: R.H. Burnside
Librettist: R.H. Burnside
Producer: Dreyfuss-Fellner Co.
Director: R.H. Burnside

Songs: Along Broadway; Anabella Jerome; Between You and Me; Divorce; Education; He's Crazy; In the Spring It's Nice to Have Someone to Love; Lily and the Rose, The; Looking for a Girl Like You; Mary Ann; Matter of Experience, A; Molly Maguire; Moonlight; Off to the Matinee; Off to the Wedding; Oh, Fifth Avenue; Oh, Romeo!; Percy; She Didn't Seem to Care; Where's the Bridegroom?

Cast: Georgia Caine; William Danforth; Fritz Williams; Peggy Wood

Notes: No New York program available. Out-of-town program used.

4360 • THREE SHOWERS
OPENED: 04/05/1920   Theatre: Harris
Musical   Broadway: 45

Composer: Turner Layton
Lyricist: Henry Creamer
Librettist: William Cary Duncan
Producer: Charles Coburn; Mrs. Charles Coburn
Director: Oscar Eagle

Choreographer: Edward P. Bower; **Costumes:** Irma Campbell; **Musical Director:** Ivan Rudisill; **Orchestrations:** Will Vodery; **Set Design:** Frank Gates; E.A. Morange

Songs: Always the Fault of the Men [1]; B Is the Note; Baby Lamb [1]; Dancing Tumble-Down [2];

He Raised Everybody's Rent but Kate's; How Wonderful You Are; If, and and But; I'll Have My Way; It Must Be Love; Love Me, Sweetheart Mine; Old Love Is the True Love, The; One of the Boys; Open Your Heart; Pussy Foot; Shower; There's a Way Out; Where Is the Love?; Work Chant; You May Be the World to Your Mother [1]

Cast: Paul Frawley; Andrew J. Lawlor Jr.; Anna Wheaton; Walter Wilson

Notes: [1] Out Baltimore 3/8/20. [2] Titled "Dancing Tumble- Tom" out Baltimore.

4361 • THREE SISTERS
OPENED: 04/09/1934   Theatre: Theatre Royal,
                                      Drury Lane
Musical   London: 45

Composer: Jerome Kern
Lyricist: Oscar Hammerstein II
Librettist: Oscar Hammerstein II
Producer: H.M. Tennant
Director: Oscar Hammerstein II; Jerome Kern

Choreographer: Ralph Reader; **Costumes:** G.E. Calthrop; **Musical Director:** Charles Prentice; **Orchestrations:** Robert Russell Bennett; **Set Design:** G.E. Calthrop

Songs: Circus Queen [4]; Funny Old House; Gaiety Chorus Girls, The; Hand in Hand; Here It Comes [1]; I Won't Dance [3]; Impression of the Derby, An; Keep Smiling; Lonely Feet [2]; My Beautiful Circus Girl; Now That I Have Springtime; Roll On, Rolling Road; Somebody Wants to Go to Sleep; There's a Joy that Steals Upon You; Three Sisters Opening (Act Two); Welcome to the Bride; What Good Are Words?; What's in the Air Tonight?; You Are Doing Very Well

Cast: Adele Dixon; Dick Francis; Charlotte Greenwood; Gladys Henson; Stanley Holloway; Victoria Hopper; Esmond Knight; Eliot Makeham

Notes: [1] Cut. [2] Used later in film SWEET ADELINE. [3] Revised in 1935 with lyric by Dorothy Fields for film ROBERTA. [4] ASCAP/Library of Congress only.

4362 • THREE TO MAKE READY
OPENED: 03/07/1946   Theatre: Adelphi
Revue   Broadway: 327

Composer: Morgan Lewis
Lyricist: Nancy Hamilton
Librettist: Nancy Hamilton
Producer: Stanley Gilkey; Barbara Payne
Director: John Murray Anderson

Choreographer: Robert Sidney; **Costumes:** Audre;
  Musical Director: Anthony Morelli;
  Orchestrations: Robert Russell Bennett; Charles
  L. Cooke; Elliot Jacoby; Walter Paul; Ted Royal;
  Hans Spialek; **Set Design:** Donald Oenslager;
  Vocal Arranger: Joe Moon

Songs: And Why Not I; Barnaby Beach; Furnished
  Bed [1]; If It's Love; It's a Nice Night for It;
  Kenosha Canoe Ballet; Lovely Lazy Kind of Day,
  A; Oh You're a Wonderful Person [2]; Old Soft
  Shoe, The; Rushing the Growler [1]; Tell Me the
  Story

Cast: Brenda Forbes; Arthur Godfrey; Gordon
  MacRae

Notes: [1] Out Boston 2/7/46. [2] Not in program.

4363 • THREE TO MAKE READY (MAGIC WITH MARY MARTIN)

OPENED: 03/29/1959   Theatre: NBC
TV Musical

Composer: Linda Melnick Rogers
Lyricist: Mary Rodgers

Musical Director: Thomas Scherman

Songs: Good Afternoon; I Took a Little Walk; It
  Takes Three to Make Music; Little Orchestra,
  The; May I Present; Middle of the Night, The;
  What Kind of Audience Are You?

Cast: Mary Martin; Dirk Sanders

4364 • THREE TWINS

OPENED: 06/15/1908   Theatre: Herald Square
Musical   Broadway: 288

Composer: Karl Hoschna
Lyricist: Otto Harbach
Librettist: Charles Dickson
Producer: Joseph M. Gaites
Director: Gus Sohlke

Source: INCOQ (Play: Mrs. R. Pacheo); **Musical
  Director:** DeWitt C. Coolman

Songs: All My Girls [1] (L: Collin Davis); At a
  Reception; Begging [3]; Boo-Hoo Tee-Hee Ta
  Ha; Cuddle Up a Little Closer, Lovey Mine;
  Dear Little Game of Guessing [2]; Fifth Avenue
  Brigade, The; Gold to Make You a Queen [2];
  Good Night, Sweetheart, Good Night; Hypnotic
  Kiss, The; I Nver Lose My Head [3]; In
  Cloudland [2]; It's Up to You to Do the Rest [3];
  Little Girl Up There, The; Little Miss
  Up-to-Date; Over There; Specialist Am I [2];
  Summer Pastimes; Three Twins [2]; We Belong
  to Old Broadway [2]; What's the Use [2]; When
  Woman, Lovely Woman, Gets Her Rights [2];
  Yama Yama Man, The (Pajama Song) (L: Collin
  Davis); You Need No Crown of Gold to Make
  You a Queen [2]

Cast: Joseph Allen; Clifton Crawford; Bessie
  McCoy

Notes: [1] Out of town 10/18/08. [2] Not used. [3]
  Sheet music only.

4365 • THREE WALTZES

OPENED: 12/25/1937   Theatre: Majestic
Musical   Broadway: 122

Composer: Oscar Straus
Lyricist: Clare Kummer
Librettist: Clare Kummer; Rowland Leigh
Producer: Messrs. Shubert
Director: Hassard Short

Source: DREI WALZER (Opera: Paul Knepler;
  Armin Robinson); **Choreographer:** Chester Hale;
  Costumes: Connie DePinna, **Musical Director:**
  Harold Levey; **Orchestrations:** Hilding
  Anderson; Conrad Salinger; Don Walker; **Set
  Design:** Watson Barratt

Songs: Ballet Rehearsal; Can-Can, The (Music
  Based On: Johann Strauss Sr.); Do You Recall?
  (Music Based On: Johann Strauss Sr.); History of
  Three Generations of Chorus Girls, The; I Some-
  times Wonder; I'll Can-Can All Day (Music
  Based On: Johann Strauss Jr.); My Heart Controls
  My Head (Music Based On: Johann Strauss Sr.);
  Olden Days, The; Only One, The (Music Based
  On: Johann Strauss Jr.); Opening (Music Based
  On: Johann Strauss Sr.); Our Last Waltz
  Together; Paree (Music Based On: Johann Strauss

Jr.); Radetzky March; Scandal (Music Based On: Johann Strauss Jr.); Sextette (Music Based On: Johann Strauss Sr.); Springtime Is in the Air (Music Based On: Johann Strauss Sr.); Three Waltzes, The; To Live Is to Love (Music Based On: Johann Strauss Jr.); Vienna Gossip (Music Based On: Johann Strauss Sr.)

Cast: Glenn Anders; Ann Andrews; Charlie Arnt; John Barker; Michael Bartlett; Kitty Carlisle; Ruth Hammond; Jayne Manners; Harry Mestayer; Rosie Moran; Victor Morley; Marion Pierce; Ivy Scott; Louis Sorin; Marguerita Sylva

4366 • THREE WISHES FOR JAMIE

OPENED: 03/21/1952   Theatre: Mark Hellinger
Musical   Broadway: 91

Composer: Ralph Blane
Lyricist: Ralph Blane
Librettist: Abe Burrows; Charles O'Neal
Producer: Albert Lewis; Arthur Lewis
Director: Abe Burrows

Source: THREE WISHES FOR JAMIE (Novel: Charles O'Neal); **Choreographer:** Ted Cappy; **Costumes:** Miles White; **Lighting Designer:** Feder; **Musical Director:** Joseph Littau; **Orchestrations:** Robert Russell Bennett; **Set Design:** George Jenkins; **Vocal Arranger:** William Ellfeldt

Songs: April Face; Army Mule Song, The; Expectant Father Dance (inst.) (C: Lee Pockriss); Girl That I Court in My Mind, The; Goin' on a Hayride; I'll Sing You a Song; It Must Be Spring; It's a Wishing World; Jamie's Responsibilities [1]; Kevin [2]; Love Has Nothing to Do with Looks (L: Charles Lederer); Magic Tree [2]; Maybe Is a Woman's Word [1]; My Heart's Darlin'; My Home's a Highway (Sunday Night Supper); Owen Roe [1]; People Talk Too Much [2]; Saint Patrick's Prayer [2]; Search, The [2]; Take Comfort [2]; 'Tis a Wonderful Thing in Nature [1]; Trottin' to the Fair; Wake, The; We're for Love; Wedding March, The; What Do I Know?; Woman's Work, A [2]

Cast: Peter Conlow; Anne Jeffreys; Charlotte Rae; John Raitt; Bert Wheeler

Notes: [1] Out San Francisco 7/30/51. [2] ASCAP/Library of Congress only.

4367 • THREE'S A CROWD

OPENED: 10/15/1930   Theatre: Selwyn
Revue   Broadway: 272

Composer: Arthur Schwartz
Lyricist: Howard Dietz
Librettist: Fred Allen; Donald Blackwell; Howard Dietz; Corey Ford; Groucho Marx; William Miles; Laurence Schwab; Arthur Sheekman
Producer: Max Gordon
Director: Hassard Short

Choreographer: Albertina Rasch; **Costumes:** Kiviette; **Musical Director:** Nicholas Kempner; **Set Design:** Albert Johnson

Songs: All the King's Horses (C/L: Eddie Brandt; C: Alec Wilder); Body and Soul (C: John Green; L: Howard Dietz; Frank Eyton; Edward Heyman; Robert Sour); Forget All Your Books [3] (C: Burton Lane); Je T'Aime; Moment I Saw You, The [1]; Night After Night; Out in the Open Air [4] (C: Burton Lane); Practising Up on You (C: Philip Charig); Right at the Start of It; Something to Remember You By [2]; Talkative Toes (C: Vernon Duke); Yaller (C: Charles M. Schwab; L: Henry Myers)

Cast: Fred Allen; California Collegians, The; Tamara Geva; Portland Hoffa; Libby Holman; Margaret Lee; Earl Oxford; Amy Revere; Clifton Webb

Notes: Fred MacMurray was a member of The California Collegians. [1] In London show THE CO-OPTIMISTS OF 1930 with lyrics also credited to Greatrex Newman. [2] Music also used for "I Have No Words" from LITTLE TOMMY TUCKER. [3] Dietz rewrote Sam Lerner's original lyric. [4] Dietz rewrote Ted Pola's original lyric.

4368 • THREEPENNY OPERA, THE (1933)

OPENED: 04/13/1933   Theatre: Empire
Musical   Broadway: 12

Composer: Kurt Weill
Lyrics Based On: Bertolt Brecht
Librettist: Gifford Cochran
Producer: Gifford Cochran; Jerrold Krimsky
Director: Francesco von Mendelssohn

Source: BEGGAR'S OPERA, THE (Opera: John Gay); **Source:** DIE DREIGROSCHENOPER

(Musical: Bertolt Brecht; Kurt Weill); **English Lyrics:** Gifford Cochran; Jerrold Krimsky; **Musical Director:** Macklin Marrow; **Orchestrations:** Kurt Weill; **Set Design:** Caspar Neber; Cleon Throckmorton

Songs: Balled of the Easy Life, The; Cry from the Dungeon; Farewell Tango; First Finale; Jealousy Duet; Legend of Mackie Messer; Love Duet; Lucy's Song; Pirate Jenny; Poor Mrs. Peachum [1] (L: Yvette Guilbert); Second Finale; Soldier's Song, The; Song of the Aimlessness of Life; Tango Ballad; Testament; Third Finale; Wedding Song

Cast: Harry Belaver; Evelyn Beresford; Robert Chisholm; Marjorie Dille; Steffi Duna; Rex Evans; George Heller; Josephine Huston; Burgess Meredith; Herbert Rudlev; Rex Weber

Notes: *See also THE THREEPENNY OPERA 1954 and 1976 as well as 3 PENNY OPERA (1989).* [1] Written for Paris production.

4369 • THREEPENNY OPERA, THE (1954)

OPENED: 03/10/1954   Theatre: Theatre de Lys
Musical   Off-Broadway: 2705

Composer: Kurt Weill
Lyrics Based On: Bertolt Brecht
Librettist: Marc Blitzstein
Producer: Carmen Capalbo; Stanley Chase
Director: Carmen Capalbo

Source: BEGGAR'S OPERA, THE (Opera: John Gay); **Source:** DIE DREIGROSCHENOPER (Musical: Bertolt Brecht; Kurt Weill); **English Lyrics:** Marc Blitzstein; **Musical Director:** Samuel Matlowsky; **Orchestrations:** Kurt Weill

Songs: Army Song; Ballad of Dependency; Ballad of Mack the Knife, The; Ballad of the Easy Life; Barbara Song; Bide-a-Wee in Soho, The; Call from the Grave; Death Message; How to Survive; Instead-of Song; Love Song; Morning Anthem; Mounted Messenger, The; Pirate Jenny; Polly's Song; Solomon Song; Tango-Ballad; Useless Song; Wedding Song; World Is Mean, The

Cast: Beatrice Arthur; John Astin; Joseph Beruh; Bernard Bogin; Paul Dooley; Lotte Lenya; Scott Merrill; Gerald Price; Charlotte Rae; Jo Sullivan; George Tyne; Martin Wolfson

Notes: The first run of this production played 94 performances. It then reopened on 9/30/55 for an additional 2,611 performances. *See also THE THREEPENNY OPERA 1933 and 1976 and 3 PENNY OPERA (1989).*

4370 • THREEPENNY OPERA, THE (1976)

OPENED: 05/01/1976   Theatre: Vivian Beaumont
Musical   Off-Broadway: 306

Composer: Kurt Weill
Lyrics Based On: Bertolt Brecht
Librettist: Ralph Manheim; John Willett
Producer: N.Y. Shakespeare Festival; Joseph Papp
Director: Richard Foreman

Source: BEGGAR'S OPERA, THE (Opera: John Gay); **Source:** DIE DREIGROSCHENOPER (Musical: Bertolt Brecht; Kurt Weill); **English Lyrics:** Ralph Manheim; John Willett; **Costumes:** Theoni V. Aldredge; **Lighting Designer:** Pat Collins; **Musical Director:** Stanley Silverman; **Set Design:** Douglas W. Schmidt

Songs: Ballad in Which Macheath Begs All Men for Forgiveness; Ballad of Gracious Living; Ballad of Immoral Earnings; Ballad of Mac the Knife; Ballad of Sexual Obsession; Barbara Song; Call from the Grave; Cannon Song; First Threepenny Finale; Jealousy Duet; Liebeslied; "No They Can't" Song; Peachum's Morning Hymn; Pirate Jenny; Polly's Lied; Second Threepenny Finale; Solomon Song; Song of the Insufficiency of Human Endeavor; Third Threepenny Finale; Wedding Song for the Less Well-Off

Cast: C.K. Alexander; Tony Azito; Roy Brocksmith; Blair Brown; Ellen Greene; Raul Julia; Caroline Kava; Elizabeth Wilson; K.C. Wilson

Notes: No songs listed in program. *See also THE THREEPENNY OPERA 1933 and 1954 as well as 3 PENNY OPERA (1989).*

4371 • 3 PENNY OPERA, THE (1989)

OPENED: 11/05/1989   Theatre: Lunt-Fontanne
Musical   Broadway: 65

Composer: Kurt Weill
Lyrics Based On: Bertolt Brecht
Librettist: Michael Feinstein

Producer: Jerome Hellman
Director: John Dexter

Source: BEGGAR'S OPERA, THE (Opera: John Gay); **English Lyrics:** Michael Feinstein; **Choreographer:** Peter Gennaro; **Costumes:** Jocelyn Herbert; **Lighting Designer:** Brian Nason; Andy Phillips; **Musical Director:** Julius Rudel; **Orchestrations:** Julius Rudel; Kurt Weill; **Set Design:** Jocelyn Herbert

Songs: Ballad of Living in Style; Ballad of Mack the Knife (Moritat); Ballad of the Prisoner of Sex; Barbara Song; Call from the Grave; Epitaph; First 3 Penny Finale; Jealousy Duet; Love Song; Lucy's Aria; March to the Gallows; Melodrama and Polly's Song; Peachum's Morning Hymn; Pimp's Ballad (Tango); Pirate Jenny; Second 3 Penny Finale; Soldiers' Song; Solomon Song; Song of Futility; Third 3 Penny Finale; Wedding Song; Why Can't They Song

Cast: Jeff Blumenkrantz; Georgia Brown; Kim Criswell; Suzanne Douglas; Ethyl Eichelberger; Alvin Epstein; Mitchell Greenberg; Larry Marshall; Maureen McGovern; Josh Mostel; Nancy Ringham; Philip Schechter; Sting; K.T. Sullivan

Notes: *See also THE THREEPENNY OPERA 1933, 1954 and 1976.*

4372 • THROUGH THE YEARS

OPENED: 01/28/1931   Theatre: Manhattan
Musical   Broadway: 20

Composer: Vincent Youmans
Lyricist: Edward Heyman
Librettist: Brian Hooker
Producer: Vincent Youmans
Director: Edgar MacGregor

Source: SMILIN' THROUGH (Play: Jane Cowl; Langdon Martin); **Choreographer:** Jack Haskell; Max Scheck; **Costumes:** John Booth; **Musical Director:** William Daly; **Orchestrations:** Deems Taylor; **Set Design:** Ward & Harvey

Songs: An Invitation; Drums in My Heart; Finaletto Act II; He and I [2]; How Happy Is the Bride; I'll Come Back to You; Invitation, An [5]; It's Every Girl's Ambition [1]; Kathleen, Mine; Kinda Like You; Love Cannot Die [3]; My Heart Is Young [3]; Road to Home, The [4]; Through

the Years; Trumpeter and the Lover, The; You're Everywhere; You're in Love [3]

Cast: Michael Bartlett; Gregory Gaye; Natalie Hall; Nick Long Jr.; Marsha Mason; Leone Neumann; Reginald Owen; Charles Winninger

Notes: Titled LOVE IS ALL in Washington, D.C. prior to New York. Titled SMILIN' THROUGH in Philadelphia 12/28/31. [1] Same music as "Daughters" cut from A NIGHT OUT. [2] Cut in rehearsal. [3] Cut during tryout. [4] Same music as "If I Told You" in WILDFLOWER, "Virginia" in RAINBOW and "Sweet Sugar Cane" in GREAT DAY. [5] ASCAP/Library of Congress only.

4373 • THUMBS UP! (1926)

OPENED: 1926
Musical   Closed out of town

Composer: Jean Schwartz
Lyricist: George Marion Jr.

Songs: Boarding House Love Call; Cottage I Call Je T'Aime; Cute Peekin' Knees; Do a Duet; Fatal Blonde; Gentlemen of the Press; Guess-Yes; I'm a Little Movie Queen; Journey's End; Just a Little Extra; Ladies, The; Laugh at Love; Never Say Never; Reba; Saturday Night; Stares that Lead to Love; Studio Stamp; Thumbs Up

Notes: No program available. Information from ASCAP and Library of Congress.

4374 • THUMBS UP! (1934)

OPENED: 12/27/1934   Theatre: St. James
Revue   Broadway: 156

Librettist: Alan Baxter; Ronald Jeans; Ballard Macdonald; H.I. Phillips; Charles Sherman
Producer: Eddie Dowling
Director: John Murray Anderson; Edward Clarke Lilley

Choreographer: Robert Alton; **Costumes:** Thomas Becher; James Morcon; Raoul Pene du Bois; James Reynolds; **Musical Director:** Gene Salzer; **Orchestrations:** David Raksin; Conrad Salinger; Hans Spialek; **Set Design:** Ted Weidhaus

Songs: Autumn in New York (C/L: Vernon Duke); Beautiful Night (C: James F. Hanley; L: Ballard Macdonald; Karl Stark); Catherine the Great

(C: Henry Sullivan); Color Blind (C: Henry Sullivan; L: Earle Crooker); Continental Honeymoon (C/L: James F. Hanley; L: Ballard Macdonald); Eileen Avourneen (C: Henry Sullivan; L: John Murray Anderson); Flamenco (C: Henry Sullivan; L: Earle Crooker); I've Gotta See a Man About His Daughter (C/L: James F. Hanley; Jean Herbert; Karl Stark); Jogging Along Thru the Park (C: James F. Hanley; L: Ballard Macdonald; Karl Stark); Lily Belle May June (C: Henry Sullivan; L: Earl Crooker); Merrily We Waltz Along (C: Henry Sullivan; L: Earle Crooker); Merry Widow Music without Words, The; Musical Chairs; My Arab Complex (C: James F. Hanley; L: Ballard Macdonald); My Girl's Gone Screwy Over Huey [1]; My Personal Rainbow (C/L: James F. Hanley; Arthur Swanstrom); Rehearsal Hall (C: Henry Sullivan); Ship's Concert, The (C: Henry Sullivan; L: Earle Crooker); Soldier of Love (C: Gerald Marks; L: Irving Caesar; Sammy Lerner); Tango Rhythm (C: Steve Child); Taste of the Sea, A (C: Henry Sullivan; L: Earle Crooker); Time and Tide; Torch Singer (What Do You Think My Heart Is Made Of?) (C: Henry Sullivan; L: Earle Crooker); Zing! Went the Strings of My Heart (C/L: James F. Hanley)

Cast: Margaret Adams; Sheila Barrett; Hugh Cameron; Bobby Clark; Jack Cole; Ray Dooley; Eddie Dowling; Paul Draper; Alice Dudley; John Fearnley; Eddie Garr; Eunice Healey; Rose King; Hal LeRoy; Irene McBride; Paul McCullough; J. Harold Murray; Barnett Parker; Pickens Sisters, The; Al Sexton; Billie Worth

Notes: Originally titled THE FATAL BLONDE. [1] Added after opening.

4375 • TICK-TACK-TOE

OPENED: 02/23/1920　Theatre: Princess
Revue　　　　　　　Broadway: 32

Composer: Herman Timberg
Lyricist: Herman Timberg
Librettist: Herman Timberg
Producer: Herman Timberg

Costumes: Homer Conant; **Musical Director:** William A. Krauth; **Set Design:** Watson Barratt

Songs: Chinese-American Rag; Dardanella Blues, The (C: John S. Black; L: Fred Fisher); Double Order of Chicken, A; Girls, Girls, Girls; Hoppy Poppy Queen; I Fell in Love with You; My Manicure Maids; Take Me Back to Philadelphia, Pa.

Cast: Pearl Eaton; Jay Gould; Flo Lewis; Herman Timberg

Notes: No program available. Newspaper review at time said show had 23 numbers.

4376 • TICKETS PLEASE (1916)

OPENED: 04/03/1916
Musical　　　　　　Closed out of town

Composer: William B. Friedlander
Librettist: Will M. Hough

Notes: Played Wheeling, West Virginia at the Victoria Theater.

4377 • TICKETS PLEASE! (1950)

OPENED: 04/27/1950　Theatre: Coronet
Revue　　　　　　　Broadway: 245

Composer: Lyn Duddy; Joan Edwards
Lyricist: Lyn Duddy; Joan Edwards
Librettist: Harry Herrmann; Ted Luce; Edmund Rice; Jack Roche
Producer: Arthur Klein
Director: Mervyn Nelson

Choreographer: Joan Mann; **Costumes:** Peggy Morrison; **Incidental Music:** Harold Hastings; Phil Ingalls; **Musical Director:** Phil Ingalls; **Orchestrations:** Ted Royal; **Set Design:** Ralph Alswang

Songs: Back at the Palace (C: Clay Warnick; L: Lucille Kallen; Mel Tolin); Darn It Baby, That's Love; Maha Roger (C: Clay Warnick; L: Lucille Kallen; Mel Tolin); Moment I Looked in Your Eyes, The; Restless; Tickets Please (C: Clay Warnick; L: Lucille Kallen; Mel Tolkin); Washington Square (C: Clay Warnick; L: Lucille Kallen; Mel Tolkin); You Can't Take It with You

Cast: Jack Albertson; Grace Hartman; Paul Hartman; Dorothy Jarnac; Larry Kert; Roger Price; Tommy Wonder

4378 • TICKLE ME

OPENED: 08/17/1920　Theatre: Selwyn
Musical　　　　　　Broadway: 207

Composer: Herbert Stothart
Lyricist: Oscar Hammerstein II; Otto Harbach
Librettist: Oscar Hammerstein II; Otto Harbach; Frank Mandel
Producer: Arthur Hammerstein
Director: William Collier

Choreographer: Bert French; **Costumes:** Charles LeMaire; **Musical Director:** Herbert Stothart; **Set Design:** Joseph Physioc

Songs: Bones [1]; Broadway Swell and Bowery Bum; Ceremony, The; Come Across [1]; Didja Ever See the Like? [1]; Famous You and Simple Me [1]; Finaletto Act I; I Don't Laugh at Love Any More; If a Wish Could Make It So; India Rubber [1]; Little Hindoo Man; Log of the Ship, The [1]; Perfect Lover, The; Safe in the Arms of Bill Hart; Sun Is Nigh, The; Tears of Love [1]; Temptation; Then Love Again; Tickle Me; Tragedy and Comedy [1]; Until You Say Goodbye; Valse du Salon; We've Got Something; You Never Know What a Kiss Can Mean [1]; You're the Type

Cast: Louise Allen; Vic Casmore; Allen Kearns; Frank Tinney; Marguerite Zender

Notes: [1] Cut.

4379 • TICKLES BY TUCHOLSKY

OPENED: 04/26/1976   Theatre: Theatre Four
Musical   Off-Broadway: 16

Composer: Kurt Tucholsky
Lyricist: Kurt Tucholsky
Librettist: Kurt Tucholsky
Producer: Primavera Productions; Norman Stephens
Director: Moni Yakim

Costumes: A. Christina Giannini; **Lighting Designer:** Spencer Mosse; **Musical Director:** Wolfgang Knittel; **Set Design:** Don Jensen; **Vocal Arranger:** Wolfgang Knittel

Songs: Anna Louisa; Christmas Shopping; Come Avec!; Compromise Soft Shoe; Epilogue; Follow Schmidt; General! General!; German Evening; Heartbeat; How to Get Rich; I'm Out; It's Your Turn; King's Regiment; Lovers; Lullaby; Over the Trenches; Rising Expectations; Song of Indifference, The; Tickles; To You I Gave My All; Waiting; War Against War

Cast: Helen Gallagher; Jerry Jarrett; Joe Masiell; Joseph Neal; Jana Robbins

Notes: Translated and adapted by Louis Golden and Harold Poor.

4380 • TIGER RAG, THE

OPENED: 02/16/1961   Theatre: Cherry Lane
Musical   Off-Broadway: 14

Composer: Kenneth Gaburo
Lyricist: Seyril Schochen
Librettist: Seyril Schochen
Producer: Lorin Ellington Price; Tira Productions
Director: Ella Gerber

Choreographer: Peter Conlow; **Costumes:** Bobb Nichols; **Lighting Designer:** Jules Fisher; **Musical Director:** Milton Seltzer; **Set Design:** Robert Soule

Songs: Apache; Cheerio, Old Boys; Flirtation Waltz; Flowery Waltz; Honeysuckle Vine; Irish Washerwoman's Lament; My Father Was a Peculiar Man; Razz-Me-Tazz-Jazz; Rhumba; Slewfoot Shuffle; Tango; Tiger Rag Blues; Travelling Song; We Were Born By Chance; What Is Good for Depression

Cast: Arthur Anderson; Nancy Andrews; Carlton Colyer; Brennan Moore; Patricia Roe

4381 • TIK TOK MAN OF OZ, THE

OPENED: 06/23/1913
Musical   Closed out of town

Composer: Louis F. Gottschalk
Lyricist: L. Frank Baum
Librettist: L. Frank Baum
Producer: Oliver Morosco
Director: Frank Stammers

Source: TIK TOK MAN OF OZ, THE (Novel: L. Frank Baum); **Musical Director:** Victor Schertzinger; **Set Design:** Robert Brunton

Songs: Apple's the Cause of It All, An [1]; Army of Oogaboo, The; Ask the Flowers to Tell You; Clockwork Man, The; Dear Old Hank; Folly!; Gardeners' Chorus; I Think an Awful Lot of You; I Want to Be Somebody's Girlie [1] (C/L: Victor Schertzinger); I've Lost My Bow; Just for Fun; Magnet of Love, The [1]; March of the White and

Gold Imps; My Wonderful Dream Girl [2]
(C: Victor Schertzinger; L: Oliver Morosco);
Rainbow Bride [1]; Shaggy Man, The; So Do I!;
Storm at Sea, A; Summer Rain; There's a Mate in
This Big World for You; Waltz Scream, The [1];
Watch Me Close; When in Trouble Come to Papa
[1]; Whirlwind, The; Work, Lads, Work!; You
Remind Me of My Old Dad

Cast: Josie Intropodi; Thomas Meegan; Lenora
Novasio; Adele Rowland; Joseph Whitehead;
Fred Woodward

Notes: [1] Sheet music only. [2] Interpolated.

4382 • TILLIE'S NIGHTMARE

OPENED: 05/05/1910   Theatre: Herald Square
Musical   Broadway: 77

Composer: A. Baldwin Sloane
Lyricist: Edgar Smith
Librettist: Edgar Smith
Producer: Lew Fields
Director: Ned Wayburn

Costumes: Melville Ellis; **Musical Director:** George
A. Nichols; **Set Design:** John H. Young

Songs: Be-Bee; Come One Come All [1]; Dream
Song [2]; Every Pretty Girl; Flight of the Air Ship;
Good Little Kiddies [2]; Heaven Will Protect the
Working Girl; Here's the Latest Thing [1]; Hustle
Bustle [1]; I Want to Bring You a Ring (C/L: John
Golden); If I Could Find Another Place Like
That [2]; I'm Little Bo Peep [2]; I'm Tight [2]; In
Paree [2]; It's Hard to Love Just One Girl All the
Time [2]; It's the Dress That Makes the Girl [1];
Jazzbo the Jazz King [1]; Life Among the Roses [2];
Life Is Only What You Make It, After All; Little
Girl Like You, A [2]; Mother Goose's School [2];
My Dainty Mermaid [2]; Old Gentlemen's Jazz [1];
On Broadway at Night [3]; Shipboard Frolics;
Shopping; Shopping Glide, The; Spook Dance;
There Goes Another One [3]; There He Goes;
They're Off [2]; Tillie's Nightmare; We're the
Noble Army [2]; Wedding Rehearsal, The; What
I Could Do on the Stage; When I Struck New
York [2]; White Light Lane

Cast: Octavia Broske; Marie Dressler; May
Montford; Horace Newman; Lottie Uart

Notes: [1] Out Wilkes-Barre 1/21/20. [2] Out
Chicago 1/2/10. [3] Out New York 10/16/11.

4383 • TIMBUKTU!

OPENED: 03/01/1978   Theatre: Mark Hellinger
Musical   Broadway: 243

Music Based On: Alexander Borodin
Composer: George Forrest; Robert Wright
Lyricist: George Forrest; Robert Wright
Librettist: Luther Davis
Producer: Luther Davis
Director: Geoffrey Holder

Source: KISMET (Play: Edward Knoblock; Charles
Lederer); **Source:** KISMET (Musical: Luther
Davis; George Forrest; Robert Wright);
Choreographer: Geoffrey Holder; **Costumes:**
Geoffrey Holder; **Lighting Designer:** Ian
Calderon; **Musical Director:** Charles H.
Coleman; **Orchestrations:** Bill Brohn; **Set
Design:** Tony Straiges

Songs: And This Is My Beloved [4]; Baubles,
Bangles and Beads [4]; Fate [4]; Fly Away (The
Kite Song) [1] (C: George Forrest; Robert
Wright); Gesticulate [4]; Golden Land, Golden
Life [3]; In the Beginning, Woman [3] (C: George
Forrest; Robert Wright); Massa Marries Tonight
(Nuptial Celebration), The (dance); My Magic
Lamp [2]; Night of My Nights [4]; Power [1]
(C: George Forrest; Robert Wright); Rahadlakum
[3] (C: George Forrest; Robert Wright); Rhymes
Have I [4]; Sands of Time [4]; Stranger in
Paradise [4]; Zubbediya [4]

Cast: Ira Hawkins; Eartha Kitt; Eleanor McCoy;
Melba Moore; Gilbert Price

Notes: Based on the musical KISMET. *See
KISMET.* [1] Cut prior to opening. Not based on
Borodin's music. [2] Cut from KISMET. [3] Not
based on Borodin's music. [4] From KISMET.

4384 TIME FOR SINGING, A

OPENED: 05/21/1966   Theatre: Broadway
Musical   Broadway: 41

Composer: John Morris
Lyricist: Gerald Freedman; John Morris
Librettist: Gerald Freedman; John Morris
Producer: Alexander H. Cohen
Director: Gerald Freedman

Source: HOW GREEN WAS MY VALLEY (Novel:
Richard Llewellyn); **Choreographer:** Donald
McKayle; **Costumes:** Theoni V. Aldredge;

Lighting Designer: Jean Rosenthal; **Musical Director:** Jay Blackton; **Orchestrations:** Don Walker; **Set Design:** Ming Cho Lee

Songs: And the Mountains Sing Back; Come You Men; Far From Home; Gone in Sorrow; Here Come Your Men; How Green Was My Valley; I Wonder If; I'm Always Wrong; I've Got Nothing to Give; Let Me Love You; Oh, How I Adore Your Name; Old Long John; Peace Come to Every Heart; Someone Must Try; Tell Her; That's What Young Ladies Do; There Is Beautiful You Are; Three Ships; Time for Singing, A; What a Good Day Is Saturday; What a Party; When He Looks at Me; When the Baby Comes; Why Would Anyone Want to Get Married

Cast: Ivor Emmanuel; Frank Griso; George Hearn; Elizabeth Hubbard; Laurence Naismith; Tessie O'Shea; Gene Rupert; Shani Wallis

4385 • TIME GOES BY

Notes: *See SARAFINA (1970).*

4386 • TIME REMEMBERED

OPENED: 11/12/1957   Theatre: Morosco
Play   Broadway: 247

Composer: Vernon Duke
Lyricist: Vernon Duke
Author: Jean Anouilh
Translator: Patricia Noyes
Producer: Playwrights' Company, The; Milton Sperling
Director: Albert Marre

Costumes: Miles White; **Lighting Designer:** Feder; **Set Design:** Oliver Smith

Songs: Ages Ago; Time Remembered

Cast: Glenn Anders; Sig Arno; Richard Burton; Helen Hayes; Le Roi Operti; Susan Strasberg

4387 • TIME, THE PLACE AND THE GIRL, THE

OPENED: 08/05/1907   Theatre: Wallack
Musical   Broadway: 32

Composer: Joseph E. Howard
Lyricist: Frank Adams; Will M. Hough
Librettist: Frank Adams; Will M. Hough

Producer: Mort H. Singer
Director: Ned Wayburn

Songs: Along Life's Highway [3] (L: G. Swarthart; I. Tressler); Blow the Smoke Away; Dixie, I Love You; Don't You Tell; First and Only [1]; I Don't Like Your Family; I Want a Thrill [3] (L: G. Swarthart; I. Tressler); It's Lonesome Tonight; Junior Miss (L: William B. Friedlander); Love Is a Will-O-the-Wisp (L: William B. Friedlander); Opening Chorus; Pop Step Melody [3] (L: I.R. Goodman); Someone Waiting for Me [3] (L: I.R. Goodman); That's What a Fellow Does When He's In Love [2] (L: Joseph E. Howard); Thursday Is My Jonah Day; Travelin' Man (L: William B. Friedlander); Uncle Sam's Best Girl [1]; Waning Honeymoon, The

Cast: Arthur Deagon; Florence Holbrook; Cecil Lean; Olive Vail

Notes: [1] Out New Bedford 9/28/07. [2] Out Wilkes-Barre 10/26/10. Written for THE FLOWER OF THE RANCH. [3] ASCAP/Library of Congress only.

4388 • TIMOTHY GRAY'S TABOO REVUE

OPENED: 1959   Theatre: Showplace, The
Musical   Nightclub

Composer: Warren B. Meyers
Lyricist: Jerry De Bono; Timothy Gray
Producer: Robert Fletcher; Timothy Gray
Director: Timothy Gray

Choreographer: Robert Haddad; **Set Design:** Robert Fletcher

Songs: Come of Age (C: Dolores Clamen); Counter Melody [1] (C: Mary Rodgers; Jay Thompson; L: Marshall Barer); Cream of Mississippi (C: David Baker; L: Sheldon Harnick); Go Away (C: Dolores Clamen); Just Plain Will (C/L: Bill Angelos; Lan O'Kun); Kaleidoscope (C: Dolores Clamen); Kismet Quick (C: Dolores Clamen); Kite, The (C: Dolores Clamen); Lollipop (C/L: Lan O'Kun); Love on the Street (L: Robert A. Bernstein); Man, A (C: Dolores Clamen); Oscar (C/L: Ralph Blane; C: Hugh Martin; L: Timothy Gray); Part of Me (L: Robert A. Bernstein); Plea for Understanding, A (C: Hugh Martin; L: Timothy Gray); Revue Hoedown (C: Dolores

Clamen); This Way Out (C: Dolores Clamen); Triple Tango (C: Dolores Clamen); Two Graces, The (C: Dolores Clamen)

Cast: Don Crichton; Sheila Smith

Notes: [1] Also in FROM A TO Z.

4389 • TINSELTOWN

OPENED: 03/20/1981   Theatre: Shepard
Musical   Los Angeles: 24

Composer: Mark Milner
Lyricist: Mark Milner
Librettist: John Vornaholt

Musical Director: Steven Applegate

Songs: Apartmento; Bozo Allegro; Buzz!!!; Commercials, Commercials; Hand Me Down My Dancin' Shoes; Life in the Theatre; SAG Card Blues; Screwing My Way to the Top; Showbiz Finale; This Could Be My Lucky Day; What About Today?; What's 3000 Miles?; Ya Gotta Have a Car

Cast: Diane Benedict; Lynda Lyons; David Pavlosky

Notes: No program available.

4390 • TINTYPES

OPENED: 04/17/1980   Theatre: John Golden
Revue   Broadway: 230

Producer: Ivan Bloch; Richmond Crinkley; Royal Pardon Productions; Larry J. Silva; Eve Skina
Director: Gary Pearle

Choreographer: Mary Kyte; **Costumes:** Jess Goldstein; **Dance Arranger:** Mel Marvin; **Lighting Designer:** Paul Gallo; **Orchestrations:** John McKinney; **Set Design:** Tom Lynch; **Vocal Arranger:** Mel Marvin; John McKinney

Songs: America the Beautiful (C: Samuel Ward; L: Katherine Lee Bates); American Beauty (inst.) (C: Joseph F. Lamb); Ay, Lye, Luy, Lye (C/L: Traditional); Ballin' the Jack [1] (C: Chris Smith; L: Jim Burris); Berthena (inst.) (C: Scott Joplin); Bill Bailey, Won't You Please Come Home (C/L: Hughie Cannon); Bird in a Gilded Cage, A (C: Harry Von Tilzer; L: Arthur Lamb); Come

Take a Trip in My Airship (C: Ren Shields; L: George Evans); Daisy Bell (C/L: Harry Dacre); El Capitan (inst.) (C: John Philip Sousa); Electricity (C: Karl Hoschna; L: Harry B. Smith); Elite Syncopation (C: Scott Joplin); Eugenia (inst.) (C: Scott Joplin); Fifty-Fifty (C: Chris Smith; L: James Burris); Hello, Ma Baby (C/L: Ida Emerson; Joseph E. Howard); Hot Time in the Old Town Tonight, A (C: Theodore M. Metz; L: Joe Hayden); I Don't Care (C: Jean Lenox; L: Harry O. Sutton); I Want What I Want When I Want It (C: Victor Herbert; L: Henry Blossom); Ida, Sweet As Apple Cider [1] (C/L: Eddie Leonard); If I Were on the Stage (Kiss Me Again) (C: Victor Herbert; L: Henry Blossom); I'll Take You Home Again, Kathleen (C: Thomas P. Westendorf); I'm Goin' to Live Anyhow, 'Til I Die (C/L: Shepard N. Edmonds); In My Merry Oldsmobile (C: Gus Edwards; L: Vincent J. Bryan); Iron Horse [1]; It's Delightful to Be Married (C: Vincent Scotto; L: Anna Held); Jonah Man (C/L: Alex Rogers); Kentucky Babe (C/L: Richard H. Buck; Adam Gelbel); Maiden with the Dreamy Eyes, The (C: Bob Cole; L: James Weldon Johnson); Meet Me in St. Louis, Louis (C: Kerry Mills; L: Andrew B. Sterling); Narcissus (inst.) (C: Ethelbert Nevin); Nobody (C: Bert Williams; L: Alex Rogers); Pastime Rag (inst.) (C: Artie Matthews); Ragtime Dance, The (inst.) (C: Scott Joplin); Ragtime Nightingale (inst.) (C: Joseph F. Lamb); She's Getting More Like the White Folks Every Day (C: Bert Williams; L: George Walker); Shine on Harvest Moon (C/L: Jack Norworth; L: Nora Bayes); Shortnin' Bread (C/L: Traditional); Smiles (C: Lee S. Roberts; L: J. Will Callahan); Solace (inst.) (C: Scott Joplin); Soldiers in the Park, The (C: Lionel Monckton; L: Harry Greenbank; Aubrey Hapwood); Sometimes I Feel Like a Motherless Child (C/L: Traditional); St. Louis Blues [1] (C/L: W.C. Handy); Stars and Stripes Forever (inst.) (C: John Philip Sousa); Streets of New York, The [1] (C: Victor Herbert; L: Henry Blossom); Strike Up the Band [1] (C: George Gershwin; L: Ira Gershwin); Ta-Ra-Ra-Boom-Dee-Ay! (C/L: Henry J. Sayers); Teddy De Roose (C: J. Fred Helf; L: Ed Moran); Then I'd Be Satisfied with Life (C/L: George M. Cohan); Toyland (C: Victor Herbert; L: Glen MacDonough); Wabash Cannonball (inst.) (C: Traditional); Wait for the Wagon (C/L: Traditional); Waltz Me Around Again, Willie (C: Ren Shields; L: Will D. Cobb); Wayfaring Stranger (C/L: Traditional); We Shall Not Be Moved (C/L: Traditional); What It Takes to

Make Me Love You-You've Got It (C: James Reese Europe; L: James Weldon Johnson); When It's All Goin' Out and Nothin' Comin' In (C: Bert Williams; L: George Walker); Yankee Doodle Boy, The (C/L: George M. Cohan); You're a Grand Old Flag (C/L: George M. Cohan)

Cast: Carolyn Mignini; Lynne Thigpen; Trey Wilson; Mary Catherine Wright; Jerry Zaks

Notes: No original songs in this show. Moved to Broadway 10/23/80 for an additional 93 performances. Run above is inclusive of both engagements. [1] Cut Washington prior to New York.

4391 • TINY TREE, THE
OPENED: 12/1975   Theatre: NBC
TV Musical

Composer: Johnny Marks
Lyricist: Johnny Marks

Songs: A Caroling We Go; I Heard the Bells on Christmas Day; (Jouyeux Noel, Buon Natale, Feliz Navidad) A Merry Merry Christmas to You; Joyous Christmas; Minuet for Clarinet; Tell It to a Turtle; To Love and Be Loved; When Autumn Comes

Voice: Buddy Ebsen; Roberta Flack

Notes: Ran five years on NBC.

4392 • TIP-TOES
OPENED: 12/28/1925   Theatre: Liberty
Musical   Broadway: 194

Composer: George Gershwin; Ira Gershwin
Librettist: Guy Bolton; Fred Thompson
Producer: Alex A. Aarons; Vinton Freedley
Director: John Harwood

Choreographer: Sammy Lee; **Costumes:** Clare; Kiviette; **Musical Director:** William Daly; **Set Design:** John Young

Songs: Finale Act I; Gather Ye Rosebuds [4]; Harbor of Dreams [4]; Harlem River Chanty [4]; It's a Great Little World! [3]; Lady Luck; Life's Too Short to Be Blue [4]; Looking for a Boy; Nice Baby! (Come to Papa!); Nightie-Night; Our Little Captain; Sweet and Low-Down [2]; That Certain Feeling; These Charming People; Tip-Toes; Waiting for the Train (Florida); We [1]; Weaken a Bit [1]; When Do We Dance?

Cast: Robert Halliday; Allen Kearns; Jeanette MacDonald; Gertrude McDonald; Queenie Smith; Andrew Tombes; Harry Watson; **Pianist:** Victor Arden; Phil Ohman

Notes: [1] Not used. [2] Titled "Blow That Sweet and Low-Down" in London. [3] Sometimes titled "Give In" in London. [4] Cut prior to opening.

4393 • TIP TOP
OPENED: 10/05/1920   Theatre: Globe
Musical   Broadway: 241

Composer: Ivan Caryll
Lyricist: Anne Caldwell
Librettist: R.H. Burnside
Producer: Charles Dillingham
Director: R.H. Burnside

Choreographer: Charles Mast; **Costumes:** O'Kane Conwell; Wilhelm; **Musical Director:** William E. MacQuinn

Songs: Beautiful Booby Prize; Cut Dance; Dance of the School Girls; Dance of the Valentines; Finders Is Keepers (and I Found You) [1] (C/L: Tom Brown; Jack Frost); Girl I've Never Met, The [1]; Girl Who Keeps Me Guessing; Give Me That Letter; Humming [1] (C: Ray Henderson; L: Louis Breau); I Don't Belong on a Farm (C: Arthur Swanstrom; L: Clark); I Want a Lily; I Want to See My Ida Hoe in Idaho (C: Bert Rule; L: Alex Sullivan); I'll Say I Love You [3] (C: Victor Jacobi; L: William Le Baron); In the Sea [3]; Keewa-Tak-A-Yaka-Holo (L: Louis Harrison); Lantern of Love, The [1]; Little Fairy in the Home; My Hortense [2]; Opening Chorus; She Knows It; Shoppers' Dance; Sweet Dreams; Tip Top; Wedding Bells (C/L: Benjamin Hapgood Burt); What Makes the Wild Waves Wild; When Shall We Meet Again (C: Richard A. Whiting; L: Raymond B. Egan); Wireless Heart, The [2] (C: Silvio Hein); Wonderful Girl- Wonderful Boy

Cast: Rosetta Duncan; Vivian Duncan; Pauline Hall; Oscar "Rags" Ragland; Helen Rich; Six Brown Brothers; Fred Stone; Violet Zell

Notes: [1] Sheet music only. [2] Out Washington, D.C. 4/16/22. [3] Out San Francisco 3/12/23.

4394 • 'TIS OF THEE

OPENED: 10/26/1940   Theatre: Maxine Elliott's
Revue   Broadway: 1

Librettist: Sam Locke
Producer: Nat Lichtman
Director: Nat Lichtman

Choreographer: Esther Junger; **Musical Director:**
Alex Saron; **Set Design:** Carl Kent

Songs: After Tonight (C: Al Moss; L: Alfred Hayes);
Brooklyn Cantata (C: George Kleinsinger; L: Mike
Stratton); Lady, The (C: Elsie Peters; L: Alfred
Hayes); Lupe (C: Alex North; L: Alfred Hayes);
Noises in the Street [1] (C: Richard Lewine;
L: Peter Barry; David Greggory); Rhythm Is Red
an' White an' Blue (C: Al Moss; L: David
Greggory); Tis of Thee (C: Alex North; L: Alfred
Hayes); Tomorrow (C: Alex North; L: Alfred
Hayes); What's Mine Is Thine (C: Al Moss;
L: Alfred Hayes); You've Got Something to Sing
About (C: Al Moss; L: Alfred Hayes)

Cast: Esther Junger; George Lloyd; Mervyn Nelson

Notes: [1] Rewritten and put into MAKE MINE
MANHATTAN.

4395 • TO BROADWAY WITH LOVE

OPENED: 04/21/1964
Revue   N.Y. World's Fair: 97

Composer: Jerry Bock
Lyricist: Sheldon Harnick
Producer: Compass Fair; George Schaefer; Angus
Wynne Jr.
Director: Morton Da Costa

Choreographer: Donald Saddler; **Costumes:**
Freddy Wittop; **Lighting Designer:** Jean
Rosenthal; **Musical Director:** Oscar Kosarin;
Orchestrations: Philip J. Lang; **Set Design:** Peter
Wolf

Songs: Beautiful Lady; 88 Rag, The (C: Colin
Romoff; L: Martin Charnin); Mata Hari Mine;
Popsicles in Paris; Remember Radio; To
Broadway with Love

Cast: Carmen Alvarez; Kelly Brown; Patti Karr;
Don Liberto; Rod Perry; Millie Slavin

Notes: Produced at the Texas Pavilion's Music
Hall. This show was presented twice daily with
two different casts.

4396 • TO LIVE ANOTHER SUMMER/ TO PASS ANOTHER WINTER

OPENED: 10/21/1971   Theatre: Helen Hayes
Revue   Broadway: 173

Composer: Dov Seltzer
Lyricist: David Paulsen
Producer: Leonard Soloway
Director: Jonathan Karmon

Choreographer: Jonathan Karmon; **Costumes:**
Lydia Pincus Gang; **Musical Director:** David
Krivoshei; **Set Design:** Neil Peter Jampolis

Songs: Better Days; Boy with the Fiddle, The (C/L:
Alexander Argov); Can You Hear My Voice?
(C: Samuel Kraus; L: George Sherman); Don't
Destroy the World; Give Me a Star (C: David
Krivoshei); Give Shalom and Sabbath to
Jerusalem; Grove of Eucalyptus, The (C: Naomi
Shemer; L: George Sherman); Ha'am Haze;
Hasidic Medley; I'm Alive (C: David Krivoshei);
Mediteranee; Noah's Ark; Sacrifice, The; Son of
Man (C/L: David Axelrod); Sorry We Won (C:
David Krivoshei); To Live Another Summer to
Pass Another Winter; What Are the Basic
Things? (L: Lillian Burstein); When My Man
Returns (C: George Moustaki)

Cast: Yona Atari; Aric Lavie; Rivka Raz

Notes: Lyrics translated by David Paulsen, Lillian
Burstein, George Sherman.

4397 • TO THE WATER TOWER

OPENED: 04/03/1963   Theatre: Second City at
                                           Square East
Revue   Off-Broadway: 210

Composer: Tom O'Horgan
Producer: Howard Alk; Bernard Sahlins; Paul Sills
Director: Paul Sills

Set Design: Ralph Alswang

Songs: Camp Let-Yourself-Go; Central Intelligence;
How to Sell a Fall-Out Shelter; Khrushchev-
Kennedy Press Conference; Looking for the

Action; Second City Theme Song; Truth About a Big Fish Story, The; Wordless Dentistry

Cast: Severn Darden; Paul Dooley; Andrew Duncan; Erin Martin; Paul Sand; Eugene Troobnick

Notes: These are songs and sketches. Scenes, dialogue and lyrics created by the company.

4398 • TO WHOM IT MAY CONCERN

OPENED: 12/16/1985   Theatre: St. Stephen's Church
Musical   Off-Broadway: 106

Composer: Carol Hall
Lyricist: Carol Hall
Librettist: Carol Hall
Producer: Bedda Roses Company
Director: Geraldine Fitzgerald

Choreographer: Michael O'Flaherty; **Lighting Designer:** Christina Giannelli; **Musical Director:** Michael O'Flaherty; **Vocal Arranger:** Michael O'Flaherty

Songs: Ain't Love Easy; Ain't Nobody Got a Bed of Roses; Blessed Be God; Dancing Bear [1]; Holy God; I Believe in God [1]; I Only Miss the Feeling (Not the Man); In the Mirror's Reflection; Jenny Rebecca [2]; Kyrie [1]; Little Plastic Man [1]; Make a Joyful Noise; Miracles; My Sort of Ex-Boyfriend; Sandy; Skateboard Acrobats; To Whom It May Concern; Truly My Soul; Walk in Love; We Believe; We Were Friends; When I Consider the Heavens; Who Will Dance with the Blind Dancing Bear

Cast: Dylan Baker; Gretchen Cryer; Al DeCristo; Louise Edeiken; Becky Gelke; George Gerden; Carol Hall; William Hardy; Michael Hirsch; Kecia Lewis-Evans; Jennifer Naimo; Michael O'Flaherty; Guy Stroman; Tamara Tunie

Notes: [1] Cut out of town. [2] Not written for this show.

4399 • TOGETHER AGAIN FOR THE FIRST TIME

OPENED: 02/27/1989   Theatre: Kaufman
Revue   Off-Broadway: 30

Composer: Frank Loesser
Lyricist: Frank Loesser
Additional Lyrics: Barry Kleinbort
Producer: Martin R. Kaurman
Director: Barry Kleinbort

Choreographer: Donald Saddler; **Costumes:** William Ivey Long; **Lighting Designer:** Ted Mather; **Musical Director:** Colin Romoff; **Set Design:** Philip Baldwin

Songs: Another Openin' Another Show [1] (C/L: Cole Porter); Anywhere I Wander [2]; Bushel and a Peck, A [3]; Can You Read My Mind [4] (C: John Williams; L: Leslie Bricusse); Can't You Just See Yourself [5] (C: Jule Styne; L: Sammy Cahn); Don't Let It Get You Down [6] (C: Burton Lane; L: E.Y. Harburg); Ev'ry Time [7] (C/L: Ralph Blane; Hugh Martin); Everything I've Got [8] (C: Richard Rodgers; L: Lorenz Hart); Family (C: Barry Kleinbort; L: Neil Kleinbort); Frank Loesser medley; Glamorous Life, The [9] (C/L: Stephen Sondheim); Heart [10] (C/L: Richard Adler; Jerry Ross); I Got Lost in His Arms [11] (C/L: Irving Berlin); I Love to Sing-A [12] (C: Harold Arlen; L: E.Y. Harburg); I Wish It So [13] (C/L: Marc Blitzstein); Inchworm [2]; I've Got a Crush on You [14] (C: George Gershwin; L: Ira Gershwin); Mack the Knife [15] (C: Kurt Weill; L: Marc Blitzstein); Mine [16] (C: George Gershwin; L: Ira Gershwin); One More Kiss [17] (C/L: Stephen Sondheim); Pack Up Your Sins [18] (C/L: Irving Berlin); Sing Something Simple [19] (C/L: Herman Hupfeld); There Is Nothin' Like a Dame [20] (C: Richard Rodgers; L: Oscar Hammerstein II); Thumbelina [2]; Travellin' Light [3]; What Is There to Say? [21] (C: Vernon Duke; L: E.Y. Harburg); What Was (C/L: Barry Kleinbort); What's Next (C/L: Barry Kleinbort); When I'm Not Near the Girl I Love [22] (C: Burton Lane; L: E.Y. Harburg); Wind Blows in My Window, The; Wonderful Copenhagen [2]; You Understand Me [23]

Cast: Emily Loesser; Jo Sullivan

Notes: [1] From KISS ME, KATE. [2] From the film HANS CHRISTIAN ANDERSEN. [3] From GUYS AND DOLLS. [4] From the film SUPERMAN. [5] From HIGH BUTTON SHOES. [6] From HOLD ON TO YOUR HATS. [7] From BEST FOOT FORWARD. [8] From BY JUPITER. [9] From A LITTLE NIGHT MUSIC. [10] From DAMN YANKEES. [11] From ANNIE GET YOUR GUN. [12] From the film THE SINGING

KID. [13] From JUNO. [14] From STRIKE UP THE BAND. [15] From THE THREEPENNY OPERA. [16] From LET 'EM EAT CAKE. [17] From FOLLIES. [18] From MUSIC BOX REVUE (SECOND EDITION). [19] From THE SECOND LITTLE SHOW. [20] From SOUTH PACIFIC. [21] From ZIEGFELD FOLLIES OF 1934. [22] From FINIAN'S RAINBOW. [23] From SENOR DISCRETION.

4400 • TOINETTE (1920)
Notes: *See ALWAYS YOU.*

4401 • 'TOINETTE (1961)
OPENED: 11/20/1961   Theatre: Theatre Marquee
Musical   Off-Broadway: 31

Composer: Dede Meyer
Lyricist: Dede Meyer
Librettist: J.J. Rodale
Producer: Bickerstaff Productions
Director: Curt Conway

Source: LA MALADE IMAGINAIRE (Play: Moliere); **Choreographer:** Harry Wolever; **Costumes:** Joe Regan; **Lighting Designer:** Don Sussman; **Musical Director:** David Shire; **Set Design:** Stuart Bishop

Songs: Beat, Little Pulse; Bonjour; Come On Outside and Get Some Air; Dr. Iatro; Even a Doctor Can Make a Mistake; Father Speaks, A; Fly Away; Honest Honore; Lullaby, A; Madly in Love with You Am I; Rags; Recitative; Small Apartment; Someone to Count On; 'Toinette; Un, Deux, Trois; Why Shouldn't I?; You're the Most Impossible Person

Cast: Paul Dooley; Tom Ingham; Joelle Jones; Logan Ramsey; Bob Randall; Ellie Wood

4402 • TOLLER CRANSTON'S THE ICE SHOW
OPENED: 05/19/1977   Theatre: Palace
Revue   Broadway: 60

Producer: Myrl A. Schreibman
Director: Myrl A. Schreibman

Choreographer: Brian Foley; **Costumes:** Miles White; **Lighting Designer:** D. Scott Linder; **Set Design:** Anthony Sabatino

Songs: Let's Hear It for Me [1]; Toller's Theme (inst.) (C: Joel Hirschhorn; Al Kasha)

Cast: Toller Cranston

Notes: Only original songs listed. [1] Written for this show.

4403 • TOM EYEN'S DIRTIEST MUSICAL
OPENED: 12/09/1975   Theatre: Truck and Warehouse
Musical   Off-Broadway

Composer: Henry Krieger
Lyricist: Tom Eyen
Librettist: Tom Eyen

Songs: Angry Boogie; Attention; Can You See; Dirty; I Am Movin'; I Love You; I See You Everywhere; Looking for Something; One More Romance; Peace; Please Be Kind; Rainbow Shines; Smile; Would You Love Me More?

Cast: Hugh Allen; Nell Carter; Alison Fraser; Madeleine LeRoux; Michelle Shay; Ray Shell

Notes: No progam available.

4404 • TOM JONES (1907)
OPENED: 11/11/1907   Theatre: Astor
Musical   Broadway: 55

Composer: Edward German
Lyricist: Charles H. Taylor
Librettist: Robert Courtneidge; A.M. Thompson
Producer: Henry W. Savage
Director: Robert Courtneidge; Edward German

Source: TOM JONES (Novel: Henry Fielding); **Costumes:** Mme. Herman; **Lighting Designer:** Joseph Wilson; **Musical Director:** Herman Perlet; **Set Design:** Walter Burridge

Songs: All for a Green Ribbon; As All the Maids [2]; Barley Mow, The; Beguile, Beguile, with Music Sweet; Benjamin Partridge a Person of Parts; Don't You Find the Weather Charming?; Dream O'Day Jill; Festina Lente [2]; For Aye, My Love; Gloss of Fashion; Hark! The Merry Marriage Bells; Here's a Paradox for Lovers; Hey Derry Down [2]; Hurry, Bustle!; I Wonder; If Love's Content; King Neptune; Let's Be Merry; Love

Maketh the Heart a Garden Fair; My Lady's Coach Has Been Attacked; On a January Morning (in Zummersetscheer); Person of Parts, A [2]; Scarlet Coat, A [2]; Today My Spinet; Uncle John Tappit; We Redcoat Soldiers Serve the King [1]; West Country Lad; Where Be My Daughter [2]; Which Is My Own True Self [2]; Wisdom Says "Festina Lente"; Wise Old Saws [2]; You Have a Pretty Wit [2]

Cast: John Bunny; Louise Gunning; William Norris; Gertrude Quinlan; Van Rensselaer Wheeler

Notes: [1] Added to post-London tour. [2] In original London version only.

4405 • TOM JONES (1969)

OPENED: 04/1969
Musical   Closed out of town

Composer: Robert Archer
Lyricist: Peter Bergman; Joseph Mathewson
Librettist: Austin Pendleton
Producer: Extension Company, The
Director: Richard Michaels

Choreographer: Mary Fariday; **Lighting Designer:** Don Abrams; **Musical Director:** Herb Kaplan; **Orchestrations:** Arthur Rubinstein

Songs: Battle for the Western Name; Bright Moon Above; Bubble Bubble; Captain Jones; Charity; Get That Will; Homecoming Cantata; Infamy; Life Like That, A; She Was a Maid; Sunlight; Thank the Lord; Trunk Packing Song; Under the Allworthy Road; Waiting

4406 • TOM JONES (1976)

OPENED: 1976
Musical   Closed out of town

Composer: Barbara Damashek
Lyricist: Larry Arrick; Barbara Damashek
Librettist: Larry Arrick

Source: TOM JONES (Novel: Henry Fielding)

Cast: James Naughton; Teri Ralston; Lea Richardson; Joy Smith

Notes: Closed Stamford, Conn. No program available.

4407 • TOM MOORE

OPENED: 08/31/1901   Theatre: Herald Square
Play   Broadway

Composer: Andrew Mack
Lyricist: Andrew Mack
Author: Theodore Burt Sayre
Producer: Rich and Harris

Songs: My Love of Long Ago; Song Games

Cast: Myron Calice; Josephine Lovett; Andrew Mack; John Napier

4408 • TOM PIPER

OPENED: 07/14/1969
Musical   Closed out of town

Composer: Edward Lasko
Lyricist: Edward Lasko
Librettist: Edward Lasko
Producer: Goodspeed Opera House
Director: Davey Marlin-Jones

Choreographer: Darwin Knight; **Costumes:** Evelyn Norton Anderson; **Lighting Designer:** John Sloat; **Musical Director:** Roy M. Rogosin; **Set Design:** Raymond T. Kurdt

Songs: Beautiful People; Before I'll Settle for Him; Chowder Ball; Civilization; Come with Me; Company Picnic; Dreams Have I; For the First Time; Give Me a Ship; Let Me Tell You About My House; My Tom; Obedience; Over and Over; Run Away; She Will Come Around; Ship Comin' In; Some Special Place for Me; That's the Way I Am; That's What a Woman Sees; Wedding Night

Cast: Dorothy Emmerson; Kathleen Freeman; Travis Hudson; Larry Kert; Peter Palmer

Notes: Goodspeed Opera House.

4409 • TOM SAWYER

OPENED: 11/21/1956   Theatre: CBS
TV Musical

Composer: Frank Luther
Lyricist: Frank Luther

Source: TOM SAWYER (Novel: Mark Twain);
    Musical Director: Ralph Norman Wilkinson

Songs: Aunt Polly's Prayer; Big Missouri, The; Girls Can't Lie; Have a Happy Holiday; He Wasn't a Bad Boy; I Gotta Whitewash; I Want to Go Home; In the Spring; It Ain't fer Me; McDougal's Cave; Missouri Meadowlark; My Friend Huckleberry Finn; My Love Has Gone Away; Please Make Up; Storm Come A' Risin'; That Lucky Boy Is Me; That's the Life for Me; There's a New Girl in Town; Time Has Come to Say Goodbye, The; We'll All Shout Together in the Mornin'; What Do You Kiss For?; Why Would You Want to Kiss Me?; You Can't Teach an Old Dog New Tricks

Cast: Rose Bampton; Jimmy Boyd; Clarence Cooper; Bennye Gatteye; John Sharpe; Song Spinners, The

Notes: Original TV musical.

4410 • TOM TAYLOR AS WOODY GUTHRIE

OPENED: 11/26/1979   Theatre: Cherry Lane
Musical   Off-Broadway: 47

Composer: Woody Guthrie
Lyricist: Woody Guthrie
Librettist: George Boyd; Michael Diamond; Tom Taylor
Producer: Michael Diamond; Harold Leventhal
Director: George Boyd

Costumes: Robert Blackman; **Lighting Designer:** Daniel Adams; **Set Design:** Robert Blackman

Cast: Tom Taylor

Notes: No original songs in this one-man show.

4411 • TOM TOM

OPENED: 1903   Theatre: La Salle
                    Chicago

Composer: Joseph E. Howard
Lyricist: Raymond W. Peck
Librettist: Raymond W. Peck

Notes: No other information available.

4412 • TOMFOOLERY

OPENED: 12/03/1981   Theatre: Top of the Gate
Revue   Off-Broadway: 27

Composer: Tom Lehrer
Lyricist: Tom Lehrer
Producer: Cameron Mackintosh; Hinks Shimberg
Director: Mary Kyte; Gary Pearle

Costumes: Ann Emonts; **Lighting Designer:** Robert Jared; **Musical Director:** Eric Stern; **Set Design:** Tom Lynch; **Vocal Arranger:** John McKinney

Songs: Be Prepared; Bright College Days; Elements, The; Fight Fiercely, Harvard; Folk Song Army, The; Hunting Song; I Got It from Agnes; I Hold Your Hand in Mine; I Wanna Go Back to Dixie; In Old Mexico; Irish Ballad; Masochism Tango; My Home Town; National Brotherhood Week; New Math; Oedipus Rex; Old Dope Peddler, The; Poisoning Pigeons; Pollution; Send the Marines; She's My Girl; Silent E; So Long Mom; Vatican Rag, The; We Will All Go Together; Wernher von Braun; When You Are Old and Grey; Who's Next

Cast: Don Correia; MacIntyre Dixon; Joy Franz; Jonathan Hadary

Notes: No original songs in this show.

4413 • TOMMY

Notes: *See THE WHO'S TOMMY.*

4414 • TOMMY ROT

OPENED: 10/20/1902   Theatre: Mrs. Osborn's
                    Playhouse
Musical   Broadway: 39

Composer: Safford Waters
Lyricist: Safford Waters
Librettist: Joseph W. Herbert; Rupert Hughes; Kirke La Shelle; Paul West

Songs: Belle of Avenue A, The [1]; Every Dog Must Have His Day and Every Puss Her Afternoon; There's a Strange Fascination About the Stage

Cast: Evelyn Nesbitt; Fletcher Norton; Blanche Ring

Notes: No program available. [1] Interpolated.

4415 • TONGUE IN CHEEK (1949)

OPENED: 03/28/1949
Revue   Closed out of town

Composer: Earl Brent
Lyricist: Earl Brent
Librettist: Charles Faber
Producer: Ross Hunter; Jacque Mapes
Director: Ross Hunter

Choreographer: Lester Horton; Bella Lewitzky;
   Costumes: Maria Donovan; **Musical Director:**
   John Lattimer; **Set Design:** Jacque Mapes; **Vocal
   Arranger:** Paul Owen

Songs: Autumn's in the Red Again; Body in the
   Trunk; Fabulous You; Girl in the Window (C/L:
   Ross Hunter); Heredity; House in the Country;
   I Call Him 'Al'; Jersey City Rhapsody; Move On
   (C/L: Buddy Pepper); Nice Little Day; Star
   without a Job (C: Earl Brent; Buddy Pepper;
   L: Ross Hunter); Tennessee (C/L: Buddy
   Pepper); World's Oldest Boy Violinist, The;
   You're Wonderful

Cast: Ross Hunter; Danny Scholl

4416 • TONGUE IN CHEEK (1958)

OPENED: 04/05/1958
Revue   Closed out of town

Composer: Edward C. Redding
Lyricist: Edward C. Redding
Librettist: Earl Carroll; Edward Collins; Herbert
   Farjeon; Peg Harig; Jay Looney; Fred Rome
Producer: Frederick Burleigh

Choreographer: Robert Ragent; **Costumes:**
   Corinne Van Dame; **Dance Arranger:** James
   Reed Lawlor; **Musical Director:** James Reed
   Lawlor; **Set Design:** Barry Buchter; Robert
   Stanger; Tom Vawter; **Vocal Arranger:** James
   Reed Lawlor

Songs: Bad-Bad-Bad; Boy Meets Girl; Finale (C/L:
   James Reed Lawlor); Grapevine, The [1];
   I Couldn't Be Happier [3] (C/L: Bud McCreery);
   I've Been to the Moon; Jefferson Davis Tyler's
   General Store [2]; Little Sambo; Love Was
   Dancing Beside Me; Mood Music (C/L: Portia
   Nelson); Opening; Since Memphis (C/L: Portia
   Nelson); Somebody's Got To; Too Many Men;
   Way of a Woman, The (C/L: Portia Nelson); We
   Who Are About to Die (C/L: Bud McCreery)

Cast: Joan Bails

Notes: [1] Also in TAKE FIVE as "Gossiping
   Grapevine." [2] Also in TAKE FIVE and FOUR
   BELOW STRIKES BACK. [3] Originally in
   SHOESTRING REVUE.

4417 • TONIGHT AT 8:30

Notes: *See FAMILY ALBUM, RED PEPPERS,
   SHADOW PLAY* and *WE WERE DANCING*, four
   musical one-acts that were part of the nine
   one-acts that comprised this show.

4418 • TONIGHT'S THE NIGHT (1914)

OPENED: 12/24/1914   Theatre: Shubert
Musical   Broadway: 108

Composer: Paul Rubens
Lyricist: Percy Greenbank; Paul Rubens
Librettist: Fred Thompson
Producer: Messrs. Shubert
Director: Austen Hurgon

Source: LES DOMINOS ROSES (Play: Delacour;
   Hennequin); **Musical Director:** Frank Tours; **Set
   Design:** Brunskill; Alfred Craven; Joseph
   Harker; Phil Harker

Songs: Any Old Night (Is a Wonderful Night) [1]
   (C: Jerome Kern; Otto Motzan; L: Schuyler
   Greene; Harry B. Smith); I Could Love You If I
   Tried; I'm a Millionaire; Only Way, The; Pink
   and White; Play Me That Tune; Please Don't Flirt
   with Me; Round the Corner; Stars; They Didn't
   Believe Me [2] (C: Jerome Kern; L: Herbert
   Reynolds); To-night's the Night

Cast: James Blakeley; Fay Compton; Lauri De
   Frece; Maurice Farkoa; George Grossmith; Leslie
   Henson

Notes: No program available. Songs from English
   and American sheet music. [1] Added to English
   production. From NOBODY HOME. [2] Added
   to English production. From THE GIRL FROM
   UTAH.

4419 • TONIGHT'S THE NIGHT (1945)

OPENED: 12/24/1945   Theatre: Shubert
Musical   Broadway: 108

Composer: Paul Rubens
Lyricist: Paul Rubens
Librettist: Fred Thompson
Producer: Messrs. Shubert
Director: Austen Hurgon

Songs: Any Old Night [2] (C: Jerome Kern; L: Otto Motzan); Boots and Shoes; Dancing Mad; I Could Love You If I Tried; I'd Like to Bring My Mother; I'm a Millionaire; Land and Water; Only Way, The; Pink and White; Round the Corner; Stars; They Didn't Believe Me [1] (C: Jerome Kern; L: Herbert Reynolds); Tonight's the Night; Too Particular; When the Boys Come Home to Tea; You Must Not Flirt with Me

Cast: Fay Compton; George Grossmith; Leslie Henson

Notes: [1] From THE GIRL FROM UTAH. Originally in NOBODY HOME with Schuyler Green and Harry B. Smith lyrics. [2] Originally in NOBODY HOME with Schuyler Green and Harry B. Smith lyrics. In London version only.

4420 • TOO MANY GIRLS

OPENED: 10/18/1939   Theatre: Imperial
Musical   Broadway: 249

Composer: Richard Rodgers
Lyricist: Lorenz Hart
Librettist: George Marion Jr.
Producer: George Abbott
Director: George Abbott

Choreographer: Robert Alton; **Costumes:** Raoul Pene du Bois; **Lighting Designer:** Jo Mielziner; **Musical Director:** Harry Levant; **Orchestrations:** Hans Spialek; **Set Design:** Jo Mielziner; **Vocal Arranger:** Hugh Martin

Songs: 'Cause We Got Cake; Give It Back to the Indians; Heroes in the Fall (L: Richard Rodgers); Hunted Stag, The [1]; I Didn't Know What Time It Was; I Like to Recognize the Tune; Look Out; Love Never Went to College; My Prince (What a Prince!); Pottawatomie; She Could Shake the Maracas; Spic and Spanish; Sweethearts of the Team, The; Tempt Me Not; Too Many Girls; You're Nearer

Cast: Desi Arnaz; Eddie Bracken; Diosa Costello; Clyde Fillmore; Van Johnson; Richard Kollmar; Mildred Law; Hal LeRoy; Hans Robert; Mary Jane Walsh; Marcy Wescott

Notes: [1] Cut prior to opening.

4421 • TOOT SWEET

OPENED: 05/07/1919   Theatre: Princess
Revue   Broadway: 45

Composer: Richard A. Whiting
Lyricist: Raymond B. Egan
Librettist: Everybody
Producer: Will Morrissey
Director: Will Morrissey

Musical Director: Hilding Anderson

Songs: America's Answer; Baby Vampire (C/L: Ray K. Moulton); Blightly Bound; Carolina; Charge of the Song Brigade; Dance de Nautica Americaine; Eyes of the Army; French Soldiers on Leave Dance; Give Him Back His Job; Je Ne Sais Pas; Just Around the Corner from Easy Street; L'Elefant Skeed; Madelon; One of the Ruins of France (C/L: Ray K. Moulton); Preliminary Skirmish; Rose of Verdun; Salvation Sal; Tout Suite; You'll Never Get a Whimper Out of Me (C/L: Will Morrissey)

Cast: May Boley; Elizabeth Brice; Lon Haskell; Will Morrissey; Sam Ward

Notes: Titled OVERSEAS REVUE in sheet music where Jack Mason was credited with direction and Elizabeth Brice was co-producer.

4422 • TOOT-TOOT!

OPENED: 03/11/1918   Theatre: Cohan
Musical   Broadway: 40

Composer: Jerome Kern
Lyricist: Berton Braley
Librettist: Edgar Allen Woolf
Producer: Henry W. Savage
Director: Edward Rose; Edgar Allen Woolf

Source: EXCUSE ME (Play: Rupert Hughes); **Choreographer:** Robert Marks; **Costumes:** Faibsey; **Lighting Designer:** Joseph Wilson; **Musical Director:** Anton Heindl; **Set Design:** Clifford Pember

Songs: Every Girl in All America; Girlie; Good-Bye and Good Luck; Honey Moon Land; I Will Knit a Suit of Dreams (Teepee); If (There's Anything You Want); If You Only Care Enough

[1] (L: Berton Braley); Indian Fox Trot; It's Greek to Me; It's Immaterial to Me; Kan the Kaiser; Last Long Mile, The (C/L: Emil Breitenfeld); Let's Go; Quarrel and Part; Runaway Colts; Shower of Rice, A; Smoke; Toot-Toot!; When You Wake Up Dancing; Yankee Doodle on the Line [1] (L: Berton Braley); You're So Cute Soldier Boy (C: Anatole Freidland; L: Edgar Allen Woolf)

Cast: Louise Allen; Louise Groody; Florence Johns; William Kent; Flora Zabelle

Notes: [1] ASCAP/Library of Congress only.

4423 • TOP BANANA
OPENED: 11/01/1951　Theatre: Winter Garden
Musical　　　　　　Broadway: 350

Composer: Johnny Mercer
Lyricist: Johnny Mercer
Librettist: Hy Kraft
Producer: Mike Sloane; Paula Stone
Director: Jack Donahue

Choreographer: Ron Fletcher; **Costumes:** Alvin Colt; **Lighting Designer:** Jo Mielziner; **Musical Director:** Harold Hastings; **Orchestrations:** Don Walker; **Set Design:** Jo Mielziner; **Vocal Arranger:** Hugh Martin

Songs: Be My Guest; Dog Is a Man's Best Friend, A; Elevator Song (Go to the Rear of the Car Please); Girl of All Nations [1]; Hail to MacCracken's; Havin' a Ball [1]; I Fought Every Step of the Way; Man of the Year This Week, The; Meet Miss Blendo; My Home Is in My Shoes; Nobody Understands Me [1]; O.K. for T.V. (You're O.K. for T.V.); Only If You're in Love; Sans Souci; Senorita Diaz [1]; Slogan Song (You Gotta Have a Slogan); That's for Sure; Top Banana; Word a Day, A (Ambiguous Means I Love You); You're So Beautiful That —

Cast: Jack Albertson; Lindy Doherty; Herbie Faye; Joey Faye; Eddie Hanley; Judy Lynn; Rose Marie; Ted Morgan; Bob Scheerer; Phil Silvers

Notes: [1] ASCAP/Library of Congress only.

4424 • TOP-HOLE
OPENED: 09/01/1924　Theatre: Fulton
Musical　　　　　　Broadway: 104

Composer: Jay Gorney
Lyricist: Owen Murphy
Librettist: Eugene Conrad; George Dill; Gladys Unger
Producer: William Caryl
Director: David Bennett

Choreographer: David Bennett; Seymour Felix; **Musical Director:** William Daly

Songs: Cheerio! (C: Lewis E. Gensler; L: Ira Gershwin); Dance Your Way to Paradise; Every Silken Lady; Every Time the Clock Ticks [2]; Golfing (C: Robert Braine; L: Eugene Conrad); Imagine Me without My You (and You without Your Me) [3] (C: Lewis E. Gensler; L: Robert Russell Bennett; Ira Gershwin); Is It Any Wonder; Love Is a Sandman (C: Robert Braine; L: Eugene Conrad); Me and You [1]; Safe in Your Heart [1]; Stardust [1]; Then You Know That You're in Love (C/L: Jay Gorney; Owen Murphy; Harry Richman); There's Always Room for a Smile [1]; There's Music in an Irish Song; Top Hole [1]; We Ran Away from School; Whistle in the Rain [1] (C: J. Fred Coots; L: McElbert Moore); You Must Come Over Eyes

Cast: Ernest Glendinning; Clare Stratton

Notes: No New York program available. [1] Out Newark 4/28/24. [2] Out New Haven 8/28/23. [3] Not used.

4425 • TOP O' THE WORLD, THE
OPENED: 10/19/1907　Theatre: Majestic
Musical　　　　　　Broadway: 156

Composer: Anne Caldwell
Lyricist: James O'Dea
Librettist: Mark Swan
Producer: J.M. Allison
Director: Frank Smithson

Choreographer: Luigi Albertierri; William Rock

Songs: After All [1]; Aurora (from Aurora, Illinois); Busy Mr. Bee; Cupid and You and I (C/L: Manuel Klein); Doll Ballet (inst.) (C: Manuel Klein); Don't You Want to Be My Bow-Wow- Wow [2]; Eccentric Dance (inst.) (C: Manuel Klein); Entrance of Aurora [2]; Finale Act I; Finale Act II; Gold, Gold, Gold; Goodbye, Dinah; Hail to Aurora; Hand Me Out a Laugh; How'd You Like to Be My Bow-Wow-Wow?; Little Brown Hen; My Dolls; My

Shaggy Old Polar Bear; O'er the Snow; One Girl, The; Opening Chorus Act I (L: Joseph W. Herbert); Opening Chorus Act II (C: Manuel Klein); Perfectly Terrible [1]; Riddle- Ma-Ree; Sailing In a Sea-Going Hack (L: Joseph W. Herbert); Side By Side [1] (C: Manuel Klein); Tinymite (C: Manuel Klein); Where Fate Shall Guide; Why Don't You?; Yankee Doodle Yarns

Cast: Kathleen Clifford; Wellington Cross; Harry Fairleigh; Bessie Franklin; Anna Laughlin; George Monroe

Notes: [1] Out Kansas City 10/11/08. [2] Vocal score only.

4426 • TOP SPEED

OPENED: 12/25/1929   Theatre: 46th Street
Musical   Broadway: 102

Composer: Harry Ruby
Lyricist: Bert Kalmar
Librettist: Guy Bolton; Bert Kalmar; Harry Ruby
Producer: Guy Bolton; Bert Kalmar; Harry Ruby
Director: John Harwood

Choreographer: John Boyle; LeRoy Prinz; **Costumes:** Kiviette; **Musical Director:** Ivan Rudisill; **Set Design:** Raymond Sovey

Songs: Dizzy Feet; Fireworks; Goodness Gracious [2]; Hot and Bothered; I'd Like to Be Liked; I'll Know and She'll Know [2]; In the Summer; Keep Your Undershirt On; Looking for the Lovelight in the Dark [2] (C: Joe Burke; L: Al Dubin); On the Border Line; Papers, The; Reaching for the Moon [2]; Sweeter Than You [1]; Try Dancing; We Want You; What Would I Care?; You Couldn't Blame Me for That

Cast: Lester Allen; Sunny Dale; Irene Delroy; Harland Dixon; Paul Frawley; Hermes Pan; Ginger Rogers

Notes: [1] Also in TWINKLE TWINKLE. [2] Sheet music only.

4427 • TOPICS OF 1923

OPENED: 11/20/1923   Theatre: Broadhurst
Revue   Broadway: 143

Composer: Al Goodman; Jean Schwartz
Lyricist: Harold Atteridge

Librettist: Harold Atteridge; Harry Wagstaff Gribble
Producer: Messrs. Shubert
Director: J.C. Huffman

Choreographer: M. Francis Weldon; **Costumes:** Travis Banton; Erte; **Musical Director:** Al Goodman; **Set Design:** Watson Barratt

Songs: American Dancers; Doing the Apache; Flowers of Evil (Garden of Evil), The (C: Jean Schwartz); Good Queen Bess (C: Bert Grant; L: Tot Seymour); I'll Stand Beneath Your Window Tonight and Whistle [2] (C/L: Jerry Benson; Jimmy McHugh; George E. Price); In the Cottage of My Heart [1]; Jazz Wedding; Just Like a Diamond (C: Jean Schwartz); Legend of the Woodland, The; Lotus Flower; Love in a Haystack [1]; Minuette, A; Oedipus Rex a la Jazz; Oh, Alice (C: Bert Grant; L: Tot Seymour); On a Beautiful Evening (C: Jean Schwartz); Opening Ensemble; Queens of Long Ago; Ran Tin Tin; When You Love (C: Bert Grant; L: Tot Seymour); Yankee Doodle Oo-la-la, The

Cast: Alice Delysia; Jay Gould; Harry McNaughton; Nat Nazzarro Jr.; Jack Pearl; Ethel Shutta

Notes: [1] Sheet music only. [2] ASCAP/Library of Congress only. Listed under TOPICS OF 1922 by ASCAP.

4428 • TOPLITZKY OF NOTRE DAME

OPENED: 12/26/1946   Theatre: Century
Musical   Broadway: 60

Composer: Sammy Fain
Lyricist: George Marion Jr.
Librettist: Jack Barnett; George Marion Jr.
Producer: William Cahn
Director: Jose Ruben

Choreographer: Robert Sidney; **Costumes:** Kenn Barr; **Musical Director:** Leon Leonardi; **Orchestrations:** Lewis Raymond; Menotti Salta; Allan Small; **Set Design:** Edward Gilbert **Vocal Arranger:** Leon Leonardi

Songs: All-American Man; Baby Let's Face It; Common Sense; I Wanna Go to City College; Let Us Gather at the Goal Line; Love Is a Random Thing; McInerney's Farm [2]; Philadelphia

Feeling [1]; Slight Case of Ecstasy, A; Wolf Time; You Are My Downfall

Cast: J. Edward Bromberg; Warde Donovan; Walter Lang; Phyllis Lynne; Frank Marlowe; Estelle Sloan; Gus Van; Betty Jane Watson

Notes: [1] Out Chicago 9/29/7. [2] ASCAP/Library of Congress only.

4429 • TOPSY AND EVA

OPENED: 12/23/1924   Theatre: Sam H. Harris
Musical   Broadway: 165

Composer: Rosetta Duncan; Vivian Duncan
Lyricist: Rosetta Duncan; Vivian Duncan
Librettist: Catherine Chisholm Cushing
Producer: Tom Wilkes
Director: Oscar Eagle

Source: UNCLE TOM'S CABIN (Novel: Harriet Beecher Stowe); **Choreographer:** Jack Holland; **Costumes:** Madam Keeler; **Musical Director:** Jerome Stewardson; **Set Design:** Dickson Morgan

Songs: Bird Dance; Cotton Time; Do-Re-Mi; Give Me Your Heart and Give Me Your Hand; Happy Go Lucky Days [3]; Heaven [1]; I Never Had a Mammy; In the Autumn [2]; Just for a Little While [3]; Kiss Me; Land of Long Ago, The; Lickin's [2]; Mariette; Moon Am Shinin'; Plantation Melodies; Rememb'ring; Sighin' [2]; Smiling Through My Tears [1]; Sweet Onion in Bermuda [1]; Ukulele Lady [1]; Um-Um-Da-Da; Uncle Tom's Cabin Blues; We'll Dance through Life Together [2]; Wedding Procession

Cast: Rosetta Duncan; Vivian Duncan; Harriet Hoctor; Basil Ruysdael; Frederick Santley

Notes: [1] Out Washington, D.C. 12/28/25. [2] Out San Francisco 7/8/23. [3] Out Newark 3/8/26.

4430 • TOREADOR, THE

OPENED: 01/06/1902   Theatre: Knickerbocker
Musical   Broadway: 146

Composer: Lionel Monckton
Lyricist: Adrian Ross
Librettist: Harry Nichols; James T. Tanner
Producer: Nixon & Zimmerman
Director: Herbert Gresham

Musical Director: Louis F. Gottschalk

Songs: Archie; Blanks [1] (L: Percy Greenbank); Espana (C: Ivan Caryll); Everybody's Awfully Good to Me (C/L: Paul A. Rubens); Governor of Villaya, The (C: Ivan Caryll); Hall of Fame, The (C: John W. Bratton; L: Robb); Hear Me, Amelia (Finale Act I) (C: Ivan Caryll); Here They Come in Glittering Glory (C: Ivan Caryll); Husband and Wife [1]; If Ever I Marry (L: Percy Greenbank); I'm Romantic (I've Always Had a Passion); It Does Amuse Me So! [1] (L: Percy Greenbank); Keep Off the Grass (L: Leslie Mayne); Language of the Flowers, The (L: Percy Greenbank); Maud [1] (C: Unknown; L: Harry B. Smith); Moon, Moon (C/L: Nat D. Mann); My Toreador (C/L: Paul Rubens); My Zoo (C: Ivan Caryll; L: Percy Greenbank); Oh, Senor, Pray (C: Ivan Caryll; L: Percy Greenbank); Punch and Judy [1] (C: Ivan Caryll; L: Percy Greenbank); Ride in the Puff-Puff, A [1] (L: Percy Greenbank); Sir Archie [1] (L: George Grossmith Jr.); Toreador's Song (I'm the Glory and Pride of the Land of Spain) (C: Ivan Caryll); We're All of Us Lovely and Young (Chorus of Bridesmaids); When I Marry Amelia [1]; Where the Gigantic Ocean Atlantic (Opening Chorus) (C: Ivan Caryll); With All the Town in Bright Array (Opening Chorus Act II) (L: Percy Greenbank); Won't It Be a Lark (We're Dear Little Girls) (C: Ivan Caryll; L: Percy Greenbank)

Cast: Melville Ellis; Christie MacDonald; Maude Raymond; Maude Richie; Queenie Vassar; Francis Wilson

Notes: [1] London vocal score only.

4431 • TOUCH

OPENED: 11/08/1970   Theatre: Village Arena
Musical   Off-Broadway: 422

Composer: Kenn Long
Lyricist: Kenn Long
Librettist: Kenn Long; Amy Saltz
Producer: Edith O'Hara; Two Arts Playhouse; Robert S. Weinstein
Director: Amy Saltz

Lighting Designer: Charles Lewis; **Musical Director:** Jim Crozier; David Rodman; **Set Design:** Robert Alexander Kates; Robert U. Taylor

Songs: Alphagenesis; City Song; Come to the
Road; Confrontation Song; Declaration; Garden
Song; Goodbyes; Guiness, Woman; Hasseltown;
I Don't Care; Maxine!; Quiet Country; Reaching,
Touching; Sitting in the Park; Susan's Song;
Tripping; Watching; Windchild (C/L: Gary
Graham)

Cast: Gerard S. Doff; Barbara Ellis; Kenn Long; Ava
Rosenblum

4432 • TOUCH AND GO
OPENED: 10/13/1949   Theatre: Broadhurst
Revue   Broadway: 176

Composer: Jay Gorney
Lyricist: Jean Kerr; Walter Kerr
Librettist: Jean Kerr; Walter Kerr
Producer: George Abbott
Director: Walter Kerr

Songs: American Primitive; Be a Mess; Broadway
Love Song; Easy Does It; Funny Little Old
World; Highbrow, Lowbrow; It'll Be All Right in
a Hundred Years; Men of the Watermark; Miss
Platt Selects Mate; Mister Brown, Miss Dupree;
Opening for Everybody, An; This Had Better Be
Love; Under the Sleeping Volcano; Wish Me
Luck

Cast: Nancy Andrews; Peggy Cass; Nathaniel Frey;
Helen Gallagher; George Hall; Pearl Lang;
Jonathan Lucas; Kyle MacDonnell; Daniel
Nagrin; Louis Nye; Dick Sykes

4433 • TOUR DE FOUR
OPENED: 06/18/1963   Theatre: Writers' Stage
Revue   Off-Broadway: 16

Composer: Larry Alexander; John Aman; Jeanne
Bargy; Albert Beach; Norman Brown; Coleman
Cohen; Carl Crow; Gerry Donovan; Ed Fearon;
Frank Gehrecke; Lee Holdridge; Jack Johnson;
James Kason; Marty Kreiner; John McKellar;
Dorothy Mendoza; Lance Mulcahy; Gratian
Ouelette; Gary Popkin; Andrew Rosenthal; Peter
Salamando; Arthur Siegel; Hugh Taliaferro; Rod
Warren; Blair Weille; Edwin Weinberg; Bruce
Williamson
Lyricist: Larry Alexander; John Aman; Jeanne
Bargy; Albert Beach; Norman Brown; June
Carroll; Coleman Cohen; Carl Crow; Gerry
Donovan; Ed Fearon; Frank Gehrecke; Jack

Johnson; James Kason; Marty Kreiner; John
McKellar; Dorothy Mendoza; Lance Mulcahy;
Gratian Ouelette; Gary Popkin; Andrew
Rosenthal; Peter Salamando; Hugh Taliaferro;
Rod Warren; Blair Weille; Edwin Weinberg;
Bruce Williamson
Librettist: Larry Alexander; John Aman; Jeanne
Bargy; Albert Beach; Norman Brown; Coleman
Cohen; Carl Crow; Gerry Donovan; Ed Fearon;
Frank Gehrecke; Jack Johnson; James Kason;
Marty Kreiner; John McKellar; Dorothy
Mendoza; Lance Mulcahy; Gratian Ouelette;
Gary Popkin; Andrew Rosenthal; Peter
Salamando; Hugh Taliaferro; Rod Warren; Blair
Weille; Edwin Weinberg; Bruce Williamson
Producer: Susan Eden; Tom Eyen; Richard Everett
Upton
Director: Tom Eyen

Costumes: Edward Charles; **Lighting Designer:**
Gene Tunezi; **Musical Director:** Natalie
Charlson

Songs: Baby John; Bus Stop; Call of the Wild;
Cooperation; Cuckoo Song; D. and D. Rag;
Fallout Shelter; Good Old Days; Hollywood Folk
Song; Letters; Lyle's Wedding; Multi-Colored
Bush; Rapid Reading Rachel; Six O'Clock; 1600
Pennsylvania Avenue; Small Town Girl; That
Certain Look; Theatres; This Time Next Year;
Tour de Four; Trio Con Brio; What I Want to Be;
Whatever Happened; You Came from Outer
Space; You Have . . .

Cast: Paul Blake; Carl Crow; Carol Fox; Lyle
O'Hara

Notes: Composers, lyricists and writers were not
differentiated. Some of these may be songs and
some sketches.

4434 • TOURISTS, THE
OPENED: 08/25/1906   Theatre: Majestic
Musical   Broadway: 132

Composer: Gustave Kerker
Lyricist: R.H. Burnside
Librettist: R.H. Burnside
Producer: Lee Shubert; Sam S. Shubert
Director: R.H. Burnside

Lighting Designer: George Morgan; **Musical
Director:** Gustave Kerker; **Set Design:** George H.
Williams

Songs: Dear Old Boston [2]; Dear Old Broadway; Different Girls; Entrance of the Rajah [3]; Game of Hearts, A; He's Gone; Here They Come; In Rang a Pang; It's Nice to Have a Sweetheart; Keep On Doing; Love Is a Wonderful Thing; Mary's Lamb; Natives; Oh, Mister Sun [1]; She Always Told the Truth; That's the Time; They Lived to Be Loved in Vain; We're the Gnomes; We're the Marriageable Daughters [3]; Wedding Procession [3]; When Love Dies [1]; When You Take a Trip; Which One Shall We Marry?; Wouldn't You Like to Know [1]

Cast: Grace LaRue; Vera Michelena; William Pruette; Julia Sanderson

Notes: [1] Sheet music only. [2] Out Boston 6/25/06. [3] Vocal selection only.

4435 • TOVARICH

OPENED: 03/18/1963   Theatre: Broadway
Musical   Broadway: 264

Composer: Lee Pockriss
Lyricist: Anne Croswell
Librettist: David Shaw
Producer: Abel Farbman; Sylvia Harris
Director: Peter Glenville

Source: TOVARICH (Play: Jacques Deval; Robert E. Sherwood); Choreographer: Herbert Ross; Costumes: Motley; Dance Arranger: Dorothea Freitag; Lighting Designer: John Harvey; Musical Director: Stanley Lebowsky; Orchestrations: Philip J. Lang; Set Design: Rolf Gerard; Vocal Arranger: Stanley Lebowsky

Songs: All for You; Grand Polonaise (dance); I Go to Bed; I Know the Feeling; Introduction Tango (dance); It Used to Be; Kukla Katusha; Lullaby for a Princess [1]; Make a Friend; Managed; Nitchevo; No! No! No!; Only One, The; Opportunity [1]; Say You'll Stay; Small Cartel, A; Stuck with Each Other; That Face; Uh-Oh!; Wilkes-Barre, Pa.; You Love Me; You'll Make an Elegant Butler (C/L: Joan Javits; Phil Springer)

Cast: Jean Pierre Aumont; Margery Gray; George S. Irving; Michael Kermoyan; Vivien Leigh; Byron Mitchell; Alexander Scourby; Louise Troy; Gene Varrone

Notes: [1] Cut prior to opening.

4436 • TOWN CLOWN, THE

OPENED: 01/06/1924   Theatre: Illinois
Musical   Chicago

Composer: Harry Ruby
Lyricist: Bert Kalmar
Librettist: Aaron Hoffman

Notes: Later revised into THE BELLE OF QUAKER TOWN and again into NO OTHER GIRL.

4437 • TOWN GOSSIP

OPENED: 1921
Revue   Closed out of town

Composer: Harold Orlob
Lyricist: George E. Stoddard; Ned Wayburn
Librettist: George E. Stoddard; Ned Wayburn
Producer: Ned Wayburn
Director: Ned Wayburn

Costumes: Shirley Barker; Alice O'Neil; Musical Director: George A. Nichols

Songs: After We're Happily Married; Argentine; Burlesque Ballet; Catch As Catch Can; Contortion Dance; Family Jewels; Golden Evenings of Autumn Time; Golden Indian, The; Good Bye School Days; Historic Kisses; I Have Something Nice; Just Like the Sunshine; Lovely Lady Nicotine; Married Life; Meow Meow Meow; My Cave Man; Picture Any Girl Can Paint, A; Polo Dance; Put and Take Top, The; Rhythmic Rhapsodies on the Piano; Riding; Seven Syncopating Sirens; Sweet Yesterday; Take It from a Happy Married Man; Teaching the Baby to Walk; Town Gossip; Trombone Symphony; Wedding Rehearsal, The

Cast: Edythe Baker; Helen Broderick; John Dooley; Lillian Fitzgerald; Vinton Freedley; Grace Moore

4438 • TOWNSHIP FEVER

OPENED: 12/19/1990   Theatre: Majestic
                             (Brooklyn)
Musical   New York: 39

Composer: Mbongeni Ngema
Lyricist: Mbongeni Ngema
Librettist: Mbongeni Ngema
Producer: Brooklyn Academy of Music; Lincoln Center Theater
Director: Mbongeni Ngema

Arrangements: Mbongeni Ngema; **Choreographer:** Mbongeni Ngema; **Costumes:** Sarah Roberts; **Lighting Designer:** Mannie Manim; **Orchestrations:** Mbongeni Ngema; **Set Design:** Sarah Roberts

Songs: Amasendenduna (chant) (C/L: Traditional); Beautiful Little Mama; Blazing Like Fire; Corruption; Daveyton; Ekufikeni (C/L: Mbongeni Ngema; Isaiah Shembe); Freedom Charter (L: Unknown); Hear My Prayer; Hohihlahla Mandela (C/L: Mbongeni Ngema; Traditional); Intombenjani (C/L: Traditional); Isidudla (C/L: Mbongeni Ngema; Traditional); Izintombi Zomjolo; Lord Is My Shepherd (L: Traditional); Meleko; Mfoka Ngema; Mngani Wamina; Nduna Ngibolekinduku (The Zulu Warriors); Ngatheth Amacala; Ngobammakhosi; Oliver Tambo; Township Fever; U Mandela Uthayihlome; Ufil Ubotha (chant); Wasiqoqela Ndawonye (C/L: Mbongeni Ngema; Traditional); Xolisinhlizyo

Cast: Sindiswa Dlathu; John Lata; David Manqele; Brian Mazibuko; Themba Mbonani; Bheki Mqadi; Bhoyi Ngema; Clara Reyes; Mamthandi Zulu

4439 • TOYLAND

OPENED: 01/08/1908
Musical   Closed out of town

Composer: Hampton Durand; Harry L. Newton
Lyricist: Harry L. Newton

Source: UNKNOWN (Musical); **Musical Director:** Harry L. Newton

Songs: And Then She Winked Her Eye; Blowing Soap Bubbles; Bogie Ogie Man, The; By the Same Old Light Above; Finale Act I; Grand Review and Finale; I Want to Be a Soldier Boy in Blue; If You Love Me As I Love You; I'll Whistle and Wait for You; I'm a Crazy Jay on Circus Day; Jumpety Jump Family; King of the Imps Am I; Love Is the Same Everywhere; Mechanical Doll Dance, The; Rain, Rain Go Away; Snuggle Up Closer to Me; Stingy; Toy Song; Witch Dance

Cast: Augusta Belle; Billie Bordon; Florence Fields; Jules Held; James H. Stewart

Notes: Program of Cedar Rapids.

4440 • TRAINED NURSES, THE

OPENED: 1914
Musical

Composer: Leo Edwards
Lyricist: Blanche Merrill
Librettist: William Le Baron
Producer: Jesse Lasky

Musical Director: Marie Mosier

Songs: Come on a Whistle; Humpty Dumpty; I Can't Believe You Really Love Me; I Love to Quarrel with You; If You Don't Want Me [1] (C/L: Irving Berlin); It Can't Be True; Kiss, Kiss; Nurses Are We; Tango Tea; We've Had a Lovely Time, So Long, Good-Bye

Cast: Henry Bergman; Mae Bronte; George W. Callahan; Gladys Clark

Notes: Vaudeville musical. Program of 6/15/14. [1] Sheet music only.

4441 • TRAITORS, THE

OPENED: 03/1913   Theatre: Lafayette
Musical   New York

Composer: Will Marion Cook
Producer: Negro Players

Notes: No other information available.

4442 • TRANSPOSED HEADS, THE

OPENED: 10/31/1986   Theatre: Lincoln Center
Musical   Off-Broadway: 4

Composer: Elliot Goldenthal
Lyricist: Sidney Goldfarb
Librettist: Sidney Goldfarb; Julie Taymor
Director: Julie Taymor

Source: TRANSPOSED HEADS, THE (Novel: Thomas Mann); **Choreographer:** Swati Gupte Bhise; Company, The; Rajika Puri; Margo Sappington; Julie Taymor; **Conductor:** Joshua Rosenblum; **Costumes:** Carol Oditz; **Lighting Designer:** Marcia Madeira; **Musical Director:** Richard Martinez; **Set Design:** Alexander Okun

Cast: Yamil Borges; Scott Burkholder; Rajika Puri; Byron Utley

Notes: No songs listed in program.

4443 • TREASURE GIRL

OPENED: 11/08/1928   Theatre: Alvin
Musical   Broadway: 69

Composer: George Gershwin
Lyricist: Ira Gershwin; Vincent Lawrence; Fred
    Thompson
Librettist: Alex A. Aarons; Vincent Lawrence
Producer: Alex A. Aarons; Vinton Freedley
Director: Bertram Harrison

Choreographer: Bobby Connolly; **Musical
    Director:** Alfred Newman

Songs: A-Hunting We Will Go; According to Mr.
    Grimes; Dead Men Tell No Tales [6]; Feeling I'm
    Falling; Finale Act I; Goodbye to the Old Love,
    Hello to the New [6]; Got a Rainbow; I Don't
    Think I'll Fall in Love Today; I Want to Marry a
    Marionette [6]; I've Got a Crush on You [3];
    K-ra-zy for You; Oh, So Nice [5]; Place in the
    Country; Skull and Bones [4]; This Particular
    Party [2]; Treasure Island; What Are We Here
    For?; What Causes That?; Where's the Boy?
    Here's the Girl!

Cast: Walter Catlett; Peggy Conklin; Constance
    Cummings; Paul Frawley; Ferris Hartman; Mary
    Hay; Gertrude Lawrence; Beryl Wallace; Clifton
    Webb; **Pianist:** Victor Arden; Phil Ohman

Notes: [1] Added after opening. [2] Not used. [3]
    Also in STRIKE UP THE BAND (1930). [4] Music
    cut from concert piece AMERICAN IN PARIS.
    [5] Cut after opening. [6] Cut prior to opening.

4444 • TREASURE ISLAND (1973)

OPENED: 08/21/1973   Theatre: Town Hall
Musical   Off-Broadway: 4

Composer: John Clifton
Lyricist: John Clifton
Librettist: Tom Tippett
Producer: N.Y. University's Town Hall;
    Performing Arts Repertory Theatre
Director: Evan Thompson

Source: TREASURE ISLAND (Novel: Robert Louis
    Stevenson); **Costumes:** Jennie Cleaver; **Set
    Design:** John Nelson

Songs: Gold; Honest Sailors; I'll Buy Me a Ship;
    Let's Be Friends; That's What I Would Do;
    Treasure Island; Yo-Ho

Cast: Joan Shepard; Bill Steele; Evan Thompson;
    Chester Thornhill

4445 • TREASURE ISLAND (1985)

Notes: *See PIECES OF EIGHT (1985).*

4446 • TREE GROWS IN BROOKLYN, A

OPENED: 04/19/1951   Theatre: Alvin
Musical   Broadway: 267

Composer: Arthur Schwartz
Lyricist: Dorothy Fields
Librettist: George Abbott; Betty Smith
Producer: George Abbott
Director: George Abbott

Source: TREE GROWS IN BROOKLYN, A (Novel:
    Betty Smith); **Choreographer:** Herbert Ross;
    Costumes: Irene Sharaff; **Lighting Designer:** Jo
    Mielziner; **Musical Director:** Max Goberman;
    Orchestrations: Robert Russell Bennett; Joe
    Glover; **Set Design:** Jo Mielziner

Songs: Bride Wore Something Old, The [1]; Call on
    Your Neighbor [1]; Don't Be Afraid; Growing
    Pains; Halloween Ballet (dance); He Had
    Refinement; If You Haven't Got a Sweetheart;
    I'll Buy You a Star; I'm Like a New Broom; Is
    That My Prince?; Look Who's Dancing; Love Is
    the Reason; Make the Man Love Me; Mine 'til
    Monday; Oysters in July [1]; Payday; That's How
    It Goes; Tuscaloosa [2]

Cast: Shirley Booth; Nathaniel Frey; Johnny
    Johnston; Marcia Van Dyke

Notes: [1] Cut prior to opening. [2] Cut prior to
    opening. Same music as "Old Enough to Love"
    in BY THE BEAUTIFUL SEA.

4447 TREEMONISHA

OPENED: 10/21/1975   Theatre: Uris
Opera   Broadway: 64

Composer: Scott Joplin
Lyricist: Scott Joplin
Librettist: Scott Joplin
Producer: Adela Holzer; Houston Grand Opera;
    Victor Lurie; James M. Nederlander
Director: Frank Corsaro

Choreographer: Louis Johnson; **Costumes:** Franco Colavecchia; **Lighting Designer:** Nananne Porcher; **Musical Director:** Gunther Schuller; **Orchestrations:** Scott Joplin; Gunther Schuller; **Set Design:** Franco Colavecchia

Songs: Abuse; Aunt Dinah Has Blowed de Horn; Bag of Luck, The; Confusion; Conjuror's Forgiven; Corn-Huskers, The; Frolic of the Bears; Going Home; Good Advice; I Want to See My Child; Real Slow Drag, A; Rescue, The; Sacred Tree, The; Superstition; Surprise; Treemonisha in Peril; Treemonisha's Bringing Up; Treemonisha's Return; Wasp Nest; We Will Rest Awhile; We Will Trust You as Our Leader; We're Goin' Around; When Villains Ramble Far and Near; Wreath, The; Wrong Is Never Right

Cast: Betty Allen; Carmen Balthrop; Kathleen Battle; Ben Harney; Kenneth Hicks; Cora Johnson; Lorna Myers; Edward Pierson; Curtis Rayam; Willard White

4448 • TRIAL HONEYMOON, A
OPENED: 1924   Theatre: La Salle
Musical   Chicago

Composer: Harold Orlob
Lyricist: Harold Orlob
Librettist: Harold Orlob

Notes: No program available.

4449 • TRIALS OF OZ, THE
OPENED: 12/19/1972
Play   Off-Broadway: 15

Composer: Mick Jagger; John Lennon; Buzzy Linhart; Yoko Ono
Lyricist: Mick Jagger; John Lennon; Buzzy Linhart; Yoko Ono
Author: Geoff Robertson
Producer: Friends of Van Wolf Prods.; Richard Scanga
Director: Jim Sharman

Costumes: Joseph G. Aulisi; **Lighting Designer:** Jules Fisher; **Set Design:** Mark Ravitz; **Vocal Arranger:** Bill Cunningham

Songs: Dirty Is the Funniest Thing I Know; Give Me Excess of It; God Save Us; If You Can't Join 'Em, Beat 'Em; Justice Game, The; Love's Still Growing, The; Masquerade Ball; Oranges and Lemons; Rupert Bear Song; Schoolboy Blues

Cast: Dallas Alinder; Greg Antonacci; Cliff DeYoung; Dan Leach; William Roerick

4450 • TRICKS
OPENED: 01/08/1973   Theatre: Alvin
Musical   Broadway: 8

Composer: Jerry Blatt
Lyricist: Lonnie Burstein
Librettist: Lonnie Burstein; Jon Jory
Producer: Herman Levin
Director: Jon Jory

Source: LES FOURBERIES DE SCAPIN (Play: Moliere); **Source:** MONSIEUR SCAPIN (Play: Moliere); **Arrangements:** Peter Howard; **Choreographer:** Donald Saddler; **Costumes:** Miles White; **Dance Arranger:** Peter Howard; **Lighting Designer:** Martin Aronstein; **Musical Director:** David Frank; **Orchestrations:** Bert De Cocteau; **Set Design:** Oliver Smith

Songs: Anything Is Possible; Believe Me; Enter Hyacinthe; Gypsy Girl; Gypsy Love [1]; Hey, Say Anything [1]; How Sweetly Simple; Life Can Be Funny; Little Bit of Trouble on the Side, A [1]; Love or Money; Man of Spirit, A; Scapin; Somebody's Doin' Somebody All the Time; Sporting Man, A; Tricks; Trouble's a Ruler; Where Is Respect; Who Was I?; Wonderful! [1]

Cast: Rene Auberjonois; Walter Bobbie; Randy Herron; Ernestine Jackson; Carolyn Mignini; Joe Morton; Christopher Murney; Shezwae Powell; Tom Toner

Notes: [1] Out Detroit 11/25/72.

4451 • TRIP TO COONTOWN, A
OPENED: 04/04/1898   Theatre: Third Avenue
Musical   Broadway: 8

Composer: Billy Johnson
Lyricist: Bob Cole

Songs: I Can Stand for Your Color, but Your Hair Won't Do [1]; I Must o' Been a Dreaming; If That's Society, Excuse Me [1]; Picking on a Chicken Bone

Cast: Camille Cassele; Bob Cole; Pauline Freeman; Billy Johnson

Notes: No program available. This show was based on a one-act mini-musical AT JOLLY COON-EY ISLAND which was part of BLACK PATTI'S TROUBADOURS (1896). [1] Added to 1901 edition.

4452 • TRIP TO JAPAN, A

OPENED: 09/04/1909   Theatre: Hippodrome
Musical   Broadway: 447

Composer: Manuel Klein
Lyricist: R.H. Burnside; Manuel Klein
Librettist: R.H. Burnside
Producer: R.H. Burnside
Director: R.H. Burnside

Choreographer: Vincenzo Romeo; **Musical Director:** Manuel Klein; **Set Design:** Arthur Voegtlin

Songs: Ballet of Jewels, The; Every Girl Loves a Uniform; Fair Flower of Japan; Good Bye; I'm Goin' to Sea; Meet Me Where the Lanterns Glow; Opening Chorus; Our Navy's the Best in the World

Cast: Chief Ki Wi; E.A. Clark; W.H. Clark; Mabel Dwight; Nanette Flack; Harry Griffith; Marceline; Albertina Rasch

4453 • TRIP TO WASHINGTON, A

OPENED: 08/18/1913   Theatre: La Salle
Musical   Chicago

Composer: Ben M. Jerome
Lyricist: Henry Blossom
Librettist: Henry Blossom
Producer: Harry Askin; Florenz Ziegfeld
Director: R.H. Burnside

Source: TEXAS STEER, A (Play: Charles H. Hoyt); **Musical Director:** Ben M. Jerome

Songs: Anybody Round Here Looking for a Scrap; Back in the Dear Old Days [1]; Best That I Can Do Is Try to Do the Best I Can, The; Chat-Chat-Chatter on the Telephone; Don't Go Too Fast Little Dearie; Every National Hymn Is Just a Rag-Time Tune; Give Us a Drink [1]; Good-Bye Forever; Good Morning; I Am a Lone-Star Girl; I Want Someone to Love; I Wonder Will You

Forget [1]; It's the Uniform that Makes the Man; I've Always Been a Lucky Little Guy; Just a Kiss and Then Goodbye (C: Charles Miller; L: George V. Hobart); Just to Keep Peace in the Family; Nobody Cares; Off to Washington!; Scandal! Scandal!; Shame, Shame, Shame; There Is Something that I Like About You; Washington Squeeze, The; We Come from Maison de la Vere; You're the Only One for Me, Dear!

Cast: Mabella Baker; Rapley Holmes; Adele Rowler; Arthur Stanford; Katherine Stevenson; Harry Von Fossen

Notes: Songs also by Harry Williams according to the program but not credited individually. May have opened on August 24. [1] Sheet music only.

4454 • TRIXIE TRUE TEEN DETECTIVE

OPENED: 12/07/1980   Theatre: Theatre de Lys
Musical   Off-Broadway: 94

Composer: Kelly Hamilton
Lyricist: Kelly Hamilton
Librettist: Kelly Hamilton
Producer: Joseph Butt; Doug Cole; Joe Novak; Spencer Tandy
Director: Bill Gile

Choreographer: Arthur Faria; **Costumes:** David Toser; **Dance Arranger:** Jimmy Roberts; **Lighting Designer:** Craig Miller; **Musical Director:** Robert Fisher; **Orchestrations:** Eddie Sauter; **Set Design:** Michael J. Hotopp; Paul de Pass; **Vocal Arranger:** Robert Fisher

Songs: In Cahoots; Juvenile Fiction; Katzenjammer Kinda Song, A; Most Popular and Most Likely to Succeed; Mr. and Mrs. Dick Dickerson; Mystery of the Moon, The; Rita from Argentina; Secret of the Tapping Shoes, The; This Is Indeed My Lucky Day; Trixie True Teen Detective!; Trixie's on the Case!; You Haven't Got Time for Love

Cast: Marianna Allen; Kathy Andrini; Alison Bevan; Keith Caldwell; Gene Lindsey; Jay Lowman; Keith Rice; Marilyn Sokol

4455 • TROISIEME AMBASSADEURS — SHOW OF 1928.

Notes: *See LA REVUE DES AMBASSADEURS.*

4456 • TROPICANA

OPENED: 05/29/1986
Musical   Off-Off-Broadway

Composer: Robert Nassif
Lyricist: Peter Napolitano
Librettist: George Abbott

Notes: No program available.

4457 • TROUBLE IN TAHITI

Notes: *See ALL IN ONE.*

4458 • TROUBLES OF 1920

OPENED: 1921
Revue

Songs: I'm My Mama's Baby Boy (C: Louis Silvers;
L: George Jessel; Roy Turk)

Notes: No other information available.

4459 • TRUCKLOAD

OPENED: 09/06/1975   Theatre: Lyceum
Musical   Broadway

Composer: Louis St. Louis
Lyricist: Wes Harris
Librettist: Hugh Wheeler
Producer: Dick Clark; Adela Holzer; Shubert
Organization
Director: Patricia Birch

Choreographer: Patricia Birch; **Costumes:** Carrie F.
Robbins; **Lighting Designer:** John Gleason;
Orchestrations: Michael Gibson; Bhen
Lanzaroni; **Set Design:** Douglas W. Schmidt;
Vocal Arranger: Carl Hall

Songs: Amelia's Theme; Bonnie's Song; Boogie
Woogie Man; Cumbia/Wedding Party; Dragon
Strikes Back; Find My Way Home; Hash House
Habit; Hello Sunshine; I Guess Everything Will
Turn Out All Right; Jesus Is My Main Man; Look at
Us; Pour Out Your Soul; Rest Stop; Ricardo's
Lament; Standing in this Phonebooth; Step-Mama;
There's Nothing Like Music; Truckload

Cast: Deborah Allen; Cheryl Barnes; Donny Burks;
Rene Enriquez; Ilene Graff; Sherry Mathis; Doug
McKeon; Laurie Prange; Louis St. Louis; Kelly
Ward

Notes: Closed in previews. Previews ended
9/11/75.

4460 • TRULY BLESSED

OPENED: 04/22/1990   Theatre: Longacre
Musical   Broadway: 33

Composer: Queen Esther Marrow
Additional Music: Reginald Royal
Lyricist: Queen Esther Marrow
Additional Lyrics: Reginald Royal
Librettist: Queen Esther Marrow
Producer: Howard Hurst; Sophie Hurst; Philip
Rose
Director: Robert Kalfin

Choreographer: Larry Vickers; **Costumes:** Andrew
B. Marlay; **Lighting Designer:** Fred Kolo;
Orchestrations: Joseph Joubert; **Set Design:** Fred
Kolo

Songs: Battle Hymn of the Republic; Come on
Children, Let's Sing; Didn't It Rain (C/L:
Traditional); Even Me; Glory Hallelujah (C/L:
Traditional); Happy Days Are Here Again
(C: Milton Ager; L: Jack Yellen); He May Not
Come When You Want Him; He's Got the Whole
World in His Hands (C/L: Traditional); His Gift
to Me; I Found the Answer; It's Amazing What
God Can Do; I've Been 'Buked; Jesus Remembers
When Others Forget; Lord, I'm Determined;
Move on Up a Little Higher; Old Ship of Zion;
On the Battlefield for My Lord; Precious Lord;
Rusty Bell; Soon I Will Be Done; St. Louis Blues
(C/L: W.C. Handy); Thank You for the Change
in My Life; Truly Blessed; Wade in the Water
(C/L: Traditional)

Cast: Lynette G. DuPre; Doug Eskew; Carl Hall;
Queen Esther Marrow; Gwen Stewart

Notes: Songs not credited in program.

4461 • TRUTH ABOUT CINDERELLA, THE

OPENED: 1975
Musical   Unproduced

Composer: Charles Strouse
Lyricist: David Rogers

Songs: Any Day's a Perfect Day for a Wedding; At
Any Age at All; At the Palace; Big Night of the

Year, The; Clumsy Waltz, The; Find the Foot; Guilt; Help Stamp Out Dirt; New Kind of Girl; Princess for the Prince, A; Ready for You; Truth About Cinderella, The

Notes: No other information available.

4462 • TRUTH ABOUT RUTH, THE

OPENED: 07/1994   Theatre: Actors' Playhouse
Musical   Off-Broadway

Composer: Brad Ellis
Lyricist: Peter Morris
Librettist: Peter Morris
Producer: Postage Stamp Xtravaganzas
Director: Phillip George

Choreographer: Phillip George; **Costumes:** Randy Carfagno; Gene Lauze; **Lighting Designer:** Mark Vogeley; **Musical Director:** Pete Blue; **Set Design:** B.T. Whitehill

Songs: Ballad of Mrs. Bluebeard, The; Bang!; Dear Ruth; Fabo Soap Jingle, The; Face the Fact; Hello! Hello!; Hit That High Note; Home Sweet Home; If I Were Beautiful; Love Nest; Low; Ruth's Hit Parade; Sermonette, The; This Is the Place to Be; Truth About Ruth; You're Unique

Cast: Ruth Fields; David Lowenstein

4463 • TRY IT, YOU'LL LIKE IT

OPENED: 03/14/1973   Theatre: Mayfair
Musical   Off-Broadway: 87

Composer: Alexander Olshenetsky
Lyricist: Jacob Jacobs
Librettist: Jacob Jacobs; Max Zalotoff
Producer: Moishe Baruch
Director: Jacob Jacobs

Lighting Designer: Peter Xantho; **Musical Director:** Michael Richardone; **Set Design:** Peter Achilles; **Vocal Arranger:** Yasha Kreizberg

Songs: A Nier Tzeit; Du Zelbege Zah; Eibig Dein; Heint Viel eich Vu Tzi Zingen; Macht a Lehaim; Mirele; Oy Ses Git; Senior Citizens; Try It, You'll Like It; Ven Sis Du Lieve; Zal Shain Shulem Zine

Cast: Nellie Casman; Jaime Lewin; Thelma Mintz

4464 • TUMBLE INN

OPENED: 03/24/1919   Theatre: Selwyn
Musical   Broadway: 128

Composer: Rudolf Friml
Lyricist: Otto Harbach
Librettist: Otto Harbach
Producer: Arthur Hammerstein
Director: Bertram Harrison

Choreographer: Bert French; **Musical Director:** Herbert Stothart

Songs: Gowns Soft and Clingy; I've Told My Love; Laugh, The; Limbo-Land; Little Chicken Fit for Old Broadway, A; Snuggle and Dream; Thoughts I Wrote on the Leaves of My Heart, The; Trousseau Ball, The; Trousseau Waltz; Valse au L'Air; Wedding Blues, The; Won't You Help Me Out?; You'll Do It All Over Again

Cast: Herbert Corthell; Johnny Ford; Peggy O'Neill; Charles Ruggles; Zelda Sears

4465 • TURN OF THE CENTURY, THE

OPENED: 1939   Theatre: Diamond Horseshoe
Musical   Nightclub

Producer: Billy Rose
Director: John Murray Anderson

Choreographer: Lauretta Jefferson; **Costumes:** Raoul Pene du Bois; **Set Design:** Albert Johnson

Songs: Lady Known As Lulu (C/L: Unknown); Let's Dream Again (C: James F. Hanley; L: Jean Herbert; Billy Rose)

Cast: Harry Armstrong; Buddy Doyle; Emma Francis; Joseph E. Howard; Beatrice Kay; Frank Libuse; Della Lind; Elizabeth Murray; Tom Patricola; Fritzi Scheff; Noble Sissle and His Orchestra; Willie Solar

Notes: No songwriters credited in program. All songs not listed in program.

4466 • TURN TO THE RIGHT

OPENED: 08/08/1981   Theatre: Wilshire Los Angeles

Producer: Buddy Ebsen

Cast: Jan Clayton

Notes: No program available.

4467 • TURNABOUT! REVUES
OPENED: 07/1941
Revue   Los Angeles

Composer: Forman Brown
Lyricist: Forman Brown

Songs: At the Drive In; Brunnhilde Rides Again; Catalog Woman; Claribel the Great; Doge's Dilemma, The; Faith, Hope and Charity; Fiji Fanny; Husband's Clock, The; I Didn't Know Where to Look; If You Can't Get in the Corners; If You Peek in My Gazebo; I'm Glad to See Your Back; Incident in Arch Street; It May Be Life; Janitor's Boy, The; Last Show, The; Linda and Her Londonderry Air; Little Fred; Lola's Saucepan; March of Rhyme; Mein Hertz; Melinda Matime; Mrs. Badger-Butts; Mrs. Pettibone's Chandelier; My New York Slip; Never Go Walking without Your Hat Pin; Please Sell No More Drink to My Father; Rat Catcher's Daughter; Ruined Maid, The; She Was Poor but Honest; Turnabout; Victory Garden; When a Lady Has a Piazza; Yashmack Song, The

Cast: Forman Brown; Bill Buck; Harry Burnett; Elsa Lanchester; Dorothy Newmann; Frances Osborne

Notes: From the Turnabout Theatre in Hollywood. Half of each show was a puppet show and the other half a live revue. The theatre finally closed in 1956 after 4,535 performances.

4468 • TUSCALOOSA'S CALLING ME . . . BUT I'M NOT GOING!
OPENED: 12/01/1975   Theatre: Top of the Gate
Revue   Off-Broadway: 429

Composer: Hank Beebe
Lyricist: Bill Heyer
Librettist: Hank Beebe; Sam Dann; Bill Heyer
Producer: Arch Lustberg; Bruce Nelson; Jerry Schlossberg
Director: Gui Andrisano; James Hammerstein

Costumes: Rome Heyer; Charles E. Hoefler; **Lighting Designer:** Charles E. Hoefler; **Musical Director:** Jeremy Harris; **Set Design:** Charles E. Hoefler

Songs: Astrology; Backwards; Central Park on a Sunday Afternoon; Cold Cash; Delicatessen; Everything You Hate Is Right Here; Fugue for a Menage a Trois; Grafitti; I Dig Myself; New York '69; New York from the Air; Only Right Here in New York City; Poor; Things Were Out; Tuscaloosa's Calling Me but I'm Not Going

Cast: Len Gochman; Patti Perkins; Renny Temple

4469 • TWANG!
OPENED: 12/20/1965   Theatre: Shaftesbury
Musical   London

Composer: Lionel Bart
Lyricist: Lionel Bart
Librettist: Lionel Bart; Harvey Orkin
Producer: John Bryan; Bernard Delfont
Director: Joan Littlewood; Burt Shevelove

Choreographer: Paddy Stone, **Costumes:** Oliver Messel; **Musical Director:** Gareth Davies; Kenneth Moule; **Set Design:** Oliver Messel

Songs: Dreamchild; Follow Your Leader; I'll Be Hanged; Make an Honest Woman of Me; Roger the Ugly; Sighs; To the Woods; Twang!!; Unseen Hands; Wanted; Welcome to Sherwood; What Makes a Star; Whose Little Girl Are You?; With Bells On; You Can't Catch Me

Cast: Kent Baker; Clive Barker; James Booth; Bernard Bresslaw; Frank Coda; George A. Cooper; Ronnie Corbett; Toni Eden; Howard Goorney; Bob Grant; Elric Hooper; Maxwell Shaw; Barbara Windsor

4470 • TWANGER
OPENED: 11/15/1972   Theatre: Van Dam
Musical   Off-Broadway: 24

Composer: Ronnie Britton
Lyricist: Ronnie Britton
Librettist: Ronnie Britton
Producer: Wayne Clark
Director: Walter Ash

Costumes: Owen H. Goldstein; **Dance Arranger:** David Wahler; **Lighting Designer:** Peter

Anderson; **Musical Director:** Lee Gillespie; **Vocal Arranger:** Gordon Harrell

Songs: Big, Big Contest; But, I Love You; Five Minutes Ago; Forest of Silver; Francis' Feast; Frogs Perform, The; Garbage-Ella [1]; Have You Seen the Princess?; Impossibility; Magic Licorice; Normal, Normal, Normal; Obey, Abide; Phyllis Frog; Potion, A; Prologue; Sister and Brother, A; Sneaky, Creepy Fellows; Tiny Light; To Win a Prince; Twanger!; Wanna Get Married

Cast: Sue Renee Bernstein; Glen M. Castello; Charles Flanagan; George Heusinger; Andrea Noel; Charles Stuart

Notes: [1] Also in GREENWICH VILLAGE FOLLIES (1976).

4471 • 'TWAS THE NIGHT BEFORE CHRISTMAS

OPENED: 12/08/1974   Theatre: CBS
TV Musical

Composer: Maury Laws
Lyricist: Jules Bass

Songs: Christmas Chimes; Even a Miracle Needs a Hand; Give Your Heart a Try

Voice: George Gobel; Joel Grey; Tammy Grimes

4472 • TWENTIETH CENTURY GIRL, THE

OPENED: 1895   Theatre: Bijou
Musical   Broadway

Composer: Ludwig Englander
Lyricist: Sydney Rosenfeld
Librettist: Sydney Rosenfeld

Notes: No other information available.

4473 • TWIDDLE-TWADDLE

OPENED: 01/11/1906   Theatre: Weber's Music
                          Hall
Revue   Broadway: 137

Composer: Maurice Levi
Lyricist: Edgar Smith
Librettist: Edgar Smith

Producer: Joseph Weber
Director: Al Holbrook

Musical Director: Maurice Levi

Songs: Butterflies of Fashion, The; Days of Forty-Nine, The; Days of My Boyhood; Hats; I Hope You'll Forgive These Tears; Little Bunch of Daisies, A; Looking for a Sure Thing [1]; My Syncopated Gypsy Maid; Next Summer in Old New York; Oh, Heigh-Ho!; Poor Little Red Papoose; Society Buds; Stories of the Stage [1]; 'Tis Dreadful! 'Tis Astonishing; 'Tis Hard to Be a Lady in a Case Like That; Venedig, Fair Venedig; When You've Pampered Your Adipose Tissue; You and the Girl You Love

Cast: Charles A. Bigelow; Marie Dressler; Trixie Friganza; Ernest Lambert; Bonnie Maginn; Joseph Weber

Notes: [1] Sheet music only.

4474 • TWIGS

OPENED: 11/14/1971   Theatre: Broadhurst
Play   Broadway: 289

Author: George Furth
Producer: Frederick Brisson
Director: Michael Bennett

Costumes: Sara Brook; **Lighting Designer:** David F. Segal; **Set Design:** Peter Larkin

Songs: Hollywood and Vine (C: Stephen Sondheim; L: George Furth)

Cast: Conrad Bain; Mark Dawson; MacIntyre Dixon; A. Larry Haines; Simon Oakland; Sada Thompson

4475 TWILIGHT ALLEY

Notes: *See BEGGAR'S HOLIDAY.*

4476 • TWINKLE TWINKLE

OPENED: 11/16/1926   Theatre: Liberty
Musical   Broadway: 167

Composer: Harry Archer
Lyricist: Harlan Thompson
Librettist: Harlan Thompson
Producer: Louis F. Werba
Director: Frank Craven

Choreographer: Julian Alfred; Harry Puck;
Costumes: Charles LeMaire; **Musical Director:**
Max Steiner; **Set Design:** P. Dodd Ackerman

Songs: Crime; Day Dreams [3] (C: Harry Ruby;
L: Bert Kalmar); Find a Girl [2]; Get a Load of
This; Hustle, Bustle; I Hate to Talk About Myself;
Practically in Love with You [2]; Reuben; Sex
Appeal [2]; Sunday Afternoon; Sweeter Than
You [1] (C: Harry Ruby; L: Bert Kalmar); Twinkle
Twinkle; We're on the Map (C: Harry Ruby;
L: Bert Kalmar); When We're Bride and Groom;
Whistle (C: Harry Ruby; L: Bert Kalmar); You
Know I Know; You're the One [2]

Cast: Joe E. Brown; Alan Edwards; Joseph Lertora;
Ona Munson; Florence Upton

Notes: [1] Also in TOP SPEED (1929). [2] Cut prior
to opening. [3] Added after opening.

4477 • TWINKLING EYES

OPENED: 05/18/1919
Musical

Composer: Richard Rodgers
Lyricist: Richard Rodgers
Librettist: Myron D. Rosenthal; Harry Strong
Producer: Brooklyn YMHA
Director: Lorenz Hart

Songs: Advertise; Ali Baba; Asiatic Angels;
Butterfly Love; Can It (L: Oscar Hammerstein
II); Dearie; I'm So Shy; Japanese Jazz; Love Is
Not in Vain; Love Me By Parcel Post
(L: Mortimer W. Rodgers); Loving Cup; Now
Listen; Out of a Job; Prisms, Plums and Prunes
(L: Benjamin Kaye); There's Always Room for
One More (L: Oscar Hammerstein II);
Twinkling Eyes; Weaknesses (L: Oscar
Hammerstein II); Wild Women's Wiles

Notes: Amateur show. Same songs as UP STAGE
AND DOWN.

4478 • TWIRLY WHIRLY

OPENED: 09/11/1902   Theatre: Weber and Fields
                          Music Hall
Musical   Broadway: 244

Composer: William T. Francis
Lyricist: Edgar Smith

Librettist: Edgar Smith
Producer: Lew Fields; Joseph Weber
Director: Lew Fields; Julian Mitchell

Costumes: Will R. Barnes; **Set Design:** John Young

Songs: After Dinner; Big Pound Cake (C/L: John T.
Kelly); Buena Senorita Am I, A; Bugaboo Man,
The; Clog Dance; Come Down Ma Evening Star
(C: John Stromberg; L: Robert B. Smith); Dream
One Dream of Me (C: William T. Francis; John
Stromberg; L: Edgar Smith); Etiquette (L: Robert
B. Smith); Gay Old Seville; Geezer (C/L:
Unknown); I Never Loved a Man As Much As
That (L: Robert B. Smith); In Stage Land; Kit;
Leader of Vanity Fair, The (L: Robert B. Smith);
Little Widow Brown; Long Green, The (L: Robert
B. Smith); Miss Pinchin's Boarding School; My
Intimate Friend (L: Wilton Lackaye; Edgar
Smith); Ping Pong (C: William T. Francis; John
Stromberg; L: Robert B. Smith); Priscilla; Romeo;
Sailing; Softly Stealing, Lanterns Gleaming;
Strike Out McCracken; Susie Woosie; Vaudeville
King, The; Ye Ho, for the Sailor's Life

Cast: Louise Allen; Mabel Barrison; Bessie Clayton;
Willie Collier; Peter Dailey; Lew Fields; Bonnie
Maginn; Lillian Russell; Fay Templeton; Joseph
Weber

4479 • TWO BOUQUETS, THE

OPENED: 05/31/1938   Theatre: Windsor
Musical   Broadway: 55

Lyricist: Eleanor Farjeon
Librettist: Eleanor Farjeon
Producer: Bela Blau; Marc Connelly
Director: Marc Connelly

Choreographer: Leslie French; Felicia Sorel;
Costumes: Raoul Pene du Bois; **Musical
Director:** Macklin Marrow; **Orchestrations:**
Ernest Irving; **Set Design:** Robert Barnhart

Songs: Against the Storm; Ah, How Capricious;
Albert Porter; Bashful Lover (C: C. Moulton);
Courses of Nature, The; Dearest Miss Bell;
Dearest Miss Flo; Fireworks, The; Fly Forth
O Gentle Dove (C: M. Pinsuti); Git on de Boat,
Chillun; Health to Dear Mama, A; Her Lilywhite
Hand; How Can We Bring the Folks Round;
I Wish I Was in Texas; I'll Tell Papa; Juanita;
Kissing; Little Champagne for Papa, A; Man You

Love, The; Oh, the Regatta; Pretty Patty Moss;
Rain Chorus; She Did the Fandango; She Loves
Thee; Sweet Blossoms (C: M. Pinsuti); Toddy's
the Drink for Me (C: Traditional); Varsovienne;
What Can I Do?; When I Was but a Bounding
Boy; White and the Pink, The; Yes or No; Young
Girl and Young Man; Youth Who Sows, The

Cast: Jane Archer; Gabrielle Brune; Leo G. Carroll;
Robert Chisholm; Alfred Drake; Leslie French;
Enid Markey; Patricia Morison; Winston
O'Keefe; Viola Roache; Robert Rounseville; John
Tyers; Marcy Wescott; Joan Wetmore

Notes: The music was written by various
uncredited Victorian composers.

4480 • 2 BY 5

OPENED: 10/18/1976   Theatre: Village Gate
Revue   Off-Broadway: 57

Composer: John Kander
Lyricist: Fred Ebb
Producer: Judy Gordon; Jack Temchin
Director: Seth Glassman

Costumes: Dan Leigh; **Lighting Designer:** Martin
Tudor; **Musical Director:** Joseph Clonick; **Set
Design:** Dan Leigh

Songs: Among My Yesterdays [4]; Broadway,
My Street [2]; Cabaret [1]; Class [9]; Home [2];
I Don't Remember You [4]; Isn't This Better [10];
Losers; Love Song (Sara Lee) [8]; Maybe This
Time [13]; Me and My Baby [9]; Mein Herr [5];
Military Man; Money Song [5]; Mr. Cellophane
[9]; My Own Best Friend [9]; New York, New
York [6]; On Stage; Only Love [7]; Quiet Thing,
A [3]; Razzle Dazzle [9]; Ring Them Bells [11];
Seeing Things [4]; Sign Here [3]; Sing Happy [3];
Ten Percent [12]; Why Can't I Speak [7];
Wilkommen [1]; World Goes Round, The [6];
Yes [2]

Cast: D'Jamin Bartlett; Kay Cummings; Daniel
Fortus; Shirley Lemmon; Scott Stevensen

Notes: [1] From CABARET. [2] From 70 GIRLS 70.
[3] From FLORA, THE RED MENACE. [4] From
THE HAPPY TIME. [5] From the film CABARET.
[6] From the film NEW YORK, NEW YORK. [7]
From ZORBA. [8] From Kaye Ballard's nightclub
act. [9] From CHICAGO. [10] From film FUNNY

LADY. [11] From TV special LIZA WITH A "Z."
[12] Cut from CHICAGO. [13] From Kaye
Ballard's nightclub act. Also later put in film
version of CABARET.

4481 • TWO BY TWO

OPENED: 11/10/1970   Theatre: Imperial
Musical   Broadway: 343

Composer: Richard Rodgers
Lyricist: Martin Charnin
Librettist: Peter Stone
Producer: Richard Rodgers
Director: Joe Layton

Source: FLOWERING PEACH, THE (Play: Clifford
Odets); **Costumes:** Fred Voelpel; **Dance
Arranger:** Trude Rittman; **Lighting Designer:**
John Gleason; **Musical Director:** Jay Blackton;
Orchestrations: Eddie Sauter; **Set Design:** David
Hays; **Vocal Arranger:** Trude Rittman

Songs: As Far As I'm Concerned [5]; Brother
Department, The [1]; Covenant, The; Death of
Me, The [3]; Ev'rything That's Gonna Be Has
Been [3]; Forty Nights [3]; Getting Married to a
Person [2]; Gitka's Song, The; Golden Ram, The;
Hey Girlie; I Can't Complain [3]; I Do Not Know
a Day I Did Not Love You; Ninety Again!; Old
Man, An; Poppa Isn't Poppa Anymore [3]; Poppa
Knows Best; Put Him Away; Something Doesn't
Happen; Something, Somewhere; Two By Two;
When It Dries; Why Me?; Without My Money [3];
You; You Couldn't Please Me More [4]; You
Have Got to Have a Rudder on the Ark

Cast: Marilyn Cooper; Joan Copeland; Harry Goz;
Madeline Kahn; Michael Karm; Danny Kaye;
Tricia O'Neil; Walter Willison

Notes: [1] Same music as "As Far As I'm
Concerned." Cut prior to opening. [2] Cut prior
to opening. Music later used as "Mama Always
Makes It Better" in I REMEMBER MAMA. [3]
Cut prior to opening. [4] Cut prior to opening.
Later in I REMEMBER MAMA. [5] Same music
as "The Brother Department."

4482 • TWO FOR FUN

OPENED: 02/13/1961   Theatre: Madison Avenue
                              Playhouse
Revue   Off-Broadway: 34

Composer: Silvio Masciarelli; Lothar Perl
Librettist: Peter Good; Jack Woodford
Producer: Madison Productions
Director: Mata & Hari

Costumes: Freddy Wittop

Songs: Have Gun, Get Gold

Cast: Georgia Caine; May DeSousa; Claude Fleming; Mata & Hari

Notes: No program available.

4483 • TWO FOR THE SHOW

OPENED: 02/08/1940   Theatre: Booth
Revue   Broadway: 124

Composer: Morgan Lewis
Lyricist: Nancy Hamilton
Librettist: Nancy Hamilton
Producer: Stanley Gilkey; Gertrude Macy
Director: John Murray Anderson; Joshua Logan

Choreographer: Robert Alton; **Costumes:** Raoul Pene du Bois; **Lighting Designer:** John Murray Anderson; **Musical Director:** Ray Kavanaugh; **Orchestrations:** Hans Spialek; Don Walker; **Set Design:** Raoul Pene du Bois; **Vocal Arranger:** Harold Cooke

Songs: All Girl Band, The; As Was and As Is [2]; At Last It's Love; Calypso Joe; Fool for Luck; House with a Little Red Barn, A; How High the Moon [2]; Teeter Totter Tessie [2]; That Terrible Tune; This Merry Christmas [1]; Where Do You Get Your Greens? [1]

Cast: Eve Arden; Alfred Drake; Brenda Forbes; Richard Haydn; Keenan Wynn

Notes: [1] Not in program. [2] Out White Plains 6/30/41.

4484 • TWO FOR TONIGHT

OPENED: 12/28/1939
Revue   Off-Broadway: 30

Composer: Berenece Kazounoff
Lyricist: John Latouche
Librettist: Ralph Berton; Mitchell Hodges
Producer: Promenaders, The
Director: Max Scheck

Costumes: Doris Roberts; **Set Design:** Edwin Vandernoot

Songs: Blase; Blues (C: John Latouche); Call of the Wild (L: Sylvia Marks); Could You Use a New Friend? (C/L: Eugene Berton; Ralph Berton); Dancing Alone (C/L: Eugene Berton; Ralph Berton); Five O'Clock (C: Bernie Wayne; L: Ben Raleigh); Home Is Where You Hang Your Hat; Masquerade (C/L: Charles Herbert); Nursery (C/L: Charles Herbert); Personal Heaven (C/L: Eugene Berton; Ralph Berton); Slap on the Greasepaint; Windows (C/L: Eugene Berton; Ralph Berton)

Cast: Charlie Herbert; Grace Herbert; Billy Sands

4485 • TWO GENTLEMEN OF VERONA

OPENED: 07/27/1971   Theatre: St. James
Musical   Broadway: 627

Composer: Galt MacDermot
Lyricist: John Guare
Librettist: John Guare; Mel Shapiro
Producer: N.Y. Shakespeare Festival; Joseph Papp
Director: Mel Shapiro

Source: TWO GENTLEMEN OF VERONA (Play: William Shakespeare); **Choreographer:** Jean Erdman; Dennis Nahat; **Costumes:** Theoni V. Aldredge; **Lighting Designer:** Lawrence Metzler; **Musical Director:** Harold Wheeler; **Set Design:** Ming Cho Lee

Songs: Bring All the Boys Back Home; Calla Lily Lady; Don't Have the Baby; Dragon Flight; Eglamour; Follow the Rainbow; Hot Lover; Howl [1]; I Am Not Interested in Love; I Love My Father; I'd Like to Be a Rose; Kidnapped; Land of Betrayal; Love Has Driven Me Sane; Love, Is That You?; Love Me; Love's Revenge; Mansion; Milkmaid; Night Letter; Pearls; Summer, Summer; Symphony; That's a Very Interesting Question; Thou, Julia, Thou Has Metamorphosed Me; Thou, Proteus, Thou Has Metamorphosed Me; Thurio's Samba; To Whom It May Concern Me; Two Gentlemen of Verona; What a Nice Idea; What Does a Lover Pack?; What's a Nice Girl Like Her; Where's North?; Who Is Sylvia? (L: William Shakespeare)

Cast: Jonelle Allen; John Bottoms; Diana Davila; Clifton Davis; Raul Julia

Notes: Moved from the Delacorte Theatre to the St. James on December 1, 1971 for an additional 614 performances. [1] Added to London production.

4486 • TWO HEARTS IN THREE-QUARTER TIME

OPENED: 07/08/1946
Musical   Closed out of town

Composer: Robert Stolz
Lyricist: Dailey Paskman
Librettist: William A. Drake
Producer: Barrie O'Daniels
Director: James Westerfield

Source: DER VERLORENE WALTZER (Musical: Robert Gilbert; Paul Knepler; J.M. Welleminsky); **Source:** TWO HEARTS IN WALTZ TIME (ZWEI HERZEN IM DREIVIERTELTAKT) (Film: Walter Reisch; Franz Schulz); **Costumes:** Kate Drain Lawson; **Musical Director:** Ray Sinatra; **Set Design:** Norman Rock

Songs: Ballet (dance); Children of the Drama; Finaletto; Give Your Bride a Kiss; Lovely Little Sister; Old Vienna; Opening; Pain of Love's First Kiss, The; Tonight with You; Two Hearts in Waltz Time; Two Times Young and Twice in Love; Wasn't It Grand; What Does My Heart Keep Saying

Cast: Edit Angold; Kenny Baker; Patricia Bowman; Fred Brookins; Pamela Caveness; Chick Chandler; Paul Craik; Thomas Glynn; Alfred Hunter; Irene Manning; John Pelletti; Thayer Roberts; Alexis Rotov; Kirby Smith

Notes: From a program of the Greek Theatre, Los Angeles.

4487 • TWO HUSBANDS AND ONE WIFE

OPENED: 1916
Musical   Closed out of town

Composer: Will Vodery
Lyricist: Frank Kennedy

Librettist: Frank Kennedy
Director: Hall Lane

Songs: Beautiful Band; Darkie's Serenade; Monterey; My Little Girl; Norway; Rag, Rag, Rag; Ragging Along; Tennessee; Virginia Rag; Wake Me Up with a Rag

Cast: Frank A. Burt; Girl Trust, The

Notes: A burlesque musical. Some of these songs were probably popular songs of the day uncredited.

4488 • TWO IF BY SEA!?

OPENED: 06/18/1971
Musical   Closed out of town

Composer: Tony Hutchins
Lyricist: Priscilla B. Dewey
Librettist: Priscilla B. Dewey; Charles Werner Moore
Director: Charles Werner Moore

Choreographer: Ronald Johnston; **Dance Arranger:** Jeff Lass; **Lighting Designer:** Michael F. Hottois; **Set Design:** Jim Stewart; **Vocal Arranger:** John Nagy

Songs: Be More Aggressive; Follow Daddy (C: John Foster); How Are You Going to Start the American Revolution?; If By Sea; Lanterns; Law Breakers; Melt It Down; News, News; Off Limits (C: John Nagy); Paul Revere (C: John Nagy); People Who Live on Islands; Some Day Soon; Stamp Act; Tea Dance; Throw the Egg; Two If By Sea, I Think! (C: Paul Lass); We Stand for Moderation; Word, The; You'll Regret Your Stand

Cast: John Scoullar

Notes: Rhode Island program used.

4489 TWO IS COMPANY

OPENED: 09/22/1915   Theatre: Lyric
Musical   Broadway: 29

Composer: Adolf Philipp
Lyricist: Edward A. Paulton; Adolf Philipp
Librettist: Edward A. Paulton; Adolf Philipp
Director: Adolf Philipp

Songs: Come with Me to Paree; Footman and the Maid, The; Free as Air; Free! Free!; I Prefer the Cat; If You But Knew What I Know; In the Land of Lorraine; La Belle Lulu; Lotus Land; Lure of the Waltz, The; Stamp Enclosed, A; Two Is Company; We Like to Whirl; You Loved Me Then

Cast: Georgia Caine; May DeSousa; Claude Fleming; Clarence Harvey; Ralph Nairn

Notes: No program available. Philipp credited the music to Jean Briquet and claimed the show was based on a play by Jean Herve. However, Briquet and Herve probably didn't exist. Paulton helped with the English language translations of book and lyrics.

4490 • TWO LITTLE BRIDES

OPENED: 04/23/1912   Theatre: Casino
Musical   Broadway: 63

Composer: Gustave Kerker
Lyricist: Arthur Anderson; Harold Atteridge; James T. Powers
Librettist: Arthur Anderson; Harold Atteridge; James T. Powers
Producer: Messrs. Shubert
Director: J.C. Huffman; William J. Wilson

Source: SCHNEEGLOCKCHEN (Musical: Julius Wilhelm; A.M. Willner); **Musical Director:** Max Hershfeld

Songs: Are We Widows, Wives or What?; Buzz on Little Busy Bees!; Corsican, The; How Do You Do?; I Like All Girls; Kiss Me Again, Bebe; Meet Me at Eight in the Hall (The Letter Song); Oh! Be Careful [1]; Oh, Honorka; Opening Chorus; Snowdrops and the Spring; So Away with Sorrow; Somehow, Sometime, Somewhere (C/L: Louis A. Hirsch); Someone I Used to Know; Waiting for Me; Waltz without a Kiss, A (L: James T. Powers); What About It?

Cast: Flavia Arcaro; Frances Cameron; Leila Hughes; James T. Powers

Notes: [1] Sheet music only.

4491 • TWO LITTLE GIRLS IN BLUE

OPENED: 05/03/1921   Theatre: Cohan
Musical   Broadway: 135

Composer: Paul Lannin; Vincent Youmans
Lyricist: Ira Gershwin [7]
Librettist: Fred Jackson
Producer: A.L. Erlanger
Director: Ned Wayburn

Choreographer: Ned Wayburn; **Costumes:** Shirley Barker; Iverson & Henneage; **Musical Director:** Charles Previn; **Orchestrations:** Stephen Jones; Paul Lannin; **Set Design:** H. Robert Law

Songs: Dolly (C: Vincent Youmans; L: Ira Gershwin; Schuyler Greene); Finale Act II (C: Vincent Youmans); Gypsy Trail, The (C: Paul Lannin; L: Irving Caesar); Happy Ending [2] (C: Paul Lannin); Here, Steward (C: Vincent Youmans); Honeymoon (When Will You Shine for Me?) (C: Paul Lannin); I'm Tickled Silly (Slapstick) (C: Paul Lannin); Just Like You (C: Paul Lannin); Little Bag of Tricks [2] (C: Paul Lannin); Make the Best of It [1] (C: Vincent Youmans); Mr. and Mrs. [4] (C: Vincent Youmans); Oh Me! Oh My! (Oh You) (C: Vincent Youmans); Orienta (C: Vincent Youmans; L: Irving Caesar; Schuyler Greene); Rice and Shoes [3] (C: Vincent Youmans; L: Ira Gershwin; Schuyler Green); She's Innocent; Silly Season, The (C: Vincent Youmans); Slapstick [1] (C: Paul Lannin); Somebody's Sunday [6] (C/L: Vernon Duke); Summertime [1] (C: Paul Lannin); There's Something About Me They Like (C: Vincent Youmans; L: Ira Gershwin; Fred Jackson); Two Little Girls in Blue (C: Vincent Youmans); Utopia [2] (C: Vincent Youmans); We're Off on a Wonderful Trip (C: Vincent Youmans); We're Off to India [8] (C: Vincent Youmans); When I'm with the Girls (C: Vincent Youmans); Who's Who with You [4] (C: Vincent Youmans); Win Some Winsome Girl [2] (C: Paul Lannin); Wonderful U.S.A. (Your Wonderful U.S.A.) (C: Paul Lannin); You Started Something (When You Came Along) [5] (C: Vincent Youmans)

Cast: Madeleine Fairbanks; Marion Fairbanks; Olin Howland; Emma Janvier; Julia Kelety; Evelyn Law; George Mack; Fred Santley; Oscar Shaw; Jack Tomson; Tommy Tomson

Notes: [1] Cut in rehearsal. [2] Cut in tryouts. [3] Called "Sweetest Girl" during tryouts. [4] Cut in tryouts. Previously in PICCADILLY TO BROADWAY. [5] Music used for "Waiting for You" from NO! NO! NANETTE! [6] Written for 1927 London version which closed out of town. [7]

Used pseudonym Arthur Francis. [8] Introduction music same as "The Silly Season." Chorus portion same music as "Win Some Winsome Girl."

4492 • TWO LOTS IN THE BRONX
OPENED: 11/1913   Theatre: Adolf Philipp
Musical   Broadway

Composer: Adolf Philipp
Lyricist: Edward Paulton; Adolf Philipp
Librettist: Edward Paulton; Adolf Philipp
Producer: Oliver Morosco

Songs: Here's to Us; I'm Fond of You-You're Fond of Me; It's Simply My Smile; Money Makes the World Go 'Round; My Darling Wife; Robbers Everywhere; Tell Me That You Love Me; 2 Lots in the Bronx

Cast: Emil Berla; Adolf Philipp; Marie Serina; Grete von Mayhof

Notes: Paulton helped with the English language lyrics and libretto.

4493 • TWO MEN AND A GIRL
OPENED: 02/13/1911
Musical   Closed out of town

Composer: Julian Edwards
Lyricist: Charles J. Campbell; Ralph M. Skinner
Librettist: Charles J. Campbell; Ralph M. Skinner
Producer: Lee Shubert; Sam S. Shubert
Director: William J. Wilson

Songs: Herman, Let's Dance That Beautiful Waltz (C: Ted Snyder; L: Irving Berlin); Wishing (C: Ted Snyder; L: Irving Berlin)

Cast: Ralph Austin; Fred Bailey

Notes: No program available. Clipping from Detroit 2/15/11 used. This was a revision of THE MOTOR GIRL. See also under that title.

4494 • TWO MUCH
OPENED: 1967   Theatre: Madeira Club
Musical   Nightclub

Author: Don Brockett; William Dyer; Joanne Pasquinelli

Cast: John Paul Hudson; Don Parks; Lily Tomlin

Notes: Provincetown, Massachusetts revue.

4495 • TWO ON AN ISLAND
OPENED: 01/25/1940   Theatre: Broadhurst
Play   Broadway: 96

Author: Elmer Rice
Producer: Playwrights' Company, The
Director: Elmer Rice

Incidental Music: Kurt Weill; **Set Design:** Jo Mielziner

Cast: Luther Adler; Howard Da Silva; Betty Field; Martin Ritt; Robert Williams

4496 • TWO ON THE AISLE
OPENED: 07/19/1951   Theatre: Mark Hellinger
Revue   Broadway: 279

Composer: Jule Styne
Lyricist: Betty Comden; Adolph Green
Librettist: Betty Comden; Adolph Green
Producer: Arthur Lesser
Director: Abe Burrows

Choreographer: Ted Cappy; **Costumes:** Joan Personette; **Dance Arranger:** Genevieve Pitot; **Lighting Designer:** Howard Bay; **Musical Director:** Herbert Greene; **Orchestrations:** Philip J. Lang; **Set Design:** Howard Bay

Songs: Catch Our Act at the Met (Vaudeville Ain't Dead); Clown, The; Everlasting; Give a Little, Get a Little; Here She Comes Now (East River Hoedown); Hold Me-Hold Me-Hold Me; How Will He Know?; If You Hadn't but You Did; Show Train; So Far, So Good [1]; There Never Was a Baby Like My Baby; Triangle (sketch)

Cast: Dolores Gray; Bert Lahr; Colette Marchand; Elliott Reid

Notes: [1] Cut prior to opening. Music from "Give Me a Song with a Beautiful Melody" from film IT'S A GREAT FEELING.

4497 • TWO ROSES, THE
OPENED: 11/21/1904   Theatre: Broadway
Musical   Broadway: 29

Composer: Ludwig Englander
Lyricist: Stanislaus Stange
Librettist: Stanislaus Stange
Producer: Charles B. Dillingham
Director: Fred G. Latham

Source: SHE STOOPS TO CONQUER (Play: Oliver Goldsmith); **Choreographer:** A.M. Holbrook; **Costumes:** Mme. Seidle; **Musical Director:** John Lund; **Set Design:** Emens & Unitt

Songs: Airy Mary; Appearances Are Deceitful; Battle on the Tiles, The; Ding Dong, Ding Dong (Finale Act I); Fairest of Roses [1]; Jack in the Box; Just Three Words; Love's Misgivings; Making of a Woman, The; Remarkable Doctor, A; Rose Marie; Simple Dimple, A; Sing Hey, Sing Ho (Opening Chorus Act II); Smile and Be Merry; Spirit of Mischief, The; There's Not a Thing I Wouldn't Do; 'Tis the Hour (Opening Chorus); What May a Lovesick Maiden Do; What's a Kiss; Why?

Cast: Josephine Bartlett; Louis Harrison; Louise LeBaron; Fritzi Scheff

Notes: No songs listed in program. [1] Vocal score only.

4498 • TWO WEEKS WITH PAY

OPENED: 06/24/1940
Revue   Closed out of town

Librettist: Peter Barry; David Greggory; Charles Sherman
Producer: Olneys, The

Choreographer: Gene Kelly; **Costumes:** Marion Herwood; **Set Design:** Lawrence L. Goldwasser; **Vocal Arranger:** Harold Cooke

Songs: All That and Heaven Too (C: Richard Lewine; L: Peter Barry; David Greggory); As Long as You're Along (C: Baldwin Bergersen; L: David Greggory); Dear Horse (C: Richard Lewine; L: Ted Fetter); Five Cent Piece (C: Richard Lewine; L: Ted Fetter); Hey Gal (C: Will Irwin; L: Peter Barry); I Would Rather Be (C: Baldwin Bergersen; L: Peter Barry; David Greggory); Jig Is Up, The (C: Richard Lewine; L: Ted Fetter); June, Moon, Spoon (C/L: Herman Hupfeld); Just Another Page in Your Diary [2] (C/L: Cole Porter); Noises in the Street (C: Richard Lewine; L: Peter Barry; David

Greggory); Now That I Know You [1] (C: Richard Rodgers; L: Lorenz Hart); Once Upon a Morning (sketch) (C: Eyck Van Goetz); Praised Be Moses (C: Charles Marvin; L: William Borden); Secret Snow (C: Baldwin Bergersen; L: Peter Barry; David Greggory); Will You Love Me on Monday Morning (C: Harold Arlen; L: Ira Gershwin; E.Y. Harburg); With You with Me (C: John Green; L: Johnny Mercer)

Cast: Remo Bufano's Puppets; Eugene Hari; Pat Harrington; Bill Johnson; Ruth Mata; Marie Nash; Earl Oxford; Hiram Sherman

Notes: [1] Same music as original deleted I'D RATHER BE RIGHT title song. [2] Cut from LEAVE IT TO ME!

4499 • TWO'S COMPANY

OPENED: 12/15/1952   Theatre: Alvin
Revue   Broadway: 91

Composer: Vernon Duke
Lyricist: Ogden Nash
Librettist: Peter DeVries; Charles Sherman
Producer: Michael Ellis; James Russo
Director: Jules Dassin

Choreographer: Jerome Robbins; **Costumes:** Miles White; **Musical Director:** Milton Rosenstock; **Orchestrations:** Clare Grundman; Don Walker; **Set Design:** Ralph Alswang

Songs: Baby Couldn't Dance; Esther (L: Sammy Cahn); Good Little Girls [2] (L: Sammy Cahn); Haunted Hot Spot; I Think You're Pretty Too [1]; It Just Occurred to Me (L: Sammy Cahn); Just Like a Man [4]; Man's Home, A (C/L: Sheldon Harnick); Merry Minuet [3] (C/L: Sheldon Harnick); Out of the Clear Blue Sky; Purple Rose; Roll Along, Sadie; Roundabout [4]; Theatre Is a Lady, The; Turn Me Loose on Broadway

Cast: David Burns; Bill Callahan; Bette Davis; Ellen Hanley; Peter Kelley; Tina Louise; Deborah Remsen; Hiram Sherman

Notes: Production under the supervision of John Murray Anderson. [1] Out Pittsburgh 1/10/52. [2] Out Detroit 10/19/52, later in THE LITTLEST REVUE. Originally written for and cut from the film APRIL IN PARIS. [3] Cut. Later used in JOHN MURRAY ANDERSON'S ALMANAC. [4] Originally in SWEET BYE AND BYE.

4500 • TZIGANE, THE

OPENED: 05/16/1895   Theatre: Abbey's
Musical   Broadway

Composer: Reginald De Koven
Lyricist: Harry B. Smith
Librettist: Harry B. Smith
Producer: Abbey; Grau; Schoeffel
Director: Max Freeman

Costumes: Mme. Seidle; **Musical Director:** Paul Steindorff; **Set Design:** Henry E. Hoyt

Cast: Jefferson De Angelis; Joseph Herbert; Clare Lane; Lillian Russell; Frederic Solomon; Hubert Wilke

Notes: No songs listed in program.

U

4501 • UBANGI CLUB FOLLIES (1935)

OPENED: 1935   Theatre: Ubangi Club
Revue   Nightclub

Composer: Andy Razaf
Lyricist: Andy Razaf
Producer: Leonard Harper

Songs: At the Reefer Smoker's Ball (C: Mildred Bailey; Andy Razaf); You Broke It Up (When You Said Dixie) (C: Duke Yellman)

Cast: Gladys Bentley; Billie Daniels; Velma Middleton

Notes: No program available. The Ubangi Club occupied the same space as the uptown Connie's Inn.

4502 • UBANGI CLUB FOLLIES (1941)

OPENED: 1941   Theatre: Ubangi Club
Revue   Nightclub

Composer: Paul Denniker
Lyricist: Andy Razaf

Songs: Get Rhythm in Your Feet; I Guess We're Gonna Get Along

Cast: Bunny Briggs; Erskine Hawkins' 'Bama State Coll.; Velma Middleton

Notes: No program available.

4503 • UBANGI CLUB REVUES

    Theatre: Ubangi Club
Revue   Nightclub

Composer: Eubie Blake
Lyricist: Andy Razaf

Songs: Boogie Woogie Bunga Boo; Conga Tap, The; Cradle of Rhythm (C: Paul Denniker); Harlem's a Garden; I'm Percy Pinchill of Harlem; Jungle Rhythm Roundup (C: Paul Denniker); Native Son, A; Red, A; Snooty, The; Sweep No More My Lady; To Arms (Dear One, Divine) (C: Paul Denniker)

Notes: Songs from various undated Ubangi Club revues.

4504 • ULYSSES AFRICANUS

OPENED: 1945

       Unproduced

Composer: Kurt Weill
Lyricist: Maxwell Anderson

Source: ULYSSES AFRICANUS (Novel: Henry Stillwell Edwards)

Songs: Big Mole [1]; Lady, You Drop Yo Feminine Wiles; Little Tin God, The [2]; Lost in the Stars [1]; Stay Well [1]; Trouble Man [1]; When I Was a Pickaninny; White Folks

Cast: Paul Robeson

Notes: Songs written for this show ended up in LOST IN THE STARS. [1] Later in LOST IN THE STARS. [2] Later in LOST IN THE STARS with lyric changed to "Little Grey House."

4505 • UMBRELLAS OF CHERBOURG, THE

OPENED: 01/02/1979   Theatre: Public
Musical   Off-Broadway: 36

Composer: Michel Legrand
Lyricist: Charles Burr; Sheldon Harnick
Librettist: Charles Burr; Sheldon Harnick
Producer: N.Y. Shakespeare Festival; Joseph Papp
Director: Andrei Serban

Source: LES PARAPLUIES DE CHERBOURG (Film: Jacques Demy; Michel Legrand); French Lyrics: Jacques Demy; Michel Legrand; French Libretto: Charles Burr; Jacques Demy;
Choreographer: Dorothy Danner; **Costumes:**

Jane Greenwood; **Dance Arranger:** Steven Margoshes; **Lighting Designer:** Ian Calderon; **Musical Director:** Steven Margoshes; **Orchestrations:** Michel Legrand; Steven Margoshes; **Set Design:** Michael H. Yeargan; **Vocal Arranger:** Michel Legrand; Steven Margoshes

Cast: Stephen Bogardus; Laurence Guittard; Marc Jordan; Dean Pitchford; Maureen Silliman

Notes: Same songs as in movie. English translation by Sheldon Harnick in association with Charles Burr.

4506 • UMPIRE, THE
OPENED: 12/02/1905   Theatre: La Salle
Musical   Chicago

Composer: Joseph E. Howard
Lyricist: Frank R. Adams; Will M. Hough
Librettist: Frank R. Adams; Will M. Hough
Producer: Mort Singer
Director: Arthur Sanders; Gus Sohlke

Songs: Big Banshee, The; Clorinda Jackson; Cross Your Heart; Drums of the Fore and Aft (L: Rudyard Kipling); I Want a Girl Like You; Let's Take a Trolley Ride; Opening Chorus; Quarterback, The; Sun That Shines on Dixieland, The; Umpire Is a Most Unhappy Man, The; You Look Awful Good to Father

Cast: Florence Holbrook; Cecil Lean; Olive Vail

4507 • UNCLE TOM'S CABIN
OPENED: 01/27/1902
Musical

Composer: Jerome Kern
Librettist: Rosewell G. Thompson
Producer: Newark Yacht Club

Songs: I Never Do a Thing Like That; Ma Blossom; Marcella; Mighty Svengali Legree, The; Opening Chorus Act II; Song of the Sheriffs; Things Have Changed from Then to Now; When Rogers Come to Town; Yo! Ho! When You're in the Chorus

Cast: Daniel Blakeman; Charles P. Gillan; Rosewell G. Thompson; Gus Troxler; Nicholas J. Tynan

Notes: Amateur show.

4508 • UNDER COVER
OPENED: 09/14/1903   Theatre: Murray Hill
Play   Broadway: 90

Composer: George Braham
Lyricist: Edward Harrigan
Author: Edward Harrigan
Producer: Liebler & Company

Musical Director: George Braham

Songs: Coon Will Follow a Band, A; Fringe of Society, The; Limerick's Running Yet; Lulu's Honeymoon; Oh, What's the Use; When Mamie Sweet Mamie's a Bride

Cast: Dan Collyer; Jane Elton; Edward Harrigan; Elizabeth King

4509 • UNDER MANY FLAGS
OPENED: 05/31/1912   Theatre: Hippodrome
Musical   Broadway: 445

Composer: Manuel Klein
Lyricist: Manuel Klein
Librettist: Carroll Fleming
Producer: Messrs. Shubert
Director: Carroll Fleming

Choreographer: William J. Wilson, **Musical Director:** Manuel Klein; **Set Design:** Arthur Voegtlin

Songs: Dear Old White House, The; Every Nation Has a Flower; Fishing; Flowers of the Nations Ballet; For Universal Peace; Home Is Where the Heart Is (Home Sweet Home); March of the Dragon; Once a Fisherman Went to Sea; Pretty Little Maiden on the Screen; Scotland Forever; Sweetheart Let's Go a Walking; Temple Bells; 'Tis Summer; Tulips with Your Color So Bright; Youngsters of the Navy

Cast: Elsie Baird; Leonard Kirtley; Albert Pellaton; Edith Singleton; Harry Truax

4510 • UNDER THE COUNTER
OPENED: 10/03/1947   Theatre: Shubert
Musical   Broadway: 27

Composer: Manning Sherwin
Lyricist: Harold Purcell
Librettist: Arthur Macrae
Producer: Lee Ephraim; Messrs. Shubert
Director: Jack Hurlbert

Choreographer: John Gregory; Jack Hurlbert; **Musical Director:** Harry Levant; **Set Design:** Clifford Pember

Songs: Ai Yi Yi; Everywhere; Let's Get Back to Glamour; Moment I Saw You, The; No-one's Tried to Kiss Me

Cast: Cicely Courtneidge; Wilfred Hyde-White

4511 • UNDER THE RED GLOBE

OPENED: 02/18/1897   Theatre: Weber & Fields
                                          Broadway Music Hall
Musical   Broadway

Composer: John Stromberg
Librettist: Joseph Herbert

Cast: Lew Fields; Joseph Weber

Notes: No program available. A burlesque on UNDER THE RED ROBE.

4512 • UNDERWORLD

OPENED: 1960
Musical   Unproduced

Composer: Jerome Moross
Lyricist: John Hollander; Lester Judson
Librettist: Moss Hart

Songs: Beer and Flowers (L: John Hollander); Cream of Society, The; It's Almost Time Now; I've Even Been in Love; Love Me (L: John Hollander); Paddy Boy; Prologue; That Extra Bit

Notes: Hollander wrote the lyrics which were polished and added to by Judson.

4513 • UNDINE

OPENED: 11/20/1911   Theatre: Winter Garden
Musical   Broadway

Composer: Manuel Klein
Lyricist: Manuel Klein
Librettist: Manuel Klein

Notes: A one-act musical.

4514 • UNFAIR TO GOLIATH

OPENED: 01/25/1970   Theatre: Cherry Lane
Musical   Off-Broadway: 73

Composer: Menachem Zur
Lyricist: Herbert Appleman
Librettist: Ephaim Kishon
Producer: Alexander Beck; Edward Schreiber
Director: Herbert Appleman; Ephaim Kishon

Costumes: Pamela Scofield; **Lighting Designer:** C. Murawski; **Musical Director:** Menachem Zur; **Set Design:** C. Murawski

Songs: Danger of Peace Is Over, The; Famous Rabbi, The; In the Reign of Chaim; Parking Meter Like Me, A; Rooster and the Hen, The; Sabra, The; Song of Sallah Shabeti, The; What Abraham Lincoln Once Said; What Kind of Baby; When Moses Spake to Goldstein

Cast: Hugh Alexander; Jim Brochu; Guy Devlin; Corinne Kason; Laura May Lewis

4515 • UNFINISHED SONG, AN

OPENED: 02/10/1991   Theatre: Provincetown
                                          Playhouse
Musical   Off-Broadway: 25

Composer: James J. Mellon
Lyricist: James J. Mellon
Librettist: James J. Mellon
Producer: Cheryl L. Fluehr; Starbuck Productions, Ltd.
Director: Simon Levy

Arrangements: Lawrence Yurman; **Costumes:** Jeffrey Ullman; **Lighting Designer:** Robert M. Wierzel; **Musical Director:** Mark Mitchell; **Set Design:** Scott Bradley

Songs: As I Say Goodbye; Balance the Plate; Being Left Out; Blonde Haired Babies; Crossing Boundaries; Frying Pan, The; Hobby Horses; How Could I Let You Leave Me; Is That Love; Keeping Score with Myself [1]; New Hampshire Nights; Remember the Ocean [1]; Things We've Collected; Tightrope [1]; Unfinished Song, An; We Were Here

Cast: Aloysius Gigl; Joanna Glushak; Robert Lambert; Ken Land; Beth Leavel

Notes: [1] Added to 2/1/95 revival in Boston.

4516 • UNSINKABLE MOLLY BROWN, THE

OPENED: 11/03/1960 Theatre: Winter Garden
Musical Broadway: 532

Composer: Meredith Willson
Lyricist: Meredith Willson
Librettist: Robert Morris
Producer: Dore Schary; Theatre Guild, The
Director: Dore Schary

Choreographer: Peter Gennaro; **Costumes:** Miles White; **Dance Arranger:** Sol Berkowitz; **Lighting Designer:** Peggy Clark; **Musical Director:** Herbert Greene; **Orchestrations:** Don Walker; **Set Design:** Oliver Smith; **Vocal Arranger:** Herbert Greene

Songs: Ambassador's Polka, The [1]; Another Big Strike [1]; Are You Sure?; Beautiful People of Denver; Belly Up to the Bar, Boys; Bon Jour (The Language Song); Chick-a-pen; Colorado, My Home [2]; Denver Police, The; Dolce Far Niente; Extra! Extra! [1]; Happy Birthday, Mrs. J.J. Brown; I Ain't Down Yet; I May Never Fall in Love with You; If I Knew; I'll Never Say No; I've Already Started In; Keep-a-Hoppin'; Leadville Johnny Brown; My Old Brass Bed; One Day at a Time [1]; Read the Label (Don't Take My Word for It Neighbor) (Get Away You Bother Me) [1]; Tomorrow [3]; Up Where the Joke's Goin' On [1]; Up Where the People Are (dance)

Cast: Tammy Grimes; Jack Harrold; Christopher Hewett; Edith Meiser; Harve Presnell; Cameron Prud'homme; Joseph Sirola

Notes: [1] Cut prior to opening. [2] Cut after opening and added to film version. [3] Cut prior to opening. Also cut from THE MUSIC MAN.

4517 • UNSUNG COLE

OPENED: 09/04/1977 Theatre: Circle Repertory
Revue Off-Broadway: 78

Composer: Cole Porter
Lyricist: Cole Porter

Producer: Circle Repertory Company
Director: Norman L. Berman

Choreographer: Dennis Grimaldi; **Costumes:** Carol Oditz; **Lighting Designer:** Arden Fingerhut; **Musical Director:** Leon Odenz; **Set Design:** Peter Harvey; **Vocal Arranger:** Norman L. Berman

Songs: Abracadabra [11]; After You, Who? [15]; Almiro [7] (L: Cole Porter; Rene Pujol); Dancin' to a Jungle Drum [9]; Down in the Depths [6]; Farming [2]; Friendship [18]; Give Me the Land [10]; Goodbye Little Dream, Goodbye [6]; Great Indoors, The [3]; I Happen to Like New York [3]; If Ever Married I'm [17]; I'm Getting Myself Ready for You [3]; I've Got Some Unfinished Business with You [2]; Just Another Page in Your Diary [12]; Kate the Great [16]; Lady Needs a Rest, A [2]; Lost Liberty Blues [7]; Love for Sale [3]; Nobody's Chasing Me [13]; Olga [8]; Ours [6]; Pick Me Up and Lay Me Down [1]; Poor Young Millionaire [5]; Queen of Terre Haute, The [4]; Red, Hot and Blue! [6]; Sing to Me Guitar [11]; Swingin' the Jinx Away [14]; Take Me Back to Manhattan [3]; Tale of an Oyster, The [4]; Thank You So Much Mrs. Lowsborough- Goodby; That's Why I Love You [4]; When the Hen Stops Laying [12]; Why Don't We Try Staying Home [4]

Cast: Gene Lindsey; Mary Louise; Maureen Moore; Anita Morris; John Sloman

Notes: No original songs in this show. [1] From STARDUST. [2] From LET'S FACE IT. [3] From THE NEW YORKERS. [4] From FIFTY MILLION FRENCHMEN. [5] Written in the 30's and used in the film AT LONG, LAST LOVE. [6] From RED, HOT AND BLUE! [7] From LA REVUE DES AMBASSADEURS. [8] From MAYFAIR AND MONTMARTRE. [9] From SEVEN LIVELY ARTS. [10] From SILK STOCKINGS. [11] From MEXICAN HAYRIDE. [12] From LEAVE IT TO ME! [13] From OUT OF THIS WORLD. [14] From BORN TO SWING. [15] From GAY DIVORCE. [16] From ANYTHING GOES. [17] From KISS ME, KATE. [18] From DUBARRY WAS A LADY. [19] From LA REVUE DES AMBASSADEURS. French lyrics by Rene Pujol.

4518 • UP AGAINST IT

OPENED: 12/04/1989 Theatre: Public
Musical Off-Broadway: 16

Composer: Todd Rundgren
Lyricist: Todd Rundgren
Librettist: Tom Ross
Producer: N.Y. Shakespeare Festival
Director: Kenneth Elliott

Source: UP AGAINST IT (Film: Joe Orton);
Choreographer: Jennifer Muller; **Costumes:** John
Glaser; **Lighting Designer:** Vivien Leone;
Musical Director: Tom Fay; **Orchestrations:**
Doug Katsaros; **Set Design:** B.T. Whitehill; **Vocal
Arranger:** Todd Rundgren

Songs: Entropy; From Hunger; If I Have to Be Alone;
Life Is a Drag; Lilly's Address; Love in Disguise;
Male and Twenty-One; Maybe I'm Better Off;
Parallel Lines; Smell of Money, The; Up Against It;
When Worlds Collide; You'll Thank Me in the End

Cast: Roger Bart; Philip Casnoff; Toni Dibuono;
Alison Fraser; Mari Nelson; Dan Tubb

4519 • UP AND DOING

OPENED: 04/17/1940   Theatre: Saville
Revue   London: 503

Composer: Richard Rodgers
Lyricist: Lorenz Hart
Librettist: Graham John
Producer: F. Firth Shepard

Songs: Falling in Love with Love [1]; Sing for Your
Supper [1]; This Can't Be Love [1]

Cast: Patricia Burke; Binnie Hale; Leslie Henson;
Stanley Holloway; Enid Lowe; Graham Payn;
Cyril Ritchard

Notes: No program available. Two runs of 171 and
332 performances. [1] From THE BOYS FROM
SYRACUSE.

4520 • UP AND DOWN

OPENED: 1922
Musical

Composer: J. Homer Tutt; Salem Tutt Whitney
Lyricist: J. Homer Tutt; Salem Tutt Whitney
Librettist: J. Homer Tutt; Salem Tutt Whitney
Producer: J. Homer Tutt; Salem Tutt Whitney

Songs: Backbiting Me; Male Vamps; Rock Me,
Daddy; We Want to Booze; When You're Crazy
Over Daddy

Cast: Blanche Calloway; Jennie Dancey; Alonzo
Fenderson; Alberta Jones; Margaret Simms;
Henry Thomson; J. Homer Tutt; Salem Tutt
Whitney

Notes: No other information available.

4521 • UP AND DOWN BROADWAY

OPENED: 07/18/1910   Theatre: Casino
Musical   Broadway: 72

Composer: Jean Schwartz
Lyricist: William Jerome
Librettist: Edgar Smith
Producer: Lee Shubert; Sam S. Shubert
Director: William J. Wilson

Costumes: Melville Ellis

Songs: Chinatown, My Chinatown; Chocolate
Soldier [2]; Come Down to Earth, My Dearie;
Dope Fiend, The (C: Melville Ellis); 1861 [2];
Everybody Is Bagpipe Crazy [1]; Ghost of Kelly,
The; Go On Your Mission [2]; Have a Smile with
Momus [2]; I Am Melpomene [2]; I Want a Lot of
Girlies, Girlies (I Want a Whole Lot of Girls); I'm
Always Happy when I'm Sad [1]; I'm the Lily;
Kellerman Girlie, The [1]; Mary Ann; Military
Glide, The; My Operatic Samson [1]; New York
Isn't Such a Bad Old Town [1]; Oh, That Beautiful
Rag (C: Ted Snyder; L: Irving Berlin); Pretty Little
Girl Inside, The; Soldier's Life Is Grand, A [1];
Spanish Fandango Rag, The (Dreamy Fandango
Tune) [2]; Sweet Italian Love [1] (C: Ted Snyder;
L: Irving Berlin); There Must Be a Girl in the
Moon [1]; Throw Up Your Hands [1]; Ticket
Speculator, The [2]; When Sist' Tetrazin' Met
Cousin Carus [2]; Where Are Your Actors [1]

Cast: Adelaide and Hughes; Irving Berlin; Emma
Carus; Eddie Foy Sr.; Ernest Hare; Oscar Shaw;
Ted Snyder; Lenore Ulric; Anna Wheaton

Notes: [1] Sheet music only. [2] Out Washington,
D.C. 10/9/10.

4522 • UP EDEN

OPENED: 11/27/1968   Theatre: Jan Hus
                               Playhouse
Musical   Off-Broadway: 8

Composer: Robert Rosenblum
Lyricist: Robert Rosenblum; Howard Schuman

Librettist: Robert Rosenblum; Howard Schuman
Producer: Jack Farren; Evan William Mandel
Director: John Bishop

Source: COSI FAN TUTTE (Opera: Wolfgang Amadeus Mozart); **Choreographer:** Patricia Birch; **Costumes:** Gordon Micunis; **Lighting Designer:** Louise Guthman; **Musical Director:** Wally Harper; **Orchestrations:** Wally Harper; Richard Hurwitz; **Set Design:** Gordon Micunis; **Vocal Arranger:** Jack Lee

Songs: Hannibal's Comin'; Haven't You Wondered; Homesick; Let Me Show You the World; Little More Like You, A; Mowla, The; No More Edens; Nothing Ever Happens Till 2 A.M.; Passin' Through; Playboy's Work Is Never Done, A; Remember Me Smiling; Virgin of Velez-Jermano, The; Was That Me Talking?; Will, The; Wishy Washy Woman

Cast: Robert Balaban; Blythe Danner; Deborah Deeble; George S. Irving; Patti Karr; Denny Shearer

4523 • UP FROM PARADISE

OPENED: 06/14/1977
Musical   Closed out of town

Composer: Stanley Silverman
Lyricist: Arthur Miller
Librettist: Arthur Miller

2:Source: CREATION OF THE WORLD AND OTHER BUSINESS, THE (Play: Arthur Miller); **Musical Director:** Gary Adams

Songs: Adorable; All Love, All Love; As Good As Paradise; Creation of Eve, The; God's Curse; Hallelujah; How Fine It Is to Name Things; I Can See the Lord in the Garden Now; If Something Leads to Good, Can It Be Bad?; I'm Lonely; I'm Me; In the Center of Your Mind Keep the Lord; It's Just Like I Was You; Lamentation; Loneliness Song, The; Mother of Mankind, The; Nothing's Left of God; Terrible Feeling, A; When Eve Is Alone

Cast: Walter Bobbie; David Patrick Kelly; Austin Pendleton; Patti Perkins; Harris Poor; Paul Ukena

Notes: No program available. Presented as part of the Kennedy Center Musical Theatre Lab.

4524 • UP IN CENTRAL PARK

OPENED: 01/27/1945   Theatre: Century
Musical   Broadway: 504

Composer: Sigmund Romberg
Lyricist: Dorothy Fields
Librettist: Dorothy Fields; Herbert Fields
Producer: Michael Todd
Director: John Kennedy

Choreographer: Lew Kessler; Helen Tamiris; **Costumes:** Grace Houston; Ernest Schrapps; **Lighting Designer:** Howard Bay **Musical Director:** Max Meth; **Orchestrations:** Don Walker; **Set Design:** Howard Bay

Songs: April Snow; Big Back Yard, The; Birds and the Bees, The; Boss Tweed; Carousel in the Park; Close As Pages in a Book; Currier and Ives; Fireman's Bride, The; It Doesn't Cost You Anything to Dream; Maypole Dance (inst.); Opening Scene III; Opening Scene V; Rip Van Winkle; Up from the Gutter; When She Walks in the Room; When the Party Gives a Party; You Can't Get Over the Wall

Cast: Noah Beery Sr.; Betty Bruce; Maureen Burke; Maureen Cannon; Wilbur Evans; Charles Irwin; Daniel Nagrin; Paul Reed; Guy Standing Jr.; Rowan Tudor

4525 • UP IN LIGHTS

OPENED: 08/01/1954
Musical   Closed out of town

Composer: William Angelas; Lan O'Kun
Librettist: William Dixon; William Levine

Notes: No other information available. Produced at Syracuse University.

4526 • UP IN MABEL'S ROOM

OPENED: 01/15/1919   Theatre: Eltinge
Play   Broadway: 229

Author: Wilson Collison; Otto Harbach
Producer: A.H. Woods
Director: Bertram Harrison

Songs: Up in Mabel's Room (C: Abner Silver; L: Alex Gerber)

Cast: John Cumberland; Hazel Dawn; Enid Markey

Notes: This song may not have been in the play but just inspired by it.

4527 • UP IN THE AIR, BOYS
OPENED: 11/29/1974   Theatre: Hartley House
Musical   Off-Off-Broadway

Composer: Robert Dahdah
Lyricist: Mary Boylan; Robert Dahdah
Librettist: Mary Boylan; Robert Dahdah
Director: Robert Dahdah

Choreographer: Robert Durkin; **Costumes:** Gene Calvin; **Musical Director:** Robert Marks

Songs: Apache Dance; Do the Heavenental; Don't Make Me Dance; Dreams Don't Mean a Thing; How Could I Forget; Laughing Daffodil; Musical Me; Reach; Top Spot; Up in the Air, Boys; Voodoo Night in Hotchkiss Corners; When Marie Antoinette Learned to Pet; You Never Change

Cast: Margaret Benczak; Peggylee Brennan; Dennis Deal; Tom Offt

4528 • UP IN THE CLOUDS
OPENED: 01/02/1922   Theatre: Lyric
Musical   Broadway: 89

Composer: Tom Johnstone
Lyricist: Will B. Johnstone
Librettist: Will B. Johnstone
Producer: Joseph M. Gaites
Director: Lawrence Marston

Choreographer: Allan K. Foster; Vaughn Godfrey; Max Scheck; **Musical Director:** Hilding Anderson

Songs: At the Fountain; Ballet of Wealth; Betsy Ross; Birth of American Fantasy Dance; Friends; Girl I Marry, The; Happiness; How Dry I Am; I See Your Face; It's a Great Life If You Don't Weaken; Jean; Last Girl Is the Best Girl, The; Look-a-Look; Movie Lesson, The; Nobody Knows; Passing of Six Months; Rum-Tum-Tiddle; Up in the Clouds; Wonderful Something

Cast: "Skeets" Gallagher; Grace Moore; June Roberts; Hal Van Rensellaer; Max Welty

4529 • UP SHE GOES
OPENED: 11/06/1922   Theatre: Playhouse
Musical   Broadway: 252

Composer: Harry Tierney
Lyricist: Joseph McCarthy
Librettist: Frank Craven
Producer: William A. Brady
Director: Frank Craven; Bert French

Source: TOO MANY COOKS (Play: Frank Craven); **Choreographer:** Bert French; **Orchestrations:** Frank Barry

Songs: Bob About a Bit; Journey's End; Lady Luck Smile on Me; Let's Kiss and Make Up; Nearing the Day; Opening Act II; Roof Tree; Settle Down, Travel Round; Strike, The; Takes a Heap of Love; Tyup; Up She Goes; Up with the Stars; Visitors, The; We'll Do the Riviera

Cast: Helen Bolton; Donald Brian; Gloria Foy; "Skeets" Gallagher; Frederick Graham

4530 • UP STAGE AND DOWN
OPENED: 03/08/1917
Musical

Composer: Richard Rodgers
Lyricist: Richard Rodgers
Librettist: Myron D. Rosenthal
Producer: Infants Relief Society
Director: Harry A. Goldberg

Choreographer: Sydney Oberfelder

Songs: Advertise; Ali Baba; Asiatic Angles; Butterfly Love; Can It (L: Oscar Hammerstein II); Dearie; I'm So Shy; Japanese Jazz; Love Is Not in Vain; Love Me By Parcel Post (L: Mortimer W. Rodgers); Loving Cup; Now Listen; Out of a Job; Prisms, Plums and Prunes (L: Benjamin Kaye); There's Always Room for One More (L: Oscar Hammerstein II); Twinkling Eyes; Weaknesses (L: Oscar Hammerstein II); Wild Women's Wiles

Notes: Amateur production. Reopened as TWINKLING EYES 5/18/19. See that entry.

4531 • UP TO DATE
OPENED: 05/15/1893   Theatre: Palmer's
Musical   Broadway

Composer: Carl Pfleuger
Lyricist: R.A. Barnet
Librettist: R.A. Barnet

Notes: No program available.

4532 • UPS-A-DAISY

OPENED: 10/08/1928   Theatre: Shubert
Musical   Broadway: 320

Composer: Lewis E. Gensler
Lyricist: Robert A. Simon
Librettist: Clifford Grey; Robert A. Simon
Producer: Lewis E. Gensler
Director: Edgar MacGregor

Source: DER HOCHTOURIST (Play: Kurt Kraatz);
  Choreographer: Earl Lindsay; **Costumes:**
  Kiviette; **Musical Director:** Gene Salzer;
  Orchestrations: Frank Black; **Set Design:** John
  Wenger

Songs: Desire Under the Alps; Give Us a Tune [1];
  Great Little Guy; Hot; I Can't Believe It's True [2];
  I've Got a Baby; Oh, How Happy We'll Be
  (L: Clifford Grey; Robert A. Simon); Oh-
  How-I-Miss-You Blues (L: Clifford Grey; Robert
  A. Simon); Opening Chorus; Sweet One;
  Sweetest of the Roses; Tell Me Who You Are;
  Ups-a-Daisy; Will You Remember? Will You
  Forget? (L: Clifford Grey; Robert A. Simon)

Cast: Luella Gear; Bob Hope; William Kent; Roy
  Royston; Marie Saxon

Notes: [1] Out Newark 10/01/28. [2] Cut.

4533 • UPSTAIRS AT O'NEAL'S

OPENED: 10/28/1982   Theatre: O'Neal's
Revue   Nightclub: 308

Producer: Martin Charnin; Michael O'Neal;
  Patrick O'Neal
Director: Martin Charnin

Choreographer: Ed Love; **Costumes:** Zoran; **Dance
  Arranger:** David Krane; **Lighting Designer:** Ray
  Recht; **Musical Director:** David Krane; **Set
  Design:** Ray Recht; **Vocal Arranger:** David Krane

Songs: All I Can Do Is Cry (C/L: Michael Abbott;
  Sarah Weeks); Ballad of Cy and Beatrice, The

(C: Paul Trueblood; L: Jim Morgan); Boy, Do We
Need It Now [1] (C/L: Charles Strouse); Cancun
(C/L: John Forster; Michael Leeds); Cover Girls
(C/L: Seth Friedman; L: David Crane; Marta
Kauffman); Feet, The (C/L: Seth Friedman;
L: David Crane; Marta Kauffman); I Furnished
My One Room Apartment (C: Stephen Hoffman;
L: Michael Mooney); Little H and Little G (C/L:
Ronald Melrose); Mommas' Turn (C/L: Douglas
Bernstein; Denis Markell); Signed, Peeled,
Delivered (C/L: Ronald Melrose); Soap
Operettas (C/L: Seth Friedman; L: David Crane;
Marta Kauffman); Soldier and the Washer-
woman, The (C/L: Ronald Melrose); Something
(C/L: Douglas Bernstein; Denis Markell); Stools
(C/L: Martin Charnin); Talkin' Morosco Blues
(C: Willie Nininger; L: Murray Horwitz);
Upstairs at O'Neal's (C/L: Martin Charnin);
We'll Be Right Back After This Message (C/L:
Douglas Bernstein; Denis Markell)

Cast: Douglas Bernstein; Randall Edwards;
  Bebe Neuwirth; Michon Peacock; Richard
  Ryder; Sarah Weeks; **Pianist:** Paul Ford;
  David Krane

Notes: [1] Written for the film THAT'S
ENTERTAINMENT PART 2.

4534 • UPTOWN . . . IT'S HOT!

OPENED: 01/29/1986   Theatre: Lunt-Fontanne
Revue   Broadway: 24

Librettist: Marion Ramsey; Jeffrey V. Thompson
Producer: Larry Magid; Allen Spivak
Director: Maurice Hines

Choreographer: Maurice Hines; **Costumes:** Ellen
  Lee; **Dance Arranger:** Thom Bridwell; Frank
  Owens; **Lighting Designer:** Marc B. Weiss;
  Musical Director: Frank Owens; **Set Design:**
  Tom McPhillips

Songs: A-Tisket A-Tasket (C: Van Alexander;
  L: Ella Fitzgerald); Ain't Too Proud to Beg
  (C/L: Eddie Holland; Norman Whitfield);
  Amazing Grace (C/L: Traditional); Be My Baby
  (C/L: Jeff Barry; Ellie Greenwich; Phil Spector);
  Blueberry Hill (C/L: Al Lewis; Vincent Rose;
  Larry Stock); Body and Soul (C: Johnny Green;
  L: Howard Dietz; Frank Eyton; Edward
  Heyman; Robert Sour); Cotton Club Stomp
  (inst.) (C: Duke Ellington); Dancin' in the

Streets (C/L: Marvin Gaye; Ivy Hunter; William Stevenson); Daybreak Express (inst.) (C: Duke Ellington); Diga Diga Doo (C: Jimmy McHugh; L: Dorothy Fields); Dinah (C: Harry Akst; L: Lewis F. Muir; Joseph Young); Do I Do (C/L: Stevie Wonder); Don't Mess with Bill (C/L: Smokey Robinson); Express (C/L: B.T. Express); Higher Ground (C/L: Stevie Wonder); His Eye Is on the Sparrow (C/L: Traditional); Ill Wind (C: Harold Arlen; L: Ted Koehler); Jim Jam Jumpin' (C: Cab Calloway); Johnny B. Goode (C/L: Chuck Berry); Jumpin' at the Woodside (inst.) (C: Count Basie); Just a Closer Walk with Thee (C/L: Traditional); Keep on Running (C/L: Stevie Wonder); Lady Be Good (C: George Gershwin; L: Ira Gershwin); Let's Get Together (inst.) (C: Chick Webb); 1999 (C/L: Prince); Old Landmark (C/L: M.A. Brunner); Proud Mary (C/L: John Fogarty); Stop in the Name of Love (C/L: Lamont Dozier; Brian Holland; Eddie Holland); Stormy Weather (C: Harold Arlen; L: Ted Koehler); Superstition (C/L: Stevie Wonder); Swing That Music (C: Louis Armstrong; L: H. Gerlach); Tap Along with Me (inst.) (C: Frank Owens); Tutti Frutti (C/L: Richard Penniman); When Your Lover Has Gone (C/L: E.A. Swan); Why Do Fools Fall in Love (C/L: Frankie Lymon); Will You Still Love Me Tomorrow (C/L: Gerry Goffin; Carole King); You Send Me (C/L: Sam Cooke)

Cast: Alisa Gyse; Lawrence Hamilton; Maurice Hines; Tommi Johnson; Marion Ramsey; Jeffrey V. Thompson

Notes: No original songs in this show.

4535 • URBAN BLIGHT

OPENED: 06/19/1988   Theatre: Manhattan Theatre Club

Revue   Off-Broadway: 12

Composer: David Shire
Lyricist: Richard Maltby Jr.
Librettist: John Augustine; John Bishop; Christopher Durang; Jules Feiffer; Larry Fishburne; Charles Fuller; Nancy Giles; A.R. Gurney; E. Katherine Kerr; Richard Maltby Jr.; David Mamet; Terrence McNally; Arthur Miller; Shel Silverstein; Ted Tally; Wendy Wasserstein; Richard Wesley; George C. Wolfe
Producer: Manhattan Theater Club
Director: Richard Maltby Jr.; John Tillinger

Choreographer: Charles Randolph-Wright; **Conductor:** Michael Skloff; **Costumes:** C.L. Hundley; **Lighting Designer:** Natasha Katz; **Set Design:** Heidi Landesman

Songs: Aerobicantata; Bill of Fare; Don't Fall for the Lights; Life Story [1]; Miss Byrd [1]; Self-Portrait (C/L: Edward Kleban); There

Cast: Larry Fishburne; Nancy Giles; E. Katherine Kerr; Oliver Platt; Faith Prince; Rex Robbins; John Rubinstein

Notes: [1] Later in CLOSER THAN EVER.

4536 • UTOPIA!

OPENED: 05/06/1963   Theatre: Folksbiene

Musical   Off-Broadway: 11

Composer: William Klenosky
Lyricist: William Klenosky
Librettist: William Klenosky
Producer: William Klenosky
Director: Cecil Reddick

Choreographer: Melinda Taintor; **Costumes:** Edith Arin; **Dance Arranger:** Stephen Lawrence; **Lighting Designer:** Gary Zeller; **Musical Director:** Stephen Lawrence; **Set Design:** Gary Zeller; **Vocal Arranger:** Stephen Lawrence

Songs: All You Need Is a Little Love; April in Siberia; Ballad of Utopia, The; Hooligan's Hop; I Can't Pretend; I Work for Pravda; Masses Are Asses, The; National Anthem of Utopia, The; Tax Collector's Soliloquy, The; Utopia Ballet; We've Got a Feeling in Our Bones; What Am I Hangin' Around For?; Why Are We Here?; You Gotta Have a Destination; You've Got the Devil in Your Eyes

Cast: Ray Gilbert; Lewis Pierce; Guje Seastrom; Vilma Vacarra

4537 • UTTER GLORY OF MORRISSEY HALL, THE

OPENED: 05/13/1979   Theatre: Mark Hellinger

Musical   Broadway: 1

Composer: Clark Gesner
Lyricist: Clark Gesner
Librettist: Clark Gesner; Nagle Jackson

Producer: H. Ridgely Bullock; Albert W. Selden; Arthur Whitelaw
Director: Nagle Jackson

Choreographer: Buddy Schwab; **Costumes:** David Graden; **Dance Arranger:** Allen Cohen; **Lighting Designer:** Howard Bay; **Musical Director:** John Lesko; **Orchestrations:** Jay Blackton; Russell Warner; **Set Design:** Howard Bay

Songs: Dance of Resignation (dance); Duet; Elizabeth's Song; Ending, The; Give Me That Key; Interlude and Gallop; Letter, The; Like a Rock [1]; Lost; Morning; Oh, Sun; Promenade; Proud, Erstwhile, Upright, Fair; Reflection; See the Blue; War, The; Way Back When; Whose Little Bird Are You [1]; You Will Know When the Time Has Come; You Would Say

Cast: Marilyn Copkey; Taina Elg; Laurie Franks; Celeste Holm; Polly Pen; Mary Saunders

Notes: [1] Out Philadelphia 11/25/77.

V

4538 • VAGABOND HERO, A
Notes: *See THE WHITE FLAME.*

4539 • VAGABOND KING, THE
OPENED: 09/21/1925   Theatre: Casino
Musical   Broadway: 511

Composer: Rudolf Friml
Lyricist: Brian Hooker
Librettist: Brian Hooker; Russell Janney;
  William H. Post
Producer: Russell Janney
Director: Max Figman

Source: IF I WERE KING (Play: Justin Huntley
  McCarthy); **Choreographer:** Julian Alfred;
  Costumes: James Reynolds; **Musical Director:**
  Anton Heindl; **Orchestrations:** Anton Heindl;
  Set Design: James Reynolds; **Vocal Arranger:**
  Anton Heindl

Songs: Ballet; Drinking Song; Finale Second Act;
  Finale Ultimo; Finaletto Act II; Huguette Waltz;
  Hunting; Lady Mary's Song to Taberie [2]
  (L: Russell Janney); Love for Sale; Love Me
  Tonight; Love Song of a Thief, The [2] (L: Russell
  Janney); Love That Cannot Be [2] (L: Russell
  Janney); Merry Gallows, The [2] (L: Russell
  Janney); Nocturne; Only a Rose; Opening Act IV
  — Scene 1; Opening Act IV — Scene 2; Scotch
  Archer's Song; Serenade; Some Day; Song of the
  Vagabonds; Te Deum Laudamus! [1]; Tomorrow;
  Vagabond King; Victory March, The [1]

Cast: Herbert Corthell; Max Figman; Dennis King;
  Carolyn Thomson

Notes: [1] Not in program. [2] Written for 1954
  revival.

4540 • VALENTINE'S DAY
                        Theatre: Manhattan
                        Theatre Club
Musical   Off-Broadway

Composer: Saul Naishtat
Lyricist: Ron Cowen

Librettist: Ron Cowen
Director: Seth Glassman

Costumes: Richard Westby-Gibson; **Lighting
  Designer:** Sari Weisman; **Musical Director:**
  Thomas Babbitt

Songs: Arizona; Biarritz and Bali; Get Up; His and
  Hers; How Do I Get Out of This; Mr. What's-
  His-Name; My Father Took Me Dancing; My
  Room and Me; People Have to Change; People
  Shouldn't Change; Sandpaper; Something for
  Nothing; Traveling Memories; Valentine's Day;
  Wonderful Dreams

Cast: Jeanne Arnold; Jerry Jarrett; Alice Playten;
  Chip Zien

4541 • VALMOUTH
OPENED: 10/06/1960   Theatre: York Playhouse
Musical   Off-Broadway: 14

Composer: Sandy Wilson
Lyricist: Sandy Wilson
Librettist: Sandy Wilson
Producer: Gene Andrewski; Barbara Griner;
  Morton Segal
Director: Vida Hope

Source: VALMOUTH (Novel: Ronald Firbank);
  Choreographer: Harry Naughton; **Conductor:**
  Jack Lee; **Costumes:** Tony Walton; **Musical
  Director:** Julian Stein; **Orchestrations:** Julian
  Stein; **Set Design:** Tony Walton

Songs: All the Girls Were Pretty; Big Best Shoes;
  Cathedral of Clemenza, The; Cry of the Peacock;
  I Loved a Man; I Will Miss You; Just Once More;
  Lady of the Manor; Little Girl Baby; Magic
  Fingers; Mustapha; My Talking Day; Niri-Esther;
  Only a Passing Phase; Pinpipi's Sob of Love;
  Valmouth; What Do I Want with Love?; What
  Then Can Make Him Come So Slow? [1]; Where
  the Trees Are Green with Parrots

Cast: William Beck; Philippa Bevans; Constance
  Carpenter; Anne Francine; Gail Jones; Gene
  Rupert; Elly Stone; Alfred Toigo

Notes: [1] Added to BBC radio version.

4542 • VAMP, THE

OPENED: 11/10/1955   Theatre: Winter Garden
Musical   Broadway: 60

Composer: John Mundy
Lyricist: John Latouche
Librettist: John Latouche; Sam Locke
Producer: Alexander Carson; Martin Cohen; Oscar Lerman
Director: David Alexander

Choreographer: Robert Alton; **Costumes:** Raoul Pene du Bois; **Musical Director:** Milton Rosenstock; **Orchestrations:** James Mundy; **Set Design:** Raoul Pene du Bois; **Vocal Arranger:** Milton Rosenstock

Songs: Delilah's Dilemma; Fan Club Chant; Flickers, The; Four Little Misfits; Have You Met Delilah?; I'm Everybody's Baby; Impossible She, The; I've Always Loved You; Keep Your Nose to the Grindstone; Little Miss Dracula [1]; Mr. Right [1]; Ragtime Romeo; Samson and Delilah; Spiel, The; That's Where a Man Fits In; Vamps, The; Who Needs Love? [1]; Why Does It Have to Be You?; Yeemy Yeemy; You're Colossal

Cast: David Atkinson; Carol Channing; Will Geer; Patricia Hammerlee; Jack Harrold; Paul Lipson; Matt Mattox; Bibi Osterwald; Steve Reeves; Robert Rippy; Jack Waldron

Notes: Titled DELILAH in out-of-town ads. [1] Out Washington, D.C. 10/18/55.

4543 • VAMP TILL READY

OPENED: 11/22/1955
Revue

Composer: Ronald Lowden
Lyricist: Richard Levinson; William Link
Librettist: Carl Leswing; Richard Levinson; William Link
Producer: Robert Wickersham
Director: Chet Cooper; Robert Wickersham

Choreographer: Walter F. Keenan; **Costumes:** Marjorie Kellberg; **Orchestrations:** Al Boss; Frank Juele; **Set Design:** Marjorie Kellberg; **Vocal Arranger:** Bruce Montgomery; Clay Warnick

Songs: Ballad of Sheriff Dunlap (C: Al Ross); Be a Vamp (C: Henning Ludlow); Charlie Chaplin Dance (inst.); Diggin' Up Dirt; Finale; I'm Great; Keep Your Dreams; Mostes' to Say the Least, The (C: Al Ross; L: Charles Roth); Party (L: T.J. Scotes); Perils of Paulette, The; Screen Test (inst.); Since You Said You're Mine; Spread Some Joy Around (L: Charles Roth); Vive Paulette (C: Henning Ludlow)

Cast: Robert M. Jaffe; Eli Subin; Alfred Toigo

Notes: Amateur show. Mask & Wig Club, University of Pennsylvania.

4544 • VANDERBILT CUP, THE

OPENED: 01/16/1906   Theatre: Broadway
Musical   Broadway: 143

Composer: Robert Hood Bowers
Lyricist: Raymond W. Peck
Librettist: Sydney Rosenfeld
Producer: Liebler and Company

Songs: Dear Old Farm; Down the Mississippi [2]; Fatal Curse of Beauty; I Can't Help Thinking of You [1] (C: Ernest R. Ball; L: Maurice J. Stonehill); If You Were I and I Were You; If You Were Lost to Me [2]; Lament of the Crusty Dames, The; Let Me Be Your House Boat Beau; Light in Girlish Eyes, The; Little Chauffeur, The; Looking for a Happy Man [1]; Love's Wireless Telephone [1]; Man with an Axe to Grind, A [2]; Ride to the Course, The [1]; So I've Been Told; Somewhere in the World (There's a Little Girl for Me); Toy Broadway, The; Vanderbilt Cup Gallop; Wine, Women and Song

Cast: Aubrey Boucicault; Charles Dow Clark; Grace Gaylor Clark; Otis Harlan; Elsie Janis; Kate Mayhew

Notes: [1] Out Cedar Rapids 11/16/06. [2] Sheet music only.

4545 • VANDERBILT REVUE, THE

OPENED: 11/03/1930   Theatre: Vanderbilt
Revue   Broadway: 13

Composer: Jimmy McHugh
Lyricist: Dorothy Fields
Librettist: Arthur Burns; James Coghlan; Edwin Gilbert; Sig Herzig; Ellis Jones; Kenyon Nicholson

Producer: Lyle D. Andrews; Lew Fields
Director: Lew Fields; Theodore Hammerstein

Choreographer: Jack Haskell; John E. Lonergan;
  Costumes: Robert Stevenson; **Musical Director:**
  Gus Salzer; **Set Design:** Ward & Harvey

Songs: Better Not Try It (C: Michael Cleary;
  L: Herb Magidson; Ned Washington); Blue
  Again; Button Up Your Heart; Cut In; Ex-Gigolo
  (C: Mario Braggiotti; L: E.Y. Harburg); Half Way
  to Heaven (C: Mario Braggiotti; L: David
  Sidney); I Give Myself Away (C: Jacques Fray;
  L: Edward Eliscu); I'm from Granada (C: Mario
  Braggiotti; L: David Sidney); I'm Plenty That
  Way Too [1] (C: Jacques Fray; L: E.Y. Harburg);
  Jackdaw of Rhiems, The (sketch) (C: Edward
  Horan); Lady of the Fan (C: Jacques Fray;
  L: Mario Braggiotti); Please Don't Take My
  Boop-a-Doop Away [1] (C: Sammy Timberg;
  L: Sammy Lerner); Then Came the War (C/L:
  Ben Black); What's My Man Gonna Be Like?
  (C/L: Cole Porter); You're the Better Half of Me

Cast: Charles Barnes; Francesca Braggiotti; Mario
  Braggiotti; Jean Carpenter; Dorothy Dixon;
  Jacques Fray; Evelyn Hoey; Tonia Ingre; Richard
  Lane; Olga Markoff; Lulu McConnell; Joe Penner;
  Gus Schilling; Teddy Walters; Franker Woods

Notes: [1] Out Newark 10/20/30.

4546 • VEILS
OPENED: 03/13/1928
Musical   Closed out of town

Librettist: Donald Heywood

Notes: No program available.

4547 • VELVET LADY, THE
OPENED: 02/03/1919   Theatre: New Amsterdam
Musical   Broadway: 136

Composer: Victor Herbert
Lyricist: Henry Blossom
Librettist: Henry Blossom; Fred Jackson
Producer: Klaw & Erlanger
Director: Edgar MacGregor; Julian Mitchell

Source: FULL HOUSE, A (Play: Fred Jackson);
  Musical Director: Frederic Stahlberg;
  Orchestrations: Victor Herbert

Songs: Any Time New York Goes Dry [1];
  Bubbles; Come Be My Wife; Dancing at the
  Wedding; Fair Honeymoon Shine On; I've
  Danced to Beat the Band; Life and Love; Little
  Girl and Boy; Logic; Merry Wedding Bells;
  Policeology [1]; Scandal; Spooky- Ookum;
  There's Nothing Too Fine for the Finest;
  Throwing the Bull; Tonight's the Night; Velvet
  Lady [2]; Way Down in Yucatan; Wedding
  Bells; What a Position for Me

Cast: Eddie Dowling; Fay Marbe; Georgia
  O'Ramey; Jed Prouty; Ernest Torrence

Notes: *See also SHE TOOK A CHANCE.* [1] Out
  Philadelphia 12/23/18. [2] ASCAP/Library of
  Congress.

4548 • VENETIAN GLASS NEPHEW, THE
OPENED: 02/23/1931   Theatre: Vanderbilt
Musical   Broadway: 8

Composer: Eugene Bonner
Lyricist: Eugene Bonner
Librettist: Ruth Hale
Producer: Walter Greenough
Director: Walter Greenough

Costumes: Brooks; **Musical Director:** Leon Barzin;
  Set Design: Edgar Bohlman; Sointu Syrjala

Cast: Lee Burgess; Gage Clarke; George Houston;
  Raymond Huntley; Dodd Mehan; Mary Silviera;
  Edgar Stehli; Louis Yaeckel

4549 • VENETIAN ROMANCE, A
OPENED: 05/02/1904   Theatre: Knickerbocker
Musical   Broadway: 31

Composer: Frederic Colt Wright
Librettist: Cornelia Osgood Taylor
Producer: Frank Perley Opera Company
Director: Al Holbrook

Songs: But Our Charms Do Not Stop Quite There

Cast: Harry MacDonough; Ignacio Martinetti

4550 • VENUS IN SILK
OPENED: 10/01/1935
Musical   Closed out of town

Composer: Robert Stolz
Lyricist: Lester O'Keefe
Librettist: Lester O'Keefe; Laurence Schwab
Producer: Laurence Schwab
Director: Zeke Colvan

Source: VENUS IN SEIDE (Musical: Alfred Grunwald; Ludwig Herzer); **Choreographer:** William Holbrook; **Costumes:** Kay Morrison; **Musical Director:** George Hirst; **Orchestrations:** George Hirst; Hans Spialek; Robert Stolz; **Set Design:** Raymond Sovey; **Vocal Arranger:** George Hirst

Songs: Baby, Play with Me; Czardas; Dance, Oh, Lonely Gypsy Maid [1]; Drag 'Em Out Dragoons; Ducky; Eyes That Are Smiling; Flame of Love; Hail, the Falcon; I Ask Not Who You Are; If I Were a Bandit; Just for You; Musical Scene; Opening; Play in Native Fashion [1]; Slave Song and Dance [1]; Sweetly I Spoke; This Life Will Roll Along; Waltz Continental; Waltz That Is Fashioned for Love, A [1]; Welcome, Happy Groom [1]; You Are the One; Zingra

Cast: Florenz Ames; Audrey Christie; Jack Cole; Alice Dudley; Gilbert Lamb; Nancy McCord; J. Harold Murray

Notes: Program Pittsburgh 10/1/35 and Washington, D.C. used. Also known as BELOVED ROGUE. [1] Added to Muny Opera (St. Louis) revival 1948.

4551 • VENUS, 1906

OPENED: 04/17/1906   Theatre: Empire
Revue   London

Composer: Jerome Kern
Lyricist: George Grossmith Jr.

Songs: Leader of the Labour Party, The; Won't You Buy a Little Canoe

Notes: Part of a longer music hall bill.

4552 • VENUS ON BROADWAY

OPENED: 10/01/1917   Theatre: Palais Royal
Revue

Composer: A. Baldwin Sloane
Director: John Murray Anderson

Notes: No other information available.

4553 • VERA VIOLETTA

OPENED: 11/20/1911   Theatre: Winter Garden
Musical   Broadway: 112

Composer: Edmund Eysler
Lyricist: Harold Atteridge
Librettist: Harold Atteridge; Leonard Liebling
Producer: Winter Garden Company

Source: VERA VIOLETTA (Musical: Edmund Eysler; Leo Stein); **Musical Director:** Samuel Lehman

Songs: Angeline from the Opera Comique (C: Louis A. Hirsch; L: Melville Gideon); Cave Man, The; Come and Dance (C: Louis A. Hirsch; L: Melville Gideon); Come Back to Me; Fifty-Seven Ways to Win a Man; Gaby Glide, The (C: Louis A. Hirsch; L: Harry Pilcer); I Want Something New to Play With; I Wonder If It's True; I've Heard That Before (C: Louis A. Hirsch; L: Melville Gideon); My Lou; Olga from the Volga; Paree, Gay Paree; Rum Tum Tiddle (C: Jean Schwartz; L: Edward Madden); That Haunting Melody (C/L: George M. Cohan); Vera Violetta; When You Hear Love's Hello [1] (C: Louis A. Hirsch; L: Harold Atteridge; E. Ray Goetz)

Cast: Barney Bernard; Gaby Deslys; Melville Ellis; Ernest Hare; Al Jolson; Annette Kellerman; Stella Mayhew; Billie Taylor; Mae West

Notes: [1] ASCAP/Library of Congress only.

4554 • VERONIQUE

OPENED: 10/30/1905   Theatre: Broadway
Musical   Broadway: 81

Composer: Andre Messager
Lyricist: Lillian Eldee; Percy Greenbank
Librettist: Henry Hamilton
Producer: Klaw & Erlanger
Director: Marcus Mayer

Source: VERONIQUE (Musical: G. Duval; Andre Messager; Albert Vanloo); **Set Design:** Ernest Gros

Songs: Ah, Well, We'll Try to Be Precise; Ah, You? Oh! Strange Situation [2]; As Along the Street We Wander; At Weddings as a General Rule; Between Us All Is O'er; Bloom of the Apple Tree, The; Come Drink a Toast to Man and Wife;

Come One and All, Haste to the Ball; Farewell, I Go, It Must Be So; Flowers of Springtime, Sweetly Scented (Opening Chorus); Garden of Love, The; Hush! Hush! She's Meditating; I Thank You for Your Welcome; I've Got a Little Hubby Now [1]; Life Is Short, My Dear Friends; Little Goose, A [2]; Now My Little Story's Ended; Now the Carriages All Are Waiting; Now Then, Where Is the Blushing Bride?; Oh, Strange Situation; Oh, What a Dainty Profession; One Day, 'Neath an Apple Tree Laden [2]; Out in the Breezy Morning Air; Please, Sir, We Want If We May; Sweet Lisette, So People Say; Swing Song, The (You Are Laughing); Take Estelle, and Veronique; Trot Here and There, Take Care, Take Care; When Not Engaged in Fighting; While I Am Waiting; You're a Charming Little Maiden

Cast: Kitty Gordon; Valli Valli; Ruth Vincent

Notes: [1] Out Boston 1/29/06. [2] British vocal score only.

4555 • VERY GOOD EDDIE

OPENED: 12/23/1915   Theatre: Princess
Musical   Broadway: 341

Composer: Jerome Kern
Lyricist: Schuyler Greene; Herbert Reynolds
Librettist: Philip Bartholomae; Guy Bolton
Producer: F. Ray Comstock; Elisabeth Marbury
Director: Frank McCormack

Source: OVER-NIGHT (Play: Philip Bartholomae); **Choreographer:** David Bennett; **Costumes:** Melville Ellis; Finchley; **Musical Director:** Max Hirschfeld; **Orchestrations:** Frank Sadler; **Set Design:** Elsie De Wolfe

Songs: Alone at Last (L: Herbert Reynolds); Alone with You (All Alone) [1] (C: Cole Porter; L: Melville Gideon); Babes in the Wood (L: Schuyler Greene; Jerome Kern); Buffo Dance (inst.); Dance Trio (inst.); Fashion Show, The; Hands Up [3]; I'd Like to Have a Million in the Bank (L: Herbert Reynolds); If I Find the Girl (L: John E. Hazzard; Herbert Reynolds); Isn't It Great to Be Married [4] (L: Schuyler Greene); I've Got to Dance [3] (L: Schuyler Greene); Nodding Roses (L: Schuyler Greene; Herbert Reynolds); Oceans of Love [3]; Old Bill Baker (Undertaker) [2] (L: Ring Lardner); Old Boy Neutral [6] (L: Schuyler Greene); On the Shore

at Le Lei Wi [5] (C: Henry Kailimai; Jerome Kern; L: Herbert Reynolds); Same Old Game, The; Some Sort of Somebody (All the Time) [7] (L: Elsie Janis); Triangle, The (scene) [9] (L: Guy Bolton); We're on Our Way (L: Schuyler Greene); Wedding Bells Are Calling Me [8] (L: Harry B. Smith); When You Wear a 13 Collar (L: Schuyler Greene)

Cast: Alice Dovey; John E. Hazzard; Ada Lewis; Helen Raymond; Oscar Shaw; Ernest Truex

Notes: [1] Added to London production. [2] Written for ZIEGFELD FOLLIES of 1915. Added after opening. [3] Cut prior to opening. [4] Same music as "Can't You See I Mean You" from 90 IN THE SHADE and "All That I Want Is Somebody to Love Me" from 90 IN THE SHADE. [5] Kern wrote verse. Kailimai wrote chorus. From MISS INFORMATION. [6] Same music as "A Little Love" from MISS INFORMATION. [7] From MISS INFORMATION. [8] From NOBODY HOME. [9] In 90 IN THE SHADE. Published in the VERY GOOD EDDIE score, might not have been in production.

4556 • VERY LITTLE FAUST AND MUCH MARGUERITE

OPENED: 08/30/1897   Theatre: Hammerstein's
                                    Olympia
Musical   Broadway: 24

Composer: Fred J. Eustis; Florimond Herve
Lyricist: Richard F. Carroll
Additional Lyrics: Clement King
Librettist: Richard F. Carroll

Cast: Florence Bell; John Belton; Richard F. Carroll; Beatrice Hamilton

Notes: No program available.

4557 • VERY WARM FOR MAY

OPENED: 11/17/1939   Theatre: Alvin
Musical   Broadway: 59

Composer: Jerome Kern
Lyricist: Oscar Hammerstein II
Librettist: Oscar Hammerstein II
Producer: Max Gordon
Director: Oscar Hammerstein II; Vincente Minnelli

Choreographer: Harry Losee; Albertina Rasch;
Costumes: Vincente Minnelli; **Musical Director:**
Robert Emmett Dolan; **Orchestrations:** Robert
Russell Bennett; **Set Design:** Vincente Minnelli;
Vocal Arranger: Ralph Blane; Hugh Martin

Songs: All in Fun; All the Things You Are;
Audition; Ballet Peculaire (inst.); Deer and the
Park Avenue Lady, The; Heaven in My Arms
(Music in My Heart); High Up in Harlem [1];
In Other Words, Seventeen; In the Heart of the
Dark; L'Histoire de Madame de la Tour; May
Tells All; Me and the Role and You [1];
Schottische Scena; Stop Dance (inst.); Strange
Case of Adam Standish, The; That Lucky Fellow
[2]; That Lucky Lady [2]

Cast: June Allyson; Eve Arden; Maxine Barat;
Helena Bliss; Donald Brian; Andre Charise; Sally
Craven; Kate Friedlich; Avon Long; Don Loper;
Grace McDonald; Frances Mercer; Richard
Quine; Hollace Shaw; Hiram Sherman; Max
Showalter; Ralph Stuart; Vera- Ellen; Jack
Whiting; Billie Worth

Notes: [1] Cut prior to opening. [2] Same music.

4558 • VIA GALACTICA

OPENED: 11/28/1972   Theatre: Uris
Musical   Broadway: 7

Composer: Galt MacDermot
Lyricist: Christopher Gore
Librettist: Christopher Gore; Judith Ross
Producer: George W. George; Nat Shapiro;
Barnard S. Strauss
Director: Peter Hall

Costumes: John Bury; **Lighting Designer:** Lloyd
Burlingame; **Musical Director:** Joyce Brown;
Orchestrations: Danny Hurd; Bhen Lanzaroni;
Horace Ott, **Set Design:** John Bury; **Vocal
Arranger:** Joyce Brown

Songs: All My Good Mornings; Children of the
Sun; Cross On Over; Dance the Dark Away!;
Different; Finale Act I; Four Hundred Girls Ago;
Gospel of Gabriel Finn; Great Forever Wagon,
The; Helen of Troy; Home [1]; Hush; Ilmar's
Tomb; Isaac's Equation; Lady Isn't Looking; Life
Wins; New Jerusalem; Other Side of the Sky,
The; Oysters; Shall We Friend; Take Your Hat
Off; Terre Haute High; Up [1]; Via Galactica; We
Are One; Worm Gene, The

Cast: Jacqueline Britt; Irene Cara; Ralph Carter;
Melanie Chartoff; Keene Curtis; James Dybas;
Raul Julia; Virginia Vestoff

Notes: [1] Cut prior to opening.

4559 • VICEROY, THE

OPENED: 04/09/1900   Theatre: Knickerbocker
Musical   Broadway: 28

Composer: Victor Herbert
Lyricist: Harry B. Smith
Librettist: Harry B. Smith
Producer: Bostonians, The; Klaw & Erlanger
Director: William H. Fitzgerald

Musical Director: Samuel L. Studley;
Orchestrations: Victor Herbert

Songs: All Men Have Their Troubles; By This Sweet
Token; Eyes of Black and Eyes of Blue; Finale Act
I; Hear Me; I See By Your Smile; I'm the Leader of
Society; In a Smuggler's Cave; Just for Today;
Love May Come, Love May Go; 'Neath the Blue
Neapolitan Sky; On My Nuptial Day; One
Fellow's Joy Is Another Fellow's Woe; Robin and
the Rose, The; Sailor's Life, A; Since I Am Queen
of the Carnival; So They Say; That's My Idea of
Love; Thy Subjects Are We; Tivolini; Viceroy; We
Come to the Lively Market Square; We'll Catch
You at Last, Tivolini!; With Military Pomp

Cast: Henry Clay Barnabee; Helen Bertram; Grace
Cameron; Henry Miller; Frank Rushworth;
Marcia Van Dresser

4560 • VICTOR/VICTORIA

OPENED: 10/25/1995   Theatre: Marquis
Musical   Broadway

Composer: Henry Mancini
Lyricist: Leslie Bricusse
Librettist: Blake Edwards
Producer: Tony Adams; Blake Edwards; Polygram
Diversified Ent.
Director: Blake Edwards

Source: VICTOR/VICTORIA (Film: Blake
Edwards); **Costumes:** Willa Kim; **Incidental
Music:** David Krane; **Lighting Designer:** Peggy
Eisenhauer; Jules Fisher; **Musical Director:** Ian
Fraser; **Orchestrations:** Billy Byers; **Set Design:**
Robin Wagner; **Vocal Arranger:** Ian Fraser

Songs: Almost a Love Song; Apache; Attitude; Chicago, Illinois [1]; Crazy World [1]; I Know Where I'm Going [2]; If I Were a Man; I've No Idea Where I'm Going (The Victoria Variations); King's Dilemma; Le Jazz Hot [1]; Living in the Shadows (C: Frank Wildhorn); Louis Says [2] (C: Frank Wildhorn); Paris By Night; Paris Makes Me Horny; Someone Else [2]; Tango, The; This Is Not Going to Change My Life [2]; Trust Me (C: Frank Wildhorn); Victor/Victoria; Victoria Variations [2]; You & Me [1]; You'd Be Surprised [2]

Cast: Julie Andrews; Michael Cripe; Hillel Gitter; Adam Heller; Gregory Jbara; Michael Nouri; Tony Roberts; Richard B. Shull; Rachel York

Notes: Still running as of publication. Wildhorn and Bricusse wrote six songs for this show of which three were accepted. [1] From score of previous film version. [2] Cut.

4561 • VICTORY CANTEEN

OPENED: 1971
Revue   Los Angeles

Composer: Richard M. Sherman
Lyricist: Robert B. Sherman

Songs: Axe the Axis Polka; Doughnuts; Happy Tomorrows; Hawks!; (They Just Can't Ration) L-O-V-E; Lafayette, We're Here!; Let's Go Native; Loose Lips (Sink Ships); My Window Full of Stars; Smoke 'Em Up, Smoke 'Em Up!; South Sea Island Rhapsody; Va-Va-Va-Vee (for Victory); Victory Canteen; We Two (Someday)

Notes: No other information available.

4562 • VICTORY GIRL, THE

OPENED: 11/16/1918
Musical   Closed out of town

Composer: Silvio Hein
Lyricist: Philip Barholomae
Librettist: Lynn Cowan; Alex Sullivan

Notes: A revision of GIRL O' MINE.

4563 • VIENNA LIFE

OPENED: 01/23/1901   Theatre: Broadway
Musical   Broadway: 35

Composer: Johann Strauss
Lyricist: Glen MacDonough
Librettist: Glen MacDonough

Source: WIENER BLUT (Musical: Victor Leon; Leo Stein; Johann Strauss)

Cast: William Blaisdell; Charles H. Drew; Raymond Hitchcock; Ethel Jackson; Julia Raymond; Amelia Stone; Maude Thomas

Notes: No other information available.

4564 • VILLAGE BLACKSMITH, THE

OPENED: 12/29/1912   Theatre: Lambs' Club
Musical   Broadway

Composer: Victor Herbert
Librettist: George V. Hobart

Notes: A one-act musical presented at the Lambs' Club.

4565 • VINCENT YOUMANS' BALLET REVUE

OPENED: 01/27/1944
Revue   Closed out of town

Composer: Ernesto Lecuona; Vincent Youmans
Lyricist: Gladys Shelley; Maria Shelton
Librettist: Eric Tatch

Choreographer: Leonide Massine; **Costumes:** John N. Booth Jr.; **Set Design:** Woodman Thompson

Songs: Black Rhapsody (C: Ernesto Lecuona)

Cast: Mason Adams; Glenn Anders; June MacLaren; Herbert Ross; Deems Taylor

Notes: Closed in Baltimore.

4566 • VINTAGE '60

OPENED: 09/12/1960   Theatre: Brooks Atkinson
Revue   Broadway: 8

Librettist: Maxwell Grant; Alan Jeffreys; Jack Wilson
Producer: Zev Bufman; David Merrick
Director: Michael Ross

Choreographer: Jonathan Lucas; **Costumes:** Fred Voelpel; **Musical Director:** Gershon Kingsley; **Orchestrations:** Allyn Ferguson; Robert Ginzler; Gershon Kingsley; John Lesko; John Mandel; Peter Matz; Sid Ramin; **Set Design:** Fred Voelpel

Songs: Afraid of Love (C/L: Alice Clark; David Morton); All American (C: David Baker; L: Sheldon Harnick); Do It in Two (C/L: Alan Jeffreys; Jack Wilson); Down in the Streets (C/L: Tommy Garlock; Alan Jeffreys); Dublin Town (C/L: Fred Ebb; Lee Goldsmith; Paul Klein); Forget Me (C: David Baker; L: Sheldon Harnick); Isms (C: David Baker; L: Sheldon Harnick); Time Is Now, The (C: Mark Bucci; L: David Rogers)

Cast: Bert Convy; Fay De Witt; Barbara Heller; Michele Lee; Dick Patterson

4567 • VIOLINS OVER BROADWAY

| | Theatre: Diamond Horseshoe |
| Revue | Nightclub |

Producer: Billy Rose
Director: John Murray Anderson

Choreographer: Esther Junger; **Costumes:** Thomas Becher; **Lighting Designer:** John Murray Anderson; **Musical Director:** Harold Sandler; **Orchestrations:** Gleb Yellin; **Set Design:** Herman Rosse; **Vocal Arranger:** Maurice Levine

Songs: Violins Over Broadway (C/L: Unknown)

Notes: No program available.

4568 • VIRGINIA (1923)

Notes: *See CAROLINE.*

4569 • VIRGINIA (1937)

OPENED: 09/02/1937   Theatre: Center
Musical   Broadway: 60

Composer: Arthur Schwartz
Lyricist: Albert Sillman
Librettist: Owen Davis; Laurence Stallings
Producer: Center Theatre, The
Director: Leon Leonidoff; Edward Clarke Lilley

Choreographer: Florence Rogge; **Costumes:** Irene Sharaff; **Musical Director:** John McManus;

Orchestrations: Hans Spialek; Will Vodery; Phil Wall; **Set Design:** Lee Simonson

Songs: Fee-Fie-Fo-Fum; Good and Lucky; Goodbye, Jonah; If You Were Someone Else; I'll Be Sittin' in de Lap o' de Lord; It's Our Duty to the King; Meet Me at the Fair; My Bridal Gown (L: Laurence Stallings; Al Stillman); My Heart Is Dancing; Old Flame Never Dies, An (L: Laurence Stallings; Al Stillman); Send One Angel Down; Virginia; We Had to Rehearse; You and I Know (L: Laurence Stallings; Al Stillman)

Cast: Avis Andrews; Mona Barrie; Bertha Belmore; Anne Booth; Patricia Bowman; Nigel Bruce; John W. Bubbles; Ford L. Buck; Ronald Graham; Lansing Hatfield; Dennis Hoey; Nora Kaye; Gene Lockhart; Billy Redfield; Gordon Richards; Valia Valentinoff

4570 • VISIONS OF 1969

OPENED: 1919
Musical

Composer: Neil Moret
Lyricist: Harry Williams
Librettist: Jack Lait
Producer: Winnie Baldwin; Percy Bronson

Notes: Vaudeville musical.

4571 • VIVA AMIGOS

OPENED: 1944
Revue

Composer: Ted Murry
Lyricist: Benny Davis

Songs: Brazilian Can-Can; Dancing to the Rhythm of Love; Viva Amigos; You Bring the Scotch and I'll Bring the Soda

Notes: No other information available. Information from ASCAP/Library of Congress.

4572 • VIVA O'BRIEN

OPENED: 10/09/1941   Theatre: Majestic
Musical   Broadway: 20

Composer: Maria Grever
Lyricist: Raymond Leveen
Librettist: Eleanor Wells; William K. Wells

Producer: Hickey, Hale & Robinson
Director: Robert Milton; William K. Wells

Choreographer: Chester Hale; **Costumes:** John N. Booth Jr.; **Musical Director:** Ray Kavanaugh; **Orchestrations:** Charles L. Cooke; **Set Design:** Clark Robinson; **Vocal Arranger:** Leonard dePaur

Songs: Broken Hearted Romeo; Carinito; Don Jose O'Brien; El Matador Terrifico; How Long?; Matador Dance; Mexican Bad Men; Mood of the Moment; Mozambamba; Our Song; Rain Ballet; Ritual Dance; Sailors, The; To Prove My Love; Wrap Me in Your Serape; Yucatana

Cast: Ruth Clayton; Victoria Cordova; Marie Nash

4573 • VIVE LA FEMME
OPENED: 1924

Songs: Chili Bom Bom (C: Walter Donaldson; L: Cliff Friend)

Notes: No other information available.

4574 • VOGUES AND VANITIES
Notes: *See PICCADILLY TO BROADWAY.*

4575 • VOGUES OF 1924
OPENED: 03/27/1924   Theatre: Shubert
Revue   Broadway: 114

Composer: Herbert Stothart
Lyricist: Clifford Grey
Librettist: Fred Thompson
Producer: Messrs. Shubert
Director: Alexander Leftwich; Frank Smithson

Choreographer: David Bennett; **Costumes:** Charles LeMaire; **Musical Director:** Alfred Newman; **Set Design:** Watson Barratt

Songs: Belle of the Ball, The; Belle of Today, The; Dressing; Eldorado; Hee-Bee Jee-Bees [1] (C: Jay Gorney; Herbert Stothart); Hush, Look Away; Katinka; Laugh and Play; Legend of the Shirt, The; Medicos; Pierrot; Rain; Spielman, The; Star of Destiny; Three Little Maids; When the Piper Plays

Cast: Fred Allen; May Boley; J. Harold Murray; Odette Myrtil; Jimmy Savo

Notes: [1] Sheet music only.

4576 • VOICE OF MCCONNELL, THE
OPENED: 12/25/1918   Theatre: Manhattan
                      Opera House
Play   Broadway: 30

Composer: George M. Cohan
Lyricist: George M. Cohan
Author: George M. Cohan
Producer: George M. Cohan; Sam H. Harris
Director: George M. Cohan; Sam Forrest

Songs: I'm True to Them All, and They're Just as True to Me [1]; Ireland, Land of My Dreams; That Tumble Down Shack in Athlone (C: Monte Carlo; Alma Sanders; L: Richard W. Pascoe); When I Look Into Your Eyes Mavourneen; You Can't Deny You're Irish

Cast: Roy Cochrane; Edna Leslie; Chauncey Olcott; Arthur Shields

Notes: [1] ASCAP/Library of Congress only.

W

4577 • W.C.

OPENED: 1971
Musical   Closed out of town

Composer: Al Carmines
Lyricist: Al Carmines
Librettist: Sam Locke; Milton Sperling
Producer: Shelly Gross; Lee Guber
Director: Richard Altman

Source: W.C. FIELDS, HIS FOLLIES AND
FORTUNES (Book: Robert Lewis Taylor);
Choreographer: Bob Herget; **Costumes:** Sara
Brook; **Dance Arranger:** John Berkman; **Lighting
Designer:** Lester Tapper; **Musical Director:**
Susan Romann; **Orchestrations:** Carlyle Hall; **Set
Design:** Peter Larkin

Songs: Being a Pal; Bring on the Booze; Chickadee
Girls, The; Dummy Juggler [2]; Fifty Years of
Making People Laugh; Greatest Comic of Them
All, The; I Knew It All the Time; I'll Follow My
Star; I'll Still Be Here; I'm a Two Way Woman [1];
I'm Through with Men; Love Can Get Your
Down; Never Give a Sucker an Even Break;
Never Trust Anyone Under Three; Old Days,
The; Philadelphia 1890; Serenade; There's a Little
Boy in Every Man; Where Is This Man? [1]; Why
Do Women Always Choose the Wrong Man?;
You Come First After Me; You Could; You've
Gotta Leave Them Laughing

Cast: Jack Bittner; Essie Borden; Virginia Martin;
Bernadette Peters; Barry Preston; Mickey
Rooney; Rudy Tronto

Notes: [1] Not in program. [2] Cut.

4578 • WAC MUSICAL

OPENED: 1944
Revue

Songs: WAC Hymn, The (C/L: Frank Loesser)

Notes: Title unknown. No other informatin
available.

4579 • WAIT A MINIM!

OPENED: 03/07/1966   Theatre: John Golden
Revue   Broadway: 457

Composer: Jeremy Taylor
Lyricist: Jeremy Taylor
Producer: Frank Productions
Director: Leon Gluckman

Choreographer: Kendrew Lascelles; Frank Staff;
Costumes: Heather MacDonald-Rouse; **Lighting
Designer:** Leon Gluckman; Frank Rembach;
Musical Director: Andrew Tracey; **Set Design:**
Frank Rembach

Songs: Ag Pleez Deddy [2]; Ajade Papa;
Amasalela; Aria; Ayama; Ballad of the Southern
Suburbs [1]; Black-White Calypso; Bold Logger,
The [1]; Butter Milk Soldier (Johnny Soldier);
Celeste Aida (C: Giuseppe Verdi); Cingoma
Chakabaruka; Confession [1]; Cool; Crow, The [2];
Cruel Youth, The [1]; Die Meistertrinker
(Deutsches Weinlied . . . Watschplattltanz);
Dingere Dingale; Dirty Old Town; Foyo;
Hammer Song; Hoe Ry Die Boere; Hush Little
Baby [1]; I Came Home [1]; I Gave My Love a
Cherry; I Know Where I'm Going; Izicatulo
Gumboot Dance; Jikel Emaweni; Jo'burg Talking
Blues [1]; Kapurapura Kupika; Last Summer;
Latirette, Le Roi a Fait Battre Tambour; Little Sir
Hugh [1]; London Talking Blues; Love Life of a
Gondolier, The; Marabi Dance Song (Chuzi
Mama/Gwabi Gwabi); Mgeniso WaMgodo
WaShambini [2]; Ndinosara Nani? (With Whom
Shall I Stay?); North of the Popo; On Guard;
Opening Knight; Out of Focus; Over the Hills;
Piece of Ground, A; Red Red Rose;
Samandoza-we!; Single Girl [1]; Sir Oswald
Sodde; Skalo-Zwi; Strangest Dream, The [1];
Subuhi Sana; Table Bay; This Is South Africa;
This Is the Land; This Is Worth Fighting For;
Tour de France; Transkei Xha Xha [2]; Vive La
Difference; Wee Copper o' Fife, The

Cast: Sarah Atkinson; Kendrew Lascelles; Michel
Martel; April Olrich; Nigel Pegram; Andrew
Tracey; Paul Tracey; Dana Valery

Notes: [1] Cut from South African production prior to Broadway. [2] Cut from London version prior to Broadway.

4580 • WAIT FOR ME WORLD

Musical   Unproduced

Composer: John Kander
Lyricist: Fred Ebb

Notes: No other information available.

4581 • WAKE UP AND DREAM

OPENED: 12/30/1929   Theatre: Selwyn
Musical   Broadway: 127

Composer: Cole Porter
Lyricist: Cole Porter
Librettist: John Hastings Turner
Producer: Charles B. Cochran
Director: Frank Collins

Choreographer: Jack Buchanan; Tilly Losch; Max Rivers; **Costumes:** Paul Colin; Marc-Henri; Oliver Messel; Ada Peacock; **Set Design:** Paul Colin; Oliver Messel; Ada Peacock

Songs: After All, I'm Only a Schoolgirl; Agua Sincopada Tango (inst.); Banjo that Man Joe Plays, The; Dance of the Crinoline Ladies; Dance of the Ragamuffins; Entrance of Emigrants [7]; Extra Man, The [9]; Fancy Our Meeting (C: Philip Charig; Joseph Meyer; L: Douglas Furber); I Dream of a Girl in a Shawl [3]; I Loved Him but He Didn't Love Me [6]; I Want to Be Raided By You [6]; I'm a Gigolo; I've Got a Crush on You; Lady I Love, The [1]; Let's Do It, Let's Fall in Love [5]; Looking at You; More Incredible Happenings (C/L: Ronald Jeans); My Louisa [2]; Night Club Opening [6]; Operatic Pills; She's Such a Comfort to Me [10] (C: Arthur Schwartz; L: Douglas Furber; Max Lief; Nathaniel Lief; Donovan Parsons); Tale of an Oyster [8]; Wait Until It's Bedtime [6]; Wake Up and Dream; What Is This Called Love?; Which [4]; Why Wouldn't I Do? (C/L: Ivor Novello; L: Desmond Carter)

Cast: Toni Birkmeyer; Sonnie Hale; Tilly Losch; Jessie Matthews; Georges Metaxa; William Stephens

Notes: [1] Cut prior to London opening (3/27/29). [2] Cut prior to London opening (3/27/29). Not

used in NYMPH ERRANT. Cut also from THE NEW YORKERS (1930). [3] Originally in HITCHY-KOO OF 1922 as "My Spanish Shawl." [4] Not used in PARIS. [5] Not in New York production. [6] Originally in PARIS. [7] Cut from FIFTY MILLION FRENCHMEN. [8] Not used. Also not used in the 9:15 REVUE and THE NEW YORKERS (1930). [9] Cut prior to London opening. Also cut from FIFTY MILLION FRENCHMEN. [10] Originally in THE HOUSE THAT JACK BUILT (1929).

4582 • WAKE UP, DARLING

OPENED: 05/02/1956   Theatre: Ethel Barrymore
Play   Broadway: 5

Author: Alec Gottlieb
Producer: Richard Cook; Gordon W. Pollock; Lee Segall
Director: Ezra Stone

Costumes: Guy Kent; **Lighting Designer:** David Ballou; **Set Design:** David Ballou

Songs: Li'l Ol' You and Li'l Ol' Me (C: Jule Styne; L: Leo Robin)

Cast: Barbara Britton; Kay Medford; Barry Nelson; Russell Nype; Richard B. Shull; Paula Trueman

4583 • WALK A LITTLE FASTER

OPENED: 12/07/1932   Theatre: St. James
Revue   Broadway: 121

Composer: Vernon Duke
Lyricist: E.Y. Harburg
Librettist: Robert McGunigle; S.J. Perelman
Producer: Courtney Burr
Director: Monty Woolley

Choreographer: Albertina Rasch; **Costumes:** Kiviette; **Musical Director:** Nicholas Kempner; **Orchestrations:** Robert Russell Bennett; Conrad Salinger; **Set Design:** Boris Aronson

Songs: April in Paris; End of a Perfect Night; Frisco Fanny (C: Henry Sullivan; L: Earle Crooker); (Manhattan's the) Loneliest Isle [1]; Mayfair (C: William Waliter; L: Rowland Leigh); Off Again, On Again; Penny for Your Thoughts, A; So Nonchalant (L: E.Y. Harburg; Charles Tobias); Speaking of Love; That's Life; Time and Tide;

Unaccustomed As I Am; Where Have We Met Before?

Cast: Charles Burr; Bobby Clark; Dave Fitzgibbon; Dorothy Fitzgibbon; Sue Hicks; Evelyn Hoey; John Hundley; Beatrice Lillie; Paul McCullough; Jerry Norris; Penny Singleton

Notes: [1] Cut.

4584 • WALK DOWN MAH STREET!

OPENED: 06/12/1968   Theatre: Players
Musical   Off-Broadway: 135

Composer: Norman Curtis
Lyricist: Patricia Taylor Curtis
Librettist: Patricia Taylor Curtis
Producer: Audience Associates, Inc.
Director: Patricia Taylor Curtis

Choreographer: Patricia Taylor Curtis; **Costumes:** Bob Rogers; **Dance Arranger:** Norman Curtis; **Lighting Designer:** Bruce D. Bassman; **Set Design:** Jack Logan; **Vocal Arranger:** Norman Curtis

Songs: Basic Black; Clean Up Your Own Backyard; Don't Have to Take It Any More; Flower Child; For Four Hundred Years; If You Want to Get Ahead; I'm Just a Statistic; Just One More Time; Lonely Girl; Someday, If We Grow Up; Teeny Bopper; Walk Down My Street; Walk, Lordy, Walk; Want to Get Retarded?; We're Today; What Shadows We Are

Cast: Denise Delapenha; Freddy Diaz; Lorraine Feather; Kenneth Frett; Vaughan Martinez; Gene Rounds

Notes: Special Material: James Taylor, Cagriel Levenson and Next Stage Theatre Co.

4585 • WALK TALL

OPENED: 07/12/1954
Revue   Closed out of town

Composer: Dean Fuller; Albert W. Selden; Ralph Strain
Lyricist: Marshall Barer; Valerie Bettis; Billings Brown
Librettist: Bud Burtson; William Engvick; Arnold B. Horwitt

Producer: Fred Miller; Martha Miller
Director: George Englund

Choreographer: Ray Harrison; **Costumes:** Robert Fletcher; **Musical Director:** Peter Matz; **Set Design:** Emanuel Gerard

Songs: Get Married Shyrlee [1] (C: Albert Selden; L: Burt Shevelove); I'll Dance You; Yesterday I Loved You

Cast: Jane Dulo; William Dwyer; June Ericson; Paul Hartman; Pat Stanley

Notes: No program available. [1] Also in SMALL WONDER and A MONTH OF SUNDAYS (1951).

4586 • WALK WITH MUSIC

OPENED: 06/04/1940   Theatre: Ethel Barrymore
Musical   Broadway: 55

Composer: Hoagy Carmichael
Lyricist: Johnny Mercer
Librettist: Guy Bolton; Parke Levy; Alan Lipscott
Producer: Ruth Selwyn; Messrs. Shubert
Director: R.H. Burnside

Source: UNKNOWN (Play: Stephen Powys); **Choreographer:** Anton Dolin; Herbert Harper; **Costumes:** Tom Lee; **Musical Director:** Joseph Littau; **Orchestrations:** Arden Cornwell; Joe Dubin; Hans Spialek; Fred Van Epps; Don Walker; Clay Warnick; **Set Design:** Watson Barratt; **Vocal Arranger:** Hugh Martin

Songs: Amazing What Love Can Do [1]; Break It Up Cinderella [3]; Darn Clever These Chinese [1]; Even If I Say It Myself; Everything Happens to Me; Friend of the Family; Give, Baby, Give [2] (C: Irving Gellers; Otis Spencer; L: Gladys Shelley); Greetings, Gates; Happy New Year to You [1]; How Nice for Me; I Like Love [2] (C/L: Hugh Martin); I Walk with Music; Love Song [1]; Newsy Bluesies [1]; Ooh! What You Said; Put Music in the Barn [1]; Rhumba Jumps!, The; Smile for the Press; Today I Am a Glamour Girl; Wait Till You See Me in the Morning [4]; Way Back in 1939 A.D.; We're Off the Wagon [1]; What'll They Think of Next?

Cast: Kitty Carlisle; Stepin Fetchit; Mitzi Green; Art Jarrett; Betty Lawford; Marty May; Frances Williams

Notes: Titled THREE AFTER THREE out of town

when it was based on a play by Guy Bolton. [1]
Out Philadelphia 12/25/39. [2] Out Detroit 1940.
[3] Revised as "Break It Now, Buck Private" in
AT EASE! [4] Revised and put into AT EASE!

4587 • WALKING DELEGATE, THE

Notes: *See THE KOREANS.*

4588 • WALKING HAPPY

OPENED: 11/26/1966   Theatre: Lunt-Fontanne
Musical   Broadway: 161

Composer: Jimmy Van Heusen
Lyricist: Sammy Cahn
Librettist: Ketti Frings; Roger O. Hirson
Producer: Cy Feuer; Ernest Martin
Director: Cy Feuer

Source: HOBSON'S CHOICE (Play: Harold
Brighouse); **Choreographer:** Danny Daniels;
Costumes: Robert Fletcher; **Dance Arranger:** Ed
Scott; **Lighting Designer:** Robert Randolph;
Musical Director: Herbert Grossman;
Orchestrations: Larry Wilcox; **Set Design:**
Robert Randolph; **Vocal Arranger:** Herbert
Grossman

Songs: Be Joyful [1]; Circle This Day on the
Calendar [2]; Clog and Grog (dance); How D'Ya
Talk to a Girl; I Don't Think I'm in Love;
I Should've Said [2]; If I Be Your Best Chance;
If Me No If — But Me No But [5]; I'll Make a
Man of the Man; It Might As Well Be Her; Joyful
Thing, A; Love Will Find a Way — They Say [3];
Man Has Got to Wear the Pants, The [5]; Most
Girls [3]; Must You Go [3]; People Who Are Nice
(No More Mr. Nice); Policeman's Whistle, A [5];
Such a Sociable Sort; There's No Love Like [3];
Think of Something Else; To Keep the Chill Off
the Bones [3]; Touch a Hair of His Head [3]; Use
Your Noggin; Very Close to Wonderful [2];
Walking Happy [4]; What Makes It Happen;
When Willie Waltzes with Me [5]; Where Was I;
Wouldn't It Break Your Heart? [5]; You're Right,
You're Right

Cast: Chad Black; Gordon Dilworth; George Rose;
Louise Troy; Gretchen Van Aken; Norman
Wisdom

Notes: [1] Not in programs. [2] Out Detroit
10/25/66. [3] ASCAP only. [4] Written for
unproduced Fred Astaire film. [5] Not used.

4589 • WALL STREET GIRL, THE

OPENED: 04/15/1912   Theatre: Cohan
Musical   Broadway: 56

Composer: Karl Hoschna
Lyricist: Benjamin Hapgood Burt
Librettist: Margaret Mayo; Edgar Selwyn
Producer: Frederic McKay
Director: Charles Winninger

Choreographer: Gus Sohlke; **Musical Director:**
William Lorraine

Songs: Chicken Pie [1]; Deedle-Dee-Dum, The
(C: Silvio Hein); Every Day [1] (C/L: Daniels;
Jones); Finale; Finale Act II (C: Nat D. Ayer;
L: A. Seymour Brown); Finale Act III (C: Karl
Hoschna; L: Benjamin Hapgood Burt); Finnegan
[2] (C: Nat D. Ayer; L: A. Seymour Brown);
Georgia Land [2] (C: Harry Carroll; L: Arthur
Fields); I Can Drink (C/L: Benjamin Hapgood
Burt); I Never Knew (C: Henry I. Marshall;
L: Stanley Murphy); I Should Have Been Born a
Boy (C: Nat D. Ayer; L: A. Seymour Brown);
I Want a Regular Man; If You Only Will [1] (C/L:
Benjamin Hapgood Burt); In Old Wall Street [2];
Indian Rag, The [3] (C: Nat D. Ayer;
L: A. Seymour Brown); Love Is a Peculiarity
(C: Al Piantadosi; L: Joseph McCarthy); Medley
of College Songs; Moving Pictures [1]; My Irish
Girl [2] (C: Henriette-Blanke Blacher; L: Alfred
Bryan); On the Quiet; Opening Chorus; Opening
Chorus Act II (C/L: Benjamin Hapgood Burt);
Spoony Land (C: M.J. Fitzpatrick; L: Edward
Madden); That Baboon Baby Dance [2] (C: Joe
Cooper; L: Dave Oppenheim); Under the Love
Tree [1] (C: Bert Grant; L: A. Seymour Brown);
Walk This Way (C: Fred Fisher; L: Grant Clarke);
Whistle It (C: Jean Schwartz; L: Alfred Bryan;
Grant Clarke); You're Exactly My Style of Girl [2]
(C: Hector McCarthy; L: Arthur Denvir); You're
Some Girl (C: Nat D. Ayer; L: A. Seymour
Brown)

Cast: Wellington Cross; Blanche Ring; Will Rogers;
Charles Winninger

Notes: [1] Out Washington, D.C. 5/1/12. [2] Sheet
music only. [3] Also in BING BOYS ON
BROADWAY.

4590 • WALTZ DREAM, A

OPENED: 01/27/1908   Theatre: Broadway
Musical   Broadway: 111

Composer: Oscar Straus
Lyricist: Joseph W. Herbert
Librettist: Joseph W. Herbert
Producer: Inter-State Amusement Co.
Director: Herbert Gresham

Source: EIN WALZERLRAUM (Musical: Felix Dormann; Leopold Jacobson; Oscar Straus); **Costumes:** F. Richard Anderson; **Set Design:** Homer Emens

Songs: Come Join in the Waltz [3]; Country Lass and a Courtly Dame, A [2]; Family's Ancient Tree, The; Finale Act II; Finale Act III; Gay Lothario, The [2] (C: Jerome Kern; L: C.H. Bovill); Hail, We Hope It's a Male [3]; Husband's Love, A; I Love and the World Is Mine (C: Charles Gilbert Spross; L: Florence Earle Coates); I'd Much Rather Stay at Home (C: Jerome Kern; L: C.H. Bovill); Just Because You Love [2] (C/L: Arthur Weld); Kissing Time; Lesson in Love, A; Life Is Love and Laughter; Love Cannot Be Bought; Love's Roundelay [2]; Love's Thoughts (C/L: Florence Duncan); Oh Joy, Let Our Song of Gladness Be Heard on Ever Side; Opening Chorus; Piccolo; Prater, The [1] (C: Ivan Caryll); Soldier Stole Her Heart, A; Sweetest Maid of All; Trumpets Blare, The; Two Is Plenty; Vienna (C: Jerome Kern; L: Adrian Ross); Wedding March and Hymn; When the Song of Love Is Heard (C: Arthur Weld)

Cast: Charles A. Bigelow; Sophie Brandt; Magda Dahl; Harry Fairleigh; Joseph W. Herbert; Edward Johnson; Josie Sadler

Notes: An English version of the original Straus songs was written by Grace Isabel Colbron and published by the Continental Publishing Company but I don't believe they were ever used on stage. [1] Out 2/15/09. [2] Sheet music only. [3] Added for revival Muny Opera, St. Louis 1938.

4591 • WALTZ OF THE STORK

OPENED: 01/05/1982   Theatre: Century
Musical   Broadway: 146

Composer: Melvin Van Peebles
Lyricist: Melvin Van Peebles
Librettist: Melvin Van Peebles
Producer: Melvin Van Peebles
Director: Melvin Van Peebles

Costumes: Bernard Johnson; **Lighting Designer:** Shirley Prendergast; **Musical Director:** Bob Carten; **Set Design:** Kert Lundell

Songs: And I Love You; Apple Sketching, The; Mother's Prayer; My Love Belongs to You; One Hundred and Fifteen; Play It As It Lays; Shoulders to Lean On; Tender Understanding (C/L: Mark Burkan; Ted Hayes); There; Weddings and Funerals (C/L: Mark Burken; Ted Hayes)

Cast: Bob Carten; C.J. Critt; Mario Van Peebles; Melvin Van Peebles

4592 • WALTZ OF THE TOREADORS

Musical   Unproduced

Composer: Harold Rome
Lyricist: Harold Rome

Source: WALTZ OF THE TOREADORS, THE (Play: Jean Anouilh)

Notes: No other information available.

4593 • WALTZ WAS BORN IN VIENNA

OPENED: 04/25/1936
Musical

Composer: Frederick Loewe
Lyricist: Earle Crooker
Librettist: Earle Crooker
Director: Donald Brian

Cast: Donald Brian

Notes: A musical skit that was part of THE LAMBS SPRING GAMBOL at the Waldorf-Astoria Hotel. There were no songs identified. See under that name for additional credits.

4594 • WALTZES FROM VIENNA
Notes: *See THE GREAT WALTZ (1934).*

4595 • WANTED

OPENED: 01/19/1972   Theatre: Cherry Lane
Musical   Off-Broadway: 79

Composer: Al Carmines
Lyricist: Al Carmines
Librettist: David Epstein
Producer: Arthur D. Zinberg
Director: Lawrence Kornfeld

Costumes: Linda Giese; **Lighting Designer:** Roger Morgan; **Musical Director:** Susan Romann; **Set Design:** Paul Zalon

Songs: As I'm Growing Older; Guns Are Fun; I Am the Man; I Do the Best I Can (L: Al Carmines; David Epstein); I Want to Blow Up the World; I Want to Ride with You (L: Al Carmines; David Epstein); Indian Benefit Ball, The; It's Love; Jailhouse Blues; Lord Is My Light, The (L: Al Carmines; David Epstein); Outlaw Man; Parasol Lady; Wahoo!; Where Have You Been Up to Now?; Whispering to You; Who's on Our Side? (L: Al Carmines; David Epstein); You Do This

Cast: Reathel Bean; Frank Coppola; June Gable; Lee Guilliatt; John Kuhner; Peter Lombard

4596 • WANTED — A WIFE
OPENED: 1917
Musical

Composer: Walter L. Rosemont
Lyricist: Darl MacBoyle
Librettist: Alan Brooks
Producer: George Choos

Costumes: Edyth Bloodgood; **Set Design:** P. Dodd Ackerman

Songs: I Am Longing, My Dearie, for You; If You Ever Want to Do Some Lovin'; Oh! I'll Be Good

Cast: Frank Harrington; Al Hinton; Charlotte Taylor

Notes: A one-act vaudeville musical in Philadelphia.

4597 • WAR BUBBLES
OPENED: 05/16/1898   Theatre: Hammerstein's Olympia
Musical   Broadway: 26

Composer: Oscar Hammerstein I
Lyricist: Oscar Hammerstein I
Librettist: Oscar Hammerstein I
Producer: Oscar Hammerstein I

Cast: Allene Crater; Oscar Figman; Lucy Nelson

Notes: No program available.

4598 • WAR-TIME WEDDING OR, IN MEXICO IN 1847, A
OPENED: 1896
Musical   Closed out of town

Composer: Oscar Weil
Librettist: C.T. Dazey; Oscar Weil
Producer: Bostonians

Musical Director: S.L. Studley

Cast: Henry Clay Barnabee; Eugene Cowles; William H. MacDonald; Alice Nielsen

Notes: No other information available.

4599 • WARS OF THE WORLD
OPENED: 09/05/1914   Theatre: Hippodrome
Musical   Broadway: 229

Composer: Manuel Klein
Lyricist: Manuel Klein
Librettist: John P. Wilson
Producer: Messrs. Shubert
Director: William J. Wilson

Costumes: Max & Mahieu; Frances M. Ziebarth; **Set Design:** Arthur Voegtlin

Songs: Baby Eyes; In Siam; Under a Gay Sombrero; When You Come Home Again, Johnny; You're Just the One I've Waited For

Cast: John Gibson; Lawrence Grant; Marceline; John P. Wilson

Notes: No program available.

4600 • WASHINGTON SQUARE
OPENED: 01/23/1947
Play   Closed out of town

Author: Augustus Goetz; Ruth Goodman Goetz
Producer: Oscar Serlin
Director: Jack Minster

Source: WASHINGTON SQUARE (Novel: Henry James); **Lighting Designer:** Donald Oenslager; **Set Design:** Donald Oenslager

Songs: Comme Tu Es Different (C/L: Dorothie Bigelow)

Cast: Peter Cookson; John Halliday; Barbara Leeds

Notes: Opened in New Haven. The play was overhauled (only Peter Cookson and the authors survived) and reopened as THE HEIRESS.

4601 • WATCH ON THE RHINE

OPENED: 01/03/1980   Theatre: John Golden
Play   Broadway: 36

Author: Lillian Hellman
Producer: Spencer H. Berlin; Marc Howard; John F. Kennedy Center; Long Wharf Theatre; Lester Osterman
Director: Arvin Brown

Costumes: Bill Walker; **Lighting Designer:** Ronald Wallace; **Set Design:** John Jensen

Songs: Soldier's Song (C/L: Thomas Fay)

Cast: Joyce Ebert; Jill Eikenberry; George Hearn; Mark McLaughlin; Jan Miner; Bobby Scott; Monica Snowden; Harris Yulin

4602 • WATCH OUT ANGEL

OPENED: 04/03/1945
Musical   Closed out of town

Composer: Josef Myrow
Lyricist: Eddie De Lange
Librettist: David Alison; Isabel Dawn
Producer: David Alison
Director: Harry Howell

Choreographer: Aida Broadhust; **Costumes:** Martingale; **Musical Director:** Charles Hathaway; **Set Design:** Richard Jackson

Songs: Co-op-hooray-shun; Don't You Believe It; Everybody Wants to Get into the Act; Five A.M. Ballet; Half a Dream to Go; I Love You but Good (L: Eddie De Lange; Jerry Seelen); It's a Great Life If You Weaken; Joyride; Out of My Mind; Publicity; Short and Sweet; That Does It [1] (L: Eddie De Lange; Jerry Seelen); To Be Young; Watch Out, Angel! (L: Eddie De Lange; Jerry Seelen); What's New in New York; Where Is the Boss

Cast: Lester Allen; Carol Haney; Marilyn Hare; Donald Kerr; Lucien Littlefield; Eden Nicholas; Jim Nolan

Notes: Program of San Francisco 4/3/45. [1] Not used.

4603 • WATCH YOUR STEP

OPENED: 12/08/1914   Theatre: New Amsterdam
Musical   Broadway: 175

Composer: Irving Berlin
Lyricist: Irving Berlin
Librettist: Harry B. Smith
Producer: Charles B. Dillingham
Director: R.H. Burnside

Source: ROUND THE CLOCK (Play: Augustin Daly); **Costumes:** Helen Dryden; Lucille; **Musical Director:** DeWitt Coolman; **Set Design:** Helen Dryden

Songs: Chatter Chatter; Come to the Land of the Argentine [1]; Homeward Bound [1]; I Hate You [1]; I Love to Have the Boys Around Me; I'm a Dancing Teacher Now; I've Gotta Go Back to Texas [1]; Lead Me to Love [1] (C: Ted Snyder); Let's Go Around the Town; Lock Me in Your Harem and Throw Away the Key [1]; Look at Them Doing It!; Metropolitan Nights; Minstrel Parade, The; Move Over; Office Hours; Old Operas in a New Way (Opera Medley); Settle Down in a One-Horse Town; Show Us How to Do the Fox Trot; Simple Melody; Syncopated Walk, The; They Always Follow Me Around; Watch Your Step [1]; What Is Love?; When I Discovered You (C/L: Irving Berlin; E. Ray Goetz); When It's Night Time in Dixie Land [1]

Cast: Elizabeth Brice; Irene Castle; Vernon Castle; Sallie Fisher; Justine Johnstone; Harry Kelly; Charles King; Elizabeth Murray; Frank Tinney

Notes: [1] Not in program. [2] Vocal score only.

4604 • WATER'S FINE, THE

OPENED: 1919
Musical

Composer: Ted Snyder
Lyricist: Sam M. Lewis; Joe Young

Songs: Boys Are Like Wonderful Toys; I'm in Love with You; In the Land of Go to Bed Early; Jazzin' the Alphabet; Shadows Always Make Me Blue; Way to Win a Girl, The; With a Little Bit of Cider Inside of Ida, Ida Was Full of Ideas

Notes: No other information available.

4605 • WAY TO KENMARE, THE
OPENED: 01/13/1906
Play   Closed out of town

Composer: Andrew Mack
Lyricist: Andrew Mack

Songs: Dan, My Darlin Dan; Legend of the Maguires, The; Rose of Kenmare, The; She Just Suits Me

Cast: Albert Andrews; George W. Deyo; Josephine Lovett; Andrew Mack

Notes: Out Cedar Rapids. No writing credits in program.

4606 • WAYWARD WAY, THE
OPENED: 09/03/1953
Musical   Closed out of town

Composer: Lorne Huycke
Lyricist: Bill Howe

Source: DRUNKARD, THE (Play: W.H. Smith)

Notes: No program available. Opened at the Hollywood Theatre Mart.

4607 • WE DID IT BEFORE
Notes: See BANJO EYES.

4608 • WE SHOULD WORRY
OPENED: 10/26/1917
Musical   Closed out of town

Composer A. Baldwin Sloane
Lyricist: Henry Blossom
Librettist: Henry Blossom

Source: UNKNOWN (Play: Charles Hoyt)

Notes: Atlantic City.

4609 • WE TAKE THE TOWN
OPENED: 02/17/1962
Musical   Closed out of town

Composer: Harold Karr
Lyricist: Matt Dubey
Librettist: Felice Bauer; Matt Dubey
Producer: Stuart Ostrow
Director: Alex Segal

Source: VIVA VILLA! (Film: Ben Hecht); **Choreographer:** Donald Saddler; **Costumes:** Motley; **Dance Arranger:** Mordecai Sheinkman; **Lighting Designer:** Tharon Musser; **Musical Director:** Colin Romoff; **Orchestrations:** Robert Russell Bennett; Hershy Kay; **Set Design:** Peter Larkin; **Vocal Arranger:** Colin Romoff

Songs: Beautiful People; Good Old Porfirio Diaz; How Does the Wine Taste?; I Don't Know How to Talk to a Lady; I Marry You; I've Got a Girl; Jesus [1]; Killing [1]; Mister Madero and Friend; Ode to a Friend; Only Girl, The; Pleadle-Eadle; Please Don't Despise Me; Poncho the Bull; Poncho's Thoughts (Little Man); Silverware; Viva Villa; We Take the Town; Wedded Man, A

Cast: Carmen Alvarez; Romney Brent; John Cullum; Mike Kellin; Robert Preston; Lester Rawlins; Kathleen Widdoes

Notes: [1] Out New Haven 2/17/62.

4610 • WE WERE DANCING
OPENED: 12/24/1936   Theatre: National
Play   Broadway: 113

Author: Noel Coward
Producer: John C. Wilson
Director: Noel Coward

Musical Director: John McManus; **Set Design:** G.E. Calthrop

Songs: We Were Dancing (C/L: Noel Coward)

Cast: Joyce Carey; Noel Coward; Gertrude Lawrence; Moya Nugent; Edward Underdown; Alan Webb

Notes: Part of TONIGHT AT 8:30.

4611 • WE'D RATHER SWITCH

OPENED: 05/02/1969   Theatre: Mermaid
Revue   Off-Broadway

Composer: Larry Crane
Lyricist: Larry Crane
Librettist: Walter Berger
Producer: Mario Manzini
Director: Robert Spelly

Choreographer: Robert Spelly; **Lighting Designer:** Donald L. Brooks; **Musical Director:** Rikki Dawn; **Set Design:** Frank Wakula

Songs: Golden Gang, The; Greatest Show on Earth; I'm Going Down the River and Have Myself a Darn Good Cry; Let's All Sing; Let's Do It All Over Again; Make Me Over; Man Is Good for Something After All, A; Man Isn't Old, A; Mod Man of Manhattan; On the Pier; Strangest Show on Earth, The; Stud Shows Us; Villains Aren't Bad Anymore; We'd Rather Switch

Cast: Robert Speller

4612 • WE'LL MEET AGAIN

Notes: *See SMILING THROUGH.*

4613 • WEBER & FIELDS JUBILEE

Revue   Broadway

Songs: Island of Roses and Love, The (C: Neil Moret; L: Earle C. Jones)

Cast: Lillian Russell

Notes: No other information available.

4614 • WEDDING DAY, THE

OPENED: 04/08/1897   Theatre: Casino
Musical   Broadway: 36

Composer: Julian Edwards
Lyricist: Stanislaus Stange
Librettist: Stanislaus Stange
Producer: Frank Murray
Director: Richard Barker

Costumes: Mme. Siedle; **Musical Director:** Julian Edwards; **Set Design:** Ernest Albert; Walter Burridge

Songs: At Last I Find in You; Come My Dearest; Confiding Woman; Days of Long Ago; Gaily Marches the Soldier; General Has Relented, The; He Never Said a Word; How I Danced Away; I Am a Simple Norman Maid; It Is Really to Good to Be True; Ladies, I Am Sorry; Life Is but Short at Best; Love's Prescription; Maid and the Officer, The; Mermaid and the Whale, The; Mon General; Nation's Pride, A; Planchette, Planchette; Rogue Lies Hid in the Wine, A; Rose Marie; Soldiers of the Parliment; This Is the Hour; Through the Years; Tomtit and the Nightingale, The; Vivandiers; Wise Little Maid, The; Woman's Tact, A

Cast: Jefferson De Angelis; Della Fox; Tom Greene; Lillian Russell

Notes: No songs listed in program. Songs from vocal score.

4615 • WEDDING OF IPHIGENIA, THE

OPENED: 12/16/1971   Theatre: Public
Musical   Off-Broadway: 139

Composer: Peter Link
Lyricist: Gretchen Cryer; Doug Dyer; Peter Link
Author: Euripides
Producer: N.Y. Shakespeare Festival; Joseph Papp
Director: Gerald Freedman

Source: IPHIGENIA (Play: Euripides)

Songs: All Greece; All Hail the King; And Now; Can't Stand in the Way of My Country; Come Let Us Dance; Crown Us with the Truth; Gate Tender; How Can I Tell My Joy?; I Was First to Call You Father; I Wonder; Last Night in a Dream; Lead Me Now; Line Is Unbroken, The; Oh, What Bridal Song; On a Ship with Fifty Oars; Only Stone; Opening; Ride on to Highest Destiny; They Sing My Marriage Song at Home; This New Land; To Greece I Gave This Body of Mine; Unhappiness Remembering; What Has Your Tongue to Tell?; Who Will Lay Hands?; Your Turn Has Come

Cast: Nell Carter; Leata Galloway; Marta Heflin; Lynda Lee Lawley; Marion Ramsey

4616 • WEDDING TRIP, THE

OPENED: 12/25/1911   Theatre: Broadway
Musical   Broadway: 48

Composer: Reginald De Koven
Lyricist: Harry B. Smith
Librettist: Fred De Gresac
Producer: Lee Shubert; Sam S. Shubert
Director: William J. Wilson

Songs: Ah, At Last; Awakened Love; Bivouac
Song; Curfew Bell Has Sounded, The; Family
Council, The; Flirtation; Fond Love [2];
Gentlemanly Brigand, The; Gypsy Kiss; Hail the
Wedding Pair; Here Is the Tunic of a Soldier;
Interrupted Love Song, The; Le Beau Sabreur;
Lesson in Love, A; Little Bride, A; Love Waltz
[2]; Marie [1]; Miraculous Cure, The; Modern
Banditti, The; Opening Ensemble; Sea Shell
Telephone, The; Soldier's Song [1]; Sweet Sixteen

Cast: Charles Angelo; Arthur Cordero; Grace
Emmons; Dorothy Jardon; George Madison;
Edward Martindel; Dorothy Morton; Christine
Nielson

Notes: [1] Sheet music only. [2] ASCAP/Library of
Congress.

4617 • WEE BIT O' SCOTCH, A

OPENED: 1970
Musical   Unproduced

Composer: Harold Rome
Lyricist: Harold Rome
Librettist: Jerome Chodorov

Source: ENGAGED (Play: W.S. Gilbert)

Songs: As the Case May Be; Belinda's Love Song;
Engaged; Farewell, My Life's True Love; Happy
Hindu Waltz; I Am Losing My Little Wren;
I Hate Her; I Intend to End It All; I Shall Be
Happy; I Shall Not Let Money Get in My Way;
Marriage; Name the Lady; Two Little Kittens;
Wee Bit o' Scotch, A; What Am I?; You Are the
Tree

4618 • WEEKEND

OPENED: 10/24/1983   Theatre: Theater at St.
                                        Peter's
Musical   Off-Broadway: 8

Composer: Roger Lax
Lyricist: Roger Lax
Librettist: Roger Lax
Producer: Mae Richard
Director: David H. Bell

Choreographer: David H. Bell; **Costumes:** Sally
Lesser; **Lighting Designer:** Toni Goldin; **Musical
Director:** Clay Fullum; **Orchestrations:** Robby
Merkin; **Set Design:** Ursula Belden

Cast: Louise Edeiken; Gregg Edelman; Justin Ross;
Carole-Ann Scott

4619 • WELCOME TO THE CLUB

OPENED: 04/13/1989   Theatre: Music Box
Musical   Broadway: 12

Composer: Cy Coleman
Lyricist: Cy Coleman; A.E. Hotchner
Librettist: A.E. Hotchner
Producer: Cy Coleman; A.E. Hotchner; William H.
Kessler Jr.; Michael M. Weatherly
Director: Peter Mark Schifter

Choreographer: Patricia Birch; **Costumes:**
William Ivey Long; **Lighting Designer:** Tharon
Musser; **Musical Director:** David Pogue;
Orchestrations: Doug Katsaros; **Set Design:**
David Jenkins; **Vocal Arranger:** Cy Coleman;
David Pogue

Songs: At My Side; Bachelors [1]; Boom Chicka
Boom [1]; By Dawn's Early Light [1];
Chickabees [1]; Combat Pay [1]; Guilty;
Holidays; Honeymoon Is Over, The [1]; I Get
Tired [1]; In the Name of Love; It Wouldn't Be
You; It's Love! It's Love!; King of the Mound [1];
Late Bloomer [1]; Let 'Em Rot [1]; Love Behind
Bars; Man of the People [1]; Meyer Chickerman;
Miami Beach; Mother-in-Law; Mrs. Meltzer
Wants the Money Now!; No Croissants [1]; Pal
Is a Pal, A [1]; Pay the Lawyer; Peace of Mind [1];
Piece of Cake, A; Place Called Alimony Jail, A;
Rap-Up, The (Alimony Rap) [1]; Rio; Single [1];
Southern Comfort; That's a Woman; To Live
Again [1]; Trouble with You, The; Two of Us,
The; Welcome to the Club [1]

Cast: Jodi Benson; Bill Buell; Sally Mayes; Marcia
Mitzman; Avery Schreiber; Marilyn Sokol; Scott
Waara; Scott Wentworth; Terri White; Samuel E.
Wright

Notes: Titled LET 'EM ROT out of town. [1] Not used.

4620 • WELL OF ROMANCE, THE
OPENED: 11/07/1930 Theatre: Craig
Musical Broadway: 8

Composer: H. Maurice Jacquet
Lyricist: Preston Sturges
Librettist: Preston Sturges
Producer: G.W. McGregor
Director: J.H. Benrimo

Choreographer: Leon Leonidoff; Florence Rogge; **Musical Director:** H. Maurice Jacquet; **Set Design:** Frank Gates; E.A. Morange

Songs: At Lovetime; Be Oh So Careful Ann; Cow's Divertissement [2]; Fare Thee Well; For You and For Me; German Country Dance [2]; Hail the King; How Can You Tell?; I Want to Be Loved By an Expert [2]; I'll Never Complain; Intermezzo [2]; Mazourka [2]; Melancholy Lady [1]; Moon's Shining Cool, The [2]; My Dream of Dreams; One Night; Rhapsody of Love; Serenade; Since You're Alone; Well of Romance, The

Cast: Lina Abarbanell; Laine Blaire; Max Figman; Howard Marsh; Tommy Monroe; Louis Sorin; Norma Terris

Notes: [1] Sheet music only. [2] Not in programs.

4621 • WELL, WELL, WELL
OPENED: 12/1928
Musical

Composer: Muriel Pollock; Arthur Schwartz
Lyricist: Max Lief; Nathaniel Lief
Librettist: Harold Atteridge; Montague Glass; Jules Eckert Goodman
Producer: Independent Prod. Company
Director: Lew Morton

Choreographer: John Boyle; Dave Gould; **Musical Director:** Harold Stern; **Set Design:** Watson Barratt

Songs: Dancing in the Moonlight; Have Pity, Sheriff; I'll Always Remember; Me 'n You; Night Life; Not Even You; Oh What a Man; Pep Up, Step Up; We Love to Go to Work; We'll Get Along; When He's Near

Cast: Virginia Barratt; Noel Francis; Fred Lightner; Jack Pearl; Jack Waterous

Notes: Program from Washington, D.C. 12/25/28. This show became PLEASURE BOUND. See that entry.

4622 • WE'RE ALL DRESSED UP AND WE DON'T KNOW HUERTO GO
OPENED: 05/22/1914
Play

Composer: Cole Porter
Lyricist: Cole Porter
Producer: Members Yale Drama Assn.

Songs: Cincinnati

Cast: Johnfritz Achelis; Lawrence Cornwell; Hay Langenheim; Phelps Newberry; Newbold Noyes; Cole Porter; Monty Woolley

Notes: Score lost except for "Cincinnati." Performed at Hotel Gibson, Cincinnati.

4623 • WE'RE CIVILIZED?
OPENED: 11/08/1962 Theatre: Jan Hus House
Musical Off-Broadway: 22

Composer: Ray Haney
Lyricist: Alfred Aiken
Librettist: Alfred Aiken
Producer: Rendell Productions
Director: Martin B. Cohen

Choreographer: Bhaskar; **Costumes:** Sonia Lowenstein; **Dance Arranger:** Michael Leonard; **Lighting Designer:** Roger Morgan; **Musical Director:** Michael Leonard; **Set Design:** Jack H. Cornwell; **Vocal Arranger:** Michael Leonard

Songs: Bad If He Does, Worse If He Don't; Brewing the Love Potion; Diversion; Everything Is Wonderful; Fertility Dance; I Like; J.B. Pictures, Inc.; Knife Dance; Lullaby Wind; Me Atahualpa; Mother Nature; Muted (C: Michael Leonard); No Place to Go; Procession; Snake Dance; Stretto; Too Old; We're Civilized; Welcome Home; Witch Song; Yankee Stay; You Can Hang Your Hat Here; You're Like

Cast: Bhaskar; Karen Black; Sally DeMay; John McLeod; Marty Ross

4624 • WEST POINT CADET, THE
OPENED: 09/30/1904   Theatre: Princess
Musical   Broadway: 4

Composer: A.M. Norden
Lyricist: A.M. Norden
Librettist: A.M. Norden
Producer: Nathaniel Roth

Source: LE NOUVEAU REGIMENT (Musical: Antoine Banes; Albert Barre; Henri Bernard; E. Martin); **Musical Director:** Jose Vandenberg

Cast: Edward Abeles; Della Fox; Joseph W. Herbert; Richie Ling; Clara Palmer

Notes: No songs listed in program.

4625 • WEST SIDE STORY
OPENED: 09/26/1957   Theatre: Winter Garden
Musical   Broadway: 732

Composer: Leonard Bernstein
Lyricist: Stephen Sondheim
Librettist: Arthur Laurents
Producer: Robert E. Griffith; Harold Prince
Director: Jerome Robbins

Choreographer: Peter Gennaro; Jerome Robbins; **Dance Arranger:** Betty Walberg; **Lighting Designer:** Jean Rosenthal; **Musical Director:** Max Goberman; **Orchestrations:** Leonard Bernstein; Irwin Kostal; Sid Ramin; **Set Design:** Oliver Smith

Songs: America; Boy Like That, A; Cool; Dance at the Gym, The (dance); Gee, Officer Krupke; I Feel Pretty; I Have a Love; Jet Song; Kids Ain't (Like Everybody Else) [1]; Maria; Mix! [1]; My Greatest Day! [1]; One Hand, One Heart; Prologue (dance); Rumble, The (dance); Something's Coming; Somewhere; This Turf Is Ours [1]; Tonight; Up to the Moon [1]

Cast: Tommy Abbott; Lee Becker; William Bramley; Mickey Calin; Martin Charnin; Marilyn Cooper; Wilma Curley; Grover Dale; Al De Sio; Reri Grist; Carmen Guiterrez; John Harkins; Arch Johnson; Larry Kert; Carol Lawrence; Ken Le Roy; Tony Mordente; Liane Plane; Chita

Rivera; Eddie Roll; Lynn Ross; Jaime Sanchez; Art Smith; Elizabeth Taylor; David Winters

Notes: Returned for an additional 249 performances on 4/27/60. The run above does not include these extra performances. [1] Cut prior to opening.

4626 • WET AND DRY
OPENED: 1920
Musical   Chicago

Composer: Jean C. Havez
Lyricist: Jean C. Havez
Producer: Max Dill; William C. Kolb

Songs: Beautiful Garden of Day Dreams; Everybody in the Town Is Sober Since My Cellar Went Dry; I'm Glad He's Irish; Let's Pretend; Love's Bouquet; Pickaninny Sam

Notes: No other information available.

4627 • WET PAINT
OPENED: 04/12/1965   Theatre: Renata
Revue   Off-Broadway: 16

Librettist: Pierre Berton; Leslie H. Carter; Tony Geiss; Stanley Handleman; Herbert Hartig; Bob Hilliard; Dolly Jonah; Lois Balk Korey; Marc London; Paul Lynde; Pat McCormick; Judith Milan; David Panich; Bob Rosenblum; Paul Sand; Howard Schulman
Producer: Lee Reynolds; Isobel Robins
Director: Michael Ross

Choreographer: Rudy Tronto; **Costumes:** Mostoller; **Dance Arranger:** Gerald Alters; **Lighting Designer:** David Moon; **Musical Director:** Gerald Alters; **Set Design:** David Moon; **Vocal Arranger:** Gerald Alters

Songs: Canary (C: Stan Davis; L: Giles O'Connor); Cantata (C: Gerald Alters; L: Herbert Hartig); Concert Encore (C/L: Sheldon Harnick); Cream in My Coffee (C: Ed Scott; L: Anne Croswell); I Know He'll Understand (C/L: Johnny Myers); Love Affair (C: Bob Kessler; L: Martin Charnin); Neville (C/L: Tony Geiss); Puns (C: Gerald Alters; L: Herbert Hartig); Showstopper (C/L: Johnny Myers); These Things I Know Are True (C/L: Jennifer Konecky); Unrequited Love March [1] (C/L: Ronny Graham)

Cast: Gene Allen; Hank Garrett; Linda Lavin; Bill McCutcheon; Isobel Robins; Paul Sand

Notes: [1] Later added to NEW FACES OF 1968.

4628 • WHAT A DAY FOR A MIRACLE

Notes: *See THE CHILDREN'S CRUSADE.*

4629 • WHAT A KILLING

OPENED: 03/27/1961   Theatre: Folksbiene
Musical   Off-Broadway: 1

Composer: George Harwell
Lyricist: Joan Anenia; George Harwell
Librettist: Fred Herbert
Producer: Jack Collins
Director: Gene Montefiore

Source: UNKNOWN (Story: Jack Waldron); **Choreographer:** Bob Hamilton; **Costumes:** Hugh Whitfield; **Dance Arranger:** Andrew Lesko; **Lighting Designer:** Robert Wightman; **Musical Director:** Andrew Lesko; **Orchestrations:** Andrew Lesko; **Set Design:** Robert Wightman

Songs: Chicago That I Knew, The; Customer Is Always Right; Face the Facts; Fools Come and Fools Go; Here I Come; I'm a Positive Guy; Laughing Out Loud; Lennie; Look at What It's Done; Nobody Cheats Big Mike; Oh, How I Love You; Out of Luck with Luck; Pride in My Work; Race, The; Rag, a Bone, a Hank of Hair, A; Rockette's Dance; Troubled Lady; What a Killing

Cast: Chanin Hale; Paul Hartman; Barney Martin; Lou Wills Jr.

4630 • WHAT DOES THE PUBLIC WANT?

Musical

Composer: Barney Gerard
Lyricist: Barney Gerard
Librettist: Barney Gerard
Director: Barney Gerard

Songs: I Wonder Why They Stare at Me; It Would Be Nice; It's Great Sport Just the Same; I've Got No Use for Opera When There's Ragtime; Red Riding Hood (C/L: Jeff T. Branen); Salvation Tess (C/L: B. Brown; Barney Gerard); San Francisco Fair (C/L: B. Brown; Barney Gerard); Up and Down (C/L: B. Brown; Barney Gerard); Virginia Rose (C/L: B. Brown; Barney Gerard); We're the Famous Impresarios (C/L: B. Brown; Barney Gerard); What Does the Public Want?; When I'm Dancing with Peg o' My Heart

Cast: Gertrude Hayes; Sam Sidman

Notes: Burlesque musical in Toledo.

4631 • WHAT EVER HAPPENED TO GEORGIE TAPPS?

OPENED: 08/12/1980   Theatre: Westwood
Playhouse
Revue   Los Angeles

Cast: Georgie Tapps

Notes: No program available.

4632 • WHAT IS LOVE?

OPENED: 07/02/1917
Musical   Closed out of town

Composer: Joseph E. Howard

Notes: Closed at the National Theatre, Washington, D.C. No other information available.

4633 • WHAT MAKES SAMMY RUN?

OPENED: 02/27/1964   Theatre: 54th St.
Musical   Broadway: 541

Composer: Ervin Drake
Lyricist: Ervin Drake
Librettist: Budd Schulberg; Stuart Schulberg
Producer: Joseph Cates
Director: Abe Burrows

Source: WHAT MAKES SAMMY RUN? (Novel: Budd Schulberg); **Choreographer:** Matt Mattox; **Costumes:** Noel Taylor; **Dance Arranger:** Arnold Goland; **Lighting Designer:** Helen Pond; Herbert Senn; **Musical Director:** Lehman Engel; **Orchestrations:** Don Walker; **Set Design:** Helen Pond; Herbert Senn; **Vocal Arranger:** Lehman Engel

Songs: Bachelor Gal [1]; Friendliest Thing, The; I Feel Humble; I See Something; Kiss Me No Kisses; Lites-Camera-Platitude; Maybe Some Other Time; Monsoon (dance); My Hometown; New Boy, A [1]; New Pair of Shoes, A; Paint a Rainbow; Room Without Windows, A; Some Days Everything Goes Wrong; Something to Live For; Sweetie [1]; Tender Spot, A; Warm Spot in My Heart, A [2]; Wedding of the Year, The; You Can Trust Me; You Help Me; You're No Good

Cast: Robert Alda; George Coe; Graciela Daniele; Arny Freeman; Sally Ann Howes; Steve Lawrence; Bernice Massi; Barry Newman; Ralph Stanley

Notes: [1] Out Philadelphia 1/64. [2] ASCAP/Library of Congress only.

4634 • WHAT NEXT?

OPENED: 06/24/1917
Musical   Closed out of town

Composer: Harry Tierney
Lyricist: Alfred Bryan
Librettist: Elmer Harris; Oliver Morosco
Producer: Oliver Morosco
Director: Fred A. Bishop

Set Design: Robert McQuinn

Songs: Angie's Patriotic Rally; Chasing the Squirrel; Cleopatra; Fame, Fame, Fame; For One Sweet Day; Get a Girl to Lead the Army; Hello Girlie; I Want a Good Girl (and I Want Her Bad); I Want You to Want Me with You; If You'll Be a Soldier, I'll Be a Red Cross Nurse; I've Got a Vegetable Garden (Garden of Liberty) (Vegetable Song); Just to Keep Expenses Down; Keep on the Right Hand Side of Father; Keep Your Eye on Little Mary Brown; Rescue, The; Routine Exercise, The; Seminary Girl, The; Send Me Back My Husband, You've Had Him Long Enough; We Do the Best That We Can; When a Pretty Peeping Ankle Peeps at You

Cast: Eva Fallon; Blanche Ring; Charles Winninger; Fannie Yantis

Notes: Program from Los Angeles 6/24/17. [1] Not in program.

4635 • WHAT'S A NICE COUNTRY LIKE YOU DOING IN A STATE LIKE THIS?

OPENED: 04/19/1973   Theatre: Upstage at
                                          Jimmy's
Revue   Off-Broadway: 477

Composer: Cary Hoffman
Lyricist: Ira Gasman
Director: Miriam Fond

Choreographer: Miriam Fond; **Costumes:** Danny Morgan; **Lighting Designer:** Richard Delahanty; **Musical Director:** Arnold Gross; **Orchestrations:** Hurbert Arnold; **Set Design:** Bill Puzo

Songs: America, You're Looking Good [1]; Bar, The; Bedroom, The; But I Love New York; Carlos, Juan and Miguel [1]; Changing Partners; Chicago; Church and State [1]; Come On, Daisy; Crime in the Streets; Daniel Boone; Dow Jones; Everybody Ought to Have a Gun; Farewell [1]; Farewell First Amendment; Fill 'Er Up [1]; Get Out of Here [1]; Girl of My Dreams [1]; Hallelujah; Hollywood; How'm I Doing? [1]; I Found the Girl of My Dreams on Broadway; I Just Pressed Button A [1]; I Like Me; I Like New York; I'm in Love With . . .; I'm Not Myself Anymore; I'm Not Taking a Chance on Love [1]; It's a Political-Satirical Revue; It's Getting Better; Johannesburg; Keeping the Peace; Kissinger und Kleindienst und Klein; Last One of the Boys, The [1]; Liberal's Lament; Liberation Tango [1]; Love Story; Mafia; Male Chauvinist Pig of Myself; Massage a Trois; Mugger's Work Is Never Done, A; Nicaragua [1]; Nuclear Winter [1]; On a Scale of One to Ten; People Are Like Porcupines; Primary Tango; Right Place at the Right Time, The; Rise and Fall of the American Empire Waltz, The; Runaways [1]; San Francisco; Street People; Take Us Back King George; Terrorist Trio [1]; Test Tube Baby; They Aren't There [1]; Things I Used to Know; Threesome; Trial of the Century; Update; Vasectomy; Watergate Suite; What the Hell [1]; What's a Nice Country Like You; Whatever Happened to the Communist Menace; Why Do I Keep Going to the Theatre?; Why Johnny?; You're Dull Johnny

Cast: Betty Buckley; Sam Freed; Bill LaVallee; Priscilla Lopez; Barry Michlin

Notes: Some sources list run as 477 performances. [1] Added for revival of 7/31/85.

4636 • WHAT'S GOING ON

OPENED: 1915
Musical

Songs: Girl You Left Behind (C: Jean Schwartz; L: William Jerome)

Notes: No other information available.

4637 • WHAT'S IN A NAME?

OPENED: 03/19/1920   Theatre: Maxine Elliott's
Musical   Broadway: 87

Composer: Milton Ager
Lyricist: John Murray Anderson; Anna Wynne O'Ryan [2]; Jack Yellen
Librettist: John Murray Anderson
Producer: John Murray Anderson

Choreographer: Michio Ito; **Costumes:** Robert E. Locher; Kay Turner; **Musical Director:** Augustus Barratt; **Orchestrations:** Maurice DePackh; Arthur Lange; **Set Design:** James Reynolds

Songs: In Fair Japan; In the Year of Fifty-Fifty [1]; Jewels of Pandora, The; My Bridal Veil; Rap-Tap-a-Tap; Strike; That Reminiscent Melody; Theatrical Blues, The; Valley of Dreams, The; What's in a Name? (Love Is Always Love); Without Kissing Love Isn't Love; Young Man's Fancy, A (Music Box Song)

Cast: James J. Corbett; Marie Gaspar; Billy B. Van; Herb Williams

Notes: [1] Sheet music only. [2] Not credited copyright records.

4638 • WHAT'S THE ODDS?

Notes: *See HONEYDEW.*

4639 • WHAT'S THE RUSH

OPENED: 1954

Composer: Charles Strouse
Lyricist: Lee Adams

Songs: Conversation; Happy Hollywood; Heart of a Girl, The; Let's Fly Away; Right Kind of Love (from the Wrong Kind of Guy); Romantic Night; Sphinx Won't Tell, The; Tame Me; To Get Us All Together; What's the Rush; When You Grow Up

Notes: No other information available. Might have been produced at Green Mansions resort.

4640 • WHAT'S UP?

OPENED: 11/11/1943   Theatre: National
Revue   Broadway: 63

Composer: Frederick Loewe
Lyricist: Alan Jay Lerner
Librettist: Alan Jay Lerner; Arthur Pierson
Producer: Mark Warnow
Director: George Balanchine; Robert H. Gordon

Choreographer: George Balanchine; **Costumes:** Grace Huston; **Musical Director:** Will Irwin; **Orchestrations:** Van Cleave; **Set Design:** Boris Aronson; **Vocal Arranger:** Bobby Tucker

Songs: From the Chimney to the Cellar; Girl is Like a Book, A; How Fly Times; Ill-Tempered Clavichord, The; Joshua; Miss Langley's School for Girls; My Last Love; Three Girls in a Boat; You Wash and I'll Dry; You've Got a Hold on Me

Cast: Larry Douglas; Lynn Gardner; Rodney McLennan; Jimmy Savo

4641 • WHEN CLAUDIA SMILES (1913)

OPENED: 04/13/1913   Theatre: Illinois
Musical   Chicago

Composer: Jean Schwartz
Lyricist: William Jerome
Librettist: Leo Ditrichstein

Notes: This show was revised for Broadway the following year. *See also WHEN CLAUDIA SMILES (1914).*

4642 • WHEN CLAUDIA SMILES (1914)

OPENED: 02/02/1914   Theatre: 39th St.
Play   Broadway: 56

Composer: Jean Schwartz
Lyricist: Anne Caldwell
Author: Anne Caldwell
Producer: Frederic McKay
Director: Charles Winninger

Source: WHEN CLAUDIA SMILES (Musical: Leo Ditrichstein; William Jerome; Jean Schwartz)

Songs: Boys All Fall for Me, The [1]; Boys, Boys, Boys; Dear Old Dinah (C: Henry Marshall; L: Stanley Murphy); Everybody Sometime Must Love Someone (C: Dave Stamper; L: Gene Buck); Flower Garden Ball, The (L: William Jerome); Grand Old Life; He's a Dear Old Pet [2] (L: William Jerome); If They'd Only Move Old Ireland Over Here; I've Got Everything I Want but You; Let Us Dance the Boston [1] (C/L: George A. Spink); Ssh! You'll Waken Mr. Doyle (C: John Golden; L: Jerome Kern; E.W. Rogers); Why Is the Ocean So Near the Shore? (C: Clarence Jones; L: Arthur Weinberg); You're My Boy

Cast: Harry Conor; Blanche Ring; Charles Winninger

Notes: *See also WHEN CLAUDIA SMILES (1913),* an earlier version of this show. [1] Out Albany 12/29/13. [2] Sheet music only.

4643 • WHEN DO THE WORDS COME TRUE

OPENED: 1971
Musical   Closed out of town

Composer: John Meyer
Lyricist: John Meyer
Librettist: John Meyer
Producer: Madeline Gilford; Gerard Oestreicher
Director: Edward Earle

Choreographer: Patti Karr; **Lighting Designer:** Don Yopp; **Musical Director:** Richard J. Leonard; **Orchestrations:** Richard J. Leonard; **Set Design:** Louis John Dezserian; **Vocal Arranger:** Richard J. Leonard

Songs: After the Holidays; Be Good to Her; But Now; Cable Car; Colder By the Hour (C: Jacques Urbont); First Thing About You, The; From Where I Stand; His Room; I'm All Yours; See You in San Diego; When Do the Word Come True; World Outside, The

Cast: David Brooks; Gloria De Haven; Jamie Donnelly; Edward Earle; Bill Gerber; Patti Karr

Notes: Closed at Bucks County Playhouse, Pennsylvania.

4644 • WHEN DREAMS COME TRUE

OPENED: 08/18/1913   Theatre: Lyric
Musical   Broadway: 64

Composer: Silvio Hein
Lyricist: Philip Bartholomae
Librettist: Philip Bartholomae
Producer: Philip Bartholomae
Director: Frank Smithson

Choreographer: Joseph Santley

Songs: America; Beautiful Bounding Sea [2]; Boy with the Violin, The; Come Along to the Movies; Come On, All Together [2]; Dear World; Dream Waltz; Giddy Up, Giddy Up, Dearie; It's Great to Be a Wonderful Detective; Laughing Water Ripple; Love Is Such a Funny Little Feeling; Love with a Capital L [3]; Minnie, Ha Ha; O.K. Two Step; There Ain't No Harm in What You Do; Town That Grows Where the Hudson Flows, The; Waltz Aviation [3]; Wedding Rehearsal; When Dreams Come True (C: Silvio Hein; Roy Webb); When the Clock Strikes One; Who's the Little Girl?; Y-O-U, Dear, Y-O-U; You're Here and I'm Here [1] (C: Jerome Kern; L: Harry B. Smith)

Cast: Joseph Santley; Amelia Summerville; May Vokes; Anna Wheaton

Notes: [1] Originally in THE LAUGHING HUSBAND. [2] Out Chicago 4/3/13. [3] Out San Antonio.

4645 • WHEN HELL FREEZES OVER I'LL SKATE

OPENED: 07/22/1983
Revue   Closed out of town

Composer: Cleavant Derricks; Clinton Derricks-Carroll
Lyricist: Linda Michelle Baron; Cleavant Derricks; Clinton Derricks-Carroll
Producer: Cocoanut Grove Playhouse; Florida Arts Council
Director: Vinnette Carroll

Choreographer: Michele Simmons; **Costumes:** William Schroder; **Dance Arranger:** George Broderick; **Lighting Designer:** Pat Simmons; **Musical Director:** George Broderick; **Orchestrations:** George Broderick; **Set Design:**

William Schroder; **Vocal Arranger:** Cleavant Derricks

Songs: Cleo's Theme; Diet; Elijah Rock; Gather to the Water; Harlem Beat; I Wanna Get to You; I'm Going Through a Change; Just Dissatisfied; Liza Jane; Lord, Hear Your Child A-Callin'; Lost in the Wilderness; Medley of Negro Spirituals; Not in the Mood for Blues; Survive; Travellin'; You Can't Get By Me

Cast: Lynne Clifton-Allen; Nora Cole; Sheila Ellis; Jamil K. Garland; L. Michael Gray; Trina Thomas

4646 • WHEN JOHNNY COMES MARCHING HOME

OPENED: 12/16/1902   Theatre: New York
Musical   Broadway: 71

Composer: Julian Edwards
Lyricist: Stanislaus Stange
Librettist: Stanislaus Stange
Producer: Whitney Opera Company
Director: A.M. Holbrook

Costumes: Caroline Seidle; **Musical Director:** William E. MacQuinn

Songs: Ariella [3]; But They Didn't; Did He, No He Didn't [2]; Drums, The; Fairyland; Flag of My Country; Good Day, Yankees!; I Could Waltz on Forever; I Was Quite Upset [3]; I'm So Upset [2]; Just Marry the Man and Be Merry; Katie, My Southern Rose; Love's Night [1]; My Honeysuckle Girl [4]; My Own United States; Of the Stars and Stripes I Am Dreaming [2]; Ootsey Tootsey [2]; Opening Chorus; Sing, Sing, Darkies, Sing; Sir Frog and Mistress Toad [3]; Spring, Sweet Spring; Swanee River, The; 'Twas Down in the Garden of Eden; What's in a Name [3]; When Our Lips In Kisses Met; While You're Thinking; Who Knows?; Years Touch Not the Heart

Cast: Thelma Fair; Julia Gifford; Maude Lambert; Homer Lind; Albert McGuckin; William G. Stewart

Notes: [1] May be "Love's Light." [2] Cut out of town. [3] Sheet music only. [4] Also referred to as "My Honeysuckle Gal."

4647 • WHEN LOVE IS YOUNG

OPENED: 10/28/1913   Theatre: Cort
Musical   Chicago

Composer: William Schroeder
Lyricist: William Cary Duncan
Librettist: Rida Johnson Young

Cast: Joe Hyams; Leila McIntyre

Notes: A sequel to THE GIRL OF MY DREAMS.

4648 • WHEN SUMMER COMES

OPENED: 02/15/1925
Musical   Closed out of town

Composer: A. Baldwin Sloane
Lyricist: Jack Arnold
Librettist: Jack Arnold
Producer: Theodore J. Hammerstein; Jerome Quinn
Director: Walter Wilson

Choreographer: Raymond Midgley; **Musical Director:** Albert Hurley

Songs: Business Man, A; Carry Me Back; Geography; I Had a Sweet, Sweet Mamma (C/L: Ruby Cowan); I've Lost My Head Over You (C/L: Asher; Razoff); I'm Lonesome for Someone Like You; Lonesome; Main Street; Papa; Peaches; Ring, Ring, Ring; Virginia Clay; Voodoo Hagamin & Hamid; Wedding Ring; What Am I Going to Say; When Summer Comes; When Summer Comes; Whoa!; You're in Love

Cast: James Barton; Nellie Fillmore; Jack McGowan; Ray Raymond

Notes: Poli's Theatre, Washington, D.C. and Easton, Pa. 2/14/25.

4649 • WHEN SWEET SIXTEEN

OPENED: 09/14/1911   Theatre: Daly's
Musical   Broadway: 12

Composer: Victor Herbert
Lyricist: George V. Hobart
Librettist: George V. Hobart
Producer: Everall & Wallach Company
Director: R.H. Burnside; George V. Hobart

Musical Director: Louis F. Gottschalk; **Orchestrations:** Victor Herbert; **Set Design:** Bernard MacDonald

Songs: Dear Old Fairyland; Fairies' Revel; Frolic of the Fairies [1]; Golden Long Ago, The; Ha! Ha!

Ha! [1]; Has Cupid Laid in Wait for You; Hearts Are Trumps; Honey Love; I Love to Read the Papers in the Morning [1]; I Want to Be a Wild, WIld Rose (The Wild Rose); I'm Not a Bit Superstitious [1]; In Fairyland; In So-So Society [1]; In the Golden Long Ago; Island of Sweet Sixteen [1]; It's Always Going to Be that Way; Lanciers (Finale Ultimo) [1]; Laughs; Little Fifi; Mah Honey Love; Man's a Man for A' That, A; Mary Drew [1]; My Toast to You; Oh! Mary You're Contrary [1]; Oh, the Things They Put in the Papers Now-a- Days [1]; Oh, Those Boys!; Opening; People Will Talk, You Know; Pourquoi?; (There's None So Sweet As) Rosalind; Since Papa Becomes a Billionaire [1]; That's Boys Your Boys [1]; There Once Was a Princess; There's Money in Graft (There's a Raft of Money in Graft! Graft! Graft!); They Follow Me Everywhere; While the Big Old World Rolls Round [1]; Wild Rose, The

Cast: Josie Intropodi; William Norris; Roy Purviance

Notes: [1] ASCAP/Library of Congress only.

4650 • WHEN WE WERE FORTY-ONE

OPENED: 06/12/1905   Theatre: New York Roof
Musical   Broadway: 66

Composer: Gus Edwards
Lyricist: Robert B. Smith
Librettist: Robert B. Smith
Director: Edward E. Rice

Choreographer: Gertrude Hoffman; Joseph Smith; **Musical Director:** Robert Hood Bowers

Songs: Advantage of a College Education, The; Brother Masons (C: Gertrude Hoffman; L: Vincent Bryan); Goddess of Rector's, The; I Am a Regular Romeo; Kindly Pass the Chloroform Along (C: Gertrude Hoffman; L: Vincent Bryan); Maiden of the Wild and Woolly West [2]; Man That Leads the Band Leads the Army, The; Meet Me Under the Wysteria; Simple Simon [2]; Sweet Kitty Kellairs [1]; Up and Down the Boardwalk; Write to Marian the Maid

Cast: Harry Bulger; Emma Carus; LaBelle Dazie; Elsie Janis; John McVeigh; Harry Meehan; Charles H. Prince

Notes: A parody of WHEN WE WERE TWENTY-ONE. Sometimes referred to as WHEN WE ARE FORTY-ONE. [1] A parody on the play SWEET KITTY BELLAIRS. [2] ASCAP/Library of Congress only.

4651 • WHEN YOU SMILE

OPENED: 10/25/1925   Theatre: National
Musical   Broadway: 49

Composer: Tom Johnstone
Lyricist: Phil Cook
Librettist: Jack Alicoate; Tom Johnstone
Producer: James P. Beury
Director: Oscar Eagle

Choreographer: Raymond Midgley; **Musical Director:** F. Wheeler Wadsworth

Songs: All Work and No Play; Buy an Extra; Gee, We Get Along; June; Keep Building Your Castles; Keep Them Guessing; Let's Dance and Make Up; Let's Have a Good Time; Naughty Eyes; Oh, What a Girl; One Little Girl; She Loves Me; Spanish Moon; When You Smile; Wonderful Rhythm; Wonderful Yesterday

Cast: Imogene Coca; Phil Cook; Carol Joyce; Philip Lord; Ray Raymond; Jack Whiting

4652 • WHERE'S CHARLEY?

OPENED: 10/11/1948   Theatre: St. James
Musical   Broadway: 792

Composer: Frank Loesser
Lyricist: Frank Loesser
Librettist: George Abbott
Producer: Cy Feuer; Ernest H. Martin; Gwen Rickard
Director: George Abbott

Source: CHARLEY'S AUNT (Play: Brandon Thomas); **Choreographer:** George Balanchine; Fred Danielli; **Costumes:** David Ffolkes; **Musical Director:** Max Goberman; **Orchestrations:** Philip J. Lang; Ted Royal; Hans Spialek; **Set Design:** David Ffolkes; **Vocal Arranger:** Garry Dolin

Songs: Argument, The [1]; At the Red Rose Cotillion; Bee, The [1]; Better Get Out of Here; Don't Introduce Me to That Angel [2]; Gossips, The; Lovelier Than Ever; Make a Miracle; My Darling, My Darling; New Ashmolean Marching

Society and Students Conservatory Band, The; Once in Love with Amy; Pernambuco; Saunter Away [1]; Serenade with Asides; Train That Brought You to Town, The [1]; Where's Charley?; Woman in His Room, A; Years Before Us, The; Your Own College Band [1]

Cast: Ray Bolger; Paul England; Jane Lawrence; Allyn Ann McLerie; Doretta Morrow; Byron Palmer

Notes: [1] Cut prior to opening. [2] Cut prior to opening. Later in stage version of HANS CHRISTIAN ANDERSEN (titled HANS ANDERSEN) under the name "Jenny Kissed Me."

4653 • WHERE'S MAMIE?

Notes: *See FIRST LADY SUITE.*

4654 • WHIRL OF NEW YORK, THE

OPENED: 06/13/1921   Theatre: Winter Garden
Musical   Broadway: 124

Composer: Al Goodman; Lew Pollack
Lyricist: Sidney D. Mitchell; Lew Morton; Edgar Smith
Librettist: Lew Morton; Edgar Smith
Producer: J.J. Shubert; Lee Shubert
Director: Lew Morton

Source: BELLE OF NEW YORK, THE (Musical: Leo Edwards; Gustave Kerker); **Choreographer:** Allan K. Foster; **Musical Director:** Al Goodman; **Set Design:** Watson Barratt

Songs: Belle of New York, The; Chain Dance; Chinese New Year's Ballet; Cora Angelique (Musical Comedy Queen) (The Queen of Musical Comedy) (C: Lew Pollack; L: Sidney D. Mitchell); Dance, Dance, Dance; Dancing Fools; Follow On; From Far Cohoes; Gee, I Wish I Had a Girl; I Do So There!; I Know That I'm in Love (C: Lew Pollack; L: Sidney D. Mitchell); Just One Good Time; La Belle Parisienne; Little Baby; Mandalay; Molly, Molly; Molly on the Trolley; Opening Chorus; Pastry Cooks, The [2]; Purity Brigadiers, The; Spirit of the Chinese Vase, The; Take Her Down to Coney and Give Her the Air [1] (C/L: Lew Pollack; Ed Rose; Richard A. Whiting); Teach Me How to Kiss; Tiffin, Tiffin; When We Are Married; Whistling

Cast: Mlle. Adelaide; Charles Dale; Louis Mann; J. Harold Murray; John T. Murray; Joe Smith

Notes: [1] Added after opening. [2] Out Boston 10/26/21.

4655 • WHIRL OF SOCIETY, THE

OPENED: 03/05/1912   Theatre: Winter Garden
Musical   Broadway: 136

Composer: Louis A. Hirsch
Lyricist: Harold Atteridge
Librettist: Harrison Rhodes
Producer: Winter Garden Company

Choreographer: William J. Wilson; **Costumes:** Melville Ellis; **Musical Director:** Samuel Lehman; **Set Design:** H. Robert Law

Songs: Billy Ballou (C/L: Will Hardy); Billy's Melody [1] (C: Joe Cooper; L: L. Wolfe Gilbert); Blow on Your Piccolo; Cinderella Waltz [1]; Come Back to Me; Cotillion, The; Fol-De-Rol-Dol-Doi (C: Jean Schwartz; L: Edward Madden); Four O'Clock Tea; Gaby Glide, The [1] (C: Louis A. Hirsch; L: Harry Pilcer); Ghost of the Violin [5] (C: Ted Snyder; L: Bert Kalmar); Hard Luck in Society [1]; Here Comes the Bride [5]; Hitchy-Koo [5] (C: Lewis F. Muir; L: Maurice Abrahams; L. Wolfe Gilbert); How Do You Do, Miss Ragtime (C/L: Louis A. Hirsch); How Do You Know?; Hypnotizing Man; I Want Something New to Play With; I Want to Be in Dixie [4] (C: Ted Snyder; L: Irving Berlin); I'm Going Back to Dixie; I'm Saving My Kisses; Lead Me to That Beautiful Band [5]; Meet Me in Peacock Alley [5]; My Sumuran Girl (C: Louis A. Hirsch; L: Al Jolson); Oh, Mister Dream Man [1]; On the Mississippi [3] (C: Harry Carroll; Arthur Fields; L: Ballard Macdonald); Opening Chorus; Oriental Rose [1] (C/L: Louis A. Hirsch); Ragtime Sextette [2] (C/L: Irving Berlin; Music Based On: Gaetano Donizetti); Ragtime Soldier Man [5] (C/L: Irving Berlin); Row, Row, Row [5] (C: James V. Monaco; L: William Jerome); Snap Your Fingers [1] (C: Harry Von Tilzer; L: William Jerome); That Society Bear [1] (C/L: Irving Berlin); Villain Still Pursued Her, The (C: Harry Von Tilzer; L: William Jerome); Which Shall I Choose

Cast: Barney Bernard; Gaby Deslys; Melville Ellis; Ernest Hare; Al Jolson; Stella Mayhew; Blossom Seeley; Billie Taylor; George White

Notes: Part one was titled THE WHIRL OF
SOCIETY, part two titled A NIGHT WITH THE
PIERROTS, part three titled THE CAPTIVE
(pantomime). [1] Sheet music only. [2] Parody of
"Chi Mi Frena" from LUCIA DI
LAMMERMOOR by Donizetti. Also in
HANKY-PANKY as "Lucia Sextette Burlesqe."
[3] Also in HANKY-PANKY. [4] Also in HULLO,
RAGTIME. [5] Not in programs.

4656 • WHIRL OF THE TOWN, THE

OPENED: 1921
Musical   Closed out of town

Songs: Any Night on Old Broadway (L: Harold
Atteridge); How'd You Like to Put Your Head
Upon My Pillow (C: Jean Schwartz; L: Alfred
Bryan); Trial of Shimmy Mae, The

Cast: Georgie Price; Mae West

Notes: *See TATTLE TALES, an earlier version of
this show. See also THE MIMIC WORLD OF 1921,
a later version.*

4657 • WHIRL OF THE WORLD, THE

OPENED: 01/10/1914   Theatre: Winter Garden
Revue   Broadway: 161

Composer: Sigmund Romberg
Lyricist: Harold Atteridge
Librettist: Harold Atteridge
Producer: Winter Garden Company
Director: William J. Wilson

Costumes: Melville Ellis

Songs: All Aboard; Amber Club, The; American
Maxixe, The; Broadway in Paree, A (C/L: Henry
Lehman); College Boy, A; Come On In the
Dancing's Fine; Dance Eccentric [1]; Dance
Extraordinaire [1]; Dance of the Fortune Wheel,
The; Dancing Romeo, A; Early Hours of the
Morn; Everybody Means It When They Say
Good-Bye; Good-Bye, London Town; Hallo!
Little Miss U.S.A. (C/L: Harry Gifford; Fred
Godfrey); How Do You Do-Good Bye; I'll Come
Back to You; Life's a Dress Parade; Lovely Trip,
A; My Cleopatra Girl; Noble Cause of Art, The;
Nobody Was in Love with Me; Oh, Allah;
Pavlova Gavotte, The; Ragtime Arabian Nights [2];

Ragtime Pinafore (C/L: Henry Lehman);
Twentieth Century Rag (C/L: Henry Lehman);
Visit, The; We Forgot the Number of the House;
What'll; Whirl of the Opera, The; Whirl of the
World, The; Why Don't You Get a Girl Like Me

Cast: Roszika Dolly; Bernard Granville; Ralph
Herz; Eugene Howard; Willie Howard; Walter C.
Kelly; Lillian Lorraine

Notes: [1] Sheet music only. [2] One source
credited the song to Henry Lehman

4658 • WHIRL-I-GIG

OPENED: 09/21/1899   Theatre: Weber & Fields'
                                          Music Hall
Musical   Broadway: 264

Composer: John Stromberg
Lyricist: Harry B. Smith
Librettist: Edgar Smith
Producer: Lew Fields; Joseph Weber

Cast: Peter F. Dailey; Lew Fields; John T. Kelly;
Bonnie Maginn; Charles J. Ross; Lillian Russell;
David Warfield; Joseph Weber

Notes: This evening included THE GIRL FROM
MARTIN'S (a burlesque of THE GIRL FROM
MAXIM'S), SAPOLIO (a burlesque of SAPPHO)
and THE OTHER WAY (a burlesque of THE
ONLY WAY).

4659 • WHISPERS ON THE WIND

OPENED: 06/03/1970   Theatre: Theatre de
                                          Lys
Musical   Off-Broadway: 9

Composer: Lor Crane
Lyricist: John B. Kuntz
Librettist: John B. Kuntz
Producer: Mitchell Fink; Bruce W. Paltrow
Director: Burt Brinckerhoff

Costumes: Joseph G. Aulisi; **Lighting Designer:**
David F. Segal; **Musical Director:** Jack Holmes;
Orchestrations: Arthur Rubenstein; **Set Design:**
David F. Segal

Songs: Apples and Raisins; Carmen Vincenzo;
Children's Games; Children's Sake, The [1]; Down
the Fields [1]; In the Mind's Eye [1]; Is There a
City?; It Won't Be Long; Midwestern Summer;

Miss Cadwallader; Neighbors; Prove I'm Really Here; Strawberries; Then in the Middle [1]; Things Are Going Nicely; Upstairs- Downstairs; Very First Girl, The [1]; Welcome, Little One; Whispers on the Wind; Why and Because

Cast: R.G. Brown; David Cryer; Nancy Dussault; Patrick Fox; Mary Louise Wilson

Notes: [1] Cut prior to opening.

4660 • WHISTLING WIZARD AND THE SULTAN OF TUFFET, THE

OPENED: 10/17/1973   Theatre: Bil Baird
Musical   Off-Broadway: 36

Composer: Bil Baird; Alan Stern
Lyricist: Bil Baird; Alan Stern
Librettist: Alan Stern
Producer: American Puppet Arts Coun.; Bil Baird
Director: Frank Sullivan; Lee Theodore

Source: WHISTLING WIZARD, THE (Television Program: Bil Baird); **Lighting Designer:** Peggy Clark; **Musical Director:** Alvy West

Puppeteer: Peter Baird; Olga Felgemacher; Jonathan E. Freeman; John O'Malley; Sean O'Malley; Bill Tost; Byron Whiting

Notes: Based on the classic TV series.

4661 • WHITE BIRDS

OPENED: 05/31/1927   Theatre: His Majesty's
Revue   London: 63

Composer: George W. Meyer
Lyricist: George W. Meyer
Librettist: Lew Leslie
Producer: Lew Leslie

Arrangements: Will Vodery; **Costumes:** Val St. Cyr; **Musical Director:** Jones; **Set Design:** John Bull

Songs: Cuddle Up; Da Da Da (The Da Da Strain); Flower of Spain; I've Got a Wonderful Girl; Sing a Little Love Song; What's to Become of the Children (C/L: Noel Coward)

Cast: Florence Brady; Maurice Chevalier; Jose Collins; Anton Dolin; Maisie Gay; Edward Lowry; Billy Mayerl; Carl Randall; Ninette de Valois

Notes: No program available.

4662 • WHITE CAT, THE

OPENED: 11/02/1905   Theatre: New Amsterdam
Musical   Broadway: 46

Composer: Ludwig Englander
Lyricist: Harry B. Smith
Librettist: Harry B. Smith
Producer: Klaw & Erlanger
Director: Herbert Gresham; Ned Wayburn

Source: WHITE CAT, THE (Musical: Arthur Collins; J. Hickory Wood); **Musical Director:** Frederic Solomon; **Set Design:** Ernest D'Auban

Songs: Antonio (C: Jean Schwartz; L: William Jerome); Catland; Cherries Ripe; Court Is Like a Chessboard, A; Dance Noveau (C: Frederic Solomon); Down the Line with Arabella (C: Jean Schwartz; L: William Jerome); Get the Money (C: Jean Schwartz; L: William Jerome); Girls and Boys; Golden Net, The; Goodbye, Maggie Doyle (C: Jean Schwartz; L: William Jerome); Graft; Henny Klein (C: Jean Schwartz; L: William Jerome); Highland Mary (C: Jean Schwartz; L: William Jerome); Kisses [1] (C: Jean Schwartz; L: William Jerome); Let the Trumpets Sound; Meet Me on the Fence Tonight (C: Jean Schwartz; L: William Jerome); My Lady of Japan (C: Jean Schwartz; L: William Jerome); Penang-Ourang- Outang, The (C/L: Philip Braham); Sailing Away; Where Broadway Meets Fifth Avenue (C/L: Keith; John Kemble); Year and a Day, A

Cast: Edgar Atchinson-Ely; Herbert Corthell; William T. Hodge; Maude Lambert; Helen Lathrop

Notes: [1] Sheet music only.

4663 • WHITE CHRYSANTHEMUM, THE

OPENED: 08/31/1905   Theatre: Criterion
Musical   London: 179

Composer: Howard Talbot
Lyricist: Arthur Anderson
Librettist: Arthur Anderson; Leedham Bantock
Producer: Frank Curzon
Director: Austen Hurgon

Costumes: Karl; **Musical Director:** Howard Talbot; **Set Design:** W.T. Hemsley

Songs: Bill's a Liar (C: Jerome Kern; L: Paul West); Butterfly and the Flower, The; I Just Couldn't Do Without You (C: Jerome Kern; L: Paul West); Latest News, The; Love of a Maid of a Man, The; Mammy's Pickaninny; O Wandering Breeze; Only Pebble on the Beach, The; You Can't Please Everybody Always

Cast: Rutland Barrington; Marie George; Lawrence Grossmith; Isabel Jay; Gracie Leigh; Henry A. Lytton; R. Morand

Notes: No program available.

4664 • WHITE EAGLE, THE
OPENED: 12/26/1927   Theatre: Casino
Musical   Broadway: 48

Composer: Rudolf Friml
Lyricist: Brian Hooker
Librettist: Brian Hooker; W.H. Post
Producer: Russell Janney
Director: Richard Boleslavsky

Source: SQUAW MAN, THE (Play: Edwin Milton Royle)

Songs: Alone (My Lover); Bad Man Number; Dance, Dance, Dance; Gather the Rose; Give Me One Hour [1]; Home for You, A; Hymn to the Sun [1]; Indian Ceremonial Music [1]; Indian Lullaby; Interlude [1]; My Heaven with You; Regimental Song; Silver Wing [1]; Smile, Darn You, Smile; Thunder Dance [1]; Winona

Cast: Lawrence D'Orsay; Blanche Fleming; Forrest Huff; Marion Keeler; Allan Prior; Fred Tilden

Notes: [1] ASCAP/Library of Congress only.

4665 • WHITE FLAME, THE
OPENED: 1939
Musical   Unproduced

Composer: Vernon Duke
Lyricist: Charles O. Locke

Songs: Bend Your Knee and Tie My Shoe; Bonjour Goodbye; Dance of the Waitresses; I Cling to You; Lisette; Shadow of Love (L: Ted Fetter; Charles O. Locke); Sport of Kings, The

4666 • WHITE HEN, THE
OPENED: 02/16/1907   Theatre: Casino
Musical   Broadway: 94

Composer: Gustave Kerker
Lyricist: Paul West
Librettist: Roderic C. Penfield
Producer: Lee Shubert; Sam S. Shubert
Director: J.C. Huffman; Julian Mitchell

Songs: At Last We're Alone, Dear; Edelweiss [1]; Everything Is Higher Nowadays; Fishing; Follow, Follow, Follow; Hands Off [1]; I'm Married Now; Keep Cool; Man Is Only a Man, A; Mountain Maids; Nothing More — Excepting You [1]; Prima Donna, The; Printemps; Smile; Swartz and Weiss [1]; That's Why the Danube Was Blue; Thrush and the Star, The; Very Well Then; Waiting for the Ride

Cast: Lotta Faust; Louise Gunning; Ralph Herz; Louis Mann

Notes: Also known as THE GIRL FROM VIENNA. [1] Sheet music only.

4667 • WHITE HORSE INN
OPENED: 10/01/1936   Theatre: Center
Musical   Broadway: 223

Composer: Ralph Benatzky
Lyricist: Irving Caesar
Librettist: David Freedman; Harry Graham
Producer: Laurence Rivers
Director: Erik Charell

Source: IM WEISSEN ROSSL (Operetta: Erik Charell; Robert Gilbert; Hans Muller); **Source:** UNKNOWN (Play: Oskar Blumenthal; Gustave Kadelburg); **Choreographer:** Max Rivers; **Costumes:** Irene Sharaff; **Musical Director:** Victor Baravalle; **Orchestrations:** Hans Spialek; **Set Design:** Ernest Stern

Songs: Alpine Symphony (inst.) (C: Adam Gelbtrunk); Arrival of Steamboat; Arrival of Tourists; Blue Eyes (C: Robert Stolz); Cowshed Rhapsody [2] (C: Adam Gelbtrunk); Good-Bye, Au Revoir, Auf Wiedersehen [1] (C: Eric Coates); High Up in the Hills; I Cannot Live Without

Your Love; I Would Love to Have You Love Me (C: Gerald Marks; L: Irving Caesar; Sammy Lerner); In a Little Swiss Chalet (C: Will Irwin; L: Norman Zeno); Leave It to Katrina (C: Jara Benes); Market Day in the Village; Rain Finale; Serenade to the Emperor; Spade Ballet; Waltz of Love, The (C: Richard Fall); We Prize Most the Things We Miss; Welcome to the Landing Stage; White Horse Inn; White Sails [2] (C: Vivian Ellis)

Cast: Kitty Carlisle; Alfred Drake; William Gaxton; Frederick Graham; Robert Halliday; Billy House; Arnold Korff; Melissa Mason; Oscar "Rags" Ragland; Carol Stone; Buster West

Notes: [1] Adapted from Coates' "Knightsbridge March." [2] ASCAP/Library of Congress only.

4668 • WHITE LIGHTS

OPENED: 10/11/1927   Theatre: Ritz
Musical   Broadway: 31

Composer: J. Fred Coots
Lyricist: Al Dubin
Librettist: Leo Donnelly; Paul Gerard Smith
Producer: James LaPenna

Choreographer: Walter Brooks; Ray Perez;
Musical Director: T.L. Jones; **Orchestrations:**
Louis Katzman

Songs: Beautiful Show Girls [1]; Better Times Are Coming (C: Jimmie Steiger; L: Dolph Singer); Deceiving Blue Bird; Don't Throw Me Down; Eyeful of You; I'll Keep on Dreaming of You (C: J. Fred Coots; Walter S. Roele); Romany Rover; Sitting in the Sun [1]; Some Other Day; Tappin' the Toe; We Are the Girls in the Chorus; White Lights

Cast: Sam Ash; Rosalie Claire; Leo Donnelly; Florence Parker; Tammany Young

Notes: Titled MITZI originally. [1] Out Stamford 08/12/27.

4669 • WHITE LILACS

OPENED: 09/10/1928   Theatre: Shubert
Musical   Broadway: 138

Music Based On: Frederic Chopin
Composer: Karl Hajos
Lyricist: J. Keirn Brennan

Librettist: Harry B. Smith
Producer: Messrs. Shubert
Director: George Marion

Source: CHOPIN (Musical: Istvan Bertha; Jeno Farago); **Choreographer:** Vaughn Godfrey; **Musical Director:** Pierre de Reeder; **Set Design:** Rollo Wayne

Songs: Adorable You (C: Maurie Rubens; L: David Goldberg); Don't Go Too Far Girls; Far Away and Long Ago; I Love Love; I Love You and I Adore You; Know When to Smile; Melodies Within My Heart; Music Call, The; Our Castle of Love (C: Sammy Timberg); Star in the Twilight; White Lilacs; Words, Music, Cash

Cast: DeWolf Hopper; Odette Myrtil; Guy Robertson

Notes: Later known as THE CHARMER.

4670 • WHITE PLUME, THE

OPENED: 12/26/1939
Musical   Closed out of town

Composer: Samuel D. Pokrass
Lyricist: Charles O. Locke
Librettist: Charles O. Locke
Producer: Messrs. Shubert
Director: George Houston; Charles O. Locke

Source: CYRANO DE BERGERAC (Play: Edmond Rostand); **Choreographer:** Natalie Kamarova; **Costumes:** Ernest Schrapps; **Set Design:** Watson Barratt

Songs: Ballade of the Duel; Bonjour Goodbye (C: Vernon Duke); Cyrano; Dance of the Waitresses (C: Vernon Duke); I Cling to You (C: Vernon Duke); Letter Duet; Lisette; Little Musketeer; Mamselle; Men of Jaloux; Minuette; My Nose; Pavanne; Play's the Thing, The; Shadow of Love (C: Vernon Duke; L: Ted Fetter; Charles O. Locke); Song of the Balcony; Song of the Gascon Cadets; Sweets to the Sweet; Tell Me of Love; What My Lips Can Never Say; World Is Young, The

Cast: Robert Chisholm; Hal Forde; Truman Gaige; George Houston; Eric Mattson; Ruby Mercer; Cornel Wilde

Notes: This show was first produced in 11/4/32 as CYRANO DE BERGERAC. It was retitled

ROXANNE before closing. Seven years later the Shuberts gave it another go as THE WHITE PLUME. This production later changed its name to A VAGABOND HERO, but it too closed before coming to New York.

4671 • WHITE SISTER, THE (1909)
OPENED: 09/27/1909　Theatre: Daly's
Play　　　　　　　　Broadway: 48

Composer: William Furst
Author: Marion Crawford; Walter Hackett
Director: Hugh Ford

Source: WHITE SISTER, THE (Novel: Marion Crawford); **Musical Director:** George Wiseman; **Set Design:** Frank Gates; E.A. Morange

Cast: Viola Allen; William Farnum; James O'Neill

Notes: No songs listed in program.

4672 • WHITE SISTER, THE (1927)
OPENED: 05/17/1927　Theatre: Wallack's
Musical　　　　　　Broadway: 7

Composer: Clement Giglio
Lyricist: Clement Giglio
Librettist: Clement Giglio

Source: WHITE SISTER, THE (Novel: Marion Crawford); **Musical Director:** Chavalier Lovreiglo

Cast: Josie Jones; Eugene Scudder

Notes: No songs listed in program. Produced in Italian on 14th St. the previous year. It was such a success it was reopened uptown for one week in English.

4673 • WHO CARES?
OPENED: 07/08/1930　Theatre: 46th Street
Revue　　　　　　　Broadway: 30

Composer: Percy Wenrich
Lyricist: Harry Clarke
Librettist: John Cantwell; Edward Clarke Lilley; Bertrand Robinson; Kenneth Webb
Producer: Satirists Inc.
Director: Edward Clarke Lilley; George Vivian

Choreographer: William Holbrook; **Musical**

Director: Irvi ng Schloss; **Set Design:** Cirker & Robbins

Songs: Believe It or Not; Broadway; Dance of the Fan; Dixieland; Heldites, The; Hunt, The; Make My Bed Down in Dixieland; Opening Number; Sun Up; Tennis; Who Cares?

Cast: Florenz Ames; John Cherry; Margaret Dale; Arthur Hartley; William Holbrook; Don Lanning; Peggy O'Neill; Olive Olsen; Robert Pitkin; Ralph Riggs; Marjorie Seltzer; Templeton Brothers

4674 • WHO IS WHO
OPENED: 02/07/1898　Theatre: Third Avenue
Musical　　　　　　Broadway: 8

Composer: Joe Kelly; Charles A. Mason

Cast: Blanche Boyer; Joe Kelly; Charles A. Mason; Georgia Tompkins

Notes: No program available.

4675 • WHO TO LOVE
Notes: *See CRY FOR US ALL.*

4676 • WHO'S TOMMY, THE
OPENED: 04/22/1993　Theatre: St. James
Musical　　　　　　Broadway: 900

Composer: Peter Townshend
Additional Music: John Entwistle; Keith Moon
Lyricist: Peter Townshend
Additional Lyrics: John Entwistle; Keith Moon
Librettist: Des McAnuff; Peter Townshend
Producer: Dodger Productions; Kardana Productions; Pace Theatrical Group
Director: Des McAnuff

Source: TOMMY (Opera: Peter Townshend); **Choreographer:** Wayne Cilento; **Costumes:** David C. Woolard; **Lighting Designer:** Chris Parry; **Musical Director:** Joseph Church; **Orchestrations:** Steve Margoshes; **Set Design:** John Arnone

Songs: Acid Queen; Amazing Journey; Captain Walker; Christmas; Cousin Kevin; Do You Think It's Alright; Eyesight to the Blind; Fiddle About; Go to the Mirror; I Believe My Own Eyes; I'm Free; It's a Boy; Listening to You; Miracle Cure; Pinball Wizard; Sally Simpson; See Me, Feel Me; Sensation; Smash the Mirror; Sparks; There's a

Doctor; Tommy Can You Hear Me; Tommy's Holiday Camp; Twenty-One; We're Not Going to Take It; We've Won; Welcome

Cast: Anthony Barrile; Maria Calabrese; Michael Cerveris; Paul Kandel; Marcia Mitzman; Buddy Smith

4677 • WHO'S WHO

OPENED: 03/01/1938   Theatre: Hudson
Revue   Broadway: 23

Librettist: Everett Marcy; Leonard Sillman
Producer: Elsa Maxwell
Director: Leonard Sillman

Costumes: Billy Livingston; **Musical Director:** Earl Busby; **Orchestrations:** Richard DuPage; **Set Design:** Mercedes

Songs: Croupier (C: Baldwin Bergersen; L: June Sillman); Dusky Debutante (C: Baldwin Bergersen; L: June Sillman); Girl with the Paint on Her Face, The (C/L: Irvin Graham); I Dance Alone (C/L: James Shelton); I Must Have a Dinner Coat (C/L: James Shelton); I Must Waltz (C: Baldwin Bergersen; L: Irvin Graham); If You Want a Kiss [1] (C: Paul McGrane; L: June Sillman); Intoxication Dance (inst.) (C: Jaroslav Jezek); It's You I Want (C: Paul McGrane; L: Al Stillman); Let Down Your Hair with a Bang (C: Baldwin Bergersen; L: June Sillman); Rinka Tinka Man (C: Lew Kessler; L: June Sillman); Skiing at Saks (C/L: Irvin Graham); Sunday Morning in June (C: Paul McGrane; L: Neville Fleeson); Train Time (C: Baldwin Bergersen; L: June Sillman); Who's Who (C: Baldwin Bergersen; L: June Sillman)

Cast: Joseph Beale; Jack Blair; June Blair; Imogene Coca; Lotte Goslar; Michael Loring; Chet O'Brien; Mort O'Brien; Oscar "Rags" Ragland; Edna Russell; James Shelton; June Sillman; Leone Sousa; Mildred Todd; Sonny Tufts; Johnnie Tunsill

Notes: [1] Sheet music only.

4678 • WHO'S WHO, BABY?

OPENED: 01/29/1968   Theatre: Players
Musical   Off-Broadway: 16

Composer: Johnny Brandon
Lyricist: Johnny Brandon
Librettist: Gerald Frank

Producer: Edmund J. Ferdinand; Charlotte Schiff
Director: Marvin Gordon

Source: WHO'S WHO (Play: Guy Bolton; P.G. Wodehouse); **Choreographer:** Marvin Gordon; **Costumes:** Alan Kimmel; **Dance Arranger:** Leslie Harley; Clark McClellan; **Lighting Designer:** John Beaumont; **Musical Director:** Leslie Harley; **Orchestrations:** Clark McClellan; **Set Design:** Alan Kimmel

Songs: Come-Along-a-Me, Babe; Drums; Feminine-inity; How Do You Stop Loving Someone?; Island of Happiness; Me; Nobody to Cry To; Nothin's Gonna Change; Syncopatin'; That'll Be the Day; That's What's Happening, Baby; There Aren't Many Ladies in the Mile End Road; Voodoo

Cast: Frank Andre; Erik Howell; Gloria Kaye; Jacqueline Mayro

4679 • WHO'S WHOM?

OPENED: 02/04/1971
Revue

Composer: Ronald Lowden
Lyricist: Stephen de Baum
Librettist: Howard Jaffe; Mark Mancini; Sandy Schussel; Frederick Swartz
Producer: Stephen Goff; Stephen de Baum
Director: Bruce Montgomery

Arrangements: Roy Straiges; **Choreographer:** Walter Keenan; **Costumes:** Stephen Goff; Stephen de Baum; **Musical Director:** William Lessig; **Set Design:** Stephen Goff; Stephen de Baum

Songs: Billy the Kid; Cocktails with Conservatives; Fantasy (C/L: Laurence Tarica); Give 'Em Hell (C: Thomas Wilson); H.M.S. Goldilocks or the Lass That Loved a Mailman (C: Bruce Montgomery); Hemlines; It's Good to Have God on Your Side (C: Roy Straiges); Lib & Let Live; Pusher, The (C: Roy Straiges); Where Are the Rich Little Poor Little Children? (C/L: Thomas Wilson); Who's Whom? (C: Seth Kane)

Cast: Bob Myer; Billy Rosenberg; Laurence Tarica

Notes: Amateur show. Mask & Wig Club, University of Pennsylvania.

4680 • WHOLE DAMN FAMILY, THE

Notes: *See LIFTING THE LID.*

4681 • WHOOP-DE-DOO

OPENED: 09/24/1903   Theatre: Weber & Fields
                                 Music Hall
Musical   Broadway: 151

Composer: William T. Francis
Lyricist: Edgar Smith
Librettist: Edgar Smith
Producer: Lew Fields; Joseph Weber
Director: Ben Teal

Set Design: John H. Young

Songs: Big Indian Chief (C: J. Rosamond Johnson; L: Bob Cole); Down By the Ocean Strand; Flowers of Dixieland, The (C: J. Rosamond Johnson; L: Bob Cole; Edgar Smith); Good Old U.S.A., The; Hoch! Hoch! Hoch!; If I Were an Actress; In Dreamland (L: Abeles); Looney Park; Maid of Timbuctoo (C: J. Rosamond Johnson; L: Bob Cole); My Goo-Goo Queen; On the Boulevard (C: A.M. Norden); Papa Wouldn't Care for That [1]; Paris on a Moonlight Night; Ragtime in Europe

Cast: Eva Allen; Marie Christie; Peter F. Dailey; Carter De Haven; Helen Du Heron; Lew Fields; John T. Kelly; Al Lewis; Jane Mandeville; Louis Mann; Maud Morris; Lillian Russell; Evie Stetson; Joe Weber

Notes: Second part of the show was called CATHERINE. [1] Out of town only.

4682 • WHOOP-UP

OPENED: 11/22/1958   Theatre: Shubert
Musical   Broadway: 56

Composer: Moose Charlap
Lyricist: Norman Gimbel
Librettist: Dan Cushman; Cy Feuer; Ernest H. Martin
Producer: Cy Feuer; Ernest H. Martin
Director: Cy Feuer

Source: STAY AWAY, JOE (Story: Dan Cushman); **Choreographer:** Onna White; **Costumes:** Anna Hill Johnstone; **Dance Arranger:** Peter Matz; **Lighting Designer:** Jo Mielziner; **Musical Director:** Stanley Lebowsky; **Orchestrations:** Philip J. Lang; **Set Design:** Jo Mielziner

Songs: Best of What This Country's Got; Caress Me, Possess Me Perfume; Chief Rocky Boy; Flattery; Girl in His Arms, The; Glenda's Place; I Wash My Hands; I'm on My Way [1]; Love Eyes; Men; Montana; Never Before; Nobody Throw Those Bull; Quarrel-tet; She or Her; Sorry for Myself; 'Til the Big Fat Moon Falls Down; What I Mean to Say; When the Tall Man Talks

Cast: Paul Ford; Susan Johnson; Julienne Marie; Danny Meehan; Estelle Parsons; Sylvia Syms; Ralph Young

Notes: [1] Cut.

4683 • WHOOPEE

OPENED: 12/04/1928   Theatre: New Amsterdam
Musical   Broadway: 407

Composer: Walter Donaldson
Lyricist: Gus Kahn
Librettist: William Anthony McGuire
Producer: Florenz Ziegfeld
Director: William Anthony McGuire

Source: NERVOUS WRECK, THE (Play: Owen Davis); **Choreographer:** Seymour Felix; Tamara Geva; **Costumes:** John Harkrider; **Musical Director:** Gus Salzer; **Set Design:** Joseph Urban

Songs: Automobile Horn Song [1] (C/L: Bennett; Carlton; Clarence Gaskill; Henry Tobias); Come West, Little Girl, Come West; Ever Since the Movies Learned to Talk [1] (C/L: Unknown); Girl Friend of a Boy Friend of Mine, A; Go Get 'Im; Gypsy Joe; Hallowe'en Whoopee Ball; Here's to the Girl of My Heart; Hungry Women [1] (C: Milton Ager; L: Jack Yellen); I Faw Down and Go Boom [1] (C/L: James Brockman; Leonard Stevens); I'll Still Belong to You (C: Nacio Herb Brown; L: Edward Eliscu); I'm Bringing a Red, Red Rose; It's a Beautiful Day Today; Love Me or Leave Me [2]; Makin' Whoopee; My Baby Just Cares for Me; My Blackbirds Are Bluebirds Now [1] (C: Cliff Friend; L: Irving Caesar); Song of the Setting Sun; Stetson; Taps; Until You Get Somebody Else; Where the Sunset Meets the Sea (Gypsy Song)

Cast: Josephine Adair; Bob Borger; Eddie Cantor; Spencer Charters; Ruth Etting; Fran Frey; Tamara Geva; Jack Gifford; Gladys Glad; George Olsen's Orchestra; Bob Rice; Jack Shaw; Ethel Shutta; Frances Upton

Notes: Closed for summer vacation after 253

performances. Reopened 8/5/1929 for 155 more. [1] Interpolated. [2] Also in SIMPLE SIMON.

4684 • WHY I LOVE NEW YORK

OPENED: 10/10/1975   Theatre: Judson Poets'
Musical   Off-Off-Broadway

Composer: Al Carmines
Lyricist: Al Carmines
Librettist: Al Carmines
Director: Leonard Peters

Costumes: Carol Oditz; **Lighting Designer:** Todd Lichtenstein; **Set Design:** Irving Cuomo

Songs: 8th Avenue; Hard-On; How Do You Love a City?; I'm Gonna Be a Star; Loneliness Trio; Love Comes in the Strangest Ways; Micritza Violetta Doanne; New York Is My Home; New York Love Is So Hard; Now and Then; Ordinary Woman; Pearl; Rags; Staten Island Barcarole; What Ever Happened to You?; Why Does Everybody in the City Put You Down; Woman Needs Approval, A

Cast: Essie Borden; Lee Guilliatt; Philip Owens; Margaret Wright

4685 • WHY THE CHICKEN?

Play

Author: John McGrath
Producer: Michael Codron
Director: Lionel Bart

Songs: Why the Chicken? (C/L: Lionel Bart)

Cast: Peter Craze; Terence Stamp

Notes: No other information available. Closed out-of-town-London.

4686 • WHY WORRY?

OPENED: 08/23/1918   Theatre: Harris
Play   Broadway: 27

Composer: Blanche Merrill
Lyricist: Blanche Merrill
Producer: A.H. Woods
Director: George Marion

Songs: I'm an Indian; I'm Bad

Cast: Fanny Brice; Charles Dale; Harry Goodwin;

Irving Kaufman; Jack Sharkey; George Sidney; Joe Smith

Notes: No songs listed in program.

4687 • WIFE HUNTERS, THE

OPENED: 11/02/1911   Theatre: Herald Square
Musical   Broadway: 36

Composer: Malvin Franklin; Anatole Friedland
Lyricist: Malvin F. Franklin; David Kemper
Librettist: Edgar Allen Woolf
Producer: Lew Fields
Director: Ned Wayburn

Choreographer: Ned Wayburn; **Musical Director:** Lee Orean Smith

Songs: All Life Is Full of Pleasure [1] (C: Anatole Friedland); Bill of Fare [1] (C: Anatole Friedland); Casey Jones [2] (C: Anatole Friedland); Down at Mammy Jinny's [1] (C: Anatole Friedland); Faint Heart Ne'er Won Fair Lady [1] (C: Anatole Friedland); Folette (C: Anatole Friedland); Girls, Girls, Keep Your Figure (C: Anatole Friedland); Honeyland; In Your Arms; Leonara (C: Anatole Friedland); Let's Take Him Home in Triumph; Little Dancing Jumping Jigger (C: Anatole Friedland); Love Waves (C: Anatole Friedland); Mammy Jinny; My Grammar Book [1] (C: Anatole Friedland); My Havana Maid (C: Anatole Friedland); On the Avenue; P.S. I Love You [1]; Pas de Seul; Picnic Club, The; Recitative; Swinging with Someone [1] (C: Anatole Friedland); Waltz of the Wild, The; Wave Crest Waltz, The

Cast: Dorothy Brenner; Emma Carus; Arthur Conrad; Edith Decker

Notes: Titled THREE MILLION DOLLARS out of town prior to New York. [1] Cut out of town. [2] Cut out of town. The famous song "Casey Jones" by T. Lawrence Seibert and Eddie Newton was written in 1909.

4688 • WIFE TAMERS, THE

OPENED: 08/08/1910
Musical   Closed out of town

Composer: Robert Hood Bowers
Lyricist: Clarence Harvey; Oliver Herford

Source: FLORIST SHOP, THE (Play: Oliver Herford)

Songs: Flannigan; I'm Looking for a Certain Little Boy [1]

Cast: Gertrude Bryan; Florence Reid; Lionel Walsh

Notes: From Atlantic City program. [1] Interpolated.

4689 • WILD AND WONDERFUL
OPENED: 12/07/1971   Theatre: Lyceum
Musical   Broadway: 1

Composer: Bob Goodman
Lyricist: Bob Goodman
Librettist: Phil Phillips
Producer: Rick Hobard; Raymonde Weil
Director: Burry Fredrik

Choreographer: Ronn Forella; **Costumes:** Frank Thompson; **Dance Arranger:** Tom Janusz; **Lighting Designer:** Neil Peter Jampolis; **Musical Director:** Tom Janusz; **Orchestrations:** Luther Henderson; **Set Design:** Stephen Hendrickson; **Vocal Arranger:** Tom Janusz

Songs: Chances; Come a Little Closer; Desmond's Dilemma; Different Kind of World, A; Fallen Angels; I Spy; Is This My Town; Jenny; Little Bits and Pieces; Moment Is Now; My First Moment; Petty Crime; She Should Have Me; Something Wonderful Can Happen; Wait for Me; Wild and Wonderful; You Can Reach the Sun

Cast: Robert Burr; Laura McDuffie; Ann Reinking; Larry Small; Ted Thurston; Walter Willison

4690 • WILD MEN
OPENED: 05/06/1993   Theatre: Westside
Musical   Off-Broadway: 59

Composer: Mark Nutter
Lyricist: Mark Nutter
Librettist: Peter Burns; Mark Nutter; Rob Riley; Tom Wolfe
Producer: James D. Stern
Director: Rob Riley

Choreographer: Jim Corti; **Costumes:** John Paoletti; **Lighting Designer:** Geoffrey Bushor; **Musical Director:** Lisa Yeargan; **Set Design:** Mary Griswold

Songs: Come Away; Get Pissed; It's You; Lookit

Those Stars; My Friend, My Father; Now I Am a Man; Ooh, That's Hot; True Value; 'Un' Song, The; We're Wild Men; What Stuart Has Planted; Wimmins

Cast: Peter Burns; David Lewman; Joe Liss; Rob Riley; George Wendt

4691 • WILD ROSE, THE (1902)
OPENED: 05/05/1902   Theatre: Knickerbocker
Musical   Broadway: 136

Composer: Ludwig Englander
Lyricist: George V. Hobart
Librettist: Harry B. Smith
Producer: George W. Lederer
Director: George W. Lederer

Choreographer: Adolph Newberger; **Costumes:** Mme. Siedle; **Set Design:** D. Frank Dodge

Songs: Cupid Is the Captain; I Sing a Little Tenor (C: Harry Linton; L: John Gilroy); Love's Young Dream; My Little Gypsy Maid [1] (C: Will Marion Cook; L: Cecil Mack; Harry B. Smith); Nancy Brown (C/L: Clifton Crawford); Soldier's Story, The; They Were All Doing the Same (C/L: Ren Shields)

Cast: Irene Bentley; Marie Cahill; Marguerite Clark; Eddie Foy Sr.; Albert Hart; Junie McCree; Evelyn Nesbitt

Notes: No songs listed in program. [1] Some sources erroneously credit the lyrics to Paul Lawrence Dunbar.

4692 • WILD ROSE, THE (1926)
OPENED: 10/20/1926   Theatre: Martin Beck
Musical   Broadway: 62

Composer: Rudolf Friml
Lyricist: Oscar Hammerstein II; Otto Harbach
Librettist: Oscar Hammerstein II; Otto Harbach
Producer: Arthur Hammerstein
Director: William J. Wilson

Choreographer: Busby Berkeley; **Costumes:** Mark Mooring; **Musical Director:** Herbert Stothart; **Set Design:** Joseph Urban

Songs: Brown Eyes; Coronation, The; Dramatico Musical Scene; How Can You Keep Your Mind on Business? [1]; I'm the Extra Man; It Was Fate; Lady of the Rose; L'Heure D'Or (One Golden Hour) [2] (L: Otto Harbach; J.B. Kantor); Love Me, Don't You?; Lovely Lady; Opening Act II; Revolution Festival; Riviera; Rumble, Rumble, Rumble [1]; That's Why I Love You [1]; We'll Have a Kingdom; Wild Rose; Won't You Come Across?

Cast: Nana Bryant; William Collier; Inez Courtney; Jerome Daley; Desiree Ellinger; Joseph Macaulay; Fuller Mellish; Len Menace; Joseph Santley; Gus Shy

Notes: [1] Out Philadelphia 10/20/26. [2] French lyrics by J.B. Kantor.

4693 • WILDCAT

OPENED: 12/16/1960 Theatre: Alvin
Musical Broadway: 171

Composer: Cy Coleman
Lyricist: Carolyn Leigh
Librettist: N. Richard Nash
Producer: Michael Kidd; N. Richard Nash
Director: Michael Kidd

Choreographer: Michael Kidd; **Costumes:** Alvin Colt; **Dance Arranger:** John Morris; **Lighting Designer:** Charles Elson; **Musical Director:** John Morris; **Orchestrations:** Robert Ginzler; Sid Ramin; **Set Design:** Peter Larkin; **Vocal Arranger:** John Morris

Songs: Ain't It Sad [1]; Angelina [1]; (We Keep) Bouncing Back for More [2]; Corduroy Road; Day I Do, The [1]; El Sombrero; Foller It Through [1]; Give a Little Whistle (and I'll Be There); Hey, Look Me Over; I Got My Man [1]; I Hear (Oil); I Like the Ladies [1]; Joe Dynamite's Dentistry Song [1]; Little What-If, Little Could-Be [1]; Once Day We Dance; Tall Hope; That's What I Want for Janie [3]; Thinkability [4]; Tippy Tippy Toes; We Have So Much in Common [1]; What Takes My Fancy; Wildcat [3]; You're a Liar; You're Far Away from Home [1]; You've Come Home

Cast: Keith Andes; Lucille Ball; Clifford David; Edith King; Al Lanti; Paula Stewart; Swen Swenson; Don Tomkins

Notes: [1] Cut prior to opening. [2] Cut prior to opening. Later in HELLZAPOPPIN 1976. [3] Cut after opening. [4] Cut prior to opening. Music

later used for "We're Heading for a Wedding" in THE WILL ROGERS FOLLIES.

4694 • WILDFLOWER

OPENED: 02/07/1923 Theatre: Casino
Musical Broadway: 477

Composer: Vincent Youmans
Lyricist: Oscar Hammerstein II; Otto Harbach
Librettist: Oscar Hammerstein II; Otto Harbach
Producer: Arthur Hammerstein
Director: Oscar Eagle

Choreographer: David Bennett; **Costumes:** Charles LeMaire; **Musical Director:** Herbert Stothart; **Orchestrations:** Robert Russell Bennett; **Set Design:** Frank Gates; E.A. Morange

Songs: April Blossoms (C: Herbert Stothart); Bambalina; Best Dance I've Had Tonight, The; Como Camel Corps, The [4]; 'Course I Will; Everything Is All Right [1]; Finale Act I; Finale Act II; Finale Act III; Friends Who Understand [1]; Girl from Casimo (C: Herbert Stothart); Good-Bye, Little Rose-Bud (C: Herbert Stothart); I Can Always Find Another Partner; If I Told You [3]; If Your Name Had Been LaRocca [4]; I'll Collaborate with You (C: Herbert Stothart); Iloveyouiloveyouiloveyou; Some Like to Hunt (C: Herbert Stothart); Spring Is Here [4]; True Love Will Never Grow Cold [1]; Wild-Flower; World's Worst Woman, The (C: Herbert Stothart); You Can Never Blame a Girl for Dreaming [2]

Cast: Evelyn Cavanagh; Jerome Daley; Edith Day; James Doyle; Esther Howard; Olin Howland; Charles Judels; Guy Robertson

Notes: [1] Cut. [2] Added after opening. [3] Cut after opening. Music used as "Virginia" in RAINBOW. [4] Added to 1926 London production.

4695 • WILL ROGERS FOLLIES, THE

OPENED: 05/01/1991 Theatre: Palace
Musical Broadway: 963

Composer: Cy Coleman
Lyricist: Betty Comden; Adolph Green
Librettist: Peter Stone
Producer: Pierre Cosette; Sam Crothers; Stewart F.

Lane; James M. Nederlander; Martin Richards; Max Weitzenhoffer
Director: Tommy Tune

Choreographer: Tommy Tune; **Costumes:** Willa Kim; **Dance Arranger:** Cy Coleman; **Lighting Designer:** Jules Fisher; **Musical Director:** Eric Stern; **Orchestrations:** Bill Byers; **Set Design:** Tony Walton; **Vocal Arranger:** Cy Coleman

Songs: Big Time, The [2]; Favorite Son; Give a Man Enough Rope; I Got You; It's a Boy!; Let's Go Flying; Look Around; Marry Me Now; My Big Mistake; My Unknown Someone; Never Met a Man I Didn't Like; No Man Left for Me; Presents for Mr. Rogers; So Long Pa; We're Heading for a Wedding [3]; Will-a-Mania; Without You

Cast: Bonnie Brackney; Tom Brackney; Vince Bruce; Keith Carradine; Dee Hoty; Cady Huffman; Dick Latessa; Gregory Peck[1]; Paul Ukena Jr.

Notes: [1] Voice on tape only. [2] Melody from an unproduced musical version of "The Wonderful O." [3] Same music as "Thinkability" cut from WILDCAT.

4696 • WILL THE MILK TRAIN RUN TONIGHT?

OPENED: 01/09/1964   Theatre: New Bowery
Musical   Off-Broadway: 8

Composer: Alyn Heim
Lyricist: Malcolm I. LaPrade
Librettist: Malcolm I. LaPrade
Producer: Jon Baisch
Director: Jon Baisch

Source: UNKNOWN (Play: Hugh Neville); **Choreographer:** Lynne Fippinger; **Costumes:** Joe Crosby; **Lighting Designer:** Joseph Kreisel; **Set Design:** Gene Czernicki

Songs: Age of Miracles; Bitter Tears; Comes the Dawn; Dearer to Me; Fall of Valor, The; Heroism; Hickory, Dickory; Honeymoon Choo-Choo; I'll Walk Alone; Nature's Serenade; No Sacrifice; Paper Matches; Prudence, Have Faith; Remember Him; Slip of a Girl, A; So Much to Be Thankful For; This Decadent Age; Three Cowards Craven; To Dream or Not to Dream; Vengeance; Villainy

Cast: Barbara Cole; Fred Jackson; Peter Lombard; Naomi Riseman

4697 • WILLIAMS & WALKER

OPENED: 03/09/1986   Theatre: American Place
Musical   Off-Broadway: 77

Librettist: Vincent D. Smith
Producer: Woodie King; New Federal Theatre
Director: Shauneille Perry

Choreographer: Lenwood Sloan; **Costumes:** Judy Dearing; **Lighting Designer:** Marc D. Malamud; **Musical Director:** Ron Metcalf; **Set Design:** Marc D. Malamud

Songs: Bon Bon Buddy (C: Will Marion Cook; L: Alex Rogers); Chocolate Drop (inst.) (C: Will Marion Cook); Constantly (C: Bert Williams; L: Barris; Smith); Everybody Wants to See the Baby (C: Bob Cole; L: James Weldon Johnson); I May Be Crazy but I Ain't No Fool (C/L: Alex Rogers); I'd Rather Have Nothin' All the Time Than Somethin' for a Little While (C: Bert Williams; L: John B. Lowitz); I'm a Jonah Man (C/L: Alex Rogers); Magnetic Rag (inst.) (C: Scott Joplin); Nobody (C: Bert Williams; L: Alex Rogers); Original Rag (inst.) (C: Scott Joplin); Save Your Money John (C/L: Les Copeland; Alex Rogers); Somebody Stole My Gal (C/L: Leo Wood)

Cast: Vondie Curtis-Hall; Ben Harney; Joe Marshall; Ron Metcalf

Notes: No original songs in this show.

4698 • WILLIE THE WEEPER

Notes: *See BALLET BALLADS.*

4699 • WILLOW PLATE, THE

OPENED: 1924
Play

Composer: Victor Herbert
Producer: Tony Sarg
Director: Tony Sarg

Songs: Chang, the Lover (inst.); Kongshee, the Mandarin's Daughter (inst.); Little Gardenhouse, The (inst.); Mandarin's Garden, The (inst.); Wedding Procession, A (inst.)

Notes: A puppet show.

4700 • WILSON MIZNER PROJECT

Musical

Songs: Life in Venetia (C/L: Stephen Sondheim)

Notes: Unfinished. No other information available.

4701 • WIND IN THE WILLOWS

OPENED: 12/19/1985   Theatre: Nederlander
Musical   Broadway: 4

Composer: William Perry
Lyricist: Robert McGough; William Perry
Librettist: Jane Iredale
Producer: Liniva Productions, Inc.; RLM
  Productions, Inc.
Director: Tony Stevens

Source: WIND IN THE WILLOWS, THE (Novel:
  Kenneth Grahame); **Choreographer:** Margery
  Beddow; **Costumes:** Freddy Wittop; **Lighting
  Designer:** Craig Miller; **Musical Director:** Robert
  Rogers; **Orchestrations:** William D. Brohn; **Set
  Design:** Sam Kirkpatrick; **Vocal Arranger:**
  Robert Rogers

Songs: Brief Encounter; Come What May; Day You
  Came Into My Life, The; Evil Weasel; Follow
  Your Instinct; Gasoline Can-Can, The; I'd Be
  Attracted; Mediterranean; Messing About in
  Boats; Moving Up in the World; S-S-Something
  Comes Over Me; That's What Friends Are For;
  When Springtime Comes to My River; Where
  Am I Now?; Wind in the Willows, The; World Is
  Waiting for Me, The; You'll Love It in Jail

Cast: Irving Barnes; P.J. Benjamin; David Carroll;
  Donna Drake; John Jellison; Nathan Lane; Vicki
  Lewis; Jackie Lowe; Nora Mae Lyng; Scott Waara

4702 • WINDY CITY (1946)

OPENED: 04/18/1946
Musical   Closed out of town

Composer: Walter Jurmann
Lyricist: Paul Francis Webster
Librettist: Philip Yordan
Producer: Harry Brandt; Richard Kollmar
Director: Edward Rivaux

Choreographer: Katherine Dunham; **Costumes:**
  Rose Bogdanoff; **Dance Arranger:** Dorothea

Freitag; **Lighting Designer:** Jo Mielziner;
  Musical Director: Charles Sanford;
  Orchestrations: Don Walker, **Set Design:** Jo
  Mielziner; **Vocal Arranger:** Clay Warnick

Songs: Don't Ever Run Away from Love; Gambler's
  Lullaby; Gentleman of the Old School [1]; Harry
  Is Only Physical [1]; It's the Better Me; It's Time
  I Had a Break; Lucky Duck [1]; Out on a Limb;
  (As the Wind Bloweth) There Goeth I; Where
  Do We Go from Here

Cast: John Conte; Susan Miller; Al Shean; Betty
  Jane Smith; Loring Smith; Frances Williams

Notes: [1] ASCAP/Library of Congress only.

4703 • WINDY CITY (1985)

OPENED: 09/18/1985
Musical   Closed out of town

Composer: Tony Macaulay
Lyricist: Dick Vosburgh
Librettist: Dick Vosburgh
Director: David H. Bell

Source: FRONT PAGE, THE (Play: Ben Hecht;
  Charles MacArthur); **Arrangements:** Kevin
  Stites; **Choreographer:** David H. Bell; **Costumes:**
  Guy Geoly; **Lighting Designer:** Jeff Davis;
  Orchestrations: David Siegel; **Set Design:**
  Michael Anania

Songs: Bensinger's Poem; Born Reporter; Circles
  'Round Us; Day I Quit This Rag, The; Hey
  Hallelujah! [1]; I Can Talk to You; Just Imagine It;
  Long Night Again Tonight [1]; Mollie Has Her
  Say; Natalie; No One Walks Out on Me [1];
  Perfect Casting [1]; Pressroom Pasa Doble;
  Round in Circles; Saturday [1]; Stamp! Stamp!
  Stamp!; Ten Years from Now; Times We Had,
  The; Wait Till I Get You on Your Own; Waltz for
  Mollie — Never Even Touched Me; Water Under
  the Bridge; Windy City

Cast: Pamela Clifford; MacIntyre Dixon; Tony
  Gilbert; Ronald Holgate; Judy Kaye; Jack Kopye;
  Jack Kyrieleison; Gary Sandy; Alan Sues

Notes: Paper Mill Playhouse, Millburn, N.J.
  Produced in London, 7/20/1982 for 250
  performances at the Victoria Palace Theatre. [1]
  Used in original British production only.

4704 • WINE, WOMEN AND SONG (0000)

Revue

Composer: Carl Schilling
Lyricist: Edward Corbett
Librettist: Edward Corbett
Producer: John W. Isham; George Paxton

Costumes: Madame Thompson; **Set Design:** Frank Gates; E.A. Morange

Songs: Along the Old Canal; Fastest Man in New York; Girls of the Midnight Matinee; I Sail the Airy Blue; Imprisoned; It Fills Me with Distress; Maidens Aquatic; Maybe You Think I Did; Old Rip Was a Flip; Pop, Pop, Pop; Rah-Rah-Rah; Tale of a Decent Married Hen; Wedding Bells Won't Ring Tonight; Whip-poor-wills

Notes: No other information available.

4705 • WINE, WOMEN AND SONG (1898)

OPENED: 09/19/1898   Theatre: Grand Opera House

Musical   Broadway: 8

Composer: Carl Schilling
Librettist: Edward Corbett
Director: George Paxton

Set Design: Frank E. Gates; Edward A. Morange

Cast: James Horan; Robert Quigley; Ruth Robinson

Notes: No program available.

4706 • WINGED VICTORY

OPENED: 11/20/1943   Theatre: 44th Street
Play   Broadway: 212

Composer: David Rose
Lyricist: David Rose
Author: Moss Hart
Producer: U.S. Army Air Forces
Director: Moss Hart

Choreographer: Leonard dePaur; **Costumes:** Howard Shoup; **Lighting Designer:** Abe Feder; **Orchestrations:** David Rose; **Set Design:** Harry Horner; **Vocal Arranger:** Leonard dePaur

Songs: Army Air Corps Song (C/L: Robert Crawford); My Dream Book of Memories; Winged Victory; You're So Nice to Remember [1] (L: Leo Robin)

Cast: Whitney Bissell; Philip Bourneuf; Red Buttons; Peter Lind Hayes; Karl Malden; Kevin McCarthy; Edward McMahon; Gary Merrill; Ray Middleton; Barry Nelson; Edmond O'Brien; George Reeves

Notes: [1] Cut prior to opening.

4707 • WINGS (1975)

OPENED: 03/16/1975   Theatre: Eastside Playhouse

Musical   Off-Broadway: 9

Composer: Robert McLaughlin; Peter Ryan
Lyricist: Robert McLaughlin; Peter Ryan
Librettist: Robert McLaughlin; Peter Ryan
Producer: Stephen Weill
Director: Robert McLaughlin

Source: BIRDS, THE (Play: Aristophanes); **Choreographer:** Nora Christiansen; **Costumes:** Shadow; **Lighting Designer:** Karl Eigsti; **Musical Director:** Larry Hochman; **Orchestrations:** Bill Brohn; **Set Design:** Karl Eigsti; **Vocal Arranger:** Bill Brohn

Songs: Call of the Birds; Comfort for the Taking; Finale; First I Propose; Great Immortals, The; How Great It Is to Be a Bird; Human Species, The; Iris the Fleet; O Sacrilege; Our Goose Is Cooked [1]; Rah Tah Tah Tio Beep Doo Doo; Take to the Air; Time to Find Something to Do; Wall Song, The; Wings; You'll Regret It!

Cast: Peter Jurasik; David Kolatch; James Howard Laurence; Stuart Pankin; Jay E. Raphael; Jerry Sroka

Notes: [1] Not in program.

4708 • WINGS (1993)

OPENED: 03/09/1993   Theatre: Public
Musical   Off-Broadway: 47

Composer: Jeffrey Lunden
Lyricist: Arthur Perlman
Librettist: Arthur Perlman
Director: Michael Maggio

Source: WINGS (Play: Arthur Kopit); **Costumes:** Birgit Rattenborg; **Lighting Designer:** Robert Christen; **Musical Director:** Bradley Vieth; **Set Design:** Linda Buchanan

Cast: William Brown; Rita Gardner; Ora Jones; Ross Lehman; Hollis Resnik; Linda Stephens

Notes: No songs listed in program.

4709 • WINKLE TOWN
OPENED: 1922
Musical   Unproduced

Composer: Richard Rodgers
Lyricist: Lorenz Hart
Librettist: Herbert Fields; Oscar Hammerstein II

Songs: Baby Wants to Dance; Comfort Me; Congratulations; Darling Will Not Grow Older [3]; Hermits, The (What Do All the Hermits Do in Springtime?) [2]; Hollyhocks of Hollywood, The; I Know You're Too Wonderful for Me; I Want a Man [4]; If I Were King [6]; I'll Always Be an Optimist; Manhattan [7]; Old Enough to Love [1]; One a Day; Since I Remember You; Three Musketeers, The [5]; We Came, We Saw, We Made 'Em!

Notes: [1] Later in DEAREST ENEMY. [2] Later in A DANISH YANKEE IN KING TUT'S COURT, TEMPLE BELLES and DEAREST ENEMY. [3] Sung in counterpoint to SILVER THREADS AMONG THE GOLD. Later in BAD HABITS OF 1925. [4] Lyrics revised for LIDO LADY and AMERICA'S SWEETHEART. [5] Later in THE GARRICK GAIETIES (1926) and in that show's 1930 touring production. [6] Later in IF I WERE KING, A DANISH YANKEE IN KING TUT'S COURT and BAD HABITS OF 1925. [7] Later in THE GARRICK GAIETIES with somewhat revised lyrics.

4710 • WINNIE THE POOH
OPENED: 10/29/1972   Theatre: Bil Baird
Musical   Off-Broadway: 44

Composer: Jack Brooks
Lyricist: Jack Brooks; A.A. Milne
Librettist: A.J. Russell
Producer: Amer. Puppet Arts Council
Director: Lee Theodore

Source: WINNIE THE POOH (Story: A.A. Milne); **Musical Director:** Alvy West; **Vocal Arranger:** Alvy West

Songs: Bear Likes Honey, A; Birthdays Are Fun; Cottleston Pie; How Sweet to Be a Cloud; Poor Little Trigger; Sing Ho for the Life of a Bear; Spring Is Spring; They've All Got Tails but Me; Tiddley Pom; Vespers

Puppeteer: Bil Baird; Peter Baird; Pady Blackwood; Olga Felgemacher; Carl Harms; Frank Sullivan; William Tost; Byron Whiting

Notes: Song list from 1960 Television special.

4711 • WINNING MISS, A
OPENED: 11/21/1908   Theatre: Garden
Musical   Chicago

Composer: William F. Peters
Lyricist: Harold Atteridge
Librettist: Harold Atteridge

Songs: I Love You for Keeps

Notes: No other information available.

4712 • WINSOME WIDOW, A
OPENED: 04/11/1912   Theatre: Moulin Rouge
Musical   Broadway: 172

Composer: Raymond Hubbell
Producer: Florenz Ziegfeld
Director: Julian Mitchell

Source: TRIP TO CHINATOWN, A (Musical: Charles H. Hoyt)

Songs: Be My Little Baby Bumble Bee (C: Henry Marshall; L: Stanley Murphy); Call Me Flo (C/L: John Golden; Jerome Kern); Could You Love a Girl Like Me? (L: Robert B. Smith); Fascinating Girl; Frisco, The; I Never Knew What Eyes Could Do Till Yours Looked Into Mine (C: Henry Marshall; L: Stanley Murphy); I Take After Dad; Pousse Cafe; Purity Brigade March; Skate Boy, The; Songs of Yesterday; String a Ring of Roses 'Round Your Rosie (C: Jean Schwartz; L: William Jerome); Teach Me Everything You Know; They Mean More; Toodle-oodle-oodle on Your Piccolo (C/L: Griffin; Murtagh); When I Waltz with You

[1] (C: Albert Gumble; L: Alfred Bryan); You're a
Regular Girl

Cast: Elizabeth Brice; Jack Clifford; Kathleen
Clifford; Dolly Sisters, The; Leon Errol; Harry
Kelly; Charles King; Charles J. Ross; Frank
Tinney; Mae West

Notes: [1] Sheet music only.

4713 • WINSOME WINNIE

OPENED: 12/01/1903   Theatre: Casino
Musical   Broadway: 56

Composer: Gustave Kerker
Lyricist: Frederick Ranken
Librettist: Frederick Ranken
Producer: Nixon & Zimmerman; Sam S. Shubert

Songs: Cities I Love (C: Edward Jakobowski);
Englishman, The (C: Edward Jakobowski;
L: Harry Paulton); Everything Is Big in Chicago;
Finale Act II; Heroes; Hola; I Don't Remember
That; I Love You Only; In the Good Old Days;
Jenny (C: Edward Jakobowski; L: Harry
Paulton); Loud Let the Bugle Sound; Maid and
the Miller, The; Miss Walker of Kalamazoo (C:
Edward Jacobowski; L: Harry Paulton);
Montenegrin Patrol (C: Edward Jacobowski; L:
Harry Paulton); Oh Maiden; Oh, The Paying
Guests
(C: Edward Jakobowski; L: Harry Paulton); Rose,
Rose, Rose (C/L: Dick Temple); Sing Song Lee;
There's a Yacht Come In; They're Looking for
Me; Two Little Doves; Winsome Winnie

Cast: Paula Edwardes; Jobyna Howland; Joseph
Miron; Helen Redmond; Julia Sanderson; Dick
Temple

4714 • WINTER GARDEN VAUDEVILLE SHOW

OPENED: 1911   Theatre: Winter Garden
Revue   Broadway

Producer: Messrs. Shubert

Songs: Sombrero Land (C: Irving Berlin; L: E. Ray
Goetz; Ted Snyder)

Cast: Dolly Jardon

Notes: No program available.

4715 • WINTER'S TALE, THE

OPENED: 07/20/1958
Play

Composer: Marc Blitzstein
Author: William Shakespeare
Producer: American Shakespeare Fest.; John
Houseman
Director: John Houseman; Jack Landau

Choreographer: George Balanchine; **Incidental
Music:** Marc Blitzstein

Songs: Shepherd's Song (When Daffodils Begin to
Peer) (L: William Shakespeare); Song of the
Glove (L: Ben Jonson); Vendor's Song (Lawn
as White as Driven Snow) (L: William
Shakespeare)

Cast: John Colicos; Richard Easton; Will Geer; Ellis
Rabb; Hiram Sherman; Inga Swenson; Nancy
Wickwire

Notes: Produced at the American Shakespeare
Festival, Stratford, Conn.

4716 • WISE CHILD, A

Musical

Composer: William Schroeder
Lyricist: Rida Johnson Young
Librettist: Rida Johnson Young
Producer: Charles Dillingham
Director: Fred G. Latham

Costumes: Mme. Francis; **Set Design:** Frank Gates;
E.A. Morange

Songs: Baby Blue; My Dear Old Daddie; Oh Joy;
Roses Say You Will, The

Cast: Vivienne Segal

Notes: No other information available.

4717 • WISE GUY, THE

OPENED: 1899
Musical   Broadway

Composer: George M. Cohan
Lyricist: George M. Cohan

Songs: Dear Little Girly Girly; Hannah's a Hummer; My Babe from Boston Town; P.S. Mr. Johnson Sends His Regards; San Francisco Sadie; Telephone Me, Baby; To Boston on Business; Who Says a Coon Can't Love

4718 • WISH YOU WERE HERE

OPENED: 06/25/1952   Theatre: Imperial
Musical   Broadway: 598

Composer: Harold Rome
Lyricist: Harold Rome
Librettist: Arthur Kober; Joshua Logan
Producer: Leland Hayward; Joshua Logan
Director: Joshua Logan

Source: HAVING WONDERFUL TIME (Play: Arthur Kober); **Choreographer:** Joshua Logan; **Costumes:** Robert Mackintosh; **Dance Arranger:** Trude Rittman; **Lighting Designer:** Jo Mielziner; **Musical Director:** Jay Blackton; **Orchestrations:** Don Walker; **Set Design:** Jo Mielziner; **Vocal Arranger:** Trude Rittman

Songs: Ain't Nature Grand [1]; Bright College Days; Camp Karefree; Certain Individuals; Could Be; Don Jose of Far Rockaway; Everybody Loves Everybody; Flattery; Glimpse of Love [1]; Goodbye Love [2]; Investigation [1]; Mix and Mingle; Relax; Shopping Around; Social Director; Summer Afternoon; There's Nothing Nicer Than People [3]; They Won't Know Me; Tripping the Light Fantastic; Where Did the Night Go?; Who Could Eat Now [1]; Wish You Were Here

Cast: Sidney Armus; Larry Blyden; Sheila Bond; Jack Cassidy; Florence Henderson; Patricia Marand; Phyllis Newman; John Perkins; Sammy Smith; Tom Tryon; Paul Valentine

Notes: Swimmers trained by Eleanor Holm Rose. [1] Cut prior to opening. [2] Cut after opening. [3] Added after opening.

4719 • WISHING WELL, THE

OPENED: 1929
Musical

Composer: Harold Garstin
Lyricist: Peter Cawthorne
Librettist: Peter Cawthorne
Producer: MacFarland Productions

Director: Peter Cawthorne

Choreographer: Marion Morgan; **Costumes:** Marion Morgan

Songs: Birdie and Ferdie; Dance of Love; Dogs; Follow Your Heart to Fairyland; Happiest Girl in the World, The; Hark to the Sound of the Horn; Healer Am I of All Sorrow, The; I Cannot Speak; I Love You; I Think I'll Go Back to Bed; Legend of the Wishing Well, The; Let's Get a Move On; Love of Mine; Peeping Tom of Coventry; Sawney Pott, the Idiot; Simple Simon; Thank God for the Homeland; This Lovely Night in June; Time for Dreams, A; Whoops-a-Daisy

Cast: Harriet Bennet; Reginald Dandy

Notes: No other information available.

4720 • WITHIN THE LOOP

OPENED: 1915
Musical

Composer: Harry Carroll
Lyricist: Ballard Macdonald

Songs: College Inn Rag, The (L: Coleman Goetz; Ballard Macdonald); Drip, Drip, Drip, Went the Waterfall; I'll Cling to You; Irish Heart, An; My Lady of the Lake; Same Little Girl; Thou Art Mine (L: Coleman Goetz; Ballard Macdonald); You Wake Up in the Morning in Chicago (L: Coleman Goetz; Ballard Macdonald)

Notes: No other information available. Possibly a Chicago show.

4721 • WITHOUT THE LAW

OPENED: 11/21/1912   Theatre: Weber and Fields
                                                  Music Hall
Musical   Broadway

Composer A. Baldwin Sloane
Lyricist: E. Ray Goetz
Librettist: Edgar Smith

Notes: One-act musical. The second half of ROLY POLY.

4722 • WIZ, THE

OPENED: 01/05/1975   Theatre: Majestic
Musical   Broadway: 1672

Composer: Charlie Smalls
Lyricist: Charlie Smalls
Librettist: William F. Brown
Producer: Ken Harper
Director: Geoffrey Holder; Gilbert Moses

Source: WONDERFUL WIZARD OF OZ, THE (Novel: L. Frank Baum); **Choreographer:** George Faison; **Costumes:** Geoffrey Holder; **Dance Arranger:** Timothy Graphenreed; **Lighting Designer:** Tharon Musser; **Musical Director:** Charles H. Coleman; Tania Leon; **Orchestrations:** Harold Wheeler; **Set Design:** Tom H. John; **Vocal Arranger:** Charles H. Coleman

Songs: Be a Lion; Ease on Down the Road; Emerald City Ballet (inst.) (C: George Faison; Timothy Graphenreed); Everybody Rejoice (Brand New Day) (C/L: Luther Vandross); Feeling We Once Had, The; Funky Monkeys; Girl Don't Cry [1]; He's the Wizard; Home; I Was Born on the Day Before Yesterday; If You Believe (Believe in Yourself); Kalidah Battle; Lion's Dream; Mean Old Lion; No Bad News; Rested Body Is a Rested Mind, A; Slide Some Oil to Me; So You Wanted to Meet the Wizard; Soon As I Get Home; Tornado Ballet (C: Timothy Graphenreed); What Would I Do If I Could Feel; Which Witch [1]; Who Do You Think You Are?; Y'All Got It!; You Can't Win [1]

Cast: Hinton Battle; Danny Beard; Dee Dee Bridgewater; Andre De Shields; Pi Douglass; Tiger Haynes; Mabel King; Esther Marrow; Stephanie Mills; Ted Ross; Clarice Taylor; Carl Earl Weaver; Ralph Wilcox

Notes: [1] Cut prior to opening.

4723 • WIZARD OF OZ, THE

OPENED: 01/21/1903   Theatre: Majestic
Musical   Broadway: 293

Composer: A. Baldwin Sloane; Paul Tietjens
Lyricist: L. Frank Baum
Librettist: L. Frank Baum
Producer: Fred R. Hamlin
Director: Julian Mitchell

Source: WONDERFUL WIZARD OF OZ, THE (Novel: L. Frank Baum); **Costumes:** W.W. Denislow; Mrs. Edward Siedle; **Musical Director:** Charles Zimmerman; **Set Design:** Walter Burridge; Fred Gibson; John Young

Songs: Alas for a Man without Brains (C: Paul Tietjens); All Aboard for Sunny Kansas (C/L: Unknown); Ball of All Nations (C: A. Baldwin Sloane; L: Edgar Smith); Carrie Barry (C: A. Baldwin Sloane; L: Glen MacDonough); Connemara Christening (C: A. Baldwin Sloane; L: Edgar Smith); Different Ways of Making Love, The [1] (C: Paul Tietjens); Guardians of the Gate, The [1] (C: Paul Tietjens); Honey Is Sweet (C: Henry Blossom; L: George Spink); How'd You Like to Like a Girl Like Me? [1] (C: Joseph S. Nathan; L: Felix F. Feist); Hurrah for Baffin's Bay [2] (C: Theodore F. Morse; L: Vincent Bryan); I Love Only One Girl in the Wide, Wide World (C: Gus Edwards; L: Will D. Cobb); I'll Be Your Honey in the Springtime [1] (C/L: Harry Freeman); In Michigan (C: A. Baldwin Sloane; L: Glen MacDonough); It Happens Every Day [1] (C: Paul Tietjens); It's Lovely to Love a Lovely Girl [1] (C: Seymour Furth; L: Edward P. Moran); Just a Simple Girl from the Prairie [1] (C: Paul Tietjens); Life in Kansas (C: Paul Tietjens); Love Is Love [1] (C: Paul Tietjens); Must You (C/L: Unknown); Niccolo's Piccolo (C: A. Baldwin Sloane; L: Glen MacDonough); On a Pay Night Evening (C: Schlinker; L: Paul West); Phantom Patrol (C: Paul Tietjens); Poppy Chorus (C: Paul Tietjens); Rosalie (C: Gus Edwards; L: Will D. Cobb); Sammy [2] (C: Edward Hutchinson; L: James O'Dea); She Really Didn't Mind the Thing at All [1] (C: Paul Tietjens); She's My Native Land (C: A. Baldwin Sloane; L: Glen MacDonough); Spanish Bolero (C: A. Baldwin Sloane; L: Edgar Smith); Star of My Native Land (C: A. Baldwin Sloane; L: Edgar Smith); That Is Love (C/L: Maurice Steinberg); That's Where She Sits All Day (C/L: Unknown); Things That We Don't Learn at School (C: A. Baldwin Sloane); Traveler and the Pie, The (C: Paul Tietjens); Wee Highland Mon (C: A. Baldwin Sloane; L: Edgar Smith); When the Circus Comes to Town (C: Bob Adams; L: James O'Dea); When We Get What's Coming to Us [1] (C: Paul Tietjens); When You Love, Love, Love (C: Paul Tietjens); Witch Behind the Man, The (C: Albert; L: Louis Weslyn)

Cast: Grace Kimball; Anna Laughlin; Dave Montgomery; Fred Stone; Bessie Wynn

Notes: This Majestic Theatre was built by the Shuberts on Columbus Circle and opened with this production. The theatre can be seen briefly in the film IT SHOULD HAPPEN TO YOU." [1] Sheet music only. [2] Added after opening.

4724 • WIZARD OF THE NILE, THE

OPENED: 11/21/1895   Theatre: Casino
Musical   Broadway

Composer: Victor Herbert
Lyricist: Harry B. Smith
Librettist: Harry B. Smith
Producer: Arthur F. Clark; Kirke La Shelle

Costumes: Mme. Seidle; **Musical Director:** Frank Palma; **Set Design:** Ernest Albert

Songs: Am I a Wizard; Bang, Bang, the Most Harmonious Sound; Cheer for the Kibosh, A; Cleopatra's Aria; Echo Song, The; Father Nile, Keep Us in Thy Care; Finale Act III; Gaze on This Face; I Adore Thee; I Am the Ruler; I Envy the Bird; I Have Been A-Maying; If I Were a King; In Dreamland; Incantation; I've Appeared Before Crowned Heads; Know Ye the Sound; Lancers; List to Our Matin Serenade; My Angeline; My Love Awaits; Nature's Song Is But a Dream; On Cleopatra's Wedding Day; Oriental March; Pure and White As the Lotus; Song of the Optimist; Star Light, Star Bright (Starlight Waltz); Stonecutters' Song (Work Away with a Song, My Boys); Strew the Way with Flor'rets Blooming; That's One Thing a Wizard Can Do; There's One Thing a Wizard Can Do; To the Pyramid; What Is Love?; When the Bugles Are Calling

Cast: Walter Allen; Frank Daniels; Dorothy Morton; Mary Palmer; Helen Redmond; Louise Royce

Notes: No songs listed in program. Songs from vocal score.

4725 • WOGGLE BUG, THE

OPENED: 06/20/1905
Musical   Closed out of town

Composer: Frederic Chapin
Lyricist: L. Frank Baum
Librettist: L. Frank Baum

Source: WOGGLE BUG BOOK, THE (Story: L. Frank Baum)

Songs: Doll and the Jumping Jack, The; Equine Paradox; Hobgoblins; Household Brigade, The; I'll Get Another Place; Mr. H.M. Woggle-Bug, T.E.; Patty Cake, Baker Man; Soldiers; Sweet Matilda; There's a Lady-Bug A'Waitin'; To the Victor Belongs the Spoils (Chewing Gum Song)

Cast: Helen Allyn; Phoebe Coyne; Blanche Deyo; Hal Godfred; Mabel Hite; Fred Mace

Notes: No program available. Produced in Chicago.

4726 • WOMAN HATERS, THE

OPENED: 10/07/1912   Theatre: Astor
Musical   Broadway: 32

Composer: Edmund Eysler
Lyricist: George V. Hobart
Librettist: George V. Hobart
Producer: A.H. Woods
Director: George Marion

Source: DIE FRAULEIN FRESSEN (Play: Carl Lindau; Leo Stein)

Songs: Come On Over Here [1] (C: Walter Kollo; L: George V. Hobart; Jerome Kern); Dance the Polka; He Will Take Me to His Heart (L: M.E. Rourke); It Was Marie; Little Girl Come Back to Me (L: M.E. Rourke)

Cast: Sallie Fisher; Joseph Santley

Notes: No songs listed in program. [1] Also in THE DOLL GIRL.

4727 • WOMAN OF THE YEAR

OPENED: 03/29/1981   Theatre: Palace
Musical   Broadway: 770

Composer: John Kander
Lyricist: Fred Ebb
Librettist: Peter Stone
Producer: Lawrence Kasha; David S. Landay; Stewart F. Lane; James M. Nederlander; Carole J. Shorenstein; Warner Theatre Productions
Director: Robert Moore

Source: WOMAN OF THE YEAR, THE (Film: Michael Kanin; Ring Lardner Jr.);
Choreographer: Tony Charmoli; **Costumes:** Theoni V. Aldredge; **Dance Arranger:** Ronald Melrose; **Lighting Designer:** Marilyn Rennagel; **Musical Director:** Donald Pippin; **Orchestrations:** Michael Gibson; **Set Design:** Tony Walton; **Vocal Arranger:** Donald Pippin

Songs: Grass Is Always Greener, The; Happy in the Morning; I Told You So; I Wrote the Book; It Isn't Working; Man About Town [1]; Nothing Personal [1]; One of the Boys; Open the Window [3]; Poker Game, The; See You in the Funny Papers; Shut Up Gerald; So What Else Is New?; Sometimes a Day Goes By; Table Talk; That's the Way It Is [1]; Two of Us, The; We're Gonna Work It Out; Who Would Have Dreamed [2]; Woman of the Year (1); Woman of the Year (2) [3]; You're Right You're Right

Cast: Lauren Bacall; Helon Blount; Roderick Cook; Marilyn Cooper; Rex Everhart; Grace Keagy; Jamie Ross

Notes: [1] Cut prior to opening. [2] Cut prior to opening then added when Raquel Welch succeeded Lauren Bacall. [3] Added for national tour after Broadway.

4728 • WOMAN-KING, THE

OPENED: 1893
Musical   Closed out of town

Composer: Ludwig Englander

Source: RAINMAKER OF SYRIA, THE (Musical: Rudolf Aronson)

Notes: Newark 11/20/1893. No other information available.

4729 • WOMB, THE

OPENED: 11/22/1986
Musical

Composer: John Pike
Additional Music: Christina Dougherty; Joseph M. Santi
Lyricist: John Pike
Librettist: John Pike
Producer: Naomi Grabel; Harold Wolpert
Director: John Pike

Costumes: Astrid Sosa; **Lighting Designer:** Ed Wilcox; **Set Design:** Ed Wilcox

Songs: Here in the Womb; Julie's Song; One More, One Less; Through the Door

Cast: Bobbi Block; Wier Harman; Lee S. Wind

Notes: Performed at the Annenberg Center Studio Theatre, Philadelphia.

4730 • WONDER BAR, THE

OPENED: 03/17/1931   Theatre: Nora Bayes
Musical   Broadway: 86

Composer: Robert Katscher
Lyricist: Irving Caesar
Librettist: Irving Caesar; Aben Kandel
Producer: Morris Gest; Messrs. Shubert
Director: William Mollison

Source: WUNDERBAR (Musical: Karl Farkas; Geza Herczeg); **Choreographer:** John Pierce; Albertina Rasch; **Costumes:** Charles LeMaire; **Musical Director:** Louis Silver; **Set Design:** Watson Barratt

Songs: Dance We All Do for Al, The [2]; Dying Flamingo, The [2]; Elizabeth; Ev'ry Day Can't Be a Sunday [3] (C/L: Al Jolson); Good Evening, Friends; I'm Falling in Love; Lenox Avenue [3] (C/L: Irving Caesar; Al Jolson; Joseph Meyer); Ma Mere [1] (C: Harry Warren; L: Irving Caesar; Al Jolson); Oh, Donna Clara (C: J. Petersburski; L: Beda; Irving Caesar); Something Seems to Tell Me [3]

Cast: Carol Chilton; Signorina Medea Columbara; Doris Groday; Al Jolson; Patsy Kelly; Wanda Lyon; Rex O'Malley; Al Segal; Vernon Steele; Maceo Thomas; Arthur Treacher; Trini

Notes: [1] Also in SWEET AND LOW. [2] Out Detroit 12/6/31. [3] Sheet music only.

4731 • WONDER YEARS, THE

OPENED: 05/25/1988   Theatre: Top of the Gate
Musical   Off-Broadway: 23

Composer: David Levy
Lyricist: David Levy
Librettist: David Holdgrive; Terry LaBolt; David Levy; Steve Liebman
Producer: Dwight Frye; Russ Thacker
Director: David Holdgrive

Choreographer: David Holdgrive; **Costumes:** Richard Schurkamp; **Lighting Designer:** Ken Billington; **Musical Director:** Keith Thompson; **Set Design:** Nancy Thun

Songs: Another Elementary School; Baby Boom Babies; First Love; Flowers from the Sixties; Gimme Get Me I Want It; Girl Most Likely, The; Me Suite, The; Monarch Notes; Pushing Thirty; Takin' Him Home to Meet Mom; Teach Me How to Fast Dance; Through You; Wonder Years, The

Cast: Adam Bryant; Meghan Duffy; Louisa Flaningam; Kathy Morath; Alan Osburn; Lenny Wolpe

Notes: No songs listed in program.

4732 • WONDERFUL LIFE, A
Musical   Closed out of town

Composer: Joe Raposo
Lyricist: Sheldon Harnick
Librettist: Sheldon Harnick
Director: Brent Wagner

Source: IT'S A WONDERFUL LIFE (Film: Frank Capra; Frances Goodrich; Albert Hackett); **Choreographer:** Tim Millett, **Conductor:** Bradley Bloom; **Lighting Designer:** Ken Yunker; **Musical Director:** Jerry DePuit; **Orchestrations:** Jerry DePuit; **Set Design:** David Leugs

Songs: Can You Find Me a House; Christmas Gifts; First Class All the Way; Good Night; I Couldn't Be with Anyone but You; If I Had a Wish; In a State; Linguine; Mystery, A; Not What I Expected; On to Pittsburgh; One of the Lucky Ones; Opening: Prayer; Panic at the Building and Loan; Precious Little; Ruth; Show Me a Suitcase; "Unborn" Sequence; Welcome a Hero; Wings; Wonderful Life, A

Cast: Mark E. Doerr; Andrew E. Lippa; Connie Sa Loutos; Edward J. Smit; Beth Spencer; Paul Winberg

Notes: Program of the Power Center of the Performing Arts used.

4733 • WONDERFUL NIGHT, A
OPENED: 10/31/1929   Theatre: Majestic
Musical   Broadway: 125

Composer: Johann Strauss
Lyricist: Fanny Todd Mitchell
Librettist: Fanny Todd Mitchell
Producer: Messrs. Shubert
Director: Jose Ruben

Source: LE REVEILLON (Story); **Costumes:** Orry Kelly; Ernest Schrapps; **Set Design:** Watson Barratt; Herbert Moore

Cast: Hal Forde; Cary Grant[1]; Robert Irving; Joseph Letora; Solly Ward

Songs: Chacun a Son Gout; Girls Must Live; Letter Song; Two in Love

Notes: The story was also the basis for DIE FLEDERMAUS. Songs not listed in program. [1] Billed as Archie Leach.

4734 • WONDERFUL TOWN
OPENED: 02/25/1953   Theatre: Winter Garden
Musical   Broadway: 559

Composer: Leonard Bernstein
Lyricist: Betty Comden; Adolph Green
Librettist: Jerome Chodorov; Joseph Fields
Producer: Robert Fryer
Director: George Abbott

Source: MY SISTER EILEEN (Play: Jerome Chodorov; Joseph Fields); **Source:** MY SISTER EILEEN (Story: Ruth McKenney); **Choreographer:** Donald Saddler; **Costumes:** Mainbocher; Raoul Pene du Bois; **Lighting Designer:** Peggy Clark; **Musical Director:** Lehman Engel; **Orchestrations:** Don Walker; **Set Design:** Raoul Pene du Bois

Songs: Ballet at the Village Vortex (dance); Christopher Street; Conga!; Conquering New York (dance) [4]; Conversation Piece (Nice Talk, Nice People); It's Love; Lallapalooza [3]; Let It Come Down [2]; Little Bit in Love, A; My Darlin' Eileen; Ohio; One Hundred Easy Ways; Pass the Football; Quiet Girl, A; Self-Expression [1]; Story of My Life, The [2]; Swing!; What a Waste; Wrong Note Rag

Cast: Edith Adams; Cris Alexander; Jordan Bentley; Dort Clark; Warren Galjour; George Gaynes; Dody Goodman; Henry Lascoe; Rosalind Russell

Notes: [1] Out New Haven 1/19/53. [2] Cut prior to opening. [3] Out New Haven 1/19/53. Same song as "Hallapalooza" cut from PETER PAN (1950). [4] Lyric cut prior to opening.

4735 • WONDERLAND
OPENED: 10/24/1905   Theatre: Majestic
Musical   Broadway: 73

Composer: Victor Herbert
Lyricist: Glen MacDonough
Librettist: Glen MacDonough
Producer: Julian Mitchell
Director: Julian Mitchell

Source: DANCING PRINCESS, THE (Story: Brothers Grimm); **Musical Director:** Carl Styx; **Orchestrations:** Victor Herbert; **Set Design:** E.G. Unitt; John Young

Songs: Barbarian Dance; Broadway Favorites; Companions of the Blade; Crew of the Peek-a-Boo, The; Eccentric Dance; From You I'll Never Part (C: Helen M. Trigg; L: Walter H. Faulkner); Hallowe'en [3]; How to Tell a Fairy Tale [1]; Hunting of the Cook, The; I and Myself and Me (L: Vincent Bryan); It's Hard to Be a Hero [2]; Jografree; Knave of Hearts, The [1]; Little Black Sheep [1]; Love's Golden Day; Minuet; Nature Class, The; Nineteen Princesses Song [2]; No Show Tonight; Only One, The; Opening Chorus Act II [1]; Oriental Dance [2]; Ossified Man, The; Popular Pauline; Tale of a Music Box Shop (Tale of a Song Box Shop); That's Why They Say I'm Crazy [1]; Until We Meet Again; Voice for It, The; When Perrico Plays; With Frame, Two Forty Nine [1]; Woman's First Thought Is a Man, A [1]; Your Heart, If You Please [1]

Cast: Sam Chip; Bessie Clayton; James Cook; Eva Davenport; Lotta Faust; James Smith; Bessie Wynn

Notes: Titled ALICE AND THE EIGHT PRINCESSES out of town. [1] Sheet music only. [2] ASCAP/Library of Congress only. [3] Vocal score only.

4736 • WONDERLAND IN CONCERT

OPENED: 12/27/1978   Theatre: Public
Musical   Off-Broadway: 3

Composer: Elizabeth Swados
Lyricist: Elizabeth Swados
Librettist: Elizabeth Swados
Producer: N.Y. Shakespeare Festival; Joseph Papp
Director: Elizabeth Swados

Source: ALICE'S ADVENTURES IN WONDERLAND (Novel: Lewis Carroll); **Source:** THROUGH THE LOOKING GLASS (Novel: Lewis Carroll); **Lighting Designer:** Jennifer Tipton

Cast: Karen Evans; Gloria Hodes; Rodney Hudson; Paul Kreppel; Joan MacIntosh; Jim McConaughty; William Parry; JoAnna Peled; Meryl Streep

Notes: *See also ALICE IN CONCERT*, a revision of this show.

4737 • WONDERWORLD

OPENED: 04/07/1964   Theatre:
                      Amphitheatre-on-the-lake
Revue   N.Y. World's Fair

Composer: Jule Styne
Lyricist: Stanley Styne
Producer: Meyer Davis
Director: Leon Leonidoff

Choreographer: Michael Kidd; **Costumes:** Alvin Colt; **Lighting Designer:** Jules Fisher; **Dance Arranger:** Peter Howard; **Orchestrations:** Meyer Davis; **Set Design:** Richard Rychtarik; Don Shirley

Songs: Age of Rock-Rock of Ages; Alfa Romeo; Coco Palm Tree Island; Good Old Fashioned Get Together; Happy Days; Independence Day Parade; Meet the Press; Welcome; Woman's Place; (The Wonder of It All) Wonderworld; Your Isle

Cast: Chita Rivera; Gretchen Wyler

4738 • WOODLAND

OPENED: 11/21/1904   Theatre: New York
Musical   Broadway: 83

Composer: Gustav Luders
Lyricist: Frank Pixley
Librettist: Frank Pixley
Producer: Henry W. Savage
Director: George Marion

Choreographer: Sam Marion; **Costumes:** Archie Gunn; **Lighting Designer:** Joe Wilson; **Musical Director:** Gustav Luders; **Set Design:** Walter Burridge; Edward La Moss

Songs: At Night, At Night; Bird and the Bottle, The [2]; Bye-Bye Baby; Cheer Boys, Cheer; Clear the Way; Dainty Little Ingenue; Execution of Prince Eagle [3]; Firefly, The [2]; If You Love Me, Lindy; Keep on Smiling; Message of Spring, The;

No Bird Ever Flew So High He Didn't Have to Light (C: Harry Bulger; L: Will D. Cobb); Old Blue Jay, The [3]; Prince Eagle's Entrance; Romance of a Bachelor Bird, The; Society; Some Day When My Dreams Come True; Tale of a Turtle Dove, The; They'll Have to Go; Time Is Flying; Valley of Hokus-Po, The; When Duty Calls; When the Heart Is Light; Will You Be My Little Bride [1]; You Never Can Tell Till You Try

Cast: Harry Bulger; Emma Carus; Helen Hale; Ida Brooks Hunt

Notes: [1] Out Boston 4/24/05. [2] Sheet music only. [3] Vocal score only.

4739 • WOODY GUTHRIE

Notes: *See TOM TAYLOR AS WOODY GUTHRIE.*

4740 • WOODY GUTHRIE'S AMERICAN SONG

OPENED: 07/31/1991
Revue   Closed out of town

Composer: Woody Guthrie
Lyricist: Woody Guthrie
Librettist: Woody Guthrie
Adaptation: Peter Glazer
Producer: Goodspeed Opera House
Director: Peter Glazer

Choreographer: Jennifer Martin; **Costumes:** Baker S. Smith; Mindy Wolfe; **Lighting Designer:** David Noling; **Musical Director:** Malcolm Ruhl; **Orchestrations:** Jeff Waxman; **Set Design:** Philipp Jung; **Vocal Arranger:** Jeff Waxman

Songs: Ain't Gonna Be Treated This Way; Better World; Bound for Glory; Deportee (Plane Wreck at Los Gatos); Do Re Mi; Dust Bowl Refugee; Dust Storm Disaster; End of My Line; Grand Coulee Dam; Hard, Ain't It Hard; Hard Travelin'; I Don't Feel at Home on the Bowery No More; Lonesome Valley; New York Town; Nine Hundred Miles; Oklahoma Hills; Pastures of Plenty; Sinking of the Reuben James, The; Talkin' Subway; This Land Is Your Land; Union Maid; Worried Man

Cast: Jane Gillman; Brian Gunter; Ora Jones; Susan Moniz; John Reeger; Malcolm Ruhl; L.J. Slavin; Christopher Walz

Notes: No songs written for this show.

4741 • WOOF, WOOF

OPENED: 12/25/1929   Theatre: Royale
Musical   Broadway: 45

Composer: Edward Pola
Lyricist: Eddie Brandt
Librettist: Estelle Hunt; Sam Summers; Cyrus Wood
Producer: William Demarest; Bernard Lohmuller
Director: William Caryl

Choreographer: Dan Healy; Leonide Massine; **Costumes:** Mabel Johnston; **Orchestrations:** Ken Macomber; **Set Designer:** Clark Robinson

Songs: Fair Weather; Girl Like You, A; I Like It; I Mean What I Say; I'll Take Care of You; Lay Your Bets; Satanic Strut; Shh!; That Certain Thing; Topple Down; Why Didn't You Tell Me; Won't I Do?; You're All the World to Me

Cast: Louise Brown; Eddie Nelson; Al Sexton; Jack Squires

4742 • WORDS AND MUSIC (1917)

OPENED: 11/24/1917   Theatre: Fulton
Revue   Broadway: 24

Composer: E. Ray Goetz
Lyricist: E. Ray Goetz
Librettist: Raymond Hitchcock
Producer: E. Ray Goetz; Raymond Hitchcock
Director: Leon Errol

Songs: Brickerty-Brackety — Tootsies; Call On Rag Doll (C: Willy White); Camouflaging (C: Jean Schwartz); Christmastide Love (C: Willy White); Dance of the Dolls; Everything Looks Rosy and Bright; First Nighters; Ginger; I May Stay Away a Little Longer; If You Hadn't Answered No (C: Harry Ruby; L: Bert Kalmar; Edgar Leslie); It's All Right If You Love (One Another) (C: Harry Ruby; L: Edgar Leslie); Ladies, The; Lady Romance; March of the Enchantress; My Broadway Butterfly (C: Willy White); New York, What's Become of You?; Nonsense; Oriental Prelude; Stop Your Camouflaging with Me (C: Jean Schwartz); They'll Be Whistling It All Over Town (C: Jean Schwartz); Wait Till the Silver Moon Rolls By; Walk Down the Avenue with Me; While We Go Marching Along [1]

Cast: Edna Aug; Elizabeth Brice; Richard Carle; Wellington Cross; Marion Davies; Gordon Dooley; William Ray

Notes: [1] Sheet music only.

4743 • WORDS AND MUSIC (1974)

OPENED: 04/16/1974   Theatre: John Golden
Revue   Broadway: 127

Composer: Jule Styne
Lyricist: Sammy Cahn
Librettist: Sammy Cahn
Producer: Alexander H. Cohen; Harvey Granat
Director: Jerry Adler

Lighting Designer: Marc B. Weiss; **Musical Director:** Richard J. Leonard; **Set Design:** Robert Randolph

Songs: All the Way [5] (C: James Van Heusen); Be My Love [6] (C: Nicholas Brodszky); Call Me Irresponsible [7] (C: James Van Heusen); Christmas Waltz, The; Come Fly with Me (C: James Van Heusen); Day By Day (C: Axel Stordahl; Paul Weston); Everybody Has the Right to Be Wrong [1] (C: James Van Heusen); Five Minutes More [8]; High Hopes [10] (C: James Van Heusen); I Fall in Love Too Easily [11]; I Guess I'll Hang My Tears Out to Dry [9]; I Only Miss Him When I Think of Him [1] (C: James Van Heusen); I Should Care [12] (C: Axel Stordahl; Paul Weston); I'll Never Stop Loving You [14] (C: Nicholas Brodszky); I'll Walk Alone [15]; It's Been a Long, Long Time; It's Magic [17]; I've Heard That Song Before [16]; Let It Snow! Let It Snow! Let It Snow!; Love and Marriage [4] (C: James Van Heusen); My Kind of Town [18] (C: James Van Heusen); Papa, Won't You Dance with Me [3]; Please Be Kind (C: Saul Chaplin); Pocket Full of Miracles [19] (C: James Van Heusen); Put 'Em in a Box [17]; Rhythm Is Our Business (C: Saul Chaplin; Jimmy Lunceford); Saturday Night (Is the Loneliest Night in the Week); Second Time Around, The [20] (C: James Van Heusen); Shake Your Head from Side to Side (C: Bob Gerow); Teach Me Tonight (C: Gene DePaul); (Love Is) The Tender Trap [21] (C: James Van Heusen); Things We Did Last Summer, The; Thoroughly Modern Millie [22] (C: James Van Heusen); Three Coins in the Fountain [23]; Time After Time [24]; Touch of Class, A [25] (C: George Barrie); Until the Real Thing Comes Along (C/L: Sammy Cahn; Saul Chaplin; L.E. Freeman); Walking Happy [2] (C: James Van Heusen); Wonder Why [13] (C: Nicholas Brodszky); You'll Never Know

Where You're Going Till You Get There [26]; You're My Girl [3]

Cast: Sammy Cahn; Kelly Garrett; Shirley Lemmon; Jon Peck

Notes: Sammy Cahn sings his own songs and discusses his career. No original songs in this show. Produced in London as THE SAMMY CAHN SONGBOOK. [1] From SKYSCRAPER. [2] From WALKING HAPPY. [3] From HIGH BUTTON SHOES. [4] From TV musical OUR TOWN. [5] From film THE JOKER IS WILD. [6] From film THE TOAST OF NEW ORLEANS. [7] From film PAPA'S DELICATE CONDITION. [8] From film THE SWEETHEART OF SIGMA CHI. [9] From GLAD TO SEE YA. [10] From film A HOLE IN THE HEAD. [11] From film ANCHORS AWEIGH. [12] From film THRILL OF ROMANCE. [13] From film RICH, YOUNG AND PRETTY. [14] From film LOVE ME OR LEAVE ME. [15] From film THREE CHEERS FOR THE BOYS. [16] From film YOUTH ON PARADE. [17] From film ROMANCE ON THE HIGH SEAS. [18] From film ROBIN AND THE SEVEN HOODS. [19] From film POCKETFUL OF MIRACLES. [20] From film HIGH TIME. [21] From film THE TENDER TRAP. [22] From film THOROUGHLY MODERN MILLIE. [23] From film THREE COINS IN THE FOUNTAIN. [24] From film IT HAPPENED IN BROOKLYN. [25] From film A TOUCH OF CLASS. [26] From film CINDERELLA JONES.

4744 • WORKING

OPENED: 05/14/1978   Theatre: 46th Street
Revue   Broadway: 25

Librettist: Stephen Schwartz
Producer: Stephen R. Friedman; Irwin Meyer
Director: Stephen Schwartz

Source: Working (Book: Studs Terkel);
Choreographer: Onna White; **Costumes:** Marjorie Slaiman; **Dance Arranger:** Michele Brourman; **Lighting Designer:** Ken Billington; **Musical Director:** Stephen Reinhardt; **Orchestrations:** Kirk Nurock; **Set Design:** David Mitchell; **Vocal Arranger:** Stephen Reinhardt

Songs: All the Livelong Day (I Hear America Singing) [2] (C/L: Stephen Schwartz; L: Walt Whitman); America Dreaming [1] (C/L: James Taylor); Brother Trucker (C/L: James Taylor); Cleanin' Women (C/L: Micki Grant); Fathers and

Sons (C/L: Stephen Schwartz); Husbands and Wives Dance (C/L: Michele Brourman); If I Could've Been (C/L: Micki Grant); It's an Art (C/L: Stephen Schwartz); Joe (C/L: Craig Carnelia); Just a Housewife (C/L: Craig Carnelia); Lovin' Al (C/L: Micki Grant); Mason, The (C/L: Craig Carnelia); Millwork (C/L: Stephen Schwartz; C: Michele Brourman); Neat to Be a Newsboy (C/L: Stephen Schwartz); Nightskate (C/L: Stephen Schwartz; C: Michele Brourman); Nobody Goes Out Anymore [1] (C/L: Craig Carnelia); Nobody Tells Me How (C: Mary Rodgers; L: Susan Birkenhead); Something to Point To (C/L: Craig Carnelia); Treasure Island Trio Dance (inst.) (C: Michele Brourman); Un Mejor Dia Vendra (C: James Taylor; L: Graciela Daniele; Matt Landers); Working Girl's Apache (dance) [1] (C: Michele Brourman)

Cast: Susan Bigelow; Steven Boockvor; Rex Everhart; Arny Freeman; Bob Gunton; David Patrick Kelly; Matt Landers; Bobo Lewis; Patti LuPone; Matthew McGrath; Lenora Nemetz; David Langston Smyrl; Lynne Thigpen

Notes: [1] Out Chicago 1/78. [2] Lyrics based on poem by Walt Whitman.

4745 • WORLD OF BLACK AND WHITE, THE

Notes: *See A REEL AMERICAN HERO.*

4746 • WORLD OF JULES FEIFFER, THE

OPENED: 07/02/1962
Revue   Closed out of town

Composer: Stephen Sondheim
Lyricist: Stephen Sondheim
Librettist: Jules Feiffer
Producer: Lewis Allen; Harry Rigby
Director: Mike Nichols

Set Designer: Don J. Remacle; **Lighting Designer:** Richard Drew; **Musical Director:** Robert Colston

Songs: Truly Content

Cast: Ronny Graham; Dorothy Loudon; Paul Sand

Notes: Part of this show was a one-act version of the story "Passionella." Jerry Bock and Sheldon

Harnick also musicalized this story as part of THE APPLE TREE.

4747 • WORLD OF PLEASURE, A (1915)

OPENED: 10/14/1915   Theatre: Winter Garden
Musical   Broadway: 116

Composer: Sigmund Romberg
Lyricist: Harold Atteridge
Librettist: Harold Atteridge
Producer: Winter Garden Company
Director: J.C. Huffman

Choreographer: Theodore Kosloff; Jack Mason; **Costumes:** Mrs. J.J. Shubert; **Musical Director:** Oscar Radin

Songs: At the Toy Shop; Dance of the Midnight Sons, The (inst.); Dance of the Squareheads (inst.); Dancing Festival, The; Danse Excentrique (inst.); Doll Dance, The (inst.); Down in Catty Corner; Employment Agency, The; Fascination; Fifth Avenue; Flights of Fancy; Girl of the Fan, The; Girlies Are Out of My Life; Good Fellows Club, The; Greatest Battle-Song of All, The (L: Harold Atteridge; Jack Wilson); I Could Go Home to a Girlie Like You; I Played My Concertina; I'll Make You Like the Town; In Arabia; In the War Against Men; Japanese Ballet; Jigaree, The; Mark Anthony; Mechanical Soldiers; Melting Pot, The; Miss Innovation; Polo Rag (inst.); Ragtime Carnival; Ragtime Pipes of Pan, The; Rosey-Posey; Shopping [1]; Syncopation (C/L: J. Leubrie Hill); Take Me Home with You; Wop Cabaret, The (C/L: John Golden)

Cast: Clifton Crawford; Sahari Djeli; Kitty Gordon; Sydney Greenstreet; Lou Holtz; Stella Mayhew

Notes: [1] Vocal score only.

4748 • WORLD OF PLEASURE (1925)

OPENED: 1925

Composer: George David Weist [1]
Lyricist: Mack Gordon; Anton F. Scibilia

Songs: Cinderella; Make Up Your Mind; Midsummer Night's Dream

Notes: No other information available. [1] Later known as George David Weiss.

4749 • WORLD OF SUZIE WONG, THE

OPENED: 10/14/1958   Theatre: Broadhurst
Play   Broadway: 508

Author: Paul Osborn
Producer: Mansfield Productions; David Merrick; Seven Arts Productions, Inc
Director: Joshua Logan

Source: WORLD OF SUZIE WONG, THE (Novel: Richard Mason); **Costumes:** Dorothy Jenkins; **Lighting Designer:** Jo Mielziner; **Set Design:** Jo Mielziner

Songs: Ding Dong Song, The [2] (C/L: Lionel Bart; L: Yao Ming); How Can You Forget [1] (C: Richard Rodgers; L: Lorenz Hart)

Cast: Sarah Marshall; France Nuyen; Ron Randell; William Shatner; Kathleen Widdoes

Notes: [1] Originally in FOOLS FOR SCANDAL. [2] Only in London production.

4750 • WORLD'S MY OYSTER, THE

OPENED: 07/31/1956   Theatre: Actors'
                                          Playhouse
Musical   Off-Broadway: 40

Composer: Lorenzo Fuller; Carley Mills
Lyricist: Lorenzo Fuller; Carley Mills
Librettist: Lorenzo Fuller; Carley Mills
Producer: Actors' Playhouse
Director: Jed Duane

Choreographer: Walter Hicks; Louis Johnson; **Costumes:** Lew Smith; **Set Design:** Henry Buckmaster

Songs: Devil Is a Man You Know, The; Finer Things of Life, The; Footprints in the Sand; Friendship Ain't No One Way Street; I Set My Heart on One Love; I Wouldn't Bother You About So Much; Just Before I Go to Sleep; Merchandise; Moola Makes the Hula Feel Much Cooler; Quiet Little Royal Household; Rich Enough to Be Rude; Shoeshine; Thing Like This, A; This Is the Life for Me; World in a Jug, The

Cast: Lorenzo Fuller; Dolores Harper; Butterfly McQueen

4751 • WRONG MR. PRESIDENT, THE

OPENED: 1913
Musical

Composer: Trevor Corwell; Russell Smith
Lyricist: J. Homer Tutt; Salem Tutt Whitney
Librettist: J. Homer Tutt; Salem Tutt Whitney
Producer: J. Homer Tutt; Salem Tutt Whitney

Musical Director: Clarence G. Wilson

Songs: All I Ask Is to Forget You; Come Out; For Honor; Have Patience, Don't Worry; Hesitation Waltz; Intruder, The; Just a Pickaninny All Dressed Up (C/L: Lewis T. Thomas); Love You Can't Forget, The; My Heart for You Pines Away (C: Russell Smith; L: Noble Sissle); Romance Espanola; Smart Set Tango; Tourists Are We; Tutt's Todalo (C/L: Lewis T. Thomas); We Welcome Thee; What You Need Is Ginger Springs; When Your Country Calls to Arms; Ye Olde Quadrille (inst.)

Cast: Greensbury Holmes; Frank Jackson; Alfred Strauder; J. Homer Tutt; Salem Tutt Whitney

Notes: No other information available.

4752 • WRONG NUMBER, THE
Notes: *See OH, WHAT A GIRL!*

Y

4753 • YANKEE CIRCUS ON MARS, A

OPENED: 04/12/1905   Theatre: Hippodrome
Musical   Broadway: 120

Composer: Jean Schwartz
Lyricist: Manuel Klein; Jean Schwartz; Harry Williams
Librettist: George V. Hobart
Producer: Elmer S. Dundy; Frederick W. Thompson
Director: Edward P. Temple

Choreographer: Sam Marion; Vincente Romeo; **Costumes:** Alfredo Edel; **Musical Director:** Manuel Klein; **Set Design:** Arthur Voegtlin

Songs: Animal King, The (C: Manuel Klein; L: George V. Hobart); Aurora Borealis (L: George V. Hobart); Bogie Man, The (L: Harry Williams); Ensemble (C: Manuel Klein; L: George V. Hobart); Entrance of Messenger from Mars (C: Manuel Klein); Entrance of Soubrette (C: Manuel Klein); Entrance of Yankee Circus (C: Manuel Klein); Get a Horse (L: Harry Williams); Grand Ensemble of Martians (C: Manuel Klein; L: George V. Hobart); Hey! Rube! (L: Stanley Crawford; Harry Williams); Hold Your Horses (L: Harry Williams); Milkmaids' Chorus (L: Manuel Klein; Harry Williams); Opening Chorus (C: Manuel Klein); Reuben Tell Your Mandy (L: Harry Williams)

Cast: James Cherry; Felix Haney; Albert Hart; Vernon Lee; Bessie McCoy; Olive North; Rio Brothers, The; Florence Sinnot; Ty Bell Sisters, The

Notes: "Dance of the Hours" from LA GIOCONDA, directed by Vincenzo Romeo was the second part of the bill. ANDERSONVILLE OR A STORY OF WILSON'S RAIDERS was the third part of the bill. This had a book by Carroll Fleming and mechanical effects by John E Corrigan. ANDERSONVILLE was replaced by THE ROMANCE OF A HINDO PRINCESS in October of 1905. It also had a book by Carroll

Fleming and starred James Cherry, Florence Sinnot and Vernon Lee who are all listed above.

4754 • YANKEE CONSUL, THE

OPENED: 02/22/1904   Theatre: Broadway
Musical   Broadway: 115

Composer: Alfred G. Robyn
Lyricist: Henry Blossom
Librettist: Henry Blossom
Producer: Henry W. Savage
Director: George Marion

Costumes: Will R. Barnes; **Musical Director:** Frank N. Darling; **Set Design:** Walter Burridge; Edward La Moss

Songs: Ain't It Funny What a Difference Just a Few Hours Make; Con-Con-Con [1]; Cupid Has Found My Heart; Gossips' Chorus; Hammers Will Go Rap, Rap, Rap, The; Hark, While I Sing to Thee! [1]; Hola!; I'd Like to Be a Soldier; In Old New York; In the Days of Old; Mermaid and the Lobster, The [1]; Mosquito and the Midge, The; My San Domingo Maid; Nine [1]; Tell Me [1]; Viva the Gay Fiesta; We Come from Proud Castilian Blood; We Were Taught to Walk Demurely; When the Goblins Are at Play [1]

Cast: William Danforth; Eva Davenport; John E. Hazzard; Raymond Hitchcock; Flora Zabelle

Notes: [1] Sheet music only.

4755 • YANKEE DOODLE SCOUTS

Musical

Composer: Gus Edwards
Lyricist: Will D. Cobb
Librettist: Thomas J. Gray
Producer: Gus Edwards
Director: Gus Edwards

Cast: Hattie Kneitel

Notes: A vaudeville musical. No other information available.

4756 • YANKEE DRUMMERS, THE

OPENED: 01/19/1908
Musical   Closed out of town

Songs: Because I'm Married Now; Honey Boy; I'd Like to Know Your Address and Your Name; In the Land of the Buffalo; In Those Boyhood Days; Insanity; Keep on Smiling; Little Bit of Everything, A; Little Bit of Now and Then; Old Fashioned Buggy Ride, An; School Days; There's Only Moon Beams; Uncle Bill

Cast: Lyman Twins; Patti Rosa; Clarence A. Sterling; Myrtle Thompson

Notes: Program of Cedar Rapids. Only cast credits in program. These may not be original songs.

4757 • YANKEE GIRL, THE

OPENED: 12/10/1910   Theatre: Herald Square
Musical   Broadway: 92

Composer: Silvio Hein
Lyricist: George V. Hobart
Librettist: George V. Hobart
Producer: Lew Fields
Director: Ned Wayburn

Songs: All, All Alone; Clap Hands [2] (C: Seymour Furth; L: Will A. Heelan); Hands Up [2] (C: J. Fred Helf; L: Arthur J. Lamb); I'll Make a Ring Around Rosie; In 1999 [1]; I've Got Rings on My Fingers or Mumbo-Jumbo-Jijjiboo-J. O'Shay [3] (C: Maurice Scott; L: F.J. Barnes; R.P. Weston); Let's Make Love Among the Roses [2] (C: Jean Schwartz; L: William Jerome); Lousiana Lizabeth; Maid of Sevilla; Nora Malone Call Me By Phone (C: Albert Von Tilzer; L: Junie McCree); Pretty Polly [2]; Tell It to Sweeney (C: Harry Von Tilzer; L: Will Dillon); That Hypnotizing Rag (C/L: C.F. Zittel); Top of the Morning, The; Where's Mama?; Whoop Daddy Ooden Dooden Day; Yankee Girl, The

Cast: Harry Gilfoil; William Halliday; Dorothy Jardon; Blanche Ring; Charles Winninger

Notes: [1] Out prior to New York. [2] Sheet music only. [3] Also in THE MIDNIGHT SONS.

4758 • YANKEE MANDARIN, THE

OPENED: 1909
Musical

Composer: Reginald De Koven
Lyricist: Edward Paulton
Librettist: Edward Paulton
Producer: F. Ray Comstock; Morris Gest

Songs: Back to New York; Dot and Carry One; Gipsy of Poughkeepsie; I Must Have a Picture of That; If I Had a Chance Like That; Oh Papa; Pocket Telephone, The; Sea Siren, The; Something Tells Me; Song of the Clock; Song of the Lantern; Sun Gold; True Blue American Boy; Two Dummies, The; Willow Pattern Plate, The

Notes: No other information available.

4759 • YANKEE PRINCE, THE

OPENED: 04/20/1908   Theatre: Knickerbocker
Musical   Broadway: 28

Composer: George M. Cohan
Lyricist: George M. Cohan
Librettist: George M. Cohan
Producer: George M. Cohan; Sam H. Harris
Director: George M. Cohan

Musical Director: Charles J. Gebest;
Orchestrations: Charles J. Gebest

Songs: A-B-C's of the U.S.A., The; American Idea, The [1]; Cohan's Rag Babe; Come on Down Town; Dancing Ceremony, The [1]; From the Land of Dreams; I Say, Flo; I'm Awfully Strong for You; I'm Going to Marry a Nobleman; M-O-N-E-Y; Nothing New Beneath the Sun [1]; Showing the Yankees London Town; Soldiers of the King; Song of the King, A; Think It Over Carefully; Tommy Atkins, You're All Right; Villains in the Play; Yankee Doodle's Come to Town; Yankee Prince March & Two-Step, The (inst.) [2]; Yankee Prince Waltz (inst.) (C: Charles J. Gebest)

Cast: George M. Cohan; Helen Cohan; Jerry Cohan; Josie Cohan; Donald Crisp; Jack Gardner; Tom Lewis

Notes: [1] Out Washington D.C. 9/20/09. [2] Sheet music only.

4760 • YANKEE PRINCESS, THE

OPENED: 10/02/1922   Theatre: Knickerbocker
Musical   Broadway: 80

Composer: Emmerich Kalman
Lyricist: B.G. DeSylva
Librettist: William Le Baron
Producer: A.L. Erlanger
Director: Fred G. Latham; Julian Mitchell

Source: DIE BAJADERE (Musical: Julius Brammer; Alfred Gruenwald; Emmerich Kalman); **Costumes:** Wilhelm; **Lighting Designer:** Tony Greshoff; **Musical Director:** William Daly

Songs: Can It Be That I'm in Love?; Eyes So Dark and Luring; Forbidden Fruit; Friendship; Husband's Only a Husband, A; I Still Can Dream; I'll Dance My Way Into Your Heart; In the Starlight; Lotus Flower; Love the Wife of Your Neighbor; My Bajadere; Roses, Lovely Roses; Stars of the Stage; Waltz Was Made for Lovers, The

Cast: Thorpe Bates; John T. Murray; Vivian Oakland; Vivienne Segal

4761 • YANKEE REGENT, THE

OPENED: 09/17/1907
Musical   Closed out of town

Composer: Ben M. Jerome
Lyricist: Chas. Adelman; Irving B. Lee
Librettist: Chas. Adelman; Irving B. Lee
Producer: H.H. Frazee

Musical Director: Ben M. Jerome

Songs: Army and Navy, The; Childhood Days; Clock in the Tower, The; Dancing Sal; Entrance of Regent; Finale Act II; Here's Looking at You; Heyday; I'm Growing Wary; Indigent Aristocrat, An; Land of the Wiener and the Wurst, The; Lilies in the Pond Are not for Me, The (L: Irving B. Lee); Mary Jane; Military, The; Opening Chorus; Proposal, The; Suppose

Cast: Elsie Baird; Thomas Burton; Osborne Clemson; Toby Lyons; Bertha Shalek; Fred Walton

Notes: Program of Cedar Rapids.

4762 • YANKEE TOURIST, A

OPENED: 08/12/1907   Theatre: Astor
Musical   Broadway: 103

Composer: Alfred G. Robyn
Lyricist: Wallace Irwin
Librettist: Richard Harding Davis
Producer: Henry W. Savage
Director: George Marion

Source: GALLOPER, THE (Play: Richard Harding Davis); **Musical Director:** John McGhie

Songs: Alabama [1]; And the World Goes On Just the Same [1] (C: Harry O. Sutton; L: Jean Lenox); Broadway Means Home to Me [1]; By the Side of the Zuyder Zee [1] (C: Bennett Scott; L: A.J. Mills); Come and Have a Smile with Me; Come in Out of the Wet [1]; Finale Act II [2]; Gee! Ain't It H — to Be Rich [1]; Glad Hand Girl, The [2]; Golden Sails; Greek Dance; Irish Lads; It's Always Nice Weather Indoors or Oh! Oh! Oh! Says Rosie [1] (C: S.R. Henry; L: Arthur J. Lamb); Longshoreman's Chanty; Love Me Enough to Remember [1]; My Volo Maid [1]; Night Before To-morow, The [2]; Opening Chorus; Opening Chorus Act III [2]; Rainbow; Saracen Song March; So Long Bill (Take Care O' Yourself) [1] (C: Alfred G. Robyn; L: Wallace Irwin); So What's the Use [1] (C/L: Edward Montagu); Steward's Song; Teddy Girl, The; Underneath a Parasol with You [1] (C/L: John B. "Swifty" Lowitz); Wal, I Swan! (Ebenezer Frye) [1] (C/L: Benjamin Hapgood Burt); What's the Use?; When a Girl Is Born to Be a Lady; When You Done Gone Broke [1]; Wouldn't You Like to Have Me for a Sweetheart?; Yankee Millionaire

Cast: Wallace Beery; Herbert Cawthorne; Eva Fallon; Raymond Hitchcock; Harry West; Flora Zabelle

Notes: [1] Sheet music only. [2] Vocal score only.

4763 • YEAH MAN

OPENED: 05/26/1932   Theatre: Park Lane
Revue   Broadway: 2

Composer: Ken Macomber; Charles Weinberg; Al Wilson
Lyricist: Ken Macomber; Charles Weinberg; Al Wilson
Librettist: Billy Mills; Leigh Whipper
Producer: Walter Campbell; Jesse Wank
Director: Walter Campbell

Choreographer: Marcus Slayter; **Musical Director:** Billy Butler; **Orchestrations:** Billy Butler; Lorenzo Caldwell; Charles Cooke

Songs: At the Barbecue; Baby, I Could Do It for You; Come to Harlem; Crazy Idea of Love; Dancin' Fool; Give Me Your Love; Gotta Get de Boat Loaded; I'm Always Happy When I'm in Your Arms; I've Got What It Takes; Mississippi Joys; Qualifications (C/L: Porter Grainger); Shady Dan; Shake Your Music; Spell of Those Harlem Nights; That's Religion (C/L: Porter Grainger)

Cast: Rose Henderson; Melodee Four, The; Billy Mills; Mantan Moreland; Eddie Rector; Marcus Slayter; Leigh Whipper; Lily Yuen

4764 • YEARLING, THE

OPENED: 12/10/1965   Theatre: Alvin
Musical   Broadway: 3

Composer: Michael Leonard
Lyricist: Herbert Martin
Librettist: Herbert Martin; Lore Noto
Producer: Lore Noto
Director: Lloyd Richards

Source: YEARLING, THE (Novel: Marjorie Kinnan Rawlings); **Choreographer:** Ralph Beaumont; **Costumes:** Ed Wittstein; **Dance Arranger:** David Baker; **Lighting Designer:** Jules Fisher; **Musical Director:** Julian Stein; **Orchestrations:** Larry Wilcox; **Set Design:** Ed Wittstein; **Vocal Arranger:** Julian Stein

Songs: Ain't He a Joy?; Bear Hunt; Boy Talk; Do What the Good Book Says [1]; Everything Beautiful; Everything in the World I Love; Fluttermill Song [1]; Growing Up Is Learning How to Say Goodbye [2]; I Love This Child [2]; I Love You [3]; I Need a Friend [3]; I'd Kick Up My Heels [3]; I'm All Smiles; In That Clearing [4]; Judgement Day [1]; Kind of a Man a Woman Needs, The; Let Him Kick Up His Heels; Little Girl [1]; Lonely Clearing; Moonshine [3]; My Pa [1]; My Prayers Have Come True [3]; Nothing More; One Promise; Planting Fever [4]; Shoot the Pig [3]; Slewfoot [3]; Some Day I'm Gonna Fly; Spring Is a New Beginning [2]; Startin' Over [3]; Teach Me How to Dance [2]; What a Happy Day; What Can I Name Him [1]; Why Did I Choose You?; You're Everything in the World I Love [4]

Cast: Carmen Alvarez; Gordon B. Clarke; Tom Fleetwood; David Hartman; Carmen Mathews; Steve Sanders; David Wayne; Dolores Wilson

Notes: [1] Cut prior to opening. [2] In CBS Radio version. [3] Added to 1985 revival in Atlanta. [4] Out Philadelphia 11/65.

4765 • YELLOW MASK, THE

OPENED: 02/08/1928   Theatre: Carlton
Musical   London: 218

Composer: Vernon Duke
Lyricist: Desmond Carter
Producer: Laddie Cliff; Julian Wylie
Director: Laddie Cliff

Choreographer: Max Rivers; **Set Designer:** Joseph and Phil Harker; Marc Henri; Hugh Gee

Songs: Bacon and the Egg, The; Blowing the Blues Away (L: Eric Little); Chinese Ballet (inst.); Chinese March (inst.); Deep Sea; Half a Kiss (L: Eric Little); I Love You So; I Still Believe in You (L: Desmond Carter; Vernon Duke); I'm Wonderful; March (inst.); Opening Chorus Act One; Some Sort of Something (L: Vernon Duke; Eric Little); Walking on Air; Yellow Mask; You Do, I Don't

Cast: Phyllis Dare; Leslie Henson; Bobby Howes

Notes: No program available.

4766 • YES, YES, YVETTE

OPENED: 10/03/1927   Theatre: Sam H. Harris
Musical   Broadway: 40

Lyricist: Irving Caesar
Librettist: William Cary Duncan; James Montgomery
Producer: H.H. Frazee

Source: NOTHING BUT THE TRUTH (Play: Frederic S. Isham); **Choreographer:** Sammy Lee; **Costumes:** Milgrim; **Musical Director:** Ben M. Jerome

Songs: Do You Love As I Love? (C: Joseph Meyer); Finale Act I; Finale Act II; For Days and Days (I Love You, I Do) [1] (C: Phil Charig); Good Morning [1] (C: Irving Caesar); How'd You Like To? (C: Stephen Jones); I'm a Little Bit Fonder of You [1] (C: Irving Caesar); My Lady (C: Ben

Jerome; L: Frank Crumit); Opening Act II; Opening Act III; Opening Chorus; Pack Up Your Blues and Smile (C: Peter De Rose; Albert Von Tilzer; L: Jo Trent); Sing, Dance and Smile (C: Philip Charig; Ben Jerome); Six O'Clock (C: Philip Charig); Two of Us, The [1]; What Kind of Boy; Woe Is Me; Yes, Yes, Yvette (C: Philip Charig); You or Nobody! (C: Irving Caesar); You're So Nice to Me

Cast: Jeanette MacDonald; Jack Whiting; Charles Winninger

Notes: [1] Sheet music only.

4767 • YESTERDAY
OPENED: 03/10/1919
Musical   Closed out of town

Composer: Reginald De Koven
Lyricist: Glen MacDonough
Librettist: Glen MacDonough
Producer: Messrs. Shubert

Songs: Bebe; Clown, The; It Isn't the Same in the Daylight; It's Paris Everywhere; Man's Forever, A; Montebanks, The (inst.); My Yesterday; Phantom Rose

4768 • YESTERDAY IS OVER
Play

Author: Mady Christians
Composer: Bill Roscoe
Lyricist: Mady Christians
Director: Margot Lewitin

Songs: The Banco Number; I'm in the Market for a Dream; Oh How I loved Him; Sawing a Woman in Half; Yesterday Is Over

Cast: Elizabeth Franz; Margot Lewitin; Lucille Patton; **Pianist:** David Tice

4769 • YIDDLE WITH A FIDDLE
OPENED: 10/28/1990   Theatre: Town Hall
Musical   Off-Broadway: 55

Composer: Abraham Ellstein
Lyricist: Isaiah Sheffer
Librettist: Isaiah Sheffer
Producer: Raymond Ariel; Lawrence Toppall
Director: Ran Avni

Source: YITL MIDN FIDL (Film: Joseph Green); **Choreographer:** Helen Butleroff; **Costumes:** Karen Hummel; **Lighting Designer:** Robert Bessoir; **Musical Director:** Lanny Meyers; **Orchestrations:** Lanny Meyers; **Set Design:** Jeffrey Schneider

Songs: Badchen's Verses; Come Gather 'Round; Hard As a Nail; Help Is on the Way!; How Can the Cat Cross the Water?; If You Wanna Dance; I'll Sing; Man to Man; Music, It's a Necessity; New Rhythm; Oh Mama, Am I in Love; Only for a Moment; Stay Home Here with Me; Take It from the Top; To Tell the Truth; Travelling First Class Style; Warsaw!; We'll Sing; Wedding Bulgar Dance (inst.); Yiddle with a Fiddle

Cast: Mitchell Greenberg; Emily Loesser; Patricia Ben Peterson; Steve Sterner

4770 • YIP! YIP! YAPHANK!
OPENED: 08/19/1918   Theatre: Century
Revue   Broadway: 32

Composer: Irving Berlin
Lyricist: Irving Berlin

Songs: Bevo [4]; Ding Dong [6]; Dream on Little Soldier Boy (L: Jean Havez); God Bless America [1]; Hello, Hello, Hello; I Can Always Find a Little Sunshine in the Y.M.C.A.; Mandy [5]; Oh! How I Hate to Get Up in the Morning [7]; Poor Little Me, I'm on K.P. [2]; Ragtime Razor Brigade; We're on Our Way to France; What a Difference a Uniform Will Make [3]

Cast: 350 Soldiers; William Bauman; Irving Berlin; Dan Healy; Sammy Lee; Benny Leonard

Notes: [1] Written as finale but cut. [2] Also known as "Kitchen Police." [3] Also known as "Ever Since I Put on a Uniform." [4] Also in ZIEGFELD FOLLIES OF 1919. [5] Also in ZIEGFELD FOLLIES OF 1919 and THIS IS THE ARMY (1942). [6] Also in THE CANARY. [7] Also in ZIEGFELD FOLLIES OF 1918 and THIS IS THE ARMY.

4771 • YO-SAN
Notes: *See CHERRY BLOSSOMS.*

4772 • YOKEL BOY
OPENED: 07/06/1939   Theatre: Majestic
Musical   Broadway: 208

Composer: Sam H. Stept
Lyricist: Lew Brown; Charles Tobias
Librettist: Lew Brown
Producer: Lew Brown
Director: Lew Brown

Choreographer: Gene Snyder; **Costumes:** Frances Feist; **Musical Director:** Al Goodman; **Set Design:** Walter Jagermann

Songs: 'Baby Wampus' Stars, The [2]; Beer Barrel Polka [1] (C: Jaromir Vejvoda; L: Lew Brown); Boy Named Lem, A; Catherine the Great; Comes Love; For the Sake of Lexington; Hollywood and Vine [2]; I Can't Afford to Dream; I Know I'm Nobody; If I Feel This Way Tomorrow [2] (C: Ray Henderson; L: Lew Brown); It's Me Again; Let's Make Memories Tonight; Ship Has Sailed, The; Time for Jukin' (C: Walter Kent); Uncle Sam's Lullaby; When the Berry Blossoms Bloom [2]

Cast: Charles Althoff; Judy Canova; Dixie Dunbar; Buddy Ebsen; Lew Hearn; Jackie Heller; Ralph Holmes; Lois January; Mark Plant; Ralph Riggs; Phil Silvers

Notes: [1] Added after opening. [2] Out Washington, D.C. 12/30/40.

4773 • YOSHE KALB

OPENED: 10/22/1972
Musical   Off-Broadway: 95

Composer: Maurice Rauch
Lyricist: Isaac Dogim
Librettist: David Licht
Producer: S. Ehrenfeld & Assoc.; Jewish Nostalgic Prods.; Harry Rothpearl
Director: David Licht

Source: YOSHE KALB (Story: Isaac Bashevis Singer); **Choreographer:** Lillian Shapero; **Costumes:** Sylvia Friedlander; **Lighting Designer:** Tom Meleck; **Musical Director:** Renee Solomon; **Set Design:** Jorday Barry

Songs: Badchen; Bwis Jolem Tanz; Chosen Doime le Meilech & Rikodle; Ein Koloheinu; Malkele's Song; Rosh Hashono; Song of Joy; Three Good Deeds, The; Trio; Tsivye's Song; Wedding Dance; Wedding Procession

Cast: Jacob Ben-Ami; Isaac Dogim; David Ellis;

Miriam Kessyn; David Opatoshu; Warren Pincus; Ruth Vool

4774 • YOU BET YOUR ASSETS

OPENED: 01/25/1979
Revue

Composer: Roy Straiges
Lyricist: Stephen de Baum
Librettist: Robert Brown; Louis Day; Sam Domsky; Paul Provenza; Stephen de Baum
Producer: Donald Fisher
Director: Bruce Montgomery

Arrangements: Bruce Montgomery; Roy Straiges; **Choreographer:** Bruce Montgomery; Robert Wilson; **Musical Director:** William Lessig; **Set Design:** Douglas Cohen; Peter Saylor

Songs: At the Casino (L: Robert Wilson; Stephen de Baum); Das Telefunken (C: Bruce Montgomery); Dow Jones Disco, The (inst.); Endangered Species, An; Fugue for Thought (C: Bruce Montgomery); Humility; Love Affair, A; Martini Rock, The; Standing Ovulation, A (C: Mark Cornfield; Murray Indick; L: Paul Provenza); Ticker Tape Caper (inst.); You Bet Your Assets

Cast: Ron Alper; Joe Fillip; Dan Helming

Notes: Amateur show. Mask & Wig Club, University of Pennsylvania.

4775 • YOU COULD BE HOME NOW

OPENED: 10/11/1992   Theatre: Public
Play   Off-Broadway: 25

Composer: Tom Judson
Lyricist: Tom Judson
Author: Ann Magnuson
Producer: N.Y. Shakespeare Festival; Women's Project & Prods.
Director: David Schweizer

Choreographer: William Fleet Lively; Jerry Mitchell; **Costumes:** Pilar Limosner; **Incidental Music:** Tom Judson; **Lighting Designer:** Heather Carson; **Set Design:** Bill Clarke

Songs: Folk Song (C/L: Ann Magnuson); West Virginia's Home to Me (C/L: Lyell B. Clay)

Cast: Ann Magnuson

4776 • YOU KNEW ME AL
Musical

Composer: Burton Hamilton
Lyricist: William A. Halloran Jr.

Songs: Bring Back that Yama Dance to Me; Garden of Love for Two; I Want the Boys Around Me (C: Burton Hamilton; Sid Marion); I'm Going Back to Mobile, Alabam'; Let Me Have a Little Corner of Your Heart (C/L: Leon De Costa); My Heart Belongs to the U.S.A.; My Little Loving Baby Mine (C: William A. Halloran Jr.)

Notes: No other information available.

4777 • YOU NEVER KNOW
OPENED: 09/21/1938   Theatre: Winter Garden
Musical   Broadway: 78

Composer: Cole Porter
Lyricist: Cole Porter
Librettist: Rowland Leigh
Producer: John Shubert; Messrs. Shubert
Director: Rowland Leigh

Source: BEI KERZENLICHT (Musical: Karl Farkas); **Source:** CANDLE LIGHT (Play: Siegfried Geyer; Robert Katscher); **Choreographer:** Robert Alton; **Costumes:** Brooks; Jenkins; Charles LeMaire; Veronica; Wilma; **Musical Director:** John McManus; Menotti Salta; **Orchestrations:** Claude Austin; Maurice DePackh; Max Hoffmann; Hans Spialek; Don Walker; **Set Design:** Watson Barratt; Albert Johnson

Songs: At Long Last Love; Au Revoir, Cher Baron; By Candlelight (1) [1]; By Candlelight (2) (C: Robert Katscher; L: Rowland Leigh); Cafe Society Set, The [2]; Don't Let It Get You Down [4]; For No Rhyme or Reason; From Alpha to Omega; Gendarmes (C: Robert Katscher; L: Rowland Leigh); Good Evening, Princesse; Ha, Ha, Ha [1]; I Am Gaston; I'll Black His Eyes [2]; I'm Back in Circulation [1]; I'm Going in for Love [1]; I'm Yours [2]; It's No Laughing Matter [1]; Ladies Room (C: Alex Fogarty; L: Edwin Gilbert); Let's Put It to Music (C: Alex Fogarty; L: Edwin Gilbert); Maria; No (You Can't Have My Heart) (C/L: Dana Suesse); One Step Ahead of Love [3]; Opening Act II; Take Yourself a Trip (C: Alex Fogarty; L: Edwin Gilbert); They Learn About Women from Me; Waiters, The [2]; What a Priceless Pleasure [5]; What Is That Tune?; What Shall I Do? (L: Rowland Leigh; Cole Porter); Yes, Yes, Yes; You Never Know

Cast: Debonairs, The; Truman Gaige; Don Harden; Grace Hartman; Paul Hartman; Libby Holman; Charles Kemper; Jean Morehead; Rex O'Malley; June Preisser; Roger Stearns; Lupe Velez; Clifton Webb; Toby Wing

Notes: [1] Not used. [2] Out New Haven 3/3/38. [3] Out Washington, D.C. 3/21/38. [4] Not used in film BREAK THE NEWS. [5] Cut.

4778 • YOU SAID IT
OPENED: 01/19/1931   Theatre: 46th Street
Musical   Broadway: 192

Composer: Harold Arlen
Lyricist: Jack Yellen
Librettist: Sid Silvers; Jack Yellen
Producer: Lou Holtz; Jack Yellen
Director: John Harwood

Choreographer: Danny Dare; **Costumes:** Kiviette; **Musical Director:** Louis Gress; **Orchestrations:** Howard Jackson; **Set Design:** Donald Oenslager; **Vocal Arranger:** Charles Henderson

Songs: Alma Mater [2]; Beatin' the Blues [2]; Best Part College Days [2]; Bright and Early [2]; Ha-Ha-Ha (Gang Song) [1] (L: Ted Koehler); If He Really Loves Me; It's Different with Me; Learn to Croon; Sweet and Hot; Tell Me with a Love Song [1] (L: Ted Koehler); They Learn About Women from Me; What Do We Care?; What'd We Come to College For?; While You Are Young; You Said It; You'll Do

Cast: Benny Baker; Peggy Bernier; Hughie Clarke; Oscar Grogan; George Haggarty; Lou Holtz; Mary Lawlor; Lyda Roberti; Slate Brothers; Stanley Smith

Notes: Special music effects: Fred Waring. [1] Not used. [2] ASCAP/Library of Congress only.

4779 • YOU TAKE IT
Musical

Composer: Dennis E. Connell
Lyricist: Dennis E. Connell

Choreographer: Estelle Murray; **Musical Director:** Elizabeth Bogan

Songs: Any Place Would Be Paradise (C/L: Joseph Vance)

Cast: James K. Young

Notes: No other information available.

4780 • YOU'D BE SURPRISED

OPENED: 1920
Musical

Composer: Richard Rodgers
Lyricist: Lorenz Hart
Librettist: Milton Bender
Producer: Akron Club
Director: Milton Bender

Musical Director: Richard Rodgers

Songs: Aphrodite; Boomerang, The; Breath of Spring, A; China; College Baby (L: Robert A. Simon); Don't Love Me Like Othello [2]; Flying the Blimp [3]; I Hate to Talk About Myself [3]; Kid, I Love You; Little Girl, Little Boy [3]; Mary, Queen of Scots [1] (L: Herbert Fields); My World of Romance; Poor Fish; Princess of the Willow Tree (L: Milton G. Bender); Spain; That Boy of Mine (L: Oscar Hammerstein II); When We Are Married (L: Milton G. Bender); You Don't Have to Be a Toreado

Cast: Dorothy Fields

Notes: Amateur production. The Hart lyrics may have been written in collaboration with Milton Bender. [1] Also in POOR LITTLE RITZ GIRL and JAZZ A LA CARTE. [2] Also in FLY WITH ME. [3] ASCAP/Library of Congress only.

4781 • YOU'LL NEVER KNOW

OPENED: 04/20/1921
Musical

Composer: Richard Rodgers
Lyricist: Lorenz Hart
Librettist: Herman Axelrod; Henry William Hanemann
Producer: Columbia University Players
Director: Herman Axelrod; Oscar Hammerstein II; Henry William Hanemann

Choreographer: Herbert Fields; **Musical Director:** Richard Rodgers; **Set Design:** Joseph Physioc

Songs: Chorus Girl Blues [2]; Don't Think That We're the Chorus of the Show [3]; I'm Broke; Jumping Jack; Just a Little Lie; Law [3]; Let Me Drink in Your Eyes [1]; Mr. Director [3]; Something Like Me [4]; Virtue Wins the Day; Watch Yourself [5]; We Take Only the Bets [3]; When I Go on the Stage; Will You Forgive Me?; You'll Never Know; Your Lullaby

Notes: Amateur production. [1] Also in POOR LITTLE RITZ GIRL. [2] Also in SAY IT WITH JAZZ and SAY MAMA. [3] ASCAP/Library of Congress only. [4] ASCAP/Library of Congress only. Also in SAY IT WITH JAZZ. [5] Also in SAY MAMA.

4782 • YOU'LL SEE STARS

OPENED: 12/29/1942   Theatre: Maxine Elliott's
Musical   Broadway: 4

Composer: Leo Edwards
Lyricist: Herman Timberg
Librettist: Herman Timberg
Producer: Dave Kramer
Director: Dave Kramer; Herman Timberg

Choreographer: Eric Victor; **Dance Arranger:** Adam Carroll; Bernard Weissman; **Musical Director:** Charles Sanford; **Orchestrations:** Adam Carroll; Bernard Weissman; **Set Design:** Perry Watkins; **Vocal Arranger:** Adam Carroll; Bernard Weissman

Songs: All You Have to Do Is Stand There; America; Betcha I Make Good; Dancing on a Rainbow; Future Stars; It Could Happen, It's Possible; Jelly Beans at Walgreens; Readin', Writin' and 'Rhythmatic; Silvery Moon; Swinging the Bhumba; Time and Time Again; What a Pretty Baby Are You

Cast: Jackie Green; Jackie Michaels; Alan Ray; Arnold Stang; Eric Victor

4783 • YOU'RE A GOOD MAN, CHARLIE BROWN

OPENED: 03/07/1967   Theatre: Theatre 80 St. Marks
Musical   Off-Broadway: 1597

Composer: Clark Gesner
Lyricist: Clark Gesner
Librettist: John Gordon [1]

Producer: Gene Persson; Arthur Whitelaw
Director: Joseph Hardy

Source: PEANUTS (Comic Strip: Charles M. Schulz); **Costumes:** Alan Kimmel; **Lighting Designer:** Jules Fisher; **Musical Director:** Joseph Raposo; **Set Design:** Alan Kimmel; **Vocal Arranger:** Joseph Raposo

Songs: Book Report; Dr. Lucy (The Doctor Is In); Happiness; Kite; Little Known Facts; My Blanket and Me; Schroeder; Snoopy; Suppertime; T.E.A.M. (The Baseball Game); You're a Good Man, Charlie Brown

Cast: Bob Balaban; Gary Burghoff; Bill Hinnant; Skip Hinnant; Karen Johnson; Reva Rose

Notes: [1] John Gordon is a pseudonym for the staff and cast of this show.

4784 • YOU'RE IN LOVE

OPENED: 02/06/1917   Theatre: Casino
Musical   Broadway: 167

Composer: Rudolf Friml
Lyricist: Edward Clark; Otto Harbach
Librettist: Edward Clark; Otto Harbach
Producer: Arthur Hammerstein
Director: Edward Clark

Choreographer: Robert Marks

Songs: Be Sure It's Light; Boola Boo (L: Otto Harbach); Buck Up; Dance of the Rose, The [1]; He Will Understand; I'm Only Dreaming; Keep Off the Grass; Love-Land (L: Otto Harbach); Married Life; Mignonette (inst.); Musical Snore, The; Opening; Pretty Lips of Velvet [1]; Snatched from the Cradle; Suck Up [2]; That's the Only Place Where Our Flag Shall Fly; Things That They Must Not Do; We'll Drift Along (Opening Chorus Act II); What's the Use of Being Lonesome [1]; Year Is a Long Long Time, A; You're in Love

Cast: Carl McCullough; Clarence Nordstrom; May Thompson

Notes: [1] Out Shubert Theatre 12/17/16. [2] ASCAP/Library of Congress only.

4785 • YOUNG ABE LINCOLN

OPENED: 04/25/1961   Theatre: Eugene O'Neill
Musical   Broadway: 93

Composer: Victor Ziskin
Lyricist: Joan Javits; Arnold Sundgaard
Librettist: John Allen; Richard N. Bernstein
Producer: Arthur Shimkin
Director: Jay Harnick

Choreographer: Rhoda Levine; **Costumes:** Fred Voelpel; **Lighting Designer:** Fred Voelpel; **Musical Director:** Victor Ziskin; **Set Design:** Fred Voelpel

Songs: Captain Lincoln March, The; Cheer Up!; Don't P-P-Point Them Guns at Me; Frontier Politics; I Want to Be a Little Frog in a Little Pond; Run, Indian, Run; Same Old Me, The; Someone You Know; Vote for Lincoln; Welcome Home Again; You Can Dance

Cast: Lou Cutell; Judy Foster; Joan Kibrig; Dan Resin; Darrell Sandeen

Notes: Opened Off-Broadway at the York Playhouse 4/3/61 for 18 performances. Moved to Broadway for 27 performances, then reopened at the York for 48 more performances.

4786 • YOUNGER MAN, OLDER WOMAN

OPENED: 10/10/1995   Theatre: Beacon
Musical   New York: 28

Composer: Douglas Knyght-Smith; Playe Scott
Lyricist: Douglas Knyght-Smith; Playe Scott
Librettist: Doug Smith; Helen Smith

Songs: Baby I'm Ready Now (C/L: Millie Jackson; Doulgas Knyght-Smith; Playe Scott); Don't Wanna B N Luv; I Wish It Would Rain Down (C/L: Phil Collins); Living with a Stranger; People in My Head (C/L: Millie Jackson; Douglas Knyght-Smith; Playe Scott); Someday We'll All Be Free (C/L: Donny Hathaway); Taking My Life Back (C/L: Millie Jackson; Jolyon Skinner); Weight of Love, The (C/L: Millie Jackson; Reynaldo Rey); When a Woman Makes Up Her Mind; You Gonna Miss Me; Young Man, Older Woman (C/L: Millie Jackson; Jolyon Skinner)

Cast: Keisha Jackson; Millie Jackson; Douglas Knyght; Kenneth "Chocolate Thunder" Montague; Reynaldo Rey

Notes: This show toured the country. No program available.

4787 • YOUNG TURK, THE

OPENED: 01/31/1910   Theatre: New York
Musical   Broadway: 32

Composer: Max Hoffmann
Lyricist: Harry Williams
Librettist: Aaron Hoffman
Producer: Klaw & Erlanger
Director: Herbert Gresham

Choreographer: Jack Mason

Songs: At Arrowhead Inn; Chauffeur, The; Did You Ever Hear That in Turkey?; I Thought I Wanted Opera; I'll Be Happy Too; Opening Act II; Parisian Glide; Proposals; Sword Is My Sweetheart True, The; Those Dear Old Wedding Bells [1]; Under the Oriental Moon

Cast: Fred Bowers; Mae Murray; Max Rogers

Notes: [1] Sheet music only.

4788 • YOUR ARMS TOO SHORT TO BOX WITH GOD

OPENED: 12/22/1976   Theatre: Lyceum
Revue   Broadway: 149

Composer: Alex Bradford; Micki Grant
Lyricist: Alex Bradford; Micki Grant
Librettist: Vinnette Carroll
Producer: Frankie Hewitt; Tom Mallow
Director: Vinnette Carroll

Source: GOSPEL ACCORDING TO ST. MATTHEW, THE (Book); **Choreographer:** Talley Beatty; **Costumes:** William Schroder; **Dance Arranger:** H.B. Barnum; **Lighting Designer:** Gilbert V. Hemsley Jr.; Richard Winkler; **Musical Director:** George Broderick; Michael Powell; **Orchestrations:** H.B. Barnum; **Set Design:** William Schroder; **Vocal Arranger:** Chapman Roberts

Songs: As Long As I Live; Band, The; Be Careful Whom You Kiss (C/L: Alex Bradford); Beatitudes; Can't No Grave Hold My Body Down (C/L: Alex Bradford); Come on Down; Didn't I Tell You (C/L: Alex Bradford); Do You Know Jesus; Everybody Has His Own Way (C/L: Alex Bradford); Give Us Barabbas; He's a Wonder; I Know I Have to Leave Here; I Love You So Much Jesus (C/L: Alex Bradford); It Was Alone; It's Too Late; Judas Dance (inst.) (C: H.B. Barnum); Just a Little Bit of Jesus Goes a Long Way; See How They Done My Lord (C/L: Alex Bradford); Something Is Wrong in Jerusalem; There's a Stranger in Town (C/L: Alex Bradford); Trial; We Are the Priests and Elders (C/L: Alex Bradford); We're Gonna Have a Good Time; When the Power Comes; Your Arms Too Short to Box with God (C/L: Alex Bradford)

Cast: Salome Bey; Clinton Derricks-Carroll; Delores Hall; Hector Jaime Mercado

4789 • YOUR OWN THING

OPENED: 01/13/1968   Theatre: Orpheum
Musical   Off-Broadway: 937

Composer: Danny Apolinar; Hal Hester
Lyricist: Danny Apolinar; Hal Hester
Librettist: Donald Driver
Producer: Zev Bufman; Dorothy Love
Director: Donald Driver

Source: TWELFTH NIGHT (Play: William Shakespeare); **Costumes:** Albert Wolsky; **Dance Arranger:** Charles Schneider; **Lighting Designer:** Tom Skelton; **Musical Director:** Charles Schneider; **Orchestrations:** Hayward Morris; **Set Design:** Robert Guerra

Songs: Apocalypse Fugue; Baby! Baby! (Somethin's Happ'nin'); Be Gentle; Come Away; Death; Do Your Own Thing; Don't Leave Me; Flowers, The; Hunca Munca; I'm Me! (I'm Not Afraid); I'm on My Way to the Top; Let It Be [1]; Middle Years, The; No One's Perfect, Dear; Now Generation, The; She Never Told Her Love; What Do I Know?; When You're Young and In Love

Cast: Danny Apolinar; Imogene Bliss; Igors Gavon; John Kuhner; Tom Ligon; Marian Mercer; Leland Palmer; Russ Thacker; Michael Valenti

Notes: [1] Added for tour 5/69.

4790 • YOURS, ANNE

OPENED: 10/13/1985   Theatre: Playhouse 91
Musical   Off-Broadway: 57

Composer: Michael Cohen
Lyricist: Enid Futterman
Librettist: Enid Futterman
Producer: John Flaxman
Director: Arthur Masella

Source: ANNE FRANK: THE DIARY OF A YOUNG GIRL (Book: Anne Frank); **Source:**

DIARY OF ANNE FRANK, THE (Play: Frances Goodrich; Albert Hackett); **Choreographer:** Helena Andreyko; **Costumes:** Judith Dolan; **Lighting Designer:** Beverly Emmons; **Musical Director:** Dan Strickland; **Orchestrations:** James Stenborg; **Set Design:** Franco Colavecchia

Songs: Dear Kitty: I Am a Woman; Dear Kitty: I Am Longing; Dear Kitty: I Am Thirteen Years Old; Dear Kitty: I Have a Nicer Side; Dear Kitty: I Still Believe; Dear Kitty: In the Night; Dear Kitty: It's a Dangerous Adventure; Dear Kitty: It's a New Year; Dear Kitty: My Sweet Secret; Dear Kitty: We Live with Fear; First Chanukah Night, The; For the Children; Hollywood; I Remember; I Think Myself Out; I'm Not a Jew; My Wife; Nightmare; Ordinary Day, An; Prologue; Schlal; She Doesn't Understand Me; Something to Get Up For; They Don't Have To; We're Here; When We Are Free; Writer, A

Cast: Betty Aberlin; Trini Alvarado; David Cady; Merwin Goldsmith; George Guidall; Hal Robinson; Ann Talman; Dana Zeller- Alexis

4791 • YOURS, EVER YOURS

Notes: *See EVER YOURS.*

4792 • YOURS IS MY HEART

OPENED: 09/05/1946   Theatre: Shubert
Musical   Broadway: 36

Composer: Franz Lehar
Lyricist: Ira Cobb; Karl Farkas; Harry Graham
Librettist: Ira Cobb; Karl Farkas; Harry Graham
Producer: Arthur Spitz
Director: Theodore Bache; Monroe Manning

Source: DAS LAND DES LACHELNS (Musical: Ludwig Herzer; Franz Lehar; Fritz Lohner-Beda); **Choreographer:** Henry Shwarze; **Costumes:** H.A. Condell; **Lighting Designer:** Milton Lowe; **Musical Director:** George Schick; **Set Design:** H.A. Condell

Songs: Beneath the Window of My Love [1]; Chinese Ceremony; Chinese Melody; Chingo-Pingo; Cup of China Tea, A; Free As the Air; Goodbye, Paree; I Love You, You Love Me [1]; Love, What Has Given You This Magic Power?; Ma Petite Cherie (The Land of Smiles); Men of China; Paris Sings Again (C: Paul

Durant); Patiently Smiling; Sad at Heart Am I [1]; Upon a Moonlight Night in May; Wedding Ceremony; You Are My Heart's Delight [1]; Yours Is My Heart Alone; Zig, Zig, Zig [1]

Cast: Stella Andreva; Alexander D'Arcy; Fred Keating; Richard Tauber; Sammy White

Notes: [1] In original London (LAND OF SMILES) or German productions.

4793 • YOURS TRULY

OPENED: 01/25/1927   Theatre: Shubert
Musical   Broadway: 127

Composer: Raymond Hubbell
Lyricist: Anne Caldwell
Librettist: Clyde North
Producer: Gene Buck
Director: Paul Dickey

Choreographer: Ralph Reader; **Costumes:** Mabel E. Johnston; **Musical Director:** Raymond Hubbell; **Set Design:** Joseph Urban

Songs: Dawn of Dreams; Don't Shake My Tree; Fearfully, Frightful Love [1]; Follow the Guide; Googly, Googly, Goos; Gunman, The [1]; High Yaller; I Want a Pal; Jade; Look at the World and Smile; Lotus Flower, The; Mary Has a Little Fair; Mayfair; Open Door Club; Quit Kiddin'; Shuffling Bill; Somebody Else; Yours Truly

Cast: Irene Dunne; Leon Errol; Jack Squires; Tiller Girls, The

Notes: [1] Sheet music only.

4794 • YVETTE

OPENED: 08/10/1916   Theatre: 39th St.
Musical   Broadway: 4

Composer: Frederick Herendeen
Lyricist: Frederick Herendeen
Librettist: Benjamin Thorpe Gilbert
Producer: Paul Benedek
Director: M. Ring

Musical Director: Arthur Gutman; **Orchestrations:** Arthur Gutman

Songs: American Beauties; Galloping Major; I Love You So; I Want All the Boys; Just One More Kiss;

Love Holds Sway; Love's Serenade; Modern Melody, A; Opening Chorus; Silly Ass; Since I Met You; Some Girls; Someone Just Like You; St. Cyr March; Summer Night; Tick-Tick; Wimmens; Wonderful Kiss

Cast: Chapine; Rose La Harte; Rena Parker; Eugene Redding

Notes: Interpolated songs by Hanley and Jackson not credited in program.

4795 • YVONNE

OPENED: 05/22/1926   Theatre: Daly's
Musical   London: 280

Composer: Vernon Duke
Lyricist: Percy Greenbank
Librettist: Percy Greenbank
Producer: George Edwardes
Director: Herbert Mason

Source: USCHI (Musical: Jean Gilbert; Leon Kastner; Alfred Moller); **Choreographer:** Fred A. Leslie; **Costumes:** De Veville; **Musical Director:** Arthur Wood

Songs: All Men Are the Same; Billing and Cooing (C: Jean Gilbert; Brother and Sister (C: Rex Kerwell; L: Percy Greenbank); Charming Weather (Opening); Day Dreams; Don't Forget the Waiter; Finale Act I (C: Jean Gilbert); Finale Act II (Jean Gilbert); I Love the Charleston (C: Edmund Eysler); It's Nicer to Be Naughty; Lucky; Magic of the Moon, The; One of the Things I Don't Profess to Know (C: Arthur Wood); Oom Ta-ra-ra (C: Marc Anthony); Opening Act II (C: Jean Gilbert); Teach Me to Dance (C: Marc Anthony; L: Harry Graham); Temperament (C: Jean Gilbert); Wake Up (C: Jean Gilbert); We Always Disagree; Yvonne (L: Jean Gilbert)

Cast: Mark Lester; Hal Sherman; Ivy Tresmand

Notes: No program available.

Z

4796 • ZAPATA

OPENED: 09/17/1980
Musical   Closed out of town

Composer: Perry Botkin Jr.; Harry Nilsson
Lyricist: Perry Botkin Jr.; Harry Nilsson
Librettist: Allan Katz
Producer: Goodspeed Opera House
Director: Bert Convy

Source: UNKNOWN (Play: Rafael Bunuel);
  Choreographer: Dan Siretta; **Costumes:** David
  Toser; **Dance Arranger:** Russell Warner;
  Lighting Designer: Peter M. Ehrnhardt; **Musical
  Director:** Lynn Crigler; **Orchestrations:** Bill
  Stafford; **Set Design:** John Jensen

Songs: Bedsprings; Big White Horse; Fiesta; I Got
  It; Mexico City; Mi Amigo; Nice Girls; Stand By
  Me; These Are the Brave; This Means War; Up
  the Revolution

Cast: Shawn Elliott; Pierre Epstein; Gary Gage;
  Larry Gelman; Stephen Hanan; Richard Karron;
  Bobbi Jo Lathan; Reni Santoni; Norman Snow

Notes: Goodspeed Opera House.

4797 • ZAZA

OPENED: 1899   Theatre: Weber & Fields'
                                      Music Hall
Musical   Broadway

Composer: John Stromberg
Lyricist: Edgar Smith
Librettist: Edgar Smith
Producer: Lew Fields; Joseph Weber

Cast: Lew Fields; Joseph Weber

Notes: No program available.

4798 • ZENDA

OPENED: 08/05/1963
Musical   Closed out of town

Composer: Vernon Duke
Lyricist: Martin Charnin
Librettist: Everett Freeman
Producer: Edwin Lester; San Francisco Civic Light
  Opera
Director: George Schaefer

Source: PRISONER OF ZENDA, THE (Novel:
  Anthony Hope); **Choreographer:** Jack Cole;
  Costumes: Miles White; **Dance Arranger:**
  Harper MacKay; **Lighting Designer:** Klaus
  Holm; **Musical Director:** Pembroke Davenport;
  Orchestrations: Irwin Kostal; **Set Design:** Harry
  Horner; **Vocal Arranger:** Irwin Kostal

Songs: Alive at Last; Alone at Night (L: Leonard
  Adelson); Announcement/Rehearsal (inst.);
  Artists (L: Sid Kuller); Athena (L: Unknown);
  Athena's Dance (inst.); Bird That Never Learned
  to Fly, A; Born at Last; Bounce; Breakfast for Two;
  Business or Pleasure; Charming Waltz (inst.);
  Come to Me; Command Performance
  (L: Unknown); Count the Stars (L: Leonard
  Adelson); Elusive Mr. Rassendyl, The (L: Leonard
  Adelson; Sid Kuller); Enchanting Girls [1] (L: Sid
  Kuller); Festive March (inst.); Flavia (inst.); For
  the Common Good of Mankind (L: Unknown);
  Gift for Each Day of the Week, A (L: Leonard
  Adelson); Gift of Love, A; Gift of Time, A
  (L: Leonard Adelson); Girls (L: Unknown); Girls
  and Rassendyl (L: Unknown); Happy Horns and
  Merry Bells (L: Leonard Adelson; Sid Kuller);
  He Wouldn't Dare; Hello!, Must Do a Show,
  Goodbye! (L: Leonard Adelson; Sid Kuller); Here
  and There; I Won't Stand in Your Way; I Wonder
  What He Meant By That (L: Leonard Adelson);
  I'll Marry a Soldier; Introducing Mr. Rassendyl
  (inst.); It Does Not (L: Leonard Adelson); It's a
  Quaint Little Custom (L: Leonard Adelson);
  Kings and Cabbages; Let Her Not Be Beautiful;
  Love Is the Worst Possible Thing; Loveless You
  and Hateful Me (L: Sid Kuller); Magic Music
  (inst.); Man Loves Me, The; Mazurka, The (inst.);
  Montage Poster (inst.); Morning You Were Born,
  The; My Heart Has Come a Tumbling Down; My
  Royal Majesty (L: Leonard Adelson; Martin
  Charnin); My Son in Law the King (L: Unknown);
  National Anthem; Never Let Them Know What's

Going On (L: Unknown); Night Is Filled with
Wonderful Sounds, The; No Ifs! No Ands! No
Buts!; No More Love; Now the World Begins
Again (L: Leonard Adelson); Old Friend
(L: Leonard Adelson); On My Own
(L: Unknown); One Night Ago (L: Unknown);
Organization (L: Leonard Adelson); Our Usual
Place (L: Unknown); Patroness of Art (L: Sid
Kuller); Pull a Rabbit Out of the Hat (L: Leonard
Adelson); Queen Mother's Crossover (inst.);
Royal Confession, A (L: Sid Kuller); Segue to
Palace (inst.); Sign on the Dotted Line (L: Leonard
Adelson); Something New (L: Leonard Adelson);
Thanks to Love (L: Leonard Adelson; Sid Kuller);
That Man Loves Me (L: Unknown); That Was
Then, Mr. Rassendyl; That's the Way It Goes
(L: Unknown); There Are Girls (L: Leonard
Adelson); There Is Nothing Like a Wedding;
There's Nothing Wrong with Marriage; There's
Room for Her; Too Beautiful Tonight
(L: Unknown); Tour de Force (L: Sid Kuller);
Train Music (inst.); Trust In Me (L: Leonard
Adelson); Turlututu (L: Vernon Duke); Verdi
Duo (inst.); Vernon Duccini (inst.); Waltz Fantasy
(inst.); We; We Just Might (L: Leonard Adelson);
Wedding March (inst.); What Does One Do?;
When Athena Dances (inst.); When You Stop and
Think; Whole Lot of Happy, A; Why Not?; Wine
Is Mine, The (L: Leonard Adelson); Words,
Words, Words! [1] (L: Sid Kuller); Yesterday's
Forgotten; You Are All That's Beautiful
(L: Unknown); You Took My Breath Away
(L: Unknown); You're Not at All Like You;
You're Not Old Enough (L: Leonard Adelson);
Zarape (Antoinette's Dance) (inst.); Zenda
(L: Leonard Adelson)

Cast: Alfred Drake; Truman Gaige; Earl
Hammond; Carmen Mathews; Chita Rivera;
Anne Rogers

Notes: [1] Same music.

4799 • ZIEGFELD A NIGHT AT THE FOLLIES

OPENED: 1991
Musical   Closed out of town

Librettist: Dallett Norris
Producer: Troika Organization, The
Director: Joe Leonardo

Arrangements: John Mezzio; David Siegel;
Choreographer: Kathryn Kendall; Costumes:

Nanzi Adzima; Theoni V. Aldredge; Lighting
Designer: Charles Houghton; Musical Director:
John Mezzio; Orchestrations: John Mezzio;
David Siegel; Set Design: Jeffrey Schneider

Songs: Destination Broadway (C: Bryon Sommers;
L: David Zippel); Do the New York (C: Ben
Oakland; L: J.P. Murray; Barry Trivers); Easy to
Love (C/L: Cole Porter); Find Me a Primitive
Man (C/L: Cole Porter); Girl for Each Month of
the Year A (C: Louis A. Hirsch; L: Channing
Pollock; Rennold Wolf); Girl on the Magazine
Cover, The (C/L: Irving Berlin); Harlem Waltz,
The (C: Walter Kent; L: Richard Jerome); Hat
Song, The (C: Maurice Levi; L: Harry B. Smith);
I Only Have Eyes for You (C: Harry Warren;
L: Al Dubin); If You Knew Susie (C: Joseph
Meyer; L: B.G. DeSylva); It's Only a Paper Moon
(C: Harold Arlen; L: E.Y. "Yip" Harburg; Billy
Rose); Lost Liberty Blues (C/L: Cole Porter);
Meet Me Tonight in Dreamland (C: Leo
Friedman; L: Beth Slater Whitson); Most
Gentlemen Don't Like Love (C/L: Cole Porter);
My Baby Just Cares for Me (C: Gus Kahn;
L: Walter Donaldson); My Old Flame (C: Arthur
Johnson; L: Sam Coslow); Object of My
Affection, The (C/L: Jimmy Grier; Coy Poe;
Pinky Tomlin); Oh, You Beautiful Doll (C: Nat D.
Ayer; L: A. Seymour Brown); Poor Butterfly
(C: John L. Golden; L: Raymond Hubbell); Pretty
Girl Is Like a Melody, A (C/L: Irving Berlin);
Shaking the Blues Away (C/L: Irving Berlin); So
Long! Oo-Long (C: Harry Ruby; L: Harry
Kalmar); Stairway to the Stars (C: Matt Malneck;
Frank Signorelli; L: Mitchell Parish); Taking a
Chance on Love (C: Vernon Duke; L: Ted Fetter;
John Latouche); They All Need a Little Hot-Cha
(C: Ray Henderson; L: Lew Brown); Too
Marvelous for Words (C: Richard A. Whiting;
L: Johnny Mercer); Toy Trumpet, The
(C: Raymond Scott; L: Sidney D. Mitchell; Lew
Pollack); What'll I Do (C/L: Irving Berlin); Who?
(C: Jerome Kern; L: Oscar Hammerstein II; Otto
Harbach); You Cannot Make Your Shimmy
Shake on Tea (C/L: Irving Berlin; Rennold Wolf);
You Stepped Out of a Dream (C: Nacio Herb
Brown; L: Gus Kahn)

Cast: Carole Cianelli; Bruce C. Ewing; Paul
Finocchiaro; A.J. Graham; Karlah Hamilton;
Catherine Hart; David Nehls; Kathy Reid; Michael
Lee Scott; Michael Shiles; Judy A. Walstrum

Notes: This show toured the country with sets and
costumes from the British show ZIEGFELD.

4800 • ZIEGFELD AMERICAN REVUE OF 1926.

Notes: *See NO FOOLIN'.*

4801 • ZIEGFELD FOLLIES OF 1907

OPENED: 07/08/1907   Theatre: Jardin de Paris
Revue   Broadway: 70

Librettist: Harry B. Smith
Producer: Florenz Ziegfeld
Director: Herbert Gresham

Choreographer: Julian Mitchell; **Costumes:** Mme. Freisinger; W.H. Matthews; **Set Design:** John H. Young

Songs: Alabama Sam [3]; Band Box Girl, The (C: Seymour Furth; L: Edgar Selden); Bridget Salome [2]; Budweiser's a Friend of Mine (C: Seymour Furth; L: Vincent Bryan); Bye, Bye Dear Old Broadway (C: Gus Edwards; L: Will D. Cobb); Cigarette [4] (C: Gertrude Hoffman; L: Vincent Bryan); Come and Float Me Freddie Dear (C: E. Ray Goetz; L: Vincent Bryan); Come Down Salomy Jane [5] (C: E. Ray Goetz; L: Vincent Bryan); Fencing Girls, The [1]; Foolish Song, A [1]; Gibson Bathing Girls, The (C: Alfred Solman; L: Paul West); Handle Me with Care (C: Jean Schwartz; L: William Jerome); Heart Breaker, The [3]; I Don't Want an Auto (C: Seymour Furth; L: William Jerome); I Think I Oughtn't Auto Any More (C: E. Ray Goetz; L: William Jerome); I Want to Be a Drummer Boy (C: Silvio Hein; L: Matt Woodward); If We Knew What the Milkman Knows [5] (C: E. Ray Goetz; L: Vincent Bryan); Imaginary Man, The [3]; In the Surf; Jiu Jitsu Waltz; Little of Everything, A [3]; Man Who Built the Subway, The [4] (C: Gertrude Hoffman; L: Vincent Bryan); Miss Ginger of Jamaica (C/L: Billy Gaston); Oh Marie [1]; On the Grand Old Sands [3] (C: Gus Edwards; L: Will D. Cobb); Pocahontas (C: Seymour Furth; L: Edgar Selden); Re-Incarnation (C: E. Ray Goetz; L: Vincent Bryan); That's How We Met the Girl [5] (C: E. Ray Goetz; L: Vincent Bryan); They All Look Alike to Mary [2]; Whistle If You Want Me Dear [3]

Cast: Nora Bayes; George Bickel; Helen Broderick; Emma Carus; Mlle. Dazie; Grace LaRue; Dave Lewis; Charles J. Ross; Marion Sunshine; Florence Tempest; Prince Tokio; Harry Watson Jr.

Notes: [1] Out Boston 9/30/07. [2] Out of town 11/4/07. [3] Out Kansas City 10/4/08. [4] Not in programs. [5] ASCAP only.

4802 • ZIEGFELD FOLLIES OF 1908

OPENED: 06/15/1908   Theatre: Jardin de Paris
Revue   Broadway: 120

Composer: Maurice Levi
Lyricist: Harry B. Smith
Librettist: Harry B. Smith
Producer: Florenz Ziegfeld
Director: Herbert Gresham

Choreographer: Julian Mitchell; **Costumes:** Alfredo Edel; Mme. Freisinger; Hafleigh; W.H. Matthews; **Lighting Designer:** Tony Greshoff; **Musical Director:** Frederic Solomon; **Set Design:** John H. Young

Songs: As You Walk Down the Strand [2]; Be Good [2]; Big Hats, The (Hat Song); Duchess of Table D'Hote; Follow the Flag [4]; Girls I Left Behind, The [4]; I Wonder If They're All True to Me [3]; International Merry Widow, The; Let's Get the Umpire's Goat [1] (C/L: Nora Bayes; Jack Norworth); Mosquito Song; Nell Brinkley Girl, The; Nothing Ever Ever Ever Hardly Ever Troubles Me (C: Albert Von Tilzer; L: Jack Norworth); Over on the Jersey Side [4] (C/L: Jack Norworth); Rajah of Broadway, The; Sextette [6]; Shine on Harvest Moon [5] (C/L: Jack Norworth; C: Nora Bayes); Since Mother Was a Girl (C: Albert Von Tilzer; L: Jack Norworth); Sing Me a Come All Ye (Like My Daddy Sang to Me) [4] (C/L: Jack Norworth; C: Nora Bayes); Society [2]; Song of the Navy [2]; Take Me 'Round in a Taxicab (C: Melville Gideon; L: Edgar Selden); That's All [2]; Titles; Wax Works [6]; When the Girl You Love Is Loving You (C: Jean Schwartz; L: William Jerome); You Will Have to Sing an Irish Song (C: Albert Von Tilzer; L: Jack Norworth)

Cast: Nora Bayes; Barney Bernard; George Bickel; Mlle. Dazie; Arthur Deagon; Rosie Green; Lee Harrison; Grace LaRue; Grace Leigh; Mae Murray; Jack Norworth; William Powers; Billie Reeves; William C. Schrode; Gertrude Vanderbilt; Florence Walton; Harry Watson; Lucy Weston

Notes: [1] Also in ZIEGFELD FOLLIES OF 1909. Some sources only credit Norworth alone. Out

Boston 4/26/09. [2] Not in programs. [3] Out Boston 4/26/09. [4] Out Boston 1/11/08. [5] Also in MISS INNOCENCE. [6] Sheet music only.

4803 • ZIEGFELD FOLLIES OF 1909
OPENED: 06/14/1909   Theatre: Jardin de Paris
Revue   Broadway: 64

Composer: Maurice Levi
Lyricist: Harry B. Smith
Librettist: Harry B. Smith
Producer: Florenz Ziegfeld
Director: Herbert Gresham; Julian Mitchell

Choreographer: Julian Mitchell; **Costumes:** Alfredo Edel; W.H. Matthews; **Musical Director:** Frederic Solomon; **Set Design:** John H. Young

Songs: And the World Keeps Rolling Along; Bathing Girls, The; Blarney (C/L: Nora Bayes; Jack Norworth); By the Light of the Silvery Moon (C: Gus Edwards; L: Edward Madden); Christy Girl, The; Come On and Play Ball with Me (C: Gus Edwards; L: Edward Madden); Dance de Maitre de Ballet; Dance of the Parisian Twist, The; Dance of the Widow Mexetexa (C: Lewis F. Muir); Dear Old Father [2] (C/L: Nora Bayes; Jack Norworth); Falling Stars (C/L: Nora Bayes; Jack Norworth); Go As Far As You Like; Greatest Navy in the World, The; Hindoo Honey; I Don't Care (C: Harry O. Sutton; L: Jean Lenox); I Wish I Was a Boy and I Wish I Was a Girl [1] (C/L: Nora Bayes; Jack Norworth); I'm After Madame Tetrazzini's Job (C/L: Gus Edwards); It's Nothing but a Bubble; Let's Get the Umpire's Goat [5] (C/L: Nora Bayes; Jack Norworth); Linger Longer, Lingerie; Love in the Springtime [4]; Mad Opera House (C/L: Nora Bayes; Jack Norworth); Madame Venus (Take a Tip from Venus); Moving Day in Jungle Town (C: Nat D. Ayer; L: A. Seymour Brown); My Cousin Carus [3] (C: Gus Edwards; L: Edward Madden); Play That Fandango Rag (C: Lewis F. Muir; L: E. Ray Goetz); Roosevelt of Germany; Rulers of the Earth; Sextette; That Aero-Naughty Girl [6]; Up! Up! Up! in My Aeroplane (C: Gus Edwards; L: Edward Madden); What Every Woman Knows

Cast: Nora Bayes; William Bonelli; Bessie Clayton; Arthur Deagon; Harry Kelly; Lillian Lorraine; Mae Murray; Jack Norworth; Eva Tanguay; Sophie Tucker; Gertrude Vanderbilt; Annabelle Whitford

Notes: [1] Also called "I'm Glad, I'm Glad." [2] Also called "Poor Old Dad." [3] From MISS INNOCENCE. [4] Not in program. [5] Cut from ZIEGFELD FOLLIES OF 1908. [6] Sheet music only.

4804 • ZIEGFELD FOLLIES OF 1910
OPENED: 06/20/1910   Theatre: Jardin de Paris
Revue   Broadway: 88

Composer: Gus Edwards
Lyricist: Harry B. Smith
Librettist: Harry B. Smith
Producer: Florenz Ziegfeld
Director: Julian Mitchell

Costumes: Crage; W.H. Matthews; **Musical Director:** Frank Darling; **Set Design:** Ernest Albert; John H. Young

Songs: Believe Me [1]; Chicken Thief Man, The; Cock of the Walk, The; Come Along Mandy; Constantly [1] (C: Bert Williams; L: James Henry Burris; Chris Smith); Cuban Glide, The [7]; Dance of the Grizzly Bear, The (C: George Botsford; L: Irving Berlin); Don't Take a Girl Down to Coney (L: Will D. Cobb); Fandango Rag [4] (C: Lewis F. Muir; L: E. Ray Goetz); Franco American Rag [7] (C/L: Unknown); Good Bye Becky Cohen [8] (C/L: Irving Berlin); I Love It Rag [7] (C: Harry Von Tilzer; L: Addison Burkhardt); I Thought He Was a Business Man [7]; I'll Get You Yet (C: Von Tilzer; L: Addison Burkhardt); I'll Lend You Everything I've Got Except My Wife [5] (C: Harry Von Tilzer; L: Jean C. Havez); I'm in Love with You [7]; In the Evening [1]; Kidland (L: Will D. Cobb); Late Hours [5]; Look Me Over Carefully and Tell Me Will I Do (L: Will D. Cobb); Lovie Joe (C: Joe Jordan; L: Will Marion Cook); Ma Blushin' Rosie [9] (C: John Stromberg; L: Edgar Smith); Mister Earth and His Comet Love (The Comet and the Earth); My Yiddish Colleen [7] (L: Edward Madden); Nix on the Glow-Worm, Lena! [6] (C: Harry Carroll; L: Ballard Macdonald); Nobody [5] (C: Bert Williams; L: Alex Rogers); Our American Colleges; Pensacola Mooch, The (C: Ford Dabney; L: Will Marion Cook); Play That Barbershop Chord [5] (C: Lewis F. Muir; L: William Tracey); Rosalie [10] (C: Gus Edwards; L: Will D. Cobb); Rosey Posey [7]; Sadie Salome Go Home [5] (C/L: Irving Berlin; Edgar Leslie); Sweet Kitty Bellairs; Swing Me High, Swing Me Low (C: Victor Hollander;

L: Ballard Macdonald); Telephone Your Riffky Issey [2]; That Horrible Hobble Skirt [5]; That Minor Strain [5] (C: Ford Dabney; L: Cecil Mack); Vision of Salome (inst.) [11] (C: Archibald. Joyce); Waltzing Lieutenant, The; What Has Become of the Girls I Used to Know (C: Gus Edwards); Woman's Dream, A; Yankiana Rag [3] (C: Ludwig Englander); You're Gwine to Get Something What You Don't Have [5] (C: Harry Von Tilzer; L: Jean Havez)

Cast: George Bickel; Fanny Brice; Lillian Lorraine; Vera Maxwell; Bobby North; Billie Reeves; Grace Tyson; Harry Watson; Bert Williams

Notes: [1] Out Nebraska 5/23/10. [2] Out Boston 2/20/11. [3] From MISS INNOCENCE. [4] From ZIEGFELD FOLLIES OF 1909. [5] Not in programs. [6] Titled "Nix on the Concertina Lena" in some programs. In program of 8/22/10 it was credited to Ball and Macdonald. ASCAP credits this song to Edwards and Smith. The sheet music credits to as above. [7] Added after opening. [8] May not be by Berlin. [9] Not in programs. From FIDDLE DEE DEE. [10] Added after opening. From THE WIZARD OF OZ. [11] Sheet music only.

4805 • ZIEGFELD FOLLIES OF 1911

OPENED: 06/26/1911   Theatre: Jardin de Paris
Revue   Broadway: 80

Composer: Raymond Hubbell; Maurice Levi
Lyricist: George V. Hobart
Librettist: George V. Hobart
Producer: Florenz Ziegfeld
Director: Julian Mitchell

Choreographer: Jack Mason; Gus Sohlke; **Costumes:** W.H. Matthews; **Set Design:** Ernest Albert; Unitt & Wickes

Songs: Bumble Bee [5] (C: James B. Blyer; L: Donnelly; Jean Havez); Cakewalk (inst.) [3] (C: Raymond Hubbell); Doggone That Chili Man [1] (C/L: Irving Berlin); Ephraham Played Upon the Piano [1] (C: Irving Berlin; L: Vincent Bryan); Girl in Pink, The (C: Raymond Hubbell); How Would You Like to Be My Pony? [3] (C: Raymond Hubbell); I'm a Crazy Daffydill (C: Jerome Kern; L: Bessie McCoy); Imitation Rag, The; It Was Me [3] (C: Seymour Furth; L: George W. Day); My Beautiful Lady [4] (C: Ivan Caryll; L: C.M.S. McLellan); New York

(You're the Best Town in Europe) (C: Raymond Hubbell; L: Raymond W. Peck); Pots and Pans [3] (C: Jean Schwartz; L: Charles Grapewin); Take Care, Little Girl, Take Care (C: Raymond Hubbell); Texas Tommy Swing (C/L: Sid Brown; Val Harris); That's Harmony [3] (C: Bert Williams; L: Grant Clarke); Turkey Gobbler's Ball [6] (C: James B. Blyer; L: Donnelly; Jean Havez); Whippoorwill (Never Again for Me) [3] (C: James Blyler; L: Fagan); Widow Wood, The (C: Maurice Levi; L: Channing Pollock; Rennold Wolf); Woodman, Woodman, Spare That Tree [1] (C: Irving Berlin; L: Vincent Bryan); You've Built a Fire Down in My Heart [2] (C/L: Irving Berlin)

Cast: Fanny Brice; Dolly Sisters, The; Leon Errol; Lillian Lorraine; Bessie McCoy; Harry Watson; George White; Bert Williams

Notes: [1] Originally in JARDIN DE PARIS. [2] Originally in JARDIN DE PARIS. Also in THE FASCINATING WIDOW. [3] Not in program. [4] Not in program. Also in THE PINK LADY. [5] This is not "Be My Little Baby Bumble Bee" by Henry Marshall and Stanley Murphy. [6] Sheet music only.

4806 • ZIEGFELD FOLLIES OF 1912

OPENED: 10/21/1912   Theatre: Moulin Rouge
Revue   Broadway: 88

Composer: Raymond Hubbell
Lyricist: Harry B. Smith
Librettist: Harry B. Smith
Producer: Florenz Ziegfeld
Director: Julian Mitchell

Costumes: Callot; **Musical Director:** Frank Darling; **Orchestrations:** Frank Saddler; **Set Design:** Ernest Albert

Songs: Beautiful, Beautiful Girl (L: John E. Hazzard); Blackberryin' To-day (C/L: Bert Williams); Borrow from Me [1]; Broadway Glide, The (C: Bert Grant; L: A. Seymour Brown); Coffee Mother Used to Make, The [1]; Daddy Has a Sweetheart and Mother Is Her Name [2] (C: Dave Stamper; L: Gene Buck); Dingle, Dingle, Dingle [1] (C: Con Conrad; Jay Whidden; L: Joe Young); Dip, Dip, Dip; Down in Dear Old New Orleans (C: Con Conrad; Jay Whidden; L: Joe Young); Good Night Nurse [1] (C: W. Raymond Walker; L: Thomas J. Gray); Good Old Circus Band; Hurry, Little Children; I Ain't No Fool [1];

I Should Worry [1]; In a Pretty Little Cottage; In a Pretty Little White House of Our Own (C: Leo Edwards; L: Blanche Merrill); Little Bit of Everything, A (C/L: Irving Berlin); Louisiana; Million, The; Mother Doesn't Know; My Landlady [1]; My Little Lady Bug [1]; Romantic Girl; Row, Row, Row (C: James V. Monaco; L: William Jerome); Society Circus Parade (C: Dave Stamper; L: Gene Buck); Society Circus Parade (inst.); Some Boy [2] (C: Dave Stamper; L: Gene Buck); Stage Door Number; That Shakespearian Rag [3] (C: Dave Stamper; L: Gene Buck; Herman Ruby); That Wonderful Tune [4] (C: Jean Schwartz; L: Grant Clarke); There's One in a Million Like You (C: Jean Schwartz; L: Grant Clarke); When You Meet Them on Broadway [1]; Yodel Song; You Gotta Keep Movin' and Dance (You Gotta Keep A' Going); You Might As Well Stay on Broadway; You Should Have Most Everything [1]; You're a Great Big, Blue-Eyed Baby Boy [1] (C/L: A. Seymour Brown); You're on the Right Road [1]

Cast: Elizabeth Brice; Leon Errol; Bernard Granville; Lillian Lorraine; Rae Samuels; Harry Watson; Bert Williams

Notes: [1] Out Philadelphia 10/7/12. [2] Not in programs. [3] Out Philadelphia 10/7/12. *See PASSING SHOW OF 1915* for "The Shakespeare Rag." [4] Sheet music only.

4807 • ZIEGFELD FOLLIES OF 1913

OPENED: 06/16/1913   Theatre: New Amsterdam
Revue   Broadway: 96

Composer: Raymond Hubbell
Lyricist: George V. Hobart
Librettist: George V. Hobart
Producer: Florenz Ziegfeld
Director: Julian Mitchell

Costumes: Schneider & Anderson; **Lighting Designer:** Frank Detering; **Musical Director:** Frank Darling; **Set Design:** Ernest Albert; Frank Gates; E.A. Morange; John H. Young

Songs: Bye and Bye You Will Miss Me [1] (C: Dave Stamper; L: Gene Buck); Cupid's Dart (C: Louis Dannenberg); Dance Classiceccentrique; Everybody Sometime Must Love Somebody (C: Dave Stamper; L: Gene Buck); Going There; Good-Bye My Tango [4]; He's So Good (C: Dave Stamper; L: Gene Buck); Hello, Honey; I Can

Live without You [3] (C: Dave Stamper; L: Gene Buck); If a Table at Rector's Could Talk (L: Will D. Cobb); In the Cradle of Love [2] (C/L: J. Leubrie Hill); Isle D'Amour (C: Leo Edwards; L: Earl Carroll); Just You and I and the Moon (C: Dave Stamper; L: Gene Buck); Katie Rooney; Little Love, a Little Kiss, A [1] (C: Leo Silesu; L: Nilson Fysher; Adrian Ross); New York, What's the Matter with You?; On Her Veranda [4] (C: Ethel Ponce; L: Phil L. Ponce); Panama; Peg O' My Heart [1] (C: Fred Fisher; L: Alfred Bryan); Ragtime Suffragette, The; Rebecca of Sunnybook Farm [3] (C: Albert Gumble; L: A. Seymour Brown); Sleep Time, My Honey; Tangoitis Dance; Turkish Trotteshness; Without You (C: Dave Stamper; L: Gene Buck); You Must Have Experience; You're Never Too Old to Love [1] (C: Albert Gumble; L: Alfred Bryan; William Jerome); You're Some Girl

Cast: Elizabeth Brice; Leon Errol; Ann Pennington; Frank Tinney; Nat Wills

Notes: [1] Out Boston 10/20/13. [2] Out Indianapolis 1/19/14. [3] Not in program. [4] Sheet music only.

4808 • ZIEGFELD FOLLIES OF 1914

OPENED: 06/01/1914   Theatre: New Amsterdam
Revue   Broadway: 112

Composer: Raymond Hubbell; Dave Stamper
Lyricist: Gene Buck
Librettist: George V. Hobart
Producer: Florenz Ziegfeld
Director: Leon Errol

Costumes: Cora MacGeachy; **Musical Director:** Frank Darling; **Set Design:** William H. Matthews

Songs: At the Ball [5] (C/L: J. Leubrie Hill); Baby Love [3] (C: Harry Von Tilzer; L: Paul Cunningham; George Whiting); Be Careful What You Do; Because I Can't Tango; Darktown Poker Club [2]; Futurist Girl, The (C: Dave Stamper); Good Night (C: Dave Stamper); Goodnight Mirster Hurdy-Gurdy Man; If You Dance Dear, I Know a Cabaret [4] (C: Raymond Hubbell; L: George V. Hobart); I'm a Statesman [3]; I'm Cured [3] (C: Bert Williams; L: Jean Havez); I've Got Him Now! (C: Dave Stamper); Keep Your Love for Me (Save Your Love for Me) [1] (C: Raymond Hubbell); Lone Star Girl, The; Man Who Wrote "The Vampire" Must Have Known

My Wife [2] (C: Bert Williams; L: Gene Buck; Earle C. Jones); My Little Pet Chicken (L: George V. Hobart); Neptune's Daughter [2] (C: Jean Schwartz; L: Grant Clarke); Night Life in Old Manhattan; Nobody Seems to Know; Nothing to Wear (C: Dave Stamper); Nut Sundae, A; Prunella Mine (C: Dave Stamper); Put Your Lovin' Arms Around Me, Dearie [2]; Rock Me in the Cradle of Love (C/L: J. Leubrie Hill); Tango Brazilian Dreams; Tangorilla; There's Something in the Air in Springtime (C: Dave Stamper); Underneath the Japanese Moon [1] (C: Walter Gustave Haenschen); When the Ragtime Army Goes Away to War (C/L: A. Seymour Brown); Wonderful Garden of Love [2] (C: Dave Stamper)

Cast: Arthur Deagon; Leon Errol; Rita Gould; Kay Laurell; Vera Michelena; Ann Pennington; Gertrude Vanderbilt; Bert Williams; Ed Wynn

Notes: [1] Added after opening. [2] Not in program. [3] ASCAP/Library of Congress only. [4] Sheet music only. [5] Originally in MY FRIEND FROM KENTUCKY.

4809 • ZIEGFELD FOLLIES OF 1915

OPENED: 06/21/1915   Theatre: New Amsterdam
Revue   Broadway: 104

Composer: Louis A. Hirsch; Dave Stamper
Lyricist: Channing Pollock; Dave Stamper; Rennold Wolf
Librettist: Gene Buck; Channing Pollock; Rennold Wolf
Producer: Florenz Ziegfeld
Director: Leon Errol; Julian Mitchell

Costumes: Lady Duff-Gordon; **Musical Director:** Frank Darling; **Set Design:** Joseph Urban

Songs: Arabia My Land of Sweet Romance [1] (C: J. Frederick Hanley; L: Bernard Granville); Bird of a Chicken, The (dance); Bowling [1]; Every-body Dance [1] (C: Dave Stamper; L: Gene Buck); Girl for Each Month in the Year, A; Hello, Frisco! (I Called You Up to Say Hello) (C: Louis A. Hirsch; L: Gene Buck); Hold Me in Your Loving Arms (C: Louis A. Hirsch; L: Gene Buck); I Can't Do Without Girls; I Love to Be Loved [1] (C: Dave Stamper; L: Gene Buck); If the Girlies Could Be Soldiers [1] (C: Dave Stamper; L: Gene Buck); I'll Be a Santa Claus to You (C: Louis A. Hirsch; L: Gene Buck); I'm a Nurse for Aching

Hearts [2] (C: Louis A. Hirsch; L: Gene Buck); I'm Neutral; In the Evening; Marie Odile (C: Louis A. Hirsch; L: Channing Pollock; Rennold Wolf); Midnight Frolic Glide (C: Dave Stamper; Will Vodery); My Little Submarine [1] (C: Dave Stamper; L: Louis A. Hirsch); My Radium Girl (C: Louis A. Hirsch; L: Gene Buck); My Zebra Lady Fair; Oriental Love; They're in the Junk Pile Now [1] (C: Dave Stamper; L: Gene Buck); Trilby [1] (C: Dave Stamper; L: Gene Buck); Twenty Years Ago; Under the Sea [2]; We'll Build a Little Home in the U.S.A. (C: Charles Elbert; L: Ward Wesley); Zebra Girl [2] (C: Dave Stamper; L: Gene Buck)

Cast: Ina Claire; Leon Errol; W.C. Fields; Bernard Granville; Justine Johnstone; Kay Laurell; Mae Murray; Ann Pennington; Carl Randall; Olive Thomas; George White; Bert Williams; Ed Wynn

Notes: [1] Sheet music only. [2] Not in programs.

4810 • ZIEGFELD FOLLIES OF 1916

OPENED: 06/12/1916   Theatre: New Amsterdam
Revue   Broadway: 104

Composer: Louis A. Hirsch
Lyricist: Gene Buck
Librettist: Gene Buck; George V. Hobart
Producer: Florenz Ziegfeld
Director: Ned Wayburn

Costumes: Lady Duff-Gordon; Cora MacGeachy; Alice O'Neil; **Musical Director:** Frank Darling; **Set Design:** Joseph Urban

Songs: Ain't It Funny What a Difference a Few Drinks Make [3] (C: Jerome Kern); Beautiful Island of Girls [4]; Dying Swan, The [5] (C: Leo Edwards; L: Blanche Merrill); Goodbye, Dear Old Bachelor Days; Hat, The [5] (C: Leo Edwards; L: Blanche Merrill); Have a Heart [3] (C: Jerome Kern); I Left Her on the Beach at Honolulu; I Want That Star [3] (L: George V. Hobart); In Florida Among the Palms [2] (C/L: Irving Berlin); I've Said Goodbye to Broadway (C: Dave Stamper); I've Saved All My Lovin' for You (C: Dave Stamper); Midnight Frolic Rag, The [3]; My Lady of the Nile (1) [1]; My Lady of the Nile (2) (C: Jerome Kern); Nijinksy [3] (C: Dave Stamper); Six Little Wives of the King; Somnambulistic Tune (C: Dave Stamper); Stop and Go; There's Ragtime in the Air (C: Dave

Stamper); Walking the Dog [1] (C: Eubie Blake; L: Noble Sissle); When the Lights Are Low [3] (C: Jerome Kern)

Cast: Don Barclay; Fanny Brice; Ina Claire; Marion Davies; W.C. Fields; Bernard Granville; Emma Haig; Sam Hardy; Justine Johnstone; Allyn King; Ann Pennington; Tot Qualters; Carl Randall; William Rock; Lilyan Tashman; Frances White; Bert Williams

Notes: Fanny Brice songs not identified in program but written by Blanche Merrill. [1] Not used. [2] Added after opening. [3] Cut after opening. [4] Music adapted from Lehar's GYPSY LOVE. [5] Not in programs. Sung by Brice.

4811 • ZIEGFELD FOLLIES OF 1917

OPENED: 06/12/1917   Theatre: New Amsterdam
Revue   Broadway: 111

Composer: Raymond Hubbell; Dave Stamper
Lyricist: Gene Buck
Librettist: Gene Buck; George V. Hobart
Producer Florenz Ziegfeld
Director: Ned Wayburn

Costumes: Lady Duff-Gordon; **Musical Director:** Frank Darling; **Set Design:** Joseph Urban

Songs: Auto Girls Song [1] (C: Raymond Hubbell); Beautiful Garden of Girls (C: Raymond Hubbell); Beautiful Girl, Goodbye (C: Dave Stamper); Can't You Hear Your Country Calling: The Spirit Calling (C: Victor Herbert); Chu, Chin, Chow (C: Dave Stamper); Egyptian [4] (C: Leo Edwards; L: Blanche Merrill); Hello, My Dearie! (C: Dave Stamper); Home Sweet Home (C/L: Ring Lardner); I Ain't Married No More [3] (C: Les Copeland; L: Rennold Wolf); I'll Be Somewhere in France (C: Raymond Hubbell); I'm So Happy (C: Turner Layton; L: Henry Creamer); Jealous Moon; Just Because You're You (Because You Are Just You) [2] (C: Jerome Kern); Just You and Me (C: Dave Stamper); Modern Maiden's Prayer, The (C: James F. Hanley; L: Ballard Macdonald); My Arabian Maid (C: Raymond Hubbell); Potato Bug, The [4] (C: Dave Stamper); Same Old Moon [4] (C: Dave Stamper); Spirit of the Garden (scene) (C: Victor Herbert); That's the Kind of Baby for Me, The (C: Jack Egan; L: Alfred Harriman); Unhappy (C: Turner Layton; L: Henry Creamer); Ziegfeld Follies Rag (C: Dave Stamper)

Cast: Fanny Brice; Walter Catlett; Dorothy Dickson; W.C. Fields; Irving Fisher; Peggy Hopkins; Carl Hyson; Allyn King; Lilyan Tashman; Bert Williams

Notes: [1] Sheet music only. [2] Originally in THE DOLL GIRL as "When Three Is Company" with lyrics by M.E. Rourke. [3] Out Philadelphia 11/5/17. [4] Not in program.

4812 • ZIEGFELD FOLLIES OF 1918

OPENED: 06/18/1918   Theatre: New Amsterdam
Revue   Broadway: 151

Composer: Louis A. Hirsch; Dave Stamper
Lyricist: Gene Buck
Librettist: Gene Buck; Rennold Wolf
Producer: Florenz Ziegfeld
Director: Ned Wayburn

Costumes: Croydon; Lady Duff-Gordon; Lucille; Schneider- Anderson; **Lighting Designer:** Ben Beerwald; **Musical Director:** Frank Darling; **Set Design:** Joseph Urban

Songs: Any Old Time at All (C: Louis A. Hirsch); Blue Devils of France (C/L: Irving Berlin); But After the Ball Was Over! (Then He Made Up for Lost Time) [1] (C/L: B.G. DeSylva; Arthur Jackson); Come on Papa [1] (C: Harry Ruby; L: Edgar Leslie); Dream, A (scene) (C: Victor Herbert); Garden of My Dreams, The (C: Louis A. Hirsch; Dave Stamper); I Want to Learn to Jazz Dance (C: Dave Stamper); If She Means What I Think She Means [1] (C: Arthur Jackson; L: B.G. DeSylva); I'm Gonna Pin My Medal on the Girl I Left Behind (C/L: Irving Berlin); I'm Making a Study of Beautiful Girls (and I'm Still in My A.B.C.'s) [1] (C/L: Eddie Cantor; Jack Glogau; Al Piantadosi); In Old Versailles (C: Louis A. Hirsch); Mine Was a Marriage of Convenience (C: Louis A. Hirsch); Oh How I Hate to Get Up in the Morning [4] (C/L: Irving Berlin); Poor Little Me; Save Your Money, John [2] (C: Eubie Blake; L: Noble Sissle); Starlight (C: Dave Stamper); Tackin' 'Em Down [1] (C: Albert Gumble; L: B.G. DeSylva); We Are the Follies [1]; We're Busy Building Boats (Ship Building Song) (C: Louis A. Hirsch); When I Hear a Syncopated Tune (C: Louis A. Hirsch); When I'm Looking at You (C: Dave Stamper); Would You Rather Be a Soldier with a Eagle on Your Shoulder or a Private with a Chicken on Your Knee? [3] (C: Archie Gottler; L: Sidney D. Mitchell)

Cast: Eddie Cantor; Frank Carter; Dolores; Fairbanks Twins, The; W.C. Fields; Joe Frisco; Harry Kelly; Allyn King; Kay Laurell; Lillian Lorraine; Marilyn Miller; Ann Pennington

Notes: [1] Sheet music only. [2] Not in program, however sheet music credits Les Copeland and Alex Rogers and places the song in the FOLLIES OF 1919. [3] Not in program. [4] Added three months after opening. Used in YIP! YIP! YAPHANK!

4813 • ZIEGFELD FOLLIES OF 1919

OPENED: 06/16/1919   Theatre: New Amsterdam
Revue   Broadway: 171

Composer: Irving Berlin
Lyricist: Irving Berlin
Librettist: Gene Buck; Dave Stamper; Rennold Wolf
Producer: Florenz Ziegfeld
Director: Ned Wayburn

Choreographer: Ned Wayburn; **Costumes:** Lady Duff-Gordon; Mme. Francis; Lucille; Cora MacGeachy; Alice O'Neil; **Lighting Designer:** Ben Beewald; **Musical Director:** Frank Darling; **Orchestrations:** Stephen Jones; **Set Design:** Joseph Urban

Songs: Bevo [2]; Bring Back Those Wonderful Days [4] (C/L: Nat Vincent; Darl MacBoyle); Checkers [4] (C: Paul Rubens; L: Billy Curtis); Circus Ballet, The (inst.) (C: Victor Herbert); Everybody Wants a Key to My Cellar [4] (L: Billy Baskette; Ed Rose); Follies Minstrel, The [5]; Follies Salad, The (C: Dave Stamper; L: Gene Buck); Goodbye Sunshine Hello Moon [7] (C: Dave Stamper; L: Gene Buck); Harem Life; How Ya' Gonna Keep 'Em Down on the Farm (After They've Seen Paree)? [4] (C: Walter Donaldson; L: Sam M. Lewis; Joe Young); I'd Rather See a Minstrel Show; I'm Sorry I Ain't Got It If I Had It You Could Have It Blues [4] (C: Ted Snyder; L: Sam M. Lewis; Joe Young); I'm the Guy Who Guards the Harem; I've Got My Captain Working for Me Now [4]; Look Out for the Bolsheviki Man [1]; Mandy [6]; My Baby's Arms (C: Harry Tierney; L: Joseph McCarthy); My Orchard of Girls [1]; My Tambourine Girl; Near Future, The; Oh, How She Can Sing [4] (C/L: Joe Schenck; Gus Van; Jack Yellen); Oh! The Last Rose of Summer [4] (C: Harry Ruby; L: Eddie Cantor; Manuel Ponce); Popular Pests,

The (C: Dave Stamper; L: Gene Buck); Pretty Girl Is Like a Melody, A; Prohibition; Save Your Money, John [1] (C: Les Copeland; L: Alex Rogers); Shimmy Town (C: Dave Stamper; L: Gene Buck); Skadatin-Dee [4] (C/L: Joe Schenck; Gus Van); Somebody [4] (C: James F. Hanley; L: Ballard Macdonald); Sweet Kisses [1] (C: Albert Von Tilzer; L: Lew Brown; Eddie Buzzell); Sweet Sixteen [5] (C: Dave Stamper; L: Gene Buck); Syncopated Cocktail, A; Tulip Time (C: Dave Stamper; L: Gene Buck); We Made the Doughnuts Over There; When the Moon Shines on the Moonshine (C: Robert Hood Bowers; L: Francis DeWitt); When They're Old Enough to Know Better It's Better to Leave Them Alone [4] (C: Harry Ruby; L: Sam M. Lewis; Joe Young); Willie or Will He Not [4] (C: Maurice Abrahams; L: Sam M. Lewis; Joe Young); World Has Gone Shimmy Mad, The [7] (C: Dave Stamper; L: Gene Buck); You Cannot Make Your Shimmy Shake on Tea (L: Irving Berlin; Rennold Wolf); You Don't Need the Wine to Have a Wonderful Time [4] (C: Harry Akst; L: Howard Rogers); You'd Be Surprised [3]

Cast: Delyle Alda; Eddie Cantor; Johnny Dooley; Ray Dooley; Eddie Dowling; Fairbanks Twins, The; Mary Hay; Marilyn Miller; Joe Schenck; John Steel; Gus Van; Bert Williams

Notes: [1] Sheet music only. [2] Sheet music only. Previously in YIP! YIP! YAPHANK! and THIS IS THE ARMY. [3] Added after opening. Later in SHUBERT GAIETIES and OH! WHAT A GIRL. [4] Not in programs. [5] Added after opening. [6] Previously in YIP! YIP! YAPHANK! and THIS IS THE ARMY. [7] ASCAP/Library of Congress only.

4814 • ZIEGFELD FOLLIES OF 1920

OPENED: 06/22/1920   Theatre: New Amsterdam
Revue   Broadway: 123

Composer: Irving Berlin
Lyricist: Irving Berlin
Producer: Florenz Ziegfeld
Director: Edward Royce

Costumes: Lady Duff-Gordon; Alice O'Neil; **Musical Director:** Frank Tours; **Orchestrations:** Maurice DePackh; Charles Grant; Victor Herbert; Stephen Jones; Frank Saddler; **Set Design:** Joseph Urban

Songs: All She'd Say Was 'Um Hum' [5] (C/L: Mac Emery; Joe Schenck; Gus Van; King Zany); Any Place Would Be Wonderful with You (C: Dave Stamper; L: Gene Buck); Bells; Chiffon Fantasie [6]; Chinese Fireworks; Come Along; Creation Scene (inst.) (C: Victor Herbert); Dancing School-Her First Lesson, The (scene) (C: Victor Herbert); Every Blossom I See Reminds Me of You (scene) [4] (C: Victor Herbert); Everybody Tells It to Sweeney [4] (C: George Fairman; L: Sidney D. Mitchell); Girls of My Dreams; Hold Me [2] (C/L: Ben Black; Art Hickman); I Found a Baby on My Doorstep [4] (C/L: Unknown); I Live in Turkey; I Was a Florodora Baby (C: Harry Carroll; L: Ballard Macdonald); I'm a Vamp from East Broadway (C/L: Irving Berlin; Bert Kalmar; Harry Ruby); I'm an Indian [5] (C: Leo Edwards; L: Blanche Merrill); It's the Smart Little Feller Who Stocked Up His Cellar, That's Getting the Beautiful Girls [5] (C: Milton Ager; L: Grant Clarke); Leg of Nations, The; Little Follies Theatre-During Intermission (sketch); Love Boat, The (C: Victor Herbert; L: Gene Buck); **Mary** and Doug (C: Dave Stamper; L: Gene Buck); My Home Town Is a One-Horse Town [4] (C: Abner Silver; L: Alex Gerber); My Midnight Frolic Girl [2] (C/L: Ben Black; Art Hickman); On Fifth Avenue-The Ziegfeld Follies Sextette; Opening; So Hard to Keep When They're Beautiful [1] (C: Harry Tierney; L: Joseph McCarthy); Sunshine and Shadows (C: Dave Stamper; L: Gene Buck); Syncopated Vamp, The; Tell Me Little Gypsy; Two Rubes [3] (C/L: Unknown); When the Right One Comes Along (C: Victor Herbert; L: Gene Buck); Where Do Mosquitos Go? [1] (C: Harry Tierney; L: Joseph McCarthy)

Cast: Delyle Alda; Fanny Brice; Jack Donahue; Ray Dooley; Mary Eaton; W.C. Fields; Bernard Granville; Art Hickman's Orchestra; Charles Mack; George Moran; Carl Randall; Jess Reed; Joe Schenck; John Steel; Gus Van; Charles Winninger

Notes: [1] Cut after opening. [2] Added after opening. [3] Added for tour. [4] Sheet music only. [5] Not in program. [6] ASCAP/Library of Congress only.

4815 • ZIEGFELD FOLLIES OF 1921

OPENED: 06/21/1921   Theatre: Globe
Revue   Broadway: 119

Librettist: Gene Buck; B.G. DeSylva; Rudolf Friml; Victor Herbert; Willard Mack; Channing Pollock; Ralph Spence
Producer: Florenz Ziegfeld
Director: George Marion

Costumes: James Reynolds; **Musical Director:** Frank Tours; **Orchestrations:** Maurice DePackh; Stephen Jones; **Set Design:** Joseph Urban

Songs: Ain't Nature Grand? [1] (C: Irving Berlin; L: Billy Rose; Ben Ryan); Allay Up (C: James F. Hanley; L: Ballard Macdonald); Birthday of the Dauphin, The (scene) (C: Victor Herbert); Bring Back My Blushing Rose (C: Rudolf Friml; L: Gene Buck); Championship of the World, The [6] (C: Victor Herbert); Come Back to Our Alley Sally (C: Dave Stamper; L: Gene Buck); Every Time I Hear a Band Play (C: Rudolf Friml; L: Gene Buck); Four Little Girls with a Future and Four Little Girls with a Past (C: Rudolf Friml; L: B.G. DeSylva); I Can't Resist Them When They're Beautiful [1]; I Hold Her Hand and She Holds Mine [1] (C: Irving Bibo; L: Billy Rose; Ben Ryan); If Plymouth Rock Had Landed on the Pilgrims Instead of the Pilgrims Landing on the Rock [2] (C: Dave Stamper; L: Channing Pollock); I'm a Hieland Lassie [3] (C: Leo Edwards; L: Blanche Merrill); In Khorossan (C: Victor Herbert; L: Gene Buck); In My Tippy Canoe [1] (C/L: Fred Fisher); In That Little Irish Home Sweet Home [6] (C: Harry Von Tilzer; L: William Jerome); In the Old Town Hall [1] (C: Ed G. Nelson; L: Howard Johnson; Harry Pease); Legend of the Cyclamen Tree, The (The Legend of the Golden Tree) (C: Victor Herbert; L: Gene Buck); My Man (C: Maurice Yvain; L: Channing Pollock); Now I Know (C: James V. Monaco; L: Grant Clarke); O'Reilly [1] (C: Ed G. Nelson; Elsie White; L: Harry Pease); Our Home Town (C: Harry Carroll; L: Ballard Macdonald); Princess of My Dreams, The (C: Victor Herbert; L: Gene Buck); Raggedy Rag (C: Dave Stamper; L: Gene Buck); Rosemary (C: Dave Stamper; L: B.G. DeSylva); Roses in the Garden [1] (C: Rudolf Friml; L: Brian Hooker); Sally, Won't You Come Back (Come Back to Our Alley, Sally?) [3] (C: Dave Stamper; L: Gene Buck); Scotch Lassie (C: Leo Edwards; L: Blanche Merrill); Second-Hand Rose (C: James F. Hanley; L: Grant Clarke); So This Is Venice [6] (C: Harry Warren; L: Edgar Leslie); Some Day the Sun Will Shine [5] (C: James V. Monaco; L: Grant Clarke); Strut Miss Lizzy (C: Turner Layton; L: Henry Creamer); Two Lovely Lying Eyes [1] (C: Rudolf

Friml; L: Gene Buck); Wang-Wang Blues [1]
(C: Henry Busse; Buster Johnson; Gustave
Mueller; L: Leo Wood); What a World This
Would Be [1] (C: Dave Stamper; L: B.G.
DeSylva); You Must Come Over (C: Jerome
Kern; L: B.G. DeSylva)

Cast: Fanny Brice; John Clarke; Ray Dooley; Mary
Eaton; W.C. Fields; Raymond Hitchcock; Mary
Lewis; Vera Michelena; Mary Milburn; Florence
O'Denishawn; Joe Schenck

Notes: [1] Sheet music only. [2] Also titled "If the
Plymouth Rock Had Landed on the Pilgrims."
[3] Not in program. [4] Brian Hooker sometimes
cocredited with lyrics in some sources, but not
ASCAP. [5] Sheet music only. ASCAP credits
this song to James F. Hanley and Grant Clarke.
[6] ASCAP/Library of Congress.

4816 • ZIEGFELD FOLLIES OF 1922

OPENED: 06/05/1922   Theatre: New Amsterdam
Revue   Broadway: 426

Composer: Louis A. Hirsch
Lyricist: Gene Buck
Librettist: Gene Buck; Ring Lardner; Ralph Spence
Producer: Florenz Ziegfeld
Director: Ned Wayburn

Choreographer: Michel Fokine; John Tiller; Ned
Wayburn; **Costumes:** Ada Fields; Cora
MacGeachy; Alice O'Neil; James Reynolds;
Musical Director: Oscar Radin; **Set Design:**
Joseph Urban

Songs: Bally-Burlesk [7]; Blunderland; Bring on the
Girls [8] (C: Dave Stamper); Come Along
(C: Turner Layton; L: Henry Creamer); Dreams
for Sale [7] (C: James F. Hanley; L: Herbert
Reynolds); Ensemble Finale (C: Louis A. Hirsch;
Dave Stamper); Everybody's Making It Now [7]
(C/L: Jimmy Duffy); Fairylands (scene) [7]
(C: Victor Herbert); Farijandis (scene) (C: Victor
Herbert); Flappers [7] (C: Dave Stamper); Four
Well Known Dames and a Guy (Song Scene) [7]
(C: Raymond Hubbell); Hello, Hello, Hello
(C: Dave Stamper); I Don't Know What I'd Do
Without You [2]; I Don't Want to Be in Dixie [2]
(C: Louis A. Hirsch; Dave Stamper); I'm
Satisfied [7]; It's Getting Dark on Old Broadway
(C: Dave Stamper); Kiss in the Dark, A [4]
(C: Victor Herbert; L: B.G. DeSylva); Lace Land
(scene) [1] (C: Victor Herbert); List'ning on Some

Radio (C: Dave Stamper); Marches (inst.) (C:
Victor Herbert); Mr. Gallagher and Mr. Shean
(C/L: Ed Gallagher; Al Shean); My Melody [3];
My Rambler Rose (C: Louis A. Hirsch; Dave
Stamper); 'Neath the South Sea Moon (C: Louis
A. Hirsch; Dave Stamper); Nobody but You [7]
(C: Louis A. Hirsch; Dave Stamper); Oh Gee! Oh
Gosh! Oh Golly! I'm in Love [2] (C: Ernest
Breuer; L: Chic Johnson; Ole Olsen); Pep It Up
(C: Dave Stamper); Sing a Song of Sunshine [5];
Sing a Swanee Song [7] (C: Louis Breau; L: Nat
Sanders); Sitting in a Corner [1]; Some Sweet Day
(C: Louis A. Hirsch; Dave Stamper); Songs I
Can't Forget (C: Louis A. Hirsch); Sunny South [7]
(C: Louis A. Hirsch); Throw Me a Kiss [6]
(C: Louis A. Hirsch; Dave Stamper; Maurice
Yvain); Weaving My Dreams (C: Victor Herbert)

Cast: Mary Eaton; Ed Gallagher; Gilda Gray; Chic
Johnson; Evelyn Law; Charles LeMaire; Lulu
McConnell; Ole Olsen; Will Rogers; Al Shean;
Tiller Girls

Notes: [1] Out Newark 5/5/24. [2] Sheet music
only. [3] Added after opening. [4] Originally in
ORANGE BLOSSOMS. [5] Not in programs. [6]
Yvain not credited in some programs. [7] Cut
after opening. [8] ASCAP credits this to Victor
Herbert.

4817 • ZIEGFELD FOLLIES OF 1923

OPENED: 10/20/1923   Theatre: New Amsterdam
Revue   Broadway: 233

Composer: Dave Stamper
Lyricist: Gene Buck
Librettist: Florenz Ziegfeld
Director: Ned Wayburn

Costumes: Erte; Evlyn McHorter; Alice O'Neil;
James Reynolds; **Musical Director:** Oscar Radin;
Set Design: Joseph Urban

Songs: As Long As He Loves Me [1] (C: James F.
Hanley; L: Lew Brown); Bebe [1] (C: Abner
Silver; L: Sam Coslow); Broadway Indians; Cane
Dance [2]; Chansonette [4] (C: Rudolf Friml;
L: Irving Caesar; Dailey Paskman; Sigmund
Spaeth); Dancing Mad [7] (C: Leo Edwards;
L: Blanche Merrill); Everlovin' Bee [2]; Fencing
(C: Victor Herbert); Fool, The (C: Lee David; L:
Benton Ley); Glorifying the Girls; Good Night [7];
Harlequin's Doll (C: Gabriel Daray); I Must Go
to Moscow [3] (C: Ernest Breuer; L: Mort Dixon;

Leon Flatow); I Want 'em Wild, Weak, Warm and Willing [8] (C/L: Eddie Cantor; Sam Coslow); I Wonder How They Get That Way [7]; I'd Love to Waltz Through Life with You (C: Victor Herbert); If I Can't Get the Sweetie I Want I Pity the Sweetie I Get [1] (C: Jean Schwartz; L: Sam M. Lewis; Joe Young); I'm a Manicurist [7] (C/L: Blanche Merrill); I'm Bugs Over You [7]; Kayo Tortoni; Lady Fair [7] (C: Rudolf Friml); Lady of the Lantern [3] (C: Victor Herbert); Legend of the Drums (C: Victor Herbert); Little Old New York (C: Victor Herbert); Lonesome Cinderella [1] (C: James F. Hanley; L: Lew Brown); Maid of Gold (C: Rudolf Friml); Mammy [7] (C: Walter Donaldson; L: Sam M. Lewis; Joe Young); Mary Rose (C: Maurice Yvain); Moonlight Ballet (inst.) [6] (C: Victor Herbert); Oh! Gee, Oh! Gosh, Oh! Golly, I'm in Love [5] (C: Ernest Breuer; L: Chic Johnson; Ole Olsen); Red Light Annie [3]; Russian Art [6] (C: Leo Edwards; L: Blanche Merrill); Shake Your Feet; So This Is Venice [3] (C: Harry Warren; L: Grant Clarke; Edgar Leslie); Springtime [6]; Steady Eddie [3]; Swanee River Blues [7]; Sweet Alice [1] (C/L: Frank Crumit); Take Those Lips Away (C: Harry Tierney; L: Joseph McCarthy); That Old Fashioned Garden of Mine [7] (C: Victor Herbert); That Society Budd (I'm a Society Bud) [7] (C: Harry Ruby; L: Bert Kalmar); Wedding Scene [7] (C: Victor Herbert); What Thrills Can There Be (L: Harry Ruskin); Why Did I Buy That Morris Chair for Morris? [8] (C/L: Bert Kalmar; Murray Kissen; Harry Ruby); You Gotta Yes 'Em to Know Them [3] (C/L: Blanche Merrill; Dave Stamper); Your Eyes Have Told Me That You Love Me [8]

Cast: Lina Basquette; Fanny Brice; Eddie Cantor; Harland Dixon; Lew Hearn; Brooke Johns; Tom Lewis; Hap Ward; Bert Wheeler; Betty Wheeler; Paul Whiteman and His Orchestra; Imogene Wilson

Notes: [1] Sheet music only. [2] Out Newark 2/23/25. [3] Not in program. [4] Not in program. Music later became "Donkey Serenade." [5] Not in program. Also in ZIEGFELD FOLLIES OF 1922. [6] Added after opening. [7] Cut after opening. [8] ASCAP/Library of Congress only.

4818 • ZIEGFELD FOLLIES OF 1924

OPENED: 06/24/1924 Theatre: New Amsterdam
Revue Broadway: 401

Composer: Harry Tierney
Lyricist: Joseph McCarthy
Librettist: William Anthony McGuire; Will Rogers
Producer: Florenz Ziegfeld
Director: Julian Mitchell

Costumes: Erte; Charles LeMaire; Miss McWhorter; James Reynolds; **Musical Director:** Victor Baravalle; **Orchestrations:** Fred Barry; Robert Russell Bennett; Raymond Hubbell; Stephen Jones; Harold Sandford; **Set Design:** Gates & Morange; Ludwig Kainer; H. Robert Law; Joseph Urban; John Wenger

Songs: Absinthe Frappe [2] (C: Victor Herbert; L: Glen MacDonough); Adoring You; All Pepped Up; Big Glass Cage, A; Biminy (C: Dave Stamper; L: Gene Buck); Ever Lovin' Bee [4] (C: Dave Stamper; L: Gene Buck); Fine Feathers Make Fine Birds [5]; Follow the Swallow [5] (C: Ray Henderson; L: Mort Dixon; Billy Rose); Garden — The Beauty Contest, A (C: Victor Herbert; Harry Tierney); Great Wide Open Spaces, The (C: Dave Stamper; L: Gene Buck); Gypsy Love Song (C: Victor Herbert); I Believe You [6] (C: Dave Stamper; L: Gene Buck); I Can't Do the Sum [1] (C: Victor Herbert; L: Glen MacDonough); If I Were on the Stage (Kiss Me Again) [3] (C: Victor Herbert; L: Henry Blossom); London Empire Girls (C: Dave Stamper); Lonely Little Melody (C: Dave Stamper; L: Gene Buck); March of the Toys [1] (C: Victor Herbert; L: Glen MacDonough); Mirage Dance, The (inst.) [4] (C: Borel Clerc; Laurent Halet); Montmartre (C: Raymond Hubbell; L: Gene Buck); Night in June, A (C: Raymond Hubbell; L: Gene Buck); Old Town Band, The; Pearl of the East (scene) (C: Raymond Hubbell); Plot, The (scene) (C: Raymond Hubbell; L: Gene Buck); Rose of My Heart (C: Albert Sirmay; L: Gene Buck); Tiller Girls Dance (inst.) (C: Victor Herbert); Toyland [1] (C: Victor Herbert; L: Glen MacDonough); You're My Happy Ending (C: James F. Hanley; L: Gene Buck)

Cast: Ray Dooley; W.C. Fields; Irving Fisher; Lupino Lane; Evelyn Law; Tom Lewis; George Olsen; Ann Pennington; James Reynolds; Will Rogers; Vivienne Segal; Tiller Girls

Notes: The number of performances includes the run of ZIEGFELD FOLLIES OF 1925 since it was basically a continuation of the 1924 edition. [1] Originally in BABES IN TOYLAND. [2] Originally in IT HAPPENED IN NORDLAND. [3] Originally in MLLE. MODISTE. [4] Added for Fall Edition and kept for ZIEGFELD FOLLIES OF 1925. [5] Not in program. [6] ASCAP list only.

4819 • ZIEGFELD FOLLIES OF 1925

OPENED: 03/10/1925   Theatre: New Amsterdam
Revue   Broadway: 223

Lyricist: Gene Buck
Librettist: W.C. Fields; J.P. McEvoy; Will Rogers
Producer: Florenz Ziegfeld
Director: Julian Mitchell

Costumes: Ben Ali Haggin; John Held Jr.; **Musical Director:** Victor Baravalle; **Orchestrations:** Fred Barry; Robert Russell Bennett; Stephen Jones; Harold Sandford; **Set Design:** Norman Bel Geddes; Gates & Morange; Ludwig Kainer; H. Robert Law; John Wenger

Songs: Bertie (C: Sigmund Romberg; L: Clifford Grey); Eddie, Be Good [2] (C: Dave Stamper); Ever Lovin' Bee [1] (C: Dave Stamper); Everybody Knows What Jazz Is (C: Werner Janssen); Home Again [2] (C: Raymond Hubbell); I'd Like to Be a Gardener in a Garden of Girls [2] (C: Raymond Hubbell); I'd Like to Corral a Gal (C: Raymond Hubbell); In the Shade of the Alamo [2] (C: Raymond Hubbell); Pearl of the East (scene) (C: Raymond Hubbell); Settle Down in a Little Town (C: Werner Janssen); Syncopating Baby (Syncopating Sadie) [2] (C: Dave Stamper); Titina (C: Leo Daniderff); Toddle Along (C: Werner Janssen); Tondelayo (C: Dave Stamper; L: Gene Buck; Jack Osterman); When Nathan Was Married to Rose of Washington Square [3] (C: Dave Stamper)

Cast: Ray Dooley; Peggy Fears; W.C. Fields; Al Oches; Will Rogers; Ethel Shutta; Tiller Girls, The

Notes: The 1925 FOLLIES is a continuation of the 1924 FOLLIES with additional cast, sketches and songs. This edition played 135 performances. The Summer Edition followed 7/6/25 for 88 performances. [1] Also in ZIEGFELD FOLLIES OF 1924. [2] Added for summer edition as was Ethel Shutta. [3] Not in programs.

4820 • ZIEGFELD FOLLIES OF 1926

Notes: *See NO FOOLIN'.* This was tour name of that show.

4821 • ZIEGFELD FOLLIES OF 1927

OPENED: 08/16/1927   Theatre: New Amsterdam
Revue   Broadway: 167

Composer: Irving Berlin
Lyricist: Irving Berlin
Librettist: Harold Atteridge; Eddie Cantor
Producer: Florenz Ziegfeld
Director: Zeke Colvan

Choreographer: Sammy Lee; Albertina Rasch; **Costumes:** John Harkrider; **Musical Director:** Frank Tours; **Orchestrations:** Ferde Grofe; Arthur Gutman; Louis Katzman; Paul Lannin; Frank Tours; Roy Webb; **Set Design:** Joseph Urban

Songs: Ev'rybody Loves My Girl [1] (C: Maurice Abrahams; L: Sam M. Lewis; Joe Young); I Want to Be Glorified; It All Belongs to Me; (Hooray, Hooray) It's Ray-Ray-Raining [1] (C: Al Sherman; L: Howard Johnson; Charles Tobias); It's Up to the Band; Jimmy; Jungle Jingle; Learn to Sing a Love Song; My Blue Heaven [2] (C: Walter Donaldson; L: George Whiting); My New York [2]; My Old Girl Is My New Girl Now; Now We Are Glorified [4]; Ooh, Maybe It's You; Rainbow of Girls; Ribbons and Bows; Shaking the Blues Away; She Don't Wanna [1] (C: Milton Ager; L: Jack Yellen); Tickling the Ivories; What Makes Me Love You? [1]; You Gotta Have 'IT' [3]

Cast: Franklin Baur; Brox Sisters, The; Eddie Cantor; Irene Delroy; Ruth Etting; Dan Healy; Claire Luce; Harry McNaughton; Frances Upton

Notes: [1] Sheet music only. [2] Not in program. [3] Not in program. A Berlin re-write of a song by Eddie Cantor. [4] Added after opening.

4822 • ZIEGFELD FOLLIES OF 1930

OPENED: 1930
Revue

Songs: You'll Give In (C: James F. Hanley; L: Joseph McCarthy)

Notes: No other information available. This song may have been written for an unproduced edition of the Follies or might have been interpolated into a touring production of a previous edition.

4823 • ZIEGFELD FOLLIES OF 1931

OPENED: 07/01/1931   Theatre: Ziegfeld
Revue   Broadway: 165

Composer: Harry Revel
Lyricist: Mack Gordon
Librettist: Gene Buck; Mark Hellinger; J.P. Murray
Producer: Florenz Ziegfeld
Director: Edward Clarke Lilley

Choreographer: Bobby Connolly; Albertina Rasch;
Costumes: John Harkrider; **Musical Director:**
Victor Baravalle; **Orchestrations:** Maurice
DePackh; Howard Jackson; Joe Jordan; Will
Vodery; **Set Design:** Joseph Urban

Songs: Bring on the Follies' Girls (C: Dave
Stamper; L: Gene Buck); Broadway Reverie
(C: Dave Stamper; L: Gene Buck); Changing of
the Guards (C: Ben Oakland; L: J.P. Murray;
Barry Trivers); Cigarettes, Cigars (C: Harry
Revel; L: Mack Gordon); Clinching the Sale
(C: Ben Oakland; L: J.P. Murray; Barry Trivers);
Dance (C: Harry Revel; L: Mack Gordon); Doin'
the New York (C: Ben Oakland; L: J.P. Murray;
Barry Trivers); Fandango Dance [2] (C: Dimitri
Tiomkin); Half Caste Woman (C/L: Noel
Coward); Help Yourself to Happiness (C: Harry
Revel; L: Mack Gordon; Harry Richman); Here
We Are in Love [1] (C: Ben Oakland; L: J.P.
Murray; Barry Trivers); Illusion in White
(C: Dimitri Tiomkin); I'm Good for Nothing but
Love (C: Bernard Maltin; L: Ballard); I'm with
You (C/L: Walter Donaldson); Legend of the
Islands (C/L: Powell; Stevens); Leonard Stokes
and Hal LeRoy (scene) (C: Dave Stamper); Let's
K'nock K'nees [5] (C: Harry Revel; L: Mack
Gordon); Mailu [4] (C: Jay Gorney; L: E.Y.
Harburg); Picture Bride, The (scene) (C: Hugo
Riesenfeld; Dave Stamper); Pink Lady Waltz
(inst.) (C: Ivan Caryll); Rhythm of the Day [6]
(C: Ben Oakland; L: J.P. Murray; Barry Trivers);
Shine on Harvest Moon [3] (C/L: Jack Norworth;
L: Nora Bayes); Tom-Tom Dance (C: Dimitri
Tiomkin); Victim of the Talkies (C: Ben Oakland;
L: J.P. Murray; Barry Trivers); Waltz (C: Dave
Stamper); Was I? (C: Chick Endor; L: Charles
Farrell); Who Paid the Rent for Mrs. Rip Van
Winkle When Rip Van Winkle Went Away
(C: Fred Fisher; L: Alfred Bryan); (I'm) Wrapped
Up in You (C: Ben Oakland; L: J.P. Murray; Barry
Trivers); You Made Me Love You (C: James V.
Monaco; L: Joseph McCarthy); Your Sunny
Southern Smile (C: Harry Revel; L: Mack
Gordon)

Cast: Faith Bacon; Edith Borden; Frank Britton;
Milt Britton; John Bubbles; Ford Buck; Arthur
Campbell; Albert Carroll; Collette Sisters, The;
Dorothy Dell; Ruth Etting; Gladys Glad; Cliff
Hall; Hal LeRoy; Mitzi Mayfair; Helen Morgan;
Pearl Osgood; Earl Oxford; Jack Pearl; Reri;
Harry Richman

Notes: [1] Sheet music only. [2] This is the name of
a song not just a dance number. [3] Originally in
ZIEGFELD FOLLIES OF 1908. [4] Hugo
Riesenfeld also credited with music by ASCAP.
[5] Not used. Later used in film THE GAY
DIVORCEE. [6] ASCAP/Library of Congress
only.

4824 • ZIEGFELD FOLLIES OF 1934

OPENED: 01/04/1934   Theatre: New Amsterdam
Revue   Broadway: 182

Composer: Vernon Duke
Lyricist: E.Y. Harburg
Librettist: Fred Allen; David Freedman; Ballard
Macdonald; H.I. Phillips; Harry Turgend
Producer: Billie Burke; Messrs. Shubert
Director: John Murray Anderson; Bobby Connolly;
Edward Clarke Lilley

Choreographer: Robert Alton; Bobby Connolly;
Costumes: Kiviette; Charles LeMaire; Billy
Livingston; Russell Patterson; Raoul Pene du
Bois, **Lighting Designer:** John Murray
Anderson; **Musical Director:** John McManus; **Set
Design:** Watson Barratt; Albert Johnson

Songs: Careful with My Heart (C: Samuel Pokrass);
Countess Dubinsky (C: Joseph Meyer; L: Ballard
Macdonald; Billy Rose); Follies Chorale
Ensemble (C: Samuel Pokrass); Goo-Goo Da Da
(Goo Goo G'Da) [5] (C: Ernest Breuer; L: Billy
Frisch; Raymond Leveen; Frank Loesser); Green
Eyes (C: Robert Emmett Dolan); House Is
Haunted, The (By the Echo of Your Last
Goodbye) [3] (C: Basil Adlam; L: Billy Rose);
I Like the Likes of You; Just a Barefoot Boy
(A'Whistlin' to His Dog) [3] (C: James F. Hanley;
L: Chris Taylor); Last Roundup, The (C/L: Billy
Hill); Moon About Town (C: Dana Suesse); Poor
Fellow [4] (C/L: Ben Oakland); Rain in My Heart
[4] (C: Louis Alter; L: Arthur Swanstrom); Rose
of Washington Square [1] (C: James F. Hanley;
L: Ballard Macdonald); Sarah, the Sunshine Girl
(C: Joseph Meyer; L: Ballard Macdonald; Billy
Rose); Shim Sham [4] (C: Louis Alter; L: Arthur

Swanstrom); Sidewalk in Paris, A [7] (C: Arthur
Swanstrom); (It's) Smart to Be Smart [4]; Soul
Saving Sadie (C: Joseph Meyer; L: Ballard
Macdonald; Billy Rose); Stop that Clock [4];
Suddenly (L: E.Y. Harburg; Billy Rose); That's
Where We Come In (C: Samuel Pokrass); Then
I'll Be Tired of You [2] (C: Arthur Schwartz); This
Is Not a Song (L: E.Y. Harburg; E. Hartman);
Time Is a Gypsy (C: Richard Myers; L: E.Y.
Harburg); To the Beat of My Heart (C: Samuel
Pokrass); Wagon Wheels (C: Peter De Rose;
L: Billy Hill); Water Under the Bridge; What Is
There to Say?; Why Am I Blue [6] (C: Peter De
Rose; L: Billy Hill); Winter Wonderland (C/L:
Felix Bernard; Dick Smith); You Oughta Be in
Pictures [3] (C: Dana Suesse; L: Edward
Heyman)

Cast: Eve Arden; Judith Barron; Betzi Beaton;
Fanny Brice; Patricia Browman; Jacques Cartier;
Robert Cummings; Buddy Ebsen; Vilma Ebsen;
Jane Froman; Eugene Howard; Willie Howard;
Ina Ray Hutton; Vivian Janis; Everett Marshall;
Victor Morley; Cherry Preisser; June Preisser;
Don Ross; Oliver Wakefield

Notes: [1] Interpolated. Originally in ZIEGFELD
FOLLIES OF 1920 and ZIEGFELD MIDNIGHT
FROLIC OF 1919. Added after opening. [2] Not
in program. [3] Added after opening. [4] Out
Boston 11/13/33. [5] Out Detroit 12/4/33. [6]
Out Detroit 11/25/34. [7] Titled "Fifth Avenue
— A Sidewalk in Paris" by ASCAP.

4825 • ZIEGFELD FOLLIES OF 1936
OPENED: 01/30/1936   Theatre: Winter Garden
Revue   Broadway: 115

Composer: Vernon Duke
Lyricist: Ira Gershwin
Librettist: David Freedman
Producer: Billie Burke; Messrs. Shubert
Director: John Murray Anderson; Edward Clarke
Lilley

Choreographer: Robert Alton; George Balanchine;
Costumes: Vincente Minnelli; **Musical Director:**
John McManus; **Orchestrations:** Robert Russell
Bennett; Conrad Salinger; Hans Spialek; Don
Walker; **Set Design:** Vincente Minnelli

Songs: Announcement for Broadway Gold Melody
Diggers of 42nd Street [1]; Are You Havin' Any
Fun [4] (C: Sammy Fain; L: Jack Yellen); Ballad of

Baby Face McGinty (Who Bit Off More Than He
Could Chew), The [3]; Better Half Knows Better,
The [1]; Dancing to the Score; Does a Duck Love
Water? [3]; Economic Situation, The (Aren't
You Wonderful); Fancy! Fancy!; Five A.M.;
Gazooka, The; He Hasn't a Thing Except Me;
Hot Number [1]; I Can't Get Started; I Used to
Be Above Love [1]; I'm Sharing My Wealth [1];
Island in the West Indies; It's a Different World;
Knife-Thrower's Wife, The [3]; Last of the
Cabbies, The [3]; Maharanee; Midnight Blue [2]
(C: Joseph Burke; L: Edgar Leslie); Modernistic
Moe (L: Ira Gershwin; Billy Rose); My Red-Letter
Day; Oh, Bring Back the Ballet Again [1]; Please
Send My Daddy Back Home [3]; Ridin' the Rails
(C: Harold Spina; L: Edward Heyman); Save
Your Yesses [1]; Sentimental Weather; Sunday
Tan [1]; That Moment of Moments; Time
Marches On!; Trailer for the 1936 Broadway
Gold Melody Diggers; Why Save for That Rainy
Day? [1]; Wishing Tree of Harlem [1]; Words
Without Music; You Don't Love Right [2] (C: Vee
Lawnhurst; L: Tot Seymour)

Cast: Eve Arden; Josephine Baker; Fanny Brice;
Hugh Cameron; Judy Canova; George Church;
Bobby Clark; Cass Daley; Ruth Fisher; Alex
Harrison; Harriet Hoctor; Bob Hope; John
Hoysradt; Stan Kavanaugh; Gypsy Rose Lee;
Duke McHale; Rodney McLennan; Nicholas
Brothers, The; Gertrude Niesen; Hugh
O'Connell; Jane Pickens; Cherry Preisser; June
Preisser; Ben Yost Varsity Eight

Notes: The cast listed is for the second edition which
opened 9/14/36 and was titled NEW ZIEGFELD
FOLLIES OF 1936-1937. The number of
performances above is for both editions. [1] Not
used. [2] Added to second edition. [3] Cut prior to
opening. [4] Added to second edition. Later in
GEORGE WHITE'S SCANDALS OF 1939.

4826 • ZIEGFELD FOLLIES OF 1943
OPENED: 04/01/1943   Theatre: Winter Garden
Revue   Broadway: 553

Composer: Ray Henderson
Lyricist: Jack Yellen
Producer: Messrs. Shubert
Director: John Murray Anderson; Arthur Pierson;
Fred de Cordova

Choreographer: Robert Alton; **Costumes:** Miles
White; **Musical Director:** John McManus;

Orchestrations: Don Walker; **Set Design:**
Watson Barratt

Songs: Advertising Song, The [1] (C/L: Harold
Rome); Back to the Farm (C: Dan White; L: Bud
Burtson); Come Up and Have a Cup of Coffee;
Hep, Hot and Solid Sweet [4]; Hindoo Serenade;
Hold That Smile; Love Songs Are Made in the
Night; Micromaniac (C/L: Harold Rome); (There
Are) New Roses Every Summer; Saga of Carmen,
The (Carmen Was); Sue Ryan (C: Dan White;
L: Bud Burtson); Swing Your Lady Mister
Hemingway; Thirty-Five Summers Ago; This Is
It; Under My Umbrella [2] (C: Vernon Duke;
L: Howard Dietz); Wedding of a Solid Sender,
The (dance) (C: Baldwin Bergersen); You're
Dreamlike [3] (C: Vernon Duke; L: Howard
Dietz)

Cast: Christine Ayers; Bil Baird; Cora Baird; Milton
Berle; Eric Blore; Imogene Carpenter; Jack Cole;
Nadine Gae; Ilona Massey; Jack McCauley; Sue
Ryan; Arthur Treacher; Tommy Wonder

Notes: [1] Added after opening. [2] Not used. Also
not used in DANCING IN THE STREETS. [3]
Not used. Also not used in SADIE THOMPSON.
[4] ASCAP/Library of Congress only.

4827 • ZIEGFELD FOLLIES OF 1956
OPENED: 04/16/1956
Revue   Closed out of town

Librettist: Ronny Graham; Arnold B. Horwitt;
Stanley Prager; David Rogers
Producer: James W. Gardiner; Richard Kollmar
Director: Christopher Hewett

Choreographer: Jack Cole; **Costumes:** Raoul Pene
du Bois; **Dance Arranger:** Hal Schaefer; **Lighting
Designer:** Peggy Clark; **Musical Director:** Anton
Coppola; **Orchestrations:** George Bassman;
Albert Sendry; **Set Design:** Raoul Pene du Bois;
Vocal Arranger: Hugh Martin

Songs: Ballad of Herman Schlepps, The (C: Albert
Hague; L: Arnold B. Horwitt); Don't Knock It
(C/L: Herbert Baker); Downtown (C: Charles
Strouse; L: Lee Adams); Faster Than Sound [1]
(C/L: Ralph Blane; Hugh Martin); Finale; Go
Bravely On (C/L: Sydney Shaw); Lady Is
Indisposed, The (C: Cy Coleman; L: Joseph
McCarthy Jr.); Miser's Serenade, The (C: Marvin
Fisher; Jack Val; L: Fred Patrick; Claude Reese);

Night the Lion Broke Loose, The (C: Milton De
Lugg; L: Chuck Sweeney); Noises in the Theatre
(C: Richard Lewine; L: Arnold B. Horwitt);
Opening Number; Runaway (C: Alton Rinker;
L: Floyd Huddleston); Small Winner (C: Albert
Hague; L: Arnold B. Horwitt); Thing About
Willie, The (C: Alton Rinker; L: Floyd
Huddleston); What It Was Was Love (C: Albert
Hague; L: Arnold B. Horwitt); When Papa
Would Waltz (C: Jerry Bock; L: Larry
Holofcener); Whip, The (C: Jerry Bock; L: Larry
Holofcener)

Cast: Tallulah Bankhead; Mae Barnes; David
Burns; Joan Diener; Timothy Gray; Carol Haney;
Larry Kert; Preshy Marker; Matt Mattox; Elliott
Reid

Notes: Irving Berlin also listed in program but not
for a specific song. [1] Later in HIGH SPIRITS.

4828 • ZIEGFELD FOLLIES OF 1957
OPENED: 03/01/1957   Theatre: Winter Garden
Revue   Broadway: 123

Librettist: Maxwell Grant; Coleman Jacoby; Alan
Jeffreys; David Rogers; Arnie Rosen
Producer: Charles Conaway; Mark Kroll
Director: John Kennedy

Choreographer: Frank Wagner; **Costumes:** Raoul
Pene du Bois; **Dance Arranger:** Rene Weigert;
Lighting Designer: Paul Morrison; **Musical
Director:** Max Meth; **Orchestrations:** Robert
Russell Bennett; Joe Glover; Bob Noelmeter; Bill
Stegmeyer; **Set Design:** Raoul Pene du Bois;
Vocal Arranger: Earl Rogers

Songs: Better Than Ever [3] (C: Richard Myers;
L: Jack Lawrence); Bring on the Girls (C: Richard
Myers; L: Jack Lawrence); Don't Tell a Soul [2]
(C: Colin Romoff; L: David Rogers); (That)
Element of Doubt (C: Sammy Fain; L: Howard
Dietz); Finale (C: Richard Myers; L: Jack
Lawrence); Follies Nocturne [2] (C/L: Bernie
Wayne); Golden Anniversary [2] (C: Richard
Myers; L: Jack Lawrence); Hazards of the
Profession [2] (C: Dean Fuller; L: Marshall Barer);
Honorable Mambo (C: Dean Fuller; L: Marshall
Barer); I Don't Wanna Rock (C: Colin Romoff;
L: David Rogers); If You Got Music (C: Colin
Romoff; L: David Rogers); Intoxication (C: Dean
Fuller; L: Marshall Barer); Lover in Me, The
(C: Philip Springer; L: Carolyn Leigh); Make Me

(C/L: Uhpio Minucci; Larry Spier; Tony Velona); Mangoes (C/L: Dee Libbey); Miss Follies (C: Colin Romoff; L: David Rogers); Miss Follies of 192 . . . (C/L: Herman Hupfeld); Music for Madame (C: Richard Myers; L: Jack Lawrence); My Late, Late Lady (C: Dean Fuller; L: Marshall Barer); Producer's Office [2] (C: Richard Myers; L: Jack Lawrence); Salesmanship (C: Philip Springer; L: Carolyn Leigh); Stay on the Subject [1] (C: Dean Fuller; L: Marshall Barer); Time Magazine [1] (C/L: Maxwell Grant; Alan Jeffreys; Jack Wilson); Two a Day on the Milky Way (C: Dean Fuller; L: Marshall Barer)

Cast: Billy De Wolfe; Harold Lang; Carol Lawrence; Beatrice Lillie; Jane Morgan

Notes: [1] Cut prior to opening. [2] Out D.C. 2/18/57. [3] ASCAP/Library of Congress only.

4829 • ZIEGFELD FOLLIES (1958)
OPENED: 09/30/1957
Revue   Closed out of town

Lyricist: David Rogers
Librettist: Eddie Davis; Coleman Jacoby; Loney Lewis; David Rogers; Arnie Rosen; Ira Wallach
Producer: Charles Conaway; Mark Kroll
Director: Mervyn Nelson

Choreographer: Bob Copsey; **Costumes:** Raoul Pene du Bois; **Lighting Designer:** Louis Popiel; **Musical Director:** Ray O'Brien; **Orchestrations:** Joe Sherman; **Set Design:** Raoul Pene du Bois

Songs: Be Bop Lullaby (C: Ralph Strain; L: Marshall Barer); Happiest Millionaires, The (C: Paul Klein; L: Fred Ebb); Honorable Mambo (C: Marshal Rosen; L: Coleman Jacoby); It's Silk, Feel It (C: Dean Fuller; L: Marshall Barer); Lonesome Is As Lonesome Does (C/L: Joe Sherman; Noel Sherman); Miss Follies (C: Colin Romoff); One More Samba (C: Gerald Alters); Parade Is Passing Me By, The (C/L: Joe Sherman; Noel Sherman); Play, Mr. Bailey (C/L: Biff Jones; Chuck Meyer); Pretty Girl Is Like a Melody, A [1] (C/L: Irving Berlin); Somebody's Keeping Score (C: Sammy Fain; L: Jackie Barnett); When Papa Would Waltz (C: Jerry Bock; L: Larry Holofcener); Ziegfeld Show, A (C: Otis Clements)

Cast: Sara Aman; Jobee Ayers; Kaye Ballard; Lord Buckley; Bob Copsey; Richard Curry; Paul

Gilbert; Patrice Helene; Lew Herbert; Jan Howard; Kitty Lester; Loney Lewis; Micki Marlo; Jimmy Roma

Notes: Program of Hanna Theatre, Cleveland, Ohio. [1] From ZIEGFELD FOLLIES OF 1919.

4830 • ZIEGFELD GIRL, THE
OPENED: 01/23/1989   Theatre: New Ziegfeld
Musical   Off-Off-Broadway: 16

Composer: Christopher Berg
Lyricist: Jordan Tinsley
Librettist: Michael Proft; Jordan Tinsley
Producer: Shoestring Follies Prod.
Director: Jordan Tinsley

Source: WHEN SHE WAS BAD (Play: H. Owen Barrie); **Arrangements:** Christopher Berg; **Choreographer:** Jordan Tinsley; **Musical Director:** Christopher Berg

Songs: Argument, The (C/L: Tom Judson); Bon Jour! (C/L: Tom Judson); Butcher, the Baker, the Candlestick Maker, The; Chocolate Covered Future [1]; Dressing Room, A [1]; Feathers; Follow Your Heart; I Don't Want to Be Hurt Again [1]; I'm a Lady!; Love in the Smoking Car; Love Is Around the Corner; Miss May; Satin, Cigarettes and Warm Brandy; Singin' the Red Hot Blues; Southern Charm [1]; Star in Heaven's Firmament, A; That Winter Was a Spring; The End [1]; Trip to Paris, A; What You're Gonna Do for Me; Why Don't We Move to Philadelphia (C/L: Tom Judson); Ziegfeld Girl, The

Cast: Joann Bright; Marla Cahan; Paul Hoffman; Ellen Mittenthal; Myka Ryan; Hans Tester; Jordan Tinsley; Victoria Trost; Michael Walsh; Michael Wilkinson

Notes: [1] Cut.

4831 • ZIEGFELD GIRLS OF 1920
OPENED: 03/08/1920   Theatre: New Amsterdam
                                Roof
Revue   Broadway: 78

Composer: Dave Stamper
Lyricist: Gene Buck
Producer: Florenz Ziegfeld
Director: Ned Wayburn

Costumes: Marie Cook; Alice O'Neil; **Musical Director:** George A. Nichols; **Set Design:** Joseph Urban

Songs: Emancipation Day; Every Telephone (Telephone Song); I'm Crazy About Somebody; Metropolitan Ladies [1] (C/L: Irving Berlin); My Man [2] (C: Maurice Yvain; L: Channing Pollock); My Rosary of Melodies [1]; Orchard of Girls (L: Rennold Wolf); We Are the Maids of the Merry Merry; When Grandpa Was a Boy; Where Are the Plays of Yesterday; Winter Beaches, The; Wonderful Girl; You Know What I Mean

Cast: Fanny Brice; W.C. Fields; John Price Jones; Allyn King; Lillian Lorraine

Notes: This show also known as ZIEGFELD'S NINE O'CLOCK REVUE. [1] Also in ZIEGFELD 9 O'CLOCK FROLIC (9TH EDITION). [2] Also in ZIEGFELD FOLLIES OF 1921, ZIEGFELD 9 O'CLOCK FROLIC (9TH EDITION) and ZIEGFELD MIDNIGHT FROLIC (2ND 1929 EDITION). James F. Hanley and Gene Buck might have had something to do with the Americanizing of this song, they're credited by ASCAP.

4832 • ZIEGFELD MIDNIGHT FROLIC (UNKNOWN EDITION)

	Theatre: New Amsterdam Roof
Revue	Broadway

Composer: Dave Stamper
Lyricist: Gene Buck
Producer: Florenz Ziegfeld

Songs: Bachelor's Dream, The; I Love to Raise the Dickens; Pharoah's Daughter

Notes: No other information available.

4833 • ZIEGFELD MIDNIGHT FROLIC (1ST EDITION)

OPENED: 03/1915	Theatre: New Amsterdam Roof
Revue	Broadway

Composer: Louis A. Hirsch; Dave Stamper
Lyricist: Gene Buck
Producer: Florenz Ziegfeld
Director: Ned Wayburn

Costumes: Cora MacGeachy; **Lighting Designer:** Tony Greshoff; **Musical Director:** George A. Nichols; **Set Design:** Joseph Urban

Songs: Gee I Only Wish I Could Make My Dreams Come True [1] (C: Dave Stamper); Girl from My Home Town, The (C: Dave Stamper); Humpty Dumpty Drag (C: Dave Stamper); I Want Someone to Make a Fuss Over Me; I'm Sober; Jungle Ball (C: Dave Stamper); My Midnight Girl; My Spooky Girl; My Tango Girl; My Ziegfeld Midnight Girl [1] (C: Dave Stamper); Red, White and Blue; Scaddle-de-Mooch [2] (C/L: Cecil Mack; Chris Smith)

Cast: Bernard Granville; Muriel Hudson; Charles Purcell

Notes: Also titled NOTHING BUT GIRLS. [1] ASCAP/Library of Congress lists only. [2] Sheet music only. This may have been in the second 1915 edition.

4834 • ZIEGFELD MIDNIGHT FROLIC (2ND EDITION)

OPENED: 09/1915	Theatre: New Amsterdam Roof
Revue	Broadway

Composer: Dave Stamper
Lyricist: Gene Buck
Producer: Florenz Ziegfeld
Director: Leon Errol

Costumes: Cora MacGeachy; **Musical Director:** George A. Nichols; **Set Design:** Joseph Urban

Songs: Bathing; Come Along; Hold Me in Your Loving Arms [1]; I Love to Be Loved; In Grandma's Day They Never Did the Fox Trot; Yankee Doodle Patriotic Tune

Cast: Sybil Carmen; Allyn King; Sue Loring; Will Rogers; Dave Stamper

Notes: Also titled JUST GIRLS (2nd of series). [1] Added after opening.

4835 • ZIEGFELD MIDNIGHT FROLIC (1916)

OPENED: 1916	
Revue	Broadway

Composer: Dave Stamper
Lyricist: Gene Buck
Producer: Florenz Ziegfeld

Songs: Don't You Wish You Were a Kid Again; Every Girl Is Fishing; Indian Fox Trot Ball; Luana Lou; My American Beauty Girl (The Melting Pot); When He Comes Back to Me; Will-of-the-Wisp

Notes: No program available. Information from ASCAP and Library of Congress.

4836 • ZIEGFELD MIDNIGHT FROLIC (5TH EDITION)

OPENED: 07/27/1917   Theatre: New Amsterdam
Roof
Revue   Broadway

Composer: Dave Stamper
Lyricist: Gene Buck
Producer: Florenz Ziegfeld
Director: Ned Wayburn

Costumes: Marie Cook; Cora MacGeachy; **Musical Director:** George A. Nichols; **Set Design:** Alice O'Neil; Joseph Urban

Songs: B-R-O-A-D-W-A-Y; Flag of Our Land; Just Girls; Midnight Zeppo, The; Mississippi; Mons. France and Miss America; My Little Belgian Maid; Sweetie Mine; They're Getting Shorter All the Time; When I Hear That Jazz Band Play

Cast: Jack McGowan; Ann Pennington; William Rock; Dorothy St. Claire; Frances White

Notes: Also titled ZIEGFELD NEW 11:30 MIDNIGHT FROLIC.

4837 • ZIEGFELD MIDNIGHT FROLIC (6TH EDITION)

OPENED: 1917   Theatre: New Amsterdam
Roof
Revue   Broadway

Composer: Dave Stamper
Lyricist: Gene Buck
Producer: Florenz Ziegfeld
Director: Ned Wayburn

Costumes: Marie Cook; Alice O'Neil; **Musical Director:** George A. Nichols

Songs: Carmen Has Nothing on Me [2]; Cutey (C/L: Leslie Stuart); Every Girl Is Doing Her Bit; Gozinto; I'm Looking for the Great White Way (I'm Looking for Old Broadway); Long, Long Ago; My Tiger Rose (C: Gene Buck); Uncle Sam Is Santa Claus to the World; We Are Going on Our Honeymoon; We Are the Bright Lights of Broadway [1]

Notes: [1] Also in 7TH EDITION. [2] Also in TAKE THE AIR. [3] Not in programs.

4838 • ZIEGFELD MIDNIGHT FROLIC (7TH EDITION)

OPENED: 1918   Theatre: New Amsterdam
Roof
Revue   Broadway

Composer: Dave Stamper
Lyricist: Gene Buck
Producer: Florenz Ziegfeld
Director: Ned Wayburn

Musical Director: George A. Nichols; **Set Design:** Joseph Urban

Songs: Becky Is Back at the Ballet [1] (C: Leo Edwards; L: Blanche Merrill); Egyptian [1] (C: Leo Edwards; L: Blanche Merrill); Here Come the Yanks; Motor Girl, The; Spring Drive, The; Swinging Along; Syncopated Frolic, A; Tackin' 'Em Down [4] (C: Albert Gumble; L: B.G. DeSylva); Try a Ring, Dear!; Victory; We Are the Bright Lights of Broadway [2]; What Do I Care [3] (C: Walter Donaldson; L: Roy Turk); You'll Find Old Dixieland in France [5] (C: George W. Meyer; L: Grant Clarke)

Cast: Gladys Buckeridge; Lillian Lorraine; Bee Palmer; Bert Williams

Notes: [1] Added after opening for the two weeks that Fanny Brice joined this show. [2] Also in the ZIEGFELD MIDNIGHT FROLIC (6th Edition). [3] ASCAP/Library of Congress only. [4] Also in ZIEGFELD FOLLIES OF 1918. [5] May be in the next 1918 edition. Sheet music only. The song was sung by Bert Williams.

4839 • ZIEGFELD MIDNIGHT FROLIC OF 1918 (B)

OPENED: 1918   Theatre: New Amsterdam
Roof
Revue   Broadway

Composer: Dave Stamper
Lyricist: Gene Buck
Producer: Florenz Ziegfeld
Director: Leon Errol

Songs: Beautiful Girl; Cane Song; Carmen; I'm Looking for Old Broadway; My Little Belgian Maid; Springtime; Sweetie Mine; Swinging Along; They're Getting Shorter All the Time; When I Hear That Jazz Band Play

Notes: No other information available except sheet music.

4840 • ZIEGFELD MIDNIGHT FROLIC (2ND 1919 EDITION)

OPENED: 10/02/1919   Theatre: New Amsterdam
                               Roof
Revue   Broadway: 171

Composer: Dave Stamper
Lyricist: Gene Buck
Producer: Florenz Ziegfeld

Songs: Baby (C: Egbert Van Alstyne; L: Gus Kahn); By Pigeon Post; I Long to Linger Longer Dearie; I Love the River and You; I'll See You in C-U-B-A [2] (C/L: Irving Berlin); It's Nobody's Business but My Own (C: Marshall Walker; L: Will Skidmore); Lonesome Alimony Blues [1] (C: James F. Hanley; L: William Tracey); Rose of Washington Square (C: James F. Hanley; L: Ballard Macdonald); Shanghai; Tipperary Mary

Cast: Fanny Brice; W.C. Fields; Allyn King; Ted Lewis; Chic Sale; Frances White

Notes: No program available. Also known as ZIEGFELD NEW 11:30 MIDNIGHT FROLIC SHOW. [1] ASCAP/Library of Congress only. [2] Also in ZIEGFELD MIDNIGHT FROLIC OF 1920 (? Edition).

4841 • ZIEGFELD MIDNIGHT FROLIC (SECOND 1919 EDITION)

OPENED: 1919   Theatre: New Amsterdam
                               Roof
Revue   Broadway

Composer: Dave Stamper
Lyricist: Gene Buck
Producer: Florenz Ziegfeld

Songs: Colonial Days; Early to Bed and To Rise Never Made Anyone Wise (C: Abner Silver; L: Alex Gerber); Shanghai; You're a Perfect Jewel to Me

Cast: Eddie Cantor

Notes: The existence of this revue is uncertain but the sheet music seems to indicate it's another edition in 1919.

4842 • ZIEGFELD MIDNIGHT FROLIC OF 1920 (? EDITION)

OPENED: 03/15/1920   Theatre: Ziegfeld Danse
                               de Follies
Revue   Broadway: 148

Composer: Dave Stamper
Lyricist: Gene Buck
Producer: Florenz Ziegfeld

Songs: All the Boys Love Mary [3] (C/L: Joe Schenck; Andrew B. Sterling; Gus Van); Beautiful Birds; Colonial Days [1]; I'll See You in C-U-B-A [2] (C/L: Irving Berlin); Rockaway Mary [1] (C: Henry Piani; Sam H. Stept; L: Ballard Macdonald); Rose of Washington Square (C: James F. Hanley; L: Ballard Macdonald); World Is Going Shimmy Mad, The

Cast: Fanny Brice; W.C. Fields; John Price Jones; Allyn King; Lillian Lorraine; Carl Randall

Notes: [1] ASCAP/Library of Congress only. [2] Also in ZIEGFELD MIDNIGHT FROLIC (2ND 1919 EDITION). [3] Sheet music only.

4843 • ZIEGFELD MIDNIGHT FROLIC (11TH EDITION)

OPENED: 02/09/1921   Theatre: Ziegfeld Danse
                               de Follies
Revue   Broadway: 29

Composer: Dave Stamper
Lyricist: Gene Buck
Producer: Florenz Ziegfeld
Director: Edward Royce

Songs: Commerce, The; Compere, The; Gondolier (L: Ballard Macdonald); I'm Gonna Do It If I

Like It; Love is Like a Mushroom; Lovelight; Metropolitan Handicap, The; Pretty Faces; Puff, Puff, Puff; Rose of My Heart (C: Albert Sirmay); Summertime; Ten Fingers of Syncopation; World Goes Bobbing Up and Down; Ziegfeld Dollies, The

Cast: Fairbanks Twins, The; Herbert Hoey

Notes: This might have also been titled ZIEGFELD 9 O'CLOCK FROLIC, as most of the Midnight Frolics were. Also titled ZIEGFELD'S NEW MIDNIGHT FROLIC.

4844 • ZIEGFELD MIDNIGHT FROLIC (16TH EDITION)

OPENED: 11/17/1921   Theatre: New Amsterdam Roof
Revue   Broadway: 123

Composer: Dave Stamper
Lyricist: Gene Buck
Producer: Florenz Ziegfeld
Director: Leon Errol

Costumes: Howard Greer; Cora MacGeachy; **Musical Director:** Gus Salzer; **Set Design:** Joseph Urban

Songs: Bouncing All Over Town; Come On, Let's Go; Dancing Shoes; Honey-Bunch [1]; Let Me Whirl to an Old Refrain; Lovelight; Masks; Sally Slide, The; Swinging Along; Violet Ray

Cast: Leon Errol; Gloria Foy; Alexander Grey; Aubrey L. Lyles; Flournoy Miller; Carl Randall; Will Rogers; Muriel Stryker

Notes: [1] ASCAP/Library of Congress only.

4845 • ZIEGFELD MIDNIGHT FROLIC (2ND 1928 EDITION)

OPENED: 12/28/1928
Revue   Broadway

Producer: Florenz Ziegfeld

Cast: Eddie Cantor; Helen Morgan; Paul Whiteman and His Orchestra

Notes: No other information available.

4846 • ZIEGFELD MIDNIGHT FROLIC (1ST 1929 EDITION)

OPENED: 01/07/1929
Revue   Broadway

Producer: Florenz Ziegfeld
Director: Seymour Felix

Costumes: John W. Harkrider; Charles LeMaire; **Set Design:** Joseph Urban

Songs: Reminiscing (C: Walter Donaldson; L: Edgar Leslie)

Cast: Paul Whiteman and His Orchestra

Notes: This consisted of songs from prior Ziegfeld shows.

4847 • ZIEGFELD MIDNIGHT FROLIC (2ND 1929 EDITION)

OPENED: 02/06/1929
Revue   Broadway

Composer: Jimmy McHugh
Lyricist: Dorothy Fields
Producer: Florenz Ziegfeld

Choreographer: Sammy Lee; **Costumes:** John W. Harkrider; Charles LeMaire; **Set Design:** Joseph Urban

Songs: Looking for Love; My Man [1] (C: Maurice Yvain; L: Channing Pollock); Squeaky Shoes; What a Whalen of a Difference Just a Few Lights Make

Cast: Paul Gregory; Helen Morgan; Lillian Roth; Paul Whiteman

Notes: [1] Also in ZIEGFELD FOLLIES OF 1921, ZIEGFELD GIRLS OF 1920, and ZIEGFELD 9 O'CLOCK FROLIC (9TH EDITION).

4848 • ZIEGFELD MIDNIGHT FROLIC (SECOND 1929 EDITION)

OPENED: 1929
Revue   Broadway

Composer: Jimmy McHugh
Lyricist: Dorothy Fields
Producer: Florenz Ziegfeld

Songs: Because I Love Nice Things; I Can't Wait; Raisin' the Roof

Notes: No other information available.

4849 • ZIEGFELD MIDNIGHT FROLIC (? EDITION)

Revue   Broadway

Composer: Dave Stamper
Lyricist: Gene Buck
Producer: Florenz Ziegfeld
Director: Ned Wayburn

Set Design: Joseph Urban

Songs: Bachelor's Dream, The; I Love to Raise the Dickens; Pharoah's Daughter; When My Sweetie Comes Back to Me

Cast: Hal Hixon; Lillian Lorraine; Bee Palmer

4850 • ZIEGFELD NEW 11:30 MIDNIGHT FROLIC

Notes: All Midnight Frolics are under ZIEGFELD MIDNIGHT FROLIC even if they were titled ZIEGFELD NEW 11:30 MIDNIGHT FROLIC.

4851 • ZIEGFELD 9 O'CLOCK FROLIC OF 1918

OPENED: 1918
Revue   Broadway

Composer: Dave Stamper
Lyricist: Gene Buck
Producer: Florenz Ziegfeld
Director: Ned Wayburn

Costumes: Alice O'Neil; **Musical Director:** George A. Nichols; **Orchestrations:** Stephen Jones; **Set Design:** Joseph Urban

Songs: Acrobatic Rag, The; After the First of July; And She Went Home in a Barrel; I Love to Linger with You; Let Me Shimmy and I'm Satisfied;

Tipperary Mary; When My Sweetie Comes Back to Me; Won't You Play the Game?; Yiddishe Wampire, A (C/L: Blanche Merrill)

Cast: Delyle Alda; Fanny Brice; Lillian Leitzell; Lillian Lorraine; Bee Palmer; George Price; Bert Williams

4852 • ZIEGFELD 9 O'CLOCK FROLIC (9TH EDITION)

OPENED: 08/02/1920
Revue   Broadway

Composer: Dave Stamper
Lyricist: Gene Buck
Producer: Florenz Ziegfeld

Costumes: Marie Cook; Alice O'Neil; **Orchestrations:** Stephen Jones, **Set Design:** Joseph Urban

Songs: Beautiful Birds; Metropolitan Ladies [1] (C/L: Irving Berlin); My Man [2] (C: Maurice Yvain; L: Channing Pollock); My Rosary of Melodies [1]

Cast: Eddie Cantor; Billy Dove; John Price Jones; Gladys Loftus

Notes: [1] Also in ZIEGFELD GIRLS OF 1920. [2] Also in ZIEGFELD FOLLIES OF 1921, ZIEGFELD GIRLS OF 1920 and ZIEGFELD MIDNIGHT FROLIC (2ND 1929 EDITION).

4853 • ZIEGFELD 9 O'CLOCK FROLIC OF 1921 (3RD EDITION)

OPENED: 02/08/1921   Theatre: Ziegfeld Danse de Follies
Revue   Broadway: 29

Composer: Harry Carroll
Lyricist: Ballard Macdonald
Producer: Florenz Ziegfeld
Director: Edward Royce

Musical Director: Max Hoffmann; **Orchestrations:** Al Dalby

Songs: Face to Face; Gondolier (C: Dave Stamper); Icy Switzerland; I'm Gonna Do It If I Like It (C: Harry Akst; L: Irving Berlin); Little Love Mill,

The; Little Red Book (C: Dave Stamper); Love Nests in France; Painted Butterfly; Two Quick Quackers (C/L: Herman Hupfeld); When Sunday Comes Around; Ziegfeld Paper Dollies

Cast: Fairbanks Twins, The; Princess White Deer; Oscar Shaw; Anna Wheaton

4854 • ZIEGFELD PALM BEACH NIGHTS

Notes: *See NO FOOLIN'.*

4855 • ZIEGFELD'S NEW MIDNIGHT FROLIC

Notes: *See ZIEGFELD MIDNIGHT FROLIC (11th Edition).*

4856 • ZIEGFELD'S NEW MIDNIGHT FROLIC

Notes: *See ZIEGFELD MIDNIGHT FROLIC (16th Edition).*

4857 • ZIEGFELD'S NINE O'CLOCK REVUE.

Notes: *See ZIEGFELD GIRLS OF 1920.*

4858 • ZIG ZAG

OPENED: 09/1922
Revue   Closed out of town

Composer: Milton Ager
Lyricist: Jack Yellen
Producer: Arthur Pearson
Director: Arthur Pearson

Choreographer: Larry Ceballos

Songs: Cartoon Town; Harry Masters, Jack Craft and Company (C: J. Fred Coots; L: Irving Caeser); Jingle Bells; (We Are the Girls in the Chorus) Please Tell Me Who Looks Good to You; Steppin' School; When the Autumn Leaves Are Falling [1] (C: Dave Stamper; L: Gene Buck); Zig Zag

Cast: Cecil Lean; Cleo Mayfield

Notes: [1] Not in programs.

4859 • ZIG ZAG ALLEY

OPENED: 1902
Musical   Closed out of town

Composer: James Gorman
Lyricist: James Gorman
Librettist: James Gorman
Producer: W.E. Flack; Walter Floyd
Director: James Gorman

Incidental Music: Karl Weixelbaum

Songs: Belles of Zig-Zag Alley; Dreaming on the Ohio; Girl with the Banjo Eyes, The; Is It Love?; Kitty Kitty; Off for Atlantic City; Pinky Panky Poo; Queen of the Alley; Sally in Our Alley (C/L: Henry Carey); Southern Nightingale, The; We Are Four Actors; When I'm an Alderman

Cast: Ella Shields; Happy Zarrow; Jolly Zeb

Notes: Closed in Chicago.

4860 • ZIP GOES A MILLION

OPENED: 1920
Musical   Closed out of town

Composer: Jerome Kern
Lyricist: B.G. DeSylva
Librettist: Guy Bolton
Producer: F. Ray Comstock; Morris Gest
Director: Oscar Eagle

Source: BREWSTER'S MILLIONS (Play: Byron Ongley; Winchell Smith); **Source:** BREWSTER'S MILLIONS (Novel: George Barr McCutcheon); **Choreographer:** Julian Mitchell; **Orchestrations:** Maurice DePackh; Frank Saddler

Songs: Bill [2]; Business of Our Own, A; Forget-Me-Not; Furnished for Monty; Give a Little Thought to Me; Hail to Monty; It's a Bother to Be a Man; Language of Love; Little Backyard Band, The; Look for the Silver Lining [1]; Man Around the House, A; Mandolin and the Man, The; Producers; Telephone Girls; When You're Smiling (What a Smile Can Do); Whip-Poor-Will [1]; You Tell 'Em

Cast: Marie Carroll; Harry Fox

Notes: [1] Later in SALLY. [2] Different lyrics than the Hammerstein/Wodehouse "Bill."

4861 • ZOOT SUIT

OPENED: 03/25/1979   Theatre: Winter Garden
Play   Broadway: 41

Composer: Lalo Guerrero
Lyricist: Lalo Guerrero
Author: Luis Valdez
Producer: Center Theatre Group; Gordon
  Davidson; Shubert Organization
Director: Luis Valdez

Choreographer: Patricia Birch; **Costumes:** Peter J.
  Hall; **Dance Arranger:** Dan Kuramoto; **Lighting
  Designer:** Dawn Chiang; **Orchestrations:** Dan
  Kuramoto; **Set Design:** Thomas A. Walsh; **Vocal
  Arranger:** Dan Kuramoto; Daniel Valdez

Songs: Los Chuchos Suaves; Vamos a Bailar; Zoot
  Suit Theme (inst.) (C: Daniel Valdez)

Cast: Charles Aidman; Roberta Delgado Esparza;
  Abel Franco; Karen Hensel; Edward James Olmos;
  Lupe Ontiveros; Tony Plana; Daniel Valdez

4862 • ZORBA

OPENED: 11/17/1968   Theatre: Imperial
Musical   Broadway: 305

Composer: John Kander
Lyricist: Fred Ebb
Librettist: Joseph Stein
Producer: Harold Prince
Director: Harold Prince

Source: ZORBA THE GREEK (Novel: Nikos
  Kazantzakis); **Choreographer:** Ron Field;
  Costumes: Patricia Zipprodt; **Dance Arranger:**
  Dorothea Freitag; **Lighting Designer:** Richard
  Pilbrow; **Musical Director:** Harold Hastings;
  Orchestrations: Don Walker; **Set Design:** Boris
  Aronson

Songs: Bells (Sousta) (dance); Bend of the Road,
  The [4]; Better Than Nothing [2]; Bouboulina [1];
  Butterfly, The; Crow, The; First Time, The;
  Goodbye, Canavaro; Grandpapa; Happy
  Birthday; I Am Free; I Have a Friend [2]; Life Is;

Mine Celebration (dance); No Boom Boom; Only
Love; That's a Beginning [5]; Top of the Hill, The
[4]; Vive la Difference; Why Can't I Speak?;
Woman [3]; Y'assou

Cast: Carmen Alvarez; Herschel Bernardi; John
  Cunningham; Al De Sio; Maria Karnilova; James
  Luisi; Lorraine Serabian

Notes: [1] Added for tour. [2] Cut prior to opening.
  [3] Added to revival. [4] Same music. [5] Added
  for tour. Contains "Why Can't I Speak?"

4863 • ZULU AND THE ZAYDA, THE

OPENED: 11/10/1965   Theatre: Cort
Play   Broadway: 179

Composer: Harold Rome
Lyricist: Harold Rome
Librettist: Theodore Mann; Dore Schary
Author: Howard Da Silva
Director: Dore Schary

Source: ZULU AND THE ZAYDA, THE (Story:
  Dan Jacobson); **Costumes:** Frank Thompson;
  Lighting Designer: Jean Eckart; William Eckart;
  Musical Director: Michael Spivakowsky;
  Orchestrations: Meyer Kupferman; **Set Design:**
  Jean Eckart; William Eckart

Songs: Biggest Men Stumble, The [2]; Cold, Cold
  Room; Crocodile Wife; Eagle Soliloquy; How
  Cold, Cold, Cold (An Empty Room); It's Good to
  Be Alive; Like the Breeze Blows; May Your Heart
  Stay Young (L'Chayim); Oisgetzaychnet (Out of
  This World); Rivers of Tears; Some Things (1);
  Some Things (2) [1]; Tkambuza (Zulu Hunting
  Song); Water Wears Down the Stone, The; Yi,
  Yi, Yi (Aye, Aye, Aye) [1]; Zulu Love Song
  (Wait for Me)

Cast: Ossie Davis; Louis Gossett; Yaphet Kotto; Joe
  Silver; Menasha Skulnik

Notes: [1] Cut prior to opening. [2]
  ASCAP/Library of Congress.

Name Index

A

Aaron, Paul *(Director)* 2618, 3824, 3900
Aarons, Alex A. *(Composer)* 246, 2465
Aarons, Alex A. *(Librettist)* 4443
Aarons, Alex A. *(Lyricist)* 246
Aarons, Alex A. *(Producer)* 1419, 1528, 1800, 1859, 1879, 1929, 2363, 2376, 3157, 3243, 3319, 3379, 3993, 4118, 4300, 4392, 4443
Aarons, Alfred E. *(Composer)* 734, 1003, 1547, 1910, 2343, 2863, 3029
Aarons, Alfred E. *(Producer)* 1003, 1547, 1910, 2374, 2714, 2863, 2899, 3063, 3319
Aarons, Ruth Hughes *(Lyricist)* 2168, 4015, 4191
Aaronson's Commanders, Irving *(Cast)* 3382
Aarseth, Art *(Composer)* 3256
Abaldo, Joseph *(Cast)* 2146
Abarbanell, Lina *(Cast)* 1309, 1756, 2603, 2667, 2903, 2926, 3978, 4187, 4620
Abbate, Charles *(Composer)* 2749
Abbate, Charles *(Lyricist)* 2749
Abbey *(Producer)* 4500
Abbott *(Costumes)* 1869
Abbott *(Set Design)* 1869
Abbott, Allen *(Lyricist)* 1244
Abbott, Annie *(Cast)* 4172
Abbott, Bud *(Cast)* 4174
Abbott, Bud *(Librettist)* 1038
Abbott, Charles *(Cast)* 1445
Abbott, Charles *(Choreographer)* 4102
Abbott, Charles *(Director)* 4102
Abbott, Eleanor *(Set Design)* 1096
Abbott, Gardner *(Cast)* 1866, 1868
Abbott, George *(Author)* 297, 2449
Abbott, George *(Director)* 32, 161, 304, 323, 372, 404, 514, 619, 957, 1158, 1227, 1273, 1280, 1310, 1382, 1422, 1672, 1886, 2014, 2258, 2311, 2582, 2797, 3015, 3097, 3113, 3278, 3283, 3288, 3351, 3353, 4312, 4420, 4446, 4652, 4734
Abbott, George *(Librettist)* 161, 323, 514, 957, 1280, 1310, 1382, 1886, 2456, 3015, 3113, 3283, 3351, 3353, 4312, 4446, 4456, 4652
Abbott, George *(Producer)* 304, 323, 372, 514, 2582, 3353, 4420, 4432, 4446
Abbott, Joan *(Cast)* 1492, 2300, 3639
Abbott, Joseph LeGrange *(Cast)* 1624
Abbott, Judith *(Producer)* 32
Abbott, Marion *(Cast)* 1538
Abbott, Merriel
    See also Abbott Dancers.
Abbott, Merriel *(Choreographer)* 787, 1275, 4025

Abbott, Michael *(Composer)* 3181, 4533
Abbott, Michael *(Librettist)* 3181
Abbott, Michael *(Lyricist)* 3181, 4533
Abbott, Michael *(Orchestrations)* 2646
Abbott, Rita *(Cast)* 3028
Abbott, Tommy *(Cast)* 4625
Abbott Dancers
    See also Merriel Abbott.
Abbott Dancers, The *(Cast)* 1491
Abbott-Dunning Inc. *(Producer)* 2311
Abboud, Mona *(Cast)* 1648
Abdallah, Leigh *(Choreographer)* 518
Abdallah's Arabs *(Cast)* 1631
Abdillah, Shion *(Cast)* 730
Abdulov, Alexander *(Cast)* 2269
Abel, Chele *(Choreographer)* 2219
Abel, Ron *(Arrangements)* 2651
Abel, Ron *(Composer)* 4171
Abel, Ron *(Dance Arranger)* 450
Abel, Ron *(Lyricist)* 4171
Abel, Ron *(Musical Director)* 450
Abel, Ron *(Vocal Arranger)* 450
Abel, Walter *(Cast)* 1187, 2821
Abeles *(Lyricist)* 4681
Abeles, Edward *(Cast)* 1593, 4624
Abelson, Robert *(Cast)* 4342
Abelson, Robert *(Lyricist)* 4342
Abene, Michael *(Dance Arranger)* 2578
Abene, Michael *(Orchestrations)* 2578
Aber, Arline *(Cast)* 4023
Aber, Charline *(Cast)* 4023
Aberlin, Betty *(Cast)* 54, 1438, 2074, 2279, 4790
Abernathy, Lee Roy *(Composer)* 4030
Abernathy, Lee Roy *(Lyricist)* 4030
Abernathy, Pat *(Composer)* 226
Able, Will B. *(Cast)* 348, 798, 1841
Abraham, F. Murray *(Cast)* 2435
Abraham, Pal *(Author)* 277
Abraham, Paul *(Composer)* 277
Abrahams, Jody *(Cast)* 4264
Abrahams, Maurice *(Composer)* 965, 2939, 3259, 3399, 3525, 4813, 4821
Abrahams, Maurice *(Lyricist)* 3399, 4655
Abrahamsen, Dan *(Lighting Designer)* 1450
Abrahamson, Eric *(Composer)* 2039
Abrahamson, Eric *(Lyricist)* 2039
Abrahamson, Manford *(Dance Arranger)* 1092
Abrahamson, Manford *(Musical Director)* 4330
Abrams, Don *(Lighting Designer)* 4405
Abrams, Larry *(Producer)* 3059

Abrams, Steve *(Producer)* 4145
Abramson, Charles H. *(Producer)* 82, 3314
Abravanel, Maurice *(Musical Director)* 1284, 2344, 2386, 3301, 3691, 4169
Abravanel, Wayne *(Musical Director)* 2197
Acaro, Flavia *(Cast)* 742, 2684
Accooe, Will *(Composer)* 352
Accooe, Will *(Lyricist)* 352
Accooe, William *(Composer)* 2465
Accurso, Aron *(Cast)* 143
Ace, Goodman *(Librettist)* 1397
Achelis, Johnfritz *(Cast)* 4622
Achilles, Peter *(Set Design)* 3669, 4463
Ackel *(Lyricist)* 2419
Acker, Mitch *(Lighting Designer)* 2759
Ackerman, Dorine *(Costumes)* 348
Ackerman, Loni *(Cast)* 1038, 1478, 3456, 4038, 4145
Ackerman, P. Dodd *(Lighting Designer)* 2601
Ackerman, P. Dodd *(Set Design)* 381, 648, 670, 717, 765, 931, 1088, 1215, 1285, 1345, 1378, 1424, 1513, 1529, 1584, 1722, 1839, 1847, 1852, 1980, 2271, 2516, 2527, 2574, 2601, 2827, 2833, 3042, 3063, 3168, 3184, 3369, 3535, 3613, 3737, 4001, 4283, 4476, 4596
Ackerman, Robert Allan *(Director)* 2146, 2437
Ackland, Joss *(Cast)* 2240
Acosta, Elizabeth *(Cast)* 949
Acres, Harry *(Composer)* 4765, 4795
Acting Company, The *(Producer)* 693
Actman, Irving *(Composer)* 398, 850, 1126, 1414, 1415, 1989, 2105, 3410, 4191
Actman, Irving *(Lyricist)* 1989
Actman, Irving *(Musical Director)* 95, 1567, 1706, 4015
Actor-Managers, The *(Producer)* 1656
Actors Studio, Inc. *(Producer)* 477
Actors' Playhouse *(Producer)* 4750
Actors-Managers Inc., The *(Producer)* 1657
Acuff, Roy *(Composer)* 655
Acuff, Roy *(Lyricist)* 655
Ada-May *(Cast)* 791
Adair, Eddie *(Composer)* 1541
Adair, Eddie *(Director)* 1541
Adair, Eddie *(Lyricist)* 1541
Adair, Frank *(Cast)* 2761
Adair, Janet *(Cast)* 487, 1643, 3404, 3405
Adair, Jean *(Cast)* 933, 3002
Adair, John *(Cast)* 919
Adair, Josephine *(Cast)* 4683
Adair, Josephine *(Lyricist)* 1689
Adair, Patricia *(Cast)* 854, 856
Adair, Tom *(Cast)* 3121
Adair, Tom *(Lyricist)* 95, 3453
Adair, Yvonne *(Cast)* 1475, 2439, 4180
Adam, Noelle *(Cast)* 3187
Adams, Becky *(Cast)* 3601
Adams, Bob *(Cast)* 186
Adams, Bob *(Composer)* 830, 1908, 1910, 4723
Adams, Bob *(Lyricist)* 830, 1316, 1910
Adams, Clifford *(Lyricist)* 1136
Adams, Daniel *(Lighting Designer)* 4410
Adams, David *(Lighting Designer)* 3814
Adams, Dianne *(Vocal Arranger)* 4139

Adams, Dick *(Composer)* 1296
Adams, Dick *(Lyricist)* 1296
Adams, Don *(Librettist)* 4268
Adams, Edith *(Cast)* 616, 759, 2484, 4734
Adams, Edward B. *(Choreographer)* 1459
Adams, Emily *(Cast)* 2124, 2220
Adams, Frank *(Librettist)* 1307, 1563, 1593, 1967, 2155, 2408, 3579, 4185, 4387
Adams, Frank *(Lyricist)* 1307, 1563, 1593, 1967, 2155, 2408, 3579, 4185, 4387
Adams, Frank R. *(Author)* 2926, 3580
Adams, Frank R. *(Librettist)* 1606, 1801, 1908, 2926, 4506
Adams, Frank R. *(Lyricist)* 1316, 1606, 1801, 1908, 2512, 2901, 2926, 4506
Adams, Franklin P. *(Lyricist)* 1357, 2559
Adams, Gary *(Musical Director)* 4523
Adams, J.B. *(Cast)* 155, 275
Adams, Lee *(Librettist)* 36, 2288
Adams, Lee *(Lyricist)* 36, 57, 64, 167, 534, 550, 602, 607, 673, 1306, 1393, 1601, 1828, 1873, 2047, 2163, 2554, 2758, 2804, 3549, 3940, 3941, 3942, 4135, 4639, 4827
Adams, Leslie *(Cast)* 207
Adams, Margaret *(Cast)* 117, 2252, 4352, 4374
Adams, Mary *(Cast)* 203, 1836
Adams, Mason *(Cast)* 4278, 4565
Adams, Maude *(Cast)* 2329, 3450
Adams, Neile *(Cast)* 223
Adams, Nick *(Cast)* 3047, 3519
Adams, Pamela *(Cast)* 840
Adams, Robert K. *(Director)* 4292
Adams, Robert K. *(Producer)* 1435
Adams, Roger *(Composer)* 596
Adams, Roger *(Dance Arranger)* 145, 367, 596, 957, 1760, 2106, 2713, 2777, 2797, 3113, 3288, 3687, 4180
Adams, Roger *(Lyricist)* 3453
Adams, Roger J. *(Librettist)* 1469
Adams, Roger J. *(Lyricist)* 1469
Adams, Samuel Hopkins *(Author)* 4312
Adams, Stanley *(Lyricist)* 166, 417, 2397, 3018, 3907, 3955
Adams, Tony *(Producer)* 4560
Adamski, Johann *(Cast)* 214
Adamson, Harold *(Lyricist)* 190, 206, 297, 1136, 1207, 1251, 1879, 3249, 3993, 4023, 4025, 4180, 4197, 4264, 4335
Adano, Ernie *(Cast)* 4157
Adderley, Nat *(Cast)* 2692
Adderley Jr., Nat *(Composer)* 1637
Adderley Jr., Nat *(Lyricist)* 1637
Addinsell, Richard *(Composer)* 55, 392, 702, 818, 1618, 2227, 3186, 3940
Addison, John *(Composer)* 920
Addison, John *(Lyricist)* 920
Ade, George *(Author)* 2430, 4017
Ade, George *(Librettist)* 772, 1230, 1870, 3154, 3268, 3437, 3943, 4201
Ade, George *(Lyricist)* 1230, 3268, 3437, 3943, 4201
Adelaide, La Petite *(Cast)* 246, 1316, 2116, 2291, 2398, 2842
Adelaide, Mlle. *(Cast)* 4654
Adelaide, Petite *(Cast)* 470
Adelaide and Hughes *(Cast)* 2939, 3087, 3395, 4521
Adelman, Chas. *(Librettist)* 4761
Adelman, Chas. *(Lyricist)* 4761

Adelson, Leonard *(Librettist)* 2925
Adelson, Leonard *(Lyricist)* 90, 1716, 2246, 2925, 3383, 3558, 4798
Ades, Hawley *(Orchestrations)* 3100
Adiarte, Patrick *(Cast)* 658, 1315
Adkins, Walter *(Cast)* 4251
Adlam, Basil *(Composer)* 4824
Adler, Bernard *(Composer)* 2840
Adler, Bruce *(Cast)* 400, 921, 1609, 2352, 3231, 3722, 4342
Adler, Bruce *(Lyricist)* 573, 1609
Adler, Celia *(Cast)* 1299
Adler, Christopher *(Lyricist)* 1865, 2196, 3936
Adler, David *(Cast)* 2108
Adler, Elsa *(Cast)* 2264
Adler, Evelyn *(Composer)* 4275
Adler, Evelyn *(Lyricist)* 4275
Adler, Felix *(Cast)* 3865
Adler, Gil *(Producer)* 1166
Adler, H. *(Composer)* 1267
Adler, H. *(Lyricist)* 1267
Adler, Hyman *(Author)* 4275
Adler, Hyman *(Cast)* 4275, 4328
Adler, Hyman *(Producer)* 4328
Adler, Jacob *(Cast)* 1639
Adler, Jerry *(Director)* 1621, 1841, 1842, 2539, 3076, 3517, 4743
Adler, Jerry *(Producer)* 1094
Adler, Julius *(Cast)* 2352
Adler, Larry *(Cast)* 787, 1322, 2301, 4023
Adler, Lou *(Producer)* 3742
Adler, Luther *(Cast)* 1299, 2228, 4495
Adler, Luther *(Director)* 1299
Adler, Marion *(Cast)* 1702
Adler, Marion *(Composer)* 1702
Adler, Marion *(Lyricist)* 1702
Adler, Peter Herman *(Musical Director)* 1085
Adler, Richard *(Composer)* 957, 1507, 2227, 2355, 2550, 2965, 3015, 3227, 3273, 3351, 3984, 4399
Adler, Richard *(Lyricist)* 957, 1507, 2227, 2355, 2550, 2965, 3227, 3273, 3351, 3984, 4399
Adler, Richard *(Producer)* 3015, 3273, 3702, 3984
Adler, Stella *(Director)* 3536
Adler, William *(Costumes)* 4250
Adnopoz, David *(Cast)* 945
Adolphus, Theodore *(Choreographer)* 82, 1476, 2479, 3823
Adrian *(Costumes)* 223, 623, 1250, 2686, 3008
Adrian *(Set Design)* 2686
Adrian, Gilbert *(Costumes)* 1484, 1691, 3007, 3144
Adrian, Henry *(Director)* 1539
Adrian, Henry *(Producer)* 1539
Adrian, Iris *(Cast)* 1979, 3131
Adrian, Louis *(Musical Director)* 2234, 2327, 3453
Adrian, Max *(Cast)* 630
Adrian, Max *(Director)* 4268
Adshead, Patricia *(Costumes)* 1903, 2146, 2320, 4288
Adzima, Nancy *(Costumes)* 2332
Adzima, Nanzi *(Costumes)* 4799
Aeromaniacs, The *(Cast)* 3121
Aerseth, Arthur E. *(Composer)* 1629
Agee, James *(Lyricist)* 2633
Agee, John *(Cast)* 3533

Ager, Milton *(Composer)* 393, 418, 487, 712, 1395, 1919, 2135, 2706, 3005, 3175, 3428, 3648, 4197, 4296, 4460, 4637, 4683, 4814, 4821, 4858
Aghayan, Ray *(Costumes)* 167, 2590
Aghayan, Ray *(Director)* 2969
Aghayan, Ray *(Librettist)* 2969
Aghayan, Ray *(Producer)* 2969
Agnese, Rita *(Cast)* 1326
Agnolucci, Mario *(Musical Director)* 2605, 4085
Agombar, Elizabeth *(Costumes)* 129
Agostini, Lucio *(Orchestrations)* 3485
Agoust, Emile *(Choreographer)* 2825
Agoust Family, The *(Cast)* 4130
Agress, Ted *(Cast)* 3928
Ahern, Will *(Cast)* 2709, 3980
Aherne, Brian *(Cast)* 1007
Ahlberg, Irene *(Cast)* 1135, 1136
Ahlert, Fred E. *(Cast)* 3153
Ahlert, Fred E. *(Composer)* 39, 428, 2161, 2308, 2939, 3726
Ahlert, Fred E. *(Lyricist)* 2308
Ahrens, Lynn *(Librettist)* 754, 2646, 3285
Ahrens, Lynn *(Lyricist)* 754, 2646, 3039, 3285
Ahronheim, Albert *(Musical Director)* 1149
Ahronheim, Albert *(Vocal Arranger)* 1149
Aibel, Douglas *(Director)* 1739
Aidman, Charles *(Cast)* 4111, 4861
Aidman, Charles *(Librettist)* 4111
Aidman, Charles *(Lyricist)* 4111
Aiello, Frank *(Cast)* 2153
Aiken, Alfred *(Librettist)* 4623
Aiken, Alfred *(Lyricist)* 4623
Aiken, D.M. *(Set Design)* 3230
Ailes, Roger *(Composer)* 2962
Ailes, Roger *(Lyricist)* 2962
Ailes, Roger *(Producer)* 2146, 2962, 3557
Ailey, Alvin *(Choreographer)* 2368, 2775
Ailey, Alvin *(Director)* 2203
Ailey American Dance Theatre, Alvin *(Cast)* 2775
Ails, Roscoe *(Cast)* 423
Aimes, Paul *(Costumes)* 3533
Aingell, Gene *(Set Design)* 3752
Ainsley, Paul *(Cast)* 2212
Ainslie, Scott *(Cast)* 900
Ainsworth, Alyn *(Orchestrations)* 1741
Airaldi, Remo *(Cast)* 3937
Aitken, G. *(Composer)* 2498
Aitken, Iaian *(Set Design)* 1079
Aitken, J. *(Cast)* 874
Akerlind, Christopher *(Lighting Designer)* 1232, 3227
Akers, Andra *(Cast)* 3444
Akers, Hattie *(Cast)* 1479
Akers, Karen *(Cast)* 1649, 3171
Ako *(Cast)* 2861
Akron Club *(Producer)* 3296, 3848, 4780
Akst, Harry *(Composer)* 26, 202, 432, 478, 622, 665, 1293, 1813, 2373, 2587, 3120, 3144, 3444, 3709, 4291, 4534, 4813, 4853
Akst, Harry *(Lyricist)* 2227
Akst, Harry *(Orchestrations)* 3006, 3007
Alan, Charles *(Director)* 3647
Alan, Charles *(Lyricist)* 3647

Alban, Manny (Orchestrations) 1273
Albani, Olga (Cast) 3117
Albee, Edward (Librettist) 521
Albeniz (Composer) 1342
Alberg, Mildred Freed (Producer) 1742
Alberghetti, Anna Maria (Cast) 44, 347, 656
Alberni, Luis (Cast) 1020, 2371, 3063
Albert (Composer) 4723
Albert, Eddie (Cast) 499, 514, 2894, 3696
Albert, Ernest (Set Design) 113, 185, 350, 357, 377, 396, 476, 559, 591, 666, 976, 1095, 1295, 1356, 1458, 1459, 1543, 1712, 1746, 1758, 1881, 2101, 2117, 2123, 2145, 2181, 2184, 2213, 2465, 2506, 2534, 2667, 2715, 2722, 2725, 2974, 3129, 3494, 3570, 3581, 3773, 3977, 4181, 4219, 4247, 4614, 4724, 4804, 4805, 4806, 4807
Albert, Nelson (Cast) 743
Alberte, Charles S. (Lyricist) 3737
Albertieri, M. (Choreographer) 2374
Albertieri, Signor (Choreographer) 1285
Albertierri, Luigi (Choreographer) 4425
Albertino, Chateau (Composer) 4154
Albertino, Chateau (Lyricist) 4154
Albertson, Coit (Cast) 960
Albertson, Frank (Cast) 3895
Albertson, Jack (Cast) 84, 1040, 2397, 2653, 2809, 4152, 4377, 4423
Albertson, Lillian (Director) 1944
Albery, Donald (Producer) 455, 1277, 1644, 2240, 3271
Albini, Felix (Author) 307, 2538, 2668
Albini, Felix (Composer) 307, 2538, 2668
Albrecht, Gretchen (Cast) 2565
Albrecht, Johanna (Cast) 4002
Albright, Frank (Conductor) 345
Albritton, Dub (Composer) 4264
Albritton, Dub (Lyricist) 4264
Albro, Arthur (Cast) 1712, 2567
Alchourron, Rodolfo (Dance Arranger) 975
Alchourron, Rodolfo (Vocal Arranger) 975
Alcorn, Mlle. (Cast) 3405
Alcott, Louisa May (Author) 2219, 2550
Alcover (Cast) 2753
Alda, Alan (Cast) 170, 615, 991, 1389
Alda, Alan (Librettist) 991
Alda, Delyle (Cast) 465, 4033, 4813, 4814, 4851
Alda, Robert (Cast) 1706, 4633
Alden, Betty (Cast) 3866
Alden, Donald (Librettist) 2841
Alden, Hazel (Cast) 165
Alden, Jane (Cast) 1492
Alden, Jerome (Librettist) 4297
Alder, Elsie (Cast) 2907
Aldredge, Theoni V. (Costumes) 54, 150, 154, 155, 160, 162, 273, 278, 287, 305, 406, 459, 721, 722, 746, 807, 1103, 1159, 1359, 1660, 1890, 1990, 2048, 2064, 2106, 2360, 2677, 2820, 2983, 3000, 3018, 3075, 3094, 3305, 3338, 3718, 3862, 4013, 4028, 4067, 4151, 4297, 4370, 4384, 4485, 4727, 4799
Aldredge, Thomas (Cast) 3094
Aldredge, Tom (Cast) 2143, 3411, 3702, 4151
Aldrich, Charles T. (Cast) 736, 1208, 2184
Aldrich, David (Composer) 1635

Aldrich, Janet (Cast) 2654, 3568
Aldrich, Richard (Producer) 3457
Alegretti, Theodore (Cast) 1862
Aleichem, Sholom (Author) 400, 1265
Alers, Yassmin (Cast) 535
Alessandrini, Gerard (Cast) 1348
Alessandrini, Gerard (Composer) 1038, 1348, 1349, 1350
Alessandrini, Gerard (Director) 1348, 1349, 1350
Alessandrini, Gerard (Lyricist) 1038, 1348, 1349, 1350
Aletter, Frank (Cast) 363
Aletter, W. (Composer) 3753
Alevy, Maurice (Director) 1046
Alevy, Maurice (Librettist) 1046
Alex, Joe (Cast) 2753
Alexander, Adinah (Cast) 3181
Alexander, Alice (Producer) 3713
Alexander, Arthur (Cast) 803
Alexander, Brooks (Musical Director) 344
Alexander, Brooks (Vocal Arranger) 344
Alexander, C.K. (Cast) 181, 4370
Alexander, Calvin (Composer) 4
Alexander, Calvin (Lyricist) 4
Alexander, Cheryl (Cast) 3136, 3169
Alexander, Cris (Cast) 98, 3278, 4734
Alexander, David (Director) 1791, 2556, 4542
Alexander, Gus (Cast) 3028
Alexander, Hugh (Cast) 4514
Alexander, Hy (Librettist) 2105
Alexander, Irene (Lyricist) 3457
Alexander, Jace (Cast) 212
Alexander, Janet (Cast) 933
Alexander, Jason (Cast) 2205, 2822, 3448, 3718
Alexander, Jason (Librettist) 2205
Alexander, Jeff (Composer) 732
Alexander, John (Cast) 3097
Alexander, Katherine (Cast) 2613
Alexander, Larry (Composer) 4433
Alexander, Larry (Librettist) 4433
Alexander, Larry (Lyricist) 973, 2279, 4433
Alexander, Melville (Lyricist) 136, 697, 904, 1292, 2387
Alexander, Melville (Producer) 2387
Alexander, Newton (Cast) 1460, 1461
Alexander, Rod (Cast) 1679, 1933, 2137, 2837, 4323
Alexander, Rod (Choreographer) 177, 520, 3934, 4337
Alexander, Sharon (Costumes) 3905
Alexander, Sheryn (Lyricist) 2288
Alexander, Van (Composer) 4534
Alf, Johnny (Composer) 2245
Alf, Johnny (Lyricist) 2245
Alfonso, Gerald (Musical Director) 3264
Alfonso, Gerald (Orchestrations) 3264
Alford, Lamar (Cast) 1595
Alford, Lamar (Composer) 4343
Alford, Lamar (Lyricist) 4343
Alford, Larry (Director) 2208
Alfred, Julian (Choreographer) 136, 336, 780, 1552, 2119, 2363, 2377, 2461, 2666, 2691, 2710, 2834, 3043, 3177, 3237, 3295, 3319, 3540, 3617, 3866, 3868, 4037, 4248, 4476, 4539
Alfred, Julian (Director) 1584, 1882, 1921, 2446, 2601, 2834, 2922, 3213, 3222, 3478, 4001

Alfred, William *(Author)* 935, 942
Alfred, William *(Librettist)* 935
Alfred, William *(Lyricist)* 935, 942
Alfred, William *(Producer)* 942
Alger, Horatio *(Author)* 4289
Alger, Joseph *(Librettist)* 3104
Ali, George *(Cast)* 591
Aliabeck *(Composer)* 710
Aliabieff *(Composer)* 710
Alicoate, Jack *(Librettist)* 4651
Alinder, Dallas *(Cast)* 4449
Alinder, Dallas *(Producer)* 4343
Alison, David *(Librettist)* 4602
Alison, David *(Producer)* 4602
Alk, Howard *(Producer)* 4397
Allan, Dennis *(Orchestrations)* 3195
Allan, Dorothy *(Cast)* 2161, 2162
Allan, Lewis *(Librettist)* 2948
Allan, Lewis *(Lyricist)* 467, 2175, 2447, 2653, 3226
Allard, Martine *(Cast)* 4286
Allard, Michel *(Cast)* 1834
Allbritton, Dub *(Composer)* 3793
Allbritton, Dub *(Lyricist)* 3793
Allen, Amelia *(Cast)* 2605
Allen, Beatrice *(Cast)* 2351
Allen, Ben G. *(Composer)* 4278
Allen, Ben G. *(Lyricist)* 4278
Allen, Betty *(Cast)* 1109, 1494, 4447
Allen, Billie *(Cast)* 2513
Allen, Charles *(Producer)* 338
Allen, Cliff *(Cast)* 1342, 3103, 3104
Allen, Cliff *(Composer)* 3103
Allen, Clifford *(Cast)* 1729
Allen, Debbie *(Cast)* 52
Allen, Debbie *(Choreographer)* 661
Allen, Deborah *(Cast)* 3656, 4459
Allen, Dennis *(Cast)* 2018
Allen, Diane *(Costumes)* 1940
Allen, Edgar *(Cast)* 3365
Allen, Edward *(Cast)* 1916
Allen, Elizabeth *(Cast)* 1060, 1456, 3761, 3931
Allen, Eva *(Cast)* 4681
Allen, Fred *(Cast)* 2545, 3405, 3532, 4367, 4575
Allen, Fred *(Librettist)* 4367, 4824
Allen, G. Brandon *(Cast)* 2993
Allen, Gaelle *(Costumes)* 299
Allen, Gene *(Cast)* 4627
Allen, Gene *(Composer)* 406
Allen, Gene *(Lyricist)* 406
Allen, George *(Composer)* 1370
Allen, Georgia *(Cast)* 3684
Allen, Gracie
    See Burns and Allen.
Allen, Harry *(Cast)* 3580
Allen, Hugh *(Cast)* 4403
Allen, Irvin *(Cast)* 434
Allen, Irving *(Cast)* 692
Allen, Jay *(Librettist)* 2047
Allen, Jay Presson *(Librettist)* 499, 3624
Allen, John *(Librettist)* 4785
Allen, Jonelle *(Cast)* 1478, 2001, 4485

Allen, Joseph *(Cast)* 3786, 4364
Allen, Josephine *(Cast)* 677, 2041
Allen, Laurette *(Cast)* 1751
Allen, Lee *(Cast)* 169
Allen, Lester *(Cast)* 1312, 1483, 1484, 1485, 1486, 2902, 3352, 3409, 3907, 4357, 4426, 4602
Allen, Lester *(Composer)* 1460
Allen, Lewis *(Librettist)* 2815
Allen, Lewis *(Producer)* 52, 150, 154, 414, 2468, 4746
Allen, Lewis M. *(Producer)* 2047
Allen, Louise *(Cast)* 102, 1368, 1516, 4378, 4422, 4478
Allen, Lynne Clifton *(Cast)* 1099
Allen, Mana *(Cast)* 3227, 3306
Allen, Margit *(Lighting Designer)* 871
Allen, Marianna *(Cast)* 4454
Allen, Marty *(Cast)* 2479
Allen, Mord *(Lyricist)* 295
Allen, Nita *(Cast)* 1835
Allen, Norma Bradley *(Author)* 3631
Allen, Norman *(Cast)* 1721
Allen, Peter *(Cast)* 2437, 4089
Allen, Peter *(Composer)* 146, 1298, 2437, 2677
Allen, Peter *(Lyricist)* 1298, 2437
Allen, Philip Richard *(Cast)* 3198
Allen, Rae *(Cast)* 957, 1116, 3274
Allen, Ralph *(Librettist)* 1970
Allen, Ralph *(Lyricist)* 1970
Allen, Ralph G. *(Librettist)* 1038, 4197
Allen, Raymond *(Cast)* 1974
Allen, Redge *(Producer)* 1734
Allen, Robert *(Composer)* 1941, 3287
Allen, Robert *(Lyricist)* 3287
Allen, Robert Lee *(Cast)* 3011
Allen, Ross *(Conductor)* 3643
Allen, Ross *(Musical Director)* 3643
Allen, Sandra *(Cast)* 4217
Allen, Scott *(Cast)* 746, 2318
Allen, Searl *(Composer)* 1340
Allen, Seth *(Cast)* 2877, 2953
Allen, Steve *(Composer)* 42, 362, 4090
Allen, Steve *(Lyricist)* 42, 362, 4090
Allen, Ted *(Librettist)* 757
Allen, Thomas S. *(Composer)* 2745
Allen, Vera *(Cast)* 216, 904, 1654, 1656, 3955
Allen, Viola *(Cast)* 4671
Allen, Vivienne *(Cast)* 4143
Allen, Walter *(Cast)* 1661, 2156, 4724
Allen, Woody *(Author)* 3516
Allen, Woody *(Cast)* 3516
Allen, Woody *(Librettist)* 1408, 1648, 3186
Allen Jr., Joseph *(Cast)* 2729
Allen-Hodgdon *(Producer)* 1721
Allers, Franz *(Musical Director)* 530, 623, 1742, 1748, 2838, 3035, 3038, 3347, 3509
Allinson, Michael *(Cast)* 62, 2617
Allison, Bernie *(Cast)* 3806
Allison, Bessie *(Cast)* 1020
Allison, Fran *(Cast)* 3496
Allison, Fred *(Lighting Designer)* 2599
Allison, J.M. *(Producer)* 4425
Allison, Karl *(Producer)* 1082, 1873

Allison, Patti (*Cast*)   135, 1997
Alloway, Jackie (*Cast*)   1841
Alloway, Jacqueline (*Cast*)   1478
Alloy, Al (*Lighting Designer*)   4214
Allvine, Glendon (*Author*)   2348
Allyn, Helen (*Cast*)   4725
Allyson, June (*Cast*)   372, 3990, 4557
Almagor, Dan (*Librettist*)   2075
Almberg, John (*Cast*)   1172
Almy, Brooks (*Cast*)   690, 1161
Aloha Maids, The (*Cast*)   1840
Aloni, Yona (*Choreographer*)   3669
Alonzo, Alicia (*Cast*)   1670, 4142
Alper, Ron (*Cast*)   4774
Alper, Steven M. (*Composer*)   3181
Alper, Steven M. (Incidental Music)   1509
Alper, Steven M. (*Musical Director*)   1509, 2229
Alper, Steven M. (*Orchestrations*)   3181
Alperin, Yankele (*Cast*)   3670, 3781
Alperin, Yankele (*Director*)   2866
Alperin, Yankele (*Lyricist*)   2866
Alpert, Larry (*Cast*)   268, 2449
Alphin, Charles (*Composer*)   4007
Alphin, Charles (*Librettist*)   4007
Alphin, Charles (*Lyricist*)   4007
Alpin, Charles (*Composer*)   4184
Alpin, Charles (*Librettist*)   4184
Alpin, Charles (*Lyricist*)   4184
Alson, Johnny (*Cast*)   3871
Alsop, Peter (*Producer*)   1813
Alston, Barbara (*Cast*)   40
Alstone, Alex (*Lyricist*)   1834
Alswang, Ralph (*Lighting Designer*)   220, 221, 911, 1567, 3321, 3452, 4018
Alswang, Ralph (*Set Design*)   673, 911, 1567, 3321, 3452, 4018, 4377, 4397, 4499
Alter, Louis (*Cast*)   3153
Alter, Louis (*Composer*)   2, 124, 288, 418, 667, 703, 1128, 1132, 1134, 1932, 3382, 3444, 3840, 4043, 4235, 4291, 4824
Alterman, Michael (*Musical Director*)   2618
Alterman, Michael (*Orchestrations*)   2618
Alters, Gerald (*Composer*)   1233, 2288, 4627, 4829
Alters, Gerald (*Dance Arranger*)   1237, 1745, 2227, 4319, 4627
Alters, Gerald (*Musical Director*)   1892, 4319, 4627
Alters, Gerald (*Orchestrations*)   534
Alters, Gerald (*Pianist*)   1892
Alters, Gerald (*Vocal Arranger*)   4319, 4627
Altfeld, Vivien (*Choreographer*)   1754
Althoff, Charles (*Cast*)   4772
Altman, A. Arthur (*Producer*)   843
Altman, Arthur (*Composer*)   4193
Altman, Arthur (*Lyricist*)   4193
Altman, H. (*Lyricist*)   907
Altman, Jean (*Producer*)   843
Altman, Richard (*Director*)   722, 4577
Altman, Ruth (*Cast*)   507, 2636
Altmann, Adolf (*Author*)   3771
Alto, Bobby (*Cast*)   4347
Alton, Robert (*Cast*)   4050

Alton, Robert (*Choreographer*)   163, 173, 383, 397, 417, 420, 601, 901, 971, 1109, 1140, 1791, 1894, 1932, 1973, 2400, 2432, 2460, 2475, 2797, 3292, 3353, 3359, 3365, 3955, 4086, 4174, 4374, 4420, 4483, 4542, 4777, 4824, 4825, 4826
Alvarado, Trini (*Cast*)   3806, 4019, 4790
Alvarez, Anita (*Cast*)   1278, 1475, 2653
Alvarez, Carmen (*Cast*)   170, 1018, 2484, 2583, 4319, 4395, 4609, 4764, 4862
Alvarez Band, Fernando (*Cast*)   858
Alvarez Orchestra, Fernando (*Cast*)   854, 856, 857
Alverez, Marie (*Cast*)   3605
Amado, Jorge (*Author*)   3838
Aman, John (*Cast*)   1761
Aman, John (*Composer*)   4433
Aman, John (*Librettist*)   4433
Aman, John (*Lyricist*)   4433
Aman, Sara (*Cast*)   4829
Amaro, Richard (*Cast*)   975
AMAS Musical Theatre (*Producer*)   1702
AMAS Repertory Theatre (*Producer*)   1816, 4192
Ambassadors, The (*Cast*)   2818
Amber, Lili (*Composer*)   3669
Amber, Lili (*Lyricist*)   3669
Ambient, Mark (*Librettist*)   178
Ambler, William (*Cast*)   283
Amdrus, Sam (*Lighting Designer*)   3278
Ameche, Don (*Cast*)   1614, 1846, 2207, 2267, 3972, 4337
Amend, Karle O. (*Set Design*)   86, 1131, 1710, 2302, 2457, 3168, 3965, 4021, 4249
Amendolia, Don (*Cast*)   785, 1161
American Allied Arts (*Producer*)   1182
American Ent. Enterprises (*Producer*)   251
American League for a free Palestine (*Producer*) 1299
American Legion (*Producer*)   3683
American Musical Theatre Festival (*Producer*)   171, 2970, 3628
American National Theatre and Academy
    See ANTA.
American Place Theatre (*Producer*)   2236, 2290, 4167
American Producing Company (*Producer*)   2639
American Puppet Arts Council
    See also Bil Baird and Arthur Cantor.
American Puppet Arts Council (*Producer*)   56, 997, 3449, 3498, 4660, 4710
American Repertory Theatre (*Producer*)   4147
American Revue Theatre (*Producer*)   2259
American Shakespeare Fest. (*Producer*)   2859, 4715
Amer. Theatre and Academy (*Producer*)   3631
American Theatre Wing, The (*Producer*)   2175, 2653
American Viennese Group (*Producer*)   3698
American Youth Theatre (*Producer*)   3226
Ames, Ed (*Cast*)   134, 928
Ames, Elliot (*Musical Director*)   3654
Ames, Florenz (*Cast*)   138, 183, 1678, 2068, 2378, 2444, 3225, 3995, 4010, 4550, 4673
Ames, Florenz (*Choreographer*)   3995
Ames, Percy (*Cast*)   1417, 1579, 3710, 4059
Ames, Roger (*Composer*)   2766
Amoretti (*Lyricist*)   2859
Amos, Herbert (*Cast*)   3945

Armstrong, Will Steven *(Lighting Designer)* 656, 2048, 2053, 2097, 2355, 4190

Armstrong, Will Steven *(Set Design)* 656, 2048, 2053, 2097, 2355, 3551, 4190

Armus, Sidney *(Cast)* 4718

Arnaud, Leo *(Musical Director)* 4316

Arnaud, Leo *(Orchestrations)* 4316

Arnaud, Leo *(Vocal Arranger)* 4316

Arnaud, Yvonne *(Cast)* 1554

Arnaz, Desi *(Cast)* 4420

Arnaz, Lucie *(Cast)* 4334

Arndt, Dennis *(Cast)* 282

Arndt, Felix *(Composer)* 2291

Arne, Thomas *(Composer)* 3450

Arnell, France *(Cast)* 2362

Arney, Randall *(Producer)* 4074

Arnheim, Gus *(Composer)* 544, 2747

Arnheim, Gus *(Lyricist)* 544

Arno, Peter *(Author)* 3131

Arno, Peter *(Costumes)* 3005, 3131

Arno, Peter *(Librettist)* 1856, 3005, 3946

Arno, Peter *(Producer)* 1856

Arno, Peter *(Set Design)* 1856

Arno, Sig *(Cast)* 1681, 2838, 4075, 4386

Arnold, Anne S. *(Costumes)* 4149

Arnold, Barry *(Librettist)* 3752

Arnold, Barry *(Lighting Designer)* 576, 583, 941, 1581, 2110, 2242, 3600, 4022

Arnold, Barry *(Set Design)* 583, 3559

Arnold, Edward *(Cast)* 2194, 4335

Arnold, Franz *(Author)* 1534

Arnold, Helen *(Cast)* 1481

Arnold, Hurbert *(Orchestrations)* 4635

Arnold, Jack *(Librettist)* 4648

Arnold, Jack *(Lyricist)* 4648

Arnold, Jean *(Author)* 3564

Arnold, Jean *(Cast)* 1023, 2804, 4268

Arnold, Jeanne *(Cast)* 798, 1764, 4540

Arnold, Ken *(Musical Director)* 2303

Arnold, Lucille *(Cast)* 202

Arnold, Malcolm *(Lyricist)* 1201

Arnold, Marshal *(Cast)* 2303

Arnold, Maurice *(Musical Director)* 362

Arnold, Maurice *(Vocal Arranger)* 362

Arnold, Phyl *(Cast)* 1333, 2467

Arnold, Robert S. *(Composer)* 4030

Arnold, Robert S. *(Lyricist)* 4030

Arnold, Seth *(Cast)* 183

Arnold, Stanley *(Composer)* 1898

Arnold, Stanley *(Lyricist)* 1898

Arnold, Tom *(Producer)* 972, 1467, 2682

Arnone, John *(Costumes)* 2784

Arnone, John *(Set Design)* 373, 2784, 3010, 4129, 4676

Arnst, Bobbe *(Cast)* 2, 1690, 2872, 3766, 3796, 3980

Arnt, Charlie *(Cast)* 4365

Aroeste, Joel *(Cast)* 114

Arons, Ellyn *(Cast)* 4136

Aronson, Boris *(Costumes)* 612

Aronson, Boris *(Set Design)* 610, 612, 832, 933, 1061, 1265, 1294, 1329, 1571, 1711, 2536, 2615, 2948, 3340, 3813, 4237, 4583, 4640, 4862

Aronson, Frances *(Lighting Designer)* 109, 992, 1872, 2177, 2746, 3010, 3368, 3666

Aronson, Henry *(Dance Arranger)* 2012, 3576, 4139

Aronson, Henry *(Musical Director)* 143, 1276, 2012, 4139, 4349

Aronson, Rudolf *(Author)* 4728

Aronstein, Martin *(Lighting Designer)* 40, 101, 302, 406, 578, 766, 956, 1045, 1074, 1158, **1478**, 1660, 1848, 2014, 2043, 2075, 2368, 2785, 2918, 2953, 2954, 2958, 3000, 3018, 3075, 3389, 3516, 3603, 3825, 4029, 4196, 4450

Arrabal, Fernando *(Author)* 237

Arrant *(Composer)* 3297

Arrant *(Lyricist)* 3297

Arrick, Larry *(Librettist)* 4406

Arrick, Larry *(Lyricist)* 4406

Arrighi, Luciana *(Set Design)* 2047

Arrnunziato, John *(Producer)* 2759

Arselli, Raimonda *(Cast)* 4273

Arsenault, Darlene *(Cast)* 2521

Arthur, Art *(Librettist)* 1930

Arthur, Beatrice *(Cast)* 1265, 2713, 2910, 2965, 3899, 3941, 4369

Arthur, Carol *(Cast)* 1891

Arthur, Daniel V. *(Director)* 2254

Arthur, Daniel V. *(Producer)* 511, 2254, 2765, 2782, 2951, 3073, 3177, 3308, 3372

Arthur, Frederick *(Author)* 1551

Arthur, George *(Lyricist)* 3322

Arthur, George K. *(Librettist)* 3605

Arthur, Gus *(Cast)* 3316

Arthur, Helen *(Cast)* 1654

Arthur, Helen-Jean *(Cast)* 3874

Arthur, Henry *(Cast)* 3713

Arthur, Jean *(Cast)* 901, 1383, 3452

Arthur, Ken *(Cast)* 1371

Arthur, Lee *(Librettist)* 522, 2029

Arthur, Paul *(Cast)* 2548

Arthur, Robert Alan *(Librettist)* 2355

Arthur Film Prods., Michael *(Producer)* 369

Arthurs, George *(Composer)* 1067, 1783, 3322

Arthurs, George *(Lyricist)* 248, 356, 1067, 1783, 2385, 2854, 3996

Artigas, Michelle *(Cast)* 595

Artists Prod. Corp. *(Producer)* 560

Artman, George *(Producer)* 600

Arvold, Mason *(Lighting Designer)* 59

Asaf, George *(Lyricist)* 964, 1852, 3259

Asaf, Michele *(Choreographer)* 535, 4139

Asbury, Claudia *(Choreographer)* 695

Asbury, Cleve *(Cast)* 1776

Asche, Oscar *(Librettist)* 758, 2802

Asche, Oscar *(Lyricist)* 758, 2802

Ascher, Leo *(Composer)* 1334, 3592

Ascher, Leo *(Librettist)* 1334

Aschinger, Brian *(Director)* 1903

Aschziger, Lowell B. *(Lighting Designer)* 1595

Ash, Randl *(Cast)* 3346

Ash, Sam *(Cast)* 796, 1026, 1065, 1944, 1962, 2005, 2939, 3258, 3405, 3995, 4054, 4668

Ash, Sam *(Composer)* 1026

Ash, Sam *(Lyricist)* 1026

Ash, Samuel *(Cast)* 2292
Ash, Walter *(Director)* 4470
Ashburn, Carroll *(Cast)* 514
Asher *(Composer)* 4648
Asher *(Lyricist)* 4648
Asher, Frances *(Cast)* 2648
Ashland, Camila *(Cast)* 2928
Ashley, Barbara *(Cast)* 283, 3326
Ashley, Christopher *(Director)* 992
Ashley, Clayton *(Librettist)* 2397
Ashley, Elizabeth *(Cast)* 2435
Ashley, J.W. *(Director)* 1248
Ashley, Mary Ellen *(Cast)* 1108, 1279, 2012
Ashley, Minnie *(Cast)* 906, 1682
Ashlyn *(Composer)* 3562
Ashlynd, Denise *(Cast)* 139
Ashman, Howard *(Director)* 1591, 2544, 4020
Ashman, Howard *(Librettist)* 245, 1591, 2544, 3666, 4020
Ashman, Howard *(Lyricist)* 245, 330, 1038, 1104, 1591, 2038, 2544, 4020
Ashton, Colleen *(Cast)* 958
Ashton, Frederick *(Choreographer)* 1366
Ashton, Linda *(Librettist)* 1107
Ashton, Linda *(Lyricist)* 1438
Ashwood, Michael *(Librettist)* 3528
Ashwood, Michael *(Producer)* 3528
Askam, Perry *(Cast)* 3385
Askin, Harry
    See also Askin-Singer Co.
Askin, Harry *(Producer)* 2326, 4103, 4453
Askin-Singer Co.
    See also Harry Askin and Mort Singer.
Askin-Singer Co. *(Producer)* 1563
Asro, Alexander *(Cast)* 2432
Assaly, Edmund *(Musical Director)* 83
Assante, Armand *(Cast)* 482
Associated Artists, Inc. *(Producer)* 3388
Associated Theatre Design *(Lighting Designer)* 251
Association of St. Louis, Municipal Theatre *(Producer)* 1476
Astaire, Adele *(Cast)* 17, 168, 294, 582, 1345, 1419, 2376, 2614, 3333, 3402, 4023
Astaire, Fred *(Cast)* 17, 168, 294, 582, 1345, 1419, 1453, 2376, 2403, 2614, 3333, 3402, 3833, 4023
Astaire, Fred *(Choreographer)* 4212
Astin, John *(Cast)* 4278, 4369
Astley, Blanche *(Cast)* 770
Astley, Edward *(Cast)* 3901
Astley, Edward *(Librettist)* 3901
Astley, Susan *(Director)* 3901
Astley, Susan *(Librettist)* 3901
Astor, Suzanne *(Cast)* 3111, 3112
Astroba, Marie *(Cast)* 4227
Atari, Yona *(Cast)* 4396
Atchinson-Ely, Edgar *(Cast)* 511, 2358, 2668, 2722, 2917, 2990, 3985, 4662
Atchison, David *(Lighting Designer)* 60, 1927
Ates, Nejla *(Cast)* 1242
Ates, Rosco *(Cast)* 3860
Atherton, Daisy *(Cast)* 2275
Atherton, Effie *(Cast)* 704

Atherton, William *(Cast)* 1999
Atkins, Boyd *(Composer)* 1813, 3840
Atkins, Boyd *(Lyricist)* 1813, 3840
Atkins, Charles *(Cast)* 1474
Atkins, Cholly *(Choreographer)* 432
Atkins, Joe *(Lighting Designer)* 460
Atkins, Roy *(Cast)* 876, 877, 3709
Atkinson, Betty *(Cast)* 2085
Atkinson, Clare *(Cast)* 1206
Atkinson, David *(Cast)* 71, 190, 223, 743, 1548, 2750, 4542
Atkinson, Don *(Cast)* 2618
Atkinson, Peggy *(Cast)* 1229
Atkinson, Sarah *(Cast)* 4579
Atlantic Overtures *(Producer)* 730
Attaway, Ruth *(Cast)* 2994
Atteridge, Harold *(Composer)* 1735
Atteridge, Harold *(Librettist)* 199, 201, 351, 391, 487, 764, 910, 965, 969, 1065, 1096, 1267, 1460, 1461, 1462, 1678, 1693, 1767, 1923, 2135, 2419, 2490, 2494, 2538, 2696, 2706, 2857, 2939, 3148, 3149, 3395, 3396, 3397, 3399, 3400, 3401, 3402, 3403, 3404, 3405, 3406, 3407, 3523, 3737, 3778, 3958, 3985, 4010, 4427, 4490, 4553, 4621, 4657, 4711, 4747, 4821
Atteridge, Harold *(Lyricist)* 199, 351, 473, 487, 551, 558, 764, 827, 910, 917, 965, 969, 1065, 1096, 1270, 1327, 1335, 1460, 1550, 1693, 1735, 1767, 1963, 2135, 2419, 2494, 2538, 2667, 2696, 2706, 2732, 2757, 2870, 2939, 3313, 3333, 3395, 3396, 3397, 3399, 3400, 3401, 3402, 3403, 3404, 3405, 3406, 3407, 3424, 3523, 3701, 3737, 3778, 3799, 3827, 3958, 3985, 4010, 4427, 4490, 4553, 4655, 4656, 4657, 4711, 4747
Attfield, Howard *(Cast)* 846
Attfield, Kitty *(Cast)* 466
Attie, Paulette *(Cast)* 3876
Attles, Joe *(Cast)* 2225
Attles, Joseph *(Cast)* 441, 576, 2203
Atwell, Lester *(Author)* 1310
Atwell, Rick *(Cast)* 2375
Atwell, Rick *(Choreographer)* 3838, 4171
Atwell, Rick *(Composer)* 4171
Atwell, Rick *(Director)* 3838, 4171
Atwell, Rick *(Lyricist)* 4171
Atwell, Roy *(Cast)* 93, 123, 124, 168, 1285, 1819, 1966, 2406, 2424, 2532, 2765, 2869, 2951, 3005, 3250, 4177
Atwell, Roy *(Lyricist)* 75, 93
Atwill, Lionel *(Cast)* 1281
Atwood, Bob *(Dance Arranger)* 941, 4337
Atwood, Bob *(Musical Director)* 941
Atwood, Robert *(Dance Arranger)* 3801
Auberjonois, Rene *(Cast)* 394, 775, 798, 4450
Aubert, Jane *(Cast)* 1461
Aubert, Jeanne *(Cast)* 111, 289, 2423, 2813, 3584
Aubrey, Monte *(Musical Director)* 679
Auden, W.H. *(Librettist)* 3441
Auden, W.H. *(Lyricist)* 3441
Audience Associates, Inc. *(Producer)* 4584
Audran, E. *(Author)* 1650
Audran, Edmond *(Author)* 2365
Audran, Edmond *(Composer)* 526, 2365
Audre *(Costumes)* 183, 2551, 4362
Audy, Robert *(Choreographer)* 2913

Audy, Robert *(Director)* 2913
Auer, Mischa *(Cast)* 2379, 2629, 2838
Auerbach, Arnold *(Cast)* 3460
Auerbach, Arnold *(Librettist)* 7, 454, 620, 1880, 2137
Auerbach, Arnold *(Lyricist)* 1957
Auerbach, Boris *(Cast)* 3336
Aug, Edna *(Cast)* 1543, 4742
Augard, Amy *(Cast)* 2524
Augarde, Adrienne *(Cast)* 1114, 3098
Augins, Charles *(Choreographer)* 1296
Augins, Charles *(Director)* 1296
Augustine, John *(Librettist)* 4535
Aulicino, Armand *(Librettist)* 3938
Aulicino, Armand *(Lyricist)* 3938
Aulisi, Joseph G. *(Costumes)* 518, 1222, 2134, 2754, 3636, 3741, 4449, 4659
Ault, Helen *(Cast)* 4234
Ault, Natalie *(Cast)* 824, 1247, 1565, 1663
Aumont, Jean Pierre *(Cast)* 4435
Aunt Jemima
    See also Tess Gardella.
Auracher, Harry *(Composer)* 1404, 2261, 3423
Auracher, Harry *(Lyricist)* 1404
Auracher, Harry *(Musical Director)* 1404
Austen, Jane *(Author)* 1290
Austen, Phyllis *(Cast)* 3605
Austin, Beth *(Cast)* 3305
Austin, Bethe B. *(Cast)* 2065
Austin, Clara *(Cast)* 2122
Austin, Claude *(Orchestrations)* 4777
Austin, Elizabeth *(Cast)* 1108, 1797
Austin, Ivy *(Cast)* 3643
Austin, Ivy *(Voice)* 56
Austin, Jennie *(Cast)* 2122
Austin, John W. *(Cast)* 818
Austin, Leslie *(Cast)* 3314
Austin, Lyn *(Producer)* 868, 1064
Austin, Pamela *(Cast)* 2364
Austin, Ralph *(Cast)* 1975, 4493
Austin, S. *(Composer)* 1296
Austin, S. *(Lyricist)* 1296
Austin-Moore, George *(Cast)* 3747
Authors Producing Co., The *(Producer)* 1434
Autry, Herman *(Composer)* 39
Avedisian, Paul *(Cast)* 1903
Aveling, Charles *(Cast)* 1593
Aveling, Claude *(Lyricist)* 351, 1537
Averell, Robert *(Cast)* 1554
Averyt, Bennet *(Set Design)* 4244
Avian, Bob *(Choreographer)* 287, 2905, 4067, 4217
Avian, Bob *(Producer)* 1103
Avilla, Manuel *(Set Design)* 3380
Avnet, Brian *(Producer)* 3903
Avni, Ran *(Director)* 2354, 4769
Avon Comedy Four *(Cast)* 3403
Awan, Adrian *(Lighting Designer)* 1711
Axe, Ronald *(Librettist)* 427, 1648
Axelrod, David *(Composer)* 3111, 4396
Axelrod, David *(Librettist)* 108, 1648, 3077, 3111, 3112
Axelrod, David *(Lyricist)* 108, 427, 1648, 3111, 3112, 4396
Axelrod, George *(Author)* 3894

Axelrod, George *(Librettist)* 63, 943, 4018
Axelrod, Herman *(Director)* 4781
Axelrod, Herman *(Librettist)* 4781
Axelrod, Herman A. *(Librettist)* 1956
Axelrod, Herman A. *(Lyricist)* 1956
Axlerod, David *(Librettist)* 2935, 3484
Axlerod, David *(Lyricist)* 2935
Axt, William P. *(Musical Director)* 2340, 3775
Axtell, Barry *(Set Design)* 275, 3211
Axton, Hoyt *(Composer)* 3739
Axton, Hoyt *(Lyricist)* 3739
Axton, Max Boren *(Composer)* 3739
Axton, Max Boren *(Lyricist)* 3739
Ayer, Ethan *(Lyricist)* 3195
Ayer, Nat D. *(Composer)* 605, 662, 1151, 2448, 2892, 3134, 3681, 3827, 3996, 4589, 4799, 4803
Ayers, Bo *(Musical Director)* 2689
Ayers, Christine *(Cast)* 2397, 4826
Ayers, Jobee *(Cast)* 4829
Ayers, Lemuel *(Costumes)* 2327, 2331, 3035, 3326, 3351, 4123
Ayers, Lemuel *(Lighting Designer)* 462
Ayers, Lemuel *(Producer)* 2331, 3326
Ayers, Lemuel *(Set Design)* 462, 2137, 2327, 2331, 3035, 3263, 3326, 3351, 4075, 4123
Ayers, Mitchell *(Vocal Arranger)* 2750
Ayler, Ethel *(Cast)* 2190, 2355
Aylesworth, Arthur *(Cast)* 2262
Aylesworth, John *(Librettist)* 1120
Aylesworth, John *(Lyricist)* 1120
Aylward, Tony *(Cast)* 871
Aylwin, Jean *(Cast)* 3322
Ayr, Michael *(Cast)* 1669
Ayres, Bob *(Musical Director)* 2611
Ayres, Mitchell *(Musical Director)* 190, 2750
Ayres, Mitchell *(Vocal Arranger)* 189
Azenberg, Emanuel *(Producer)* 39, 40, 1325, 1620, 1633, 2205, 4062, 4210, 4334, 4342
Azenberg, Karen *(Choreographer)* 3601
Azenberg, Karen *(Director)* 3601
Azenzer, Arthur *(Musical Director)* 2043
Azito, Tony *(Cast)* 1638, 1755, 4370
Aznavour, Charles *(Composer)* 2245, 2558
Aznavour, Charles *(Lyricist)* 2245

B

B and M Productions *(Producer)* 1766
B.F. Concerts *(Producer)* 922
B.T. Express *(Composer)* 4534
B.T. Express *(Lyricist)* 4534
BMC Productions *(Producer)* 4205
BQE Dancers *(Cast)* 4347
Baba *(Costumes)* 128
Babatunde, Obba *(Cast)* 1103, 2173, 2513, 3690
Babb, Kevin *(Cast)* 828
Babb, Roger *(Cast)* 1715
Babbitt, Thomas *(Musical Director)* 4540
Babcock, Donald *(Cast)* 4186

Baker, David *(Composer)* 823, 868, 1047, 2168, 2227, 2288, 2804, 3473, 3940, 3941, 4028, 4153, 4388, 4566
Baker, David *(Dance Arranger)* 134, 823, 1061, 1310, 3577, 3702, 4764
Baker, David *(Producer)* 1047
Baker, Dylan *(Cast)* 4398
Baker, Edythe *(Cast)* 391, 1831, 1923, 2135, 3291, 4437
Baker, Evelyn *(Composer)* 470, 675, 1043
Baker, Gale *(Cast)* 2969
Baker, Herbert *(Composer)* 4827
Baker, Herbert *(Librettist)* 3499
Baker, Herbert *(Lyricist)* 1817, 4827
Baker, Jack *(Choreographer)* 1884
Baker, Jennifer *(Cast)* 4160
Baker, Joe Don *(Cast)* 477
Baker, Joseph *(Arrangements)* 3667
Baker, Josephine *(Cast)* 740, 4825
Baker, Kenny *(Cast)* 3301, 4486
Baker, Kent *(Cast)* 4469
Baker, Lenny *(Cast)* 2058, 3370
Baker, Mabel *(Cast)* 2978
Baker, Mabella *(Cast)* 527, 4453
Baker, Marilyn Cantor *(Producer)* 2657
Baker, Mildred *(Cast)* 3857
Baker, Paul *(Composer)* 226
Baker, Phil *(Cast)* 201, 203, 418, 622, 1395, 3008, 3149, 3406, 3523, 3594
Baker, Phil *(Composer)* 565, 1687, 3149, 3523
Baker, Phil *(Lyricist)* 3149
Baker, R. Melville *(Librettist)* 1374, 1573
Baker, R. Melville *(Lyricist)* 639
Baker, R.M. *(Librettist)* 2902
Baker, R.M. *(Lyricist)* 2902
Baker, Raymond *(Cast)* 2152
Baker, Rita *(Director)* 778
Baker, Robert M. *(Librettist)* 639
Baker, Robert M. *(Lyricist)* 639
Baker, Robert Michael *(Cast)* 549
Baker, Robert N. *(Lyricist)* 3033
Baker, Russell *(Librettist)* 1955, 4338
Baker, Sam *(Cast)* 3093
Baker, Scott *(Cast)* 2783
Baker, Susan *(Cast)* 4160
Baker, Theodore *(Lyricist)* 1589
Baker, Word *(Director)* 496, 1245, 2074, 2418, 3209
Baker-Bergen, Stuart *(Cast)* 54
Bakst, Leon *(Costumes)* 165, 2802
Bakst, Leon *(Set Design)* 396
Bakula, Scott *(Cast)* 2171, 2754, 3760, 4349
Bal, Jeanne *(Cast)* 1456
Balaban, Bob *(Cast)* 4783
Balaban, Bob *(Director)* 1575
Balaban, Cherry *(Composer)* 2288
Balaban, Cherry *(Lyricist)* 2288
Balaban, Robert *(Cast)* 4522
Balanchine, George *(Choreographer)* 247, 514, 612, 791, 911, 1101, 2061, 2379, 2597, 2859, 2909, 2985, 3283, 3767, 4075, 4640, 4652, 4715, 4825
Balanchine, George *(Director)* 612, 4640
Balding, Ivor David *(Producer)* 2663

Baldomero, Brian R. *(Cast)* 2905
Baldoni, Gail *(Costumes)* 760
Baldwin, Alec *(Cast)* 3884
Baldwin, Brooks *(Cast)* 693
Baldwin, Clive *(Cast)* 2235, 2436
Baldwin, George *(Cast)* 433
Baldwin, George *(Librettist)* 433
Baldwin, Islish *(Composer)* 1978
Baldwin, Islish *(Lyricist)* 1978
Baldwin, James *(Author)* 105, 477
Baldwin, John *(Composer)* 3739
Baldwin, John *(Lyricist)* 3739
Baldwin, Philip *(Set Design)* 4399
Baldwin, Tallmadge *(Cast)* 4103
Baldwin, Winnie *(Cast)* 2818
Baldwin, Winnie *(Producer)* 4570
Baleff, Ariel *(Costumes)* 1892
Baleff, Ariel *(Set Design)* 1892
Balemar Productions *(Producer)* 3902
Balfe, M.W. *(Composer)* 1897
Balfe, Michael *(Composer)* 1710
Balfour, William *(Cast)* 3219
Balieff, Nikita *(Cast)* 710, 839
Balin, Edmund *(Choreographer)* 600, 1047, 2288
Balk, H. Wesley *(Director)* 2001
Ball, Ernest R. *(Composer)* 310, 591, 1751, 1803, 1897, 2154, 231 0, 2498, 2662, 2990, 3642, 3753, 3827, 3910, 3981, 4544
Ball, George *(Cast)* 2578
Ball, Jonathan *(Cast)* 2416
Ball, Lucille *(Cast)* 4693
Ball, Michael *(Cast)* 211
Ball, Samuel C. *(Costumes)* 3711
Ball, Samuel C. *(Set Design)* 3711
Ball, Thomas *(Composer)* 4240
Ball, Thomas *(Producer)* 4240
Ballantine, Carl *(Cast)* 2965
Ballantine, Paul *(Composer)* 2140
Ballard *(Lyricist)* 4823
Ballard, Beverly *(Cast)* 2018
Ballard, Bob *(Orchestrations)* 2095, 2096
Ballard, Clint *(Composer)* 3111
Ballard, Clinton *(Composer)* 280
Ballard, F.D. *(Composer)* 3455
Ballard, F.D. *(Lyricist)* 3455
Ballard, Hank *(Composer)* 3739
Ballard, Hank *(Lyricist)* 3739
Ballard, Kay *(Cast)* 2925, 3925
Ballard, Kaye *(Author)* 1873
Ballard, Kaye *(Cast)* 322, 656, 759, 1018, 1600, 1873, 2294, 3524, 3696, 3788, 4323, 4829
Ballard, Kaye *(Composer)* 2294
Ballard, Kaye *(Lyricist)* 1873, 2294
Ballard, Lucinda *(Costumes)* 85, 117, 153, 657, 1456, 1670, 1749, 1894, 2144, 2615, 2817, 3036, 3972, 3989, 4095, 4143, 4169
Ballard, Pat *(Composer)* 3645, 4170, 4264
Ballard, Pat *(Lyricist)* 3645, 4170, 4264
Ballard Jr., Clint *(Composer)* 3671, 3925, 4264
Ballard Jr., Clint *(Lyricist)* 4264

Ballard Jr., Clint *(Orchestrations)* 3671
Ballard Jr., Clint *(Vocal Arranger)* 3671
Ballet Concepts *(Producer)* 4172
Ballou, David *(Costumes)* 3938
Ballou, David *(Lighting Designer)* 4582
Ballou, David *(Set Design)* 2664, 3619, 3938, 4582
Balmain, Pierre *(Costumes)* 1762
Balsam, Martin *(Cast)* 2464, 3210
Balthrop, Carmen *(Cast)* 4447
Balzar, George *(Librettist)* 180
Bamboschek, Giuseppe *(Musical Director)* 3219
Bambrelli, Maria *(Cast)* 2115
Bamford, George *(Composer)* 1978
Bamford, George *(Lyricist)* 1978
Bampton, Rose *(Cast)* 4409
Bancroft, Anne *(Cast)* 2073
Bancroft, George *(Cast)* 765
Bane, Paula *(Cast)* 620, 3893
Banes, Antoine *(Author)* 4624
Bangs, Charles Kendrick *(Lyricist)* 2724
Bangs, John Kendrick *(Author)* 2005
Bangs, John Kendrick *(Librettist)* 2399
Bangs, John Kendrick *(Lyricist)* 2399
Bankey, Chris *(Orchestrations)* 36
Bankey, Christopher *(Orchestrations)* 1813, 2208, 2790
Bankhead, Tallulah *(Cast)* 1416, 2510, 4059, 4827
Banks, Ada *(Cast)* 2979
Banks, Ernie *(Cast)* 1073
Banks, Larry *(Composer)* 3695
Banks, Larry *(Lyricist)* 3695
Banks, Leslie *(Cast)* 2591, 3451, 4207
Banner, John *(Cast)* 1413, 1681
Bannister, Albert *(Director)* 3457, 3596
Bannister, Albert *(Producer)* 3596, 3860
Bannister, Frank *(Lyricist)* 1836
Banome, Nino *(Lyricist)* 1436
Bantock, Leedham *(Author)* 1526
Bantock, Leedham *(Composer)* 906
Bantock, Leedham *(Librettist)* 353, 4663
Banton, Travis *(Costumes)* 910, 1250, 1577, 4427
Bantry, Bryan *(Producer)* 1873
Baral, Vicki *(Lighting Designer)* 2470
Baral, Vicki *(Set Design)* 2470, 2702, 3643
Barand, Robert *(Cast)* 3970
Baranov, Alvin B. *(Producer)* 1884, 4199
Baranova, Irina *(Cast)* 1336
Baranski, Christine *(Cast)* 829, 3142
Barasch, Norman *(Author)* 3874
Barat, Maxine *(Cast)* 4557
Baravalle, Victor *(Musical Director)* 25, 78, 126, 376, 582, 672, 773, 827, 841, 1551, 1625, 2816, 3014, 3144, 3146, 3699, 3735, 3949, 4150, 4667, 4818, 4819, 4823
Barbary Coast Prod. *(Producer)* 302
Barbeau, Adrienne *(Cast)* 1664, 4124
Barber, Ada Lytton *(Cast)* 1795
Barber, Bernie *(Composer)* 3614
Barber, Bernie *(Lyricist)* 3614
Barber, Ellen *(Cast)* 1418
Barber, Vivian *(Cast)* 1514
Barbier *(Costumes)* 201, 3150, 4170

Barbosa *(Costumes)* 3139
Barbour, Dave *(Composer)* 3428
Barbour, Joyce *(Cast)* 1202, 2238, 2570, 2788, 3556, 3634, 4010, 4118, 4327
Barbour, Nina *(Cast)* 1183
Barcelo, Randy *(Costumes)* 550, 1116, 1236, 2212, 2687, 2790, 2992, 3159, 3169, 3873, 3903
Barcelo, Randy *(Set Design)* 2790
Barclay, Don *(Cast)* 125, 1587, 2827, 3170, 3252, 4810
Barclay, Jered *(Choreographer)* 3902
Barclay, Jered *(Director)* 3902
Barclay, John *(Cast)* 689
Barclay, William *(Set Design)* 1589, 3667, 3724
Barclift, Nelson *(Cast)* 2057
Barclift, Nelson *(Choreographer)* 189, 2057, 4340
Bard, Robert *(Cast)* 3104
Bardaretto, Burrell *(Cast)* 1629
Barde, Andre *(Author)* 25, 2637
Barde, Andre *(Librettist)* 1309
Barefield, Eddie *(Musical Director)* 898
Barefield, Edward *(Orchestrations)* 242
Barer, Marshall *(Librettist)* 3288
Barer, Marshall *(Lyricist)* 1408, 1818, 1873, 2246, 2357, 2535, 2663, 3108, 3286, 3288, 3524, 3551, 3889, 4388, 4585, 4828, 4829
Bargy, Jeanne *(Composer)* 1697, 4433
Bargy, Jeanne *(Dance Arranger)* 1697
Bargy, Jeanne *(Librettist)* 4433
Bargy, Jeanne *(Lyricist)* 1697, 4433
Bargy, Jeanne *(Vocal Arranger)* 1697
Barholomae, Philip *(Lyricist)* 4562
Bari, Charles *(Cast)* 1258
Barie, B.J. *(Cast)* 3668
Barilum, Trudy *(Costumes)* 1347
Baring-Gould, Sabine *(Lyricist)* 3259
Barkan, M. *(Composer)* 4193
Barkan, M. *(Lyricist)* 4193
Barkdull, Leo *(Librettist)* 2114
Barker, Albert *(Librettist)* 2817
Barker, Clive *(Cast)* 4469
Barker, Edith *(Cast)* 191, 1445
Barker, Howard *(Costumes)* 249, 2522
Barker, Howard *(Producer)* 2522, 2664
Barker, Howard *(Set Design)* 2522
Barker, Jack *(Cast)* 799, 3184, 3819
Barker, Jean *(Cast)* 3544
Barker, John *(Cast)* 294, 1339, 2602, 3352, 4365
Barker, Marguerite Abbott *(Producer)* 1244
Barker, Richard *(Director)* 45, 476, 618, 727, 995, 1030, 1305, 1473, 1720, 2233, 2502, 2548, 2733, 3582, 4125, 4614
Barker, Ronnie *(Cast)* 3630
Barker, Shirley *(Costumes)* 1587, 1847, 2378, 2519, 4437, 4491
Barker, Shirley *(Set Design)* 1685
Barker, William *(Cast)* 2111
Barklie, Lance *(Librettist)* 348
Barklie, Lance *(Producer)* 348
Barlow, Anna Marie *(Librettist)* 101, 1727
Barlow, Howard *(Musical Director)* 1654, 1655
Barmark, Ira *(Librettist)* 1369

Barnabee, Henry Clay (*Cast*)   2345, 2697, 3570, 3736, 3881, 4559, 4598

Barnard, Armand (*Librettist*)   2782

Barnes (*Costumes*)   998

Barnes, Billy (*Cast*)   412, 3447

Barnes, Billy (*Composer*)   316, 407, 408, 410, 411, 412, 413, 450, 1341, 2080, 2969, 3447, 3499, 4057

Barnes, Billy (*Librettist*)   2969

Barnes, Billy (*Lyricist*)   316, 407, 408, 410, 411, 412, 413, 450, 2080, 2969, 3447, 3499, 4057

Barnes, Billy (*Musical Director*)   411, 413

Barnes, Billy (*Producer*)   413

Barnes, Binnie (*Cast*)   2547

Barnes, Charles (*Cast*)   4545

Barnes, Charles (*Composer*)   3594

Barnes, Charles (*Lyricist*)   3594

Barnes, Cheryl (*Cast*)   4459

Barnes, Eric (*Arrangements*)   3004

Barnes, Eric (*Musical Director*)   3004

Barnes, Eric (*Orchestrations*)   3004

Barnes, F.J. (*Lyricist*)   2858, 4757

Barnes, Gregg (*Costumes*)   3346, 4193

Barnes, Harry (*Choreographer*)   3228

Barnes, Irving (*Cast*)   1385, 4701

Barnes, Johnny (*Cast*)   1109

Barnes, Mae (*Cast*)   108, 603, 1989, 3660, 4827

Barnes, Marjorie (*Cast*)   1671, 2284

Barnes, May (*Cast*)   1050

Barnes, Paul (*Lighting Designer*)   1993

Barnes, Paul (*Set Design*)   1993, 2313

Barnes, T. Roy (*Cast*)   3333, 3672

Barnes, Terry (*Cast*)   2285

Barnes, Theo (*Cast*)   755

Barnes, Theo (*Costumes*)   755

Barnes, Tom (*Set Design*)   1412

Barnes, Wade (*Composer*)   3630

Barnes, Wade (*Librettist*)   3630

Barnes, Wade (*Lyricist*)   3630

Barnes, Will R. (*Composer*)   336

Barnes, Will R. (*Costumes*)   175, 185, 378, 712, 968, 1095, 1118, 1176, 1208, 1264, 1459, 1525, 1631, 1753, 1758, 1868, 1925, 1926, 2041, 2385, 2917, 2919, 2938, 3081, 3268, 3337, 3578, 3626, 3732, 3951, 4201, 4478, 4754

Barnes, Will R. (*Lyricist*)   336

Barnes, William C. (*Cast*)   255

Barnes, William C. (*Lyricist*)   255

Barnet, R.A. (*Director*)   761

Barnet, R.A. (*Librettist*)   306, 761, 1213, 2181, 2902, 2906, 3047, 3951, 4353, 4531

Barnet, R.A. (*Lyricist*)   306, 761, 2906, 3047, 4531

Barnett, Eileen (*Cast*)   2969, 3641

Barnett, Jack (*Composer*)   1120

Barnett, Jack (*Librettist*)   4428

Barnett, Jack (*Lyricist*)   1120

Barnett, Jackie (*Composer*)   1120

Barnett, Jackie (*Lyricist*)   1120, 4829

Barnett, Mary (*Cast*)   4291

Barnett, Mary (*Choreographer*)   4147

Barnett, Randy (*Musical Director*)   602

Barnett, Rose (*Cast*)   3951

Barnett, Stanley (*Producer*)   1380

Barnett, Zoe (*Cast*)   60, 2854, 3681

Barney, Alice (*Librettist*)   2943

Barney, Ariel (*Producer*)   2502

Barnhart, Robert (*Set Design*)   3457, 4479

Barnum, H.B. (*Composer*)   4788

Barnum, H.B. (*Dance Arranger*)   593, 4788

Barnum, H.B. (*Orchestrations*)   52, 593, 4788

Barnum, H.B. (*Vocal Arranger*)   52

Baron, Art (*Cast*)   4076

Baron, Christy (*Cast*)   3227

Baron, Evalyn (*Cast*)   394, 1256, 1897, 2049, 3631, 3644, 3858

Baron, Linda Michelle (*Lyricist*)   4645

Baron, Marie (*Cast*)   1079

Baron, Maurice (*Orchestrations*)   3639

Baron, Sandy (*Cast*)   1471

Barone, John (*Cast*)   3463

Barovick, Fred (*Orchestrations*)   137

Barr, Edna (*Cast*)   2640

Barr, George (*Librettist*)   627

Barr, Kenn (*Costumes*)   1571, 2751, 2940, 3947, 4428

Barr, Michael (*Composer*)   1107

Barr, Richard (*Producer*)   72, 1662, 2678, 4233

Barraclough, Sydney (*Cast*)   2506

Barrat, Maxine (*Cast*)   3292

Barratt, Augustus (*Composer*)   **1240**, 1519, 1544, 1852, 2180, 2546, 3031, 3402, 3618

Barratt, Augustus (*Lyricist*)   1240, 1544, 1852, 2180, 2816, 3618

Barratt, Augustus (*Musical Director*)   1565, 1780, 1852, 2056, 2399, 2524, 2546, 2603, 3031, 3618, 3978, 4219, 4637

Barratt, Virginia (*Cast*)   4621

Barratt, Watson (*Costumes*)   1506

Barratt, Watson (*Librettist*)   199

Barratt, Watson (*Lighting Designer*)   1506

Barratt, Watson (*Set Design*)   110, 138, 184, 199, 200, 201, 202, 203, 204, 324, 391, 463, 487, 495, 659, 718, 764, 771, 814, 905, 948, 969, 1033, 1096, 1207, 1219, 1384, 1460, 1461, 1462, 1506, 1557, 1678, 1693, 1799, 1836, 1992, 2115, 2135, 2293, 2384, 2396, 2397, 2419, 2540, 2546, 2595, 2602, 2622, 2628, 2637, 2706, 2747, 2757, 2789, 2808, 2816, 2843, 2870, 2939, 2947, 3011, 3012, 3056, 3064, 3084, 3148, 3149, 3150, 3152, 3170, 3258, 3310, 3402, 3403, 3405, 3406, 3407, 3410, 3523, 3573, 3586, 3680, 3778, 3974, 3985, 4010, 4025, 4121, 4170, 4188, 4213, 4352, 4365, 4375, 4427, 4575, 4586, 4621, 4654, 4670, 4730, 4733, 4777, 4824, 4826

Barre (*Author*)   3237

Barre, Albert (*Author*)   4624

Barre, Gabriel (*Cast*)   147, 1353, 3456, 3695, 4139

Barre, Gabriel (*Director*)   1969, 2224, 3377

Barre, Stella (*Cast*)   3122

Barreca, Chris (*Set Design*)   789

Barrett, Alan (*Costumes*)   2047

Barrett, Brent (*Cast*)   589, 784, 3544

Barrett, Christopher (*Cast*)   16

Barrett, Gene (*Cast*)   1269, 3669

Barrett, James Lee (*Author*)   3928

Barrett, James Lee (*Librettist*)   3928

Barrett, Joe (*Cast*)   508, 1172

Barrett, John (*Cast*)   2124

Barrett, Leslie *(Cast)* 3059
Barrett, Lester *(Lyricist)* 1430
Barrett, Mace *(Cast)* 1567, 4272
Barrett, Nancy *(Cast)* 3482
Barrett, Sheila *(Cast)* 1693, 4374
Barrett, William E. *(Author)* 2583
Barrett Jr., Oscar *(Producer)* 3213
Barri, Bebe *(Choreographer)* 2972
Barri, Maud Lillian *(Cast)* 2502
Barrie, Alexandra *(Cast)* 459
Barrie, Ann *(Cast)* 3822
Barrie, Barbara *(Cast)* 262, 832, 1977, 2859, 3871
Barrie, George *(Composer)* 4743
Barrie, Gracie *(Cast)* 1493, 3955, 4177
Barrie, H. Owen *(Author)* 4830
Barrie, James *(Author)* 2680
Barrie, James M. *(Author)* 2329, 3439, 3450, 3451, 3453, 3454, 3472, 3779
Barrie, James M. *(Composer)* 3450
Barrie, James M. *(Librettist)* 3452, 3453
Barrie, James M. *(Lyricist)* 3450
Barrie, Leslie *(Cast)* 163
Barrie, Mona *(Cast)* 4569
Barrile, Anthony *(Cast)* 4676
Barrillet, Pierre *(Author)* 98
Barrington, Rutland *(Cast)* 4663
Barrington, Rutland *(Lyricist)* 906
Barris *(Lyricist)* 4697
Barris, Harry *(Composer)* 1425
Barris, Harry *(Lyricist)* 1425
Barrison, Mabel *(Cast)* 250, 472, 1054, 1316, 2408, 2649, 3566, 4478
Barron, David *(Cast)* 451, 1258, 2654, 3864
Barron, Evelyn *(Producer)* 4286
Barron, Judith *(Cast)* 4824
Barron, P.J. *(Librettist)* 353
Barrosa, A.E. *(Set Design)* 703
Barrow, Bernard *(Director)* 4124
Barrow, P.J. *(Lyricist)* 353
Barrow, Patrick *(Composer)* 3828
Barrow, Patrick *(Lyricist)* 3828
Barrow, Ting *(Lighting Designer)* 3111
Barrows, Fred *(Cast)* 696
Barrows, Richard *(Cast)* 1085, 2658
Barrows, William *(Cast)* 263
Barruschee, Leo *(Choreographer)* 396
Barry, Carolyne *(Director)* 2046
Barry, Frank *(Orchestrations)* 670, 2308, 2380, 2461, 3719, 3946, 4529
Barry, Fred *(Orchestrations)* 4818, 4819
Barry, Gene *(Cast)* 454, 1577, 1748, 2360, 3767, 4114, 4331
Barry, Jeff *(Composer)* 1383, 2427, 3739, 4193, 4534
Barry, Jeff *(Lyricist)* 1383, 2427, 3739, 4193, 4534
Barry, Jimmie *(Cast)* 3323
Barry, John *(Composer)* 2539, 2568
Barry, Jorday *(Set Design)* 4773
Barry, Julian *(Librettist)* 2196
Barry, Katie *(Cast)* 2716
Barry, Leonard *(Cast)* 1502
Barry, Michael *(Cast)* 1657
Barry, Mrs. Jimmy *(Cast)* 3323

Barry, Peter *(Librettist)* 4498
Barry, Peter *(Lyricist)* 2707, 3698, 4394, 4498
Barry, Philip *(Author)* 1762, 3468
Barry, Robert *(Lighting Designer)* 759
Barry, Rod *(Cast)* 3112
Barry, Rodd *(Cast)* 3111
Barry, Suzanne *(Cast)* 2011
Barry Sisters *(Cast)* 862
Barrymore, Ethel *(Cast)* 17, 2855, 4230
Barrymore, John *(Cast)* 515, 3686, 4185
Barrymore, Lionel *(Cast)* 2403
Barsky, Barbara *(Cast)* 871
Barsony, Rosy *(Cast)* 277
Barstow, Edith *(Choreographer)* 3715
Barstow, Richard *(Choreographer)* 304, 3107
Barstow, Richard *(Director)* 3715
Bart, Lionel *(Cast)* 2572
Bart, Lionel *(Composer)* 455, 874, 1089, 1277, 2368, 2572, 2682, 3271, 4469, 4685, 4749
Bart, Lionel *(Director)* 455, 4685
Bart, Lionel *(Librettist)* 455, 3271, 4469
Bart, Lionel *(Lyricist)* 455, 874, 1089, 1277, 2368, 2563, 2572, 2682, 3271, 4469, 4685, 4749
Bart, Roger *(Cast)* 4518
Barte, Leon *(Cast)* 4166
Bartel, Paul *(Librettist)* 1149
Bartel, Paul *(Screenwriter)* 1149
Bartels, Louis John *(Cast)* 1297
Bartes, John *(Cast)* 1047
Bartfeld, Carl *(Librettist)* 4328
Barth, Gene *(Costumes)* 2887
Barth, Lee *(Lyricist)* 3155
Bartholomae, Donald *(Librettist)* 4167
Bartholomae, Philip *(Author)* 2342, 4283, 4555
Bartholomae, Philip *(Librettist)* 1557, 1685, 2342, 2884, 3300, 3333, 4555, 4644
Bartholomae, Philip *(Lyricist)* 1557, 1685, 2884, 3300, 3333, 4644
Bartholomae, Philip *(Producer)* 2884, 4644
Bartlett, D'Jamin *(Cast)* 482, 1581, 2536, 4114, 4480
Bartlett, Harry *(Cast)* 3026
Bartlett, Josephine *(Cast)* 2697, 4497
Bartlett, Lisbeth *(Cast)* 264
Bartlett, Michael *(Cast)* 1329, 4365, 4372
Bartley, Dallas *(Composer)* 1296
Bartley, Dallas *(Lyricist)* 1296
Bartley, Nailbro *(Author)* 1796
Barto, Betty Lou *(Cast)* 206
Barton, Dewey *(Cast)* 1840
Barton, Earl *(Choreographer)* 2742
Barton, Fred *(Cast)* 1348
Barton, Fred *(Musical Director)* 1348, 2022
Barton, James *(Cast)* 397, 532, 1033, 2419, 3179, 3347, 3403, 3407, 3778, 3984, 4235, 4648
Barton, Julien *(Director)* 938
Barton, Mary *(Cast)* 2085
Barton, Steve *(Cast)* 3464, 3682
Barton, William *(Lyricist)* 1392
Bartow, Arthur *(Cast)* 2584, 3876
Bartsch, Michael *(Cast)* 1701
Barty, Billy *(Cast)* 1730

Baruch, Hugo (Costumes)   742
Baruch, Hugo (Set Design)   3092
Baruch, Moishe (Producer)   3669, 4463
Baruch, Steven (Producer)   992, 4031, 4076
Barzell, Wolfe (Cast)   4191
Barzin, Leon (Musical Director)   4548
Barzman, Ben (Librettist)   2809, 4316
Barzman, Sol (Librettist)   2809, 4316
Basie, Count (Composer)   4534
Basile, Frank (Producer)   2852
Baskcomb, A.W. (Cast)   1454, 2788
Baskerville, Priscilla (Cast)   1291, 4091
Baskette, Billy (Composer)   3401
Baskette, Billy (Lyricist)   4813
Baskette, Jimmie (Cast)   443, 1980, 1984
Basotina, James (Cast)   3938
Basquette, Lina (Cast)   4817
Bass, Emory (Cast)   2659, 3427, 3897
Bass, George Houston (Lyricist)   3001
Bass, Jules (Director)   928
Bass, Jules (Lyricist)   928, 2941, 3833, 4471
Bass, Jules (Producer)   928, 2941
Bass, Paul (Cast)   2690, 3054
Bass, R. (Composer)   4193
Bass, R. (Lyricist)   4193
Bass, Ralph (Composer)   4264
Bass, Ralph (Lyricist)   4264
Basse, Eli (Librettist)   4180
Bassett, John A. (Librettist)   2249
Bassett, John A. (Lyricist)   2249
Bassett, Peter (Cast)   3432
Bassman, Bruce D. (Lighting Designer)   4584
Bassman, George (Composer)   2809
Bassman, George (Musical Director)   2975
Bassman, George (Orchestrations)   59, 1706, 2809, 4827
Bataille, Henri (Lyricist)   4240
Batchelder, William H. (Lighting Designer)   1075
Batchelor, Ruth (Lyricist)   3619
Batchelor, W.H. (Composer)   45, 175, 1466
Batchelor, William H. (Musical Director)   1374
Bateman, Edgar (Lyricist)   3857
Bateman, James (Lyricist)   932
Bateman, R. (Composer)   4193
Bateman, R. (Lyricist)   4193
Bates, Blanche (Cast)   1502
Bates, Charles (Cast)   1646
Bates, Charles (Lyricist)   2135
Bates, Edna (Cast)   2184
Bates, Jerome Preston (Cast)   2239
Bates, Katherine Lee (Lyricist)   4390
Bates, Kathy (Cast)   3010
Bates, Lulu (Cast)   420, 1237, 1300, 3113
Bates, Peg Leg (Cast)   445, 886
Bates, Sally (Cast)   2739
Bates, Thorpe (Cast)   1610, 4760
Batie, Franklyn (Cast)   391, 1462
Batt, Bryan (Cast)   4217
Batt, Mike (Lyricist)   3464
Batten, Tom (Cast)   3279
Batterberry, Michael (Director)   1370
Batterberry, Michael (Producer)   1370

Battie, Franklyn (Cast)   3401
Battis, Emery (Cast)   951, 3195
Battista, Lloyd (Cast)   1377, 2320
Battista, Miriam (Cast)   1342, 1979
Battista, Miriam (Librettist)   4015
Battista, Miriam (Lyricist)   4015
Battle, Edwin (Cast)   1099, 2970
Battle, Hinton (Cast)   2905, 3932, 4091, 4286, 4722
Battle, Joseph (Cast)   303
Battle, Kathleen (Cast)   4447
Battles, George (Cast)   2302
Battles, John (Cast)   85, 3278, 4337
Bauduc, Ray (Composer)   964
Bauer, Felice (Librettist)   4609
Bauer, George (Arrangements)   382
Bauer, George (Composer)   4153
Bauer, George (Dance Arranger)   4153
Bauer, George (Librettist)   4153
Bauer, George (Lyricist)   4153
Bauer, George (Musical Director)   382, 2439, 4153
Bauer, George (Pianist)   2439
Bauer, George (Vocal Arranger)   4153
Bauer, Julius (Author)   2732
Baughan, Terry (Cast)   809
Baughman, Renee (Cast)   746
Baum, Bernie (Composer)   4264
Baum, Bernie (Lyricist)   4264
Baum, Gene (Lighting Designer)   177
Baum, Joanne (Cast)   3811
Baum, L. Frank (Author)   4381, 4722, 4723, 4725
Baum, L. Frank (Librettist)   4381, 4723, 4725
Baum, L. Frank (Lyricist)   4381, 4723, 4725
Baum, Marilyn (Director)   3034
Baum, Susan J. (Cast)   2055
Baum, Vicki (Author)   223, 1649
Bauman, John (Musical Director)   3824
Bauman, William (Cast)   4770
Baur, Franklin (Cast)   4821
Bautier, Michele (Cast)   4137
Bavaar, Tony (Cast)   3347
Bavan, Yolande (Cast)   756, 1809, 2236, 2433, 3824, 4035
Bawtree, Michael (Director)   599
Baxley, Barbara (Cast)   3918
Baxt, George (Librettist)   2554
Baxter, Alan (Librettist)   622, 2475, 3365, 4374
Baxter, George (Cast)   2595
Baxter, Gladys (Cast)   948, 3573
Baxter, Rebecca (Cast)   2199
Baxter, Skippy (Cast)   4143
Baxtresser, Suzanne (Cast)   1715
Bay, Howard (Costumes)   1959, 2727
Bay, Howard (Director)   206
Bay, Howard (Lighting Designer)   935, 1300, 1336, 1577, 1730, 1959, 2679, 2727, 2748, 2864, 3016, 3612, 3831, 4496, 4524, 4537
Bay, Howard (Set Design)   206, 653, 901, 935, 1300, 1336, 1577, 1730, 1959, 2175, 2234, 2510, 2679, 2727, 2748, 2755, 2850, 2864, 3016, 3180, 3301, 3536, 3612, 3831, 4058, 4117, 4496, 4524, 4537
Bayer, Carole
   See also Carole Bayer Sager.

Belt, Madeline *(Cast)* 1989, 2034

Belton, John *(Cast)* 4556

Belushi, John *(Cast)* 3077

Belushi, John *(Librettist)* 3076

Belzer, Rick *(Lighting Designer)* 172, 1732, 2759

Ben-Ami, Jacob *(Cast)* 4773

Ben-Ari, Neal *(Cast)* 721

Ben-Zali, Daniel *(Cast)* 3015

Benatzky, Ralph *(Author)* 795, 2610, 2808

Benatzky, Ralph *(Composer)* 659, 795, 2419, 2610, 2808, 4667

Benatzky, Ralph *(Lyricist)* 2808

Benavente, Jacinto *(Author)* 3412

Benavente, Joseph *(Musical Director)* 138

Benbow, William M. *(Cast)* 4112

Benbow, William M. *(Producer)* 4112

Benchley, Nathaniel *(Librettist)* 4039

Benchley, Robert *(Cast)* 3008

Benchley, Robert *(Librettist)* 1357

Benczak, Margaret *(Cast)* 4527

Benda, G.K. *(Costumes)* 133, 702, 704

Bendel, Henri *(Costumes)* 2216

Bendell, Alfred *(Musical Director)* 3237

Bender, Milton *(Director)* 3130, 4780

Bender, Milton *(Librettist)* 4780

Bender, Milton G. *(Composer)* 3296

Bender, Milton G. *(Director)* 3296

Bender, Milton G. *(Lyricist)* 4780

Bendix *(Composer)* 3981

Bendix, Charles *(Composer)* 2952

Bendix, Max *(Choreographer)* 102

Bendix, Max *(Composer)* 742

Bendix, Max *(Musical Director)* 670, 3537, 4119

Bendix, Theodore *(Composer)* 830

Bendix, Theodore *(Musical Director)* 4012

Beneboch, Julian *(Musical Director)* 2407

Beneby, Lehman *(Cast)* 10, 4055

Benedek, Paul *(Producer)* 4794

Benedict, Diane *(Cast)* 4389

Benedict, Gail *(Cast)* 1075

Benes, Jara *(Composer)* 702, 4667

Benet, Laura *(Librettist)* 2653

Benet, Stephen Vincent *(Author)* 2229, 3888

Benham, Earl *(Cast)* 801, 803, 1154

Beniades, Ted *(Cast)* 1354, 4028

Benjamin, Bennie *(Composer)* 3695

Benjamin, Bennie *(Lyricist)* 3695

Benjamin, Carla *(Cast)* 922

Benjamin, Fred *(Choreographer)* 4089

Benjamin, Joseph *(Librettist)* 3725

Benjamin, P.J. *(Cast)* 143, 699, 2289, 3838, 4091, 4701

Benjamin School for Girls *(Producer)* 738, 2102, 3595

Bennet, Harriet *(Cast)* 4719

Bennett *(Composer)* 4683

Bennett *(Lyricist)* 4683

Bennett, Alan *(Cast)* 384

Bennett, Alan *(Librettist)* 384

Bennett, Arnold *(Author)* 989

Bennett, Bernie *(Composer)* 4260

Bennett, Bernie *(Lyricist)* 4260

Bennett, David *(Arrangements)* 132

Bennett, David *(Choreographer)* 21, 133, 381, 930, 994, 1011, 1096, 1128, 1131, 1132, 1308, 1588, 1603, 1829, 1911, 2174, 2264, 2387, 2430, 2570, 2628, 2638, 2686, 2739, 2757, 2972, 3063, 3193, 3207, 3246, 3254, 3508, 3538, 3623, 3712, 3772, 4012, 4212, 4345, 4424, 4555, 4575, 4694

Bennett, David *(Director)* 380, 2739, 2960, 4424

Bennett, Evelyn *(Cast)* 1617

Bennett, Florence *(Cast)* 116

Bennett, George J. *(Lyricist)* 1694

Bennett, Harry Gordon *(Set Design)* 966, 3336

Bennett, Joan *(Cast)* 2267

Bennett, Johnstone *(Cast)* 1259

Bennett, Jordan *(Cast)* 949

Bennett, Joseph *(Composer)* 3178

Bennett, Joseph *(Lyricist)* 3178

Bennett, Keith Robert *(Cast)* 1890

Bennett, Leo *(Composer)* 2358

Bennett, Mark *(Composer)* 2037, 2488

Bennett, Mark *(Lyricist)* 2488

Bennett, Matthew *(Cast)* 838, 2046

Bennett, Meg *(Cast)* 1664

Bennett, Michael *(Cast)* 269, 4190

Bennett, Michael *(Choreographer)* 287, 746, 798, 832, 1103, 1329, 1846, 2248, 3603, 3869

Bennett, Michael *(Director)* 287, 746, 1103, 1329, 3852, 3869, 4474

Bennett, Michael *(Librettist)* 3869

Bennett, Michael *(Producer)* 287, 1103

Bennett, Milton *(Composer)* 3695

Bennett, Milton *(Lyricist)* 3695

Bennett, Richard *(Cast)* 1267

Bennett, Robert Russell *(Composer)* 372, 1283, 1932, 3583

Bennett, Robert Russell *(Dance Arranger)* 3703

Bennett, Robert Russell *(Incidental Music)* 1749

Bennett, Robert Russell *(Lyricist)* 3703, 4424

Bennett, Robert Russell *(Orchestrations)* 44, 82, 85, 111, 134, 153, 163, 189, 216, 294, 363, 462, 466, 512, 603, 623, 653, 672, 759, 773, 901, 930, 961, 1109, 1202, 1225, 1278, 1315, 1322, 1342, 1453, 1493, 1528, 1534, 1564, 1662, 1679, 1689, 1745, 1800, 1811, 1879, 1932, 1979, 2103, 2115, 2137, 2187, 2201, 2252, 2268, 2312, 2331, 2423, 2475, 2479, 2569, 2595, 2597, 2638, 2691, 2777, 2786, 2847, 3014, 3038, 3113, 3214, 3225, 3263, 3274, 3291, 3326, 3359, 3365, 3379, 3386, 3505, 3622, 3674, 3687, 3699, 3703, 3735, 3743, 3772, 3850, 3949, 3993, 4001, 4058, 4077, 4095, 4096, 4150, 4212, 4234, 4267, 4314, 4323, 4337, 4361, 4362, 4366, 4446, 4557, 4583, 4609, 4694, 4818, 4819, 4825, 4828

Bennett, Robert Russell *(Vocal Arranger)* 3703

Bennett, Russell

See also Robert Russell Bennett.

Bennett, Sid *(Lighting Designer)* 3932

Bennett, Stanley *(Musical Director)* 691, 981

Bennett, Stanley *(Vocal Arranger)* 691

Bennett, Terry *(Set Design)* 564

Bennett, Thomas *(Choreographer)* 1866

Bennett, Virgil *(Choreographer)* 3877

Bennett, Virgil *(Director)* 1550, 1556

Bennett, Wilda *(Cast)* 168, 1210, 1527, 2666, 3006, 3304, 3727

Berle, Milton (*Composer*)   924, 1415, 1892
Berle, Milton (*Lyricist*)   924, 3822, 3926
Berle, Milton (*Producer*)   3895
Berlin, Irving (*Cast*)   1399, 3006, 3153, 4340, 4521, 4770
Berlin, Irving (*Composer*)   25, 60, 79, 94, 149, 153, 207, 376, 545, 619, 627, 683, 789, 799, 805, 959, 1042, 1208, 1225, 1247, 1298, 1327, 1398, 1399, 1416, 1488, 1501, 1519, 1598, 1685, 1686, 1738, 1793, 1813, 1920, 1927, 2184, 2205, 2261, 2294, 2301, 2363, 2525, 2597, 2894, 2983, 3006, 3007, 3008, 3009, 3031, 3079, 3096, 3175, 3258, 3395, 3412, 3627, 3658, 3665, 3791, 3827, 3917, 3926, 3946, 3962, 4045, 4131, 4144, 4148, 4153, 4154, 4158, 4159, 4206, 4264, 4340, 4399, 4440, 4603, 4655, 4714, 4770, 4799, 4804, 4805, 4806, 4810, 4812, 4813, 4814, 4815, 4821, 4829, 4831, 4840, 4842, 4852
Berlin, Irving (*Librettist*)   1225
Berlin, Irving (*Lyricist*)   25, 60, 79, 94, 149, 153, 179, 207, 376, 511, 545, 619, 627, 683, 789, 799, 805, 959, 1042, 1208, 1225, 1247, 1298, 1327, 1398, 1399, 1416, 1488, 1501, 1523, 1550, 1598, 1685, 1686, 1738, 1793, 1813, 1920, 1927, 2184, 2205, 2232, 2294, 2301, 2363, 2525, 2597, 2894, 2983, 3006, 3007, 3008, 3009, 3031, 3079, 3096, 3175, 3258, 3395, 3412, 3627, 3658, 3665, 3791, 3827, 3917, 3926, 3946, 3962, 4045, 4131, 4144, 4148, 4153, 4154, 4158, 4159, 4206, 4264, 4340, 4399, 4440, 4493, 4521, 4603, 4655, 4770, 4799, 4804, 4805, 4806, 4810, 4812, 4813, 4814, 4821, 4829, 4831, 4840, 4842, 4852, 4853
Berlin, Irving (*Producer*)   2894
Berlin, Spencer H. (*Producer*)   4601
Berlind, Roger (*Producer*)   154, 393, 450, 775, 1262, 2205, 3015, 3175, 3411, 3702, 3718, 4091
Berlind, Roger S. (*Producer*)   3171
Berliner, Rudolf (*Musical Director*)   1746
Berlinger, Warren (*Cast*)   550
Berman, David (*Cast*)   3908
Berman, M. (*Costumes*)   972
Berman, Marjorie (*Cast*)   3631
Berman, Norman L. (Additional Music)   4176
Berman, Norman L. (*Director*)   4517
Berman, Norman L. (*Musical Director*)   4176
Berman, Norman L. (*Orchestrations*)   4176
Berman, Norman L. (*Vocal Arranger*)   2320, 4176, 4517
Berman, Shelley (*Cast*)   1237, 1567
Berman and Sons, Max (*Costumes*)   408
Bern, Mina (*Cast*)   2356, 2421, 4342
Bernal, Barry K. (*Cast*)   2905
Bernard, Ada (*Cast*)   618, 2343
Bernard, Barney (*Cast*)   506, 2358, 4553, 4655, 4802
Bernard, Ben (*Director*)   439
Bernard, Ben (*Lyricist*)   439
Bernard, Ben (*Producer*)   439
Bernard, Billy (*Lyricist*)   3241
Bernard, Felix (*Composer*)   25, 3955, 4824
Bernard, Felix (*Lyricist*)   4824
Bernard, Francis (*Cast*)   3490
Bernard, Henri (*Author*)   4624
Bernard, Loraine (*Cast*)   1521
Bernard, Lygia (*Costumes*)   2275
Bernard, Mitchell (*Lyricist*)   747
Bernard, Nan (*Cast*)   4120

Bernard, Olive P. (*Set Design*)   2040
Bernard, Peter (*Composer*)   377
Bernard, Peter (*Lyricist*)   377
Bernard, Sam (*Cast*)   68, 208, 350, 351, 666, 683, 976, 1523, 1537, 1578, 1793, 1926, 2725, 3006, 3085, 3489, 3710, 3753, 3976
Bernard, Sam (*Director*)   364
Bernard, Sam (*Librettist*)   364, 3144
Bernard, Tristan (*Author*)   2025, 2497
Bernard Jr., Sam (*Lyricist*)   364
Bernardi, Herschel (*Cast*)   269, 4862
Bernauer, Rudolf (*Author*)   1561, 2469, 2794, 4121
Bernauer, Rudolph (*Author*)   742
Bernhard, Arnold (*Producer*)   1776
Bernie, Al (*Cast*)   242, 622, 855
Bernie, Ben (*Cast*)   1859, 2739
Bernie, Ben (*Composer*)   393, 3905
Bernie, Ben (*Lyricist*)   3905
Bernier, Buddy (*Composer*)   1296
Bernier, Buddy (*Lyricist*)   1296, 3647
Bernier, Peggy (*Cast*)   4778
Berns, Bert (*Composer*)   3695
Berns, Bert (*Lyricist*)   3695
Bernstein, Aline (*Cast*)   1655
Bernstein, Aline (*Costumes*)   1652, 1653, 1654, 1655, 1656, 1657, 2510, 3691
Bernstein, Aline (*Set Design*)   1652, 1654, 1655, 1656, 1657
Bernstein, B. (*Cast*)   907
Bernstein, Douglas (*Cast*)   262, 2790, 3960, 4533
Bernstein, Douglas (*Composer*)   262, 3181, 3960, 4533
Bernstein, Douglas (*Librettist*)   262, 1832, 3181, 3960
Bernstein, Douglas (*Lyricist*)   262, 3181, 3960, 4533
Bernstein, Elmer (*Composer*)   2010, 2014, 2820
Bernstein, Elmer (*Incidental Music*)   3453
Bernstein, Ira (*Producer*)   1497, 1611, 3175
Bernstein, Leonard (*Composer*)   72, 599, 630, 1214, 1294, 2205, 2411, 2677, 2775, 3018, 3278, 3452, 3967, 4004, 4008, 4625, 4734
Bernstein, Leonard (*Incidental Music*)   2411
Bernstein, Leonard (*Lyricist*)   72, 599, 630, 1294, 2411, 2677, 2775, 3278, 3452
Bernstein, Leonard
   See also The Revuers
Bernstein, Leonard (*Orchestrations*)   630, 3278, 4625
Bernstein, Lisa (*Cast*)   4309
Bernstein, Richard N. (*Librettist*)   4785
Bernstein, Robert A. (*Librettist*)   90
Bernstein, Robert A. (*Lyricist*)   4388
Bernstein, Rube (*Librettist*)   1532
Bernstein, Sid (*Producer*)   2248, 2440
Bernstein, Stanley (*Producer*)   2440
Bernstein, Sue Renee (*Cast*)   4470
Berr, Georges (*Author*)   2808, 3251, 3494
Berra, Mabel (*Cast*)   1197
Berri, Beth (*Cast*)   2180, 2308
Berri, Maude Lillian (*Cast*)   2035, 4201
Berrington & Berrington (*Cast*)   986
Berry, Ada (*Cast*)   3202
Berry, Chu (*Composer*)   887
Berry, Chu (*Lyricist*)   887
Berry, Chuck (*Composer*)   3739, 4534

Bishop, Randy (*Lyricist*) 3690
Bishop, Sir Henry Rowley (*Composer*) 1425
Bishop, Stuart (*Librettist*) 2169, 3920, 4243
Bishop, Stuart (*Producer*) 3920
Bishop, Stuart (*Set Design*) 4401
Bishop, Thom (*Composer*) 494
Bishop, Thom (*Librettist*) 494
Bishop, Thom (*Lyricist*) 494
Bissell, Gene (*Composer*) 2913
Bissell, Gene (*Lyricist*) 2913
Bissell, Gene P. (*Composer*) 3112
Bissell, Gene P. (*Lyricist*) 3112
Bissell, Marian (*Librettist*) 3845
Bissell, Richard (*Author*) 3351
Bissell, Richard (*Librettist*) 3351, 3845
Bissell, Whitney (*Cast*) 55, 4706
Bissing (*Producer*) 1504
Bissing, H. (*Lighting Designer*) 1403
Bisson, Alexandre (*Author*) 1347, 3146
Bittan, Roy (*Musical Director*) 1769
Bittner, Jack (*Cast*) 31, 599, 3835, 4155, 4577
Bittner, Julius (*Orchestrations*) 1680
Bixby, Frank (*Cast*) 1501
Bixby, Johnathan (*Costumes*) 2198
Bizet, Georges (*Author*) 653
Bizet, Georges (*Composer*) 653
Bjornson, Maria (*Costumes*) 211
Bjornson, Maria (*Set Design*) 211, 3464
Blacher, Henriette-Blanke (*Composer*) 4589
Black, Ben (*Composer*) 2088, 4545, 4814
Black, Ben (*Lyricist*) 2088, 4545, 4814
Black, Chad (*Cast*) 4588
Black, David (*Director*) 4114
Black, David (*Producer*) 1139, 1256, 1478, 2659, 3824
Black, Don (*Librettist*) 4217
Black, Don (*Lyricist*) 211, 299, 2539, 2820, 3930, 4068,
    4138, 4217, 4301
Black, Frank (*Composer*) 1112, 2045
Black, Frank (*Orchestrations*) 4532
Black, John S. (*Composer*) 4375
Black, Johnny (*Composer*) 1686
Black, Johnny S. (*Composer*) 25
Black, Karen (*Cast*) 2297, 4623
Black, Malcolm (*Director*) 3491
Black, Max (*Cast*) 1439
Black, Robert (*Cast*) 1439
Black, Valerie (*Cast*) 3321
Black Patti Troubadours (*Producer*) 982
Black-Brown, Shirley (*Cast*) 166, 2427
Blackbirds Productions (*Producer*) 3704
Blackburn, Charles (*Cast*) 3469
Blackburn, Charles (*Costumes*) 491, 3469, 3542
Blackburn, Clarice (*Cast*) 2268
Blackburn, Mary (*Costumes*) 1266
Blackburn, Ticia (*Costumes*) 4205
Blackfriars' Guild (*Producer*) 2661
Blackhurst, Klea (*Cast*) 3641
Blackman, Charles (*Musical Director*) 4237
Blackman, Jack (*Lighting Designer*) 2278, 2306, 2657
Blackman, Jack (*Set Design*) 2278, 2306, 2657
Blackman, Robert (*Costumes*) 282, 4410

Blackman, Robert (*Set Design*) 4410
Blackman, Teddy (*Director*) 1772
Blackmer, Sidney (*Cast*) 2967, 4043
Blackmon, Ted (*Producer*) 1772
Blackmon, Teddy (*Director*) 1981, 1982
Blackmore, Peter (*Author*) 3816
Blackston, Phyllis (*Choreographer*) 3756
Blackstone, Nan (*Cast*) 1448, 3172
Blackton, Jack (*Cast*) 1770, 2284
Blackton, Jay
    See also Jacob Schwartzdorf.
Blackton, Jay (*Composer*) 4035
Blackton, Jay (*Dance Arranger*) 3234
Blackton, Jay (*Musical Director*) 134, 153, 223, 603, 619,
    751, 1478, 1564, 1616, 1760, 2064, 2137, 2449, 2894,
    2898, 2983, 3108, 3234, 3263, 3687, 3702, 3931, 4214,
    4384, 4481, 4718
Blackton, Jay (*Orchestrations*) 4537
Blackton, Jay (*Vocal Arranger*) 603, 1478, 1564, 2064,
    2983, 3234, 3687, 3931
Blackwell, Carlyle (*Cast*) 1718, 3975
Blackwell, Charles (*Librettist*) 4286
Blackwell, Charles (*Producer*) 40
Blackwell, Donald (*Librettist*) 2105, 3861, 4367
Blackwell, Otis (*Composer*) 3695, 3739
Blackwell, Otis (*Lyricist*) 3695, 3739
Blackwell, Robert (*Composer*) 3695
Blackwell, Robert (*Lyricist*) 3695
Blackwood, Pady (*Puppeteer*) 997, 4710
Blaine, Martin (*Producer*) 2167
Blaine, Rose (*Cast*) 851
Blaine, Vivian (*Cast*) 853, 1190, 1706, 3845
Blair, Barbara (*Cast*) 1492
Blair, Frank (*Cast*) 476
Blair, Jack (*Cast*) 3104, 4677
Blair, Jimmy (*Cast*) 2167
Blair, Joyce (*Cast*) 299
Blair, June (*Cast*) 3104, 4677
Blair, Milton (*Cast*) 96
Blair, Milton J. (*Lyricist*) 96
Blair, Nicholas (*Librettist*) 3375
Blair, Pamela (*Cast*) 374, 746, 1082, 1915, 2318, 3666, 4196
Blair, Richard (*Cast*) 272, 366, 1091, 1436, 1438, 2279
Blair, Tony (*Cast*) 117
Blaire, Laine (*Cast*) 608, 4620
Blaisdell, William (*Cast*) 311, 4563
Blake, Ann-Marie (*Cast*) 2689
Blake, Arthur (*Cast*) 4332
Blake, Bob (*Cast*) 2085
Blake, Curtis (*Cast*) 3987
Blake, Eubie
    See also Eubie Blake and His Orchestra
Blake, Eubie (*Cast*) 740, 1984, 3963, 3966
Blake, Eubie (*Composer*) 133, 318, 393, 432, 443, 740, 792,
    1052, 1063, 1174, 1198, 1328, 1765, 1917, 1989, 2151,
    2570, 2856, 3020, 3144, 3512, 3905, 3963, 3965, 3966,
    4154, 4253, 4281, 4503, 4810, 4812
Blake, Eubie (*Director*) 740
Blake, Eubie (*Librettist*) 498
Blake, Eubie (*Lyricist*) 3144, 4281
Blake, Eubie (*Musical Director*) 443, 740, 3963, 3965, 3993

Bloom, Ken (*Director*)   528, 1155, 3165, 3997
Bloom, Ken (*Librettist*)   2541, 3997
Bloom, Ken (*Lighting Designer*)   3997
Bloom, Ken (*Producer*)   528, 1155, 3165, 3329, 3997
Bloom, Ken (*Set Design*)   3997
Bloom, Leo (*Cast*)   2876
Bloom, Rube (*Composer*)   420, 446, 447, 882, 888, 3705, 4137
Bloomfield, Harry (*Producer*)   3536
Bloomfield, Maggie (*Lyricist*)   4
Bloomgarden, Kermit (*Producer*)   162, 933, 1456, 2106, 2146, 2411, 2961, 3016, 3210
Bloomingdale, Alfred (*Producer*)   84, 1889
Blore, Douglas (*Cast*)   4302
Blore, Eric (*Cast*)   138, 1113, 1453, 1856, 1859, 2277, 2526, 4826
Blore, Eric (*Lyricist*)   133, 702, 4327
Blossom, Henry (*Author*)   1961
Blossom, Henry (*Composer*)   4723
Blossom, Henry (*Librettist*)   68, 126, 307, 1162, 1335, 1578, 2723, 2915, 3304, 3567, 3590, 3675, 3921, 4017, 4453, 4547, 4608, 4754
Blossom, Henry (*Lyricist*)   68, 126, 307, 683, 1162, 1335, 1578, 2025, 2723, 2906, 2915, 3304, 3567, 3590, 3675, 3685, 3820, 3921, 4017, 4311, 4390, 4453, 4547, 4608, 4754, 4818
Blossom, Roberts (*Cast*)   3309
Blount, Helon (*Cast*)   941, 1060, 1319, 1329, 2961, 3067, 3619, 3725, 4727
Blount Jr., Roy (*Librettist*)   1038
Blow, Sidney (*Author*)   4302
Blow, Sidney (*Director*)   4302
Blow, Sidney (*Librettist*)   3237, 4302
Blue, Ben (*Cast*)   1494
Blue, Peggie (*Cast*)   166, 2754
Blue, Pete (*Musical Director*)   4462
Bluestone, Henry (*Composer*)   1415
Blum, Joel (*Cast*)   1120, 1146
Blum, Robert (*Author*)   2808
Blumberg, David A. (*Producer*)   1832
Blume, Norman A. (*Cast*)   2760
Blumenfeld, Robert (*Cast*)   4288
Blumenkrantz, Jeff (*Cast*)   4371
Blumenstock, I.L. (*Librettist*)   4324
Blumenstock, I.L. (*Lyricist*)   4324
Blumenthal, A.C. (*Producer*)   3014
Blumenthal, Oskar (*Author*)   4667
Bluth (*Director*)   1093
Bluth, Fred (*Librettist*)   1093
Bluth, Fred (*Lyricist*)   1093
Blyden, Larry (*Cast*)   170, 1315, 1373, 1406, 2178, 3273, 4718
Blyer, James B. (*Composer*)   4805
Blyler, James (*Composer*)   2857, 4805
Blythe (*Costumes*)   1251
Boak, Mike (*Set Design*)   2477
Boardman, Chris (*Orchestrations*)   695
Bobbie, Walter (*Cast*)   1093, 1380, 4450, 4523
Bobby, Anne Marie (*Cast*)   119, 171, 4020
Bobley, Peter (*Producer*)   1289
Boccaccio, Giovanni (*Author*)   482, 1017, 2931
Bock (*Lyricist*)   4247

Bock, Jerry (*Composer*)   160, 170, 270, 390, 483, 635, 673, 1190, 1265, 1280, 1471, 1848, 2205, 2246, 2589, 2726, 2804, 2987, 3018, 3097, 3780, 3890, 3918, 4260, 4273, 4312, 4395, 4827, 4829
Bock, Jerry (*Incidental Music*)   1471
Bock, Jerry (*Librettist*)   170
Bock, Jerry (*Lyricist*)   2677, 2987
Bock, W.E. (*Composer*)   1535
Bodanzky, Robert (*Author*)   93, 307, 902, 967, 1199, 1455, 1712, 2334, 2947, 4010
Bodenheim, Maxwell (*Librettist*)   1244
Boder, Lada (*Cast*)   4217
Bodo, Yakov (*Cast*)   2866
Bodry, Penelope (*Cast*)   1053, 1216
Boesky, Billy (*Composer*)   1232
Boesky, Billy (*Librettist*)   1232
Boesky, Billy (*Lyricist*)   1232
Bogaev, Paul (*Conductor*)   4217
Bogaev, Paul (*Musical Director*)   211, 721, 4138
Bogan, Elizabeth (*Musical Director*)   4779
Bogard, Michael (*Lighting Designer*)   4129
Bogardus, Janet (*Choreographer*)   1291
Bogardus, Stephen (*Cast*)   1161, 1234, 1258, 2746, 4505
Bogart, Andrew (*Cast*)   1521
Bogart, Humphrey (*Cast*)   2060
Bogart, Neil (*Producer*)   1289
Bogart, Paul (*Director*)   1200, 1744, 3496
Bogdanoff, Rose (*Costumes*)   2748, 4702
Boggs, Gail (*Cast*)   2648, 2962
Bogin, Abba (*Dance Arranger*)   3725
Bogin, Abba (*Musical Director*)   157, 1273, 1698, 2994, 3110
Bogin, Abba (*Orchestrations*)   157, 461
Bogin, Abba (*Vocal Arranger*)   157, 3696, 3725
Bogin, Bernard (*Cast*)   4369
Bogok, Gusti (*Cast*)   2440
Bohannon, M.T. (*Cast*)   3348
Bohemians, The (*Producer*)   1685, 1686, 1688, 1689, 1691, 1692, 1693
Bohlman, Edgar (*Set Design*)   4548
Bohmler, Craig (*Composer*)   1702
Bohmler, Craig (*Lyricist*)   1702
Bohmler, Craig (*Musical Director*)   1702
Bohmler, Craig (*Orchestrations*)   1702
Bohmler, Craig (*Vocal Arranger*)   1702
Bohnen, Roman (*Cast*)   2228
Bohner, Aloys (*Costumes*)   3737
Bois, Curt (*Cast*)   3536
Bois, Curt (*Director*)   4316
Bois, Curt (*Producer*)   4316
Bojar, Alvin (*Producer*)   3018
Boland, Clay (*Composer*)   18, 750, 1885, 3150, 3870, 3914
Boland, Clay (*Director*)   1885
Boland, Clay (*Lyricist*)   18, 898, 3150
Boland, Clay (*Orchestrations*)   18, 750
Boland, Clay (*Vocal Arranger*)   18, 750
Boland, Mary (*Cast*)   1225, 2252
Boland Jr., Clay (*Lyricist*)   18
Bolasni, Saul (*Costumes*)   911
Bolcom, William (*Composer*)   1122
Bold, Richard (*Cast*)   1134, 1460, 1461, 1485, 1486, 1487
Boldi, J.B. (*Composer*)   1569

Boris, Ruthanna *(Choreographer)* 2234
Bormann, James *(Cast)* 2661
Bormet, Garry *(Director)* 2783
Bormet, Garry *(Librettist)* 2783
Bormet, Garry *(Lyricist)* 2783
Borne, Hal *(Composer)* 59, 673, 1892, 2259, 3683
Borne, Hal *(Lyricist)* 3683
Borne, Hal *(Orchestrations)* 2259
Borne, Hal *(Vocal Arranger)* 2259
Borodin, A. *(Composer)* 1963
Borodin, Alexander *(Music Based On)* 2327, 4383
Boros, Ferike *(Cast)* 1098
Boros, Frank J. *(Costumes)* 916, 2472, 3830, 3909
Boros, Frank J. *(Set Design)* 916, 2472, 3830, 3909
Borow, Rena Berkowicz *(Librettist)* 4082
Borowitz, Katherine *(Cast)* 2440
Borts, Joanne *(Cast)* 1609
Bosco, Philip *(Cast)* 345, 932, 1076, 2028, 3309
Bosen, Harry *(Costumes)* 3380
Bosley, Tom *(Cast)* 330, 1158, 1280, 3210
Boss, Al *(Incidental Music)* 1604, 4303
Boss, Al *(Orchestrations)* 18, 750, 1604, 4303, 4543
Boss, Al *(Vocal Arranger)* 18, 1604
Bostock, Claude W. *(Librettist)* 1502
Boston, Steve *(Composer)* 1637
Boston, Steve *(Lyricist)* 1637
Boston Cadet Corps *(Producer)* 2902
Bostonians *(Producer)* 2345, 4032, 4598
Bostonians, The *(Producer)* 2697, 4559
Bostwick, Barry *(Cast)* 807, 1664, 2001, 3142, 3733, 4089
Bosveld, Alice *(Cast)* 2124
Boswell, William *(Composer)* 2069
Boswell, William *(Musical Director)* 2069
Boswell, William *(Vocal Arranger)* 2069
Bosworth, Patricia *(Cast)* 3984
Botari, Michael *(Costumes)* 3576
Botari, Michael *(Set Design)* 3576
Botemps, Arna *(Author)* 4123
Botkin Jr., Perry *(Arrangements)* 928
Botkin Jr., Perry *(Composer)* 4796
Botkin Jr., Perry *(Lyricist)* 4796
Botkin Jr., Perry *(Musical Director)* 928
Botsford, George *(Composer)* 1531, 4804
Bottari, Michael *(Costumes)* 4146
Botto, Louis *(Composer)* 3186
Botto, Louis *(Librettist)* 3108
Botto, Louis *(Lyricist)* 272, 1107, 1363, 3186, 3890
Bottomley, Roland *(Cast)* 1453, 3344
Bottoms, John *(Cast)* 963, 1086, 2877, 4485
Botwin, Shirley *(Composer)* 2876
Boublil, Alain *(Librettist)* 2442, 2905
Boublil, Alain *(Lyricist)* 2905
Boucher, Dolores *(Cast)* 3
Boucicault, Aubrey *(Cast)* 1994, 2326, 2673, 4544
Boucicault, Aubrey *(Composer)* 1994
Boucicault, Aubrey *(Lyricist)* 1994
Boucicault, Dion *(Author)* 191, 298, 4173
Boucicault, Dion G. *(Director)* 2871
Boucree, Gladys *(Cast)* 4254
Boudreau, Robin *(Cast)* 109
Boudreaux, Darleen *(Cast)* 1075

Bougla, Charles *(Cast)* 449, 641, 982
Boulanger, Daniel *(Author)* 2318
Boulden, Alice *(Cast)* 1275
Boulton, Milo *(Cast)* 1846
Bourchier, Arthur *(Producer)* 1805
Bouret, Grace *(Lyricist)* 318
Bourne, Matthew *(Choreographer)* 730
Bourneuf, Philip *(Cast)* 1286, 2894, 3292, 4706
Bousard, Joe *(Cast)* 3571
Bousard, Joe *(Musical Director)* 3527
Boutelje, Phil *(Composer)* 831
Bouton, Mabel *(Cast)* 3199
Boutsikaris, Dennis *(Cast)* 1418
Bouvier, Adine *(Cast)* 906
Bouvier, Yvonne *(Cast)* 4174
Bova, Joe *(Cast)* 3288
Bova, Joseph *(Cast)* 825, 1359, 1991
Bovill, C.H. *(Librettist)* 3213
Bovill, C.H. *(Lyricist)* 396, 1318, 1454, 1569, 2498, 3213, 3433, 4590
Bowab, John *(Producer)* 1273, 2681, 3876
Bowan, Sybil *(Cast)* 1127
Bowden, Charles *(Producer)* 72
Bowden, Jonny *(Musical Director)* 140, 1161, 2852
Bowden, Jonny *(Vocal Arranger)* 1161
Bowen, Paul H. *(Lighting Designer)* 1750
Bowen, Paul H. *(Set Design)* 1750
Bowen, Thomas *(Lighting Designer)* 1377
Bower, Edward *(Choreographer)* 1404
Bower, Edward P. *(Choreographer)* 4360
Bower, Joy *(Orchestrations)* 3110
Bowers, Bobby *(Cast)* 508
Bowers, Charles B. *(Cast)* 3566
Bowers, Charles H. *(Cast)* 457, 947, 1535
Bowers, Clent *(Cast)* 1289, 1776
Bowers, Fred *(Cast)* 4787
Bowers, Frederick *(Composer)* 2316
Bowers, Frederick V. *(Cast)* 811
Bowers, Frederick V. *(Composer)* 811, 4130
Bowers, Kenneth *(Cast)* 372
Bowers, Kenny *(Cast)* 153, 1577
Bowers, Robert Hood *(Composer)* 219, 326, 545, 617, 687, 1142, 1144, 1327, 2025, 2126, 2574, 2695, 2770, 3236, 3681, 3771, 3977, 4115, 4119, 4544, 4688, 4813
Bowers, Robert Hood *(Lyricist)* 2574
Bowers, Robert Hood *(Musical Director)* 75, 1230, 2025, 2574, 2695, 2900, 3236, 3304, 3771, 3977, 4158, 4650
Bowers, Robert Hood *(Orchestrations)* 2040
Bowers, Teresa *(Cast)* 1496
Bowes, Major Edward *(Producer)* 638
Bowie, David *(Composer)* 3739
Bowie, David *(Lyricist)* 3739
Bowie, John *(Cast)* 3983
Bowie, Pat *(Cast)* 4074
Bowler, Walter S. *(Cast)* 1866
Bowles, Anthony *(Musical Director)* 920
Bowman, Laura *(Cast)* 3904
Bowman, Patricia *(Cast)* 622, 3639, 4486, 4569
Bowman, Rob *(Dance Arranger)* 690
Bowman, Rob *(Musical Director)* 690, 1172
Bowman Productions *(Producer)* 1045

Braggiotti, Francesca (Cast)   4545
Braggiotti, Mario (Cast)   4545
Braggiotti, Mario (Composer)   4545
Braggiotti, Mario (Lyricist)   4545
Bragiotti, S. Herbert (Cast)   3680
Braham, Dave (Composer)   114, 1776, 2428, 3266
Braham, Dave (Incidental Music)   4239
Braham, Dave (Lyricist)   114
Braham, George (Composer)   4508
Braham, George (Musical Director)   4508
Braham, George F. (Composer)   516
Braham, George F. (Lyricist)   516
Braham, Harry (Cast)   3883
Braham, Harry (Composer)   1148
Braham, Harry (Musical Director)   687, 1148, 1501
Braham, Horace (Cast)   993
Braham, John (Composer)   476
Braham, John (Lyricist)   476
Braham, John J. (Composer)   175
Braham, John J. (Musical Director)   175, 2779, 3828, 3887
Braham, Lionel (Cast)   2802
Braham, Philip (Composer)   133, 700, 702, 1569, 2570, 2972, 4154, 4302, 4327, 4662
Braham, Philip (Lyricist)   605, 702, 2972, 4154, 4662
Braham, Philip (Musical Director)   133, 704, 2570
Brahms, Johannes (Composer)   1589
Braine, Robert (Composer)   4424
Brainin, Jerome (Composer)   4131
Brainin, Jerome (Lyricist)   4131
Brainsfather, Bruce (Librettist)   377
Braithwaite, Clara (Cast)   3857
Braley, Berton (Composer)   1132
Braley, Berton (Lyricist)   1132, 4422
Brambell, Wilfred (Cast)   2304
Bramble, Mark (Director)   1253
Bramble, Mark (Librettist)   305, 1171, 1253, 1359, 1660, 3208, 3485, 4261
Bramley, William (Cast)   4625
Brammel, David (Cast)   1079
Brammer, Julius (Author)   905, 1113, 1530, 2424, 3051, 4760
Brammer, Julius (Librettist)   771, 1113
Brammer, Julius (Lyricist)   393
Branch, Billy (Cast)   4174
Branch, Gretchen (Cast)   27, 444
Branch, James (Cast)   2393
Branch, Nick (Composer)   1201
Branch, Susan (Costumes)   1832
Brand, David (Cast)   3568
Brand, Georgiana (Cast)   3495
Brand, Gibby (Cast)   669, 2289, 2993, 3411, 3666
Brand, John (Cast)   762
Brand, John E. (Cast)   727
Brand, Max (Author)   1027
Brand, Oscar (Composer)   1158, 2018, 2248
Brand, Oscar (Lyricist)   1158, 2018, 2248
Brand, Phoebe (Cast)   2228
Brandeaux, Pal'mere (Choreographer)   203, 1836, 2238, 3168, 3573
Brandeaux, Pal'mere (Director)   242, 398
Brandeaux, Pal'mere (Producer)   242, 849
Brandell, William (Director)   1397

Brander, Arthur (Composer)   1655, 3898
Brander, Arthur (Lyricist)   3898
Brandfon, Joe (Composer)   1722
Brandfon, Joe (Lyricist)   1722
Brandl, Johann (Composer)   2824
Brando, Marlon (Cast)   1299
Brandon, Charles A. (Costumes)   3224
Brandon, Charles A. (Lighting Designer)   3224
Brandon, Charles A. (Set Design)   3204, 3224
Brandon, Joclyn (Author)   1551
Brandon, John (Composer)   3752
Brandon, John (Lyricist)   3752
Brandon, Johnny (Cast)   2608
Brandon, Johnny (Composer)   415, 766, 1816, 2616, 3427, 3932, 4192, 4678
Brandon, Johnny (Librettist)   2616, 4192
Brandon, Johnny (Lyricist)   415, 766, 1198, 1816, 2616, 3427, 3932, 4192, 4678
Brandt, Denise (Cast)   2098
Brandt, Eddie (Composer)   4367
Brandt, Eddie (Lyricist)   4367, 4741
Brandt, Harry (Producer)   4702
Brandt, Jerry (Producer)   1637
Brandt, Mike (Composer)   1216
Brandt, Mike (Lyricist)   1216
Brandt, Sophie (Cast)   4590
Brandt Sisters (Cast)   1782
Brandywine Orchestra, Nat (Cast)   849
Brandzel, Robert (Musical Director)   3711
Brandzel, Robert (Orchestrations)   3711
Brandzel, Robert (Vocal Arranger)   3711
Branen, Jeff T. (Composer)   295, 4630
Branen, Jeff T. (Lyricist)   295, 830, 3073, 3396, 4181, 4630
Brantley, Marion (Cast)   4253
Brasington, Alan (Cast)   2820, 3909
Brass, Stacey Lynn (Cast)   3757
Brassard, Gail (Costumes)   3227, 4136
Brasser, Victoria (Cast)   2674
Braswell, Adrienne (Cast)   914
Braswell, Adrienne (Composer)   914
Braswell, Adrienne (Librettist)   914
Braswell, Adrienne (Lyricist)   914
Braswell, Charles (Cast)   832, 3815
Braswell, John (Director)   300, 654
Braswell, John (Lyricist)   300
Bratt, J. (Lyricist)   2421
Bratton, John W. (Composer)   591, 702, 719, 737, 1464, 1925, 2261, 2465, 2722, 2990, 3134, 3229, 3422, 3753, 3856, 3857, 3882, 3951, 4130, 4430
Bratton, John W. (Lyricist)   702, 3753
Braun, Eugene (Lighting Designer)   2023, 2024, 2098, 2099, 4143
Braun, Gene (Lighting Designer)   4180
Braun, Ralph (Cast)   2784
Braunstein, Alan (Cast)   2212, 3456
Braunstein, Lester (Producer)   1205
Braxton, Brenda (Cast)   4031
Bray, Bonnie (Cast)   1781
Bray, David (Cast)   1781
Brayfield, Doug (Lyricist)   1159
Brayton, Jude (Librettist)   37

Brayton, Jude *(Lyricist)* 37
Breau, Louis *(Composer)* 2857, 2972, 4816
Breau, Louis *(Lyricist)* 4393
Breaux, Marc *(Cast)* 309, 1029, 2484
Breaux, Marc *(Choreographer)* 1061, 2626, 2874, 4034
Brecher, Irving *(Author)* 2805
Brecht, Bertolt *(Author)* 1214, 4368, 4369, 4370
Brecht, Bertolt *(Librettist)* 1755
Brecht, Bertolt *(Lyricist)* 369, 1755, 3840
Brecht, Bertolt *(Lyrics Based On)* 4368, 4369, 4370, 4371
Bredin, Patricia *(Cast)* 1386, 1887
Bredschneider, Willie *(Composer)* 1561
Bredschneider, Willy *(Author)* 2794
Bredt, James *(Composer)* 1761
Breen, Grace *(Cast)* 1162
Breen, Harry *(Lyricist)* 1560
Breen, Jerry *(Lyricist)* 2512
Breen, Margaret *(Cast)* 1113
Breen, Nellie *(Cast)* 1027, 1513
Breen, Robert *(Director)* 1385
Breffort, Alexandre *(Author)* 2150
Bregman, Buddy *(Musical Director)* 3800
Breier, Edward F. *(Composer)* 1626, 3552
Breier, Edward F. *(Lyricist)* 1626, 3552
Breitenbach, Robert *(Librettist)* 1608
Breitenfeld, Emil *(Composer)* 4422
Breitenfeld, Emil *(Lyricist)* 4422
Brel, Jacques *(Composer)* 2188, 3338
Brel, Jacques *(Lyricist)* 2188, 3338
Bremseth, Lloyd *(Cast)* 2332
Brendel, El *(Cast)* 1923, 2870
Brennan, A. St. John *(Lyricist)* 1743
Brennan, Eileen *(Cast)* 908, 1828, 2522, 4186
Brennan, Frederick Hazlett *(Librettist)* 2679
Brennan, J. Keirn *(Additional Lyrics)* 718
Brennan, J. Keirn *(Composer)* 1026
Brennan, J. Keirn *(Librettist)* 3150
Brennan, J. Keirn *(Lyricist)* 202, 495, 551, 718, 1026, 1461, 1462, 1751, 1803, 2310, 2636, 2662, 3012, 3150, 3238, 3415, 3642, 3680, 4189, 4669
Brennan, James *(Cast)* 2250
Brennan, James *(Lyricist)* 3443
Brennan, James A. *(Composer)* 487
Brennan, James A. *(Lyricist)* 487
Brennan, Jay
  See also Savoy & Brennan
Brennan, Jay *(Cast)* 201, 1281, 1686, 1780
Brennan, Jimmy *(Cast)* 3743
Brennan, Maureen *(Cast)* 2235, 4137
Brennan, Nan *(Cast)* 4206
Brennan, Nora *(Choreographer)* 3076
Brennan, Peggylee *(Cast)* 4527
Brennan, Tom *(Director)* 71
Brenner, Dorothy *(Cast)* 4687
Brenner, Janet *(Producer)* 784
Brenner, Ruth *(Costumes)* 2545
Brenner, S.M. *(Librettist)* 1521
Brenner, S.M. *(Lyricist)* 1521
Brent, Earl *(Composer)* 4047, 4415
Brent, Earl *(Lyricist)* 544, 4047, 4415
Brent, Romney *(Cast)* 1446, 1447, 2459, 2545, 4609

Brent, Romney *(Director)* 2379, 3214
Brent, Romney *(Librettist)* 3214
Brentano, Felix *(Director)* 2985, 3767
Brentano, Felix *(Producer)* 2985
Brentano, Lowell *(Author)* 4105
Brentano, Lowell *(Librettist)* 1670
Bresbey, Eugene W. *(Author)* 3050
Bresler, Jerry *(Composer)* 1296, 4114
Bresler, Jerry *(Lyricist)* 1296
Breslin, Tom *(Cast)* 3019
Breslin, Tommy *(Cast)* 1010, 2305, 3846, 3900
Bresslaw, Bernard *(Cast)* 4469
Brest, Arthur G. *(Director)* 4009
Brett, Jason *(Producer)* 2470
Brett, Simon *(Librettist)* 3930
Bretton, Elise *(Composer)* 4273
Bretton, Elise *(Lyricist)* 4273
Bretton, Elise *(Vocal Arranger)* 1813, 3897, 4252
Breuer, Ernest *(Composer)* 4816, 4817, 4824
Breuer, Kurt *(Author)* 3012
Breuer, Lee *(Director)* 1636
Breuer, Lee *(Librettist)* 1636
Breuer, Lee *(Lyricist)* 1636
Breuler, Robert *(Cast)* 4074
Brevis, Skip *(Dance Arranger)* 338
Brevis, Skip *(Musical Director)* 338
Brevis, Skip *(Vocal Arranger)* 338
Brewer, Robert *(Director)* 962
Brewerton, Henry R. *(Librettist)* 6
Brewerton, Henry R. *(Lyricist)* 6
Brewster, Townsend *(Author)* 3522
Brian, Antony *(Cast)* 841
Brian, Donald *(Cast)* 354, 579, 910, 1067, 1356, 1527, 1544, 1851, 2517, 2761, 2836, 3153, 3996, 4258, 4529, 4557, 4593
Brian, Donald *(Composer)* 2761, 3996
Brian, Donald *(Director)* 4593
Brian, Donald *(Lyricist)* 2761, 3996
Briant, Roy *(Cast)* 2274
Briants, The *(Cast)* 1973
Briar, Suzanne *(Cast)* 4288
Brice, Carol *(Cast)* 1474, 1662, 3837
Brice, Elizabeth *(Cast)* 598, 2232, 2900, 2914, 2966, 3085, 4017, 4044, 4285, 4421, 4603, 4712, 4742, 4806, 4807
Brice, Elizabeth *(Composer)* 4017
Brice, Elizabeth *(Lyricist)* 4017
Brice, Fanny *(Cast)* 418, 1281, 1944, 1963, 3009, 4235, 4686, 4804, 4805, 4810, 4811, 4814, 4815, 4817, 4824, 4825, 4831, 4840, 4842, 4851
Brice, Fanny *(Costumes)* 418
Brice, Fanny *(Librettist)* 1944
Brice, Fanny *(Lyricist)* 3926
Brice, Fanny *(Producer)* 568
Brice, Lew *(Cast)* 123, 124, 418, 2696, 3396, 3397, 4148
Brice, Monte *(Lyricist)* 3717
Brick, Eva *(Cast)* 1733
Brickell, Beth *(Cast)* 1674
Brickhill, Joan *(Choreographer)* 2805
Brickhill-Burke Prods. *(Producer)* 2805
Bricklayers, The *(Cast)* 3121
Bricklin, Jonathan *(Cast)* 319

Brickman, Marshall *(Librettist)* 2913, 4167
Bricusse, Leslie *(Composer)* 3454, 3482, 3731, 3846, 4160
Bricusse, Leslie *(Librettist)* 2198, 3731, 3846, 4160
Bricusse, Leslie *(Lyricist)* 2198, 3454, 3482, 3731, 3846, 3878, 3879, 4160, 4399, 4560
Bridge, Andrew *(Lighting Designer)* 211, 1296, 3464, 4217
Bridge Theatre Prod. Co. *(Producer)* 564
Bridges, Kenneth *(Cast)* 1634
Bridges, Mark *(Costumes)* 1732
Bridgewater, Dee Dee *(Cast)* 3175, 4722
Bridwell, Thom *(Composer)* 2908
Bridwell, Thom *(Dance Arranger)* 2908, 4534
Bridwell, Thom *(Musical Director)* 2908
Bridwell, Thom *(Vocal Arranger)* 2908
Bridwell, Thomas *(Musical Director)* 3932
Brigate, Edward *(Composer)* 3739
Brigate, Edward *(Lyricist)* 3739
Brigati, E. *(Composer)* 4193
Brigati, E. *(Lyricist)* 4193
Brigel, Stockton *(Cast)* 2279
Briggs, Bunny *(Cast)* 432, 4502
Briggs, Casey *(Cast)* 1172
Briggs, Clare *(Librettist)* 199
Briggs, John R. *(Composer)* 3517
Briggs, John R. *(Lyricist)* 3517
Briggs, Matt *(Cast)* 462, 2311
Briggs, Rita *(Lyricist)* 3908
Briggs, Tom *(Librettist)* 4146
Brigham, Constance *(Cast)* 72
Brighouse, Harold *(Author)* 4588
Bright, Joann *(Cast)* 4830
Bright, Joe *(Cast)* 1499
Bright, Joe *(Librettist)* 1499
Bright, Richard S. *(Producer)* 1914
Brightman, Sarah *(Cast)* 3464
Brightman, Stanley *(Author)* 2972
Brighton, Hilda *(Lyricist)* 702
Brill, E.S. *(Composer)* 1318
Brill, E.S. *(Lyricist)* 1318
Brill, Fran *(Cast)* 3684
Brill, Klaus *(Cast)* 3698
Brill, Leighton K. *(Librettist)* 288
Brill, Leighton K. *(Lyricist)* 288
Brill, Marty *(Cast)* 171
Brill, Marty *(Lyricist)* 615
Brinckerhoff, Burt *(Cast)* 2297
Brinckerhoff, Burt *(Director)* 4659
Brindley, Madge *(Cast)* 635
Brink, Robert *(Director)* 1092
Brinkley, Grace *(Cast)* 1323, 1693, 1856, 3225
Briquet, Jean *(Composer)* 20, 1565
Brisebois, Danielle *(Cast)* 150
Brisker, Yankl *(Lyricist)* 1609
Brisson, Carl *(Cast)* 1352
Brisson, Frederick *(Producer)* 798, 957, 958, 1471, 2260, 3113, 3351, 4038, 4474
Brit, Browley *(Composer)* 1296
Brit, Browley *(Lyricist)* 1296
Brita, Inga *(Cast)* 2091
Britt, Jacqueline *(Cast)* 2775, 2874, 4558
Britt, Kelly *(Cast)* 3752

Brittan, Robert *(Lyricist)* 3656
Britton, Barbara *(Cast)* 4582
Britton, Dorothy *(Cast)* 1135
Britton, Florence *(Cast)* 3596
Britton, Frank *(Cast)* 4823
Britton, Jeff *(Producer)* 426, 535, 669, 1974, 2231, 2785, 2801
Britton, John *(Producer)* 692
Britton, Milt *(Cast)* 4823
Britton, Pamela *(Cast)* 530
Britton, Ronnie *(Composer)* 1508, 1695, 1978, 4470
Britton, Ronnie *(Director)* 1695
Britton, Ronnie *(Librettist)* 1508, 1695, 4470
Britton, Ronnie *(Lyricist)* 1508, 1695, 1978, 4470
Britz, John R. *(Musical Director)* 543
Bro, Judith *(Cast)* 2285
Broad, Jay *(Director)* 3684
Broad, Jay *(Librettist)* 3517, 3684
Broadbent, Aida *(Choreographer)* 1711
Broadhurst, George *(Author)* 1014, 1519
Broadhurst, George *(Librettist)* 1118, 1519, 1794, 2383
Broadhurst, George *(Lyricist)* 1118, 1519, 1794, 2383
Broadhurst, George *(Producer)* 1118, 1794, 2383
Broadhust, Aida *(Choreographer)* 4602
Broadway Productions *(Producer)* 3380
Brochu, Jim *(Cast)* 4514
Brock, Heinie *(Cast)* 2085, 2088
Brockbank, Harrison *(Composer)* 1502
Brockbank, Harrison *(Lyricist)* 1502
Brockett, Don *(Author)* 4494
Brockman, James *(Composer)* 805, 2261, 4683
Brockman, James *(Lyricist)* 2261, 4683
Brockmeier, William *(Cast)* 1508
Brocksmith, Roy *(Cast)* 4252, 4370
Broderick, George *(Dance Arranger)* 4645
Broderick, George *(Musical Director)* 1970, 4645, 4788
Broderick, George *(Orchestrations)* 4645
Broderick, George *(Vocal Arranger)* 1970
Broderick, Helen *(Cast)* 48, 207, 294, 1137, 1272, 1563, 3144, 3254, 3466, 3478, 3617, 4437, 4801
Broderick, James *(Cast)* 2680
Broderick, William *(Cast)* 1260
Brodszky, Nicholas *(Composer)* 2458, 4743
Brodszky, Nicholas *(Incidental Music)* 2458
Brody, Lee *(Cast)* 3946, 4166
Brody, Lee *(Composer)* 1342, 4152
Brody, Lee *(Librettist)* 4174
Brody, Lee *(Lyricist)* 1342, 4152
Brody, Leo *(Producer)* 2580
Brody, Max *(Author)* 2761
Brody, Miksa *(Author)* 4258
Brody, Miska *(Author)* 2907
Broecker, Tom *(Costumes)* 1291
Brohn, Bill *(Composer)* 485
Brohn, Bill *(Musical Director)* 3201
Brohn, Bill *(Orchestrations)* 669, 1638, 2318, 2332, 2433, 2754, 2877, 3743, 3876, 4383, 4707
Brohn, Bill *(Vocal Arranger)* 3619, 4707
Brohn, William D. *(Musical Director)* 3908
Brohn, William D. *(Orchestrations)* 496, 921, 2205, 2905, 3544, 3682, 3862, 4701
Brohn, William David *(Orchestrations)* 589

Broich, Madame *(Costumes)* 377
Brokaw, Mark *(Director)* 240
Bromberg, J. Edward *(Cast)* 2450, 4428
Bromfield, Valri *(Cast)* 1575
Bron, Eleanor *(Cast)* 1195
Bronell, Barbara *(Cast)* 2492
Bronfman, Edgar M. *(Producer)* 535, 4252
Bronfman Jr., Edgar *(Producer)* 546
Bronson, Edna *(Cast)* 1295
Bronson, Percy *(Cast)* 2347, 2383
Bronson, Percy *(Producer)* 4570
Bronte, Mae *(Cast)* 4440
Brook, Peter *(Director)* 2000, 2150, 3445
Brook, Sara *(Costumes)* 181, 2043, 2278, 2941, 3427, 4474, 4577
Brooke, Clifford *(Director)* 465, 680, 1011, 1142, 1281, 1580, 1794, 2387
Brooke, J. Clifford *(Director)* 1266, 1557, 2684, 3043
Brooke, J. Clifford *(Librettist)* 2684
Brooke, John *(Cast)* 3168
Brooke, Walter *(Cast)* 225
Brooke, William *(Librettist)* 2069
Brooker, Gary *(Composer)* 3739
Brooker, Gary *(Lyricist)* 3739
Brookfield, Charles H.E. *(Librettist)* 356
Brookins, Fred *(Cast)* 4486
Brooklyn Academy of Music *(Producer)* 4438
Brooklyn YMHA *(Producer)* 4477
Brooks *(Costumes)* 567, 689, 2034, 2071, 3069, 3243, 3860, 3907, 4548, 4777
Brooks, Alan *(Librettist)* 4596
Brooks, Alfred *(Composer)* 3224
Brooks, Arthur D. *(Costumes)* 968, 1867
Brooks, Arthur D. *(Set Design)* 1867
Brooks, Charles *(Choreographer)* 2976
Brooks, David *(Cast)* 462, 530, 1880, 2983, 3389, 3831, 3947, 4643
Brooks, David *(Director)* 72, 298
Brooks, David Allen *(Cast)* 3198
Brooks, Donald *(Costumes)* 127, 652, 958, 1049, 1227, 1310, 2874, 3020, 3187, 3274, 3603
Brooks, Donald L. *(Lighting Designer)* 4611
Brooks, Donald L. *(Set Design)* 1304
Brooks, Dudley *(Musical Director)* 4199
Brooks, Eleanor *(Cast)* 1118
Brooks, Florence *(Cast)* 3417
Brooks, Georgia *(Cast)* 1118
Brooks, Harry *(Composer)* 39, 432, 1980, 3020, 4033
Brooks, Irving *(Cast)* 2407
Brooks, Jack *(Composer)* 4710
Brooks, Jack *(Lyricist)* 4710
Brooks, Jeff *(Cast)* 3142
Brooks, Juanita *(Cast)* 4127
Brooks, Lawrence *(Cast)* 596, 3064, 3725, 4075
Brooks, Leon *(Cast)* 676
Brooks, Louis *(Costumes)* 972
Brooks, Marion *(Cast)* 1192
Brooks, Marion *(Director)* 1192
Brooks, Marion *(Librettist)* 1192
Brooks, Marion A. *(Librettist)* 3358
Brooks, Marjorie *(Cast)* 133, 3139

Brooks, Matt *(Librettist)* 1397, 1494, 1930, 1931
Brooks, Mel *(Cast)* 1389
Brooks, Mel *(Librettist)* 64, 943, 3107, 3286, 3934
Brooks, Phyllis *(Cast)* 3359
Brooks, Shelton *(Cast)* 567, 1058, 3513
Brooks, Shelton *(Composer)* 1813, 3297, 4197
Brooks, Shelton *(Lyricist)* 1813, 3297, 4197
Brooks, Tyler *(Cast)* 136
Brooks, Walter *(Choreographer)* 1174, 1270, 1335, 1747, 2309, 3533, 4668
Brooks, Walter *(Director)* 1308, 1513, 1587, 1747, 2516, 2557, 2807, 3042, 3252, 3511, 3963, 3965
Brooks, Walter *(Producer)* 2807
Broome, John *(Choreographer)* 4160
Broomfeld & Greeley *(Cast)* 2640
Broones, Martin *(Composer)* 46, 1780, 3391, 3796
Broones, Martin *(Lyricist)* 3796
Brophy, Edmund *(Producer)* 4243
Broske, Octavia *(Cast)* 3251, 4382
Brosset, Colette *(Cast)* 2364
Brosset, Colette *(Choreographer)* 2362, 2364
Brosten, Harve *(Producer)* 3272, 3760
Brothers, Bowman *(Lyricist)* 2996
Brothers, Carla *(Cast)* 2239
Brothers, Howard *(Composer)* 3405
Brothers, Howard *(Lyricist)* 3405
Brotherson, Eric *(Cast)* 383, 1475, 3036, 3526
Brougham, St. John *(Composer)* 2509
Broughton, Philip *(Composer)* 1191, 3172
Broun, Heywood *(Cast)* 3783, 3946
Broun, Heywood *(Librettist)* 3946
Broun, Heywood *(Producer)* 3946
Broun, Heywood Hale *(Cast)* 3874
Brourman, Michele *(Composer)* 1804, 4744
Brourman, Michele *(Dance Arranger)* 4744
Brourman, Michele *(Lyricist)* 4744
Brower, Jay *(Musical Director)* 945
Brower, Jay *(Orchestrations)* 945, 1408
Browman, Patricia *(Cast)* 4824
Brown, A. Seymour *(Cast)* 2481
Brown, A. Seymour *(Composer)* 257, 736, 1901, 4806, 4808
Brown, A. Seymour *(Librettist)* 21, 1692
Brown, A. Seymour *(Lyricist)* 21, 257, 608, 662, 736, 1151, 1901, 2448, 2696, 2782, 2892, 3134, 3681, 4589, 4799, 4803, 4806, 4807, 4808
Brown, Ada *(Cast)* 567, 2817
Brown, Agnes *(Cast)* 3736
Brown, Agnes Cain *(Cast)* 3774
Brown, Al W. *(Composer)* 1582, 1963, 2538, 2732, 3396
Brown, Al W. *(Lyricist)* 1582
Brown, Albert W. *(Composer)* 3396
Brown, Alex *(Lyricist)* 1713
Brown, Alice *(Cast)* 2009, 4182
Brown, Aline *(Cast)* 1056
Brown, Allan *(Producer)* 164
Brown, Ann Wiggins *(Cast)* 1416
Brown, Anne *(Cast)* 3541
Brown, Anthony *(Director)* 2225
Brown, Arvin *(Director)* 951, 4601
Brown, B. *(Composer)* 4630
Brown, B. *(Lyricist)* 4630

Brown, Babe (Cast)   1906
Brown, Barry (Producer)   2360, 3787
Brown, Barry M. (Producer)   3515
Brown, Bessie (Cast)   676
Brown, Bill (Cast)   128
Brown, Billings (Lyricist)   4585
Brown, Billy (Cast)   4183
Brown, Blaine (Cast)   676
Brown, Blair (Cast)   4370
Brown, Bob (Puppeteer)   2726
Brown, Calvin (Librettist)   3849
Brown, Candy (Cast)   723
Brown, Charles (Lyricist)   2922
Brown, Charles D. (Cast)   587, 3365
Brown, Charles D. (Lyricist)   2485
Brown, Charles H. (Lyricist)   2485, 3981
Brown, Claudia (Costumes)   1169
Brown, Daisy (Cast)   3041
Brown, Daniel (Cast)   314, 1959
Brown, Dave (Composer)   1256
Brown, Dave (Orchestrations)   140
Brown, David (Cast)   4149
Brown, David (Producer)   227
Brown, Dewey (Cast)   1773, 1981, 2561
Brown, Domer C. (Composer)   552
Brown, Earl (Vocal Arranger)   16, 2969
Brown, Eddy (Composer)   3754
Brown, Edna (Cast)   4339
Brown, Esther (Cast)   3599
Brown, Fleta Ian (Lyricist)   1802
Brown, Fleta Ian (Composer)   4094
Brown, Flo (Cast)   554, 2034
Brown, Forman (Cast)   4467
Brown, Forman (Composer)   4467
Brown, Forman (Lyricist)   1415, 1680, 1681, 1959, 2838, 3013, 3772, 4467
Brown, Gaye (Cast)   874
Brown, George (Lyricist)   1415, 2077
Brown, George R. (Lyricist)   398, 1415
Brown, Georgia (Cast)   42, 652, 3271, 3792, 4371
Brown, Gerard (Author)   2239
Brown, Grace (Costumes)   4047
Brown, Harry (Cast)   3881
Brown, Harry (Composer)   2990
Brown, Harry (Lyricist)   2990
Brown, Helen (Cast)   3480
Brown, Honey (Cast)   2302
Brown, Ian (Cast)   4173
Brown, Ida (Cast)   43, 254
Brown, Jack (Lighting Designer)   367
Brown, Jack (Set Design)   415, 1809
Brown, James (Composer)   3695, 3739, 4193
Brown, James (Lyricist)   3695, 3739, 4193
Brown, Jason (Cast)   2658
Brown, Jason Robert (Arrangements)   3125, 3456
Brown, Jason Robert (Musical Director)   3125, 3456
Brown, Jason Robert (Orchestrations)   2224, 3125
Brown, Jean (Cast)   3821
Brown, Jeffrey (Cast)   2039
Brown, Jessie (Cast)   581
Brown, Joe David (Author)   3364

Brown, Joe E. (Cast)   381, 642, 911, 2214, 4476
Brown, Johnny (Cast)   1601
Brown, Joyce (Musical Director)   52, 278, 3610, 4558
Brown, Joyce (Vocal Arranger)   1289, 3656, 4558
Brown, Ka-Ron (Cast)   3830
Brown, Kay (Cast)   837
Brown, Kelly (Cast)   722, 1614, 4395
Brown, Kid (Cast)   2984
Brown, Kid (Producer)   2984
Brown, Kitty (Cast)   981
Brown, L. Russell (Composer)   2235, 4197
Brown, L. Russell (Lyricist)   2235, 4197
Brown, L. Slade (Producer)   64, 534, 607, 1993, 2248, 2898, 3788, 4002
Brown, Leroy (Cast)   3022
Brown, Leroy (Composer)   3022
Brown, Leroy (Lyricist)   3022
Brown, Lester (Cast)   1563
Brown, Lester (Director)   909, 2944
Brown, Lew (Cast)   3153
Brown, Lew (Composer)   391, 2189, 2308, 3376, 3926
Brown, Lew (Director)   622, 4177, 4772
Brown, Lew (Librettist)   622, 924, 1323, 1492, 1979, 4177, 4772
Brown, Lew (Lyricist)   202, 391, 393, 573, 622, 665, 1215, 1293, 1323, 1339, 1460, 1486, 1488, 1489, 1490, 1491, 1492, 1628, 1688, 1692, 1813, 1919, 1929, 1979, 2066, 2111, 2189, 2308, 2467, 2489, 2706, 2734, 2857, 3020, 3297, 3376, 3489, 3535, 3926, 3969, 3973, 4177, 4253, 4345, 4772, 4799, 4813, 4817
Brown, Lew (Producer)   622, 4177, 4772
Brown, Lewis (Costumes)   2218, 3001
Brown, Lottie (Cast)   2021
Brown, Louise (Cast)   642, 2382, 3650, 4741
Brown, Lydia (Cast)   489
Brown, Mae (Cast)   981
Brown, Mae (Choreographer)   981
Brown, Mae (Composer)   981
Brown, Mae (Librettist)   981
Brown, Mae (Lyricist)   981
Brown, Marjorie (Cast)   1871
Brown, Mark A. (Lyricist)   1055
Brown, Martin (Cast)   2966
Brown, Martin (Librettist)   3382
Brown, Martin (Lyricist)   2334
Brown, Martin G. (Lyricist)   2825
Brown, Max (Producer)   1029, 1634, 2874
Brown, Max J. (Producer)   594, 2583
Brown, Maxine (Cast)   2950
Brown, Michael (Composer)   272, 427, 943, 1023, 1045, 1049, 1107, 1362, 1363, 2294, 2554, 2988, 3107, 3108, 3889, 4268
Brown, Michael (Director)   1045, 2988
Brown, Michael (Librettist)   1045, 2988
Brown, Michael (Lyricist)   272, 427, 943, 1023, 1045, 1049, 1107, 1362, 1363, 2000, 2294, 2554, 2988, 3107, 3108, 3889, 4268
Brown, Michael (Producer)   2630
Brown, Nacio Herb (Composer)   393, 487, 544, 1138, 1943, 1944, 1946, 3139, 3992, 4267, 4683, 4799
Brown, Nacio Herb (Lyricist)   1298

Brown, Norman *(Composer)* 4433
Brown, Norman *(Librettist)* 4433
Brown, Norman *(Lyricist)* 4433
Brown, Patrika *(Lighting Designer)* 482, 1498, 1769
Brown, Pendleton *(Cast)* 4089
Brown, Peter *(Composer)* 3739
Brown, Peter *(Lyricist)* 3739
Brown, R.A. *(Composer)* 2481
Brown, R.A. *(Lyricist)* 2481
Brown, R.G. *(Cast)* 1436, 1438, 2279, 3110, 4659
Brown, R.G. *(Librettist)* 1436, 3110
Brown, Ralph *(Cast)* 432
Brown, Raymond *(Composer)* 1148
Brown, Raymond *(Lyricist)* 1148
Brown, Rita *(Costumes)* 3066
Brown, Robert *(Librettist)* 4774
Brown, Robert F. *(Librettist)* 750
Brown, Ronnie *(Cast)* 2039
Brown, Roo *(Cast)* 4
Brown, Rose *(Cast)* 1987
Brown, Russ *(Cast)* 957, 1323
Brown, Ruth *(Cast)* 105, 432, 4127
Brown, Sherman *(Producer)* 2264
Brown, Sid *(Composer)* 4805
Brown, Sid *(Lyricist)* 4805
Brown, Steve *(English Lyrics)* 4176
Brown, Steve *(Librettist)* 1897
Brown, Steve *(Lyricist)* 669, 840, 1249, 1897, 4261
Brown, Susan *(Cast)* 3807
Brown, Tom *(Cast)* 1208, 2979
Brown, Tom *(Composer)* 1154, 4393
Brown, Tom *(Lyricist)* 4393
Brown, Troy *(Cast)* 4256
Brown, Vanessa *(Cast)* 3894
Brown, W. *(Librettist)* 4242
Brown, W. *(Lyricist)* 4242
Brown, W.P. *(Musical Director)* 3049
Brown, Warwick *(Set Design)* 3286
Brown, Will P. *(Composer)* 1540
Brown, Will P. *(Lyricist)* 1540
Brown, William *(Cast)* 4708
Brown, William *(Lyricist)* 1049
Brown, William F. *(Composer)* 3889
Brown, William F. *(Librettist)* 272, 427, 550, 1049, 2018, 3112, 3479, 4722
Brown, William F. *(Lyricist)* 427, 3479, 3889
Brown, William P. *(Composer)* 1301
Brown, William P. *(Lyricist)* 1301
Brown, Zoe *(Costumes)* 3902
Brown Jr., J. Terry *(Producer)* 71
Brown Jr., Oscar *(Cast)* 2245
Brown Jr., Oscar *(Composer)* 578, 2245, 2306
Brown Jr., Oscar *(Director)* 578
Brown Jr., Oscar *(Librettist)* 578, 2245, 2306
Brown Jr., Oscar *(Lyricist)* 578, 2245, 2306
Browne *(Composer)* 246
Browne *(Lyricist)* 246
Browne, Bothwell *(Cast)* 2893
Browne, Bothwell *(Choreographer)* 2893
Browne, Bothwell *(Costumes)* 2893
Browne, Irene *(Cast)* 841, 1564

Browne, J. Albert *(Musical Director)* 929, 3712
Browne, L.A. *(Librettist)* 3593
Browne, Leslie *(Cast)* 3682
Browne, Lester *(Cast)* 1292
Browne, Lester *(Director)* 1292
Browne, Lewis Allen *(Librettist)* 3344, 3580
Browne, Porter Emerson *(Librettist)* 1559
Browne, Richard *(Cast)* 4035
Browne, Roscoe Lee *(Cast)* 3060
Browne, Simon *(Cast)* 456
Browne, Tyrone *(Cast)* 3522
Browne, Walter *(Author)* 1210
Browne, Walter *(Librettist)* 2929
Browne, Walter *(Lyricist)* 2929
Browne, William Maynadier *(Librettist)* 4103
Browne, Winifred *(Cast)* 2334
Browning, Billy *(Cast)* 3025
Browning, Connie *(Cast)* 2571
Browning, Ivan Harold *(Cast)* 740
Browning, Joe *(Cast)* 4290
Browning, Kirk *(Director)* 3287
Browning, Robert *(Cast)* 4102
Browning, Susan *(Cast)* 394, 832, 1049, 1634, 2219, 3927
Brownlee, Frank *(Director)* 2778
Brownlow, Wallace *(Cast)* 2632
Brox Sisters, The *(Cast)* 799, 3006, 3008, 3009, 4821
Bruant, Aristide *(Composer)* 3386
Brubeck, Dave *(Composer)* 2611
Bruce, Allan *(Cast)* 1676
Bruce, Betty *(Cast)* 857, 1889, 2458, 4058, 4524
Bruce, Carol *(Cast)* 95, 1060, 1846, 2458, 2597, 3121, 3138
Bruce, Dan *(Cast)* 1563
Bruce, Doun *(Composer)* 4303
Bruce, Eddie *(Cast)* 4021
Bruce, Jack *(Composer)* 3739
Bruce, Jack *(Lyricist)* 3739
Bruce, Judy *(Cast)* 194
Bruce, Michael *(Composer)* 3739
Bruce, Michael *(Lyricist)* 3739
Bruce, Nigel *(Cast)* 2348, 4154, 4569
Bruce, Shelley *(Cast)* 150, 556, 2578
Bruce, Thomas
    See also Tom Jones.
Bruce, Vince *(Cast)* 4695
Bruce, Virginia *(Cast)* 111, 4023
Bruck, Arnold *(Producer)* 2754
Bruder, Patsy *(Cast)* 2556
Brugger, George *(Cast)* 3537
Brugiere, Emil *(Composer)* 308
Bruhns, Arthur *(Composer)* 906
Brumage, Bruce H. *(Costumes)* 2783
Brumley, Albert E. *(Composer)* 4030
Brumley, Albert E. *(Lyricist)* 4030
Brumm, Carol *(Cast)* 1883
Brummel, Barbara *(Cast)* 3557
Brummel, David *(Cast)* 1510
Brummel, Harry S. *(Cast)* 3270
Brummel, Harry S. *(Composer)* 3270
Brummel, Harry S. *(Lyricist)* 3270
Brun, George L. *(Composer)* 4201
Brunce, David *(Cast)* 114

Brune, Gabrielle *(Cast)* 4479
Brune, Paul *(Costumes)* 3380
Brune, Phebe *(Cast)* 4077
Bruneau, Ralph *(Cast)* 1077
Brunetti, Ted *(Cast)* 240
Brunner, M.A. *(Composer)* 4534
Brunner, M.A. *(Lyricist)* 4534
Brunner, Roslyn *(Costumes)* 3667
Bruno, Albert *(Cast)* 2788
Bruno, Jean *(Cast)* 2590
Bruns, Philip *(Cast)* 461, 3889
Brunskill *(Set Design)* 4418
Brunton, John *(Lighting Designer)* 3006
Brunton, Robert *(Set Design)* 3562, 4381
Brush, Bob *(Composer)* 1289
Brusie, Judson D. *(Librettist)* 2062, 2576
Brusie, Judson D. *(Lyricist)* 2576
Bruskin, Perry *(Cast)* 3226
Bruskin, Perry *(Director)* 3226
Bruskin, Perry *(Producer)* 1740
Brustein, Robert *(Librettist)* 3937
Bryan *(Composer)* 1327
Bryan *(Lyricist)* 736, 2493, 3747
Bryan, Al *(Lyricist)* 965
Bryan, Alfred *(Composer)* 1247, 3827, 3926
Bryan, Alfred *(Lyricist)* 208, 351, 405, 684, 822, 965, 1065,
    1154, 1174, 1247, 1334, 1626, 1784, 1799, 1823, 1951,
    1963, 1992, 1998, 2336, 2706, 2856, 2939, 2974, 3018,
    3020, 3149, 3403, 3404, 3429, 3432, 3926, 3962, 3985,
    4589, 4634, 4656, 4712, 4807, 4823
Bryan, C.D.B. *(Librettist)* 3530
Bryan, Frank *(Composer)* 2481
Bryan, Frank *(Lyricist)* 2481
Bryan, Gertrude *(Cast)* 2495, 3433, 4001, 4688
Bryan, John *(Producer)* 4469
Bryan, Vincent *(Composer)* 1327
Bryan, Vincent *(Librettist)* 2724, 3545
Bryan, Vincent *(Lyricist)* 48, 954, 1118, 1243, 1307, 1327,
    1472, 1526, 1569, 1845, 2111, 2335, 2800, 2974, 3191,
    3268, 3313, 3387, 3545, 3626, 3745, 3773, 3855, 3856,
    3857, 4014, 4650, 4723, 4735, 4801, 4805
Bryan, Vincent J. *(Lyricist)* 4390
Bryan, Wayne *(Cast)* 112, 3743
Bryan, Wayne *(Director)* 1262
Bryant, Adam *(Cast)* 4731
Bryant, Anita *(Cast)* 1261
Bryant, Ben *(Cast)* 280, 1736
Bryant, Boudleaux *(Composer)* 3739
Bryant, Boudleaux *(Lyricist)* 3739
Bryant, David C. *(Director)* 80, 3471
Bryant, Felice *(Composer)* 3739
Bryant, Felice *(Lyricist)* 3739
Bryant, Francis *(Author)* 21
Bryant, Francis *(Composer)* 2675
Bryant, Francis *(Lyricist)* 2675
Bryant, George *(Composer)* 1995
Bryant, Gerald *(Lyricist)* 2168
Bryant, Glenn *(Cast)* 653
Bryant, Hugh *(Cast)* 920
Bryant, Katie *(Cast)* 1421
Bryant, Marie *(Cast)* 341, 2259

Bryant, Nana *(Cast)* 834, 1110, 4692
Bryant, Willie *(Cast)* 467, 2712
Bryce, Peter C. *(Director)* 870
Brydon, Eugene *(Director)* 2103
Bryer, Vera *(Cast)* 1855, 2392
Bryggman, Larry *(Cast)* 2918
Bryk, Hugo *(Musical Director)* 2317
Brymer *(Costumes)* 3002
Brymn, J. Tim *(Composer)* 9, 434
Brymn, James *(Composer)* 2044
Brymn, James *(Lyricist)* 2044
Brymn, James T. *(Composer)* 1758, 1909, 2029, 3358
Brymn, Tim *(Composer)* 1050, 3614
Brymn, Tim *(Lyricist)* 1050
Brymn, Tim *(Musical Director)* 2557, 3614
Bryne, Barbara *(Cast)* 1787
Brynner, Yul *(Cast)* 1959, 2312, 2655
Bryon, Lord *(Lyricist)* 2633
Bryson, Arthur *(Cast)* 925, 1989
Bua, Gene *(Cast)* 729
Bubbles, John *(Cast)* 3541, 4823
Bubbles, John W.
    See also Buck & Bubbles.
Bubbles, John W. *(Cast)* 4569
Bucalossi, Ernest *(Composer)* 1537
Bucci, Mark *(Composer)* 19, 3110, 4566
Bucci, Mark *(Lyricist)* 19, 3110
Bucci, Mark *(Orchestrations)* 3110
Buchanan, Jack *(Cast)* 133, 383, 702, 4320
Buchanan, Jack *(Choreographer)* 702, 4320, 4581
Buchanan, Jack *(Director)* 702, 4320
Buchanan, Jack *(Producer)* 4320
Buchanan, Linda *(Set Design)* 158, 4708
Buchanan, Thompson *(Author)* 2649
Buchbinder, Bernhard *(Author)* 1522
Buchen, Walter *(Cast)* 96
Buchen, Walter *(Lyricist)* 96
Buchholz, Fred *(Lighting Designer)* 1402, 2787, 3608
Buchholz, Fred *(Set Design)* 1402
Buchner, Georg *(Author)* 979
Buchs, Sherri *(Costumes)* 3202
Buchter, Barry *(Set Design)* 4416
Buck, Bill *(Cast)* 4467
Buck, Dennis *(Composer)* 3302
Buck, Ford *(Cast)* 3541, 4823
Buck, Ford L.
    See also Buck & Bubbles.
Buck, Ford L. *(Cast)* 4569
Buck, Gene *(Composer)* 4271, 4837
Buck, Gene *(Librettist)* 3179, 4809, 4810, 4811, 4812,
    4813, 4815, 4816, 4823
Buck, Gene *(Lyricist)* 152, 335, 993, 1124, 1154, 2126,
    2446, 2570, 3179, 4206, 4271, 4642, 4806, 4807, 4808,
    4809, 4810, 4811, 4812, 4813, 4814, 4815, 4816, 4817,
    4818, 4819, 4823, 4831, 4832, 4833, 4834, 4835, 4836,
    4837, 4838, 4839, 4840, 4841, 4842, 4843, 4844, 4849,
    4851, 4852, 4858
Buck, Gene *(Producer)* 4271, 4793
Buck, Pearl S. *(Librettist)* 751
Buck, Randy *(Librettist)* 3568
Buck, Richard H. *(Composer)* 4390

Buck, Richard H. *(Lyricist)*   4390
Buck, Susan Hum *(Costumes)*   963
Buck & Bubbles
   See also John W. Bubbles and Ford Buck.
Buck & Bubbles *(Cast)*   443, 1983, 3657
Buck Jr., Fred C. *(Vocal Arranger)*   1839
Buckeridge, Gladys *(Cast)*   4838
Buckhantz, Allan A. *(Director)*   1766
Buckley, Betty *(Cast)*   280, 661, 678, 3070, 3897, 4635
Buckley, Candy *(Cast)*   3456
Buckley, Dennis *(Cast)*   2212
Buckley, Emerson *(Musical Director)*   1474
Buckley, Hal *(Cast)*   3890
Buckley, John *(Producer)*   346
Buckley, Lord *(Cast)*   4829
Buckley, May *(Cast)*   1806
Buckley, Ralph *(Cast)*   3606
Buckley, Ralph *(Librettist)*   3557
Buckley, Robert A. *(Producer)*   209
Buckmaster, Henry *(Set Design)*   4750
Buckner, Martin *(Choreographer)*   528
Bucks County Playhouse *(Producer)*   2169
Bucksey, Colin *(Director)*   682
Budd, Julie *(Cast)*   3311
Buele, Carol H. *(Costumes)*   1412
Buell, Bill *(Cast)*   4619
Buell, Mabel *(Set Design)*   447, 2613, 3511, 3860
Buell, Mabel A. *(Set Design)*   444, 563, 1270, 4204
Buell, William *(Cast)*   922
Bufano, Remo *(Cast)*   1244
Bufano, Rocco *(Director)*   1977
Bufano, Rocco *(Lyricist)*   1977
Bufano's Puppets, Remo *(Cast)*   4498
Buffalo Bills, The *(Cast)*   3016
Buffaloe, Katherine *(Cast)*   2250
Buffano, Jules *(Cast)*   860, 862
Buffano, Jules *(Composer)*   1120
Buffano, Jules *(Lyricist)*   1120
Bufman, Zev *(Producer)*   578, 1289, 2208, 2218, 2242, 3136, 3231, 3428, 4019, 4566, 4789
Buhrer, Suzanne *(Cast)*   3318
Buhrer, Suzanne *(Composer)*   2294, 3318
Buhrer, Suzanne *(Librettist)*   3318
Buhrer, Suzanne *(Lyricist)*   2294, 3318
Bulger, Harry *(Cast)*   215, 604, 804, 2324, 2964, 3154, 4650, 4738
Bulger, Harry *(Composer)*   215, 604, 2724, 4738
Bulger, Harry *(Librettist)*   604
Bulger, Harry *(Lyricist)*   215, 604
Bulger, Harry *(Producer)*   215
Bull, D. Thomas *(Composer)*   3450
Bull, F. *(Set Design)*   4302
Bull, John *(Librettist)*   4154
Bull, John *(Set Design)*   4661
Bull, Peter *(Cast)*   3482
Bullins, Ed *(Librettist)*   4162
Bullock, Donna *(Cast)*   2241, 3544
Bullock, H. Ridgely *(Producer)*   4537
Bullock, Lou *(Cast)*   624
Bullock, Ridgely *(Producer)*   828
Bullock, Turner *(Librettist)*   3365, 3986

Bullock, Walter *(Librettist)*   1679
Bullock, Walter *(Lyricist)*   1679
Bulmash, Jay S. *(Producer)*   3760
Buloff, Joseph *(Cast)*   1269, 3263
Buloff, Joseph *(Director)*   1269
Bumpass, Rodger *(Cast)*   3076
Bunce, Alan *(Cast)*   868
Bunch, Jack *(Director)*   302
Bundsmann, Anton *(Director)*   3104
Bundy, Laura *(Cast)*   3811
Bunin, Shmuel *(Director)*   2811
Bunker, Ralph *(Cast)*   1565, 3481
Bunn, Alfred *(Author)*   1710
Bunn, Alfred *(Lyricist)*   1897
Bunnage, Avis *(Cast)*   874
Bunny, John *(Cast)*   235, 1148, 1318, 3265, 4404
Bunson, Bertha M. *(Cast)*   3480
Bunt, George *(Choreographer)*   1108, 2026, 2231, 2375, 3688
Bunuel, Rafael *(Author)*   4796
Bunyan, Vashti *(Composer)*   1736
Bunyan, Vashti *(Lyricist)*   1736
Buono, Victor *(Cast)*   2742
Burbridge, Edward *(Set Design)*   578, 1592, 2218, 2415, 2719, 3001, 3690, 3840
Burch, Cassie *(Cast)*   813
Burch, Edwin *(Composer)*   2206, 2761
Burch, Edwin *(Lyricist)*   2206
Burch, Fred *(Librettist)*   119
Burch, Fred *(Lyricist)*   119
Burch, Shelly *(Cast)*   3171
Burdick, David *(Cast)*   674
Burdon, Albert *(Cast)*   1202
Burdon, Eric *(Composer)*   3695
Burdon, Eric *(Lyricist)*   3695
Burge, Gregg *(Cast)*   4068, 4091
Burge, Gregg *(Choreographer)*   838
Burger, John *(Composer)*   2162
Burger, Lt. Fairfax *(Cast)*   1972
Burgess, Anthony *(Librettist)*   946
Burgess, Anthony *(Lyricist)*   946
Burgess, Dorothy *(Cast)*   608
Burgess, Gelett *(Lyricist)*   3611
Burgess, Granville *(Librettist)*   838
Burgess, Grover *(Cast)*   2228
Burgess, Kendall *(Composer)*   3084
Burgess, Lee *(Cast)*   4548
Burghoff, Gary *(Cast)*   4783
Burgie, Irving *(Composer)*   279
Burgie, Irving *(Librettist)*   279
Burgie, Irving *(Lyricist)*   279
Burgoyne, Ollie *(Cast)*   2942
Burk, Bobby *(Lyricist)*   364
Burkan, Mark *(Composer)*   4591
Burkan, Mark *(Lyricist)*   4591
Burke, Albert *(Cast)*   1267
Burke, Billie *(Cast)*   100, 152, 2206, 2624, 2871, 3768
Burke, Billie *(Producer)*   4824, 4825
Burke, Charles *(Cast)*   2694
Burke, Charles A. *(Cast)*   4125
Burke, Deirdre *(Costumes)*   3926
Burke, Dorothea *(Choreographer)*   1110

Burke, Joe *(Composer)*   417, 1134, 2460, 4426
Burke, Johnny *(Cast)*   1823
Burke, Johnny *(Composer)*   1076, 1255, 4255
Burke, Johnny *(Lyricist)*   657, 1076, 1255, 1296, 3091, 4255
Burke, Joseph *(Composer)*   173, 1134, 4825
Burke, Joseph A. *(Composer)*   3958
Burke, Louis *(Director)*   2805
Burke, Marie *(Cast)*   1680, 3307
Burke, Maureen *(Cast)*   4524
Burke, Melville *(Director)*   1215
Burke, Patricia *(Cast)*   1763, 3756, 4519
Burke, Sonny *(Composer)*   59, 3905
Burke, Thomas *(Lyricist)*   1871
Burke, Tom *(Composer)*   1780
Burke, Willi *(Cast)*   3279
Burke, Wilma *(Cast)*   932
Burken, Mark *(Composer)*   4591
Burken, Mark *(Lyricist)*   4591
Burker, Maidie *(Cast)*   822
Burkhardt, Addison *(Composer)*   8, 1609
Burkhardt, Addison *(Librettist)*   2596, 3293, 3805, 4247
Burkhardt, Addison *(Lyricist)*   8, 248, 470, 830, 1593,
    1609, 2408, 2596, 2869, 2892, 3387, 3746, 3805, 4094,
    4247, 4804
Burkhardt, Gerry *(Cast)*   921
Burkholder, Scott *(Cast)*   4442
Burks, Donnie *(Cast)*   415
Burks, Donny *(Cast)*   4459
Burks, Hattie *(Cast)*   1026, 1911, 2216
Burleigh, Frederick *(Producer)*   382, 2483, 4416
Burlingame, Lloyd *(Lighting Designer)*   280, 2563, 3491,
    3863, 4329, 4558
Burlingame, Lloyd *(Set Design)*   1727, 2297, 2563, 3491,
    3863, 4318
Burmester, Leo *(Cast)*   2442, 3643
Burnaby, David *(Lyricist)*   4327
Burnaby, Davy *(Cast)*   700
Burnaby, Davy *(Composer)*   700
Burnaby, Davy *(Lyricist)*   700
Burnand, Francis C. *(Librettist)*   727
Burnell, Buster *(Choreographer)*   3264
Burnell, Helen *(Cast)*   2004
Burnett, Carol *(Cast)*   1227, 3288
Burnett, Frances Hodgson *(Author)*   3862
Burnett, Francis Hodgson *(Author)*   1255
Burnett, Harry *(Cast)*   4467
Burnett, Howard J. *(Producer)*   583
Burnett, Martha *(Cast)*   848
Burnette, Brevard *(Cast)*   290
Burney, Steve *(Cast)*   1256
Burnier, Jeannine *(Cast)*   407
Burns, Annelu *(Lyricist)*   1972
Burns, Arthur *(Librettist)*   2726, 4545
Burns, Catherine *(Cast)*   3309
Burns, David *(Cast)*   59, 404, 520, 673, 1061, 1225, 1422,
    1811, 1828, 2626, 2653, 2707, 2729, 3016, 3036, 3214,
    3326, 3535, 3563, 4499, 4827
Burns, George
    See also Burns and Allen.
Burns, George E. *(Producer)*   1924
Burns, Helen *(Cast)*   3818

Burns, Jack *(Librettist)*   3454
Burns, Jeanne *(Composer)*   879
Burns, Jeanne *(Lyricist)*   879
Burns, Peter *(Cast)*   4690
Burns, Peter *(Librettist)*   4690
Burns, Ralph *(Composer)*   964
Burns, Ralph *(Orchestrations)*   16, 393, 521, 534, 723, 868,
    964, 989, 1060, 1227, 1420, 1601, 1842, 1991, 2097, 2106,
    2523, 2874, 3187, 3273, 3473, 3506, 3524, 3564, 3925,
    4060, 4180, 4238, 4334
Burns, Robert *(Lyricist)*   1897, 3450
Burns, Sandy *(Cast)*   4231
Burns, Sandy *(Librettist)*   4231
Burns, Sandy *(Producer)*   4231
Burns and Allen *(Cast)*   3153
Burnside, Molly *(Cast)*   266
Burnside, R.H. *(Cast)*   425
Burnside, R.H. *(Director)*   126, 246, 335, 355, 378, 396,
    712, 735, 736, 773, 930, 968, 1178, 1208, 1243, 1395,
    1524, 1534, 1535, 1536, 1631, 1667, 1753, 1768, 1866,
    1867, 1868, 1901, 1932, 2139, 2184, 2394, 2399, 2403,
    2666, 2848, 2917, 3052, 3144, 3486, 3681, 3790, 3883,
    4025, 4044, 4054, 4113, 4150, 4158, 4178, 4345, 4359,
    4393, 4434, 4452, 4453, 4586, 4603, 4649
Burnside, R.H. *(Librettist)*   286, 378, 396, 588, 712, 736,
    968, 1208, 1246, 1534, 1631, 1753, 1869, 1901, 2139,
    2184, 2897, 3052, 3486, 3883, 4054, 4113, 4150, 4345,
    4359, 4393, 4434, 4452
Burnside, R.H. *(Lyricist)*   248, 378, 396, 968, 1208, 1246,
    1534, 1631, 1753, 1867, 1868, 1901, 2184, 2897, 3486,
    3883, 4054, 4359, 4434, 4452
Burnside, R.H. *(Musical Director)*   1524
Burnside, R.H. *(Producer)*   286, 1246, 1464, 1534, 4113,
    4345, 4452
Burnson, George *(Cast)*   2085, 2841
Burr, Charles *(Cast)*   4583
Burr, Charles *(Composer)*   1770, 3280, 4262
Burr, Charles *(French Libretto)*   4505
Burr, Charles *(Librettist)*   4505
Burr, Charles *(Lyricist)*   1770, 1959, 3280, 4262, 4505
Burr, Courtney *(Producer)*   1775, 3874, 3894, 4583
Burr, Donald *(Cast)*   1814, 2747, 3931
Burr, Henry *(Composer)*   560
Burr, Henry *(Lyricist)*   560
Burr, Robert *(Cast)*   269, 3468, 4689
Burrell, Deborah *(Cast)*   1103, 2173
Burrell, John *(Director)*   3452
Burrell, Pamela *(Cast)*   3682, 4176
Burrell, Teresa *(Cast)*   1970, 2283, 3628
Burrell, Terry *(Cast)*   4255
Burrell-Cleveland, Deborah *(Cast)*   1890
Burress, William *(Cast)*   2543, 3122, 3529, 4119
Burridge, Walter *(Set Design)*   906, 1433, 2117, 2233,
    2315, 2515, 2592, 2723, 2724, 2836, 3437, 3943, 4201,
    4404, 4614, 4723, 4738, 4754
Burris, James *(Cast)*   434, 1087, 1909
Burris, James *(Lyricist)*   1909, 4390
Burris, James Henry *(Lyricist)*   1544, 4804
Burris, Jim *(Cast)*   254, 984
Burris, Jim *(Composer)*   146
Burris, Jim *(Lyricist)*   146, 4390

Burroughs, Don *(Cast)* 1391, 3026
Burrow, David *(Cast)* 3802
Burrows, Abe *(Director)* 629, 1290, 1760, 2019, 3845, 4366, 4496, 4633
Burrows, Abe *(Librettist)* 629, 1290, 1706, 1842, 2019, 3845, 3972, 4366
Burrows, Ann *(Costumes)* 1378
Burrows, Joe *(Librettist)* 3133
Burrows, Joe *(Lyricist)* 1121
Burstein, Lillian *(Lyricist)* 4396
Burstein, Lonnie *(Librettist)* 1786, 4450
Burstein, Lonnie *(Lyricist)* 1786, 4450
Burstein, Mike *(Cast)* 2811
Burstein, Pesach *(Cast)* 2811, 3669
Burstein, Pesach *(Director)* 3669
Burstein, Pesach *(Librettist)* 3669
Burstyn, Mike *(Cast)* 36
Burt, Benj. Hapgood *(Composer)* 75, 379
Burt, Benj. Hapgood *(Lyricist)* 93, 246, 335, 379, 606, 627, 675
Burt, Benjamin H. *(Lyricist)* 425
Burt, Benjamin Hapggod *(Composer)* 2765
Burt, Benjamin Hapgood *(Composer)* 712, 772, 1518, 1553, 1566, 1901, 2892, 2906, 2951, 3229, 3753, 3882, 4283, 4393, 4589, 4762
Burt, Benjamin Hapgood *(Librettist)* 425, 1312, 2922, 4333
Burt, Benjamin Hapgood *(Lyricist)* 75, 379, 712, 1312, 1518, 1553, 1901, 2184, 2671, 2765, 2892, 2922, 2951, 3229, 3753, 3857, 3882, 4283, 4393, 4589, 4762
Burt, Flo *(Cast)* 764
Burt, Frank A. *(Cast)* 4487
Burt, Frederic *(Cast)* 4066
Burt, Harriet *(Cast)* 2056, 2213
Burt, Laura *(Cast)* 976
Burt, Sadie *(Cast)* 3396
Burt, Willie *(Costumes)* 874, 2572
Burton, Brenda *(Costumes)* 2676
Burton, Donald *(Cast)* 3598
Burton, Ebbie *(Cast)* 986
Burton, Eugene *(Composer)* 2032, 3410
Burton, Eugene *(Lyricist)* 2032, 3410
Burton, Frederick *(Cast)* 1020
Burton, Hal *(Lyricist)* 3891
Burton, Irving *(Cast)* 757
Burton, Jenny *(Cast)* 3724
Burton, Kate *(Cast)* 1077
Burton, Kenneth *(Composer)* 637, 1678, 3382
Burton, Miriam *(Cast)* 2000
Burton, Nat *(Lyricist)* 3018, 4027
Burton, Richard *(Cast)* 623, 4386
Burton, Robert *(Cast)* 1342, 4166
Burton, Thomas *(Cast)* 4761
Burton, Val *(Composer)* 1947, 3173
Burton, Val *(Lyricist)* 1947, 3173
Burtson, Bud *(Librettist)* 4585
Burtson, Bud *(Lyricist)* 673, 2397, 4826
Burwell, Cliff *(Composer)* 4137
Bury, John *(Costumes)* 3780, 4558
Bury, John *(Lighting Designer)* 2196, 3259
Bury, John *(Set Design)* 1277, 2196, 3259, 3780, 4558
Busby, Earl *(Musical Director)* 163, 1528, 2637, 3379, 4677

Busby, Georgia *(Cast)* 4239
Busby, Michelle *(Cast)* 2521
Busch, Charles *(Author)* 3606
Busch, Charles *(Cast)* 3606
Busch, Lou *(Orchestrations)* 127
Busch, Mae *(Cast)* 3332
Bushar, George *(Producer)* 814
Bushe Company *(Producer)* 3725
Bushkin, Joe *(Composer)* 4255
Bushman, Francis X. *(Cast)* 3626
Bushor, Geoffrey *(Lighting Designer)* 4690
Busia, Akosua *(Cast)* 3001
Busley, Jessie *(Cast)* 1680
Busling, Elfreda *(Cast)* 639
Busse, Henry *(Composer)* 4815
Bussert, Anna *(Cast)* 1455
Bussert, Meg *(Cast)* 3600, 3908
Bussert, Victoria *(Director)* 1510
Bussins, Jack *(Composer)* 314
Bussins, Jack *(Librettist)* 314
Bussins, Jack *(Lyricist)* 314
Bustle, Jonathan *(Cast)* 99
Butcher, George *(Dance Arranger)* 105
Buterbaugh, Keith *(Cast)* 2674
Butler, A.F. *(Cast)* 1560
Butler, Artie *(Musical Director)* 845
Butler, Bill *(Costumes)* 580
Butler, Billy *(Musical Director)* 467, 1984, 4763
Butler, Billy *(Orchestrations)* 4763
Butler, Bruce *(Cast)* 2272
Butler, Buddy *(Lighting Designer)* 2719
Butler, Daws *(Voice)* 2092, 2093
Butler, Edward L. *(Producer)* 1152
Butler, Gregory *(Cast)* 1630, 4055
Butler, James *(Choreographer)* 322
Butler, John *(Choreographer)* 1237, 1742, 2556
Butler, Mark Anthony *(Cast)* 3806
Butler, Michael *(Producer)* 1717, 3690
Butler, Nellie *(Cast)* 4165
Butler, Paul Lindsay *(Lighting Designer)* 916, 4251
Butler, Ralph *(Lyricist)* 2798
Butler, Rhoda *(Cast)* 808, 1249
Butler, Rick *(Lighting Designer)* 696
Butler, Rick *(Set Design)* 696
Butler Jr., Sam *(Cast)* 1636
Butleroff, Helen *(Choreographer)* 1092, 2197, 4769
Butt, Alfred *(Producer)* 3398
Butt, Billy *(Lyricist)* 2689, 3637
Butt, Dan *(Lighting Designer)* 790, 1047
Butt, Jennifer *(Cast)* 2442
Butt, Joseph *(Producer)* 1813, 4454
Butterfield, Everett *(Director)* 728
Butterworth, Charles *(Cast)* 86, 123, 901, 1322, 1617, 4234
Butterworth, Michael *(Author)* 2646
Buttkay, Akos *(Author)* 3537
Button, Dick *(Cast)* 1742
Button, Dick *(Choreographer)* 2097
Button, Dick *(Director)* 2097
Button, Dick *(Producer)* 1062, 2097
Button, Jeanne *(Costumes)* 112, 496, 1383, 1406, 1500, 3209, 3733, 3876, 3960

Buttons, Red *(Cast)*   304, 1744, 1930, 4706
Buttons, Red *(Voice)*   3793
Buttram, Jan *(Cast)*   1249
Buzzell, Eddie *(Cast)*   1027, 1516, 1617, 3185, 4249
Buzzell, Eddie *(Librettist)*   2382
Buzzell, Eddie *(Lyricist)*   4813
Buzzi, Ruth *(Cast)*   249, 272, 1438, 4238
Bybell, Patricia *(Cast)*   85
Byck, Dann *(Producer)*   166
Byers, Bill *(Musical Director)*   499
Byers, Bill *(Orchestrations)*   322, 547, 695, 746, 1068, 1298,
   1699, 3126, 3444, 3846, 4020, 4695
Byers, Billy *(Orchestrations)*   775, 1633, 4560
Byers, Ralph *(Cast)*   3456
Byng, Douglas *(Cast)*   791, 792, 1877, 3291, 4154
Byrd, Anthony D. *(Cast)*   982
Byrd, Debra *(Cast)*   1713
Byrd, Joe *(Cast)*   14, 435
Byrd, Joseph *(Cast)*   27
Byrd, Sam *(Producer)*   2225
Byrde, Edye *(Cast)*   4162
Byrne, Barbara *(Cast)*   2143, 4210
Byrne, Beatrice *(Choreographer)*   1972
Byrne, C.A. *(Librettist)*   2157
Byrne, C.A. *(Lyricist)*   2157
Byrne, Charles Alfred *(Librettist)*   2156
Byrne, Charles Wilson *(Librettist)*   3199
Byrne, Gaylea *(Cast)*   71
Byrne, Gypsy *(Cast)*   2271
Byrne, J. Edmund *(Producer)*   3860
Byrne, John *(Set Design)*   2988
Byrne, Kiki *(Costumes)*   4160
Byrnes, James *(Composer)*   3222
Byrnes, James *(Musical Director)*   3222
Byrns, Harold *(Orchestrations)*   999
Byron, Arthur *(Cast)*   2202, 3917
Byron, Ben B. *(Cast)*   540
Byron, Bert *(Cast)*   538
Byron, Betty *(Cast)*   4322
Byron, George *(Cast)*   2077, 3104
Byron, Helen *(Cast)*   3065
Byron-Kirk, Keith *(Cast)*   494

C

C.T.A. *(Lyricist)*   123
CHS Productions *(Producer)*   2416, 3178
CSC Repertory *(Producer)*   3853
Cabell, Robert W. *(Composer)*   3561
Cabell, Robert W. *(Librettist)*   3561
Cabell, Robert W. *(Lyricist)*   3561
Cabot, Ceil *(Cast)*   1023, 1107, 3484, 3889, 4065, 4268
Cabot, Tony *(Musical Director)*   961
Caccia, Roger *(Cast)*   2364
Cacoyannis, Michael *(Director)*   2659
Cacoyannis, Michael *(Translator)*   2659
Cadby, Peter *(Composer)*   4153
Cadby, Peter *(Lyricist)*   4153
Caddick, David *(Musical Director)*   3464, 4138, 4217

Caddick, Edward *(Cast)*   455, 1277
Cadenhead, Ian *(Lighting Designer)*   1017
Caderette, Christine *(Musical Director)*   533
Cadiff, Andrew *(Director)*   572, 2702, 4349
Cadiff, Andrew *(Librettist)*   572
Cadman, Ethel *(Cast)*   178, 822
Cady, David *(Cast)*   4790
Caesar, Adolph *(Cast)*   1671
Caesar, Arthur *(Librettist)*   1690
Caesar, Irving *(Cast)*   1396
Caesar, Irving *(Composer)*   1396, 1481, 2706, 2818, 3036,
   3721, 4212, 4730, 4766
Caesar, Irving *(Librettist)*   376, 969, 1396, 1492, 1690,
   2112, 2567, 3036, 3179, 3907, 4730
Caesar, Irving *(Lyricist)*   124, 146, 292, 376, 381, 393, 465,
   487, 545, 638, 702, 773, 969, 1026, 1120, 1179, 1193,
   1396, 1432, 1481, 1491, 1626, 1688, 1689, 1690, 1691,
   1859, 1920, 1923, 2112, 2180, 2336, 2363, 2385, 2387,
   2567, 2594, 2606, 2706, 2757, 2813, 2818, 3020, 3036,
   3140, 3144, 3157, 3170, 3172, 3179, 3184, 3249, 3319,
   3443, 3500, 3532, 3540, 3639, 3662, 3721, 3762, 3953,
   3985, 4104, 4212, 4235, 4249, 4276, 4374, 4491, 4667,
   4683, 4730, 4766, 4817, 4858
Caesar, Irving *(Producer)*   3036
Caesar, Jimmy *(Cast)*   92
Caesar, Robert *(Cast)*   600
Caesar, Sid *(Cast)*   2523, 2707, 4287
Caffey, Marion J. *(Cast)*   2790
Cagney, James *(Cast)*   1656, 1657, 3508
Cagney, James *(Choreographer)*   1656
Cagney, James *(Voice)*   281
Cahan, Abraham *(Author)*   3722
Cahan, Marla *(Cast)*   4830
Cahill, Alfred *(Cast)*   1613
Cahill, James *(Cast)*   775
Cahill, Marie *(Cast)*   511, 1213, 1599, 2160, 2254, 2274,
   2765, 2827, 2938, 2951, 3073, 3131, 3177, 3308, 3820,
   4130, 4353, 4691
Cahill, Marie *(Composer)*   2765
Cahill, Marie *(Lyricist)*   2765
Cahill, Paul *(Cast)*   941
Cahill, William *(Lyricist)*   2765
Cahn, Cathy *(Cast)*   4034
Cahn, Sammy *(Cast)*   4743
Cahn, Sammy *(Composer)*   1813, 4743
Cahn, Sammy *(Librettist)*   4743
Cahn, Sammy *(Lyricist)*   51, 172, 432, 486, 664, 820, 889,
   1577, 1658, 1659, 1813, 1886, 1982, 2076, 2183, 2205,
   2443, 2554, 2583, 2737, 3160, 3324, 3683, 3832, 3844,
   4013, 4342, 4399, 4499, 4588, 4743
Cahn, William *(Producer)*   4428
Caillavet, G. *(Author)*   2624
Cain, John E. *(Cast)*   45, 537, 540
Cain, Sibol *(Cast)*   653
Cain, Viola *(Cast)*   3308
Caine, Georgia *(Cast)*   20, 317, 1123, 1375, 2533, 2592,
   2668, 2844, 2889, 2966, 3218, 3437, 3710, 3750, 3820,
   3943, 4023, 4359, 4482, 4489
Caine, William *(Lyricist)*   356
Caird, John *(Director)*   730, 2442
Caird, John *(Librettist)*   730

Carey, Macdonald *(Cast)* 2386
Carey, Michael *(Composer)* 1501
Carey, Michael *(Lyricist)* 1501
Carey, Robert *(Cast)* 3606
Carfagno, Randy *(Costumes)* 4462
Carine, Martha *(Cast)* 767
Cariou, Len *(Cast)* 167, 958, 2536, 4233, 4297
Carl, George *(Cast)* 1326
Carl, Joseph *(Set Design)* 972
Carlbach, Schlomo *(Composer)* 1609
Carle, Cynthia *(Cast)* 2152
Carle, Richard *(Cast)* 21, 560, 804, 1066, 1213, 1220,
    1538, 1682, 2116, 2261, 2374, 2398, 2695, 2714, 2770,
    2793, 3131, 3177, 4161, 4218, 4311, 4742
Carle, Richard *(Choreographer)* 2040
Carle, Richard *(Composer)* 121, 506, 2261, 2695, 2770,
    4115, 4161
Carle, Richard *(Director)* 2040, 2261, 2695, 4311
Carle, Richard *(Librettist)* 506, 2040, 2261, 2695, 2714,
    2770, 2793, 4115, 4161, 4311
Carle, Richard *(Lyricist)* 506, 560, 2040, 2261, 2374, 2529,
    2695, 2714, 2770, 2793, 4115, 4161, 4311
Carle, Richard *(Producer)* 2695, 2770, 2793, 4115
Carle, Virginia *(Cast)* 3803
Carleton, Arthur *(Cast)* 1206
Carleton, Carle *(Composer)* 4283
Carleton, Claire *(Cast)* 536
Carleton, W.P. *(Cast)* 3566
Carleton, W.T. *(Cast)* 1178, 2803, 2914, 3575
Carleton, Will *(Librettist)* 141, 2222
Carleton, Will *(Lyricist)* 141, 2222
Carleton, William *(Cast)* 2399
Carleton, William *(Librettist)* 668
Carleton, William P. *(Cast)* 4293
Carleton, William T. *(Cast)* 1576, 4353
Carleton Jr., Wm. P. *(Cast)* 2716
Carlin, Tony *(Cast)* 1739
Carlini, John *(Orchestrations)* 4076
Carlisle, Gertie *(Cast)* 2543, 3422, 4293
Carlisle, Kevin *(Choreographer)* 1729
Carlisle, Kitty *(Cast)* 689, 1933, 4365, 4586, 4667
Carlisle, Louise *(Cast)* 1165
Carlo, Monte *(Composer)* 606, 728, 1132, 1174, 2005,
    2595, 3580, 4283, 4576
Carlo, Monte *(Lyricist)* 606, 728, 1132, 1174, 2005, 2595,
    3069, 3252, 3580, 4283
Carlo Studios *(Set Design)* 4328
Carlos, Laurie *(Cast)* 1344
Carlson, Deborah *(Cast)* 198, 2968
Carlson, Richard *(Cast)* 621, 4142
Carlson, Violet *(Cast)* 3680, 4188, 4234
Carlton *(Composer)* 4683
Carlton *(Lyricist)* 4683
Carlton, Bob *(Director)* 2654, 3695
Carlton, Bob *(Librettist)* 3695
Carlton, Carle *(Composer)* 230, 2371, 3369
Carlton, Carle *(Director)* 2371, 3369
Carlton, Carle *(Lyricist)* 2371
Carlton, Carle *(Producer)* 2371, 3369, 4283
Carlton, Carle *(Set Design)* 2371
Carlton, Graeme *(Choreographer)* 3490

Carlton, Harry *(Composer)* 4264
Carlton, Harry *(Lyricist)* 605, 4264
Carlton, Sidney *(Librettist)* 2938
Carlton, Will *(Director)* 3951
Carlton, William *(Lyricist)* 2062
Carlysle, Lynn *(Cast)* 3338
Carmel, Kate *(Costumes)* 788, 3162
Carmel, Kate *(Set Design)* 788
Carmello, Carolee *(Cast)* 198, 992, 1822
Carmen, Sybil *(Cast)* 4834
Cameron, Grace *(Cast)* 2505
Carmichael, Bill *(Cast)* 1348
Carmichael, Hoagy *(Composer)* 39, 59, 213, 3444, 3955,
    4137, 4586
Carmichael, Patricia *(Director)* 3565, 3764
Carminati, Tullio *(Cast)* 1670, 3014
Carmines, Al *(Cast)* 755, 1229, 1958, 2110, 2220
Carmines, Al *(Composer)* 624, 755, 1229, 1426, 1958,
    2110, 2124, 2220, 2243, 2478, 2579, 3418, 3602, 4577,
    4595, 4684
Carmines, Al *(Director)* 1229, 2220
Carmines, Al *(Librettist)* 624, 755, 1229, 1426, 2220, 2243,
    2478, 2579, 4684
Carmines, Al *(Lyricist)* 624, 755, 1229, 1426, 2124, 2220,
    2243, 2478, 2579, 3418, 4577, 4595, 4684
Carmines, Al *(Musical Director)* 2220, 3418, 3602
Carmines, Al *(Orchestrations)* 2579
Carmines, Al *(Pianist)* 3418
Carmines, Al *(Vocal Arranger)* 2579
Carmody, John *(Cast)* 1795
Carnahan, Kirsti *(Cast)* 2333
Carnegie, Hattie *(Costumes)* 2386, 3243, 3335
Carnelia, Craig *(Cast)* 4358
Carnelia, Craig *(Composer)* 1038, 2152, 3181, 4358, 4744
Carnelia, Craig *(Lyricist)* 1038, 2152, 3181, 4358, 4744
Carnes, Kathleen *(Cast)* 153
Carney, Alan *(Cast)* 1242
Carney, Art *(Cast)* 192, 193
Carney, George *(Cast)* 1618
Carney, Grace *(Cast)* 135, 1076, 3059
Carney, Harry *(Composer)* 875, 885, 895, 4091
Carnovsky, Morris *(Cast)* 1237, 2228, 2450, 2859
Carol, Hope *(Cast)* 3002
Carol, Jacqueline *(Cast)* 1695
Carothers, A.J. *(Librettist)* 589
Carousel Group, Inc. *(Producer)* 2692
Carpenter, Carleton *(Cast)* 2227
Carpenter, Constance *(Cast)* 133, 702, 703, 834, 1763,
    3011, 3243, 4335, 4541
Carpenter, E.J. *(Librettist)* 3025
Carpenter, Edward Childs *(Author)* 763
Carpenter, Edward Childs *(Librettist)* 2002, 2813
Carpenter, Edward Childs *(Lyricist)* 763
Carpenter, Francis *(Cast)* 2257
Carpenter, Freddie *(Choreographer)* 972
Carpenter, Frederick *(Cast)* 1333
Carpenter, Imogene *(Cast)* 4826
Carpenter, J.E. *(Composer)* 1897
Carpenter, J.E. *(Lyricist)* 1897
Carpenter, Jean *(Cast)* 4545
Carpenter, John A. *(Librettist)* 2508

Carpenter, John A. *(Lyricist)* 2508
Carpenter, Larry *(Director)* 3598, 4139
Carpenter, Larry *(Producer)* 33
Carpenter, Thelma *(Cast)* 145, 2137, 2817, 3966
Carr, Alexander *(Cast)* 1464, 1728, 2596
Carr, Allan *(Producer)* 2360
Carr, Charmian *(Cast)* 1200
Carr, F. Osmond *(Composer)* 1905, 2131
Carr, George *(Cast)* 1466
Carr, George H. *(Cast)* 2316
Carr, Henry *(Director)* 1887
Carr, Jack *(Cast)* 27, 653
Carr, Jack *(Librettist)* 345
Carr, Jimmie *(Musical Director)* 2296
Carr, Kenneth *(Cast)* 3636
Carr, Lawrence *(Producer)* 603, 1273, 1991, 2713, 3687,
    3913, 4238
Carr, Leon *(Composer)* 3863, 4264
Carr, Leon *(Lyricist)* 4264
Carr, Michael *(Additional Music)* 2572
Carr, Tottie *(Cast)* 1445
Carra, Lawrence *(Director)* 825, 2339, 4191
Carra, Lawrence *(Librettist)* 825
Carra, Lawrence *(Producer)* 2339
Carradine, John *(Cast)* 1422
Carradine, Keith *(Cast)* 1372, 4695
Carrafa, John *(Choreographer)* 647
Carras, Nicholas *(Orchestrations)* 1766
Carre, Albert *(Author)* 1347
Carre fils, Michel *(Author)* 25
Carrere, Fernando *(Set Design)* 2091
Carrick, Hartley *(Lyricist)* 758
Carrillo, Leo *(Cast)* 1228
Carrington, Katherine *(Cast)* 1196, 1225, 1448, 3014
Carrington, Will *(Cast)* 434
Carrol, W.F. *(Librettist)* 3348
Carroll, Adam *(Dance Arranger)* 4782
Carroll, Adam *(Orchestrations)* 4782
Carroll, Adam *(Pianist)* 138, 2545
Carroll, Adam *(Vocal Arranger)* 4782
Carroll, Albert *(Cast)* 125, 1357, 1448, 1651, 1652, 1653,
    1654, 1655, 1656, 1657, 4823
Carroll, Albert *(Choreographer)* 1357, 1652, 1653
Carroll, Albert *(Composer)* 1651
Carroll, Albert *(Dance Arranger)* 1651
Carroll, Albert *(Librettist)* 621
Carroll, Albert *(Lyricist)* 1651, 1652, 1654, 1655, 1657
Carroll, Barbara *(Cast)* 2797
Carroll, Bob *(Cast)* 3577, 3683
Carroll, Carroll *(Librettist)* 1448
Carroll, Carroll *(Lyricist)* 720
Carroll, Chris *(Cast)* 3557
Carroll, Danny *(Cast)* 249, 287, 1359, 1478, 3186
Carroll, David *(Cast)* 721, 1649, 2359, 4701
Carroll, David-James *(Cast)* 2785, 3231, 3743, 3888, 4114
Carroll, Diahann *(Cast)* 2000, 3187
Carroll, Earl *(Composer)* 628, 1129, 1130, 2939, 3395,
    3562, 3662, 3812, 4037
Carroll, Earl *(Director)* 1126, 1127, 1128, 1130, 1131,
    1132, 1134, 1135, 1136, 1137, 1138, 1312, 3002
Carroll, Earl *(Librettist)* 1130, 1138, 2619, 3002, 4416

Carroll, Earl *(Lyricist)* 60, 351, 628, 1129, 1130, 1138, 1309,
    2619, 2939, 3332, 3395, 3562, 3662, 3812, 3827, 4037, 4807
Carroll, Earl *(Producer)* 1125, 1126, 1127, 1128, 1129,
    1130, 1131, 1132, 1134, 1135, 1136, 1137, 1138, 1281,
    1312, 2020, 3002
Carroll, Eddie *(Cast)* 2436
Carroll, Georgia *(Cast)* 2597
Carroll, Gladys *(Costumes)* 4152
Carroll, Harry *(Cast)* 2696
Carroll, Harry *(Composer)* 351, 448, 965, 1209, 1270, 1486,
    1694, 1738, 1777, 1778, 1920, 1963, 2494, 2696, 3246,
    3354, 3397, 4589, 4655, 4720, 4804, 4814, 4815, 4853
Carroll, Harry *(Lyricist)* 448, 1209
Carroll, Harry *(Producer)* 3246
Carroll, Helena *(Cast)* 3482
Carroll, Irving *(Musical Director)* 268
Carroll, James *(Costumes)* 858
Carroll, Jane *(Cast)* 2430
Carroll, Joan *(Cast)* 3359
Carroll, John *(Cast)* 2742
Carroll, June
    See also June Sillman.
Carroll, June *(Cast)* 817, 3107
Carroll, June *(Librettist)* 2103, 3105
Carroll, June *(Lyricist)* 679, 817, 1878, 2103, 2294, 2772,
    3105, 3107, 3108, 3110, 3111, 3112, 3178, 3320, 3880,
    3890, 3941, 4433
Carroll, Lambert *(Librettist)* 1207
Carroll, Leo G. *(Cast)* 2786, 4100, 4479
Carroll, Lewis *(Author)* 52, 54, 55, 56, 57, 58, 593, 4736
Carroll, Lewis *(Lyricist)* 55
Carroll, Marie *(Cast)* 3043, 3230, 4860
Carroll, Nancy *(Cast)* 391, 910, 3072
Carroll, Pat *(Cast)* 673, 2742, 4273
Carroll, Pauline *(Composer)* 448
Carroll, Pauline *(Lyricist)* 448
Carroll, R.F. *(Lyricist)* 539
Carroll, Richard *(Cast)* 47, 976, 3049, 3199
Carroll, Richard *(Composer)* 3022
Carroll, Richard *(Director)* 541, 1912, 3025
Carroll, Richard *(Lyricist)* 47, 3022
Carroll, Richard F. *(Author)* 2326
Carroll, Richard F. *(Cast)* 523, 2350, 4556
Carroll, Richard F. *(Director)* 3022
Carroll, Richard F. *(Librettist)* 4556
Carroll, Richard F. *(Lyricist)* 4556
Carroll, Richard F. *(Producer)* 2518
Carroll, Robert *(Cast)* 3013
Carroll, Ronn *(Cast)* 373, 921, 2346, 2542, 3517, 3718
Carroll, Sidney *(Librettist)* 2772, 3108
Carroll, Vinnette *(Director)* 52, 1072, 4645, 4788
Carroll, Vinnette *(Librettist)* 52, 593, 4788
Carry, Louis *(Cast)* 2737
Carson, Alexander *(Producer)* 4542
Carson, Doris *(Cast)* 672, 2636, 3283, 4179
Carson, Heather *(Lighting Designer)* 1509, 4775
Carson, Irwin *(Composer)* 3714
Carson, Jack *(Cast)* 1204
Carson, James B. *(Cast)* 292, 1308
Carson, Jean *(Cast)* 2608
Carson, Jeannie *(Cast)* 461, 1815, 2550, 3630

Carson, Mindy *(Cast)*   483
Carson, Sue *(Cast)*   865, 1341
Carson, Susan Dawn *(Cast)*   4055, 4217
Carten, Bob *(Cast)*   4591
Carten, Bob *(Musical Director)*   4591
Carten, Kenneth *(Cast)*   3885
Carter *(Librettist)*   1995
Carter *(Lyricist)*   1995
Carter, Alice E. *(Costumes)*   2908
Carter, Benjamin *(Cast)*   344
Carter, Claire *(Lighting Designer)*   2988
Carter, Desmond *(Composer)*   2376
Carter, Desmond *(Librettist)*   1110, 2323, 2547
Carter, Desmond *(Lyricist)*   700, 791, 834, 921, 1338,
    1680, 1681, 1756, 1855, 2004, 2323, 2376, 2547, 3430,
    3569, 4027, 4207, 4212, 4300, 4320, 4581, 4765
Carter, Dixie *(Cast)*   2838, 3902
Carter, Frank *(Cast)*   3868, 4812
Carter, Frank *(Composer)*   3333
Carter, Genna *(Cast)*   366
Carter, Jack *(Cast)*   649, 2987
Carter, Janis *(Cast)*   1109
Carter, Joey *(Cast)*   3110
Carter, Joey *(Librettist)*   3110
Carter, Joey *(Lyricist)*   3110
Carter, Lavada *(Cast)*   3965
Carter, Leslie H. *(Librettist)*   4627
Carter, Lincoln J. *(Producer)*   1185
Carter, Louise *(Cast)*   2826
Carter, Nell *(Cast)*   39, 314, 1116, 2898, 4089, 4403, 4615
Carter, Ralph *(Cast)*   1116, 2290, 3656, 4558
Carter, Robert Peyton *(Cast)*   2383
Carter, Rosanna *(Cast)*   2133
Carter, Sidney *(Lyricist)*   220
Carter, Stanley *(Lyricist)*   2389
Carter, Terry *(Cast)*   2355, 2994
Carter, Vicki *(Musical Director)*   1198, 2027
Carter-Waddell, Joan *(Cast)*   1874
Carthay, Dan *(Cast)*   1136, 2300
Carthe, Dan *(Choreographer)*   3409
Cartier, Deidre *(Costumes)*   461, 1761
Cartier, Jacques *(Cast)*   1603, 4824
Cartier, Jeanne *(Cast)*   3865
Cartwright, Charles *(Director)*   2819
Cartwright, Peggy *(Cast)*   125
Carty Jr., Edward M. *(Lighting Designer)*   4149
Carucci, Frank *(Director)*   843
Carus, Emma *(Cast)*   1021, 1505, 1728, 2324, 2803, 2851,
    4521, 4650, 4687, 4738, 4801
Caruso, Dee *(Librettist)*   272, 427, 1049, 1648, 3186,
    4153, 4268
Caruso, Fran *(Costumes)*   1978
Carver, Brent *(Cast)*   2333
Carvill, Rosemary *(Costumes)*   1386
Carwell, T.L. *(Composer)*   987
Cary, Addison *(Choreographer)*   497
Cary, Claiborne *(Cast)*   73, 198, 339, 4028
Caryl, William *(Director)*   2540, 4240, 4741
Caryl, William *(Producer)*   4424
Caryll, Fred *(Librettist)*   3434
Caryll, Fred *(Lyricist)*   3434

Caryll, Ivan *(Author)*   351, 3322, 4115
Caryll, Ivan *(Composer)*   351, 627, 719, 736, 770, 1114,
    1123, 1313, 1527, 1537, 1540, 1569, 1992, 2184, 2336,
    2374, 2497, 2498, 2500, 2760, 2844, 3020, 3092, 3098,
    3251, 3313, 3322, 3362, 3494, 3803, 3948, 3976, 3999,
    4115, 4393, 4430, 4590, 4805, 4823
Caryll, Ivan *(Musical Director)*   1114, 3098
Caryll, Ivan *(Orchestrations)*   2336
Casale, Glenn *(Director)*   2651
Casanave, Carolyn *(Cast)*   140, 583
Cascio, Gigi *(Lighting Designer)*   679
Cascone, Michael *(Cast)*   2630
Case, Allen *(Cast)*   649, 1729, 3288, 3696
Case, Mary *(Puppeteer)*   56, 3449
Case, Ronald *(Costumes)*   3576, 4146
Case, Ronald *(Set Design)*   3576
Case, Russ *(Musical Director)*   3490
Case, Russ *(Orchestrations)*   3490
Casella, Martin *(Librettist)*   3364
Casella, Matt *(Director)*   3364
Casey, Charles E. *(Composer)*   3220
Casey, Charles E. *(Lyricist)*   3220
Casey, Dorothy *(Cast)*   2253
Casey, Gene *(Composer)*   2026, 3318
Casey, Gene *(Librettist)*   3318
Casey, Gene *(Lyricist)*   2026, 3318
Casey, Gene *(Orchestrations)*   3318
Casey, Jan *(Composer)*   2026
Casey, Jan *(Librettist)*   2026
Casey, Kenneth *(Composer)*   3905
Casey, Kenneth *(Lyricist)*   3905
Casey, Michael *(Costumes)*   107, 1638, 2737
Casey, Warren *(Composer)*   1664
Casey, Warren *(Librettist)*   1664
Casey, Warren *(Lyricist)*   1664
Cash, Estelle *(Cast)*   254
Cash, Nat *(Choreographer)*   1328, 1989, 3361
Cash, Rosalind *(Cast)*   1592
Casher, Izidor *(Cast)*   3336
Casher, Jennie *(Cast)*   3336
Cashman, Edward *(Composer)*   821, 2641
Cashman, Edward *(Dance Arranger)*   345
Cashman, Edward *(Lyricist)*   821
Cashman, Edward *(Musical Director)*   345
Cashone, Regina *(Cast)*   4168
Casler, Richard *(Lighting Designer)*   161, 937, 3684
Casler, Richard *(Set Design)*   937
Casman, Nellie *(Cast)*   4463
Casman, Nellie *(Composer)*   1279
Casman, Nellie *(Lyricist)*   1279, 4342
Casmore, Vic *(Cast)*   4378
Casmore, Victor *(Cast)*   2747, 3170
Casnoff, Philip *(Cast)*   496, 721, 2269, 2320, 3944, 4518
Cason, Barbara *(Cast)*   272, 427, 3235
Cass, Byrle *(Director)*   1918
Cass, Carol *(Cast)*   2177
Cass, Lee *(Cast)*   71, 1698, 1993, 2961
Cass, Peggy *(Cast)*   98, 4432
Cass, Ronald *(Composer)*   392, 3890
Cass, Ronnie *(Composer)*   3186
Cass, Ronnie *(Lyricist)*   3186

Chadal, Georges *(Cast)* 1743
Chadman, Christopher *(Cast)* 723, 964, 3506, 3741
Chadman, Christopher *(Choreographer)* 2307, 2820
Chadwick, Cyril *(Cast)* 1197, 3011
Chadwick, George Whitefield *(Composer)* 1210
Chadwick, Ida May *(Cast)* 3369
Chaflin, Paul *(Costumes)* 2900
Chaikin, Shami *(Cast)* 1715
Chakraband, B. *(Composer)* 2850
Chakraband, B. *(Lyricist)* 2850
Chalfonte, Lucille *(Cast)* 1688
Chaliapine, Lydia *(Cast)* 839
Chalif, Louis *(Choreographer)* 3219
Challis, William *(Orchestrations)* 1384
Chalmers, Anthony *(Lyricist)* 3940
Chalmers, Cary *(Set Design)* 2759
Chalmers, H. Hilbert *(Librettist)* 1752
Chalmers, Thomas *(Cast)* 1196
Chalzel, Leo *(Cast)* 1352, 1973
Chamber, Peter *(Cast)* 294
Chamberlain, Douglas *(Cast)* 3066
Chamberlain, Richard *(Cast)* 521
Chamberlin, Ida Hoyt *(Composer)* 1182
Chamberlin, Ida Hoyt *(Librettist)* 1182
Chamberlin, Ida Hoyt *(Lyricist)* 1182
Chamberlin, Ida Hoyt *(Set Design)* 1182
Chamberlin, Kevin *(Cast)* 4030
Chamberlyn, A.H. *(Producer)* 613, 1021, 2959, 3047, 3566
Chambers, David *(Director)* 1684, 1914
Chambers, Ernest *(Librettist)* 1107, 1878, 3954
Chambers, Ernest A. *(Lyricist)* 427
Chambers, H. Kellett *(Librettist)* 375
Chambers, Howard *(Cast)* 310
Chambers, Marilyn *(Cast)* 2426
Chambers, Peter *(Cast)* 672
Chambers, Ralph *(Cast)* 619
Chambers, Ralph W. *(Cast)* 536
Chambers, Robert *(Producer)* 2522, 2664
Chambers, Robert W. *(Author)* 2145
Chambers, Robert W. *(Librettist)* 2145
Chambers, Robert W. *(Lyricist)* 2145
Chambers-Ketchum, Annie *(Lyricist)* 3020
Chaminade *(Composer)* 77
Chaminade *(Lyricist)* 77
Champagne, Michael *(Director)* 430
Champagne, Michael *(Lyricist)* 430
Champion, Gower *(Cast)* 2379, 4174, 4287, 4346
Champion, Gower *(Choreographer)* 550, 607, 656, 1359, 1764, 1828, 2050, 2439, 2660, 2705, 3741, 4018, 4196, 4287, 4346
Champion, Gower *(Director)* 550, 607, 656, 1359, 1764, 1828, 2050, 2660, 3564, 3741, 4196, 4346
Champion, Marge *(Cast)* 1205, 1298, 4346
Chan, Don *(Arrangements)* 4251
Chan, Eric *(Cast)* 3944
Chance, Anna *(Cast)* 1641
Chandler, Anna *(Cast)* 1337
Chandler, Byron *(Producer)* 375, 2929
Chandler, Chick *(Cast)* 4486
Chandler, Evelyn *(Cast)* 2086
Chandler, Helen *(Cast)* 2396

Chandler, Richard *(Author)* 1383
Chandler, Richard *(Producer)* 681
Chandler, Stan *(Cast)* 1353
Chandler, Stephen *(Costumes)* 4332
Chandler, Wilfred *(Lyricist)* 1066
Chaney, Jan *(Cast)* 3543
Chaney, Lon *(Cast)* 432
Chaney, Stewart *(Costumes)* 1679, 2379, 3104, 3916
Chaney, Stewart *(Lighting Designer)* 1679
Chaney, Stewart *(Set Design)* 842, 1101, 1679, 2255, 2311, 2379, 2400, 2985, 3104, 3895, 3916, 4180, 4214
Channing, Carol *(Cast)* 658, 1389, 1475, 1828, 2072, 2439, 2590, 3180, 3954, 4230, 4542
Chansky, Dorothy *(Cast)* 4172
Chansky, Dorothy *(Librettist)* 564
Chansky, Dorothy *(Lyricist)* 564
Chansky, Dorothy *(Producer)* 564
Chapel, C.M. *(Composer)* 2286, 4094
Chapin, Carl *(Cast)* 3986
Chapin, Eleanor *(Choreographer)* 4157
Chapin, Frederic *(Composer)* 1351, 2694, 3738, 4725
Chapin, Frederic *(Librettist)* 2694
Chapin, Frederic *(Lyricist)* 2694
Chapin, Fredric *(Composer)* 4161
Chapin, Harry *(Cast)* 3159
Chapin, Harry *(Composer)* 900, 2470, 3159
Chapin, Harry *(Lyricist)* 900, 2470, 3159
Chapin, Sandy *(Composer)* 2470
Chapin, Sandy *(Lyricist)* 2470
Chapin, Stephen *(Cast)* 3159
Chapin, Stephen *(Dance Arranger)* 2470
Chapin, Stephen *(Musical Director)* 2470, 3159
Chapin, Stephen *(Vocal Arranger)* 2470
Chapin, Tom *(Cast)* 3159
Chapin, Tom *(Dance Arranger)* 2470
Chapin, Tom *(Musical Director)* 900
Chapin, Tom *(Orchestrations)* 2470
Chapin, Tom *(Vocal Arranger)* 2470
Chapine *(Cast)* 2867, 3776, 4794
Chaplin, Charlie *(Composer)* 4264
Chaplin, Charlie *(Lyricist)* 4264
Chaplin, Saul *(Composer)* 432, 490, 889, 1658, 1659, 1813, 1982, 4743
Chaplin, Saul *(Lyricist)* 1813, 4342, 4743
Chaplin, Sydney *(Cast)* 363, 1420, 4190
Chapman, David *(Costumes)* 2426, 3684, 4089
Chapman, David *(Lighting Designer)* 2426, 4124
Chapman, David *(Set Design)* 840, 1289, 1713, 2231, 2426, 2433, 2687, 3018, 3075, 3517, 3684, 4124
Chapman, Edwin *(Cast)* 2500
Chapman, Elmer B. *(Musical Director)* 3877
Chapman, Frank *(Cast)* 3168
Chapman, Gary *(Cast)* 393, 4003
Chapman, J.S. *(Additional Music)* 761
Chapman, Michael *(Director)* 1348
Chapman, Stella *(Cast)* 129
Chapman, Topsy *(Cast)* 1425, 3297
Chapman, Topsy *(Vocal Arranger)* 1425
Chapman, William *(Cast)* 177, 630, 1698
Chappell, Delos *(Producer)* 818
Chappell, George S. *(Librettist)* 824

Chappell, George S. *(Lyricist)* 824
Chappell, Helen *(Cast)* 2153
Chappell, Vickie *(Cast)* 2784
Chappelle, Chappie *(Cast)* 1019
Chappelle, Chappy *(Cast)* 2009, 4198
Chappelle, Frederic *(Composer)* 2571, 3500
Charell, Erik *(Author)* 4667
Charell, Erik *(Director)* 4256, 4667
Charell, Erik *(Librettist)* 4256
Charell, Erik *(Producer)* 4256
Charig, Phil *(Composer)* 1395, 1397, 1690, 2392, 3255, 3861, 4766
Charig, Phil *(Lyricist)* 1397
Charig, Philip *(Composer)* 86, 123, 204, 673, 1215, 1336, 1892, 2246, 2277, 3168, 3352, 3532, 3946, 4235, 4320, 4367, 4581, 4766
Charioteers, The *(Cast)* 1840
Charise, Andre *(Cast)* 3699, 4557
Charisse, Zan *(Cast)* 915
Charkham, David *(Cast)* 635
Charlap, Moose *(Composer)* 58, 786, 837, 1298, 2205, 2304, 2313, 3453, 3940, 4682
Charlap, Moose *(Lyricist)* 58
Charles, Edward *(Costumes)* 4433
Charles, Hughie *(Composer)* 4027
Charles, Hughie *(Lyricist)* 4027
Charles, Jacques *(Lyricist)* 1176, 3905
Charles, Keith *(Cast)* 681
Charles, Lee *(Cast)* 2556
Charles, Milton *(Composer)* 200
Charles, Ray
   See also Ray Charles Choir.
Charles, Ray *(Vocal Arranger)* 3428
Charles, Robert *(Choreographer)* 2661
Charles, Vicki
   See also Vicki Cummings.
Charles, Walter *(Cast)* 211, 754, 2360, 2766
Charles Choir, Ray
   See also Ray Charles.
Charles Choir, Ray *(Cast)* 2182
Charlip, Remy *(Choreographer)* 2236
Charlip, Remy *(Costumes)* 2236
Charlip, Remy *(Set Design)* 2236
Charlot, Andre *(Director)* 133
Charlot, Andre *(Producer)* 703, 3521, 3827
Charlotte *(Cast)* 396
Charlson, Natalie *(Dance Arranger)* 1727
Charlson, Natalie *(Musical Director)* 249, 4433
Charlton, Richard *(Producer)* 920
Charmoli, Tony *(Choreographer)* 58, 145, 1119, 1326, 2313, 4727
Charmoli, Tony *(Producer)* 1257
Charnas, Fran *(Choreographer)* 74
Charnas, Fran *(Director)* 74
Charnas, Fran *(Librettist)* 74
Charney, Jordan *(Cast)* 1736
Charney, Suzanne *(Cast)* 108
Charnin, Martin *(Cast)* 1567, 4625
Charnin, Martin *(Composer)* 1233, 3181, 4533
Charnin, Martin *(Director)* 150, 154, 155, 262, 278, 299, 1289, 2230, 3018, 3075, 3181, 4136, 4533

Charnin, Martin *(Librettist)* 1233, 3181
Charnin, Martin *(Lyricist)* 150, 154, 155, 278, 602, 1233, 1257, 1289, 1370, 1991, 2064, 2288, 2368, 2777, 3018, 3181, 3484, 3615, 3889, 4048, 4395, 4481, 4533, 4627, 4798
Charnin, Martin *(Producer)* 4533
Charnin, Sasha *(Cast)* 2230, 3181
Charsky, Boris *(Producer)* 796
Charters, Spencer *(Cast)* 1368, 4683
Chartoff, Melanie *(Cast)* 2633, 4558
Chase, Arlene *(Cast)* 2430
Chase, Chaz *(Cast)* 288, 1889, 3822
Chase, Chevy *(Cast)* 3077
Chase, Chevy *(Librettist)* 3076
Chase, Colin *(Cast)* 1404
Chase, Ilka *(Cast)* 759, 2301, 3699
Chase, Lloyd *(Composer)* 796
Chase, Lloyd *(Librettist)* 796
Chase, Lloyd *(Lyricist)* 796
Chase, Mary *(Author)* 2993, 3846
Chase, Pauline *(Cast)* 3322
Chase, Stanley *(Producer)* 1385, 4369
Chase, William P. *(Composer)* 2665
Chase, William P. *(Lyricist)* 2665
Chasemore, Arthur *(Costumes)* 476
Chasen, Dave *(Cast)* 1275, 1932
Chasin, Susan *(Cast)* 2124
Chastain, Don *(Cast)* 2163, 2992, 3187
Chatelaine, Stella *(Cast)* 1647
Chatrian *(Author)* 1401
Chatterton, Ruth *(Cast)* 2691
Chatto, Tom *(Cast)* 1277
Chaucer, Geoffrey *(Author)* 634, 1500
Chaykin, Maury *(Cast)* 2429
Cheek, Jean *(Cast)* 105
Chekhov, Anton *(Author)* 1620
Chelsea Productions *(Producer)* 2180
Chelsea Theatre Center *(Producer)* 599, 1037, 1684, 1897, 4176
Chelsi, Laurence *(Cast)* 3920
Chenault, Cory *(Costumes)* 3004
Chenault, Lawrence *(Cast)* 1499
Cheney, Ed *(Cast)* 2423
Cheng, Kam *(Cast)* 2905
Chermayeff, S. *(Costumes)* 703
Chermayeff, S. *(Set Design)* 703
Chernis, Jay *(Composer)* 2169
Cherpakov, Gary *(Composer)* 2676, 3239
Cherpakov, Gary *(Lyricist)* 2676, 3239
Cherry, James *(Cast)* 3745, 3751, 4753
Cherry, John *(Cast)* 4227, 4673
Cherry, Paul *(Librettist)* 3389
Cherry, Paul *(Lyricist)* 3389
Chesnutt, Jim *(Set Design)* 3239
Chester, Alfred "Slick" *(Cast)* 2720
Chester, Eddie *(Cast)* 202
Chetwyn, Robert *(Director)* 4329
Chevalier, Louis *(Cast)* 2552
Chevalier, Maurice *(Cast)* 1396, 4661
Chew, Christopher *(Cast)* 3306
Chew, Ray *(Composer)* 1637
Chew, Ray *(Lyricist)* 1637

Chiang, Dawn *(Lighting Designer)* 4861
Chiari, Walter *(Cast)* 1456
Chiasson, Gilles *(Cast)* 1804
Chicago Federal Theatre *(Producer)* 4254
Chicas, Roy *(Cast)* 535
Chief Iron Shell *(Cast)* 2413
Chief Ki Wi *(Cast)* 4452
Chiffarelli, Albert *(Orchestrations)* 2298
Chihara, Paul *(Composer)* 3944
Chijo, Antonio Torroella *(Composer)* 3755, 4206
Child, Alan
    See also Lawrence Langner.
Child, Alan *(Librettist)* 689
Child, Marilyn *(Cast)* 1229, 3111
Child, Steve *(Composer)* 4374
Children of Eden, Ltd. *(Producer)* 730
Childs, Jennifer *(Cast)* 264
Childs, Reginald *(Musical Director)* 1267
Chilton, Carol *(Cast)* 4730
Chilvers, Hugh *(Cast)* 1682, 1851, 3176
Chilvers, Thomas *(Composer)* 2515
Chiment, Marie Anne *(Costumes)* 2846
Chimola, George *(Lyricist)* 1689
Ching, William *(Cast)* 85
Chinn, Lori Tan *(Cast)* 282
Chip, Sam *(Cast)* **4735**
Chipmonck *(Lighting Designer)* 3742
Chisholm, Hazel *(Composer)* 2476
Chisholm, Robert *(Cast)* 1603, 1894, 2636, 3390, 4368, 4479, 4670
Chivot *(Author)* 1650
Chivot, Henri *(Author)* 1305
Chocolateers, The *(Cast)* 467, 886
Choder, Jill *(Cast)* 482, 1842
Chodorov, Jerome *(Author)* 2267, 4734
Chodorov, Jerome *(Director)* 751
Chodorov, Jerome *(Librettist)* 59, 1119, 1548, 2053, 3273, 3563, 4617, 4734
Chodosh, Richard *(Composer)* 3186
Chodosh, Richard B. *(Composer)* 4173
Choos, George *(Producer)* 1223, 1839, 2503, 2972, 4596
Chopin, Frederic *(Music Based On)* 745, 3536, 4669
Choraleers, The *(Cast)* 1423
Chorpenning, Ruth *(Cast)* 1448
Chotin, Andre *(Set Design)* 1244
Choyce, Root *(Lighting Designer)* 914
Chris, Marilyn *(Cast)* 2422
Chrisdie, Charles *(Costumes)* 1395
Chrisman, Richard *(Cast)* 2703
Chrispijn, Rob *(Lyricist)* 1865
Christen, Robert *(Lighting Designer)* 158, 4074, 4708
Christenberry Jr., Charles W. *(Director)* 1918
Christians, Mady *(Author)* 4768
Christians, Mady *(Composer)* 4768
Christians, Mady *(Lyricist)* 4768
Christians, William *(Costumes)* 159
Christiansen, Nora *(Choreographer)* 4707
Christianson, Bob *(Musical Director)* 251
Christianson, Bob *(Orchestrations)* 251
Christie, Audrey *(Cast)* 297, 1112, 1879, 2061, 2709, 3907, 4550

Christie, Frank M. *(Cast)* 542
Christie, George Stuart *(Cast)* 1098
Christie, Irene *(Cast)* 117
Christie, Ken *(Vocal Arranger)* 117
Christie, Marice *(Cast)* 3573
Christie, Marie *(Cast)* 4681
Christine, Henri *(Author)* 3466
Christine, Henri *(Composer)* 2356, 3079, 3466, 3467
Christine, Lily *(Cast)* 2850, 4180
Christine, Marilyn *(Choreographer)* 2104
Christine, Mrs. *(Composer)* 998
Christine, P.H. *(Composer)* 377, 1066, 2385, 3177, 3387
Christmas, David *(Cast)* 956, 1591
Christmas, Eric *(Cast)* 3818
Christofferson, Nancy *(Costumes)* 3418
Christopher, Don *(Lyricist)* 2599
Christopher, Gavin *(Composer)* 1298
Christopher, Gavin *(Lyricist)* 1298
Christopher, Kevin *(Cast)* 4332
Christopher, Paula *(Cast)* 4294
Christopher, Tony *(Composer)* 1159
Christopher, Tony *(Librettist)* 1159
Christopher, Tony *(Lyricist)* 1159
Christy, Chandler *(Cast)* 1460
Christy, Harold *(Lyricist)* 3032
Christy, Lew *(Cast)* 102
Chryst, Gary *(Cast)* 146
Church, George *(Cast)* 4825
Church, Harden *(Composer)* 680
Church, Jordan *(Cast)* 2676
Church, Joseph *(Composer)* 1201
Church, Joseph *(Musical Director)* 674, 1201, 4676
Church, Sandra *(Cast)* 1709
Church, Stanley *(Cast)* 278
Churchill, Benton *(Cast)* 2121
Churchill, Caryl *(Author)* 785, 3884
Churchill, E.P. *(Producer)* 1556
Churchill, Frank *(Author)* 4035
Churchill, Frank *(Composer)* 4035
Churchill, Stuart *(Cast)* 4340
Chute, B.J. *(Author)* 1698
Cianelli, Carole *(Cast)* 4799
Ciannelli, Eduardo *(Cast)* 97, 3772
Ciccone, Sandra *(Cast)* 2521
Ciesla, Diane *(Cast)* 760
Cilento, Wayne *(Cast)* 393, 746, 964, 3444
Cilento, Wayne *(Choreographer)* 140, 253, 2208, 3548, 4676
Cina, John *(Musical Director)* 2375
Cina, John *(Vocal Arranger)* 2375
Cindy Lou *(Cast)* 155
Cindy Pritzker, Inc. *(Producer)* 3992
Cinko, Paula *(Cast)* 3619
Cioffi, Charles *(Cast)* 496
Circle Production Co. *(Producer)* 2826
Circle Repertory Company *(Producer)* 1268, 1346, 4517
Circle Repertory Theatre *(Producer)* 3034
Circle in the Square *(Producer)* 147, 788, 1222, 4109
Cirker & Robbins *(Set Design)* 288, 423, 1251, 2636, 4673
Cissel, Chuck *(Cast)* 746
Citadel Theatre *(Producer)* 3485
City Center, The *(Producer)* 148, 3018

Ciucicini, Signor *(Lyricist)* 3567
Claflin, Rick *(Lighting Designer)* 2776
Claghorn, Senator
　See also Kenny Delmar.
Claghorn, Senator *(Cast)* 1899
Claire, Helen *(Cast)* 4214
Claire, Ina *(Cast)* 1327, 2261, 2390, 3618, 4809, 4810
Claire, Marion *(Cast)* 1680
Claire, Rosalie *(Cast)* 4668
Claire, Stella *(Cast)* 194
Clamen, Dolores *(Composer)* 4388
Clancy, Elizabeth Hope *(Costumes)* 3853
Clapton, Eric *(Composer)* 3739
Clapton, Eric *(Lyricist)* 3739
Clare *(Costumes)* 4392
Clare, Henry *(Lyricist)* 3523
Clare, Johnne *(Cast)* 1267
Clare, Joseph *(Set Design)* 1576
Clare, Sidney *(Composer)* 3770
Clare, Sidney *(Lyricist)* 1137, 1692, 2857, 2870, 3020, 3249
Claret, Gaston *(Composer)* 839
Claribol *(Composer)* 77
Claribol *(Lyricist)* 77
Clark *(Lyricist)* 4393
Clark, Alexander *(Cast)* 132, 354, 1021, 1580, 1613, 2374, 2914, 2922, 3078, 3082, 3590, 3681, 3805, 4236
Clark, Alexander *(Librettist)* 3290
Clark, Alice *(Composer)* 4566
Clark, Alice *(Lyricist)* 4566
Clark, Arthur F. *(Producer)* 4724
Clark, Bessie *(Cast)* 1499
Clark, Bobby
　See also Clark & McCullough.
Clark, Bobby *(Cast)* 206, 1856, 2234, 2402, 2403, 2847, 3426, 3659, 4131, 4174, 4179, 4374, 4583, 4825
Clark, Bobby *(Director)* 2850
Clark, Bobby *(Librettist)* 2850
Clark, Bryan *(Cast)* 1914
Clark, Buddy *(Cast)* 532
Clark, Capt. Anson *(Cast)* 1972
Clark, Charles Dow *(Cast)* 1360, 4544
Clark, Cheryl *(Cast)* 723
Clark, Cumberland *(Composer)* 605
Clark, Cumberland *(Lyricist)* 605
Clark, Dick
　See also Dick Clark Inc.
Clark, Dick *(Producer)* 4459
Clark, Dort *(Cast)* 363, 1749, 4734
Clark, E.A. *(Cast)* 4452
Clark, Eddie *(Choreographer)* 1003
Clark, Edward *(Director)* 1335, 1424, 1551, 3258, 4784
Clark, Edward *(Librettist)* 765, 1424, 1551, 1961, 2527, 3258, 3369, 4784
Clark, Edward *(Lyricist)* 765, 1424, 1551, 2527, 3258, 3332, 4784
Clark, Edwin A. *(Cast)* 4046
Clark, Eva *(Cast)* 2768, 3323, 3662, 3842, 4211
Clark, Fred *(Cast)* 3761
Clark, Fred *(Choreographer)* 2457
Clark, Fred *(Director)* 2457
Clark, Gilbert *(Costumes)* 2180

Clark, Gladys *(Cast)* 4045, 4148, 4440
Clark, Grace Gaylor *(Cast)* 4544
Clark, Grant *(Lyricist)* 1058
Clark, Helen *(Cast)* 2363
Clark, Hilda *(Cast)* 1896, 3582
Clark, James Nisbet *(Cast)* 793
Clark, James Nisbet *(Lighting Designer)* 2188
Clark, John F. *(Cast)* 2991
Clark, Keith *(Cast)* 1137
Clark, Kenneth *(Composer)* 2481
Clark, Kenneth *(Lyricist)* 2481
Clark, Kenneth S. *(Composer)* 2481, 3134, 3710, 4026, 4094
Clark, Kenneth S. *(Lyricist)* 2481, 3134, 3710, 4094
Clark, Lillion *(Cast)* 1352
Clark, Marguerite *(Cast)* 336, 350, 1768, 2317, 2724, 2982, 3129, 3486, 4691
Clark, Norman *(Librettist)* 3861
Clark, Peggy *(Costumes)* 1546, 2175
Clark, Peggy *(Lighting Designer)* 56, 95, 98, 189, 269, 341, 363, 411, 607, 649, 657, 943, 989, 1119, 1315, 1369, 1564, 1886, 2217, 2234, 2268, 2327, 2615, 2680, 2987, 3019, 3108, 3188, 3347, 3371, 3453, 3498, 3509, 3815, 3845, 3954, 4323, 4516, 4660, 4734, 4827
Clark, Peggy *(Set Design)* 943
Clark, Rudy *(Composer)* 3695
Clark, Rudy *(Lyricist)* 3695
Clark, Thais *(Cast)* 3297
Clark, Tony *(Cast)* 1229
Clark, W.H. *(Cast)* 1351, 2126, 2139, 3504, 4452
Clark, Wayne *(Producer)* 1508, 4470
Clark & McCullough
　See also Bobby Clark and Paul McCullough.
Clark & McCullough *(Cast)* 3007, 3009
Clark Bros. *(Cast)* 1423
Clarke *(Composer)* 3322
Clarke, Alex *(Cast)* 4222
Clarke, Alexander *(Cast)* 2159, 2500
Clarke, Bert *(Composer)* 1342
Clarke, Bert *(Lyricist)* 1342
Clarke, Bill *(Set Design)* 4775
Clarke, Caitlin *(Cast)* 4295
Clarke, Charlene *(Cast)* 2521
Clarke, Corson *(Cast)* 1523
Clarke, Della *(Cast)* 2008
Clarke, Edwin A. *(Cast)* 3093
Clarke, Gage *(Cast)* 4548
Clarke, George *(Composer)* 1342
Clarke, George *(Lyricist)* 1342
Clarke, Gordon *(Cast)* 3986
Clarke, Gordon B. *(Cast)* 4764
Clarke, Grant *(Composer)* 3737
Clarke, Grant *(Lyricist)* 432, 478, 487, 558, 805, 1058, 1154, 1334, 1735, 1763, 2462, 2923, 3031, 3525, 3737, 3827, 3973, 4033, 4589, 4805, 4806, 4808, 4814, 4815, 4817, 4838
Clarke, Harry *(Cast)* 735, 1033, 1558, 1882, 2331, 2455, 3580, 4206, 4285, 4293
Clarke, Harry *(Composer)* 2373
Clarke, Harry *(Librettist)* 184, 2540, 2747, 4025
Clarke, Harry *(Lyricist)* 627, 2174, 2373, 2402, 2405, 2747, 4673

Clugston, Glen (*Musical Director*) 227, 3925
Clugston, Glen (*Orchestrations*) 227
Clugston, Glen (*Vocal Arranger*) 3925
Clurman, Harold (*Director*) 3505
Clurman, Harold (*Producer*) 2450
Clute, Chester (*Cast*) 3130
Clutsam, G.A. (*Orchestrations*) 1680
Clyburn, Rose (*Cast*) 3987
Clyde, June (*Cast*) 297, 1973
Coates, Dorothy Love (*Composer*) 3987
Coates, Dorothy Love (*Lyricist*) 3987
Coates, Eric (*Choreographer*) 703
Coates, Eric (*Composer*) 4667
Coates, Florence Earle (*Lyricist*) 4590
Coates, Norman (*Lighting Designer*) 3136, 3576
Cobb, Earl (*Composer*) 4273
Cobb, George L. (*Composer*) 1888, 2696
Cobb, Ira (*Librettist*) 4792
Cobb, Ira (*Lyricist*) 4792
Cobb, Irvin (*Librettist*) 1417
Cobb, John S. (*Producer*) 90
Cobb, Lee J. (*Cast*) 2228
Cobb, Will D. (*Composer*) 3999
Cobb, Will D. (*Lyricist*) 8, 326, 511, 1391, 1434, 1464,
    1526, 1703, 1704, 1900, 1910, 1919, 1998, 2803, 2835,
    2858, 2885, 2974, 2990, 3322, 3387, 3855, 4079, 4181,
    4209, 4390, 4723, 4738, 4755, 4801, 4804, 4807
Cobb Jr., Henry Ives (*Set Design*) 1784, 2532
Cobey, Louis (*Composer*) 3140
Coburn, Charles (*Cast*) 377, 563, 1235
Coburn, Charles (*Producer*) 1235, 4360
Coburn, D.L. (*Author*) 2230
Coburn, Mrs. Charles (*Cast*) 377, 563, 1235
Coburn, Mrs. Charles (*Producer*) 4360
Coburn, Richard (*Composer*) 1120
Coburn, Richard (*Lyricist*) 1120, 3246
Coca, Imogene (*Cast*) 70, 621, 1322, 1342, 1448, 3103,
    3104, 3279, 3800, 3946, 4166, 4651, 4677
Coccia, Aurelia (*Choreographer*) 350
Coccia, Aurelio (*Choreographer*) 3348
Cochran, C.B. (*Producer*) 453, 1153
Cochran, Charles (*Producer*) 2462, 2788
Cochran, Charles B. (*Producer*) 700, 841, 1202, 1338,
    1763, 3214, 3291, 3467, 3597, 4154, 4341, 4581
Cochran, Dorcas (*Lyricist*) 1138
Cochran, Gifford (*English Lyrics*) 4368
Cochran, Gifford (*Librettist*) 4368
Cochran, Gifford (*Producer*) 4368
Cochrane, James (*Costumes*) 3495
Cochrane, Jeannetta (*Costumes*) 346
Cochrane, June (*Cast*) 834, 1446, 1529
Cochrane, Roy (*Cast*) 4576
Cochren, Felix E. (*Costumes*) 105
Cochren, Felix E. (*Set Design*) 2133
Coco, James (*Cast*) 546, 991, 1864, 2553, 4318
Coco, Jim (*Cast*) 2511
Cocoanut Grove Playhouse (*Producer*) 4645
Cocteau, Jean (*Set Design*) 2611
Coda, Alfred (*Cast*) 2393
Coda, Frank (*Cast*) 4469
Codron, Michael (*Producer*) 4329, 4685

Coe, Fred (*Producer*) 1497, 2313, 3324
Coe, George (*Cast*) 832, 1232, 2713, 2935, 3279, 4633
Coe, John (*Cast*) 2236, 2368
Coe, Peter (*Director*) 3271, 3482, 4002
Coes, G. (*Composer*) 476
Coffin, Frederick (*Cast*) 1591, 3000, 4019
Coffin, Gene (*Costumes*) 3816
Coffin, Maurice (*Musical Director*) 1989
Coggin, Barbara (*Cast*) 164, 3671
Coghill, Nevill (*Librettist*) 634
Coghill, Nevill (*Lyricist*) 634
Coghlan, James (*Librettist*) 3861, 4545
Coghlan, Rosalind (*Cast*) 1501
Cogley, Edward F. (*Composer*) 405
Cogley, Edward F. (*Lyricist*) 405
Cogswell, Bill (*Composer*) 4264
Cogswell, Bill (*Lyricist*) 4264
Cohan, Cora (*Choreographer*) 459
Cohan, George M. (*Author*) 403, 1271, 2730, 4576
Cohan, George M. (*Cast*) 1399, 1480, 1640, 1826, 1968,
    2068, 2517, 2525, 2829, 3153, 3809, 4759
Cohan, George M. (*Choreographer*) 805
Cohan, George M. (*Composer*) 115, 403, 800, 801, 803,
    804, 805, 964, 1271, 1356, 1478, 1480, 1527, 1640, 1826,
    1968, 1988, 2415, 2493, 2517, 2525, 2533, 2730, 2829,
    2964, 2975, 3018, 3020, 3153, 3723, 3791, 3809, 4277,
    4390, 4553, 4576, 4717, 4759
Cohan, George M. (*Director*) 115, 800, 803, 804, 805,
    1271, 1356, 1399, 1480, 2517, 2525, 2533, 2730, 3809,
    4277, 4576, 4759
Cohan, George M. (*Librettist*) 115, 403, 800, 801, 803,
    804, 805, 1356, 1480, 1640, 1826, 1968, 2517, 2525, 2533,
    2730, 2829, 3723, 3809, 4277, 4759
Cohan, George M. (*Lyricist*) 115, 403, 800, 801, 803, 804,
    805, 964, 1271, 1356, 1478, 1480, 1527, 1640, 1826, 1968,
    1988, 2415, 2493, 2517, 2525, 2533, 2730, 2829, 2964,
    2975, 3018, 3020, 3153, 3723, 3791, 3809, 4277, 4390,
    4553, 4576, 4717, 4759
Cohan, George M. (*Producer*) 115, 335, 403, 800, 801,
    802, 803, 804, 805, 1271, 1360, 1598, 1803, 1826, 2525,
    2533, 2730, 2767, 2829, 3218, 3529, 3685, 3791, 4277,
    4576, 4759
Cohan, Helen (*Cast*) 1480, 1640, 1968, 2517, 2525,
    3809, 4759
Cohan, Jerry (*Cast*) 1480, 1640, 1968, 2517, 2525,
    3809, 4759
Cohan, John C. (*Producer*) 2551
Cohan, Josephine (*Cast*) 3749
Cohan, Josie (*Cast*) 1640, 3809, 4759
Cohen, Alexander (*Producer*) 1841
Cohen, Alexander H. (*Director*) 826
Cohen, Alexander H. (*Producer*) 220, 221, 270, 532, 826,
    1000, 1012, 1621, 1842, 2064, 2072, 2705, 3226, 3564,
    3798, 4384, 4743
Cohen, Allen (*Composer*) 3557
Cohen, Allen (*Dance Arranger*) 4537
Cohen, Allen (*Lyricist*) 3557
Cohen, Coleman (*Composer*) 4433
Cohen, Coleman (*Librettist*) 4433
Cohen, Coleman (*Lyricist*) 4433
Cohen, Darren R. (*Musical Director*) 3227

Cohen, David *(Composer)* 459
Cohen, Douglas *(Set Design)* 4774
Cohen, Douglas J. *(Composer)* 1510
Cohen, Douglas J. *(Librettist)* 1510
Cohen, Douglas J. *(Lyricist)* 1510
Cohen, Douglas J. *(Vocal Arranger)* 1510
Cohen, Hanoch *(Composer)* 2421
Cohen, Harold *(Composer)* 2397
Cohen, Harry R. *(Composer)* 1795
Cohen, Jay *(Producer)* 166
Cohen, Jay J. *(Producer)* 2133
Cohen, Joyce *(Cast)* 1037
Cohen, Julie *(Cast)* 455
Cohen, Lawrence D. *(Librettist)* 661
Cohen, Margery *(Cast)* 369, 599, 4145
Cohen, Martin *(Producer)* 4542
Cohen, Martin B. *(Director)* 4623
Cohen, Martin B. *(Producer)* 751
Cohen, Michael *(Composer)* 1438, 2913, 3112, 4790
Cohen, Michael *(Dance Arranger)* 2913
Cohen, Michael *(Musical Director)* 366
Cohen, Michael *(Orchestrations)* 2913
Cohen, Michael *(Pianist)* 366, 1436, 2279, 2913
Cohen, Michael *(Vocal Arranger)* 2913
Cohen, N.D. *(Cast)* 1624
Cohen, Phil *(Composer)* 1126
Cohen, Robert *(Lyricist)* 387
Cohen, S.A. *(Lighting Designer)* 1637
Cohen, Sol *(Composer)* 2943
Cohen, Steve *(Orchestrations)* 4107
Cohen, Ze-eva *(Choreographer)* 2918
Cohenour, Patti *(Cast)* 394, 1068, 2359, 3070, 3464
Cohn, Al *(Orchestrations)* 3018, 3656, 4091
Cohn, Max *(Costumes)* 1513
Cohn, Sam *(Producer)* 1354
Coile, Bob *(Lyricist)* 2493
Coini, Jacques *(Director)* 824, 1743, 3081
Coit-Wright, Fredrick *(Composer)* 1518
Cokas, Nicholas *(Cast)* 1804
Cokayne, A.H. *(Musical Director)* 2222
Coke, Peter *(Author)* 3900
Colavecchia, Franco *(Costumes)* 4447
Colavecchia, Franco *(Set Design)* 4447, 4790
Colbin, Rod *(Cast)* 2664
Colby, Archie *(Librettist)* 1533
Colby, Jack *(Cast)* 288
Colby, Marion *(Cast)* 2809, 3351
Colby, Michael *(Librettist)* 705, 1757, 2647, 2993, 3201
Colby, Michael *(Lyricist)* 705, 1757, 2647, 2993, 3201
Colby, Robert *(Composer)* 1727
Colby, Robert *(Lyricist)* 1727
Coldrey, Jeff *(Composer)* 296
Coldrey, Jeff *(Lyricist)* 296
Cole *(Composer)* 1076
Cole, Barbara *(Cast)* 4696
Cole, Barbara *(Choreographer)* 2641
Cole, Beatrice *(Author)* 2629
Cole, Bob *(Cast)* 633, 3676, 3945, 4451
Cole, Bob *(Composer)* 982, 2029, 2035, 2044, 2111, 2325, 2765, 2892, 2951, 3073, 3945, 4390, 4697
Cole, Bob *(Librettist)* 3676, 3945

Cole, Bob *(Lyricist)* 217, 352, 633, 982, 1188, 1535, 1537, 2035, 2044, 2111, 2123, 2493, 2506, 2805, 2892, 2964, 2974, 3073, 3676, 3820, 3945, 3999, 4014, 4451, 4681
Cole, Bob *(Producer)* 633
Cole, Charles W. *(Cast)* 1274
Cole, Christopher *(Set Design)* 3178
Cole, Cosy *(Cast)* 653
Cole, Doris *(Producer)* 467
Cole, Doug *(Producer)* 4454
Cole, Jack
    See also Jack Cole and His Dancers.
Cole, Jack *(Cast)* 59, 680, 2786, 4374, 4550, 4826
Cole, Jack *(Choreographer)* 59, 84, 657, 1076, 1373, 1422, 2190, 2295, 2327, 2679, 2727, 2777, 4058, 4798, 4827
Cole, Jack *(Director)* 1076, 2295
Cole, Kay *(Cast)* 746, 3277, 3651, 3903, 4034
Cole, Kay *(Choreographer)* 456, 1737
Cole, Kay *(Librettist)* 456
Cole, Lester *(Cast)* 3436
Cole, Louis *(Cast)* 500
Cole, Nat "King" *(Composer)* 39
Cole, Nat "King" *(Lyricist)* 39
Cole, Nora *(Cast)* 2968, 4645
Cole and His Dancers, Jack
    See also Jack Cole.
Cole and His Dancers, Jack *(Cast)* 397
Coleman, Charles *(Cast)* 478
Coleman, Charles H. *(Dance Arranger)* 1762
Coleman, Charles H. *(Musical Director)* 4383, 4722
Coleman, Charles H. *(Vocal Arranger)* 4722
Coleman, Cy *(Composer)* 229, 305, 327, 775, 1023, 1038, 1097, 1168, 1648, 1708, 1842, 1955, 2058, 2227, 2294, 2297, 2473, 2523, 2804, 3279, 3428, 3869, 3936, 4167, 4238, 4337, 4338, 4619, 4693, 4695, 4827
Coleman, Cy *(Dance Arranger)* 1955, 2058, 3869, 4695
Coleman, Cy *(Librettist)* 2473
Coleman, Cy *(Lyricist)* 4619
Coleman, Cy *(Producer)* 305, 4619
Coleman, Cy *(Vocal Arranger)* 305, 775, 1955, 2058, 4619, 4695
Coleman, Dan *(Cast)* 2314
Coleman, David *(Composer)* 1120
Coleman, David *(Lyricist)* 1120
Coleman, Don *(Lighting Designer)* 484, 4244
Coleman, Ed Lea *(Cast)* 2113
Coleman, Gladys *(Cast)* 1602
Coleman, Hamilton *(Composer)* 4092
Coleman, Hamilton *(Director)* 4092
Coleman, Hamilton *(Librettist)* 4092
Coleman, Hamilton *(Lyricist)* 4092
Coleman, Herbert *(Cast)* 2591
Coleman, Jim *(Musical Director)* 3734
Coleman, Jim *(Vocal Arranger)* 3734
Coleman, Larry *(Cast)* 4220
Coleman, Larry *(Composer)* 4264
Coleman, Lillian *(Cast)* 246, 3578, 3747
Coleman, Marilyn B. *(Cast)* 40
Coleman, Shepard *(Musical Director)* 1828, 1846, 3259, 4186
Coleman, Shepard *(Vocal Arranger)* 1828, 1846
Coleman, Ted *(Composer)* 263

Comden, Betty *(Screenwriter)* 3992
Comedian's Guild *(Producer)* 3173
Comelli *(Costumes)* 334, 902, 1561, 2974, 3156, 3663
Comelli, A. *(Costumes)* 4187
Comfort, Vaughn *(Cast)* 801, 803
Comor, Henry *(Cast)* 2278
Comor, Henry *(Director)* 2278
Comor, Henry *(Librettist)* 2278
Comor, Henry *(Lyricist)* 2633
Company, The *(Choreographer)* 4442
Company, The *(Librettist)* 3997
Compass Fair *(Producer)* 4395
Complex IV *(Producer)* 2925
Compton, Betty *(Cast)* 123, 827, 1272, 1419, 1929, 3243
Compton, Fay *(Cast)* 4418, 4419
Compton, Francis *(Cast)* 2275
Compton, Frank *(Lyricist)* 675
Comstock, F. Ray *(Director)* 1246
Comstock, F. Ray *(Producer)* 25, 165, 295, 336, 684, 710, 758, 1246, 1588, 1975, 2340, 2430, 2698, 2802, 2979, 3193, 3230, 3245, 3250, 3535, 3775, 4555, 4758, 4860
Comstock, Frances *(Cast)* 3292
Conant, Homer *(Costumes)* 208, 764, 1065, 2794, 2856, 3333, 3865, 3958, 3985, 4056, 4375
Conant, Homer *(Set Design)* 764, 2794, 2856
Conaway, Charles *(Producer)* 4828, 4829
Conaway, Jeff *(Cast)* 3136
Conaway, Joe *(Producer)* 2027
Condell, H.A. *(Costumes)* 4792
Condell, H.A. *(Set Design)* 309, 4792
Conderman, Susan *(Cast)* 1978
Condon, Dennis *(Lighting Designer)* 2436
Condon, Eva *(Cast)* 1894
Condon, Kate *(Cast)* 3560, 3736
Condon, Kate *(Composer)* 1178
Condos, Frank *(Cast)* 1135
Condos, Harry *(Cast)* 1135
Condray, Peggy *(Cast)* 919
Cone, Tom *(Author)* 1872
Conforti, Gino *(Cast)* 1369, 2727, 3612, 3918, 4028
Conforti, Robert *(Cast)* 821
Conforti, Tom *(Producer)* 3905
Conforti, Tony *(Producer)* 2759
Confrey, Zez *(Composer)* 3261
Congdon, James *(Cast)* 253
Congreve, William *(Author)* 2607
Conkey, Thomas *(Cast)* 371, 3323
Conklin, Bill *(Librettist)* 3217
Conklin, Bill *(Lyricist)* 597, 3217
Conklin, John *(Costumes)* 1786, 3702, 3835
Conklin, John *(Set Design)* 808, 945, 1017, 1786, 2590, 3195, 3468, 3702, 3835
Conklin, Peggy *(Cast)* 2545, 4443
Conkwright, Anna *(Costumes)* 1555
Conlee, John Ellison *(Cast)* 2038
Conley, Larry *(Composer)* 1241
Conley, Matt *(Cast)* 2017
Conley, Robert *(Choreographer)* 3939
Conley, Robert *(Set Design)* 239
Conley, Shannon *(Cast)* 1232
Conlow, Peter *(Cast)* 108, 4270, 4366

Conlow, Peter *(Choreographer)* 4380
Conlow, Peter *(Director)* 73
Conmee, Marie *(Cast)* 2682
Conn, Harry *(Librettist)* 1492
Conn, Irving *(Composer)* 3008
Connaughton, Kevin *(Lighting Designer)* 4106
Connell, Dennis E. *(Composer)* 4779
Connell, Dennis E. *(Lyricist)* 4779
Connell, Gordon *(Cast)* 394, 1107, 1828, 2033, 2659, 3484, 4190
Connell, Gordon *(Composer)* 2294
Connell, Gordon *(Lyricist)* 2294
Connell, Gordon *(Musical Director)* 3615
Connell, Gordon *(Pianist)* 1023, 4268
Connell, Jane *(Cast)* 921, 1012, 1023, 1081, 1093, 1094, 1354, 2659, 2713, 2798, 3108, 3186, 3484, 3615, 3788, 4310
Connell, Tom *(Lyricist)* 4328
Connelli, Regina *(Cast)* 1560
Connelly, David *(Cast)* 4074
Connelly, Edward *(Cast)* 252
Connelly, Marc *(Author)* 647
Connelly, Marc *(Cast)* 4278
Connelly, Marc *(Director)* 1357, 3699, 4479
Connelly, Marc *(Librettist)* 102, 216, 317, 1357, 1819, 2020, 2402, 3783, 3861, 4335
Connelly, Marc *(Lyricist)* 102, 317, 1901, 2698
Connelly, Marc *(Producer)* 3546, 4479
Connelly, Reg *(Composer)* 4027
Connelly, Reg *(Lyricist)* 1135, 1136, 4027
Conner, Bruce *(Cast)* 1897
Conners, Jack *(Choreographer)* 3137
Connolly, Bobby *(Choreographer)* 111, 289, 1027, 1145, 1323, 1339, 1387, 1419, 1628, 1879, 1965, 1979, 2253, 2342, 2813, 3117, 3796, 3953, 4118, 4267, 4443, 4823, 4824
Connolly, Bobby *(Director)* 2366, 3584, 4087, 4824
Connolly, Bobby *(Producer)* 289, 3584, 4087
Connolly, Don *(Cast)* 680
Connolly, Edward J. *(Cast)* 228
Connolly, Joseph *(Composer)* 1873
Connolly, Joseph *(Lyricist)* 1873
Connolly, Marc *(Author)* 80, 317
Connolly, Patrick *(Composer)* 3695
Connolly, Patrick *(Lyricist)* 3695
Connor, Joseph *(Composer)* 2148
Connor, Joseph *(Lyricist)* 2148
Connor, Maureen *(Costumes)* 2746
Connor, Peggy *(Composer)* 702
Connor, Peggy *(Lyricist)* 2570
Connor, Zoe *(Cast)* 3752
Connors, Barry *(Author)* 3415
Connors, Barry *(Librettist)* 3415
Connors, Edgar *(Cast)* 2942
Connors, Frankie *(Cast)* 851
Connors, Jack *(Choreographer)* 1182, 1314, 2112
Connors, Kevin *(Composer)* 3568
Connors, Kevin *(Director)* 3568
Connors, Kevin *(Lyricist)* 3568
Connors & Bennett *(Set Design)* 3130
Conoly, Joseph *(Composer)* 3022

Conoly, Joseph (*Lyricist*) 3022
Conoly, Joseph (*Producer*) 3022
Conor, Harry (*Cast*) 457, 472, 694, 1226, 1240, 1522, 1543, 2390, 2649, 2760, 3308, 4165, 4642
Conor, Harry (*Composer*) 436
Conor, Harry (*Lyricist*) 436
Conrad, Art (*Composer*) 1223
Conrad, Art (*Lyricist*) 1223
Conrad, Arthur (*Cast*) 1824, 4687
Conrad, Arthur (*Choreographer*) 1824
Conrad, Con (*Composer*) 103, 123, 124, 200, 381, 391, 487, 545, 827, 1154, 1689, 2302, 2342, 2467, 2818, 2856, 2857, 2950, 3032, 4033, 4271, 4806
Conrad, Con (*Director*) 2302
Conrad, Con (*Lyricist*) 487, 545, 827, 1689, 2302, 2342, 2818, 2856, 3770, 4033
Conrad, Con (*Producer*) 2302
Conrad, Constance (*Composer*) 2580
Conrad, Eddie (*Cast*) 1460
Conrad, Eddie (*Composer*) 3717
Conrad, Eddie (*Lyricist*) 1693, 3148, 3717
Conrad, Edith (*Cast*) 4351
Conrad, Eugene (*Librettist*) 557, 1127, 1135, 2400, 3380, 3822, 4424
Conrad, Eugene (*Lyricist*) 557, 4424
Conradt, Mark (*Librettist*) 1676
Conreid, Hans (*Cast*) 1257, 3900, 4278
Conried, Hans (*Cast*) 629, 928
Conrow, Jonathan (*Producer*) 3020
Conroy, Frances (*Cast*) 1575
Conroy, Frank (*Cast*) 1560, 2510, 3768
Conroy, Pat (*Author*) 838
Consentino, Nicholas (*Author*) 2946
Conte, John (*Cast*) 85, 2837, 4702
Continental Music Halls (*Producer*) 431
Continentals, The (*Cast*) 216
Continer, Anthony (*Set Design*) 27
Contreras, Ray (*Cast*) 1053, 2970, 3806
Contrucci, Lance (*Librettist*) 3076
Converse, C.C. (*Composer*) 2046
Converse, C.C. (*Lyricist*) 2046
Converse, Frank (*Cast*) 1999
Converse, Harry E. (*Producer*) 1515
Convy, Bert (*Cast*) 322, 411, 610, 1265, 2958, 3210, 4566
Convy, Bert (*Director*) 4796
Conway, Bert (*Cast*) 3180
Conway, Curt (*Cast*) 3180, 3226
Conway, Curt (*Director*) 4237, 4401
Conway, Daniel (*Set Design*) 1915
Conway, Gary (*Cast*) 1750
Conway, Gordon (*Costumes*) 703, 706, 3583
Conway, Lizzie (*Cast*) 3270
Conway, Shirl (*Cast*) 3509
Conwell, O'Kane (*Costumes*) 136, 1536, 1922, 3146, 4393
Conwit, Phil (*Lyricist*) 3986
Coogan, Jack (*Lyricist*) 1063
Coogan, Joe (*Librettist*) 932
Cook, Barbara (*Cast*) 630, 1300, 1456, 1662, 1744, 3016, 3509, 3918, 4060
Cook, Carole (*Cast*) 1359, 2011
Cook, Cecil (*Composer*) 1537

Cook, Charles Emerson (*Director*) 3774
Cook, Charles Emerson (*Librettist*) 3774
Cook, Charles Emerson (*Lyricist*) 1394, 1397, 3673, 3774
Cook, Christopher (*Cast*) 752
Cook, Gregory (*Cast*) 1695
Cook, Harold (*Cast*) 1973
Cook, Hartwell (*Choreographer*) 2942
Cook, Howard (*Musical Director*) 1502
Cook, James (*Cast*) 4735
Cook, Jill (*Cast*) 964, 1665, 3444, 3548
Cook, Joe (*Additional Dialogue*) 1932
Cook, Joe (*Cast*) 1129, 1130, 1275, 1396, 1726, 1921, 1932, 2020, 2161, 2162, 3426, 3648
Cook, Joe (*Librettist*) 1275, 4035
Cook, Joe (*Lyricist*) 4035
Cook, Joe (*Producer*) 1932
Cook, John H. (*Composer*) 2111
Cook, Judy (*Costumes*) 2076
Cook, Louise (*Cast*) 1772
Cook, Marie (*Costumes*) 683, 3538, 3652, 4831, 4836, 4837, 4852
Cook, Olga (*Cast*) 463, 3407, 4209
Cook, Patrick (*Librettist*) 647
Cook, Patrick (*Lyricist*) 647
Cook, Peter (*Cast*) 384, 1621
Cook, Peter (*Librettist*) 384, 1621
Cook, Peter (*Lyricist*) 1621
Cook, Peter (*Producer*) 1195
Cook, Phil (*Cast*) 4651
Cook, Phil (*Composer*) 3511
Cook, Phil (*Librettist*) 3511
Cook, Phil (*Lyricist*) 1533, 2927, 3511, 4651
Cook, Ray (*Musical Director*) 2196, 3967
Cook, Ray (*Vocal Arranger*) 2949
Cook, Richard (*Producer*) 4582
Cook, Roderick (*Cast*) 1564, 2295, 3235, 4727
Cook, Roderick (*Director*) 3235
Cook, Roderick (*Librettist*) 3196
Cook, Roderick (*Lyricist*) 4134
Cook, Victor Trent (*Cast*) 3757, 4031
Cook, Virginia (*Composer*) 4030
Cook, Virginia (*Lyricist*) 4030
Cook, W.A. (*Cast*) 449
Cook, Will A. (*Cast*) 641, 982, 1050, 2127
Cook, Will A. (*Librettist*) 2127
Cook, Will Marion (*Composer*) 9, 295, 511, 633, 783, 988, 1535, 2111, 2127, 2210, 2254, 2990, 3089, 3129, 4088, 4098, 4441, 4691, 4697
Cook, Will Marion (*Lyricist*) 26, 511, 2127, 2881, 2990, 3089, 3129, 4804
Cook, Will Marion (*Musical Director*) 295, 783
Cook, Will Marion (*Orchestrations*) 9
Cook, Will Marion (*Producer*) 3089
Cook Jr., Elisha (*Cast*) 1831
Cook Jr., Joe (*Cast*) 557, 4340
Cooke, Charles (*Orchestrations*) 3813, 3907, 4763
Cooke, Charles L. (*Composer*) 3985, 4281
Cooke, Charles L. (*Lyricist*) 4281
Cooke, Charles L. (*Musical Director*) 567
Cooke, Charles L. (*Orchestrations*) 70, 341, 507, 567, 612, 1336, 1748, 1987, 2748, 3966, 4086, 4362, 4572

Cooke, Charles L. *(Vocal Arranger)*   2379
Cooke, Edmund Vance *(Composer)*   998
Cooke, Emerson *(Librettist)*   2350
Cooke, Harold *(Vocal Arranger)*   4483, 4498
Cooke, Leonard *(Lyricist)*   632
Cooke, Malcolm *(Producer)*   2754
Cooke, Rose *(Cast)*   472
Cooke, Sam *(Composer)*   4534
Cooke, Sam *(Lyricist)*   4534
Cooksey, Curtis *(Cast)*   1036
Cookson, Peter *(Cast)*   629, 4600
Cookson, Peter *(Producer)*   840
Cool, Walter *(Composer)*   2661
Cool, Walter *(Director)*   2393, 2661
Cool, Walter *(Librettist)*   2661
Cool, Walter *(Lyricist)*   2661
Cooley, Dennis *(Cast)*   2164
Cooley, Eddie *(Composer)*   3428
Cooley, Eddie *(Lyricist)*   3428
Cooley, Lee *(Director)*   2551
Cooley, Lee *(Librettist)*   2551
Coolidge, Philip *(Cast)*   3989
Coolman, DeWitt *(Composer)*   1151
Coolman, DeWitt *(Lyricist)*   1151
Coolman, DeWitt *(Musical Director)*   60, 3332, 3755, 4603
Coolman, DeWitt C. *(Musical Director)*   1151, 4364
Coombs, Frank T. *(Cast)*   2962
Coombs, J. Parker *(Cast)*   236, 3093
Coombs, J.P. *(Cast)*   3504
Coombs, Kristi *(Cast)*   2754
Cooms, Robert *(Composer)*   1897
Cooms, Robert *(Lyricist)*   1897
Cooney, Kevin *(Cast)*   373
Cooney, Warren *(Lyricist)*   467
Coons, Cheri *(Lyricist)*   3461
Cooper, Adrienne *(Cast)*   4082
Cooper, Alice *(Composer)*   3739
Cooper, Alice *(Lyricist)*   3739
Cooper, Ashley *(Cast)*   3993
Cooper, Bob *(Cast)*   420
Cooper, Chester R. *(Director)*   1604, 4303
Cooper, Chet *(Director)*   4543
Cooper, Chet *(Producer)*   4093
Cooper, Christopher *(Cast)*   282
Cooper, Chuck *(Cast)*   105, 240
Cooper, Clarence *(Cast)*   4409
Cooper, Dick *(Cast)*   2092, 2094, 2095
Cooper, Dulcie *(Cast)*   2175
Cooper, Edward *(Composer)*   700
Cooper, Frank Kemble *(Cast)*   3328
Cooper, Fred *(Lyricist)*   1342
Cooper, George *(Composer)*   1897
Cooper, George *(Lyricist)*   1897
Cooper, George A. *(Cast)*   4469
Cooper, Harry *(Cast)*   1738, 3081, 3525
Cooper, Harry *(Composer)*   1738
Cooper, Hy *(Librettist)*   1539
Cooper, Irving *(Producer)*   290, 488
Cooper, James E. *(Librettist)*   2912
Cooper, Jane *(Cast)*   1493
Cooper, Joe *(Composer)*   505, 1400, 1738, 2696, 4589, 4655

Cooper, Judith *(Costumes)*   2001
Cooper, Lillian Kemble *(Cast)*   1921
Cooper, Lou *(Cast)*   2373
Cooper, Lou *(Composer)*   2447, 3226
Cooper, Lou *(Musical Director)*   2447, 3226
Cooper, Mabel *(Cast)*   116
Cooper, Marilyn *(Cast)*   287, 1427, 1709, 1729, 2048, 2651, 3088, 3456, 4481, 4625, 4727
Cooper, Maurice *(Cast)*   4254
Cooper, Max *(Producer)*   826
Cooper, Melville *(Cast)*   649, 1284, 1711, 2252, 2464, 2547, 2705, 3291
Cooper, Melville *(Director)*   1817
Cooper, Neil *(Costumes)*   1508
Cooper, Opal *(Cast)*   984
Cooper, Pamela *(Lighting Designer)*   2427
Cooper, Patricia *(Author)*   3631
Cooper, Peggy *(Cast)*   2368
Cooper, Randi *(Cast)*   2676
Cooper, Robert M. *(Director)*   576
Cooper, Robert M. *(Producer)*   576
Cooper, Roy *(Cast)*   634
Cooper, Sara Lou *(Cast)*   1697
Cooper, Susan *(Author)*   1372
Cooper, Susan *(Lyricist)*   1372
Cooper, Theodore *(Lighting Designer)*   4314
Cooper, Theodore *(Set Design)*   4314
Cooper, Tod *(Musical Director)*   2195
Cooper, Violet Kemble *(Cast)*   3974
Cooper & Rector *(Producer)*   4282
Cooper-Cliffe, H. *(Cast)*   3219
Cooper-Hecht, Gail *(Costumes)*   2420, 3811, 4342
Cooper-Hecht, Gail *(Lighting Designer)*   2012
Cooperman, Alvin *(Librettist)*   786
Cooperman, Alvin *(Lyricist)*   786
Coopersmith, Jerome *(Librettist)*   170, 278, 1168, 2777, 3498
Coote, Henry *(Cast)*   371
Coote, Robert *(Cast)*   58, 3038
Coots, J. Fred *(Composer)*   200, 201, 208, 274, 320, 551, 667, 885, 886, 887, 1033, 1300, 1460, 1461, 1693, 1829, 1939, 2135, 2263, 2273, 2669, 2789, 2843, 3020, 3148, 3175, 3721, 3821, 3833, 4000, 4087, 4104, 4249, 4264, 4424, 4668, 4858
Coots, J. Fred *(Lyricist)*   883, 884, 897
Copani, Peter *(Composer)*   1282, 4168
Copani, Peter *(Director)*   4168
Copani, Peter *(Librettist)*   1282, 4168
Copani, Peter *(Lyricist)*   1282, 4168
Cope, Foster *(Orchestrations)*   2083, 2089, 2090, 2092, 2093, 2094
Copeland, A.A. *(Cast)*   1995
Copeland, Arnold *(Composer)*   4047
Copeland, Arnold *(Lyricist)*   4047
Copeland, Carolyn Rossi *(Director)*   1509
Copeland, Carolyn Rossi *(Producer)*   2224
Copeland, Joan *(Cast)*   4060, 4481
Copeland, Les *(Composer)*   1531, 4697, 4811, 4813
Copeland, Les *(Lyricist)*   4697
Copeland, Nick *(Cast)*   4291
Copeland, Nick *(Librettist)*   4291

Copkey, Marilyn (*Cast*) 4537
Copland, Aaron (*Composer*) 3441
Copley, Johnathan (*Librettist*) 2426
Coppe, Carlo (*Choreographer*) 45
Coppel, Alec (*Author*) 3234
Coppicus, F.C. (*Producer*) 2567, 3441
Coppin, Grace (*Cast*) 1286
Copping, C.S. (*Orchestrations*) 584
Coppola, Anton (*Musical Director*) 507, 519, 2556,
    3107, 3798, 3972, 4827
Coppola, Anton (*Vocal Arranger*) 519
Coppola, Frank (*Cast*) 4595
Copsey, Bob (*Cast*) 4829
Copsey, Bob (*Choreographer*) 4829
Coral, Tito (*Cast*) 1979
Corato, Lou (*Cast*) 3697
Corbet, Frank (*Cast*) 994
Corbett, Edward (*Librettist*) 4704, 4705
Corbett, Edward (*Lyricist*) 4704
Corbett, James J. (*Cast*) 1065, 4637
Corbett, Leonora (*Cast*) 3390
Corbett, Michael (*Cast*) 2783
Corbett, Ronnie (*Cast*) 4469
Corbin, Ramilles (*Cast*) 730
Corbin, Roso (*Costumes*) 1341
Corby, Mabelina (*Composer*) 575
Corday, Leo (*Composer*) 4264
Corday, Leo (*Lyricist*) 4264
Corden, Henry (*Voice*) 57
Corden, Julia (*Cast*) 3732
Corder, Leeta (*Cast*) 1513
Cordero, Arthur (*Cast*) 4616
Cordettes, The (*Cast*) 197
Cordner, Blaine (*Cast*) 1839
Cordova, Victoria (*Cast*) 189, 4572
Corey, Herb (*Lyricist*) 1697
Corey, Irwin (*Cast*) 1300, 1748, 1811, 3140
Corey, Madison (*Producer*) 102, 1663
Corey, Wendell (*Cast*) 2175, 2187
Corin (*Lyricist*) 1520
Corin, Joel P. (*Composer*) 1318, 4012
Cork, J. Frank (*Musical Director*) 2601, 2789, 3860
Corkill, Cathy (*Cast*) 832
Corlett, Irene (*Cast*) 601
Corley, Al (*Cast*) 4294
Corley, Nick (*Cast*) 754, 2230
Corley, Pat (*Cast*) 477
Corliss, E.W. (*Composer*) 2906, 3951, 4353
Corliss, Edward W. (*Composer*) 306, 761, 3047, 3951
Corliss, William (*Cast*) 104
Cormack, Rennie (*Composer*) 543
Corman, Paul (*Cast*) 4172
Corman, Roger (*Author*) 2544
Corn, Belmont (*Set Design*) 1957
Corneal, Joran (*Cast*) 838
Corneille, Rosaline (*Cast*) 1333
Cornell, Katharine (*Cast*) 1007, 1294
Cornell, Katharine (*Producer*) 1294
Cornett, Ewel (*Composer*) 1781
Cornett, Ewel (*Director*) 1781
Cornfield, Mark (*Composer*) 4774

Cornwall, Ardon (*Orchestrations*) 4256
Cornwell, Arden (*Orchestrations*) 4586
Cornwell, Eric (*Lighting Designer*) 430, 3249
Cornwell, Jack H. (*Set Design*) 2322, 3217, 4623
Cornwell, Lawrence (*Cast*) 4622
Corona, Sandra (*Composer*) 3103
Correia, Don (*Cast*) 1298, 3444, 3499, 3992, 4412
Corrigan, Nancy (*Cast*) 1916
Corrigan, William (*Director*) 2550
Corrin, George (*Lighting Designer*) 2339
Corrine (*Cast*) 734, 2481, 3746
Corrod, Vinny (*Cast*) 1742
Corry, James (*Costumes*) 2177
Corsaro, Frank (*Director*) 2173, 4447
Cort, Harry (*Producer*) 1173
Cort, Harry L. (*Librettist*) 735, 1587, 2214, 2270, 2491, 3915
Cort, Harry L. (*Lyricist*) 735, 2214, 2270, 2491
Cort, Harry L. (*Producer*) 82, 1378, 3533
Cort, Irene (*Cast*) 3528
Cort, John (*Producer*) 47, 118, 735, 1266, 1308, 1309,
    1580, 1587, 1707, 2214, 2270, 2491, 2774, 2931, 3590,
    3754, 3776, 3915, 4226
Cortelyou, Winthrop (*Composer*) 2330, 3692
Cortez, Billy (*Cast*) 290
Corthell, Herbert (*Cast*) 78, 110, 201, 276, 628, 910, 929,
    1270, 1433, 1519, 1524, 3396, 3729, 3866, 4178, 4464,
    4539, 4662
Corti, Jean (*Composer*) 2188
Corti, Jim (*Cast*) 158, 599
Corti, Jim (*Choreographer*) 4690
Cortner, Jack (*Orchestrations*) 3564
Corto, Diana (*Cast*) 1848
Corwell, T.L. (*Cast*) 3062
Corwell, T.L. (*Composer*) 2792
Corwell, Taylor L. (*Composer*) 2013, 3040
Corwell, Trevor (*Composer*) 4751
Corwin, Norman (*Librettist*) 2653
Corwin, Norman (*Lyricist*) 3226
Cory, Kenneth (*Cast*) 314
Cosette, Pierre (*Producer*) 4695
Cosler, Charles (*Set Design*) 908
Coslow, Sam (*Composer*) 794, 1381, 1638, 2593, 3756, 4817
Coslow, Sam (*Lyricist*) 200, 487, 794, 1343, 1381, 2593,
    2987, 3406, 3756, 4240, 4799, 4817
Cossart, Ernest (*Cast*) 971, 1569, 1680
Costa, Bill (*Musical Director*) 1697
Costa, Bill (*Orchestrations*) 1697
Costa-Greenspon, Muriel (*Cast*) 2017
Costello, Bartley (*Lyricist*) 694, 1907, 2662
Costello, Bartley C. (*Lyricist*) 310
Costello, Diosa (*Cast*) 4420
Costello, Dolores (*Cast*) 1485, 1487
Costello, Helene (*Cast*) 1487
Costello, John (*Cast*) 283
Costello, Julian (*Cast*) 2013, 3241
Costello, Lou (*Cast*) 4174
Costello, Lou (*Librettist*) 1038
Costello, Shirley (*Choreographer*) 2482
Costello, Ward (*Cast*) 2411
Coster, Nicholas (*Cast*) 3217
Coster, Nicolas (*Cast*) 2185

Costigan, James *(Cast)* 322
Costigan, James *(Librettist)* 322
Costigan, James *(Lyricist)* 322
Costigan, Ken *(Director)* 3939
Costigan, Ken *(Producer)* 3939
Costing, Stephen *(Cast)* 451, 3864
Cota, Keith *(Cast)* 1761
Cothran, Robert *(Set Design)* 1970
Cotsirilos, Stephanie *(Cast)* 169, 1684
Cotten, Joseph *(Cast)* 979, 2257
Cottle, Mitzi *(Composer)* 2483
Cottle, Mitzi *(Lyricist)* 2483
Cotton, Robert F. *(Cast)* 2117
Cotton Club, The *(Producer)* 875
Cottrell, Bessie *(Cast)* 3446
Coudray, Peggy *(Cast)* 2108, 3986
Coudy, Doug *(Director)* 854, 855, 857, 859, 860, 864, 865
Coudy, Douglas *(Choreographer)* 1734, 1948
Coudy, Douglas *(Director)* 851, 853, 856, 858, 861, 862
Coughlin, Bruce *(Musical Director)* 2152
Coughlin, Bruce *(Orchestrations)* 158, 992, 2152, 2651
Coullet, Rhonda *(Cast)* 2992, 3733
Coulon, F. *(Lyricist)* 3148
Coulouris, George *(Cast)* 490, 2257
Coulter, Ned *(Cast)* 3908
Counsel, John *(Director)* 1644
Counsell, Elizabeth *(Cast)* 2196
Coupe-Frankel, Diane *(Choreographer)* 2388
Cournoyer, Jerry *(Arrangements)* 2611
Courtenay, William *(Cast)* 2698
Courtland, Jerome *(Cast)* 1300, 4180
Courtleigh, William *(Cast)* 2765
Courtneidge, Charles *(Cast)* 1333
Courtneidge, Cicely *(Cast)* 1467, 2004, 2467, 4510
Courtneidge, Robert *(Director)* 4404
Courtneidge, Robert *(Librettist)* 246, 954, 4404
Courtney, Alex *(Cast)* 247
Courtney, C.C. *(Cast)* 1139, 3824
Courtney, C.C. *(Composer)* 1139, 3824
Courtney, C.C. *(Director)* 1139
Courtney, C.C. *(Librettist)* 1139, 3824
Courtney, C.C. *(Lyricist)* 1139, 3824
Courtney, Florence *(Cast)* 1176
Courtney, Inez *(Cast)* 111, 1628, 1932, 3532, 4050, 4118, 4240, 4692
Courtney, Margaret *(Author)* 2201
Courtney, Ragan *(Cast)* 1139
Courtney, Ragan *(Composer)* 1139
Courtney, Ragan *(Librettist)* 1139
Courtney, Ragan *(Lyricist)* 1139
Courtney Sisters *(Cast)* 1124
Courts, Randy *(Composer)* 1509, 2185, 2229, 2241
Courts, Randy *(Lyricist)* 1509, 2185, 2229, 2241
Cousins, Derek *(Set Design)* 634
Covan and Florence *(Cast)* 1057
Coventry, Gerald *(Director)* 737, 3176, 3228
Coventry, Gerard *(Director)* 3488, 3805
Cover, A.D. *(Cast)* 674
Cover, Frankie *(Cast)* 1383
Coverdale, Minerva *(Cast)* 1835
Coverly, Robert *(Composer)* 311

Covert, Earl *(Cast)* 3415
Covington, Robert *(Cast)* 1632
Cowan, Edie *(Choreographer)* 2544
Cowan, Irv *(Producer)* 3428
Cowan, Jerome *(Cast)* 207, 3801, 3845
Cowan, Lynn *(Librettist)* 4562
Cowan, Marge *(Producer)* 3428
Cowan, Rubey *(Lyricist)* 1922
Cowan, Ruby *(Composer)* 2457, 4648
Cowan, Ruby *(Lyricist)* 2457, 4648
Cowan, Stanley *(Composer)* 2085, 2086, 2087
Cowan, Stanley *(Lyricist)* 2085, 2086, 2087
Coward, Noel *(Author)* 1238, 1787, 1891, 3678, 3906, 4610
Coward, Noel *(Cast)* 134, 1238, 2570, 3597, 3678, 3906, 4341, 4610
Coward, Noel *(Composer)* 133, 146, 429, 702, 841, 1238, 1564, 2570, 3018, 3020, 3196, 3235, 3339, 3597, 3678, 3815, 3885, 3906, 4335, 4341, 4610, 4661, 4823
Coward, Noel *(Director)* 429, 841, 1238, 1891, 3339, 3597, 3678, 3815, 3885, 3906, 4610
Coward, Noel *(Librettist)* 429, 841, 2570, 3005, 3339, 3815, 3885, 4335, 4341
Coward, Noel *(Lyricist)* 133, 146, 429, 702, 841, 1238, 1564, 2570, 3018, 3020, 3196, 3235, 3339, 3597, 3678, 3815, 3885, 3906, 4335, 4341, 4610, 4661, 4823
Coward, Noel *(Producer)* 3597
Cowart, Sheri *(Cast)* 695
Cowen, Ron *(Librettist)* 4540
Cowen, Ron *(Lyricist)* 4540
Cowl, Jane *(Author)* 4372
Cowl, Jane *(Cast)* 1434
Cowles, Albert *(Librettist)* 2380
Cowles, Chandler *(Cast)* 620, 4018
Cowles, Eugene *(Cast)* 252, 511, 2345, 2765, 3570, 3773, 3881, 3994, 4598
Cox, Baby *(Cast)* 1980
Cox, Catherine *(Cast)* 253, 2171, 3015, 3299, 3661, 3909, 4055
Cox, Christopher *(Composer)* 459
Cox, Christopher *(Lyricist)* 459
Cox, Eddie *(Cast)* 2494
Cox, Eddie *(Composer)* 3399
Cox, Eddie *(Lyricist)* 3399
Cox, Eugene *(Set Design)* 4092
Cox, Gertrude "Baby" *(Cast)* 2034
Cox, Hazel *(Cast)* 2893
Cox, Ida *(Composer)* 146, 478
Cox, Ida *(Lyricist)* 146, 478
Cox, Jimmy *(Composer)* 478
Cox, Jimmy *(Lyricist)* 478
Cox, Palmer *(Costumes)* 571
Cox, Palmer *(Librettist)* 571
Cox, Richard *(Cast)* 54, 3515
Cox, Ronny *(Cast)* 1955
Cox, Tony *(Arrangements)* 949
Cox, Veanne *(Cast)* 3076, 3960, 4020
Cox, Wally *(Cast)* 961, 1815
Cox, Wally *(Librettist)* 961
Cox, William *(Dance Arranger)* 135, 3015
Cox, William *(Musical Director)* 135, 1427
Cox, William *(Vocal Arranger)* 3015

Coxon, Eric *(Cast)* 475

Coyero, Monica *(Cast)* 2115

Coyle, Bruce W. *(Musical Director)* 3600, 4279

Coyle, Bruce W. *(Vocal Arranger)* 4279

Coyne, Joe *(Cast)* 2123

Coyne, Joseph *(Cast)* 1627, 3052, 3092, 3154, 3753, 4044, 4130

Coyne, Phoebe *(Cast)* 4725

Crabbe, Buster *(Cast)* 3100

Crabtree, Don *(Cast)* 374, 1029, 1237, 1359, 3294

Crabtree, Howard *(Cast)* 2022

Crabtree, Howard *(Costumes)* 2022

Crabtree, Paul *(Director)* 4314

Cracraft, Tom Adrian *(Set Design)* 1871, 3907

Craddock & Shandney *(Cast)* 500

Crage *(Costumes)* 4804

Craig, Bradford *(Choreographer)* 1993

Craig, Casey *(Cast)* 4022

Craig, David *(Librettist)* 868

Craig, David *(Lyricist)* 868, 943, 2168, 3473, 4153

Craig, David *(Vocal Arranger)* 1734

Craig, Dick *(Cast)* 2023, 2024

Craig, Helen *(Cast)* 3104

Craig, Joel *(Cast)* 4279

Craig, Richard *(Cast)* 2098, 2099

Craig, Virginia *(Cast)* 2583

Craig, Walter *(Lyricist)* 637

Craig, William *(Lyricist)* 3382

Craig Jr., Richy *(Cast)* 1874

Craig Jr., Richy *(Librettist)* 1874

Craik, Paul *(Cast)* 4486

Crain, Stephen *(Cast)* 3517

Cramer, Augustus *(Cast)* 2938

Crandall, Charles D. *(Lyricist)* 114

Crandall, Courtney *(Composer)* 1862

Crandall, Victoria *(Producer)* 2219

Crandell, Elizabeth *(Cast)* 3011

Crane, A. Wilbur *(Costumes)* 591, 2722

Crane, Bettymae *(Cast)* 1840

Crane, Beverly *(Cast)* 1840

Crane, David *(Librettist)* 4, 198, 2197, 3448

Crane, David *(Lyricist)* 4, 198, 2197, 3448, 4533

Crane, Harold *(Cast)* 3575, 4206

Crane, Irving *(Lyricist)* 3986

Crane, Larry *(Composer)* 4611

Crane, Larry *(Lyricist)* 4611

Crane, Les *(Cast)* 4291

Crane, Lor *(Composer)* 4659

Crane, Thurston *(Cast)* 3674

Crane, Virginia *(Cast)* 3255

Cranko, John *(Director)* 920

Cranko, John *(Lyricist)* 920

Cranston, Deborah *(Cast)* 455

Cranston, Toller *(Cast)* 4402

Cranton, Hal *(Author)* 596

Crashaw, Richard *(Lyricist)* 2633

Crater, Allene *(Cast)* 45, 2184, 2502, 2906, 3675, 4597

Crave, Warren *(Lighting Designer)* 991

Craven, Alfred *(Set Design)* 4418

Craven, Alfred E. *(Set Design)* 4327

Craven, Frank *(Author)* 4529

Craven, Frank *(Cast)* 1536, 1598

Craven, Frank *(Director)* 4476, 4529

Craven, Frank *(Librettist)* 1536, 4529

Craven, Frank *(Lyricist)* 1360, 1536, 1588, 3146, 3372

Craven, Hawes *(Set Design)* 3098, 3625, 4354

Craven, Richard *(Librettist)* 427

Craven, Richard *(Lyricist)* 1370

Craven, Sally *(Cast)* 4557

Craven, Sydney *(Cast)* 1606

Craver, Mark *(Composer)* 3261

Craver, Mark *(Lyricist)* 3261

Craver, Mike *(Arrangements)* 4030

Craver, Mike *(Cast)* 3261, 3641

Craver, Mike *(Composer)* 3261, 3641, 4030

Craver, Mike *(Librettist)* 3261, 3641

Craver, Mike *(Lyricist)* 3261, 3641, 4030

Craver, Mike *(Musical Director)* 4030

Crawford, Ann *(Musical Director)* 1903

Crawford, Boyd *(Cast)* 4256

Crawford, Cheryl *(Librettist)* 1300

Crawford, Cheryl *(Producer)* 530, 681, 807, 1383, 1571, 1928, 2007, 2201, 2615, 3301, 3347, 3691, 3696

Crawford, Clifton *(Cast)* 30, 1240, 1374, 1852, 2056, 2213, 2964, 3031, 3048, 3424, 3618, 3867, 4364, 4747

Crawford, Clifton *(Composer)* 627, 639, 1240, 1573, 1852, 2465, 2906, 2964, 3031, 3047, 3048, 3400, 3424, 3618, 4691

Crawford, Clifton *(Librettist)* 2056, 3867

Crawford, Clifton *(Lyricist)* 627, 639, 1240, 1573, 1852, 2056, 2465, 2964, 3031, 3047, 3048, 3400, 3424, 3618, 3867, 4691

Crawford, Clifton *(Producer)* 2056

Crawford, Douglas *(Producer)* 2563

Crawford, Ellen *(Cast)* 1059

Crawford, Gary *(Librettist)* 1159

Crawford, Jayne *(Cast)* 1938

Crawford, Kathryn *(Cast)* 2222, 3131

Crawford, Lew *(Choreographer)* 439, 2720

Crawford, Marion *(Author)* 4671, 4672

Crawford, Michael *(Additional Music)* 1159

Crawford, Michael *(Cast)* 1159, 3464

Crawford, Mimi *(Cast)* 3634

Crawford, Neil *(Producer)* 1644

Crawford, Robert *(Composer)* 4706

Crawford, Robert *(Lyricist)* 4706

Crawford, Stanley *(Lyricist)* 4753

Crawley, Sayre *(Cast)* 55

Cray, Richard *(Cast)* 747

Crayon *(Set Design)* 1898

Craze, Peter *(Cast)* 4685

Creamer, Henry *(Cast)* 4182

Creamer, Henry *(Composer)* 432, 1965, 2009, 4037

Creamer, Henry *(Director)* 1019

Creamer, Henry *(Librettist)* 4182

Creamer, Henry *(Lyricist)* 2, 432, 513, 563, 724, 1019, 1128, 1132, 1334, 1460, 1468, 1965, 2009, 2135, 2302, 2757, 2796, 3020, 3297, 3337, 3840, 3985, 4054, 4104, 4182, 4360, 4811, 4815, 4816

Creamer, Henry S. *(Lyricist)* 511, 1087

Crean, Richard *(Musical Director)* 1202

Creatore, Luigi *(Composer)* 825, 2230, 2681, 4022

Creatore, Luigi *(Librettist)* 825, 2230, 2681

Crumit, Frank (Cast)   380, 1686, 3144, 4283
Crumit, Frank (Composer)   3144, 4817
Crumit, Frank (Lyricist)   3144, 3622, 4283, 4766, 4817
Crump, Owen (Director)   3683
Crusar, Don (Composer)   1304
Crutchfield, Buddy (Cast)   2737
Cryer, David (Cast)   181, 823, 2674, 2775, 3209, 3542, 4173, 4659
Cryer, David (Producer)   3209
Cryer, Gretchen (Cast)   474, 2074, 2523, 3294, 4398
Cryer, Gretchen (Composer)   1737, 2074
Cryer, Gretchen (Director)   1169
Cryer, Gretchen (Librettist)   1169, 2074, 2418, 3209, 3927
Cryer, Gretchen (Lyricist)   496, 1169, 1737, 2074, 2418, 3209, 3927, 4615
Crystal, Raphael (Composer)   2354
Crystal, Raphael (Musical Director)   2354
Crystal, Raphael (Orchestrations)   2354
Crystall, Jeanne (Cast)   2090
Csaszar, Lou Ann (Cast)   2737
Cuadro Productions (Producer)   3286
Cuccioli, Robert (Cast)   131, 2198
Cuervo, Alma (Cast)   682, 2152, 3631
Cukor, George (Cast)   1026
Culbertson, Sandy (Cast)   2097
Culkin, Joan (Costumes)   1371
Cullen, Countee (Librettist)   4123
Cullen, David (Orchestrations)   211, 678, 730, 3464, 3944, 4068, 4138, 4217
Cullen, Michael (Cast)   2704
Cullinan, Ralph (Librettist)   648
Cullman, Joan (Producer)   652, 1149, 3299, 3718
Cullum, John (Cast)   134, 623, 1369, 2199, 3274, 3279, 3928, 4609
Cullum, John (Director)   3671
Culver, Dick (Cast)   1754
Cumberland, John (Cast)   3481, 4526
Cumby, Billy (Cast)   2942, 3528
Cumming, Don (Cast)   4291
Cumming, Howard T. (Cast)   2287
Cumming, Richard (Musical Director)   35, 3938
Cummings, Agnes (Cast)   1155
Cummings, Constance (Cast)   4443
Cummings, Gretel (Cast)   1958
Cummings, Joanne (Producer)   4272
Cummings, Kay (Cast)   4480
Cummings, Robert (Cast)   1137, 4824
Cummings, Roy (Cast)   3406
Cummings, Vicki (Cast)   966, 1856, 3138, 3314, 4214
Cunningham, Arthur (Cast)   734, 2358
Cunningham, Beau (Cast)   283
Cunningham, Bill (Dance Arranger)   3636
Cunningham, Bill (Musical Director)   1002
Cunningham, Bill (Vocal Arranger)   4449
Cunningham, Billy (Dance Arranger)   2451
Cunningham, Billy (Musical Director)   2451
Cunningham, Billy (Vocal Arranger)   2451
Cunningham, Cecil (Cast)   1267, 3775
Cunningham, Charles (Cast)   3349
Cunningham, Davis (Cast)   4142
Cunningham, George (Choreographer)   1836, 1944

Cunningham, George (Director)   3349
Cunningham, Jo Ann (Cast)   3249
Cunningham, John (Cast)   147, 491, 832, 945, 1797, 2599, 3195, 3491, 4862
Cunningham, Joy (Cast)   914
Cunningham, Joy (Librettist)   914
Cunningham, Margo (Cast)   2682
Cunningham, Paul (Lyricist)   1687, 4808
Cunningham, Robert (Cast)   2937
Cunningham, Scott (Cast)   3937
Cunnningham, Arthur (Cast)   340
Cuomo, Irving (Set Design)   4684
Cuomo, Jimmy (Set Design)   2968
Cupero, Edward V. (Composer)   3545
Cupero, Edward V. (Musical Director)   3545
Curcio, Armando (Author)   1354
Curiale, James (Composer)   4171
Curiale, James (Lyricist)   4171
Curiel, Gonzalo (Composer)   1840
Curlee, Karen (Cast)   4264
Curley, George (Cast)   1245
Curley, George (Lighting Designer)   2935, 3186
Curley, Wilma (Cast)   4625
Curley Company, The (Producer)   941
Curnock, Richard (Cast)   3756
Curran, Frank (Cast)   3312
Curran, Gerard (Cast)   114
Curran, Homer (Author)   4075
Curran, Homer (Librettist)   2679
Curran, Homer (Producer)   2679
Curran, Keith (Cast)   2283, 2305, 2790, 2968
Curran, Michael (Cast)   139
Currie (Producer)   1118, 2383
Currie, Donal (Producer)   4243
Currie, Richard (Lighting Designer)   2037, 2488
Currier, Terrence (Cast)   2199
Curry, J. Dan (Cast)   3318
Curry, John (Cast)   3598
Curry, Richard (Cast)   4829
Curry, Steve (Cast)   1717
Curry, Tim (Cast)   3039, 3742
Curry, Virgil (Cast)   128, 157, 1436, 4243
Curti (Composer)   3981
Curtin, Jane (Cast)   3565
Curtin, Jane (Librettist)   3565
Curtis, Ann (Costumes)   2798
Curtis, Billy (Lyricist)   1241, 4813
Curtis, Donna (Cast)   2375
Curtis, Francis I. (Producer)   3914
Curtis, June (Producer)   2754
Curtis, Keene (Cast)   273, 807, 3780, 4558
Curtis, Mann (Lyricist)   2227
Curtis, Norman (Composer)   4584
Curtis, Norman (Dance Arranger)   4584
Curtis, Norman (Vocal Arranger)   4584
Curtis, Patricia Taylor (Choreographer)   4584
Curtis, Patricia Taylor (Director)   4584
Curtis, Patricia Taylor (Librettist)   4584
Curtis, Patricia Taylor (Lyricist)   4584
Curtis-Hall, Vondie (Cast)   1103, 2852, 4697
Curty, Gene (Composer)   2472

Curty, Gene *(Librettist)* 2472
Curty, Gene *(Lyricist)* 2472
Curzon, Frank *(Librettist)* 276
Curzon, Frank *(Producer)* 4663
Curzon, George *(Cast)* 635, 2486
Cushing, Bartley *(Director)* 2155
Cushing, C.C.S. *(Librettist)* 3839
Cushing, C.C.S. *(Lyricist)* 3839
Cushing, Catherine Chisholm *(Author)* 2206, 2412
Cushing, Catherine Chisholm *(Librettist)* 385, 1580, 2412, 2756, 4429
Cushing, Catherine Chisholm *(Lyricist)* 102, 385, 1580, 2412
Cushing, J.D. *(Composer)* 4047
Cushing, Tom *(Librettist)* 3325
Cushman, Dan *(Author)* 4682
Cushman, Dan *(Librettist)* 4682
Cushman, Nancy *(Cast)* 1010
Cusseaux, Zulema *(Dance Arranger)* 2195
Cutell, Lou *(Cast)* 4785
Cutler, Ben *(Cast)* 1286
Cutler, Robert F. *(Producer)* 3292
Cutter, Murray *(Orchestrations)* 2258
Cutting, Ernest *(Musical Director)* 1529, 3042, 3849
Cutts, Patricia *(Cast)* 2295
Cuvillier, Charles *(Author)* 2486
Cuvillier, Charles *(Composer)* 25, 1309, 2486
Cypher, Jon *(Cast)* 759, 798, 2727, 3564, 3612, 3931
Cypkin, Diane *(Cast)* 400, 2866
Cyrus, Jim *(Cast)* 164, 3557
Czajka, Mariusz *(Cast)* 2846
Czaroulch *(Composer)* 710
Czaroulch *(Lyricist)* 710
Czernicki, Gene *(Set Design)* 4696
Czettel, Ladislas *(Costumes)* 1817, 2948, 3767
Czinner, Paul *(Producer)* 3335

D

Dabdoub, Jack *(Cast)* 177, 753, 1092, 2012, 2565, 2573
Dabney, Ford *(Composer)* 2111, 3193, 3660, 4253, 4804
Dabney, Ford *(Lyricist)* 2415
Dabney, Ford T. *(Composer)* 1909
Dabney, Sheila *(Cast)* 54
Daboll, W.S. *(Cast)* 1193
Da Costa, Morton *(Director)* 2681, 3016, 3020, 3188, 3509, 3837, 3956, 4395
Da Costa, Morton *(Librettist)* 3720, 3837
Da Costa, Morton *(Lyricist)* 3720
Dacre, Harry *(Composer)* 662, 3989, 4109, 4390
Dacre, Harry *(Lyricist)* 662, 3989, 4109, 4390
Daffodil Productions *(Producer)* 4102
Dagand, Henry *(Lyricist)* 1836
Daggett, Robert *(Producer)* 2560
Dagmar *(Cast)* 98
Dagnall, E. *(Cast)* 3092
Dahdah, Robert *(Composer)* 941, 4527
Dahdah, Robert *(Director)* 941, 4527
Dahdah, Robert *(Librettist)* 941, 4527

Dahdah, Robert *(Lyricist)* 941, 4527
Dahl, Gail *(Lighting Designer)* 319
Dahl, Magda *(Cast)* 4590
Dahlia, Helen *(Cast)* 1923
Dailey, Dan *(Cast)* 4142
Dailey, Peter *(Cast)* 2123, 4478
Dailey, Peter F. *(Cast)* 677, 688, 1925, 2041, 2493, 2835, 3560, 4658, 4681
Dailey, Robert *(Cast)* 1531
Daily, Pat *(Producer)* 1589
Dalby, Al *(Orchestrations)* 4853
Dalby, Alfred *(Musical Director)* 2040
Dalby, Alfred *(Orchestrations)* 2040, 3006, 3007, 3973
Dalby, Alfred *(Vocal Arranger)* 2446
D'Alby, Pierre *(Costumes)* 1075
Dale, Billy *(Cast)* 2749
Dale, Charles
    See also Smith & Dale.
Dale, Charles *(Cast)* 17, 532, 1132, 3264, 3968, 4204, 4654, 4686
Dale, Chester *(Choreographer)* 138
Dale, Cynthia *(Cast)* 3066
Dale, Fern *(Cast)* 1337
Dale, Glen *(Cast)* 1027
Dale, Grover *(Cast)* 98, 1233, 1698, 1721, 2484, 3815, 4019, 4625
Dale, Grover *(Choreographer)* 406, 2320, 2687, 2702, 2925, 3280, 3869
Dale, Grover *(Director)* 2320, 2687
Dale, Harry *(Cast)* 3093, 4113
Dale, Jack *(Composer)* 1337
Dale, Jack *(Lyricist)* 1337
Dale, James E. *(Orchestrations)* 1120
Dale, Janet *(Cast)* 2474
Dale, Jim *(Cast)* 305, 3598
Dale, Karen Lynn *(Cast)* 3544
Dale, Margaret *(Cast)* 2386, 3766, 4673
Dale, Mary *(Cast)* 2992
Dale, Maryon *(Cast)* 364
Dale, Sunny *(Cast)* 4426
Dale, Violet *(Cast)* 2695
Daley, Cass *(Cast)* 4825
Daley, George *(Producer)* 2925
Daley, Jerome *(Cast)* 4692, 4694
Daley, John W. *(Musical Director)* 1887
Daley, Mary Pat *(Librettist)* 932
Dall, Evelyn *(Cast)* 3365
Dallas, Lorna *(Cast)* 2169
Dallas, Walter *(Director)* 2932
Dallavo, John *(Lyricist)* 1251
Dallin, Jacques *(Dance Arranger)* 924
Dallin, Jacques *(Orchestrations)* 924
Dallin, Jacques *(Vocal Arranger)* 924
Dalton, Doris *(Cast)* 3895
Dalton, Dorothy *(Cast)* 165
Daly, Ambrose *(Cast)* 2502
Daly, Arnold *(Cast)* 515, 1535
Daly, Arnold *(Costumes)* 1250
Daly, Arnold *(Director)* 515
Daly, Augustin
    See also Augustin Daly Musical Co.

Daly, Augustin (*Author*) 4603
Daly, Augustin (*Director*) 1470, 3803
Daly, Augustin (*Producer*) 770, 906, 1429, 1470, 3803
Daly, Bill (*Musical Director*) 4235
Daly, Dan (*Cast*) 357, 613, 2181, 2398, 2824, 2842, 3129, 3784
Daly, Joseph M. (*Composer*) 545
Daly, Lucy (*Cast*) 1646, 1798, 3205
Daly, Nellie (*Cast*) 2035
Daly, Orlando (*Cast*) 3079
Daly, Robert (*Cast*) 115
Daly, Thomas (*Cast*) 3154
Daly, William (*Composer*) 745, 1129, 1208, 1345, 2112, 2180, 2336, 3323, 3649, 3866, 4300
Daly, William (*Musical Director*) 168, 1129, 1345, 1487, 1488, 1489, 1490, 2444, 3243, 3923, 3953, 4178, 4372, 4392, 4424, 4760
Daly, William (*Orchestrations*) 3225, 3243, 3379, 4267
Daly, William Harrigan (*Orchestrations*) 787
Daly, William J. (*Musical Director*) 379
Daly Musical Co., Augustin
  See also Augustin Daly.
Daly Musical Co., Augustin (*Producer*) 3828
Dam, H.J. (*Librettist*) 3948
Dam, H.J.W. (*Librettist*) 3625
Damashek, Barbara (*Composer*) 3631, 4406
Damashek, Barbara (*Director*) 3631
Damashek, Barbara (*Librettist*) 3631
Damashek, Barbara (*Lyricist*) 3631, 4406
D'Amboise, Charlotte (*Cast*) 661, 2205, 4068
d'Amboise, Christopher (*Cast*) 4068
D'Amboise, Jacques (*Cast*) 1933, 3934
D'Amboise, Jacques (*Choreographer*) 3763
D'Ambricourt, Adrienne (*Cast*) 1391
Damerel, George (*Cast*) 1801
Damita, Lily (*Cast*) 1481, 4087
D'Amore, L'Alba (*Lyricist*) 1285
Damon, Cathryn (*Cast*) 823, 1237, 1310, 1373, 3863, 3956
Damon, Stuart (*Cast*) 842, 1060, 1408, 2150
Damone, Vic (*Cast*) 974, 4155
Damrosch, Walter (*Composer*) 1083
Dana, Barbara (*Cast*) 1190
Dana, Bill (*Librettist*) 1023, 3484
Dana, Bill (*Voice*) 57
Dana, Dick "Gabby" (*Cast*) 2850
Dana, F. Mitchell (*Lighting Designer*) 908, 2245, 2305, 2654
Dana, Frederick (*Composer*) 1627
Danby, Charles (*Cast*) 2398
Dance (*Composer*) 737
Dance (*Lyricist*) 737
Dance, George (*Director*) 2398
Dance, George (*Librettist*) 737, 1540, 2374, 2398
Dance, George (*Lyricist*) 737, 2374
Danceny, Robert (*Author*) 511
Dancer, Earl (*Director*) 26, 435, 2640, 2881
Dancer, Earl (*Librettist*) 2881
Dancer, Earl (*Lyricist*) 2881
Dancer, Earl (*Producer*) 26, 435, 2881
Dancey, Jennie (*Cast*) 4520
Dancey, John (*Choreographer*) 2720
Dancing Duchess Company (*Producer*) 968

d'Ancona, Miranda (*Producer*) 101
d'Ancourt, Grenet (*Author*) 3362
Dancrey, Anne (*Cast*) 3396
Dancy, John (*Choreographer*) 1499
Dancy, Virginia (*Set Design*) 2776
Dandora Associates (*Costumes*) 4106
Dandridge, Dorothy (*Cast*) 2259, 4256
Dandridge, Etta (*Cast*) 4256
Dandridge, Vivian (*Cast*) 4256
Dandridge Sisters, The (*Cast*) 887
Dandy, Jess (*Cast*) 2745, 3096
Dandy, Jess (*Lyricist*) 2745
Dandy, Reginald (*Cast*) 4719
Dane, Clemence (*Author*) 589
Dane, Clemence (*Director*) 818
Dane, Clemence (*Librettist*) 818
Dane, Clemence (*Lyricist*) 818
Dane, Rita (*Cast*) 3537
Danford, Andrea (*Cast*) 74
Danforth, Will (*Cast*) 1768, 2101
Danforth, William (*Cast*) 20, 104, 824, 1016, 1335, 1538, 1565, 2317, 2528, 2698, 2906, 2974, 4359, 4754
D'Angelo, Beverly (*Cast*) 3741
Dangerfield, Fred (*Set Design*) 175
Dangerfield, Frederick (*Set Design*) 45, 2733
Dangler, Anita (*Cast*) 790
Daniderff, Leo (*Composer*) 3617, 4819
Daniele, Graciela (*Cast*) 723, 1329, 3603, 4633
Daniele, Graciela (*Choreographer*) 54, 112, 756, 975, 1633, 1822, 1914, 3070, 3285, 3718, 4019
Daniele, Graciela (*Director*) 756, 975, 1822, 3285, 4019
Daniele, Graciela (*Librettist*) 756, 975
Daniele, Graciela (*Lyricist*) 4744
Danielle, Marlene (*Cast*) 2544
Danielle, Martha (*Cast*) 3702
Danielli, Fred (*Choreographer*) 4652
Daniels (*Composer*) 4589
Daniels (*Lyricist*) 4589
Daniels, Bebe (*Cast*) 1939
Daniels, Billie (*Cast*) 4501
Daniels, Billy (*Cast*) 1601, 2817
Daniels, Danny (*Cast*) 372, 404, 2707, 4169
Daniels, Danny (*Choreographer*) 64, 154, 1369, 1891, 1892, 1990, 2064, 2617, 3940, 4286, 4588
Daniels, Danny (*Director*) 2617
Daniels, David (*Cast*) 298, 3491, 3509
Daniels, Frank (*Cast*) 104, 353, 2101, 2906, 3229, 3755, 3882, 4293, 4724
Daniels, Frank (*Producer*) 104
Daniels, Jeff (*Cast*) 1268
Daniels, M.W. (*Composer*) 306, 3951
Daniels, Marc (*Director*) 868, 3473
Daniels, Sharon (*Cast*) 451, 3864
Daniels, Stan (*Composer*) 392, 3890, 4038
Daniels, Stan (*Lyricist*) 392, 3890, 4038
Daniels, Walker (*Cast*) 1500
Daniels, William (*Cast*) 3274, 3897
Danilova, Alexandra (*Cast*) 1680, 3234, 4075
Danko, Harold (*Composer*) 2784
Danks, H.P. (*Composer*) 1897
Danks, H.P. (*Lyricist*) 1897

Dann, Larry *(Cast)* 456, 874
Dann, Roger *(Cast)* 3756
Dann, Sam *(Librettist)* 4468
Dannenberg, Louis *(Composer)* 4807
Danner, Blythe *(Cast)* 594, 2777, 3468, 4522
Danner, Braden *(Cast)* 2442, 4138
Danner, Dorothy *(Choreographer)* 4505
Danner, Dorothy *(Director)* 3864
Dano, Royal *(Cast)* 1278
Dansicker, Michael *(Composer)* 3277
Dansicker, Michael *(Dance Arranger)* 3277
Dansicker, Michael *(Musical Director)* 74
Dansicker, Michael *(Orchestrations)* 74
Dansicker, Michael *(Vocal Arranger)* 3277
D'Antalffy, Desdit *(Orchestrations)* 3639
Dante, Nicholas *(Librettist)* 746
Dante, Ron *(Composer)* 406
Dante, Ron *(Lyricist)* 406
Dante, Ron *(Producer)* 39
D'Antonakis, Fleury *(Cast)* 1060
Dantuono, Mike *(Cast)* 4244
Danyliw, Annastasia *(Cast)* 2521
Danziger, Harry Lee *(Musical Director)* 1618
Da Pron, Louis *(Choreographer)* 2496
D'Aquuila, Kenny *(Cast)* 556
Daray, Gabriel *(Composer)* 4817
Darcel, Denise *(Cast)* 3381
D'Arcy, Alexander *(Cast)* 4792
D'Arcy, Bette *(Cast)* 1470
Darcy, Jacques *(Costumes)* 3005
D'Arcy, Mary *(Cast)* 262, 3992, 4210
Darcy, Maurice *(Cast)* 2101, 2711
D'Arcy, Pattie *(Cast)* 1402
Darcy, Pattie *(Cast)* 338, 2427
D'Arcy, Richard *(Choreographer)* 3954
Darden, Severn *(Cast)* 4397
Dare, Ada *(Cast)* 357, 1576, 1599
Dare, Danny *(Cast)* 132, 1297
Dare, Danny *(Choreographer)* 1980, 2545, 4234, 4235, 4291, 4331, 4778
Dare, Danny *(Director)* 1395, 1949, 1950, 1951, 2809
Dare, Danny *(Librettist)* 2809
Dare, Dorothy *(Cast)* 111, 787, 1856, 4177
Dare, Phyllis *(Cast)* 2467, 4765
Dare, Violet *(Cast)* 1307
Dare, Zena *(Cast)* 650
Daresford Prod. Company *(Producer)* 1248
Darewski, Herman *(Composer)* 208, 377, 1153, 1430, 1763, 1963, 2571, 3663, 3710, 3779, 4017
Darewski, Hermann E. *(Composer)* 3259
Darewski, Max *(Composer)* 396, 1208, 1733, 1805
Darewski, Max *(Lyricist)* 1588
Darian, Anita *(Cast)* 1648, 3696, 3938
Darion, Joe *(Librettist)* 2811, 3934
Darion, Joe *(Lyricist)* 50, 2106, 2727, 2811, 3226, 3934, 4264
D'Arle, Yvonne *(Cast)* 905
Darling, Candy *(Cast)* 3671
Darling, Clifton *(Cast)* 247
Darling, Denver *(Composer)* 1296
Darling, Denver *(Lyricist)* 1296
Darling, Eddie *(Producer)* 1811

Darling, Frank *(Musical Director)* 2770, 4804, 4806, 4807, 4808, 4809, 4810, 4811, 4812, 4813
Darling, Frank N. *(Musical Director)* 4754
Darling, James *(Director)* 1544, 2770
Darling, Jean *(Cast)* 660, 2751
Darling, Robert E. *(Lighting Designer)* 157
Darling, Robert E. *(Set Design)* 157
Darmon, Leonie *(Cast)* 2029
D'Armond, Frank *(Composer)* 3822
D'Armond, Isabel *(Cast)* 1563
d'Arnell, Nydia *(Cast)* 1603
D'Arnell, Nydia *(Cast)* 1756
Darnell, Robert *(Cast)* 2043
Darnley, Herbert *(Composer)* 2986
Darnley, Herbert *(Librettist)* 2986
Darrah, James *(Cast)* 1146
Darrieux, Danielle *(Cast)* 101
Darrow, Harry *(Set Design)* 1785
Darrow, Harry Silverglat *(Lighting Designer)* 3688
Darrow, Harry Silverglat *(Set Design)* 3688
Darrow, Jason *(Lyricist)* 1427
Darrow, Richard *(Cast)* 2051
D'Arville, Camille *(Cast)* 355, 995, 2673
d'Arville, Camille *(Cast)* 3834
D'Arville, Camille *(Producer)* 2673
Darvis, Charlie *(Composer)* 478
Darvis, Charlie *(Lyricist)* 478
Darway, Chris *(Composer)* 4171
Darway, Chris *(Lyricist)* 4171
Dash, Irwin *(Composer)* 4197
Dash, Irwin *(Lyricist)* 4197
Dash, Julian *(Composer)* 3018
Da Silva, Howard *(Adaptation)* 3280
Da Silva, Howard *(Author)* 4863
Da Silva, Howard *(Cast)* 55, 919, 1091, 1280, 2027, 2357, 2653, 3263, 3897, 3947, 4495
Da Silva, Howard *(Director)* 31, 3280, 3831
Dassin, Jules *(Director)* 2106, 2679, 4499
Dassin, Jules *(Librettist)* 2106
D'Auban, Ernest *(Choreographer)* 2035, 2964, 2974
D'Auban, Ernest *(Director)* 1975
D'Auban, Ernest *(Set Design)* 4662
D'Auban, John *(Choreographer)* 205
Daugherty, Doc *(Composer)* 432
Dave and Tressie *(Cast)* 3512
Davenport *(Composer)* 2162
Davenport *(Lyricist)* 2162
Davenport, David *(Lyricist)* 3484
Davenport, Eva *(Cast)* 1078, 1392, 1783, 2548, 3363, 3790, 4735, 4754
Davenport, Harry *(Cast)* 357, 968, 1021, 1537, 1543, 2117, 2160, 2326, 2465, 3784, 3839
Davenport, Johnny *(Composer)* 3428
Davenport, Johnny *(Lyricist)* 3428
Davenport, Marie *(Cast)* 1078
Davenport, Millie *(Costumes)* 1235
Davenport, Pembroke *(Composer)* 70, 1091, 2458
Davenport, Pembroke *(Lyricist)* 2458
Davenport, Pembroke *(Musical Director)* 31, 177, 651, 1791, 2053, 2295, 2331, 2357, 2582, 2748, 3046, 3280, 3326, 3371, 3947, 4337, 4798

de Baum, Stephen *(Composer)* 4093
de Baum, Stephen *(Costumes)* 4679
de Baum, Stephen *(Librettist)* 4093, 4774
de Baum, Stephen *(Lyricist)* 4093, 4679, 4774
de Baum, Stephen *(Producer)* 4679
de Baum, Stephen *(Set Design)* 4679
de Bear, Archibald *(Producer)* 3634
DeBecker, Nesta *(Cast)* 310
de Benedictis, Richard *(Dance Arranger)* 269, 1060, 1227
de Benedictis, Richard *(Pianist)* 1648
De Bere, Elsie *(Cast)* 3673
de Boer, Ed *(Set Design)* 1865
De Bono, Jerry *(Lyricist)* 4388
de Botton, Yvette *(Cast)* 3463
de Broca, Philippe *(Author)* 2318
de Brugada, Philippe *(Cast)* 1695
de Caillaux, Pierre *(Composer)* 703
de Caillaux, Pierre *(Orchestrations)* 703
de Caillavet, A. *(Author)* 1066
DeCardi, Laura *(Cast)* 2768
De Carlo, Yvonne *(Cast)* 1329
de Cervantes, Miguel *(Author)* 2727, 3829
De Cocteau, Bert *(Orchestrations)* 4450
de Cordoba, Pedro *(Cast)* 1904, 3177, 3812
de Cordova, Fred *(Director)* 4826
deCordova, Fred *(Director)* 383
De Cormier, Robert *(Musical Director)* 1745, 4061
De Cormier, Robert *(Vocal Arranger)* 1745, 2618, 3294
DeCosta, Harry *(Composer)* 2308
DeCosta, Harry *(Lyricist)* 2308, 3297
De Costa, Leon *(Composer)* 458, 1270, 2107, 2351, 2613, 3344, 4776
De Costa, Leon *(Librettist)* 458, 2351
De Costa, Leon *(Lyricist)* 458, 1270, 2351, 2613, 3344, 4776
De Costa, Leon *(Producer)* 3344
De Costa, Viola *(Cast)* 2717
DeCottons *(Author)* 613
de Courville, Albert *(Director)* 3500
de Courville, Albert *(Librettist)* 2571, 3500, 3649, 3663
de Courville, Albert *(Lyricist)* 2571, 3663
de Courville, Albert *(Producer)* 2571, 3500, 3649, 3663
de Croisset, Francois *(Author)* 3312
DeCristo, Al *(Cast)* 3463, 3792, 4398
De Falla, Manuel *(Composer)* 1112
DeFaria, Walt *(Producer)* 499
DeFelice, Harold *(Producer)* 1038
de Feure, George *(Set Design)* 3827
de Filippo, Eduardo *(Author)* 1354
DeFlers, R. *(Author)* 2624
de Fleurs *(Author)* 1066
DeFore, Don *(Cast)* 3647
De Frece, Lauri *(Cast)* 4418
DeFrece, Lauri *(Cast)* 2509
de Freitas, Lois *(Cast)* 1883
de Freitas, Lois *(Librettist)* 1883
DeGaston, Gallie *(Cast)* 554
De Gaston, Zudora *(Cast)* 981
de Gerald, Guy *(Costumes)* 1333
De Gerald, Guy *(Costumes)* 133, 2004, 2467
De Gerald, Guy *(Set Design)* 133
DeGerde, Oliver *(Composer)* 377

DeGerde, Oliver *(Lyricist)* 377
de Gray, Sidney *(Cast)* 2938
De Gresac, Fred *(Author)* 3312
De Gresac, Fred *(Librettist)* 1183, 1308, 3312, 3613, 4250, 4616
De Gresac, Fred *(Lyricist)* 3613, 4250
De Grey, Sydney *(Cast)* 2986
De Grey, Sydney *(Cast)* 2986
de Groot, Myra *(Cast)* 3890
de Guzman, Jossie *(Cast)* 652, 1439, 2648, 3806
de Hartog, Jan *(Author)* 2050
De Haven, Carter *(Cast)* 60, 1147, 1212, 1553, 1738, 1911, 2885, 3396, 3626, 4681
De Haven, Carter *(Director)* 1553
De Haven, Carter *(Librettist)* 1942
De Haven, Carter *(Lyricist)* 1212, 2978
De Haven, Carter *(Producer)* 1946
De Haven, Charles *(Cast)* 4063
De Haven, Gloria *(Cast)* 1786, 2975, 3899, 4643
De Haven, Rose *(Cast)* 1147
De Haven, Rose *(Composer)* 1147
de Jari, M. *(Cast)* 1131
de Jari, M. *(Composer)* 1132
de Jari, M. *(Lyricist)* 1132
DeJesus, Luchi *(Orchestrations)* 2742
De Karlo, Sergio *(Cast)* 2458
De Karlo, Sergio *(Composer)* 4110
De Karlo, Sergio *(Lyricist)* 4110
DeKnight, Jimmy *(Composer)* 3739
DeKnight, Jimmy *(Lyricist)* 3739
de Knight, Rene *(Vocal Arranger)* 2817
De Koven, Reginald *(Composer)* 49, 336, 559, 934, 1260, 1375, 1570, 1602, 1768, 1849, 1896, 2209, 2345, 2506, 2697, 2725, 2733, 3363, 3621, 3673, 3732, 3736, 4187, 4500, 4616, 4758, 4767
De Koven, Roger *(Cast)* 1196, 2411, 4176
de la Fontaine, Gerald *(Cast)* 4256
De Lange, Eddie *(Lyricist)* 445, 850, 851, 1808, 3914, 4091, 4256, 4602
de Lange, Louis *(Librettist)* 833, 2515, 2963, 3550, 4236
de la Passardiere, Guy *(Producer)* 3551
de la Pena, George *(Cast)* 756, 3682
de Lappe, Gemze *(Choreographer)* 793
de Lappe, Gemze *(Cast)* 1635, 2268, 3473
DeLaurier, Julie *(Cast)* 4294
de Lavallade, Carmen *(Cast)* 1406, 1991
de Lavallade, Carmen *(Choreographer)* 1406
De Laurentis, Semina *(Cast)* 1426, 1785, 2243, 2579, 3211
De Leo, Don *(Cast)* 404
de Leon, Jack *(Producer)* 129
DeLeon, Michael *(Cast)* 4096
DeLeon, Noel *(Cast)* 4096
De Leon, Walter *(Composer)* 545
De Leon, Walter *(Librettist)* 1033, 1058, 1839, 3655
DeLiagre, Alfred *(Producer)* 1600
DeLiagre Jr., Alfred *(Producer)* 2355, 3457
de Lima, C.A. *(Director)* 2527
de Lima, C.A. *(Librettist)* 2407
De Lisle, Rouget *(Composer)* 4023
De Lisle, Rouget *(Lyricist)* 4023
De Lon, Jack *(Cast)* 108, 1237, 2201

DeVries, Peter *(Lyricist)* 3107
DeWalbe, F. *(Costumes)* 1230
DeWitt *(Composer)* 604
De Witt, Fay *(Cast)* 1300, 3178, 3381, 3940, 3942, 4566
DeWitt, Francis *(Librettist)* 3236
DeWitt, Francis *(Lyricist)* 545, 1144, 2261, 2564, 3236, 4813
De Witt, Josie *(Cast)* 215
De Witte, Daisy *(Cast)* 3842
DeWolf, Ward *(Cast)* 2385De Wolfe, Billy *(Cast)* 1389, 2227, 4828
De Wolfe, Elsie *(Set Design)* 3193, 4555
De Wolfe, Mme. *(Costumes)* 1900
DeYoung, Cliff *(Cast)* 4151, 4449
de Zulueta, Pedro *(Composer)* 2761
Deacon, Richard *(Cast)* 1040
Deagle, Tessie *(Cast)* 516
Deagon, Arthur *(Cast)* 1083, 1901, 2315, 2533, 3437, 3772, 4387, 4802, 4803, 4808
Deagrave, Charles *(Cast)* 284
Deaker, Thomas *(Cast)* 1995
Deal, Bordon *(Author)* 2248
Deal, Dennis *(Cast)* 4527
Deal, Dennis *(Choreographer)* 3178
Deal, Dennis *(Composer)* 3178
Deal, Dennis *(Director)* 3178
Deal, Dennis *(Librettist)* 3178
Deal, Dennis *(Lyricist)* 3178
Deal, Dennis *(Orchestrations)* 3178
Deal, Dennis *(Vocal Arranger)* 3178
Dean, Basil *(Director)* 3451, 4207
Dean, Eddie *(Cast)* 3512
Dean, Eddie *(Lyricist)* 4260
Dean, Gerri *(Cast)* 2796, 3825
Dean, Hazel *(Cast)* 1343
Dean, J. *(Composer)* 1713
Dean, J. *(Lyricist)* 1713
Dean, Laura *(Cast)* 674, 1077, 1258, 3448
Dean, Norman *(Composer)* 239
Dean, Norman *(Librettist)* 239
Dean, Norman *(Lyricist)* 239
Dean, Norman *(Orchestrations)* 239
Dean, Rita *(Cast)* 4046
Dean, Virginia L. *(Producer)* 2735
Deane, Barbara *(Cast)* 1454
Deane, Berna *(Cast)* 324, 2602
Deane, Michael Howell *(Cast)* 2372
Deane, Sydney *(Cast)* 1313, 2343, 3049
Dearborn Theatre Company *(Producer)* 4311
Dearborn Theatre Management *(Producer)* 1351
Dearing, Judy *(Costumes)* 1099, 1344, 2007, 2237, 2908, 2932, 3285, 3599, 3840, 4255, 4697
Deas, Lawrence *(Choreographer)* 691, 3963
Deasy, Mary *(Author)* 2958
Deaves, Ada *(Cast)* 45, 4161
Debenham, Cecily *(Cast)* 2509
Debenham, Cicely *(Cast)* 1733
Debenham & Freebody *(Costumes)* 292
Debin, David *(Lyricist)* 3636
Debonaires, The *(Cast)* 2458
Debonairs, The *(Cast)* 383, 4777
Decareau, Dick *(Cast)* 2674

Decker, Edith *(Cast)* 1783, 3771, 4687
Decker, Gertrude *(Cast)* 4092
Decker, John *(Set Design)* 1244
Decker, Lindsey *(Set Design)* 1609
Decker, Paul *(Cast)* 1565, 4351
Decks, Barbara *(Cast)* 2608
Dedrickson, Tracy *(Lighting Designer)* 2022
Dee, Pauline *(Cast)* 2005, 3069
Dee, Sandra *(Composer)* 4193
Dee, Sandra *(Lyricist)* 4193
Dee, Sylvia *(Composer)* 3695
Dee, Sylvia *(Lyricist)* 304, 3261, 3695
Deeble, Deborah *(Cast)* 4522
Deedee *(Cast)* 3860
Deegan, John Michael *(Lighting Designer)* 3568, 4246
Deel, Sandra *(Cast)* 4096
Deems, Mickey *(Cast)* 59, 2288, 2523, 3788
Deep River Boys *(Cast)* 4256
Deerin, Oliver *(Lyricist)* 2180
Deering, Jane *(Cast)* 1140
Deering, Olive *(Cast)* 1196, 3180
Dees, Billy *(Composer)* 3695
Dees, Billy *(Lyricist)* 3695
Dekker, Albert *(Cast)* 2228
Dekker, Thomas *(Author)* 3939
Dekker, Thomas *(Lyricist)* 3450
Del Bondio, J.H. *(Producer)* 1670
Del Bondio, John H. *(Producer)* 1874
Del Duca Jr., Lennie *(Cast)* 2759
Del Rossi, Angelo *(Producer)* 3734, 3851
Delacour *(Author)* 4418
Delafield, Anne *(Cast)* 3451
Delahanty, Richard *(Lighting Designer)* 4635
Delamater, A.G. *(Producer)* 3033
Delamater, G. *(Director)* 1098
Delaney, Edward *(Set Design)* 972, 1467
Delaney, William M. *(Lyricist)* 114
Delapenha, Denise *(Cast)* 4584
Delerue, Georges *(Composer)* 1865
Delettre, Jean *(Composer)* 839, 4137
Delf, Harry *(Cast)* 804, 1132, 1685, 2216, 2854, 3652, 4208
Delf, Harry *(Composer)* 4053, 4208
Delf, Harry *(Librettist)* 4053, 4208
Delf, Harry *(Lyricist)* 4053, 4208
Delfont, Bernard *(Producer)* 1619, 1621, 2682, 3482, 4469
Dell, Claudia *(Cast)* 1460
Dell, Dorothy *(Cast)* 4291, 4823
Dell, Gabriel *(Cast)* 145, 162, 237, 1354, 1892
Dell, Marlene *(Cast)* 788
Dell'Isola, Salvatore *(Musical Director)* 85, 145, 1315, 2797, 3505, 4096
Delmar, Elaine *(Cast)* 2204
Delmar, Ethel *(Cast)* 3652
Delmar, Harry *(Director)* 1336
Delmar, Harry *(Producer)* 1779
Delmar, Kenny
See also Senator Claghorn.
Delmar, Kenny *(Cast)* 4314
Delmet, Paul *(Composer)* 3386
Delroy, Irene *(Cast)* 1339, 1404, 1689, 1691, 1859, 3783, 4426, 4821

Delsener, Ron *(Producer)*   1512, 2558
Delta Rhythm Boys *(Cast)*   497, 2817
Delu, Dahl *(Lighting Designer)*   2618
Delysia, Alice *(Cast)*   25, 910, 2788, 3583, 4154, 4427
Demarest, Frances *(Cast)*   473, 1424, 1530, 1578, 1593, 1712, 2424, 2667, 3397, 3399, 3400
Demarest, Margaret *(Cast)*   116
Demarest, William *(Cast)*   1126, 1136, 3973
Demarest, William *(Producer)*   4741
Demas, Carole *(Cast)*   1664, 2018, 2958, 3763
Demetriou, Claude *(Composer)*   1296
Demetriou, Claude *(Lyricist)*   1296
Demick, Ken *(Lighting Designer)*   4047
Demidoff, Alexander *(Choreographer)*   910
Deming, Will J. *(Cast)*   1584
Demmher, Edward *(Lighting Designer)*   378
Dempsey *(Composer)*   938
Dempsey *(Lyricist)*   938
Dempsey, Jerome *(Cast)*   1406, 3070
Dempsey, Mark *(Cast)*   2777, 3233
Dempster, Robert *(Cast)*   3730
Dempster, Roger *(Cast)*   2317
Demy, Jacques *(Author)*   4505
Demy, Jacques (French Libretto)   4505
Demy, Jacques (French Lyrics)   4505
Denaker, Susan *(Cast)*   456
Denby, Edwin (Adaptation)   3441
Denby, Edwin *(Choreographer)*   2344
Denby, Edwin *(Lyricist)*   3441
Dench, Judi *(Cast)*   1619
Denee, Charles *(Composer)*   1021, 2543
Denere, Billy *(Cast)*   917
Denes, Oskar *(Cast)*   277
Denham, George W. *(Cast)*   250
Denise, Patricia *(Cast)*   3
Denislow, W.W. *(Costumes)*   4723
Denison, Robert G. *(Cast)*   840
Dennam, Barry *(Cast)*   3186
Dennehy, Dennis *(Choreographer)*   696, 705, 2420, 2472, 2993, 4246
Dennen, Barry *(Cast)*   2212
Denney, Nicholas *(Cast)*   2572
Denni, Gwynne *(Lyricist)*   1756
Denni, Lucien *(Composer)*   1756, 3617
Dennigan, Gib *(Librettist)*   2584
Denniker, Paul *(Composer)*   725, 1981, 3707, 3782, 4502, 4503
Denniker, Paul *(Lyricist)*   3707
Denning, Frank *(Orchestrations)*   2397
Denning, Nancy *(Cast)*   2332
Denning, Nancy Ann *(Cast)*   518
Dennis, Carol *(Cast)*   2932, 3724
Dennis, Inez *(Cast)*   1057, 2942
Dennis, Inez *(Composer)*   1057
Dennis, Inez *(Director)*   4231
Dennis, Patrick *(Author)*   2523, 2713
Dennis, Patrick *(Librettist)*   1622
Dennis, Robert *(Composer)*   1370
Dennis, Robert *(Orchestrations)*   1977
Dennis, Ronald *(Cast)*   746
Dennis, Sandy *(Cast)*   160

Denniston, Leslie *(Cast)*   869, 1762
Denny, Christopher *(Dance Arranger)*   33
Denny, Dodo *(Cast)*   348
Denny, George *(Cast)*   3714
Denny, Harry *(Cast)*   1343
Denny, Harry *(Composer)*   1343
Denny, Harry *(Lyricist)*   1343
Denny, Reginald *(Cast)*   3403
Denslow, W.W. *(Librettist)*   3422
Denslow, W.W. *(Set Design)*   3422
Denton, Clara J. *(Lyricist)*   3631
Denton, Jimmy *(Composer)*   3178
Denton, Jimmy *(Lyricist)*   3178
Denver Theatre Center *(Producer)*   3631
Denvir, Arthur *(Lyricist)*   4589
Denys, Marguerite *(Cast)*   132
Depp, Harry *(Cast)*   1230, 2025, 2497
Deppe, Lois *(Cast)*   1251, 1667, 1836
Derain, Andre *(Costumes)*   792
Derain, Andre *(Set Design)*   792
Derbas, Frank *(Choreographer)*   1194
Derbil, Albert *(Cast)*   385
Derefinko, Rod *(Musical Director)*   681, 2674
Derosa, Rob *(Cast)*   1418
Derr, Richard *(Cast)*   3509
Derricks, Cleavant *(Cast)*   52, 393, 593, 1103, 3757
Derricks, Cleavant *(Composer)*   4645
Derricks, Cleavant *(Lyricist)*   4645
Derricks, Cleavant *(Vocal Arranger)*   593, 1103, 4645
Derricks-Carroll, Clinton *(Cast)*   52, 4788
Derricks-Carroll, Clinton *(Composer)*   4645
Derricks-Carroll, Clinton *(Lyricist)*   4645
Derro, John *(Costumes)*   4018
Derwent, Clarence *(Cast)*   1711, 2396, 2655, 4357
Derwent, Clarence *(Director)*   4275
Derx, Hallam B. *(Lighting Designer)*   3539
Deshe, A. *(Producer)*   2147
Designers Circle *(Set Design)*   3427
Deslys, Gaby *(Cast)*   351, 1963, 2538, 3098, 3701, 3779, 4158, 4553, 4655
Desmond, Dan *(Cast)*   1406
Desmond, Denny *(Cast)*   673
Desmond, Ferral *(Cast)*   2711
Desmond, Florence *(Cast)*   703, 792, 2103, 4341
Desmond, Johnny *(Cast)*   98, 3845, 4155
Desmond, Mary *(Cast)*   77
Despo *(Cast)*   2106, 2536
Despotovich, Nada *(Cast)*   1915
Desrocher, Tom *(Cast)*   3169
Destazio, Brian *(Cast)*   1959
Desvallieres, Maurice *(Author)*   4298
Detering, Frank *(Lighting Designer)*   902, 1199, 4271, 4807
Detling, Rose *(Cast)*   2486
Detric *(Lighting Designer)*   4198
Detweiler, Lowell *(Costumes)*   2953
Detweiler, Lowell *(Set Design)*   4139
Deuth, Celeste *(Cast)*   834
Deutsch, Adolph *(Musical Director)*   1856, 2258
Deutsch, Adolph *(Orchestrations)*   207, 2258, 3379
Deutsch, Helen *(Author)*   656
Deutsch, Helen *(Lyricist)*   2182

Deutsch, Nicholas (*Orchestrations*) 3235
Deval, Jacques (*Author*) 2753, 4435
Deval, Jacques (*Librettist*) 2753
Deval, Jacques (*Lyricist*) 369, 2753
Devane, William (*Cast*) 1383
Devere, William (*Cast*) 998
Devere, William (*Composer*) 436, 998
Devere, William (*Lyricist*) 436
Devin, Richard (*Lighting Designer*) 35, 2332, 3195
Devin, Richard (*Set Design*) 2332
Devine, Elizabeth (*Cast*) 1897
Devine, Erick (*Cast*) 2542
Devine, Jeanne (*Cast*) 3491
Devine, Jerry (*Cast*) 2814
Devine, Jerry (*Librettist*) 127
Devine, Jerry (*Producer*) 127
Devine, Loretta (*Cast*) 393, 550, 828, 1103, 1638, 2692, 2908
Devlin, Guy (*Cast*) 4514
Devlin, John (*Cast*) 406
Devlin, Sandra (*Choreographer*) 1974, 3491, 4318
Devlin, Sandra (*Director*) 366, 1438, 2279
Dew, Edward (*Cast*) 2103
Dewey, Earle S. (*Cast*) 2238
Dewey, Frances (*Cast*) 3103, 3946
Dewey, Priscilla B. (*Librettist*) 4488
Dewey, Priscilla B. (*Lyricist*) 4488
Dexter, Joan (*Cast*) 2447
Dexter, John (*Director*) 1060, 3299, 4371
Dexter, Rose (*Cast*) 3104
Dexter, Van (*Cast*) 790
Deykarhanova, Mesdames (*Cast*) 710
Deyle, John (*Cast*) 3764
Deyo, Blanche (*Cast*) 75, 767, 2835, 2848, 2902, 4044, 4725
Deyo, George W. (*Cast*) 4605
Dezina, Kate (*Cast*) 2132
Dezserian, Louis John (*Set Design*) 4643
Dhery, Robert (*Cast*) 2364
Dhery, Robert (*Director*) 2362, 2364
Dhery, Robert (*Librettist*) 2362, 2364
Dhery, Robert (*Lyricist*) 2364
Di Giovanni, Paul (*Cast*) 932
Di Leone, Leon (*Lighting Designer*) 1903
DiGiovanni, Paul (*Lyricist*) 932
DiLuca, Dino (*Cast*) 2000
Diamini, Khumbuzle (*Cast*) 3836
Diamini, Ntomb'khona (*Cast*) 3836
Diamond, Eddie (*Choreographer*) 3173
Diamond, Eddie (*Director*) 1947, 3173
Diamond, I.A.L. (*Author*) 3603, 4196
Diamond, I.A.L. (*Librettist*) 59
Diamond, I.A.L. (*Lyricist*) 673, 1892, 2246
Diamond, Jack (*Cast*) 2331
Diamond, Michael (*Librettist*) 4410
Diamond, Michael (*Producer*) 4410
Diamond, Neil (*Composer*) 964
Diamond, Neil (*Lyricist*) 964
Diard, Fatimah (*Cast*) 2345
Diard, William (*Cast*) 2977
Dias, Susan (*Lyricist*) 4244

Diaz, Freddy (*Cast*) 4584
Diaz, Nancy (*Cast*) 4172
Dibuono, Toni (*Cast*) 4518
Dick, Paul (*Composer*) 2055
Dick, Paul (*Lyricist*) 2055
Dick Clark Inc.
See also Dick Clark.
Dick Clark Inc. (*Producer*) 3739
Dickens, Charles (*Author*) 752, 753, 754, 828, 869, 2474, 2980, 2982, 3070, 3143, 3271, 3481, 3482, 4155
Dickens, Matthew (*Cast*) 4217
Dickinson, Emily (*Lyricist*) 2124
Dicker, Dorothy (*Producer*) 974
Dickerson, Dudley (*Cast*) 2561
Dickerson, Glenda (*Director*) 3690
Dickerson, Jennie (*Cast*) 1565
Dickerson, Jenny (*Cast*) 3582
Dickerson Orchestra, Carroll (*Cast*) 3707
Dickey, Annamary (*Cast*) 85, 1476, 1948, 3703, 3823
Dickey, Paul (*Director*) 3772, 4793
Dickey, Paul (*Librettist*) 2891
Dickson, Charles (*Author*) 531
Dickson, Charles (*Cast*) 2824, 2842, 4298
Dickson, Charles (*Librettist*) 531, 1629, 3256, 4364
Dickson, Charles (*Lyricist*) 1629
Dickson, Dorothy (*Cast*) 17, 334, 611, 650, 1557, 2412, 3740, 3791, 4159, 4811
Didjah, Belle (*Cast*) 1710
Diehl, Crandall (*Cast*) 3696
Diehl, Otto F. (*Lighting Designer*) 142
Diem, Charles J. (*Cast*) 1902
Diener, Joan (*Cast*) 223, 935, 1959, 2327, 2357, 2727, 3612, 4018, 4827
Dietrichstein, Leo
See also Leo Ditrichstein.
Dietz, Carl (*Cast*) 2567
Dietz, Howard (*Director*) 1322, 3699
Dietz, Howard (*Librettist*) 216, 294, 383, 971, 1322, 1357, 2545, 2827, 3540, 3699, 3813, 4287, 4367
Dietz, Howard (*Lyricist*) 213, 216, 294, 347, 383, 432, 844, 971, 1011, 1322, 1338, 1357, 1448, 1456, 1657, 1763, 1855, 1971, 2137, 2187, 2201, 2246, 2301, 2545, 2653, 2743, 2827, 2989, 3020, 3243, 3540, 3699, 3709, 3813, 3861, 3905, 3955, 4159, 4287, 4367, 4534, 4826, 4828
Dietz, Susan (*Producer*) 2702
Diffen, Ray (*Costumes*) 1959, 2617
Diggs, Dudley (*Cast*) 971
Diggs, Dudley (*Lyricist*) 1446
Dill, George (*Librettist*) 4424
Dill, Max (*Cast*) 3520, 3531
Dill, Max (*Producer*) 3425, 3520, 3531, 4626
Dill, Max M. (*Cast*) 2062, 2576, 3349, 3425
Dill, Max M. (*Director*) 2576
Dill, Max M. (*Producer*) 2062, 2576
Dill, Mollie (*Cast*) 3945
Dille, David (*Costumes*) 338, 3724
Dille, Marjorie (*Cast*) 110, 4368
Dillea, Herbert (*Musical Director*) 187
Dilley, Dorothy (*Cast*) 2342, 3236
Dillingham, Charles (*Cast*) 4039

Dillingham, Charles *(Producer)* 168, 252, 378, 379, 736, 930, 1151, 1175, 1208, 1230, 1555, 1625, 1723, 1753, 1901, 2184, 2638, 2666, 2671, 2891, 2915, 3103, 3254, 3268, 3295, 3332, 3451, 3567, 3675, 3768, 3923, 4017, 4150, 4158, 4212, 4293, 4393, 4716

Dillingham, Charles B. *(Producer)* 396, 582, 627, 632, 683, 773, 1536, 1631, 2025, 2394, 2614, 2885, 2900, 3144, 3146, 3229, 3617, 3721, 3882, 3924, 3968, 4497, 4603

Dillon, Denny *(Cast)* 1775, 3060

Dillon, Gwladys *(Choreographer)* 4327

Dillon, Harry *(Composer)* 2025

Dillon, J.J. *(Composer)* 3220

Dillon, J.J. *(Lyricist)* 3220

Dillon, Mia *(Cast)* 1787

Dillon, Richard *(Cast)* 1163

Dillon, Will *(Composer)* 543

Dillon, Will *(Lyricist)* 543, 1613, 4757

Dillon, William *(Lyricist)* 4197

Dilworth, Gordon *(Cast)* 3038, 4214, 4588

Dilworth, Hugh *(Cast)* 2190

Dimitrov, Olga *(Costumes)* 3846

Dinehart, Allan *(Cast)* 3768

Dinehart, Allan *(Director)* 123, 124, 2827

Dingenary, Gene *(Producer)* 101, 4173

Dingle, Charles *(Cast)* 2894

Dingle, Tom *(Cast)* 1826, 2601, 3433, 4208

Dinroe, Dorothy *(Cast)* 344

Dinroe, Dorothy A. *(Composer)* 3522

DioGuardi, Joseph *(Producer)* 2754

Dippel, Andreas *(Producer)* 2619

Dishy, Bob *(Cast)* 1047, 1310, 1408

Disipio, Fred *(Producer)* 3739

Dissell, Betty *(Cast)* 80

Ditrichstein, Leo *(Author)* 179, 4642

Ditrichstein, Leo *(Cast)* 179, 1594, 4125

Ditrichstein, Leo *(Librettist)* 1888, 4641

Ditsch, James *(Cast)* 643

Dittman, Dean *(Cast)* 3279, 3696

Dix, Beulah Marie *(Author)* 1096, 3730

Dix, Frank *(Author)* 1975

Dix, Lillian *(Cast)* 998, 2996

Dix, Richard *(Cast)* 2059

Dix, Tommy *(Cast)* 372

Dixey, Henry E. *(Cast)* 586, 758, 1465, 3887

Dixey, Henry E. *(Director)* 3887

Dixey, Henry E. *(Librettist)* 3887

Dixie Nightingales *(Cast)* 1772

Dixon, Adele *(Cast)* 346, 383, 3168, 4361

Dixon, Dorothy *(Cast)* 1492, 2960, 4545

Dixon, Ed *(Cast)* 599, 949, 2320, 4136

Dixon, Gale *(Cast)* 798

Dixon, Harland
    Part of team of Dodge & Dixon.

Dixon, Harland *(Cast)* 627, 965, 1625, 2308, 2403, 2734, 3243, 3650, 4426, 4817

Dixon, Harland *(Choreographer)* 703

Dixon, Harold *(Cast)* 3166

Dixon, Harry *(Cast)* 1492

Dixon, Heather *(Composer)* 4264

Dixon, Heather *(Lyricist)* 4264

Dixon, Jean *(Cast)* 2265

Dixon, Jerry *(Cast)* 1296, 3285

Dixon, Julius *(Composer)* 4264

Dixon, Julius *(Lyricist)* 4264

Dixon, Lee *(Cast)* 1814, 1894, 3138, 3263

Dixon, MacIntyre *(Cast)* 679, 2072, 2663, 3330, 4412, 4474, 4703

Dixon, Mildred *(Cast)* 892

Dixon, Mort *(Lyricist)* 418, 1359, 1813, 2423, 4235, 4817, 4818

Dixon, Roy *(Librettist)* 4227

Dixon, Roy *(Lyricist)* 4227

Dixon, Will *(Cast)* 1479, 2791

Dixon, William *(Librettist)* 4525

Djeli, Sahari *(Cast)* 4747

Dlathu, Sindiswa *(Cast)* 4438

D'Lugoff, Art *(Producer)* 3297, 3987

D'Lugoff, Burt *(Producer)* 3297, 3987

D'Lugoff, Burt Charles *(Producer)* 2306

Dlugos, Gregory J. *(Musical Director)* 2420

Doane, Frank *(Cast)* 830, 1529, 1743, 1994, 3251, 3466, 3924

Doane, Melanie *(Cast)* 580

Dobbins, Tim *(Puppeteer)* 56, 3449

Dobbs, George *(Cast)* 4352

Dobbs, George *(Choreographer)* 3148

Dobos, Viola *(Cast)* 2140

Dobson, James *(Cast)* 2175

Dobson, West *(Producer)* 2372

Docherty, Peter *(Set Design)* 3967

Dockery, Leslie *(Choreographer)* 338

Dockery, Leslie *(Director)* 2272

Docket, Larry *(Cast)* 3359

Dockstader, Lew *(Cast)* 2710, 3545, 4054

Dockstader, Lew *(Director)* 3545

Dockstader, Lew *(Producer)* 3545

Doctor, Rubin *(Composer)* 1609

Doctor, Rubin *(Lyricist)* 1609

Doda, Dan *(Director)* 806

Dodd, Clare *(Cast)* 4023

Dodd, John *(Lighting Designer)* 2134

Dodd, Johnny *(Lighting Designer)* 4011

Dodd, Malcolm *(Cast)* 2164

Dodd, Rory *(Cast)* 3741

Dodds, Malcolm *(Vocal Arranger)* 4091

Dodds and the Tunedrops, Malcolm *(Cast)* 898

Dodge, Anna Bacon *(Composer)* 364

Dodge, D. Frank
    See also Dodge & Castle.

Dodge, D. Frank *(Set Design)* 113, 175, 350, 357, 457, 523, 559, 561, 737, 976, 1021, 1243, 1392, 1469, 1540, 2116, 2123, 2179, 2347, 2398, 2695, 2725, 3129, 3732, 3790, 3820, 3856, 3951, 4098, 4236, 4250, 4691

Dodge, Jerry *(Cast)* 1478, 1828, 2660, 3294, 3835

Dodge, Jerry *(Director)* 3876

Dodge, Marcia Milgrom *(Choreographer)* 494, 784, 2477, 2542, 3227

Dodge, Marcia Milgrom *(Director)* 3227

Dodge, Mary Mapes *(Source Author)* 1742

Dodge & Castle
    See also D. Frank Dodge and William Castle.

Dodge & Castle *(Set Design)* 1626, 2373, 3048

Dodger Productions *(Producer)* 394, 1402, 1636, 3862, 4676

Dodger Productions, Inc. *(Producer)* 3608

Dods, Marcus *(Musical Director)* 455, 2682

Dodson, A.E. *(Director)* 3948

Dodson, Colleen *(Cast)* 2783

Dody, Dan *(Choreographer)* 185, 1032, 1457

Dody, Dan *(Composer)* 1032

Dody, Dan *(Lyricist)* 1032

Dody, Sam *(Cast)* 1824

Dody, Sam *(Librettist)* 1824

Doe, Joe *(Librettist)* 3417

Doemland, Ann *(Cast)* 2124

Doermann, Felix *(Author)* 1334

Doermann, Felix *(Librettist)* 1309, 1334

Doerr, Mark E. *(Cast)* 4732

Doerr, Mary *(Cast)* 303

Doff, Gerard S. *(Cast)* 4431

Dogim, Isaac *(Cast)* 4773

Dogim, Isaac *(Lyricist)* 4773

Dohanos, Peter *(Lighting Designer)* 1194

Dohanos, Peter *(Set Design)* 1194, 2551

Dohanos, Stevan *(Set Design)* 4047

Doherty, Lindy *(Cast)* 4423

Dolan, Gerald *(Composer)* 966

Dolan, Judith *(Costumes)* 1038, 2242, 2822, 3456, 4272, 4790

Dolan, Robert Emmett *(Composer)* 1373, 3584, 4314, 4824

Dolan, Robert Emmett *(Musical Director)* 44, 798, 1352, 1973, 2268, 2597, 2786, 4557

Dolan, Robert Emmett *(Vocal Arranger)* 1322

Dolgoy, Sholem *(Lighting Designer)* 1120

Dolin, Anton *(Cast)* 703, 2140, 3893, 4661

Dolin, Anton *(Choreographer)* 1128, 4586

Dolin, Garry *(Vocal Arranger)* 4652

Dolin, Gerald *(Composer)* 1945, 4021

Dolin, Gerald *(Lyricist)* 1945

Dolin, Gerald *(Musical Director)* 4021

Doll, Roy *(Composer)* 1134

Doll, Roy *(Lyricist)* 1134

Dollar, William *(Choreographer)* 1670

Dolloff, William *(Producer)* 1971

Dolly, Edward *(Choreographer)* 1805, 2788, 3467

Dolly, Edward *(Director)* 2788, 3467

Dolly, Helen *(Cast)* 4231

Dolly, Roszika *(Cast)* 1151, 1904, 2469, 2825, 4657

Dolly, Yancsi *(Cast)* 1151, 1904, 1963, 2696, 2825

Dolly Sisters
   See also Roszika Dolly and Yansci Dolly.

Dolly Sisters *(Choreographer)* 3467

Dolly Sisters, The *(Cast)* 1690, 4712, 4805

Dolman, Richard *(Cast)* 1855, 2392

Dolores *(Cast)* 910, 4812

Domino, Antoine "Fats" *(Composer)* 3739

Domino, Antoine "Fats" *(Lyricist)* 3739

Domsky, Sam *(Librettist)* 4774

Don, Robin *(Set Design)* 299

DonHowe, Gwyda *(Cast)* 550, 1797, 3763

Donaggio, Pino *(Composer)* 4193

Donaggio, Pino *(Lyricist)* 4193

Donaghey, Frederick *(Librettist)* 1524, 2596

Donaghey, Frederick *(Lyricist)* 2596

Donaghy, Harry *(Composer)* 1722

Donaghy, Harry *(Lyricist)* 1722

Donahue, Gus *(Orchestrations)* 2084

Donahue, Jack *(Cast)* 136, 317, 2855, 2927, 3766, 3907, 4087, 4212, 4814

Donahue, Jack *(Choreographer)* 180, 277, 1251, 2234, 2540, 2987, 3907

Donahue, Jack *(Composer)* 1267

Donahue, Jack *(Director)* 2234, 2987, 3801, 3893, 4423

Donahue, Jack *(Librettist)* 3584, 4087

Donahue, Jack *(Lyricist)* 1267

Donahue, James *(Cast)* 2284

Donahue Sales Corporation *(Producer)* 2988

Donald, Donald K. *(Producer)* 432, 3643

Donaldson, Arthur *(Cast)* 3578, 4236

Donaldson, John *(Cast)* 3314

Donaldson, Norma *(Cast)* 3619

Donaldson, Walter *(Composer)* 123, 391, 393, 487, 1084, 1154, 1395, 1638, 2342, 2385, 2706, 3018, 3020, 3175, 3405, 3717, 3783, 3973, 3980, 3985, 3989, 4023, 4037, 4249, 4322, 4573, 4683, 4813, 4817, 4821, 4823, 4838, 4846

Donaldson, Walter *(Lyricist)* 1395, 1638, 3175, 3783, 3980, 3989, 4023, 4037, 4799, 4823

Donaldson, Wharton *(Cast)* 4093

Donath, Ludwig *(Cast)* 3918

Dondlinger, Mary Jo *(Lighting Designer)* 147, 809, 1510, 1630, 1737

Donegan, Francis X. *(Cast)* 1529

Donehue, Vincent J. *(Cast)* 2202

Donehue, Vincent J. *(Director)* 2201, 4095

Donen, Stanley *(Cast)* 323, 372, 3353

Donen, Stanley *(Director)* 3682

Doner, Kitty *(Cast)* 969, 3737, 3985

Doner, Ted *(Cast)* 771, 969, 1944, 2135

Donizetti, Gaetano *(Author)* 3197

Donizetti, Gaetano (Music Based On) 3197, 4655

Donklin, Willis P. *(Cast)* 1957

Donlevy, Brian *(Cast)* 1916, 2475, 3650

Donley, Robert *(Cast)* 3671

Donlin, Mike *(Cast)* 687

Donn, Berta *(Cast)* 4328

Donnelly *(Lyricist)* 4805

Donnelly, Arthur *(Cast)* 2857

Donnelly, Candice *(Costumes)* 2945

Donnelly, Dorothy *(Director)* 3540

Donnelly, Dorothy *(Librettist)* 463, 1240, 1309, 1831, 3056, 3063, 3540, 4188

Donnelly, Dorothy *(Lyricist)* 463, 1831, 3020, 3056, 3063, 3540, 4188

Donnelly, Elsie *(Cast)* 1833

Donnelly, Harry *(Composer)* 1120

Donnelly, Harry *(Lyricist)* 1120

Donnelly, Jamie *(Cast)* 1478, 3742, 3743, 4643

Donnelly, Ken *(Librettist)* 3019

Donnelly, Leo *(Cast)* 913, 4668

Donnelly, Leo *(Librettist)* 3701, 4668

Donnelly, Leo *(Lyricist)* 3701

Donnelly, Ruth *(Cast)* 208, 1598

Donner, Vyvyan *(Costumes)* 1027

Donnet, Mary *(Cast)* 2049
Donnolly, Candice *(Costumes)* 3853
D'Onofrio, Benny *(Cast)* 2521
D'Onofrio, Rip *(Cast)* 985
Donovan, Gerry *(Composer)* 4433
Donovan, Gerry *(Librettist)* 4433
Donovan, Gerry *(Lyricist)* 4433
Donovan, Joe *(Choreographer)* 3651
Donovan, Joe *(Director)* 3651
Donovan, King *(Cast)* 2057
Donovan, Linda *(Cast)* 1380
Donovan, Maria *(Costumes)* 4415
Donovan, Nancy *(Cast)* 2610
Donovan, Walter *(Composer)* 3589
Donovan, Warde *(Cast)* 853, 3837, 4428
Dooley, Gordon *(Cast)* 1134, 1488, 4742
Dooley, John *(Cast)* 4437
Dooley, John *(Composer)* 1924
Dooley, John *(Librettist)* 1924
Dooley, John *(Lyricist)* 1924
Dooley, Johnny *(Cast)* 1486, 1552, 2264, 2298, 2491, 3401, 3478, 4813
Dooley, Paul *(Cast)* 1091, 1233, 4369, 4397, 4401
Dooley, Ray *(Cast)* 582, 827, 1134, 1920, 3144, 3179, 3968, 4374, 4813, 4814, 4815, 4818, 4819
Dooley, Sean *(Cast)* 3125
Doolittle, James A. *(Producer)* 3954
Doran, Johnny *(Cast)* 1222
Doran, Mr. *(Cast)* 1743
Dore, Daniel *(Composer)* 224
Dore, Daniel *(Lyricist)* 224
Dore, Daniel *(Musical Director)* 1910, 2538
Dore, Demaris *(Cast)* 3556
Dore, Lynn *(Cast)* 3172
Dorff, Steve *(Arrangements)* 2651
Dorff, Steve *(Composer)* 2651
Dorfman, Andrew *(Musical Director)* 3739
Dorfman, Nat *(Librettist)* 444, 447, 787, 2140, 3705
Dorfman, Robert *(Cast)* 109, 3198
Dorfmunder, Dieter *(Lyricist)* 154
Dorman, Edna *(Cast)* 2795
Dormann, Felix *(Author)* 3771, 4590
Dormeuil, Edmee *(Cast)* 4302
Dormont, Frances *(Costumes)* 4047
Dorn, Margaret *(Composer)* 459
Doro, Marie *(Cast)* 405, 1537, 2952
Doro, Marie *(Composer)* 2498
Doro, Marie *(Lyricist)* 2498
Dorothy, Isabelle *(Cast)* 2571
Dorr, Dorothy *(Cast)* 3805
Dorsell, Sabry *(Cast)* 188
Dorsett, Flora *(Cast)* 2771
Dorsey, Abner *(Cast)* 1366
Dorsey, Frances *(Cast)* 2083
Dorsey, Jimmy *(Cast)* 1207, 1528
Dorsey, Kent *(Lighting Designer)* 4193
Dorsey, Tommy *(Cast)* 1207
Dorsey, Tommy *(Composer)* 1825

Dorsey, Tommy *(Lyricist)* 1825
Dorsey, Will *(Composer)* 2984
D'Orso, Wisa *(Cast)* 2288, 2983, 3204
Dossert, Frank *(Composer)* 4012
Dossett, John *(Cast)* 1377, 1822
Dotrice, Roy *(Cast)* 1787
Dotson, Deborah *(Cast)* 2993
Doty, Charles *(Librettist)* 4044
Doty, Dan *(Director)* 513
Doty, David *(Cast)* 373
Doucet, Catherine *(Cast)* 3415
Doucette, David *(Costumes)* 2482
Dougall, Bernard *(Lyricist)* 2204, 3735
Dougherty, Byrd *(Composer)* 2959, 2978
Dougherty, Byrd *(Musical Director)* 782
Dougherty, Christina *(Additional Music)* 4729
Dougherty, Dan *(Composer)* 700
Dougherty, Dennis *(Set Design)* 1977
Dougherty, George *(Composer)* 1523
Dougherty, George Byrd *(Composer)* 1523
Dougherty, J.P. *(Cast)* 1785, 3169, 3757, 3873
Dougherty, Joseph *(Librettist)* 3039
Douglas, Bob *(Cast)* 601
Douglas, C. Noel *(Lyricist)* 2990
Douglas, C.N. *(Lyricist)* 694
Douglas, Charles Noel *(Librettist)* 15
Douglas, Charles Noel *(Lyricist)* 15, 250, 1532, 3753, 3857
Douglas, Fred *(Cast)* 2111
Douglas, George *(Cast)* 3158
Douglas, Gilbert *(Cast)* 2059
Douglas, Jerry *(Librettist)* 3763
Douglas, Jerry *(Lyricist)* 3763
Douglas, Kirk *(Cast)* 1089
Douglas, Larry *(Cast)* 1860, 2312, 4640
Douglas, Louis *(Choreographer)* 26
Douglas, Malcolm *(Composer)* 571
Douglas, Melvyn *(Cast)* 1416, 2268, 2450
Douglas, Melvyn *(Producer)* 620
Douglas, Milton *(Cast)* 2813
Douglas, Noel *(Lyricist)* 3753
Douglas, Suzanne *(Cast)* 4371
Douglas, Wade *(Set Design)* 1009
Douglas, Walter *(Cast)* 1513
Douglas, Warren *(Librettist)* 362
Douglas, Warren *(Lyricist)* 362
Douglas, William *(Cast)* 2023
Douglass, Jane *(Composer)* 348
Douglass, Jane *(Dance Arranger)* 348
Douglass, Jane *(Musical Director)* 348
Douglass, Jane *(Vocal Arranger)* 348
Douglass, Louis *(Cast)* 3089
Douglass, Louis *(Director)* 3528
Douglass, Louis *(Lyricist)* 3528
Douglass, Pi *(Cast)* 1497, 3871, 4722
Douglass, Stephen *(Cast)* 957, 1600, 2705, 3294, 3801
Douthitt, Wilfred *(Cast)* 2486
Douthitt, Wilfred *(Lyricist)* 2486
Dova, Ben *(Cast)* 4174
Dova, Nina *(Cast)* 2052
Dove, Billy *(Cast)* 4852

Dove, Julius (Set Design)   97
Dovey, Alice (Cast)   1735, 3193, 3265, 3362, 3494, 3579, 3627, 4185, 4203, 4555
Dovey, Ethel (Cast)   88
Dow, Susan (Cast)   3555
Dowd, M'el (Cast)   623
Dowdy, Helen (Cast)   2994, 3541
Dowe, Julius (Set Design)   3081
Dowell, Coleman (Composer)   34, 4292
Dowell, Coleman (Librettist)   4292
Dowell, Coleman (Lyricist)   4292
Dowell, Edgar (Composer)   1876, 3514
Dowell, Edgar (Lyricist)   1876
Dowell, J. Edgar (Composer)   1658
Dowell, J. Edgar (Lyricist)   1658
Dowling, Doris (Cast)   323
Dowling, Eddie (Cast)   1965, 3153, 3821, 3968, 4374, 4547, 4813
Dowling, Eddie (Composer)   1965
Dowling, Eddie (Director)   717, 2504, 3321
Dowling, Eddie (Librettist)   1965, 3821, 3968
Dowling, Eddie (Lyricist)   1965, 3968
Dowling, Eddie (Producer)   717, 2504, 3321, 4374
Dowling, Edward (Cast)   79
Dowling, Edward (Producer)   79
Dowling, Edward Duryea (Director)   383, 1763, 1840, 2301, 4086, 4174
Dowling, Edward Duryea (Librettist)   4174
Dowling, Edward Duryea (Lighting Designer)   4086
Dowling, M.L. (Costumes)   1392, 1540
Dowling, Vincent (Librettist)   451
Downey, Morton (Cast)   173, 1215, 1416, 2366, 2460, 4178
Downie, Barbara (Cast)   283
Downing, David (Cast)   1592, 1671, 3522
Downs, Johnny (Cast)   180, 1930, 4177
Downs, Michael E. (Set Design)   1832, 2237
Downs, Sarah (Cast)   1757
Downs, Stephen (Composer)   1262
Downs, Stephen (Librettist)   1262
Downs, Stephen (Lyricist)   1262
Downs Jr., Edward R. (Producer)   3015
Doyle, Arthur Conan (Author)   270
Doyle, Buddy (Cast)   4465
Doyle, David (Cast)   1860
Doyle, David (Director)   339
Doyle, James (Cast)   627, 965, 3252, 4694
Doyle, Ted (Cast)   821
Doyle, William (Musical Director)   4193
Doyle & Dixon (Cast)   558, 683, 1963, 4158
Dozer, David (Librettist)   3527
Dozier, Lamont (Composer)   146, 3739, 4193, 4534
Dozier, Lamont (Lyricist)   146, 3739, 4193, 4534
Dozzel, Master (Cast)   1192
Drabble, Richard (Cast)   456
Drabinsky, Garth H. (Producer)   550
Drake, Alfred (Adaptation)   3280
Drake, Alfred (Cast)   23, 31, 247, 341, 1435, 1511, 2295, 2327, 2331, 3263, 3280, 3292, 3989, 4166, 4479, 4483, 4667, 4798
Drake, Alfred (Director)   911, 1091, 2464, 2563

Drake, Alfred (Librettist)   1091, 2464, 3798
Drake, David (Cast)   3346
Drake, Donna (Cast)   484, 746, 4701
Drake, Ervin (Composer)   204, 1848, 4091, 4633
Drake, Ervin (Librettist)   1848
Drake, Ervin (Lyricist)   204, 1848, 3905, 4091, 4633
Drake, Milton (Composer)   478, 2060
Drake, Milton (Lighting Designer)   4318
Drake, Milton (Lyricist)   478, 2060, 3374
Drake, Ronald (Cast)   461, 4244
Drake, William A. (Librettist)   4486
Drakeley, Ray (Cast)   23
Draper, Alexander (Cast)   3853
Draper, Kate (Cast)   1000
Draper, Paul (Cast)   1416, 2406, 2504, 3594, 4374
Draper, Paul (Choreographer)   1474
Drayton, Mary (Cast)   3647
Drayton, Otto (Librettist)   3692
Drayton, Thaddius (Cast)   2557
Drean, Robert (Director)   1347
Dregely, Gabriel (Author)   2526
Dreiser, Theodore (Author)   3831
Drescher, Otto (Orchestrations)   1343
Dreskin, William (Composer)   3448
Dresselhuys, Lorraine Manville (Producer)   3703
Dresser, Forrest J. (Cast)   1868
Dresser, Louise (Cast)   8, 558, 632, 1526, 1569, 1613, 1784, 1826, 2782, 3740
Dresser, Richard (Author)   1915
Dressler, Eric (Cast)   1215
Dressler, Marie (Cast)   77, 506, 683, 969, 1728, 1881, 1994, 2316, 2324, 2398, 2673, 2725, 2904, 3404, 3755, 4125, 4382, 4473
Dressler, Marie (Costumes)   77
Dressler, Marie (Director)   77
Dressler, Marie (Librettist)   77
Drew, Bernard (Librettist)   2275
Drew, Bill (Cast)   3439
Drew, Charles H. (Cast)   4563
Drew, Doris (Voice)   57
Drew, George (Costumes)   3059
Drew, Georgie (Costumes)   1834
Drew, John (Cast)   17
Drew, Louise (Cast)   17, 2624
Drew, Maurice (Cast)   3910
Drew, Richard (Lighting Designer)   4746
Drexler, Rosalyn (Librettist)   1958
Drexler, Rosalyn (Lyricist)   1958
Dreyer, Bob (Cast)   1883
Dreyer, Dave (Composer)   393, 1404, 1643, 3020, 3149
Dreyer, Dave (Lyricist)   1404
Dreyfuss, Henry (Costumes)   2739
Dreyfuss, Henry (Director)   839
Dreyfuss, Henry (Lighting Designer)   3946
Dreyfuss, Henry (Set Design)   672, 715, 1275, 1440, 1929, 2739, 3946, 4177
Dreyfuss-Fellner Co. (Producer)   4359
Drischell, Ralph (Cast)   3671
Driscoll, Clara (Librettist)   2848
Drivas, Robert (Cast)   1294
Drivas, Robert (Director)   546, 2435, 3428

Driver, Donald *(Choreographer)* 3231
Driver, Donald *(Director)* 547, 2218, 3231, 4789
Driver, Donald *(Librettist)* 3231, 4789
Driver, Donald *(Lyricist)* 3231
Driver, John *(Cast)* 3330, 3858
Driver, John *(Composer)* 3711, 3858
Driver, John *(Director)* 729, 3858, 3909, 4297
Driver, John *(Librettist)* 729, 3711, 3858, 3944
Driver, John *(Lyricist)* 3711, 3858, 3944
Drix, Walter *(Composer)* 1413
Drotos, Ron *(Arrangements)* 4255
Drowne, Edwin S. *(Cast)* 1274
Druce, Hubert *(Director)* 4284
Druce, Olga *(Cast)* 2946
Drum, Leonard *(Cast)* 2288, 3215, 4107
Drummond, David K. *(Producer)* 4246
Drummond, Jack *(Cast)* 2664
Drummond, Nolan *(Costumes)* 337
Drury, Charles *(Musical Director)* 418, 1460, 1486, 1494, 3091, 4271
Drury, Hazel *(Cast)* 1603
Drury, Ian *(Lyricist)* 3884
Dryden, Helen *(Costumes)* 4603
Dryden, Helen *(Set Design)* 4603
Dryer, Jay *(Orchestrations)* 2018
Dryer, Jerome Jay *(Orchestrations)* 1059
Dryer, Jerome Jay *(Vocal Arranger)* 1059
Du Clos, Danielle *(Cast)* 211
Du Clos, Deanna *(Cast)* 211
Du Heron, Helen *(Cast)* 4681
Du Shon, Jean *(Cast)* 478
DuBois, Geraldine *(Cast)* 856
DuBois, Jeannette *(Cast)* 1601
duBois, Raul Pene
  See Pene du Bois, Raoul.
DuBois, William *(Author)* 2060
DuMont, William *(Cast)* 489
DuMouchel, Michael *(Set Design)* 3004
DuPage, Richard *(Orchestrations)* 4677
DuPre, Lynette G. *(Cast)* 4460
DuVal, Billy *(Lyricist)* 4322
Duane, Jed *(Director)* 4750
Dubberley, Robert E. *(Producer)* 1255
Dubens, A. *(Costumes)* 1610
Duberman, Martin *(Librettist)* 4089
Dubey, Matt *(Librettist)* 4029, 4609
Dubey, Matt *(Lyricist)* 860, 1760, 3108, 4029, 4609
Dubin, Al *(Lyricist)* 397, 543, 702, 1359, 1687, 2301, 2400, 2662, 2772, 3018, 3020, 3916, 3958, 4131, 4174, 4197, 4235, 4271, 4426, 4668, 4799
Dubin, Charles S. *(Director)* 1933
Dubin, Joe *(Orchestrations)* 4586
Dubinsky, Barney *(Cast)* 3480
Dubinsky, Barney *(Producer)* 3480
Dubinsky, M.M. *(Cast)* 3480
Dubinsky, M.M. *(Producer)* 3480
Duchin, Eddie *(Cast)* 3153
Duckworth, Dortha *(Cast)* 1310, 1698, 3271
Duddy, Lyn *(Composer)* 197, 858, 4193, 4264, 4377
Duddy, Lyn *(Lyricist)* 197, 858, 859, 4114, 4193, 4264, 4377

Dudley, Alice *(Cast)* 680, 4374, 4550
Dudley, Bide *(Librettist)* 608, 815, 2780, 3222, 4194
Dudley, Bide *(Lyricist)* 815, 2549, 2780, 3222, 4194
Dudley, Bide *(Producer)* 4194
Dudley, Bronson *(Cast)* 4166
Dudley, Ethel *(Cast)* 2524
Dudley, Grace *(Cast)* 1537
Dudley, John *(Set Design)* 3207
Dudley, Mrs. S.H. *(Cast)* 1909
Dudley, S.H. *(Cast)* 1087, 1909
Dudley, S.H. *(Director)* 1909
Dudley, S.H. *(Lyricist)* 434
Dudley, S.H. *(Producer)* 986, 1087
Dudley, Sherman H. *(Cast)* 434
Dudley, Sherman H. *(Librettist)* 434
Dudley, Sherman H. *(Producer)* 434
Duer, Fred *(Set Design)* 450
Dufault, Buddy *(Orchestrations)* 817
Duff, J.C. *(Director)* 906, 2361
Duff, J.C. *(Producer)* 767
Duff, Michael *(Composer)* 3461
Duff-Gordon, Lady *(Costumes)* 4809, 4810, 4811, 4812, 4813, 4814
Duffield, Blanche *(Cast)* 307
Duffrey, J.H. *(Cast)* 3771
Duffy, Anna Nichols *(Author)* 4120
Duffy, Anna Nichols *(Lyricist)* 4120
Duffy, Gordon *(Composer)* 1766
Duffy, Henry *(Producer)* 46, 2479, 3013, 3415
Duffy, Herbert *(Cast)* 1036
Duffy, James *(Lyricist)* 1538
Duffy, Jimmy *(Composer)* 2296, 4816
Duffy, Jimmy *(Librettist)* 2296
Duffy, Jimmy *(Lyricist)* 2296, 4816
Duffy, John *(Composer)* 1977
Duffy, John *(Lyricist)* 1977
Duffy, John *(Orchestrations)* 1977
Duffy, Meghan *(Cast)* 4731
Duffy, William *(Producer)* 2296
Duggan, Louis *(Composer)* 1632
Duggan, Thomas *(Cast)* 3973
Duggan, Thomas *(Librettist)* 3973
Dukas, Paul *(Composer)* 193
Duke, Bill *(Cast)* 40
Duke, Edward *(Cast)* 3429
Duke, Irving Milton *(Set Design)* 2069
Duke, Milton *(Costumes)* 4102
Duke, Milton *(Lighting Designer)* 4102
Duke, Milton *(Set Design)* 4102
Duke, Patty *(Cast)* 3287
Duke, Robert *(Librettist)* 2103
Duke, Stuart *(Lighting Designer)* 549, 838, 2224, 2651, 4055
Duke, Vernon
  See also Vernon Dukelsky.
Duke, Vernon *(Composer)* 125, 213, 297, 478, 503, 612, 664, 924, 971, 1035, 1048, 1448, 1792, 1818, 2077, 2161, 2187, 2293, 2301, 2379, 2554, 3074, 3307, 3383, 3493, 3813, 3946, 3955, 4237, 4287, 4367, 4374, 4386, 4399, 4491, 4499, 4583, 4665, 4670, 4765, 4795, 4798, 4799, 4824, 4825, 4826

Duke, Vernon *(Lyricist)* 478, 612, 924, 3493, 4374, 4386, 4491, 4765, 4798

Duke, Vernon *(Orchestrations)* 2187, 3813

Duke, Vernon *(Vocal Arranger)* 3813, 4237

Dukelsky, Vernon
See also Vernon Duke.

Dukelsky, Vladimir *(Composer)* 3955

Dukes, Ashley *(Author)* 2731

Dukes, David *(Cast)* 2607

Dulac, Edward *(Costumes)* 3467

Dulac, Edward *(Set Design)* 3467

Dulchin, Edwin *(Librettist)* 2674

Dulchin, Edwin *(Lyricist)* 2633, 2674

Dulin, Michael *(Set Design)* 1508

Dull, Harry *(Lyricist)* 1340

Dull, Harry *(Producer)* 1340

Dullea, Keir *(Cast)* 594

Dulo, Jane *(Cast)* 180, 4585

Dumakude, Thuli *(Cast)* 1719

Dumakude, Thuli *(Choreographer)* 1719

Dumakude, Thuli *(Vocal Arranger)* 1719

Dumaresq, William *(Librettist)* 2033, 2153

Dumaresq, William *(Lyricist)* 2033, 2153

Dumas, Alexandre *(Author)* 168, 3047, 4357

du Maurier, George *(Author)* 4230

du Maurier, Gerald *(Author)* 4229

Dumbells, The *(Cast)* 388

Dumbrille, Douglas *(Cast)* 3584, 3586, 4357

Dumke, Ralph *(Cast)* 2985, 3813

Dumont, Frank *(Librettist)* 3028

Dumont, Frank *(Lyricist)* 3024

Dumont, Margaret *(Cast)* 142, 799, 1368, 1584, 2479, 4299

Dumont, Marie *(Cast)* 349

Dumrose, Boyd *(Lighting Designer)* 3988

Dumrose, Boyd *(Set Design)* 3988

Duna, Steffi *(Cast)* 4368

Dunaway, Faye *(Cast)* 942

Dunbar, Dixie *(Cast)* 2475, 4772

Dunbar, Paul Laurence *(Librettist)* 633, 783, 2210

Dunbar, Paul Laurence *(Lyricist)* 783, 1803, 2111, 2210, 2662

Duncan, A. Clark *(Set Design)* 3318

Duncan, Andrew *(Cast)* 4397

Duncan, Augustin *(Cast)* 2504

Duncan, Augustin *(Director)* 827

Duncan, Doris *(Cast)* 1314, 3349

Duncan, Florence *(Composer)* 4590

Duncan, Florence *(Lyricist)* 4590

Duncan, Harold *(Composer)* 3104

Duncan, Ina *(Cast)* 4198

Duncan, Isadora *(Cast)* 1470

Duncan, Jessica *(Cast)* 1466

Duncan, Laura *(Cast)* 2175, 3885

Duncan, Rosetta
See also Duncan Sisters.

Duncan, Rosetta *(Cast)* 1065, 4393, 4429

Duncan, Rosetta *(Composer)* 4429

Duncan, Rosetta *(Lyricist)* 4429

Duncan, Sandy *(Cast)* 634, 1298, 3499

Duncan, Stuart *(Producer)* 825, 1595, 4022

Duncan, Todd *(Cast)* 612, 2591, 3541, 4207

Duncan, Vivian
See also Duncan Sisters.

Duncan, Vivian *(Cast)* 1065, 4393, 4429

Duncan, Vivian *(Composer)* 4429

Duncan, Vivian *(Lyricist)* 4429

Duncan, William Cary *(Composer)* 1432, 2112

Duncan, William Cary *(Librettist)* 468, 640, 1266, 1911, 2112, 2273, 2291, 2768, 2927, 2943, 3580, 3613, 3692, 3770, 3791, 4213, 4218, 4226, 4276, 4360, 4766

Duncan, William Cary *(Lyricist)* 468, 1266, 1733, 1911, 2112, 2273, 2291, 2623, 2768, 3249, 3613, 3770, 3791, 4213, 4218, 4226, 4647

Duncan Sisters
See also Rosetta Duncan and Vivian Duncan.

Duncan Sisters, The *(Cast)* 3923

Dundes, Alan *(Composer)* 4041

Dundy, Elmer S. *(Producer)* 4046, 4753

Dunham, By *(Lyricist)* 4204

Dunham, Clarke *(Lighting Designer)* 2018, 2801

Dunham, Clarke *(Set Design)* 171, 576, 1186, 1699, 2018, 2420, 2801, 4272, 4349

Dunham, David *(Director)* 2051

Dunham, Joan *(Producer)* 708

Dunham, Katherine *(Cast)* 612, 651

Dunham, Katherine *(Choreographer)* 467, 651, 3427, 4702

Dunham, Ronald *(Cast)* 52

Dunham Dancers, Katherine *(Cast)* 467

Dunkel, Eugene *(Set Design)* 1286, 1342, 1546, 3082

Dunkle, Nancy *(Cast)* 932

Dunlay, William *(Cast)* 2181

Dunlay, Willie *(Cast)* 1550

Dunleavy, Timothy *(Costumes)* 2555

Dunlop, Geoffrey *(Translator)* 979

Dunn, Arthur *(Cast)* 1213, 2029, 2518

Dunn, Cesar *(Author)* 1368

Dunn, Edward *(Lyricist)* 583

Dunn, Edward Delaney *(Author)* 3472

Dunn, Edward Delaney *(Librettist)* 659, 1033, 2419

Dunn, Edward Delaney *(Lyricist)* 659, 2419, 3472, 3680

Dunn, Elaine *(Cast)* 673, 2227

Dunn, Griffin *(Cast)* 829

Dunn, Jack *(Cast)* 673

Dunn, James *(Cast)* 2975, 3359

Dunn, James *(Producer)* 1754

Dunn, Josephine *(Cast)* 4267

Dunn, Kathy *(Cast)* 4095

Dunn, Mrs. Edward Delaney *(Lyricist)* 3472

Dunn, Ralph *(Cast)* 3351, 3898, 4312

Dunn, Vera *(Cast)* 163

Dunne, Irene *(Cast)* 773, 780, 1121, 2637, 3924, 4249, 4793

Dunne, John W. *(Producer)* 782

Dunne, Stephan *(Cast)* 3539

Dunning, Philip *(Author)* 2311

Dunning, Philip *(Director)* 387

Dunning, Philip *(Librettist)* 387

Dunning, Philip *(Lyricist)* 387

Dunnock, Mildred *(Cast)* 807, 937, 2655

Dunsmore, John *(Cast)* 1650, 1710

Dunsmore, John H. *(Composer)* 3627

E

Earle, Edward (Composer) 1017

Earle, Edward (Dance Arranger) 4243

Earle, Edward (Director) 4643

Earle, Florence (Cast) 2567

Earle, Fred (Composer) 675

Earle, Fred (Lyricist) 675

Earle, Harry (Cast) 1213

Earle, Ronald Hamilton (Cast) 1707

Earle, Virginia (Cast) 350, 666, 770, 1543, 1599, 2116, 2123, 2398, 2481, 3129, 3883

Earley, Candice (Cast) 2114

Earley, J.B. (Composer) 806

Early, Dan (Director) 3167

Easen, Otto (Cast) 4006

Easley, Holmes (Set Design) 705

East, Ed (Composer) 3407

East, Ed (Lyricist) 3407

Easterbrook, Randall (Cast) 3019

Eastham, Dickinson and Richard Eastham are the same person.

Eastham, Dickinson (Cast) 4096

Eastham, Richard (Cast) 1815

Eastman, Gretchen (Cast) 2145, 3729

Eastman, Joan (Cast) 1974

Eastman, Nikki (Set Design) 1834

Eastman, Virginia (Cast) 3434

Eastmond, Barry (Musical Director) 2133

Easton, Jack (Conductor) 4028

Easton, Jack (Musical Director) 400

Easton, Richard (Cast) 3818, 4715

Easton, Sidney (Cast) 2021

Easton, Sidney (Composer) 3709

Easton, Sidney (Lyricist) 3709

Eastright, Bob (Librettist) 1880

Eastwood, Gini (Cast) 1769

Eaton, Bob (Author) 2440

Eaton, Bob (Director) 2440

Eaton, Charles (Cast) 3451

Eaton, Doris (Cast) 1215, 1943, 3185

Eaton, Mary (Cast) 1297, 2308, 2638, 3333, 4814, 4815, 4816

Eaton, Pearl (Cast) 1131, 3924, 4375

Eaton, Sally (Cast) 1717

Eaton Associates (Producer) 3527

Eaves (Costumes) 1251, 1710, 3082, 4328

Ebb, Fred (Composer) 3615, 4566

Ebb, Fred (Librettist) 723, 2958, 3900

Ebb, Fred (Lyricist) 16, 131, 392, 610, 723, 826, 1038, 1310, 1408, 1585, 1605, 1764, 1770, 1787, 2333, 2558, 2677, 2958, 3615, 3718, 3900, 4480, 4566, 4580, 4727, 4829, 4862

Eben, Al (Cast) 3501

Eberhard, Deac (Orchestrations) 855, 864

Eberhard, Eliot G. (Orchestrations) 858

Eberhard, Eliot G. "Deac" (Orchestrations) 857

Eberhard, Leslie (Composer) 1873, 2294

Eberhard, Leslie (Librettist) 2235

Eberhard, Leslie (Lyricist) 1873, 2294

Ebersole, Christine (Cast) 1684, 1776

Ebert, Franz (Cast) 1608

Ebert, Joyce (Cast) 951, 4601

Ebony Jo-Ann (Cast) 1236

Ebsen, Buddy (Cast) 1322, 4772, 4824

Ebsen, Buddy (Producer) 4466

Ebsen, Buddy (Voice) 4391

Ebsen, Vilma (Cast) 383, 1322, 4824

Eburne, Maude (Cast) 1667, 2605

Eck, Marsha Louis (Set Design) 1222, 2925

Eckart, Jean (Costumes) 759, 957, 1280, 3288, 3696

Eckart, Jean (Lighting Designer) 32, 483, 868, 1227, 1280, 1745, 2449, 2484, 3097, 3918, 4863

Eckart, Jean (Producer) 3288

Eckart, Jean (Set Design) 32, 162, 483, 759, 868, 957, 1158, 1227, 1273, 1280, 1310, 1600, 1729, 1745, 1860, 2449, 2484, 2556, 2643, 2681, 2713, 2965, 3097, 3288, 3696, 3876, 3918, 4863

Eckart, William (Costumes) 759, 957, 1280, 3288, 3696

Eckart, William (Lighting Designer) 32, 483, 868, 1227, 1280, 1745, 2449, 2484, 3097, 3918, 4863

Eckart, William (Producer) 3288

Eckart, William (Set Design) 32, 162, 483, 759, 868, 957, 1158, 1227, 1273, 1280, 1310, 1600, 1729, 1745, 1860, 2449, 2484, 2556, 2643, 2681, 2713, 2965, 3097, 3288, 3696, 3876, 3918, 4863

Eckhart, Lois (Cast) 1493

Eckley, Dan (Choreographer) 1814, 2447, 2748

Eckstein, George (Producer) 408, 411

Eckstein, William (Composer) 1154

Ecton, Robert (Cast) 488, 3704

Eda-Young, Barbara (Cast) 3309

Eddinger, Lawrence (Cast) 2967, 3618

Eddington, Paul (Cast) 2240

Eddleman, Jack (Cast) 1092, 1676, 3234

Eddy, David (Lyricist) 227

Eddy, Eddie (Set Design) 2207

Ede, George (Cast) 2607, 3468

Edegran, Lars (Arrangements) 1425

Edegran, Lars (Orchestrations) 3297

Edegran, Lars (Vocal Arranger) 1425

Edeiken, Louise (Cast) 1496, 4398, 4618

Edeken, Louise (Cast) 2372

Edel, Alfredo (Costumes) 286, 1318, 3093, 3753, 4046, 4113, 4753, 4802, 4803

Edell, Ruth (Cast) 4021

Edelman, Gregg (Cast) 147, 775, 1496, 3411, 4618

Edelman, Herbert (Cast) 269, 1842

Edelshtat, David (Lyricist) 1609

Eden, Sidney (Producer) 3925

Eden, Susan (Producer) 4433

Eden, Toni (Cast) 4469

Edens, Roger (Cast) 1528

Edens, Roger (Composer) 3992

Edens, Roger (Vocal Arranger) 4267

Eder, Linda (Cast) 2198, 4229

Ederle, Gertrude (Cast) 173

Edgar, David (Author) 2474

Edgar, Kate (Musical Director) 3695

Edgerton, Sandy (Cast) 450

Edgewood Productions, Inc. (Producer) 3991

Edington, May (Author) 3048

Ediss, Connie (Cast) 178, 1526, 1561, 1613, 3098, 3948

Edlin, Teddy (Cast) 2788

Edmead, Wendy *(Cast)* 107, 678, 3456
Edmond, Grace *(Cast)* 1532, 3251
Edmonds, Charles *(Composer)* 1687
Edmonds, Louis *(Cast)* 630, 1017, 1194, 3788
Edmonds, Shepard N. *(Composer)* 4390
Edmonds, Shepard N. *(Lyricist)* 4390
Edmonton Jounal *(Producer)* 3485
Edmunds, Kate *(Set Design)* 699, 4216
Edouin, Willie *(Cast)* 1313, 1537
Edouin, Willie *(Director)* 1313
Edson, Eda *(Director)* 1337
Edvina, Louise *(Cast)* 1805
Edward, Carlo *(Musical Director)* 1016
Edward, Felix *(Director)* 2376
Edward Spector Prod. Inc. *(Producer)* 3874
Edwardes, Felix *(Producer)* 2389
Edwardes, George *(Author)* 3322
Edwardes, George *(Director)* 1429
Edwardes, George *(Producer)* 1114, 1537, 3098, 4354, 4795
Edwardes, Kathleen *(Cast)* 2747
Edwardes, Paula *(Cast)* 1021, 2181, 3581, 3951, 4713
Edwards, Alan *(Cast)* 2376, 2829, 3540, 3980, 4033, 4345, 4476
Edwards, Ben *(Lighting Designer)* 1383, 2450
Edwards, Ben *(Set Design)* 747, 1383, 3610
Edwards, Blake *(Author)* 4560
Edwards, Blake *(Director)* 4560
Edwards, Blake *(Librettist)* 4560
Edwards, Blake *(Producer)* 4560
Edwards, Bobby *(Cast)* 2456
Edwards, Bobby *(Composer)* 1244
Edwards, Bobby *(Lyricist)* 1244
Edwards, Brandt *(Cast)* 746
Edwards, Bucky *(Cast)* 985
Edwards, Carlo *(Musical Director)* 1218
Edwards, Cliff *(Cast)* 1493, 2376, 2403, 2405, 2870, 4212, 4290
Edwards, Cliff *(Composer)* 2376, 4212
Edwards, Cliff *(Lyricist)* 2376, 4212
Edwards, Cuddles *(Cast)* 1703
Edwards, David *(Cast)* 430
Edwards, Frank *(Cast)* 1004
Edwards, Gail *(Cast)* 337
Edwards, Gail *(Composer)* 337
Edwards, Gail *(Librettist)* 337
Edwards, Gail *(Lyricist)* 337
Edwards, George *(Lyricist)* 1308
Edwards, Glynn *(Cast)* 1277
Edwards, Gus *(Cast)* 2493, 2781, 3153
Edwards, Gus *(Composer)* 8, 470, 522, 557, 1243, 1391, 1434, 1703, 1704, 1900, 1910, 1919, 1925, 1998, 2096, 2493, 2747, 2781, 2803, 2826, 2892, 2974, 2990, 3327, 3387, 3397, 3855, 3856, 3857, 4079, 4181, 4209, 4390, 4650, 4723, 4755, 4801, 4803, 4804
Edwards, Gus *(Director)* 1703, 4755
Edwards, Gus *(Librettist)* 1703, 1704
Edwards, Gus *(Lyricist)* 2096, 2493, 2781, 2892, 3999, 4803
Edwards, Gus *(Producer)* 557, 2781, 3327, 3855, 4755
Edwards, Henry Stillwell *(Author)* 4504

Edwards, Jack *(Cast)* 1447
Edwards, James *(Composer)* 3739, 4264
Edwards, James *(Lyricist)* 3739, 4264
Edwards, Joan *(Composer)* 197, 858, 859, 4377
Edwards, Joan *(Lyricist)* 197, 858, 4377
Edwards, John *(Lyricist)* 3381
Edwards, Julian *(Composer)* 355, 523, 1071, 1401, 1458, 1521, 1523, 1594, 1910, 2233, 2632, 2673, 2899, 2929, 2966, 3585, 4493, 4614, 4646
Edwards, Julian *(Director)* 1458
Edwards, Julian *(Librettist)* 2673
Edwards, Julian *(Musical Director)* 2673, 4614
Edwards, Leo *(Composer)* 326, 419, 473, 522, 539, 773, 1998, 2696, 2834, 2856, 3009, 3399, 3969, 4440, 4782, 4806, 4807, 4810, 4811, 4814, 4815, 4817, 4838
Edwards, Leo *(Lyricist)* 2696, 3009, 3926, 4654
Edwards, Lotta *(Cast)* 538
Edwards, Marcelle *(Cast)* 1137
Edwards, Michael *(Composer)* 4137
Edwards, Michele *(Costumes)* 624, 2243
Edwards, Nazig *(Cast)* 3239
Edwards, Paula *(Cast)* 2361
Edwards, Randall *(Cast)* 4533
Edwards, Richard *(Cast)* 1337
Edwards, Robert W. *(Composer)* 3384
Edwards, Robert W. *(Musical Director)* 3384
Edwards, S. *(Composer)* 4193
Edwards, S. *(Lyricist)* 4193
Edwards, Sam *(Cast)* 3865
Edwards, Samuel *(Cast)* 2350
Edwards, Sherman *(Composer)* 3897, 4273, 4337
Edwards, Sherman *(Lyricist)* 3897, 4273
Edwards, Snitz *(Cast)* 436, 1888, 2543
Edwards, Tom *(Librettist)* 474
Edwards, Zelda *(Cast)* 3157
Edwards and Edwards *(Cast)* 3804
Edwin, David *(Librettist)* 2771
Efron, Marshall *(Cast)* 3000
Egan, Jack *(Composer)* 4811
Egan, John *(Composer)* 1221, 3540
Egan, Raymond B. *(Lyricist)* 46, 324, 393, 709, 1127, 1689, 1935, 2574, 2856, 2946, 3404, 3430, 3783, 3842, 4393, 4421
Egan, Robert *(Director)* 282
Egan, Susan *(Cast)* 330
Egbert, June *(Cast)* 2602
Egen, Von *(Composer)* 364
Eggerth, Marta *(Cast)* 808, 1894, 3536
Eggett, Charles *(Composer)* 3332
Eglevsky, Andre *(Cast)* 1670
Egnos, Bertha *(Composer)* 2147
Egnos, Bertha *(Director)* 2147
Egnos, Bertha *(Librettist)* 2147
Ehlert, Matt *(Lighting Designer)* 2416
Ehman, Don *(Lighting Designer)* 4030
Ehrenfeld & Assoc., S. *(Producer)* 4773
Ehrenreich, Jake *(Cast)* 2237
Ehrhardt, Bess *(Cast)* 2086
Ehrhardt, Peter M. *(Lighting Designer)* 915, 2026, 2578, 3671
Ehrle, John *(Cast)* 1275

Elliott, Jack *(Lyricist)* 2165, 3683
Elliott, Jack *(Orchestrations)* 786
Elliott, James W. *(Producer)* 670
Elliott, Kenneth *(Director)* 3606, 4518
Elliott, Kenneth *(Lyricist)* 3606
Elliott, Kenneth *(Producer)* 3606
Elliott, Mariana *(Lighting Designer)* 2288
Elliott, Patricia *(Cast)* 2536
Elliott, Paul *(Producer)* 580
Elliott, Robert *(Librettist)* 272
Elliott, Shawn *(Cast)* 775, 4796
Elliott, Sumner Locke *(Librettist)* 2313
Elliott, Verne *(Director)* 2413
Elliott, William *(Composer)* 774, 3197
Elliott, William *(Conductor)* 2359
Elliott, William *(Producer)* 2698
Elliott, Zo *(Composer)* 3259
Ellis, Anita *(Cast)* 1315
Ellis, Antonia *(Cast)* 2702
Ellis, Barbara *(Cast)* 4431
Ellis, Brad *(Cast)* 1350
Ellis, Brad *(Composer)* 4462
Ellis, Brad *(Musical Director)* 1350
Ellis, C.J. *(Lyricist)* 2970
Ellis, Charles T. *(Cast)* 668
Ellis, Charles T. *(Composer)* 668
Ellis, Charles T. *(Librettist)* 668
Ellis, Charles T. *(Lyricist)* 668
Ellis, Chris *(Lighting Designer)* 2798
Ellis, David *(Cast)* 4773
Ellis, Edith *(Librettist)* 2623
Ellis, Evelyn *(Cast)* 467
Ellis, Gene *(Librettist)* 1884
Ellis, Harold *(Librettist)* 470
Ellis, James *(Cast)* 3056
Ellis, John *(Cast)* 2841
Ellis, Larry *(Cast)* 1380
Ellis, Leigh *(Cast)* 611
Ellis, Mary *(Cast)* 715, 972, 3772
Ellis, Maurice *(Cast)* 1987
Ellis, Melville *(Cast)* 965, 1403, 1464, 1963, 2891, 3313,
    3747, 3999, 4430, 4553, 4655
Ellis, Melville *(Composer)* 8, 737, 934, 2825, 2869, 3220,
    3730, 3747, 4154, 4521
Ellis, Melville *(Costumes)* 60, 68, 75, 276, 351, 353,
    558, 965, 1218, 1522, 1578, 1613, 1793, 1963, 2232,
    2317, 2334, 2358, 2696, 2732, 2825, 2854, 2858, 3237,
    3265, 3396, 3397, 3424, 3701, 3865, 4382, 4521, 4555,
    4655, 4657
Ellis, Melville *(Dance Arranger)* 965, 3397
Ellis, Melville *(Lyricist)* 737, 3220
Ellis, Michael *(Director)* 4273
Ellis, Michael *(Producer)* 911, 4499
Ellis, Perry *(Costumes)* 3181
Ellis, Philip *(Orchestrations)* 27
Ellis, Philip *(Vocal Arranger)* 1840
Ellis, Ray *(Dance Arranger)* 3863
Ellis, Ray *(Orchestrations)* 1227
Ellis, Ray *(Vocal Arranger)* 3863
Ellis, Rina *(Cast)* 3669
Ellis, Scott *(Cast)* 1897, 3718

Ellis, Scott *(Director)* 131
Ellis, Sheila *(Cast)* 1103, 4645
Ellis, Toni *(Cast)* 444
Ellis, Vivian *(Composer)* 129, 453, 605, 700, 791, 834,
    1333, 2004, 2547, 2976, 4207, 4667
Ellis, Vivian *(Lyricist)* 129, 791, 2976, 4207
Ellis, Walker *(Cast)* 4284
Ellison, Ben *(Lyricist)* 2640
Ellison, Bob *(Librettist)* 2072
Ellison, Sydney *(Director)* 205, 1522, 2486, 3031,
    3092, 3156
Ellmore Sisters *(Cast)* 2991
Ellsler, Effie *(Cast)* 1517
Ellsner, Joseph *(Lighting Designer)* 396, 1901
Ellstein, Abe *(Composer)* 423, 1279
Ellstein, Abe *(Lyricist)* 1279
Ellstein, Abe *(Musical Director)* 423
Ellstein, Abe *(Orchestrations)* 423
Ellstein, Abraham *(Composer)* 1609, 1679, 2751,
    3670, 4769
Ellstein, Abraham *(Lyricist)* 3670
Ellstein, Abraham *(Musical Director)* 2751
Ellstein, Abraham *(Orchestrations)* 2751
Ellsworth, Eugene *(Composer)* 3073
Ellsworth, Eugene *(Lyricist)* 3073
Ellsworth, Olin *(Composer)* 314
Ellsworth, Olin *(Librettist)* 314
Ellsworth, Olin *(Lyricist)* 314
Ellsworth, Ursula *(Cast)* 2639
Elm City Four, The *(Cast)* 1491
Elmer, George *(Producer)* 944
Elmo, Monte *(Cast)* 1388
Elmore, Steve *(Cast)* 832, 956, 1184, 3075, 3476, 4019
Elmslie, Kenward *(Author)* 774
Elmslie, Kenward *(Librettist)* 1662, 2565
Elmslie, Kenward *(Lyricist)* 237, 392, 774, 1362, 1662,
    2554, 2565, 2678
Elsass, Jeff *(Cast)* 1757
Elsie, Lily *(Cast)* 475
Elsner, Edward *(Director)* 375, 2330, 2967, 3898, 4218
Elsner, Edward *(Producer)* 2330
Elsner, Joseph *(Lighting Designer)* 1208, 1753
Elsom, Isobel *(Cast)* 30
Elson, Anita *(Cast)* 1805
Elson, Charles *(Lighting Designer)* 1290, 2364, 3691, 4693
Elston, Robert *(Cast)* 4111, 4278
Eltinge, Julian *(Cast)* 800, 913, 929, 1177, 1247, 1947,
    2986, 3166, 3173
Eltinge, Julian *(Costumes)* 929
Eltinge, Julian *(Lyricist)* 929, 3425
Elton, Jane *(Cast)* 4508
Elton, William *(Orchestrations)* 3018
Elward, James *(Lyricist)* 932
Elwell *(Set Design)* 1814
Elwin, Maurice *(Lyricist)* 2798
Elzy, Ruby *(Cast)* 1251, 2225, 3541
Embs, Lisa *(Cast)* 2555
Emden, H. *(Set Design)* 2974
Emden, Henry *(Set Design)* 2964
Emens, Homer
    See also Emens & Unitt.

Epstein, I.L. *(Dance Arranger)* 3495
Epstein, I.L. *(Vocal Arranger)* 3495
Epstein, Julius J. *(Author)* 663, 3843
Epstein, Julius J. *(Librettist)* 2057, 3843, 4323
Epstein, L.I. *(Musical Director)* 2257
Epstein, Philip G. *(Author)* 663, 3843
Epstein, Philip G. *(Librettist)* 2057, 4323
Epstein, Pierre *(Cast)* 282, 1190, 1591, 3497, 3602, 4796
Equity Players *(Producer)* 1221
Erckmann *(Author)* 1401
Ercole, Joe *(Composer)* 2285
Ercole, Joe *(Orchestrations)* 2285
Erdman, Ernie *(Composer)* 487, 3404
Erdman, Ernie *(Lyricist)* 487, 3404
Erdman, Jean *(Cast)* 790
Erdman, Jean *(Choreographer)* 4485
Erdman, Jean *(Director)* 790
Erdman, Jean *(Librettist)* 790
Erickson, Leif *(Cast)* 1894, 3493, 4323
Ericson, June *(Cast)* 1362, 3286, 4065, 4585
Erlanger, A.L.
    See also Erlanger Prods., Klaw & Erlanger and Klaw
    & Erlanger Opera Co.
Erlanger, A.L. *(Producer)* 527, 571, 605, 1399, 1643, 1756,
    1965, 2181, 4491, 4760
Erlanger, Alene *(Librettist)* 2739
Erlanger Prods.
    See also A.L. Erlanger, Klaw & Erlanger, Klaw &
    Erlanger Opera Co.
Erlanger Productions *(Producer)* 4043
Erlich, Sam *(Lyricist)* 1824, 1900
Ernie, Val *(Musical Director)* 1889
Ernotte, Andre *(Director)* 829, 1589, 3667, 4216
Ernst, Leila *(Cast)* 2103, 3353
Ernster, Mary *(Cast)* 158
Ernstoff, Jeffrey *(Composer)* 1146
Ernstoff, Jeffrey *(Lyricist)* 1146
Errico, Melissa *(Cast)* 147
Errol, Leon *(Cast)* 425, 683, 959, 1281, 1647, 1919, 1920,
    2403, 2594, 3819, 4712, 4793, 4805, 4806, 4807, 4808,
    4809, 4844
Errol, Leon *(Choreographer)* 78
Errol, Leon *(Composer)* 1117, 1647
Errol, Leon *(Director)* 468, 683, 1919, 1920, 3593, 4033,
    4742, 4808, 4809, 4834, 4839, 4844
Errol, Leon *(Librettist)* 1117, 1647
Errol, Leon *(Lyricist)* 1117, 1647
Errolle, Martha *(Cast)* 2234, 3390
Ershova *(Cast)* 710
Ersi, Elsa *(Cast)* 568
Erskine, Howard *(Producer)* 160
Erte *(Costumes)* 201, 910, 1146, 1485, 1486, 1487, 1488,
    1489, 1490, 1491, 2734, 3150, 4427, 4817, 4818
Erte *(Set Design)* 1146, 2364
Ertegun, Ahmet *(Producer)* 3636
Erwin, Ralph *(Composer)* 2382
Erwin, Stuart *(Cast)* 1679, 3153
Escudero, Vicente *(Orchestrations)* 839
Eskew, Doug *(Cast)* 1296, 4460
Eskew, Jack *(Orchestrations)* 3126
Eskow, Jerome *(Director)* 615, 1319, 3224

Eskow, Jerome *(Librettist)* 1319
Esmond, Annie *(Cast)* 2891
Esmond, Jill *(Cast)* 3597
Esparza, Roberta Delgado *(Cast)* 4861
Espero, Sidonie *(Cast)* 2698
Espinosa, Kelland *(Choreographer)* 3156, 3583
Esposito, Giancarlo *(Cast)* 1073, 2898, 3869
Esposito, Larry *(Musical Director)* 1377
Esposito, Larry *(Vocal Arranger)* 1377
Esposito, Laurence J. *(Musical Director)* 2783
Esposito, Mark *(Cast)* 2416
Essen, Viola *(Cast)* 1948
Essex, Francis *(Lyricist)* 392, 3186
Essler, Fred *(Cast)* 1413
Estabrook, Howard *(Cast)* 2891
Estey, Carol *(Cast)* 181, 1116, 2785
Estey, Robert *(Dance Arranger)* 4102
Estey, Robert *(Musical Director)* 2657, 4102
Estey, Robert *(Vocal Arranger)* 2657, 4102
Estey, Suellen *(Cast)* 597, 825, 1435, 3871, 4022
Estin, Amelia *(Cast)* 1004
Estrin, Melvyn J. *(Producer)* 2242
Esudero, Vicente *(Cast)* 839
Etchison, Gregory *(Set Design)* 1347
Etheridge, Dorothy *(Cast)* 3013
Etra, Will *(Composer)* 3076
Etting, Ruth *(Cast)* 3172, 3980, 4683, 4821, 4823
Ettinger, Daniel *(Set Design)* 3346
Ettlinger, Don *(Librettist)* 101
Eugene, Max C. *(Composer)* 1123, 2986
Eugene Productions *(Producer)* 2207
Eugster, Carl *(Composer)* 2042
Eugster, Carl *(Lyricist)* 2042
Euklewitz, Abel *(Producer)* 3983
Eula, Joe *(Costumes)* 1637
Eureka *(Cast)* 2037, 2488
Euripides *(Author)* 4615
Europe, James Reese *(Composer)* 434, 2025, 2493,
    2964, 3193, 3676, 3945, 3963, 4390
Europe, James Reese *(Lyricist)* 434, 1198, 2025,
    2493, 2964
Eustis, Fred *(Musical Director)* 561
Eustis, Fred J. *(Arrangements)* 3228
Eustis, Fred J. *(Composer)* 476, 3228, 4556
Eustis, Fred J. *(Musical Director)* 3228
Eustis, Frederick *(Composer)* 2963
Eustis, Frederick J. *(Composer)* 625, 976, 2543
Eustis, Frederick J. *(Musical Director)* 976
Evanko, Ed *(Cast)* 634, 2618, 3702
Evans, Al *(Musical Director)* 1286, 1546
Evans, Alan *(Cast)* 2451
Evans, Albert *(Composer)* 3178, 3346
Evans, Albert *(Lyricist)* 2861, 3178
Evans, Albert *(Orchestrations)* 3178
Evans, Albert *(Vocal Arranger)* 3178
Evans, Alfred *(Musical Director)* 3410
Evans, Barbara *(Cast)* 194
Evans, Bobby *(Cast)* 447
Evans, Bruce Balfour *(Lyricist)* 2401
Evans, Charles *(Cast)* 3392, 3943
Evans, Charles *(Set Design)* 413

Evans, Charles E. *(Cast)* 4333

Evans, Craig *(Lighting Designer)* 1258, 1591, 2544, 3125

Evans, David *(Arrangements)* 81

Evans, David *(Composer)* 4, 424

Evans, David *(Librettist)* 424

Evans, David *(Musical Director)* 81, 1510, 1822, 1832

Evans, David *(Vocal Arranger)* 1510, 1832

Evans, Dell *(Cast)* 2455

Evans, Dickie *(Cast)* 1002

Evans, Don *(Librettist)* 2692

Evans, Don *(Lyricist)* 2692

Evans, Don *(Musical Director)* 3970

Evans, Edith *(Cast)* 4152, 4291

Evans, Frank *(Lyricist)* 260

Evans, Freida *(Costumes)* 4157

Evans, Frieda *(Set Design)* 2067

Evans, G. Douglas *(Cast)* 834

Evans, George *(Cast)* 800, 801

Evans, George *(Composer)* 662, 1021

Evans, George *(Lyricist)* 4390

Evans, George "Honey Boy" *(Cast)* 803

Evans, George "Honey Boy" *(Composer)* 1226, 1686, 2978

Evans, George "Honey Boy" *(Lyricist)* 1226, 1686

Evans, Greek *(Cast)* 1182, 3012, 4077, 4271

Evans, Gwyllum *(Cast)* 4244

Evans, Harry *(Librettist)* 2105

Evans, Harvey *(Cast)* 155, 162, 1329, 1478, 3902

Evans, Helena *(Librettist)* 1756

Evans, Helena *(Lyricist)* 1756

Evans, Karen *(Cast)* 1053, 3162, 3806, 4736

Evans, Margie *(Cast)* 202, 1462

Evans, Maurice *(Cast)* 277, 4312

Evans, Maurice *(Producer)* 3188

Evans, Peter *(Cast)* 3339

Evans, Ray *(Composer)* 3182, 3841, 4197, 4321

Evans, Ray *(Lyricist)* 2057, 2449, 3182, 3234, 3841, 4197, 4274, 4321

Evans, Raymond *(Cast)* 2611

Evans, Rex *(Cast)* 700, 1475, 3064, 4368

Evans, Rex *(Composer)* 700

Evans, Sandy *(Cast)* 861

Evans, Sticks *(Musical Director)* 3983

Evans, Thomas *(Choreographer)* 998

Evans, Tudor *(Cast)* 3339

Evans, W.J. *(Set Design)* 2482

Evans, Warwick *(Cast)* 460

Evans, Wilbur *(Cast)* 603, 2847, 4524

Evans, William Kendall *(Lyricist)* 115

Evelyn, John *(Cast)* 429

Evelyn, Judith *(Cast)* 3335

Everage, Kenneth *(Costumes)* 2006

Everall & Wallach Company *(Producer)* 4649

Everard, George *(Composer)* 2986

Everest, John *(Lyricist)* 1035

Everett, Frances *(Cast)* 4253

Everett, Paul *(Lighting Designer)* 1201, 1897

Everett, Tanya *(Cast)* 1265

Everett, Timmy *(Cast)* 2556, 3696

Everhard, Eliot G. *(Orchestrations)* 860

Everhart, Rex *(Cast)* 259, 1955, 3188, 3644, 4013, 4278, 4312, 4727, 4744

Everly, Jack *(Musical Director)* 1633

Everly, Phil *(Composer)* 3739

Everly, Phil *(Lyricist)* 3739

Everson, Patricia Ann *(Cast)* 3987

Everton, Paul *(Cast)* 834

Everybody *(Librettist)* 4421

Evett, Benjamin *(Cast)* 3937

Ewell, Lois *(Cast)* 2836

Ewell, Tom *(Cast)* 3138, 3894, 4018, 4214

Ewing, Bruce C. *(Cast)* 4799

Ewing, Marjorie *(Producer)* 137

Ewing, Max *(Composer)* 1652, 1655, 1656, 1657

Ewing, Max *(Lyricist)* 1656, 1657

Ewing, Sherman *(Producer)* 137

Excell, E.O. *(Composer)* 3261

Excell, E.O. *(Lyricist)* 3261

Extension Company, The *(Producer)* 4405

Eyck, Ten *(Costumes)* 1352

Eyen, Tom *(Director)* 2307, 3636, 4433

Eyen, Tom *(Librettist)* 1103, 2307, 3636, 4403

Eyen, Tom *(Lyricist)* 1103, 2307, 4403

Eyen, Tom *(Producer)* 4433

Eysler, Edmund *(Author)* 473, 2424, 2603, 4553

Eysler, Edmund *(Composer)* 473, 2262, 2424, 2603, 4553, 4726, 4795

Eysler, Edward *(Author)* 2262

Eysler, Edward *(Lyricist)* 3753

Eythe, William *(Cast)* 2439, 2464, 3326

Eythe, William *(Director)* 520

Eythe, William *(Producer)* 2439

Eyton, Frank *(Librettist)* 4174

Eyton, Frank *(Lyricist)* 432, 1618, 3139, 3905, 4367, 4534

Ezell, John *(Set Design)* 1439

F

F.W. Woolworth Company *(Producer)* 2988

F.W.M. Producing Group *(Producer)* 4068

FPC *(Producer)* 2018

Faber, Charles *(Librettist)* 4415

Faber, Ron *(Cast)* 1064, 2646

Fabian, Robert *(Producer)* 1256

Fabiani, Joel *(Cast)* 2607

Fabray, Nanette *(Cast)* 58, 183, 225, 1886, 2187, 2453, 2615, 2705, 2809, 2983, 3036

Fabrizi, Aldo *(Cast)* 3798

Factora, Marshall *(Cast)* 114

Faded Glory *(Costumes)* 843

Fagan *(Lyricist)* 4805

Fagan, Barney *(Cast)* 3968

Fagan, Barney *(Choreographer)* 2722

Fagan, Barney *(Composer)* 191, 604, 1897

Fagan, Barney *(Lyricist)* 191, 1897

Fagan, Garth *(Choreographer)* 3628

Fagan, Garth *(Director)* 3628

Fagan, J.B. *(Librettist)* 129

Fagan, Joan *(Cast)* 1076

Fagan, Scott *(Composer)* 4089
Fagan, Scott *(Lyricist)* 4089
Fagerbakke, Bill *(Cast)* 262
Fagin, Gary S. *(Orchestrations)* 3175
Faibsey *(Costumes)* 2900, 3230, 3400, 3737, 4422
Fain, Sammy *(Author)* 616
Fain, Sammy *(Cast)* 447
Fain, Sammy *(Composer)* 59, 145, 190, 447, 512, 616, 673, 710, 751, 1034, 1207, 1300, 1494, 1813, 1840, 2234, 2246, 2772, 2850, 3046, 3166, 3178, 3356, 3404, 3713, 3739, 3789, 3916, 4010, 4060, 4086, 4137, 4428, 4825, 4828, 4829
Fair, Thelma *(Cast)* 2986, 4646
Fairbanks, Ethel *(Cast)* 77
Fairbanks, Gladys *(Cast)* 3686
Fairbanks, Madeleine *(Cast)* 86, 1747, 1780, 2818, 4491
Fairbanks, Marion *(Cast)* 1643, 4491
Fairbanks, Nola *(Cast)* 2023, 2024, 2099, 3151
Fairbanks Jr., Douglas *(Cast)* 635, 1243
Fairbanks Twins, The *(Cast)* 1489, 3007, 3243, 4812, 4813, 4843, 4853
Fairbrother, Sydney *(Cast)* 333, 1454
Fairchild, Charlotte *(Cast)* 3439
Fairchild, Edgar *(Cast)* 622, 931
Fairchild, Edgar *(Composer)* 2105, 2396, 3130
Fairleigh, Harry *(Cast)* 3753, 4425, 4590
Fairman, George *(Composer)* 4814
Faison, George *(Cast)* 3610
Faison, George *(Choreographer)* 166, 789, 1072, 2949, 3991, 4004, 4722
Faison, George *(Composer)* 3991, 4722
Faison, George *(Director)* 166, 789, 3991, 4004
Faison, George *(Librettist)* 166, 789, 3991
Faison, George *(Lyricist)* 166, 3991
Faison, Sandy *(Cast)* 150, 699, 2152
Falabella, John *(Costumes)* 426, 900, 1797, 3444, 4279
Falabella, John *(Set Design)* 426, 478, 900, 1797, 2177, 3444, 4279
Falana, Lola *(Cast)* 108, 1063
Falco, Anthony *(Cast)* 3126
Falconer, Helen *(Cast)* 736, 2184
Falconer, Sheila *(Choreographer)* 3429
Falk, Eleanor *(Cast)* 4242
Falk, Henri *(Author)* 3079
Falk, Lee *(Librettist)* 1754
Falk, Willy *(Cast)* 2754, 2905
Falkenburg, Jinx *(Cast)* 1931
Fall, Leo *(Author)* 1067, 1555, 2249, 2469, 2666, 3996
Fall, Leo *(Composer)* 1066, 1067, 1197, 1555, 2249, 2469, 2666, 3778, 3996
Fall, Richard *(Composer)* 710, 1067, 4667
Fallon, Eva *(Cast)* 256, 1003, 1151, 1975, 2603, 2854, 2929, 3590, 3613, 4056, 4187, 4634, 4762
Fallon, Larry *(Dance Arranger)* 692
Fallon, Larry *(Musical Director)* 3428
Fallon, Larry *(Orchestrations)* 692, 1809, 3869
Fallon, Larry *(Vocal Arranger)* 692
Falls, Arlene *(Costumes)* 2159, 2347, 3068
Falls, Charles B. *(Set Design)* 1685
Falls, Robert *(Director)* 494
Famous People Players *(Producer)* 2521

Fanale, Susan *(Cast)* 1757
Fanchon, Miss *(Choreographer)* 2085
Fanchon, Miss *(Costumes)* 3842
Fanchon, Miss *(Director)* 2085, 2086, 2087
Fanchon & Marco
    See also Miss Fanchon and Marco.
Fanchon & Marco *(Cast)* 3842, 4211
Fanchon & Marco *(Composer)* 3842, 4211
Fanchon & Marco *(Director)* 4211
Fanchon & Marco *(Librettist)* 4211
Fanchon & Marco *(Lyricist)* 3842, 4211
Fanchon & Marco *(Producer)* 3842, 4128, 4211
Fanchonetti, Marie *(Cast)* 1565
Fancy, Richard *(Cast)* 3992
Fantasy Factory, The *(Producer)* 1450, 2776
Faraday, P. Michael *(Director)* 1554
Faraday, P. Michael *(Producer)* 1554
Farago, Geza *(Costumes)* 4154
Farago, Geza *(Set Design)* 4154
Farago, Jeno *(Author)* 2622, 4669
Farber, Mitch *(Orchestrations)* 3126
Farber, Sandy *(Producer)* 249, 1380, 4186
Farbman, Abel *(Producer)* 4435
Farer, Ronnie *(Cast)* 674
Fargue, Annie *(Producer)* 3739
Faria, Arthur *(Cast)* 1497, 4196
Faria, Arthur *(Choreographer)* 547, 583, 4162, 4454
Faria, Arthur *(Director)* 583, 4162
Faria, Scott *(Director)* 1159
Fariday, Mary *(Choreographer)* 4405
Farina, Marilyn *(Cast)* 3211
Faris, Alexander *(Musical Director)* 299, 3756
Faris, Alexander *(Vocal Arranger)* 299
Farjeon, Eleanor *(Librettist)* 4479
Farjeon, Eleanor *(Lyricist)* 4479
Farjeon, Herbert *(Librettist)* 2227, 2483, 4153, 4416
Farjeon, Herbert *(Lyricist)* 3107, 4153
Farkas, Carl *(Author)* 3756
Farkas, Jonathan *(Producer)* 3718
Farkas, Karl *(Author)* 4730, 4777
Farkas, Karl *(Director)* 2755
Farkas, Karl *(Librettist)* 2755, 4792
Farkas, Karl *(Lyricist)* 2755, 4792
Farkoa, Maurice *(Cast)* 1095, 2825, 2891, 4354, 4418
Farleigh, Harry *(Cast)* 3820
Farley, Alice *(Costumes)* 2970
Farley, Edward *(Composer)* 393, 1813
Farley, Edward *(Lyricist)* 393
Farley, J.J. *(Cast)* 1636
Farley, Morgan *(Cast)* 4284
Farnham, Hilda *(Costumes)* 691
Farnum, Dustin *(Cast)* 3759
Farnum, Franklyn *(Cast)* 1606
Farnum, Hilda *(Costumes)* 1876
Farnum, William *(Cast)* 4671
Farr, Kimberly *(Cast)* 572, 1762, 2953, 2962, 3925
Farr, Lowell *(Musical Director)* 3215
Farrar, Tony *(Cast)* 3105
Farrell, Anthony B. *(Producer)* 67, 1791
Farrell, Anthony Brady *(Producer)* 145, 183, 4314
Farrell, Charles *(Cast)* 4207

Farrell, Charles *(Lyricist)* 4823
Farrell, Genevieve *(Lyricist)* 574
Farrell, Isabelle *(Cast)* 4243, 4337
Farrell, Kevin *(Musical Director)* 550
Farrell, Peter *(Cast)* 2153
Farrell, W.H. *(Composer)* 3953
Farrell, W.H. *(Lyricist)* 3953
Farrell, William H. *(Composer)* 1120
Farrell, William H. *(Lyricist)* 1120
Farren, Jack *(Producer)* 4522
Farrington, Frank *(Cast)* 1553
Farrow, Mia *(Cast)* 3454
Farwell, Tommy *(Cast)* 304
Fashion Productions *(Producer)* 1250
Fasman, Barry *(Composer)* 1298
Fasman, Barry *(Lyricist)* 1298
Fassell, Otto *(Cast)* 3639
Fata, Wesley *(Choreographer)* 2945, 3136, 3169, 3873
Fatone, Charles *(Costumes)* 1018
Faulkner, Rex *(Cast)* 1337
Faulkner, Virginia *(Librettist)* 70
Faulkner, Virginia *(Lyricist)* 70
Faulkner, Walter H. *(Lyricist)* 4735
Faun, Florence *(Cast)* 3130
Faussett, Hudson *(Director)* 3810
Faussett, Hudson *(Producer)* 3810
Faust, Allen *(Orchestrations)* 3126
Faust, Lotta *(Cast)* 666, 1526, 2465, 2858, 2869, 4666, 4735
Faversham, William *(Cast)* 3974
Faversham, William *(Director)* 3974
Fawcett, George *(Cast)* 1501
Fay, Elfie *(Cast)* 349
Fay, Frank *(Cast)* 199, 1378, 1557, 1779, 2104, 2214, 3258, 3402, 3662, 4291
Fay, Frank *(Composer)* 2104
Fay, Frank *(Director)* 1378, 4291
Fay, Frank *(Librettist)* 1378, 2104, 4291
Fay, Frank *(Lyricist)* 2104, 4291
Fay, Frank *(Producer)* 4291
Fay, Gus *(Cast)* 116, 332, 2107
Fay, Meagen *(Cast)* 2065
Fay, Patricia *(Cast)* 991
Fay, Sally *(Composer)* 3181
Fay, Sally *(Lyricist)* 3181
Fay, Thomas *(Arrangements)* 951
Fay, Thomas *(Composer)* 4601
Fay, Thomas *(Dance Arranger)* 4019
Fay, Thomas *(Lyricist)* 4601
Fay, Thomas *(Musical Director)* 951, 4109
Fay, Tom *(Arrangements)* 4027
Fay, Tom *(Dance Arranger)* 1699, 2702, 2822, 3718
Fay, Tom *(Musical Director)* 2702, 4027, 4518
Fay, Vivian *(Cast)* 1481, 2813
Faye, Alice *(Cast)* 1492
Faye, Francis *(Cast)* 204
Faye, Herbie *(Cast)* 4423
Faye, Joey *(Cast)* 84, 98, 843, 1112, 1699, 1842, 1886, 2523, 2653, 2657, 3900, 3990, 4180, 4423
Fazakas, Franz *(Puppeteer)* 2726
Fazan, Eleanor *(Choreographer)* 194, 1644

Fazan, Eleanor *(Director)* 1644
Fazioli, Billy *(Composer)* 1154
Fearnley, John *(Cast)* 4374
Fearnley, John *(Director)* 4153
Fearnley, John *(Producer)* 2680
Fearon, Ed *(Composer)* 4433
Fearon, Ed *(Librettist)* 4433
Fearon, Ed *(Lyricist)* 2279, 4433
Fears, Peggy *(Cast)* 1784, 3179, 3796, 4819
Fears, Peggy *(Producer)* 3014
Feaster, Carl *(Composer)* 3739, 4264
Feaster, Carl *(Lyricist)* 3739, 4264
Feaster, Claude *(Composer)* 4264
Feaster, Claude *(Lyricist)* 4264
Feather, Lorraine *(Cast)* 4584
Fechheimer, Richard *(Lyricist)* 627, 1175
Fechheimer, Richard B. *(Cast)* 1632
Fechheimer, Richard B. *(Librettist)* 1632
Fechheimer, Richard B. *(Lyricist)* 1632
Fechner, Dianina *(Cast)* 710
Feder *(Lighting Designer)* 223, 477, 507, 622, 623, 652, 1063, 1366, 1614, 1634, 1698, 1931, 3038, 3104, 3274, 3495, 3899, 4366, 4386
Feder *(Set Design)* 477, 507
Feder, Abe *(Lighting Designer)* 4706
Federal Theatre Project *(Producer)* 1337
Fedor, Marck Adrian *(Producer)* 3311
Fehlhaber, Fred R. *(Producer)* 161
Feiffer, Jules *(Author)* 170
Feiffer, Jules *(Librettist)* 2611, 3233, 4535, 4746
Feiffer, Jules *(Lyricist)* 2611
Feigay, Paul *(Producer)* 404, 490, 1062, 1742, 2097, 3278
Feigenbaum, Ziske *(Composer)* 1609
Fein, Lupin *(Composer)* 875, 885
Fein, Lupin *(Lyricist)* 885, 2540
Feiner, Harry *(Set Design)* 760
Feiner, Herman *(Author)* 4352
Feingold, Michael *(Lyricist)* 369
Feinstein, Michael (English Lyrics) 4371
Feinstein, Michael *(Librettist)* 4371
Feirce, Louis *(Cast)* 2008
Feist, Felix F. *(Lyricist)* 1318, 1520, 4012, 4723
Feist, Frances *(Costumes)* 447, 4772
Fekaris, Dino *(Composer)* 3739
Fekaris, Dino *(Lyricist)* 3739
Feld, Eliot *(Cast)* 3831
Feld, Kenneth *(Producer)* 3840
Felder, Clarence *(Cast)* 3684, 4295
Feldkamp, Walter *(Composer)* 3103
Feldman, Al *(Composer)* 887
Feldman, Al *(Lyricist)* 887
Feldman, Dick *(Director)* 192
Feldman, Jack *(Composer)* 829, 2022, 2677
Feldman, Jack *(Librettist)* 846
Feldman, Jack *(Lyricist)* 829, 846, 2022, 2677
Feldman, Peter *(Cast)* 1056
Feldon, Barbara *(Cast)* 944
Feldshuh, Tovah *(Cast)* 518, 946, 1832, 3743, 3838, 4167
Feldstein, Robert D. *(Producer)* 2876, 3988, 4292
Felgemacher, Olga *(Puppeteer)* 56, 997, 3449, 3498, 4660, 4710

Felix, Edmund (*Costumes*) 139

Felix, Hugo (*Author*) 2667

Felix, Hugo (*Composer*) 2412, 2667, 2756, 3431, 3534, 3537, 3618, 3829, 4248, 4285

Felix, Hugo (*Lyricist*) 3829

Felix, Seymour (*Choreographer*) 200, 391, 1461, 1780, 1831, 1916, 2135, 3084, 3407, 3436, 3766, 3980, 4010, 4177, 4208, 4424, 4683

Felix, Seymour (*Director*) 1267, 1831, 4846

Feller, Sid (*Musical Director*) 928

Fellini, Federico (*Author*) 1189, 2368, 3171, 4238

Fellows, Don (*Cast*) 1471

Fellows, Edith (*Cast*) 2595

Femia, Tommy (*Cast*) 2022

Fender, Harry (*Cast*) 2594

Fenderson, Alonzo (*Cast*) 291, 980, 984, 1050, 1960, 2013, 2942, 4520

Fenholt, Jeff (*Cast*) 2212

Fenn, Frederick (*Librettist*) 1554

Fenn, Jean (*Cast*) 1369

Fenning, Stephen (*Cast*) 4034

Fenstock, Belle (*Composer*) 417, 3140

Fenton, Frank (*Cast*) 3219

Fenton, Mabel (*Cast*) 1505, 1900, 4044

Fenwick, Herbert (*Cast*) 1610

Fenwick, Irene (*Cast*) 94

Fenwick, John (*Dance Arranger*) 1255

Fenwick, John (Music Adaptation) 1255

Fenwick, John (*Musical Director*) 148

Fenwick, John (*Orchestrations*) 148, 1255, 3818

Fenwick, John (*Vocal Arranger*) 1255

Feranda, Fredda (*Orchestrations*) 27

Ferber, Edna (*Author*) 3787, 3837, 3949

Ferden, Dennis (*Cast*) 3539

Ferdinand, Edmund J. (*Producer*) 4678

Ferdos (*Librettist*) 1995

Ferdos (*Lyricist*) 1995

Ferguson, Allyn (*Orchestrations*) 786, 4566

Ferguson, Elsie (*Cast*) 1537, 2885

Ferguson, Lester (*Cast*) 2910

Ferguson, Lorena (*Cast*) 421

Ferguson, Robert V. (*Cast*) 2662

Ferland, Danielle (*Cast*) 2143, 3368, 3377

Fernandez, Bijou (*Cast*) 2068

Fernandez, Jose (*Librettist*) 1164, 1236

Ferrante, Elena (*Cast*) 3169

Ferrari, Gustave (*Musical Director*) 758

Ferrat, Jean (*Composer*) 1865

Ferrat, Jean (*Lyricist*) 1865

Ferre, Cliff (*Choreographer*) 3683

Ferrer, Jose (*Cast*) 1564, 4073

Ferrer, Jose (*Director*) 652, 2268, 3234

Ferrer, Jose (*Librettist*) 3234, 4073

Ferrer, Richard (*Set Design*) 3653

Ferris (*Composer*) 4093

Ferris (*Lyricist*) 4093

Ferris, Chet (*Costumes*) 1348

Festa, James (*Cast*) 1004

Fetchit, Stepin (*Cast*) 4586

Fetter, Ted (*Cast*) 1448, 2252

Fetter, Ted (*Lyricist*) 173, 397, 557, 612, 1191, 1286,

1546, 2460, 2707, 2940, 3082, 3861, 3914, 3955, 4335, 4498, 4665, 4670, 4799

Fetzko, Donald C. (*Producer*) 1046

Feuer, Cy (*Director*) 2064, 2523, 3972, 4013, 4588, 4682

Feuer, Cy (*Librettist*) 4682

Feuer, Cy (*Producer*) 16, 507, 629, 1706, 2019, 2523, 3972, 4013, 4588, 4652, 4682

Feuer, Howard (*Producer*) 4019

Feuer, Jed (*Composer*) 1149

Feuer, Jed (*Vocal Arranger*) 1149

Fevrier, Henri (*Composer*) 165

Feydeau, Georges (*Author*) 1538, 1993, 3156

Feyder, Jacques (*Author*) 657

Ffolkes, David (*Costumes*) 95, 530, 1300, 3895, 4015, 4652

Ffolkes, David (*Set Design*) 4652

Fiander, Lewis (*Cast*) 2047

Fibich, Felix (*Choreographer*) 2866, 3670, 3781

Fichandler, Zelda (*Producer*) 2579

Fickett, Homer (*Librettist*) 3104

Fidler, Samuel (*Musical Director*) 1397

Fieg, Jonathan (*Cast*) 3806

Fieger, Addy (*Composer*) 692, 1010

Field, Alice (*Producer*) 140

Field, B. Eugene (*Director*) 489

Field, Betty (*Cast*) 4495

Field, Billy (*Composer*) 1298

Field, Billy (*Lyricist*) 1298

Field, Daniel Thomas (*Set Design*) 3764

Field, Grace (*Cast*) 2528, 2931, 3679

Field, Leonard (*Producer*) 3563

Field, Robin (*Cast*) 4102

Field, Ron (*Choreographer*) 167, 610, 615, 1298, 2318, 3210, 3644, 4862

Field, Ron (*Director*) 167, 1298, 2318, 3499

Field, Sylvia (*Cast*) 3324

Fielding, Harold (*Producer*) 1616, 1721, 1741

Fielding, Henry (*Author*) 2563, 4404, 4406

Fielding, Jerry (*Arrangements*) 1326

Fielding, Marjery (*Choreographer*) 3594, 3975, 4117, 4265

Fielding, Marjery (*Composer*) 3594

Fielding, Marjery (*Director*) 3375

Fielding, Marjery (*Lyricist*) 3594

Fielding, May (*Cast*) 762

Fields, Ada (*Costumes*) 1484, 3443, 3723, 4816

Fields, Al (*Cast*) 3133

Fields, Arthur (*Composer*) 1738, 4655

Fields, Arthur (*Lyricist*) 3401, 3589, 4589

Fields, Benny (*Cast*) 1693

Fields, Bertha A. (*Costumes*) 2264

Fields, Chip (*Cast*) 1073

Fields, Clare (*Cast*) 3181

Fields, Dolly (*Cast*) 1457

Fields, Dorothy (*Cast*) 738, 3153, 3595, 3639, 3848, 4780

Fields, Dorothy (*Librettist*) 153, 183, 603, 2453, 2847, 3687, 4058, 4524

Fields, Dorothy (*Lyricist*) 39, 183, 393, 432, 441, 442, 603, 787, 892, 893, 894, 895, 1168, 1827, 1928, 2140, 2204, 2267, 2294, 2297, 2372, 2772, 3428, 3639, 3687, 3704, 3709, 3869, 3905, 3946, 3993, 4142, 4152, 4197, 4238, 4446, 4524, 4534, 4545, 4847, 4848

Fields, Florence *(Cast)* 4439
Fields, Frank *(Composer)* 3938
Fields, Frank *(Orchestrations)* 3938
Fields, Herbert
    See also Herbert Richard Lorenz.
Fields, Herbert *(Cast)* 2574
Fields, Herbert *(Choreographer)* 1321, 1446, 1447, 4781
Fields, Herbert *(Director)* 978, 2102, 2193, 3595, 3848,
    4058, 4304
Fields, Herbert *(Librettist)* 111, 153, 183, 603, 711,
    834, 978, 1013, 1109, 1272, 1447, 1529, 1827, 1916,
    1944, 2453, 2847, 3131, 3379, 3436, 3556, 3687, 4058,
    4524, 4709
Fields, Herbert *(Lyricist)* 978, 3538, 3595, 4780
Fields, Herbert *(Producer)* 3359
Fields, Joe *(Cast)* 40, 1672
Fields, Joseph *(Author)* 2267, 4734
Fields, Joseph *(Librettist)* 1315, 1475, 1548, 2653, 4734
Fields, Joseph *(Producer)* 1315
Fields, Lew *(Cast)* 8, 60, 182, 258, 301, 465, 677, 940,
    1217, 1264, 1526, 1827, 1845, 1900, 1926, 1927, 2041,
    2160, 2574, 2814, 2900, 3265, 3303, 3632, 3639, 3755,
    4033, 4148, 4203, 4478, 4511, 4658, 4681, 4797
Fields, Lew *(Director)* 1689, 1690, 1916, 4478, 4545
Fields, Lew *(Librettist)* 1690, 2574, 3538
Fields, Lew *(Producer)* 8, 60, 182, 301, 677, 711, 834, 940,
    1188, 1217, 1264, 1526, 1529, 1578, 1738, 1827, 1845,
    1916, 1926, 1927, 2160, 2232, 2262, 2814, 2858, 2869,
    3096, 3265, 3303, 3436, 3525, 3538, 3556, 3575, 3632,
    3773, 4033, 4203, 4206, 4228, 4382, 4478, 4545, 4658,
    4681, 4687, 4757, 4797
Fields, Nat *(Cast)* 2232
Fields, Nelson *(Costumes)* 2573
Fields, Richard *(Producer)* 3927
Fields, Ronnie *(Choreographer)* 3725
Fields, Ruth *(Cast)* 4462
Fields, Sol *(Director)* 3384
Fields, W.C. *(Cast)* 288, 827, 1134, 1485, 1731, 2403,
    3540, 4809, 4810, 4811, 4812, 4814, 4815, 4818, 4819,
    4831, 4840, 4842
Fields, W.C. *(Librettist)* 1134, 1485, 4819
Fier, Newman *(Composer)* 1395
Fier, Newman *(Lyricist)* 1395
Fierstein, Harvey *(Cast)* 1304
Fierstein, Harvey *(Librettist)* 1304, 2360, 2437
Fierstein, Harvey *(Lyricist)* 1304
Fifth Avenue Productions *(Producer)* 154, 1636
Figman, Max *(Cast)* 523, 1110, 1599, 2309, 3117,
    4539, 4620
Figman, Max *(Director)* 3673, 4539
Figman, Max *(Librettist)* 47
Figman, Oscar *(Cast)* 1259, 1308, 2293, 2489,
    3431, 4597
Fillip, Joe *(Cast)* 4774
Fillmore, Clyde *(Cast)* 1225, 4420
Fillmore, Nellie *(Cast)* 4648
Fillmore, Russell *(Cast)* 3415
Fillmore, Russell *(Director)* 2479, 3415
Fimberg, Hal *(Librettist)* 3, 2259
Fimberg, Hal *(Lyricist)* 2259
Finch, R. Thomas *(Set Design)* 1978

Finchley *(Costumes)* 2148, 2569, 4555
Finck, Henry *(Cast)* 697
Finck, Herman *(Composer)* 186, 1176, 1544, 1845,
    2891, 3020, 3096, 3259, 3397, 3398
Finck, Herman *(Lyricist)* 3259
Findlay, Agnes *(Cast)* 235, 2716, 3363
Findlay, Diane *(Cast)* 825, 4022
Findlay, Hal *(Musical Director)* 2640
Findlay, Thomas *(Cast)* 4066
Findley, Danielle *(Cast)* 154
Fine, Laura *(Director)* 760
Fine, Sylvia *(Composer)* 2453, 4166
Fine, Sylvia *(Lyricist)* 2453, 4166
Finger, Leonard *(Producer)* 583
Finger, Thelma *(Producer)* 4005
Fingerhut, Arden *(Lighting Designer)* 54, 474,
    1684, 1715, 1787, 2877, 3277, 4294, 4517
Fingleton, Anthony *(Producer)* 3555
Fink, Mitchell *(Producer)* 4659
Finkbinder, T.G. *(Cast)* 1155
Finkel, Alicia *(Costumes)* 2375
Finkel, Alicia *(Set Design)* 2375
Finkel, Barry *(Cast)* 198, 2654
Finkel, Barry *(Choreographer)* 2654
Finkel, Elliot *(Composer)* 1279
Finkel, Elliot *(Musical Director)* 3669
Finkel, Fyvush *(Cast)* 1279
Finkelstein, Norman *(Lighting Designer)* 4243
Finkelstein, Richard *(Set Design)* 114
Finkle, David *(Composer)* 3181
Finkle, David *(Lyricist)* 2043, 2075, 2279, 2913,
    3181, 3479
Finklehoffe, Fred *(Librettist)* 1879
Finklehoffe, Fred F. *(Author)* 2805
Finklehoffe, Fred F. *(Director)* 145
Finklehoffe, Fred F. *(Librettist)* 447
Finklehoffe, Fred F. *(Producer)* 145, 1205
Finletter, Gretchen *(Librettist)* 1448
Finley, Grace *(Cast)* 148
Finley, Pat *(Cast)* 1697
Finn, Robyn *(Cast)* 2578
Finn, Terry *(Cast)* 2822
Finn, William *(Composer)* 109, 1234, 2132, 2746, 3757
Finn, William *(Librettist)* 1234, 2132, 2746, 3757
Finn, William *(Lyricist)* 109, 975, 1234, 2132, 2746, 3757
Finn Productions, Jeffrey *(Producer)* 4016
Finner, Leigh *(Cast)* 2784
Finnerty, Mary Sue *(Cast)* 3743
Finney, Mary *(Cast)* 1290, 1760
Finocchiaro, Paul *(Cast)* 4799
Fiocca, Richard *(Musical Director)* 1450
Fiocca, Richard *(Orchestrations)* 1450
Fiocca, Richard *(Vocal Arranger)* 1450
Fiordellsi, Angelina *(Cast)* 1785
Fiore, Roland *(Musical Director)* 3064
Fiorentino, Imero *(Lighting Designer)* 3159
Fiorini, Lando *(Cast)* 3798
Fiorito, Ted *(Composer)* 393, 3962
Fiorito, Ted *(Lyricist)* 487, 3962
Fippinger, Lynne *(Choreographer)* 4696
Firbank, Ronald *(Author)* 4541

First, Harry *(Cast)* 1531
First All Children's Th. *(Producer)* 3164
First Durante Tour Company *(Producer)* 1120
Firth, Shephard *(Librettist)* 2389
Firth, Tazeena *(Costumes)* 1211
Firth, Tazeena *(Set Design)* 1068, 1211
Fischer, Clifford C. *(Producer)* 822, 3121, 3594
Fischer, Robert *(Cast)* 1680
Fischer, Robert C. *(Cast)* 2786, 4234
Fischer, William S. *(Composer)* 2332
Fischoff, George *(Composer)* 1497, 3571, 3851
Fish, Donald *(Cast)* 2676
Fishback, Cliff *(Composer)* 226
Fishback, John *(Lighting Designer)* 3557
Fishback, John *(Producer)* 3557
Fishbein, Zenon *(Musical Director)* 2178
Fishburne, Larry *(Cast)* 4535
Fishburne, Larry *(Librettist)* 4535
Fisher, Al *(Choreographer)* 1971
Fisher, Alex *(Cast)* 4177
Fisher, Alfred *(Cast)* 2119
Fisher, Alice *(Cast)* 830, 1417, 3488, 4148
Fisher, Bruce *(Composer)* 3739
Fisher, Bruce *(Lyricist)* 3739
Fisher, Bud *(Author)* 3021, 3024, 3026, 3028
Fisher, Bud *(Librettist)* 3021
Fisher, Carrie *(Cast)* 682
Fisher, Donald *(Producer)* 4774
Fisher, Doris *(Composer)* 1773, 1951
Fisher, Doris *(Lyricist)* 1773
Fisher, Fred *(Composer)* 39, 89, 351, 393, 822, 917, 965,
    1065, 1246, 1773, 1963, 2336, 2706, 2826, 2857, 3086,
    3429, 3432, 3926, 3980, 4589, 4807, 4815, 4823
Fisher, Fred *(Lyricist)* 25, 39, 393, 917, 965, 1154, 1773,
    2706, 2857, 3086, 3926, 4375, 4815
Fisher, Gary *(Lyricist)* 3901
Fisher, Grace *(Cast)* 2112, 2619
Fisher, Ham *(Author)* 3025
Fisher, Ham *(Librettist)* 2653
Fisher, Harrison *(Cast)* 1399
Fisher, Harrison *(Dance Arranger)* 280
Fisher, Harrison *(Musical Director)* 280, 564, 4172
Fisher, Harrison *(Orchestrations)* 1435
Fisher, Harry *(Cast)* 8, 2160, 2358, 2428, 2858
Fisher, Harry S. *(Cast)* 1902
Fisher, Irving *(Cast)* 683, 805, 959, 1533, 2373, 2637,
    3179, 3819, 3962, 4811, 4818
Fisher, Irving *(Lyricist)* 2373, 2587
Fisher, Irving *(Pianist)* 3133
Fisher, J.W. *(Producer)* 652
Fisher, John C. *(Director)* 3976
Fisher, John C. *(Producer)* 246, 248, 1016, 1313, 1579,
    2716, 2803, 3588, 3976
Fisher, Jules *(Lighting Designer)* 71, 162, 298, 373, 393,
    424, 594, 634, 723, 754, 756, 964, 1018, 1060, 1195, 1319,
    1427, 1441, 1596, 1649, 1697, 1717, 1721, 1727, 1761,
    1822, 1841, 1864, 1891, 1974, 2200, 2212, 2360, 2437,
    2558, 2568, 2617, 2659, 2728, 2874, 2925, 3039, 3217,
    3338, 3482, 3506, 3602, 3636, 3644, 3725, 3739, 3741,
    3788, 3869, 3903, 4019, 4068, 4089, 4111, 4380, 4449,
    4560, 4695, 4737, 4764, 4783

Fisher, Jules *(Producer)* 964, 975, 3718, 3739
Fisher, Linda *(Costumes)* 262, 482, 1372, 2290, 3195
Fisher, Lola *(Cast)* 1623
Fisher, M. Anthony *(Producer)* 394, 2143
Fisher, Madelyn *(Cast)* 3025
Fisher, Marvin *(Composer)* 4827
Fisher, Marvin *(Lyricist)* 4153
Fisher, Mary *(Costumes)* 292
Fisher, Mary L. *(Lyricist)* 474
Fisher, Max *(Musical Director)* 3173
Fisher, Nelle *(Cast)* 2707, 3947
Fisher, Nelle *(Choreographer)* 3664, 3810
Fisher, Rick *(Lighting Designer)* 3884
Fisher, Robert *(Musical Director)* 4454
Fisher, Robert *(Vocal Arranger)* 4454
Fisher, Ruth *(Cast)* 4825
Fisher, Sallie *(Cast)* 405, 744, 1199, 1801, 2347, 2923,
    3579, 3882, 4185, 4293, 4603, 4726
Fisher, Snow *(Cast)* 26
Fisher, Susie *(Cast)* 2493
Fisher, Sydney *(Composer)* 4303
Fisher, William Arms *(Composer)* 1813
Fisher, William Arms *(Lyricist)* 1813
Fisher Theatre Foundation *(Producer)* 699, 1897, 2783
Fisher and His Orchestra, Max *(Cast)* 1947
Fiske, George *(Cast)* 2159
Fiske, Robert *(Cast)* 3048
Fistos, John *(Cast)* 1740
Fitch, Bob *(Cast)* 937
Fitch, Clyde *(Author)* 324, 325, 472, 642, 643, 1897,
    2494, 3056
Fitch, Clyde *(Director)* 472
Fitch, George *(Lyricist)* 637
Fitch, Robert *(Cast)* 150, 798, 1059, 2590, 2660,
    2887, 3603
Fite, Mark *(Cast)* 778
Fitt, Tom *(Vocal Arranger)* 74
Fitts, Dudley *(Author)* 1636
Fitz *(Composer)* 3566
Fitz *(Lyricist)* 3566
Fitz, Erica *(Cast)* 4329
FitzPatrick, Eileen *(Cast)* 99
Fitzgerald, Ara *(Choreographer)* 1589, 2648
Fitzgerald, Aubrey *(Lyricist)* 1537
Fitzgerald, Ella *(Composer)* 887
Fitzgerald, Ella *(Lyricist)* 887, 4534
Fitzgerald, F. Scott *(Author)* 1451
Fitzgerald, Geraldine *(Cast)* 951, 4175
Fitzgerald, Geraldine *(Director)* 4398
Fitzgerald, Geraldine *(Librettist)* 951, 4175
Fitzgerald, Kathy *(Cast)* 4255
Fitzgerald, Lillian *(Cast)* 125, 467, 1773, 2835, 4437
Fitzgerald, Robert *(Author)* 1636
Fitzgerald, William H. *(Director)* 4559
Fitzgerald Jr., Louis *(Cast)* 934
Fitzgerald Jr., Louis *(Librettist)* 934
Fitzgibbon, Bert *(Composer)* 4094
Fitzgibbon, Bert *(Lyricist)* 4094
Fitzgibbon, Dave *(Cast)* 2467, 4320, 4583
Fitzgibbon, David E. *(Director)* 1880
Fitzgibbon, Dorothy *(Cast)* 3849, 4335, 4583

Fitzhugh, Ellen *(Additional Lyrics)*   146
Fitzhugh, Ellen *(Cast)*   2703
Fitzhugh, Ellen *(Lyricist)*   1038, 1186, 1699, 1861, 1872, 3364
Fitzhugh, Ida *(Cast)*   1183, 1305
Fitzhugh, Louise *(Author)*   4286
Fitzhugh, Venita *(Cast)*   1544, 2761
Fitziu, Anna *(Cast)*   308
Fitziu, Anna *(Lyricist)*   3137
Fitzpatrick, Allen *(Cast)*   2185
Fitzpatrick, Any *(Cast)*   2521
Fitzpatrick, Colleen *(Cast)*   3411
Fitzpatrick, Jim *(Cast)*   760
Fitzpatrick, M.J. *(Composer)*   4589
Fitzpatrick, Margaret *(Cast)*   1445
Fitzsimmons, Robert *(Cast)*   3871
Five Blind Boys of Alabama *(Cast)*   1636
Flack, Nanette *(Cast)*   286, 378, 1631, 1831, 2407, 3192, 4452
Flack, Roberta *(Voice)*   4391
Flack, W.E. *(Producer)*   4859
Flagg, Fannie *(Cast)*   1750, 2279
Flagg, Fannie *(Librettist)*   2279
Flagg, James Montgomery *(Librettist)*   199
Flaherty, Hugh *(Choreographer)*   1912
Flaherty, Stephen *(Composer)*   2646, 3039, 3285
Flaherty, Stephen *(Musical Director)*   3960
Flaiano, Ennio *(Author)*   3171, 4238
Flanagan, Bud *(Cast)*   1763
Flanagan, Bud *(Composer)*   4027
Flanagan, Bud *(Lyricist)*   4027
Flanagan, Charles *(Cast)*   4470
Flanders, Michael *(Cast)*   220, 221
Flanders, Michael *(Lyricist)*   220, 221
Flanders, Richard *(Cast)*   1347
Flaningam, Louisa *(Cast)*   143, 2289, 2346, 2579, 3517, 4731
Flash, Serge *(Cast)*   2077
Flatow, Leon *(Composer)*   3401
Flatow, Leon *(Lyricist)*   4817
Flatt, Ernest *(Choreographer)*   223, 1227, 2163, 2590, 4197
Flatt, Ernest O. *(Choreographer)*   1970
Flatt, Ernest O. *(Director)*   1120, 1970
Flaxman, John *(Producer)*   3871, 4790
Fleeson, Neville *(Composer)*   3005
Fleeson, Neville *(Lyricist)*   608, 1516, 1961, 3005, 4050, 4677
Fleetwood, Tom *(Cast)*   4764
Fleishman, Philip *(Composer)*   3802
Fleitas, Allison *(Composer)*   1604, 4303
Fleitas, Allison *(Lyricist)*   1604, 4303
Fleming, Blanche *(Cast)*   1447, 4664
Fleming, Carroll *(Author)*   3998
Fleming, Carroll *(Director)*   188, 4509
Fleming, Carroll *(Librettist)*   188, 3504, 4509
Fleming, Carroll *(Lyricist)*   3998
Fleming, Claude *(Cast)*   4482, 4489
Fleming, Conn *(Librettist)*   3671, 4252
Fleming, Conn *(Lyricist)*   3671
Fleming, Eugene *(Cast)*   1890, 4255

Fleming, Fred *(Musical Director)*   385, 1656, 1657, 4208
Fleming, Peggy *(Cast)*   2094
Flesh, Ed *(Set Design)*   600
Fless, Scott *(Cast)*   1732
Fletcher, Allen *(Director)*   255
Fletcher, Bramwell *(Cast)*   2396, 2680
Fletcher, Charles *(Cast)*   1593
Fletcher, Dusty *(Cast)*   1251
Fletcher, George *(Composer)*   1340, 2771
Fletcher, George *(Lyricist)*   2771
Fletcher, Jack *(Cast)*   127, 367, 1023, 1049, 1094, 1362, 1841, 2590, 2659, 3497, 4065, 4153, 4156, 4197, 4310
Fletcher, Joe *(Composer)*   1343
Fletcher, Joe *(Lyricist)*   1343
Fletcher, Juanita *(Cast)*   977, 1882, 2527
Fletcher, Percy *(Musical Director)*   292
Fletcher, Percy *(Orchestrations)*   758
Fletcher, Percy E. *(Composer)*   2802
Fletcher, Robert *(Costumes)*   935, 1237, 1294, 1373, 1727, 1745, 1891, 2019, 2168, 2357, 2523, 3210, 3273, 4585, 4588
Fletcher, Robert *(Producer)*   1891, 4388
Fletcher, Robert *(Set Design)*   1891, 4388
Fletcher, Ron *(Choreographer)*   315, 4423
Fletcher, Susann *(Cast)*   1633, 2205
Flett, Sharon *(Cast)*   3066
Flick, Pat *(Cast)*   760
Flick, Pat C. *(Librettist)*   512
Flick, Patsy *(Cast)*   622
Flicker, Theodore J. *(Director)*   2067, 3094
Flicker, Theodore J. *(Librettist)*   3094
Flicker, Theodore J. *(Producer)*   2067
Flickinger, Brad *(Orchestrations)*   1630
Flink, Stanley *(Producer)*   3818
Flinn, Brook *(Composer)*   2039
Flinn, Denny Martin *(Cast)*   302, 3956, 4196
Flinn, Denny Martin *(Choreographer)*   4002
Flinn, Dylan *(Lyricist)*   2039
Flint, Shelby *(Cast)*   499
Flippen, Jay C. *(Cast)*   1678, 1831, 2263, 2653, 3342, 3861, 4265
Flood, Peter *(Producer)*   3927
Florell, Walter *(Costumes)*   341, 2985
Florell, Walter *(Director)*   848
Florelle *(Cast)*   2753
Florence, Kathryn *(Cast)*   3952
Florenz, Paul *(Choreographer)*   4021
Florenz & Alvarez *(Cast)*   1950
Florida Arts Council *(Producer)*   4645
Florida Atlantic University *(Producer)*   2027
Flovie, Mlle. *(Librettist)*   3203
Flower, Belle *(Cast)*   2275
Flower, Chris *(Set Design)*   3629
Flowers, Martha *(Cast)*   1385
Flowerton, Consuelo *(Cast)*   1110, 2444, 2813
Floyd, Gene *(Cast)*   2094
Floyd, Walter *(Producer)*   4859
Fludd III, Quitman *(Cast)*   1164, 3279
Fludd III, Quitman D. *(Cast)*   1063
Fluehr, Cheryl L. *(Producer)*   4515
Fluty, Rex *(Set Design)*   2027

Flynn, Elinor *(Cast)* 1342
Flynn, Jimmy *(Lyricist)* 3614
Flynn, John *(Composer)* 3322
Flynn, John H. *(Composer)* 2835, 2858
Flynn, Kitty *(Cast)* 1531, 3821
Flynn, Marie *(Cast)* 697, 1519, 1606, 2854, 3344, 3866
Flynn, Maryellen *(Producer)* 908
Flynn, Susan *(Cast)* 484, 549
Flynn, Terrance *(Cast)* 647
Fodor, Joleen *(Cast)* 249, 1676
Foerster, Frederick H. *(Composer)* 6
Fogarty, Alex *(Composer)* 3103, 3104, 4777
Fogarty, Alexander *(Composer)* 637
Fogarty, John *(Composer)* 4534
Fogarty, John *(Lyricist)* 4534
Fogarty, John C. *(Composer)* 3739
Fogarty, John C. *(Lyricist)* 3739
Fokine, Michel *(Cast)* 3153
Fokine, Michel *(Choreographer)* 165, 1656, 4816
Folden, Lewis *(Set Design)* 2704
Foldes, Lew *(Cast)* 660
Foley, Brian *(Choreographer)* 4402
Foley, Ellen *(Composer)* 2427
Foley, Ellen *(Lyricist)* 2427
Foley, John *(Cast)* 3608
Foley, John *(Composer)* 3608
Foley, John *(Lyricist)* 3608
Foley, John *(Musical Director)* 4030
Foley Jr., Daniel G. *(Composer)* 1604
Foley Jr., Daniel G. *(Lyricist)* 18, 1604
Folger Theatre Group *(Producer)* 699
Follis, Dorothy *(Cast)* 1962
Follmann Jr., Joseph F. *(Musical Director)* 18, 750, 1885
Folmer, Wallace Walter *(Cast)* 3647
Folsom, Bobby *(Cast)* 1131
Fond, Miriam *(Choreographer)* 871, 4635
Fond, Miriam *(Director)* 871, 4635
Fonda, Henry *(Cast)* 1471, 2060, 3103
Fonda, Jane *(Cast)* 2144
Fong, Joseph *(Cast)* 595
Fonson *(Author)* 94
Fontaine, Gene *(Cast)* 4021
Fontaine, Joel *(Set Design)* 2354
Fontaine, Robert L. *(Author)* 1764
Fontana, Georges *(Cast)* 3975
Fontanne, Lynn *(Cast)* 1416, 2121, 3328
Food Industries, The *(Producer)* 2175
Foote, Don *(Costumes)* 227
Foote, Gene *(Cast)* 723, 3506
Foote, Gene *(Choreographer)* 3561
Foote, Gene *(Director)* 3561
Foote, Horton *(Librettist)* 1616
Foote, Jay *(Composer)* 128, 1049
Foran, William *(Cast)* 2311
Foray, June *(Voice)* 2015
Forbes, Barbara *(Costumes)* 549, 2199
Forbes, Brenda *(Author)* 3764
Forbes, Brenda *(Cast)* 989, 3292, 4362, 4483
Forbes, Donna Liggitt *(Cast)* 2043, 4022
Forbes, Edward *(Cast)* 1871
Forbes, Elliot *(Composer)* 1231

Forbes, Esther *(Author)* 823
Forbes, Grace *(Cast)* 2492
Forbes, Hazel *(Cast)* 3980
Forbes, Kathryn *(Author)* 2064
Forbes, Ralph *(Cast)* 2691
Forbes-Robinson, Beatrice *(Cast)* 2952
Forcen, Ida *(Cast)* 982
Forchion, Raymond George *(Cast)* 2027
Ford, Anna *(Cast)* 2254
Ford, Chip *(Cast)* 3928
Ford, Constance *(Cast)* 3845
Ford, Corey *(Librettist)* 1322, 1932, 4367
Ford, David *(Cast)* 3897
Ford, Frank *(Producer)* 3931
Ford, George *(Producer)* 1013
Ford, Harry *(Director)* 1013
Ford, Helen *(Cast)* 97, 711, 1013, 1345, 1516, 1670, 1819, 3185, 3436, 4248
Ford, Henry *(Cast)* 475
Ford, Hugh *(Director)* 1501, 4671
Ford, Inez *(Cast)* 1922
Ford, Joan *(Lyricist)* 1614
Ford, Joe Taylor *(Librettist)* 2415
Ford, John *(Director)* 1076
Ford, Johnny *(Cast)* 4464
Ford, Johnny *(Choreographer)* 2277
Ford, Lena Guilbert *(Lyricist)* 3259
Ford, Nancy *(Additional Music)* 1439
Ford, Nancy *(Arrangements)* 1169, 1439
Ford, Nancy *(Composer)* 944, 1169, 1737, 2074, 2418, 3209, 3927
Ford, Nancy *(Lyricist)* 1737
Ford, Nancy *(Orchestrations)* 2074
Ford, Nancy *(Vocal Arranger)* 3209
Ford, Paul *(Cast)* 2267, 3097, 4682
Ford, Paul (Pianist) 4533
Ford, Phyllis *(Cast)* 3810
Ford, Rodney *(Costumes)* 2654
Ford, Rodney *(Set Design)* 2654, 3695
Ford, Ruth *(Cast)* 979, 1662, 1775, 4256
Ford, Steven *(Musical Director)* 1073
Ford, Tom *(Composer)* 1131, 1132, 3172
Ford, Tom *(Lyricist)* 1131, 1132
Ford, Vesta *(Cast)* 985
Ford, Walter *(Lyricist)* 1925, 3951, 4130
Ford, Wrena *(Composer)* 477
Ford's Theatre Society *(Producer)* 3318, 4162
Forde, Hal *(Cast)* 20, 207, 787, 1493, 1530, 1780, 1962, 2005, 2402, 2567, 2696, 2927, 3230, 3236, 4670, 4733
Forde, Hal *(Director)* 3290
Forde, Larry *(Director)* 1637, 3261
Forde, Stanley *(Cast)* 2363, 2373, 2730, 3420, 3580, 3581
Fordin, Wolff *(Costumes)* 331
Forella, Ronn *(Cast)* 1990
Forella, Ronn *(Choreographer)* 692, 4689
Foreman, Richard *(Director)* 1064, 4370
Foreman, Richard *(Lyricist)* 1064
Foreman, Richard *(Set Design)* 1064
Fores, J.F. *(Cast)* 3797
Forestieri, Lou *(Orchestrations)* 562
Forestieri, Marcel *(Cast)* 534

Fownes, Henry *(Producer)* 1848

Fox, Carol *(Cast)* 4433

Fox, Chester *(Producer)* 3169, 3873

Fox, Della *(Cast)* 1305, 2515, 2548, 3360, 3744, 4614, 4624

Fox, Dorothy *(Cast)* 3365, 3990

Fox, Ed *(Producer)* 1658

Fox, Edna *(Vocal Arranger)* 2453

Fox, Elizabeth *(Cast)* 2455

Fox, Fontaine *(Librettist)* 199

Fox, Frederick *(Lighting Designer)* 3874, 3894

Fox, Frederick *(Set Design)* 23, 1815, 2395, 2707, 2751, 3314, 3841, 3874, 3894, 3947

Fox, George *(Cast)* 2902

Fox, Harry *(Cast)* 1332, 1488, 1963, 2696, 3246, 3395, 3783, 4158, 4860

Fox, Herschel *(Cast)* 2421

Fox, James *(Set Design)* 1458

Fox, Janet *(Cast)* 1342, 1894, 3931

Fox, Jay *(Choreographer)* 1450

Fox, Kevin *(Cast)* 1969

Fox, Lou *(Composer)* 1658

Fox, Lou *(Lyricist)* 1658

Fox, Manheim *(Producer)* 4091

Fox, Maxine *(Producer)* 1664, 3330

Fox, Nancy *(Cast)* 3888

Fox, Patrick *(Cast)* 459, 4659

Fox, Patrick *(Composer)* 459

Fox, Patrick *(Lyricist)* 459

Fox, Patrick *(Musical Director)* 459

Fox, Rick *(Musical Director)* 460, 1079

Fox, Sonny *(Producer)* 4272

Fox, William *(Cast)* 3974

Fox, William *(Producer)* 1531

Fox Theatricals *(Producer)* 2198

Foy, Bryan *(Composer)* 2363

Foy, Cathy *(Cast)* 4076

Foy, Edwin *(Cast)* 4181

Foy, Gloria *(Cast)* 381, 771, 4050, 4529, 4844

Foy, Ken *(Set Design)* 533, 535

Foy, Kenneth *(Set Design)* 3548, 3722, 4136

Foy Jr., Eddie *(Cast)* 216, 672, 1076, 1395, 1577, 2975, 3182, 3273, 3314, 3351, 3721, 3801, 3953, 4023

Foy Sr., Eddie *(Cast)* 175, 476, 1123, 1994, 2974, 2978, 3228, 3313, 3332, 3488, 4521, 4691

Foyer, Bernie *(Producer)* 3895

Fracht, J. Albert *(Librettist)* 227

Fraction, Edward *(Cast)* 4254

Fradkin, Phil *(Musical Director)* 4292

Fradrich, James *(Composer)* 3201

Fradrich, James *(Librettist)* 3201

Fradrich, James *(Musical Director)* 1508

Fradrich, James *(Orchestrations)* 2776

Fradrich, James *(Vocal Arranger)* 1508

Fradrich, Jim *(Musical Director)* 1412

Fradrich, Jim *(Orchestrations)* 1412

Fradrich, Jim *(Vocal Arranger)* 1412

Fram, Joel *(Musical Director)* 2224

Frame, Grazina *(Cast)* 455

Franbau, Ella *(Cast)* 1657

France, Millard *(Set Design)* 2455

France, Richard *(Cast)* 603, 1567

France, Wesley *(Lighting Designer)* 209

Francell, Jacqueline *(Cast)* 2323

Frances, Arlene *(Cast)* 2653

Franceschina, John *(Musical Director)* 708, 2114

Franceschina, John *(Vocal Arranger)* 314

Franchi, Sergio *(Cast)* 1060

Francillion *(Costumes)* 3924

Francine, Anne *(Cast)* 550, 603, 2653, 2898, 4035, 4541

Francioli, Signor *(Choreographer)* 357, 2116

Franciosa, Massimo *(Librettist)* 3798

Francis, Adele *(Cast)* 2895

Francis, Alfred *(Composer)* 2619

Francis, Allan *(Producer)* 1762

Francis, Arlene *(Cast)* 979, 2060

Francis, Arthur
  See also Ira Gershwin.

Francis, Dick *(Cast)* 277, 4341, 4361

Francis, Dorothy *(Cast)* 930, 2622, 4212

Francis, Emma *(Cast)* 4465

Francis, Helen *(Cast)* 524

Francis, James *(Director)* 1274

Francis, Mamie *(Cast)* 2413

Francis, May *(Cast)* 1114

Francis, Mme. *(Costumes)* 152, 396, 2667, 2923, 4195, 4283, 4296, 4716, 4813

Francis, Noel *(Cast)* 4621

Francis, W.T. *(Composer)* 675, 954, 1067, 1569, 1927, 2515, 3753, 3856, 3857, 3951

Francis, W.T. *(Lyricist)* 3857

Francis, W.T. *(Musical Director)* 1067, 1569, 2341, 3092, 3322

Francis, William *(Cast)* 1590

Francis, William T. *(Composer)* 675, 1318, 3790, 4478, 4681

Francis, William T. *(Musical Director)* 675, 3790, 3857

Francisco, William *(Choreographer)* 3925

Francisco, William *(Composer)* 3835

Francisco, William *(Director)* 3763, 3835, 3925

Franck, Nelly *(Cast)* 1413

Franck, Nelly *(Composer)* 3698

Francks, Don *(Cast)* 2304

Franco, Abel *(Cast)* 4861

Franco, Ramon *(Cast)* 4205

Frandsen, Erik *(Cast)* 4076

Frandsen, Erik *(Composer)* 4076

Frandsen, Erik *(Librettist)* 4076

Frandsen, Erik *(Lyricist)* 4076

Frangipane, Ronald *(Orchestrations)* 406

Frank, Allen *(Cast)* 3495

Frank, Anne *(Author)* 4790

Frank, Arthur *(Musical Director)* 2169

Frank, Ben *(Cast)* 2321

Frank, Benno D. *(Director)* 3439

Frank, David *(Musical Director)* 3902, 4450

Frank, David *(Orchestrations)* 3902

Frank, Dottie *(Cast)* 3111

Frank, Doug *(Composer)* 2754

Frank, Doug *(Lyricist)* 2754

Frank, Erle *(Costumes)* 3185

Frank, Gerald (*Librettist*)   4678
Frank, Gerri-Ann (*Cast*)   1269, 2356
Frank, Judy (*Cast*)   3209
Frank, Larry (*Composer*)   1380
Frank, Larry (*Librettist*)   1380
Frank, Larry (*Lyricist*)   1380
Frank, Melvin (*Author*)   652
Frank, Melvin (*Librettist*)   2301, 2484
Frank, Melvin (*Producer*)   2484
Frank, Paul (*Author*)   2594
Frank, Ruella (*Choreographer*)   729
Frank, Sherman (*Musical Director*)   837, 3493, 3551
Frank, Willie (*Producer*)   2168
Frank, Yasha (*Director*)   1744, 3495
Frank, Yasha (*Librettist*)   1744, 3495, 3496
Frank Productions (*Producer*)   634, 1698, 3016, 3526, 4579
Frankel, Gene (*Director*)   3159
Frankel, Jerry (*Producer*)   2198
Frankel, Kenneth (*Director*)   753, 4109
Frankel, Leo (*Cast*)   340
Frankel, Richard (*Producer*)   573, 992, 4031, 4076
Frankel, Scott (*Musical Director*)   4067
Franken, Steve (*Cast*)   408
Franklin, Barbara (*Cast*)   3818
Franklin, Bessie (*Cast*)   2966, 4425
Franklin, Bonnie (*Cast*)   167, 752, 1093
Franklin, Edgar S. (*Author*)   2527
Franklin, Frederic (*Cast*)   4075
Franklin, Harold B. (*Producer*)   839, 841, 3699
Franklin, Hazel (*Cast*)   2089
Franklin, Irene (*Cast*)   1687, 1735, 3313, 3401, 4203, 4234
Franklin, Irene (*Lyricist*)   2816, 4203, 4234
Franklin, J.E. (*Librettist*)   3599
Franklin, J.E. (*Lyricist*)   3599
Franklin, Judy (*Cast*)   752
Franklin, Malvin (*Composer*)   1014, 4687
Franklin, Malvin (*Lyricist*)   1014
Franklin, Malvin (*Musical Director*)   1014
Franklin, Malvin F. (*Composer*)   60, 1911, 2574, 4033
Franklin, Malvin F. (*Lyricist*)   4687
Franklin, Malvin M. (*Composer*)   2486, 2574, 4033
Franklin, Nat (*Cast*)   1647
Franklin, Tony (*Cast*)   1053, 1103
Franklin, William (*Cast*)   651, 4254
Franklyn, Beth (*Cast*)   3910
Franklyn, Blanche (*Lyricist*)   1404
Franks, Danny (*Lighting Designer*)   658
Franks, Dobbs (*Musical Director*)   2322
Franks, Laurie (*Cast*)   1435, 4232, 4537
Fransworth, Scott (*Librettist*)   1884
Franz, Al (*Cast*)   319
Franz, Elizabeth (*Cast*)   4768
Franz, Joy (*Cast*)   212, 2049, 2143, 2988, 3019, 4412
Franzell, Carlotta (*Cast*)   653
Fraser, Alec (*Cast*)   2514
Fraser, Alex (*Cast*)   3663
Fraser, Alison (*Cast*)   338, 2746, 3760, 3862, 4403, 4518
Fraser, Ann (*Cast*)   1648
Fraser, George (*Composer*)   1887
Fraser, Ian (*Dance Arranger*)   3846
Fraser, Ian (*Musical Director*)   695, 3454, 3482, 4560

Fraser, Ian (*Orchestrations*)   4160
Fraser, Ian (*Vocal Arranger*)   3482, 3846, 4560
Fraser, J.A. (*Librettist*)   3298
Fraser, Jane (*Cast*)   3353
Fraser, Jean (*Lyricist*)   1134
Fraser, Ronald (*Cast*)   2362
Fraser, Sally (*Cast*)   752
Fraser-Simpson, Harold (*Composer*)   2698, 3634
Fratantoni, Diane (*Cast*)   275
Fratti, Mario (*Librettist*)   3171
Frawley, James (*Cast*)   162
Frawley, Mark (*Cast*)   3239
Frawley, Paul (*Cast*)   638, 815, 1819, 1856, 2336, 2734, 3006, 3222, 4212, 4360, 4426, 4443
Frawley, T. Daniel (*Director*)   3562
Frawley, William (*Cast*)   608, 1859, 2709, 2833, 3924, 4087, 4276, 4299
Fray, Jacques (*Cast*)   4545
Fray, Jacques (*Composer*)   3172, 4545
Frazee, H.H. (*Director*)   3048, 3184
Frazee, H.H. (*Producer*)   1746, 2145, 2261, 2667, 2670, 3048, 3184, 4761, 4766
Frazee, Jane
   See also Frazee Sisters.
Frazee, Jane (*Cast*)   2460
Frazee, Marion (*Costumes*)   2789
Frazee Sisters, The
   See also Jane Frazee.
Frazee Sisters, The (*Cast*)   417, 420
Frazier, Grenoldo (*Cast*)   2932
Frazier, Grenoldo (*Composer*)   2932
Frazier, Grenoldo (*Lyricist*)   2932
Frazier, Michael (*Producer*)   1186, 1425, 1699, 1865, 2702, 4347
Fredena Productions (*Producer*)   1596
Frederic, Helen (*Cast*)   3586
Frederick, Helena (*Cast*)   4311
Frederick, Jean (*Lyricist*)   200
Frederick, Lee (*Cast*)   117
Frederick, Pauline (*Cast*)   2160, 3588, 3745
Fredericks, Charles (*Cast*)   3013
Fredericks, Chester (*Cast*)   1461, 4209
Fredericks, Rita (*Producer*)   482
Fredericks, William (*Cast*)   2055
Frederickson, Carl (*Composer*)   2115
Fredhoven, Hans (*Pianist*)   3290
Fredhoven, John (*Musical Director*)   1670
Fredrik, Burry (*Director*)   1017, 4689
Fredrik, Burry (*Producer*)   3565, 3787
Free Space Ltd. (*Producer*)   2968
Freeborn, Cassius (*Cast*)   3384
Freeborn, Cassius (*Composer*)   1907, 2717, 3910
Freeborn, Cassius (*Musical Director*)   1922, 2485, 3910
Freed, Alan (*Composer*)   4264
Freed, Alan (*Lyricist*)   4264
Freed, Arthur (*Composer*)   69, 196, 544, 1298, 1777, 1942, 1944, 1946, 3349
Freed, Arthur (*Lyricist*)   69, 196, 393, 544, 1638, 1777, 1942, 1944, 1946, 2215, 3349, 3973, 3992
Freed, Cathy (*Cast*)   2092
Freed, Ralph (*Lyricist*)   3175, 3374

Freed, Sam *(Cast)*   4635
Freedley, Vinton *(Cast)*   977, 1174, 1345, 2897, 3319, 4437
Freedley, Vinton *(Composer)*   1863
Freedley, Vinton *(Director)*   3379
Freedley, Vinton *(Producer)*   163, 612, 971, 1419, 1528, 1679, 1683, 1800, 1859, 1929, 2187, 2376, 2432, 2453, 3243, 3379, 3674, 3993, 4118, 4392, 4443
Freedley Jr., Vinton *(Cast)*   4039
Freedman, Betty *(Librettist)*   3527
Freedman, Danny *(Cast)*   1695
Freedman, David *(Librettist)*   376, 418, 2475, 3955, 4235, 4667, 4824, 4825
Freedman, Gerald *(Choreographer)*   1439
Freedman, Gerald *(Director)*   112, 693, 807, 1439, 1456, 1660, 2726, 3733, 3825, 4089, 4384, 4615
Freedman, Gerald *(Librettist)*   2097, 4384
Freedman, Gerald *(Lyricist)*   2097, 4384
Freedman, Louis *(Librettist)*   343
Freedman, Max *(Composer)*   3739
Freedman, Max *(Lyricist)*   3739
Freedman, Melvin H. *(Librettist)*   3697
Freedman, Melvin H. *(Lyricist)*   3697
Freedman, Robert M. *(Orchestrations)*   550, 952, 1914, 2689, 2898, 3088, 3656, 4288
Freeman, Arny *(Cast)*   1991, 2975, 3000, 3175, 4633, 4744
Freeman, Bud
   See also Bud Freeman's Summa Cum Laude Band.
Freeman, Bud *(Author)*   339
Freeman, Bud *(Librettist)*   339
Freeman, Bud *(Lyricist)*   339
Freeman, Charles K. *(Director)*   4075
Freeman, Charles K. *(Librettist)*   616
Freeman, Damita Jo *(Cast)*   3515
Freeman, Everett *(Librettist)*   4798
Freeman, Gladys *(Cast)*   4220
Freeman, Grace *(Cast)*   906, 3759
Freeman, H. Lawrence *(Composer)*   645, 3358
Freeman, Harry *(Composer)*   4723
Freeman, Harry *(Lyricist)*   4723
Freeman, Howard *(Cast)*   1991, 2344
Freeman, Jay *(Musical Director)*   4006
Freeman, Jonathan E. *(Cast)*   3498
Freeman, Jonathan E. *(Puppeteer)*   4660
Freeman, K. Todd *(Producer)*   4074
Freeman, Kathleen *(Cast)*   2057, 4408
Freeman, L.E. *(Composer)*   1813, 4743
Freeman, L.E. *(Lyricist)*   1813, 4743
Freeman, Louis *(Librettist)*   2352
Freeman, Max *(Cast)*   1193, 1553, 3784
Freeman, Max *(Director)*   457, 559, 639, 734, 1594, 1896, 2179, 2326, 2507, 2632, 2673, 2963, 3732, 3784, 4236, 4500
Freeman, Max *(Librettist)*   2507
Freeman, Morgan *(Cast)*   166, 1636
Freeman, Pauline *(Cast)*   4451
Freeman, Stan *(Composer)*   2053, 2626
Freeman, Stan *(Lyricist)*   2053, 2626
Freeman, Steven *(Musical Director)*   3202
Freeman, Stu *(Cast)*   1769
Freeman, Vera *(Cast)*   3467
Freeman, Virginia *(Choreographer)*   143, 699

Freeman Jr., Al *(Cast)*   477, 1671, 2306, 2583
Freeman's Summa Cum Laude Band, Bud
   See also Bud Freeman.
Freeman's Summa Cum Laude, Bud *(Cast)*   4256
Frees, Paul *(Cast)*   928, 3833
Freidland, Anatole *(Composer)*   4422
Freiman, L. *(Author)*   3669
Freirson, Andrea *(Cast)*   3285
Freisinger, Mme. *(Costumes)*   379, 1469, 2159, 3078, 3519, 4801, 4802
Freitag, Dorothea (Arrangements)   3656
Freitag, Dorothea *(Cast)*   3900
Freitag, Dorothea *(Composer)*   722, 2772
Freitag, Dorothea *(Dance Arranger)*   1012, 1441, 1892, 2075, 2318, 2772, 2804, 4435, 4702, 4862
Freitag, Dorothea *(Musical Director)*   722, 840, 2772, 2918, 3186, 3940
Freitag, Dorothea (Orchestrations)   722, 3940
Freitag, Dorothea (Pianist)   1892, 2439, 3186
Freitag, Dorothea (Vocal Arranger)   2439, 2772, 3186
Freitas, Richard *(Composer)*   1046
Freitas, Richard *(Musical Director)*   1046
Freitas, Richard *(Orchestrations)*   1046
Fremont, Rob *(Composer)*   3476
Fremont, Rob *(Librettist)*   3476
French, Adelaide *(Librettist)*   3344
French, Arthur *(Cast)*   40, 1592, 2719
French, Bert *(Choreographer)*   385, 465, 728, 1174, 1580, 1794, 2216, 2276, 2494, 2549, 2569, 2698, 2756, 3006, 4378, 4464, 4529
French, Bert *(Costumes)*   3712
French, Bert *(Director)*   560, 1582, 1819, 1961, 4283, 4529
French, Charles K. *(Cast)*   2029
French, Harold *(Cast)*   2467
French, Hugh *(Cast)*   3885
French, Jack *(Musical Director)*   2558, 3936
French, Larry *(Cast)*   2703
French, Leslie *(Cast)*   4479
French, Leslie *(Choreographer)*   4479
French, Pauline *(Cast)*   1851
French, Percy *(Cast)*   1013
French, Rick *(Lyricist)*   95
French, T.R. *(Producer)*   1576
Freschi, Bob *(Cast)*   1955
Fresco, Al *(Cast)*   3361
Fresnay, Pierre *(Cast)*   841, 3216
Frett, Kenneth *(Cast)*   4584
Freund, Julius *(Author)*   3627
Frey, Blanche *(Cast)*   1457
Frey, Fran *(Cast)*   4683
Frey, Fran *(Orchestrations)*   3381
Frey, Fran *(Vocal Arranger)*   3381
Frey, Hugo *(Composer)*   1173, 1308, 3313
Frey, Hugo *(Musical Director)*   88, 1593, 2835
Frey, Leonard *(Cast)*   790, 2568
Frey, Nathaniel *(Cast)*   957, 1158, 1280, 1614, 3918, 4432, 4446
Freydberg, James B. *(Producer)*   253, 4349
Freyer, Frederick *(Composer)*   647
Freyer, Frederick *(Vocal Arranger)*   647
Freyman, Evelyn *(Producer)*   1734

Friberg, Carl (*Composer*) 3112
Frick, Mr. (*Cast*) 2083, 2084
Frick and Frack (*Cast*) 2085, 2086, 2088, 2089, 2090
Friebus, Florida (*Cast*) 55
Friebus, Florida (*Librettist*) 55
Friebus, Theodore (*Cast*) 3560
Fried, Barbara (*Lyricist*) 1955, 4338
Fried, Kenneth (*Composer*) 1836
Fried, Kenneth (*Lyricist*) 1836
Fried, Martin (*Musical Director*) 637
Fried, Walter (*Producer*) 2450
Friedberg, Billy (*Librettist*) 2554
Friedberg, William (*Librettist*) 23, 743, 1815, 2837, 3841
Friedland, Anatol (*Composer*) 2858
Friedland, Anatole (*Composer*) 558, 904, 1065, 1292, 1334, 3446, 4687
Friedlander, Sylvia (*Costumes*) 4773
Friedlander, William B. (*Choreographer*) 1404
Friedlander, William B. (*Composer*) 1343, 1404, 2238, 2706, 2818, 2950, 3083, 3508, 4376
Friedlander, William B. (*Director*) 2238, 2818, 2950, 3168, 3489, 4100
Friedlander, William B. (*Librettist*) 2818
Friedlander, William B. (*Lyricist*) 1343, 1404, 2238, 2706, 2818, 2950, 3508, 4387
Friedlander, William B. (*Producer*) 2238, 3489, 3508, 4100
Friedlich, Kate (*Cast*) 4018, 4557
Friedman, Alan (*Composer*) 1233, 1436, 1438, 2279, 3484
Friedman, Alan (*Lyricist*) 1436, 1438, 2279
Friedman, Allan Jay (*Composer*) 3908
Friedman, Arthur (*Cast*) 283
Friedman, Bruce Jay (*Author*) 2965
Friedman, Bruce Jay (*Librettist*) 2965
Friedman, Charles (*Director*) 653, 2225, 3035, 3501, 3990, 4169
Friedman, Charles (*Librettist*) 3035, 3501, 3990
Friedman, Charles (*Lyricist*) 3035, 3501
Friedman, Charles (*Producer*) 3800
Friedman, David (*Librettist*) 2402
Friedman, David (*Musical Director*) 172, 508, 1591, 2242, 2283, 2539, 3838
Friedman, David (*Orchestrations*) 1786
Friedman, David (*Vocal Arranger*) 330, 508, 1591, 2539, 3838
Friedman, Gary William (*Author*) 4216
Friedman, Gary William (*Composer*) 535, 669, 1714, 2422, 2801, 3515, 4216, 4272
Friedman, Gary William (*Dance Arranger*) 2801
Friedman, Gary William (*Orchestrations*) 2801, 4216, 4272
Friedman, Gary William (*Vocal Arranger*) 535, 2801, 3515, 4216, 4272
Friedman, Joel Phillip (*Composer*) 3448
Friedman, Kim (*Director*) 2953
Friedman, Leo (*Composer*) 3581, 4799
Friedman, Lewis (*Producer*) 2470, 2852
Friedman, Louis (*Lyricist*) 2419
Friedman, Martin (*Lighting Designer*) 2633
Friedman, Peter (*Cast*) 2607
Friedman, Samuel J. (*Producer*) 2110

Friedman, Seth (*Composer*) 3448, 4533
Friedman, Seth (*Librettist*) 3448
Friedman, Seth (*Lyricist*) 3448, 4533
Friedman, Stephen R. (*Producer*) 150, 1955, 4744
Friedman, Susan (*Cast*) 2354
Friedman, Tracy (*Choreographer*) 2470, 2852
Friedman, Tracy (*Director*) 2852
Frieman, Max (*Director*) 2515
Friend, Cliff (*Composer*) 297, 391, 487, 1136, 1481, 1491, 2066, 2857, 3489, 3532, 3623, 4607, 4683
Friend, Cliff (*Lyricist*) 391, 487, 1136, 1491, 1643, 1689, 2857, 3623, 3907, 4322, 4573
Friend, John Edward (*Costumes*) 1885
Friend, John Edward (*Set Design*) 1885
Friend, William (*Cast*) 1646
Friends of Van Wolf Prods. (*Producer*) 4449
Fries, Catherine (*Cast*) 1059
Friesen, Dick (Arrangements) 2095
Friesen, Dick (*Composer*) 2084, 2092, 2093, 2094, 2095, 2096
Friesen, Dick (*Lyricist*) 2084, 2092, 2093, 2094, 2095, 2096
Friesen, Dick (*Orchestrations*) 2084, 2092
Friesen, John (*Orchestrations*) 2096
Friganza, Trixie (*Cast*) 115, 350, 628, 694, 2365, 2851, 3005, 3087, 3313, 3395, 4247, 4473
Frilling, Ednor (*Cast*) 1267
Friml, Rudolf (*Composer*) 102, 152, 234, 288, 385, 468, 765, 1033, 1285, 1442, 1580, 1888, 2121, 2264, 2292, 2340, 2549, 2636, 3011, 3020, 3172, 3179, 3424, 3772, 4063, 4357, 4464, 4539, 4664, 4692, 4784, 4815, 4817
Friml, Rudolf (*Librettist*) 4815
Friml, William (*Composer*) 1754, 2234
Frings, Ketti (*Author*) 135
Frings, Ketti (*Librettist*) 135, 4588
Friquet, Jules (*Musical Director*) 1902
Frisby, Terence (*Author*) 4329
Frisch, Billy (*Composer*) 1065
Frisch, Billy (*Lyricist*) 1065, 4824
Frisco, Joe (*Cast*) 1134, 1395, 4812
Frisco, Joe (*Librettist*) 1134
Fritzke, Michael (*Cast*) 2356
Froehlich, Rico (*Cast*) 108, 223, 519, 2961, 3696
Frohman, Charles (*Producer*) 100, 178, 205, 675, 719, 954, 1066, 1067, 1318, 1454, 1537, 1538, 1543, 1544, 1559, 1569, 1806, 1905, 2131, 2206, 2329, 2341, 2424, 2498, 2526, 2624, 2761, 2871, 2889, 2952, 3049, 3079, 3092, 3322, 3658, 3710, 3753, 3779, 3857, 3948, 3996, 4219, 4258, 4354
Frohman, Daniel (*Producer*) 515, 2315
Frolich, Otto (*Musical Director*) 1834
Froman, Jane (*Cast*) 204, 2301, 4824
Froman, Jay (*Cast*) 1754
Frondale, Pierre (*Librettist*) 165
Frontiere, Dominic (*Orchestrations*) 3428
Frontiere, Georgia (*Producer*) 3428
Froos, Sylvia (*Cast*) 1462
Frost, Jack (*Composer*) 2298, 4393
Frost, Jack (*Lyricist*) 560, 4197, 4393
Frost, Russell (*Cast*) 1556
Frost, Sue (*Producer*) 595, 1997, 2289

Frost, Thomas *(Lyricist)* 2824
Frothingham, George *(Cast)* 3570, 3736, 3881
Frothingham, George B. *(Cast)* 1768, 2697
Fry, Alex *(Composer)* 1062
Fry, Christopher *(Author)* 1294
Fry, Stephen *(Librettist)* 2798
Frye, Dwight *(Cast)* 4001
Frye, Dwight *(Producer)* 4731
Frye, Edward *(Cast)* 4253
Fryer, Robert *(Producer)* 603, 723, 1068, 1991, 2713, 2822, 3687, 3837, 3913, 4233, 4238, 4734
Fuchs, Isadore *(Author)* 3625
Fuchs, Leo *(Cast)* 343
Fuchs, Peter *(Musical Director)* 1974
Fuchs, Peter *(Vocal Arranger)* 1974
Fuerst, Jim *(Lyricist)* 3110
Fujii, Timm *(Cast)* 3340
Fuller, Charles *(Librettist)* 4535
Fuller, Dean *(Composer)* 943, 1734, 2168, 2246, 3108, 3286, 3524, 4029, 4585, 4828, 4829
Fuller, Dean *(Dance Arranger)* 2680
Fuller, Dean *(Librettist)* 3288, 4029
Fuller, Dean *(Lyricist)* 3286
Fuller, Dean *(Vocal Arranger)* 1734, 4029
Fuller, Edward *(Cast)* 3986
Fuller, Frances *(Cast)* 1850, 2060
Fuller, James *(Composer)* 3695
Fuller, James *(Lyricist)* 3695
Fuller, Jerry *(Composer)* 3695
Fuller, Jerry *(Lyricist)* 3695
Fuller, Larry *(Choreographer)* 461, 1068, 1211, 1638, 1837, 2152, 2198, 2822, 3279, 4233
Fuller, Larry *(Director)* 1638, 1837, 2598
Fuller, Lorenzo *(Cast)* 1278, 2331, 4750
Fuller, Lorenzo *(Composer)* 2580, 4102, 4750
Fuller, Lorenzo *(Dance Arranger)* 2580
Fuller, Lorenzo *(Librettist)* 4750
Fuller, Lorenzo *(Lyricist)* 4102, 4750
Fuller, Lorenzo *(Musical Director)* 2580
Fuller, Lorenzo *(Vocal Arranger)* 2580
Fuller, Molly *(Cast)* 1599
Fuller, Paul *(Musical Director)* 2896
Fuller, Paul Fairfax *(Composer)* 2896
Fuller, Paul Fairfax *(Librettist)* 2896
Fuller, Paul Fairfax *(Lyricist)* 2896
Fuller, Penny *(Cast)* 167, 3702
Fullerton, Joyce *(Cast)* 1201
Fullum, Clay *(Dance Arranger)* 3780
Fullum, Clay *(Musical Director)* 583, 599, 1809, 1914, 2134, 2418, 4618
Fullum, Clay *(Orchestrations)* 2418
Fullum, Clay *(Vocal Arranger)* 599
Fulton, Maude *(Cast)* 632, 1417, 2779, 3313, 3738
Funking, Bob *(Producer)* 2231
Fuqua, Harvey *(Composer)* 4264
Fuqua, Harvey *(Lyricist)* 4264
Fuqua, V.C. *(Lighting Designer)* 2663, 3551
Furber, Douglas *(Author)* 2972
Furber, Douglas *(Cast)* 133, 702
Furber, Douglas *(Librettist)* 1333, 2004, 2798, 3139, 4320

Furber, Douglas *(Lyricist)* 25, 133, 292, 702, 704, 1333, 2004, 2570, 2798, 3139, 3532, 3924, 4320, 4581
Furlow, Brown *(Composer)* 2560
Furlow, Brown *(Lyricist)* 2560, 4273
Furman, Ariel *(Cast)* 2811
Furman, John *(Cast)* 1871
Furse, Roger *(Costumes)* 3482
Furst, William *(Composer)* 1305, 2156, 2548, 3199, 4671
Furth, George *(Author)* 4474
Furth, George *(Cast)* 1363
Furth, George *(Librettist)* 16, 832, 2822
Furth, George *(Lyricist)* 4474
Furth, Seymour *(Composer)* 539, 1464, 1523, 2498, 2869, 2996, 3085, 3203, 3313, 3387, 3417, 3753, 4094, 4104, 4723, 4757, 4801, 4805
Furth, Seymour *(Lyricist)* 3085
Futrelle, Virginia *(Cast)* 378
Futterman, Enid *(Librettist)* 3544, 4790
Futterman, Enid *(Lyricist)* 3544, 4790
Fyfe, Jim *(Cast)* 2437, 3598
Fyffe, Will *(Cast)* 1137
Fyleman, Rose *(Lyricist)* 4335
Fysher, Nilson *(Lyricist)* 4807

G

Gabel, Martin *(Cast)* 270, 979, 2257
Gabel, Martin *(Librettist)* 4141
Gaberman, Alexander *(Cast)* 3456
Gabhardt, George *(Lighting Designer)* 1299
Gable, Christopher *(Cast)* 1619
Gable, June *(Cast)* 829, 1002, 2375, 3080, 3195, 4595
Gable, Martin *(Cast)* 4141
Gabler, Milt *(Composer)* 1296, 4264
Gabler, Milt *(Lyricist)* 1296, 4264
Gabor, Eva *(Cast)* 3816
Gabriel, Master *(Cast)* 591, 2461, 2534, 4242
Gabrielle, Caryl *(Librettist)* 1010
Gabrielle, Caryl *(Lyricist)* 1010
Gabrielson, Frank *(Librettist)* 2105, 2475, 3365
Gabrielson, Frank *(Lyricist)* 1710
Gabrilov, Alexander *(Choreographer)* 1691
Gaburo, Kenneth *(Composer)* 4380
Gaby, Frank *(Cast)* 200, 551, 1461, 1462, 3133
Gaby, Frank *(Producer)* 1462
Gae, Nadine *(Cast)* 3292, 4826
Gaebler, Mary *(Cast)* 753
Gage, Gary *(Cast)* 1093, 4062, 4796
Gage, Lila *(Cast)* 616
Gagel, Frederick *(Composer)* 1661, 2963
Gagliano, Frank *(Author)* 3370
Gagliano, Frank *(Lyricist)* 3370
Gagnon, Roland *(Musical Director)* 1755, 4004
Gaige, Crosby *(Producer)* 1187, 1196, 2060
Gaige, Truman *(Cast)* 110, 948, 1119, 1511, 3011, 3837, 4670, 4777, 4798
Gail, Janet *(Cast)* 2682
Gaillard, Francis *(Cast)* 526

Gaines, David *(Musical Director)*   3181
Gaines, Frederick *(Librettist)*   2001
Gaines, Frederick *(Lyricist)*   2001
Gaines, Lee *(Lyricist)*   2259, 4091
Gaines, Muriel *(Cast)*   467
Gaines, Sam *(Cast)*   3041
Gaites, Joseph *(Director)*   4269
Gaites, Joseph M. *(Producer)*   531, 1088, 1183, 1558, 2291, 2623, 3613, 4269, 4322, 4364, 4528
Gaither, David S. *(Set Design)*   2423
Gaither, Gant *(Producer)*   3899
Gal, Riki *(Cast)*   1075
Galantich, Tom *(Cast)*   2674
Galarno, Bill *(Librettist)*   1347
Galde, Anthony *(Cast)*   3576
Gale, Edwin *(Lyricist)*   2402
Gale, Jack *(Orchestrations)*   314, 2598
Gale, Nita *(Cast)*   27
Gale, Sandra *(Cast)*   4335
Gale Quadruplets, The *(Cast)*   1323, 1492
Galjour, Warren *(Cast)*   4734
Gallagher, David *(Composer)*   2022
Gallagher, Dick *(Composer)*   1785
Gallagher, Dick *(Librettist)*   2022
Gallagher, Dick *(Lyricist)*   1785, 2022
Gallagher, Ed *(Cast)*   1432, 3771, 4816
Gallagher, Ed *(Composer)*   4816
Gallagher, Ed *(Lyricist)*   4816
Gallagher, Edward *(Cast)*   1404, 2112
Gallagher, Helen *(Cast)*   404, 530, 935, 1791, 1886, 2049, 2705, 2877, 2928, 3543, 3893, 4238, 4279, 4379, 4432
Gallagher, Jennifer *(Set Design)*   1740
Gallagher, Larry *(Director)*   338
Gallagher, Larry *(Librettist)*   338
Gallagher, Laura *(Cast)*   2076
Gallagher, Micky *(Composer)*   3884
Gallagher, Peter *(Cast)*   1068
Gallagher, Richard "Skeets" *(Cast)*   2638
Gallagher, Skeets *(Cast)*   773, 1884, 1939, 2691, 2757, 3434, 4528, 4529
Gallardo, Edward *(Librettist)*   3456
Gallaudet, John *(Cast)*   1440, 1856
Gallegher, John *(Librettist)*   1108
Gallegher, John *(Lyricist)*   1108
Gallegly, David *(Cast)*   508
Gallen, Judy *(Set Design)*   2945
Gallico, Paul *(Author)*   656, 2989, 3287
Gallico, Paul *(Librettist)*   2909
Gallico, Robert *(Composer)*   4336
Galligan, David *(Director)*   450
Gallimore, Catherine *(Cast)*   202
Gallin, Sandy *(Producer)*   695
Gallis, Paul *(Set Design)*   949
Gallo, Paul *(Lighting Designer)*   212, 775, 829, 921, 1418, 2359, 3070, 4020, 4390
Galloway, Jane *(Cast)*   4358
Galloway, Leata *(Cast)*   2033, 3741, 4089, 4615
Galloway, Louise *(Cast)*   1852, 2639, 3655
Gallup, Sammy *(Lyricist)*   67, 2227
Galonka, Arlene *(Cast)*   4270
Galster, Robert *(Set Design)*   817

Galvin, Gene *(Costumes)*   3239
Gam, Rita *(Cast)*   4329
Gamache, Laurie *(Cast)*   589, 3682
Gambarelli, Maria *(Cast)*   858
Gammon, James *(Cast)*   2468
Gampel, Chris *(Cast)*   1294
Ganeau, Wilda *(Cast)*   293
Gang, Lydia Pincus *(Costumes)*   4396
Gangi, Jamie Dawn *(Cast)*   3461
Gannaway, Lynne *(Choreographer)*   426, 2285
Gannaway, Lynne *(Director)*   4176
Ganne, Louis *(Author)*   1743
Ganne, Louis *(Composer)*   466
Ganne, M. Louis *(Composer)*   1743
Gannon, Kim *(Lyricist)*   3895
Gannon, Paul *(Cast)*   2085, 2086, 2087, 2089, 2091
Ganon, David *(Director)*   2488
Ganor, Warwick *(Cast)*   3176
Gant, H.C. *(Librettist)*   1541
Gant, Rosemary *(Lighting Designer)*   1435
Gantry, Don *(Cast)*   1184
Gantvoort, Carl *(Cast)*   2546
Garber, Victor *(Cast)*   212, 3852, 4233
Garde, Betty *(Cast)*   32, 3263, 4043
Gardella, Tess *(Cast)*   1484, 2504, 3949
Gardenia, Vincent *(Cast)*   287
Gardenier, Ed *(Lyricist)*   3745, 3747, 3748, 3749, 3855
Gardes, George *(Cast)*   1915
Gardiner, Frank *(Cast)*   1121, 1466
Gardiner, James W. *(Producer)*   180, 3509, 4827
Gardiner, Reginald *(Cast)*   216, 3955
Gardiner, Reginald *(Librettist)*   216
Gardner, Aaron *(Producer)*   1878
Gardner, Ann *(Cast)*   634
Gardner, Brenda *(Cast)*   3059
Gardner, Gary *(Librettist)*   2783
Gardner, Gary *(Lyricist)*   2783
Gardner, Helene *(Cast)*   4212
Gardner, Henry D. *(Cast)*   1274
Gardner, Herb *(Librettist)*   3299
Gardner, Herb *(Lyricist)*   3299
Gardner, Hy *(Producer)*   1880
Gardner, Jack *(Cast)*   356, 742, 1318, 2667, 4277, 4759
Gardner, Lynn *(Cast)*   4640
Gardner, Nat *(Composer)*   1982
Gardner, Rick *(Cast)*   2114
Gardner, Rita *(Cast)*   1237, 1245, 2578, 3161, 4244, 4708
Gardner, Robert *(Composer)*   4093
Gardner, Robert *(Lyricist)*   4093
Gardner, Sam *(Cast)*   1479, 3040
Gardner, William H. *(Lyricist)*   2415
Gardner, Worth *(Composer)*   35
Gardner, Worth *(Director)*   3987
Garey, James R. *(Director)*   263, 1902
Garfein, Jack *(Director)*   1571, 3984
Garfield, David *(Cast)*   1736
Garfield, John *(Cast)*   2228, 4152
Garfinkle, Louis *(Librettist)*   2925
Gargan, Edward *(Cast)*   1225
Gari, Brian *(Composer)*   2420
Gari, Brian *(Lyricist)*   2420

Gari, Janet *(Composer)* 2657
Garin, Michael *(Cast)* 4076
Garin, Michael *(Composer)* 3076, 4076
Garin, Michael *(Librettist)* 4076
Garin, Michael *(Lyricist)* 3076, 4076
Garinei, Pietro *(Director)* 3798
Garinei, Pietro *(Librettist)* 3798
Garinei, Pietro *(Lyricist)* 3798
Garing, A.J. *(Musical Director)* 378, 1208, 1753
Garland, Jamil K. *(Cast)* 4645
Garland, Joe *(Composer)* 3018
Garland, Nicholas *(Director)* 1195
Garland, Patricia *(Cast)* 746
Garland, Robert *(Librettist)* 621
Garlid, Karl *(Cast)* 2124
Garlock, Tommy *(Composer)* 4566
Garlock, Tommy *(Lyricist)* 4153, 4566
Garn, Jack *(Choreographer)* 293
Garn, Jack *(Director)* 293
Garner, Jay *(Cast)* 374, 1161, 1634, 2319, 2360, 3684
Garner, Josie *(Costumes)* 4251
Garnett, Chip *(Cast)* 2539
Garnett, David *(Author)* 211
Garon, Jay *(Producer)* 33
Garr, Eddie *(Cast)* 2405, 2467, 4177, 4374
Garr, Stanton *(Cast)* 3004
Garrambone, Joe *(Cast)* 4168
Garreau, Claude *(Vocal Arranger)* 3966
Garrett, Betty *(Cast)* 339, 620, 2187, 2400, 2447, 2653, 2805, 3226, 4058, 4111
Garrett, Bob *(Composer)* 4171
Garrett, Bob *(Lyricist)* 4171
Garrett, Hank *(Cast)* 4627
Garrett, Joy *(Cast)* 1498
Garrett, Kelly *(Cast)* 2962, 3159, 4743
Garrett, Russell *(Cast)* 3346
Garrick, Beulah *(Cast)* 869, 2268
Garrick, David *(Author)* 1071
Garrick, John *(Cast)* 2540
Garrick, Kathy *(Cast)* 450
Garringer, Nelson *(Lyricist)* 3479
Garrison, David *(Cast)* 1000, 1597, 1914, 4034
Garrison, Sean *(Cast)* 1727, 1990
Garsia, Marston *(Cast)* 1610
Garson, M. *(Composer)* 4193
Garson, Toby *(Lyricist)* 2657
Garstin, Harold *(Composer)* 4719
Garth, Caswell *(Author)* 1680
Garth, Caswell *(Librettist)* 2547
Gartlan, Anne *(Cast)* 564
Gartlan, George H. *(Composer)* 2763, 2779, 4120
Gartlan, George H. *(Lyricist)* 2763
Garvie, Eddie *(Cast)* 1247, 1248, 1569, 2491, 2567, 3581, 4025
Garvie, Edward *(Cast)* 1925, 2695
Garwood, Patti *(Musical Director)* 3461
Gary, Harold *(Cast)* 2106, 2449
Gary, Romain *(Author)* 3792
Gary, Ted *(Cast)* 4142
Gary, Ted *(Choreographer)* 4287
Garza, Ronald *(Cast)* 4138

Garza, Troy *(Choreographer)* 1371, 1637
Gascoine, Jill *(Cast)* 3454
Gaskill, Clarence *(Composer)* 883, 896, 1131, 1378, 2296, 4683
Gaskill, Clarence *(Lyricist)* 437, 883, 896, 1131, 1378, 1460, 2296, 4683
Gasman, Ira *(Librettist)* 2473
Gasman, Ira *(Lyricist)* 2473, 4167, 4635
Gaspar, Marie *(Cast)* 4637
Gaspard, Ray *(Producer)* 2049
Gaspard, Raymond L. *(Producer)* 3901
Gasper, Eddie *(Cast)* 2523, 3526
Gasper, Eddie *(Choreographer)* 1273
Gass, Kyle *(Composer)* 655
Gaston, Billy *(Composer)* 246, 697, 2576, 3685, 4801
Gaston, Billy *(Lyricist)* 246, 697, 2576, 3685, 4801
Gaston, Ken *(Producer)* 181, 1809
Gaston, Lydia *(Cast)* 3682
Gaston, Penny *(Cast)* 3939
Gaston, William *(Lyricist)* 1780
Gatchell Jr., R. Tyler *(Producer)* 131
Gates, Aaron *(Producer)* 4183
Gates, Charles *(Cast)* 2492
Gates, Frank
   See also Gates & Morange.
Gates, Frank *(Set Design)* 185, 376, 577, 749, 815, 1501, 1625, 1667, 2515, 2768, 2819, 2884, 3519, 3650, 3772, 3865, 3868, 4234, 4360, 4620, 4671, 4694, 4704, 4716, 4807
Gates, Frank E. *(Set Design)* 1243, 2326, 3228, 3774, 4705
Gates, Larry *(Cast)* 1200
Gates, Lewis *(Lyricist)* 4094
Gates, Terry *(Set Design)* 4003
Gates & Morange
   See also Frank E. Gates and E.A. Morange.
Gates & Morange *(Set Design)* 3073, 3675, 4818, 4819
Gateson, Marjorie *(Cast)* 458, 1345, 1784, 2378, 2497, 2519, 2527, 2546, 2614, 3236, 3345, 4241
Gathers, Helen *(Composer)* 4264
Gathers, Helen *(Lyricist)* 4264
Gatteye, Bennye *(Cast)* 4409
Gatti, A. & S. *(Producer)* 719
Gattinguer, Robert *(Composer)* 3827
Gatts, George M. *(Producer)* 452
Gaudin, Kevin *(Cast)* 2735
Gaughan, Jack *(Musical Director)* 1171
Gaumont, Irving *(Producer)* 3966
Gaus, Robert T. *(Producer)* 2611
Gauthier, Katherine *(Cast)* 1657
Gautier, Dick *(Cast)* 607
Gavault, Paul *(Author)* 613, 4285, 4327
Gavault, Paul *(Librettist)* 4285
Gavon, Igors *(Cast)* 1216, 3020, 3427, 3564, 4196, 4789
Gawthorne, Peter *(Cast)* 3583
Gaxton, William *(Cast)* 69, 163, 834, 1272, 1948, 2402, 2432, 2444, 2597, 2888, 3007, 3091, 3225, 3371, 4667
Gay *(Composer)* 2454
Gay *(Lyricist)* 2454
Gay, Alden *(Cast)* 1013
Gay, Byron *(Composer)* 69, 1687, 1819, 1966, 3246
Gay, Byron *(Lyricist)* 1687, 1819, 3246

Gay, John *(Author)*   341, 4368, 4369, 4370, 4371
Gay, John *(Lyricist)*   1589
Gay, Maisie *(Cast)*   704, 791, 2570, 3500, 4258, 4661
Gay, Noel *(Composer)*   2148, 2798, 4027
Gay, Noel *(Lyricist)*   2148, 2798
Gaye, Gregory *(Cast)*   4372
Gaye, Marvin *(Composer)*   4534
Gaye, Marvin *(Lyricist)*   4534
Gaylord, Al E. *(Musical Director)*   1271
Gaynes, Edmund *(Cast)*   2579, 3696
Gaynes, George
    See also George Jongeyans.
Gaynes, George *(Cast)*   616, 1122, 3696, 4734
Gaynor, Charles *(Composer)*   382, 2148, 2168, 2439,
    2483, 3954, 4230
Gaynor, Charles *(Director)*   3954
Gaynor, Charles *(Librettist)*   382, 2168, 2439, 2483, 3954
Gaynor, Charles *(Lyricist)*   382, 2148, 2168, 2439, 2483,
    3954, 4153, 4230
Gaynor, Jane *(Producer)*   39
Gaynor, Janet *(Cast)*   1775
Gaynor, Mitzi *(Cast)*   2234
Gaze, Hal *(Composer)*   2341
Gaze, Hal *(Lyricist)*   2341
GeBauer, Judy *(Librettist)*   3688
Gear, Florence *(Cast)*   939
Gear, Luella *(Cast)*   901, 924, 1453, 2475, 2620, 3064,
    3283, 3310, 3540, 3622, 4174, 4532
Geary, Arthur *(Cast)*   2747
Geary, Joyce *(Lyricist)*   90
Gebest, Charles *(Composer)*   604
Gebest, Charles J. *(Composer)*   335, 3685, 4759
Gebest, Charles J. *(Musical Director)*   335, 804, 805, 1640,
    1826, 2533, 2767, 2829, 3218, 3685, 3809, 4759
Gebest, Charles J. *(Orchestrations)*   115, 1271, 2517, 3809,
    4277, 4759
Gebirtig, M. *(Composer)*   4342
Gebirtig, M. *(Lyricist)*   4342
Gebirtig, Mordechai *(Composer)*   2356
Gebirtig, Mordechai *(Lyricist)*   2356
Gee, George *(Cast)*   2323
Gee, Hugh *(Set Designer)*   4765
Gee, Kevin John *(Cast)*   595
Gee, Lottie *(Cast)*   740, 3676, 3963
Geer, Kevin *(Cast)*   1304
Geer, Shippen *(Lyricist)*   1370
Geer, Shippen *(Producer)*   1370
Geer, Will *(Cast)*   919, 1977, 2653, 2859, 3294, 3990,
    4542, 4715
Geffen, David *(Producer)*   678, 2544
Geffen Records *(Producer)*   1103
Gehman, Richard *(Lyricist)*   600
Gehrecke, Frank *(Composer)*   4433
Gehrecke, Frank *(Director)*   1697
Gehrecke, Frank *(Librettist)*   1697, 4433
Gehrecke, Frank *(Lyricist)*   1697, 4433
Gehrue, Mayme *(Cast)*   666, 2324
Geidt, Jeremy *(Cast)*   1195, 1406
Geiger *(Composer)*   2419
Geiger *(Lyricist)*   2419
Geise, Sugar *(Cast)*   1938

Geiss, Tony *(Composer)*   4627
Geiss, Tony *(Librettist)*   3479, 4627
Geiss, Tony *(Lyricist)*   2913, 3112, 4627
Geissmann, Bob *(Set Design)*   4047
Geist, Lisa *(Cast)*   1159
Geistinger, Marie *(Cast)*   3896
Gelb, Philip *(Set Design)*   2476
Gelbart, Larry *(Librettist)*   775, 837, 1422, 3046
Gelbel, Adam *(Composer)*   4390
Gelbel, Adam *(Lyricist)*   4390
Gelber, Stanley Jay *(Composer)*   2599
Gelbert, Franklin *(Producer)*   2439
Gelbtrunk, Adam *(Composer)*   4667
Geld, Gary *(Composer)*   135, 3610, 3928
Gelfand, Carol *(Cast)*   832
Gelfer, Steven *(Cast)*   678
Gelfman, Sam W. *(Producer)*   2067
Gelke, Becky *(Cast)*   4398
Geller, Bruce *(Librettist)*   71, 2556
Geller, Bruce *(Lyricist)*   71, 2556, 3889
Geller, Helen *(Cast)*   3641
Gellers, Irving *(Composer)*   4586
Gelman, Larry *(Cast)*   4796
Gemignani, Paul *(Composer)*   2607
Gemignani, Paul *(Musical Director)*   212, 754, 921, 1038,
    1068, 1184, 1699, 2143, 2205, 2822, 3015, 3279, 3340,
    3411, 3718, 4020, 4210, 4233
Gemignani, Paul *(Orchestrations)*   1038
Gene *(Costumes)*   876
Genee, Adeline *(Cast)*   256, 4094
Genee, Richard *(Author)*   689, 3150, 3151
Genevieve *(Cast)*   3841
Gennaro, Liza *(Choreographer)*   2766
Gennaro, Peter *(Cast)*   183, 363, 1706, 3351, 3563
Gennaro, Peter *(Choreographer)*   150, 155, 269, 299,
    652, 1280, 2217, 2643, 2983, 3299, 3899, 4371,
    4516, 4625
Genni, Gwynne *(Lyricist)*   3617
Geno, Alton *(Choreographer)*   778
Genovese, Gen *(Author)*   596
Genovese, Gen *(Librettist)*   596
Genovese, Gen *(Lyricist)*   596
Genovese, Gen *(Producer)*   596
Gensler, Lewis *(Composer)*   317
Gensler, Lewis E. *(Composer)*   289, 317, 391, 393, 642,
    1357, 1440, 1689, 1923, 3622, 3623, 4424, 4532
Gensler, Lewis E. *(Producer)*   289, 1275, 1440, 4532
Genteel, Grace *(Cast)*   4191
Gentile, Pietro *(Cast)*   1950
Gentry, Derek *(Cast)*   3227
Gentry, Minnie *(Cast)*   40
Genus, Karl *(Director)*   3543
Geoffreys, Stephen *(Cast)*   2033
Geoly, Guy *(Costumes)*   3734, 4703
George, Andre *(Cast)*   2735
George, Betty *(Cast)*   145
George, Bob *(Orchestrations)*   2074
George, Charles *(Composer)*   1584, 2492
George, Charles *(Costumes)*   2492
George, Charles *(Director)*   2492
George, Charles *(Librettist)*   1584, 2492

Ghoshal, Kurnar *(Cast)* 1603

Ghostley, Alice *(Cast)* 52, 72, 759, 1047, 1474, 2556, 2611, 3107, 3831, 3913

Giacosa, Giuseppe *(Librettist)* 2359

Giagni, D.J. *(Choreographer)* 171, 212, 1776, 3448

Giamatti, Bartlett *(Cast)* 945

Giampa, W.J. *(Set Design)* 1450

Gianfrancesco, Edward T. *(Set Design)* 1258, 1591, 2544

Gianiotis, Anna *(Cast)* 3539

Giannelli, Christina *(Lighting Designer)* 4398

Giannini, A. Christina *(Costumes)* 1171, 4172, 4379

Gianono, Joe *(Orchestrations)* 674

Gianono, Joseph *(Orchestrations)* 146, 1149, 2208

Giasco, Kitty *(Cast)* 1824

Gibb, Barry *(Composer)* 3739

Gibb, Barry *(Lyricist)* 3739

Gibb, Maurice *(Composer)* 3739

Gibb, Maurice *(Lyricist)* 3739

Gibb, Robin *(Composer)* 3739

Gibb, Robin *(Lyricist)* 3739

Gibberson, Bill *(Cast)* 1815

Gibbings, Jim *(Lighting Designer)* 3841

Gibbons, Carroll *(Composer)* 418

Gibbs, Georgia *(Cast)* 2653

Gibbs, Lloyd *(Cast)* 4088

Gibbs, Nancy *(Cast)* 4302

Gibbs, Sheila *(Cast)* 3285

Gibney, Susan *(Cast)* 1232

Gibson, B.G. *(Cast)* 3903

Gibson, Corine *(Cast)* 986

Gibson, Fred *(Set Design)* 4723

Gibson, Joanne *(Cast)* 1249

Gibson, Joe *(Composer)* 2856

Gibson, Joe *(Lyricist)* 2856

Gibson, John *(Cast)* 4599

Gibson, Judy *(Cast)* 3741, 3876

Gibson, Julie *(Cast)* 242

Gibson, Madeline *(Cast)* 4341

Gibson, Michael *(Dance Arranger)* 2146

Gibson, Michael *(Orchestrations)* 146, 535, 757, 1146, 1164, 1172, 1510, 1638, 2333, 2689, 2702, 2737, 2805, 3060, 3126, 3305, 3330, 3577, 3718, 3792, 4459, 4727

Gibson, Michael *(Vocal Arranger)* 1510, 2146, 2728

Gibson, Tanya *(Cast)* 432

Gibson, Virginia *(Cast)* 1681, 1760

Gibson, William *(Author)* 3869

Gibson, William *(Librettist)* 1601, 3643

Gibson, William *(Lyricist)* 3643

Gideon, I.E. *(Producer)* 1995

Gideon, Melville *(Cast)* 3310

Gideon, Melville *(Composer)* 208, 336, 511, 1153, 1327, 1523, 1613, 1801, 2892, 3213, 3310, 3701, 3827, 4802

Gideon, Melville *(Lyricist)* 201, 377, 1523, 4302, 4553, 4555

Gideon, Melville *(Producer)* 3310

Gideon, Melville T. *(Composer)* 3061

Gideon, Steve *(Cast)* 3178

Giehse, Theodore *(Director)* 3441

Giehse, Therese *(Cast)* 3441

Gielgud, Sir John *(Narrator)* 3454

Gierasch, Stefan *(Cast)* 4095

Giersberg, Max *(Author)* 82

Giese, Linda *(Costumes)* 4595

Gifford, Harry *(Composer)* 336, 2334, 3755, 4206, 4657

Gifford, Harry *(Lyricist)* 2334, 3755, 4206, 4657

Gifford, Jack *(Cast)* 4683

Gifford, Julia *(Cast)* 1248, 4646

Giftos, Elaine *(Cast)* 3112

Gigl, Aloysius *(Cast)* 4515

Giglio, Clement *(Composer)* 4672

Giglio, Clement *(Librettist)* 4672

Giglio, Clement *(Lyricist)* 4672

Gignoux, Regis *(Author)* 2669

Gilb, Melinda *(Cast)* 261, 3992, 4193

Gilb, Melinda *(Librettist)* 4193

Gilbert, Alan *(Cast)* 4096

Gilbert, Barbara *(Cast)* 3124

Gilbert, Benjamin Thorpe *(Librettist)* 4794

Gilbert, Bert *(Cast)* 2701

Gilbert, Billy *(Cast)* 596, 1711, 2182

Gilbert, Billy *(Librettist)* 596

Gilbert, Craig P. *(Librettist)* 1862

Gilbert, Edward *(Costumes)* 3105

Gilbert, Edward *(Lighting Designer)* 1204

Gilbert, Edward *(Set Design)* 67, 70, 1204, 1930, 2098, 2099, 2103, 3105, 3335, 4166, 4428

Gilbert, Edwin *(Librettist)* 3104, 4545

Gilbert, Edwin *(Lyricist)* 3103, 3104, 4777

Gilbert, Franklin *(Producer)* 2680

Gilbert, Fred *(Composer)* 1301

Gilbert, Fred *(Lyricist)* 1301

Gilbert, George *(Producer)* 1290, 2987

Gilbert, Gloria *(Cast)* 289, 1423, 4174

Gilbert, H. *(Author)* 2610

Gilbert, Hy *(Lyricist)* 3851

Gilbert, James *(Composer)* 1644

Gilbert, James *(Lyricist)* 1644

Gilbert, Jean *(Author)* 12, 1554, 2293, 2384, 2923, 3529, 4795

Gilbert, Jean *(Composer)* 184, 965, 1534, 1554, 2293, 2384, 2385, 2747, 2922, 2923, 3237, 3529, 3627, 3680, 4170, 4795

Gilbert, Jean *(Lyricist)* 4795

Gilbert, John *(Composer)* 2747

Gilbert, John D. *(Librettist)* 3228

Gilbert, John D. *(Lyricist)* 3228

Gilbert, L. Wolfe *(Lyricist)* 433, 558, 710, 1065, 1334, 1400, 1531, 2415, 2486, 3018, 3259, 3614, 3995, 4655

Gilbert, Lisa *(Cast)* 3002

Gilbert, Lorenz *(Cast)* 1624

Gilbert, Lou *(Cast)* 1122, 2319

Gilbert, Maud *(Cast)* 175

Gilbert, Melvin B. *(Choreographer)* 761

Gilbert, Mercedes *(Cast)* 488

Gilbert, Olive *(Cast)* 650, 972

Gilbert, Paul *(Cast)* 2742, 4829

Gilbert, Ray *(Cast)* 4536

Gilbert, Ray *(Lyricist)* 4264

Gilbert, Robert *(Author)* 2610, 4486, 4667

Gilbert, Tony *(Cast)* 4703

Gilbert, W.S. *(Author)* 345, 1948, 2817, 2861, 4617

Gilbert, W.S. *(Librettist)* 1905, 1987, 4254

Gilbert, W.S. *(Lyricist)* 1905, 1987, 2348, 2977, 3280, 4254
Gilbert, W.S. *(Music Based On)* 2817
Gilbert, Willie *(Librettist)* 1991, 2019
Gilder, Vanessa K. *(Cast)* 3522
Gile, Bill *(Director)* 2877, 3080, 4454
Gile, William *(Director)* 2026
Giler, Bernie *(Author)* 1539
Giles, Anthony *(Librettist)* 3197
Giles, Anthony *(Lyricist)* 3197
Giles, Nancy *(Cast)* 2790, 4535
Giles, Nancy *(Librettist)* 4535
Gilfether, Daniel *(Cast)* 1445, 3759, 4239
Gilfoil, Harry *(Cast)* 2465, 4165, 4181, 4757
Gilford, Jack *(Cast)* 59, 610, 1422, 2809, 3286, 3288, 3761
Gilford, Madeline *(Producer)* 4643
Gilk, Hirsh *(Lyricist)* 1740
Gilkey, Stanley *(Producer)* 3292, 4362, 4483
Gill, Brenden *(Librettist)* 2357
Gill, Gus *(Librettist)* 3024
Gill, Michael *(Producer)* 784
Gill, Ray *(Cast)* 583
Gill, William *(Cast)* 3856
Gill, William *(Librettist)* 3887
Gill, William *(Set Design)* 3047
Gillan, Charles P. *(Cast)* 4507
Gillen, Frank *(Composer)* 1223
Gillen, Frank *(Lyricist)* 1223
Gillespie, Arthur *(Composer)* 2286
Gillespie, Arthur *(Librettist)* 1173, 3877
Gillespie, Arthur *(Lyricist)* 1054, 1212, 1316, 2793, 3877
Gillespie, Christina *(Cast)* 71, 1194
Gillespie, Conor *(Cast)* 2229
Gillespie, Frank M. *(Choreographer)* 463, 659
Gillespie, Frank M. *(Director)* 1667
Gillespie, H.L. *(Producer)* 2532
Gillespie, Haven *(Lyricist)* 885, 1137, 1939, 3020, 3175, 3833
Gillespie, Lee *(Dance Arranger)* 1978
Gillespie, Lee *(Musical Director)* 1978, 4470
Gillespie, Marion *(Lyricist)* 293, 377
Gillespie, Robert *(Director)* 1256
Gillespie, T. *(Cast)* 1604
Gillespie, Tinker *(Cast)* 1010
Gillette, Anita *(Cast)* 64, 656, 2217, 2304, 2983, 3497, 3810
Gillette, Bobby *(Cast)* 3946
Gillette, Priscilla *(Cast)* 1600, 3326, 3691
Gillette, Ruth *(Cast)* 1460
Gillette, Viola *(Cast)* 1518, 1975
Gillette, William *(Author)* 1270
Gilliam, Michael *(Lighting Designer)* 450
Gilliam, Philip *(Lighting Designer)* 4220
Gilliam, Philip *(Set Design)* 4022, 4220
Gillian, Allie *(Cast)* 2520
Gilligan, Helen *(Cast)* 4179
Gilliland, Helen *(Cast)* 3680
Gilliland, Jane *(Producer)* 4173
Gillingwater, Claude *(Cast)* 509, 1555, 2915
Gillins, Bobby *(Cast)* 1421
Gillins, George *(Composer)* 1421
Gillman, Jane *(Cast)* 4740

Gillmore, Ruth *(Cast)* 1357
Gillsepie, Arthur *(Librettist)* 2635
Gillsepie, Arthur *(Lyricist)* 2635
Gilman, D. *(Costumes)* 3580
Gilman, Eliot *(Orchestrations)* 2785
Gilman, Mabel *(Cast)* 2117, 3784
Gilman, Mabelle *(Cast)* 666, 2917
Gilman, Mme. *(Costumes)* 2557, 2601
Gilman, Sondra *(Producer)* 4091
Gilmore, Douglas *(Author)* 1939
Gilmore, Margalo *(Cast)* 3453, 3815
Gilmore, Mary *(Cast)* 1538
Gilmore, Paul *(Cast)* 224, 515
Gilmore, Paul *(Director)* 3192
Gilmore, W.H. *(Director)* 1391, 2526, 2757, 3079, 3323, 3382, 3466, 3472
Gilmour, David *(Composer)* 3739
Gilpin, Charles *(Cast)* 645, 2520
Gilpin, Charles *(Composer)* 525, 2490
Gilpin, Charles *(Lyricist)* 525, 2490
Gilpin, Charles A. *(Cast)* 2044
Gilrod, Louis *(Lyricist)* 573, 1609
Gilroy, Frank *(Author)* 139, 1510
Gilroy, John *(Cast)* 2592
Gilroy, John *(Librettist)* 2851
Gilroy, John *(Lyricist)* 470, 2465, 2851, 4691
Gimbel, Norman *(Composer)* 863, 4193
Gimbel, Norman *(Lyricist)* 837, 863, 3940, 3941, 4193, 4264, 4682
Gimble, Harriet *(Cast)* 1686
Gimpel, Erica *(Cast)* 119
Gindi, Roger Alan *(Producer)* 2171
Gingold, Hermione *(Cast)* 1119, 1290, 1408, 2168, 2227, 2536, 4153
Gingold, Hermione *(Librettist)* 2168, 2483, 4153
Gingold, Hermione *(Lyricist)* 2168, 2227, 4153
Ginnes, Abram S. *(Librettist)* 2449
Ginzler, Robert *(Orchestrations)* 64, 519, 607, 837, 1076, 1237, 1567, 1709, 2019, 2150, 3210, 3234, 4566, 4693
Ginzler, Robert *(Vocal Arranger)* 837
Gioe, Salvatore *(Musical Director)* 817
Giono, Jean *(Author)* 273
Giordano, Frank *(Cast)* 1498
Giordano, Gus *(Choreographer)* 3925
Giovanni *(Lyricist)* 4264
Giovannini, Sandro *(Director)* 3798
Giovannini, Sandro *(Librettist)* 3798
Giovannini, Sandro *(Lyricist)* 3798
Giradot, Etienne *(Cast)* 2827
Girard, Dixie *(Cast)* 396
Girard, Eddie *(Cast)* 2181
Girard, Harry *(Composer)* 47
Girard, Teddy *(Cast)* 1153
Giraudoux, Jean *(Author)* 1012
Girdler, Deb G. *(Cast)* 3306
Girio, Cesar *(Costumes)* 3144
Girl Friends, The *(Cast)* 1950
Girl Trust, The *(Cast)* 4487
Girlando, Paul J. *(Composer)* 1710
Girls from the Follies, The *(Cast)* 806
Girolami, Peter *(Set Design)* 2611

Giroux, Germaine *(Cast)* 4105
Girvin, T. Galen *(Cast)* 3539
Gish, Lillian *(Cast)* 161, 3020
Gisondi, John *(Lighting Designer)* 33
Gittens, Hugh *(Director)* 3814
Gitter, Chaim *(Lighting Designer)* 3654
Gitter, Hillel *(Cast)* 4560
Gittler, Barbara *(Producer)* 2195
Givot, George *(Cast)* 125, 223, 1061, 1126, 2847, 3153, 3379
Gizienski, George *(Lighting Designer)* 1262
Gizienski, George *(Set Design)* 1262
Glad, Gladys *(Cast)* 3766, 4683, 4823
Glade, Carol *(Cast)* 249
Glade, Coe *(Cast)* 3639
Gladke, Peter *(Cast)* 190
Gladstein, Renee *(Costumes)* 3781
Glaser, C.J.M. *(Composer)* 3977
Glaser, C.J.M. *(Musical Director)* 3977
Glaser, John *(Costumes)* 4518
Glaser, Lulu *(Cast)* 727, 947, 1030, 1071, 1292, 1522, 1720, 2282, 2502, 2566, 2671, 2835, 2885, 2886, 2914, 3566, 4236
Glaser, Lulu *(Composer)* 1292
Glaser, Michael *(Cast)* 594
Glaser and Company, Lulu *(Producer)* 4236
Glass, George *(Musical Director)* 1647
Glass, Montague *(Librettist)* 2407, 4621
Glassman, Seth *(Director)* 4480, 4540
Glassman, Stephen *(Librettist)* 406
Glave, Jeffrey *(Set Design)* 2388
Glawson, Carol *(Lighting Designer)* 2573
Glazener, Janet *(Musical Director)* 2208, 3277
Glazer, Benjamin *(Lyricist)* 2487
Glazer, Peter *(Adaptation)* 4740
Glazer, Peter *(Director)* 4740
Glazier, Marie *(Cast)* 2518
Gleason, Helen *(Cast)* 1384, 3152
Gleason, Jackie *(Cast)* 95, 204, 1336, 4270
Gleason, James *(Cast)* 42, 2403, 3562
Gleason, James *(Librettist)* 3648
Gleason, Joanna *(Cast)* 2058, 2143, 3142
Gleason, John *(Lighting Designer)* 135, 1380, 2362, 2590, 3309, 3330, 3468, 3515, 3787, 4459, 4481
Gleason, Thomas *(Cast)* 603
Gleason, William *(Librettist)* 843
Gleason, William *(Lyricist)* 843
Glecker, Robert *(Cast)* 1979
Gleeson, Colette *(Cast)* 1741
Glendenning, John *(Cast)* 1553
Glendinning, Ernest *(Cast)* 1517, 2070, 2537, 2922, 2950, 4085, 4424
Glendinning, Jessie *(Cast)* 2613
Glenn, "Happy" Julius *(Cast)* 641
Glenn, Julius *(Cast)* 2127
Glenn, Nettie *(Cast)* 3945
Glenn-Smith, Michael *(Cast)* 681, 3469
Glenville, Peter *(Director)* 4270, 4435
Glenville, Shaun *(Cast)* 3472
Glick, Ben *(Set Design)* 1514
Glickman, Stanley A. *(Producer)* 74

Glickman, Will *(Librettist)* 59, 483, 743, 2267, 2439, 2837, 2987, 3509
Glines, John *(Composer)* 1590
Glines, John *(Director)* 4157
Glines, John *(Librettist)* 1590
Glines, John *(Lyricist)* 1590
Glines, John *(Producer)* 2022
Glines, The *(Producer)* 2022
Glist, Alan *(Producer)* 3926
Glist, Kathi *(Producer)* 3926
Glitter, Jimmy *(Composer)* 2580
Glogau, Jack *(Composer)* 60, 2189, 4812
Glogau, Jack *(Lyricist)* 4812
Glopen, Joe *(Cast)* 4107
Glosser, Daniel *(Musical Director)* 1346
Glover, Beth *(Cast)* 484, 3568
Glover, Corey *(Cast)* 1232
Glover, Cyd *(Cast)* 432
Glover, Ernest *(Set Design)* 2841
Glover, J.M. *(Composer)* 2035, 2964, 4014
Glover, J.M. *(Lyricist)* 2964
Glover, Joe *(Orchestrations)* 98, 177, 180, 1091, 1336, 2103, 2554, 2556, 3108, 3234, 3371, 3813, 4337, 4446, 4828
Glover, John *(Cast)* 3871
Glover, Ralph *(Cast)* 711, 3131
Glover, Rita *(Set Design)* 2496
Glover, S. *(Composer)* 1897
Glover, S. *(Lyricist)* 1897
Glover, Savion *(Cast)* 432, 2200
Glover, William *(Cast)* 2650
Glover, William *(Director)* 2650
Glover, William *(Librettist)* 2650
Gloves, W.F. *(Arrangements)* 45
Gluck, J. *(Composer)* 4193
Gluck, J. *(Lyricist)* 4193
Gluck, M. Senia *(Choreographer)* 1131, 2330
Gluck, Marvin A. *(Author)* 2578
Gluck, Wally *(Producer)* 1722
Gluckman, Leon *(Director)* 4579
Gluckman, Leon *(Lighting Designer)* 4579
Glushak, Joanna *(Cast)* 2470, 4515
Glynn, Carlin *(Cast)* 374
Glynn, Thomas *(Cast)* 4486
Gobel, George *(Cast)* 2449
Gobel, George *(Voice)* 4471
Goberman, Max *(Musical Director)* 404, 2563, 2864, 3278, 4446, 4625, 4652
Gochman, Len *(Cast)* 1010, 4468
Gockel, Fred *(Cast)* 239
Godard, Charles *(Composer)* 364
Godard, Flora *(Costumes)* 2547
Goddard, Charles W. *(Librettist)* 2891
Goddard, Gary *(Composer)* 1159
Goddard, Gary *(Lyricist)* 1159
Goddard, Malcolm *(Choreographer)* 3445
Goddard, Mark *(Cast)* 16
Goddard, Willoughby *(Cast)* 3271
Godfred, Hal *(Cast)* 4725
Godfrey *(Lyricist)* 4154
Godfrey, Arthur *(Cast)* 197, 4362

Godfrey, Arthur E. *(Musical Director)* 2976
Godfrey, Fred *(Composer)* 4657
Godfrey, Fred *(Lyricist)* 4657
Godfrey, Jeff *(Composer)* 3397
Godfrey, Jeff *(Lyricist)* 965
Godfrey, Lynnie *(Cast)* 1198
Godfrey, Mostyn *(Cast)* 1610
Godfrey, Roy *(Cast)* 1386
Godfrey, Vaughn *(Choreographer)* 1710, 2071, 4322,
    4328, 4528, 4669
Godkin, Paul *(Cast)* 283, 1670, 1886, 4142
Godkin, Paul *(Choreographer)* 283, 4323
Godowsky, Leopold *(Composer)* 4033
Godreau, Miguel *(Cast)* 1012
Godreau, Miguel *(Choreographer)* 3830
Godreau, Miguel *(Director)* 3830
Godwin, Howard *(Composer)* 662, 1415
Goëckner, Anton *(Musical Director)* 982
Goehr, Rudolph *(Orchestrations)* 1748
Goehring, George *(Composer)* 2375, 3695
Goehring, George *(Lyricist)* 3695
Goering, Hal *(Composer)* 393
Goetz, Augustus *(Author)* 4600
Goetz, Coleman *(Lyricist)* 965, 1084, 4720
Goetz, E. Ray *(Composer)* 60, 208, 470, 913, 954, 1391,
    1464, 1735, 1919, 1920, 1927, 2456, 2526, 3052, 3079,
    3096, 3191, 3313, 3382, 3525, 4044, 4148, 4206, 4603,
    4742, 4801
Goetz, E. Ray *(Director)* 3131
Goetz, E. Ray *(Librettist)* 1920
Goetz, E. Ray *(Lyricist)* 60, 201, 208, 336, 802, 910,
    913, 960, 1063, 1153, 1247, 1391, 1464, 1485, 1486,
    1613, 1626, 1735, 1738, 1835, 1845, 1919, 1920, 1927,
    2262, 2456, 2526, 2782, 2892, 3052, 3079, 3096, 3175,
    3382, 3466, 3478, 3525, 3575, 3715, 3716, 3737, 3755,
    4033, 4044, 4148, 4206, 4553, 4603, 4714, 4721, 4742,
    4803, 4804
Goetz, E. Ray *(Producer)* 208, 1272, 1335, 1391, 3079,
    3131, 3382, 3478, 4742
Goetz, Ruth Goodman *(Author)* 4600
Goetzl, Anselm *(Composer)* 165, 3770, 3791, 4066
Goetzl, Anselm *(Musical Director)* 2486
Goetzl, Anselm *(Producer)* 3770
Goff, Charles *(Cast)* 3682
Goff, Jerry *(Cast)* 4179
Goff, Stephen *(Costumes)* 4679
Goff, Stephen *(Producer)* 4679
Goff, Stephen *(Set Design)* 4093, 4679
Goffin, Gerry *(Composer)* 3739, 4193, 4534
Goffin, Gerry *(Lyricist)* 3739, 4193, 4534
Goggie *(Costumes)* 2709
Goggin, Dan *(Cast)* 1770
Goggin, Dan *(Choreographer)* 275
Goggin, Dan *(Composer)* 275, 546, 1770, 2435, 3211
Goggin, Dan *(Director)* 275, 3211
Goggin, Dan *(Librettist)* 275, 3211
Goggin, Dan *(Lyricist)* 275, 3211
Goggin, Victoria *(Cast)* 3671
Gogotsky, N. *(Composer)* 464
Gohl, James F. *(Set Design)* 1500
Gohman, Don *(Composer)* 101, 4273

Going, John *(Director)* 1079, 2565
Goland, Arnold *(Dance Arranger)* 249, 1864, 4186, 4633
Goland, Arnold *(Orchestrations)* 249, 1380, 2522, 4186
Goland, Arnold *(Vocal Arranger)* 249, 4186
Gold, Al *(Cast)* 3946
Gold, Annabelle *(Cast)* 3505
Gold, Belle *(Cast)* 1519
Gold, David *(Cast)* 1094
Gold, David *(Musical Director)* 874
Gold, Ernest *(Composer)* 2075, 3261
Gold, Joe *(Composer)* 2856
Gold, W. *(Composer)* 4193
Gold, W. *(Lyricist)* 4193
Gold, Zisha *(Cast)* 2811
Goldberg, David *(Lyricist)* 1657, 4669
Goldberg, Diana *(Cast)* 3559
Goldberg, Harry *(Producer)* 926, 927
Goldberg, Harry A. *(Director)* 4530
Goldberg, Jack *(Producer)* 3614
Goldberg, Jerry *(Composer)* 1873
Goldberg, Jerry *(Lyricist)* 1873
Goldberg, Jerry *(Musical Director)* 2925, 3988
Goldberg, Jerry *(Vocal Arranger)* 2925
Goldberg, Leonard *(Producer)* 181
Goldberg, Leonard J. *(Producer)* 1809
Goldberg, Rube *(Librettist)* 199, 3005, 3810, 4047
Goldberg, Rube *(Lyricist)* 1689
Goldberg, Russell *(Cast)* 484
Goldblatt, Hanan *(Cast)* 1075
Goldblum, Jeff *(Cast)* 2949
Goldby, Derek *(Director)* 1848
Golden, Annie *(Cast)* 212, 2427, 3076
Golden, E. *(Composer)* 1688
Golden, E. *(Lyricist)* 1688
Golden, Edward *(Composer)* 2349
Golden, Edward *(Librettist)* 2349
Golden, Edward *(Lyricist)* 2349
Golden, Ernie *(Composer)* 203, 1134, 1687
Golden, Ernie *(Lyricist)* 203, 1134
Golden, Grace *(Cast)* 311
Golden, John *(Composer)* 632, 782, 960, 1009, 1151, 1360,
    1588, 2025, 2254, 2904, 3332, 3372, 3737, 4017, 4219,
    4258, 4382, 4642, 4712, 4747
Golden, John *(Librettist)* 782, 1360, 1588
Golden, John *(Lyricist)* 396, 632, 712, 736, 782, 1151,
    1208, 1360, 1538, 1566, 1588, 1901, 2025, 2254, 2891,
    2904, 3332, 3737, 4258, 4382, 4712, 4747
Golden, John *(Producer)* 1009
Golden, John L. *(Composer)* 1430, 1455, 4799
Golden, John L. *(Lyricist)* 396, 1455
Golden, Lee *(Cast)* 2654
Golden, Ray *(Composer)* 59, 1892, 2246, 2742, 2962
Golden, Ray *(Director)* 1892, 2246, 2962
Golden, Ray *(Librettist)* 2742, 2809, 3255
Golden, Ray *(Lyricist)* 59, 673, 1892, 2246, 2259, 2742,
    2962, 3255
Golden, Ray *(Producer)* 59, 2246
Golden, Richard *(Cast)* 1355
Golden Glow Unlimited, Ltd. *(Producer)* 2704
Goldenberg, Billy *(Composer)* 287, 973, 1298
Goldenberg, Billy *(Dance Arranger)* 2449

Goldenberg, William (*Composer*) 2279
Goldenberg, William (*Dance Arranger*) 1846, 1891, 3294
Goldenthal, Elliot (*Composer*) 4442
Goldfaden, Abraham (*Composer*) 1279
Goldfaden, Abraham (*Lyricist*) 1279
Goldfarb, Sidney (*Librettist*) 4442
Goldfarb, Sidney (*Lyricist*) 4442
Goldin, Al (*Producer*) 820
Goldin, Toni (*Lighting Designer*) 3239, 4618
Golding, Samuel R. (*Librettist*) 563
Goldman, Byron (*Producer*) 594, 1634, 2205, 2874
Goldman, Donald H. (*Producer*) 2731
Goldman, Harold (*Composer*) 1448
Goldman, Harold (*Librettist*) 4152
Goldman, Harold (*Lyricist*) 1448, 3103
Goldman, James (*Librettist*) 1200, 1237, 1329
Goldman, James (*Lyricist*) 1237
Goldman, Jerry (*Librettist*) 1233, 3484
Goldman, Kathleen (*Librettist*) 4152
Goldman, Louis S. (*Producer*) 461
Goldman, Robert (*Lyricist*) 1290
Goldman, Sherwin M. (*Producer*) 1609, 3088
Goldman, William (*Librettist*) 1237
Goldman, William (*Lyricist*) 1237
Goldmark, Leo (*Author*) 995
Goldmark, Leo (*Librettist*) 3896
Goldmark, Leo (*Lyricist*) 3896
Goldner, Charles (*Cast*) 1548
Goldner, Charles (*Director*) 346
Goldner, George (*Composer*) 166
Goldner, George (*Lyricist*) 166
Goldoni, Carlo (*Author*) 225, 2464, 2910, 4244
Goldsmith, Abe (*Librettist*) 1233, 3484
Goldsmith, Beatrice (*Lyricist*) 3226
Goldsmith, C. Gerald (*Producer*) 935
Goldsmith, Eleanor (*Costumes*) 1278, 2137, 2629, 4314
Goldsmith, George (*Author*) 1783
Goldsmith, Lee (*Composer*) 4566
Goldsmith, Lee (*Librettist*) 3902, 3925
Goldsmith, Lee (*Lyricist*) 1408, 3902, 3925, 4566
Goldsmith, Merwin (*Cast*) 36, 171, 198, 2359, 3666, 3702, 4790
Goldsmith, Oliver (*Author*) 2650, 3215, 3302, 4497
Goldsmith, Ted (*Composer*) 1342
Goldsmith, Ted (*Lyricist*) 1342
Goldstein, Hy (*Cast*) 3501
Goldstein, Jerome (*Dance Arranger*) 268
Goldstein, Jerome (*Vocal Arranger*) 268
Goldstein, Jess (*Costumes*) 595, 699, 784, 2766, 3277, 4390
Goldstein, Joel (*Producer*) 105
Goldstein, Jonathan (*Cast*) 1232
Goldstein, Nat (*Composer*) 2363
Goldstein, Nat (*Lyricist*) 2363
Goldstein, Owen H. (*Costumes*) 4470
Goldstein, Ted (*Set Design*) 624
Goldstone, Bob (*Arrangements*) 573
Goldstone, Bob (*Dance Arranger*) 1092
Goldstone, Bob (*Musical Director*) 573, 647, 843, 1092, 3817
Goldstone, Bob (*Orchestrations*) 1092, 1739

Goldstone, Bob (*Vocal Arranger*) 1092
Goldstone, Nat (*Producer*) 462
Goldstone, Robert (*Dance Arranger*) 3764
Goldstone, Robert (*Vocal Arranger*) 3764
Goldsworthy, John (*Cast*) 3865
Goldwasser, Lawrence L. (*Set Design*) 1862, 2610, 4174, 4498
Golladlay, Nancy (*Lighting Designer*) 1978
Golman, Daniel A. (*Producer*) 1059
Goloboff, Mim (*Cast*) 1757
Golomb, Sheldon (*Cast*) 2322
Golonka, Arlene (*Cast*) 3612
Golub, Solomon (*Composer*) 1279
Golub, Solomon (*Lyricist*) 1279
Gomez (*Cast*) 2105
Gomez, Vincente (*Cast*) 7
Gomez and Winona (*Cast*) 662
Gon, Zamira (*Choreographer*) 1299
Gondra, Arthur (*Librettist*) 4110
Gontard, G.V. (*Producer*) 4316
Gonzalez, Ernesto (*Cast*) 3711
Gonzalez, Raoul (*Composer*) 2288, 2580
Gonzalez, Raoul (*Lyricist*) 2288
Good, Jack (*Cast*) 796, 1225, 1414, 1836
Good, Peter (*Librettist*) 4482
Goodacre, Ralph (*Set Design*) 3173
Goodall, Howard (*Composer*) 1903
Goodchild, Tim (*Set Design*) 456, 1296
Goode, Herbert (*Composer*) 3946
Goode, Herbert (*Lyricist*) 3946
Goode, Jack (*Cast*) 1711
Goode, Mort (*Lyricist*) 2260
Goode, Richard (*Cast*) 3871
Goodelle, Niela (*Cast*) 2105
Goodfriend, Oscar (*Musical Director*) 3357
Goodhall, Elizabeth (*Cast*) 93, 4133
Goodhart, Al (*Composer*) 544
Goodhart, William (*Author*) 1471
Goodhart, William (*Lyricist*) 1471
Goodhue, Willis Maxwell (*Librettist*) 625
Goodhue, Willis Maxwell (*Lyricist*) 625
Goodings, Sally (*Cast*) 878
Goodjohn, Arlouine (*Cast*) 283
Goodman, Al (*Cast*) 3153
Goodman, Al (*Composer*) 201, 659, 905, 969, 1033, 1460, 2384, 2419, 2489, 2832, 3148, 3405, 4010, 4427, 4654
Goodman, Al (*Incidental Music*) 3404
Goodman, Al (*Musical Director*) 216, 294, 622, 771, 910, 969, 1096, 1322, 1323, 1339, 1894, 1931, 2135, 2475, 2622, 2870, 3011, 3117, 3131, 3407, 3584, 4427, 4654, 4772
Goodman, Al (*Orchestrations*) 2135, 3117
Goodman, Alfred (*Composer*) 199, 659, 1033, 1460, 3084
Goodman, Alfred (*Musical Director*) 391, 487, 718, 1481, 1492, 1628, 1979, 2813, 3179, 3405, 3406, 3586, 3778, 3921, 3985, 4104, 4142, 4177
Goodman, Alfred (*Orchestrations*) 199, 441, 4142
Goodman, Arthur (*Librettist*) 227
Goodman, Aubrey (*Composer*) 4041
Goodman, Aubrey (*Librettist*) 4041
Goodman, Aubrey (*Lyricist*) 4041

Goodman, Benny
See also Benny Goodman Sextette and Benny
Goodman's Orchestra.
Goodman, Benny *(Cast)* 1528, 2402, 3893, 4256
Goodman, Benny *(Composer)* 146, 432, 4137, 4256
Goodman, Bill *(Cast)* 2676
Goodman, Bob *(Composer)* 4689
Goodman, Bob *(Lyricist)* 4689
Goodman, Charles *(Composer)* 4030
Goodman, Charles *(Lyricist)* 4030
Goodman, Dody *(Cast)* 1362, 2590, 2898, 3366, 3940,
    3941, 4047, 4734
Goodman, Doug *(Producer)* 166
Goodman, Douglas F. *(Producer)* 4
Goodman, Frank *(Composer)* 2587
Goodman, Frank *(Lyricist)* 2587
Goodman, I.R. *(Lyricist)* 4387
Goodman, John *(Cast)* 394
Goodman, Jules Eckert *(Librettist)* 4621
Goodman, Kenneth Sawyer *(Author)* 1797
Goodman, Lee *(Cast)* 657, 961, 2898, 4038
Goodman, Lee *(Librettist)* 961
Goodman, Paul *(Librettist)* 2236
Goodman, Paul *(Lyricist)* 2236
Goodman, Philip *(Producer)* 1011, 1297, 3540, 3650, 3659
Goodman, Susan *(Cast)* 2442
Goodman, Susan *(Composer)* 2039
Goodman, Tommy *(Dance Arranger)* 3972
Goodman, Tommy *(Orchestrations)* 2554
Goodman Sextette, Benny
See also Benny Goodman and Benny Goodman's
Orchestra.
Goodman Sextette, Benny *(Cast)* 4256
Goodman Theater *(Producer)* 158
Goodman Theatre *(Producer)* 494
Goodman's Orchestra, Benny
See also Benny Goodman and Benny Goodman Sextette.
Goodman's Orchestra, Benny *(Cast)* 1387
Goodmanson, Tim *(Set Design)* 484
Goodrich, Ace *(Cast)* 4141
Goodrich, Ace *(Choreographer)* 4141
Goodrich, Ace *(Composer)* 4141
Goodrich, Ace *(Librettist)* 4141
Goodrich, Ace *(Lyricist)* 4141
Goodrich, Bruce *(Set Design)* 3926
Goodrich, D. Parsons *(Musical Director)* 1568
Goodrich, Edna *(Cast)* 2715, 3805
Goodrich, Frances *(Author)* 1207, 3142, 4732, 4790
Goodrich, Francis *(Author)* 3888
Goodrow, Garry *(Cast)* 3077
Goodsight, Larry *(Lyricist)* 3601
Goodspeed Opera House *(Producer)* 198, 544, 595, 647,
    838, 915, 1276, 1496, 1630, 1665, 1804, 1969, 1997, 2026,
    2230, 2289, 2542, 2578, 2993, 3667, 3671, 4055, 4136,
    4255, 4408, 4740, 4796
Goodwin, Bill *(Set Design)* 2080
Goodwin, Doug *(Musical Director)* 1615
Goodwin, Harry *(Cast)* 4686
Goodwin, J. Cheever *(Author)* 3689
Goodwin, J. Cheever *(Librettist)* 45, 175, 995, 1030, 1090,
    1305, 1518, 1576, 2361, 2592, 2936, 3199, 3360, 4014

Goodwin, J. Cheever *(Lyricist)* 613, 934, 1090, 1188,
    1305, 2361, 2936, 2974, 3744, 3745, 4014
Goodwin, Joe *(Composer)* 1532
Goodwin, Joe *(Lyricist)* 879, 1391, 1686, 1963, 2214, 2448,
    2706, 3137, 3500, 3958, 4290
Goodwin, John *(Composer)* 319
Goodwin, John *(Librettist)* 319, 3103
Goodwin, John *(Lyricist)* 319
Goodwin, Thelma *(Cast)* 4352
Goodwin, Theodore *(Lyricist)* 1654
Goolden, Richard *(Cast)* 1857
Goorney, Howard *(Cast)* 4469
Goralik, Mordecai *(Set Design)* 3984
Gorbea, Carlos *(Composer)* 696
Gorbea, Carlos *(Librettist)* 696
Gorbea, Carlos *(Lyricist)* 696
Gorcey, Bernard *(Cast)* 97, 718, 4077
Gordon, Al
See also Al Gordon's Dogs.
Gordon, Alex *(Librettist)* 1864
Gordon, Alvin J. *(Cast)* 1957
Gordon, Arthur *(Composer)* 1974
Gordon, Barry H. *(Musical Director)* 3019
Gordon, Ben *(Lyricist)* 715
Gordon, Bert *(Cast)* 1931
Gordon, Bert *(Composer)* 2168
Gordon, Bob *(Orchestrations)* 2083, 2092, 2093
Gordon, Bruce *(Cast)* 3210
Gordon, Charles *(Producer)* 568
Gordon, Dan *(Dance Arranger)* 1924
Gordon, David *(Choreographer)* 3937
Gordon, David *(Director)* 3937
Gordon, David P. *(Set Design)* 264
Gordon, Don *(Set Design)* 4332
Gordon, Everett *(Musical Director)* 1596
Gordon, Gloria *(Cast)* 831
Gordon, Hayes *(Cast)* 4018
Gordon, Irving *(Composer)* 4131
Gordon, Irving *(Lyricist)* 4131
Gordon, John *(Librettist)* 4783
Gordon, Jon *(Arrangements)* 2735
Gordon, Jon *(Cast)* 4076
Gordon, Judith *(Producer)* 1914
Gordon, Judy *(Producer)* 305, 1890, 4480
Gordon, Katherine *(Cast)* 1640
Gordon, Kitty *(Cast)* 88, 1183, 1523, 2358, 2387, 3092,
    4554, 4747
Gordon, Lady Duff *(Costumes)* 2900
Gordon, Lawrence *(Producer)* 4019, 4020
Gordon, Leon *(Librettist)* 465
Gordon, Mack *(Librettist)* 4177
Gordon, Mack *(Lyricist)* 244, 478, 1207, 1251, 1298, 1302,
    1395, 2747, 2808, 3175, 3249, 3343, 3639, 4023, 4025,
    4748, 4823
Gordon, Margaret *(Cast)* 3450
Gordon, Marie *(Composer)* 2168, 2288, 3110
Gordon, Mark *(Librettist)* 1581
Gordon, Marvin *(Choreographer)* 766, 1596, 4678
Gordon, Marvin *(Director)* 766, 2657, 4678
Gordon, Marvin *(Librettist)* 4172
Gordon, Marvin *(Lyricist)* 4172

Gouraud, Powers *(Lyricist)* 1461
Gourlay, John *(Cast)* 1392
Gout, Alan *(Musical Director)* 2474
Govatos, Marguerite *(Costumes)* 985
Govatos, Marguerite *(Set Design)* 985
Govern, Alonzo *(Lyricist)* 2720
Gowers, Patrick *(Composer)* 1195, 1857
Gowers, Patrick *(Lyricist)* 1195
Goyen, William *(Librettist)* 35
Goyen, William *(Lyricist)* 35
Goyle, Jack *(Cast)* 1343
Goz, Harry *(Cast)* 171, 721, 4481
Graae, Jason *(Cast)* 1258, 1353, 1832, 2283, 3272, 3960, 4137
Grabel, Naomi *(Producer)* 4729
Grable, Betty *(Cast)* 362, 1109, 1416
Grace, Michael *(Composer)* 2227
Grace, Michael L. *(Librettist)* 4034
Grace, Timothy *(Cast)* 2817
Grace, Wayne *(Cast)* 732
Grace Costumes *(Costumes)* 2294
Grad, Peter *(Producer)* 2043
Grade, Lord *(Producer)* 2822, 4138
Graden, David *(Costumes)* 456, 1591, 4034, 4264, 4537
Graden, David *(Set Design)* 4034
Grady, Don *(Composer)* 1159
Grady, Don *(Musical Director)* 1159
Grady, Lotte *(Cast)* 645
Grady, Lottie *(Cast)* 2044, 2840, 2979, 3979
Grady, Thomas J. *(Director)* 2303
Grady, Tom *(Composer)* 541
Grael, Barry *(Cast)* 2052
Grael, Barry Alan *(Cast)* 4173
Grael, Barry Alan *(Librettist)* 2052, 4173
Grael, Barry Alan *(Lyricist)* 3186, 4173
Graf, Herbert *(Director)* 1817
Graf, James M. *(Producer)* 3069
Graff, George *(Lyricist)* 1751
Graff, Grace *(Cast)* 3255
Graff, Ilene *(Cast)* 2058, 4459
Graff, Kurt *(Cast)* 3255
Graff, Randy *(Cast)* 4, 775, 1161, 2305, 2442
Graff, Todd *(Cast)* 119, 253
Graff Jr., George *(Lyricist)* 310, 2154, 3642, 3910
Grafton, Gerald *(Composer)* 3098
Grafton, Gerald *(Lyricist)* 3098
Grafton, Gloria *(Cast)* 2258, 2311, 3861
Grafton, Portia *(Cast)* 3584
Graham, A.J. *(Cast)* 4799
Graham, Boyd *(Cast)* 2477
Graham, Boyd *(Librettist)* 2477
Graham, Boyd *(Lyricist)* 1149, 2477
Graham, Deborah *(Cast)* 3760, 4034
Graham, Fred *(Cast)* 2497
Graham, Frederick *(Cast)* 2594, 4529, 4667
Graham, Gary *(Composer)* 4431
Graham, Gary *(Lyricist)* 4431
Graham, H. Gordon *(Director)* 3986
Graham, Harry *(Author)* 4010
Graham, Harry *(Composer)* 2392

Graham, Harry *(Librettist)* 2509, 4010, 4258, 4667, 4792
Graham, Harry *(Lyricist)* 466, 1121, 1618, 2293, 2384, 2392, 2509, 2698, 2798, 4258, 4792, 4795
Graham, Hedley Gordon *(Director)* 3255
Graham, Irvin *(Composer)* 63, 70, 621, 924, 943, 2772, 3104, 3108, 4677
Graham, Irvin *(Librettist)* 3104
Graham, Irvin *(Lyricist)* 63, 70, 621, 924, 943, 2772, 3108, 4677
Graham, John McDougal *(Librettist)* 4039
Graham, June *(Choreographer)* 2680
Graham, Larry *(Lyricist)* 1713
Graham, Martha
    See also Martha Graham and Her Dance Group.
Graham, Mose *(Cast)* 4112
Graham, R.E. *(Cast)* 1313, 2836
Graham, Rachael *(Cast)* 2805
Graham, Richard *(Cast)* 3837
Graham, Robert *(Composer)* 3103
Graham, Ronald
    Not the same as Ronny Graham.
Graham, Ronald *(Cast)* 514, 601, 1101, 1109, 1476, 2379, 4569
Graham, Ronny
    Not the same as Ronald Graham.
Graham, Ronny *(Cast)* 108, 154, 2168, 2230, 3107, 3111, 4060, 4268, 4746
Graham, Ronny *(Choreographer)* 3111
Graham, Ronny *(Composer)* 679, 1363, 1648, 2168, 2772, 3107, 3110, 3111, 3112, 3941, 4268, 4627
Graham, Ronny *(Director)* 1648, 2935, 3111
Graham, Ronny *(Librettist)* 2168, 2772, 3107, 3110, 3111, 3112, 3181, 4827
Graham, Ronny *(Lyricist)* 519, 679, 1363, 1648, 2168, 2772, 3107, 3110, 3111, 3112, 3484, 3941, 4268, 4627
Graham, Ronny *(Producer)* 1648
Graham, Stephen *(Producer)* 2468
Graham, William *(Cast)* 2522
Graham and Her Dance Group, Martha *(Cast)* 3639
Graham-Dent, Nellie *(Cast)* 2549
Graham-Geraci, Phillip *(Producer)* 2630
Grahame, Kenneth *(Author)* 4701
Grahame, Sheilah *(Cast)* 3291
Grainer, Ron *(Composer)* 3734
Grainger, Percy *(Composer)* 1989
Grainger, Porter *(Cast)* 2645
Grainger, Porter *(Composer)* 39, 432, 567, 1251, 1499, 1960, 1984, 2645, 3808, 4763
Grainger, Porter *(Librettist)* 2645
Grainger, Porter *(Lyricist)* 39, 432, 567, 1251, 1499, 1960, 1984, 2645, 4763
Grammer, Sidney *(Cast)* 841
Grammis, Adam *(Choreographer)* 1082
Granat, Frank *(Producer)* 160, 367
Granat, Harvey *(Producer)* 4743
Granat, Louis *(Cast)* 2842
Granat, Richard *(Cast)* 1990
Granata, Dona *(Costumes)* 3311, 4004
Grand, Murray *(Composer)* 722, 1362, 1370, 1622, 3107, 3108, 3110, 3111, 3112, 3178, 3286, 4153
Grand, Murray *(Librettist)* 4153

Gray, L. Michael *(Cast)* 4645
Gray, Lawrence *(Cast)* 2423
Gray, Len *(Lyricist)* 500
Gray, Margery *(Cast)* 4312, 4435
Gray, Margery *(Voice)* 56, 3498
Gray, Oliver *(Cast)* 2295
Gray, Patricia *(Librettist)* 2553
Gray, Ralph *(Musical Director)* 3270
Gray, Roger *(Choreographer)* 1458
Gray, Roger *(Librettist)* 3086, 3137
Gray, Roger *(Lyricist)* 1780, 2403
Gray, Rudolf *(Cast)* 14
Gray, Scott *(Costumes)* 1644
Gray, T.J. *(Librettist)* 3006
Gray, Thomas *(Librettist)* 3087
Gray, Thomas *(Lyricist)* 3087
Gray, Thomas J. *(Librettist)* 560, 1686, 4195, 4755
Gray, Thomas J. *(Lyricist)* 909, 1911, 3087, 4195, 4806
Gray, Timothy *(Cast)* 4827
Gray, Timothy *(Composer)* 1891, 2148, 3302
Gray, Timothy *(Director)* 4332, 4388
Gray, Timothy *(Librettist)* 1891, 3302
Gray, Timothy *(Lyricist)* 1891, 2148, 2608, 2705, 3302, 4332, 4388
Gray, Timothy *(Producer)* 4332, 4388
Gray, Timothy *(Vocal Arranger)* 1891
Gray, William *(Director)* 3270
Gray, William *(Producer)* 3270
Grayhorn, Joseph *(Composer)* 2067
Grayhorn, Joseph *(Lyricist)* 2067
Grayhorn, Joseph *(Producer)* 2067
Grayson, Lee *(Orchestrations)* 2074
Grayson Jr., Milton B. *(Cast)* 2372
Graziano, Stephen *(Composer)* 2477
Greaza, Walter N. *(Cast)* 3335
Grec, George *(Producer)* 1785
Greco, Lois *(Cast)* 3539
Gredy, Pierre *(Author)* 98
Greeley, Aurora *(Cast)* 554
Green, Adolph
    See also The Revuers.
Green, Adolph *(Cast)* 490, 3278
Green, Adolph *(Librettist)* 167, 363, 404, 490, 599, 1068, 1227, 3278, 3279, 3992, 4008, 4190, 4496
Green, Adolph *(Lyricist)* 363, 404, 490, 599, 1038, 1061, 1068, 1227, 1729, 2073, 2076, 2205, 2452, 2590, 2677, 3278, 3279, 3452, 3453, 3845, 3992, 4008, 4167, 4190, 4496, 4695, 4734
Green, Adolph *(Screenwriter)* 3992
Green, Adoph *(Lyricist)* 3453
Green, Amanda *(Cast)* 2197, 3926
Green, Bernard *(Composer)* 3622
Green, Bernard *(Lyricist)* 3622
Green, Billy *(Cast)* 3605
Green, Bud *(Composer)* 3926, 3962
Green, Bud *(Lyricist)* 418, 1425, 1460, 2141, 2587, 3382, 3907, 3926, 3962, 4240
Green, Burton *(Cast)* 1735, 3401, 4203
Green, Burton *(Composer)* 2816, 4203
Green, Cliff *(Cast)* 813
Green, Cora *(Cast)* 1772, 3614, 4182

Green, Daisy *(Cast)* 1313
Green, Dennis *(Librettist)* 1104
Green, Dennis *(Lyricist)* 1591, 1714
Green, Doe Doe *(Cast)* 1960
Green, Eddie *(Cast)* 439, 1987
Green, Eddie *(Composer)* 2796, 3297
Green, Eddie *(Librettist)* 439, 1980
Green, Eddie *(Lyricist)* 2796, 3297
Green, Eugene *(Cast)* 643
Green, Gerald *(Author)* 4060
Green, H.F. *(Cast)* 3113
Green, H.J. *(Composer)* 1535
Green, Howard J. *(Librettist)* 1446
Green, J. Ed *(Cast)* 645, 982, 3797
Green, J. Ed *(Director)* 645, 2044, 3358
Green, J. Ed *(Librettist)* 645
Green, J. Ed *(Producer)* 645, 2044, 3358, 3797
Green, Jack *(Composer)* 1486
Green, Jackie *(Cast)* 4782
Green, Jane *(Cast)* 1691, 2857
Green, John *(Cast)* 982, 3153
Green, John *(Composer)* 323, 1856, 3905, 4152, 4367, 4498
Green, John *(Musical Director)* 4152
Green, Johnny *(Composer)* 418, 432, 1879, 2772, 3002, 3980, 4159, 4534
Green, Johnny *(Musical Director)* 601, 1879
Green, Johnny *(Vocal Arranger)* 601
Green, Joseph *(Cast)* 361
Green, Joseph *(Screenwriter)* 4769
Green, Laura *(Producer)* 4309
Green, Laurence *(Cast)* 2467
Green, Marion *(Cast)* 152, 1110, 2068, 2937
Green, Martyn *(Cast)* 634, 2977, 3496, 3913, 4155
Green, Martyn *(Director)* 2977
Green, Martyn *(Librettist)* 2977
Green, Milton *(Vocal Arranger)* 483
Green, Mitzi *(Cast)* 247, 404, 2447, 4586
Green, Morris *(Director)* 1110, 1275, 4299
Green, Morris *(Producer)* 1110, 1275, 1440, 1690, 2112, 3185, 3648
Green, Norma *(Cast)* 3180
Green, Paul *(Author)* 2573
Green, Paul *(Librettist)* 2228
Green, Paul *(Lyricist)* 369, 2228
Green, Phil *(Composer)* 2608
Green, Phil *(Orchestrations)* 2608
Green, R. *(Cast)* 1604
Green, Robert *(Lighting Designer)* 3067
Green, Robert *(Set Design)* 3067
Green, Rosie *(Cast)* 4802
Green, Ruby *(Cast)* 1385
Green, Sarah *(Cast)* 449, 641
Green, Schuyler *(Lyricist)* 1607, 4491
Green, Scott *(Director)* 4309
Green, Sylvan *(Composer)* 3605
Green, Teddy *(Cast)* 989
Green, Wayne *(Musical Director)* 3164
Green & Blyer *(Cast)* 684
Green Jr., Isaac *(Librettist)* 2595
Green and Roberta, Tim *(Cast)* 1421

Greenbank, Harry *(Composer)* 1429
Greenbank, Harry *(Lyricist)* 205, 770, 1429, 1470, 1682, 2938, 3803, 3828, 3999, 4390
Greenbank, Percy *(Author)* 4115
Greenbank, Percy *(Composer)* 30, 1470
Greenbank, Percy *(Librettist)* 4795
Greenbank, Percy *(Lyricist)* 30, 178, 353, 470, 767, 906, 1123, 1537, 1538, 1544, 1561, 1626, 2293, 2524, 2844, 3049, 3052, 3098, 3313, 3322, 3618, 3976, 4115, 4354, 4418, 4430, 4554, 4795
Greenbaum, Hyman *(Musical Director)* 3214
Greenberg, Edward *(Director)* 2838
Greenberg, Edwin *(Composer)* 3490
Greenberg, Edwin *(Librettist)* 3490
Greenberg, Edwin *(Lyricist)* 3490
Greenberg, Mitchell *(Cast)* 2142, 2754, 4371, 4769
Greenberg, Rob *(Director)* 1232
Greenberg, Rocky *(Cast)* 3162
Greenberg, Steven A. *(Producer)* 2172
Greenblatt, Kenneth D. *(Producer)* 1649, 1699, 2360, 3171
Greenblatt, Nat *(Librettist)* 62
Greenblatt, Nat *(Producer)* 62
Greenburg, Dan *(Author)* 2016
Greenburg, Dan *(Librettist)* 3233
Greene, Alan *(Composer)* 159, 2580
Greene, Alan *(Lyricist)* 159, 2580
Greene, Bradford *(Composer)* 3713
Greene, Clay M. *(Librettist)* 476, 2117, 2548, 3689, 3976
Greene, Clay M. *(Lyricist)* 235, 476, 687, 3689
Greene, Ellen *(Cast)* 2539, 2544, 3636, 4370
Greene, Evie *(Cast)* 1114
Greene, Frank *(Cast)* 3772
Greene, H.C. *(Director)* 2271
Greene, H.C. *(Librettist)* 2271
Greene, H.C. *(Producer)* 2271
Greene, Harrison *(Cast)* 1206
Greene, Herbert *(Musical Director)* 162, 1456, 2961, 3016, 3210, 4496, 4516
Greene, Herbert *(Producer)* 3016, 3210
Greene, Herbert *(Vocal Arranger)* 162, 363, 1456, 1706, 1748, 3016, 3210, 3837, 3972, 4018, 4516
Greene, Herman *(Cast)* 4254
Greene, I.M. *(Composer)* 1179
Greene, James *(Cast)* 1086
Greene, Jo *(Composer)* 1296
Greene, Jo *(Lyricist)* 1296
Greene, Lyn *(Cast)* 212
Greene, Marge *(Director)* 2388
Greene, Marge *(Librettist)* 2388
Greene, Marion *(Cast)* 3778
Greene, Milton *(Composer)* 2246
Greene, Milton *(Dance Arranger)* 3204
Greene, Milton *(Lyricist)* 2246
Greene, Milton *(Musical Director)* 483, 673, 1265, 1408, 2246, 3204, 3780
Greene, Milton *(Orchestrations)* 2246
Greene, Milton *(Vocal Arranger)* 1265, 1408, 3204, 3780
Greene, Ruby *(Cast)* 1251
Greene, Schuyler *(Lyricist)* 543, 913, 1559, 1588, 1784, 2309, 2373, 2587, 2696, 3184, 3193, 3658, 4418, 4491, 4555

Greene, Tom *(Cast)* 4614
Greener, Dorothy *(Cast)* 1596, 2246, 3664, 3940, 3941, 3942
Greenfield, Debra *(Cast)* 562, 2759
Greenfield, George T. *(Cast)* 1867
Greenfield, H. *(Composer)* 4193
Greenfield, H. *(Lyricist)* 4193
Greenfield, Howard *(Composer)* 4264
Greenfield, Howard *(Lyricist)* 4264
Greenfield, Lillian *(Costumes)* 3662
Greenfield, T. *(Set Design)* 2488
Greenhalgh, Edward *(Cast)* 1373
Greenhouse, Joel *(Librettist)* 1785
Greenhut, Andrew *(Lighting Designer)* 1002
Greenhut, Andrew *(Set Design)* 1002
Greenleaf, Augusta *(Cast)* 3675
Greenleaf, Mace *(Cast)* 1157
Greenough, Walter *(Director)* 4548
Greenough, Walter *(Producer)* 4548
Greenspon, Muriel *(Cast)* 3215
Greenstein, Michael *(Director)* 3670, 3781
Greenstreet, Sydney *(Cast)* 2377, 2669, 2686, 3652, 3735, 4747
Greentrack Entertainment *(Producer)* 3178
Greenville Company, The *(Producer)* 3217
Greenwald, Joseph *(Cast)* 1352
Greenwald, Robert *(Director)* 2796
Greenwald, Tom *(Librettist)* 2224
Greenwald, Tom *(Lyricist)* 2224
Greenwich, Ellie *(Cast)* 2427
Greenwich, Ellie *(Composer)* 2427, 3739, 4193, 4534
Greenwich, Ellie *(Lyricist)* 2427, 3739, 4193, 4534
Greenwich Musical Guild *(Producer)* 3605
Greenwich Village Players *(Producer)* 2203
Greenwich Villagers, *(Producer)* 293
Greenwood, Barrett *(Cast)* 2533, 3677
Greenwood, Charlotte *(Cast)* 1780, 2446, 2461, 2489, 2732, 3007, 3326, 3395, 3396, 3562, 3796, 4037, 4361
Greenwood, Jane *(Costumes)* 1955, 1999, 2075, 2359, 3411, 3577, 3900, 4505
Greenwood, Joan *(Cast)* 2313
Greenwood, Lottie *(Cast)* 3748
Greenwood, Michael *(Cast)* 3227
Greer, Howard *(Costumes)* 1688, 1689, 1944, 2180, 4844
Greer, Howard *(Set Design)* 1688
Greer, Jean *(Cast)* 3654
Greer, Jesse *(Composer)* 567, 771, 1128, 1132, 1134, 1778, 1779, 3342, 3796, 3849, 3907, 3973
Gregg, Bud (Pianist) 3914
Gregg, Hubert *(Composer)* 4027
Gregg, Hubert *(Lyricist)* 4027
Gregg, Jess *(Librettist)* 915
Gregg, Mitchell *(Cast)* 3187
Gregg, Norma *(Composer)* 2
Gregg, Norma *(Lyricist)* 2
Greggory, David *(Librettist)* 1413, 4498
Greggory, David *(Lyricist)* 2707, 3698, 4394, 4498
Gregorio, Rose *(Cast)* 2218
Gregory, Dave *(Librettist)* 1987
Gregory, David *(Librettist)* 3501
Gregory, David *(Lyricist)* 2162, 2167, 2447

Grimball, Elizabeth B. (Director) 2739
Grimes, Rollin (Cast) 953
Grimes, Scott (Cast) 695
Grimes, Tammy (Cast) 98, 499, 1359, 1427, 1507,
    1891, 1933, 2554, 2674, 3020, 4216, 4516
Grimes, Tammy (Voice) 4471
Grimm, Brothers (Author) 1727, 4106, 4735
Grimwood, Herbert (Cast) 2802
Griner, Barbara (Producer) 4541
Grinnage, Jack (Cast) 407, 410, 413
Grisham, Walter (Director) 2168
Grisman, Sam H. (Director) 2009
Grisman, Sam H. (Producer) 919, 1352, 4276
Grismer, Joseph R. (Director) 235
Grismer, Joseph R. (Producer) 235
Griso, Frank (Cast) 4384
Grist, Reri (Cast) 309, 4625
Griswold, Mary (Set Design) 4690
Grizzard, George (Cast) 3196
Groberg, Susan (Choreographer) 3997
Groday, Doris (Cast) 1387, 4730
Grodin, Charles (Director) 1974
Grodin, Charles (Librettist) 1974
Grodin, Charles (Lyricist) 1974
Groenendaal, Cris (Cast) 2766, 3411, 3464, 4210, 4233
Groener, Harry (Cast) 678, 921, 1776, 2152, 3231
Grofe, Ferde (Composer) 3639
Grofe, Ferde (Orchestrations) 444, 447, 787, 3639, 4821
Grogan, Oscar (Cast) 4778
Grollner, Jerry (Lighting Designer) 2969
Gromelski, Brad (Producer) 3539
Grona, Van (Choreographer) 1539
Groneman, Sammy (Author) 2075
Groniec, Katarzyna (Cast) 2846
Groody, Helen (Cast) 1378, 1582
Groody, Louise (Cast) 17, 186, 1266, 1625, 1916, 3146,
    3184, 3295, 4422
Grooney, E. (Musical Director) 617
Grooney, Ernest G. (Musical Director) 370, 2126
Gropman, David (Set Design) 414, 3175
Gropper, Milton Herbert (Librettist) 4280
Gros, Ernest (Set Design) 113, 618, 675, 749, 1067, 1090,
    1165, 1543, 1905, 2029, 2117, 2233, 2309, 2548, 2624,
    2723, 2952, 3144, 3450, 3745, 3751, 3753, 3857, 3948,
    4066, 4353, 4554
Gros, Ernest M. (Set Design) 357, 527, 770, 3360, 3582
Grose, Robert Paine (Set Design) 991
Gross, Arnie (Arrangements) 3561
Gross, Arnold (Dance Arranger) 2785, 2822, 2925, 4197
Gross, Arnold (Musical Director) 1010, 2284,
    2785, 4635
Gross, Arnold (Orchestrations) 829
Gross, Arnold (Vocal Arranger) 2785
Gross, Charles (Vocal Arranger) 1878
Gross, Edward (Producer) 4123
Gross, Michael (Cast) 3468
Gross, Milt (Librettist) 2809
Gross, Shelly
    See also Guber & Gross Productions.
Gross, Shelly (Producer) 534, 1837, 2590, 3427,
    3931, 4577

Gross Associates, Lee (Producer) 146
Grosser, Maurice (Librettist) 1366
Grossman (Lyricist) 4291
Grossman, Allen (Producer) 1082
Grossman, Bernard (Lyricist) 2446, 2489, 2832
Grossman, Bill (Choreographer) 962
Grossman, Hal (Producer) 4090
Grossman, Herbert (Composer) 1136
Grossman, Herbert (Musical Director) 101, 935, 1094,
    2568, 3731, 4588
Grossman, Herbert (Vocal Arranger) 101, 1094,
    2568, 4588
Grossman, Larry (Composer) 1038, 1068, 1146, 1186,
    1634, 1699, 2874, 3186, 3364, 3637, 4034
Grossman, Larry (Lyricist) 1038, 3186, 3516
Grossman, Larry (Vocal Arranger) 146
Grossman, Shirley (Composer) 3530
Grossman, Shirley (Lyricist) 3530
Grossmith, Edward (Lyricist) 913
Grossmith, George (Author) 3157, 4115
Grossmith, George (Cast) 334, 611, 1318, 1561, 2392,
    2808, 3583, 3584, 3857, 4327, 4418, 4419
Grossmith, George (Director) 611
Grossmith, George (Librettist) 334, 611, 1067, 3156, 3157,
    3569, 4327, 4551
Grossmith, George (Lyricist) 334, 611, 1067, 1318, 2498,
    3322, 3494, 4115
Grossmith, George (Producer) 334, 611, 3569, 4327
Grossmith, Lawrence (Cast) 672, 2620, 3193, 3974, 4663
Grossmith, Lawrence (Lyricist) 3193
Grossmith Jr., George (Cast) 3098, 3948
Grossmith Jr., George (Librettist) 3433
Grossmith Jr., George (Lyricist) 1569, 3098, 3313,
    4115, 4430
Group Theatre (Producer) 2228
Grout, James (Cast) 1721
Grouya, Ted (Composer) 2259
Grove, Betty Ann (Cast) 1478, 2064
Grover, Kit (Set Design) 3329
Grover, Stanley (Cast) 2449, 2651, 2983, 3123
Gruber, Franz (Composer) 3259
Grubman, Patty (Producer) 2318
Grudeff, Marian (Composer) 270, 1841
Grudeff, Marian (Librettist) 1107
Grudeff, Marian (Lyricist) 270, 1841
Gruenbaum, Fritz (Author) 12
Gruenberg, Louis (Composer) 3754
Gruenewald, Tom (Director) 2731
Gruenwald, Alfred (Author) 1113, 4760
Gruenwald, Alfred (Librettist) 1113, 2985
Gruenwald, Tom (Director) 3527
Grunbaum, Alfred (Author) 2334
Grunbaum, Fritz (Author) 1067, 2886, 3839
Grundman, Clare (Orchestrations) 1094, 2439, 3473,
    3954, 4499
Grundmann, Tim (Composer) 528, 1004, 1155, 3165,
    3329, 3997
Grundmann, Tim (Dance Arranger) 528, 1155,
    3329, 3997
Grundmann, Tim (Librettist) 528, 1004, 1155, 3165,
    3329, 3997

Gwillim, Jack *(Cast)*   181
Gwin, Byrne *(Cast)*   3224
Gwynne, Fred *(Cast)*   135, 1860, 2150, 2553, 2953
Gwyther, Geoffrey *(Cast)*   466, 3307
Gwyther, Geoffrey *(Composer)*   3719
Gwyther, Geoffrey *(Lyricist)*   702, 3719
Gyarmathy, Michel *(Costumes)*   1326
Gyarmathy, Michel *(Producer)*   1326
Gyarmathy, Michel *(Set Design)*   1326
Gyde, Courier *(Composer)*   1213
Gyngell, Paul *(Cast)*   661
Gynt, Kaj *(Librettist)*   3660
Gyse, Alisa *(Cast)*   4534

H

H.M. Tennent *(Producer)*   66
Haack, Morton *(Costumes)*   2707
Haagensen, Erik *(Librettist)*   1276, 2012, 3221
Haagensen, Erik *(Lyricist)*   1276, 2012, 3221, 4004
Haakon, Paul *(Cast)*   117, 216, 689, 1973, 2402, 2847, 3011, 3683, 3955, 4110
Haakon, Paul *(Choreographer)*   2847, 3683, 4110
Haas, Helen A. *(Costumes)*   1378
Haas, Holly *(Set Design)*   3209
Haas, Hugo *(Cast)*   2679
Haase, Oscar *(Composer)*   2701
Haatainen, Christina *(Costumes)*   3752
Habbema, Eddy *(Director)*   949
Haber, Carl *(Director)*   562
Haber, John L. *(Director)*   1037, 1402
Haber, John L. *(Librettist)*   1402
Haber, John L. *(Producer)*   1402
Haber, Louis *(Composer)*   447, 3705
Haberman, Linda *(Choreographer)*   424, 2230
Hack, Moe *(Lighting Designer)*   2175
Hack, Monroe *(Director)*   4273
Hack, Monroe B. *(Director)*   467
Hack, Monroe B. *(Producer)*   4273
Hackady, Hal *(Composer)*   456, 3516
Hackady, Hal *(Librettist)*   90, 3708
Hackady, Hal *(Lyricist)*   90, 101, 456, 1146, 1634, 2874, 3111, 3112, 3637, 3708, 4034, 4297
Hacker, Linda *(Set Design)*   198, 1804, 1873, 3034
Hacker, Phil M. *(Lyricist)*   331
Hacker, Seymour *(Producer)*   2220
Hacket, George *(Arrangements)*   2094
Hackett, Albert *(Author)*   1207, 3142, 3888, 4732, 4790
Hackett, Buddy *(Cast)*   2053
Hackett, George *(Arrangements)*   2092, 2093
Hackett, George *(Musical Director)*   2083, 2091, 2092, 2093, 2094, 2095
Hackett, George *(Orchestrations)*   2085, 2089, 2090, 2092
Hackett, Hal *(Cast)*   490
Hackett, Jeanne *(Costumes)*   1779
Hackett, Jeanne *(Lyricist)*   1779
Hackett, Joan *(Cast)*   3389
Hackett, Lester *(Producer)*   600

Hackett, Raymond *(Cast)*   423
Hackett, Ron *(Cast)*   2572
Hackett, W. Broderick *(Set Design)*   2910
Hackett, Walter *(Author)*   4671
Hackforth, Norman *(Composer)*   703, 2168, 2227
Hackforth, Norman *(Lyricist)*   2168, 2227
Hackman, Gene *(Cast)*   160
Hackney, John C. *(Composer)*   1604
Hadary, Jonathan *(Cast)*   212, 829, 1591, 4412
Haddad, Robert *(Choreographer)*   2977, 3186, 4388
Haddon, Peter *(Cast)*   704
Haddow, Jeffrey *(Cast)*   3858
Haddow, Jeffrey *(Composer)*   3858
Haddow, Jeffrey *(Librettist)*   3858
Haddow, Jeffrey *(Lyricist)*   3858
Hadjidakis, Manos *(Composer)*   2106
Hadley, Bob *(Producer)*   239
Hadley, Henry *(Composer)*   3073, 3147
Hadley, Henry *(Musical Director)*   3147
Hadley, Jonathan *(Cast)*   3568, 4325
Haenschen, Walter *(Orchestrations)*   3179
Haenschen, Walter Gustave *(Composer)*   1654, 4808
Haffner, Karl *(Author)*   689
Hafleigh *(Costumes)*   4802
Hafner, Julia J. *(Cast)*   788
Hafner, Tom *(Cast)*   3555
Hagan, Aaron *(Arrangements)*   2065
Hagan, Aaron *(Musical Director)*   2065, 2241
Hagan, Howard *(Cast)*   319, 3697
Hageman, Maurice *(Librettist)*   1459
Hagen, Earle *(Composer)*   1713
Hagen, Gay *(Cast)*   3318
Hagen, John Milton *(Composer)*   293
Hagen, John Milton *(Lyricist)*   293
Hager, Clyde *(Cast)*   2300
Hager, Frederick W. *(Composer)*   2964
Hager, Louis Busch *(Producer)*   1402, 1636, 3429, 3608
Hagerman, Maurice *(Librettist)*   1758
Hagerman, Maurice *(Lyricist)*   1758
Hagerty, Julie *(Cast)*   2945
Haggard, Stephen *(Cast)*   818
Haggart, Bob *(Composer)*   964, 4255
Haggart, Bobby *(Orchestrations)*   1336
Haggarty, George *(Cast)*   4778
Haggin, Ben Ali *(Costumes)*   3768, 4819
Haggins, Jon *(Costumes)*   3522
Haggott, John *(Director)*   1284
Haggott, John *(Librettist)*   1284
Hagler, Stan *(Lyricist)*   90
Hagman, Larry *(Cast)*   3094
Hague, Aaron *(Musical Director)*   533
Hague, Aaron *(Orchestrations)*   533
Hague, Albert *(Composer)*   615, 961, 1273, 1306, 1567, 1832, 2015, 2168, 2898, 3123, 3509, 3687, 3694, 4827
Hague, Albert *(Dance Arranger)*   2898
Hague, Albert *(Vocal Arranger)*   2898
Haig, Emma *(Cast)*   1920, 3006, 3323, 4300, 4810
Haig, Peter *(Cast)*   2918
Haigh, Kenneth *(Cast)*   2682
Haight, Reba *(Cast)*   222
Haight Jr., George *(Librettist)*   3086

Haile, Evans *(Musical Director)* 3864
Haimsohn, George *(Librettist)* 956
Haimsohn, George *(Lyricist)* 956
Hain, William *(Cast)* 1110, 3735
Hainert, Henry *(Cast)* 2762
Haines, A. Larry *(Cast)* 1471, 3603, 4474
Haines, H.E. *(Composer)* 246
Haines, Herbert E. *(Composer)* 333, 675, 1043
Haines, Jim *(Lyricist)* 757
Haines, Louis *(Cast)* 1388
Haines, Will E. *(Composer)* 1066, 3820
Haines, Will E. *(Lyricist)* 3820
Hairston, William *(Librettist)* 2203
Hajos, Karl *(Composer)* 110, 3078, 4669
Hajos, Karl *(Music Adaptation)* 110
Hajos, Karl *(Musical Director)* 4226
Hajos, Karl *(Orchestrations)* 110, 4226
Hajos, Mitzi *(Cast)* 1849, 2358, 3537, 3621, 3839
Hakesworth, Jenny *(Librettist)* 1253
Haldane, Harry *(Lyricist)* 2042
Haldane, Harry M. *(Composer)* 1766
Haldeman, Ed *(Librettist)* 3683
Hale, Alan *(Cast)* 2574
Hale, Binnie *(Cast)* 2976, 4519
Hale, Bobby *(Cast)* 396
Hale, Chanin *(Cast)* 4629
Hale, Charles *(Cast)* 1196
Hale, Chester *(Cast)* 3006, 3431
Hale, Chester
    See also Chester Hale Girls.
Hale, Chester *(Choreographer)* 1384, 1693, 1694, 1779,
    1780, 2005, 2078, 2140, 2504, 2628, 2691, 2947, 3002,
    3012, 3150, 3431, 3680, 4365, 4572
Hale, Creighton *(Cast)* 977
Hale, Diana *(Cast)* 92
Hale, George *(Choreographer)* 1528, 3225, 3379, 3674,
    4179
Hale, George *(Director)* 63, 3966
Hale, George *(Lyricist)* 1411
Hale, George *(Producer)* 1411, 1931, 2379
Hale, Georgie *(Cast)* 608, 1690, 2706
Hale, Georgie *(Choreographer)* 1136, 1800, 3131
Hale, Georgie *(Director)* 1800
Hale, Georgie *(Producer)* 1825
Hale, Helen *(Cast)* 3437, 4738
Hale, John *(Cast)* 1135, 1137
Hale, Louise Closser *(Cast)* 1221, 3382, 3799
Hale, Richard *(Cast)* 165
Hale, Ruth *(Librettist)* 4548
Hale, Sonnie *(Cast)* 1202, 3291, 4581
Hale, Tom *(Arrangements)* 914
Hale, Walter *(Cast)* 3050
Hale Girls, Chester
    See also Chester Hale.
Hale Girls, Chester *(Cast)* 3150
Haleloke *(Cast)* 197
Halet, Laurent *(Composer)* 4818
Halevy, Ludovic *(Author)* 653, 2507
Haley, Jack *(Cast)* 1339, 1387, 1396, 1460, 1461, 1894,
    2137, 3783, 4267
Haley Sisters, The *(Cast)* 1911

Haliday, Bryant *(Producer)* 2772
Hall, Adelaide *(Cast)* 441, 567, 880, 1028, 2190, 2608,
    3808, 4207
Hall, Adrian *(Director)* 35, 3725
Hall, Annette *(Cast)* 2559
Hall, Bettina *(Cast)* 163, 672, 2545, 2808, 4352
Hall, Cameron *(Cast)* 814
Hall, Carl *(Cast)* 4460
Hall, Carl *(Vocal Arranger)* 4459
Hall, Carlyle *(Orchestrations)* 823, 935, 1730, 4577
Hall, Carol *(Cast)* 4398
Hall, Carol *(Composer)* 4, 373, 374, 1389, 1630, 4398
Hall, Carol *(Librettist)* 4, 4398
Hall, Carol *(Lyricist)* 4, 373, 374, 1389, 1630,
    3364, 4398
Hall, Charles Edward *(Cast)* 3637
Hall, Cliff *(Cast)* 1860, 3379, 4823
Hall, Cliff *(Lyricist)* 3241
Hall, Davis *(Director)* 1702
Hall, Delores *(Cast)* 374, 1116, 2134, 2372, 3159,
    3871, 4788
Hall, Donald *(Cast)* 954
Hall, Dorothy *(Cast)* 1323, 4100
Hall, George *(Cast)* 44, 620, 759, 809, 1023, 1194, 2439,
    3914, 4329, 4432
Hall, George *(Librettist)* 3914
Hall, Glenn *(Cast)* 2340, 2385, 2670
Hall, Grayson *(Cast)* 1755, 4190
Hall, Gus *(Cast)* 449
Hall, Harrison *(Producer)* 3168
Hall, Howard *(Lyricist)* 510
Hall, Jessie Mae *(Cast)* 938
Hall, John *(Cast)* 2285
Hall, John *(Composer)* 2954
Hall, John T. *(Composer)* 3626
Hall, Josephine *(Cast)* 41, 734, 1540, 2302, 2343, 2374,
    2714, 2863, 3790
Hall, Juanita *(Cast)* 1315, 2000, 2750, 4096, 4123
Hall, Kate *(Cast)* 447
Hall, Laura Nelson *(Cast)* 1210
Hall, Lewis *(Composer)* 114
Hall, Lisa *(Cast)* 2055
Hall, Margaret *(Cast)* 1891
Hall, Marie *(Cast)* 1703
Hall, Mollie *(Cast)* 264
Hall, Natalie *(Cast)* 277, 2348, 3011, 3014, 4352, 4372
Hall, Owen *(Author)* 351, 3976
Hall, Owen *(Librettist)* 205, 351, 1313, 1429, 1470, 1537,
    1682, 2498, 2803, 3882
Hall, Owen *(Lyricist)* 2498, 3882
Hall, Pamela *(Cast)* 1012
Hall, Pauline *(Cast)* 1193, 4393
Hall, Peter *(Director)* 2196, 4558
Hall, Peter J. *(Costumes)* 4861
Hall, Phil *(Musical Director)* 3517, 3708
Hall, Phil *(Vocal Arranger)* 3517
Hall, Porter *(Cast)* 536
Hall, Ralston *(Cast)* 2229
Hall, Ronnie *(Cast)* 3124
Hall, Steve *(Cast)* 2759
Hall, Steven F. *(Cast)* 809

Hall, Teddy *(Composer)* 532
Hall, Teddy *(Lyricist)* 532, 1840
Hall, Terry *(Composer)* 3739
Hall, Terry *(Lyricist)* 3739
Hall, Thurston *(Cast)* 1391, 1784, 3304
Hall, William D. *(Librettist)* 3797
Hall Johnson Choir *(Cast)* 467
Hall Jr., Barrie Lee *(Orchestrations)* 3628
Hallam, Basil *(Cast)* 3398
Hallelujah Quartette *(Cast)* 2640
Hallem, Henry *(Cast)* 1473
Haller, Herman *(Author)* 659
Haller, Tobias *(Cast)* 1635
Halley, Sharon *(Choreographer)* 1171, 2651
Halley Jr., Ben *(Cast)* 1914
Hallick, Ned *(Lighting Designer)* 426, 3123
Halliday, Andy *(Cast)* 3606
Halliday, Buzz *(Cast)* 1567, 3204, 3615
Halliday, Francis *(Cast)* 2972
Halliday, Heller *(Cast)* 3453
Halliday, Hildegarde *(Cast)* 1446, 1447, 1448,
    3064, 3103
Halliday, John *(Cast)* 1144, 4105, 4600
Halliday, Richard *(Producer)* 2201, 3453, 4095
Halliday, Robert *(Cast)* 1027, 3011, 3117, 3584,
    4392, 4667
Halliday, Will *(Cast)* 3348
Halliday, William *(Cast)* 4757
Halligan, William *(Director)* 79, 3796
Halligan, William *(Producer)* 79
Hallor, Edith *(Cast)* 2430
Halloran Jr., William A. *(Composer)* 4776
Halloran Jr., William A. *(Lyricist)* 4776
Hallow, John *(Cast)* 3126
Hally, Martha *(Costumes)* 140
Halperin, Nan *(Cast)* 2516, 2706, 4104
Halpern, Jeff *(Musical Director)* 992
Halpin, Helen *(Cast)* 673
Halpin, Luke *(Cast)* 4270
Halstead, Edgar *(Cast)* 1230
Halston *(Costumes)* 16
Halt, Spaulding *(Lyricist)* 720
Halvertson, Lynn *(Cast)* 3561
Hambitzer, Charles *(Composer)* 2623, 3692
Hamblen, Bernard *(Composer)* 717
Hambleton, John *(Costumes)* 2061, 2068, 2225, 2821,
    3990, 4142
Hambleton, T. Edward *(Producer)* 2958, 3288
Hamblin, Bernard *(Composer)* 3481
Hamblin, Bernard *(Lyricist)* 3481
Hamburger, Jay *(Lyricist)* 1595
Hamerman, Marc *(Producer)* 2055
Hamill, Harriet *(Cast)* 266
Hamill, Katherine *(Cast)* 4179
Hamill, Mark *(Cast)* 1776
Hamill, Stuart *(Librettist)* 303
Hamilton, Al *(Costumes)* 1880
Hamilton, Al *(Set Design)* 1880
Hamilton, Beatrice *(Cast)* 4556
Hamilton, Bob *(Choreographer)* 2246, 3801, 4629
Hamilton, Burton *(Composer)* 4776

Hamilton, Caroline *(Cast)* 3570
Hamilton, Christian *(Librettist)* 2617
Hamilton, Cosmo *(Author)* 675, 3481, 3974
Hamilton, Cosmo *(Librettist)* 333, 356, 675, 1043, 1309,
    2025, 4133
Hamilton, Gertrude *(Cast)* 2698
Hamilton, Gloria *(Cast)* 2439
Hamilton, Grace *(Cast)* 199, 4121
Hamilton, Hale *(Author)* 1009
Hamilton, Hale *(Cast)* 1009
Hamilton, Hamtree *(Cast)* 2540
Hamilton, Harry *(Lyricist)* 1429
Hamilton, Henry *(Librettist)* 1114, 2524, 3857, 4554
Hamilton, Henry *(Lyricist)* 1114, 1429, 1454
Hamilton, Holly *(Cast)* 3814
Hamilton, James *(Cast)* 2780
Hamilton, James *(Set Design)* 1637
Hamilton, John F. *(Cast)* 3224
Hamilton, Karlah *(Cast)* 4799
Hamilton, Kelly *(Composer)* 962, 4454
Hamilton, Kelly *(Librettist)* 962, 4454
Hamilton, Kelly *(Lyricist)* 962, 4454
Hamilton, Laura *(Cast)* 1228, 3222, 3396, 3652
Hamilton, Lawrence *(Cast)* 3724, 4534
Hamilton, Les *(Cast)* 2086
Hamilton, Margaret *(Cast)* 823, 1614, 2496, 3287
Hamilton, Marion *(Cast)* 792
Hamilton, Morris *(Composer)* 1128, 1132, 1134,
    2545, 4335
Hamilton, Nancy *(Cast)* 3103, 3292
Hamilton, Nancy *(Composer)* 2294
Hamilton, Nancy *(Librettist)* 3103, 3292, 4362, 4483
Hamilton, Nancy *(Lyricist)* 2294, 3103, 3104, 3292,
    3453, 4362, 4483
Hamilton, Ord *(Composer)* 203, 3020
Hamilton, Ord *(Lyricist)* 203
Hamilton, Patrick *(Cast)* 1732
Hamilton, Peter *(Choreographer)* 339, 2168, 2339
Hamilton, Roger *(Cast)* 3506
Hamilton, Spike *(Cast)* 2850
Hamilton, Thomas *(Cast)* 207
Hamilton, W. Franklin *(Set Design)* 2159
Hamilton, William *(Cast)* 402, 1080
Hamlin, Fred R. *(Producer)* 250, 2160, 4723
Hamlin, Stephen *(Lighting Designer)* 945
Hamlisch, Marvin *(Composer)* 427, 746, 1436, 1437, 1633,
    2038, 2196, 3181, 3936, 4019, 4020, 4334
Hamlisch, Marvin *(Dance Arranger)* 1611, 1846, 2874
Hammel, T.A. *(Composer)* 3022
Hammel, T.A. *(Lyricist)* 3022
Hammer, Jack *(Composer)* 3695, 3739
Hammer, Jack *(Lyricist)* 3695, 3739
Hammer, Mark *(Cast)* 3000
Hammer, Robert *(Vocal Arranger)* 1924
Hammerlee, Patricia *(Cast)* 3107, 3899, 4542
Hammerschlag, Peter *(Librettist)* 1413
Hammerstein, Alice *(Lyricist)* 4273
Hammerstein, Arthur *(Director)* 97
Hammerstein, Arthur *(Lyricist)* 4056
Hammerstein, Arthur *(Producer)* 97, 288, 468, 953,
    1424, 1603, 1617, 1888, 2216, 2292, 2636, 2708, 2768,

Hanley, Matthew *(Cast)* 2886
Hanlon, Bert *(Cast)* 1267
Hanlon, Bert *(Composer)* 1267, 1992
Hanlon, Bert *(Librettist)* 3861
Hanlon, Bert *(Lyricist)* 1267, 1919
Hanlon, Harry *(Cast)* 1563
Hanlon Jr., George *(Librettist)* 574
Hanlon Jr., George *(Lyricist)* 574
Hann, Walter *(Set Design)* 333, 2524
Hanna, William A. *(Set Design)* 584
Hannan, Walter F. *(Lyricist)* 4163
Hanneford, Poodles *(Cast)* 771, 2258
Hanneford Family *(Cast)* 1631
Hanneford Family, The *(Cast)* 1753
Hanning, Geraldine *(Cast)* 3697
Hansberry, Lorraine *(Author)* 3656
Hansberry, Lorraine *(Director)* 2306
Hanscombe, Harry *(Cast)* 4313
Hansen, Judith *(Cast)* 3606
Hansen, Kim *(Cast)* 2521
Hansen, Mike *(Composer)* 4278
Hansen, Mike *(Lyricist)* 4278
Hansen, Steve *(Puppeteer)* 56, 3449
Hanson, Dave *(Librettist)* 3076
Hanson, Dorothy *(Cast)* 1153
Hanson, Gladys *(Cast)* 2206, 2802
Hanson, Grace *(Cast)* 537
Happ, William *(Librettist)* 2560
Happy Medium Theatre *(Producer)* 1081
Hapwood, Aubrey *(Lyricist)* 4390
Harary, Nettie *(Cast)* 3501
Harbach, Otto *(Author)* 4526
Harbach, Otto *(Composer)* 2549
Harbach, Otto *(Librettist)* 381, 468, 672, 929, 930, 1027, 1088, 1247, 1248, 1285, 1352, 1476, 1598, 1603, 1617, 1888, 2180, 2216, 2264, 2292, 2308, 2342, 2425, 2549, 2638, 2667, 2767, 2927, 3170, 3184, 3218, 3254, 3735, 3772, 4077, 4212, 4228, 4378, 4464, 4692, 4694, 4784
Harbach, Otto *(Lyricist)* 288, 381, 468, 497, 531, 672, 903, 930, 1027, 1088, 1247, 1248, 1285, 1352, 1476, 1558, 1598, 1603, 1617, 1788, 1888, 2180, 2204, 2216, 2292, 2340, 2342, 2372, 2425, 2549, 2638, 2667, 2767, 2806, 3020, 3170, 3184, 3218, 3249, 3254, 3475, 3735, 3772, 4077, 4212, 4228, 4364, 4378, 4464, 4692, 4694, 4784, 4799
Harbert, James *(Composer)* 2080
Harbert, James *(Lyricist)* 2080
Harbert, James *(Orchestrations)* 2080
Harbert, Jim *(Composer)* 2080
Harbert, Jim *(Lyricist)* 2080
Harbord, Carl *(Cast)* 841
Harburg, E.Y. *(Author)* 2234
Harburg, E.Y. *(Composer)* 418
Harburg, E.Y. *(Director)* 462, 1300
Harburg, E.Y. *(Librettist)* 1278, 1300, 2190, 2234, 2475
Harburg, E.Y. *(Lyricist)* 12, 125, 213, 289, 418, 462, 467, 732, 839, 989, 1126, 1135, 1278, 1298, 1300, 1448, 1609, 1672, 1674, 1745, 1763, 1931, 1973, 2076, 2190, 2204, 2234, 2294, 2372, 2475, 3018, 3103, 3940, 3946, 3955, 3980, 4152, 4159, 4399, 4498, 4545, 4583, 4823, 4824
Harburg, E.Y. "Yip" *(Lyricist)* 4799

Harcourt, William J. *(Cast)* 3567
Hardeen, Theo *(Cast)* 1840
Harden, Don *(Cast)* 2105, 4777
Harding *(Composer)* 2493
Harding *(Lyricist)* 2493
Harding, John *(Musical Director)* 2029
Harding, May *(Cast)* 1537
Hards, Ira *(Director)* 780, 2569, 2686, 3623, 4204
Hardt-Warden, Bruno *(Author)* 4010, 4352
Hardwick, Cheryl *(Composer)* 4, 944, 1575
Hardwick, Cheryl *(Dance Arranger)* 1737
Hardwick, Cheryl *(Musical Director)* 1737
Hardwick, Cheryl *(Orchestrations)* 1737
Hardwick, Cheryl *(Vocal Arranger)* 1737
Hardwick, Mark *(Arrangements)* 4030
Hardwick, Mark *(Cast)* 3261, 3608
Hardwick, Mark *(Composer)* 3261, 3608, 3641, 4030
Hardwick, Mark *(Librettist)* 3261, 3641
Hardwick, Mark *(Lyricist)* 3608, 3641, 4030
Hardwicke, Catherine *(Set Design)* 655
Hardy, Jim *(Lighting Designer)* 2051
Hardy, Joseph *(Cast)* 1383
Hardy, Joseph *(Director)* 1511, 3516, 4173, 4783
Hardy, Mark *(Cast)* 2250
Hardy, Patricia *(Cast)* 3815
Hardy, Sam *(Cast)* 627, 3590, 3727, 4810
Hardy, Sam B. *(Cast)* 2309
Hardy, Stephani *(Cast)* 3181
Hardy, Thomas *(Author)* 962
Hardy, Will *(Composer)* 4655
Hardy, Will *(Lyricist)* 4655
Hardy, William *(Cast)* 198, 4398
Hare, Betty *(Cast)* 3214, 3339
Hare, David *(Librettist)* 2346
Hare, Ernest *(Cast)* 1783, 3395, 3399, 3424, 3701, 3958, 4521, 4553, 4655
Hare, Lumsden *(Cast)* 2206
Hare, Marilyn *(Cast)* 4602
Hare, Robertson *(Cast)* 3139
Haresfoot Club *(Producer)* 96
Haresfoot Club, The *(Producer)* 390
Harewood, Dorian *(Cast)* 518, 2898
Harford, W. *(Set Design)* 719, 2514
Hargate, Bill *(Costumes)* 2928, 4292, 4319
Hargate, Bill *(Set Design)* 127, 4319
Hargate, William *(Costumes)* 1047
Hargrave, Roy *(Cast)* 4105
Hargrave, Roy *(Director)* 2187
Hargrave, William *(Cast)* 3822, 4291
Hargreaves, Reginald *(Librettist)* 700
Hargreaves, William *(Composer)* 353
Hargreaves, William *(Lyricist)* 353
Hargreeves, William *(Composer)* 1148
Hargreeves, William *(Lyricist)* 1148
Hari, Eugene *(Cast)* 4498
Hari, Otto *(Cast)* 4166
Harig, Peg *(Librettist)* 4416
Harig, Peg *(Lyricist)* 2483
Haring, Forrest C. *(Producer)* 1874
Hariton, Gerry *(Lighting Designer)* 2470
Hariton, Gerry *(Set Design)* 2470, 2702, 3643

Harker, Joseph *(Set Design)* 165, 277, 292, 334, 466, 758, 2389, 2392, 2524, 2802, 2844, 3098, 3139, 3625, 4327, 4354, 4418, 4765

Harker, Phil *(Set Design)* 165, 277, 292, 334, 466, 758, 2389, 2392, 2802, 3098, 3139, 4327, 4418, 4765

Harker, W. Vere *(Musical Director)* 4302

Harkins, Evelyn *(Cast)* 4092

Harkins, John *(Cast)* 4625

Harkins, Mary Thomasine *(Costumes)* 81

Harkleroad, Mary *(Cast)* 2028

Harkrider, John *(Costumes)* 2453, 3014, 3179, 3719, 3949, 3953, 4023, 4683, 4821, 4823

Harkrider, John W. *(Costumes)* 4357, 4846, 4847

Harlan, Otis *(Cast)* 436, 559, 561, 968, 998, 1095, 1327, 1543, 2495, 3177, 3433, 4130, 4544

Harlan, Otis *(Composer)* 436

Harlan, Otis *(Lyricist)* 436

Harlan, Scott *(Cast)* 1161

Harland, Robert *(Cast)* 1185

Harlekyn U.S.A. Company *(Producer)* 1865

Harlem Producing Company *(Producer)* 1499

Harlem Productions *(Producer)* 2645

Harley, John F. *(Director)* 1466

Harley, John F. *(Lyricist)* 476, 1466

Harley, Leslie *(Dance Arranger)* 4678

Harley, Leslie *(Musical Director)* 4678

Harley, Margot *(Cast)* 1194

Harley, Margot *(Producer)* 942, 3733

Harling, W. Frank *(Composer)* 1020, 3849

Harling, W. Frank *(Lyricist)* 3849

Harling, W. Franke *(Composer)* 1244, 1780, 1819, 2987

Harlon, Beatrice *(Cast)* 2303

Harlowe, Beatrice *(Cast)* 539

Harman, Barry *(Director)* 3272, 3760

Harman, Barry *(Librettist)* 3272, 3760

Harman, Barry *(Lyricist)* 3272, 3760

Harman, Paul *(Cast)* 3926

Harman, Wier *(Cast)* 4729

Harmon, April *(Cast)* 2467

Harmon, Erv *(Cast)* 1709

Harmon, Jane *(Producer)* 209

Harmon, Johnny *(Cast)* 766

Harmon, Keith *(Cast)* 643

Harmon, Lucille *(Cast)* 3842

Harmon, Peggy *(Lyricist)* 1589

Harmon, Steve *(Cast)* 2657

Harms, Carl *(Lighting Designer)* 3449

Harms, Carl *(Puppeteer)* 997, 4710

Harney, Ben *(Cast)* 518, 572, 1103, 4447, 4697

Harney, Ben *(Composer)* 2796

Harney, Ben *(Lyricist)* 2796

Harnick, Jay *(Director)* 2197, 2231, 4785

Harnick, Sheldon *(Additional Lyrics)* 98, 949, 3913

Harnick, Sheldon *(Composer)* 1092, 1892, 2227, 2246, 2288, 2554, 2611, 2677, 2804, 3107, 3941, 4499, 4627

Harnick, Sheldon *(Librettist)* 170, 643, 1092, 3107, 3941, 4505, 4732

Harnick, Sheldon *(Lyricist)* 56, 160, 170, 192, 270, 483, 635, 643, 753, 1092, 1190, 1265, 1280, 1389, 1848, 1892, 2205, 2227, 2246, 2288, 2554, 2589, 2611, 2726, 2804, 2839, 3018, 3097, 3107, 3498, 3543, 3702, 3780, 3918,

3940, 3941, 4028, 4312, 4388, 4395, 4499, 4505, 4566, 4627, 4732

Harnick, Sheldon *(Voice)* 56

Harnley, Leslie *(Composer)* 1370

Harnley, Leslie *(Dance Arranger)* 3427

Harnley, Leslie *(Musical Director)* 1370

Harp, William *(Set Design)* 2560

Harper, Billy *(Cast)* 2520

Harper, Dolores *(Cast)* 2000, 4750

Harper, Don *(Orchestrations)* 2689

Harper, Helen *(Cast)* 1906

Harper, Herbert *(Choreographer)* 4586

Harper, Jessica *(Cast)* 1064

Harper, Ken *(Producer)* 4722

Harper, Leonard *(Director)* 1980

Harper, Leonard *(Producer)* 725, 1986, 2561, 3707, 3782, 4501

Harper, Richard *(Lighting Designer)* 1282

Harper, Richard *(Set Design)* 1282

Harper, Robert Alan *(Set Design)* 3600

Harper, Valerie *(Cast)* 1585, 4190, 4270

Harper, Ves *(Costumes)* 2203

Harper, Ves *(Lighting Designer)* 2203

Harper, Wally *(Additional Music)* 1649

Harper, Wally *(Arrangements)* 544

Harper, Wally *(Composer)* 1298, 2148, 2171, 2754, 3876

Harper, Wally *(Dance Arranger)* 373, 832, 1000, 2584, 3018, 3039, 3060, 3088, 4038, 4114

Harper, Wally *(Musical Director)* 1000, 1660, 3171, 4002, 4522

Harper, Wally *(Orchestrations)* 544, 2584, 4522

Harper, Wally *(Vocal Arranger)* 373, 1000

Harper, William *(Orchestrations)* 2766

Harper and Blanks *(Cast)* 3512

Harra, Henrietta *(Costumes)* 2395

Harrell, Gordon *(Dance Arranger)* 2134, 2360, 2542, 3682

Harrell, Gordon *(Orchestrations)* 2134

Harrell, Gordon *(Vocal Arranger)* 4470

Harrell, Gordon Lowry *(Dance Arranger)* 393, 964, 1146, 1842, 4297

Harrell, Gordon Lowry *(Musical Director)* 775, 964, 3169, 3741, 3873, 3903

Harrell, Gordon Lowry *(Vocal Arranger)* 393, 964, 3741, 3903

Harrigan, Edward *(Author)* 4508

Harrigan, Edward *(Cast)* 2428, 3266, 4508

Harrigan, Edward *(Composer)* 114, 516

Harrigan, Edward *(Librettist)* 2428, 3266

Harrigan, Edward *(Lyricist)* 114, 516, 1776, 3266, 4508

Harrigan, James *(Cast)* 215

Harrigan, Mary *(Cast)* 345

Harriman, Alfred *(Lyricist)* 4811

Harriman, P. Chelsea *(Costumes)* 3600

Harrington, Bobby *(Cast)* 187

Harrington, Delphi *(Cast)* 272

Harrington, Frank *(Cast)* 4596

Harrington, Giles *(Cast)* 3068

Harrington, Hamtree *(Cast)* 207, 447, 691, 1058, 3614, 4182

Harrington, Helen *(Cast)* 3622

Harrington, Laura *(Librettist)* 2766

Harrington, Laura (*Lyricist*)   2766
Harrington, Pat (*Cast*)   619, 1204, 3359, 4131, 4498
Harrington, Robert (*Cast*)   3453
Harris, Al (*Orchestrations*)   3046
Harris, Albert (*Director*)   2674, 4137
Harris, Albert (*Librettist*)   2674
Harris, Ann (*Composer*)   4011
Harris, Ann (*Lyricist*)   4011
Harris, Arthur (*Orchestrations*)   1045, 2689, 2737
Harris, Barbara (*Cast*)   170, 1122, 3274
Harris, Ben (*Composer*)   2009
Harris, Ben (*Lyricist*)   2009
Harris, Bud (*Composer*)   621, 1342, 3104
Harris, Charlene (*Cast*)   593
Harris, Charles (*Cast*)   1401
Harris, Charles K. (*Composer*)   3926, 3949
Harris, Charles K. (*Lyricist*)   2247, 3926, 3949
Harris, Clifford (*Lyricist*)   333, 675, 1208, 1538, 1588, 2498, 2698, 3827, 3882
Harris, Daniel (*Cast*)   1352
Harris, Diane (*Lyricist*)   4108
Harris, Diane David (*Lyricist*)   2998
Harris, Donald (*Set Design*)   2796
Harris, Donny (*Cast*)   206
Harris, Elmer (*Librettist*)   2832, 3562, 4037, 4634
Harris, Eva (*Cast*)   2984
Harris, Frank (*Author*)   1256
Harris, Frederic (*Dance Arranger*)   4011
Harris, Frederic (*Vocal Arranger*)   4011
Harris, Gary (*Lighting Designer*)   2908
Harris, Hazel (*Cast*)   203
Harris, Henry B. (*Producer*)   1, 1327, 1835, 3618, 4012
Harris, Holly (*Cast*)   2615
Harris, Howard (*Composer*)   1402
Harris, Howard (*Dance Arranger*)   1402
Harris, Howard (*Librettist*)   1898
Harris, Howard (*Musical Director*)   1402
Harris, Howard (*Vocal Arranger*)   1402
Harris, James Berton (*Costumes*)   35, 3653
Harris, Jayne Anne (*Cast*)   4011
Harris, Jayne Anne (*Choreographer*)   4011
Harris, Jeannie (*Cast*)   1619
Harris, Jed (*Director*)   933
Harris, Jeff (*Composer*)   157
Harris, Jeff (*Librettist*)   157
Harris, Jeff (*Lyricist*)   157
Harris, Jeremiah (*Producer*)   1159
Harris, Jeremy (*Musical Director*)   1108, 4468
Harris, Jeremy (*Vocal Arranger*)   1108
Harris, Jimmy (*Composer*)   3178
Harris, Jimmy (*Lyricist*)   3178
Harris, Joseph (*Producer*)   1068, 1273, 2726, 3944
Harris, Joseph P. (*Producer*)   1497, 1611, 2713, 3175, 4238
Harris, Julian (*Cast*)   1592
Harris, Julie (*Cast*)   2411, 4013
Harris, Lawrence (*Lyricist*)   621, 1342, 3104
Harris, Lew (*Orchestrations*)   1494
Harris, Lionel (*Composer*)   392
Harris, Lottie (*Cast*)   4339
Harris, Lulu Belle (*Cast*)   4011
Harris, Lulu Belle (*Choreographer*)   4011

Harris, Margaret (*Musical Director*)   105
Harris, Mrs. Henry B. (*Producer*)   4050
Harris, Niki (*Cast*)   1000
Harris, Paul (*Cast*)   1385
Harris, Phil (*Cast*)   3153
Harris, Ralph (*Cast*)   3361
Harris, Robert (*Cast*)   2582
Harris, Robert H. (*Cast*)   1373
Harris, Rosemary (*Cast*)   1787, 3787
Harris, Sam (*Composer*)   337
Harris, Sam (*Librettist*)   337
Harris, Sam (*Lyricist*)   337
Harris, Sam (*Producer*)   115, 121, 802, 1480, 1598, 1803, 1826, 1961, 2068, 2252, 2517, 2537, 3529, 4105
Harris, Sam H. (*Director*)   3009
Harris, Sam H. (*Producer*)   142, 207, 335, 536, 800, 801, 803, 804, 805, 1225, 1271, 1360, 1395, 1399, 1968, 2194, 2265, 2386, 2444, 2525, 2729, 2730, 2821, 3007, 3008, 3009, 3225, 3685, 3791, 4277, 4576, 4759
Harris, Scott (*Director*)   36, 2229
Harris, Steve (*Director*)   4264
Harris, Sylvia (*Producer*)   4435
Harris, Timmy (*Lighting Designer*)   2284
Harris, Tom (*Cast*)   1664, 4184
Harris, Val (*Composer*)   4805
Harris, Val (*Lyricist*)   4805
Harris, Wes (*Lyricist*)   4459
Harris, William (*Producer*)   1142, 1627
Harris Jr., William (*Librettist*)   4012
Harris Jr., William (*Lyricist*)   4012
Harris Jr., William (*Producer*)   2121
Harrison, Alex (*Cast*)   4825
Harrison, Bertram (*Director*)   381, 1584, 1819, 1904, 3849, 3850, 3860, 3993, 4443, 4464, 4526
Harrison, Gregory (*Cast*)   3364
Harrison, Gregory (*Producer*)   450
Harrison, Lee (*Cast*)   1926, 2123, 3744, 3745, 3747, 3750, 4094, 4802
Harrison, Lee (*Producer*)   3681
Harrison, Llewellyn (*Lighting Designer*)   3901
Harrison, Llewellyn (*Set Design*)   1073
Harrison, Louis (*Cast*)   627, 1246, 1505, 1576, 1728, 1793, 2209, 2324, 2481, 2592, 2666, 3053, 4125, 4497
Harrison, Louis (*Director*)   2675
Harrison, Louis (*Librettist*)   559, 2156, 2865
Harrison, Louis (*Lyricist*)   559, 976, 1026, 1246, 2184, 4393
Harrison, Louis B. (*Cast*)   252, 1602
Harrison, Madeline (*Cast*)   4285
Harrison, Muriel (*Cast*)   2366
Harrison, Paul Carter (*Author*)   1671
Harrison, Peter (*Set Design*)   2229, 4030
Harrison, Ray (*Cast*)   3278, 3326, 3947
Harrison, Ray (*Choreographer*)   1408, 2522, 3217, 3543, 4186, 4585
Harrison, Ray (*Director*)   2522
Harrison, Rex (*Cast*)   3038
Harrison, Ruth (*Cast*)   4177
Harrison, Seth (*Producer*)   4343
Harrison, Stafford (*Composer*)   3690
Harrison, Stafford (*Librettist*)   3690

Harvey, Peter (Costumes)   956, 1974, 2663, 3389
Harvey, Peter (Set Design)   956, 1216, 1974, 2284,
   2663, 2935, 3389, 3615, 3902, 4167, 4517
Harvey, Richard (Cast)   283
Harvey, Robert (Cast)   2225
Harvey, Roslyn (Lyricist)   2447, 3226
Harvey, Walter H.
   See also Ward & Harvey.
Harvey, Walter H. (Set Design)   3613
Harwell, George (Composer)   4629
Harwell, George (Lyricist)   4629
Harwood, H.M. (Librettist)   4327
Harwood, James (Cast)   1697
Harwood, Jill (Cast)   3764
Harwood, John (Director)   466, 931, 1297, 1529, 1992,
   2180, 2392, 2613, 3243, 3307, 3532, 3659, 3719, 4300,
   4392, 4426, 4778
Harwood, Ronald (Librettist)   1619
Hasbrook, Ethelberta (Lyricist)   1747
Hascall, Lon (Cast)   2298, 3403
Hasen, Irwin (Librettist)   3810
Haskell, Charles (Cast)   86
Haskell, David (Cast)   1595
Haskell, Jack (Cast)   2983
Haskell, Jack (Choreographer)   201, 568, 611, 711, 1297,
   1529, 1929, 3310, 3532, 3611, 4050, 4077, 4372, 4545
Haskell, Jimmie (Orchestrations)   3515
Haskell, Jimmie (Vocal Arranger)   3515
Haskell, Lon (Cast)   4421
Haskins, James (Cast)   2754
Hasomeris, Nick (Cast)   4016
Hassall, Christopher (Librettist)   650
Hassall, Christopher (Lyricist)   972
Hassell, George (Cast)   203, 324, 711, 948, 1530,
   1626, 1735, 1827, 2620, 2788, 3310, 3402, 3406,
   3407, 3799, 4188
Hassert, Bernard (Costumes)   3173
Hassler, Simon (Musical Director)   2428
Hastings, Basil Macdonald (Librettist)   3663
Hastings, Frederick (Cast)   77
Hastings, Hal (Musical Director)   270, 610, 1329, 1422,
   1507, 2368, 2550, 3113, 3288, 3351
Hastings, Harold (Dance Arranger)   1010
Hastings, Harold (Incidental Music)   4377
Hastings, Harold (Musical Director)   161, 657, 832, 957,
   1280, 1310, 2163, 2536, 3871, 3918, 4312, 4423, 4862
Hastings, Harold (Vocal Arranger)   1010
Hastings, J.B. (Musical Director)   1153, 2788,
   3291, 4154
Hastings, John (Lighting Designer)   198, 2171
Hastings, Lew (Librettist)   1340
Hasting's, Sue
   See also Sue Hasting's Marionettes.
Hastings, Tom (Cast)   2069
Hastings' Marionettes, Sue (Cast)   125, 216, 1973
Hasty Pudding Club (Producer)   1231, 4039
Hatch, Eric (Author)   3055
Hatch, Frank (Director)   1881
Hatch, James (Composer)   1319
Hatch, James (Librettist)   1319
Hatch, James (Lyricist)   1319

Hatch, Joel (Cast)   155
Hatch, Riley (Cast)   830
Hatch, Tony (Composer)   626, 4193
Hatch, Tony (Lyricist)   626, 4193
Hatcher, James (Director)   1750
Hatcher, James (Producer)   1750
Hatcher, Mary (Cast)   4314
Hatcher, Tom (Cast)   2144
Hateley, Linzi (Cast)   661
Hatfield, Lansing (Cast)   3813, 4569
Hatfield, Mark (Cast)   456
Hathaway, Charles (Musical Director)   4602
Hathaway, Donny (Composer)   4786
Hathaway, Donny (Lyricist)   4786
Hathaway, Gus (Cast)   3165
Hatten, Tom (Cast)   408
Hatvany, Lila (Author)   3152
Hauer, Mary Elizabeth (Librettist)   2784
Hauer, Mary Elizabeth (Lyricist)   2784
Hauerbach, Otto
   See Otto Harbach.
Hauptman, William (Librettist)   394
Hauptmann, Elisabeth (Author)   1755
Hauser, Franklin (Composer)   3219
Hauser, Kim (Cast)   544, 3718
Havel, Arthur (Cast)   2271
Havel, Morton (Cast)   2271
Havel, Tommy (Cast)   2271
Havens, Patricia (Costumes)   1862
Havens, Richie (Producer)   3814
Haverstick, Madame (Costumes)   764
Havez, Jean (Librettist)   3701
Havez, Jean (Lyricist)   538, 1703, 1704, 3327, 3701,
   4770, 4804, 4805, 4808
Havez, Jean C. (Composer)   4626
Havez, Jean C. (Librettist)   3842
Havez, Jean C. (Lyricist)   1531, 4626, 4804
Havez, Lou (Lyricist)   3397
Havoc, June (Cast)   1352, 1397, 2847, 2859, 2975,
   3353, 3813
Havoc, June (Director)   3788
Hawkes, Albert (Lighting Designer)   1654
Hawkins, Erskine
   See Erskine Hawkins and His Band and Erskine
   Hawkins' `Bama State Coll.
Hawkins, Ira (Cast)   1970, 3792, 4162, 4383
Hawkins, John (Composer)   634
Hawkins, John (Orchestrations)   634
Hawkins, John (Set Design)   711
Hawkins, June (Cast)   653, 4123
Hawkins, Lynette (Cast)   3991
Hawkins, Michael (Cast)   2599
Hawkins, Rick (Librettist)   2651
Hawkins, Stanley (Cast)   1118, 2399, 3951
Hawkins, Tom (Composer)   1978
Hawkins, Tom (Lyricist)   1978
Hawkins, Walter (Composer)   3987
Hawkins, Walter (Lyricist)   3987
Hawkins, Wood (Cast)   3605
Hawkins Jr., John (Costumes)   834
Hawkins Jr., John (Set Design)   834

Heller, Jayne *(Cast)* 3505
Heller, Randee *(Cast)* 2043
Heller, Richard *(Composer)* 4041
Heller, Richard *(Librettist)* 4041
Heller, Richard *(Lyricist)* 4041
Hellerman, Fred *(Composer)* 3112
Hellinger, Mark *(Cast)* 3153
Hellinger, Mark *(Librettist)* 1979, 4823
Hellman, Jerome *(Producer)* 4371
Hellman, Lillian *(Adaptation)* 2411
Hellman, Lillian *(Author)* 2510, 3691, 4601
Hellman, Lillian *(Librettist)* 630, 2653
Hellman, Lillian *(Lyricist)* 630
Helm, Mornay D. *(Orchestrations)* 1686
Helm, Thomas *(Conductor)* 2798
Helm, Thomas *(Musical Director)* 1298
Helm, Tom *(Musical Director)* 2861
Helming, Dan *(Cast)* 4774
Helmond, Katherine *(Cast)* 1999
Helms, Edwin I. *(Composer)* 3611
Helmsley, Estelle *(Cast)* 2994
Helmsley, W. *(Set Design)* 3092
Helpmann, Robert *(Cast)* 808, 4159
Helpmann, Robert *(Librettist)* 1809
Helward, Dale *(Cast)* 942
Heming, Percy *(Cast)* 3569
Heming, Violet *(Cast)* 1318, 2211
Hemion, Dwight *(Director)* 3454
Hemion, Dwight *(Producer)* 3454
Hemmer, Carl *(Choreographer)* 86, 1013, 1121, 2669
Hemmer, Carl *(Director)* 86
Hemphill, A. Marcus *(Author)* 2133
Hemphill, Barry *(Cast)* 344
Hemsley, Sherman *(Cast)* 3610
Hemsley, W.T. *(Set Design)* 4663
Hemsley, Winston De Witt *(Cast)* 597, 1729, 3741, 4003
Hemsley Jr., Gilbert V. *(Lighting Designer)* 808, 828, 946, 2058, 2260, 2775, 3088, 4197, 4788
Hendee, Harold *(Cast)* 2613
Henderson, Al *(Librettist)* 4110
Henderson, Charles *(Cast)* 1971
Henderson, Charles *(Composer)* 3645, 4170
Henderson, Charles *(Lyricist)* 3131, 3645, 4170
Henderson, Charles *(Vocal Arranger)* 2258, 4778
Henderson, David *(Producer)* 45
Henderson, F.A. *(Cast)* 761
Henderson, Fletcher
    See also Fletcher Henderson and His Orchestra.
Henderson, Fletcher *(Musical Director)* 925, 926
Henderson, Fletcher *(Orchestrations)* 4256
Henderson, Florence *(Cast)* 1242, 1564, 1681, 2550, 4718
Henderson, Isabel *(Cast)* 1710
Henderson, John *(Cast)* 554
Henderson, Katherine *(Cast)* 500
Henderson, L.D. *(Cast)* 2721
Henderson, Luther *(Composer)* 2200
Henderson, Luther *(Dance Arranger)* 432, 519, 1222, 1289, 1315, 1420, 1611, 1729, 2053, 2195, 2513, 3610, 4162
Henderson, Luther *(Incidental Music)* 1063
Henderson, Luther *(Music Adaptation)* 2200

Henderson, Luther *(Musical Director)* 2692
Henderson, Luther *(Orchestrations)* 341, 432, 1061, 1063, 1222, 1289, 1762, 1991, 2195, 2200, 2513, 3280, 3610, 3743, 4003, 4038, 4162, 4689
Henderson, Luther *(Vocal Arranger)* 432, 1222, 2195, 2513, 3610, 3743, 4162
Henderson, Marcia *(Cast)* 3452
Henderson, Ray *(Cast)* 3153
Henderson, Ray *(Composer)* 202, 391, 393, 1215, 1323, 1339, 1425, 1488, 1489, 1490, 1491, 1492, 1493, 1628, 1688, 1813, 1929, 1979, 2467, 2734, 3020, 3241, 3297, 3850, 3936, 4152, 4177, 4345, 4393, 4772, 4799, 4818, 4826
Henderson, Ray *(Dance Arranger)* 410
Henderson, Ray *(Director)* 4177
Henderson, Ray *(Librettist)* 1979, 4177
Henderson, Ray *(Musical Director)* 408, 410, 4163
Henderson, Ray *(Producer)* 3850, 4177
Henderson, Ray *(Vocal Arranger)* 410
Henderson, Rose *(Cast)* 4763
Henderson, Slim *(Cast)* 500
Henderson, W.C. *(Composer)* 3024
Henderson and His Orchestra, Fletcher
    See also Fletcher Henderson.
Henderson and His Orchestra, Fletcher *(Cast)* 925
Hendra, Tony *(Director)* 3077
Hendra, Tony *(Librettist)* 3077, 4029
Hendra, Tony *(Lyricist)* 3077
Hendra, Tony *(Orchestrations)* 3077
Hendra, Tony *(Producer)* 3077
Hendra, Tony *(Vocal Arranger)* 3077
Hendricks, Jon *(Cast)* 1710
Hendricks, Jon *(Composer)* 1296, 3178
Hendricks, Jon *(Lyricist)* 1296, 3178
Hendrickson, Hugh *(Cast)* 2089
Hendrickson, Ned *(Producer)* 348
Hendrickson, Stephen *(Set Design)* 4689
Hendry, Tom *(Lyricist)* 1064
Heneker, David *(Composer)* 194, 1721, 2240, 3429
Heneker, David *(Librettist)* 2150
Heneker, David *(Lyricist)* 194, 1721, 2150, 2240, 3429
Henie, Sonja *(Librettist)* 2024
Henie, Sonja *(Producer)* 1782, 2023, 2098, 2099, 2161, 2162, 4143
Henkins, Hezekiah *(Composer)* 3297
Henkins, Hezekiah *(Lyricist)* 3297
Henley, Bob *(Librettist)* 3916
Hennequin *(Author)* 4418
Hennequin, Maurice *(Author)* 68, 1527, 2824, 3254, 3363, 3784, 4213
Henner, Marilu *(Cast)* 3330
Hennes, Tom *(Lighting Designer)* 3311
Henning, Doug *(Cast)* 2687, 2820
Henning, Leo *(Cast)* 539
Henning, Magnus *(Composer)* 3441
Henning, Magnus *(Musical Director)* 3441
Henning, Pat *(Cast)* 3287
Hennings, John E. *(Cast)* 1121
Henri, F. *(Composer)* 560
Henrikson, Eve *(Costumes)* 239
Henrique, Luis *(Composer)* 2245

Henrique, Luis *(Lyricist)* 2245
Henry, B.C. *(Composer)* 306
Henry, Chad *(Composer)* 140
Henry, Chad *(Lyricist)* 140
Henry, Donna Jean *(Cast)* 2483
Henry, Eleanor *(Cast)* 1882, 2489
Henry, Grace *(Librettist)* 1863
Henry, Grace *(Lyricist)* 1128, 1132, 1134, 1281,
    2545, 4335
Henry, John *(Choreographer)* 3752
Henry, Judith *(Producer)* 105
Henry, Leonard *(Composer)* 702
Henry, Marc *(Librettist)* 4154
Henry, O. *(Author)* 1306, 1507, 1508, 1509, 3221
Henry, O. *(Librettist)* 2559
Henry, Peggie *(Cast)* 4220
Henry, S.R. *(Composer)* 2527, 4762
Henry, Suzanne *(Cast)* 2764
Henry B. Harris Estate *(Producer)* 2486
Hensel, Christopher *(Cast)* 3202
Hensel, Karen *(Cast)* 4861
Henshaw, Hal *(Set Design)* 1644
Henshaw, John E. *(Cast)* 308, 639, 2725
Henske, Judy *(Cast)* 1596
Henson, Gladys *(Cast)* 3885, 4361
Henson, Leslie *(Cast)* 129, 334, 2389, 3139, 3156, 3569,
    4327, 4418, 4419, 4519, 4765
Henson, Leslie *(Director)* 844, 3139
Henson, Leslie *(Producer)* 346, 3139
Hepburn, Katharine *(Cast)* 798
Herbert, A.J. *(Cast)* 1858, 2446
Herbert, A.P. *(Librettist)* 453
Herbert, A.P. *(Lyricist)* 453, 1763
Herbert, Charles *(Composer)* 4484
Herbert, Charles *(Lyricist)* 4484
Herbert, Charlie *(Cast)* 3255, 4484
Herbert, Evelyn *(Cast)* 1962, 2622, 2813, 3056, 3117,
    3584, 3586, 4150
Herbert, Fred *(Librettist)* 4629
Herbert, Fred *(Producer)* 1076
Herbert, Gene *(Composer)* 532
Herbert, Gene *(Lyricist)* 532
Herbert, Grace *(Cast)* 3255, 4484
Herbert, H.E. *(Cast)* 2871
Herbert, Jean *(Composer)* 4374
Herbert, Jean *(Lyricist)* 1126, 1989, 4374, 4465
Herbert, Jocelyn *(Costumes)* 4371
Herbert, Jocelyn *(Set Design)* 4371
Herbert, Joseph *(Cast)* 1355, 2507, 2592, 3732, 4500
Herbert, Joseph *(Director)* 2317
Herbert, Joseph *(Librettist)* 4511
Herbert, Joseph W. *(Author)* 1962
Herbert, Joseph W. *(Cast)* 8, 45, 335, 379, 1540,
    2160, 2506, 2715, 2848, 2886, 3237, 3313, 3820,
    3994, 4590, 4624
Herbert, Joseph W. *(Composer)* 3193
Herbert, Joseph W. *(Director)* 1351, 2538, 2668, 2715,
    3673, 3679, 4194
Herbert, Joseph W. *(Librettist)* 8, 336, 1111, 1246, 1613,
    1962, 1963, 2538, 2668, 2715, 2956, 3313, 4044, 4194,
    4414, 4590

Herbert, Joseph W. *(Lyricist)* 8, 93, 195, 336, 1111, 1962,
    2668, 2715, 2855, 2886, 2938, 4044, 4425, 4590
Herbert, Lew *(Cast)* 4829
Herbert, Lillian *(Cast)* 1462
Herbert, Victor *(Author)* 251, 3773
Herbert, Victor *(Composer)* 48, 104, 136, 250, 251, 252,
    638, 683, 763, 947, 1016, 1095, 1096, 1098, 1111, 1162,
    1183, 1355, 1394, 1397, 1552, 1599, 1711, 1851, 2101,
    2160, 2370, 2394, 2404, 2465, 2481, 2534, 2670, 2855,
    2882, 2885, 2900, 2915, 3043, 3081, 3122, 3172, 3265,
    3304, 3312, 3319, 3567, 3570, 3590, 3675, 3704, 3773,
    3783, 3819, 3881, 3994, 4010, 4017, 4070, 4250, 4293,
    4390, 4547, 4559, 4564, 4649, 4699, 4724, 4735, 4811,
    4812, 4813, 4814, 4815, 4816, 4817, 4818
Herbert, Victor *(Librettist)* 4815
Herbert, Victor *(Music Based On)* 1711
Herbert, Victor *(Orchestrations)* 1016, 1111, 1183, 2670,
    2885, 2915, 3081, 3304, 3312, 3590, 3675, 3773, 4250,
    4293, 4547, 4559, 4649, 4735, 4814
Herberth, Hans *(Cast)* 1413
Herbold, Lisa *(Cast)* 2488
Herbst, Jeffrey *(Cast)* 690
Herbstritt, Larry *(Arrangements)* 2651
Herczeg, Geza *(Author)* 4730
Herczeg, Geza *(Librettist)* 2985
Herczeq, Franz *(Author)* 3974
Hereford, Kathryn *(Cast)* 3721, 4023
Herendeen, Fred *(Librettist)* 3069, 3314
Herendeen, Fred *(Lyricist)* 1920, 2774, 3314
Herendeen, Frederick *(Composer)* 4794
Herendeen, Frederick *(Librettist)* 82, 1560, 3605
Herendeen, Frederick *(Lyricist)* 82, 1173, 3605, 4794
Herford, Beatrice *(Cast)* 2456
Herford, Oliver *(Author)* 4688
Herford, Oliver *(Librettist)* 2603
Herford, Oliver *(Lyricist)* 2603, 4688
Herget, Bob *(Cast)* 3664
Herget, Bob *(Choreographer)* 624, 842, 1237, 1435,
    3956, 4060, 4577
Heritage Project, Inc., The *(Producer)* 1903
Herk, I.H. *(Director)* 1032
Herk, I.H. *(Producer)* 1032
Herko, Fred *(Cast)* 1958
Herlein, Lillian *(Cast)* 3773
Herlie, Eileen *(Cast)* 64, 4270
Herman, Al *(Cast)* 1947, 3173
Herman, Danny *(Choreographer)* 158
Herman, George *(Cast)* 930
Herman, George *(Composer)* 2028
Herman, George *(Librettist)* 2028
Herman, George *(Lyricist)* 2028
Herman, Harold *(Librettist)* 1539
Herman, Jerry *(Composer)* 367, 1000, 1012, 1408, 1660,
    1828, 2052, 2208, 2360, 2660, 2664, 2713, 2864, 3018,
    3161, 3366, 3840, 3942
Herman, Jerry *(Director)* 2052, 3161, 3366
Herman, Jerry *(Lyricist)* 367, 1000, 1012, 1408, 1660,
    1828, 2052, 2208, 2360, 2660, 2664, 2713, 2864, 3018,
    3161, 3366, 3840, 3942
Herman, John *(Producer)* 1991
Herman, Mme. *(Costumes)* 4404

Hezer, Ludwig *(Author)* 1384
Hi-Hatters, The *(Cast)* 2259
Hiatt, Jessie *(Cast)* 3158
Hibbert, Edward *(Cast)* 3598
Hibbert, Geoffrey *(Cast)* 346, 507
Hibiscus Productions *(Producer)* 4011
Hickey, Bill *(Cast)* 134
Hickey, Ed *(Cast)* 376
Hickey, John *(Lighting Designer)* 338
Hickey, John *(Musical Director)* 3730
Hickey, John *(Set Design)* 338
Hickey, William *(Cast)* 1018
Hickey Jr., John *(Producer)* 2296
Hickey, Hale & Robinson *(Producer)* 4572
Hicklin, Margery *(Cast)* 3569
Hicklin, Walter *(Costumes)* 2477, 4358
Hickman, Alfred *(Director)* 2527
Hickman, Annie *(Costumes)* 2970
Hickman, Art
    See also Art Hickman's Orchestra.
Hickman, Art *(Composer)* 4814
Hickman, Art *(Lyricist)* 4814
Hickman, Charles *(Director)* 2608
Hickman, George *(Composer)* 3103
Hickman, George *(Lyricist)* 3103
Hickman, Leo *(Composer)* 1296
Hickman, Leo *(Lyricist)* 1296
Hickman's Orchestra, Art
    See also Art Hickman.
Hickman's Orchestra, Art *(Cast)* 4814
Hickok, John *(Cast)* 789, 2065
Hicks, Bill *(Cast)* 1037
Hicks, Charles K. *(Musical Director)* 3026
Hicks, J. *(Set Design)* 4302
Hicks, James *(Cast)* 552
Hicks, Juanita *(Cast)* 552
Hicks, Julian *(Set Design)* 4014
Hicks, Kenneth *(Cast)* 4447
Hicks, Marva *(Cast)* 4127
Hicks, Munson *(Cast)* 482
Hicks, Munson *(Director)* 251, 2289
Hicks, Russell *(Cast)* 82
Hicks, Seymour *(Author)* 675, 1188, 2991
Hicks, Seymour *(Cast)* 333, 719, 1454, 3948
Hicks, Seymour *(Director)* 333, 1454
Hicks, Seymour *(Librettist)* 333, 675, 719, 1043, 1123, 1454, 2509, 3803
Hicks, Seymour *(Musical Director)* 719
Hicks, Seymour *(Producer)* 2509
Hicks, Sue *(Cast)* 4583
Hicks, Walter *(Choreographer)* 4750
Hicks and Brooks *(Set Design)* 2974
Hidalgo, Allen *(Cast)* 1236
Hide, Eugene *(Set Design)* 2630
Hidey, Hal *(Musical Director)* 339, 407
Hidey, Hal *(Orchestrations)* 339
Hidlay, William *(Cast)* 2511
Hidlay, William *(Choreographer)* 2511
Higgens, Joel *(Cast)* 135
Higginbotham, Irene *(Composer)* 498

Higgins, Billy *(Cast)* 899
Higgins, Colin *(Author)* 1775
Higgins, Douglas *(Set Design)* 2607
Higgins, Joel *(Cast)* 3928
Higgins, John Michael *(Cast)* 3076
Higgins, Michael *(Cast)* 2411
Higgins, Peter *(Cast)* 1387
Higgins, Steven *(Lyricist)* 2039
High John Prods. *(Producer)* 578
Highley, Ronald *(Cast)* 643
Hight, Pearl *(Cast)* 3254
Hightower, Robert *(Cast)* 601
Higlen, David *(Cast)* 564
Hiken, Gerald *(Cast)* 747, 1047, 3094, 4176, 4229
Hiken, Nat *(Librettist)* 95, 2554, 2653
Hiken, Nat *(Lyricist)* 95
Hilb, Emil *(Composer)* 2249
Hildebrand, Fred *(Cast)* 2490, 4209
Hilder *(Cast)* 1181
Hilditch, Doris *(Cast)* 325
Hilferty, Susan *(Costumes)* 1161
Hill, Alex *(Composer)* 3782
Hill, Alex *(Lyricist)* 3782
Hill, Alexander *(Composer)* 432, 2034
Hill, Alexander *(Lyricist)* 2034
Hill, Annabelle *(Cast)* 2331
Hill, Arthur *(Cast)* 4060
Hill, Bette Cerf *(Producer)* 4074
Hill, Billy *(Composer)* 3596, 4824
Hill, Billy *(Lyricist)* 3457, 3596, 4824
Hill, Bobby *(Cast)* 1072
Hill, Craig *(Cast)* 752
Hill, Dule *(Cast)* 2542
Hill, Erin *(Cast)* 1969
Hill, Errol *(Author)* 2719
Hill, Errol *(Lyricist)* 2719
Hill, George B. *(Cast)* 96
Hill, George B. *(Lyricist)* 96
Hill, George Roy *(Director)* 1698, 1846
Hill, Graham *(Author)* 1783
Hill, Gus *(Producer)* 537, 538, 539, 540, 541, 542, 3021, 3022, 3026, 3028, 3030
Hill, Homer *(Set Design)* 4047
Hill, J. Leubrie *(Cast)* 295, 984, 2979, 3041, 3797
Hill, J. Leubrie *(Composer)* 295, 983, 984, 2979, 3041, 3399, 4747, 4807, 4808
Hill, J. Leubrie *(Director)* 984
Hill, J. Leubrie *(Librettist)* 3041
Hill, J. Leubrie *(Lyricist)* 983, 984, 1835, 2111, 2979, 3041, 3399, 4747, 4807, 4808
Hill, J. Leubrie *(Producer)* 983, 984, 3041
Hill, Jack *(Librettist)* 1880
Hill, Jack *(Lyricist)* 1880
Hill, James *(Cast)* 2111
Hill, Joe *(Composer)* 1609
Hill, Joe *(Lyricist)* 1609
Hill, John-Edward *(Producer)* 3448
Hill, Ken *(Cast)* 874
Hill, Ken *(Librettist)* 3462
Hill, Ken *(Lyricist)* 3462

Hill, Leitha *(Cast)* 876, 877, 880, 3709
Hill, Ralston *(Cast)* 2415, 4173
Hill, Richard *(Composer)* 634
Hill, Richard *(Orchestrations)* 634
Hill, Ruby *(Cast)* 4123
Hill, Teddy
  See also Teddy Hill Orchestra.
Hill, Teddy *(Musical Director)* 897
Hill, Valerie *(Cast)* 4309
Hill Orchestra, Teddy
  See also Teddy Hill.
Hill Orchestra, Teddy *(Cast)* 3782
Hillbrandt, James *(Cast)* 282
Hillebrand, Fred *(Cast)* 4269
Hillebrand, Fred *(Composer)* 2406
Hillebrand, Fred *(Lyricist)* 2406
Hiller, J. Sebastian *(Composer)* 830, 4026
Hiller, J.S. *(Lyricist)* 185
Hiller, J.S. *(Musical Director)* 3360
Hiller, John S. *(Musical Director)* 1165
Hiller, John Sebastian *(Composer)* 830
Hiller, John Sebastian *(Musical Director)* 3488
Hiller, Rose *(Cast)* 455
Hilliam, B.C. *(Author)* 325
Hilliam, B.C. *(Composer)* 325, 579, 1175, 3317
Hilliam, B.C. *(Librettist)* 3593
Hilliam, B.C. *(Lyricist)* 325, 579, 3317, 3593
Hilliam, B.C. *(Musical Director)* 579
Hilliard, Bob *(Composer)* 854
Hilliard, Bob *(Librettist)* 4627
Hilliard, Bob *(Lyricist)* 137, 854, 856, 857, 861, 862,
  1791, 2076, 2850, 3683, 4193
Hilliard, Mack *(Producer)* 3434
Hilliard, Mark *(Producer)* 1368
Hillias, Peg *(Cast)* 3452
Hillman *(Composer)* 1627
Hillman *(Lyricist)* 1627
Hillman, B. *(Cast)* 3062
Hillman, George *(Cast)* 941
Hillman, Gerald Paul *(Lyricist)* 3688
Hillman, Gerald Paul *(Producer)* 3688
Hillman, Nancy Tribush *(Director)* 3688
Hills, Alice *(Cast)* 2532
Hilton, James *(Author)* 3913
Hilton, James *(Librettist)* 3913
Hilton, James *(Lyricist)* 3913
Himber, Richard *(Composer)* 1899
Himber, Richard *(Lyricist)* 1899
Himber, Richard *(Producer)* 1899
Himber Orchestra, Richard *(Cast)* 1899
Hindman, James *(Cast)* 789
Hinds, Ernie *(Cast)* 985
Hinds, Ernie *(Set Design)* 985
Hindus, Milton *(Lyricist)* 3698
Hines, Altona *(Cast)* 1366
Hines, Babe *(Cast)* 90, 98, 961
Hines, Earl
  See also Earl Hines Orchestra.
Hines, Elizabeth *(Cast)* 2263, 2533, 2601, 2757, 2931,
  3218, 3868

Hines, Gregory *(Cast)* 828, 1198, 2200, 2415, 4091
Hines, Gregory *(Choreographer)* 2200
Hines, Jack *(Lyricist)* 3405
Hines, Jackson *(Cast)* 2340
Hines, John *(Cast)* 3855
Hines, Johnny *(Cast)* 2270
Hines, Maurice *(Cast)* 534, 1198, 4534
Hines, Maurice *(Choreographer)* 3840, 4534
Hines, Maurice *(Director)* 4534
Hines, Nat C. *(Cast)* 1836
Hines, Patrick *(Cast)* 946, 1985
Hines Orchestra, Earl *(Cast)* 725
Hingle, Pat *(Cast)* 477, 1571, 3871
Hinkle, Velma *(Cast)* 1556
Hinkley, Brett *(Cast)* 655
Hinnant, Bill *(Cast)* 73, 945, 1107, 1380, 1590, 2617,
  3479, 4041, 4783
Hinnant, Skip *(Cast)* 4783
Hinton, Al *(Cast)* 4596
Hipkens, Robert *(Cast)* 4076
Hipkens, Robert *(Composer)* 4076
Hipkens, Robert *(Librettist)* 4076
Hipkens, Robert *(Lyricist)* 4076
Hipp, Paul *(Cast)* 580
Hippen, Lynn *(Cast)* 251
Hirsch, Hugo *(Author)* 2567
Hirsch, Hugo *(Composer)* 2567
Hirsch, John *(Costumes)* 941
Hirsch, John *(Lyricist)* 1064
Hirsch, Ken *(Composer)* 952
Hirsch, Louis *(Composer)* 1613, 1663
Hirsch, Louis A. *(Composer)* 186, 258, 381, 822, 1464,
  1523, 1598, 1663, 1688, 1689, 1793, 2334, 2538, 2767,
  2854, 2869, 2892, 2926, 3045, 3085, 3218, 3250, 3395,
  3652, 3701, 3868, 4094, 4490, 4553, 4655, 4799, 4809,
  4810, 4812, 4816, 4833
Hirsch, Louis A. *(Lyricist)* 186, 3395, 4490, 4655, 4809
Hirsch, Michael *(Cast)* 4398
Hirsch, Walter *(Composer)* 487
Hirsch, Walter *(Lyricist)* 393, 487, 1658
Hirschfeld, Abe *(Producer)* 3576
Hirschfeld, Al *(Librettist)* 4237
Hirschfeld, Max *(Musical Director)* 250, 694, 1543, 1555,
  1582, 1588, 1962, 2160, 2213, 2534, 2670, 2886, 3078,
  3193, 3230, 3245, 3675, 4555
Hirschfeld, Susan *(Costumes)* 2993, 4139
Hirschhorn, Joel *(Composer)* 869, 3888, 4402
Hirschhorn, Joel *(Librettist)* 869
Hirschhorn, Joel *(Lyricist)* 869, 3888
Hirschhorn, Naomi Caryl *(Cast)* 4111
Hirschhorn, Naomi Caryl *(Composer)* 4111
Hirschhorn, Robert *(Musical Director)* 2049
Hirschman, Herbert *(Director)* 939
Hirsh, George *(Cast)* 2164
Hirson, Roger O. *(Librettist)* 3506, 4588
Hirst, George *(Composer)* 1176
Hirst, George *(Lyricist)* 2747
Hirst, George *(Musical Director)* 799, 1414, 1476, 1948,
  2747, 3823, 4550
Hirst, George *(Orchestrations)* 4550

Hirst, George *(Vocal Arranger)* 4550
Hiss, Anthony *(Author)* 1402
Hitchcock, Raymond *(Cast)* 335, 352, 379, 586, 1148, 1433, 1780, 1919, 1920, 1921, 1922, 1923, 2277, 2315, 2730, 3662, 3685, 4187, 4353, 4563, 4754, 4762, 4815
Hitchcock, Raymond *(Librettist)* 4742
Hitchcock, Raymond *(Producer)* 1335, 1920, 1921, 1922, 4742
Hite, Mabel *(Cast)* 687, 1518, 2826, 4725
Hite, Mabel *(Composer)* 687
Hite, Mabel *(Lyricist)* 687
Hixon, Hal *(Cast)* 684, 4849
Hlela, Betty-Boo *(Cast)* 2147
Hlophe, Bongani *(Cast)* 209
Hoadley, Helen *(Cast)* 1863
Hoagland, Carleton *(Producer)* 3717
Hoare, Douglas *(Author)* 4302
Hoare, Douglas *(Librettist)* 3237, 4302
Hoare, Douglas *(Lyricist)* 4302
Hoare, Ken *(Additional Material)* 1857
Hoban, Stella *(Cast)* 3400
Hoban et Jeanne *(Costumes)* 2467
Hobard, Rick *(Producer)* 3763, 4689
Hobart, George V. *(Author)* 69, 399, 1014, 1218, 2176, 2274, 2710, 2878, 2990, 2996
Hobart, George V. *(Director)* 1218, 2461, 4085, 4649
Hobart, George V. *(Librettist)* 29, 69, 88, 228, 258, 511, 559, 579, 632, 830, 1430, 1566, 1688, 1731, 1921, 1925, 2209, 2324, 2336, 2408, 2461, 2835, 2863, 2865, 2878, 2882, 2895, 2904, 2951, 3006, 3007, 3090, 3332, 3529, 3820, 4085, 4317, 4564, 4649, 4726, 4753, 4757, 4805, 4807, 4808, 4810, 4811
Hobart, George V. *(Lyricist)* 29, 88, 126, 228, 258, 354, 465, 511, 559, 830, 1151, 1430, 1728, 2209, 2324, 2336, 2835, 2863, 2865, 2878, 2951, 2964, 2996, 3090, 3122, 3129, 3265, 3529, 3746, 3747, 3749, 3820, 4026, 4070, 4085, 4453, 4649, 4691, 4726, 4753, 4757, 4805, 4807, 4808, 4810
Hobart, Rose *(Cast)* 2060
Hobbs, Jack *(Cast)* 334
Hobbs, Robert *(Cast)* 133, 2140
Hobson, I.M. *(Cast)* 109, 958
Hochhauser, Jeff *(Librettist)* 4325
Hochhauser, Jeff *(Lyricist)* 4325
Hochman, Larry *(Composer)* 3202
Hochman, Larry *(Dance Arranger)* 3202
Hochman, Larry *(Musical Director)* 1059, 3666, 4707
Hochman, Larry *(Orchestrations)* 2420
Hochman, Larry *(Vocal Arranger)* 1059, 3202, 3666
Hockwald, Arthur *(Producer)* 4184
Hoctor, Harriet *(Cast)* 2, 1137, 1932, 3953, 3980, 4357, 4429, 4825
Hoctor, Harriet *(Choreographer)* 1932
Hodapp, Ann *(Cast)* 1256, 1590
Hoder, Mark *(Musical Director)* 42
Hodes, Gloria *(Cast)* 788, 4736
Hodge, William T. *(Cast)* 1095, 4662
Hodges, Ann *(Cast)* 3187
Hodges, Eddie *(Cast)* 3016
Hodges, Elijah *(Cast)* 1385
Hodges, John *(Lyricist)* 1026

Hodges, John King *(Librettist)* 1863
Hodges, John King *(Lyricist)* 1863
Hodges, Johnnie *(Composer)* 4091
Hodges, Johnnie *(Lyricist)* 4091
Hodges, Johnny *(Composer)* 895
Hodges, Joy *(Cast)* 1101, 2068, 2219, 3091
Hodges, Mitchell *(Librettist)* 4484
Hodges, Raymond *(Composer)* 1026
Hodgkins, Gene *(Composer)* 697
Hodgkins, Gene *(Lyricist)* 697
Hodgkinson, Guy *(Set Design)* 874, 2572
Hodgson, Red *(Composer)* 393
Hodgson, Red *(Lyricist)* 393, 1813
Hodley, Henry *(Composer)* 2855
Hodshire, Allan *(Director)* 1697
Hodshire, Allan *(Producer)* 1697
Hoebee, Mark S. *(Choreographer)* 3461
Hoefler, Charles E. *(Costumes)* 4468
Hoefler, Charles E. *(Lighting Designer)* 2173, 4468
Hoefler, Charles E. *(Set Design)* 2173, 4468
Hoey, Bill *(Cast)* 3392
Hoey, Dennis *(Cast)* 2293, 4569
Hoey, Evelyn *(Cast)* 1272, 2366, 4545, 4583
Hoey, Herbert *(Cast)* 4843
Hoey, William F. *(Cast)* 1301
Hoff, Edwin H. *(Cast)* 2345
Hoff, Fred *(Musical Director)* 659, 728, 1710, 1819, 2112, 2739, 3207, 4328
Hoff, Louise *(Cast)* 1408, 2910
Hoff, Louise *(Composer)* 4153
Hoff, Louise *(Lyricist)* 4153
Hoff, Robin *(Cast)* 1427
Hoffa, Portland *(Cast)* 4300, 4367
Hoffenstein, Samuel *(Librettist)* 1453
Hoffert, Paul *(Composer)* 1500
Hoffert, Paul *(Orchestrations)* 1500
Hoffman, Aaron *(Librettist)* 349, 358, 1531, 2314, 2448, 3134, 3185, 3519, 3520, 3531, 3748, 3855, 4436, 4787
Hoffman, Aaron *(Lyricist)* 2299
Hoffman, Aaron S. *(Lyricist)* 248, 3073
Hoffman, Al *(Composer)* 544, 4264
Hoffman, Al *(Lyricist)* 4264
Hoffman, Armin *(Pianist)* 412
Hoffman, Avi *(Cast)* 1609, 3722, 4082
Hoffman, Avi *(Director)* 4082
Hoffman, Avi Ber *(Cast)* 1279
Hoffman, Bena *(Choreographer)* 3590
Hoffman, Bill *(Librettist)* 2357
Hoffman, Bill *(Set Design)* 131
Hoffman, Cary *(Composer)* 4635
Hoffman, Dustin *(Cast)* 2218
Hoffman, E.A. *(Composer)* 3631
Hoffman, E.A. *(Lyricist)* 3631
Hoffman, Ferdi *(Cast)* 1284
Hoffman, G. Wayne *(Cast)* 1732
Hoffman, Gertrude
See also Gertrude Hoffman Girls.
Hoffman, Gertrude *(Cast)* 558, 959, 1829, 1968, 2209, 3387, 3609
Hoffman, Gertrude *(Choreographer)* 201, 2800, 2951, 3148, 3149, 3409, 4650

Hollins, Mabel H. *(Lyricist)* 1
Hollins, Maud *(Cast)* 2233, 2673
Hollis, Tommy *(Cast)* 3368
Hollister, David *(Composer)* 1233, 2288
Hollister, David *(Dance Arranger)* 4292
Hollister, David *(Orchestrations)* 2887, 4292
Hollmann, Erica *(Costumes)* 2285
Holloway, Joan *(Cast)* 3800, 3913
Holloway, Stanley *(Cast)* 842, 844, 1089, 3038, 3156, 4361, 4519
Holloway, Sterling *(Cast)* 1446, 1447, 1448, 2032
Holloway, Sterling *(Librettist)* 1448
Hollywood, Daniel *(Producer)* 3097
Hollywood Alliance *(Producer)* 2809
Holm, Celeste *(Cast)* 462, 2144, 2182, 3263, 4191, 4537
Holm, Eleanor *(Cast)* 173, 417, 3100
Holm, Hanya *(Choreographer)* 161, 283, 623, 751, 1600, 2331, 2464, 2948, 3035, 3038, 3326, 3496, 3696, 4048
Holm, Hanya *(Director)* 4048
Holm, John Cecil *(Author)* 297, 2449
Holm, John Cecil *(Librettist)* 372, 971
Holm, Klaus *(Lighting Designer)* 842, 1076, 1600, 2554, 2556, 3473, 4798
Holm, Klaus *(Set Design)* 2554
Holman, Bill *(Orchestrations)* 3428
Holman, Libby *(Cast)* 1446, 2545, 2827, 3086, 3650, 3699, 4367, 4777
Holmes, Ben *(Cast)* 1461
Holmes, Ben *(Director)* 1836
Holmes, Greenberg *(Cast)* 1906
Holmes, Greensbury *(Cast)* 4751
Holmes, J. Merrill *(Cast)* 1036
Holmes, Jack *(Composer)* 392, 597, 679, 1049, 1107, 1408, 3110, 3217, 3889, 3890, 4310
Holmes, Jack *(Conductor)* 1380
Holmes, Jack *(Dance Arranger)* 1380, 1408, 2522, 3110
Holmes, Jack *(Librettist)* 392, 597
Holmes, Jack *(Lyricist)* 392, 679, 1049, 1107, 1408, 3110, 3889, 3890, 4310
Holmes, Jack *(Musical Director)* 3217, 4173, 4659
Holmes, Jack *(Pianist)* 392
Holmes, Jack *(Vocal Arranger)* 2522, 4173
Holmes, Jerry *(Cast)* 2011
Holmes, Leroy *(Composer)* 2072
Holmes, Leroy *(Musical Director)* 2072
Holmes, Lucy *(Cast)* 1347
Holmes, Michael *(Musical Director)* 319
Holmes, Michael *(Orchestrations)* 319
Holmes, Ralph *(Cast)* 4772
Holmes, Rapley *(Cast)* 4453
Holmes, Roy *(Lighting Designer)* 2809
Holmes, Rupert *(Composer)* 3070
Holmes, Rupert *(Librettist)* 3070
Holmes, Rupert *(Lyricist)* 3070
Holmes, Rupert *(Orchestrations)* 3070
Holmes, Scott *(Cast)* 1038, 2204, 3718
Holmes, Taylor *(Cast)* 1756, 1992, 2068, 2858, 3850, 4064
Holmes, Vernon *(Musical Director)* 392
Holmes, Violet *(Choreographer)* 107, 2689, 2737, 3126, 3637, 3638

Holmes a Court, Peter *(Producer)* 1232
Holofcener, Larry *(Composer)* 2987, 3186
Holofcener, Larry *(Lyricist)* 673, 2246, 2987, 3186, 3890, 4260, 4273, 4827, 4829
Holpit, Penny *(Set Design)* 3960
Holse, Glenn *(Set Design)* 411
Holst, Edouard *(Composer)* 3176
Holt, Calvin *(Cast)* 673
Holt, Fritz *(Director)* 3444
Holt, Fritz *(Producer)* 2360, 2677, 3515, 3787
Holt, Henry *(Cast)* 1523
Holt, Shannon *(Cast)* 655
Holt, Stella *(Producer)* 70, 71
Holt, Vivian *(Cast)* 1799
Holt, Will *(Author)* 4216
Holt, Will *(Cast)* 2246, 3970
Holt, Will *(Composer)* 33, 3970, 4318
Holt, Will *(Librettist)* 823, 2796, 3330, 3515, 3970, 4216, 4318
Holt, Will *(Lyricist)* 33, 823, 2801, 3015, 3338, 3515, 3970, 4216, 4272, 4318
Holter, Bill *(Cast)* 3530
Holter, Bob *(Composer)* 1677
Holton, Robert *(Composer)* 1878
Holtz, Lou *(Cast)* 622, 1396, 1482, 1483, 2734, 3153, 3416, 3594, 4300, 4747, 4778
Holtz, Lou *(Director)* 1396
Holtz, Lou *(Producer)* 4778
Holtz Sr., Gregory *(Cast)* 2239
Holtzman, Jonathan *(Composer)* 1372, 1669
Holtzman, Jonathan *(Lyricist)* 1372, 1669
Holtzman, Jonathan *(Musical Director)* 1372
Holtzman, Jonathan *(Orchestrations)* 1372
Holtzman, Willy *(Librettist)* 2007
Holtzman, Willy *(Lyricist)* 451
Holzer, Adela *(Producer)* 518, 1116, 3169, 3873, 4447, 4459
Holzer, Jane *(Cast)* 1637
Holzer, Peter *(Producer)* 1116
Holzman, Winnie *(Librettist)* 424
Holzman, Winnie *(Lyricist)* 4, 424
Home, Cyril Morton *(Composer)* 2763
Home, Cyril Morton *(Lyricist)* 2763
Home Town Quartet, The *(Cast)* 1507
Homer *(Author)* 1816, 1959
Honan, Mark *(Cast)* 533, 760
Honeg *(Lyricist)* 4264
Honey, George *(Cast)* 1392
Hong, Arabella *(Cast)* 1315
Honrath, Donald *(Composer)* 3103
Hood, Basil *(Librettist)* 1178, 1392, 1473, 2514, 2836, 3588, 3777
Hood, Basil *(Lyricist)* 356, 902, 1473, 1569, 3588
Hood, Janet *(Dance Arranger)* 1371
Hood, Janet *(Musical Director)* 1371
Hood, Janet *(Vocal Arranger)* 1371
Hood, Noel *(Cast)* 325
Hood, Thomas *(Lyricist)* 2633
Hook, James *(Composer)* 3450
Hook, Nina Warner *(Librettist)* 2168, 4153
Hooker, Brian *(Librettist)* 3219, 3323, 4372, 4539, 4664

Hooker, Brian *(Lyricist)* 710, 1235, 2264, 2756, 3020, 3219, 3323, 3649, 4300, 4539, 4664, 4815

Hooker, Michael S. *(Lighting Designer)* 3925

Hooks, Robert *(Cast)* 1729

Hooper, Claire *(Cast)* 1836

Hooper, Elric *(Cast)* 4469

Hooper, Lewis *(Choreographer)* 2383

Hooper, Lewis *(Director)* 830, 1313

Hoover, J. *(Composer)* 4193

Hoover, J. *(Lyricist)* 4193

Hope, Anthony *(Author)* 3586, 3595, 4798

Hope, Bob *(Cast)* 289, 3153, 3674, 3735, 3850, 3968, 4023, 4532, 4825

Hope, Dorothy *(Cast)* 3451

Hope, Edward *(Author)* 3919

Hope, Edward *(Librettist)* 1447

Hope, Maidie *(Cast)* 3213

Hope, Peggy *(Cast)* 1687, 2888

Hope, Vida *(Director)* 507, 4541

Hopkins, Anthony *(Composer)* 3761

Hopkins, Anthony *(Director)* 1623

Hopkins, Anthony *(Lyricist)* 3761

Hopkins, Anthony *(Producer)* 1623

Hopkins, Arthur *(Author)* 587

Hopkins, Arthur *(Director)* 587, 1020, 1517, 2211, 3686

Hopkins, Arthur *(Lyricist)* 3686

Hopkins, Arthur *(Producer)* 587, 1020, 1517, 2211

Hopkins, Bruce *(Cast)* 1426

Hopkins, Bruce *(Director)* 1785

Hopkins, Kaitlin *(Cast)* 2229

Hopkins, Ken *(Orchestrations)* 2850

Hopkins, Kenyon *(Musical Director)* 3287

Hopkins, Linda *(Cast)* 432, 2134, 2796, 3610

Hopkins, May *(Cast)* 77

Hopkins, Miriam *(Cast)* 1215, 2516

Hopkins, Peggy *(Cast)* 4811

Hoppenstein, Reuben *(Producer)* 1079

Hopper, DeWolf *(Cast)* 340, 698, 1090, 1165, 1208, 1264, 1768, 1926, 1975, 2403, 2469, 2724, 2782, 2982, 3360, 3401, 3486, 3639, 4033, 4054, 4669

Hopper, DeWolf *(Producer)* 2982, 4054

Hopper, Edna Wallace *(Cast)* 8, 749, 1090, 1271, 1313, 1557, 2261, 3976

Hopper, Irma *(Composer)* 3849

Hopper, Irma *(Lyricist)* 3849

Hopper, Victoria *(Cast)* 4361

Hopwood, Aubrey *(Lyricist)* 1313, 3803

Hopwood, Avery *(Author)* 2526, 3079, 3812, 3860

Hopwood, Avery *(Librettist)* 2070, 2254, 4064

Hopwood, Avery *(Lyricist)* 719, 2254, 4064

Horan, Edward *(Composer)* 3500, 4545

Horan, Edward A. *(Composer)* 82

Horan, James *(Cast)* 4705

Horchow, Roger *(Producer)* 921

Hord, Parker *(Librettist)* 4200

Horen, Michael *(Set Design)* 1761

Horn, Barbara Lee *(Producer)* 3956

Horn, Frank *(Cast)* 3170

Horne, C. Morton *(Cast)* 2760

Horne, Lena *(Cast)* 447, 854, 880, 882, 2190

Horne, Marie *(Composer)* 353

Horne, William *(Cast)* 1817

Horner, Carrie *(Cast)* 2064

Horner, Chuck *(Librettist)* 2657

Horner, Harry *(Costumes)* 2202, 3647

Horner, Harry *(Lighting Designer)* 1791

Horner, Harry *(Set Design)* 297, 1791, 2202, 2386, 2453, 3046, 3138, 3647, 3698, 4131, 4706, 4798

Horner, Louise *(Cast)* 510

Horner, Paul *(Composer)* 3428

Horner, Richard *(Producer)* 2965, 3743

Hornez, Andre *(Lyricist)* 2356

Hornsbee, Leonard *(Musical Director)* 1561

Hornsby, Joe *(Composer)* 4278

Hornsby, Joe *(Lyricist)* 4278

Hornsey, Leonard *(Musical Director)* 184, 351, 1534, 1855, 3573, 4320

Hornung, Richard *(Costumes)* 3136

Horovitz, Israel *(Author)* 2954

Horovitz, Israel *(Lyricist)* 2954

Horowitz, Charles *(Librettist)* 3030

Horowitz, David *(Vocal Arranger)* 4343

Horowitz, Herschel *(Composer)* 3530

Horowitz, Jimmy *(Composer)* 2759

Horowitz, Jimmy *(Lyricist)* 2759

Horowitz, Jimmy *(Orchestrations)* 2759

Horowitz, Jimmy *(Vocal Arranger)* 2759

Horton, Edward Everett *(Cast)* 1119, 2837

Horton, John *(Cast)* 171, 4109

Horton, Josiah T.S. *(Librettist)* 3471

Horton, Lester *(Choreographer)* 3947, 4415

Horton, Robert *(Cast)* 3294

Horton, Ron *(Cast)* 4220

Horton, Vaughn *(Composer)* 1296, 4264

Horton, Vaughn *(Lyricist)* 1296, 4264

Horvath, Jan *(Cast)* 3125, 3464

Horwitt, Arnold *(Librettist)* 2422

Horwitt, Arnold *(Lyricist)* 2422

Horwitt, Arnold B. *(Librettist)* 620, 1567, 2137, 2707, 4585, 4827

Horwitt, Arnold B. *(Lyricist)* 180, 1567, 2707, 3501, 3509, 4827

Horwitz, Charles *(Librettist)* 2316

Horwitz, Charles *(Lyricist)* 2316

Horwitz, Murray *(Director)* 1713

Horwitz, Murray *(Librettist)* 1713

Horwitz, Murray *(Lyricist)* 39, 4533

Hosbein, James *(Cast)* 871

Hoschna, Karl *(Composer)* 15, 361, 531, 1088, 1151, 1247, 1558, 2261, 2291, 2667, 3475, 3574, 3977, 4364, 4390, 4589

Hoschna, Karl *(Orchestrations)* 559

Hoschna, Karl L. *(Composer)* 1532

Hoshour, Robert *(Cast)* 3760

Hosier, Beverly *(Cast)* 2439

Hoskins, Ray *(Cast)* 2572

Hosmer *(Cast)* 1181

Hosmer, Lucius *(Composer)* 2350, 3774

Hossack, Grant *(Musical Director)* 2240

Hotchner, A.E. *(Librettist)* 4619

Hotchner, A.E. *(Lyricist)* 4619

Hotchner, A.E. *(Producer)* 4619

Hotopp, Michael *(Costumes)* 3280
Hotopp, Michael *(Lighting Designer)* 944
Hotopp, Michael *(Set Design)* 944, 3280, 4286
Hotopp, Michael J. *(Costumes)* 251
Hotopp, Michael J. *(Lighting Designer)* 31, 778
Hotopp, Michael J. *(Set Design)* 31, 251, 2114, 2171, 3231, 4454
Hott, Jordan *(Producer)* 956, 4029
Hottois, Michael F. *(Lighting Designer)* 4488
Hoty, Dee *(Cast)* 373, 775, 2578, 3448, 4695
Houck, Ted *(Cast)* 3764
Houdina, Mary Jane *(Cast)* 1329
Houdina, Mary Jane *(Choreographer)* 2142, 4288
Houdini, Harry *(Cast)* 712, 1208
Hough, Will M. *(Librettist)* 1307, 1524, 1563, 1593, 1606, 1801, 1908, 1966, 1967, 2155, 2408, 3083, 3508, 3579, 4185, 4376, 4387, 4506
Hough, Will M. *(Lyricist)* 1307, 1316, 1563, 1593, 1801, 1908, 1966, 1967, 2155, 2408, 2512, 2575, 2901, 2922, 3508, 3579, 4185, 4387, 4506
Houghton, Charles *(Lighting Designer)* 4799
Houghton, Norris *(Producer)* 3288
Hould-Ward, Ann *(Costumes)* 1776, 2143, 2230, 2283, 2643, 3448
Hould-Ward, Anne *(Costumes)* 330, 4210
Housam, Robert *(Author)* 1517
House, Billy *(Cast)* 3002, 4667
House, Billy *(Composer)* 2637
House, Eric *(Cast)* 3066
House, Estelle *(Cast)* 149
House, Ron *(Cast)* 1166
Houseman, A.E. *(Lyricist)* 2633
Houseman, John *(Director)* 1366, 2655, 4715
Houseman, John *(Producer)* 919, 942, 979, 2257, 2859, 3733, 4715
Housman, Laurence *(Author)* 738
Houston, Cissy *(Cast)* 4272
Houston, Elizabeth *(Cast)* 2105
Houston, Ethel Dufre *(Cast)* 307, 4250
Houston, George *(Cast)* 680, 711, 948, 1281, 2813, 3219, 4548, 4670
Houston, George *(Director)* 4670
Houston, George *(Librettist)* 2841
Houston, George *(Lyricist)* 2841
Houston, Grace *(Costumes)* 620, 1941, 2024, 4524
Houston Grand Opera *(Producer)* 4447
Hoven, Louise *(Cast)* 518
Hovenden, Peggy *(Cast)* 1342
Howard, Ada *(Cast)* 2896
Howard, Alan *(Cast)* 2322
Howard, Andree *(Choreographer)* 325
Howard, Bart *(Composer)* 943, 1107, 1370, 2227, 3484, 4268
Howard, Bart *(Lyricist)* 943, 1107, 1370, 2227, 3484, 4268
Howard, Bruce *(Cast)* 1366
Howard, Charles *(Cast)* 2122
Howard, Charlotte *(Cast)* 2682
Howard, Cindi *(Cast)* 2965
Howard, Don *(Cast)* 1126
Howard, Elizabeth *(Composer)* 459
Howard, Esther *(Cast)* 3117, 4212, 4300, 4694

Howard, Eugene *(Cast)* 289, 1489, 1490, 1491, 1492, 1493, 1494, 3395, 3399, 3402, 3405, 3958, 4657, 4824
Howard, Eugene *(Lyricist)* 3404
Howard, Florence *(Cast)* 1806
Howard, Frederick *(Cast)* 2623
Howard, Frederick *(Librettist)* 2402
Howard, Garland *(Cast)* 691, 981
Howard, Garland *(Choreographer)* 981
Howard, Garland *(Composer)* 981
Howard, Garland *(Librettist)* 691, 981
Howard, Garland *(Lyricist)* 981
Howard, George *(Cast)* 3753
Howard, George Bronson *(Librettist)* 558
Howard, George W. *(Cast)* 3887
Howard, Gus *(Cast)* 1145, 3823
Howard, Jack *(Cast)* 117
Howard, Jan *(Cast)* 4829
Howard, Jerry *(Cast)* 2097
Howard, Joe (Joseph E.)
   See also Joseph E. Howard Amusement Co.
Howard, Joe *(Composer)* 1967, 3579, 3949
Howard, Joe *(Lyricist)* 3949
Howard, Joe *(Producer)* 24
Howard, John *(Cast)* 1791
Howard, Joseph E. *(Cast)* 1054, 1316, 1560, 2155, 2408, 3975, 4465
Howard, Joseph E. *(Composer)* 472, 548, 733, 1054, 1263, 1307, 1316, 1405, 1560, 1563, 1593, 1606, 1897, 1908, 2108, 2155, 2247, 2408, 2512, 2600, 2635, 2649, 2901, 3057, 3367, 4071, 4185, 4247, 4387, 4390, 4411, 4506, 4632
Howard, Joseph E. *(Director)* 1593, 1908
Howard, Joseph E. *(Librettist)* 1054, 1316
Howard, Joseph E. *(Lyricist)* 472, 1054, 1263, 1316, 1405, 1563, 1593, 1606, 1897, 1908, 2408, 2600, 2649, 2740, 4387, 4390
Howard, Joseph E. *(Producer)* 1593
Howard, Ken *(Cast)* 3603, 3869, 3897, 4004
Howard, Madeline *(Cast)* 1218
Howard, Marc *(Producer)* 4601
Howard, May *(Cast)* 2842
Howard, Mel *(Producer)* 432
Howard, Michael *(Director)* 3215
Howard, Noel *(Costumes)* 1296
Howard, Olin *(Cast)* 2489
Howard, Peter *(Arrangements)* 4450
Howard, Peter *(Dance Arranger)* 150, 154, 181, 656, 723, 921, 1660, 1828, 1848, 1860, 2014, 2048, 2368, 2874, 3731, 3897, 4190, 4252, 4255, 4288, 4450, 4737
Howard, Peter *(Musical Director)* 150, 154, 253, 305, 826, 958, 1776, 1848, 2014, 2142, 2204, 2422, 3564, 3897, 4252
Howard, Peter *(Producer)* 3845
Howard, Peter *(Vocal Arranger)* 2014, 3731, 4288
Howard, Richard *(Translator)* 237
Howard, Shafter *(Composer)* 1912
Howard, Shafter *(Librettist)* 1912
Howard, Shafter *(Lyricist)* 1912
Howard, Shemp *(Cast)* 3409
Howard, Sidney *(Author)* 2961
Howard, Sidney *(Librettist)* 2655
Howard, Sonny *(Cast)* 863

Howard, Tom *(Cast)* 1440, 1689, 1691, 2300, 3648, 4023
Howard, Tom *(Librettist)* 1058, 1692
Howard, William *(Musical Director)* 2587
Howard, Willie *(Cast)* 289, 924, 1489, 1490, 1491, 1492, 1493, 1494, 1528, 2506, 3036, 3395, 3399, 3402, 3405, 3410, 3594, 3958, 4010, 4657, 4824
Howard, Willie *(Lyricist)* 3404
Howard Amusement Co., Joseph E.
  See also Joe (Joseph E.) Howard.
Howard Amusement Co., Joseph E. *(Producer)* 1316
Howarth, Anthony *(Lyricist)* 4041
Howden, Philip *(Set Design)* 1454, 4765
Howe, Bill *(Lyricist)* 4606
Howe, Bob *(Choreographer)* 3967
Howe, E.T. *(Musical Director)* 2517
Howe, George *(Cast)* 700
Howe, Julia Ward *(Lyricist)* 2203, 3020
Howe, Junius *(Producer)* 2963
Howe, Margaret *(Cast)* 2682
Howe, Michael *(Musical Director)* 3318
Howe, William *(Composer)* 3940
Howell, Erik *(Cast)* 4678
Howell, Harry *(Director)* 4602
Howell, Lottice *(Cast)* 1020
Howell, Rita *(Cast)* 1924
Howell, Thomas *(Lyricist)* 95
Howell, Thomas B. *(Lyricist)* 4273
Hower, Frank *(Vocal Arranger)* 1839
Howerd, Frankie *(Cast)* 635
Howes, Basil *(Cast)* 792, 2366, 2976
Howes, Bobby *(Cast)* 66, 475, 2976, 4765
Howes, Sally Ann *(Cast)* 1507, 2355, 4633
Howland, Beth *(Cast)* 832, 1891
Howland, Jason *(Vocal Arranger)* 2198
Howland, Jobyna *(Cast)* 17, 1335, 1613, 1731, 2282, 2844, 2904, 3395, 3799, 4713
Howland, Katherine *(Cast)* 48
Howland, Olin *(Cast)* 340, 2276, 3323, 3923, 4491, 4694
Howland, Olin *(Choreographer)* 1448
Howse, Lola *(Cast)* 2451
Hoy, Toots *(Cast)* 1821
Hoyer, Roy *(Cast)* 138, 4150
Hoylen, Tony *(Cast)* 2852
Hoysradt, John *(Cast)* 3325, 4825
Hoyt, Charles *(Author)* 3392, 4608
Hoyt, Charles *(Librettist)* 3392
Hoyt, Charles H. *(Author)* 4165, 4453, 4712
Hoyt, Charles H. *(Composer)* 436, 998
Hoyt, Charles H. *(Director)* 998, 4165
Hoyt, Charles H. *(Librettist)* 436, 998
Hoyt, Charles H. *(Lyricist)* 436, 4165
Hoyt, Charles H. *(Producer)* 436, 998, 4165
Hoyt, Grace *(Cast)* 934
Hoyt, Harry *(Lyricist)* 811
Hoyt, Henry E. *(Set Design)* 175, 476, 559, 727, 770, 906, 1193, 1213, 1470, 1576, 1594, 2156, 2507, 2725, 2936, 3732, 4353, 4500
Hoyt, Howard *(Producer)* 145, 4180
Hoyt, Lon *(Cast)* 3739
Hoyt, Peggy *(Costumes)* 780
Hruba, Vera *(Cast)* 2078

Hsiung, S.I. *(Author)* 2396
Hsiung, S.I. *(Director)* 2396
Huara, Helba *(Cast)* 3149
Hubbard, Bruce *(Cast)* 2648
Hubbard, Elizabeth *(Cast)* 2064, 2563, 4384
Hubbell, Raymond *(Composer)* 8, 41, 126, 246, 256, 378, 396, 712, 824, 993, 1177, 1208, 1228, 1243, 1525, 1534, 1588, 1631, 1753, 1780, 1901, 1920, 2232, 2328, 2347, 2716, 2723, 2848, 2858, 2897, 2919, 2921, 3096, 3144, 3617, 3685, 3805, 3977, 4054, 4085, 4345, 4359, 4712, 4793, 4805, 4806, 4807, 4808, 4811, 4816, 4818, 4819
Hubbell, Raymond *(Lyricist)* 4799
Hubbell, Raymond *(Musical Director)* 396, 712, 1228, 1901, 3617, 4793
Hubbell, Raymond *(Orchestrations)* 4818
Huber, Lon *(Cast)* 3318
Huber, Paul *(Cast)* 3131, 3584
Huber Marionettes, The *(Cast)* 589
Hubert, Hugh *(Cast)* 3533
Hubert, Hugh W. *(Composer)* 1457
Hubert, Hugh W. *(Lyricist)* 1457
Hubert, Janet L. *(Cast)* 678
Hubert, Rene *(Costumes)* 650, 2622, 2838
Huddleston, David *(Cast)* 1289
Huddleston, Floyd *(Lyricist)* 3683, 3966, 4827
Hudgins, Johnny *(Cast)* 441, 1989, 2462
Hudson, Charles *(Cast)* 159, 1676, 2284
Hudson, Helen *(Cast)* 1486, 1487
Hudson, Joe *(Composer)* 4171
Hudson, Joe *(Lyricist)* 4171
Hudson, John Paul *(Cast)* 4494
Hudson, Muriel *(Cast)* 4833
Hudson, Rodney *(Cast)* 54, 109, 1053, 4736
Hudson, Rodney Scott *(Cast)* 789
Hudson, Travis *(Cast)* 547, 915, 1500, 1660, 3110, 3551, 4292, 4408
Hudson, Walter *(Cast)* 647, 1785
Hudson, Will *(Composer)* 445, 4137
Hudson, Will *(Lyricist)* 2161
Hudson Guild Theatre *(Producer)* 962
Hudson Productions Co. *(Producer)* 1584
Huey, Richard *(Cast)* 462, 3990
Huff, Carrie *(Cast)* 4198
Huff, Forrest *(Cast)* 351, 487, 561, 1578, 1731, 2390, 2825, 3776, 3985, 4333, 4664
Huff, L. *(Composer)* 4193
Huff, L. *(Lyricist)* 4193
Huffine, Charles *(Orchestrations)* 341, 620
Huffman, Cady *(Cast)* 393, 2199, 4695
Huffman, J.C. *(Director)* 75, 202, 391, 463, 487, 545, 764, 771, 905, 910, 965, 969, 1065, 1096, 1111, 1218, 1240, 1461, 1526, 1613, 1678, 1693, 1923, 2262, 2281, 2282, 2293, 2334, 2358, 2419, 2602, 2628, 2649, 2684, 2696, 2706, 2732, 2747, 2843, 2869, 2884, 2914, 2939, 3051, 3056, 3063, 3085, 3096, 3148, 3170, 3237, 3333, 3397, 3399, 3400, 3401, 3402, 3403, 3404, 3405, 3406, 3407, 3424, 3586, 3680, 3730, 3737, 3778, 3958, 3962, 3985, 4121, 4188, 4427, 4490, 4666, 4747
Huffman, J.C. *(Librettist)* 248
Huffman, J.C. *(Producer)* 3586
Huffman, Mike *(Musical Director)* 1279

Hughes, Allen Lee (*Lighting Designer*) 140, 595, 1004, 3001, 3285, 3631, 4127
Hughes, Barnard (*Cast*) 499, 1186, 1620, 3000
Hughes, Dickson (*Cast*) 4232
Hughes, Dickson (*Composer*) 1408
Hughes, Dickson (*Librettist*) 4232
Hughes, Dickson (*Lyricist*) 1408, 4232
Hughes, Felix (*Cast*) 1866
Hughes, J.J. (*Choreographer*) 2371
Hughes, John (*Choreographer*) 1513
Hughes, Langston (*Author*) 2513, 3001
Hughes, Langston (*Composer*) 2203
Hughes, Langston (*Librettist*) 309, 2203, 2259, 2653, 3315, 3983
Hughes, Langston (*Lyricist*) 309, 369, 2203, 2275, 3001, 3315, 3983, 4169, 4273
Hughes, Leila (*Cast*) 2701, 2922, 3053, 3672, 4490
Hughes, Michael (*Composer*) 1023
Hughes, Revella (*Cast*) 290, 488, 1989, 3808
Hughes, Rhetta (*Cast*) 105
Hughes, Richard B. (*Lighting Designer*) 348
Hughes, Richard B. (*Set Design*) 348
Hughes, Rosamond (*Composer*) 1026
Hughes, Rupert (*Author*) 4422
Hughes, Rupert (*Librettist*) 311, 1226, 4414
Hugill, J. Randall (*Choreographer*) 1630
Hugill, J. Randall (*Director*) 1630
Hugo, Victor (*Author*) 2037, 2442, 3208
Huhn, Bruno (*Composer*) 1502
Huhn, Bruno (*Lyricist*) 1502
Hulbert, Claude (*Cast*) 3569
Hulbert, Jack (*Cast*) 1333, 2467, 2509
Hulbert, Jack (*Choreographer*) 1333, 2392
Hulbert, Jack (*Director*) 1333, 1467, 2004, 2467
Hulbert, Jack (*Producer*) 475, 1333, 2467
Hulburt, Claude (*Lyricist*) 4300
Hulett, Otto (*Cast*) 1448
Hull, Henry (*Cast*) 2121
Hull, Katherine (*Choreographer*) 2426
Hull, Shelley (*Cast*) 100, 763
Hull, Warren (*Cast*) 3648
Humans, Maria (*Costumes*) 924
Humason, Sally (*Librettist*) 1448, 3914
Hume, Edward (*Cast*) 1316
Hume, Michael J. (*Cast*) 1201
Hume, Nancy (*Cast*) 4297
Humes, Bibi (*Cast*) 3668
Hummel, Karen (*Costumes*) 2354, 4769
Hummel, Mark (*Dance Arranger*) 1146, 1298, 1633, 2208, 2437, 2820, 3637
Hummel, Mark (*Musical Director*) 534, 1289
Hummel, Mark (*Vocal Arranger*) 534
Humphrey, Cavada (*Cast*) 206, 4191
Humphrey, Doris
 See also Doris Humphrey Group.
Humphrey, Doris (*Choreographer*) 3989
Humphrey, Doris (*Director*) 309
Humphrey, James Luther (*Director*) 810
Humphrey, Jay (*Cast*) 2095
Humphrey Group, Doris
 See also Doris Humphrey.

Humphrey Group, Doris (*Cast*) 125
Humphreys, Joseph (*Director*) 1090
Humphries, Barry (*Author*) 2006
Humphries, Barry (*Cast*) 2006, 2682, 3271
Humphries, Barry (*Composer*) 2006
Humphries, Barry (*Director*) 2006
Humphries, Barry (*Lyricist*) 2006
Humphries, Ernest J. (*Set Design*) 292
Hundley, C.L. (*Costumes*) 4535
Hundley, John (*Cast*) 4118, 4583
Hungerford, Edward (*Librettist*) 3647
Hungerford, Edward (*Producer*) 3647
Hunnewell, Clyde (*Cast*) 1357
Hunt, Allen (*Director*) 3318
Hunt, Carl (*Director*) 385
Hunt, Carl (*Producer*) 385
Hunt, Don (*Composer*) 3922
Hunt, Don (*Lyricist*) 3922
Hunt, Dorothy (*Set Design*) 1244
Hunt, E. Howard (*Librettist*) 328
Hunt, Edward A. (*Musical Director*) 4166
Hunt, Estelle (*Librettist*) 4741
Hunt, Grady (*Costumes*) 410
Hunt, Ida Brooks (*Cast*) 48, 742, 4738
Hunt, Leigh (*Lyricist*) 2633
Hunt, Linda (*Cast*) 1186
Hunt, Lois (*Cast*) 596
Hunt, Pamela (*Choreographer*) 2416
Hunt, Pamela (*Director*) 2416
Hunt, Peter (*Director*) 1497, 1634, 3897
Hunt, Peter (*Lighting Designer*) 1122, 1786, 3196, 3835
Hunt, William (*Composer*) 4273
Hunt, William (*Lyricist*) 4273
Hunt, William E. (*Director*) 2372, 4220
Hunter, Alberta (*Cast*) 691, 897, 1981, 2712
Hunter, Alberta (*Composer*) 478
Hunter, Alberta (*Lyricist*) 478
Hunter, Alfred (*Cast*) 4486
Hunter, Alison McLellan (*Costumes*) 1207, 1219, 2540
Hunter, Anne (*Cast*) 1546
Hunter, Barbara (*Cast*) 3082
Hunter, Charles A. (*Librettist*) 3358
Hunter, Chas. A. (*Lyricist*) 3676
Hunter, Eddie (*Cast*) 444, 2009, 3054
Hunter, Eddie (*Librettist*) 2009, 3054
Hunter, Frank (*Librettist*) 3847
Hunter, Frank (*Lyricist*) 2193, 3847
Hunter, George (*Director*) 4273
Hunter, Glenn (*Cast*) 4118
Hunter, Ian McLellan (*Librettist*) 1373
Hunter, Ivy (*Composer*) 4534
Hunter, Ivy (*Lyricist*) 4534
Hunter, James (*Cast*) 1391
Hunter, JoAnn M. (*Cast*) 2905, 3944
Hunter, Kevin (*Cast*) 2055
Hunter, Kim (*Cast*) 2230
Hunter, Louise (*Cast*) 1603
Hunter, Mary (*Director*) 283, 651, 1679, 2948
Hunter, Nina (*Cast*) 2009

Hunter, Robert (*Musical Director*) 658, 3954
Hunter, Robert (*Orchestrations*) 3954
Hunter, Ross (*Cast*) 4415
Hunter, Ross (*Composer*) 4415
Hunter, Ross (*Director*) 4415
Hunter, Ross (*Lyricist*) 4415
Hunter, Ross (*Producer*) 4415
Hunter, Tab (*Cast*) 1742
Hunter, Timothy (*Lighting Designer*) 3346, 4031
Hunter, Walt (*Cast*) 4216
Hunting, John (*Cast*) 1340
Hunting, Lew (*Cast*) 1340
Hunting, Mollie (*Cast*) 1340
Hunting, Tony (*Cast*) 1340
Huntley, Fred (*Cast*) 3588
Huntley, G.P. (*Cast*) 1453, 1922, 2341, 3431, 4354
Huntley, Raymond (*Cast*) 4548
Hup, Irving (*Composer*) 2857
Hup, Irving (*Lyricist*) 2857
Hupfeld, Herman (*Cast*) 3153
Hupfeld, Herman (*Composer*) 2, 203, 961, 1207, 1219,
    1481, 1763, 1874, 2545, 2843, 3002, 3172, 3409, 3861,
    3955, 4335, 4399, 4498, 4828, 4853
Hupfeld, Herman (*Lyricist*) 2, 203, 961, 1207, 1219,
    1481, 1763, 1874, 2545, 2843, 3002, 3172, 3409, 3861,
    3955, 4335, 4399, 4498, 4828, 4853
Hurd, Danny (*Orchestrations*) 4558
Hurd, Earl (*Author*) 4035
Hurdle, Lawrence (*Director*) 3105
Hurgon, Austen (*Director*) 2341, 2760, 4017, 4327,
    4418, 4419, 4663
Hurgon, Austen (*Librettist*) 1197, 2889
Hurgon, Austen (*Lyricist*) 1197
Hurgon, Austen (*Producer*) 1610
Hurlbert, Jack (*Cast*) 2004
Hurlbert, Jack (*Choreographer*) 4510
Hurlbert, Jack (*Director*) 4510
Hurlbert, Jack (*Producer*) 2004
Hurlburt, Jack (*Cast*) 605
Hurlburt, William J. (*Librettist*) 2528
Hurlbut, Gladys (*Librettist*) 1894
Hurley, Albert (*Musical Director*) 4648
Hurley, Arthur (*Director*) 1027, 1283
Hurley, Brian (*Cast*) 2992
Hurley, Edwin (*Librettist*) 1989
Hurley, Laurel (*Cast*) 3151
Hurok, Sol (*Producer*) 2775
Hurry, Leslie (*Costumes*) 2682
Hurst, David (*Cast*) 623
Hurst, Fannie (*Author*) 1496
Hurst, Gregory S. (*Director*) 2199, 3932
Hurst, Howard (*Producer*) 4460
Hurst, James (*Cast*) 278
Hurst, Sophie (*Producer*) 4460
Hurston, Zora Neale (*Author*) 3001
Hurt, Marybeth (*Cast*) 2607, 2953
Hurt, William (*Cast*) 1268, 1669
Hurtig, Joe (*Director*) 1457, 1824, 2720
Hurtig, Joe (*Producer*) 1457, 2223, 2720
Hurtig, Jules (*Director*) 2122, 2800
Hurtig, Jules (*Producer*) 2122, 2281

Hurtig & Seamon (*Producer*) 2111, 3337
Hurwit, Lawrence (*Composer*) 3902
Hurwitz, Deborah (*Dance Arranger*) 484
Hurwitz, Deborah (*Musical Director*) 484
Hurwitz, Deborah (*Orchestrations*) 484
Hurwitz, Richard (*Orchestrations*) 4522
Husmann, Ron (*Cast*) 64, 1280, 2584, 2626, 4312
Hussar, E. (*Composer*) 2684
Hussey, James (*Cast*) 3400
Hussey, James (*Lyricist*) 2870
Hussey, Jimmy (*Cast*) 376, 3617, 4290
Hussey, Jimmy (*Librettist*) 4290
Hussey, Jimmy (*Lyricist*) 4290
Hussey, Jimmy (*Producer*) 4290
Huston, Grace (*Costumes*) 4640
Huston, Jon (*Orchestrations*) 4089
Huston, Josephine (*Cast*) 1137, 2475, 3379, 4368
Huston, Philip (*Cast*) 1546
Huston, Walter (*Cast*) 2344
Hutch, Willie (*Composer*) 3739
Hutch, Willie (*Lyricist*) 3739
Hutcheson, David (*Cast*) 1387
Hutchins, Emory (*Cast*) 3657
Hutchins, Emory (*Producer*) 1288
Hutchins, Harriet (*Cast*) 2300
Hutchins, Tony (*Composer*) 4488
Hutchinson, E.S. (*Composer*) 560
Hutchinson, E.S. (*Lyricist*) 3026
Hutchinson, E.S.S. (*Lyricist*) 3021
Hutchinson, Ed (*Choreographer*) 473, 2602, 3024
Hutchinson, Ed (*Composer*) 3155
Hutchinson, Edward (*Choreographer*) 537, 538, 1557,
    2587, 3026, 3865
Hutchinson, Edward (*Composer*) 2303, 3026, 4723
Hutchinson, Edward (*Director*) 540
Hutchinson, Edward (*Lyricist*) 540, 3203
Hutchinson, Edward (*Producer*) 3203
Hutchinson, Georgia (*Cast*) 813
Hutchinson, Josephine (*Cast*) 55
Hutchinson, Kathryn (*Cast*) 2025
Hutchinson, Leslie (*Pianist*) 791, 3291
Hutchinson, Mark Michael (*Cast*) 460
Hutchinson, Mary (*Cast*) 1971
Hutson, Eric (*Cast*) 2798
Hutton, Betty (*Cast*) 3359, 3841
Hutton, Bill (*Cast*) 450, 1262, 2242
Hutton, C.A. (*Cast*) 251
Hutton, Ina Ray (*Cast*) 2813, 4824
Huycke, Lorne (*Composer*) 4606
Hwarng, Wern-Ying (*Costumes*) 2046
Hyams, Barry (*Cast*) 2813
Hyams, Joe (*Cast*) 4647
Hyams, John (*Cast*) 350, 968, 1558, 2374, 3045, 3488
Hyatt, Maggie (*Composer*) 459
Hyde, Bruce (*Cast*) 634
Hyde, James (*Producer*) 2991
Hyde, R.N. (*Costumes*) 1162
Hyde, Raymond Newton (*Costumes*) 102
Hyde, Victor (*Choreographer*) 1964
Hyde-White, Wilfred (*Cast*) 4510
Hydes, Watty (*Composer*) 1078

Hydes, Watty *(Musical Director)*   178, 2675, 3229, 3882, 3999
Hyer, June *(Cast)*   2664
Hyers, Frank *(Cast)*   3359
Hyland, Al *(Lyricist)*   1964
Hyland, Lily *(Composer)*   1652, 1653, 1654, 1656, 1657
Hyland, Lily *(Incidental Music)*   1653
Hylands, Fred *(Composer)*   331
Hylands, Fred *(Musical Director)*   331
Hylands, Scott *(Cast)*   42
Hyldorf, Joan *(Cast)*   2099
Hylton, Jack *(Producer)*   3798
Hylton Sisters, The *(Cast)*   4174
Hyman, Dick *(Orchestrations)*   4197
Hyman, Earle *(Cast)*   2236, 3188
Hyman, Fracaswell *(Cast)*   1201
Hyman, Jack *(Composer)*   2476
Hyman, Jack *(Lyricist)*   2476
Hyman, Joseph *(Producer)*   2707
Hyman, Larry *(Choreographer)*   450
Hyman, Mac *(Author)*   3188
Hyman, Phyllis *(Cast)*   4091
Hyman, Robert *(Cast)*   2242
Hyman, Sarah Ellis *(Author)*   3898
Hymer, John B. *(Author)*   1142, 2872
Hymes *(Choreographer)*   349
Hymes, Phil *(Lighting Designer)*   2551
Hynd, Ghrett *(Costumes)*   1636
Hynes, John *(Cast)*   1220
Hyperion Productions *(Producer)*   3654
Hyslop, Jeff *(Cast)*   148
Hyson, Carl *(Cast)*   17, 685, 1557, 2412, 2960, 3740, 3791, 4811
Hyson, Carl *(Choreographer)*   3569
Hytner, Nicholas *(Director)*   2905

I

I, Robert *(Lyricist)*   1713
Ianni, Richard *(Cast)*   2055
Ibert, Jacques *(Composer)*   2178
Ibrahim, El Tahra *(Cast)*   2735
Idare *(Costumes)*   4341
Idare & Cie *(Costumes)*   2392
Idare & Co. *(Costumes)*   1610
Ide, Bernard *(Lyricist)*   1884
Ide, Letitia *(Cast)*   125
Ide, Richard *(Cast)*   2556
Ideal Extravaganza Company *(Producer)*   476
Idoine, Christopher M. *(Set Design)*   83
Ihmsen, Josephine *(Composer)*   2454
Ihmsen, Josephine *(Lyricist)*   2454
Ikeda, Thomas *(Cast)*   2861
Illica, Luigi *(Librettist)*   2359
Illmann, Margaret *(Cast)*   3682
Immerman, Connie *(Producer)*   1980, 1981
Immerman, George *(Producer)*   1980
Immerman, Joseph *(Producer)*   2904
Imperato, Carlo *(Cast)*   3806

Improvisation, The *(Producer)*   2069
Independent Prod. Company *(Producer)*   4621
Indick, Murray *(Composer)*   4774
Infants Relief Society *(Producer)*   4530
Ing, Alvin *(Cast)*   3340, 4002
Inga, Laura *(Costumes)*   1757
Ingalls, James F. *(Lighting Designer)*   494, 2033
Ingalls, Phil *(Incidental Music)*   4377
Ingalls, Phil *(Musical Director)*   137, 4377
Inge, William *(Author)*   716, 1990, 3925
Ingham, Barrie *(Cast)*   869
Ingham, Tom *(Cast)*   4401
Inghram, Rose *(Cast)*   3536
Ingle, Doug *(Composer)*   3261
Ingle, Doug *(Lyricist)*   3261
Ingle, John *(Cast)*   2630
Inglesi, Ricky *(Cast)*   2084, 2094, 2096
Inglett, Donald *(Costumes)*   3889
Ingraham, Herbert *(Composer)*   470, 3977
Ingraham, Herbert *(Lyricist)*   470, 3977
Ingraham, Roy *(Composer)*   1311, 1938
Ingram, Michael *(Cast)*   2229, 3555, 3838
Ingram, Rex *(Cast)*   612, 2355, 3990, 4123
Ingram, Tad *(Cast)*   3682
Ingre, Tonia *(Cast)*   4545
Inkijinoff *(Cast)*   2753
Inman, Billy *(Cast)*   1964
Innerarity, Memrie *(Cast)*   788, 1813
Institute of Musical Art *(Producer)*   978, 2193, 3847
Institutional Radio Choir *(Cast)*   1636
Insull, Sigrid *(Costumes)*   809, 4244
Inter-State Amusement Co. *(Producer)*   4590
Inter-Theatre Arts, Inc. *(Producer)*   720
Interludes *(Producer)*   2100
International Artistic Prods., Inc. *(Producer)*   2356
Intropidi, Josephine *(Cast)*   947
Intropodi, Ethel *(Cast)*   2669, 2914, 3746
Intropodi, Josie *(Cast)*   1220, 1266, 1375, 1851, 2291, 2424, 2461, 2665, 2914, 2931, 3746, 4161, 4236, 4381, 4649
Investors Production Co. *(Producer)*   2278
Ionesco, Eugene *(Additional Materal)*   1857
Ionesco, Eugene *(Author)*   2017, 2146
Irby, Iva *(Cast)*   2448
Iredale, Jane *(Librettist)*   4701
Iredale, Martin *(Cast)*   2509
Ireland, Joe *(Cast)*   4220
Irizarry, Vincent *(Cast)*   2440
Irvin, Rea *(Set Design)*   199
Irvine, Mabel *(Cast)*   2326
Irving, Ernest *(Musical Director)*   792
Irving, Ernest *(Orchestrations)*   4479
Irving, George S. *(Cast)*   161, 519, 825, 869, 1475, 1933, 2064, 2150, 2563, 2797, 2798, 3221, 3263, 3602, 3934, 4038, 4323, 4435, 4522
Irving, George S. *(Voice)*   56, 3449
Irving, Isabel *(Cast)*   2778
Irving, John *(Cast)*   1194
Irving, Laurence *(Costumes)*   4207
Irving, Laurence *(Set Design)*   4207
Irving, Margaret *(Cast)*   1027, 4174
Irving, Robert *(Cast)*   4733

Irving, Washington *(Author)* 239, 2100, 2344, 3720, 4015
Irwin, Bill *(Cast)* 1298
Irwin, Charles *(Cast)* 2, 3086, 4524
Irwin, Flo *(Cast)* 1465, 1582
Irwin, Fred *(Librettist)* 116
Irwin, Fred *(Producer)* 116
Irwin, Marc *(Conductor)* 2992
Irwin, May *(Cast)* 8, 352, 934, 1357, 1501, 2675, 2990, 2996, 3189, 3917, 3999
Irwin, May *(Composer)* 2990, 2996
Irwin, May *(Lyricist)* 2990
Irwin, May *(Producer)* 2996, 3999
Irwin, Robin *(Cast)* 4325
Irwin, Virginia *(Director)* 2076
Irwin, Virginia *(Librettist)* 2076
Irwin, Wallace *(Librettist)* 1083
Irwin, Wallace *(Lyricist)* 1083, 1318, 1417, 4762
Irwin, Will *(Composer)* 70, 1127, 1342, 1657, 1874, 3105, 3365, 3409, 3543, 3638, 3955, 3990, 4086, 4235, 4335, 4498, 4667
Irwin, Will *(Librettist)* 2655
Irwin, Will *(Lyricist)* 3638
Irwin, Will *(Musical Director)* 180, 1336, 2103, 2554, 3543, 3638, 4314, 4640
Irwin, Will *(Vocal Arranger)* 3638
Iscove, Rob *(Choreographer)* 869
Iscove, Rob *(Director)* 869
Isen, Richard *(Composer)* 1276
Isham, Frederic *(Author)* 4299, 4766
Isham, Frederic *(Librettist)* 2180
Isham, John W. *(Producer)* 4704
Ishee, Suzanne *(Cast)* 2654
Isherwood, Christopher *(Author)* 610
Ishii, Leslie *(Cast)* 3944
Island Stage *(Producer)* 2076
Isley, B. *(Composer)* 4193
Isley, B. *(Lyricist)* 4193
Isley, O. *(Composer)* 4193
Isley, O. *(Lyricist)* 4193
Isley, R. *(Composer)* 4193
Isley, R. *(Lyricist)* 4193
Isquith, Louis *(Director)* 2845
Isquith, Louis *(Producer)* 2845
Israel, Neil *(Director)* 3370
Israel, Robert *(Set Design)* 3937
Israel, William *(Lyricist)* 387
Issa, Paul *(Lyricist)* 3636
Ito, Michio *(Choreographer)* 718, 1689, 3662, 4637
Ito, Teiji *(Composer)* 790
Ivanek, Zeljko *(Cast)* 785
Ivanoff, Alexander *(Lyricist)* 3686
Ivanoff, Alexandra *(Dance Arranger)* 788
Ivanoff, Alexandra *(Musical Director)* 788
Ivanoff, Alexandra *(Vocal Arranger)* 788
Iverson & Henneage *(Costumes)* 2376, 4491
Ives, Burl *(Cast)* 514, 3497, 3794, 3989, 4340
Ives, Charles *(Composer)* 1589
Ivey, Dana *(Cast)* 4210
Ivey, Judith *(Cast)* 1575
Ivey, Scott K. *(Cast)* 4055
Ivins, Perry *(Director)* 266

Ivins, Perry *(Lyricist)* 266
Ivor-Szinngey, Stephen *(Librettist)* 3791

J

J.D. Steele Singers, The *(Cast)* 1636
Jabara, Paul *(Cast)* 1717, 3636
Jabara, Paul *(Composer)* 1298, 3636
Jabara, Paul *(Librettist)* 3636
Jabara, Paul *(Lyricist)* 1298, 3636
Jablons, Karen *(Cast)* 99, 181, 2132
Jablonski, Carl *(Choreographer)* 808
Jablonski, Peter *(Lyricist)* 4137
Jac-Lewis *(Costumes)* 2610
Jack, Angel *(Cast)* 4011
Jack, Angel *(Costumes)* 4011
Jack, Angel *(Set Design)* 4011
Jack, Burt M. *(Cast)* 2771
Jackel, Paul *(Cast)* 81, 1509
Jackman, Hope *(Cast)* 1619, 3271
Jackness, Andrew *(Set Design)* 829
Jacks, Susan *(Cast)* 4172
Jackson *(Costumes)* 998
Jackson, "Poppa" Charlie *(Composer)* 3001
Jackson, "Poppa" Charlie *(Lyricist)* 3001
Jackson, Al *(Librettist)* 1533
Jackson, Alfred *(Librettist)* 3489
Jackson, Arthur *(Composer)* 3399, 4812
Jackson, Arthur *(Lyricist)* 545, 1345, 1482, 1483, 1484, 1873, 1911, 2363, 2376, 3399, 4812
Jackson, Brady *(Cast)* 444
Jackson, Brian *(Costumes)* 1255
Jackson, Brian *(Set Design)* 1255
Jackson, Byron *(Cast)* 2077
Jackson, C. *(Composer)* 1319
Jackson, C. *(Librettist)* 1319
Jackson, C. *(Lyricist)* 1319
Jackson, Charlie *(Composer)* 3297
Jackson, Charlie *(Lyricist)* 3297
Jackson, Danny *(Composer)* 819
Jackson, Danny *(Librettist)* 819
Jackson, Danny *(Lyricist)* 819
Jackson, David *(Cast)* 1649
Jackson, Donald *(Cast)* 2094
Jackson, Eddie
    See also Clayton, Jackson, & Durante.
Jackson, Eddie *(Cast)* 848, 858, 860, 3131, 3953
Jackson, Emma *(Cast)* 291, 980, 1906
Jackson, Ernestine *(Cast)* 572, 3656, 3661, 4450
Jackson, Ethel *(Cast)* 470, 1994, 2543, 2836, 4563
Jackson, Eugene *(Cast)* 2415
Jackson, Frank *(Cast)* 1479, 3040, 4751
Jackson, Frank *(Director)* 815
Jackson, Fred *(Author)* 3921, 4547
Jackson, Fred *(Cast)* 4696
Jackson, Fred *(Librettist)* 1345, 2363, 3307, 4491, 4547
Jackson, Fred *(Lyricist)* 4491
Jackson, Gary *(Composer)* 146, 1638, 3739
Jackson, Gary *(Lyricist)* 146, 1638, 3739

Jackson, Glenda (Cast)   3445

Jackson, Helen
  See Helen Jackson Girls.

Jackson, Howard (Composer)   4291

Jackson, Howard (Orchestrations)   1492, 4291, 4335, 4778, 4823

Jackson, J.W. (Choreographer)   292

Jackson, Jerry (Choreographer)   3888

Jackson, Jo (Cast)   344

Jackson, Jo (Librettist)   344

Jackson, Joe (Cast)   117, 959, 1631, 2696

Jackson, Keisha (Cast)   4786

Jackson, Laura Mae (Lighting Designer)   3280

Jackson, Lemuel (Cast)   1050

Jackson, Leonard (Cast)   2290

Jackson, Margaret (Cast)   4184

Jackson, Marlene (Cast)   2091

Jackson, Melinda (Cast)   2735

Jackson, Millie (Cast)   4786

Jackson, Millie (Composer)   4786

Jackson, Millie (Lyricist)   4786

Jackson, Nagle (Cast)   272, 427

Jackson, Nagle (Director)   83, 2305, 4537

Jackson, Nagle (Librettist)   83, 4537

Jackson, Papa Charlie (Composer)   26, 3709

Jackson, Papa Charlie (Lyricist)   26, 3709

Jackson, R. (Composer)   4242

Jackson, Richard (Lighting Designer)   2104

Jackson, Richard (Set Design)   941, 2104, 4602

Jackson, Robert (Cast)   828, 3656

Jackson, Shirley (Cast)   344

Jackson, Tod (Choreographer)   13, 1045, 2785

Jackson, Tod (Director)   2785

Jackson, Tony (Composer)   3400

Jackson, Zaidee (Cast)   3660

Jackson Jr., Joe (Cast)   2077

Jackson Jr., Oliver (Cast)   4076

Jacob, Bill (Composer)   2217

Jacob, Bill (Lyricist)   2217

Jacob, Jackie (Cast)   2356

Jacob, Jackie (Lyricist)   2356

Jacob, Norman (Cast)   1304

Jacob, Patti (Composer)   2217

Jacob, Patti (Lyricist)   1261, 2217

Jacob, Steven (Cast)   1732

Jacobi, Georgio (Dance Arranger)   45

Jacobi, Lou (Cast)   1227, 3273

Jacobi, Paula (Author)   19

Jacobi, Victor (Author)   2761, 4258

Jacobi, Victor (Composer)   168, 364, 1723, 2614, 2761, 3658, 4258, 4393

Jacobowski, Edward
  See Edward Jakobowski.

Jacobs, Al (Composer)   1953

Jacobs, Al (Lyricist)   1953

Jacobs, Hal (Set Design)   3161

Jacobs, Harvey (Author)   1075

Jacobs, Harvey (Librettist)   107, 1075

Jacobs, Iona (Cast)   1556

Jacobs, Ira (Musical Director)   1130, 3511

Jacobs, Jacob (Cast)   343, 3559

Jacobs, Jacob (Director)   3559, 4463

Jacobs, Jacob (Librettist)   4463

Jacobs, Jacob (Lyricist)   343, 1609, 3559, 4342, 4463

Jacobs, Jacob (Producer)   343, 3559

Jacobs, Jim (Composer)   1664

Jacobs, Jim (Librettist)   1664

Jacobs, Jim (Lyricist)   1664

Jacobs, Louis (Librettist)   3947

Jacobs, Pat (Composer)   2039

Jacobs, Pat (Lyricist)   2039

Jacobs, Paul (Cast)   3077

Jacobs, Paul (Composer)   3077

Jacobs, Paul (Musical Director)   3077

Jacobs, Sally (Set Design)   3445

Jacobs, Sander (Producer)   1649

Jacobs, Will (Cast)   2962

Jacobson (Author)   967

Jacobson, Dan (Author)   4863

Jacobson, Helen (Producer)   1319

Jacobson, Henrietta (Cast)   2352, 3900

Jacobson, Henrietta (Choreographer)   2352, 3559

Jacobson, Henrietta (Set Design)   2352

Jacobson, Hy (Lyricist)   268

Jacobson, Hymie (Composer)   4342

Jacobson, Hymie (Lyricist)   4342

Jacobson, Irving (Cast)   1190, 2352, 2727, 3612

Jacobson, John (Composer)   2784

Jacobson, John (Musical Director)   2784

Jacobson, Kenneth (Composer)   1990, 3956

Jacobson, Leopold (Author)   742, 2293, 4590

Jacobus, Robert (Lighting Designer)   4047

Jacoby, Coleman (Librettist)   3524, 4828, 4829

Jacoby, Coleman (Lyricist)   4829

Jacoby, Elliot (Orchestrations)   1898, 3091, 3278, 4362

Jacoby, Mark (Cast)   3734

Jacoby, Scott (Cast)   732, 1611

Jacquemot, Ray (Cast)   1085

Jacquet, H. Maurice (Composer)   3978, 4620

Jacquet, H. Maurice (Musical Director)   4620

Jaffe, George (Additional Lyrics)   2275

Jaffe, Howard (Composer)   4093

Jaffe, Howard (Librettist)   4679

Jaffe, Howard (Lyricist)   4093

Jaffe, Joan (Cast)   696

Jaffe, Moe (Composer)   18

Jaffe, Moe (Librettist)   3150

Jaffe, Moe (Lyricist)   18, 551, 750, 2540, 3150, 3523

Jaffe, Robert M. (Cast)   4543

Jaffe, Sam (Cast)   1196, 1396, 2194, 2653

Jaffe, Sam (Librettist)   1446

Jaffee, Lynne (Cast)   3501

Jagermann, Walter (Set Design)   1493, 4256, 4772

Jagger, Mick (Composer)   3739, 4449

Jagger, Mick (Lyricist)   3739, 4449

Jahan, Marine (Cast)   484

Jaime (Author)   4115

Jaimes, Ray (Orchestrations)   3234

Jaimes, Raymond (Orchestrations)   2449

Jakobowski, Edward (Author)   1193, 3625

Jakobowski, Edward (Composer)   1030, 1193, 3625, 4713

Jakobs, Ned (Producer)   2005

Jakubovic, Jaroslav *(Musical Director)* 3167
Jamal, Sati *(Cast)* 1671
Jamerson, Thomas *(Cast)* 2839
James, Alex *(Composer)* 1132
James, Alex *(Lyricist)* 1132
James, Arthur *(Composer)* 1919
James, Arthur *(Lyricist)* 1919
James, Bob *(Composer)* 3871
James, Byron *(Cast)* 2302
James, Carolyne *(Cast)* 643
James, Dan *(Author)* 462
James, David *(Costumes)* 3010
James, Don *(Composer)* 2082, 2482
James, Don *(Lyricist)* 2082, 2482
James, Don *(Musical Director)* 757
James, Don *(Orchestrations)* 2482
James, Dorothea *(Cast)* 3584
James, Ethel *(Cast)* 2984
James, Graham *(Cast)* 455
James, Hal *(Producer)* 823, 1729, 2727, 3280
James, Harry *(Composer)* 509, 4091
James, Harry *(Lyricist)* 4091
James, Harry *(Musical Director)* 2378, 2446, 2461, 4037
James, Henry *(Author)* 101, 4600
James, Henry *(Composer)* 3562
James, Henry *(Lyricist)* 3562
James, Hilary *(Cast)* 1804
James, Ida *(Cast)* 2817
James, Jessica *(Cast)* 556, 4180
James, Julia *(Cast)* 4327
James, Lester *(Cast)* 3366, 4318
James, Miller *(Cast)* 2263
James, Olga *(Cast)* 2987
James, Paul *(Lyricist)* 1134, 1275, 1448, 2545, 3172, 3849
James, Philip *(Musical Director)* 3043
James, Polly *(Cast)* 1721, 2047
James, Ray *(Cast)* 2522
James, Ray *(Choreographer)* 1924
James, Rian *(Author)* 1359
James, Stephanie Renee *(Cast)* 3724
James, Stephen *(Cast)* 1000, 1684, 3175
James, Ted *(Librettist)* 3479
James, Toni-Leslie *(Costumes)* 756, 789, 1822, 2200
James-Mark *(Orchestrations)* 3195
Jameson, House *(Cast)* 3097
Jameson, Joyce *(Cast)* 407, 408, 410, 411, 412, 413, 1341
Jamison, Betsy *(Cast)* 2177
Jamison, Judith *(Cast)* 2775, 4091
Jamison, Marshall *(Director)* 603
Jampolis, Neil Peter *(Lighting Designer)* 259, 432, 1164, 1775, 1955, 2142, 3318, 3752, 3763, 3846, 3956, 4162, 4689
Jampolis, Neil Peter *(Set Design)* 1139, 1353, 2142, 2474, 3485, 3661, 3846, 4396
Janas, Mark *(Composer)* 2573
Janas, Mark *(Lyricist)* 2573
Janas, Mark *(Musical Director)* 2573
Jane, Mary *(Cast)* 2216
Janes, Alan *(Librettist)* 580
Janet Sisters, The *(Cast)* 560
Jani, Robert F. *(Director)* 2689, 3126

Jani, Robert F. *(Producer)* 107, 2689, 2737, 3126, 3637, 4035
Janik, Ada *(Dance Arranger)* 3019
Janik, Ada *(Orchestrations)* 3019
Janik, Ada *(Vocal Arranger)* 3019
Janine *(Costumes)* 3827
Janis, Beverly *(Cast)* 2275
Janis, Conrad *(Cast)* 1204, 2246
Janis, Elsie *(Cast)* 683, 1175, 1176, 1230, 2025, 2394, 2891, 3398, 4017, 4544, 4650
Janis, Elsie *(Composer)* 1176, 3332, 3617
Janis, Elsie *(Director)* 1175, 3103
Janis, Elsie *(Librettist)* 1175, 3617
Janis, Elsie *(Lyricist)* 683, 1175, 1176, 2891, 3332, 3617, 4017, 4555
Janis, Vivian *(Cast)* 4824
Jankel, Chas *(Composer)* 3884
Jankowski, Steven *(Composer)* 1377
Jannath, Heba *(Lyricist)* 1989
Janney, Allison *(Cast)* 1169
Janney, Leon *(Cast)* 2304, 3365, 3526
Janney, Russell *(Librettist)* 3219, 4539
Janney, Russell *(Lyricist)* 3219, 4539
Janney, Russell *(Producer)* 2756, 3219, 3829, 4539, 4664
Janowski, Robert *(Cast)* 2846
Jans, Harry
   See also Jans & Whelan.
Jans, Harry *(Cast)* 2140, 2636
Jans & Whelan
   See also Harry Jans and Harold Whelan.
Jans & Whalen *(Cast)* 1693
Jansen, Marie *(Cast)* 2824
Jansen, Robert *(Cast)* 3682
Janssen, Werner *(Composer)* 495, 1780, 2378, 2446, 2461, 2519, 2564, 2605, 2637, 3137, 4819
Jansson, A.L. *(Lyricist)* 2159
January, Lois *(Cast)* 4772
Janus, Billy *(Composer)* 487
Janus, Billy *(Lyricist)* 487
Janusz, Tom *(Dance Arranger)* 4689
Janusz, Tom *(Musical Director)* 1216, 4689
Janusz, Tom *(Orchestrations)* 1216
Janusz, Tom *(Vocal Arranger)* 4689
Janvier, Emma *(Cast)* 102, 1271, 2592, 2793, 2892, 3176, 4115, 4491
Janvier, Marcel *(Author)* 904
Jarboe, Richard *(Composer)* 1732
Jarboe, Richard *(Librettist)* 1732
Jarboe, Richard *(Lyricist)* 1732
Jardon, Dolly *(Cast)* 4714
Jardon, Dorothy *(Cast)* 968, 1295, 2358, 2826, 3362, 3525, 3701, 4616, 4757
Jardon, Dorothy *(Composer)* 545
Jardon, Dorothy *(Lyricist)* 545
Jared, Robert *(Lighting Designer)* 4216, 4412
Jarick Prods. Ltd. *(Producer)* 2354
Jarnac, Dorothy *(Cast)* 1811, 2554, 4377
Jarnagin, Jerry *(Composer)* 4234
Jarno, Georges *(Composer)* 1522
Jaroslow, Ruth *(Cast)* 2236, 2965, 4318
Jarratt, Howard *(Cast)* 3035

Jarrett, Art *(Cast)* 1979, 4586
Jarrett, Arthur *(Cast)* 3220
Jarrett, Daniel *(Cast)* 1157, 3220
Jarrett, Jerry *(Cast)* 2195, 2231, 2422, 4379, 4540
Jarvis, Graham *(Cast)* 2953, 3742
Jarvis, Scott *(Cast)* 2433
Jarvis, Sidney *(Cast)* 1851, 2025
Jasien, Deborah *(Set Design)* 2199
Jason, Michael *(Cast)* 2212
Jason, Mitchell *(Cast)* 1227, 1649, 2231, 4038
Jason, Will *(Composer)* 1947, 3173
Jason, Will *(Lyricist)* 1947, 3173
Jatim, Arthur *(Author)* 831
Javits, Joan *(Composer)* 4435
Javits, Joan *(Lyricist)* 1993, 3966, 4435, 4785
Javits, Marion *(Producer)* 1736
Jaxson, Frankie *(Cast)* 3528
Jay, Isabel *(Cast)* 4663
Jay-Thorpe *(Costumes)* 3860, 4299
Jaycox, Martin *(Cast)* 1636
Jayne, Estelle *(Cast)* 1493
Jayson, Paul *(Cast)* 1341
Jbara, Gregory *(Cast)* 1785, 3598, 4560
Jeanmaire *(Cast)* 1548
Jeans, Ronald *(Composer)* 605, 4581
Jeans, Ronald *(Director)* 703
Jeans, Ronald *(Librettist)* 605, 703, 704, 792, 1128, 1338, 2004, 2467, 2483, 2570, 3005, 3291, 4374
Jeans, Ronald *(Lyricist)* 133, 702, 1448, 2570, 4581
Jebe, Halfdau *(Producer)* 1117
Jecko, Timothy *(Cast)* 3908
Jefferson, C.B. *(Producer)* 571
Jefferson, Lauretta *(Choreographer)* 420, 2187, 2460, 4465
Jefferson, William *(Composer)* 352
Jefferson, William *(Lyricist)* 352
Jeffrey, Alan *(Lyricist)* 4264
Jeffrey, Allan *(Composer)* 4264
Jeffrey, Clare *(Costumes)* 3818
Jeffrey, Howard *(Choreographer)* 786, 1497
Jeffrey Betancourt Prods. *(Producer)* 3311
Jeffreys, Alan *(Composer)* 4153, 4566, 4828
Jeffreys, Alan *(Librettist)* 4566, 4828
Jeffreys, Alan *(Lyricist)* 4153, 4566, 4828
Jeffreys, Anne *(Cast)* 1415, 2837, 3064, 4169, 4366
Jeffries, Herb *(Cast)* 2259
Jeffries, Jay *(Lyricist)* 1346, 4137
Jeffries, Will *(Cast)* 2783
Jellison, John *(Cast)* 212, 2440, 4701
Jenbach, Bela *(Author)* 473, 1121, 2486, 2509, 2538, 2668
Jenkins *(Costumes)* 163, 2376, 3314, 4777
Jenkins, Allen *(Cast)* 4058
Jenkins, Daniel *(Cast)* 2229
Jenkins, Daniel H. *(Cast)* 394
Jenkins, David *(Set Design)* 140, 474, 573, 951, 2648, 3555, 3743, 4137, 4619
Jenkins, Dorothy *(Costumes)* 4749
Jenkins, Frank *(Cast)* 2791
Jenkins, George *(Choreographer)* 2847
Jenkins, George *(Lighting Designer)* 84, 145, 180, 1205, 1471, 2750, 3801, 4278, 4337

Jenkins, George *(Set Design)* 84, 145, 180, 190, 1140, 1205, 1471, 2201, 2591, 2750, 2817, 3371, 3801, 4278, 4337, 4366
Jenkins, Gordon *(Composer)* 95, 478, 2677
Jenkins, Gordon *(Lyricist)* 2677, 3992
Jenkins, Gordon *(Musical Director)* 3955
Jenkins, Gordon *(Orchestrations)* 95, 3428, 3955
Jenkins, Gordon *(Vocal Arranger)* 95
Jenkins, John *(Cast)* 945
Jenkins, Joseph *(Arrangements)* 2028
Jenkins, Sharon *(Choreographer)* 35
Jenkins, W.E.C. *(Cast)* 1202
Jenks, Mrs. Donald F. *(Cast)* 1972
Jenks Jr., Almet F. *(Director)* 3547
Jenks Jr., Almet F. *(Librettist)* 3547
Jenn, Myvanwy *(Cast)* 2064
Jennings, Don *(Musical Director)* 287, 652, 1406
Jennings, John *(Composer)* 3725
Jennings, John *(Lyricist)* 3725
Jennings, Ken *(Cast)* 754, 1649, 2542, 2790, 4233
Jennings, Mary *(Choreographer)* 587
Jennings, P. O'Malley *(Cast)* 617
Jens, Alaric *(Composer)* 1059
Jens, Alaric *(Lyricist)* 1059
Jens, Salome *(Cast)* 2075, 4005
Jensbach, Bela *(Author)* 3727
Jensen, Carol-Leigh *(Cast)* 3067
Jensen, Don *(Costumes)* 2017, 2616
Jensen, Don *(Set Design)* 692, 2017, 2616, 3568, 4379
Jensen, Donald *(Costumes)* 793
Jensen, Donald *(Set Design)* 793
Jensen, John *(Set Design)* 946, 4601, 4796
Jensen, Rick *(Musical Director)* 2305
Jergens, Adele *(Cast)* 1109, 2432
Jerome, Ben *(Composer)* 1524, 1535, 1793, 2029, 2869, 2922, 3622, 4766
Jerome, Ben *(Lyricist)* 2974
Jerome, Ben M. *(Composer)* 248, 2159, 2596, 2851, 2869, 2978, 3745, 3786, 4324, 4453, 4761
Jerome, Ben M. *(Musical Director)* 2922, 2966, 2978, 3786, 4453, 4761, 4766
Jerome, Helen *(Author)* 1290
Jerome, Jerome K. *(Author)* 3652
Jerome, Jerome K. *(Composer)* 2056
Jerome, M.K. *(Composer)* 714, 2194, 3683
Jerome, Richard *(Lyricist)* 4799
Jerome, Timothy *(Cast)* 809, 1649, 2169, 2798, 2949, 3456, 3565
Jerome, William *(Author)* 2991, 4642
Jerome, William *(Composer)* 3951
Jerome, William *(Lyricist)* 115, 379, 685, 688, 712, 737, 800, 910, 1151, 1188, 1208, 1247, 1403, 1579, 1731, 1735, 1868, 1901, 1910, 1926, 1927, 1963, 2119, 2209, 2481, 2498, 2566, 2892, 2956, 2964, 2974, 2991, 3031, 3259, 3313, 3332, 3488, 3525, 3537, 3560, 3685, 3710, 3882, 3977, 4014, 4130, 4148, 4181, 4317, 4521, 4636, 4641, 4642, 4655, 4662, 4712, 4757, 4801, 4802, 4806, 4807, 4815
Jerry, Philip *(Cast)* 975
Jessel, George *(Cast)* 431, 504, 1396, 1416, 1889, 2194, 3406, 3962, 4235

Jessel, George *(Composer)* 504
Jessel, George *(Costumes)* 504
Jessel, George *(Librettist)* 504, 1889
Jessel, George *(Lyricist)* 504, 4458
Jessel, George *(Producer)* 1819
Jessel, George *(Set Design)* 504
Jessel, Leon *(Composer)* 710
Jessel, Ray *(Composer)* 3890
Jessel, Ray *(Lyricist)* 3890
Jessel, Raymond *(Composer)* 270, 392, 1107, 1841
Jessel, Raymond *(Lyricist)* 270, 392, 1107, 1841, 2064
Jessop, George H. *(Librettist)* 3049, 3912
Jessop, George H. *(Lyricist)* 3049
Jessup, Stanley *(Cast)* 3170
Jessye, Eva *(Vocal Arranger)* 1366, 3541
Jeter, Michael *(Cast)* 54, 1164, 1649
Jethro, Phil *(Cast)* 2212
Jewell, Clara Alene *(Cast)* 3176
Jewell, Violet *(Cast)* 2465
Jewett, John *(Librettist)* 2168
Jewett, Tom *(Set Design)* 2275
Jewish Nostalgic Prods. *(Producer)* 400, 1269, 4773
Jewish Repertory Theater *(Producer)* 2354
Jezek, Jaroslav *(Composer)* 4677
Jiler, John *(Librettist)* 240
Jiler, John *(Lyricist)* 240
Jillian, Ann *(Cast)* 4197
Jillson, Joyce *(Cast)* 3731
Jines, Henry *(Cast)* 552
Joannest, Gerard *(Composer)* 2188
Jochim, Keith *(Cast)* 31, 1164, 3280
Jockin, H. DeSilva *(Composer)* 1722
Jockin, H. DeSilva *(Lyricist)* 1722
Jockin, Henry *(Composer)* 1722
Jockin, Henry *(Lyricist)* 1722
Joffe, Bob *(Lyricist)* 567
Johanis, Rudolf *(Composer)* 3432
Johann, Cameron *(Cast)* 3171
Johanson, Jane *(Cast)* 1120
Johanson, Robert *(Choreographer)* 2861, 3734
Johanson, Robert *(Composer)* 81
Johanson, Robert *(Director)* 81, 2861, 3734, 3851
Johanson, Robert *(Lyricist)* 81
Johansson, Don *(Choreographer)* 2764
John, Elton *(Composer)* 3739
John, Elton *(Lyricist)* 3739
John, Graham *(Librettist)* 466, 4519
John, Graham *(Lyricist)* 466, 605, 1733, 1780, 1805, 2392, 3721, 4170
John, Mary W. *(Producer)* 1010
John, Michael *(Cast)* 3702
John, Tom H. *(Set Design)* 1298, 1380, 1478, 2754, 3428, 3871, 3956, 4722
John F. Kennedy Center *(Producer)* 699, 808, 958, 1186, 1959, 2260, 2435, 2702, 2775, 3231, 3631, 3643, 4601
Johnakins, Leslie *(Composer)* 432
Johns, Al *(Composer)* 295, 2979, 2990
Johns, Al *(Lyricist)* 2979
Johns, Barter *(Musical Director)* 3948
Johns, Brooke *(Cast)* 827, 2180, 3489, 4817
Johns, Clay *(Cast)* 4332

Johns, Florence *(Cast)* 4422
Johns, Glynis *(Cast)* 172, 2536
Johns, Kenneth *(Librettist)* 1710
Johns, Kurt *(Cast)* 721
Johns, Martin *(Set Design)* 2798
Johnson *(Composer)* 2111
Johnson, A. David *(Cast)* 528, 1155, 3165, 3329, 3997
Johnson, Adel *(Cast)* 3041
Johnson, Alan *(Choreographer)* 146, 278, 1289, 2437, 3936, 4038
Johnson, Alan *(Director)* 146, 3936
Johnson, Alan *(Musical Director)* 1291
Johnson, Albert *(Lighting Designer)* 125, 924, 1539
Johnson, Albert *(Producer)* 117
Johnson, Albert *(Set Design)* 117, 125, 173, 207, 294, 383, 397, 417, 420, 662, 924, 1225, 1494, 1539, 1670, 1680, 2225, 2258, 2413, 2432, 2444, 2475, 3036, 3381, 3699, 3966, 3989, 4367, 4465, 4777, 4824
Johnson, Alice *(Cast)* 2515
Johnson, Allie *(Cast)* 1421
Johnson, Arch *(Cast)* 4625
Johnson, Arnold *(Composer)* 1126, 1858, 2401, 4137
Johnson, Arnold *(Director)* 2401
Johnson, Arnold *(Musical Director)* 4291
Johnson, Arte *(Cast)* 3941
Johnson, Arthur *(Composer)* 4799
Johnson, Arthur *(Vocal Arranger)* 3009
Johnson, Bayn *(Cast)* 941
Johnson, Ben *(Cast)* 1218
Johnson, Benny *(Choreographer)* 4253
Johnson, Bernard *(Choreographer)* 1816
Johnson, Bernard *(Costumes)* 40, 166, 576, 952, 1074, 1198, 1592, 1816, 2513, 2719, 3656, 3932, 4591
Johnson, Bill *(Cast)* 297, 999, 4058, 4498
Johnson, Bill *(Choreographer)* 645
Johnson, Billy *(Cast)* 4451
Johnson, Billy *(Composer)* 217, 2964, 3999, 4451
Johnson, Billy *(Lyricist)* 2029, 2325, 2964
Johnson, Bobby *(Cast)* 3104
Johnson, Buddy *(Composer)* 1495
Johnson, Buddy *(Lyricist)* 1495
Johnson, Buster *(Composer)* 4815
Johnson, Cameron *(Set Design)* 1887
Johnson, Carroll *(Cast)* 3545
Johnson, Charlie *(Composer)* 39
Johnson, Charlie *(Lyricist)* 39
Johnson, Charles
    See Charles Johnson's Orchestra.
Johnson, Chic *(Cast)* 1423, 1840, 2400, 3380, 3381, 4086, 4816
Johnson, Chic *(Composer)* 1423
Johnson, Chic *(Director)* 1423
Johnson, Chic *(Librettist)* 1840, 2400, 3381, 4086
Johnson, Chic *(Lyricist)* 1423, 3381, 4816, 4817
Johnson, Chic *(Producer)* 901, 1840, 2400, 3381, 4174
Johnson, Choo Choo *(Cast)* 1140
Johnson, Christine *(Cast)* 660
Johnson, Cora *(Cast)* 4447
Johnson, Danny *(Set Design)* 520
Johnson, Doug *(Director)* 3608
Johnson, Doug *(Set Design)* 3608

Jones, Leilani (Cast)   1699
Jones, Leslie Julian (Cast)   3877
Jones, Leslie Julian (Composer)   4027, 4153
Jones, Leslie Julian (Lyricist)   4027, 4153
Jones, Lyman (Cast)   3539
Jones, Olive (Cast)   689
Jones, Ora (Cast)   4708, 4740
Jones, Pattie Darcy (Cast)   4031
Jones, Quincy (Composer)   3126
Jones, Quincy (Musical Director)   1385
Jones, Quincy (Orchestrations)   3126
Jones, Reed (Cast)   107, 146, 678, 3517
Jones, Richard (Composer)   1342
Jones, Richard (Lyricist)   1342
Jones, Rick (Composer)   626
Jones, Rick (Lyricist)   626
Jones, Robert (Author)   2623
Jones, Robert (Costumes)   558
Jones, Robert Earl (Cast)   1636, 3001
Jones, Robert Edmond (Costumes)   1624, 2655
Jones, Robert Edmond (Lighting Designer)   971, 1817,
   2655, 2981
Jones, Robert Edmond (Set Design)   971, 1623, 1624,
   1817, 2187, 2211, 2655, 2967, 2981, 3639, 3686
Jones, Robert Owen (Cast)   643
Jones, Robin (Librettist)   4041
Jones, Shirley (Cast)   1389, 2681
Jones, Shrimp (Musical Director)   2462
Jones, Sidney (Composer)   205, 1429, 1470, 1544, 1682,
   2317, 2803, 3049, 3828
Jones, Simon (Cast)   3598
Jones, Sissieretta (Cast)   641, 982, 2127
Jones, Stephen (Composer)   642, 2263, 2302, 2757, 3540,
   4276, 4766
Jones, Stephen (Lyricist)   642
Jones, Stephen (Orchestrations)   2, 317, 545, 582, 1154,
   1625, 1667, 1827, 1916, 1921, 1948, 2180, 2376, 2378,
   3006, 3007, 3008, 3009, 4249, 4267, 4491, 4813, 4814,
   4815, 4818, 4819, 4851, 4852
Jones, Steve (Orchestrations)   3179
Jones, Steven (Costumes)   3272, 3760
Jones, T.C. (Cast)   2772, 3108
Jones, T.L. (Musical Director)   4668
Jones, Thomas (Composer)   1637
Jones, Thomas (Lyricist)   1637
Jones, Tom (Cast)   1245, 1701, 3542
Jones, Tom (Director)   681
Jones, Tom (Librettist)   681, 808, 809, 1245, 1363, 1439,
   1701, 2050, 2288, 3469
Jones, Tom (Lyricist)   491, 681, 807, 808, 809, 1023,
   1245, 1362, 1363, 1364, 1439, 1701, 2050, 2244, 2288,
   3294, 3469, 3479, 3484, 3542, 3940
Jones, Tom (Musical Director)   622, 1207, 1448, 1493,
   1836, 3409
Jones, Trevor (Lyricist)   3605
Jones, Walker (Cast)   3853
Jones, Walter (Cast)   75, 694, 1516, 2398, 2725, 2835,
   2902, 3154, 3237
Jones, Walton (Director)   3175
Jones, Walton (Librettist)   3175
Jones III, Frederick (Costumes)   2180

Jones III, Frederick (Set Design)   2180
Jones Jr., George (Cast)   2225
Jongerius, Gerard (Set Design)   1865
Jongeyans, George
   See also George Gaynes.
Jongeyans, George (Cast)   3326
Jons, Joelle (Cast)   298
Jonsen, Tommy (Choreographer)   3825
Jonson, Ben (Author)   1373
Jonson, Ben (Lyricist)   4715
Jonson, Bill (Dance Arranger)   911
Joplin, Scott (Composer)   573, 4196, 4390, 4447, 4697
Joplin, Scott (Librettist)   4447
Joplin, Scott (Lyricist)   4447
Joplin, Scott (Orchestrations)   4447
Jordan, Bert (Cast)   4150
Jordan, Chas. (Cast)   3480
Jordan, Clarence (Author)   900
Jordan, Dale (Lighting Designer)   1169
Jordan, Dorothy (Cast)   1447
Jordan, G. Adam (Director)   157
Jordan, Glenn (Director)   4141
Jordan, Hal (Composer)   3763
Jordan, Joe (Composer)   295, 567, 1019, 1251, 2044,
   2721, 3797, 4182, 4804
Jordan, Joe (Lyricist)   295, 500, 567
Jordan, Joe (Musical Director)   1251, 4182
Jordan, Joe (Orchestrations)   444, 567, 4823
Jordan, Joseph (Orchestrations)   3860
Jordan, Jules (Cast)   2814
Jordan, Leslie (Cast)   2046
Jordan, Leslie (Librettist)   2046
Jordan, Louis (Composer)   1296
Jordan, Louis (Lyricist)   1296
Jordan, Marc (Cast)   170, 652, 695, 825, 989, 1775,
   2523, 3015, 4062, 4114, 4505
Jordan, Richard (Cast)   1471
Jordon, Dale F. (Lighting Designer)   3463
Jordon, Dale F. (Set Design)   3463
Jory, Jon (Director)   4450
Jory, Jon (Librettist)   4450
Josea, Joe (Composer)   4264
Josea, Joe (Lyricist)   4264
Joseloff, Stanley (Lyricist)   417, 662
Joseph (Costumes)   3974
Joseph, Bob (Composer)   3557
Joseph, Bob (Lyricist)   3557
Joseph, Edmund (Composer)   3533
Joseph, Edmund (Librettist)   2640, 3533
Joseph, Edmund (Lyricist)   3533
Joseph, Irving (Musical Director)   2218
Joseph, Jackie (Cast)   410, 411, 412, 1257
Joseph, Peter (Composer)   298
Joseph, Peter (Costumes)   2248
Joseph, Robert L. (Producer)   3035
Joslyn, Allyn (Cast)   1283
Joslyn, Betsy (Cast)   1068, 2542, 4233
Jossey, William (Cast)   1185
Jossey, William (Composer)   1185
Jossey, William (Director)   1185
Jossey, William (Librettist)   1185

Jossey, William *(Lyricist)* 1185
Jouannest, Gerard *(Composer)* 2188
Joubert, Joseph *(Orchestrations)* 4460
Jourge *(Costumes)* 1938
Jowitt, John *(Composer)* 4153
Jowitt, John *(Lyricist)* 2168, 4153
Joy *(Costumes)* 945
Joy, Bernie *(Lighting Designer)* 3920
Joy, James Leonard *(Set Design)* 1099, 1496, 1665, 2250, 2542, 4146
Joy, Leonard John *(Set Design)* 2230
Joy, Nicholas *(Cast)* 3014
Joy, Robert *(Cast)* 1787
Joy, Signa *(Cast)* 518
Joyce, Archibald *(Lyricist)* 3562
Joyce, Archibald. *(Composer)* 4804
Joyce, Baby *(Cast)* 2720
Joyce, Carol *(Cast)* 584, 1971, 4651
Joyce, Elaine *(Cast)* 4196
Joyce, Emmett *(Cast)* 715
Joyce, Frances *(Cast)* 1126
Joyce, James *(Author)* 790
Joyce, Joe *(Cast)* 3346
Joyce, Paddy *(Cast)* 1277
Joyce, Peggy Hopkins *(Cast)* 1129
Joyce, Phyllis *(Cast)* 1733
Joyce, Yootha *(Cast)* 2572
Joyner, B.B. *(Cast)* 3904
Jozefowicz, Janusz *(Cast)* 2846
Jozefowicz, Janusz *(Choreographer)* 2846
Jozefowicz, Janusz *(Director)* 2846
Jozefowicz, Janusz *(Librettist)* 2846
Jozwick, Jim *(Set Design)* 2289
Jscherey & Hully *(Cast)* 202
Jubilee Singers, The *(Cast)* 1836, 1980
Judd, Carl *(Cast)* 3537
Judd, Charles *(Costumes)* 703, 3139
Judd, Rebecca *(Cast)* 3862
Jude, Patrick *(Cast)* 699, 1637, 1715, 2759, 3136
Jude, Patrick *(Vocal Arranger)* 2759
Judels, Charles *(Cast)* 1345, 2343, 2595, 2832, 3265, 4694
Judels, Charles *(Director)* 202, 1460, 1461, 2843, 3149
Judels, May *(Director)* 4143
Judge, Arline *(Cast)* 3861
Judge, Count Wellington *(Cast)* 2147
Judge, Ian *(Director)* 3429
Judge, Jack *(Composer)* 736, 965, 3020, 3259
Judge, Jack *(Lyricist)* 3020, 3259
Judge, Jane *(Cast)* 2876
Judge, Peter *(Costumes)* 700
Judson, Alice *(Cast)* 559, 698, 2524
Judson, Lester *(Composer)* 722
Judson, Lester *(Librettist)* 722
Judson, Lester *(Lyricist)* 722, 4512
Judson, Tom *(Composer)* 4775, 4830
Judson, Tom *(Incidental Music)* 4775
Judson, Tom *(Lyricist)* 4775, 4830
Judson Poets' Theatre *(Producer)* 1958, 2110
Judy, James *(Cast)* 171, 674, 1510
Juele, Frank *(Musical Director)* 1604
Juele, Frank *(Orchestrations)* 4543

Juielle, Don *(Musical Director)* 4249
Jujamcyn Productions *(Producer)* 652, 3175
Jujamcyn Theaters *(Producer)* 589, 775, 1649, 2143, 3862, 4031
Juke, Guy *(Additional Dialogue)* 264
Jule, Charles *(Composer)* 3258
Jule, Charles *(Librettist)* 2511
Julia, Raul *(Cast)* 2319, 3171, 3370, 4370, 4485, 4558
Julian, Doris *(Librettist)* 315
Julian, Doris *(Producer)* 315
Julian-Jones, Leslie *(Lyricist)* 3108
Juliana *(Cast)* 3069
Juliano, Frank *(Cast)* 3539
Julien, Jay *(Producer)* 2173
Jullis Productions *(Producer)* 3938
Jun, Rose Marie (Voice) 56
June, Roma *(Cast)* 4053
Jung, Philipp *(Set Design)* 424, 784, 2674, 2677, 4740
Junge, Alexa *(Librettist)* 4136
Junge, Alexa *(Lyricist)* 4136
Junger, Esther *(Cast)* 2475, 3365, 4394
Junger, Esther *(Choreographer)* 4117, 4394, 4567
Junior, John *(Cast)* 1501, 3189
Junker, Hans *(Cast)* 3896
Juracek, Judy *(Set Design)* 99
Jurasik, Peter *(Cast)* 4707
Jurist, Irma *(Composer)* 1892, 3664, 4018
Jurist, Irma *(Dance Arranger)* 1930
Jurist, Irma (Pianist) 2175
Jurman, Karl (Conductor) 2470
Jurman, Karl *(Musical Director)* 373
Jurmann, Walter *(Composer)* 464, 4702
Jurmann, Walter *(Producer)* 2259
Jury, Paul *(Musical Director)* 580
Justice, Jimmy *(Composer)* 3830
Justice, Jimmy *(Lyricist)* 3830
Justice, Jimmy *(Musical Director)* 3830
Justus, William *(Producer)* 4332

K

Kabler, James *(Producer)* 2754
Kaczorowski, Peter *(Lighting Designer)* 573, 3937, 4076
Kadelburg, Gustave *(Author)* 4667
Kadison, Luba *(Librettist)* 1269
Kadison, Luba *(Lyricist)* 1269
Kadison, Phil *(Composer)* 4273
Kadison, Philip *(Composer)* 95
Kadogo, Aku *(Cast)* 1344
Kadokawa, Haruki *(Producer)* 3944
Kaempfert, Bert *(Composer)* 4264
Kaempfert, Bert *(Lyricist)* 4264
Kagan, Richard *(Producer)* 1633, 4019
Kagan, Richard M. *(Producer)* 4020
Kahal, Irving *(Lyricist)* 173, 512, 662, 1126, 1207, 1343, 1813, 2413, 2772, 3356, 3523, 3713, 3789, 4086
Kahan, Judy *(Cast)* 2536, 3565
Kahan, Judy *(Librettist)* 3565
Kahl, Leona *(Librettist)* 1244

Kahn, Grace LeRoy
  See also Grace LeRoy.
Kahn, Grace LeRoy *(Composer)*   2158, 2261
Kahn, Gus *(Composer)*   487, 3985, 4799
Kahn, Gus *(Lyricist)*   123, 393, 544, 921, 965, 1026, 1626,
  1629, 1689, 1823, 1935, 2158, 2204, 2261, 2274, 2342,
  2706, 3018, 3020, 3246, 3249, 3400, 3405, 3430, 3650,
  3842, 3953, 3980, 3985, 3989, 3992, 4683, 4799, 4840
Kahn, Herman *(Composer)*   452
Kahn, Herman *(Lyricist)*   452
Kahn, Madeline *(Cast)*   366, 2279, 2913, 3112, 3279,
  3602, 4481
Kahn, Marvin *(Composer)*   855, 864, 865
Kahn, Michael *(Director)*   1383, 1864, 4318
Kahn, Mme. *(Costumes)*   1852, 3051
Kahn, Roger Wolfe *(Composer)*   124, 1859, 3172
Kahn, Stanley *(Director)*   2089
Kahn, Stanley D. *(Cast)*   2090
Kahn, Stanley D. *(Choreographer)*   2091
Kahn, Stanley D. *(Director)*   2083
Kahn, Sy *(Composer)*   4055
Kahn, Sy *(Lyricist)*   4055
Kahn, Theodore *(Set Design)*   567, 4198
Kahn Jr., E.J. *(Author)*   1776
Kailimai, Henry *(Composer)*   2891, 4555
Kainer, Ludwig *(Set Design)*   4818, 4819
Kaitz, Emily *(Composer)*   914
Kaitz, Emily *(Lyricist)*   914
Kalbuss, F. *(Author)*   2540
Kalcheim, Lee *(Librettist)*   2043
Kaldenberg, Keith *(Cast)*   2961
Kalegi, Sylvia *(Costumes)*   3527
Kales, Arthur F. *(Librettist)*   3423
Kales, Arthur F. *(Lyricist)*   3423
Kalfin, Robert *(Director)*   599, 1276, 1755, 1897, 2012,
  4176, 4460
Kalfin, Robert *(Librettist)*   1897
Kaliban, Bob *(Cast)*   367, 837, 1648
Kalich, Jacob *(Cast)*   2352, 3336
Kalich, Jacob *(Director)*   2352, 3336
Kalich, Jacob *(Librettist)*   2352, 3336
Kalich, Jacob *(Producer)*   423
Kalil-Ogly *(Cast)*   3170
Kalioujny, Alexandre *(Cast)*   1548
Kalish, Larry *(Producer)*   2173
Kaliz, Armand *(Cast)*   2025, 2328, 4080, 4104
Kaliz, Armand *(Composer)*   4080
Kaliz, Armand *(Lyricist)*   4104
Kaliz, Armand *(Producer)*   4104
Kallaghan, Kathie *(Choreographer)*   1346
Kallan, Randi *(Cast)*   4102
Kallen, Lucille *(Author)*   2578
Kallen, Lucille *(Librettist)*   4153
Kallen, Lucille *(Lyricist)*   4377
Kallini, Joseph *(Cast)*   2432
Kallman, Dick *(Cast)*   3895
Kalman, Emmerich *(Author)*   1113, 1455, 1852, 2509,
  2907, 3727, 3839, 4760
Kalman, Emmerich *(Composer)*   771, 905, 1113, 1121,
  1455, 1603, 1788, 1852, 2509, 2755, 2907, 2909, 3020,
  3385, 3727, 3839, 4760

Kalmanov, H. *(Librettist)*   3559
Kalmar, Bert *(Author)*   2467
Kalmar, Bert *(Cast)*   79, 581, 1396, 2485
Kalmar, Bert *(Composer)*   2392, 4814, 4817
Kalmar, Bert *(Librettist)*   1396, 1889, 1935, 1944, 3009,
  3659, 3924, 4426
Kalmar, Bert *(Lyricist)*   142, 176, 358, 545, 581, 930, 1297,
  1368, 1617, 1686, 1688, 1691, 1819, 1873, 1889, 1944,
  2373, 2392, 2638, 2696, 2706, 2857, 3020, 3144, 3185,
  3293, 3399, 3583, 3617, 3659, 3695, 3827, 3926, 4033,
  4249, 4426, 4436, 4476, 4655, 4742, 4814, 4817
Kalmar, Bert *(Producer)*   4426
Kalmar, Harry *(Lyricist)*   4799
Kalmar Jr., Bert *(Composer)*   943
Kalmar Jr., Bert *(Lyricist)*   943
Kaly Dancers, Chandra *(Cast)*   849
Kaman, Michael *(Composer)*   3690
Kamaroff, George *(Composer)*   2397
Kamarova, Mlle. *(Costumes)*   3410
Kamarova, Natalie *(Choreographer)*   204, 2397, 4670
Kamen, Michael *(Composer)*   3690
Kamen, Michael *(Lyricist)*   3690
Kamen, Michael *(Musical Director)*   3690
Kami, Virginia *(Cast)*   3174
Kaminsky, Helen *(Lyricist)*   2476
Kamlot, Robert *(Producer)*   1194
Kamnetz, Eddie *(Composer)*   3241
Kanapoff, Finshl *(Composer)*   4342
Kanapoff, Finshl *(Lyricist)*   4342
Kandel, Aben *(Librettist)*   4730
Kandel, Paul *(Cast)*   3162, 4676
Kander, John *(Composer)*   16, 131, 610, 723, 826, 1038,
  1237, 1310, 1585, 1605, 1764, 1787, 2333, 2558, 2677,
  3110, 3718, 3900, 4480, 4580, 4727, 4862
Kander, John *(Dance Arranger)*   1709, 2150
Kander, John *(Incidental Music)*   3097
Kane, Anthony *(Producer)*   4272
Kane, Arleen *(Producer)*   4272
Kane, Donna *(Cast)*   2805
Kane, Edward *(Cast)*   4142
Kane, Francis *(Cast)*   4076
Kane, Gail *(Cast)*   2662
Kane, Helen *(Cast)*   1617, 3149, 3907
Kane, Lyda *(Cast)*   537
Kane, Seth *(Composer)*   4679
Kane, Sonny *(Lyricist)*   2168
Kane, Trish *(Cast)*   4309
Kane, Whitford *(Cast)*   1651
Kane Triplets, The *(Cast)*   1993
Kanfer, Stefan *(Composer)*   2067
Kanfer, Stefan *(Librettist)*   2067
Kanfer, Stefan *(Lyricist)*   2067
Kanin, Fay *(Author)*   1699
Kanin, Fay *(Librettist)*   1456, 1699
Kanin, Garson *(Author)*   820, 1061
Kanin, Garson *(Director)*   820, 1061, 1420, 4152
Kanin, Garson *(Librettist)*   1061
Kanin, Michael *(Author)*   4727
Kanin, Michael *(Librettist)*   1456
Kanin, Myer *(Set Design)*   439
Kann, Manny *(Cast)*   214

Keenan, Walter *(Choreographer)* 18, 750, 4093, 4679

Keenan, Walter F. *(Choreographer)* 1604, 1885, 4303, 4543

Keene *(Composer)* 4255

Keene, Dick *(Cast)* 3352, 4118

Keene, Elizabeth *(Cast)* 2768

Keene, Lew *(Cast)* 3513

Keene, Margaret *(Cast)* 2768

Keene, Richard *(Cast)* 1831, 3006

Keener, Suzanne *(Cast)* 3431

Keeth, Trevor *(Cast)* 112

Kehr, Don *(Cast)* 119, 2033

Keifert *(Orchestrations)* 4227

Keiffer, Lester *(Composer)* 2986

Keightley, Cyril *(Cast)* 2624

Keil, Mary *(Producer)* 4139

Keim, Adelaide *(Cast)* 4313

Keir, Andrew *(Cast)* 2682

Keitel, Harvey *(Cast)* 2468

Keith *(Composer)* 1246, 4662

Keith *(Lyricist)* 1246, 4662

Keith, A.L. *(Composer)* 3079

Keith, A.L. *(Lyricist)* 3079

Keith, B.F. *(Producer)* 1703

Keith, David *(Cast)* 3671

Keith, Ian *(Cast)* 3974

Keith, Isham *(Cast)* 1286

Keith, Kenneth *(Composer)* 4104

Keith, Kenneth *(Lyricist)* 953

Keith, Laurence *(Cast)* 1891

Keith, Lester *(Composer)* 1433, 2716

Kelety, Julia *(Cast)* 97, 1722, 2056, 4491

Kelk, Jackie *(Cast)* 2797

Kellaher, Ed *(Librettist)* 13

Kellam *(Set Design)* 3562

Kellaway, Cecil *(Cast)* 1698

Kellberg, Marjorie *(Costumes)* 4543

Kellberg, Marjorie *(Set Design)* 4543

Keller, J. *(Composer)* 4264

Keller, J. *(Lyricist)* 4264

Keller, Jeff *(Cast)* 754, 3448

Keller, Sheldon *(Author)* 652

Kellerman, Annette *(Cast)* 149, 2919, 2921, 4553

Kellerman, Annette *(Director)* 149

Kellerman, Sally *(Cast)* 521

Kellerman Girls, The *(Cast)* 149

Kellermann, Susan *(Cast)* 2945

Kellette, John William *(Composer)* 3402

Kellette, John William *(Lyricist)* 3402

Kelley, Barry *(Cast)* 3263

Kelley, Clarence *(Composer)* 890

Kelley, Clarence *(Lyricist)* 890

Kelley, Gene *(Cast)* 4273

Kelley, Janey *(Cast)* 319

Kelley, Louise *(Cast)* 2587, 2814, 3304

Kelley, Peter *(Cast)* 4499

Kellin, Mike *(Cast)* 1955, 2450, 3505, 4609

Kellin, Orange *(Arrangements)* 1425

Kellin, Orange *(Musical Director)* 1425

Kellin, Orange *(Orchestrations)* 3297

Kellogg, Christine *(Cast)* 450

Kellogg, Lynn *(Cast)* 1717

Kellogg, Marjorie *(Costumes)* 1684

Kellogg, Marjorie *(Set Design)* 374, 1684, 3825, 4109

Kellogg, Marjorie Bradley *(Set Design)* 1172

Kellogg, Peter *(Librettist)* 147

Kellogg, Peter *(Lyricist)* 147

Kellogg, Shirley *(Cast)* 3663

Kelly *(Composer)* 436

Kelly *(Lyricist)* 436, 515

Kelly, Al *(Cast)* 3410

Kelly, Alice *(Cast)* 3205

Kelly, Brian *(Cast)* 2360

Kelly, Constance *(Librettist)* 4153

Kelly, David Patrick *(Cast)* 1086, 2440, 3903, 4523, 4744

Kelly, David Paul *(Cast)* 2152

Kelly, Frank *(Cast)* 2515

Kelly, Frank *(Librettist)* 3346

Kelly, Frank *(Lyricist)* 3346

Kelly, Fred *(Cast)* 2275

Kelly, Fred *(Choreographer)* 2275, 4237

Kelly, Frederic N. *(Choreographer)* 3064

Kelly, Gene *(Cast)* 2183, 2432, 3292, 3353

Kelly, Gene *(Choreographer)* 372, 3166, 4498

Kelly, Gene *(Director)* 786, 1315, 2183

Kelly, Gene *(Producer)* 2183

Kelly, George *(Director)* 2

Kelly, George *(Librettist)* 2

Kelly, Georgia *(Cast)* 3820

Kelly, Glen *(Composer)* 2861

Kelly, Glen *(Dance Arranger)* 330, 754, 3708

Kelly, Glen *(Incidental Music)* 754

Kelly, Gregory *(Cast)* 3855

Kelly, Harry *(Cast)* 199, 405, 1003, 1543, 1910, 1912, 2343, 2534, 2856, 2900, 3258, 3319, 4603, 4712, 4803, 4812

Kelly, Horace L. *(Director)* 4149

Kelly, Jean *(Cast)* 2143

Kelly, Joe *(Cast)* 4674

Kelly, Joe *(Composer)* 4674

Kelly, John T. *(Cast)* 421, 677, 687, 1926, 1927, 2041, 4658, 4681

Kelly, John T. *(Composer)* 2116, 4478

Kelly, John T. *(Lyricist)* 4478

Kelly, Kate *(Cast)* 1346

Kelly, Kitty *(Cast)* 2768, 3069

Kelly, Martha *(Costumes)* 1377

Kelly, Moiya *(Cast)* 2608

Kelly, Nell *(Cast)* 4170

Kelly, Orry *(Costumes)* 1491, 1533, 1722, 3170, 3342, 3954, 4733

Kelly, Pat *(Cast)* 1337

Kelly, Patsy *(Cast)* 1126, 1135, 1137, 1322, 1779, 4345, 4730

Kelly, Paul *(Cast)* 3172

Kelly, Paula *(Cast)* 52, 3454

Kelly, Perry J. *(Producer)* 3045

Kelly, Ritamarie *(Cast)* 1785

Kelly, Sean *(Librettist)* 1038, 3077

Kelly, Sean *(Lyricist)* 3077

Kelly, Tom *(Composer)* 687

Kelly, Walter C. *(Cast)* 1667, 3229, 3958, 4657

Kelsey, Carlton *(Composer)* 4010
Kelsey, Carlton *(Musical Director)* 1747, 3342, 4010
Kelsey, Karl F. *(Musical Director)* 2763
Kelso, Louis *(Cast)* 1469, 3994
Kelso, Maym *(Cast)* 1469, 2040
Kelton, Gene *(Cast)* 287
Kelton, Pert *(Cast)* 1110, 1297, 1698, 3016, 3138, 4212
Kelton, Pert *(Composer)* 4212
Kelton, Pert *(Lyricist)* 4212
Kemble, John *(Composer)* 1246, 4662
Kemble, John *(Lyricist)* 1246, 1433, 2716, 2986, 4662
Kemmerling, Michael *(Cast)* 1201
Kemp, Bobby *(Cast)* 982
Kemp, Emme *(Lyricist)* 576
Kemp, Ethel *(Lyricist)* 576
Kemp, Henry *(Cast)* 2976
Kemp, Mae *(Cast)* 3200
Kemper, Charles *(Cast)* 4777
Kemper, Dave *(Lyricist)* 295
Kemper, David *(Lyricist)* 3357, 4687
Kempinski, Thomas *(Cast)* 455
Kempner, Nicholas *(Composer)* 3540, 4170
Kempner, Nicholas *(Musical Director)* 86, 1667, 3184, 4367, 4583
Kempson, Voigt *(Choreographer)* 922
Kempson, Voigt *(Director)* 922
Kenbrovin, Jean *(Composer)* 3402
Kenbrovin, Jean *(Lyricist)* 3402
Kendall, Don *(Composer)* 2281
Kendall, Henry *(Cast)* 703, 704, 3079
Kendall, Kathryn *(Choreographer)* 4799
Kendall, Kuy *(Cast)* 1962
Kendall, Kuy *(Choreographer)* 1378, 1962, 3962
Kendall, Lottie *(Cast)* 4007
Kendall, Pat *(Cast)* 4154
Kendall, Tom *(Cast)* 4007
Kendall, William *(Cast)* 383, 4320
Kendirck, D. Polly *(Costumes)* 2224
Kendis, James *(Composer)* 8, 1518, 1963, 4010
Kendis, James *(Lyricist)* 8, 2263, 4010
Kendrick, Rexford *(Cast)* 2145
Kener, David *(Cast)* 4082
Kenneally, Nina *(Producer)* 209
Kennedy *(Composer)* 2493
Kennedy *(Lyricist)* 2493
Kennedy, Arthur *(Cast)* 933
Kennedy, Bob *(Cast)* 1539, 2275
Kennedy, Cheryl *(Cast)* 2240
Kennedy, Clayton *(Choreographer)* 2286
Kennedy, Francis *(Cast)* 132, 353, 2155, 3679
Kennedy, Frank *(Librettist)* 3203, 4487
Kennedy, Frank *(Lyricist)* 592, 4487
Kennedy, Harold J. *(Director)* 1884
Kennedy, James *(Lyricist)* 3605
Kennedy, Jay *(Orchestrations)* 3126
Kennedy, Jimmy *(Composer)* 4027, 4109
Kennedy, Jimmy *(Lyricist)* 4027
Kennedy, John *(Director)* 137, 204, 2847, 4524, 4828
Kennedy, John *(Producer)* 616, 2928
Kennedy, Madge *(Cast)* 1472, 3540
Kennedy, Matt *(Librettist)* 3137

Kennedy, Mimi *(Cast)* 1985
Kennedy, Sandy *(Cast)* 2312
Kennedy, Tara *(Cast)* 2064
Kennedy, Zona *(Cast)* 239
Kennedy-Fox, Dorothy *(Cast)* 1342, 3103
Kennel, Louis *(Costumes)* 1046
Kennel, Louis *(Lighting Designer)* 1046
Kennel, Louis *(Set Design)* 1046, 1235, 2946
Kennel & Entwhistle *(Set Design)* 2380
Kenneny, A. *(Librettist)* 4106
Kenneny, A. *(Lyricist)* 4106
Kenneny, C.E. *(Composer)* 4106
Kenneny, C.E. *(Director)* 4106
Kenneny, C.E. *(Librettist)* 4106
Kenneny, C.E. *(Lyricist)* 4106
Kenneny, C.E. *(Orchestrations)* 4106
Kenner, Chris *(Composer)* 3739
Kenner, Chris *(Lyricist)* 3739
Kenneth-John Productions *(Producer)* 253, 1038, 2208, 3718
Kenneth-Mark Productions *(Producer)* 3060, 4295
Kennett, Karl *(Lyricist)* 1038
Kenney, Doug *(Lyricist)* 3077
Kenney, Ed *(Cast)* 1315, 4337
Kenney, James C. *(Cast)* 392
Kenney, Kay *(Author)* 1939
Kenney, Kay *(Librettist)* 110, 2947
Kenney, Kay *(Lyricist)* 2947
Kennon, Skip *(Cast)* 1872
Kennon, Skip *(Composer)* 451, 1258, 1861, 1872
Kennon, Skip *(Lyricist)* 451, 1258
Kennon, Skip *(Musical Director)* 451, 3557
Kenny, Charles *(Lyricist)* 364, 3409, 3907, 4264
Kenny, Gerard *(Composer)* 3055
Kenny, Nick *(Lyricist)* 4091, 4264
Kenny, Sean *(Costumes)* 2563, 3271
Kenny, Sean *(Lighting Designer)* 786, 2563, 3731, 4160
Kenny, Sean *(Set Design)* 455, 786, 2682, 3271, 3482, 3731, 4160
Kenny, Walter *(Director)* 2896
Keno, Joe *(Cast)* 1796, 3855
Kent, Arthur *(Composer)* 3261
Kent, Billy *(Cast)* 228, 349
Kent, Carl *(Composer)* 924
Kent, Carl *(Lyricist)* 924
Kent, Carl *(Set Design)* 4394
Kent, Charlotte *(Composer)* 924, 943, 1136, 2105, 2545, 4235
Kent, Charlotte *(Librettist)* 3986
Kent, Charlotte *(Lyricist)* 924, 943, 1136, 2105, 2294, 2545, 4235
Kent, Eleanor *(Cast)* 1707
Kent, Gordon *(Composer)* 3688
Kent, Gordon *(Orchestrations)* 3688
Kent, Gordon *(Vocal Arranger)* 3688
Kent, Guy *(Costumes)* 1204, 2313, 2449, 4582
Kent, Jeff *(Composer)* 2427
Kent, Jeff *(Lyricist)* 2427
Kent, Lennie *(Cast)* 1718
Kent, Lucille *(Cast)* 1703

Key, Francis Scott (*Lyricist*)   117, 1897, 3739
Key, Tom (*Cast*)   900
Key, Tom (*Librettist*)   900
Keyava, Stan (*Composer*)   1884
Keyava, Stan (*Musical Director*)   1884
Keyes, Bert (*Composer*)   593
Keyes, Bert (*Orchestrations*)   593
Keyes, Daniel (*Author*)   699
Keyes, Daniel (*Cast*)   751, 1974, 2578, 3653
Keyes, Evelyn (*Cast*)   2302
Keyes, George (*Cast*)   2413
Keyes, James (*Composer*)   3739, 4264
Keyes, James (*Lyricist*)   3739, 4264
Keys, Nelson (*Lyricist*)   1733
Khalaf, Ramzi (*Cast*)   647, 4107
Khumalo, Leleti (*Cast*)   3836
Khuzwayo, Mhlathi (*Cast*)   3836
Kiam, Omar (*Costumes*)   2981
Kibbee, Roland (*Librettist*)   1959
Kibby, William (*Lighting Designer*)   255
Kibrig, Joan (*Cast*)   4785
Kidd, Johnny (*Composer*)   3695
Kidd, Johnny (*Lyricist*)   3695
Kidd, Kathleen (*Cast*)   1657
Kidd, Michael (*Cast*)   3563, 3647
Kidd, Michael (*Choreographer*)   183, 521, 629, 1029,
    1278, 1706, 1860, 1930, 2484, 2615, 3563, 3780,
    4013, 4190, 4693, 4737
Kidd, Michael (*Director*)   367, 946, 1029, 1633, 2484,
    3780, 4190, 4693
Kidd, Michael (*Producer*)   2484, 4693
Kidder, Edward (*Author*)   3998
Kidder, Edward E. (*Author*)   1148
Kiefert, Carl (*Composer*)   284
Kiefert, Carl (*Orchestrations*)   1962
Kiehl, William (*Cast*)   2992
Kiepura, Jan (*Cast*)   1416, 3536
Kilbride, Percy (*Cast*)   1672
Kilburn, Terry (*Director*)   2057
Kiley, Richard (*Cast*)   753, 1848, 2053, 2327, 2727,
    2940, 3187, 3612, 3687
Kilgallen, Dorothy (*Librettist*)   1101
Kilgore, Robert (*Orchestrations*)   2441
Kilgour, Garfield (*Lyricist*)   733
Kilgour, Joseph (*Cast*)   94
Killalea, J. Edward (*Lyricist*)   1803
Killeen, Marilyn (*Cast*)   4276
Killian, Scott (*Composer*)   2441
Killian, Scott (*Lyricist*)   2441
Killian, Scott (*Orchestrations*)   2441
Killian, Victor (*Cast*)   536
Kilpatrick, James (*Cast*)   3317
Kilpatrick, Joan (*Costumes*)   2220
Kilroy & Britton (*Producer*)   917
Kilty, Jack (*Cast*)   2161, 2162, 4143
Kilty, Jerome (*Author*)   1007
Kilty, Jerome (*Director*)   1007
Kim, Randy (*Cast*)   2290
Kim, Willa (*Costumes*)   180, 589, 695, 964, 1112, 1354,
    1634, 2260, 2437, 2659, 3309, 3602, 4068, 4091,
    4560, 4695

Kim, Willa (*Set Design*)   1122
Kim Loo Sisters, The (*Cast*)   1494
Kimball, Grace (*Cast*)   4723
Kimball, John (*Producer*)   2651
Kimball, Steve (*Producer*)   3817
Kimborough, Emily (*Author*)   3320
Kimbrough, Charles (*Cast*)   83, 832, 1787, 2607,
    3299, 4210
Kimbrough, Mary Jane (*Cast*)   83
Kimmel, Alan (*Costumes*)   4678, 4783
Kimmel, Alan (*Set Design*)   2416, 2962, 4678, 4783
Kimmins, Ken (*Cast*)   1346
Kimmins, Kenneth (*Cast*)   1273
Kinch, Myra (*Choreographer*)   2610
Kind, Roslyn (*Cast*)   4347
Kindl, Ruth (*Cast*)   382
Kindley, Jeff (*Author*)   2152
Kindley, Jeffrey (*Librettist*)   2152
King, Alexander (*Librettist*)   2948
King, Allyn (*Cast*)   2950, 4208, 4810, 4811, 4812, 4831,
    4834, 4840, 4842
King, Beula (*Author*)   3860
King, Billy (*Cast*)   676, 1838
King, Billy (*Librettist*)   1838
King, Billy (*Producer*)   676, 1838
King, Calvin (*Choreographer*)   1632
King, Carlton (*Cast*)   1220
King, Carole (*Composer*)   3668, 3739, 4193, 4534
King, Carole (*Lyricist*)   3739, 4193, 4534
King, Carrie (*Cast*)   731, 980, 2013
King, Charles (*Cast*)   397, 685, 1484, 1626, 1916, 2174,
    2298, 2533, 2869, 3131, 3179, 3396, 3556, 3860, 3975,
    4017, 4050, 4603, 4712
King, Charles (*Composer*)   4017
King, Charles (*Lyricist*)   4017
King, Clement (*Additional Lyrics*)   4556
King, Cory (*Cast*)   838
King, Denis (*Composer*)   3598
King, Dennis (*Cast*)   44, 1384, 2061, 3457, 3772, 3913,
    3916, 4357, 4539
King, Dennis (*Producer*)   3916
King, Donna (*Cast*)   678
King, Ed (*Composer*)   1159
King, Edith (*Cast*)   1384, 3048, 3837, 4693
King, Elizabeth (*Cast*)   4508
King, Everett (*Producer*)   942
King, Hattie (*Cast*)   2720
King, Jack (*Composer*)   733
King, Jane (*Cast*)   2446
King, John (*Cast*)   801, 803
King, John Michael (*Cast*)   161, 652, 1786, 2563, 3038
King, Larry L. (*Author*)   374
King, Larry L. (*Librettist*)   373, 374
King, Lawrence (*Costumes*)   599
King, Lawrence (*Set Design*)   599
King, Mabel (*Cast*)   1074, 2173, 4722
King, Mary (*Cast*)   2446
King, Mazie (*Cast*)   3348
King, Michael (*Cast*)   2797
King, Michael (*Puppeteer*)   2726
King, Mollie (*Cast*)   465, 1626, 3396

King, Nellie (Cast)   1626, 3237
King, Patsy (Cast)   1337
King, Pee Wee (Composer)   4264
King, Pee Wee (Lyricist)   4264
King, Peggy (Cast)   1742, 2182
King, Pete (Musical Director)   3487
King, Pete (Vocal Arranger)   1879
King, Peter (Lighting Designer)   4130
King, Robert A. (Composer)   638, 3989
King, Robert A. (Lyricist)   3989
King, Rose (Cast)   2, 1889, 4374
King, Rufus (Librettist)   3002
King, Rufus F. (Cast)   2287, 3378
King, Sidney (Composer)   2455
King, Sidney (Lyricist)   2455
King, Stephen (Author)   661
King, Stoddard (Lyricist)   3259
King, Walter Woolf (Cast)   2786
King, Wayne (Composer)   200
King, William (Director)   985
King, Wilson (Lighting Designer)   922
King, Woodie (Producer)   4697
King & King (Cast)   202
King Jr., Woodie (Producer)   1344, 3599
King Sisters, The (Cast)   2214
Kingsburry, Lillian (Cast)   1283
Kingsbury, George A. (Producer)   1274
Kingsford, Walter (Cast)   4075
Kingsley, Evelyn (Cast)   1269
Kingsley, Gershon (Dance Arranger)   1194, 2322, 3615
Kingsley, Gershon (Musical Director)   615, 1319, 1993, 2075, 2364, 4566
Kingsley, Gershon (Orchestrations)   1194, 1319, 1676, 1974, 1993, 4566
Kingsley, Gershon (Vocal Arranger)   615, 1194, 1319, 2075, 3615
Kingsley, Herbert (Composer)   3212, 4273
Kingsley, Herbert (Musical Director)   4273
Kinkin, Ethel (Cast)   524
Kinkman, Tamara (Set Design)   1903
Kinney, Ray (Cast)   1840
Kinney, Sharon (Choreographer)   2132
Kinoy, Ernest (Librettist)   269, 1503, 1611, 3497
Kinsely, Dan (Lighting Designer)   2354
Kinser-Lau, Patrick (Cast)   3340
Kinsey, Bennett (Cast)   1002
Kinsey, Tony (Composer)   1195
Kinsey, Tony (Lyricist)   1195
Kinsley, Dorothy (Author)   3888
Kinsley, Herbert (Composer)   467
Kinzy, Rebecca (Cast)   4112
Kipling, Rudyard (Author)   647, 2283, 2970
Kipling, Rudyard (Lyricist)   1502, 4506
Kipness, Joseph (Producer)   167, 1886, 2053, 2058, 2134, 2318, 2362, 2364, 3299, 3741, 3869, 3947, 4323
Kirby (Lyricist)   3941
Kirby, Gerald (Cast)   4302
Kirby, Gerald (Producer)   4302
Kirby, John Mason (Producer)   4062
Kirby, Johnny (Cast)   2496
Kirby, Langford (Cast)   3092

Kirby, Maurice B. (Lyricist)   1455
Kirby, Maurice Brown (Librettist)   1455
Kirby, Maurice Brown (Lyricist)   1455
Kirchner, Raphael (Costumes)   683
Kirk, Andy
    See also Andy Kirk and His Clouds of Joy.
Kirk, Andy (Composer)   432, 890
Kirk, Andy (Lyricist)   890
Kirk, Deanna (Composer)   1232
Kirk, Deanna (Lyricist)   1232
Kirk, George (Cast)   1322, 3170, 3699
Kirk, Jody (Cast)   1754
Kirk, Joe (Cast)   1938
Kirk, Lisa (Cast)   85, 1955, 2331, 2660
Kirk, William (Lyricist)   2495
Kirk and His Clouds of Joy, Andy
    See also Andy Kirk.
Kirk and His Clouds of Joy, Andy (Cast)   890
Kirkbride, Bradford (Cast)   4194
Kirke, Hazel (Cast)   2145, 2262, 3258, 3729, 3755
Kirkeby, Ed (Lyricist)   39
Kirkland (Composer)   432
Kirkland (Lyricist)   432
Kirkland, Jack (Producer)   1352, 4331
Kirkland, Leroy (Composer)   3178
Kirkland, Leroy (Lyricist)   3178
Kirkpatrick, John (Director)   2275
Kirkpatrick, Sam (Costumes)   3088
Kirkpatrick, Sam (Set Design)   3088, 4701
Kirkpatrick, Sidney (Cast)   646, 3904
Kirksbride, Bradford (Cast)   3593
Kirkwood, James (Cast)   961
Kirkwood, James (Librettist)   746, 961
Kirkwood, Kathleen (Director)   303
Kirkwood, Kathleen (Lighting Designer)   303
Kirkwood, Kathleen (Producer)   303
Kirs, William F. (Composer)   123
Kirsch, Carolyn (Cast)   746
Kirschner, Jan (Lyricist)   3076
Kirsh, Bob (Cast)   2038
Kirsten, Dorothy (Cast)   1670, 1681
Kirtland, Louise (Cast)   2479, 2813, 3907, 4299
Kirtley, Leonard (Cast)   4509
Kirwin, Terry (Cast)   2643
Kisco, Charley (Composer)   3933
Kiser, Terry (Cast)   2953, 3370, 3927
Kishon, Ephaim (Director)   4514
Kishon, Ephaim (Librettist)   2421, 4514
Kissen, Murray (Composer)   4817
Kissen, Murray (Lyricist)   4817
Kitsopoulos, Constantine (Conductor)   3628
Kitsopoulos, Constantine (Musical Director)   949
Kitt, Eartha (Cast)   916, 2994, 3107, 3427, 3934, 4383
Kiviette (Costumes)   294, 383, 441, 642, 672, 740, 971, 1011, 1225, 1339, 1387, 1419, 1481, 1528, 1628, 1800, 1856, 1859, 1929, 2187, 2298, 2376, 2382, 2444, 2475, 2939, 2972, 3144, 3172, 3222, 3735, 3946, 3973, 3993, 4118, 4177, 4267, 4322, 4367, 4392, 4426, 4532, 4583, 4778, 4824
Klages, Raymond (Lyricist)   567, 771, 1128, 1132, 1134, 1136, 1778, 3821, 3849

Klain, Margery (*Producer*) 992
Klapis, Ralph (*Cast*) 643
Klaris, Harvey J. (*Producer*) 785, 3171, 4286
Klassen, Ben (*Cast*) 4006
Klausen, Ray (*Set Design*) 826
Klausner, Brachah (*Costumes*) 1358
Klausner, Terri (*Cast*) 1589, 1737, 2470, 4091
Klaussner, Josh (*Composer*) 1232
Klaussner, Josh (*Lyricist*) 1232
Klavan, Walter (*Cast*) 3845
Klaw, Joseph
   See also Klaw & Erlanger.
Klaw, Joseph (*Producer*) 4053
Klaw, Marc (*Producer*) 527, 571, 2181
Klaw, Marcus
   See also Klaw & Erlanger and Klaw & Erlanger
   Opera Co.
Klaw, Marcus (*Producer*) 1026
Klaw & Erlanger
   See also A.L. Erlanger, Erlanger Prods., Klaw &
   Erlanger Opera Co., Marcus Klaw and Joseph Klaw.
Klaw & Erlanger (*Producer*) 186, 256, 405, 749, 902, 1199,
   1228, 1356, 1388, 1403, 1527, 1650, 1731, 2029, 2035,
   2119, 2123, 2465, 2481, 2493, 2497, 2534, 2566, 2723,
   2830, 2907, 2964, 2974, 3251, 3328, 3362, 3422, 3494,
   3652, 3727, 3744, 3745, 3747, 3749, 3751, 3921, 3977,
   4014, 4547, 4554, 4559, 4662, 4787
Klaw & Erlanger Opera Co. (*Producer*) 1375
Kleban, Ed (*Composer*) 2677
Kleban, Ed (*Lyricist*) 2677
Kleban, Edward (*Composer*) 4535
Kleban, Edward (*Lyricist*) 746, 4535
Kleiman, Harlan P. (*Producer*) 1786
Klein, A. Edward (*Lighting Designer*) 2393
Klein, A. Edward (*Set Design*) 2393
Klein, A.A. (*Cast*) 1316
Klein, Alan (*Composer*) 874
Klein, Alan (*Lyricist*) 874
Klein, Albert (*Librettist*) 1829
Klein, Alfred (*Cast*) 1165
Klein, Allen Edward (*Lighting Designer*) 2661
Klein, Allen Edward (*Set Design*) 2661
Klein, Amanda (*Costumes*) 10
Klein, Arthur (*Producer*) 4377
Klein, Charles (*Author*) 1434
Klein, Charles (*Librettist*) 698, 913, 1165, 2824, 2982,
   3673, 3790
Klein, Charles (*Lyricist*) 698, 1165
Klein, Hermann (*Lyricist*) 2982
Klein, John (*Orchestrations*) 3813
Klein, Joseph (*Musical Director*) 3330
Klein, Joy (*Producer*) 2598
Klein, Lou (*Lyricist*) 1963
Klein, Manuel (*Composer*) 106, 188, 236, 719, 1041, 1535,
   1557, 1875, 1882, 1975, 2139, 2174, 2724, 2982, 3093,
   3486, 3504, 3642, 4046, 4113, 4425, 4452, 4509, 4513,
   4599, 4753
Klein, Manuel (*Librettist*) 236, 3093, 4513
Klein, Manuel (*Lyricist*) 106, 188, 236, 1557, 2139, 2724,
   3093, 3504, 3642, 4046, 4113, 4425, 4452, 4509, 4513,
   4599, 4753

Klein, Manuel (*Musical Director*) 1031, 1975, 2139, 2982,
   4113, 4452, 4509, 4753
Klein, Maurice (*Composer*) 3663
Klein, Maxine (*Director*) 518, 2332
Klein, Maxine (*Librettist*) 518, 2332
Klein, Maxine (*Lyricist*) 2332
Klein, Paul (*Composer*) 1408, 2958, 4566, 4829
Klein, Paul (*Lyricist*) 4566
Klein, Randy (*Composer*) 2177
Klein, Randy (*Dance Arranger*) 2177
Klein, Randy (*Orchestrations*) 2177
Klein, Randy (*Vocal Arranger*) 2177
Klein, Robert (*Cast*) 170, 2954, 3112, 4334
Klein, Robert (*Librettist*) 3112
Klein, Sally (*Cast*) 2822
Kleinbort, Barry (*Additional Lyrics*) 4399
Kleinbort, Barry (*Composer*) 139, 2294, 3587, 4399
Kleinbort, Barry (*Director*) 2294, 4399
Kleinbort, Barry (*Librettist*) 139, 3587
Kleinbort, Barry (*Lyricist*) 139, 2294, 3587, 4399
Kleinbort, Neil (*Lyricist*) 4399
Kleinecke, August (*Musical Director*) 115, 568, 2262,
   2405, 2406, 2665, 2858, 2884, 2919, 3137, 4206, 4277
Kleinman, Sy (*Composer*) 673, 2246
Kleinman, Sy (*Lyricist*) 673, 2246
Kleinman, Sy (*Producer*) 673
Kleinschmitt, Carl (*Librettist*) 544
Kleinsinger, George (*Composer*) 50, 1416, 3226,
   3934, 4394
Kleinsinger, George (*Orchestrations*) 3934
Klemperer, Werner (*Cast*) 3577
Klenner, John (*Orchestrations*) 266
Klenosky, William (*Composer*) 4536
Klenosky, William (*Librettist*) 4536
Klenosky, William (*Lyricist*) 4536
Klenosky, William (*Producer*) 4536
Kletter, Debra (*Lighting Designer*) 4358
Kletter, Debra J. (*Lighting Designer*) 2477, 2764
Klimczewska, Violetta (*Cast*) 2846
Kline, Kevin (*Cast*) 962, 3279
Kline, Marvin (*Director*) 92
Kline, Norman (*Lyricist*) 3112
Klotz, Florence (*Costumes*) 546, 775, 1068, 1205, 1329,
   1699, 1775, 2163, 2208, 2333, 2435, 2536, 3097, 3279,
   3340, 3428, 3644, 3792, 3967
Kluger, Bruce (*Librettist*) 2285
Kluger, Bruce (*Lyricist*) 2285
Kluger, Bruce (*Producer*) 2285
Klugman, Jack (*Cast*) 1709
Klugman, Kate (*Cast*) 2784
Knaiz, Judy (*Cast*) 1436
Knapheis, M. (*Lyricist*) 1609
Knapp, Dorothy (*Cast*) 1129, 1132, 1134, 1281, 1387
Knapp, Eleanor (*Cast*) 2727
Knapp, Marjorie (*Cast*) 4131
Knapp, Sarah (*Cast*) 1509, 3181
Knauer, Max (*Musical Director*) 2917
Knee, Allan (*Librettist*) 2420
Kneebone, Tom (*Cast*) 3818
Kneeland, Richard (*Cast*) 1010
Kneitel, Hattie (*Cast*) 4755

Kolo, Fred *(Set Design)*   1276, 4460
Koloc, Bonnie *(Cast)*   2033
Kolodner, Arnie *(Cast)*   3606
Komack *(Composer)*   2754
Komack *(Lyricist)*   2754
Komack, Jimmie *(Cast)*   3524, 4005
Komack, Jimmy *(Cast)*   957
Komisarjevskaia *(Cast)*   710
Komisarjevsky, Theodore *(Costumes)*   1805
Komisarjevsky, Theodore *(Director)*   1805, 3699
Komisarjevsky, Theodore *(Set Design)*   1805
Komolova, Valentina *(Costumes)*   2269
Kondolf, George *(Producer)*   3255
Konecky, Isobel Robins *(Producer)*   699
Konecky, Jennifer *(Composer)*   4627
Konecky, Jennifer *(Lyricist)*   4627
Konrardy, Nancy *(Costumes)*   3076
Kook, Edward F. *(Producer)*   2618
Kookoolis, Joseph Martinez *(Composer)*   4089
Koontz, Porter *(Cast)*   1004
Kopit, Arthur *(Author)*   1186, 4708
Kopit, Arthur *(Librettist)*   3171, 3465
Kopp, Norma *(Cast)*   2101
Kopp, William G. *(Composer)*   3220
Kopp, William G. *(Lyricist)*   3220
Koppell, Al *(Lyricist)*   1989
Kopyc, Frank W. *(Cast)*   3539
Kopye, Jack *(Cast)*   4703
Korbich, Eddie *(Cast)*   212, 1149, 2230, 2416
Koreto, Paul *(Librettist)*   1436, 2279
Koreto, Paul *(Lyricist)*   2913
Korey, Alexandra *(Cast)*   109, 451, 1258
Korey, Alix *(Cast)*   36, 2185, 3757
Korey, Lois *(Librettist)*   1363
Korey, Lois Balk *(Librettist)*   4627
Korf, Gene R. *(Producer)*   131
Korff, Arnold *(Cast)*   4667
Korie, Michael *(Lyricist)*   451
Korman, Jess J. *(Composer)*   2067
Korman, Jess J. *(Lyricist)*   2067
Kornblum, I.B. *(Composer)*   465, 733, 3057
Kornblum, I.B. *(Lyricist)*   733
Kornfeld, Lawrence *(Director)*   1958, 2110, 2236, 2579, 3418, 3602, 4595
Kornfeld, Robert *(Librettist)*   3697
Kornfeld, Robert *(Lyricist)*   3697
Korngold, Erich Wolfgang *(Composer)*   225, 1817, 3767
Korngold, Erich Wolfgang *(Music Adaptation)*   1681
Korngold, Erich Wolfgang *(Musical Director)*   1817, 3767
Korngold, Erich Wolfgang *(Orchestrations)*   1680
Koroll, Gary *(Composer)*   2321
Koron, Barry *(Musical Director)*   2993
Korthaze, Richard *(Cast)*   723, 964, 3506
Kortlander, Max *(Composer)*   3402, 3535
Kosarin, Michael *(Dance Arranger)*   992, 2643, 2790
Kosarin, Michael *(Musical Director)*   330, 2790, 3862
Kosarin, Michael *(Vocal Arranger)*   2790, 3862
Kosarin, Oscar *(Musical Director)*   634, 1764, 3389, 3900, 4060, 4395
Kosarin, Oscar *(Orchestrations)*   3234, 3389
Kosarin, Oscar *(Vocal Arranger)*   1764, 3900

Kosary, Emma *(Cast)*   184
Koski, Hilary *(Composer)*   146
Koski, Hilary *(Lyricist)*   146
Kosloff, Alexis *(Choreographer)*   758, 1460, 2622, 4212
Kosloff, Theodore *(Choreographer)*   3395, 3399, 3865, 4747
Koslow, Pamela *(Producer)*   2200
Kosta, Tessa *(Cast)*   17, 659, 758, 2412, 2830, 3580, 3593, 3778, 3791, 4077
Kostal, Irwin *(Arrangements)*   1815, 3841
Kostal, Irwin *(Musical Director)*   1742
Kostal, Irwin *(Orchestrations)*   23, 299, 869, 1280, 1369, 1422, 1511, 1742, 2355, 2850, 3702, 3815, 3888, 4312, 4625, 4798
Kostal, Irwin *(Vocal Arranger)*   4798
Kostalik-Boussom, Linda *(Choreographer)*   4358
Kostelanetz, Andre *(Vocal Arranger)*   1322
Koster & Bial *(Producer)*   1466
Kostka, Karol *(Cast)*   2977
Kotai, Ralph *(Set Design)*   661
Kotchetovsky *(Choreographer)*   3407
Kotchoff, Ted *(Director)*   2682
Kotite, Tony *(Director)*   1149
Kotlowitz, Dan *(Lighting Designer)*   2372
Kotto, Yaphet *(Cast)*   4863
Kourkoulos, Nikos *(Cast)*   2106
Kovachy, Ed *(Cast)*   3714
Kowal, James *(Dance Arranger)*   975
Kowal, James *(Musical Director)*   975
Kowal, James *(Vocal Arranger)*   975
Kowal, Marsha *(Costumes)*   2470
Kowalski, George W. *(Cast)*   1632
Kozak, Greg *(Cast)*   2521
Kraatz, Kurt *(Author)*   2914, 3529, 4532
Kraber, Gerrit Tony *(Cast)*   2228
Kraber, Tony *(Cast)*   1546
Krachmalnick, Samuel *(Musical Director)*   630, 649, 1766
Krachmalnick, Samuel *(Vocal Arranger)*   1766
Kraft, Beatrice *(Cast)*   2837
Kraft, Helen *(Author)*   3304
Kraft, Hy *(Author)*   615, 1979
Kraft, Hy *(Librettist)*   615, 4152, 4423
Kraft, Hy *(Lyricist)*   4152
Kraft, Randy *(Pianist)*   3914
Kragen, Ken *(Producer)*   2470
Krakeur, Richard W. *(Director)*   709
Krakeur, Richard W. *(Producer)*   2757
Krakeur II, Jacques *(Composer)*   1952
Krakeur II, Jacques *(Lyricist)*   1952
Krakowski, Jane *(Cast)*   1649, 4138
Krall, Heidi *(Cast)*   961
Kramer, Alex *(Composer)*   1296
Kramer, Alex *(Lyricist)*   1296
Kramer, Allan *(Producer)*   407
Kramer, Arthur *(Lyricist)*   3501
Kramer, Dave *(Director)*   4782
Kramer, Dave *(Producer)*   4782
Kramer, Joel *(Cast)*   669
Kramer, Larry *(Author)*   3198
Kramer, Leo *(Librettist)*   3810
Kramer, Les *(Lyricist)*   3810

Kramer, Terry Allen *(Producer)* 1635, 2058, 2798, 3142, 4197

Krancer, Elliot *(Lighting Designer)* 4153

Krane, David *(Composer)* 1120

Krane, David *(Dance Arranger)* 652, 808, 1120, 1970, 2333, 4533

Krane, David *(Incidental Music)* 4560

Krane, David *(Musical Director)* 2633, 4533

Krane, David *(Orchestrations)* 131, 1665

Krane, David *(Pianist)* 4533

Krane, David *(Vocal Arranger)* 1120, 4533

Kranth, William *(Musical Director)* 1337

Krany, Ben *(Director)* 4273

Krasny, Diana *(Producer)* 162

Krass, Michael *(Costumes)* 2038, 2646

Kratzinger, Ernest *(Musical Director)* 2085, 2086, 2087, 2088

Kraus, Philip *(Cast)* 3927

Kraus, Samuel *(Composer)* 4396

Krause, Albert *(Musical Director)* 256, 1613, 4236

Krause, Jay *(Set Design)* 2246

Krause, Marc *(Cast)* 1609

Kraushaar, Arnold A. *(Set Design)* 2377

Krauss, Marvin A. *(Producer)* 2360, 2820, 3644

Krausz, Diane F. *(Producer)* 1832

Krausz, Michael *(Composer)* 1044

Krausz, Rob *(Librettist)* 1832

Krauth, William A. *(Musical Director)* 4375

Kravat, Jerry *(Producer)* 2790

Krawford, Gary *(Cast)* 1079, 1158

Krebs, Cela *(Cast)* 3314

Krebs, Eric *(Director)* 4288

Krebs, Eric *(Producer)* 549, 1279, 1719, 2320, 2654, 3722, 4288

Kreck, Karl *(Composer)* 2

Kreck, Karl *(Lyricist)* 2

Kreffert, Charles *(Orchestrations)* 728

Kreiner, Marty *(Composer)* 4433

Kreiner, Marty *(Librettist)* 4433

Kreiner, Marty *(Lyricist)* 4433

Kreis, Robert *(Composer)* 328

Kreis, Robert *(Lyricist)* 328

Kreisel, Betty *(Costumes)* 2742

Kreisel, Joseph *(Lighting Designer)* 4696

Kreisler, Fritz *(Composer)* 168, 3698, 3703

Kreisler, Fritz *(Lyricist)* 3698

Kreizberg, Yasha *(Vocal Arranger)* 4463

Kren, Jean *(Author)* 1925

Krenn, L. *(Author)* 4181

Krenz, Frank *(Costumes)* 4027, 4076

Kreppel, Paul *(Cast)* 1832, 4736

Kresley, Ed *(Composer)* 2279, 2913

Kress, Helmy *(Orchestrations)* 207

Kressin, Lianne *(Cast)* 3557

Kressyn, Miriam *(Cast)* 343, 400, 1269

Kretzmer, Herbert *(Lyricist)* 2442

Kreuder, Peter *(Composer)* 3441

Krick, Cynthia *(Costumes)* 1781

Krieger, Henry *(Composer)* 1103, 1253, 3034, 4286, 4403

Krieger, Henry *(Lyricist)* 1253

Krimsky, Jerrold *(English Lyrics)* 4368

Krimsky, Jerrold *(Producer)* 3003, 3082, 4368

Krimsky, John *(Producer)* 920, 1286, 1546, 3003, 3082

Krimsley, John *(Producer)* 1195

Kristen, Ilene *(Cast)* 1510, 2790

Kristen, Karen *(Choreographer)* 3527

Kristofer, Lou *(Choreographer)* 3439

Kristofferson, Kris *(Cast)* 2241

Kristofferson, Kris *(Composer)* 914

Kristofferson, Kris *(Lyricist)* 914

Kristy, Carol *(Cast)* 2650, 2962

Krivoshei, David *(Composer)* 4396

Krivoshei, David *(Musical Director)* 1075, 4396

Kroeger, Berry *(Cast)* 3913

Kroeger, Perry Arthur *(Composer)* 4171

Kroeger, Perry Arthur *(Librettist)* 3873

Kroeger, Perry Arthur *(Lyricist)* 3873, 4171

Kroeger, Perry Arthur *(Set Design)* 4107

Krofft, Marty *(Director)* 2443

Krofft, Marty *(Producer)* 2443

Krofft, Sid *(Cast)* 3380

Krofft, Sid *(Director)* 2443

Krofft, Sid *(Producer)* 2443

Krogstad, Bob *(Orchestrations)* 2689

Kroll, Bernice *(Composer)* 3664

Kroll, Louis *(Musical Director)* 2419, 2619, 3580, 4352

Kroll, Louis *(Orchestrations)* 3580

Kroll, Mark *(Producer)* 4828, 4829

Kroll, William *(Composer)* 2193, 3847

Kroll, William *(Musical Director)* 2193

Krone, Gerard *(Producer)* 3491

Kronenberger, Louis J. *(Author)* 2674

Krones, Fred R. *(Producer)* 478

Krones, Michael *(Lighting Designer)* 626

Krones, Michael *(Set Design)* 626

Kronyack, Nick *(Lighting Designer)* 965, 3397

Kroopf, Milton *(Librettist)* 1321

Kroschell, Joan *(Cast)* 1761

Krueger, Martin *(Lighting Designer)* 45

Kruger, George *(Musical Director)* 293

Kruger, Jerrie *(Cast)* 1938

Krumgold, Sigmund *(Composer)* 978

Krumgold, Sigmund *(Lyricist)* 2193

Krummer, Roy *(Composer)* 1342

Krupa, Gene *(Cast)* 1528

Krupa, Gene *(Composer)* 3444

Krupska, Dania *(Cast)* 629

Krupska, Dania *(Choreographer)* 649, 1745, 1848, 2012, 2961, 3702, 3798, 3895, 3941, 4319

Krupska, Dania *(Director)* 4319

Krusader, Goldie *(Cast)* 1703

Kruschen, Jack *(Cast)* 2048

Kruse, Werner *(Composer)* 3441

Krushin, Jeff *(Composer)* 1159

Kubala, Michael *(Cast)* 146, 921, 2205, 2754

Kuchiki, Sashi *(Cast)* 2080

Kuczewski, Ed *(Cast)* 1450, 2776

Kuczewski, Ed *(Librettist)* 1450, 2776

Kughn, Richard *(Producer)* 2142

Kuhlman, Ron *(Cast)* 746

Kuhn, Judy *(Cast)* 721, 2442, 2766, 3070, 3644

L

Lannin, Paul *(Orchestrations)* 1916, 3157, 3650, 4023, 4491, 4821

Lanning, Don *(Cast)* 4673

Lanning, Jerry *(Cast)* 147, 302, 369, 1040, 2713, 3368, 3902

Lannon, David *(Lyricist)* 4039

Lanouette *(Costumes)* 762

Lansbury, Angela *(Cast)* 162, 1012, 2713, 3564, 4233

Lansbury, Edgar *(Producer)* 547, 825, 1184, 1595, 2583, 2687, 3159, 3602

Lansing, Charlotte *(Cast)* 1145

Lantern Productions *(Producer)* 3476

Lanti, Al *(Cast)* 4693

Lantz, Robert *(Producer)* 2295, 3094

Lantzy, Tom *(Cast)* 4172

Lanyer, Charles *(Cast)* 54

Lanzaroni, Bhen *(Musical Director)* 2018

Lanzaroni, Bhen *(Orchestrations)* 2018, 4459, 4558

Lapine, James *(Director)* 1234, 2143, 2746, 3411, 4210

Lapine, James *(Librettist)* 1234, 2143, 3411, 4210

Larabee, Louise *(Cast)* 4028

Laraia, Frank *(Producer)* 1785

Lardner, Ring *(Author)* 2265

Lardner, Ring *(Composer)* 4811

Lardner, Ring *(Librettist)* 1357, 2265, 3172, 4816

Lardner, Ring *(Lyricist)* 2265, 4023, 4555, 4811

Lardner Jr., Ring *(Author)* 4727

Lardner Jr., Ring *(Librettist)* 1373

Larimer, Bob *(Composer)* 593

Larimer, Bob *(Librettist)* 593

Larimer, Bob *(Lyricist)* 593

Larimer, Robert *(Composer)* 2322

Larimer, Robert *(Lyricist)* 2322

Larkey, Joan *(Lighting Designer)* 2731, 2941

Larkey, Joan *(Set Design)* 2731, 3824

Larkin, Eddie *(Choreographer)* 4316

Larkin, Peter *(Set Design)* 259, 393, 546, 547, 964, 1077, 1290, 1614, 1698, 1955, 3108, 3188, 3210, 3453, 3718, 3913, 4474, 4577, 4609, 4693

Larkins, Ellis *(Cast)* 3551

Larned, Mel *(Cast)* 3941

Larner, Elizabeth *(Cast)* 2798

Larrimore, Francine *(Cast)* 4063

Larrimore, Martha *(Cast)* 1600

Larry, Sheldon *(Director)* 1082

Larsen, Carl *(Librettist)* 3527

Larsen, Liz *(Cast)* 1732, 3708

Larsen, William *(Cast)* 1012, 1245, 3491

Larson, Bev *(Cast)* 2049

Larson, Dennis *(Cast)* 499

Larson, G. *(Composer)* 4193

Larson, G. *(Lyricist)* 4193

Larson, Liz *(Cast)* 4139

Larson, Peter *(Cast)* 3555

Larson, Peter *(Composer)* 572

Larson, Peter *(Dance Arranger)* 1059, 3060

Larson, Peter *(Lyricist)* 572

Larson, Peter *(Orchestrations)* 3555, 4062

Larson, Rick *(Cast)* 669

Lascelles, Kendrew *(Cast)* 4579

Lascelles, Kendrew *(Choreographer)* 4579

Lascelles, Kendrew *(Composer)* 3690

Lascelles, Kendrew *(Librettist)* 3690

Lascelles, Kendrew *(Lyricist)* 3690

Lasco, Morry *(Composer)* 1296

Lasco, Morry *(Lyricist)* 1296

Lascoe, Henry *(Cast)* 656, 2975, 3761, 3972, 4734

Lasha, Joseph *(Lyricist)* 3357

Lasher, Albert C. *(Producer)* 1081

Laska, Edward *(Composer)* 224, 246, 515, 1088, 1123

Laska, Edward *(Lyricist)* 224, 246, 1088, 1123, 2372, 3710

Lasker, Harvey *(Director)* 3264

Lasker, Harvey *(Librettist)* 3264

Lasker, Harvey *(Lyricist)* 3264

Lasker, Harvey *(Producer)* 3264

Laskey, Charles *(Cast)* 2061, 2597

Lasko, Edward *(Composer)* 4408

Lasko, Edward *(Librettist)* 4408

Lasko, Edward *(Lyricist)* 4408

Lasky, Jesse *(Lyricist)* 2826

Lasky, Jesse *(Producer)* 1, 326, 1124, 1327, 1835, 2126, 4440

Lasky, Jesse L. *(Producer)* 617, 4045

Lass, Jeff *(Dance Arranger)* 4488

Lass, Paul *(Composer)* 4488

Lassar, Al *(Musical Director)* 977

Lasser, Brian *(Composer)* 583, 2783, 3181

Lasser, Brian *(Director)* 2783

Lasser, Brian *(Lyricist)* 2783

Lasser, Louise *(Cast)* 1846

Lassie Company *(Producer)* 2412

Laszlo, Miklos Nikolaus *(Author)* 3918

Lata, John *(Cast)* 4438

Latell, Blanche *(Cast)* 3254

Latessa, Dick *(Cast)* 109, 1038, 1104, 1329, 3469, 3491, 3644, 4695

Latessa, Richard *(Cast)* 2887

Latham, Bradley *(Cast)* 2689

Latham, Cynthia *(Cast)* 3687

Latham, Fred G. *(Director)* 168, 252, 582, 627, 632, 659, 1033, 1151, 1162, 1183, 1230, 1285, 1555, 1723, 1851, 2622, 2670, 2915, 3084, 3146, 3295, 3304, 3567, 3590, 3675, 3685, 3923, 4001, 4010, 4250, 4258, 4497, 4716, 4760

Latham, Stacy *(Cast)* 2689

Lathan, Bobbi Jo *(Cast)* 4796

Lathram, Elizabeth *(Cast)* 729

Lathrop, Alton *(Cast)* 1671

Lathrop, Helen *(Cast)* 4662

Latimer, William *(Cast)* 643

Latouche, John *(Adaptation)* 3441

Latouche, John *(Author)* 3003

Latouche, John *(Cast)* 3441

Latouche, John *(Composer)* 924, 4484

Latouche, John *(Librettist)* 341, 1600, 4542

Latouche, John *(Lyricist)* 34, 283, 297, 315, 341, 599, 612, 630, 924, 1600, 1754, 1873, 2077, 2294, 2379, 2554, 2948, 3003, 3212, 3441, 3501, 3536, 3551, 3703, 3986, 4280, 4484, 4542, 4799

Latta, Richard *(Lighting Designer)* 3178

Lattimer, John *(Musical Director)* 4415
Lattimer, John *(Vocal Arranger)* 3493
Lauber, Liza *(Cast)* 119
Lauchaume, Aime *(Composer)* 934, 2465, 3566
Lauchaume, Aime *(Musical Director)* 2465
Lauder, Harry *(Cast)* 1829
Lauder, Willie *(Cast)* 1829
Lauderdale, Jim *(Cast)* 900
Laufer, Murray *(Set Design)* 148, 3818
Laughlin, Alvin *(Director)* 1967
Laughlin, Anna *(Cast)* 350, 1558, 1912, 2710, 3129,
    4425, 4723
Laughlin, Jane *(Cast)* 190
Laughlin, Sharon *(Cast)* 2918
Laun, Louis *(Librettist)* 4018
Laurell, Kay *(Cast)* 4808, 4809, 4812
Lauren, Lilyan *(Cast)* 3130
Laurence, James Howard *(Cast)* 4707
Laurence, Jeanne *(Costumes)* 3622
Laurence, Larry
    See also Enzo Stuarti.
Laurence, Larry *(Cast)* 189
Laurence, Paula *(Cast)* 1112, 1744, 2255, 2464, 3301,
    3986, 4058
Laurence, Vincent *(Author)* 2121
Laurens, Marie *(Cast)* 2842
Laurents, Arthur *(Author)* 1060, 1184, 2144
Laurents, Arthur *(Cast)* 2479
Laurents, Arthur *(Director)* 162, 424, 1184, 2048, 2144,
    2360, 2677, 3142
Laurents, Arthur *(Librettist)* 162, 1060, 1709, 1729,
    2677, 3142, 4625
Laurents, Arthur *(Lyricist)* 2677
Laurie, Joe *(Cast)* 3333
Laurie Jr., Joe *(Cast)* 3511
Laurier, Jay *(Cast)* 3467
Laurillard, Edward *(Producer)* 4327
Lautner, Joe *(Cast)* 2339
Lauze, Gene *(Costumes)* 4462
Lavalle, Pat *(Cast)* 1104
Lavella, Gertrude *(Cast)* 539
Lavendero, Leo S. *(Director)* 4041
Laver, James *(Librettist)* 4174
Laverdet *(Set Design)* 700, 703, 2570, 3827, 4341
Laverty, Johnny *(Cast)* 817
Laverty, W.A. *(Cast)* 727
Lavie, Aric *(Cast)* 4396
Lavin, Julian C. *(Lighting Designer)* 1640
Lavin, Linda *(Cast)* 1237, 1370, 1438, 1993, 2163,
    2663, 4627
Lavine, Audrey *(Cast)* 451, 1813
Lavine, W. Robert *(Costumes)* 2217
Lavino, Edwin M. *(Librettist)* 525
Law, Alex *(Orchestrations)* 2092, 2093
Law, Evelyn *(Cast)* 376, 2594, 4491, 4816, 4818
Law, H. Robert *(Set Design)* 60, 472, 712, 968, 1631, 1735,
    1829, 1868, 1920, 2148, 2174, 2276, 2298, 2351, 2363,
    2587, 2696, 2869, 2893, 2931, 3538, 3618, 3737, 4012,
    4491, 4655, 4818, 4819
Law, Jenny Lou *(Cast)* 382, 1363, 2168, 2439

Law, Mildred *(Cast)* 4420
Lawford, Betty *(Cast)* 4586
Lawford, Ernest *(Cast)* 2624, 3450
Lawford, Peter *(Cast)* 3800
Lawler, Anderson *(Producer)* 1679
Lawless, Sue *(Cast)* 3939
Lawless, Sue *(Director)* 484, 708, 944, 2114, 3548, 3722
Lawless, Tommy *(Set Design)* 2089
Lawley, Lynda Lee *(Cast)* 4615
Lawlor, C.B. *(Composer)* 3968
Lawlor, Frank *(Cast)* 102, 1274
Lawlor, James Reed *(Composer)* 3664, 4416
Lawlor, James Reed *(Dance Arranger)* 3664, 4416
Lawlor, James Reed *(Lyricist)* 4416
Lawlor, James Reed *(Musical Director)* 3067, 3664, 4416
Lawlor, James Reed *(Orchestrations)* 3067
Lawlor, James Reed *(Vocal Arranger)* 4416
Lawlor, Mary *(Cast)* 931, 1628, 1827, 3184, 3622,
    3723, 4778
Lawlor Jr., Andrew *(Cast)* 1013
Lawlor Jr., Andrew J. *(Cast)* 4360
Lawn, Sand *(Dance Arranger)* 2651
Lawn, Sand *(Musical Director)* 1258, 3249
Lawn, Sand *(Vocal Arranger)* 3249
Lawner, Mordecai *(Cast)* 3644
Lawnhurst, Vee *(Composer)* 4204, 4825
Lawrence, Alfred S. *(Composer)* 2334
Lawrence, Alfred S. *(Lyricist)* 2334
Lawrence, Bert *(Librettist)* 2809
Lawrence, Beth *(Composer)* 2754
Lawrence, Beth *(Lyricist)* 2754
Lawrence, Bob *(Cast)* 417, 2258, 4214
Lawrence, Carol *(Cast)* 3107, 3837, 3913, 4190,
    4625, 4828
Lawrence, Charles *(Cast)* 488, 3069, 3172
Lawrence, Clara *(Cast)* 1565
Lawrence, David *(Cast)* 3365
Lawrence, David *(Orchestrations)* 1832
Lawrence, Donald *(Composer)* 3987
Lawrence, Donald *(Lyricist)* 3987
Lawrence, Donald *(Musical Director)* 3987
Lawrence, Eddie *(Cast)* 363, 3931
Lawrence, Eddie *(Librettist)* 2304
Lawrence, Eddie *(Lyricist)* 2304
Lawrence, Elliot *(Composer)* 1205, 2368
Lawrence, Elliot *(Musical Director)* 170, 607, 1497,
    1601, 1611, 1860, 2019, 4196
Lawrence, Elliot *(Orchestrations)* 3018, 3564
Lawrence, Elliot *(Vocal Arranger)* 170, 1497, 1611,
    1860, 4196
Lawrence, Elliott *(Composer)* 2452
Lawrence, Francis *(Composer)* 1231
Lawrence, Gertrude *(Cast)* 133, 702, 1238, 2140, 2312,
    2386, 2570, 3214, 3243, 3597, 3678, 3906, 4443, 4610
Lawrence, Jack *(Composer)* 924, 2053
Lawrence, Jack *(Lyricist)* 911, 924, 2053, 3816, 4828
Lawrence, Jane *(Cast)* 4652
Lawrence, Jerome *(Author)* 2713
Lawrence, Jerome *(Librettist)* 1012, 2582, 2713, 3913
Lawrence, Jerome *(Lyricist)* 1048, 3913

Lehr, Fred *(Cast)* 2853
Lehr, Wilson *(Librettist)* 1507, 2550
Lehrer, Tom *(Composer)* 4412
Lehrer, Tom *(Lyricist)* 4412
Lehue, John *(Director)* 322
Leib, Dick *(Dance Arranger)* 3019
Leib, Dick *(Orchestrations)* 3019
Leib, Dick *(Vocal Arranger)* 3019
Leib, Mani *(Lyricist)* 4342
Leib, Russell *(Librettist)* 2785
Leibell, Richard *(Cast)* 4232
Leiber, Jerry *(Composer)* 964, 3428, 3739, 4031
Leiber, Jerry *(Lyricist)* 599, 964, 1214, 3428, 3739, 4031
Leibman, Harriet *(Costumes)* 2020
Leibman, Ron *(Cast)* 3197
Leigh *(Composer)* 710, 1318
Leigh *(Lyricist)* 710
Leigh, Carol *(Cast)* 603
Leigh, Carolyn *(Librettist)* 2072
Leigh, Carolyn *(Lyricist)* 614, 743, 1023, 1097, 1189,
    1298, 1451, 1648, 1708, 1815, 1842, 2010, 2014, 2072,
    2205, 2294, 2523, 2688, 2804, 2837, 3453, 3485, 3637,
    3940, 4019, 4061, 4268, 4337, 4693, 4828
Leigh, Dan *(Costumes)* 4480
Leigh, Dan *(Lighting Designer)* 164
Leigh, Dan *(Set Design)* 164, 337, 4480
Leigh, Fred W. *(Composer)* 4027
Leigh, Fred W. *(Lyricist)* 675, 2858, 4027
Leigh, Grace *(Cast)* 4802
Leigh, Gracie *(Cast)* 4663
Leigh, Jaime *(Cast)* 1496
Leigh, Lesley *(Cast)* 4113
Leigh, Leslie *(Cast)* 617
Leigh, Lisle *(Cast)* 1907
Leigh, Mary *(Cast)* 2366
Leigh, Mitch *(Composer)* 36, 172, 757, 935, 1730, 1959,
    2727, 3612, 3838, 3844
Leigh, Mitch *(Producer)* 935
Leigh, Paul *(Lyricist)* 3208
Leigh, Rowland *(Author)* 1506
Leigh, Rowland *(Director)* 1110, 1414, 1506, 3064, 4777
Leigh, Rowland *(Librettist)* 1110, 1414, 2610, 3011, 3064,
    3152, 4365, 4777
Leigh, Rowland *(Lyricist)* 700, 702, 703, 791, 797, 1110,
    1414, 1506, 2610, 3011, 3064, 3152, 4583, 4777
Leigh, Vivien *(Cast)* 4435
Leigh, Walter *(Composer)* 4153
Leigh, Walter *(Librettist)* 4153
Leight, Warren *(Librettist)* 2790
Leight, Warren *(Lyricist)* 2790
Leighton, Dot *(Cast)* 1532
Leighton, Isabel *(Librettist)* 2293, 2818, 3532
Leighton, Mauri *(Cast)* 898
Leighton, Rose *(Cast)* 1080, 1576
Leisek, Liz *(Cast)* 3561
Leiser, Henri *(Producer)* 2395
Leiserowitz, Jacob *(Composer)* 1609
Leisten, Annette *(Lyricist)* 251
Leitheed, Mike *(Cast)* 3606
Leitzell, Lillian *(Cast)* 4851

Leland, Dawn *(Cast)* 3997
Lellon, Charles A. *(Director)* 2749
Lelong, Lucien *(Costumes)* 702
Lemac, Linda *(Choreographer)* 107, 2689, 2737, 3126, 3637
Leman, Harry N. *(Musical Director)* 1678
Lemarque, Francis *(Composer)* 3107
Lemarque, Francis *(Lyricist)* 3107
Lembeck, Harvey *(Cast)* 3473
Lembeck, Michael *(Cast)* 140
Lemberg, Stephen H. *(Composer)* 2195
Lemberg, Stephen H. *(Librettist)* 2195
Lemberg, Stephen H. *(Lyricist)* 2195
Lemberg, Steve *(Composer)* 1713
Lemberg, Steve *(Lyricist)* 1713
Lemming, Geo. A. *(Cast)* 1562
Lemmon, Shirley *(Cast)* 4480, 4743
Lemonier, Tom *(Composer)* 295, 2111, 3753, 3797
Lemos, Murray *(Composer)* 2164
Lemos, Murray *(Lyricist)* 2164
Lenert, Marguerite *(Cast)* 35
Lengsfelder, Hans *(Composer)* 4091
Lengsfelder, Hans *(Lyricist)* 3905, 4091
Lengson, Jose *(Costumes)* 1146, 3637
Lengyil, Melchoir *(Librettist)* 3829
Lenn, Robert *(Cast)* 153, 283
Lenn, Robert *(Musical Director)* 4243
Lennart, Isobel *(Librettist)* 1420
Lennon, John *(Author)* 3903
Lennon, John *(Composer)* 3739, 3903, 3936, 4193, 4449
Lennon, John *(Librettist)* 3233
Lennon, John *(Lyricist)* 3739, 3903, 3936, 4193, 4449
Lennon, Rusell *(Cast)* 2448
Lennox, Annie *(Composer)* 1713
Lennox, Fred *(Cast)* 2695, 3582
Lennox, Gilbert *(Librettist)* 346
Lennox, Jane *(Cast)* 604
Lennox, Vera *(Cast)* 1618, 3569
Lennox, William *(Librettist)* 1270
Lenoir, Jean *(Composer)* 839
Lenoir, Jean *(Lyricist)* 839
Lenox, Adriane *(Cast)* 338
Lenox, Jean *(Composer)* 4390
Lenox, Jean *(Lyricist)* 1148, 1246, 4762, 4803
Lenya, Lotte *(Cast)* 610, 1196, 1284, 2678, 4369
Lenzberg, Jules *(Musical Director)* 3168
Leo, Frank *(Composer)* 1783, 3882
Leo, Frank *(Lyricist)* 1783, 3882
Leogrande, Ernest *(Librettist)* 3527
Leon, Daisy *(Cast)* 3423
Leon, Felix (Adaptation) 3280
Leon, Frederic A. *(Director)* 284
Leon, Geoff *(Lyricist)* 583
Leon, Harry *(Composer)* 3820
Leon, Harry *(Lyricist)* 3820
Leon, Joseph *(Cast)* 2235, 2838
Leon, Lillian *(Cast)* 1515
Leon, Tania *(Conductor)* 2033
Leon, Tania *(Musical Director)* 4722
Leon, Victor *(Author)* 1555, 1852, 2701, 2836, 2837,
    2838, 3308, 4563

Leonard, Benny *(Cast)* 1923, 4770
Leonard, Billie *(Cast)* 292, 680, 1534
Leonard, Charles *(Librettist)* 2259
Leonard, Eddie *(Cast)* 800, 2481, 3166, 3754, 4098
Leonard, Eddie *(Composer)* 4390
Leonard, Eddie *(Director)* 977
Leonard, Eddie *(Lyricist)* 3754, 4390
Leonard, Eddie *(Producer)* 977
Leonard, Jack *(Cast)* 3738
Leonard, John F. *(Cast)* 3348
Leonard, Leon *(Cast)* 1308
Leonard, Lu *(Cast)* 519, 1094, 1456, 1745
Leonard, Michael *(Composer)* 2016, 3551, 4623, 4764
Leonard, Michael *(Dance Arranger)* 4623
Leonard, Michael *(Musical Director)* 4623
Leonard, Michael *(Orchestrations)* 1664
Leonard, Michael *(Vocal Arranger)* 4623
Leonard, Parker *(Cast)* 340
Leonard, Patrick A. *(Producer)* 680
Leonard, Queenie *(Cast)* 752, 3214, 4341
Leonard, Richard J. *(Musical Director)* 956, 1761, 4643, 4743
Leonard, Richard J. *(Orchestrations)* 1761, 4643
Leonard, Richard J. *(Vocal Arranger)* 956, 4643
Leonard, Robert Z. *(Producer)* 3421
Leonard, Roger *(Cast)* 1010
Leonard, Susanne *(Cast)* 113
Leonard, Suzanne *(Cast)* 3625
Leonardi, Leon *(Musical Director)* 462, 905, 2496, 4123, 4428
Leonardi, Leon *(Vocal Arranger)* 4123, 4428
Leonardo, Joe *(Director)* 3461, 4799
Leonardo, Joseph *(Director)* 1597, 2171
Leonardo, Joseph *(Librettist)* 1377, 1597
Leonardos, Urylee *(Cast)* 415
Leone, Henry *(Cast)* 2518
Leone, John *(Cast)* 240, 533
Leone, Vivien *(Lighting Designer)* 1740, 4518
Leong, Terry *(Costumes)* 3125
Leong, Terry *(Set Design)* 3125
Leonidoff, Leon *(Choreographer)* 3172, 4620
Leonidoff, Leon *(Director)* 117, 177, 1843, 2161, 2162, 3989, 4569, 4737
Leonora, Lily *(Choreographer)* 377
Lepane Amusement Co. *(Producer)* 1795
Lepere, William H. *(Librettist)* 2179
Leporaka, Zoya *(Choreographer)* 3224
Lerch, Stuart *(Cast)* 3329
Lerman, April *(Cast)* 3668
Lerman, Oscar *(Producer)* 4542
Lerman, Oscar S. *(Producer)* 751
Lerman, Rhonda *(Author)* 1169
Lerman, Rhonda *(Librettist)* 1169
Lerner, Alan Jay *(Cast)* 4039
Lerner, Alan Jay *(Composer)* 1231, 2611, 4039
Lerner, Alan Jay *(Director)* 958
Lerner, Alan Jay *(Librettist)* 530, 623, 652, 798, 958, 999, 1231, 1511, 2479, 2568, 2615, 3018, 3038, 3274, 3347, 4004, 4640
Lerner, Alan Jay *(Lyricist)* 369, 530, 623, 652, 798, 958,

999, 1231, 1511, 2401, 2568, 2615, 3018, 3038, 3055, 3274, 3347, 4004, 4039, 4640
Lerner, Alan Jay *(Producer)* 623, 3274
Lerner, Alan Jay *(Screenwriter)* 1511
Lerner, Gene *(Librettist)* 369
Lerner, Gene *(Lyricist)* 369
Lerner, Gene *(Producer)* 369
Lerner, Sam *(Lyricist)* 1930, 3036
Lerner, Sammy *(Composer)* 3036
Lerner, Sammy *(Lyricist)* 203, 431, 3036, 4374, 4545, 4667
Leroux, Gaston *(Author)* 3462, 3463, 3464, 3465
Leroux, Xaver *(Composer)* 3148
Leroux, Xaver *(Lyricist)* 3148
Leroy, Nat *(Librettist)* 539, 541
Lertora, Joseph *(Cast)* 4328, 4476
Les Quat' Jeudis *(Cast)* 3954
Lesan, David *(Cast)* 3365
Lesan, David *(Librettist)* 2105, 3365, 3986
Leser, Tina *(Costumes)* 3390
Leska, Elene *(Cast)* 4064
Lesker, Lorraine *(Producer)* 4015
Lesko, Andrew *(Dance Arranger)* 4629
Lesko, Andrew *(Musical Director)* 4629
Lesko, Andrew *(Orchestrations)* 4629
Lesko, John *(Musical Director)* 842, 1359, 1435, 1730, 1842, 2050, 2201, 2681, 3018, 3020, 4013, 4038, 4244, 4537
Lesko, John *(Orchestrations)* 4566
Lesko, John *(Vocal Arranger)* 1359, 2681, 3018
Leslee, Ray *(Composer)* 240, 4129
Leslee, Ray *(Lyricist)* 240
Leslee, Ray *(Musical Director)* 4129
Lesley, Charlotte *(Cast)* 2485
Leslie, Bert *(Cast)* 3087, 3322
Leslie, Diane *(Composer)* 843
Leslie, Doree *(Cast)* 3980
Leslie, Earl *(Cast)* 2135
Leslie, Eddie *(Cast)* 364
Leslie, Edgar *(Composer)* 4804
Leslie, Edgar *(Lyricist)* 173, 379, 417, 418, 487, 558, 965, 1613, 1813, 2373, 2460, 3175, 3293, 3399, 3525, 3705, 3737, 3827, 3840, 3977, 4235, 4742, 4804, 4812, 4815, 4817, 4825, 4846
Leslie, Edna *(Cast)* 4576
Leslie, Fred *(Cast)* 133, 4249
Leslie, Fred *(Choreographer)* 334, 466, 4795
Leslie, Fred A. *(Cast)* 3649
Leslie, Fred A. *(Choreographer)* 2976
Leslie, Henry *(Composer)* 1065
Leslie, Henry *(Lyricist)* 1065
Leslie, Lew *(Choreographer)* 787, 3783
Leslie, Lew *(Director)* 441, 443, 444, 447, 787, 1058, 2140, 3704, 3705
Leslie, Lew *(Librettist)* 444, 447, 787, 1058, 2140, 3705, 4661
Leslie, Lew *(Producer)* 441, 443, 445, 447, 787, 1058, 2140, 2462, 3513, 3514, 3704, 4661
Leslie, Lew *(Vocal Arranger)* 445
Leslie, Michael *(Cast)* 2970, 3169
Leslie, Norma *(Cast)* 132

Leslie, Sylvia (*Cast*)   841
Leslie-Smith, Kenneth (*Composer*)   4207
Lessac, Arthur (*Vocal Arranger*)   3989
Lesser, Arthur (*Producer*)   95, 2362, 4496
Lesser, Sally (*Costumes*)   2544, 4618
Lesser, Sally I. (*Costumes*)   3695
Lessey, George A. (*Cast*)   3220
Lessig, William (*Musical Director*)   4093, 4679, 4774
Lessing, Edith Maida (*Lyricist*)   1738
Lessing, Madge (*Cast*)   976, 1228, 2116, 2181, 2543, 2936
Lessner, George (*Composer*)   2985, 4015
Lessner, George (*Orchestrations*)   2985, 3152, 4015
Lester, Alfred (*Cast*)   1153
Lester, Edwin (*Producer*)   223, 1119, 1369, 1511, 1681, 1711, 2234, 2327, 3453, 4075, 4798
Lester, Florence (*Cast*)   1163
Lester, Hugh (*Lighting Designer*)   699
Lester, Jerry (*Cast*)   323, 1138, 1950, 2187
Lester, Kitty (*Cast*)   4829
Lester, Mark (*Cast*)   466, 4795
Lester, Noble Lee (*Composer*)   2239
Lester, Noble Lee (*Lyricist*)   2239
Lester Ltd. (*Costumes*)   787
Leswing, Carl (*Director*)   4093
Leswing, Carl (*Librettist*)   4543
Leterrier, Eugene (*Author*)   1576, 1720
Letora, Joseph (*Cast*)   728, 4733
Lett, Robert (*Cast*)   2025
Letters, Will (*Composer*)   2232
Letters, Will (*Lyricist*)   2232
Leugs, David (*Set Design*)   4732
Levans, Daniel (*Choreographer*)   533
Levant, Harry (*Musical Director*)   189, 514, 1539, 2068, 2140, 2847, 3036, 3353, 4420, 4510
Levant, Lila (*Librettist*)   4102
Levant, Lila (*Lyricist*)   4102
Levant, Oscar (*Cast*)   587
Levant, Oscar (*Composer*)   3721
Levant, Oscar (*Musical Director*)   121
Leve, Sam (*Librettist*)   615
Leve, Sam (*Set Design*)   615
Leve, Samuel (*Lighting Designer*)   596
Leve, Samuel (*Set Design*)   323, 596, 2257
Leveen, Raymond (*Lyricist*)   4572, 4824
Leveilee, Claude (*Composer*)   1596
Levene, Sam (*Cast*)   615, 1706, 2449, 3577, 3787
Levenson, Jeanine (*Dance Arranger*)   3862
Levenson, Jeanine (*Musical Director*)   595
Levenson, Keith (*Arrangements*)   533
Levenson, Keith (*Librettist*)   4136
Levenson, Keith (*Lyricist*)   4136
Levenson, Keith (*Musical Director*)   155
Levenson, Keith (*Orchestrations*)   155, 595
Levenson, Lew (*Lyricist*)   1855, 2545
Leventhal, Harold (*Producer*)   4410
Leventhal, Jules J. (*Producer*)   1506
Leveridge, Lynn Ann (*Cast*)   4244
Levering, Nancy (*Producer*)   101
Levey, Ethel (*Cast*)   1480, 1584, 1640, 2517, 2755, 3085, 3809, 4214

Levey, Harold (*Composer*)   1691, 1692, 1796, 2628, 2686, 3655
Levey, Harold (*Musical Director*)   924, 1796, 2628, 2686, 4365
Levey, Harold A. (*Composer*)   780, 2377, 2691
Levey, Harold A. (*Musical Director*)   780, 2691
Levi, Maurice (*Additional Music*)   215
Levi, Maurice (*Composer*)   1327, 1881, 3744, 3745, 3751, 4094, 4473, 4799, 4802, 4803, 4805
Levi, Maurice (*Musical Director*)   3744, 4473
Levi, Richard (*Choreographer*)   747
Levin, Chaim (*Cast*)   2866
Levin, Charles (*Cast*)   1406, 3937
Levin, Herman (*Producer*)   454, 490, 620, 1475, 1564, 2626, 3038, 4450
Levin, Ira (*Author*)   3188
Levin, Ira (*Librettist*)   1094
Levin, Ira (*Lyricist*)   1094
Levin, Maurice L. (*Lyricist*)   1957
Levin, Sylvan (*Musical Director*)   1548
Levine, Bill (*Librettist*)   272, 427, 1049, 4268
Levine, David (*Composer*)   147
Levine, Irwin (*Composer*)   2235, 4197
Levine, Irwin (*Lyricist*)   2235, 4197
Levine, Joseph E. (*Producer*)   2304
Levine, Louis (*Composer*)   3605
Levine, Maurice (*Musical Director*)   596, 868, 1300, 2591, 2680, 3934
Levine, Maurice (*Producer*)   4272
Levine, Maurice (*Vocal Arranger*)   652, 868, 1300, 4567
Levine, Rhoda (*Choreographer*)   1662, 1857, 1977, 2067, 2563, 2599, 4785
Levine, Sam (*Producer*)   2051
Levine, Susan (*Cast*)   3601
Levine, Wally (*Musical Director*)   2052
Levine, William (*Librettist*)   1648, 4525
Levinsky, Walt (*Dance Arranger*)   482
Levinsky, Walt (*Orchestrations*)   482, 2231
Levinsky, Walt (*Vocal Arranger*)   482
Levinson, Fred (*Producer*)   3444
Levinson, J.J. (*Producer*)   2330
Levinson, Leonard (*Lyricist*)   1944, 1946
Levinson, Leonard I. (*Librettist*)   2985
Levinson, Leonard Louis (*Librettist*)   3703
Levinson, Richard (*Composer*)   3076
Levinson, Richard (*Librettist*)   2820, 4303, 4543
Levinson, Richard (*Lyricist*)   3076, 4543
Levinson, Sam (*Cast*)   863
Levister, Alonzo (*Composer*)   3112
Levister, Alonzo (*Orchestrations*)   2306
Levit, Ben (*Director*)   109, 264, 1872
Levitas, Willard (*Producer*)   1200, 3273
Levitch, Sula (*Composer*)   4260
Levitt, Barry (*Musical Director*)   4255, 4272
Levitt, Barry (*Orchestrations*)   4255
Levitt, Barry (*Vocal Arranger*)   4255
Levy, Abe (*Producer*)   3357
Levy, Abraham (*Producer*)   2549
Levy, Al (*Cast*)   3501
Levy, Arnold H. (*Producer*)   2375

Lewis, Vicki (*Cast*)   140, 494, 583, 1092, 4034, 4171, 4701
Lewis, Walter (*Set Design*)   26
Lewis, Walter H. (*Composer*)   1220
Lewis, William J. (*Composer*)   4104
Lewis & MacCoughtry (*Set Design*)   1505, 2675
Lewis Jr., Alde (*Cast*)   393
Lewis Jr., J.C. (*Composer*)   3933
Lewis Jr., J.C. (*Lyricist*)   3933
Lewis and Gordon (*Producer*)   2194
Lewis-Evans, Kecia (*Cast*)   3285, 4398
Lewisohn, Irene (*Cast*)   1654
Lewitin, Margot (*Cast*)   4768
Lewitin, Margot (*Director*)   4768
Lewitzky, Bella (*Choreographer*)   4415
Lewman, David (*Cast*)   4690
Ley, Benton (*Lyricist*)   1690, 4817
Leybourne, George (*Composer*)   1897
Leybourne, George (*Lyricist*)   1897
Leyden, Jimmy (*Orchestrations*)   520
Leyden, Jimmy (*Vocal Arranger*)   520
Leyden, Leo (*Cast*)   2798
Leyden, Norman (*Orchestrations*)   1864
Leys, Bryan D. (*Librettist*)   3004
Leyton, Drue (*Cast*)   1871
Liandre, Lil (*Choreographer*)   2653
Libbey, Dee (*Composer*)   4828
Libbey, Dee (*Lyricist*)   4828
Libby, J. Aldrich (*Cast*)   2157
Libertini, Richard (*Cast*)   679, 2663
Liberto, Don (*Cast*)   2339, 2582, 4395
Liberto, Don (*Choreographer*)   2103
Libin, Paul (*Producer*)   298, 2220
Libowitsky, Hervig (*Set Design*)   2142
Librandi, Geraldine (*Cast*)   81
Libuse, Frank (*Cast*)   2400, 4465
Lichine, David (*Choreographer*)   323, 3536
Licht, David (*Director*)   4773
Licht, David (*Librettist*)   4773
Lichtefeld, Michael (*Choreographer*)   1258, 2185, 3862
Lichtenstein, Todd (*Lighting Designer*)   4684
Lichtman, Nat (*Director*)   4394
Lichtman, Nat (*Producer*)   4394
Lieb, Dick (*Orchestrations*)   1146
Lieb, Francis (*Cast*)   1707, 4161
Lieb, Francis (*Producer*)   2062
Lieb, Francis K. (*Cast*)   617
Lieb, Gil (*Vocal Arranger*)   74
Lieb, Lora (*Cast*)   326
Lieberman, Maurice (*Librettist*)   3847
Lieberson, Goddard (*Composer*)   1342
Liebert, Dick (*Composer*)   532
Liebgold, Leon (*Cast*)   2356, 3781
Liebler & Company (*Producer*)   1501, 2760, 2819, 4544, 4508
Liebling, Howard (*Lyricist*)   427, 1436, 1437, 3479
Liebling, Leonard (*Librettist*)   118, 1522, 4553
Liebling, Leonard (*Lyricist*)   118, 1522
Liebman, Harriet (*Costumes*)   2789
Liebman, Max (*Composer*)   2453

Liebman, Max (*Director*)   23, 1815, 1933, 2707, 3841, 4166, 4287
Liebman, Max (*Librettist*)   2105, 3841, 4166
Liebman, Max (*Lyricist*)   2140, 2453
Liebman, Max (*Producer*)   23, 743, 1815, 1933, 2837, 3841, 3947, 4287
Liebman, Steve (*Librettist*)   4731
Lieder, Rose (*Cast*)   1286
Liederman, Susan (*Producer*)   4074
Lief, Arthur (*Musical Director*)   298
Lief, Max (*Lyricist*)   1136, 1657, 1693, 1855, 1874, 2105, 2637, 3409, 3523, 3849, 3946, 4291, 4335, 4581, 4621
Lief, Nathaniel (*Lyricist*)   1136, 1657, 1693, 1855, 1874, 2105, 2637, 3409, 3523, 3849, 3946, 4291, 4335, 4581, 4621
Liepman, Joan (*Lighting Designer*)   4145
Lieurance, Thurlow (*Composer*)   3840
Liff, Samuel (*Director*)   4273
Lifshey, Oscar (*Musical Director*)   1221
Lifshitz, Max (*Musical Director*)   1695
Light, James (*Cast*)   421
Lightfoot, J.E. (*Cast*)   9
Lightfoot, James (*Cast*)   1909
Lightner, Fred (*Cast*)   4621
Lightner, Winnie (*Cast*)   1460, 1461, 1485, 1486, 1487, 1779
Ligon, Tom (*Cast*)   4789
Lilley, Edward Clarke (*Director*)   145, 814, 948, 1127, 1231, 1323, 1539, 1856, 1979, 2140, 2413, 2709, 3292, 3584, 3955, 4039, 4374, 4569, 4673, 4823, 4824, 4825
Lilley, Edward Clarke (*Librettist*)   4673
Lilley, Joseph (*Vocal Arranger*)   1931
Lilley, Joseph J. (*Composer*)   3444
Lilley, Joseph J. (*Musical Director*)   1893
Lillian, Isodore (*Composer*)   1609
Lillian, Isodore (*Lyricist*)   1609
Lilliard, James A. (*Cast*)   500
Lillie, Beatrice (*Cast*)   133, 216, 702, 703, 1763, 1891, 2137, 3254, 3521, 3885, 3893, 3924, 3955, 4335, 4341, 4583, 4828
Lillie, Muriel (*Composer*)   702, 1733
Lillis Jr., Joseph H. (*Producer*)   843
Lilly, Andrea (*Costumes*)   4003
Lilo (*Cast*)   629, 3551
Lim, Debbie (*Cast*)   2521
Lime Trio, The (*Cast*)   662
Limon, Jose (*Cast*)   125, 207, 3767
Limon, Jose (*Choreographer*)   1880, 3735
Limosner, Pilar (*Costumes*)   4775
Lincke, Paul (*Composer*)   1526, 2858, 4094, 4228
Lincke, Paul (*Lyricist*)   1526, 2858
Lincoln, Harry J. (*Composer*)   1443
Lincoln Center Theater (*Producer*)   756, 3001, 3039, 3468, 3836, 4438
Lind, Betty (*Choreographer*)   4273
Lind, Christina (*Cast*)   153, 3990
Lind, Della (*Cast*)   3975, 4174, 4465
Lind, Homer (*Cast*)   1515, 4646
Lind, Oona (*Cast*)   562
Lindau, Carl (*Author*)   2262, 2495, 2603, 4181, 4726

Linden, Hal *(Cast)* 1158, 2106, 2617, 3780, 3800, 4060
Linder, D. Scott *(Lighting Designer)* 4402
Linder, Helen *(Cast)* 1608
Linder, Jack *(Producer)* 1036, 4204
Linder, Mark *(Author)* 4204
Linderman, Ed *(Additional Music)* 4062
Linderman, Ed *(Cast)* 549
Linderman, Ed *(Musical Director)* 2146
Lindholm, Robert *(Cast)* 622
Lindley, Donald *(Lyricist)* 1131
Lindon, Michael *(Lyricist)* 2388
Lindsay, Carl *(Author)* 132
Lindsay, Earl *(Choreographer)* 202, 288, 1177, 1460, 1678, 2298, 2636, 2789, 3344, 3968, 3973, 4532
Lindsay, Earl *(Composer)* 1678
Lindsay, Earl *(Director)* 3344
Lindsay, Howard *(Author)* 3919, 4180, 4278
Lindsay, Howard *(Cast)* 759, 1357
Lindsay, Howard *(Director)* 163, 1357, 1453, 1973, 3674, 3919
Lindsay, Howard *(Librettist)* 163, 619, 1683, 1760, 1973, 2983, 3674, 4095
Lindsay, John *(Composer)* 60
Lindsay, Robert *(Cast)* 2798
Lindsay, Walter C. *(Producer)* 1562
Lindsay-Hogg, Michael *(Director)* 3198
Lindsey, Gene *(Cast)* 518, 1596, 4454, 4517
Lindsey, Kathleen *(Producer)* 3136
Lindsey, Mort *(Orchestrations)* 269
Lindsey, Robert Nassif *(Additional Dialogue)* 1969
Lindsey, Robert Nassif *(Composer)* 1969, 3306
Lindsey, Robert Nassif *(Librettist)* 3306
Lindsey, Robert Nassif *(Lyricist)* 1969, 3306
Lindup, David *(Orchestrations)* 4160
Lines, Harry *(Set Design)* 2195
Ling, Richie *(Cast)* 252, 308, 1154, 1594, 2507, 3768, 3994, 4624
Ling, Ritchie *(Cast)* 1521
Lingard, William *(Composer)* 1897
Lingard, William *(Lyricist)* 1897
Lingard, William Horace *(Lyricist)* 3989
Linhart, Buzzy *(Composer)* 4449
Linhart, Buzzy *(Lyricist)* 4449
Liniva Productions, Inc. *(Producer)* 4701
Link, Harry *(Composer)* 39, 478, 1813
Link, Harry *(Lyricist)* 478
Link, Peter *(Cast)* 3824
Link, Peter *(Composer)* 1139, 1620, 2318, 2659, 3000, 3724, 3824, 4615
Link, Peter *(Librettist)* 3824
Link, Peter *(Lyricist)* 2659, 3000, 3724, 3824, 4615
Link, William *(Librettist)* 2820, 4303, 4543
Link, William *(Lyricist)* 4543
Linkey, Henry *(Cast)* 2694
Linley, Betty *(Cast)* 3596
Linn, Bambi *(Cast)* 660, 1679, 2048, 2837
Linn, Ben *(Librettist)* 3203
Linn, Diana *(Cast)* 2267
Linn, John *(Cast)* 3446
Linn, Margaret *(Cast)* 1999

Linn, Ralph *(Cast)* 660, 2484, 2797
Linn, Ralph *(Choreographer)* 2910
Linn, Ray *(Composer)* 2084, 2096
Linn, Ray *(Lyricist)* 2084, 2096
Linn, Ray *(Vocal Arranger)* 2084, 2096
Linn Jr., Ray *(Vocal Arranger)* 2092, 2094, 2095
Linn-Baker, Mark *(Cast)* 54, 1015, 1077, 2787
Linne, Hans *(Composer)* 2710
Linne, Hans *(Musical Director)* 2710
Linne, Hans S. *(Composer)* 8, 2261
Linne, Hans S. *(Musical Director)* 2261, 2667, 4285
Linnit & Dunfee *(Producer)* 1386
Linsenmann, George W. *(Composer)* 427
Linthicum, Lotta *(Cast)* 4050
Linti, Arnoldo *(Cast)* 3639
Linton, Bill *(Cast)* 62
Linton, Harry *(Author)* 3068
Linton, Harry *(Composer)* 2465, 4691
Linton, W. *(Composer)* 4193
Linton, W. *(Lyricist)* 4193
Linz *(Composer)* 2162
Linz *(Lyricist)* 2162
Linzberg, Julius *(Musical Director)* 1482
Lion, Margo *(Producer)* 2200
Lion Theatre Company *(Producer)* 3010
Lionel Productions *(Producer)* 3898
Liotta, Jerome *(Lighting Designer)* 2067
Lipman, Clara *(Cast)* 1540, 4298
Lipner, Nancy *(Cast)* 3764
Lippa, Andrew *(Composer)* 2224
Lippa, Andrew *(Dance Arranger)* 1630
Lippa, Andrew *(Librettist)* 2224
Lippa, Andrew *(Orchestrations)* 1630
Lippa, Andrew E. *(Cast)* 4732
Lippen, Renee *(Cast)* 3564
Lipper, Arthur *(Producer)* 3822
Lipper Productions *(Producer)* 3987
Lippman, Sidney *(Composer)* 304
Lippmann, Arthur *(Lyricist)* 1207
Lippmann, Robert *(Composer)* 1956
Lippmann, Robert K. *(Composer)* 4308
Lipscott, Alan *(Librettist)* 2301, 3713, 4586
Lipson, Ann K. *(Composer)* 3654
Lipson, Ann K. *(Lyricist)* 3654
Lipson, Arthur *(Cast)* 2262, 3740
Lipson, Paul *(Cast)* 657, 4542
Lipton *(Composer)* 246
Lipton *(Lyricist)* 246
Lipton, Celia *(Cast)* 2227, 2680
Lipton, Dan *(Composer)* 2528, 3193
Lipton, Dan *(Lyricist)* 2528, 3827
Lipton, George *(Cast)* 153
Lipton, Holly T. *(Cast)* 3167
Lipton, James *(Librettist)* 2887, 3210, 3931
Lipton, James *(Lyricist)* 327, 2887, 3210, 3931
Lipton, Richard *(Producer)* 1229
Lisa, Luba *(Cast)* 656, 1841, 2053, 4332
Lisanby, Charles *(Costumes)* 71
Lisanby, Charles *(Set Design)* 71, 2689, 3637
Liss, Joe *(Cast)* 4690

Lissauer, John *(Orchestrations)*   1770
Lissauer, Robert *(Producer)*   1770
Lister, Lance *(Cast)*   3291
Lister, Laurie *(Director)*   194
Liston, Dave *(Cast)*   2013
Lisz, Gary *(Costumes)*   908
Litel, John B. *(Cast)*   2148
Lithgow, John *(Cast)*   4109
Litomy, Leslie *(Cast)*   3082, 3990
Litomy, Leslie *(Vocal Arranger)*   1286
Litt, Jim *(Musical Director)*   922
Littau, Frank *(Composer)*   1481
Littau, Frank *(Lyricist)*   1481
Littau, Joseph *(Musical Director)*   653, 660, 2615, 3152,
   3895, 4366, 4586
Litten, Jim *(Cast)*   2472, 3743
Little, Cleavon *(Cast)*   2218, 3610
Little, Eric *(Lyricist)*   605, 4765, 4795
Little, George A. *(Composer)*   879, 3405
Little, George A. *(Lyricist)*   567, 879, 3405
Little, J. *(Composer)*   3953
Little, Little Jack *(Composer)*   3375
Little Billie *(Cast)*   804
Little Billy *(Cast)*   2
Little Jr., Bascom *(Composer)*   1342
Little Prince Productions *(Producer)*   2539
Little Theatre Playes *(Producer)*   524
Littlefield, Carl *(Choreographer)*   1941
Littlefield, Carl *(Director)*   1941
Littlefield, Catherine *(Choreographer)*   117, 924,
   1284, 1336, 1423, 1931, 2023, 2024, 2098, 2099,
   2161, 2162, 4143
Littlefield, Catherine *(Director)*   1782, 2023, 2024,
   2098, 2099, 4143
Littlefield, Emma *(Cast)*   1746, 4277
Littlefield, James *(Lyricist)*   1782
Littlefield, Lucien *(Cast)*   4602
Littler, Emile *(Lyricist)*   3756
Littler, Emile *(Producer)*   3756
Littlewood, Joan *(Director)*   874, 1277, 2572, 3259, 4469
Littlewood, Joan *(Librettist)*   3259
Liturgy of the Roman Mass *(Lyricist)*   2775
Litvinoff, Si *(Producer)*   2047
Litwack, Ned C. *(Producer)*   1811
Litwin, Burton L. *(Producer)*   4091, 4137
Litz, Katherine *(Cast)*   283, 2243
Litz, Katherine *(Choreographer)*   283, 2243
Lively, DeLee *(Cast)*   4031
Lively, William Fleet *(Choreographer)*   1997, 2674, 4775
Lively and Yiddish Co., The *(Producer)*   2421
Livent (U.S.) Inc. *(Producer)*   2333
Liveright *(Producer)*   1283
Liverpool, Charles *(Cast)*   646
Livings, George *(Cast)*   643
Livingston, Billy *(Costumes)*   63, 67, 622, 853, 854, 856,
   857, 858, 859, 860, 864, 865, 1476, 2023, 2024, 2098,
   2400, 2475, 3138, 3365, 3907, 4058, 4677, 4824
Livingston, Fudd *(Orchestrations)*   612, 1827
Livingston, Jay *(Composer)*   2057, 2449, 3182, 3234, 3841,
   4197, 4321

Livingston, Jay *(Lyricist)*   2057, 2449, 3182, 3234, 3841,
   4197, 4274, 4321
Livingston, Jerry *(Composer)*   532, 1040, 1716, 1951, 2182,
   2925, 3558
Livingston, Jerry *(Lyricist)*   1040
Livingston, Johnny *(Cast)*   641
Livingston, Robert H. *(Director)*   1279, 2018, 2801,
   3871, 4272
Livingston, Robert H. *(Librettist)*   1279
Llewellyn, Dorothy *(Cast)*   637
Llewellyn, Richard *(Author)*   4384
Lloyd, Bernard *(Cast)*   2240
Lloyd, Christopher *(Cast)*   1755
Lloyd, Evans *(Composer)*   295, 830, 4181
Lloyd, Evans *(Lyricist)*   295
Lloyd, Florence *(Cast)*   2131
Lloyd, George *(Cast)*   3292, 4394
Lloyd, Henry *(Composer)*   364
Lloyd, Jack *(Cast)*   185
Lloyd, Jack *(Lyricist)*   2148
Lloyd, Jay *(Cast)*   4273
Lloyd, John Robert *(Lighting Designer)*   90
Lloyd, John Robert *(Set Design)*   90
Lloyd, Kevin *(Cast)*   3111
Lloyd, Norman *(Cast)*   2257
Lloyd, Norman *(Director)*   1600
Lloyd, Pat *(Cast)*   1257
Lloyd, Violet *(Cast)*   3213
Lloyd Webber, Andrew *(Composer)*   211, 678, 1211, 2212,
   2242, 3464, 4068, 4138, 4217, 4301
Lloyd Webber, Andrew *(Librettist)*   211, 3464
Lloyd Webber, Andrew *(Orchestrations)*   211, 678, 1211,
   2212, 3464, 4068, 4138, 4217
Lloyd-King, Richard *(Cast)*   730
Loane, Mary *(Cast)*   3931
Lobato, Eber *(Composer)*   2356
Lobato, Eber *(Lyricist)*   2356
Lobban, Lynn *(Cast)*   3631
Lobel, Adrianne *(Set Design)*   2320, 3060, 3411
Loblov, Bela *(Musical Director)*   266
Lobos, Alan *(Cast)*   239
Local 840, U.A.W. *(Producer)*   985
Locatelli, Basillio *(Author)*   825
Locher, Robert E. *(Costumes)*   1686, 2180, 4637
Locher, Robert E. *(Set Design)*   1686
Lochner, Robert E. *(Set Design)*   2788
Locke, Charles *(Lyricist)*   3290
Locke, Charles O. *(Director)*   4670
Locke, Charles O. *(Librettist)*   948, 4670
Locke, Charles O. *(Lyricist)*   948, 1836, 4665, 4670
Locke, Edward *(Author)*   1098
Locke, Edward *(Cast)*   3050
Locke, Edward *(Librettist)*   2602
Locke, Edward *(Lyricist)*   1098
Locke, R. *(Lyricist)*   670
Locke, Ralph *(Cast)*   125, 3248
Locke, Sam *(Librettist)*   2447, 3226, 4394, 4542, 4577
Locke, Shamus *(Producer)*   649
Locke, W.J. *(Author)*   2952
Locker, Robert E. *(Costumes)*   2788, 3005

Long, Kenn (Cast)   4431
Long, Kenn (Composer)   4431
Long, Kenn (Librettist)   4431
Long, Kenn (Lyricist)   4431
Long, Lois (Composer)   924
Long, Lois (Lyricist)   924
Long, Ray (Cast)   3914
Long, Shorty (Cast)   2961
Long, Sumner Arthur (Author)   3097
Long, Tamara (Cast)   956, 2590
Long, Walter (Cast)   512, 1336
Long, William Ivey (Costumes)   119, 212, 544, 754,
   921, 1186, 1873, 2307, 2702, 3171, 3175, 4020, 4031,
   4399, 4619
Long Jr., Nick (Cast)   324, 1338, 2342, 2569, 2597, 2990,
   3850, 3924, 4170, 4226, 4372
Long Wharf Theatre (Producer)   4109, 4601
Longbottom, Robert (Choreographer)   3346
Longbottom, Robert (Director)   3346
Longpre, Guy (Cast)   2097
Longstaffe, Ernest (Musical Director)   1610
Longstreet, Stephen (Author)   1886
Longstreet, Stephen (Librettist)   1886
Lonner, Mara (Costumes)   562
Lonsdale, Frederick (Author)   2698
Lonsdale, Frederick (Librettist)   276, 379, 2293, 2317,
   2384, 2392, 2698, 2937
Lonsdale, Harold (Composer)   2341, 3322
Loomis, Frederick (Cast)   1185
Loomis, Joe (Cast)   981
Loomis Sisters, The (Cast)   1481, 1492
Looney, Jay (Librettist)   4416
Loos, Anita (Author)   715, 1475, 1749, 1750, 4043
Loos, Anita (Director)   4043
Loos, Anita (Librettist)   98, 1475, 1596, 1750, 3172, 3349
Loper, Don (Cast)   3292, 4557
Loper, Don (Costumes)   847
Loper, Don (Director)   847
Lopez, Jess (Cast)   214
Lopez, Lilian (Lyricist)   576
Lopez, Paul (Costumes)   2482
Lopez, Perry N. (Composer)   722
Lopez, Priscilla (Cast)   521, 746, 1000, 2659, 3197, 4635
Lopez, Vincent (Cast)   2601
Lopez, Vincent (Musical Director)   3100
Lopez and His Orchestra, Vincent (Cast)   1690, 3717
Loquasto, Santo (Costumes)   109, 693, 1633, 1649, 3838
Loquasto, Santo (Set Design)   109, 496, 693, 952, 1633,
   2318, 2435, 3838, 3992, 4151
Lor, Denise (Cast)   3811
Loraine, Oscar (Musical Director)   2298
Lorber, Martha (Cast)   4352
Lord, Arthur (Lyricist)   1946
Lord, Frederick (Cast)   3157
Lord, Frederick (Choreographer)   1855
Lord, Helen (Cast)   2906
Lord, Mindret (Librettist)   3103, 3104
Lord, Philip (Cast)   1387, 1856, 2747, 4651
Lord, Philip (Librettist)   1447
Lord, Robert (Lyricist)   1944, 1946

Lord, Sylvia (Cast)   679
Loredo, Armando (Composer)   3495
Loredo, Armando (Lyricist)   3495
Lorenz, Fred (Cast)   3698
Lorenz, Herbert Richard
   See also Herbert Fields, Richard Rodgers and
   Lorenz Hart.
Lorenz, Herbert Richard (Author)   2814
Lorenz, Herbert Richard (Composer)   2814
Lorenz, Herbert Richard (Lyricist)   2814
Lorenz, Mort (Cast)   2335
Loretta, Dee (Cast)   2216
Lorette, Mariette (Choreographer)   396, 1901
Lorick, Robert (Lyricist)   546, 1770, 4286
Lorin, Will (Composer)   2167, 3874
Loring, Ernest (Choreographer)   1681
Loring, Estelle (Cast)   2940
Loring, Eugene (Choreographer)   596, 653, 3972
Loring, Eugene (Director)   596
Loring, Michael (Cast)   3990, 4677
Loring, Sue (Cast)   4834
Lorne, Marion (Cast)   961
Lorraine, Betty (Cast)   861
Lorraine, Lillian (Cast)   468, 2494, 2892, 3222, 3332,
   4657, 4803, 4804, 4805, 4806, 4812, 4831, 4838, 4842,
   4849, 4851
Lorraine, Roy (Cast)   2514
Lorraine, Ted (Cast)   473, 2419, 2816, 2856, 2966,
   3333, 3962
Lorraine, William (Composer)   1274, 2454, 3437, 3560
Lorraine, William (Musical Director)   2454, 3045, 4589
Lorraine and Walton (Cast)   684
Lortel, Lucille (Producer)   3615
Lorwin, Liza (Producer)   1636
Los Angeles Civic Light Opera (Producer)   1369
Losch, Tilly (Cast)   294, 4581
Losch, Tilly (Choreographer)   429, 1440, 4341, 4581
Losee, Harry (Choreographer)   216, 2300, 4557
Lotito, Mark (Cast)   2229
Lott, Lawrence (Cast)   3198
Lotti, Antonio (Composer)   1589
Loud, David (Dance Arranger)   131
Loud, David (Musical Director)   131, 3368
Loudon, Dorothy (Cast)   150, 154, 287, 826, 1273, 2208,
   2568, 3196, 3210, 4746
Loughrane, Basil (Cast)   2351
Loughrey, J.B. (Lyricist)   954, 1569
Louiguy (Composer)   2356
Louis, Jean (Costumes)   3493
Louis, Murray (Choreographer)   2441
Louis, Murray (Director)   2441
Louise, Mary (Cast)   483, 1319, 4192, 4517
Louise, Merle (Cast)   705, 832, 2143, 2333, 2360,
   4233, 4319
Louise, Tina (Cast)   1227, 2227, 4499
Louys, Pierre (Author)   165
Love, Clarence (Musical Director)   1248
Love, Darlene (Cast)   661, 2427
Love, Dorothy (Director)   692
Love, Dorothy (Librettist)   692

Luescher, Mark A. *(Producer)*   2528, 2886, 4119
Luetters, Ray *(Cast)*   1903
Luftig, Hal *(Producer)*   261
Lugg, William *(Cast)*   1454
Lugosi, Bela *(Cast)*   3002
Luigs, Jim *(Librettist)*   992
Luigs, Jim *(Lyricist)*   992
Luisi, James *(Cast)*   1060, 4238, 4862
Lukas, Paul *(Cast)*   619
Luke, Keye *(Cast)*   1315
Luker, Rebecca *(Cast)*   3464, 3862
Lum, Alvin *(Cast)*   757, 775, 3201
Lumet, Baruch *(Cast)*   1196
Lumet, Sidney *(Cast)*   1196, 1299
Lumet, Sidney *(Director)*   1742, 2975, 3210
Lumet, Sidney *(Producer)*   2975
Luna, Barbara *(Cast)*   4096
Lunceford, Jimmy *(Composer)*   432, 4743
Lunceford and His Orchestra, Jimmy *(Cast)*   880, 882
Lund, Alan *(Choreographer)*   148, 1255, 3818
Lund, Alan *(Director)*   148, 1255
Lund, Art *(Cast)*   521, 1076, 2961, 3224, 4090
Lund, Blanche *(Choreographer)*   3818
Lund, Erika *(Cast)*   3
Lund, Hettice *(Cast)*   3777
Lund, John *(Cast)*   1140, 3105
Lund, John *(Composer)*   68
Lund, John *(Librettist)*   3105
Lund, John *(Lyricist)*   3105
Lund, John *(Musical Director)*   68, 252, 2915, 3567, 4497
Lundborg, Arne *(Set Design)*   2105
Lundell, Kert *(Set Design)*   40, 518, 1074, 1596, 3159, 4089, 4591
Lundell, Kurt *(Set Design)*   3741, 4004
Lunden, Jeffrey *(Composer)*   158, 4708
Lundy, Pat *(Cast)*   2616
Luner, Fritz *(Librettist)*   1043
Luner, Fritz *(Lyricist)*   1043
Luneska, Gene *(Cast)*   1430
Lupino, Barry *(Cast)*   3737
Lupino, Stanley *(Cast)*   3084, 3163, 3467
Lurenz, Betty *(Costumes)*   2436
Lurie, Carol *(Cast)*   1068
Lurie, Victor *(Producer)*   4447
Lusby, Ruby *(Lyricist)*   3155
Lusby, Vernon *(Cast)*   3294
Lusby, Vernon *(Choreographer)*   392, 681, 1018
Lusby, Vernon *(Director)*   392
Lusk, Milton *(Composer)*   968, 1868, 1869, 1870
Lusk, Milton W. *(Composer)*   115, 1867, 4115
Lussier, Laura *(Cast)*   1391
Lussier, R. Robert *(Lighting Designer)*   344
Lussier, R. Robert *(Producer)*   3939
Lustberg, Arch *(Cast)*   3530
Lustberg, Arch *(Director)*   3530
Lustberg, Arch *(Producer)*   1072, 3530, 4468
Lustig, Alexander *(Additional Music)*   3670
Lustig, Alexander *(Composer)*   2866
Lustig, I. *(Composer)*   2421

Luther, Frank *(Composer)*   4409
Luther, Frank *(Librettist)*   204
Luther, Frank *(Lyricist)*   4409
Luther, Harry H. *(Lyricist)*   2902
Lutken, David M. *(Cast)*   1969
Lutkus III, Frank Charles *(Cast)*   544
Luttrell, Helen *(Cast)*   929
Lutvak, Steven *(Composer)*   1740
Lutvak, Steven *(Incidental Music)*   1740
Lutvak, Steven *(Lyricist)*   1740
Lutyens, Edith *(Costumes)*   933
Lutz, Meyer *(Composer)*   175, 1537
Lux, Lillian *(Cast)*   2811, 3669
Luz, Franc *(Cast)*   2544
Lydecker, George *(Cast)*   1538, 2730, 3193, 3308, 3748
Lydercker, George *(Cast)*   2407
Lydiard, Robert *(Cast)*   164
Lyding, George *(Musical Director)*   1803
Lyle, Jack *(Cast)*   1759
Lyles, Aubrey L. *(Cast)*   697, 988, 1488, 1667, 1678, 2302, 3089, 3660, 3808, 3963, 4198, 4844
Lyles, Aubrey L. *(Composer)*   813
Lyles, Aubrey L. *(Director)*   3660
Lyles, Aubrey L. *(Librettist)*   813, 988, 1960, 2044, 2302, 2721, 3089, 3337, 3808, 3963
Lyles, Aubrey L. *(Lyricist)*   813, 2044
Lyles, Aubrey L. *(Producer)*   813, 1960
Lylleton, Trevor *(Composer)*   1000
Lyman, Abe
   See also Abe Lyman Orchestra and Abe Lyman and His Californians.
Lyman, Abe *(Composer)*   544, 3149
Lyman, Abe *(Lyricist)*   544
Lyman, Abe *(Musical Director)*   1951
Lyman, Dorothy *(Director)*   908
Lyman, Tommy *(Composer)*   452
Lyman, Tommy *(Lyricist)*   452
Lyman Orchestra, Abe
   See also Abe Lyman and Abe Lyman and His Californians.
Lyman Orchestra, Abe *(Cast)*   851
Lyman Twins *(Cast)*   4756
Lyman and His Californians, Abe
   See also Abe Lyman and Abe Lyman Orchestra.
Lyman and His Californians, Abe *(Cast)*   2460
Lymon, Frankie *(Composer)*   166, 3739, 4534
Lymon, Frankie *(Lyricist)*   166, 3739, 4534
Lynch, Hal *(Cast)*   4111
Lynch, Louise Teddy *(Cast)*   3103
Lynch, Michael *(Cast)*   2205
Lynch, Teddy *(Cast)*   1342
Lynch, Thomas *(Set Design)*   146, 3039
Lynch, Tom *(Set Design)*   1164, 4390, 4412
Lynch Jr., Kenneth *(Cast)*   1924
Lynd, Helen *(Cast)*   1136, 2105, 3650, 4209
Lyndal, Percy *(Cast)*   531
Lynde, Janice *(Cast)*   3368
Lynde, Paul *(Cast)*   607, 817, 1047, 3107, 3800
Lynde, Paul *(Director)*   3108
Lynde, Paul *(Librettist)*   3107, 3108, 3110, 4627

M

Mack, William B. *(Cast)*   1434
Mack, Willie *(Cast)*   2853
Mack Choir, Cecil
   See also Cecil Mack and Cecil Mack's Southland
   Singers.
Mack Choir, Cecil *(Cast)*   443, 444, 3704, 3705
Mack's Southland Choir
   See Cecil Mack and Cecil Mack Choir.
Mack's Southland Singers, Cecil *(Cast)*   488
Mackay, Edward *(Cast)*   1210
Mackay, Wm. Wellington *(Librettist)*   415
Mackay Production Co. *(Producer)*   3672
Mackaye, Dorothy *(Cast)*   3772, 4077
Mackeben, Theo *(Orchestrations)*   1110
Mackenberg, Charles *(Orchestrations)*   4141
Mackenzie, Len *(Composer)*   3175
Mackenzie, Len *(Lyricist)*   3175
Mackenzie, Will *(Cast)*   1721, 2958, 3000, 3018
Mackey, Bill *(Cast)*   1959
Mackey, Percival *(Orchestrations)*   3139
Mackie, Bob *(Costumes)*   373, 407, 2590, 2969, 3515
Mackie, Bob *(Librettist)*   2969
Mackie, Bob *(Producer)*   2969
Mackintosh, Cameron *(Producer)*   678, 1296, 2442, 2544,
   2905, 3464, 4068, 4412
Mackintosh, Robert *(Costumes)*   507, 594, 1184,
   1273, 1993, 2014, 2415, 2713, 2898, 2987, 3931,
   3972, 4114, 4718
Mackintosh, Woods *(Set Design)*   3806
Macklin, Albert *(Cast)*   1077
Macklin, Clara *(Cast)*   2274
Maclagan, T. *(Composer)*   3989
Macloon, Louis *(Producer)*   1944
Macnichol, Lizzie *(Cast)*   2326, 3732
Macomber, Ken *(Arrangements)*   3528
Macomber, Ken *(Composer)*   4763
Macomber, Ken *(Lyricist)*   4763
Macomber, Ken *(Musical Director)*   444
Macomber, Ken *(Orchestrations)*   441, 443, 444, 447,
   787, 4741
Macrae, Arthur *(Librettist)*   2227, 2483, 4510
Macrae, Arthur *(Lyricist)*   392, 2227, 3186, 3940
Mactayne, C.S. *(Librettist)*   4194
Macy, Bill *(Cast)*   3233
Macy, Gertrude *(Producer)*   3292, 4483
Madden, Danny *(Cast)*   3724
Madden, Danny *(Vocal Arranger)*   3724
Madden, Donald *(Cast)*   1290
Madden, Edward *(Composer)*   1523, 3926
Madden, Edward *(Librettist)*   598
Madden, Edward *(Lighting Designer)*   2027
Madden, Edward *(Lyricist)*   371, 598, 675, 913, 1247,
   1318, 1523, 1613, 1704, 1793, 2215, 2358, 2495, 2576,
   2826, 2869, 2892, 2978, 3073, 3327, 3519, 3737, 3748,
   4553, 4589, 4655, 4803, 4804
Madden, Edward J. *(Lyricist)*   2858
Madden, George *(Conductor)*   985
Madden, Harry *(Author)*   2311
Madden, Jeanne *(Cast)*   2344
Madden, Sharon *(Cast)*   1346

Maddern, Merle *(Cast)*   1221
Maddern, Richard *(Composer)*   476
Maddock & Hart *(Producer)*   3207
Maddox, Web *(Lyricist)*   805
Maddux, Frances *(Cast)*   1874
Maddux, James *(Cast)*   1781
Madeira, Marcia *(Lighting Designer)*   785, 2648, 2754,
   3060, 3171, 3598, 4442
Madera, J. *(Composer)*   4193
Madera, J. *(Lyricist)*   4193
Madero, Ralph *(Lighting Designer)*   2173
Madigan, Betty *(Cast)*   4155
Madison, Coressa *(Cast)*   3657
Madison, Ellen *(Producer)*   135
Madison, George *(Cast)*   4616
Madison Productions *(Producer)*   4482
Madison Square Garden *(Producer)*   754
Maeder, Fred G. *(Librettist)*   644
Maganini, Margaretta *(Costumes)*   1590
Magee, Patrick *(Cast)*   3445
Magee, Sherry *(Musical Director)*   1874
Mages, Libby Adler *(Producer)*   1059
Maggart, Brandon *(Cast)*   108, 167, 1841, 1842, 2072,
   2590, 3019, 3111, 3112, 3299, 3548, 3615, 4167
Maggio, Michael *(Director)*   158, 4708
Maggio, Ross *(Arrangements)*   1337
Magid, Karen *(Cast)*   3539
Magid, Larry *(Producer)*   4534
Magidson, Herb *(Composer)*   1134
Magidson, Herb *(Lyricist)*   1134, 1481, 1494, 2850,
   4083, 4545
Magidson, Herbert *(Lyricist)*   1481
Maginn, Bonnie *(Cast)*   1264, 1881, 1926, 2974, 4473,
   4478, 4658
Magito, Suria *(Arrangements)*   972
Magnes, Alex *(Musical Director)*   3130
Magness, Marilyn *(Choreographer)*   2689
Magnusen, Michael *(Cast)*   1262
Magnuson, Ann *(Author)*   4775
Magnuson, Ann *(Cast)*   4775
Magnuson, Ann *(Composer)*   4775
Magnuson, Ann *(Lyricist)*   4775
Magoon Jr., Eaton *(Composer)*   1809, 4337
Magoon Jr., Eaton *(Librettist)*   1809, 4337
Magoon Jr., Eaton *(Lyricist)*   1809, 4337
Maguire, Fred *(Cast)*   1610
Maguire, George F. *(Cast)*   4244
Maguire, Michael *(Cast)*   2442
Maguire, Sylvester *(Librettist)*   3748
Mahaffey, Valerie *(Cast)*   1256
Mahan, Kevin *(Lighting Designer)*   3641
Mahard, Fran *(Set Design)*   3714
Maher, Joseph *(Cast)*   3787, 4109
Maher, William Michael *(Director)*   1412
Mahieu
   See also Max & Mahieu.
Mahieu *(Costumes)*   984, 1343, 1718, 1840, 1984, 2071,
   2302, 2330, 2587, 3342, 4198, 4275
Mahieu, Hilaire *(Costumes)*   2455
Mahin, John Lee *(Author)*   647

Manning, Ruth *(Cast)* 2925
Manning, Sylvia *(Choreographer)* 1871
Mannings, Allan *(Librettist)* 2554
Manocherian, Jennifer *(Producer)* 3960
Manocherian, Jennifer R. *(Producer)* 1832
Manoff, Dinah *(Cast)* 2427
Manola, Marion *(Cast)* 1401
Manqele, David *(Cast)* 4438
Mansfield, Laurie *(Producer)* 580
Mansfield, Scott *(Composer)* 2426
Mansfield, Scott *(Director)* 2426
Mansfield, Scott *(Librettist)* 2426
Mansfield, Scott *(Lyricist)* 2426
Mansfield, Scott *(Producer)* 4145
Mansfield Productions *(Producer)* 4749
Manson, Alan *(Cast)* 620
Manson, Bevan *(Arrangements)* 4082
Mansur, Byrd *(Cast)* 4147
Mansur, Susan *(Cast)* 3811
Mantell, June *(Cast)* 2709
Mantia, Buddy *(Cast)* 4347
Mantovani *(Musical Director)* 129, 3339
Manulis, John Bard *(Director)* 1669
Manulis, Martin *(Director)* 1112
Manulis, Martin E. *(Cast)* 1957
Manuscript Prods. *(Producer)* 253
Manville, Lorraine *(Cast)* 3511
Manzano, Sonia *(Cast)* 1595
Manzini, Mario *(Producer)* 4611
Mao, Freddy *(Cast)* 3340
Mapes, Jacque *(Producer)* 4415
Mapes, Jacque *(Set Design)* 4415
Maple, Audrey *(Cast)* 1285, 1629, 1851, 3084
Marand, Patricia *(Cast)* 2163, 4718
Marascalco, John *(Composer)* 3695
Marascalco, John *(Lyricist)* 3695
Marba, Joseph S. *(Cast)* 929
Marbe, Fay *(Cast)* 910, 2567, 2684, 4547
Marble, Anna *(Composer)* 3073
Marble, Anna *(Lyricist)* 3073
Marble, Carolyn *(Cast)* 3643
Marble, Dan *(Cast)* 4322
Marbury, Elisabeth *(Producer)* 1557, 2620, 3193, 3849, 3865, 4555
Marc, Peter *(Cast)* 450
Marc Henri *(Set Design)* 3291
Marc-Henri *(Cast)* 4341
Marc-Henri *(Costumes)* 4581
Marc-Henri *(Set Design)* 133, 700, 703, 704, 791, 1610, 2570, 3827, 4320, 4765
Marc-Michel *(Author)* 2178, 4319
Marceline *(Cast)* 188, 236, 378, 3093, 4046, 4113, 4452, 4599
March, Bill *(Cast)* 1508
March, David L. *(Producer)* 1255
March, Fredric *(Cast)* 121, 752, 2653, 2814
March, Ursula *(Cast)* 2454
Marchand, Colette *(Cast)* 4496
Marchand, Susan *(Cast)* 1635
Marchante, Marion *(Cast)* 3170

Marchetti, Filiberto *(Choreographer)* 175
Marchetti, H. *(Choreographer)* 2938
Marco
    See also Fanchon & Marco.
Marco *(Director)* 4128
Marco, Maria *(Cast)* 2407
Marco, Sano *(Composer)* 2580
Marcone, Lance *(Cast)* 1695
Marcovicci, Andrea *(Cast)* 695, 3088
Marcus, A.B. *(Producer)* 2749
Marcus, D. Frank *(Composer)* 290, 488
Marcus, D. Frank *(Librettist)* 290, 488
Marcus, D. Frank *(Lyricist)* 290, 488
Marcus, Daniel *(Cast)* 1702
Marcus, Linda *(Lyricist)* 328
Marcus, Madame *(Costumes)* 792
Marcus, Ruth *(Cast)* 2321
Marcus, Sol *(Composer)* 3695
Marcus, Sol *(Lyricist)* 3695
Marcy, Everett *(Librettist)* 70, 3104, 4677
Marcy, Everett *(Lyricist)* 621, 3103, 3104
Marcy, George *(Cast)* 406, 2554
Marden, Ben *(Producer)* 3726
Mardirosian, Tom *(Cast)* 3039
Marek, Mary Ann *(Cast)* 2356
Marek, Rochelle *(Cast)* 4157
Maresch, Harold *(Producer)* 3046
Margetson, Arthur *(Cast)* 189, 3390
Margo, Philip F. *(Composer)* 2785
Margo, Philip F. *(Lyricist)* 2785
Margolies, Abe *(Producer)* 2075, 2440
Margoshes, Steve *(Dance Arranger)* 2953, 3651
Margoshes, Steve *(Musical Director)* 2953, 3651
Margoshes, Steve *(Orchestrations)* 4031, 4676
Margoshes, Steve *(Vocal Arranger)* 2953, 3651
Margoshes, Steven *(Composer)* 1236
Margoshes, Steven *(Dance Arranger)* 1737, 4505
Margoshes, Steven *(Musical Director)* 1236, 2754, 4505
Margoshes, Steven *(Orchestrations)* 171, 394, 583, 753, 1236, 1737, 2643, 2754, 3944, 4505
Margoshes, Steven *(Vocal Arranger)* 583, 753, 1737, 2754, 4505
Margosian, Linda *(Costumes)* 99
Marguerite, Mlle.
    See also La Petite Marguerite.
Marguerite, Mlle. *(Cast)* 1962
Margulies, David *(Cast)* 3577
Margulies, Ellen *(Cast)* 4325
Mari, Floria *(Cast)* 2322
Maricle, Marijane *(Cast)* 607
Marie, Julienne *(Cast)* 699, 1060, 1373, 4682
Marie, Rose *(Cast)* 4423
Marik, Carol *(Choreographer)* 2783
Marineau, Barbara *(Cast)* 430
Mariners, The *(Cast)* 197
Marino, F. *(Lyricist)* 4264
Marion, David *(Choreographer)* 4064
Marion, Frank *(Choreographer)* 2896
Marion, George *(Cast)* 48, 1663, 2506, 3363

Marren, Howard (*Composer*)   1496, 2598, 3377, 3544
Marrow, Esther (*Cast*)   166, 2692, 3991, 4722
Marrow, Macklin (*Musical Director*)   4368, 4479
Marrow, Queen Esther (*Cast*)   1172, 4460
Marrow, Queen Esther (*Composer*)   4460
Marrow, Queen Esther (*Librettist*)   4460
Marrow, Queen Esther (*Lyricist*)   4460
Mars, Anthony (*Author*)   1553
Mars, Antony (*Author*)   3784
Mars, Antony (*Librettist*)   1212
Mars Bonfire (*Composer*)   3695
Mars Bonfire (*Lyricist*)   3695
Marsden, Frank (*Set Design*)   1356
Marsden, Richard (*Set Design*)   1576
Marsh, Diane (*Choreographer*)   63
Marsh, Howard (*Cast*)   463, 718, 1663, 1686, 3949,
  4188, 4620
Marsh, John (*Author*)   1257
Marsh, Mary (*Cast*)   2739
Marsh, Roy K. (*Composer*)   2856
Marsh, Roy K. (*Lyricist*)   2856
Marsh, Vera (*Cast*)   111, 1145, 1387, 3365
Marshall, Amelia (*Cast*)   1776
Marshall, Armina (*Author*)   183
Marshall, Austin (*Cast*)   2068
Marshall, Boots (*Choreographer*)   1499
Marshall, Boyd (*Cast*)   1796, 2377
Marshall, Capt. Robert (*Author*)   138
Marshall, Donna (*Cast*)   602
Marshall, E.G. (*Cast*)   933, 2553, 3075
Marshall, Eric (*Cast*)   791
Marshall, Ethel (*Cast*)   1479, 2791, 2792
Marshall, Everett (*Cast*)   622, 662, 1492, 2813,
  3100, 4824
Marshall, George (*Cast*)   3409
Marshall, George Preston (*Producer*)   3356
Marshall, Henry (*Composer*)   3384, 4642, 4712
Marshall, Henry (*Librettist*)   3384
Marshall, Henry (*Lyricist*)   3384
Marshall, Henry I. (*Composer*)   2667, 4017, 4589
Marshall, Iris (*Cast*)   512
Marshall, James R. (*Cast*)   4227
Marshall, Jay (*Cast*)   2615
Marshall, Joe (*Cast*)   4697
Marshall, Kathleen (*Choreographer*)   4255
Marshall, Ken (*Cast*)   259
Marshall, Larry (*Cast*)   393, 550, 828, 2134, 2648, 2775,
  2953, 3231, 3628, 3741, 4147, 4371
Marshall, Madeline (*Cast*)   2157
Marshall, Mort (*Cast*)   1475, 1709, 2523, 3497, 3526,
  4018, 4029
Marshall, Pat (*Cast*)   1782, 2987
Marshall, Patricia (*Cast*)   999
Marshall, Peter L. (*Cast*)   4013
Marshall, Red (*Cast*)   70, 2850
Marshall, Rob (*Cast*)   146, 3070
Marshall, Rob (*Choreographer*)   2333, 3456
Marshall, Sarah (*Cast*)   4749
Marshe, Vera (*Cast*)   289
Marsicano, Mary (*Costumes*)   696

Marsolais, Ken (*Producer*)   1589, 2415
Marston, Lawrence (*Director*)   1722, 2490, 2814,
  4322, 4528
Marston, Richard (*Set Design*)   1030, 1305, 2123, 2493,
  2500, 2502, 4125
Martel, Janece (*Cast*)   3669
Martel, Michel (*Cast*)   4579
Martel, Tom (*Cast*)   1769
Martel, Tom (*Composer*)   1769
Martel, Tom (*Lyricist*)   1769
Martel, William (*Cast*)   227
Martell, Fred (*Cast*)   2023
Martell, Karla (*Author*)   225
Martell, Philip (*Musical Director*)   1386, 2608
Martelle, Thomas (*Cast*)   1248
Martens, George (*Musical Director*)   1187
Martens, Mme. (*Costumes*)   1080
Marti Band, Frank (*Cast*)   862
Marti Orchestra, Frank (*Cast*)   847, 849, 855, 859,
  860, 861, 863
Martin (*Set Design*)   4291
Martin, Andrea (*Cast*)   3039
Martin, Angel (*Cast*)   4168
Martin, Angela (*Cast*)   1478
Martin, Ann-Ngaire (*Cast*)   3277
Martin, Barbara (*Cast*)   2097
Martin, Barney (*Cast*)   190, 723, 2651, 4629
Martin, Bernard (*Lyricist*)   488
Martin, Bob (*Vocal Arranger*)   1886
Martin, Daisy (*Cast*)   1087
Martin, David (*Composer*)   3983
Martin, David (*Orchestrations*)   3983
Martin, Dean (*Cast*)   853, 857
Martin, Denis (*Cast*)   3339
Martin, Dolores (*Cast*)   1278
Martin, E. (*Author*)   4624
Martin, Ellen (*Cast*)   2988
Martin, Elliot (*Producer*)   1776, 3097
Martin, Erin (*Cast*)   4397
Martin, Ernest (*Producer*)   507, 629, 1706, 2019, 2523,
  3972, 4013, 4588
Martin, Ernest H. (*Librettist*)   4682
Martin, Ernest H. (*Producer*)   16, 4652, 4682
Martin, Ethel (*Choreographer*)   693, 3871, 4145
Martin, Evelyn (*Cast*)   3369
Martin, Frank (*Director*)   1377
Martin, Fred (*Producer*)   2580
Martin, George N. (*Cast*)   3070
Martin, Helen (*Cast*)   3610
Martin, Herb (*Lyricist*)   2320, 4288
Martin, Herbert (*Librettist*)   4764
Martin, Herbert (*Lyricist*)   2016, 3551, 4764
Martin, Hugh (*Cast*)   1973, 2597, 4174
Martin, Hugh (*Composer*)   372, 1628, 1742, 1891, 2148,
  2535, 2582, 2608, 2705, 2805, 3175, 4289, 4332, 4388,
  4399, 4586, 4827
Martin, Hugh (*Librettist*)   1891
Martin, Hugh (*Lyricist*)   372, 1628, 1742, 1891, 2148,
  2582, 2608, 2705, 2805, 3175, 4289, 4332, 4399,
  4586, 4827

Matthews, Inez *(Cast)* 2591
Matthews, Jessie *(Cast)* 133, 1128, 1202, 3291, 4581
Matthews, Jon *(Cast)* 3806
Matthews, Julian *(Producer)* 215
Matthews, Junius *(Cast)* 1651, 1657
Matthews, Karen *(Costumes)* 1872
Matthews, Lester *(Cast)* 2392
Matthews, Robert *(Cast)* 793
Matthews, Roger *(Cast)* 3963
Matthews, Tom *(Cast)* 4011
Matthews, W. *(Costumes)* 1285
Matthews, W.H. *(Costumes)* 1357, 2670, 2691, 2756, 4801, 4802, 4803, 4804, 4805
Matthews, William H. *(Costumes)* 378, 712, 1134, 1208, 1281, 1378, 1552, 1900, 1901, 2922, 3978, 4012
Matthews, William H. *(Set Design)* 4808
Matthews, William Henry *(Costumes)* 683, 1016, 3525, 4247
Matthews Jr., William Henry *(Costumes)* 1524
Mattioli, Louis *(Librettist)* 4146
Mattison, Johnny *(Choreographer)* 3860
Mattox, Matt *(Cast)* 2679, 3288, 3496, 3845, 4542, 4827
Mattox, Matt *(Choreographer)* 2201, 2551, 3493, 3845, 4633
Mattson, Eric *(Cast)* 660, 4670
Mature, Victor *(Cast)* 2386, 4287
Matz, Peter *(Arrangements)* 3275
Matz, Peter *(Dance Arranger)* 98, 2190, 3187, 3286, 3815, 4682
Matz, Peter *(Musical Director)* 3187, 3275, 3286, 3815, 4585
Matz, Peter *(Orchestrations)* 147, 339, 373, 1649, 1729, 3126, 4566
Matz, Peter *(Vocal Arranger)* 98, 3286
Matz, Theodore A. *(Composer)* 3297
Matz, Theodore A. *(Lyricist)* 3297
Matzanauer, Adrienne *(Cast)* 2475
Maubourg, Jeanne *(Cast)* 2486
Mauceri, John *(Musical Director)* 4068
Maugham, Dora *(Cast)* 1275
Maugham, Somerset *(Author)* 1144
Maul, Betty *(Cast)* 1104
Maule, Brad *(Cast)* 2969
Maultsby, Carl *(Dance Arranger)* 2173
Maultsby, Carl *(Vocal Arranger)* 1816, 4192
Maurer, Michael *(Director)* 2142, 3752
Maurer, Michael *(Librettist)* 3752
Maurette, Marcelle *(Author)* 161
Maurice, Albert *(Composer)* 3856
Maurice, Marcus *(Cast)* 3568
Maurice, May *(Cast)* 2008
Maury, Richard *(Director)* 3110
Maury, Richard *(Librettist)* 2246, 3108, 3110, 3941
Maury, Richard *(Lyricist)* 3108, 3110
Mavin Productions *(Producer)* 1059
Mawin Productions *(Producer)* 3965
Max & Mahieu
    See also Mahieu.
Max & Mahieu *(Costumes)* 335, 3308, 4250, 4599
Maxcellas, The *(Cast)* 3822

Maxim, John *(Cast)* 2362
Maxmen, Mimi *(Costumes)* 1279, 3722
Maxmen, Mimi *(Set Design)* 1279
Maxson, Bob *(Choreographer)* 2084, 2096
Maxson, Bob *(Director)* 2084, 2096
Maxson, Helen *(Choreographer)* 2084, 2095, 2096
Maxson, Helen *(Director)* 2084, 2096
Maxson, Ruby *(Cast)* 2088
Maxwell, Arthur *(Cast)* 63, 2439, 2797
Maxwell, Chris *(Choreographer)* 3134
Maxwell, Edwin *(Director)* 4284
Maxwell, Elsa *(Composer)* 665
Maxwell, Elsa *(Producer)* 4677
Maxwell, Frank *(Cast)* 2680
Maxwell, Marilyn *(Cast)* 3091
Maxwell, Michael *(Producer)* 626
Maxwell, Mitchell *(Director)* 140, 747
Maxwell, Mitchell *(Producer)* 140, 478, 747
Maxwell, Vera *(Cast)* 4804
Maxwell, Vera *(Choreographer)* 968
Maxwell, William *(Cast)* 1646
May, Ada *(Cast)* 791, 3719
May, Billy *(Orchestrations)* 3428
May, Bobby *(Cast)* 4006
May, Deborah *(Cast)* 1402
May, Earl C. *(Cast)* 4076
May, Edna *(Cast)* 357, 675, 1543, 2788, 3092, 3834, 3857
May, Florence *(Cast)* 2291
May, Helen *(Cast)* 3446
May, Jane *(Cast)* 675
May, Maggie *(Cast)* 4354
May, Marty *(Cast)* 153, 372, 1423, 2401, 3381, 4586
May, Olive *(Cast)* 3388
May, Val *(Director)* 2240
May, William *(Producer)* 2754
Maye, Edythe *(Cast)* 1944
Mayehoff, Eddie *(Cast)* 3703
Mayer, Don *(Lyricist)* 3942
Mayer, Edwin Justus *(Author)* 1283, 1284
Mayer, Edwin Justus *(Librettist)* 1284
Mayer, George *(Set Design)* 1435
Mayer, Hy *(Costumes)* 1210, 4064
Mayer, Jeremy *(Cast)* 3318
Mayer, Jo *(Lighting Designer)* 2968, 3167
Mayer, Joseph *(Composer)* 2392, 3946, 4249
Mayer, Marcus *(Director)* 4554
Mayer, Michael *(Director)* 2038
Mayer, Ray *(Cast)* 297, 4152, 4291
Mayer, Timothy S. *(Librettist)* 3060
Mayerl, Billy *(Cast)* 4661
Mayerl, Billy *(Composer)* 702
Mayers, Lloyd *(Dance Arranger)* 4091
Mayers, Lloyd *(Vocal Arranger)* 4091
Mayerson, Frederic H. *(Producer)* 2143, 3862, 4031
Mayes, Sally *(Cast)* 784, 992, 4619
Mayfair, Mitzi *(Cast)* 622, 3955, 4267, 4823
Mayfair Productions *(Producer)* 1939
Mayfield, Cleo *(Cast)* 86, 473, 480, 577, 2135, 2587, 2732, 2900, 4858

Mayfield, Julian *(Cast)* 2591
Mayfield, Kathryn *(Cast)* 3104, 3415, 3860
Mayfield, Menlo *(Librettist)* 293
Mayfield, Menlo *(Lyricist)* 293
Mayfield, Percy *(Composer)* 1713
Mayfield, Percy *(Lyricist)* 1713
Mayhall, Jerry *(Arrangements)* 2077
Mayhew, Billy *(Composer)* 39
Mayhew, Billy *(Lyricist)* 39
Mayhew, Kate *(Cast)* 4544
Mayhew, Stella *(Cast)* 830, 1403, 1836, 1916, 2232, 2358, 2371, 2481, 2722, 4553, 4655, 4747
Mayhood, Orville *(Musical Director)* 2387
Mayhood, Orville L. *(Lyricist)* 3738
Maynard, Charles A. *(Director)* 2825, 3569
Maynard, Dorothy *(Cast)* 385, 3319
Maynard, Edwin *(Cast)* 1563
Maynard, Ruth *(Cast)* 3271
Mayne, Frank *(Cast)* 3323
Mayne, Leslie *(Lyricist)* 2844, 3098, 3313, 3322, 3803, 4115, 4430
Mayo, Don *(Cast)* 1510
Mayo, Fred *(Composer)* 1626
Mayo, Harry *(Cast)* 953
Mayo, Joan *(Costumes)* 2633
Mayo, Margaret *(Author)* 1904, 3534, 3740
Mayo, Margaret *(Librettist)* 3534, 3740, 4589
Mayo, Margaret *(Lyricist)* 3534
Mayo, Sam *(Composer)* 1763
Mayo, Sam *(Lyricist)* 1763
Mayon, John *(Cast)* 2498
Mayro, Jacqueline *(Cast)* 181, 766, 1709, 2278, 4678
Mayson, Edward *(Composer)* 3248
Mazel Musicals *(Producer)* 3926
Mazibuko, Brian *(Cast)* 4438
Mazier, Eddie *(Cast)* 3545
Mazin, Stan *(Choreographer)* 1262
Mazursky, Paul *(Cast)* 3940
Mazursky, Paul *(Director)* 2288
Mazzeo, Roger *(Cast)* 240
Mazzie, Marin *(Cast)* 3411
Mbonani, Themba *(Cast)* 4438
McAfee, Don *(Composer)* 1676
McAliece, F.J. *(Lighting Designer)* 722
McAlister, David *(Cast)* 3429
McAllen, Kathleen Rowe *(Cast)* 158
McAllister, Blue *(Cast)* 444, 3704
McAloney, Michael *(Producer)* 3846
McAnuff, Des *(Composer)* 1015, 2429
McAnuff, Des *(Director)* 394, 1015, 2429, 4676
McAnuff, Des *(Librettist)* 1015, 2429, 4676
McAnuff, Des *(Lyricist)* 1015, 2429
McAnuff, Des *(Vocal Arranger)* 1015
McArdle, Andrea *(Cast)* 150, 4138, 4146
McArdle, John *(Cast)* 1561
McArt, Jan *(Cast)* 190
McArt, Jan *(Producer)* 3576
McArthur, Edwin *(Composer)* 3720
McArthur, Edwin *(Musical Director)* 616
McArthur, Neil *(Orchestrations)* 1296

McAteer, Kathryn *(Cast)* 2142, 2790
McAuliffe, Jason *(Cast)* 1346
McAuliffe, Jason *(Composer)* 1346
McAuliffe, Jerry *(Cast)* 3423
McAvoy, Dan *(Cast)* 830, 2974, 3820
McAvoy, Dan *(Composer)* 2974
McAvoy, J.P. *(Author)* 3953
McBain, Allison *(Cast)* 2620
McBride, Edith Ethel *(Cast)* 1526
McBride, Irene *(Cast)* 2068, 4374
McBride, Ora *(Cast)* 2977
McBroom, Amanda *(Composer)* 4, 1804
McBroom, Amanda *(Librettist)* 1804
McBroom, Amanda *(Lyricist)* 4, 1804
McCabe, James *(Orchestrations)* 1962
McCabe, James C. *(Orchestrations)* 3403
McCall, Janet *(Cast)* 793
McCall, Marti *(Composer)* 1713
McCall, Marti *(Lyricist)* 1713
McCall, Nancy *(Cast)* 1813
McCallion, Joseph *(Cast)* 1014
McCamm, James *(Lighting Designer)* 3683
McCamm, James *(Set Design)* 3683
McCandless, Stanley *(Lighting Designer)* 3703
McCane, Mabel *(Cast)* 1560, 1562, 3866
McCane, Mabel *(Lyricist)* 548
McCann, Elizabeth I. *(Producer)* 2474
McCann, Elizabeth Ireland *(Producer)* 3142
McCann, Gene *(Cast)* 4332
McCann, Geraldine *(Cast)* 4125
McCarroll, Earl *(Cast)* 81
McCarroll, Earl *(Librettist)* 81
McCarroll, Ernest *(Cast)* 4220
McCarron, Charles *(Composer)* 3297
McCarron, Charles *(Lyricist)* 965, 1063, 3297, 3737
McCarron, Charles A. *(Composer)* 370
McCarron, Charles A. *(Lyricist)* 370
McCarry, Charles E. *(Set Design)* 1969, 2046, 2224, 4347
McCarter Theatre Company *(Producer)* 2305
McCarthy, Bob *(Lighting Designer)* 1269
McCarthy, Charles *(Cast)* 1283
McCarthy, Dorothy *(Cast)* 2382
McCarthy, Hector *(Composer)* 4589
McCarthy, Jeff *(Cast)* 533, 4020
McCarthy, Joe *(Lyricist)* 1963
McCarthy, Joseph *(Composer)* 4153
McCarthy, Joseph *(Lyricist)* 25, 89, 501, 560, 685, 931, 965, 1065, 1208, 1334, 1501, 1582, 1873, 1963, 2148, 2308, 3100, 3246, 3396, 3719, 3737, 3791, 4529, 4589, 4813, 4814, 4817, 4818, 4822, 4823
McCarthy, Justin Huntley *(Author)* 2670, 3219, 4539
McCarthy, Justin Huntley *(Librettist)* 2670
McCarthy, Justin Huntley *(Lyricist)* 2670
McCarthy, Kevin *(Cast)* 3841, 4706
McCarthy, Lawrence *(Librettist)* 2394
McCarthy, Margaret *(Cast)* 2382
McCarthy, Mary *(Cast)* 4015
McCarthy, Tom *(Cast)* 264
McCarthy, W.J. *(Cast)* 2258

McCarthy, William *(Cast)* 689, 3924
McCarthy Jr., Joseph *(Lyricist)* 2227, 4827
McCarthy Sisters, The *(Cast)* 1489
McCartney, Ellen *(Costumes)* 240
McCartney, Mary *(Librettist)* 164
McCartney, Paul *(Author)* 3903
McCartney, Paul *(Composer)* 3739, 4193
McCartney, Paul *(Librettist)* 3903
McCartney, Paul *(Lyricist)* 3739, 3903, 4193
McCarty, Ernest *(Composer)* 2051
McCarty, Ernest *(Lyricist)* 2051
McCarty, Mary *(Cast)* 454, 723, 1329, 2894, 4018
McCarty, Mary *(Composer)* 2294
McCarty, Mary *(Lyricist)* 2294
McCarty, Michael *(Cast)* 2318
McCarver, Bamboo *(Cast)* 2845
McCary, Ernest *(Orchestrations)* 2051
McCauley, Jack *(Cast)* 1440, 1475, 1874, 1886, 3409, 3955, 4174, 4826
McCauley, John *(Cast)* 1916
McCauley, Judith *(Cast)* 2219
McChesney, Ernest *(Cast)* 3767
McClain, Florence *(Additional Lyrics)* 1821
McClain, Florence *(Additional Music)* 1821
McClain, Florence *(Cast)* 2113
McClain, George *(Cast)* 1479, 1909
McClain, Marcia *(Cast)* 426, 1086
McClain, Saundra *(Cast)* 828
McClanahan, Rue *(Cast)* 2218
McClaskie, Alden *(Cast)* 3028
McCleary, Michael *(Composer)* 1134
McCleary, R.C. *(Set Design)* 719, 1454, 2964, 2974, 4014
McCleery, R.C. *(Musical Director)* 1610
McClellan, Clark *(Dance Arranger)* 4678
McClellan, Clark *(Musical Director)* 766, 2616
McClellan, Clark *(Orchestrations)* 415, 766, 4678
McClellan, Clark *(Vocal Arranger)* 415, 2616
McClellan, George B. *(Producer)* 976
McClellan, Jack *(Librettist)* 2380
McClelland, Kay *(Cast)* 775, 2143
McClelland, Keith *(Orchestrations)* 941
McClendon, Afi *(Cast)* 3285
McClendon, Rue *(Cast)* 1020
McClennahan, Charles *(Set Design)* 1425
McClennon, George *(Cast)* 3200, 3965
McClintic, Guthrie *(Director)* 2712, 2994
McClintic, Guthrie *(Producer)* 1007, 2712
McCloud *(Composer)* 655
McCloud *(Lyricist)* 655
McClure, Bob *(Cast)* 2357
McClure, Edna *(Cast)* 308
McColl, Mitzi *(Cast)* 4230
McCollin, A.W.F. *(Cast)* 402
McComas, Carroll *(Cast)* 3422
McComb, Malcolm *(Lyricist)* 1874, 4235
McConaughty, Jim *(Cast)* 4736
McConnell *(Composer)* 1925
McConnell *(Lyricist)* 1925
McConnell, Lula *(Cast)* 3407

McConnell, Lulu *(Cast)* 289, 931, 3436, 3538, 4033, 4545, 4816
McConnell, Ty *(Cast)* 840, 1012, 1249, 2633, 3602
McConrad, Guthrie *(Director)* 557
McCord, Nancy *(Cast)* 82, 324, 2786, 4550
McCorder, Lucille *(Costumes)* 4271
McCorkle, David *(Cast)* 2220
McCormack, Danny *(Cast)* 3025, 3026
McCormack, Frank *(Director)* 110, 2888, 3147, 4148, 4555
McCormick, Andrew A. *(Producer)* 1896
McCormick, Dolly *(Cast)* 1980
McCormick, Frank *(Director)* 2489
McCormick, Michael *(Cast)* 705, 2333, 3853
McCormick, Myron *(Cast)* 3188, 4096
McCormick, Pat *(Librettist)* 4627
McCormick, Pearl *(Cast)* 3361
McCormick, Robert *(Cast)* 2654, 3695
McCourt, Sean *(Cast)* 1969
McCown, Ellen *(Cast)* 1698
McCoy, Bessie
   See also Bessie McCoy Davis.
McCoy, Bessie *(Cast)* 1151, 2715, 2900, 4115, 4364, 4753, 4805
McCoy, Bessie *(Lyricist)* 4805
McCoy, Eleanor *(Cast)* 4383
McCoy, Frank *(Director)* 1275, 1440
McCoy, Joe *(Composer)* 3428
McCoy, Joe *(Lyricist)* 3428
McCoy, Kerry *(Musical Director)* 2436
McCoy, Michael *(Composer)* 1232
McCoy, Nellie *(Cast)* 2715, 3977
McCoy, R. *(Composer)* 1296
McCoy, R. *(Lyricist)* 1296
McCracken, Joan *(Cast)* 404, 462, 596, 961, 2797, 3263
McCrane, Paul *(Cast)* 1053
McCree, Junie *(Cast)* 228, 246, 1563, 1728, 1746, 2710, 2851, 3883, 4098, 4222, 4691
McCree, Junie *(Composer)* 3313
McCree, Junie *(Librettist)* 1746, 2710, 3026
McCree, Junie *(Lyricist)* 246, 1120, 1746, 2261, 2667, 2710, 3313, 4757
McCreery, Bud *(Cast)* 3940
McCreery, Bud *(Composer)* 272, 1023, 1049, 1362, 1363, 2554, 2804, 3186, 3484, 3615, 3940, 3941, 3942, 4047, 4416
McCreery, Bud *(Librettist)* 2554, 2804
McCreery, Bud *(Lyricist)* 272, 1023, 1049, 1362, 1363, 2554, 2804, 3186, 3484, 3615, 3940, 3941, 3942, 4047, 4416
McCreery, Bud *(Producer)* 4156
McCreery, Bud *(Vocal Arranger)* 2804
McCullers, Carson *(Author)* 1222
McCullers, Carson *(Librettist)* 1222
McCulloh, Barbara *(Cast)* 2354
McCullough, Carl *(Cast)* 628, 2119, 4784
McCullough, Paul
   See also Clark & McCullough.
McCullough, Paul *(Cast)* 1856, 2403, 3426, 3659, 4179, 4374, 4583

McCutcheon, Bill *(Cast)*   825, 1648, 2018, 3108, 3186, 3942, 4627

McCutcheon, George Barr *(Author)*   4860

McCutcheon, John T. *(Costumes)*   4201

McCutcheon, Wallace *(Cast)*   1131, 1199, 1569, 1849, 3621, 3681, 4017

McCutcheon, Wallace *(Choreographer)*   968

McDaniel *(Composer)*   432

McDaniel *(Lyricist)*   432

McDaniel, John *(Dance Arranger)*   589

McDaniel, John *(Musical Director)*   589

McDaniel, John *(Vocal Arranger)*   589

McDaniel, Keith *(Cast)*   2427

McDaniel, William Foster *(Arrangements)*   1099

McDaniel, William Foster *(Musical Director)*   1099

McDermott, Keith *(Cast)*   1775

McDermott, Michelle *(Cast)*   2676

McDermott, W.J. *(Cast)*   1758

McDevitt, Bob *(Producer)*   280

McDonald, Bill *(Choreographer)*   62

McDonald, Gertrude *(Cast)*   1419, 3254, 4335, 4392

McDonald, Grace *(Cast)*   3292, 4557

McDonald, James *(Composer)*   4062

McDonald, James *(Librettist)*   4062

McDonald, James *(Lyricist)*   4062

McDonald, Joe *(Composer)*   3739

McDonald, Joe *(Lyricist)*   3739

McDonald, Marie *(Cast)*   1565

McDonald, Ray *(Cast)*   247, 3390

McDonald, Sadie *(Cast)*   3228

McDonald, Tanny *(Cast)*   2229

McDonald, W.H. *(Cast)*   3570, 3881

McDonough, Glen *(Author)*   2795

McDonough, Harry *(Cast)*   175

McDowall, Roddy *(Cast)*   623, 928, 3188

McDowell, Bob *(Arrangements)*   2416

McDowell, Bob *(Musical Director)*   2416

McDowell, John *(Cast)*   202

McDuffie, Laura *(Cast)*   4689

McElhinay, Rick *(Cast)*   2320

McElroy, Jackie *(Cast)*   3505

McElroy, Michael *(Cast)*   1890

McElwaine, James *(Musical Director)*   2441

McElwaine, James *(Orchestrations)*   1589, 2441, 4139

McEnroe, Robert E. *(Librettist)*   1076

McEvoy, J.P. *(Librettist)*   86, 123, 125, 827, 3179, 4142, 4819

McEvoy, J.P. *(Lyricist)*   123, 124, 827

McEwen, Odetta *(Cast)*   1046

McEwen, Walter *(Cast)*   3948

McFadden *(Composer)*   2133

McFadden *(Lyricist)*   2133

McFarland, C.K. *(Cast)*   914

McFarland, C.K. *(Librettist)*   914

McGail, Paul *(Cast)*   782

McGarity, Jerry *(Cast)*   992

McGarrahan, Jerry *(Musical Director)*   1957

McGee, Corliss *(Set Design)*   2032

McGee, Richard Dwight *(Costumes)*   3329

McGee, Rusty *(Composer)*   3853

McGee, Rusty *(Lyricist)*   3853

McGee, Truly *(Choreographer)*   1987, 3121

McGee, Truly *(Director)*   1934

McGhee, Brownie *(Cast)*   3983

McGhee, John *(Musical Director)*   2698

McGhie, John *(Musical Director)*   48, 276, 968, 1111, 2145, 2292, 2430, 2502, 2532, 2701, 2724, 3177, 3773, 3943, 4250, 4762

McGibeney, Donald *(Composer)*   3768

McGill, Alma *(Cast)*   3357

McGill, Bruce *(Cast)*   3060

McGill, Everett *(Cast)*   3764

McGillin, Howard *(Cast)*   2359, 3070

McGinley, Phyllis *(Lyricist)*   3178, 4018

McGinn, Frank *(Cast)*   3230

McGinn, Walter *(Cast)*   1864

McGinness, Joe *(Author)*   3871

McGiveney *(Cast)*   3629

McGiveney, Michael *(Librettist)*   3629

McGiver, John *(Cast)*   1674

McGlennon, George *(Cast)*   1983

McGonigal, William *(Director)*   516

McGough, Robert *(Lyricist)*   4701

McGourty, Patricia *(Costumes)*   394, 669, 1015, 1077, 1402, 3555, 3608, 4022

McGovern, Dennis *(Cast)*   1635

McGovern, Maureen *(Cast)*   4019, 4371

McGowan, Jack *(Cast)*   1485, 2268, 2494, 2767, 3723, 4269, 4648, 4836

McGowan, Jack *(Director)*   4177

McGowan, Jack *(Librettist)*   1137, 1800, 3850, 4177, 4240

McGowan, Jack *(Producer)*   3850

McGowan, Jane *(Cast)*   2085

McGowan, John *(Author)*   1215, 3993

McGowan, John *(Director)*   3379

McGowan, John *(Librettist)*   921, 1323, 1528, 1929, 3005

McGrane, Don *(Orchestrations)*   3166

McGrane, Paul *(Composer)*   2099, 4143, 4677

McGrane, Paul *(Conductor)*   507

McGrath, George *(Cast)*   1064, 3418

McGrath, John *(Author)*   4685

McGrath, Mark *(Cast)*   1092

McGrath, Matthew *(Cast)*   4744

McGrath, Michael *(Cast)*   4255

McGrath, Paul *(Cast)*   3816

McGrath, Thomas *(Cast)*   3450

McGraw, Martha *(Cast)*   3450

McGraw, William *(Cast)*   1085

McGreevey, Annie *(Cast)*   2687, 2949, 4288

McGregor, Dion *(Lyricist)*   1107

McGregor, G.W. *(Producer)*   4620

McGroder, Carol *(Producer)*   1581

McGroder, Jack *(Costumes)*   319

McGroder, Jack *(Set Design)*   319

McGuckin, Albert *(Cast)*   4646

McGuinn, Roger *(Composer)*   3695

McGuinn, Roger *(Lyricist)*   3695

McGuire, Biff *(Additional Dialogue)*   3630

McGuire, Biff *(Cast)*   339, 961, 1766, 2234, 3630, 4096

McGuire, Dorothy *(Cast)*   4256

McGuire, Paul C. *(Set Design)* 2928
McGuire, William Anthony *(Director)* 376, 1404, 3721, 3766, 4023, 4357, 4683
McGuire, William Anthony *(Librettist)* 376, 1404, 1667, 2308, 2872, 3721, 3766, 3953, 4023, 4357, 4683, 4818
McGuire III, John Thomas *(Cast)* 2658
McGunigle, Brian *(Librettist)* 3714
McGunigle, Robert *(Librettist)* 4583
McGurn, Ned *(Choreographer)* 1137, 2068, 2444, 3002, 3104, 3990
McHale, Duke *(Cast)* 247, 3584, 4825
McHorter, Evlyn *(Costumes)* 3511, 4817
McHugh, Augustin *(Librettist)* 1875, 1882, 2174
McHugh, Burke *(Cast)* 1697
McHugh, David *(Composer)* 1282
McHugh, Frank *(Cast)* 993, 1215, 3953
McHugh, James *(Lyricist)* 4303
McHugh, Jimmy *(Cast)* 3153, 3639
McHugh, Jimmy *(Composer)* 39, 206, 432, 441, 442, 487, 787, 892, 893, 894, 895, 1460, 1827, 2140, 2301, 3018, 3444, 3639, 3704, 3709, 3905, 3946, 3993, 4010, 4131, 4174, 4180, 4197, 4427, 4534, 4545, 4847, 4848
McHugh, Jimmy *(Lyricist)* 4427
McIlmoyle, Jean *(Cast)* 1466
McIlvane, Thomas *(Costumes)* 1640
McInerney, Bernie *(Cast)* 942
McIntosh, Hattie *(Cast)* 2111, 2979, 4088
McIntyre, Dianne *(Choreographer)* 1161, 1671, 3001
McIntyre, Frank *(Cast)* 495, 1691, 3251, 3622, 3775, 4001, 4213
McIntyre, Gerry *(Cast)* 549, 3285
McIntyre, Jack *(Cast)* 3604
McIntyre, James
 See also McIntyre & Heath.
McIntyre, James *(Cast)* 110, 1731, 1799, 3677
McIntyre, John *(Cast)* 2119
McIntyre, Leila *(Cast)* 968, 1558, 2493, 2964, 3045, 4647
McIntyre, Molly *(Cast)* 1221
McIntyre & Heath
 See also Tom Heath and James McIntyre.
McIntyre & Heath *(Cast)* 1823, 3958
McIver, Ray *(Librettist)* 1592
McIver, Ray *(Lyricist)* 1592
McKay, Frederic *(Producer)* 543, 4589, 4642
McKay, Kay *(Cast)* 203, 2808
McKay, Neil *(Choreographer)* 2147
McKay, Windsor *(Author)* 2534
McKaye, Dorothea *(Cast)* 3868
McKayle, Donald *(Choreographer)* 1063, 1601, 2075, 2306, 3656, 4091, 4384
McKayle, Donald *(Director)* 1063, 2415, 3656
McKean, Verd *(Arrangements)* 1883
McKean, Verd *(Musical Director)* 1883
McKechnie, Donna *(Cast)* 155, 746, 832, 944, 1158, 2072, 3018, 3603, 4146
McKee *(Producer)* 998
McKee, Frank *(Producer)* 48, 1521, 1925, 4130, 4165
McKee, Jeanellen *(Producer)* 2288
McKee, John *(Cast)* 1520
McKee, John *(Director)* 2377, 2564, 2605, 3868

McKee, Julia *(Director)* 2446
McKee, Lonette *(Cast)* 1289
McKee, Tom *(Lyricist)* 242
McKeever, Jacquelyn *(Cast)* 649, 3234
McKellar, John *(Composer)* 4433
McKellar, John *(Librettist)* 2305, 4433
McKellar, John *(Lyricist)* 2305, 4433
McKenna, Boots *(Choreographer)* 1127, 1414, 2397, 3822
McKenna, J.P. *(Composer)* 2996
McKenna, J.P. *(Lyricist)* 2996
McKenna, Kenneth *(Cast)* 2821
McKenna, Philip C. *(Producer)* 3918
McKenna, Virginia *(Cast)* 3454
McKenna, William *(Lyricist)* 3729
McKenna, William C. *(Lyricist)* 2232
McKenna, William J. *(Composer)* 592
McKennan, Arnett *(Lyricist)* 814
McKenney, John *(Musical Director)* 1418
McKenney, Ruth *(Author)* 4734
McKenzie, Alice *(Cast)* 3978
McKenzie, Branice *(Cast)* 3905
McKenzie, Branice *(Composer)* 3905
McKenzie, Branice *(Lyricist)* 3905
McKenzie, Herbert *(Cast)* 929
McKenzie, Julia *(Cast)* 2682, 3967
McKenzie, Julia *(Director)* 4067
McKeon, Doug *(Cast)* 4459
McKeon, Joseph H. *(Lyricist)* 2825
McKernon, John *(Lighting Designer)* 1425
McKie, Shirley *(Cast)* 344
McKinley, Mary *(Costumes)* 1010, 2297, 2962
McKinley, Philip William *(Cast)* 2861
McKinley, Philip William *(Director)* 3708
McKinley, Tom *(Costumes)* 4349
McKinney, John *(Composer)* 3010
McKinney, John *(Dance Arranger)* 1776, 2993
McKinney, John *(Librettist)* 1897
McKinney, John *(Orchestrations)* 705, 1776, 1897, 3368, 4390
McKinney, John *(Vocal Arranger)* 198, 1776, 4390, 4412
McKinney, Julian Jean *(Cast)* 1876
McKinney, Nina Mae *(Cast)* 289, 882, 4281
McKinney, Tom *(Cast)* 1092
McKinnon, Fred *(Lighting Designer)* 1815
McKinnon, Rik *(Cast)* 2092, 2094, 2095
McKneely, Joey *(Choreographer)* 4031
McKnight, Thomas *(Composer)* 1448
McKnight, Thomas *(Lyricist)* 1448
McKnight, Tom *(Additional Dialogue)* 1840
McKnight, Tom *(Librettist)* 4174
McKuen, Rod *(Cast)* 499
McKuen, Rod *(Composer)* 499
McKuen, Rod *(Lyricist)* 499
McLain, John *(Lighting Designer)* 114, 496, 1609, 2970, 2992, 3169, 3873, 3908, 4109, 4171
McLane, Derek *(Set Design)* 1291, 1822
McLane, Lorenzo *(Cast)* 471
McLaren, Ivor *(Cast)* 2004

Meade *(Set Design)* 1869
Meade, Ada *(Cast)* 3658
Meade, Norman *(Composer)* 3739
Meade, Norman *(Lyricist)* 3739
Meade, Tom *(Cast)* 537
Meade, Tommy *(Cast)* 543
Meader, George *(Cast)* 672, 2255
Meadows, Hunt *(Cast)* 3997
Meadows, Kristen *(Cast)* 1256
Meadows, Michael *(Set Design)* 1816
Meara, Anne *(Cast)* 1999, 2804
Meara, Anne *(Librettist)* 4
Mears, DeAnn *(Cast)* 1017
Mears, Elizabeth *(Cast)* 2253
Mears, John Henry *(Librettist)* 2960
Mears, John Henry *(Lyricist)* 560, 685, 2960
Mears, John Henry *(Producer)* 2253
Mears, Stannard *(Author)* 1831
Meat Loaf *(Cast)* 2953, 3651, 3741, 3742
Medford, Don *(Producer)* 1754
Medford, Kay *(Cast)* 90, 607, 1420, 2227, 4582
Medley, Cassandra *(Librettist)* 4
Medoff, Mark *(Author)* 2704
Medoff, Mark *(Lyricist)* 2704
Mee, Kirk *(Director)* 973
Meech, Cliff *(Lyricist)* 2122
Meech, George J. *(Cast)* 2761
Meegan, Patrick *(Composer)* 533
Meegan, Thomas *(Cast)* 4381
Meehan, Aileen *(Cast)* 3185
Meehan, Danny *(Cast)* 1420, 1427, 4028, 4682
Meehan, Harry *(Cast)* 117, 1286, 3003, 3082, 4650
Meehan, John *(Director)* 1484, 3185, 3723
Meehan, Thomas *(Librettist)* 36, 150, 154, 155, 2064, 3181
Meehan, Thomas *(Lyricist)* 2662
Meehan Jr., John *(Librettist)* 1817, 3767
Meek, Donald *(Cast)* 1598, 2537, 2981, 3063, 3207
Meek, Joe *(Composer)* 3695
Meek, Joe *(Lyricist)* 3695
Meek, Kate *(Cast)* 2624
Meeker, George *(Cast)* 2253
Meeker, Jesse *(Dance Arranger)* 619
Meers, Paul *(Cast)* 3709
Megley, Macklin *(Director)* 1352
Megrue, Roi Cooper *(Author)* 126
Megrue, Roi Cooper *(Librettist)* 126
Mehan, Dodd *(Cast)* 4548
Mehler, Jack *(Lighting Designer)* 2038
Mehr, Rachel *(Costumes)* 2322
Meier, Ron *(Cast)* 3561
Meighan, Thomas *(Cast)* 41, 425
Meilhac, Henri *(Author)* 653, 2507
Meisel, Bella *(Composer)* 4342
Meisel, Bella *(Lyricist)* 4342
Meiser, Edith *(Cast)* 1446, 1447, 1448, 2453, 3436, 4516
Meiser, Edith *(Librettist)* 1446
Meiser, Edith *(Lyricist)* 1446
Meisner, Sanford *(Cast)* 1446, 2228

Meiss, Edwin *(Librettist)* 3104
Meister, Norman *(Cast)* 337
Meit, Marvin R. *(Producer)* 140, 747
Mekka, Eddie *(Cast)* 2472
Melanie *(Composer)* 13
Melanie *(Lyricist)* 13
Melchior, Lauritz *(Cast)* 177
Mele, Rande *(Cast)* 2704
Meleck, Tom *(Lighting Designer)* 400, 4773
Melfi, Leonard *(Author)* 4294
Melfi, Leonard *(Librettist)* 781, 3233
Melford, Austin *(Cast)* 3156
Melford, Austin *(Librettist)* 700, 3310
Melford, Austin *(Lyricist)* 3310
Melford, Jack *(Cast)* 2976
Melford, Quentin *(Author)* 2972
Melin, Frank *(Director)* 3822
Melis, Jose *(Composer)* 4264
Mell, Marisa *(Cast)* 2777
Mellin, Robert *(Lyricist)* 4264
Mellish, Fuller *(Cast)* 3056, 4692
Mellish, Harold *(Cast)* 3436
Mellish, Mary *(Cast)* 3078
Mellish Jr., Fuller *(Cast)* 3436, 3556
Mello, Al *(Dance Arranger)* 2626
Mellon, Edward *(Musical Director)* 1632
Mellon, Edward *(Vocal Arranger)* 1632
Mellon, James J. *(Choreographer)* 1279
Mellon, James J. *(Composer)* 4515
Mellon, James J. *(Librettist)* 4515
Mellon, James J. *(Lyricist)* 4515
Mellor, Tom *(Composer)* 2334, 3755, 4206
Mellor, Tom *(Lyricist)* 2334, 3755, 4206
Mellow, Stephen *(Producer)* 2018
Melnick, Daniel *(Producer)* 2304
Melnick, Linda Rodgers *(Composer)* 4363
Melnick, Marjorie *(Director)* 564
Melnotte, Violet *(Producer)* 2570
Melodee Four, The *(Cast)* 4763
Melrose, Ron *(Dance Arranger)* 16
Melrose, Ronald *(Composer)* 1371, 4533
Melrose, Ronald *(Dance Arranger)* 146, 2754, 3444, 4727
Melrose, Ronald *(Lyricist)* 4533
Melrose, Ronald *(Musical Director)* 146, 4034
Melrose, Ronald *(Orchestrations)* 4034
Melrose, Walter *(Composer)* 478, 2200
Melrose, Walter *(Lyricist)* 478, 1063
Melso, Chino *(Cast)* 4205
Melson, Joe *(Composer)* 3695
Melson, Joe *(Lyricist)* 3695
Meltzer, Robert *(Lyricist)* 2748
Melville, Alan *(Librettist)* 2168, 3107
Melville, Alan *(Lyricist)* 1408, 1467, 2168, 2227, 3107, 4153
Melville, Emile *(Cast)* 3432
Melville, Herman *(Author)* 406
Melville, Rose *(Cast)* 604, 3998
Melville, Rose *(Composer)* 3998
Melville, Rose *(Lyricist)* 3998

Melville, Winnie *(Cast)* 3583
Melvin, Murray *(Cast)* 3259
Members Yale Drama Assn.
See also Yale University Dramatic Assn.
Members Yale Drama Assn. *(Producer)* 4622
Members of the 385th Inf. *(Producer)* 214
Menace, Len *(Cast)* 4692
Menchell, Ivan *(Librettist)* 4027
Menchen, Joseph *(Lighting Designer)* 1459,
3585, 3951
Menchen, Joseph C. *(Lighting Designer)* 737
Mencher, Murray *(Composer)* 1127
Mendelsohn, David *(Orchestrations)* 2610
Mendelson, Gary *(Cast)* 3601
Mendelssohn, Felix *(Music Based On)* 4256
Mendoza, David *(Musical Director)* 2023, 2024, 2098,
2099, 2161, 2162, 4143
Mendoza, Dorothy *(Composer)* 4433
Mendoza, Dorothy *(Librettist)* 4433
Mendoza, Dorothy *(Lyricist)* 4433
Mendum, Georgia Drew *(Cast)* 1563, 2922
Menefee, Pete *(Costumes)* 2796, 3637
Menendez, Brad *(Cast)* 1757
Menken, Alan *(Composer)* 171, 245, 330, 754, 1038,
1591, 2038, 2171, 2307, 2544, 3448, 3557, 3666
Menken, Alan *(Director)* 3666
Menken, Alan *(Lyricist)* 3557, 3666
Menkes *(Costumes)* 3034
Mennefee, Pete *(Costumes)* 3936
Mensoff, Richard *(Lighting Designer)* 2913
Mentel, Jim *(Composer)* 3076
Mentel, Jim *(Lyricist)* 3076
Menten, Dale F. *(Composer)* 2001
Menten, Dale F. *(Lyricist)* 2001
Menten, Dale F. *(Musical Director)* 2001
Menzies, Angus *(Cast)* 3885
Meorz, Otto C.A. *(Orchestrations)* 968
Meranus, Norman *(Composer)* 2511
Meranus, Norman *(Lyricist)* 2511
Mercado, Hector *(Cast)* 2775
Mercado, Hector Jaime *(Cast)* 678, 1063, 3830, 4788
Mercardo, Ralph *(Producer)* 2356
Mercedes *(Set Design)* 621, 4677
Mercer, Beryl *(Cast)* 1357
Mercer, Frances *(Cast)* 4557
Mercer, Johnny *(Composer)* 3178, 3837, 4423
Mercer, Johnny *(Lyricist)* 125, 146, 213, 446, 447,
478, 964, 1359, 1373, 1385, 1448, 1619, 2204, 2484,
2611, 3175, 3178, 3352, 3385, 3428, 3705, 3837, 3840,
3888, 3905, 4091, 4123, 4131, 4291, 4314, 4423, 4498,
4586, 4799
Mercer, Mabel *(Cast)* 1318
Mercer, Marian *(Cast)* 128, 1436, 1993, 3110, 3111,
3195, 3603, 4789
Mercer, Ruby *(Cast)* 1352, 4670
Mercer, Will *(Composer)* 4098
Mercer, Will *(Lyricist)* 4098
Mercier, G.W. *(Costumes)* 674, 1700
Mercier, G.W. *(Set Design)* 674, 1700, 1739
Mercier, Rene *(Composer)* 1343, 4240

Mercouri, Melina *(Cast)* 2106, 2659
Mercury Theatre *(Producer)* 189, 919
Meredith, Burgess *(Cast)* 55, 1416, 1748, 2306,
3919, 4368
Meredith, Burgess *(Director)* 477, 1748, 2450
Meredith, Lee *(Cast)* 3019
Meredith, Morley *(Cast)* 751
Merimee, Prosper *(Author)* 653
Merkel, Una *(Cast)* 4270
Merkerson, S. Epatha *(Cast)* 166, 1099
Merkin, Robby *(Dance Arranger)* 2852
Merkin, Robby *(Orchestrations)* 474, 690, 1161, 1873,
2544, 2598, 2852, 4618
Merkin, Robby *(Vocal Arranger)* 474, 2852
Merkyl, John *(Cast)* 1014, 2387, 3323
Merle, Margaret *(Cast)* 3172
Merle, Sandi *(Composer)* 4347
Merle, Sandi *(Lyricist)* 4347
Merley, Heinz *(Author)* 3012
Merlin, F.S. *(Librettist)* 568
Merlin, Frank *(Cast)* 3874
Merlin, Frank *(Producer)* 4253
Merlin, Frank S. *(Director)* 670, 4021
Merlin, Joanna *(Cast)* 1265, 3927
Merlin, Ving *(Musical Director)* 84, 2397
Merlin, Ving *(Orchestrations)* 2397
Merlo, Michael *(Composer)* 4264
Merlo, Michael *(Lyricist)* 4264
Merman, Ethel *(Cast)* 153, 163, 619, 1109, 1416, 1492,
1528, 1709, 1760, 3359, 3674, 4058, 4142, 4267
Merman, Ethel *(Voice)* 3793
Merola, Gaetano *(Composer)* 93
Merola, Gaetano *(Musical Director)* 1285, 1530, 3051,
3081, 4133
Merriam, Eve *(Author)* 2134
Merriam, Eve *(Librettist)* 788
Merriam, Eve *(Lyricist)* 2134
Merrick, David *(Producer)* 34, 273, 521, 656, 1029, 1061,
1242, 1359, 1373, 1709, 1764, 1828, 1990, 2014, 2048,
2050, 2150, 2190, 2297, 2364, 2660, 2777, 3259, 3271,
3294, 3445, 3482, 3516, 3603, 3731, 3761, 4160, 4190,
4196, 4270, 4566, 4749
Merrick, Mike *(Producer)* 869
Merrick, Walt *(Composer)* 1296
Merrick, Walt *(Lyricist)* 1296
Merrigal, Alice *(Costumes)* 2393, 2661
Merrill, Blanche *(Composer)* 815, 3009, 3617, 4686,
4817, 4851
Merrill, Blanche *(Lyricist)* 70, 473, 815, 1704, 1944, 1946,
2180, 2696, 3009, 3345, 3399, 3617, 4440, 4686, 4806,
4810, 4811, 4814, 4815, 4817, 4838, 4851
Merrill, Bob *(Composer)* 521, 656, 1645, 1739, 1828, 1846,
1873, 3113, 3577, 4196, 4264, 4270
Merrill, Bob *(Librettist)* 1645, 1739, 3564, 3577
Merrill, Bob *(Lyricist)* 521, 656, 974, 1420, 1645, 1739,
1828, 1846, 1873, 2076, 2980, 3113, 3564, 3577, 3682,
4196, 4264, 4270
Merrill, Gary *(Cast)* 4340, 4706
Merrill, Howard *(Producer)* 3234
Merrill, Louis G. *(Composer)* 1624

Merrill, Marcia Lee *(Choreographer)* 345
Merrill, Paul *(Cast)* 564
Merrill, Scott *(Cast)* 4369
Merriman, Leo *(Musical Director)* 1758, 2328, 2335
Merritt, Theresa *(Cast)* 1222, 1616, 3001, 3321
Merson, Billy *(Composer)* 1963
Merson, Billy *(Lyricist)* 1963
Merson, Marc *(Producer)* 134
Mertz, Paul *(Vocal Arranger)* 1839
Merzvinsky, Edward *(Producer)* 1164
Meskill, Jack *(Composer)* 1136
Meskill, Jack *(Lyricist)* 1136
Messager, Andre *(Author)* 2524, 4554
Messager, Andre *(Composer)* 2524, 2937, 3079, 4554
Messel, Oliver *(Cast)* 4341
Messel, Oliver *(Costumes)* 791, 1511, 2000, 4469, 4581
Messel, Oliver *(Set Design)* 791, 2000, 4341, 4469, 4581
Messick, Don *(Voice)* 57
Mestayer, Harry *(Cast)* 3011, 4365
Metaxa, Georges *(Cast)* 503, 672, 1805, 3699, 4581
Metcalf, Ron *(Cast)* 4697
Metcalf, Ron *(Musical Director)* 4697
Metcalf, Ronald P. *(Musical Director)* 3724
Metcalf, Steven *(Composer)* 1093
Metcalf, Steven *(Musical Director)* 1093
Metcalfe, Edward *(Cast)* 2071
Metezl, Lothar *(Lyricist)* 3698
Meth, Max *(Musical Director)* 202, 203, 204, 206, 289, 341, 612, 971, 1101, 1342, 1577, 1679, 1693, 1799, 2187, 2432, 2453, 3170, 3365, 3850, 3899, 3990, 4267, 4335, 4524, 4828
Metheny, Russell *(Set Design)* 528, 1004, 1155, 2651, 3165
Methot, Mayo *(Cast)* 1667, 4083
Methven, Florence *(Composer)* 377
Metropolitan Stage Prods. *(Producer)* 2222
Metz, Janet *(Cast)* 1234
Metz, Theodore *(Composer)* 2796
Metz, Theodore M. *(Composer)* 662, 1425, 2415, 4390
Metzl, Beatrice *(Lyricist)* 2751
Metzl, Ervine *(Set Design)* 4047
Metzl, Lothar *(Librettist)* 1413
Metzl, Lothar *(Lyricist)* 2751, 3036, 3698
Metzler, Lawrence *(Lighting Designer)* 2375, 4485
Meyer, Adolf *(Producer)* 606
Meyer, Charles *(Cast)* 1078
Meyer, Chuck *(Composer)* 4829
Meyer, Chuck *(Lyricist)* 4829
Meyer, Dede *(Composer)* 3920, 4157, 4401
Meyer, Dede *(Lyricist)* 3920, 4157, 4401
Meyer, Dede *(Producer)* 3920
Meyer, Deed *(Composer)* 1347
Meyer, Deed *(Lyricist)* 1347
Meyer, Don *(Composer)* 4273
Meyer, Don *(Lyricist)* 4273
Meyer, Donna *(Costumes)* 962
Meyer, George *(Composer)* 3031, 4033
Meyer, George W. *(Composer)* 959, 1058, 1334, 1405, 1626, 1763, 2448, 2462, 2856, 3018, 3175, 3737, 3827, 4033, 4661, 4838

Meyer, George W. *(Lyricist)* 2462, 4661
Meyer, Henry *(Lyricist)* 4249
Meyer, Henry *(Producer)* 3907
Meyer, Irwin *(Producer)* 150, 1955, 4744
Meyer, John *(Composer)* 1436, 1648, 3484, 3890, 4643
Meyer, John *(Librettist)* 1363, 4643
Meyer, John *(Lyricist)* 1436, 1648, 2279, 2913, 3484, 3890, 4643
Meyer, Joseph *(Composer)* 124, 292, 391, 487, 702, 1296, 1460, 1859, 1923, 2112, 2238, 2277, 2382, 2392, 2972, 3020, 3103, 3104, 3149, 3444, 3662, 3953, 3966, 4235, 4249, 4320, 4581, 4730, 4766, 4799, 4824
Meyer, Joseph *(Lyricist)* 1296, 4730
Meyer, Joseph *(Orchestrations)* 2636
Meyer, Leo *(Composer)* 3926
Meyer, Leo *(Costumes)* 3302
Meyer, Leo *(Set Design)* 3302
Meyer, Leo W. *(Composer)* 3926
Meyer, Leo W. *(Lyricist)* 3926
Meyer, Paul *(Musical Director)* 2393
Meyer, Pieter *(Costumes)* 208, 4283
Meyer, Richard *(Composer)* 2976
Meyer, Sol *(Lyricist)* 2077, 2078
Meyer, Stan *(Set Design)* 330
Meyerhoff, Tom O. *(Producer)* 2852
Meyerovitch, D. *(Composer)* 1609
Meyerovitch, D. *(Lyricist)* 1609
Meyerowitz, David *(Composer)* 1279
Meyerowitz, David *(Lyricist)* 1279
Meyerowitz, Jan *(Composer)* 309
Meyers, Bubsy *(Composer)* 1296
Meyers, Bubsy *(Lyricist)* 1296
Meyers, Lanny *(Arrangements)* 3926
Meyers, Lanny *(Composer)* 1736, 3926
Meyers, Lanny *(Dance Arranger)* 1974, 3217
Meyers, Lanny *(Librettist)* 4167
Meyers, Lanny *(Lyricist)* 1736, 3926
Meyers, Lanny *(Musical Director)* 3722, 3926, 4167, 4769
Meyers, Lanny *(Orchestrations)* 3112, 3217, 4769
Meyers, Lanny *(Vocal Arranger)* 3217
Meyers, Nicholas *(Arrangements)* 793
Meyers, Nicholas *(Composer)* 169, 793
Meyers, Timothy *(Cast)* 1664
Meyers, Warren B. *(Composer)* 4388
Meyers, Zeke *(Lyricist)* 465, 733, 3057
Mezzio, John *(Arrangements)* 4799
Mezzio, John *(Musical Director)* 4799
Mezzio, John *(Orchestrations)* 4799
Mgt. III Prods. *(Producer)* 634
Mhlongo, Ndaba *(Conductor)* 3836
Michael, Margaret *(Librettist)* 1270
Michael, Patricia *(Cast)* 3429
Michael, Paul *(Cast)* 3988
Michaelis, Lisa *(Cast)* 3136
Michaelis, Robert *(Cast)* 1610
Michaels, Bert *(Cast)* 2660, 3564
Michaels, Bert *(Choreographer)* 1730, 2433
Michaels, Edwin *(Cast)* 3495
Michaels, Frankie *(Cast)* 2713

Michaels, Gloria *(Cast)* 2511
Michaels, Jackie *(Cast)* 4782
Michaels, Jerryn *(Lighting Designer)* 1508
Michaels, Laura *(Cast)* 2962
Michaels, Lorne *(Librettist)* 1512
Michaels, Lorne *(Producer)* 1512
Michaels, Patricia *(Librettist)* 2754
Michaels, Richard *(Director)* 4405
Michaels, Sidney *(Author)* 1730
Michaels, Sidney *(Librettist)* 367, 1634, 1730
Michaels, Sidney *(Lyricist)* 367, 1730
Michaels, Steve *(Composer)* 4347
Michaels, Steve *(Lyricist)* 4347
Michaels, Steve *(Musical Director)* 4347
Michel, Henry *(Cast)* 4096
Michel, Scott *(Author)* 4005
Michel, Werner *(Composer)* 1413, 3698
Michel, Werner *(Librettist)* 1413
Michel, Werner *(Lyricist)* 3036, 3698
Michele, Linda *(Cast)* 2742
Michelena, Kate *(Cast)* 1682
Michelena, Vera *(Cast)* 1308, 1417, 1519, 1555, 1570, 1967, 2490, 2605, 2832, 3087, 4269, 4434, 4808, 4815
Michell, Keith *(Cast)* 129, 2150
Michelle, Melanie *(Cast)* 1978
Michener, James A. *(Author)* 3851, 4096
Michi *(Costumes)* 861, 862, 1918
Michlin, Barry *(Cast)* 4635
Michon, Joe *(Cast)* 3172
Michon, Pete *(Cast)* 3172
Micunis, Gordon *(Costumes)* 4522
Micunis, Gordon *(Set Design)* 1837, 2219, 4522
Middleton, George *(Librettist)* 3532
Middleton, Ray *(Cast)* 117, 153, 752, 1899, 2344, 2615, 2727, 3612, 3735, 4706
Middleton, Raymond *(Cast)* 1494
Middleton, Velma *(Cast)* 497, 4501, 4502
Midgley, Fanny *(Cast)* 1388
Midgley, Raymond *(Choreographer)* 948, 1533, 2749, 2827, 3580, 3680, 4648, 4651
Miele, Elizabeth *(Lyricist)* 1918
Miele, Elizabeth *(Producer)* 1918
Mielziner, Jo *(Lighting Designer)* 64, 153, 304, 514, 629, 651, 751, 961, 1242, 1278, 1284, 1497, 1706, 1709, 1749, 1760, 2312, 2411, 2583, 2777, 2797, 2898, 2940, 2961, 2983, 3234, 3353, 3505, 3897, 3972, 4015, 4169, 4420, 4423, 4446, 4682, 4702, 4718, 4749
Mielziner, Jo *(Producer)* 1760
Mielziner, Jo *(Set Design)* 64, 85, 153, 273, 304, 372, 514, 601, 603, 629, 651, 660, 689, 751, 961, 1242, 1278, 1284, 1453, 1497, 1706, 1709, 1749, 1760, 1874, 1894, 1948, 2061, 2252, 2312, 2344, 2411, 2504, 2545, 2583, 2618, 2777, 2797, 2821, 2898, 2940, 2961, 2983, 3225, 3234, 3283, 3353, 3505, 3861, 3897, 3972, 3990, 4015, 4096, 4142, 4169, 4235, 4335, 4420, 4423, 4446, 4495, 4682, 4702, 4718, 4749
Mieszkuc, Ruth *(Producer)* 4127
Migenes, Julia *(Cast)* 1265
Migliani *(Lyricist)* 4137, 4264
Mignini, Carolyn *(Cast)* 4390, 4450

Mikesell, Emily *(Cast)* 3641
Miklaszewska, Agata *(Librettist)* 2846
Miklaszewska, Agata *(Lyricist)* 2846
Miklaszewska, Maryna *(Librettist)* 2846
Miklaszewska, Maryna *(Lyricist)* 2846
Milan, Joe *(Choreographer)* 157
Milan, Judith *(Librettist)* 4627
Milazzo, Ann Marie *(Arrangements)* 1700
Milazzo, Ann Marie *(Cast)* 2237
Milazzo, Ann Marie *(Musical Director)* 1700
Milbank, Stephen *(Dance Arranger)* 1739
Milbank, Stephen (Incidental Music) 1739
Milbank, Stephen *(Musical Director)* 1739
Milbank, Stephen *(Vocal Arranger)* 1739
Milbro Productions *(Producer)* 3718
Milburn, Ann *(Cast)* 1533, 2490, 4010
Milburn, Mary *(Cast)* 1461, 1552, 2491, 2927, 3921, 4249, 4815
Milch, David H. *(Choreographer)* 264
Milchan, Arnon *(Producer)* 2173
Miles, Bernard *(Librettist)* 2563
Miles, Dean *(Cast)* 4110
Miles, Sara *(Cast)* 146
Miles, Sherman *(Composer)* 4153
Miles, Sylvia *(Cast)* 2172
Miles, Sylvia *(Librettist)* 2172
Miles, Sylvia *(Lyricist)* 2172
Miles, William *(Director)* 3916
Miles, William *(Librettist)* 3861, 4367
Miley, Bubber *(Cast)* 4235
Miley, Bubber *(Composer)* 432, 875, 885, 895, 4235
Milford, Jim *(Producer)* 534
Milford, Kim *(Cast)* 2555, 3741, 3742, 4216
Milford, Penelope *(Cast)* 3928
Milgrim *(Costumes)* 2342, 3556, 4766
Milgrim, Lynn *(Cast)* 3370
Milhelm, Margot *(Composer)* 4291
Milhelm, Margot *(Lyricist)* 4291
Milholland, Bruce *(Author)* 3279
Milikin, Paul *(Cast)* 3544
Militello, Anne *(Lighting Designer)* 3661, 4082
Militello, Anne E. *(Lighting Designer)* 2468
Milk, Ed *(Librettist)* 1880
Millar, Gertie *(Cast)* 3098
Millaud, Albert *(Author)* 2824
Millay, Edna St. Vincent *(Lyricist)* 1648
Mille, Antoinette *(Cast)* 4251
Mille, E.P. *(Cast)* 3480
Miller *(Composer)* 3382
Miller *(Lyricist)* 3382
Miller, Albert G. *(Librettist)* 2496
Miller, Albert G. *(Lyricist)* 2168, 2496
Miller, Alex *(Composer)* 933
Miller, Alex *(Lyricist)* 933
Miller, Alice Duer *(Author)* 706, 2263, 2691, 3735
Miller, Alice Duer *(Lyricist)* 706
Miller, Amy *(Cast)* 1059
Miller, Ann *(Cast)* 1494, 4197
Miller, Arthur *(Author)* 933, 3157, 4523
Miller, Arthur *(Librettist)* 3157, 4523, 4535

Miller, Arthur *(Lyricist)* 4523
Miller, Barbara *(Set Design)* 2599
Miller, Beth *(Cast)* 3388
Miller, Bill *(Cast)* 3742
Miller, Bill *(Choreographer)* 3124
Miller, Bob *(Cast)* 2052
Miller, Bob *(Librettist)* 3217
Miller, Bob *(Lyricist)* 597, 3217
Miller, Buzz *(Cast)* 177, 519, 2797, 3351, 3687
Miller, Buzz *(Choreographer)* 793, 4216
Miller, Carlton *(Cast)* 3461
Miller, Cathy *(Cast)* 2095
Miller, Charles *(Composer)* 4453
Miller, Charles *(Orchestrations)* 378, 577, 2809
Miller, Court *(Cast)* 1289
Miller, Craig *(Lighting Designer)* 305, 1665, 2283, 2542,
    3760, 4027, 4454, 4701
Miller, Edward *(Cast)* 249
Miller, Edward A. *(Producer)* 4249
Miller, Elinor *(Cast)* 3938
Miller, Everett *(Composer)* 1448
Miller, Flournoy *(Cast)* 443, 697, 988, 1488, 1667, 1678,
    3660, 3808, 3966, 4198, 4281, 4844
Miller, Flournoy *(Director)* 1668, 3660
Miller, Flournoy *(Librettist)* 443, 988, 3808, 3963, 3966
Miller, Flournoy *(Producer)* 1668
Miller, Flournoy E. *(Cast)* 813, 1192, 1960, 2302, 3089,
    3963, 3965
Miller, Flournoy E. *(Librettist)* 813, 1192, 1960, 2302,
    2721, 2807, 3089, 3337, 3965, 4199
Miller, Flournoy E. *(Lyricist)* 813, 1198, 1917, 2151, 2338,
    2807, 4199
Miller, Flournoy E. *(Producer)* 813, 1960
Miller, Fred *(Producer)* 4585
Miller, Gilbert *(Producer)* 1203, 2937, 3382
Miller, Gladys *(Cast)* 2148
Miller, Glenn *(Cast)* 1528
Miller, Glenn *(Composer)* 4137
Miller, Gregory *(Cast)* 2133
Miller, Harry *(Composer)* 1897
Miller, Harry *(Lyricist)* 1897
Miller, Helen *(Composer)* 2134
Miller, Helen *(Vocal Arranger)* 2134
Miller, Henry *(Cast)* 4559
Miller, Henry *(Director)* 2154, 3910
Miller, Henry *(Producer)* 2691, 2778
Miller, Hugh *(Cast)* 2747, 3481
Miller, Irvin C. *(Cast)* 43, 489, 552, 553, 554, 813,
    1050, 2557, 2984
Miller, Irvin C. *(Director)* 489, 554, 3614, 4281
Miller, Irvin C. *(Librettist)* 43, 471, 489, 552, 553, 554,
    1050, 2557, 2984, 3614
Miller, Irvin C. *(Lyricist)* 471, 2984
Miller, Irvin C. *(Producer)* 43, 471, 489, 498, 552, 553,
    554, 739, 813, 1028, 1050, 2151, 2984, 3614, 4281
Miller, J.E. *(Cast)* 2763
Miller, James M. *(Costumes)* 778
Miller, Jenia *(Costumes)* 1604
Miller, Jim *(Cast)* 2056
Miller, John *(Cast)* 2058

Miller, John *(Composer)* 6
Miller, John *(Musical Director)* 2058
Miller, Jonathan *(Cast)* 384
Miller, Jonathan *(Librettist)* 384
Miller, Joseph E. *(Lyricist)* 3052
Miller, Karen D. *(Costumes)* 2132
Miller, Lawrence *(Set Design)* 785, 3171
Miller, Margot *(Costumes)* 3167
Miller, Marilyn *(Cast)* 207, 1240, 3397, 3399, 3451,
    3766, 3819, 3958, 4023, 4212, 4812, 4813
Miller, Marilyn *(Producer)* 1342
Miller, Marilyn Suzanne *(Librettist)* 1512, 1575
Miller, Marilyn Suzanne *(Lyricist)* 1575
Miller, Martha *(Producer)* 4585
Miller, Midge *(Cast)* 2296
Miller, Midge *(Choreographer)* 1989
Miller, Midgie *(Cast)* 3533
Miller, Mitch *(Producer)* 1864
Miller, Patsy Ruth *(Librettist)* 3013
Miller, Paul *(Lighting Designer)* 275
Miller, Paula *(Cast)* 2228
Miller, Quintard *(Cast)* 553
Miller, Quintard *(Director)* 553
Miller, Quintard *(Librettist)* 1057
Miller, Quintard *(Producer)* 1057
Miller, Ray *(Cast)* 2258
Miller, Ray *(Composer)* 1154
Miller, Rev. Earl F. *(Cast)* 1636
Miller, Richard A. *(Set Design)* 1072
Miller, Robert *(Set Design)* 1049
Miller, Robert Strong *(Costumes)* 1969, 3601
Miller, Robin *(Librettist)* 956, 3429
Miller, Robin *(Lyricist)* 722, 956
Miller, Roger *(Composer)* 394
Miller, Roger *(Lyricist)* 394
Miller, Ron *(Librettist)* 952
Miller, Ron *(Lyricist)* 716, 952, 3485
Miller, Ronald *(Librettist)* 3734
Miller, Ronald *(Lyricist)* 3734
Miller, Sharron *(Cast)* 1770
Miller, Shelley *(Lyricist)* 1389
Miller, Sidney *(Cast)* 3846
Miller, Sidney *(Lyricist)* 2259
Miller, Skedge *(Cast)* 3920
Miller, Stanley *(Composer)* 2401
Miller, Susan *(Cast)* 323, 1138, 4702
Miller, Taps *(Cast)* 447, 3965
Miller, Timothy *(Costumes)* 169
Miller, Tod *(Cast)* 4124
Miller, Walter C. *(Director)* 499
Miller, William Henry *(Director)* 2662
Miller, William P. *(Producer)* 155
Miller, Woods *(Cast)* 216, 1136, 2300, 3002
Miller, Wynne *(Cast)* 600
Miller & Mantan *(Cast)* 882
Miller Brothers, The *(Cast)* 2034
Miller-Moffatt *(Lighting Designer)* 2219
Millership, Florrie *(Cast)* 1332
Millership, Lillian *(Cast)* 1332
Millett, Tim *(Choreographer)* 4732

Millham, Margot *(Composer)* 1932
Millham, Margot *(Lyricist)* 1932
Millhollin, James *(Cast)* 3837
Milligan, Tuck *(Cast)* 916
Millikin, Robert *(Cast)* 2944
Millington, Gertrude *(Cast)* 3679
Millocker, Carl *(Composer)* 340, 1110
Mills, A.J. *(Lyricist)* 4762
Mills, Annette *(Lyricist)* 1840
Mills, Bertha *(Cast)* 2040
Mills, Billy *(Cast)* 26, 4763
Mills, Billy *(Librettist)* 4763
Mills, C. Richard *(Set Design)* 3599
Mills, Carley *(Composer)* 3914, 4750
Mills, Carley *(Librettist)* 4750
Mills, Carley *(Lyricist)* 90, 969, 3914, 4750
Mills, Carley *(Vocal Arranger)* 2453
Mills, Eleanor *(Cast)* 166
Mills, F.A. *(Composer)* 1247
Mills, Florence *(Cast)* 1058, 1666, 2148, 2462, 3513
Mills, George *(Cast)* 3286
Mills, Grant *(Cast)* 2821
Mills, Harry *(Cast)* 526
Mills, Irving *(Cast)* 2972
Mills, Irving *(Composer)* 437, 883, 885, 896, 4091, 4137
Mills, Irving *(Lyricist)* 437, 445, 875, 881, 883, 885, 886, 896, 1125, 3018, 3020, 4091
Mills, Jerry *(Cast)* 2044, 2302, 2840
Mills, Jerry *(Director)* 646, 2127
Mills, Jim *(Cast)* 2511
Mills, John *(Cast)* 1619
Mills, Kerry *(Composer)* 662, 1246, 1247, 1535, 2415, 2805, 3905, 4390
Mills, Kerry *(Lyricist)* 2805, 3905
Mills, Maude *(Cast)* 925
Mills, Richard M. *(Producer)* 1619
Mills, Shirley *(Cast)* 1257
Mills, Stephan *(Cast)* 4352
Mills, Stephanie *(Cast)* 4722
Mills Brothers
    See also Four Mills Brothers.
Mills Brothers *(Cast)* 3153
Millstein, Jack *(Producer)* 956
Millward, Jessie *(Cast)* 1553
Milne, A.A. *(Author)* 4710
Milne, A.A. *(Lyricist)* 3634, 4710
Milner, Mark *(Composer)* 4389
Milner, Mark *(Lyricist)* 4389
Milner, Ron *(Director)* 1073
Milner, Ron *(Librettist)* 1073
Milner & Gehard *(Producer)* 1332
Milton, Billy *(Cast)* 1342, 4341
Milton, Burt *(Lyricist)* 1539
Milton, Frank *(Producer)* 1775
Milton, Katie *(Cast)* 3979
Milton, Robert *(Author)* 706
Milton, Robert *(Director)* 763, 913, 2020, 2121, 2385, 2891, 3177, 3219, 3230, 3245, 3246, 3250, 3436, 3775, 3812, 3866, 4572
Milton, Robert *(Producer)* 706, 1187

Milton, Robert *(Set Design)* 3250
Milward, Jo *(Author)* 2476
Milwaukee Repertory Theatre *(Producer)* 83
Minami, Roger *(Cast)* 16
Mindell, Fanin *(Costumes)* 3686
Mineo, John *(Cast)* 964, 975, 3299, 3330, 3506, 4196
Mineo, John *(Choreographer)* 337
Mineo, John *(Director)* 337
Mineo, Sal *(Cast)* 44
Miner, Jan *(Cast)* 1017, 1383, 4601
Miner, Raynard *(Composer)* 146, 1638
Miner, Raynard *(Lyricist)* 146, 1638
Miner, Renard *(Composer)* 3739
Miner, Renard *(Lyricist)* 3739
Miner, Worthington *(Director)* 1850, 2060, 3283, 3699
Minevitch, Borrah *(Cast)* 1617, 4235
Ming, Yao *(Lyricist)* 4749
Minick, Wendell *(Producer)* 3764
Mink, Gary *(Cast)* 2037
Mink, Louise *(Cast)* 4185
Minkoff, Fran *(Lyricist)* 3112
Minkovsky *(Composer)* 1609
Minkowski, Giack *(Composer)* 4032
Minkus, Barbara *(Cast)* 427, 1158
Minnelli, Liza *(Cast)* 16, 974, 1310, 2558, 3718
Minnelli, Vincente *(Costumes)* 216, 443, 1110, 1135, 1136, 1137, 3955, 4557, 4825
Minnelli, Vincente *(Director)* 216, 2777, 3955, 4557
Minnelli, Vincente *(Librettist)* 961
Minnelli, Vincente *(Set Design)* 216, 1110, 1136, 1137, 1973, 3955, 4557, 4825
Minoff, Tammy *(Cast)* 1633
Minskoff, Jerome *(Producer)* 393, 958, 1730, 1842, 2754
Minskoff, Maggie *(Producer)* 1842, 2598
Minster, Jack *(Director)* 4600
Minter, Mary Miles
    See Miss Minter.
Minter, Miss *(Cast)* 3025
Minton Jr., David M. *(Composer)* 4037
Minturn, Harry *(Director)* 4254
Mintz, Eli *(Cast)* 2218, 2925
Mintz, Thelma *(Cast)* 4463
Mintzer, Bill *(Lighting Designer)* 2195
Mintzer, Helen *(Producer)* 1785
Mintzer, William *(Lighting Designer)* 166, 1198, 1216, 1590, 1914, 2579, 3656
Minucci, Uhpio *(Composer)* 4828
Minucci, Uhpio *(Lyricist)* 4828
Minzey, Frank *(Composer)* 3998
Minzey, Frank *(Lyricist)* 3998
Mio, Tesore *(Cast)* 680
Miracle Expressions, Inc. *(Producer)* 2784
Miranda, Carmen *(Cast)* 4086, 4174
Miranda, Evan *(Cast)* 3806
Miranda, Sylvia *(Cast)* 1282
Mirande, Yves *(Author)* 468, 3295
Miron, J.C. *(Cast)* 1030, 1720, 3585
Miron, Joseph *(Cast)* 1417, 2335, 4713
Miron, Joseph C. *(Cast)* 694, 727, 1458, 1521
Mironchik, James *(Musical Director)* 4082

Mironchik, Jim *(Musical Director)*   3561
Mirvish, David *(Producer)*   580, 3846
Mirvish, Edwin *(Producer)*   3846
Misita, Michael *(Cast)*   1329
Miss Faun *(Cast)*   2294
Missimi, Dominic *(Choreographer)*   1701
Missimi, Dominic *(Director)*   1701
Missimi, Nancy *(Costumes)*   1701, 3461
Mistinguett *(Cast)*   2135
Mistretta, Sal *(Cast)*   3279
Mitch Leigh Company, The *(Producer)*   757
Mitchell, Abbie *(Cast)*   295, 2510, 3089, 3358, 3541
Mitchell, Abbie *(Librettist)*   3089
Mitchell, Adrian *(Adaptation)*   3445
Mitchell, Arthur *(Cast)*   3196
Mitchell, Barbara *(Cast)*   3615
Mitchell, Billy *(Producer)*   2942
Mitchell, Brian *(Cast)*   2702
Mitchell, Brian *(Composer)*   2702
Mitchell, Bryon *(Cast)*   937
Mitchell, Byron *(Cast)*   4435
Mitchell, Cameron *(Cast)*   2202
Mitchell, David *(Set Design)*   36, 150, 154, 169, 305,
   534, 807, 958, 1159, 1372, 1776, 1890, 2058, 2064,
   2360, 2437, 3577, 3628, 4744
Mitchell, Doris *(Cast)*   1566, 2059
Mitchell, Fanny Todd *(Librettist)*   138, 495, 3012, 4733
Mitchell, Fanny Todd *(Lyricist)*   4733
Mitchell, Frank *(Cast)*   1136
Mitchell, Georges *(Author)*   1743
Mitchell, Georges *(Librettist)*   1743
Mitchell, Grant *(Author)*   3349
Mitchell, Howard Johnstone *(Librettist)*   2901
Mitchell, James *(Cast)*   404, 530, 656, 2556, 2660
Mitchell, Jerry *(Choreographer)*   4775
Mitchell, John Cameron *(Cast)*   1822, 3862
Mitchell, Joni *(Composer)*   3739
Mitchell, Joni *(Lyricist)*   3739
Mitchell, Joseph *(Author)*   269
Mitchell, Julian *(Choreographer)*   186, 208, 740, 827, 902,
   1199, 1228, 1527, 1796, 2497, 2567, 2830, 2907, 2927,
   3251, 3323, 3494, 3585, 3627, 3723, 3727, 3921, 3977,
   4212, 4226, 4258, 4801, 4802, 4803, 4860
Mitchell, Julian *(Director)*   8, 175, 215, 250, 256, 425, 468,
   740, 953, 993, 1264, 1355, 1360, 1526, 1543, 1643, 1849,
   1900, 1919, 1926, 2041, 2101, 2160, 2328, 2767, 2835,
   2892, 2960, 3218, 3387, 3443, 3500, 3585, 3652, 3775,
   3791, 3994, 4053, 4094, 4293, 4478, 4547, 4666, 4712,
   4723, 4735, 4760, 4803, 4804, 4805, 4806, 4807, 4809,
   4818, 4819
Mitchell, Julian *(Producer)*   250, 2160, 4735
Mitchell, Kitty *(Cast)*   2963
Mitchell, Lauren *(Cast)*   154, 2143
Mitchell, Loften *(Librettist)*   576
Mitchell, Loften *(Lyricist)*   576
Mitchell, Margaret *(Author)*   1616
Mitchell, Mark *(Musical Director)*   494, 4515
Mitchell, Mary-Jennifer *(Cast)*   3077
Mitchell, Mel *(Lyricist)*   855, 864
Mitchell, Melanie *(Cast)*   4264

Mitchell, Millard *(Cast)*   2629
Mitchell, Norma *(Librettist)*   1692
Mitchell, Robert *(Orchestrations)*   2573
Mitchell, Robert *(Set Design)*   757
Mitchell, Robert D. *(Set Design)*   172
Mitchell, Ruth *(Cast)*   1921
Mitchell, Ruth *(Producer)*   2163, 2536
Mitchell, Sidney D. *(Lyricist)*   1687, 1847, 1920, 2856,
   4033, 4104, 4654, 4799, 4812, 4814
Mitchell, Thomas *(Cast)*   1791, 2309, 3686
Mitchell, Thomas *(Director)*   216, 622, 1939, 4059
Mitchell, Vontress *(Cast)*   3937
Mitchell & Durant *(Cast)*   1491
Mitgang, Norman *(Librettist)*   486
Mitgang, Norman *(Lyricist)*   485
Mittenthal, Ellen *(Cast)*   4830
Mittoo, Jackie *(Composer)*   3690
Mittoo, Jackie *(Lyricist)*   3690
Mitzi *(Cast)*   2377, 2669, 2686, 3084
Mitzman, Marcia *(Cast)*   721, 4619, 4676
Mixon, Tom *(Cast)*   600, 1837, 2052, 2288
Mizner, Wilson *(Librettist)*   822
Mizzy, Vic *(Composer)*   447, 524, 4006
Mlotek, Chana *(Lyricist)*   4342
Mlotek, Chane *(Lyricist)*   1609
Mlotek, Zalmen *(Additional Music)*   3937
Mlotek, Zalmen *(Dance Arranger)*   1609
Mlotek, Zalmen *(Librettist)*   4342
Mlotek, Zalmen *(Lyricist)*   573, 1609
Mlotek, Zalmen *(Musical Director)*   1609, 3937, 4342
Mlotek, Zalmen *(Vocal Arranger)*   1609
Mobley, Mary Ann *(Cast)*   3210
Mobley, Ross *(Musical Director)*   380, 1584
Modick, Murray *(Cast)*   3501
Modugno, Domenic *(Composer)*   4137
Modugno, Dominic *(Composer)*   4264
Modugno, Dominic *(Lyricist)*   4264
Moehl, Robert *(Composer)*   2676
Moeller, Friedrich Wilhelm *(Composer)*   4264
Moffat, John *(Lighting Designer)*   600
Moffatt, Harold *(Cast)*   3225
Moffett, D.W. *(Cast)*   3198
Mofletti, Duke *(Composer)*   497
Mofletti, Duke *(Lyricist)*   497
Mohr, Joseph *(Lyricist)*   3259
Moir, Ronald *(Cast)*   80
Moise, Solo *(Cast)*   2866
Moiseiwitsch, Tanya *(Costumes)*   453
Moiseiwitsch, Tanya *(Set Design)*   453
Mokae, Zakes *(Cast)*   4074
Molaskey, Jessica *(Cast)*   158
Moliere *(Author)*   127, 649, 1091, 2877, 3853, 3956,
   4401, 4450
Molina, Alex *(Cast)*   2578
Molinaro, Thom *(Cast)*   1056
Molineaux, Constance *(Cast)*   3910
Moll, Billy *(Composer)*   1965
Moll, Billy *(Lyricist)*   1965
Moll, William *(Lyricist)*   2238
Mollenhauer, E.R. *(Musical Director)*   762

Moller, Alfred *(Author)* 4795
Mollison, Clifford *(Cast)* 1855
Mollison, William *(Director)* 1207, 2547, 2808, 3216, 4730
Mollison, William *(Producer)* 3216, 3583
Molloy, J.L. *(Composer)* 1897
Molloy, J.L. *(Lyricist)* 1897
Molloy, Molly *(Cast)* 791
Molly, Michael *(Set Design)* 4172
Molnar, Ferenc *(Author)* 660, 2487, 2614, 2705
Molyneux, Edward *(Costumes)* 2570
Momand, Pop *(Author)* 2303
Moms Company *(Producer)* 2932
Monaco, James *(Composer)* 1813
Monaco, James V. *(Composer)* 25, 418, 487, 1334, 1738, 1779, 1873, 1963, 3259, 3396, 3737, 4033, 4255, 4655, 4806, 4815, 4823
Monaco, James V. *(Lyricist)* 25
Monagas, Lionel *(Cast)* 2690, 2720, 2881
Monahan, Dick *(Cast)* 1889
Monaster, Nate *(Librettist)* 4060
Monat, Phil *(Lighting Designer)* 131, 1589, 1739, 1969, 2046, 2852, 2861, 3667, 3722, 3724, 4347
Monckton, Lionel *(Author)* 3322, 4115
Monckton, Lionel *(Composer)* 178, 351, 767, 770, 906, 1470, 1538, 1569, 1626, 1682, 1994, 2341, 2844, 3020, 3098, 3313, 3322, 3618, 3803, 3828, 3948, 3999, 4115, 4390, 4430
Monckton, Lionel *(Lyricist)* 178, 1569, 3322, 3618, 3803, 4115
Monehan, Joseph *(Cast)* 2497
Monferdini, Carole *(Cast)* 788
Monica, Corbett *(Cast)* 32
Moniz, Susan *(Cast)* 4740
Monk, Debra *(Cast)* 212, 3142, 3261, 3608
Monk, Debra *(Composer)* 3261, 3608
Monk, Debra *(Librettist)* 3261
Monk, Debra *(Lyricist)* 3261, 3608
Monk, Isabell *(Cast)* 1636
Monk, Julius *(Director)* 272, 1049, 1107, 1363, 3479, 4156
Monk, Julius *(Producer)* 272, 427, 1023, 1049, 1107, 1362, 1363, 1364, 3484, 4065, 4156, 4268
Monk, Robby *(Lighting Designer)* 3548, 4176
Monk, Terence *(Cast)* 1616, 3763
Monkhouse, Gladys *(Costumes)* 378, 712, 1208, 3923
Monkhouse, Harry *(Cast)* 1429
Monkman, Dorothy *(Cast)* 3213
Monkman, Phyllis *(Cast)* 704, 2389, 3156, 4159
Monks, Chris *(Composer)* 4295
Monks Jr., John *(Librettist)* 447, 1879
Monnot, Marguerite *(Author)* 2150
Monnot, Marguerite *(Composer)* 2150
Monroe, Bruce *(Set Design)* 314
Monroe, Dale *(Cast)* 722
Monroe, George *(Cast)* 60, 902, 1919, 2858, 2869, 3096, 3397, 3399, 3958, 4206, 4425
Monroe, George W. *(Cast)* 2995
Monroe, Lucy *(Cast)* 117, 1839, 3219, 3532
Monroe, Tommy *(Cast)* 4620
Montagne, Louise *(Cast)* 3228

Montagu, Edward *(Composer)* 4762
Montagu, Edward *(Lyricist)* 4762
Montague, Edward *(Lyricist)* 3581
Montague, J. *(Lyricist)* 675
Montague, J.J. *(Composer)* 954
Montague, J.J. *(Lyricist)* 954
Montague, James *(Lyricist)* 2793
Montague, James R. *(Lyricist)* 2793
Montague, Kenneth "Chocolate Thunder" *(Cast)* 4786
Montalban, Ricardo *(Cast)* 58, 2190, 3899
Montano, Robert *(Cast)* 139
Monte, Barbara *(Cast)* 406
Monte Carlo Girls, The *(Cast)* 61
Montefiore, Gene *(Director)* 4629
Montel, Michael *(Director)* 1665, 2100
Monterey, Carlotta *(Cast)* 1250
Montero, Gus *(Dance Arranger)* 2472
Montero, Gus *(Vocal Arranger)* 2472
Montevecchi, Liliane *(Cast)* 1638, 1649, 3171
Montford, May *(Cast)* 4382
Montgomery, Andre *(Cast)* 3181
Montgomery, Barbara *(Cast)* 2133, 4286, 4343
Montgomery, Bruce *(Arrangements)* 4774
Montgomery, Bruce *(Choreographer)* 4774
Montgomery, Bruce *(Composer)* 127, 4679, 4774
Montgomery, Bruce *(Director)* 4679, 4774
Montgomery, Bruce *(Lyricist)* 127
Montgomery, Bruce *(Vocal Arranger)* 4543
Montgomery, Dave *(Cast)* 736, 1543, 2394, 3268, 3675, 4723
Montgomery, Dick *(Cast)* 653
Montgomery, Douglass *(Cast)* 3168
Montgomery, Frank *(Cast)* 1821, 2113
Montgomery, Frank *(Choreographer)* 2009, 3200, 3657
Montgomery, Frank *(Composer)* 1821, 2113, 3022
Montgomery, Frank *(Dance Arranger)* 1821
Montgomery, Frank *(Director)* 1983
Montgomery, Frank *(Librettist)* 2113
Montgomery, Frank *(Lyricist)* 1821, 2113, 3022
Montgomery, Frank *(Musical Director)* 3022
Montgomery, Frank *(Producer)* 1821, 2113
Montgomery, Garth *(Composer)* 3175
Montgomery, Garth *(Lyricist)* 3175
Montgomery, I.M. *(Author)* 148
Montgomery, James *(Author)* 1598, 2148, 3246, 4299
Montgomery, James *(Director)* 1598
Montgomery, James *(Librettist)* 773, 1582, 2148, 3246, 4766
Montgomery, Janice Lynn *(Cast)* 3825
Montgomery, John *(Choreographer)* 2633
Montgomery, Louis *(Cast)* 4242
Montgomery, Mabel *(Cast)* 4125
Montgomery, Richard *(Set Design)* 4147
Montgomery, Robert *(Cast)* 266
Montgomery, Robert *(Librettist)* 1684
Montgomery, Robert *(Lighting Designer)* 1255
Montgomery, Robert *(Lyricist)* 1684
Montgomery, Ron *(Lighting Designer)* 1079
Montgomery, Ronald *(Lighting Designer)* 148
Montgomery, William *(Cast)* 1738, 3525

Monti, Mili *(Cast)* 2504
Montresor, Beni *(Costumes)* 1060
Montresor, Beni *(Set Design)* 1060, 3644
Montrose, Helen *(Cast)* 3712
Montrose, Muriel *(Cast)* 2467, 4341
Moody, David *(Cast)* 578
Moon, David *(Lighting Designer)* 4627
Moon, David *(Set Design)* 4627
Moon, Edna *(Cast)* 3821
Moon, Joe *(Vocal Arranger)* 4362
Moon, Keith *(Additional Lyrics)* 4676
Moon, Keith *(Additional Music)* 4676
Moon, Marjorie *(Producer)* 2133
Mooney, Hal *(Musical Director)* 2588
Mooney, Michael *(Lyricist)* 4533
Mooney, Robert *(Cast)* 760
Moor, James *(Choreographer)* 3110
Moore *(Composer)* 2133
Moore *(Lyricist)* 2133
Moore, Ada *(Cast)* 2000
Moore, Al *(Cast)* 3704
Moore, Allen *(Vocal Arranger)* 4055
Moore, Brennan *(Cast)* 4380
Moore, Carroll *(Author)* 3874
Moore, Charles H. *(Cast)* 9
Moore, Charles Werner *(Director)* 4488
Moore, Charles Werner *(Librettist)* 4488
Moore, Charlotte *(Cast)* 2607, 2805
Moore, Constance *(Cast)* 601
Moore, Dana *(Cast)* 975
Moore, Dennie *(Cast)* 1145, 1672, 2504, 3850
Moore, Donald C. *(Cast)* 3764
Moore, Dudley *(Cast)* 384, 1621
Moore, Dudley *(Composer)* 384, 1621
Moore, Dudley *(Librettist)* 384, 1621
Moore, Dudley *(Lyricist)* 384, 1621
Moore, Elsie *(Cast)* 1560
Moore, Fleecie *(Composer)* 1296
Moore, Fleecie *(Lyricist)* 1296
Moore, Florence *(Cast)* 17, 202, 1691, 1738, 1826,
 2140, 3006, 3008, 3400, 3409, 3525
Moore, Frank F. *(Cast)* 2834
Moore, Garry *(Narrator)* 2975
Moore, George Austin *(Cast)* 558, 1403, 1650,
 1920, 3749
Moore, George Leon *(Cast)* 2532
Moore, Gladys *(Cast)* 2858
Moore, Grace *(Cast)* 1110, 1922, 3008, 3009,
 4437, 4528
Moore, Herbert *(Set Design)* 136, 4248, 4733
Moore, J.C. *(Composer)* 3631
Moore, J.C. *(Lyricist)* 3631
Moore, James *(Cast)* 1192, 2451
Moore, James *(Choreographer)* 3111
Moore, John *(Cast)* 2348
Moore, John H. *(Composer)* 666
Moore, John H. *(Lyricist)* 666
Moore, John J. *(Lighting Designer)* 2016
Moore, John J. *(Set Design)* 2728
Moore, Joseph *(Vocal Arranger)* 3543

Moore, Judith *(Cast)* 2654
Moore, Julian *(Librettist)* 2150
Moore, Julian *(Lyricist)* 2150
Moore, Karen *(Cast)* 1709
Moore, Kenny *(Composer)* 1713
Moore, Kenny *(Lyricist)* 1713
Moore, Larry *(Orchestrations)* 139
Moore, Laura *(Cast)* 1473
Moore, Marshall *(Director)* 4014
Moore, Mary Tyler *(Cast)* 521, 1040
Moore, Maureen *(Cast)* 314, 602, 1059, 1291, 4517
Moore, Mavor *(Composer)* 3110
Moore, Mavor *(Librettist)* 1255
Moore, Mavor *(Lyricist)* 1255, 3110
Moore, McElbert *(Composer)* 2780
Moore, McElbert *(Librettist)* 12, 1747, 2780, 3511
Moore, McElbert *(Lyricist)* 274, 1033, 1747, 1829, 2135,
 2780, 3148, 4000, 4104, 4424
Moore, Melba *(Cast)* 1717, 2133, 3610, 4383
Moore, Melton *(Cast)* 3365
Moore, Monette *(Cast)* 1322, 2645
Moore, Monica *(Cast)* 601, 2595
Moore, Napier *(Librettist)* 2105
Moore, Pauline *(Cast)* 2309, 3002
Moore, Percival *(Composer)* 515
Moore, Percival *(Lyricist)* 515
Moore, Phil *(Composer)* 2748
Moore, Phil *(Musical Director)* 4003
Moore, Phil *(Orchestrations)* 4003
Moore, Raymond *(Producer)* 621
Moore, Richard *(Lighting Designer)* 4232
Moore, Richard *(Set Design)* 4232
Moore, Robert *(Director)* 345, 2590, 3603, 4334, 4727
Moore, Sam *(Librettist)* 4314
Moore, Stanley *(Set Design)* 129, 1644
Moore, Thomas *(Lyricist)* 2633
Moore, Tim *(Cast)* 439, 441, 445, 447, 1251, 2645, 3705
Moore, Tom *(Director)* 1664, 3330
Moore, Tom *(Set Design)* 2037
Moore, Tony *(Cast)* 2737
Moore, Victor *(Cast)* 86, 163, 1356, 1419, 1746,
 1800, 1929, 1948, 2402, 2432, 2444, 2597, 3091,
 3225, 3243, 3584, 4277
Moore, William *(Orchestrations)* 2271
Moore & Megley *(Producer)* 2927
Moorehead, Agnes *(Cast)* 58, 1511, 3493
Moorehead, Jean *(Cast)* 2400
Mooring, Mark *(Costumes)* 317, 1013, 1027, 1603,
 1617, 1691, 1916, 3436, 4077, 4692
Mooser, George *(Director)* 3425
Mopsy *(Costumes)* 2018
Morales, Mark *(Cast)* 107
Moran, Alan *(Composer)* 2023, 2024
Moran, E.P. *(Lyricist)* 1963, 2111, 2299, 3387, 3753
Moran, Ed *(Lyricist)* 805, 4104, 4390
Moran, Edward P. *(Lyricist)* 2498, 2996, 3313,
 4094, 4723
Moran, George *(Cast)* 1128, 1132, 4814
Moran, Lois *(Cast)* 2444, 3225
Moran, Rosie *(Cast)* 3860, 4365

Moran & Mack *(Cast)*   1690, 3179
Morand, R. *(Cast)*   4663
Morando, Estelle *(Librettist)*   3907
Morange, E.A.
   See also Gates & Marange.
Morange, E.A. *(Set Design)*   185, 376, 577, 749, 815, 1243,
   1501, 1625, 1667, 2768, 2819, 2884, 3228, 3519, 3650,
   3772, 3774, 3865, 3868, 4234, 4360, 4620, 4671, 4694,
   4704, 4716, 4807
Morange, Edward A. *(Set Design)*   2326, 4705
Moras, Alan *(Musical Director)*   1814
Morath, Kathryn *(Cast)*   54
Morath, Kathy *(Cast)*   3142, 3221, 3600, 4731
Moray, Stella *(Cast)*   346
Morcon, James *(Costumes)*   4374
Mordecai, David *(Conductor)*   2447
Mordecai, James *(Cast)*   3986, 4253
Mordente, Lisa *(Cast)*   2759, 3515
Mordente, Tony *(Cast)*   2484, 4625
Mordente, Tony *(Choreographer)*   1864
Morder, Georgio *(Composer)*   3739
Morder, Georgio *(Lyricist)*   3739
Mordhorst, Gunda *(Cast)*   791
Mordkin, Michael *(Choreographer)*   3699
More, Julian *(Librettist)*   194, 1644, 2949, 3792
More, Julian *(Lyricist)*   194, 1644, 2949, 3792
Morea, Robert *(Cast)*   4157
Morehead, Jean *(Cast)*   4777
Morehouse, Harold *(Producer)*   2640
Moreland, Mantan *(Cast)*   439, 441, 443, 3965, 3993, 4763
Morell, Peter *(Director)*   27
Morelli, Anthony *(Musical Director)*   4362
Morelli, Toni *(Musical Director)*   4117
Moreno, Rita *(Cast)*   1441
Morenzic, Leon *(Cast)*   4147
Morenzie, Leon *(Cast)*   793
Mores, Mariano *(Composer)*   2356
Moret, Neil *(Composer)*   685, 1531, 1927, 2747, 2960,
   3297, 4351, 4570, 4613
Moret, Neil *(Lyricist)*   1531, 1927, 3297
Moretty, C.R. *(Composer)*   1678
Morey, Larry *(Author)*   4035
Morey, Larry *(Composer)*   2083, 2089, 2090, 2091
Morey, Larry *(Lyricist)*   2083, 2089, 2090, 2091, 4035
Morgan, Agnes *(Cast)*   1651, 1653, 1655, 1657
Morgan, Agnes *(Director)*   1651, 1653, 1654, 1655, 1656,
   1657, 1871
Morgan, Agnes *(Librettist)*   1652, 1653, 1654, 1655, 1656,
   1657, 2732
Morgan, Agnes *(Lyricist)*   1652, 1653, 1654, 1655, 1656,
   1657, 1871
Morgan, Al *(Librettist)*   3234
Morgan, Carey *(Composer)*   1063, 1176, 1687, 2700
Morgan, Cass *(Cast)*   1402, 1737, 2346, 2359, 3608
Morgan, Cass *(Composer)*   3608
Morgan, Cass *(Lyricist)*   3608
Morgan, Claudia *(Cast)*   2729
Morgan, Danny *(Costumes)*   1770, 3764, 4635
Morgan, Denise *(Cast)*   838
Morgan, Dickson *(Director)*   3072

Morgan, Dickson *(Set Design)*   4429
Morgan, Elizabeth *(Cast)*   1176
Morgan, Frank *(Cast)*   294, 1283, 1847, 1874, 3048,
   3740, 3766
Morgan, Gary *(Cast)*   2318
Morgan, George *(Lighting Designer)*   4434
Morgan, Helen *(Cast)*   123, 1488, 2459, 3949, 4234, 4823,
   4845, 4847
Morgan, Henry *(Librettist)*   59
Morgan, J.L. *(Composer)*   1063
Morgan, James *(Set Design)*   147, 451, 549, 809, 1092,
   1510, 1630, 1737, 2565, 3202, 3864, 4027
Morgan, Jane *(Cast)*   4828
Morgan, Jim *(Lyricist)*   4533
Morgan, L. *(Producer)*   292
Morgan, Marion *(Choreographer)*   4719
Morgan, Marion *(Costumes)*   4719
Morgan, Merlin *(Composer)*   2698
Morgan, Merlin *(Lyricist)*   379
Morgan, Miles *(Lighting Designer)*   2168
Morgan, Mme. *(Costumes)*   1984
Morgan, Mrs. Edmund Nash *(Author)*   4313
Morgan, Priscilla *(Cast)*   2474
Morgan, Ralph *(Cast)*   2121
Morgan, Robert *(Lighting Designer)*   547
Morgan, Roger *(Lighting Designer)*   807, 825, 900, 1222,
   1512, 1635, 2064, 2172, 2236, 2290, 2539, 2798, 3418,
   4114, 4167, 4595, 4623
Morgan, Roger *(Set Design)*   1116
Morgan, Russ *(Composer)*   4137
Morgan, Stuart
   See Stuart Morgan Dancers.
Morgan, Ted *(Cast)*   4423
Morgan, W. Aston *(Composer)*   553
Morgan, Wallace *(Author)*   1318
Morgan, William T. *(Cast)*   2310
Morgan Dancers, Stuart *(Cast)*   1889
Morgan Jr., Charles S. *(Choreographer)*   2390, 4250
Morganstern, C. William *(Producer)*   3342
Morgenstern, Christopher *(Lyricist)*   1589
Morgenstern, Sam *(Dance Arranger)*   3215
Morgenstern, Sam *(Orchestrations)*   3215
Morgenstern, Sam *(Vocal Arranger)*   3215
Moriarty, George *(Lyricist)*   545
Moriarty, Michael *(Producer)*   4003
Morick, Jeanine *(Cast)*   674
Morin, Terry *(Composer)*   2580
Morinelli, Patricia *(Producer)*   1638
Morison, Patricia *(Cast)*   84, 2331, 4479
Moritz, Al *(Composer)*   467
Moritz, Al *(Lyricist)*   467
Morley, Al *(Producer)*   407, 413
Morley, Angela *(Orchestrations)*   695, 1619
Morley, Carol *(Cast)*   128, 1436, 3548, 4029, 4330
Morley, Jay *(Costumes)*   2234
Morley, Karen *(Cast)*   298
Morley, Ruth *(Costumes)*   4, 171, 615, 747, 1864, 2173,
   3908, 4167
Morley, Victor *(Cast)*   1123, 1663, 2619, 2813, 3043, 3177,
   4115, 4365, 4824

Morley, Victor *(Director)* 3069
Morne, Maryland *(Cast)* 2121
Morningstar, Carter *(Costumes)* 339
Morningstar, Carter *(Lighting Designer)* 339, 3941
Morningstar, Carter *(Set Design)* 339, 3941
Morosco, Leslie *(Producer)* 2564
Morosco, Oliver *(Director)* 628, 2605, 4037
Morosco, Oliver *(Librettist)* 628, 2461, 2832, 2955, 3562, 4037, 4634
Morosco, Oliver *(Lyricist)* 2605, 2955, 4381
Morosco, Oliver *(Producer)* 233, 422, 628, 763, 2378, 2446, 2461, 2489, 2519, 2605, 2832, 2955, 3432, 3562, 3812, 4037, 4381, 4492, 4634
Moross, Jerome *(Composer)* 283, 1474, 1600, 1873, 2294, 3365, 4512
Moross, Jerome *(Librettist)* 1474
Moross, Jerome *(Orchestrations)* 1600, 3365
Morreale, Enrico *(Musical Director)* 1071, 2936
Morrell, Don *(Cast)* 1836
Morris, Anita *(Cast)* 1955, 2687, 3171, 3636, 3869, 4517
Morris, Bobby *(Cast)* 3410
Morris, Chester *(Cast)* 2967
Morris, David *(Cast)* 1275, 3283, 4142
Morris, Edward *(Pianist)* 366, 2279
Morris, Edward *(Producer)* 2913
Morris, Edwin H. *(Producer)* 3940
Morris, Garrett *(Cast)* 40, 1081, 1729, 2075, 3309
Morris, Gary *(Cast)* 2359
Morris, George *(Director)* 1514
Morris, George *(Librettist)* 1514
Morris, George *(Lyricist)* 1514
Morris, Hayward *(Orchestrations)* 4789
Morris, Howard *(Cast)* 44, 1475
Morris, I.N. *(Librettist)* 2779
Morris, Janet S. *(Costumes)* 143
Morris, Jeremiah *(Director)* 2043
Morris, Jeremiah *(Librettist)* 2043
Morris, Joe *(Cast)* 2631
Morris, John *(Arrangements)* 635
Morris, John *(Composer)* 2097, 4384
Morris, John *(Dance Arranger)* 64, 270, 363, 607, 868, 1290, 1567, 1742, 2355, 2568, 3159, 3473, 3505, 3931, 4693
Morris, John *(Incidental Music)* 2660
Morris, John *(Librettist)* 4384
Morris, John *(Lyricist)* 2097, 4273, 4384
Morris, John *(Musical Director)* 64, 635, 2097, 2553, 4693
Morris, John *(Orchestrations)* 3075
Morris, John *(Pianist)* 1047
Morris, John *(Vocal Arranger)* 1991, 4693
Morris, June *(Choreographer)* 4163
Morris, Kenny *(Cast)* 1377
Morris, Kenny *(Lyricist)* 1377
Morris, Lynne *(Choreographer)* 2962
Morris, Mary *(Cast)* 2476
Morris, Maud *(Cast)* 4681
Morris, McKay *(Cast)* 121, 165
Morris, Mickey *(Cast)* 2655
Morris, Mildred *(Cast)* 3450

Morris, Nat *(Cast)* 1116
Morris, Peter *(Cast)* 2022
Morris, Peter *(Librettist)* 2022, 4462
Morris, Peter *(Lyricist)* 2022, 4462
Morris, Phil *(Producer)* 2271
Morris, Ramsey *(Librettist)* 2675
Morris, Richard *(Director)* 1369
Morris, Richard *(Librettist)* 1369, 1605
Morris, Robert *(Librettist)* 4516
Morris, Seymour *(Lyricist)* 637
Morris, Thomas *(Composer)* 1687
Morris, William *(Set Design)* 302
Morris, William E. *(Cast)* 4105
Morris, William E. *(Director)* 3995
Morris Jr., William *(Director)* 1411
Morrisey, Bob *(Cast)* 171, 2146, 3643
Morrisey, J. *(Composer)* 1957
Morrison, Alex *(Cast)* 3406
Morrison, Ann *(Cast)* 1589, 2822, 3429
Morrison, Dorothy *(Cast)* 4021
Morrison, Ethel *(Cast)* 1235
Morrison, Florence *(Cast)* 2373, 3623
Morrison, Kay *(Costumes)* 2786, 4550
Morrison, Lee *(Director)* 1014, 3605
Morrison, Lee *(Producer)* 1014
Morrison, Paul *(Costumes)* 4153
Morrison, Paul *(Lighting Designer)* 249, 630, 920, 1766, 2144, 3094, 3984, 4005, 4186, 4828
Morrison, Paul *(Set Design)* 249, 3094, 4005
Morrison, Peggy *(Costumes)* 4377
Morrison, Priestley *(Director)* 1098
Morrison, Priestly *(Director)* 1135, 1177, 1345
Morrison, Sam *(Composer)* 4204
Morrison, Van *(Composer)* 3695
Morrison, Van *(Lyricist)* 3695
Morrison, Wayne *(Composer)* 1637
Morrison, Wayne *(Lyricist)* 1637
Morrison, William *(Cast)* 119
Morrison Jr., Charles T. *(Set Design)* 4163
Morrissey *(Composer)* 1963
Morrissey *(Lyricist)* 1963
Morrissey, Paul *(Director)* 2728
Morrissey, Will *(Cast)* 598, 2296, 4421
Morrissey, Will *(Composer)* 78, 598, 2296, 2397, 3133, 3399, 3410, 3533, 3891, 4421
Morrissey, Will *(Director)* 598, 1989, 3133, 3533, 4421
Morrissey, Will *(Librettist)* 78, 598, 1989, 2296, 3133, 3533, 3822
Morrissey, Will *(Lyricist)* 78, 443, 598, 1328, 1989, 2296, 2397, 3133, 3399, 3410, 3533, 3822, 4421
Morrissey, Will *(Producer)* 398, 598, 1328, 3133, 4421
Morrow, Doretta *(Cast)* 23, 1933, 2312, 2327, 3947, 4652
Morrow, Helen *(Cast)* 1871
Morrow, Karen *(Cast)* 1597, 1662, 2053, 2072, 2075, 2248, 3018, 3871, 3988
Morrow, Macklin *(Musical Director)* 818
Morrow, Milo *(Costumes)* 2918, 3825
Morrow, Rob *(Cast)* 747
Morscher, Sepp *(Musical Director)* 1020
Morse, Barry *(Director)* 3818

Morse, Carl F. *(Cast)*   1868
Morse, Harry M. *(Cast)*   800
Morse, John A. *(Cast)*   3329
Morse, John A. *(Lyricist)*   2039
Morse, John P. *(Cast)*   1556
Morse, Josephine *(Cast)*   1707
Morse, Muriel *(Producer)*   4318
Morse, Richard *(Cast)*   73
Morse, Robert *(Cast)*   1389, 2019, 3845, 4038, 4196, 4270
Morse, Robert G. *(Composer)*   3047
Morse, Robin *(Cast)*   534
Morse, Stacy *(Costumes)*   2970
Morse, Theodore *(Composer)*   246, 675, 1907, 2576, 2826, 2974, 3030, 3519
Morse, Theodore *(Director)*   2954
Morse, Theodore F. *(Composer)*   2974, 3073, 4723
Morse, Tilda *(Choreographer)*   1370
Morse, Woolson *(Composer)*   1090, 2592, 3360
Morse, Woolson *(Librettist)*   762
Morsell, Fred *(Cast)*   3059
Mortimer, Charles *(Composer)*   4171
Mortimer, Charles *(Lyricist)*   4171
Mortimer, Jeannie *(Cast)*   300
Mortimer, Nellie *(Cast)*   402
Mortiz, Dave *(Composer)*   4171
Mortiz, Dave *(Lyricist)*   4171
Morton, Brooks *(Cast)*   1848, 3725
Morton, Clara *(Cast)*   399, 522
Morton, David *(Composer)*   4566
Morton, David *(Lyricist)*   4566
Morton, Dorothy *(Cast)*   175, 1682, 3199, 4616, 4724
Morton, Edna *(Cast)*   3041
Morton, Edward *(Librettist)*   3828
Morton, Emma *(Cast)*   2113
Morton, Fred *(Composer)*   1120
Morton, Fred *(Lyricist)*   1120
Morton, Frederic *(Author)*   3780
Morton, George "Shadow" *(Composer)*   2427
Morton, George "Shadow" *(Lyricist)*   2427
Morton, Gregory *(Cast)*   1119
Morton, Harry K. *(Cast)*   332, 905, 2605, 2622, 3532, 4170
Morton, Harry K. *(Composer)*   905
Morton, Hugh *(Librettist)*   113, 357, 1543, 1579, 2116, 4298
Morton, Hugh *(Lyricist)*   357, 982, 1543, 1579, 4044
Morton, Hughie *(Musical Director)*   2457
Morton, James C. *(Cast)*   558, 1935, 2834, 3434
Morton, James J. *(Cast)*   1835, 2826
Morton, Jelly Roll *(Music Based On)*   2200
Morton, Joe *(Cast)*   1970, 3231, 3564, 3656, 3824, 4450
Morton, Kate *(Cast)*   399, 522
Morton, Lew *(Choreographer)*   2107, 3372
Morton, Lew *(Director)*   684, 718, 2602, 2637, 2856, 3012, 3150, 3523, 3573, 4621, 4654
Morton, Lew *(Librettist)*   4654
Morton, Lew *(Lyricist)*   4654
Morton, Lewis *(Choreographer)*   2254
Morton, Lewis *(Director)*   2293, 2893, 3163, 3701, 3981
Morton, Mark *(Set Design)*   2993

Morton, Martha *(Cast)*   1134
Morton, Michael *(Librettist)*   4285
Morton, Moe *(Producer)*   3933
Morton, Paul *(Cast)*   399, 522
Morton, Richard *(Composer)*   3229
Morton, Richard *(Lyricist)*   3229
Morton, Sam *(Cast)*   399, 522
Morton, Tommy *(Cast)*   2439, 2554
Morton, William K. *(Cast)*   4248
Morton, Winn *(Costumes)*   190, 1158, 2097, 2657, 2750, 3112, 3371, 3928, 4029
Morton, Winn *(Set Design)*   3112
Mosby, Marion *(Cast)*   178, 2494
Mosconi, Charles *(Choreographer)*   431, 3290
Moscowitz, Jennie *(Cast)*   4083
Mosel, Tad *(Librettist)*   2664
Moseley, Peggy *(Cast)*   1492, 1493
Moser, Barbara *(Cast)*   2464
Moser, Margo *(Cast)*   1730
Moses, Burke *(Cast)*   330
Moses, Gilbert *(Director)*   40, 4004, 4722
Moses, Harry *(Producer)*   1366
Moses & Hamilton *(Set Design)*   1313, 2803
Mosher, Sue *(Cast)*   261
Mosher, Susan *(Cast)*   4193
Mosier, Enid *(Cast)*   2000
Mosier, Marie *(Musical Director)*   4440
Mosiman, Marnie *(Cast)*   3764
Moss *(Composer)*   3747
Moss, Al *(Composer)*   2167, 4394
Moss, Anguss *(Lighting Designer)*   314
Moss, Arnold *(Cast)*   23, 1329
Moss, Earl *(Arrangements)*   2077
Moss, Herbert M. *(Producer)*   1744, 3496
Moss, Jeffrey *(Composer)*   1082
Moss, Jeffrey *(Librettist)*   1082
Moss, Jeffrey *(Lyricist)*   1082
Moss, Jeffrey B. *(Costumes)*   400, 1269
Moss, Jeffrey B. *(Director)*   2790
Moss, Jeffrey B. *(Set Design)*   400, 1269
Moss, Jo *(Cast)*   1951
Moss, Joe *(Producer)*   1949, 1950
Moss, Kathi *(Cast)*   1664
Moss, Kurt *(Composer)*   3530
Moss, Larry *(Cast)*   2913
Moss, Lawrence John *(Cast)*   4038
Moss, Paul *(Producer)*   1657
Moss, Paula *(Cast)*   1344
Moss, Paula *(Choreographer)*   1344
Moss Empires Ltd. *(Producer)*   4320
Moss and Fry *(Cast)*   1404
Mosse, Spencer *(Lighting Designer)*   1249, 1439, 3653, 4379
Mosser, Jack *(Additional Music)*   3381
Mosser, Jack *(Costumes)*   3381
Most, Earle *(Orchestrations)*   3639
Mostel, Josh *(Cast)*   3039, 4167, 4371
Mostel, Joshua *(Cast)*   2877
Mostel, Kate *(Cast)*   3299
Mostel, Zero *(Cast)*   341, 1265, 1422, 2653, 3286

Mostel, Zero *(Librettist)* 2653
Mostoller *(Costumes)* 4627
Mostyn, Hadden *(Cast)* 995
Moten, Etta *(Cast)* 1251
Mothersbaugh, Mark *(Composer)* 3739
Mothersbaugh, Mark *(Lyricist)* 3739
Motion Pictures Artists Co. *(Producer)* 4152
Motley *(Costumes)* 270, 367, 629, 651, 1748, 2355, 2464, 2894, 2961, 3294, 3347, 3452, 3453, 3813, 3934, 4096, 4155, 4435, 4609
Motley *(Set Design)* 1748
Motown *(Producer)* 952
Motteaux, Peter Anthony *(Lyricist)* 2633
Motts, Robert *(Producer)* 3979
Motzan, Otto *(Composer)* 1266, 2696, 2922, 3193, 3400, 3401, 3958, 4418
Motzan, Otto *(Lyricist)* 3400, 4419
Mouezy-Eon *(Librettist)* 3769
Moulan, Eugene *(Cast)* 4333
Moulan, Frank *(Cast)* 178, 902, 1228, 1650, 1851, 2035, 2276, 2527, 3593, 3627, 3996, 4201
Moule, Kenneth *(Musical Director)* 4469
Moulton, C. *(Composer)* 4479
Moulton, Harold *(Cast)* 55
Moulton, Ray K. *(Composer)* 4421
Moulton, Ray K. *(Lyricist)* 4421
Mountain, Vince *(Set Design)* 2198
Mourning, Inez *(Choreographer)* 2436
Moustaki, George *(Composer)* 4396
Moveing Day Company *(Producer)* 4198
Mowatt, Anna Cora *(Author)* 1249
Mowbray, Alan *(Cast)* 1190
Mowell, Shelley *(Composer)* 3664, 3940, 3942
Mowry, Greg *(Cast)* 4138
Moyen *(Costumes)* 3524
Moyer, Edythe *(Cast)* 1728
Moylan, Mary Ellen *(Cast)* 3841
Mozart, Wolfgang Amadeus *(Author)* 4522
Mozart, Wolfgang Amadeus *(Composer)* 221
Mqadi, Bheki *(Cast)* 209, 4438
Msomi, Mandla *(Cast)* 1719
Msomi, Welcome *(Composer)* 1719
Msomi, Welcome *(Director)* 1719
Msomi, Welcome *(Librettist)* 1719
Msomi, Welcome *(Lyricist)* 1719
Mucci, David *(Cast)* 580
Muchison, Kenneth M. *(Composer)* 824
Mudie, Alan *(Cast)* 178
Mudie, Leonard *(Cast)* 1144
Mueller, Gustave *(Composer)* 4815
Mueller, Karl *(Cast)* 1413
Mueller, Mark *(Librettist)* 595
Mueller, Mark *(Lyricist)* 595
Mueller, Zizi *(Musical Director)* 654
Mueltzer *(Costumes)* 1712
Muenz, Richard *(Cast)* 721, 784, 3577, 4004
Muffatti, S. Todd *(Set Design)* 973
Muhammed Ali
  See Cassius Clay.
Muhsam, Erich *(Librettist)* 3441

Muhsam, Erich *(Lyricist)* 3441
Muir, Gavin *(Cast)* 715
Muir, Lewis F. *(Composer)* 433, 558, 1531, 2415, 3259, 4655, 4803, 4804
Muir, Lewis F. *(Lyricist)* 4534
Muir, William *(Director)* 2946
Mulaney, Jan *(Composer)* 2289
Mulcahy, Lance *(Composer)* 1978, 2305, 3389, 3890, 3909, 4246, 4433
Mulcahy, Lance *(Librettist)* 4433
Mulcahy, Lance *(Lyricist)* 1978, 3890, 4433
Mulgrew, J.P. *(Librettist)* 538
Mulgrew, James P. *(Librettist)* 2303
Mulgrew, John P. *(Librettist)* 537, 540
Mulhern, Michael *(Cast)* 2861
Mullally, W.S. *(Arrangements)* 1913
Mullaly, Harry G. *(Musical Director)* 2952
Mulle, Ida *(Cast)* 571
Mullen *(Composer)* 2493
Mullen, Charles E. *(Composer)* 917
Mullen, J.B. *(Composer)* 2481
Mullen, J.B. *(Lyricist)* 2481
Mullen, Joseph *(Costumes)* 266
Mullen, Joseph *(Set Design)* 266
Muller, Ernst *(Composer)* 3600
Muller, Ernst *(Lyricist)* 3600
Muller, Hans *(Author)* 4667
Muller, Jennifer *(Choreographer)* 1015, 1236, 4518
Muller, Romeo *(Author)* 2941
Muller, Romeo *(Librettist)* 928, 2941
Muller-Norden, Alfred *(Composer)* 1188
Muller-Norden, Alfred *(Lyricist)* 1188
Mulligan, Charles *(Producer)* 1314
Mulligan, Gerry *(Composer)* 1750
Mulligan, Ralph *(Costumes)* 1962, 3006, 3007, 3008, 3770
Mulligan, Richard *(Cast)* 1205
Mulligan, Robert J. *(Cast)* 3353
Mullins, Melinda *(Cast)* 3884
Mulvey, Ben *(Cast)* 953
Mumford, Ethel Watts *(Lyricist)* 1009
Munce, Howard *(Librettist)* 4047
Mundin, Herbert *(Cast)* 133, 702, 1128, 2392
Mundy, James *(Orchestrations)* 4542
Mundy, John *(Composer)* 2464, 3989, 4542
Mundy, Meg *(Cast)* 1680, 1973, 3468
Munford, Gordon *(Musical Director)* 239
Muni, Paul *(Cast)* 223
Munier, Leon *(Lighting Designer)* 3059
Munier, Leon *(Set Design)* 3059
Munnik, Rob *(Lighting Designer)* 1865
Munoz, Rodney *(Costumes)* 2065
Munro, BIll *(Composer)* 1685
Munroe, Walter *(Cast)* 3219, 3536
Munsel, Patrice *(Cast)* 2838, 3020, 4155
Munshin, Jules *(Cast)* 7, 454, 620, 1456, 3954
Munson, Eddie *(Composer)* 3754
Munson, Ona *(Cast)* 1482, 1929, 1932, 2734, 4476
Muntz, Elsie *(Composer)* 3827
Munz, Louis G. *(Composer)* 3073
Mura, Corinna *(Cast)* 2847

Murawski, C. *(Lighting Designer)*   840, 4514
Murawski, C. *(Set Design)*   1612, 3928, 4514
Mure, Glenn *(Cast)*   922
Murfitt, Mary *(Cast)*   3261
Murfitt, Mary *(Librettist)*   3261
Murger, Henri *(Author)*   2359
Murin, David *(Costumes)*   424, 474, 478, 533, 690, 1172, 1258, 1635
Murney, Christopher *(Cast)*   4450
Murphy, Brian *(Cast)*   3259
Murphy, C.W. *(Composer)*   246, 1148, 1544, 2232, 2528, 2858, 3193
Murphy, C.W. *(Lyricist)*   1148, 1544, 2232, 2528, 3144
Murphy, Danny *(Cast)*   3158
Murphy, Donna *(Cast)*   1377, 1822, 3070, 3411, 3598, 3960, 4076
Murphy, Edward *(Choreographer)*   3912
Murphy, Frank "Rags" *(Composer)*   2349
Murphy, Frank "Rags" *(Librettist)*   2349
Murphy, Frank "Rags" *(Lyricist)*   2349
Murphy, George *(Cast)*   3225, 3735, 3946
Murphy, George *(Director)*   2496
Murphy, George P. *(Cast)*   2448
Murphy, Jeanette *(Cast)*   449
Murphy, John Daly *(Cast)*   1368, 1501, 3866
Murphy, Judy *(Cast)*   2124
Murphy, Lyle *(Composer)*   2084
Murphy, Lyle *(Lyricist)*   2084
Murphy, Lyle *(Orchestrations)*   2084, 2093, 2095, 2096
Murphy, Owen *(Composer)*   1131, 2870, 3648, 3655, 3677, 4104, 4424
Murphy, Owen *(Librettist)*   3655
Murphy, Owen *(Lyricist)*   317, 1131, 1440, 1690, 1691, 1692, 1780, 1932, 2020, 2308, 2870, 3648, 3655, 3677, 4104, 4424
Murphy, Pixie *(Cast)*   2608
Murphy, Ralph *(Lyricist)*   1314
Murphy, Reggie *(Cast)*   531
Murphy, Rosemary *(Cast)*   160
Murphy, Stanley *(Composer)*   1501
Murphy, Stanley *(Lyricist)*   1501, 2667, 2922, 3396, 4017, 4589, 4642, 4712
Murphy, William *(Cast)*   750
Murphy III, William *(Producer)*   3539
Murray, Alan *(Choreographer)*   388
Murray, Alfred *(Librettist)*   2844
Murray, Alfred *(Lyricist)*   1313
Murray, Art *(Librettist)*   4
Murray, Braham *(Choreographer)*   1736
Murray, Braham *(Director)*   1619, 1736
Murray, Brian *(Director)*   1787
Murray, Carl *(Cast)*   4220
Murray, Charles *(Cast)*   2884
Murray, Charles A. *(Librettist)*   4215
Murray, Chas. A. *(Cast)*   187
Murray, Don *(Cast)*   4029
Murray, Edgar *(Cast)*   4247
Murray, Elizabeth *(Cast)*   804, 1212, 1629, 1888, 2601, 2667, 2671, 4465, 4603
Murray, Estelle *(Choreographer)*   4779

Murray, Frank *(Producer)*   4614
Murray, Fred *(Lighting Designer)*   4296
Murray, George *(Librettist)*   728
Murray, J. Harold *(Cast)*   642, 659, 670, 735, 1145, 1225, 2706, 2857, 3404, 3719, 4121, 4374, 4550, 4575, 4654
Murray, J.K. *(Cast)*   175, 2673
Murray, J.P. *(Librettist)*   4823
Murray, J.P. *(Lyricist)*   1932, 4799, 4823
Murray, J.S. *(Director)*   1910
Murray, Jack *(Composer)*   1722
Murray, Jack *(Librettist)*   3986
Murray, Jack *(Lyricist)*   1722
Murray, James *(Cast)*   1910
Murray, Jan *(Cast)*   3013
Murray, John *(Composer)*   4152
Murray, John *(Director)*   4152
Murray, John *(Lyricist)*   124, 4152
Murray, John T. *(Cast)*   764, 3174, 3399, 3958, 4133, 4654, 4760
Murray, Kathleen *(Cast)*   2339
Murray, Ken *(Cast)*   1127, 2459
Murray, Lyn *(Vocal Arranger)*   1278, 2453, 3359, 4256
Murray, Mae *(Cast)*   256, 1849, 2025, 2884, 3153, 3421, 3975, 4787, 4802, 4803, 4809
Murray, Mary *(Cast)*   3172
Murray, Mary Gordon *(Cast)*   **4**, **474**, 2346, 3517
Murray, Michael *(Cast)*   2661
Murray, Pat *(Cast)*   214
Murray, Paul *(Producer)*   1333, 2467
Murray, Peg *(Cast)*   162, 610, 1184, 1709, 3918, 4060
Murray, S. Barkley *(Cast)*   251
Murray, Ted *(Composer)*   847
Murray, Wynn *(Cast)*   70, 117, 247, 514, 2379
Murray Singers, The, Lyn *(Cast)*   1278
Murril, Herbert *(Composer)*   3441
Murry, Jules *(Director)*   224
Murry, Jules *(Producer)*   939
Murry, Ted *(Composer)*   24, 867, 3145, 4265, 4571
Murtagh *(Composer)*   4712
Murtagh *(Lyricist)*   4712
Muse, Clarence *(Composer)*   3840
Muse, Clarence *(Lyricist)*   3840
Musel, Bob *(Composer)*   2653
Musel, Bob *(Lyricist)*   2653
Music Maker, Inc. *(Orchestrations)*   2727
Music Maker, Inc. *(Vocal Arranger)*   2727
Music Makers, Inc. *(Dance Arranger)*   2727
Music Theatre of Lincoln Center *(Producer)*   2838
Music Theater Workshop *(Producer)*   451, 1092, 3864
Musical Theater Works *(Producer)*   10, 3811
Musicworks Inc. *(Orchestrations)*   2007
Musky, Jane *(Set Design)*   3136
Musser, Tharon *(Lighting Designer)*   16, 160, 167, 287, 461, 521, 746, 1103, 1273, 1294, 1310, 1329, 1359, 1601, 1620, 1633, 1729, 1860, 2208, 2304, 2536, 2660, 2681, 2713, 2796, 2820, 2949, 2965, 3175, 3210, 3288, 3340, 3862, 3934, 4004, 4067, 4297, 4334, 4609, 4619, 4722
Muzio, Gloria *(Director)*   573
Myer, Bob *(Cast)*   4679
Myerberg, Michael *(Producer)*   309, 2655

Myers, Damar *(Costumes)* 1884
Myers, Edward *(Costumes)* 3490
Myers, Edward *(Librettist)* 2748
Myers, Edward *(Lyricist)* 2748
Myers, Henry *(Author)* 732
Myers, Henry *(Composer)* 732
Myers, Henry *(Librettist)* 732, 1617, 1711, 1745, 4331
Myers, Henry *(Lyricist)* 303, 1448, 1477, 2447, 2545,
    2809, 2810, 2823, 2933, 3005, 3130, 4249, 4331, 4367
Myers, Henry *(Producer)* 4331
Myers, Joanna *(Cast)* 4102
Myers, John Bernard *(Producer)* 1498
Myers, Johnny *(Composer)* 2580, 4627
Myers, Johnny *(Lyricist)* 4627
Myers, Lorna *(Cast)* 4447
Myers, Louise *(Cast)* 1961
Myers, Margot *(Cast)* 1357
Myers, Nancy *(Cast)* 427
Myers, Pamela *(Cast)* 832, 3871
Myers, Peter *(Composer)* 392, 2168
Myers, Peter *(Librettist)* 2168
Myers, Peter *(Lyricist)* 392, 2168, 3186, 3890
Myers, Richard *(Composer)* 86, 125, 577, 605, 1137, 1448,
    1691, 1839, 1856, 2976, 3002, 3172, 3352, 3816, 4170,
    4291, 4824, 4828
Myers, Stan *(Orchestrations)* 2089
Myers, Stanley *(Composer)* 1195
Myers, Stanley *(Lyricist)* 392, 1195
Myers, Stanley *(Musical Director)* 1644
Mylett, Jeffrey *(Cast)* 1595, 4343
Myrow, Josef *(Composer)* 851, 1125, 1298, 1808, 4602
Myrtil, Odette *(Cast)* 551, 672, 2622, 2680, 3837,
    4575, 4669
Myrtil, Odette *(Costumes)* 2496
Mysels, George *(Lyricist)* 1046
Mysteria, Princess *(Cast)* 471

N

N.E.T.W.O.R.K. *(Producer)* 916
N.I.M. and A. Co. *(Producer)* 4007
N.N.N. Company *(Producer)* 275
N.Y. City Center *(Producer)* 1474
N.Y. Shakespeare Festival *(Producer)* 54, 169, 282, 459,
    655, 746, 1015, 1053, 1055, 1344, 1575, 1715, 2033, 2237,
    2239, 2359, 2429, 2441, 2648, 2877, 2918, 2953, 3000,
    3197, 3198, 3276, 3456, 3757, 3806, 3825, 3830, 4151,
    4370, 4485, 4505, 4518, 4615, 4736, 4775
N.Y. State Theatre Inst. *(Producer)* 114
N.Y. University's Town Hall *(Producer)* 4444
N.Y. World's Fair Co *(Producer)* 117
Nabel, Bill *(Cast)* 36
Nabokov, Vladimir *(Author)* 2568
Nadeau, Nicky *(Set Design)* 544, 2443
Nadel, Arlene *(Cast)* 3684
Nadel, E.K. *(Producer)* 2298
Nadler, Arch *(Producer)* 593
Nadler, Mark *(Cast)* 3641, 3926

Nador, Mihaly *(Author)* 2622
Nadoud, Serge *(Cast)* 2753
Nagle, Jeri *(Choreographer)* 2028
Nagler, A.N. *(Author)* 3703
Nagrin, Daniel *(Cast)* 153, 3226, 3509, 4432, 4524
Nagy, John *(Composer)* 4488
Nagy, John *(Vocal Arranger)* 4488
Nahat, Dennis *(Choreographer)* 2260, 4485
Naify, Marshall *(Producer)* 2001
Naimo, Jennifer *(Cast)* 3377, 4398
Nainby, Robert *(Cast)* 3098
Nairn, Ralph *(Cast)* 4489
Naishtat, Saul *(Composer)* 4540
Naismith, Laurence *(Cast)* 406, 1860, 4384
Najimy, Kathy *(Director)* 261
Najimy, Kathy *(Producer)* 261
Naldi, Nita *(Cast)* 3402, 3975
Namanworth, Phillip *(Lyricist)* 1279
Namara, Madame *(Cast)* 93
Namara, Marguerite *(Cast)* 3152
Namuth, Harold *(Composer)* 1957
Nankwill, Guy *(Lyricist)* 4104
Napier, John *(Cast)* 4407
Napier, John *(Costumes)* 678, 2474, 4138
Napier, John *(Set Design)* 678, 730, 2442, 2474,
    2905, 4138, 4217
Napier, Nina *(Cast)* 2292
Napoli, Jeanne *(Composer)* 2754
Napoli, Jeanne *(Lyricist)* 2754
Napolitano, Peter *(Lyricist)* 4456
Nappo, Carmen *(Composer)* 1934
Nardo, Eric *(Composer)* 1250
Narmore, Eugene *(Composer)* 1637
Narmore, Eugene *(Lyricist)* 1637
Nash, Florence *(Cast)* 48, 2889
Nash, George *(Cast)* 1434
Nash, John *(Director)* 523, 2345
Nash, Marie *(Cast)* 924, 2068, 4498, 4572
Nash, Mary *(Cast)* 1570
Nash, N. Richard *(Author)* 1571
Nash, N. Richard *(Librettist)* 1764, 3294, 3838, 4693
Nash, N. Richard *(Lyricist)* 3838
Nash, N. Richard *(Producer)* 4693
Nash, Ogden *(Librettist)* 1874, 3301
Nash, Ogden *(Lyricist)* 192, 193, 369, 1792, 1874, 2554,
    3075, 3301, 3449, 4237, 4499
Nash, Robert *(Cast)* 2809
Nash, Ron *(Director)* 1732, 2055
Nason, Brian *(Lighting Designer)* 4371
Nassau, Paul *(Composer)* 1158, 1233, 1766, 2248, 3108
Nassau, Paul *(Lyricist)* 1158, 1233, 1766, 2248, 3108, 3112
Nassif, Robert *(Composer)* 4456
Nassif-Lindsey, Robert
    See Lindsay, Robert Nassif.
Nathan, Adele Gutman *(Author)* 2348
Nathan, Caspar *(Lyricist)* 3402
Nathan, Joseph *(Composer)* 688, 3384
Nathan, Joseph *(Lyricist)* 3384
Nathan, Joseph S. *(Composer)* 1520, 4723
Nathan, L & H *(Costumes)* 972, 3139

Nathan, Robert *(Author)* 2237, 3544
Nathan, Stephen *(Cast)* 1595
Nathan Jr., Alfred *(Composer)* 2739, 3783
National CIO War Prods. *(Producer)* 2748
Nations, Curt *(Set Design)* 1766
Natwick, Mildred *(Cast)* 1294, 3900, 4142
Naudain, May *(Cast)* 1526
Naughton, Amanda *(Cast)* 2038, 3377, 3757
Naughton, Bill *(Author)* 2297
Naughton, Harry *(Choreographer)* 4541
Naughton, James *(Cast)* 775, 2058, 4406
Naumkin, Yuri *(Cast)* 2269
Navarre, Jay *(Composer)* 673, 2246
Navarro, Jesus *(Cast)* 2407
Navasio, Lenora *(Cast)* 1360
Navon, Ruthi *(Cast)* 1075
Naylor, Ian *(Cast)* 2451
Naylor, Ian *(Choreographer)* 2451
Nayor, Ed *(Director)* 62
Nayor, Ed *(Librettist)* 62
Nazareth, Ernesto *(Composer)* 3397
Nazhad, Eric *(Producer)* 3690
Nazzarro, Nat *(Producer)* 1983, 3657
Nazzarro Jr., Nat *(Cast)* 969, 3069, 3137, 3397, 3405, 3406, 4427
Neal, Joseph *(Cast)* 169, 793, 4379
Neal, Joseph *(Librettist)* 1560
Neal, Joseph *(Lyricist)* 1560
Neal, Kathleen *(Cast)* 540
Neale, Grant *(Cast)* 2488
Nealy *(Musical Director)* 4220
Nealy, Milton Craig *(Cast)* 1296, 3285
Nease, Byron *(Cast)* 430
Neber, Caspar *(Set Design)* 4368
Nedbal, Oscar *(Composer)* 3424
Nederlander, Charlene *(Producer)* 3142, 4295
Nederlander, Gladys *(Producer)* 1633
Nederlander, James M. *(Producer)* 547, 695, 958, 975, 1068, 1633, 1660, 1699, 2360, 2437, 2798, 2820, 3142, 3171, 3299, 3682, 3869, 4295, 4447, 4695, 4727
Nederlander, Joseph Z. *(Producer)* 2142
Nederlander Organization *(Producer)* 1645, 3936
Neeley, Ted *(Cast)* 3903
Neenan, Audrie *(Cast)* 942
Neff, Clad *(Musical Director)* 2771
Neff, Hildegarde *(Cast)* 3972
Neff, Morty *(Lyricist)* 1046
Negro Ensemble Company *(Producer)* 1592, 1671, 2272, 2719
Negro Players *(Producer)* 4441
Negulesco, Dusky *(Lyricist)* 3383
Nehls, David *(Cast)* 4799
Neiburg, Al J. *(Lyricist)* 1951
Neidlinger, W.H. *(Composer)* 4236
Neil, Fred *(Composer)* 3739
Neil, Fred *(Lyricist)* 3739
Neil, Grace *(Cast)* 3952
Neil, Julian *(Director)* 1201
Neil, Roger *(Cast)* 3858
Neil, Roger *(Dance Arranger)* 3688

Neil, Roger *(Musical Director)* 3688
Neil, Roger *(Vocal Arranger)* 3858
Neill, Jeffrey K. *(Choreographer)* 159, 164, 3697
Neill, Jeffrey K. *(Director)* 164, 3697
Neilson, Alice *(Cast)* 1355, 3881
Neilson, Evelyn *(Cast)* 325
Neilson, Francis *(Librettist)* 2370, 3570
Neiman, Harold *(Musical Director)* 200
Nell Jr., Edward *(Cast)* 3117
Nelligan, Kate *(Cast)* 3884
Nelova, Dorissa *(Cast)* 289
Nelson, Arvid *(Lighting Designer)* 408
Nelson, Barry *(Cast)* 16, 1273, 4582, 4706
Nelson, Bob *(Cast)* 199
Nelson, Bruce *(Producer)* 4468
Nelson, Ed G. *(Composer)* 567, 1626, 4815
Nelson, Ed G. *(Lyricist)* 567
Nelson, Eddie *(Cast)* 1152, 4741
Nelson, Edgar *(Cast)* 94
Nelson, Gail *(Cast)* 602, 3018, 4002
Nelson, Gene *(Cast)* 1329, 1341, 2439, 3018
Nelson, Gene *(Choreographer)* 1341
Nelson, Gene *(Director)* 1341
Nelson, Joan Marie *(Cast)* 821
Nelson, John *(Set Design)* 3802, 4444
Nelson, John L. *(Composer)* 815
Nelson, John L. *(Lyricist)* 815
Nelson, Keith *(Lighting Designer)* 459
Nelson, Kenneth *(Cast)* 1245, 2288, 2626, 3161, 3788, 3835, 3895
Nelson, Lee Mark *(Cast)* 589
Nelson, Lucy *(Cast)* 4597
Nelson, Mari *(Cast)* 4518
Nelson, Mervyn *(Cast)* 2748, 3105, 4394
Nelson, Mervyn *(Director)* 943, 1834, 3863, 4377, 4829
Nelson, Mervyn *(Producer)* 943
Nelson, Nan-Lynn *(Cast)* 3806
Nelson, Novella *(Cast)* 1977, 3610
Nelson, Ozzie
  See Ozzie Nelson and His Orchestra.
Nelson, Portia *(Author)* 4330
Nelson, Portia *(Cast)* 273, 1600
Nelson, Portia *(Composer)* 90, 1023, 4153, 4330, 4416
Nelson, Portia *(Librettist)* 4330
Nelson, Portia *(Lyricist)* 90, 1023, 4153, 4330, 4416
Nelson, Ralph *(Director)* 44, 759, 2267
Nelson, Ralph *(Producer)* 2583
Nelson, Richard *(Librettist)* 721
Nelson, Richard *(Lighting Designer)* 572, 674, 682, 692, 789, 826, 1015, 1093, 1298, 1776, 1924, 2143, 2320, 2687, 2702, 3204, 3231, 3305, 3448, 3695, 4038, 4210, 4255
Nelson, Richard *(Set Design)* 4002
Nelson, Rick *(Cast)* 3275
Nelson, Rowland *(Cast)* 1957
Nelson, Rudolph *(Author)* 2886
Nelson, Rudolph *(Composer)* 2886
Nelson, Steve *(Lyricist)* 3793
Nelson and His Orch., Ozzie *(Cast)* 397
Nemerov, Howard *(Author)* 4278
Nemetz, Lee *(Director)* 3938

Ney, Richard *(Lyricist)* 3543
Neyman, Al *(Producer)* 205
Ngema, Bhoyi *(Cast)* 209, 4438
Ngema, Mbongeni *(Arrangements)* 4438
Ngema, Mbongeni *(Author)* 209
Ngema, Mbongeni *(Choreographer)* 4438
Ngema, Mbongeni *(Composer)* 3836, 4438
Ngema, Mbongeni *(Dance Arranger)* 3836
Ngema, Mbongeni *(Director)* 209, 3836, 4438
Ngema, Mbongeni *(Librettist)* 3836, 4438
Ngema, Mbongeni *(Lyricist)* 3836, 4438
Ngema, Mbongeni *(Orchestrations)* 4438
Ngema, Mbongeni *(Vocal Arranger)* 3836
Ngema, Nhlanhla *(Cast)* 3836
Nhlanhla, Thandekile *(Cast)* 3836
Niblo, Fred *(Cast)* 3749
Niblo, Fred *(Producer)* 3809
Nicander, Edwin *(Cast)* 1623
Nicastro, Michelle *(Cast)* 2820
Nice, Emily *(Cast)* 1833
Nice, Nellie *(Cast)* 1833
Nicholas, Anna *(Cast)* 846
Nicholas, Eden *(Cast)* 4602
Nicholas, Fayard
    See also The Nicholas Brothers.
Nicholas, Fayard *(Cast)* 247, 4123
Nicholas, Fayard *(Choreographer)* 432
Nicholas, Harold
    See also The Nicholas Brothers.
Nicholas, Harold *(Cast)* 247, 1385, 4123
Nicholas Brothers, The
    See also Fayard Nicholas and Harold Nicholas.
Nicholas Brothers, The *(Cast)* 446, 859, 875, 876, 877, 884, 885, 887, 4825
Nicholes, Bud *(Lighting Designer)* 3161
Nicholls, Allan *(Cast)* 3903
Nicholls, Horatio *(Composer)* 200
Nichols, Alberta *(Composer)* 138, 444, 1461, 1874, 2140, 3680, 3704
Nichols, Anne *(Author)* 1751, 2281, 2763
Nichols, Anne *(Cast)* 2310
Nichols, Anne *(Librettist)* 1751, 2489, 2605
Nichols, Anne *(Lyricist)* 2763
Nichols, Anne *(Producer)* 3922
Nichols, Barbara *(Cast)* 2246, 2449
Nichols, Beatrice *(Cast)* 4284
Nichols, Beverely *(Composer)* 791
Nichols, Beverely *(Librettist)* 791
Nichols, Beverely *(Lyricist)* 791
Nichols, Billy *(Composer)* 4167
Nichols, Billy *(Lyricist)* 4167
Nichols, Bobb *(Costumes)* 4380
Nichols, George *(Composer)* 3998
Nichols, George A. *(Composer)* 768, 2642
Nichols, George A. *(Lyricist)* 768
Nichols, George A. *(Musical Director)* 1927, 2642, 2990, 3723, 4195, 4382, 4437, 4831, 4833, 4834, 4836, 4837, 4838, 4851
Nichols, Harry *(Librettist)* 3803, 4430
Nichols, Joy *(Cast)* 1567

Nichols, Mike *(Director)* 170, 3624, 4129, 4746
Nichols, Mike *(Producer)* 52, 150, 414
Nichols, Nichelle *(Cast)* 2306
Nichols, Peter *(Author)* 3598
Nichols, Peter *(Lyricist)* 3598
Nichols, Peter *(Screenwriter)* 1497
Nichols, Red
    See Red Nichols Orchestra.
Nichols III, George *(Producer)* 4018
Nichols Orchestra, Red *(Cast)* 1528, 4179
Nicholson, John *(Cast)* 2802
Nicholson, John *(Director)* 2108
Nicholson, Kenyon *(Author)* 3138
Nicholson, Kenyon *(Librettist)* 4545
Nicholson, Paul *(Cast)* 2358
Nicholson, William *(Costumes)* 4154
Nicholson, William *(Set Design)* 4154
Nichtern, Claire *(Producer)* 298, 2218
Nick and Arnold *(Producer)* 817
Nickelodeon Family Classics *(Producer)* 754
Nickerson, Charles *(Cast)* 2113
Nickerson, Dawn *(Cast)* 3725
Nickerson, Denise *(Cast)* 2568
Nicodemus *(Cast)* 2597, 4256
Nicol, Lesslie *(Cast)* 2731
Nicol, Megg *(Cast)* 456
Nicola, James *(Director)* 1104
Nicolai *(Author)* 2841
Nicoll, Charles *(Choreographer)* 2876
Nido, Estaban Rio
    See Stephen Sondheim.
Nieburg, Al *(Lyricist)* 432
Niederhorn, Joe *(Cast)* 2094
Niehaus, Lennie *(Arrangements)* 2611
Nielsen, Alice *(Cast)* 2340, 3994, 4598
Nielsen Opera Company, Alice *(Producer)* 3994
Nielson, Christine *(Cast)* 276, 1738, 4616
Nieman, Harry *(Musical Director)* 201, 1461
Niemeyer, Joseph *(Cast)* 1606
Niesen, Gertrude *(Cast)* 622, 1336, 3409, 4825
Nightingale, Bill *(Cast)* 3539
Nigro, Robert *(Director)* 2152, 2542
Nikardi Productions *(Producer)* 1046
Nikko Producing Company *(Producer)* 3963
Nikolais, Alwin *(Choreographer)* 2441
Nikolais, Alwin *(Director)* 2441
Nikolais, Alwin *(Lighting Designer)* 2441
Nikolais, Alwin *(Set Design)* 2441
Niles, Barbara *(Cast)* 518, 1104
Niles, Marion *(Cast)* 1539
Niles, Mary Ann *(Cast)* 961, 2275, 2496, 4047
Niles, Mary Ann *(Choreographer)* 4047
Nilley, Florence *(Cast)* 1661
Nilo *(Costumes)* 1107, 1697, 3161, 3366
Nilsen, Harry *(Cast)* 1606
Nilsson, Harry *(Composer)* 4796
Nilsson, Harry *(Lyricist)* 4796
Nilsson, Walter *(Cast)* 1840
Nimura, Yeichi *(Choreographer)* 2655
Nininger, Willie *(Composer)* 4533

Northrup, Theodore H. *(Lyricist)*   1157
Norton, Coe *(Cast)*   4292
Norton, Edgar *(Cast)*   511, 2695, 3085, 3578
Norton, Fletcher *(Cast)*   1003, 1910, 2119, 2715, 3134, 4414
Norton, Frederick *(Composer)*   333, 758, 2701
Norton, Frederick *(Lyricist)*   333, 758, 2701
Norton, George *(Composer)*   1535
Norton, Jack *(Cast)*   1131
Norton, Mary *(Author)*   499
Norton, May *(Cast)*   749
Norton, Richard *(Producer)*   1149
Norton, Ruby *(Cast)*   1285, 1308, 1424, 3207
Norton and Margot, Harold *(Cast)*   897
Nortzar Productions *(Producer)*   1425
Norvo, Jimmy *(Cast)*   3500
Norvo, Red *(Cast)*   3893
Norwick, Douglas *(Choreographer)*   474, 556, 3666, 4272
Norworth, Jack *(Cast)*   8, 2232, 2528, 3222, 3755, 3779, 4802, 4803
Norworth, Jack *(Composer)*   2232, 2528, 2892, 3222, 3755, 4206, 4390, 4802, 4803, 4823
Norworth, Jack *(Librettist)*   3222
Norworth, Jack *(Lyricist)*   8, 1038, 2232, 2528, 2892, 3222, 3755, 4206, 4390, 4802, 4803, 4823
Norworth, Jack *(Producer)*   3222
Noto, Lore *(Librettist)*   4764
Noto, Lore *(Producer)*   1245, 4764
Noto, Tony *(Cast)*   4041
Nouri, Michael *(Cast)*   3088, 4560
Nova, Marta *(Cast)*   1244
Novak, Joe *(Producer)*   4454
Novasio, Lenora *(Cast)*   3434, 4381
Novello, Don *(Cast)*   1512
Novello, Don *(Librettist)*   1512
Novello, Ivor *(Cast)*   650, 972
Novello, Ivor *(Composer)*   133, 582, 650, 702, 703, 791, 972, 1467, 1610, 2004, 2570, 3020, 3259, 3924, 4154, 4327, 4581
Novello, Ivor *(Librettist)*   972, 1467
Novello, Ivor *(Lyricist)*   650, 702, 4581
Novis, Donald *(Cast)*   2258, 2636
Novotna, Jarmila *(Cast)*   1742, 1817
Novy, Nita *(Cast)*   1775
Nowak, Christopher *(Set Design)*   1872, 3608
Noyes, Newbold *(Cast)*   2287, 3378, 4622
Noyes, Patricia *(Translator)*   4386
Noyes, Thomas *(Producer)*   868
Nudelman, M. *(Librettist)*   2421
Nugent, Elliott *(Producer)*   3894
Nugent, Frank *(Author)*   1076
Nugent, Kitty *(Cast)*   2904
Nugent, Maude *(Composer)*   688, 1188
Nugent, Maude *(Lyricist)*   688
Nugent, Moya *(Cast)*   841, 1238, 3214, 3339, 3678, 3885, 3906, 4610
Nugent, Nelle *(Producer)*   2474
Nugent, Reita *(Cast)*   2976
Nunn, Trevor *(Director)*   211, 678, 721, 2442, 2474, 4138, 4217

Nunn, Trevor *(Lyricist)*   678
Nunn, Wayne *(Cast)*   1560
Nunsense Theatrical Co. *(Producer)*   3211
Nurock, Kirk *(Arrangements)*   2970
Nurock, Kirk *(Composer)*   2970
Nurock, Kirk *(Musical Director)*   3927
Nurock, Kirk *(Orchestrations)*   3824, 4744
Nurock, Kirk *(Vocal Arranger)*   251, 2970, 3927
Nurok, Robert *(Musical Director)*   3415
Nusbaum, Jane C. *(Producer)*   1729
Nussbaum, Joseph *(Orchestrations)*   2258, 3342
Nussbaum, Mike *(Director)*   1059
Nutter, Eileen *(Librettist)*   2034
Nutter, Mark *(Composer)*   4690
Nutter, Mark *(Librettist)*   4690
Nutter, Mark *(Lyricist)*   4690
Nuyen, France *(Cast)*   4749
Nyberg, David *(Orchestrations)*   275
Nye, April Ann *(Composer)*   4030
Nye, April Ann *(Lyricist)*   4030
Nye, Bill *(Librettist)*   4125
Nye, Carrie *(Cast)*   945, 1721
Nye, Louis *(Cast)*   2137, 4432
Nygh, Anna *(Choreographer)*   1166
Nyitray, Emil *(Author)*   2818, 3184
Nyitray, Emil *(Librettist)*   3048
Nyman, Betty Anne *(Cast)*   153, 851
Nype, Russell *(Cast)*   619, 1614, 2375, 3691, 4279, 4582

O

O'Brian, Hugh *(Cast)*   1257
O'Brien, Chester *(Choreographer)*   1342
O'Brien, Chet *(Cast)*   4677
O'Brien, Edmond *(Cast)*   4706
O'Brien, Eileen *(Cast)*   99
O'Brien, Gypsy *(Cast)*   1144, 2059
O'Brien, Jack *(Director)*   3088
O'Brien, Jack *(Librettist)*   3871
O'Brien, Jack *(Lyricist)*   3871
O'Brien, John J. *(Lyricist)*   543
O'Brien, Margaret *(Cast)*   2550
O'Brien, Marietta *(Cast)*   202
O'Brien, Michael Miguel *(Cast)*   3874
O'Brien, Mort *(Cast)*   4677
O'Brien, Ray *(Musical Director)*   4829
O'Brien, Richard *(Composer)*   3742
O'Brien, Richard *(Librettist)*   3742
O'Brien, Richard *(Lyricist)*   3742
O'Brien, Ritz *(Cast)*   3742
O'Brien, Sylvia *(Cast)*   1010
O'Brien, Timothy *(Costumes)*   1211
O'Brien, Timothy *(Set Design)*   1068, 1211
O'Brien, Virginia *(Cast)*   2020, 2301, 2492, 3434, 3723
O'Casey, Sean *(Author)*   2268, 3612
O'Casey, Sean *(Librettist)*   3612
O'Casey, Sean *(Lyricist)*   3612
O'Connell, Hugh *(Cast)*   1225, 4825

Oliver, Barrie *(Cast)*   700, 3131, 3605
Oliver, Barrie *(Choreographer)*   700
Oliver, Barrie *(Librettist)*   3605
Oliver, Don *(Cast)*   344
Oliver, Edna May *(Cast)*   1723, 3043, 3230, 3949, 4178
Oliver, Ike *(Cast)*   1316
Oliver, Joseph "King" *(Composer)*   1063
Oliver, King *(Composer)*   2200, 3840
Oliver, King *(Lyricist)*   3840
Oliver, Rochelle *(Cast)*   1184
Oliver, Roland *(Librettist)*   1343, 1629, 3256
Oliver, Roland *(Lyricist)*   1629, 3256
Oliver, Stephen *(Composer)*   2474
Oliver, Stephen *(Lyricist)*   2474
Oliver, Sy *(Musical Director)*   108
Oliver, Sy *(Orchestrations)*   3110, 3234
Oliver, Thelma *(Cast)*   766, 1319, 4238
Olivier, Laurence *(Cast)*   3597
Olman, Abe *(Composer)*   1334, 2856
Olmos, Edward James *(Cast)*   4861
Olneys, The *(Producer)*   1814, 4498
Olon, John *(Director)*   4246
Olrich, April *(Cast)*   4579
Olsen, Bob (Set *Design)*   3814
Olsen, George
  See also George Olsen and His Orchestra/
  Olsen's Orchestra.
Olsen, George *(Cast)*   2308, 4818
Olsen, Harry B. *(Composer)*   37, 1629, 3256
Olsen, Harry B. *(Musical Director)*   37, 3256
Olsen, Irene *(Cast)*   953, 1733
Olsen, J.C. *(Cast)*   1423
Olsen, Morry *(Composer)*   3314
Olsen, Morry *(Lyricist)*   3314
Olsen, Ole *(Cast)*   1423, 1840, 2400, 3380, 3381,
  4086, 4816
Olsen, Ole *(Composer)*   1423
Olsen, Ole *(Director)*   1423
Olsen, Ole *(Librettist)*   1840, 2400, 3381, 4086
Olsen, Ole *(Lyricist)*   1423, 3381, 4816, 4817
Olsen, Ole *(Producer)*   901, 1840, 2400, 3381, 4174
Olsen, Olive *(Cast)*   1136, 2808, 4673
Olsen, Robert *(Cast)*   4030
Olsen and His Orchestra/Olsen's Orchestra, George
  See also George Olsen.
Olsen and His Orchestra, George *(Cast)*   1628
Olsen's Orchestra, George *(Cast)*   4683
Olshanetsky, Alexander *(Composer)*   573, 1279, 1609
Olshanetsky, Alexander *(Lyricist)*   573, 1609
Olshenetsky, Alexander *(Composer)*   4463
Olson, Marcus *(Cast)*   212, 3411
Olson, Nancy *(Cast)*   3874
Olson, Scott *(Lyricist)*   3894
Olsson, Jack *(Composer)*   345
Olsson, Jack *(Lyricist)*   345
Olvis, William *(Cast)*   649, 3035
Omer, Costas *(Producer)*   4332
Omeron, Guen *(Cast)*   3151
Omeron, Gueneth *(Cast)*   2841
Ongley, Byron *(Author)*   577, 4860

Ongley, Byron *(Director)*   1520
Ono, Yoko *(Composer)*   3125, 4449
Ono, Yoko *(Librettist)*   3125
Ono, Yoko *(Lyricist)*   3125, 4449
Onrubia, Cynthia *(Cast)*   678
Ontiveros, Lupe *(Cast)*   4861
Onuki, Haru *(Cast)*   396
Opalach, Dorothy *(Musical Director)*   669
Opatoshu, David *(Cast)*   223, 400, 519, 3972, 4773
Opatoshu, David *(Director)*   400
Opatoshu, David *(Librettist)*   400
Opel, Nancy *(Cast)*   2038, 3448, 4210, 4297
Open Window, The *(Composer)*   3233
Open Window, The *(Lyricist)*   3233
Operti, Albert *(Set Design)*   2543
Operti, Le Roi *(Cast)*   919, 1343, 2610, 2729, 4386
Ophir, Shai K. *(Cast)*   1358
Ophir, Shai K. *(Director)*   1358
Ophir, Shai K. *(Librettist)*   1358
Ophir, Shai K. *(Lyricist)*   1358
Oppenheim, Dave *(Composer)*   1952
Oppenheim, Dave *(Lyricist)*   567, 1738, 1938, 1949,
  1950, 1952, 1953, 1963, 3375, 4335, 4589
Oppenheim, David *(Lyricist)*   1311
Oppenheim, E. Phillips *(Librettist)*   1153
Oppenheim, James *(Lyricist)*   1609
Oppenheimer, Alan *(Cast)*   4217
Oppenheimer, George S. *(Librettist)*   961, 2739
Oppenheimer, George S. *(Lyricist)*   2739
Oppenheimer, J. *(Producer)*   4275
Opper, Frederick Burr *(Author)*   1758, 1759
Opsahl, Jason *(Cast)*   3708
Oram, Harold L. *(Producer)*   344
Orange *(Costumes)*   2884
Orange, Fredi *(Cast)*   3814
Orbach, Jerry *(Cast)*   656, 723, 1245, 1359, 3603
Orbach, Ron *(Cast)*   2470
Orbison, Roy *(Composer)*   3695
Orbison, Roy *(Lyricist)*   3695
Orchard, Julian *(Cast)*   3482
Orczy, Baroness *(Author)*   3491
Ordonneau, Maurice *(Author)*   1994, 2365, 2667, 2723
Ordynski, Richard *(Director)*   1309
Orefice, Frank *(Librettist)*   242
Orenstein, Larry *(Composer)*   732
Orezzoli, Hector *(Costumes)*   432
Orezzoli, Hector (Set *Design)*   432
Orfaly, Alexander *(Cast)*   3711
Original Dixieland Jass Band *(Composer)*   3297
Orkin, Harvey *(Librettist)*   4469
Orlando, Phil *(Vocal Arranger)*   1924
Orlob, Harold *(Composer)*   1, 144, 246, 248, 638, 1307,
  1513, 1718, 1801, 1920, 2270, 2491, 2774, 2901, 3052,
  3087, 3207, 3395, 3579, 3672, 4226, 4276, 4437, 4448
Orlob, Harold *(Librettist)*   2270, 2709, 4448
Orlob, Harold *(Lyricist)*   1307, 1593, 1718, 2270, 2709,
  2901, 3395, 4448
Orlob, Harold *(Producer)*   1513, 1718
Orloff, Penny *(Cast)*   1068
Orlova, Gay *(Cast)*   3002

Orme, Gordon *(Cast)* 3103
Ormes, Alberta *(Cast)* 1909
Ormiston, George *(Cast)* 3111
Ormont, Dave *(Lyricist)* 673
Ormont, David *(Lyricist)* 1892
Ormston, George *(Set Design)* 796
Ornadel, Cyril *(Composer)* 1313, 3482
Ornbo, Robert *(Lighting Designer)* 832, 2047
Orr, Ann *(Cast)* 1531, 3923
Orr, Clifford *(Lyricist)* 3005
Orr, Forrest *(Cast)* 3674
Orr, Mary *(Author)* 167
Orr, William P. *(Producer)* 2328
Ortega, Eva *(Cast)* 3885
Ortega, Kenny *(Choreographer)* 2754
Ortega, Kenny *(Director)* 2754
Orth, Louise *(Cast)* 1919
Ortmann, Will *(Additional Music)* 718
Ortmann, Will *(Composer)* 718, 1935, 1944, 3430, 3783, 4189
Ortmann, Will *(Lyricist)* 1944
Orton, Chip *(Lyricist)* 1638
Orton, Joe *(Screenwriter)* 4518
Ory, Kid *(Composer)* 3297
Osato, Sono *(Cast)* 283, 3278, 3286, 3301
Osborn, Hubert *(Author)* 1916
Osborn, Paul *(Author)* 4749
Osborn, Paul *(Librettist)* 1990
Osborne, Frances *(Cast)* 4467
Osborne, Loraine *(Cast)* 1535
Osborne, Nat *(Composer)* 231, 1407, 1517, 1824, 2274
Osborne, Nat *(Librettist)* 231
Osborne, Vivienne *(Cast)* 3974
Osburn, Alan *(Cast)* 4731
Osburne, Oran *(Cast)* 1029
Oscar, Brad *(Cast)* 2198
Oscar, Gail *(Cast)* 871
Oscar, Henry *(Cast)* 4207
Osgood, Pearl *(Cast)* 1323, 4823
Oshins, Jules *(Cast)* 4340
Oshrin, Harry *(Producer)* 4276
Oshrin, Sidney S. *(Producer)* 2052
Osser, Glenn *(Arrangements)* 1744
Osser, Glenn *(Musical Director)* 1744, 2522, 3496
Osser, Glenn *(Orchestrations)* 1146, 1864, 3126
Osterman, Jack *(Cast)* 202, 3148, 3409, 4021
Osterman, Jack *(Lyricist)* 202, 4819
Osterman, Lester *(Producer)* 630, 1227, 1891, 2965, 2987, 3299, 3741, 3743, 3780, 3845, 4060, 4601
Ostermann, Curt *(Lighting Designer)* 962, 1496, 1997, 3764
Osterwald, Bibi *(Cast)* 108, 1237, 1507, 1600, 3914, 3989, 4156, 4542
Ostranger, A.A. *(Set Design)* 1112
Ostrov, Dmitri *(Director)* 1710
Ostrov, Dmitri *(Producer)* 1710
Ostrow, Stuart *(Director)* 1860, 4252
Ostrow, Stuart *(Producer)* 119, 170, 1214, 1860, 2949, 3506, 3897, 4252, 4609
Otero, Emma *(Cast)* 1414

Otis, Elita Proctor *(Cast)* 2770, 3613
Otis, Phoebe *(Cast)* 4332
Ott, Horace *(Dance Arranger)* 1116
Ott, Horace *(Orchestrations)* 1116, 4558
Ott, Horace *(Vocal Arranger)* 1116
Ott, Joseph *(Cast)* 559, 2865
Ott, Matthew *(Cast)* 1213
Ott, Matthew *(Librettist)* 2934
Ott, Matthew *(Lyricist)* 2934
Ott, Phil *(Composer)* 2934
Ott, Phil *(Librettist)* 1964
Ott, Phil *(Producer)* 1964
Ott & Wallin *(Producer)* 2934
Otto, Arthur *(Cast)* 361
Otto, Ernest *(Cast)* 361
Otto, Frank *(Cast)* 2265
Otto, Liz *(Cast)* 2051
Otvos, A. Dorian *(Composer)* 2972, 3369
Otvos, A. Dorian *(Librettist)* 622, 1493, 1692, 3172
Oudin, Eugene *(Cast)* 1080
Ouelette, Gratian *(Composer)* 4433
Ouelette, Gratian *(Librettist)* 4433
Ouelette, Gratian *(Lyricist)* 4433
Oumansky, Alexander *(Choreographer)* 2413, 3008
Oursler, Fulton *(Author)* 4105
Ousley, Robert *(Cast)* 4233
Ouspenskaya, Maria *(Cast)* 2211
Outcault, R.E. *(Author)* 591
Ouzounian, Richard *(Director)* 426
Ouzounian, Richard *(Lyricist)* 426
Overholt, Miles *(Librettist)* 2454
Overman, Lynne *(Cast)* 1961, 1979, 2281, 4213
Overstreet, Benton *(Composer)* 4231
Overstreet, William *(Composer)* 1838
Overstreet, William Benton *(Additional Music)* 1499
Overton, Frank *(Cast)* 4191
Overton, Jane *(Cast)* 1013
Owen, Alun *(Librettist)* 2682
Owen, Delos *(Composer)* 4240
Owen, Delos *(Librettist)* 4240
Owen, Garry *(Cast)* 2896
Owen, Guy *(Cast)* 4143
Owen, Hayden *(Musical Director)* 1098
Owen, J. Edwin *(Librettist)* 3316
Owen, John *(Director)* 4041
Owen, John *(Librettist)* 4041
Owen, Margaret *(Cast)* 1098
Owen, Nancy *(Cast)* 4149
Owen, Paul *(Vocal Arranger)* 4415
Owen, Reginald *(Cast)* 4357, 4372
Owen, Wallace *(Cast)* 2274
Owens, Daniel *(Librettist)* 2513
Owens, Flo *(Cast)* 395
Owens, Frank *(Composer)* 3905, 4171, 4534
Owens, Frank *(Dance Arranger)* 3905, 4171, 4534
Owens, Frank *(Lyricist)* 3905, 4171
Owens, Frank *(Musical Director)* 3905, 4534
Owens, Frank *(Orchestrations)* 4171
Owens, Frank *(Vocal Arranger)* 3905
Owens, Frederick B. *(Cast)* 4031

P

Palmer, Winthrop *(Author)* 2887
Palmer, Winthrop *(Producer)* 2887
Palsson's Supper Club *(Producer)* 430
Paltrow, Bruce W. *(Producer)* 4659
Palumbo, Gene *(Composer)* 1638
Palumbo, Gene *(Musical Director)* 1638
Palumbo, Gene *(Vocal Arranger)* 1638
Pan, Hermes *(Cast)* 1747, 4426
Pan, Hermes *(Choreographer)* 206
Panama, Norman *(Librettist)* 2301, 2484
Panama, Norman *(Producer)* 2484
Panaro, Hugh *(Cast)* 3682
Panetta, George *(Author)* 2322
Panetta, George *(Librettist)* 2322
Pangborn, Franklin *(Cast)* 4230
Panich, David *(Librettist)* 1233, 2288, 4627
Panis, Reuben *(Costumes)* 2294
Pankey, Anna Cook *(Cast)* 3797
Pankin, Stuart *(Cast)* 4707
Panko, Tom *(Choreographer)* 1611, 3204
Panko, Tom *(Director)* 1002
Pankow, John *(Cast)* 3884
Pantages, Rodney *(Producer)* 2640
Paoletti, John *(Costumes)* 4690
Pape, Joan *(Cast)* 1914
Paper Mill Playhouse *(Producer)* 3851
Papez & Zwack *(Cast)* 2086
Papp, Joseph *(Director)* 54, 169, 2918
Papp, Joseph *(Producer)* 54, 282, 459, 746, 1015, 1053,
    1344, 1575, 1715, 2033, 2074, 2239, 2359, 2648,
    2877, 2918, 2953, 3000, 3070, 3198, 3276, 3806, 3825,
    3830, 3884, 4151, 4370, 4485, 4505, 4615, 4736
Papp Yiddish Theater, Joseph *(Producer)* 4082
Pappas, Evan *(Cast)* 1120, 3039
Pappas, Theodore *(Choreographer)* 829, 1038, 1872,
    3368
Pappas, Theodore *(Director)* 3368
Pappen, Delmar *(Cast)* 2396
Paragon Park Prods. *(Producer)* 573
Parallel Productions *(Producer)* 1216
Paramount Pictures *(Producer)* 1649
Paramount Theatre Prods. *(Producer)* 3060
Pardo, Eddie *(Cast)* 2490
Parell, Nancy *(Cast)* 3479
Parent, Gail *(Composer)* 3112
Parent, Gail *(Librettist)* 2590, 3111, 3112
Parent, Gail *(Lyricist)* 3112
Parent, Nicole *(Cast)* 2364
Parenteau, Zoel *(Composer)* 102, 1335, 2309
Parenteau, Zoel J. *(Composer)* 1901
Paret, Frank *(Musical Director)* 1626
Parichy, Dennis *(Lighting Designer)* 374, 942, 1669,
    2152, 2440
Paris, Judith *(Choreographer)* 874
Paris, Norman *(Musical Director)* 2988
Paris, Norman *(Orchestrations)* 1045, 4191
Parise, Tony *(Choreographer)* 275, 3346
Parise, Tony *(Director)* 275
Parisette, Mildred *(Cast)* 2813
Parish, Mitchell *(Lyricist)* 445, 447, 710, 839, 881,

1138, 1813, 1939, 2077, 2161, 2178, 3020, 3354, 3950,
    4091, 4137, 4264, 4799
Park, John *(Cast)* 118, 830, 1469, 1962, 2335, 2770,
    2844, 3437, 3786, 4285
Park, John B. *(Cast)* 132
Park, Michael *(Cast)* 1822, 4031
Park, Phil *(Lyricist)* 4027
Park, R. Vincent *(Librettist)* 3136
Park, R. Vincent *(Producer)* 3136
Park Avenue Synogogue *(Producer)* 4304
Parker, Barnett *(Cast)* 910, 4374
Parker, Dell *(Cast)* 512
Parker, Dorothy *(Author)* 1861
Parker, Dorothy *(Cast)* 1218
Parker, Dorothy *(Librettist)* 1357, 3946
Parker, Dorothy *(Lyricist)* 630, 2633, 3783
Parker, E. Huntington *(Costumes)* 4332
Parker, Flora *(Cast)* 60, 1212, 1523, 1911, 2974, 3626
Parker, Florence *(Cast)* 4668
Parker, Frank *(Cast)* 197, 1336
Parker, George D. *(Author)* 2613
Parker, George D. *(Director)* 2976
Parker, Harry Doel *(Librettist)* 4223
Parker, Howard *(Choreographer)* 2737, 3126
Parker, Jimmie *(Cast)* 553
Parker, Lem B. *(Librettist)* 631, 917
Parker, Lem B. *(Lyricist)* 917
Parker, Lew *(Cast)* 127, 145, 180, 1397, 1528,
    3823, 4299
Parker, Loria *(Cast)* 139
Parker, Lotta *(Cast)* 2524
Parker, Lou *(Cast)* 2709
Parker, Louis N. *(Author)* 2756
Parker, Rena *(Cast)* 4794
Parker, Robert *(Cast)* 2937
Parker, Ross *(Cast)* 2364
Parker, Ross *(Composer)* 4027
Parker, Ross *(English Lyrics)* 2364
Parker, Ross *(Lyricist)* 4027
Parker, Roxann *(Cast)* 1262, 3318
Parker, Stewart *(Author)* 4109
Parker, Stewart *(Lyricist)* 4109
Parker, Walter Coleman *(Librettist)* 2631
Parker Jr., R. *(Composer)* 1298
Parker Jr., R. *(Lyricist)* 1298
Parks, Bernice *(Cast)* 341, 3947, 4117
Parks, Beverly *(Costumes)* 2692
Parks, Don *(Cast)* 4494
Parks, Don *(Librettist)* 2219, 2288
Parks, Don *(Lyricist)* 272, 1408, 2219
Parks, Hildy *(Producer)* 1000, 2064
Parks, John *(Choreographer)* 2513
Parks, Larry *(Cast)* 339
Parks, Melvin *(Cast)* 3103, 3104
Parks, Michael *(Cast)* 1709
Parks, Robert *(Cast)* 2483
Parks, Trina *(Cast)* 692
Parlato, Dennis *(Cast)* 1785, 1822
Parnell, Jack *(Conductor)* 3454
Parnis, Molly *(Composer)* 72

Parr, Albert *(Cast)*   2697, 3073, 3883
Parr-Davies, Harry *(Composer)*   4027
Parrinello, Richard *(Musical Director)*   3888, 4029
Parrish, Elizabeth *(Cast)*   2360, 2522, 3195, 3725
Parrish, Robert *(Cast)*   1987
Parry, Chris *(Lighting Designer)*   4676
Parry, Frederick *(Director)*   2951
Parry, Sally E. *(Producer)*   3697
Parry, William *(Cast)*   212, 1053, 1510, 1630, 2142, 2346, 3411, 3903, 4736
Parry, William *(Director)*   2374
Parson, William *(Musical Director)*   1987, 4018, 4058
Parson, William *(Vocal Arranger)*   4058
Parsons, Chauncey *(Cast)*   202
Parsons, Donovan *(Lyricist)*   700, 702, 792, 2004, 2789, 2843, 4581
Parsons, Estelle *(Cast)*   237, 339, 1171, 1760, 3484, 4682
Parsons, Geoffrey *(Composer)*   4264
Parsons, Geoffrey *(Lyricist)*   4264
Parsons, George *(Cast)*   1271, 2525
Parsons, Jennifer *(Cast)*   3631
Parsons, Joseph *(Cast)*   1631
Partington, Jeanne *(Costumes)*   3940
Parva, Cynthia *(Cast)*   3548
Pascal, Fran *(Librettist)*   1478
Pascal, John *(Librettist)*   1478
Pascal, Milton *(Composer)*   1397
Pascal, Milton *(Lyricist)*   95, 204, 673, 1207, 1336, 1397, 1892, 2105, 2246, 2396
Pascaud, Mme. *(Costumes)*   208
Pascoe, Richard W. *(Lyricist)*   4576
Pasekoff, Marilyn *(Cast)*   518, 1349, 3600
Paskman, Dailey *(Composer)*   710
Paskman, Dailey *(Lyricist)*   710, 2121, 4486, 4817
Pasquinelli, Joanne *(Author)*   4494
Passman, Ray *(Composer)*   2580
Passman, Ray *(Lyricist)*   2580
Patch, William *(Cast)*   382
Patch, William Moore *(Producer)*   1882, 2174, 4248
Patek, Patrick J. *(Producer)*   131
Paterson, Vincent *(Choreographer)*   2333
Patinkin, Mandy *(Cast)*   1211, 2346, 2429, 3862, 4210
Paton, Alan *(Author)*   2591
Patrelle, Francis *(Choreographer)*   3565
Patrick, Dennis *(Cast)*   1837
Patrick, Fred *(Lyricist)*   4827
Patrick, John *(Author)*   347, 2626
Patrick, John *(Librettist)*   2626
Patrick, Lee *(Cast)*   423, 2265
Patrick, Nigel *(Cast)*   1205
Patrick, Robert *(Author)*   3034
Patrick, Robert *(Lyricist)*   3034
Patricola, Tom *(Cast)*   1486, 1487, 1488, 1489, 1490, 1932, 2460, 4465
Patricola Jr., Tom *(Cast)*   3264
Patron, Elias *(Cast)*   1269
Patston, Doris *(Cast)*   324, 1384, 2293, 2628, 4025
Patten, Caymichael *(Director)*   3661
Patterson, Chuck *(Cast)*   2692

Patterson, Dianthia *(Cast)*   2059
Patterson, Dick *(Cast)*   410, 1227, 4020, 4566
Patterson, Elizabeth *(Cast)*   1850
Patterson, Helen *(Cast)*   2271
Patterson, James *(Composer)*   1964
Patterson, Lorna *(Cast)*   140
Patterson, Neva *(Cast)*   3841, 3894
Patterson, Raymond *(Cast)*   2992, 3169, 3739
Patterson, Robert *(Set Design)*   1604, 4303
Patterson, Russell *(Costumes)*   289, 1342, 1440, 1932, 4824
Patterson, Russell *(Musical Director)*   643
Patterson, Russell *(Producer)*   289, 3810
Patterson, Russell *(Set Design)*   289, 1342, 1493, 1932
Patterson, Ruth Cleary *(Composer)*   3810
Patterson, Ruth Cleary *(Musical Director)*   3810
Patterson, Stark *(Cast)*   711
Patterson, Vaughn *(Set Design)*   2197
Patton, Lucille *(Cast)*   169, 2368, 4768
Patton, Mal *(Cast)*   4184
Patton, Will *(Cast)*   2468
Paul, Agnes *(Cast)*   1220, 1720
Paul, Alan *(Cast)*   1664
Paul, Betty *(Cast)*   2680
Paul, Bobby *(Composer)*   3722
Paul, Cedar *(Librettist)*   2202
Paul, Eden *(Librettist)*   2202
Paul, Gene *(Lyricist)*   702
Paul, Tina *(Cast)*   975
Paul, Tina *(Choreographer)*   975, 1739, 3142, 4264
Paul, Walter *(Orchestrations)*   180, 1336, 2103, 4123, 4362
Paulee, Mona *(Cast)*   2664, 2961
Paulette, Larry *(Cast)*   2451
Pauley, Pat *(Cast)*   2097
Pauling, Lowman *(Composer)*   4264
Pauling, Lowman *(Lyricist)*   4264
Paull, Harry *(Cast)*   904
Paull, Morgan *(Cast)*   3111
Paulsen, David *(Lyricist)*   4396
Paulson, Kay *(Cast)*   512
Paulton, Edward *(Author)*   1193, 2336
Paulton, Edward *(Director)*   1078
Paulton, Edward *(Librettist)*   20, 517, 955, 1078, 1193, 1301, 1875, 2495, 2867, 3071, 3627, 4200, 4492, 4758
Paulton, Edward *(Lyricist)*   20, 465, 517, 1193, 1301, 1308, 1875, 1882, 2174, 2495, 2587, 2867, 3627, 4200, 4492, 4758
Paulton, Edward A. *(Author)*   4322
Paulton, Edward A. *(Composer)*   2495
Paulton, Edward A. *(Librettist)*   233, 717, 1565, 2387, 2665, 2854, 3051, 3052, 3581, 4489
Paulton, Edward A. *(Lyricist)*   233, 717, 1041, 1565, 2495, 2665, 2854, 3051, 3581, 3855, 4489
Paulton, Harry *(Cast)*   1080
Paulton, Harry *(Director)*   1193
Paulton, Harry *(Librettist)*   1078, 1301
Paulton, Harry *(Lyricist)*   1301, 4713
Paulton, Jack *(Cast)*   1626
Pavell, Barbara *(Cast)*   3920

Perley Opera Company, Frank *(Producer)* 4549
Perlino, Hilda *(Cast)* 1989
Perlman, Arthur *(Librettist)* 158, 4708
Perlman, Arthur *(Lyricist)* 158, 4708
Perlman, Max *(Composer)* 2356
Perlman, Max *(Lyricist)* 2356
Perlmutter *(Composer)* 907
Perlmutter, Arnold *(Composer)* 1609
Perlmutter, Arnold *(Lyricist)* 1609
Perr, Harvey *(Librettist)* 3902
Perrault, Charles *(Author)* 759
Perren, Frederick J. *(Composer)* 3739
Perren, Frederick J. *(Lyricist)* 3739
Perri, Valerie *(Cast)* 3277
Perrin *(Composer)* 1627
Perrin *(Lyricist)* 1627
Perrin, Adrian S. *(Choreographer)* 584, 3192
Perrin, Adrian S. *(Director)* 3192
Perrin, Margaret *(Composer)* 272
Perrin, Nat *(Librettist)* 2640
Perrin, Sam *(Librettist)* 180
Perrin, Sidney *(Composer)* 813
Perrin, Sidney L. *(Composer)* 719
Perrin, Sidney L. *(Lyricist)* 719
Perrin, Sydney L. *(Composer)* 719
Perrin, Sydney L. *(Lyricist)* 719
Perrineau, Harold *(Cast)* 240
Perrineau Jr., Harold *(Cast)* 1236
Perry, Alan D. *(Producer)* 261
Perry, Barbara *(Cast)* 1748, 2103
Perry, E. Martin *(Musical Director)* 2764
Perry, Elaine *(Cast)* 3180
Perry, Irene *(Cast)* 618
Perry, Jaime *(Cast)* 2239
Perry, John Bennett *(Cast)* 280, 2941, 2962
Perry, Karen *(Costumes)* 2239
Perry, Katheryn *(Cast)* 444, 888
Perry, Keith *(Cast)* 3364
Perry, Lynnette *(Cast)* 747, 1649, 3125
Perry, Marsha *(Cast)* 166
Perry, Robert E. *(Director)* 1930
Perry, Robert E. *(Producer)* 1892
Perry, Rod *(Cast)* 952, 3111, 3112, 4395
Perry, Sara *(Cast)* 1806
Perry, Shauneille *(Director)* 3599, 4697
Perry, Shauneille *(Librettist)* 952
Perry, Steve *(Cast)* 2278
Perry, Steven *(Set Design)* 4082
Perry, William *(Cast)* 843
Perry, William *(Composer)* 4701
Perry, William *(Lyricist)* 4701
Perry/Wood Company *(Producer)* 27
Perryman, Al *(Choreographer)* 105
Perschk, Max *(Composer)* 4228
Pershing, D'Vaughn *(Musical Director)* 3742
Persoff, Nehemiah *(Cast)* 3452
Personette, Joan *(Costumes)* 1840, 4006, 4496
Persson, Gene *(Director)* 3653
Persson, Gene *(Producer)* 4034, 4783
Persson, Ruby *(Cast)* 3653

Pertwee, Jon *(Cast)* 4329
Pertwee, Michael *(Librettist)* 814
Perugini, Sidmund *(Cast)* 2179
Peskanov, Alexander *(Composer)* 456
Peter, Fred *(Pianist)* 214
Peter, Rene *(Author)* 511, 3079
Peters, Bernadette *(Cast)* 941, 956, 1478, 1633,
    2143, 2368, 2660, 3439, 4068, 4210, 4577
Peters, Beth *(Cast)* 2650
Peters, Brandon *(Cast)* 1283
Peters, Brock *(Cast)* 483, 2355
Peters, Burt *(Composer)* 2232
Peters, Clarke *(Librettist)* 1296
Peters, Elsie *(Composer)* 4394
Peters, Joan *(Costumes)* 2970
Peters, Lauri *(Cast)* 1290, 4095
Peters, Leonard *(Director)* 1418, 4684
Peters, Mason *(Producer)* 1515
Peters, Michael *(Cast)* 406, 3610, 4003
Peters, Michael *(Choreographer)* 828, 1103, 2427
Peters, Michael *(Director)* 2427
Peters, N. *(Cast)* 1604
Peters, Paul *(Librettist)* 3365
Peters, Paul *(Lyricist)* 3365
Peters, Roger *(Producer)* 1787
Peters, Shannon Reyshard *(Cast)* 535
Peters, Stephanie *(Composer)* 3688
Peters, Stephanie *(Lyricist)* 3688
Peters, W.H. *(Composer)* 3399
Peters, William F. *(Composer)* 934, 1767, 2145, 2893,
    3399, 3820, 3866, 4711
Peters, William Frederick *(Composer)* 2793, 3033, 3613
Petersburski, J. *(Composer)* 4730
Peterson, Aleigh *(Choreographer)* 3966
Peterson, Don *(Composer)* 2288
Peterson, Eric *(Cast)* 414
Peterson, Eric *(Composer)* 414
Peterson, Eric *(Lyricist)* 414
Peterson, Erika *(Cast)* 1222
Peterson, Kurt *(Cast)* 273, 599, 1012, 1329
Peterson, Lenka *(Cast)* 3631
Peterson, Margorie *(Cast)* 1131
Peterson, Mary *(Costumes)* 275
Peterson, Nora *(Choreographer)* 3476, 3817
Peterson, Patricia Ben *(Cast)* 4769
Pether, Henry E. *(Composer)* 675, 1544, 3268
Petherbridge, Edward *(Cast)* 2474
Petina, Irra *(Cast)* 161, 630, 1918, 2679, 4075
Petit, Charles *(Author)* 711
Petrayer, Sophia *(Cast)* 1531
Petricoff, Elaine *(Cast)* 1770, 3711
Petrides, Avra *(Lyricist)* 459
Petrie, Dan *(Director)* 4155
Petrie, Daniel *(Director)* 2958
Petrie, George *(Cast)* 1546
Petrie, H.W. *(Composer)* 1301
Petrillo, Stephen *(Lighting Designer)* 760
Petro, Michael *(Cast)* 2243
Petroff, Boris *(Director)* 831
Petroff, Boris *(Producer)* 831

Picon, Molly (Composer) 3336
Picon, Molly (Lyricist) 1279
Picture, Kay (Cast) 2300, 2432
Pidgeon, Walter (Cast) 3617, 4059, 4270
Piech, Jennifer (Cast) 2654
Pierantozzi, Victor (Cast) 4243
Pierce, Betty (Cast) 2174
Pierce, Billy (Choreographer) 1202, 1722, 4043
Pierce, Charlie (Composer) 3962
Pierce, Charlie (Lyricist) 3962
Pierce, Frank (Cast) 1224
Pierce, Jo Carol (Librettist) 264
Pierce, Jo Carol (Lyricist) 264
Pierce, John (Choreographer) 966, 1546, 1862, 2808, 4730
Pierce, Lewis (Cast) 4536
Pierce, Marion (Cast) 4365
Pierce, Wendell (Cast) 3628
Pierce, Wesley (Cast) 203
Pierlot, Francis (Cast) 294, 2344
Pierlot, Frank (Cast) 2771
Pierpont, J.S. (Composer) 3175
Pierpont, J.S. (Lyricist) 3175
Pierre, Christopher (Cast) 2908
Pierre, Jacques (Producer) 1177
Pierre, Mabelle (Cast) 1248
Pierre, Olivier (Cast) 1256
Pierro, Christina (Cast) 328
Pierson, Arthur (Director) 4826
Pierson, Arthur (Librettist) 3290, 4640
Pierson, Edward (Cast) 4447
Pierson, Harold (Cast) 4238
Pierson, Rita (Cast) 2025
Pierson, Thomas (Musical Director) 518, 946, 1116
Pierson, Thomas (Orchestrations) 599, 3927
Pierson, William (Cast) 4022
Piffi, Henry (Librettist) 3
Piggot, J.W. (Librettist) 2341
Piggot, J.W. (Lyricist) 2341
Pigliavento, Debra (Choreographer) 2737
Pigliavento, Michele (Cast) 2372
Pigott, Colin (Set Design) 2204
Pigott, J.W. (Author) 2341
Pike, John (Composer) 4729
Pike, John (Director) 4729
Pike, John (Librettist) 4729
Pike, John (Lyricist) 4729
Pilbrow, Richard (Lighting Designer) 589, 3780, 3927, 4252, 4862
Pilbrow, Richard (Producer) 1619
Pilcer, Harry (Cast) 263, 351, 1307, 1801, 1835, 1963, 2538, 3500, 4158
Pilcer, Harry (Choreographer) 1472
Pilcer, Harry (Lyricist) 2538, 4553, 4655
Pilgrim, Chris (Composer) 1865
Piller, Heinar (Director) 3066
Pils, Jacques (Cast) 3756
Pinaud, Lena (Cast) 909
Pinchot, Rosamond (Cast) 1196
Pincus, Henry (Producer) 2717

Pincus, Warren (Cast) 4773
Pincus, Warren (Producer) 2993
Pine, Lester (Librettist) 2246
Pinelli, Tullio (Author) 3171, 4238
Pinero, Arthur Wing (Author) 100, 2871
Pinero, Arthur Wing (Lyricist) 2871
Pinero, Miguel (Author) 4205
Pink, Wal (Librettist) 2571, 3500, 3663
Pink, Wal (Lyricist) 3663
Pinkard, Fred (Cast) 2075
Pinkard, Maceo (Composer) 489, 554, 2204, 2557, 3361, 3905, 3962, 4104
Pinkard, Maceo (Lyricist) 2557, 3361, 3905
Pinkard, Maceo (Producer) 3361
Pinkham, Richard (Librettist) 3916
Pinkins, Tonya (Cast) 2200
Pinkney, Mikell (Director) 2133
Pinkney, Scott (Lighting Designer) 2704
Pinsuti, M. (Composer) 4479
Pinto, Cola (Cast) 2114
Pinza, Ezio (Cast) 1242, 4096
Piontek, Michael (Cast) 1997
Pip (Author) 208
Piper, John (Set Design) 920
Piper Jr., Ralph (Composer) 2239
Piper Jr., Ralph (Lyricist) 2239
Pippin, Don (Composer) 669, 840, 2688, 2689, 3637
Pippin, Don (Musical Director) 1146, 3637, 3869
Pippin, Don (Vocal Arranger) 840, 1146, 2713, 3869, 4297
Pippin, Donald (Arrangements) 3682
Pippin, Donald (Composer) 1249, 2737
Pippin, Donald (Dance Arranger) 145, 1249
Pippin, Donald (Musical Director) 167, 367, 746, 1012, 1373, 2360, 2660, 2713, 2737, 3126, 3271, 3294, 3682, 4727
Pippin, Donald (Orchestrations) 1002, 1093
Pippin, Donald (Vocal Arranger) 167, 367, 550, 746, 1002, 1012, 1249, 1373, 1660, 2360, 2660, 4727
Piquet, Rolf (Composer) 3443
Pirkle, Mac (Director) 4055
Pirkle, Mac (Librettist) 4055
Piron, A.J. (Composer) 1063, 3297
Piron, A.J. (Lyricist) 1063, 3297
Pirosh, Robert (Librettist) 3893
Piscariello, Frederick A. (Composer) 722
Piscariello, Frederick A. (Lyricist) 722
Pistone, Charles (Cast) 647, 1510
Pitchford, Dean (Cast) 3817, 4505
Pitchford, Dean (Lyricist) 661, 1236
Pitilli, Lawrence (Composer) 1282
Pitkin, Robert (Cast) 1278, 1888, 3345, 4673
Pitkin, William (Costumes) 597, 825
Pitkin, William (Set Design) 597, 825, 837, 1010, 1474, 2144
Pitot, Genevieve (Dance Arranger) 483, 619, 629, 842, 1029, 1094, 1564, 1679, 2137, 2331, 2357, 2484, 2556, 2864, 3837, 3913, 4090, 4496
Pitou, Augustus (Author) 1445, 3267, 3759, 4239
Pitou, Augustus (Director) 1445, 3267, 3759, 4239, 4313

Pitou, Augustus *(Producer)* 1157, 1163, 1907, 2662, 2763, 3220, 3267, 3642, 4120, 4313
Pitou Jr., Augustus *(Director)* 2186
Pitou Jr., Augustus *(Producer)* 2186, 2310
Pitou Sr., Augustus *(Author)* 2186, 2310
Pitou Sr., Augustus *(Director)* 2310
Pitt, Charles D. *(Director)* 4227
Pitts, Tom *(Composer)* 2856
Pitts, Tom *(Lyricist)* 2856
Pitts. Civic Light Opera *(Producer)* 2651
Pixley, Frank *(Librettist)* 586, 1313, 1650, 1707, 2315, 2745, 3578, 4738
Pixley, Frank *(Lyricist)* 586, 1650, 1707, 2315, 2745, 3578, 4738
Pixley, Gus *(Cast)* 187, 250
Pizzolla, Astor *(Composer)* 975
Placzek, Ron *(Set Design)* 556, 3311
Plain Jane Incorporated *(Producer)* 3511
Plaisted, T.S. *(Set Design)* 1193
Plamstierna-Weiss, Gunilla *(Costumes)* 3445
Plana, Tony *(Cast)* 4861
Plane, Liane *(Cast)* 4625
Planquette, Robert *(Author)* 3372
Planquette, Robert *(Composer)* 102, 3372
Plant, Mark *(Cast)* 4772
Plate, Jennie *(Cast)* 1499
Platt, Edward *(Cast)* 3234
Platt, George Foster *(Director)* 2779
Platt, Howard *(Cast)* 1169
Platt, Livingston *(Costumes)* 1935
Platt, Livingston *(Set Design)* 2, 1935, 2121, 2342, 3185, 3248, 3849
Platt, Marc *(Cast)* 323, 2252, 2379, 2680, 3263
Platt, Maxwell *(Director)* 293
Platt, Oliver *(Cast)* 2945, 4535
Platt, William *(Cast)* 263
Platzman, Eugene *(Composer)* 710
Platzman, Eugene *(Lyricist)* 710
Plautus *(Author)* 514, 1422
Players Club of Columbia U. *(Producer)* 1724, 1725
Players Ring, The *(Producer)* 2057
Playfair, Arthur *(Cast)* 1554
Playfair, Nigel *(Producer)* 325
Playhouse Square Center *(Producer)* 1636
Playkill Productions, Inc. *(Producer)* 1348
Playten, Alice *(Cast)* 1291, 1828, 1846, 3077, 3271, 3602, 4540
Playwrights Horizons *(Producer)* 109, 212, 829, 1234, 1872, 2185, 2746, 3368, 4210, 4358
Playwrights' Company, The *(Producer)* 2268, 2344, 2591, 4169, 4386, 4495
Plaza Theatre *(Producer)* 2643
Pleasence, Donald *(Cast)* 1089
Pleininger, Carl *(Composer)* 1608
Pleis, Jack *(Composer)* 2168
Plimmer, Harry *(Cast)* 3481
Plimpton, Martha *(Cast)* 119
Plimpton, Shelley *(Cast)* 1717, 3162
Plohn, Edmund *(Producer)* 4284
Ploner, George *(Lyricist)* 272

Plotnick, Jack *(Cast)* 3926
Plowman, Cory *(Cast)* 810
Plowman, Justin *(Cast)* 810
Plowman, Pat *(Author)* 810
Plowman, Travis *(Cast)* 810
Plumer, Lincoln *(Cast)* 3529
Plummer, Amanda *(Cast)* 54, 2468
Plummer, Christopher *(Cast)* 946, 1620, 2411
Plummer, H. Joseph *(Cast)* 821
Plunkett, Blanche *(Cast)* 1720
Plunkett, Charles *(Cast)* 976
Plunkett, M.W. *(Producer)* 388
Plunkett, Maryann *(Cast)* 81, 2798
Plunkett, Paul *(Cast)* 1561
Pober, Leon *(Composer)* 339
Pockriss, Lee *(Composer)* 614, 838, 1194, 1451, 4193, 4260, 4261, 4264, 4366, 4435
Pockriss, Lee *(Lyricist)* 4193, 4264
Poddany, Eugene *(Musical Director)* 2015
Poddubiuk, Christina *(Costumes)* 1120
Podell, Jules *(Producer)* 857, 858, 863
Podell, Rick *(Cast)* 597, 2579, 2962
Poe, Aileen *(Cast)* 1227, 2684, 3538, 3898
Poe, Coy *(Composer)* 1813, 4799
Poe, Coy *(Lyricist)* 1813, 4799
Pogany, Willy *(Costumes)* 2684, 2900
Pogany, Willy *(Set Design)* 2005, 2666, 2684, 3622
Pogue, David *(Musical Director)* 4619
Pogue, David *(Vocal Arranger)* 4619
Pohl, Richard *(Author)* 2538, 2668
Poindexter, H.R. *(Lighting Designer)* 1616, 3015
Pointing, Audrey *(Cast)* 429
Points, Ruth *(Costumes)* 2483
Poiret, Jean *(Author)* 2360, 3624
Poiret, Jules *(Costumes)* 4327
Poiret, Paul *(Costumes)* 25, 208, 582, 1712, 3312
Poiret, Paul *(Set Design)* 25, 582
Pokrass, Dmitiri *(Composer)* 1740
Pokrass, Samuel *(Composer)* 948, 3409, 4824
Pokrass, Samuel D. *(Composer)* 4670
Pola, Edward *(Composer)* 4741
Polacheck, Charles *(Cast)* 3180
Polacheck, Charles *(Director)* 1085
Polachek, Leon *(Musical Director)* 399
Polakov, Lester *(Costumes)* 924, 3698
Polakov, Lester *(Set Design)* 620
Polanco, Iraida *(Cast)* 696
Poland, Albert *(Producer)* 300, 3209, 4074
Polcsa, Juliet *(Costumes)* 2846, 2852
Poldine, Leo *(Librettist)* 1448
Polechek, Leon *(Musical Director)* 433
Polen, Linda *(Cast)* 626
Polenz, Robert *(Cast)* 169, 729
Poleo, Dom *(Lighting Designer)* 1878
Polk, Gordon *(Cast)* 1760
Polk, Jeffrey *(Cast)* 1159
Polk, Oscar *(Cast)* 536, 1225, 4256
Polla, W.C. *(Composer)* 1646
Polla, William *(Composer)* 2857
Polla, William C. *(Composer)* 2481

Posluns, Leah *(Producer)* 1079
Posnak, Charles *(Composer)* 364
Posner, Kenneth *(Lighting Designer)* 2229, 3811
Posner, Lee *(Librettist)* 439
Post, August *(Lyricist)* 3686
Post, Douglas *(Composer)* 3667
Post, Douglas *(Librettist)* 3667
Post, Douglas *(Lyricist)* 3667
Post, J. *(Composer)* 4193
Post, J. *(Lyricist)* 4193
Post, W. *(Composer)* 1342
Post, W.H. *(Author)* 4249
Post, W.H. *(Director)* 60, 2574, 4053, 4351
Post, W.H. *(Librettist)* 4664
Post, William H. *(Director)* 1270, 1472
Post, William H. *(Librettist)* 354, 2264, 3729, 4539
Postage Stamp Xtravaganzas *(Producer)* 4462
Postell, Steve *(Composer)* 1232
Postell, Steve *(Musical Director)* 1232
Poston, Tom *(Cast)* 837
Pot, Pan and Skillet *(Cast)* 2259
Pothier, Charles *(Lyricist)* 4240
Potok, Chaim *(Author)* 747
Potter, Chandler *(Set Design)* 2483
Potter, Clare *(Costumes)* 3894
Potter, Edward *(Cast)* 1342
Potter, H.C. *(Director)* 649, 1219
Potter, Henry C. *(Cast)* 3325
Potter, Jane *(Cast)* 4030
Potter, L.S. *(Composer)* 3828
Potter, L.S. *(Lyricist)* 3828
Potter, Maude *(Cast)* 3877
Potter, Paul *(Author)* 3866
Potter, Paul *(Librettist)* 1312, 3626, 3857, 4125
Potter, Paul *(Lyricist)* 1312, 1318
Potter, Paul M. *(Librettist)* 2732
Potter, Paul M. *(Lyricist)* 2732
Potter, S. *(Composer)* 1429
Pottle, Sam *(Cast)* 4041
Pottle, Sam *(Composer)* 73, 108, 427, 1049, 1648, 2935, 3111, 3112, 4041
Pottle, Sam *(Dance Arranger)* 2935
Pottle, Sam *(Librettist)* 3111
Pottle, Sam *(Lyricist)* 3111
Pottle, Sam *(Musical Director)* 2663, 2935
Pottle, Sam *(Pianist)* 4041
Pottle, Sam *(Producer)* 3186
Pottle, Sam *(Vocal Arranger)* 2935
Potts, David *(Set Design)* 3932, 4205
Potts, Nancy *(Costumes)* 52, 942, 1059, 1662, 1717, 1977, 2368, 3468, 3651, 3871, 3991
Pought, Emma Ruth *(Composer)* 4264
Pought, Emma Ruth *(Lyricist)* 4264
Pought, Jannie *(Composer)* 4264
Pought, Jannie *(Lyricist)* 4264
Pound, Courtice *(Composer)* 758
Pound, Courtice *(Lyricist)* 758
Pounds, Courtice *(Cast)* 719
Pounds, Louie *(Cast)* 2514
Pounds, Toots *(Cast)* 3157

Pourcel, F. *(Composer)* 4193
Pourcel, F. *(Lyricist)* 4193
Powell *(Composer)* 4823
Powell *(Lyricist)* 4823
Powell, Addison *(Cast)* 3577
Powell, Anthony *(Costumes)* 4217
Powell, Dawn *(Librettist)* 2379
Powell, Dick *(Cast)* 2371
Powell, Eddie *(Orchestrations)* 207
Powell, Edgar *(Composer)* 291
Powell, Edgar *(Lyricist)* 291
Powell, Edward *(Orchestrations)* 680, 1322, 1672, 2444, 3002, 4267
Powell, Edward B. *(Orchestrations)* 1137
Powell, Eleanor *(Cast)* 216, 1275, 1339, 1481, 1979, 3310
Powell, Felix *(Composer)* 964, 1852, 1919, 3259
Powell, Gary *(Arrangements)* 914
Powell, Jack *(Cast)* 1932, 2423
Powell, Jane *(Cast)* 1257, 3800
Powell, Janet *(Cast)* 3651
Powell, Jerry *(Composer)* 62, 128, 366, 1120, 1637, 2913, 3111, 3112, 3124
Powell, Jerry *(Lyricist)* 1120, 1637, 3111
Powell, Lovelady *(Cast)* 1990, 3725
Powell, Michael *(Author)* 3682
Powell, Michael *(Musical Director)* 4788
Powell, Shezwae *(Cast)* 730, 4450
Power, Chosei Funahara *(Composer)* 3739
Power, Chosei Funahara *(Lyricist)* 3739
Power, Udana *(Cast)* 1616
Power Productions *(Producer)* 705
Power Sr., Tyrone *(Cast)* 758
Powers, Amy *(Lyricist)* 760
Powers, Arthur Augustus *(Lyricist)* 1392
Powers, Augustus *(Lyricist)* 1392
Powers, George *(Cast)* 1913, 4007
Powers, Georgia *(Cast)* 2361
Powers, James T. *(Author)* 2378
Powers, James T. *(Cast)* 470, 770, 1783, 2213, 2519, 2803, 2844, 3588, 3828, 3834, 4490
Powers, James T. *(Librettist)* 1783, 2519, 4490
Powers, James T. *(Lyricist)* 1783, 2519, 4490
Powers, John *(Orchestrations)* 92
Powers, John R. *(Author)* 1059
Powers, John R. *(Librettist)* 1059
Powers, Leona *(Cast)* 3713
Powers, Manila *(Cast)* 202, 3680
Powers, Margot *(Cast)* 2057
Powers, Neva Rae *(Cast)* 2318, 2616
Powers, T. *(Composer)* 4193
Powers, T. *(Lyricist)* 4193
Powers, Tom *(Cast)* 2605, 3230
Powers, Tony *(Composer)* 2427
Powers, Tony *(Lyricist)* 2427
Powers, W.H. *(Cast)* 2494
Powers, William *(Cast)* 4802
Powys, Stephen *(Author)* 4586
Poynter, Edward *(Cast)* 1368
Prager, Stanley *(Cast)* 3351

Prager, Stanley *(Director)* 519, 2449, 2874, 3273, 3286, 3900

Prager, Stanley *(Librettist)* 4827

Prange, Laurie *(Cast)* 4459

Pransky, John *(Producer)* 268, 4323

Prather, Tom Ross *(Director)* 3067

Pratt, Alvin Ronn *(Cast)* 1671

Pratt, Charles E. *(Composer)* 1897

Pratt, Charles E. *(Lyricist)* 1897

Pratt, John *(Costumes)* 1370, 2582, 4254

Pratt, Ron *(Set Design)* 3752

Pratt, Thomas Charles *(Costumes)* 2104

Praxis Group *(Producer)* 1377

Preble, Ed *(Librettist)* 2423

Precarious Productions *(Producer)* 3970

Preisser, Cherry *(Cast)* 4824, 4825

Preisser, June *(Cast)* 901, 4777, 4824, 4825

Premice, Josephine *(Cast)* 576, 2190, 3524

Premus, Judy *(Cast)* 3926

Prendergast, Shirley *(Lighting Designer)* 105, 1073, 2513, 4591

Prentice, Amelia *(Cast)* 549

Prentice, Charles *(Composer)* 702

Prentice, Charles *(Musical Director)* 277, 475, 650, 791, 972, 2392, 4361

Prentice, Charles *(Orchestrations)* 841, 972

Prentice, Keith *(Cast)* 3815

Presburg, Jacques *(Composer)* 3258

Presburg, Jacques *(Orchestrations)* 3258

Presbury, Eugene *(Director)* 2824

Presnell, Harve *(Cast)* 154, 155, 1674, 4516

Press, Brian *(Cast)* 330

Press, Jacques *(Lyricist)* 1937

Press, Richard *(Producer)* 166

Pressburger, Emeric *(Author)* 3682

Pressel, Marc *(Musical Director)* 2212

Pressley, Brenda *(Cast)* 131

Pressman, Aaron *(Musical Director)* 3495

Pressman, Kenneth *(Lyricist)* 2633

Preston, Barry *(Cast)* 576, 4577

Preston, Billy *(Composer)* 3739

Preston, Billy *(Lyricist)* 3739

Preston, J. David *(Librettist)* 1231

Preston, Morgan *(Librettist)* 1231

Preston, Rob *(Lyricist)* 3908

Preston, Robert *(Cast)* 367, 2050, 2660, 3016, 3577, 4609

Preston, Robert W. *(Composer)* 1978

Preston, Robert W. *(Lyricist)* 1978

Preston, Robert W. *(Musical Director)* 1581, 4145

Preston, Tony *(Librettist)* 3814

Preston-Smith, Roger *(Choreographer)* 3764

Previn, Andre *(Composer)* 798, 1619

Previn, Charles *(Musical Director)* 186, 1527, 1686, 2180, 2363, 2684, 2907, 3157, 3225, 3538, 3727, 4491

Prewitt, Arrington *(Lyricist)* 47

Pribor, Richard *(Dance Arranger)* 2705

Pribor, Richard *(Musical Director)* 1341, 4346

Priborsky, Richard *(Musical Director)* 1257

Price, Allan *(Cast)* 3650

Price, Alonzo *(Cast)* 3532, 3951

Price, Alonzo *(Director)* 606, 1533, 2768, 3978, 4056, 4209

Price, Alonzo *(Librettist)* 606, 3978, 4056

Price, Alonzo *(Lyricist)* 3978, 4056

Price, Chilton *(Composer)* 4264

Price, Chilton *(Lyricist)* 4264

Price, Don *(Choreographer)* 2284, 2759

Price, Don *(Director)* 2284, 2759

Price, Edwin *(Director)* 3828

Price, George *(Cast)* 764, 1703, 4851

Price, George E. *(Composer)* 4427

Price, George E. *(Lyricist)* 4104, 4427

Price, Georgie *(Cast)* 1395, 1396, 4083, 4104, 4656

Price, Georgie *(Composer)* 4083

Price, Gerald *(Cast)* 1242, 2178, 4369

Price, Gilbert *(Cast)* 1119, 1319, 2203, 3159, 3602, 3731, 4002, 4004, 4383

Price, Henry *(Cast)* 2839

Price, John *(Cast)* 2795

Price, Lonny *(Cast)* 171, 1120, 2822, 3644

Price, Lonny *(Director)* 838

Price, Lonny *(Lyricist)* 1120

Price, Lorin *(Producer)* 1478

Price, Lorin E. *(Producer)* 3869, 3956

Price, Lorin Ellington *(Producer)* 4380

Price, Mark deSolla *(Producer)* 4279

Price, Mme. Helene *(Costumes)* 1014

Price, Paul B. *(Cast)* 3217

Price, Roger *(Cast)* 4377

Price, Roger *(Librettist)* 3107

Price, Tim Rose *(Lyricist)* 2346

Price, Tom *(Composer)* 1298

Price, Tom *(Lyricist)* 1298

Price, Vincent *(Cast)* 989

Pride, Malcolm *(Costumes)* 1619

Pride, Malcolm *(Set Design)* 1619

Priest, Janet *(Cast)* 2485, 2695, 3855

Priestley, J.B. *(Author)* 1618

Priestley, J.B. *(Librettist)* 1618

Prima, Louis *(Composer)* 146, 964

Primary Stages *(Producer)* 2065

Primavera Productions *(Producer)* 3522, 4379

Primont, Marian *(Cast)* 1897

Primrose, Joe *(Composer)* 445

Primrose, Joe *(Lyricist)* 445

Primrose Sisters *(Cast)* 1824

Primus, Barry *(Cast)* 1064

Prince *(Composer)* 4534

Prince *(Lyricist)* 4534

Prince, Charles *(Cast)* 354, 1728, 2324, 3423, 4185

Prince, Charles A. *(Musical Director)* 3063

Prince, Charles H. *(Cast)* 1505, 2865, 4650

Prince, Daisy *(Cast)* 3456

Prince, Faith *(Cast)* 1234, 1665, 2205, 2643, 3142, 4535

Prince, Graham *(Composer)* 432

Prince, Graham *(Lyricist)* 432

Prince, Harold *(Director)* 270, 610, 832, 1038, 1068, 1186, 1211, 1237, 1329, 1699, 2163, 2333, 2536, 2607, 2822, 3279, 3340, 3456, 3464, 3702, 3792, 3918, 4233, 4862

Prince, Harold *(Producer)* 610, 832, 957, 1265, 1280, 1310, 1329, 1422, 1699, 2163, 2417, 2536, 2822, 3113, 3340, 3351, 3918, 3967, 4312, 4625, 4862
Prince, Hughie *(Composer)* 1539, 3739
Prince, Hughie *(Lyricist)* 1539
Prince, Jack *(Cast)* 1029
Prince, Robert *(Composer)* 4060
Prince, Robert *(Dance Arranger)* 1721, 1990, 4060
Prince, Robert *(Orchestrations)* 1227
Prince, William *(Conductor)* 2027
Prince-Joseph, Bruce *(Musical Director)* 2910
Princess White Deer *(Cast)* 4853
Princess White Durrah *(Cast)* 1421
Pringle, Marjorie *(Cast)* 815, 1549
Printemps, Yvonne *(Cast)* 841, 3216
Prinz, Eddie *(Choreographer)* 1138, 3173
Prinz, Eddie *(Director)* 1947, 3173
Prinz, LeRoy *(Choreographer)* 1126, 1135, 1281, 1462, 1667, 1799, 3978, 4291, 4426
Prinz, LeRoy *(Director)* 2640, 3683
Prior, Allan *(Cast)* 1667, 2293, 2622, 3407, 4664
Prior, Thomas W. *(Lyricist)* 331
Priscilla, Victor *(Lyricist)* 621
Pritchard, John *(Composer)* 3186
Pritchard, Mark *(Set Design)* 874, 2572
Pritchard, Ted *(Cast)* 1092, 3018
Pritchett, James *(Cast)* 3815
Pritchett, John *(Composer)* 392
Pritchett, John *(Lyricist)* 392
Pritchett, Liz *(Cast)* 1766
Probst, Gerry *(Cast)* 3104
Probst, Robert *(Musical Director)* 1467
Prochaska, Bobby *(Cast)* 580
Prochnik, Bruce *(Cast)* 3271
Proctor, Catherine *(Cast)* 1144
Proctor, David *(Cast)* 3693
Proctor, Ethelyn *(Cast)* 1479
Proctor, Phil *(Composer)* 3076
Proctor, Phil *(Lyricist)* 3076
Proctor, Philip *(Cast)* 127
Proctor, Warren *(Cast)* 3472
Producers Associates *(Producer)* 1414
Producers Circle *(Producer)* 229
Producers Circle 2, The *(Producer)* 3279
Producers Circle Co. *(Producer)* 3792
Proett, Daniel *(Set Design)* 3076
Proft, Michael *(Librettist)* 4830
Program Devlopment Co. *(Producer)* 4127
Proia, Alexandre *(Cast)* 756
Prokofiev, Serge *(Composer)* 192
Prokofiev, Serge *(Music Based On)* 3449
Promenaders, The *(Producer)* 4484
Prophet Company, The *(Producer)* 3568
Proser, Monte *(Producer)* 850, 1811, 1886
Prosper and Maret *(Cast)* 1460
Prosser, Julie *(Cast)* 2027
Prostak, Edward *(Cast)* 2689
Proud, Peter *(Set Design)* 362
Prouty, Jed *(Cast)* 78, 1566, 2291, 2907, 3304, 3866, 4054, 4058, 4547

Provenza, Paul *(Librettist)* 4774
Provenza, Paul *(Lyricist)* 4774
Provenza, Rosario *(Set Design)* 2932
Provost, William *(Composer)* 924
Prucell, Charles *(Cast)* 1309
Prud'homme, Cameron *(Cast)* 603, 3113, 4516
Prudhomme Prod. Ltd. *(Producer)* 105
Pruette, William *(Cast)* 48, 737, 742, 1088, 1783, 2665, 2671, 2915, 3053, 3679, 3732, 4434
Prunczik, Karen *(Cast)* 1359
Pruneau, Phillip *(Librettist)* 4090
Prussian, E.D. *(Composer)* 1535
Pruyn, William *(Dance Arranger)* 3840
Pruyn, William *(Vocal Arranger)* 3840
Pryce, Jonathan *(Cast)* 2905
Prymus, Ken *(Cast)* 2250, 3628
Pryor, Arthur *(Composer)* 3268
Pryor, Marjorie *(Cast)* 2131
Pryor, Roger *(Cast)* 4178
Pryor, Roger *(Librettist)* 1856
Psacharopoulos, Nikos *(Director)* 945, 3195
Ptaszynski, Andre *(Producer)* 3695
Public Players, Inc. *(Producer)* 319
Puccini, Giacomo *(Author)* 595
Puccini, Giacomo *(Composer)* 2359, 3079
Puck, Eva *(Cast)* 1529, 1689, 1823, 2148, 2814, 3949
Puck, Harry *(Cast)* 2569, 2637, 2669, 2833, 3042, 4240, 4283, 4352
Puck, Harry *(Choreographer)* 2637, 2833, 4476
Puehringer, F. *(Composer)* 2895
Puerner, Charles *(Musical Director)* 1576
Puerto Rican Travelling Th. *(Producer)* 696
Pugh, E.E. *(Cast)* 14
Pugh, Ed *(Cast)* 26
Pugh, Ted *(Cast)* 708, 1786
Puig, Manuel *(Author)* 2333
Pujol, Rene *(French Lyrics)* 2366
Pujol, Rene *(Lyricist)* 4517
Pulen, Sim *(Cast)* 1388
Pulitzer, Walter *(Composer)* 2624
Pulitzer, Walter *(Lyricist)* 2624
Pullman, Kate *(Cast)* 3754
Pully, B.S. *(Cast)* 1706
Purcell, Charles *(Cast)* 1013, 1602, 2253, 2684, 2794, 2939, 3051, 3254, 3538, 3562, 3712, 3770, 3907, 4833
Purcell, Gertrude *(Author)* 4284
Purcell, Gertrude *(Cast)* 2816
Purcell, Gertrude *(Librettist)* 2277, 2490, 2637, 2669, 4352
Purcell, Gertrude *(Lyricist)* 4284
Purcell, Harold *(Lyricist)* 4510
Purcell, Jack *(Cast)* 859
Purcell, John H. *(Cast)* 2126
Purchese, Donald *(Musical Director)* 1857
Purdham, David *(Cast)* 2539
Purdom, Ralph *(Cast)* 73, 2750, 3371
Purdy, Richard *(Cast)* 629
Puri, Rajika *(Cast)* 4442
Puri, Rajika *(Choreographer)* 4442
Purinton, Jock *(Lighting Designer)* 92

Purinton, Jock *(Set Design)*   92
Purnell, Carrie *(Cast)*   552
Pursley, David *(Cast)*   1229
Purviance, Roy *(Cast)*   3045, 4649
Purvis, James *(Cast)*   2795
Pusey, Charles A. *(Cast)*   1213
Pusilo, Robert *(Costumes)*   344, 840
Puzo, Bill *(Set Design)*   4635
Pysher, Ernie *(Cast)*   3159

Q

Qrezzoli, Hector *(Director)*   432
Quackenbush, Karyn *(Cast)*   789, 1630
Quadri, Therese *(Cast)*   3597
Quality Amusement Company *(Producer)*   254
Qualters, Tot *(Cast)*   684, 736, 2706, 2856, 2857, 3866, 4810
Quaney, Barbara *(Cast)*   2067, 2935
Quartermaine, Leon *(Cast)*   3779
Quartet Productions *(Producer)*   3835
Quayle, Anna *(Cast)*   4160
Quayle, Anthony *(Cast)*   1294
Quayle, Anthony *(Director)*   1294
Quesenbery, Whitney *(Lighting Designer)*   1719, 4288
Questel, Mae *(Cast)*   269
Quick, George *(Cast)*   2838
Quick, Louise *(Cast)*   1273
Quick, Louise *(Choreographer)*   2426
Quigley, Erin *(Costumes)*   4074
Quigley, Herb *(Orchestrations)*   4256
Quigley, Jack *(Dance Arranger)*   302
Quigley, Jack *(Vocal Arranger)*   302
Quigley, Martin *(Librettist)*   2928
Quigley, Robert *(Cast)*   4705
Quillan, Joe *(Librettist)*   297
Quilley, Dennis *(Cast)*   129, 1644
Quilter, Roger *(Composer)*   4154
Quin, Mike *(Librettist)*   2809
Quine, Richard *(Cast)*   4557
Quinlan, Dan *(Cast)*   1823, 3677
Quinlan, Gertrude *(Cast)*   1845, 2315, 4201, 4404
Quinlan, John *(Cast)*   2666
Quinn, Aidan *(Cast)*   2468
Quinn, Anthony *(Cast)*   2450
Quinn, Colleen *(Cast)*   533
Quinn, Florence *(Cast)*   2716
Quinn, James *(Composer)*   1059
Quinn, James *(Lyricist)*   1059
Quinn, Jerome *(Producer)*   4648
Quinn, Marie *(Cast)*   2310
Quinn, Michael *(Cast)*   3113
Quinn, Patricia *(Cast)*   477, 2207
Quinn, Patrick *(Cast)*   1597
Quinson, Gustave *(Author)*   468
Quintero, Jose *(Director)*   1427, 3551
Quintero, Jose *(Librettist)*   1427
Quinton, Dolores *(Producer)*   2754

Quinton, Everett *(Cast)*   2037, 2488
Quinton, Everett *(Costumes)*   2037
Quinton, Everett *(Director)*   2037
Quinton, Everett *(Librettist)*   2037, 2488
Quinton, Everett *(Lyricist)*   2037, 2488
Quixano, Dave *(Cast)*   2587
Quong, Rose *(Cast)*   1315

R

RLM Productions, Inc. *(Producer)*   4701
Rabb, Ellis *(Cast)*   2859, 3787, 4715
Rabb, Ellis *(Director)*   1662, 3468, 3787
Rabe, David *(Cast)*   4151
Rabe, David *(Lyricist)*   4151
Rabinowitz, Harry *(Musical Director)*   4301
Rabiroff, Jacques *(Musical Director)*   2379, 3916
Rachael, Anne *(Cast)*   3824
Racheff, James *(Librettist)*   10
Racheff, James *(Lyricist)*   10
Rachel Productions *(Producer)*   3831
Rachmaninoff, Sergei *(Music Based On)*   161
Rackerby, Donald *(Cast)*   80
Rackmil, Gladys *(Producer)*   1645, 2435, 2677, 3444, 3515
Racolin, Alexander E. *(Producer)*   2110
Racolin, Dina *(Producer)*   2110
Radaelli *(Cast)*   2140
Radcliffe, Carrie *(Cast)*   2675
Radford, Dave *(Lyricist)*   3737
Radford, Robert *(Cast)*   3992
Radin, Al *(Musical Director)*   2843
Radin, Oscar *(Musical Director)*   463, 684, 764, 1065, 1111, 1343, 1522, 1920, 1929, 2358, 2373, 2666, 2668, 2696, 2732, 2825, 2856, 3246, 3397, 3399, 3400, 3401, 3403, 3525, 3680, 3958, 4747, 4816, 4817
Radin, Oscar *(Orchestrations)*   965, 2282, 2378, 2519, 2684, 3006, 3395, 3403, 3650, 3737
Radio City Mu. Hall *(Producer)*   107
Radio City Music Hall *(Producer)*   2737, 3126, 3638, 4035
Radio City Music Hall Prod. *(Producer)*   1298
Radio City Music Hall Prods *(Producer)*   1146, 1638
Radio Rogues, The *(Cast)*   1840
Radner, Gilda *(Cast)*   1512
Radner, Gilda *(Librettist)*   1512
Radner, Gilda *(Lyricist)*   1512
Rado, James (Cast)   1717, 1736
Rado, James *(Composer)*   3651
Rado, James *(Librettist)*   1717, 3651
Rado, James *(Lyricist)*   1717, 3651
Rado, James *(Producer)*   3651
Rado, Ted *(Librettist)*   3651
Rado, Ted *(Producer)*   3651
Radomski, James *(Composer)*   932
Radomski, James *(Lyricist)*   932
Radomski, Jim *(Cast)*   932
Radomski, Jim *(Composer)*   932
Radomski, Jim *(Lyricist)*   932
Radomsky, Saul *(Set Design)*   2949

Rae, Charlotte *(Cast)*   2484, 2554, 2954, 3482, 3497, 3564, 4366, 4369
Rae, Florence *(Cast)*   2083
Rae, Olive *(Cast)*   2514
Rae, Phyllis *(Cast)*   3924
Rael, Elsa *(Lyricist)*   2633
Raft, Dick *(Cast)*   3403
Raft, George *(Cast)*   773, 1416, 3342, 3403
Rafter, Adele *(Cast)*   2697
Rafter, Frank *(Set Design)*   175, 284, 1213, 1392, 1540, 2500, 2543, 2938, 2986
Ragent, Robert *(Choreographer)*   4416
Raggio, Lisa *(Cast)*   1637
Ragland, Oscar "Rags" *(Cast)*   930, 2184, 2978, 3131, 3172, 3359, 4150, 4267, 4393, 4667, 4677
Ragni, Gerome *(Cast)*   1717, 1736
Ragni, Gerome *(Librettist)*   1116, 1717
Ragni, Gerome *(Lyricist)*   1116, 1717
Rago, Jerry *(Cast)*   2573
Ragotzy, Jack *(Director)*   2322
Ragusa, Michele *(Cast)*   3926
Rahn, Muriel *(Cast)*   309, 818, 3807, 4256
Rahn, Patsy *(Cast)*   2618
Raiff, Stan *(Producer)*   705
Raiken, Larry *(Cast)*   3722, 3926
Railey, Thomas *(Librettist)*   513
Railey, Thomas *(Lyricist)*   3065, 3268
Raine, Lola *(Cast)*   1693, 3649
Rainer, Louise *(Cast)*   1506
Raineri, Orestes *(Set Design)*   3995
Raines, John *(Librettist)*   2720
Raines, Quinton *(Director)*   314
Raines, Ron *(Cast)*   451, 808
Rainey, Joel *(Musical Director)*   496
Rainey, Ma *(Composer)*   3297
Rainey, Ma *(Lyricist)*   3297
Rainger, Frank *(Choreographer)*   628
Rainger, Frank *(Director)*   3621
Rainger, Frank M. *(Director)*   2222
Rainger, Ralph *(Cast)*   931
Rainger, Ralph *(Composer)*   2032, 2545, 3138, 3172, 4291
Rainger, Ralph *(Lyricist)*   1638
Rainger, Ralph *(Pianist)*   138, 2545
Rains, Claude *(Cast)*   3287
Raisa *(Composer)*   819
Raisa *(Librettist)*   819
Raisa *(Lyricist)*   819
Raison, Milton *(Producer)*   3946
Raiter, Frank *(Cast)*   3227
Raitt, James *(Arrangements)*   1353, 3346
Raitt, James *(Composer)*   4137
Raitt, James *(Dance Arranger)*   2420, 2805
Raitt, James *(Musical Director)*   1353, 3346, 4137
Raitt, James *(Orchestrations)*   3346, 4137
Raitt, James *(Vocal Arranger)*   2420, 4137
Raitt, John *(Cast)*   657, 660, 2248, 2679, 2742, 3020, 3182, 3351, 4366
Raker, Lorin *(Cast)*   3623
Rakov, Theresa *(Cast)*   1660
Raksin, David *(Composer)*   2103

Raksin, David *(Orchestrations)*   216, 2809, 3104, 3365, 4374
Raleigh, Ben *(Composer)*   4193
Raleigh, Ben *(Lyricist)*   4193, 4484
Raleigh, Cecil *(Librettist)*   2500, 4219
Raleigh, Cecil *(Lyricist)*   2500
Raleigh, R. *(Composer)*   4193
Raleigh, R. *(Lyricist)*   4193
Raleigh, Sir Walter *(Lyricist)*   2633
Raleigh, Stuart W. *(Musical Director)*   1439
Raley, Wade *(Cast)*   3668
Rall, Tommy *(Cast)*   615, 619, 935, 2268, 2582, 2864, 2894, 4018
Ralph, Cecil *(Author)*   1806
Ralph, Harry B. *(Lyricist)*   2923
Ralph, Jessie *(Cast)*   215, 1904
Ralph, Julia *(Cast)*   1356, 1911
Ralph, Sheryl Lee *(Cast)*   1103, 3690
Ralston, Alfred *(Dance Arranger)*   3259
Ralston, Alfred *(Vocal Arranger)*   3259
Ralston, Curt *(Cast)*   164
Ralston, Teri *(Cast)*   273, 832, 1955, 2536, 2651, 4406
Rambeau, Edward *(Cast)*   1809
Rambeau, Marjorie *(Cast)*   3812
Rambo, David *(Composer)*   2022
Rambo, David *(Lyricist)*   2022
Ramer, Jack *(Librettist)*   2051
Ramer, Jack *(Lyricist)*   2051
Ramin, Jordan *(Composer)*   2584
Ramin, Sid *(Composer)*   32
Ramin, Sid *(Lyricist)*   32
Ramin, Sid *(Orchestrations)*   837, 1422, 1567, 1709, 2048, 2205, 2355, 3682, 4004, 4020, 4090, 4566, 4625, 4693
Ramin, Sid *(Vocal Arranger)*   837, 2584
Ramirez, Ramiro *(Composer)*   3830
Ramirez, Ramiro *(Librettist)*   3830
Ramirez, Ramiro *(Lyricist)*   3830
Ramirez, Ray *(Cast)*   2580
Ramirez, Roger *(Composer)*   478
Ramirez, Roger *(Lyricist)*   478
Rampino, Lewis D. *(Costumes)*   1439, 3015
Ramsay, Remak *(Cast)*   1736, 2260, 2626, 3142
Ramsey, Gordon *(Cast)*   652, 2114
Ramsey, John *(Producer)*   2332
Ramsey, Kevin *(Cast)*   432, 1296, 2250, 4127
Ramsey, Logan *(Cast)*   4401
Ramsey, Marion *(Cast)*   1198, 1699, 2775, 2898, 3636, 3739, 4089, 4534, 4615
Ramsey, Marion *(Librettist)*   4534
Ramsey, Stanley *(Cast)*   576
Ramsey, Van Broughton *(Costumes)*   871
Ramsey, Will *(Cast)*   434
Rand, Lionel *(Orchestrations)*   4131
Rand, Sally *(Cast)*   662, 2460, 2636
Randall, Andre *(Cast)*   1137
Randall, Bob *(Cast)*   4401
Randall, Bob *(Librettist)*   2687
Randall, Carl *(Cast)*   17, 905, 924, 1688, 2403, 2540, 2855, 3009, 3245, 3379, 4085, 4213, 4335, 4661, 4809, 4810, 4814, 4842, 4844

Reddie, J. Milton *(Lyricist)* 4253
Reddin, Keith *(Cast)* 1915
Redding, Earl *(Cast)* 3024
Redding, Edward C. *(Composer)* 722, 1363, 1892, 4268, 4416
Redding, Edward C. *(Lyricist)* 722, 1363, 1892, 4268, 4416
Redding, Edward C. *(Pianist)* 4156
Redding, Eugene *(Cast)* 1551, 4794
Redding, Otis *(Composer)* 146, 3695, 3739, 4193
Redding, Otis *(Lyricist)* 146, 3695, 3739, 4193
Reddon, Nancy *(Cast)* 2069
Redfarn, Roger *(Director)* 846
Redfield, Adam *(Cast)* 4252
Redfield, Billy *(Cast)* 4569
Redfield, Harry C. *(Musical Director)* 1722
Redfield, Henry *(Orchestrations)* 3907
Redfield, Liza *(Musical Director)* 112, 169, 699, 1194, 1222, 2231, 2887, 2918, 4090
Redfield, Liza *(Orchestrations)* 2918
Redfield, Liza *(Vocal Arranger)* 4090
Redfield, William *(Cast)* 134, 304, 1116, 3326
Redfield, William *(Orchestrations)* 3580, 4206
Redfield, William M. *(Orchestrations)* 606
Redford, Harry *(Composer)* 1208
Redford, Harry *(Lyricist)* 1208
Redford, Jeff *(Cast)* 2650
Redford, William *(Cast)* 2300
Redgrave, Lynn *(Cast)* 1842
Redgrave, Michael *(Cast)* 635, 1089, 3800
Redlin, Richard *(Producer)* 4193
Redman, Don *(Cast)* 2000
Redman, Scott *(Director)* 4172
Redman Orchestra, Don *(Cast)* 1986
Redman and His Orchestra, Don *(Cast)* 1772
Redmond, Helen *(Cast)* 104, 2101, 4713, 4724
Redmond, John *(Composer)* 875, 885, 886
Redmond, John *(Lyricist)* 875, 4091
Redmond, Marge *(Cast)* 3473
Redmond, Rita *(Cast)* 2834
Redpath, Olive *(Cast)* 2963
Redstone, Willie *(Author)* 3157
Redstone, Willie *(Musical Director)* 3156, 4327
Redwine, Skip *(Composer)* 1380
Redwine, Skip *(Dance Arranger)* 1018
Redwine, Skip *(Librettist)* 1380
Redwine, Skip *(Lyricist)* 1380
Redwine, Skip *(Musical Director)* 1018, 3788
Redwine, Skip *(Vocal Arranger)* 1018
Ree, Max *(Costumes)* 3009
Reece, Kathryn *(Cast)* 1182, 1235
Reed *(Composer)* 3297
Reed *(Lyricist)* 3297
Reed, Alaina *(Cast)* 4, 1198, 2132, 3903
Reed, Alan *(Cast)* 2653
Reed, Alfred *(Orchestrations)* 63
Reed, Alyson *(Cast)* 302, 958, 1597, 1638, 2754, 3231
Reed, Bobby *(Cast)* 508, 2488
Reed, Carl *(Producer)* 1935, 3849

Reed, Dave *(Composer)* 1925
Reed, Dave *(Lyricist)* 1925, 3981
Reed, Florence *(Cast)* 758, 1144
Reed, Harry *(Cast)* 3337
Reed, Jess *(Cast)* 4814
Reed, Jessie *(Cast)* 3402
Reed, Jozella *(Cast)* 3636
Reed, Lou *(Composer)* 3739
Reed, Lou *(Lyricist)* 3739
Reed, Luther *(Author)* 1009
Reed, Mabel *(Cast)* 3417
Reed, Maggi-Meg *(Cast)* 3169
Reed, Mark *(Author)* 3457
Reed, Michael *(Composer)* 2148
Reed, Michael *(Lyricist)* 2148
Reed, Michael *(Musical Director)* 1741
Reed, Michael *(Orchestrations)* 1256, 1741
Reed, Napoleon *(Cast)* 653
Reed, Nat *(Composer)* 567
Reed, Nat *(Lyricist)* 567
Reed, Paul *(Cast)* 657, 1706, 1860, 2019, 3016, 3603, 4524
Reed, Pauline *(Costumes)* 2111
Reed, Roland *(Cast)* 526
Reed, Samuel *(Cast)* 2025
Reed, Stuart *(Librettist)* 947
Reed, Vivian *(Cast)* 576, 1890, 2173
Reed, William L. *(Composer)* 1887
Reed Jr., Dave *(Composer)* 675, 1537, 2261, 2675, 3313, 4014, 4130
Reed Jr., Dave *(Lyricist)* 310, 591, 675, 1537, 2261, 2675, 3313, 3753, 4014, 4130
Reeder, George *(Cast)* 134, 2484
Reeder, James *(Cast)* 3318
Reeger, John *(Cast)* 1439, 4740
Reehling, Joyce *(Cast)* 1268
Reeker, Cecelia *(Composer)* 725
Rees, Roger *(Cast)* 2474
Rees, Vernon *(Cast)* 2682
Reese, Bob *(Producer)* 411
Reese, Claude *(Lyricist)* 4827
Reese, Della *(Cast)* 2415
Reese, Oliver *(Cast)* 1462
Reeves, Al *(Composer)* 3982
Reeves, Al *(Director)* 3982
Reeves, Al *(Librettist)* 3982
Reeves, Al *(Lyricist)* 3982
Reeves, Billie *(Cast)* 4802, 4804
Reeves, Cheryl *(Cast)* 2037
Reeves, D.W. *(Composer)* 938
Reeves, D.W. *(Lyricist)* 938
Reeves, George *(Cast)* 4706
Reeves, Peter *(Lyricist)* 949, 4138
Reeves, Steve *(Cast)* 4542
Reeves-Smith, H. *(Cast)* 1680, 3432
Refregier, Anton *(Set Design)* 3441
Refugee Artists Group, The *(Producer)* 1413
Regal, Henry *(Cast)* 1154
Regan, J.D. *(Lighting Designer)* 344
Regan, Jay *(Cast)* 3973

Regan, Joe *(Costumes)* 4401
Regan, Joe *(Producer)* 4294
Regan, Patti *(Cast)* 410, 412, 413, 1341, 3186
Regan, Sylvia *(Author)* 1269
Regan, Sylvia *(Librettist)* 1679, 2751
Regan, Walter *(Cast)* 765, 2148
Regay, Pearl *(Cast)* 638, 1027, 1485, 3772
Rehan, Ada *(Cast)* 762
Reich, Adina *(Set Design)* 3670, 3781
Reich, Herbert *(Librettist)* 2288
Reich, Holly *(Cast)* 1155
Reicher, Frank *(Director)* 2487, 4077
Reichert, Heinz *(Author)* 463, 1680, 2886
Reichner, Bickley *(Composer)* 2772
Reichner, Bickley *(Lyricist)* 1885, 2772, 3103,
    3104, 3870
Reichner, S. Bickley *(Lyricist)* 18
Reid, Alexander *(Costumes)* 661
Reid, Carl Benton *(Cast)* 2510
Reid, Elliott *(Cast)* 1408, 4496, 4827
Reid, Florence *(Cast)* 1455, 4688
Reid, Hal *(Librettist)* 1520
Reid, Hugh L. *(Set Design)* 284
Reid, Hugh Logan *(Set Design)* 1429, 2500
Reid, James Allen *(Composer)* 2876
Reid, James Allen *(Director)* 2876
Reid, James Allen *(Librettist)* 2876
Reid, James Allen *(Lyricist)* 2876
Reid, James Allen *(Producer)* 2876
Reid, John *(Costumes)* 2055
Reid, Kathy *(Cast)* 4799
Reid, Keith *(Composer)* 3739
Reid, Keith *(Lyricist)* 3739
Reid, M.W. *(Cast)* 1149
Reid, Stephen O. *(Producer)* 2477
Reiff, Linda *(Choreographer)* 3164
Reigert, Peter *(Cast)* 682
Reilley, Victor *(Cast)* 3286
Reilly, C. *(Author)* 3481
Reilly, Charles Nelson *(Cast)* 1233, 1828, 2019,
    3161, 3366, 4013
Reilly, Frank C. *(Producer)* 3481
Reilly, Jacqueline *(Cast)* 164
Reilly, William *(Choreographer)* 83
Reillys, Five *(Cast)* 1973
Reimherr, George *(Cast)* 3078
Rein, Martin *(Producer)* 4137
Reina *(Set Design)* 914
Reina, Mark *(Cast)* 3936
Reine *(Costumes)* 1989
Reiner, Carl *(Author)* 1190, 4038
Reiner, Carl *(Cast)* 59, 2137, 3563
Reiner, Ethel Linder *(Producer)* 630
Reinhardt, Gottfried *(Librettist)* 1817, 3536, 3767
Reinhardt, Heinrich *(Author)* 3613, 4119
Reinhardt, Heinrich *(Composer)* 3613, 4119
Reinhardt, Max *(Director)* 225, 1196
Reinhardt, Max *(Librettist)* 3767
Reinhardt, Stephen *(Choreographer)* 825

Reinhardt, Stephen *(Dance Arranger)* 1581
Reinhardt, Stephen *(Musical Director)* 2687, 4744
Reinhardt, Stephen *(Orchestrations)* 1581
Reinhardt, Stephen *(Vocal Arranger)* 1581, 4744
Reinking, Ann *(Cast)* 146, 964, 1634, 3330, 4689
Reinking, Ann *(Choreographer)* 1169
Reisch, Michele *(Costumes)* 705
Reisch, Walter *(Author)* 3972, 4486
Reisch, Walter *(Lyricist)* 3946
Reisen, A. *(Composer)* 1279
Reisen, A. *(Lyricist)* 1279
Reisenfeld, Hugo *(Composer)* 380
Reisenfeld, Hugo *(Musical Director)* 1199
Reisfeld, Bert *(Composer)* 4264
Reisfeld, Bert *(Lyricist)* 4264
Reisig, Theodore *(Set Design)* 1218, 2986, 3081
Reisig-Dove *(Set Design)* 1285
Reisman, Jane *(Lighting Designer)* 127, 432, 1353, 2134
Reisman, Joe *(Dance Arranger)* 2443
Reisman, Joe *(Musical Director)* 2443
Reisman, Joe *(Orchestrations)* 2443
Reisman, Joe *(Vocal Arranger)* 2443
Reisman's Orchestra, Leo *(Cast)* 1625
Reismueller, Ross *(Musical Director)* 1959
Reisner, C. Francis *(Lyricist)* 3401
Reiss, Martin *(Lighting Designer)* 3110
Reiss, Martin *(Set Design)* 3110
Reissa, Eleanor *(Cast)* 3697, 3722, 4082, 4342
Reissa, Eleanor *(Choreographer)* 4082, 4342
Reissa, Eleanor *(Director)* 4342
Reissa, Eleanor *(Lyricist)* 1609
Reiter, Tom *(Costumes)* 1510
Reiter, Val *(Cast)* 1282
Reitman, Ivan *(Director)* 2820
Reitman, Ivan *(Producer)* 2687, 2820
Reizner, June *(Composer)* 272, 1049, 1364, 2913, 3479
Reizner, June *(Lyricist)* 272, 1049, 1364, 2913, 3479
Relkin, Edwin A. *(Producer)* 3336
Relyea, Marjorie *(Cast)* 284, 1313
Remacle, Don J. *(Set Designer)* 4746
Remaily, Robin *(Composer)* 3309
Remaily, Robin *(Lyricist)* 3309
Rembach, Frank *(Lighting Designer)* 4579
Rembach, Frank *(Set Design)* 4579
Remick, Lee *(Cast)* 162
Remlinger, William *(Lighting Designer)* 3753
Remos, Susanne *(Choreographer)* 3226
Remsen, Deborah *(Cast)* 4499
Remus, Jorie *(Cast)* 1878
Renard, Jules *(Author)* 3760
Renaud, Andre *(Cast)* 1137
Renaud, Andre *(Composer)* 1137
Renaud, William *(Cast)* 3369
Renault, Paul *(Cast)* 1500
Rendell Productions *(Producer)* 4623
Renderer, Scott *(Cast)* 4295
Rene, Leon
    See also Leon Rene's Lucky Day Band.
Rene, Leon *(Composer)* 2640, 3840
Rene, Leon *(Lyricist)* 3840

Rice, Andy *(Director)* 86
Rice, Andy *(Librettist)* 1483, 1485, 1778, 3796
Rice, Blanche *(Cast)* 2836
Rice, Bob *(Cast)* 4683
Rice, E.E. *(Composer)* 830, 1392, 2543
Rice, Edmund *(Librettist)* 4377
Rice, Edward E. *(Composer)* 1213, 2938, 2986, 3887
Rice, Edward E. *(Director)* 2500, 4650
Rice, Edward E. *(Producer)* 284, 783, 1392, 1540, 1994, 2316, 2500, 2938, 2986, 3887, 3951
Rice, Elmer *(Author)* 1097, 1933, 4013, 4495
Rice, Elmer *(Director)* 4495
Rice, Elmer *(Librettist)* 4169
Rice, Elmer *(Lyricist)* 4169
Rice, Fanny *(Cast)* 222
Rice, Felix *(Composer)* 1966
Rice, Florence D. *(Cast)* 2265
Rice, Gitz *(Cast)* 1502, 3137
Rice, Gitz *(Composer)* 208, 1502, 1551, 2698, 3137, 3328, 3593
Rice, Gitz *(Lyricist)* 1502, 3328
Rice, J. Clifford *(Cast)* 1836
Rice, John C. *(Cast)* 1301
Rice, Keith *(Cast)* 4454
Rice, Lillian *(Cast)* 2394
Rice, Michael *(Conductor)* 1785
Rice, Michael *(Dance Arranger)* 1638
Rice, Michael *(Musical Director)* 275, 1785, 3211
Rice, Michael *(Orchestrations)* 275
Rice, Peter *(Costumes)* 101, 3429, 3482
Rice, Peter *(Set Design)* 101, 3429
Rice, Sam *(Composer)* 2693
Rice, Sam *(Lyricist)* 2693
Rice, Sarah *(Cast)* 4233
Rice, Susan *(Librettist)* 1630
Rice, Tim *(Lyricist)* 330, 721, 1211, 2212, 2242
Rice Jr., Andy *(Cast)* 288
Rice and Prevost *(Cast)* 800
Rich, Buddy *(Cast)* 3255
Rich, Charles T. *(Producer)* 1627
Rich, Charlie *(Composer)* 3608
Rich, Charlie *(Lyricist)* 3608
Rich, Chuck *(Composer)* 914
Rich, Chuck *(Lyricist)* 914
Rich, Doris *(Cast)* 3687
Rich, Freddie
    See Freddie Rich and His Orchestra.
Rich, Helen *(Cast)* 4393
Rich, Irene *(Cast)* 206
Rich, James *(Cast)* 2555
Rich, John *(Director)* 1040
Rich, Max *(Composer)* 1481, 2300
Rich, Max *(Lyricist)* 1481
Rich, Nancy *(Cast)* 2968
Rich, Ron *(Cast)* 578
Rich, Sylvan *(Composer)* 72
Rich, Tony *(Cast)* 74
Rich, Vinnie *(Composer)* 4171
Rich, Vinnie *(Lyricist)* 4171
Rich and Harris *(Producer)* 191, 4407

Rich and His Orchestra, Freddie *(Cast)* 2459
Richard, Emily *(Cast)* 2474
Richard, Gene *(Choreographer)* 265
Richard, Mae *(Lyricist)* 944, 4279
Richard, Mae *(Producer)* 4618
Richard, Thomas *(Cast)* 2886
Richardone, Michael *(Musical Director)* 4463
Richards, Al *(Cast)* 443
Richards, Al *(Choreographer)* 443, 444, 1251
Richards, Carol *(Cast)* 2496
Richards, Don *(Lyricist)* 2288
Richards, Donald *(Cast)* 95, 1278
Richards, Evan *(Cast)* 869
Richards, George *(Cast)* 1259
Richards, Gordon *(Cast)* 4569
Richards, Houston *(Cast)* 163
Richards, Jess *(Cast)* 2633, 3019, 3688
Richards, Jess *(Vocal Arranger)* 74
Richards, Jim *(Cast)* 2968
Richards, Keith *(Composer)* 3739
Richards, Keith *(Lyricist)* 3739
Richards, Lloyd *(Director)* 2053, 4764
Richards, Martin *(Producer)* 1068, 1649, 1699, 2360, 2790, 4233, 4695
Richards, Marty *(Producer)* 3792
Richards, Reve *(Costumes)* 2630, 2776
Richards, Sal *(Cast)* 4347
Richards, Sal *(Director)* 4347
Richards, Thomas D. *(Cast)* 1292
Richardson, Barbara *(Cast)* 1371
Richardson, Claibe *(Composer)* 392, 942, 1049, 1362, 1662, 2565, 2611, 2678, 3468, 3479, 3484, 3787, 3940
Richardson, Claibe *(Lyricist)* 3468, 3479, 3484, 3787
Richardson, George T. *(Librettist)* 2543
Richardson, Ian *(Cast)* 3445
Richardson, Jane *(Cast)* 3775
Richardson, Jazzlips *(Cast)* 443, 1980
Richardson, Jim *(Cast)* 225
Richardson, Lea *(Cast)* 4406
Richardson, Lea *(Musical Director)* 952
Richardson, Robert E. *(Producer)* 415, 2616
Richardson, Ron *(Cast)* 394
Richardson, Walter *(Cast)* 27, 435, 1499, 2111
Richel, George *(Cast)* 2800
Richert, Wanda *(Cast)* 1359
Richett, Edward *(Composer)* 1655
Richie, Adele *(Cast)* 613, 737, 2324, 4044
Richie, Maude *(Cast)* 4430
Richler, Mordecai *(Author)* 171
Richler, Mordecai *(Librettist)* 171
Richman, Arthur *(Author)* 2789
Richman, Harry *(Cast)* 1395, 1416, 1481, 1489, 1490, 1825, 2140, 3121, 3153, 3623, 3850, 4823
Richman, Harry *(Composer)* 3020, 3297, 3623, 4424
Richman, Harry *(Lyricist)* 3443, 3623, 4424, 4823
Richmond, Elizabeth *(Cast)* 4136
Richmond, June *(Cast)* 180, 887
Richmond, Wynn *(Cast)* 1733
Richter, Carolyn *(Cast)* 1754
Richter, Carolyn *(Librettist)* 280

Richter, Carolyn *(Lyricist)* 280
Richter, Joseph *(Musical Director)* 2804
Richter, Joseph *(Vocal Arranger)* 2804
Richter, Will *(Cast)* 227
Rickabaugh, Clive *(Set Design)* 4254
Rickard, Dick *(Author)* 4035
Rickard, Earl *(Cast)* 3649
Rickard, Gwen *(Producer)* 4652
Rickenback, Don *(Arrangements)* 2076
Rickenback, Don *(Cast)* 2076
Rickenback, Don *(Musical Director)* 2076
Ricker, Benjamin F. *(Director)* 750
Ricketts, Bob *(Additional Music)* 1499
Ricketts, Bob *(Composer)* 1960
Ricketts, Bob *(Lyricist)* 1960
Ricketts, Robert W. *(Orchestrations)* 3022
Ricketts, Tom *(Director)* 2986
Rickey, Al *(Musical Director)* 90
Rickman, Allen Lewis *(Cast)* 4325
Rickman, Carl *(Librettist)* 567
Riddell, Richard *(Lighting Designer)* 394, 4147
Riddle, George *(Cast)* 1581
Riddle, Nelson *(Arrangements)* 3841
Riddle, Nelson *(Cast)* 3324
Riddle, Nelson *(Musical Director)* 3324
Riddle, Richard *(Composer)* 915
Riddle, Richard *(Lyricist)* 915
Rideamus, Edward *(Author)* 659
Ridge, Antonia *(Lyricist)* 4264
Ridge, John David *(Costumes)* 869, 3370
Ridges, Stanley *(Cast)* 425, 993, 1174, 3729, 3819
Ridiculous Theatrical Co. *(Producer)* 2037
Rieffel, Lisa *(Cast)* 3643
Riegel, Eden *(Cast)* 4107
Riehl, Bob *(Cast)* 239
Riemueller, Ross *(Musical Director)* 1511
Riesenfeld, Hugo *(Composer)* 2830, 4823
Riesenfeld, Hugo *(Musical Director)* 2403, 2830, 3627
Rieser, Terry *(Choreographer)* 1797, 2289
Riffle, Miles *(Cast)* 214
Rigby, Harry *(Producer)* 808, 1635, 1721, 1729, 2058, 2705, 4197, 4746
Rigdon, Kevin *(Set Design)* 4074
Rigg, Diana *(Cast)* 808
Riggs, Lynn *(Author)* 3263
Riggs, Ralph *(Cast)* 1183, 1476, 2444, 2597, 3137, 3225, 3263, 3365, 3590, 3955, 4673, 4772
Riggs, Ralph *(Choreographer)* 2351, 3236
Riggs, Ralph *(Costumes)* 1183
Riggs, Stanley *(Cast)* 495
Riggs, T. Lawrason *(Librettist)* 3378, 3865
Rigsby, Gordon *(Director)* 3273
Riha, Bobby *(Cast)* 2183
Riley *(Cast)* 3142
Riley, Betsy *(Musical Director)* 114
Riley, Eric *(Cast)* 3285
Riley, James *(Set Design)* 4038
Riley, Larry *(Cast)* 1038, 1099, 1402, 3909
Riley, Lary *(Cast)* 550
Riley, Michael *(Composer)* 393, 1813

Riley, Michael *(Lyricist)* 393
Riley, Rob *(Cast)* 4690
Riley, Rob *(Director)* 4690
Riley, Rob *(Librettist)* 4690
Riley, Sid *(Musical Director)* 2253
Riley, Thomas W. *(Producer)* 356
Rimsky-Korsakov *(Music Based On)* 23
Rinal *(Cast)* 471
Rinehimer, John *(Conductor)* 3136
Rinehimer, John *(Dance Arranger)* 3136
Rinehimer, John *(Orchestrations)* 3136
Rinehimer, John *(Vocal Arranger)* 3136
Ring, Blanche *(Cast)* 8, 17, 457, 543, 560, 1021, 1226, 1464, 1910, 1912, 2005, 2209, 2213, 2835, 2858, 3153, 3166, 3403, 3713, 3882, 4179, 4414, 4589, 4634, 4642, 4757
Ring, M. *(Director)* 4794
Ring, Michael *(Choreographer)* 1624
Ringgold, Jennie *(Cast)* 2044
Ringham, Nancy *(Cast)* 1169, 4371
Ringle, Dave *(Composer)* 1343, 3989
Ringle, Dave *(Lyricist)* 1343, 3989
Ringwald, Roy *(Vocal Arranger)* 3100
Rinker, Al *(Composer)* 3683
Rinker, Alton *(Composer)* 4827
Rinker, Kenneth *(Choreographer)* 4252
Rio Brothers, The *(Cast)* 4753
Rios, Augie *(Cast)* 3837
Ripley, Alice *(Cast)* 4217
Ripley, Constance *(Costumes)* 125, 294, 672, 1322, 1672, 3365, 3674, 3699
Ripley, Madame *(Costumes)* 2986
Ripley, Patricia *(Cast)* 2617
Ripple, Pacie *(Cast)* 3117
Rippy, Robert *(Cast)* 4542
Riscoe, Arthur *(Lyricist)* 3500
Riseman, Naomi *(Cast)* 4696
Riser, P. *(Composer)* 1713
Riser, P. *(Lyricist)* 1713
Rising, Lawrence *(Author)* 1904
Riskin, Irving *(Orchestrations)* 2397
Risque, W.H. *(Author)* 3976
Risque, W.H. *(Librettist)* 3098
Risque, W.H. *(Lyricist)* 3098, 3976
Riss, Sheldon *(Producer)* 3668
Ritchard, Cyril *(Cast)* 44, 844, 974, 1745, 2182, 2313, 2389, 3020, 3453, 3617, 3634, 3731, 4196, 4519
Ritchard, Cyril *(Director)* 1745, 2227
Ritchie, Adele *(Cast)* 68, 1030, 1243, 1246, 1579, 2733, 3049, 4353
Ritchie, Bill *(Cast)* 185
Ritchie, Robert G. *(Producer)* 1879
Riter, Joseph *(Producer)* 102
Ritholz Associates *(Set Design)* 2804
Ritman, William *(Costumes)* 3810
Ritman, William *(Lighting Designer)* 1354, 2322, 3810
Ritman, William *(Set Design)* 1047, 1354, 3186, 3305, 3516, 3810
Ritt, Martin *(Cast)* 3180, 4495
Ritter, Tex *(Cast)* 4163

Roberts, Nelson *(Producer)* 1912
Roberts, Pernell *(Cast)* 1616, 2777
Roberts, R.A. *(Cast)* 1465, 1627
Roberts, R.A. *(Director)* 1627, 1925
Roberts, R.A. *(Lyricist)* 3065
Roberts, R.A. *(Producer)* 3065
Roberts, Rachel *(Cast)* 2682
Roberts, Ralph *(Cast)* 2411, 3157, 3214, 3890
Roberts, Ralph *(Lyricist)* 1569, 2341, 3322
Roberts, Rhoda *(Lyricist)* 1990, 3956
Roberts, Roy *(Cast)* 657
Roberts, Ruth *(Lighting Designer)* 1256, 1873,
    2598, 4205
Roberts, Sarah *(Costumes)* 3836, 4438
Roberts, Sarah *(Set Design)* 3836, 4438
Roberts, Thayer *(Cast)* 4486
Roberts, Tony *(Cast)* 4196, 4560
Robertson, Alene *(Cast)* 155
Robertson, Geoff *(Author)* 4449
Robertson, Guy *(Cast)* 82, 771, 953, 1680, 2628, 2747,
    3170, 3443, 3713, 3823, 3868, 4077, 4170, 4669, 4694
Robertson, Guy *(Lyricist)* 2747
Robertson, J. Robbie *(Composer)* 3739
Robertson, J. Robbie *(Lyricist)* 3739
Robertson, Jane *(Cast)* 3636
Robertson, Liz *(Cast)* 958, 2204
Robertson, Patrick *(Set Design)* 1386
Robertson, R.A. *(Lyricist)* 1159
Robertson, Ronnie *(Cast)* 2097, 3287
Robertson, Ross *(Cast)* 2492
Robertson, Scott *(Cast)* 262
Robertson, Will *(Director)* 4193
Robertson, Will *(Producer)* 4193
Robertston, Warren *(Cast)* 1046
Robeson, Paul *(Cast)* 2225, 4504
Robey, Ken *(Producer)* 1898
Robi, Armand *(Composer)* 1314
Robi, Armand *(Director)* 1314
Robi, Armand *(Librettist)* 1314
Robin, Gil *(Composer)* 964
Robin, Jean-Claude *(Costumes)* 1713
Robin, Leo *(Additional Lyrics)* 2976
Robin, Leo *(Composer)* 1916
Robin, Leo *(Lyricist)* 2, 86, 393, 464, 577, 605, 663,
    1475, 1548, 1691, 1839, 1916, 2076, 2253, 2277, 2367,
    2372, 2392, 2590, 2976, 3020, 3138, 3249, 3683, 3800,
    3946, 4291, 4582, 4706
Robin, Sid *(Composer)* 1296
Robin, Sid *(Lyricist)* 1296
Robins, Edward H. *(Cast)* 2432, 2444, 3225
Robins, Isobel *(Cast)* 4627
Robins, Isobel *(Producer)* 4627
Robins, J.J. *(Lyricist)* 3103
Robins, Kenneth *(Librettist)* 2441
Robins, Kenneth *(Lyricist)* 2441
Robinson, A. *(Lyricist)* 3946
Robinson, Adelaide *(Cast)* 340
Robinson, Andre *(Cast)* 3814
Robinson, Ann *(Cast)* 2817
Robinson, Anna *(Cast)* 1392

Robinson, Armin *(Author)* 2610, 4365
Robinson, Bartlett *(Cast)* 3082
Robinson, Bertrand *(Director)* 3713
Robinson, Bertrand *(Librettist)* 4673
Robinson, Bill *(Cast)* 70, 441, 444, 445, 497, 567,
    883, 1416, 1984, 1987, 2817, 3153
Robinson, Bill "Bojangles" *(Cast)* 888
Robinson, Blondie *(Cast)* 1821
Robinson, Cardew *(Cast)* 3630
Robinson, Charles *(Author)* 3138
Robinson, Charles *(Cast)* 2853
Robinson, Charles *(Director)* 2853
Robinson, Charles *(Librettist)* 2853
Robinson, Charles *(Lyricist)* 2853
Robinson, Charles *(Producer)* 2853
Robinson, Cheryl *(Cast)* 1616
Robinson, Christine *(Costumes)* 2204
Robinson, Clarence *(Cast)* 2302, 3709
Robinson, Clarence *(Choreographer)* 883, 897, 2302
Robinson, Clarence *(Director)* 875, 883
Robinson, Clark *(Lighting Designer)* 418, 1779, 2423
Robinson, Clark *(Set Design)* 557, 568, 1013, 1127, 1691,
    1692, 1779, 1780, 2300, 3005, 3006, 3007, 3008, 3009,
    3172, 3431, 3436, 3735, 3850, 4572, 4741
Robinson, David *(Composer)* 1298
Robinson, David *(Costumes)* 3568
Robinson, David *(Lyricist)* 1298
Robinson, Doug *(Cast)* 382
Robinson, Earl *(Composer)* 467, 1674, 1840, 2175,
    2447, 3831, 3986
Robinson, Earl *(Librettist)* 3831
Robinson, Earl *(Lyricist)* 1840
Robinson, Edward G. *(Cast)* 1283
Robinson, Edward G. *(Musical Director)* 3944, 4288
Robinson, Florence *(Cast)* 1491, 1806
Robinson, Hal *(Cast)* 4790
Robinson, J. Russel *(Composer)* 481, 565, 1129, 2308,
    2706, 2856, 3513, 4271
Robinson, J. Russel *(Lyricist)* 2706, 2856, 3953, 4271
Robinson, Jack (Director) 1337
Robinson, Jack *(Librettist)* 1337
Robinson, Lilla Cayley *(Lyricist)* 1526
Robinson, Mabel *(Choreographer)* 2173, 2692
Robinson, Martin P. *(Cast)* 2544
Robinson, Meghan *(Cast)* 3606
Robinson, Muriel *(Composer)* 3557
Robinson, Muriel *(Lyricist)* 3557
Robinson, Phyllis *(Lyricist)* 935
Robinson, Richard *(Composer)* 2913
Robinson, Richard *(Lyricist)* 2913
Robinson, Roberta *(Cast)* 294
Robinson, Roger *(Cast)* 105, 2852
Robinson, Ruth *(Cast)* 4705
Robinson, Smokey *(Composer)* 4534
Robinson, Smokey *(Lyricist)* 4534
Robinson, Walter *(Cast)* 3450
Robinson, Wayne *(Arrangements)* 928
Robinson, Wayne *(Orchestrations)* 2443
Robinson, William *(Composer)* 166
Robinson, William *(Lyricist)* 166

Rogers, Ann *(Cast)*   1733
Rogers, Anne *(Cast)*   4798
Rogers, Ben *(Cast)*   2028
Rogers, Bob *(Costumes)*   4584
Rogers, Buddy *(Cast)*   1979
Rogers, Buddy *(Director)*   1604
Rogers, Cynthia *(Cast)*   1286, 1448
Rogers, David *(Cast)*   1236
Rogers, David *(Librettist)*   699, 2168, 4827, 4828, 4829
Rogers, David *(Lyricist)*   602, 699, 2168, 2288, 3110, 4461, 4566, 4828, 4829
Rogers, Dick *(Composer)*   1539
Rogers, Dick *(Lyricist)*   1539, 1713
Rogers, Don Loring *(Cast)*   1782
Rogers, Doug *(Choreographer)*   2016, 3159, 4124
Rogers, E.W. *(Lyricist)*   4642
Rogers, Earl *(Vocal Arranger)*   4828
Rogers, Ed *(Composer)*   2991
Rogers, Ed *(Lyricist)*   2991
Rogers, Emmett *(Producer)*   3188, 4278
Rogers, Eric *(Orchestrations)*   3271, 3482
Rogers, Ferne *(Cast)*   3677
Rogers, Frederick *(Cast)*   1316
Rogers, Ginger *(Cast)*   1528, 3493, 4426
Rogers, Gus *(Cast)*   3744, 3745, 3746, 3747, 3748, 3749, 3750, 3751
Rogers, Gus *(Producer)*   3748
Rogers, Hilda *(Cast)*   2690, 3054
Rogers, Howard *(Lyricist)*   4813
Rogers, Howard E. *(Lyricist)*   2856
Rogers, Howard Emmett *(Director)*   2636
Rogers, Howard Emmett *(Librettist)*   684, 2636, 2856
Rogers, Jaime *(Cast)*   1601
Rogers, Jaime *(Choreographer)*   1158
Rogers, James D. *(Cast)*   345
Rogers, Jay *(Cast)*   2022
Rogers, Jay *(Composer)*   1506
Rogers, Jay *(Lyricist)*   1506
Rogers, Jo Jean *(Cast)*   2597
Rogers, John P. *(Cast)*   801, 803
Rogers, Lavinia *(Cast)*   254, 295
Rogers, Louis T. *(Producer)*   3241
Rogers, Marshall *(Cast)*   2881
Rogers, Max *(Cast)*   1738, 3525, 3744, 3745, 3746, 3747, 3748, 3749, 3750, 3751, 4787
Rogers, Max *(Producer)*   3748
Rogers, Mickie *(Cast)*   3264
Rogers, Paul *(Cast)*   1864
Rogers, Phyllis *(Cast)*   2597
Rogers, Ralph *(Cast)*   1833
Rogers, Ric *(Lighting Designer)*   2239
Rogers, Robert *(Arrangements)*   1590, 3111
Rogers, Robert *(Dance Arranger)*   2898
Rogers, Robert *(Musical Director)*   1590, 3111, 3491, 4701
Rogers, Robert *(Orchestrations)*   1590
Rogers, Robert *(Vocal Arranger)*   4701
Rogers, Shoshanna *(Cast)*   1500
Rogers, Stanley *(Cast)*   1462
Rogers, Vivien *(Cast)*   3031

Rogers, Will *(Cast)*   792, 1735, 2403, 3087, 4345, 4589, 4816, 4818, 4819, 4834, 4844
Rogers, Will *(Librettist)*   4818, 4819
Rogerson, Bob *(Cast)*   1349
Rogerson, Clarence *(Musical Director)*   353, 1783, 1912, 2745, 4313
Rogge, Florence *(Choreographer)*   4569, 4620
Rogness, Peter *(Set Design)*   261, 3561
Rogoff, Renee *(Cast)*   2483
Rogosin, Roy *(Musical Director)*   3643
Rogosin, Roy M. *(Composer)*   3629
Rogosin, Roy M. *(Director)*   3629
Rogosin, Roy M. *(Librettist)*   3629
Rogosin, Roy M. *(Musical Director)*   4408
Rohrer, Andy *(Cast)*   3653
Roland, Steve *(Cast)*   3294, 3889
Rolfe, Wendy A. *(Costumes)*   1232
Rolfing, Tom *(Cast)*   1377
Rolin, Judi *(Cast)*   58
Roll, Eddie *(Cast)*   4090, 4625
Roll, Edward *(Choreographer)*   3612
Rolle, Esther *(Cast)*   1074, 1592, 2719
Roller, Olga *(Cast)*   2665
Rollins, Jack *(Composer)*   3793
Rollins, Jack *(Producer)*   3112
Rollins, Pierce *(Lyricist)*   3530
Rollins, Rowena *(Cast)*   597, 843
Rollins, Sherwood *(Composer)*   1231
Rollins, Sherwood *(Lyricist)*   1231
Rollit, George *(Lyricist)*   3976
Rollnick, William D. *(Producer)*   757
Rolph, Marti *(Cast)*   1329, 3817
Rolt, Bernard *(Composer)*   719, 954, 1537, 2724, 2964, 3313
Rolt, Bernard *(Lyricist)*   719, 954, 1537, 3313
Roma, Caro *(Cast)*   2848
Roma, Caro *(Composer)*   2415
Roma, Jimmy *(Cast)*   4829
Romagnoli, Joe *(Cast)*   3548
Romaguera, Joaquin *(Cast)*   2674, 4233
Romaine, George *(Cast)*   335
Romaine, Margaret *(Cast)*   2854
Romaine, W.L. *(Cast)*   2724, 3486
Roman, Bob *(Cast)*   1017
Roman, Lawrence *(Author)*   3338
Roman, Martin *(Composer)*   1358
Roman, Paul Reid *(Cast)*   1729
Romann, Susan *(Cast)*   1249
Romann, Susan *(Conductor)*   3602
Romann, Susan *(Musical Director)*   1249, 2579, 4577, 4595
Romano, Cathi *(Cast)*   2580
Romano, Jane *(Cast)*   483
Romano, Tom *(Lyricist)*   3810
Romanoff, Prince Michael *(Cast)*   3850
Romay, Lina *(Cast)*   2850
Romberg, Sigmund *(Cast)*   3153
Romberg, Sigmund *(Composer)*   152, 200, 201, 463, 473, 480, 487, 718, 910, 965, 969, 1027, 1065, 1096, 1145, 1334, 1335, 1352, 1530, 1548, 1735, 1852, 2135,

2384, 2594, 2601, 2602, 2684, 2696, 2757, 2786, 2794, 2813, 2816, 2939, 3018, 3020, 3051, 3056, 3063, 3064, 3117, 3170, 3253, 3333, 3397, 3400, 3401, 3402, 3403, 3406, 3407, 3538, 3586, 3737, 3766, 3769, 3778, 3799, 3958, 3985, 4121, 4188, 4214, 4350, 4524, 4657, 4747, 4819

Romberg, Sigmund *(Producer)* 2601, 2684

Rome, Fred *(Librettist)* 4416

Rome, Harold *(Composer)* 5, 59, 454, 620, 1029, 1242, 1616, 1763, 2048, 2130, 2447, 2504, 2653, 2718, 2850, 3018, 3074, 3178, 3501, 3563, 3761, 3990, 4009, 4099, 4131, 4141, 4174, 4323, 4592, 4617, 4718, 4826, 4863

Rome, Harold *(Incidental Music)* 3761

Rome, Harold *(Librettist)* 3990

Rome, Harold *(Lyricist)* 5, 59, 454, 620, 1029, 1242, 1616, 1763, 2048, 2130, 2362, 2447, 2504, 2653, 2718, 2850, 3018, 3074, 3178, 3501, 3563, 3761, 3986, 3990, 4009, 4099, 4131, 4141, 4174, 4323, 4592, 4617, 4718, 4826, 4863

Romeo, John *(Cast)* 114

Romeo, Max *(Composer)* 3690

Romeo, Max *(Lyricist)* 3690

Romeo, Signor *(Choreographer)* 3570

Romeo, Vincente *(Choreographer)* 4753

Romeo, Vincenzo *(Cast)* 286

Romeo, Vincenzo *(Choreographer)* 3093, 4046, 4452

Romeo, Vincenzo *(Director)* 286

Romeo Jr., Vincent *(Cast)* 3093

Romer, Leila *(Cast)* 4046

Romero, Alex *(Choreographer)* 1760, 3524

Romero, Cesar *(Cast)* 4043, 4170

Romero, Miguel *(Set Design)* 2953

Romilli, G. *(Composer)* 1281

Romilli, G. *(Lyricist)* 1281

Romoff, Colin *(Composer)* 4395, 4828, 4829

Romoff, Colin *(Dance Arranger)* 2965

Romoff, Colin *(Musical Director)* 1227, 2355, 2777, 2965, 3577, 4399, 4609

Romoff, Colin *(Pianist)* 3845

Romoff, Colin *(Vocal Arranger)* 2777, 2965, 3577, 4609

Romoff, Wood *(Cast)* 2838, 3918

Romoff, Woody *(Cast)* 3526

Romshinsky, Joseph *(Composer)* 573

Ron, Shoshana *(Cast)* 2421

Ronald, Landon *(Composer)* 3976

Rondell, Gloria *(Cast)* 3104

Ronell, Ann *(Composer)* 478, 901, 933, 2841, 3946

Ronell, Ann *(Lyricist)* 478, 901, 933, 2841, 3946

Ronn, E. *(Lyricist)* 3617

Ronstadt, Linda *(Cast)* 2359

Rooney *(Composer)* 1318

Rooney, Katie *(Cast)* 3024

Rooney, Mickey *(Cast)* 2975, 3496, 3833, 4197, 4577

Rooney, Mickey *(Composer)* 2259, 4197

Rooney, Mickey *(Lyricist)* 4197

Rooney, Mickey *(Voice)* 3793

Rooney, Pat *(Cast)* 994, 1395, 1505, 2403, 2601, 2851, 2865, 2964, 3166, 3717, 3745, 3751, 3911, 4265

Rooney, Pat *(Choreographer)* 3748

Rooney, Pat *(Director)* 994, 3717, 3911

Rooney, Sherry *(Cast)* 2235

Rooney, Wallace *(Cast)* 3441

Rooney III, Pat *(Cast)* 994

Rooney Sr., Pat *(Cast)* 1706

Roos, Casper *(Cast)* 181, 1060, 2142, 2874, 3928

Roos, Delmar *(Cast)* 3490

Roos, Joanna *(Librettist)* 2948

Roos, Patricia *(Cast)* 946

Roos, William *(Librettist)* 206, 911, 2850

Root, Lynn *(Librettist)* 612

Roovray, Verna *(Lyricist)* 3248

Ropes, Bradford *(Author)* 1359

Rork, Samuel E. *(Producer)* 1274, 3574

Rosa, Dennis *(Choreographer)* 3544, 3908

Rosa, Dennis *(Director)* 808, 3544, 3908

Rosa, Dennis *(Librettist)* 3544

Rosa, Patti *(Cast)* 4756

Rosaire, Robert *(Cast)* 396

Rosalie *(Cast)* 922

Rosato, Mary Lou *(Cast)* 693, 3733

Roscoe, Bill *(Composer)* 4768

Roscoe, Bill *(Lyricist)* 4768

Rose, Alice *(Cast)* 2995

Rose, Billy *(Composer)* 418, 2311, 3926

Rose, Billy *(Director)* 418

Rose, Billy *(Librettist)* 2653, 3100

Rose, Billy *(Lyricist)* 39, 173, 393, 397, 417, 418, 419, 420, 662, 702, 1126, 1667, 1672, 1779, 1873, 2204, 2413, 2460, 2706, 3018, 3020, 3100, 3149, 3166, 3179, 3249, 3342, 3796, 3926, 3975, 3980, 4235, 4264, 4465, 4799, 4815, 4818, 4824, 4825

Rose, Billy *(Producer)* 173, 397, 417, 418, 653, 662, 1267, 1672, 2258, 2413, 2460, 3166, 3893, 3975, 4235, 4465, 4567

Rose, Charles J. *(Cast)* 677

Rose, Charlie *(Cast)* 2113

Rose, David *(Composer)* 3683, 4706

Rose, David *(Lighting Designer)* 914

Rose, David *(Lyricist)* 4706

Rose, David *(Musical Director)* 3683

Rose, David *(Orchestrations)* 4706

Rose, Ed *(Composer)* 4654

Rose, Ed *(Lyricist)* 830, 1334, 1573, 4654, 4813

Rose, Edward *(Author)* 452

Rose, Edward *(Director)* 349, 361, 4422

Rose, Edward *(Producer)* 2543

Rose, Fred *(Composer)* 3404

Rose, Fred *(Lyricist)* 3404

Rose, George *(Cast)* 634, 798, 958, 2553, 3070, 4588

Rose, Gilberg *(Costumes)* 1244

Rose, Helen *(Costumes)* 2085, 2086, 2087, 2088, 2089, 2090, 2091

Rose, Howard *(Producer)* 4137

Rose, Jack *(Cast)* 3407

Rose, Jack *(Composer)* 924

Rose, Jack *(Lyricist)* 924

Rose, Jerry *(Choreographer)* 1781

Rose, Julian *(Cast)* 2119

Rose, L. Arthur *(Librettist)* 2798

Rose, L. Arthur *(Lyricist)* 2798

Rose, Lew *(Cast)*   3232
Rose, Lew *(Director)*   3232
Rose, Lew *(Librettist)*   3232
Rose, Lew *(Lyricist)*   3232
Rose, Louisa *(Librettist)*   300
Rose, Louisa *(Lyricist)*   300
Rose, Margot *(Cast)*   2074
Rose, Michael *(Musical Director)*   1256
Rose, Morris *(Producer)*   465
Rose, Patrick *(Cast)*   426
Rose, Patrick *(Composer)*   426
Rose, Philip *(Director)*   105, 135, 828, 3059, 3610
Rose, Philip *(Librettist)*   105, 828, 3610, 3928
Rose, Philip *(Producer)*   135, 519, 615, 3610, 3928, 4460
Rose, Ralph *(Director)*   567
Rose, Reva *(Cast)*   4783
Rose, S. Lee *(Choreographer)*   2780
Rose, Sam *(Choreographer)*   2, 290, 1929
Rose, Stephen *(Composer)*   164
Rose, Susan R. *(Producer)*   2242
Rose, Vincent *(Composer)*   487, 1120, 1126, 1136,
   3246, 3739, 3985, 4284, 4534
Rose, Vincent *(Lyricist)*   1120, 1417, 4534
Rose Marie *(Cast)*   1040, 3153, 4117
Rosebach, Sophie *(Set Design)*   2739
Rosebrook, Leon *(Composer)*   3973
Rosebrook, Leon *(Musical Director)*   1513, 2371,
   2519, 3973, 4213
Rosebrook, Leon *(Orchestrations)*   3973
Rosegarten, Rory *(Producer)*   2420
Roseleigh, Jack *(Director)*   1795
Roselle, William *(Cast)*   834, 1502, 1523
Rosemont, Norman *(Producer)*   1094
Rosemont, Walter L. *(Composer)*   2503, 2972, 4596
Rosemont, Walter L. *(Dance Arranger)*   2972
Rosemont, Walter L. *(Vocal Arranger)*   2972
Rosen, Arnie *(Librettist)*   4828, 4829
Rosen, Arnold *(Librettist)*   3524
Rosen, Burt *(Producer)*   1089
Rosen, Louis *(Composer)*   494
Rosen, Louis *(Librettist)*   494
Rosen, Louis *(Lyricist)*   494
Rosen, Marshal *(Composer)*   4829
Rosen, Sam *(Lyricist)*   90
Rosenbaum, Edward *(Producer)*   2780
Rosenberg, Billy *(Cast)*   4679
Rosenberg, Irene *(Librettist)*   3305
Rosenberg, Irene *(Lyricist)*   3305
Rosenberg, J.B. *(Librettist)*   3105
Rosenberg, J.B. *(Lyricist)*   3105
Rosenberg, Jan *(Musical Director)*   705, 3080
Rosenberg, Victor I. *(Producer)*   2643
Rosenblat, Barbara *(Cast)*   2646
Rosenblatt, Marcell *(Cast)*   3227
Rosenbloom, Jonathan *(Lighting Designer)*   1757
Rosenbloom, Jonathan *(Set Design)*   1757
Rosenblum, Ava *(Cast)*   4431
Rosenblum, Bob *(Librettist)*   4627
Rosenblum, Joshua *(Conductor)*   4442
Rosenblum, Robert *(Composer)*   4522

Rosenblum, Robert *(Librettist)*   4522
Rosenblum, Robert *(Lyricist)*   4522
Rosenburg, Sophie *(Costumes)*   1250
Rosener, George *(Author)*   4100
Rosener, George *(Director)*   2300, 3011
Rosener, George *(Librettist)*   199, 2300
Rosenfeld, Carl *(Director)*   1608
Rosenfeld, Carl *(Producer)*   1608
Rosenfeld, Grace *(Producer)*   3966
Rosenfeld, Hilary *(Costumes)*   1053, 1985, 2648,
   2787, 3806, 4294
Rosenfeld, Lois F. *(Producer)*   305, 3992
Rosenfeld, M.H. *(Composer)*   2952
Rosenfeld, Moishe *(Librettist)*   4342
Rosenfeld, Moishe *(Lyricist)*   573, 1609, 4342
Rosenfeld, Moishe *(Producer)*   1609
Rosenfeld, Stephen *(Director)*   3557
Rosenfeld, Stephen *(Librettist)*   3557
Rosenfeld, Sydney *(Composer)*   4046, 4222
Rosenfeld, Sydney *(Librettist)*   526, 976, 1464, 1728,
   1746, 1975, 2261, 2324, 2914, 2917, 3308, 3394, 3753,
   3776, 4046, 4222, 4472, 4544
Rosenfeld, Sydney *(Lyricist)*   526, 1464, 1505, 1746, 1975,
   2324, 2914, 2917, 3308, 3753, 3776, 4046, 4222, 4472
Rosenfeld, Sydney *(Producer)*   2324
Rosenfeld, Theodore *(Producer)*   1608
Rosenfield, Maurice *(Producer)*   305, 3992
Rosenstock, Milton *(Composer)*   3075
Rosenstock, Milton *(Musical Director)*   304, 363, 629, 823,
   943, 1278, 1420, 1475, 1709, 1886, 1990, 1991, 2217,
   2583, 2590, 2705, 3846, 4160, 4190, 4340, 4499, 4542
Rosenstock, Milton *(Vocal Arranger)*   1990, 2217, 4542
Rosenthal, Andrew *(Composer)*   4433
Rosenthal, Andrew *(Librettist)*   4433
Rosenthal, Andrew *(Lyricist)*   4433
Rosenthal, Chayele *(Cast)*   3559
Rosenthal, Harry *(Cast)*   2265
Rosenthal, Harry *(Composer)*   292, 3532, 3614, 3762
Rosenthal, Harry *(Musical Director)*   1396
Rosenthal, Jack *(Author)*   299
Rosenthal, Jack *(Librettist)*   299
Rosenthal, Jean *(Lighting Designer)*   170, 270, 322, 610,
   837, 1007, 1012, 1029, 1265, 1383, 1422, 1456, 1764,
   1828, 1990, 2000, 2050, 2106, 2190, 2201, 3687, 3767,
   3837, 4095, 4270, 4384, 4395, 4625
Rosenthal, Jean *(Set Design)*   322, 837, 1383
Rosenthal, Laurence *(Composer)*   3931
Rosenthal, Laurence *(Dance Arranger)*   1076, 1614,
   3016, 4270
Rosenthal, Leo *(Producer)*   2754
Rosenthal, Myron D. *(Librettist)*   4477, 4530
Rosenthal, Nancy *(Producer)*   1775
Roset, Val *(Choreographer)*   1539
Rosey, George *(Composer)*   2286
Rosey, George *(Librettist)*   2286
Rosey, Joseph *(Lyricist)*   3856, 3857
Rosing, Vladimir *(Director)*   1681
Rosko *(Cast)*   119
Rosley, Adrian *(Cast)*   4023, 4328
Rosner, Paul *(Lyricist)*   3890, 3940

Rosoff, Charles *(Composer)*   1138, 2253, 2392

Ross, Adrian *(Author)*   1384, 4115

Ross, Adrian *(Librettist)*   2131

Ross, Adrian *(Lyricist)*   284, 351, 379, 659, 767, 770, 902, 906, 1067, 1114, 1153, 1470, 1537, 1544, 1561, 1569, 1626, 1682, 1783, 2131, 2317, 2761, 2836, 2844, 2937, 3098, 3313, 3322, 3618, 3828, 3857, 3948, 3996, 3999, 4115, 4285, 4327, 4430, 4590, 4807

Ross, Al *(Composer)*   4543

Ross, Alan *(Cast)*   943

Ross, Allan *(Cast)*   1781

Ross, Allie *(Musical Director)*   26, 441

Ross, Annie *(Cast)*   920

Ross, Arthur *(Librettist)*   2809

Ross, Beverly *(Composer)*   4264

Ross, Beverly *(Lyricist)*   4264

Ross, Budd *(Cast)*   2895

Ross, Charles *(Cast)*   1900

Ross, Charles J. *(Cast)*   1264, 2041, 2603, 2835, 4044, 4658, 4712, 4801

Ross, Clarke *(Producer)*   3252

Ross, David *(Director)*   2178

Ross, David *(Producer)*   2178

Ross, Diana *(Cast)*   1389

Ross, Diane *(Choreographer)*   345

Ross, Don *(Cast)*   4824

Ross, Don *(Librettist)*   204

Ross, Don *(Producer)*   204

Ross, Eliza *(Cast)*   62

Ross, Eliza *(Librettist)*   1648

Ross, Hank *(Musical Director)*   2320

Ross, Herbert *(Cast)*   341, 3947, 4565

Ross, Herbert *(Choreographer)*   98, 162, 170, 483, 1060, 1456, 2000, 2048, 2304, 3274, 4435, 4446

Ross, Herbert *(Director)*   2304

Ross, Howard *(Cast)*   652, 3469, 4004

Ross, Howard *(Composer)*   3020

Ross, Howard *(Lyricist)*   3020

Ross, Hugh *(Musical Director)*   283, 1600

Ross, Jack *(Director)*   4106

Ross, Jamie *(Cast)*   181, 272, 427, 1045, 2199, 2563, 3235, 3439, 4727

Ross, Jerry *(Cast)*   1101

Ross, Jerry *(Composer)*   957, 2227, 3351, 4399

Ross, Jerry *(Lyricist)*   957, 2227, 3351, 4399

Ross, Joe *(Cast)*   98, 483, 937, 1511, 4319

Ross, Jonathan *(Cast)*   3485

Ross, Judith *(Librettist)*   4558

Ross, Justin *(Cast)*   1371, 1637, 2953, 3181, 4618

Ross, King *(Orchestrations)*   3946

Ross, Lynn *(Cast)*   4625

Ross, Mae *(Cast)*   2089

Ross, Marilyn *(Cast)*   1300

Ross, Martin *(Cast)*   2026, 2584

Ross, Marty *(Cast)*   4623

Ross, Michael *(Director)*   1993, 4566, 4627

Ross, Robert *(Cast)*   4142

Ross, Robert *(Director)*   901, 1546, 2817

Ross, Roy *(Cast)*   1109

Ross, Sandra *(Lighting Designer)*   2272

Ross, Shirley *(Cast)*   1894

Ross, Stanley Stephen *(Composer)*   695

Ross, Stanley Stephen *(Librettist)*   695

Ross, Stanley Stephen *(Lyricist)*   695

Ross, Stephen *(Lighting Designer)*   3066

Ross, Stuart *(Choreographer)*   674, 1353, 1813

Ross, Stuart *(Director)*   1353, 1813

Ross, Stuart *(Librettist)*   1353, 1813, 4139

Ross, Ted *(Cast)*   578, 952, 3610, 3656, 4722

Ross, Tom *(Librettist)*   4518

Ross, William *(Producer)*   1740

Rosse, Frederick *(Composer)*   2317, 3882

Rosse, Frederick *(Lyricist)*   3882

Rosse, Herman *(Set Design)*   1672, 1827, 4567

Rossen, Debbie *(Cast)*   2521

Rossetti, Christina *(Author)*   1589

Rossetti, Christina *(Lyricist)*   1589, 2633

Rossi, Tony *(Cast)*   2676

Rossini, Giochino *(Composer)*   4342

Rossini, Giochino *(Music Based On)*   225

Rossiter, Len *(Cast)*   1386

Rossiter, P.T. *(Producer)*   3236

Rossiter, Will *(Arrangements)*   2552

Rost, Leo *(Librettist)*   2759

Rost, Leo *(Lyricist)*   2759

Rostand, Edmond *(Author)*   945, 946, 947, 948, 949, 1245, 4073, 4670

Rosten, Leo *(Author)*   1158, 2422

Roston, Karen *(Costumes)*   1512, 2142, 2195

Rotante, Ted *(Choreographer)*   2992

Rotenberg, David *(Director)*   3136

Rotenberg, David *(Librettist)*   3136

Roter, Ted *(Cast)*   2321

Roter, Ted *(Librettist)*   2321

Roth, Ann *(Costumes)*   374, 1194, 1441, 2053, 3516, 3564, 3610, 3787, 3869, 3992, 4334

Roth, Charles *(Lyricist)*   4543

Roth, Daryl *(Producer)*   261, 784, 992, 3142

Roth, Don *(Librettist)*   2834

Roth, Jack *(Cast)*   860, 862

Roth, Lillian *(Cast)*   1134, 1136, 2048, 3342, 3900, 4847

Roth, Lillian *(Composer)*   1134

Roth, Lillian *(Lyricist)*   1134

Roth, Michael *(Musical Director)*   1015

Roth, Michael *(Vocal Arranger)*   1015

Roth, Michael S. *(Musical Director)*   2787

Roth, Michael S. *(Vocal Arranger)*   2787

Roth, Murray *(Lyricist)*   1685, 1686, 2706, 3400

Roth, Nat *(Producer)*   618, 2515, 2548

Roth, Nathaniel *(Producer)*   4624

Roth, Robert Jess *(Director)*   330

Roth, Wolfgang *(Set Design)*   3543, 4176

Rothafel, Samuel "Roxy" *(Producer)*   3639

Rothlein, Arlene *(Choreographer)*   3418

Rothman, Bernard *(Producer)*   3499

Rothpearl, Harry *(Producer)*   400, 1269, 4773

Rothweiler Jr., Larry N. *(Musical Director)*   4107

Rotondaro, Stephen *(Costumes)*   3178

Rotondi, Michael G. *(Cast)*   139

Rotov, Alexis (Cast)   4486

Rott, Bernard (Composer)   1579

Roudenko, Lubov (Cast)   153

Roullier, Ron (Composer)   3697

Roulston, Allison (Lyricist)   128, 1049

Roundabout Theater Company (Producer)   572, 3598, 4175

Rounds, David (Cast)   273, 1373, 1872, 2935, 3780, 4330

Rounds, David (Director)   4330

Rounds, David (Set Design)   4330

Rounds, Gene (Cast)   4584

Rounseville, Robert (Cast)   247, 630, 1894, 2344, 2727, 3612, 3647, 4479

Rourke, M.E.
    See also Herbert Reynolds.

Rourke, M.E. (Librettist)   506

Rourke, M.E. (Lyricist)   121, 506, 954, 1066, 1067, 1151, 1152, 1246, 1455, 1464, 1519, 1538, 1569, 1613, 1888, 2282, 2317, 2341, 2358, 2469, 2498, 2761, 2793, 2952, 3177, 3322, 3679, 3710, 3996, 4115, 4219, 4726

Rousseau, Emil (Cast)   4092

Roussimoff, Ari (Cast)   2356

Roussin, Andre (Author)   3338

Routledge, Patricia (Cast)   134, 989, 2617, 3846, 4004

Roven, Glen (Composer)   4, 1638

Roven, Glen (Dance Arranger)   1082

Roven, Glen (Lyricist)   1638

Roven, Glen (Musical Director)   4197

Rovin, Robert (Cast)   366, 2913, 3551

Rowan, James (Cast)   3840

Rowe, Caryl (Cast)   407

Rowe, Eleanor (Cast)   2814

Rowe, Hansford (Cast)   2026, 2346, 3992

Rowe, Josephine V. (Lyricist)   2662

Rowland, Adele (Cast)   17, 1318, 1793, 1852, 2040, 2119, 2292, 2334, 2385, 2695, 2793, 3193, 3304, 3672, 4115, 4381

Rowland, Betty (Composer)   1637

Rowland, Betty (Lyricist)   1637

Rowland, Julia (Cast)   917

Rowland, Rowena (Cast)   3410

Rowland, Steve (Cast)   2053

Rowland, William (Cast)   1502

Rowland & Clifford Amus. Co (Producer)   3316

Rowlands, Gena (Cast)   63

Rowler, Adele (Cast)   4453

Rowles, Polly (Cast)   3187, 4114

Rowley, Bill (Cast)   3708

Rowley, Eddie (Cast)   77

Rowley, J. Henry (Costumes)   1459, 1900

Rowser, Bertin (Composer)   535

Rowser, Bertin (Director)   535

Rowser, Bertin (Lyricist)   535

Rox, John (Composer)   70, 1342, 2227, 3108

Rox, John (Lyricist)   70, 1342, 2168, 2227, 3108

Roxolo, Conrado N. (Author)   1046

Roy, Lillian (Composer)   632

Roy, Neil (Cast)   2238

Roy, Sheila (Cast)   790

Roy, Vernon (Lyricist)   675, 954, 3753

Roy, William (Cast)   262, 272

Roy, William (Composer)   272, 427, 1049, 1107, 1363, 2357, 2680, 3110, 3439, 3484, 3889, 4134

Roy, William (Librettist)   3439

Roy, William (Lyricist)   272, 1107, 1363, 2680, 3439, 3484, 3889

Roy, William (Musical Director)   262, 272, 427, 3889

Roy, William (Orchestrations)   1049

Roy, William (Pianist)   1049, 1107, 3484, 3889

Roy, William (Vocal Arranger)   272, 1049, 1107, 1363, 3889

Royal, Charles (Cast)   3005

Royal, Mathew J. (Librettist)   235

Royal, Reginald (Additional Lyrics)   4460

Royal, Reginald (Additional Music)   4460

Royal, Reginald (Musical Director)   1296

Royal, Ted (Orchestrations)   90, 153, 180, 189, 206, 483, 507, 530, 1045, 1109, 1300, 1494, 1539, 1706, 1760, 1930, 2000, 2103, 2187, 2227, 2453, 2479, 2707, 2817, 2940, 2987, 3036, 3091, 3107, 3108, 3110, 3278, 3347, 3801, 3895, 4015, 4018, 4058, 4123, 4362, 4377, 4652

Royal, Ted (Vocal Arranger)   1539

Royal Pardon Productions (Producer)   4390

Royce, Edward (Choreographer)   333, 683, 1066, 1454, 2614, 3819

Royce, Edward (Director)   152, 168, 379, 627, 684, 685, 765, 815, 1598, 1625, 1784, 2070, 2148, 2308, 2336, 2340, 2412, 2424, 2430, 2594, 2614, 2761, 2829, 3230, 3245, 3250, 3312, 3740, 3819, 3924, 4814, 4843, 4853

Royce, Edward (Librettist)   3246

Royce, Edward (Lyricist)   3246

Royce, Edward (Producer)   577, 765, 3312

Royce, Jack (Lyricist)   390

Royce, Louise (Cast)   4724

Royce, Shirley (Cast)   764

Royce, Stanley (Composer)   3238

Royce, William (Director)   1966

Royce Jr., E.W. (Choreographer)   2514

Roye, Dorothy (Cast)   711

Roye, Ruth (Cast)   3589

Royle, Edwin Milton (Author)   4664

Royle, Edwin Milton (Director)   2765

Royle, Edwin Milton (Librettist)   2765, 2951

Royle, Edwin Milton (Lyricist)   2951

Roynton, Helen (Cast)   734

Royon (Composer)   1869

Royston, Roy (Cast)   791, 2263, 3431, 4025, 4532

Rozario, Bob (Musical Director)   2969

Rozario, Bob (Orchestrations)   2969

Rozovsky, M. (Composer)   4176

Rozovsky, Mark (Author)   4176

Rubel, Reverand Hines (Composer)   3104

Ruben, Aaron (Director)   1567

Ruben, Jose (Cast)   672, 3680

Ruben, Jose (Director)   82, 324, 672, 1352, 2786, 4428, 4733

Rubens, Bernice (Author)   2065

Rubens, Hugo (Composer)   2255

Rubens, Maurie (Composer)   201, 202, 545, 551, 1113,

1460, 1461, 1462, 1678, 1693, 1836, 2293, 2637, 2669,
2747, 2789, 2843, 3012, 3084, 3148, 3150, 3523, 3680,
4010, 4669
Rubens, Maurie *(Musical Director)* 2540
Rubens, Paul *(Author)* 3052
Rubens, Paul *(Composer)* 30, 276, 379, 470, 906, 954,
1188, 1313, 1391, 1472, 1526, 1537, 1538, 1544, 1561,
1666, 2495, 2526, 2761, 2889, 2901, 3052, 3079, 3259,
3313, 3387, 3828, 3856, 3857, 4219, 4354, 4418, 4419,
4430, 4813
Rubens, Paul *(Librettist)* 2889, 4219, 4354
Rubens, Paul *(Lyricist)* 30, 276, 379, 470, 954, 1188, 1313,
1391, 1537, 1538, 2761, 2889, 2901, 3052, 3259, 3313,
3387, 3856, 3857, 4219, 4354, 4418, 4419, 4430
Rubens, Paul A. *(Composer)* 1537, 2844, 4430
Rubens, Paul A. *(Lyricist)* 2844, 3857, 4219, 4430
Rubens, Walter *(Composer)* 4354
Rubenstein, Arthur *(Orchestrations)* 4659
Rubenstein, Arthur B. *(Composer)* 496, 1634
Rubenstein, Barbara *(Cast)* 576
Rubenstein, Carol *(Lighting Designer)* 3209
Rubenstein, Marty *(Vocal Arranger)* 2804
Rubenstein, Steve *(Producer)* 963
Rubin, Arthur *(Cast)* 2295
Rubin, Arthur *(Producer)* 36, 695, 975, 2437
Rubin, Benny *(Cast)* 1722
Rubin, Benny *(Choreographer)* 1722
Rubin, Charles *(Librettist)* 109
Rubin, Cyma *(Producer)* 1063
Rubin, Pedro *(Cast)* 3719
Rubin, Ruth *(Composer)* 1609
Rubin, Ruth *(Lyricist)* 1609
Rubin, Steven *(Set Design)* 1732, 3760
Rubinek, Saul *(Cast)* 2429
Rubins, Josh *(Composer)* 572
Rubins, Josh *(Librettist)* 572
Rubins, Josh *(Lyricist)* 572
Rubinstein, Arthur *(Musical Director)* 1441
Rubinstein, Arthur *(Orchestrations)* 2599, 4405
Rubinstein, Arthur B. *(Incidental Music)* 1634
Rubinstein, Arthur B. *(Musical Director)* 1634
Rubinstein, John *(Cast)* 3506, 4535
Rubinstein, Ruth *(Cast)* 3501
Ruby, Cyrus *(Lyricist)* 3248
Ruby, Harry *(Author)* 2467
Ruby, Harry *(Cast)* 79, 1396
Ruby, Harry *(Composer)* 142, 176, 358, 545, 1297, 1368,
1617, 1686, 1688, 1691, 1819, 1873, 1889, 1944, 2373,
2392, 2638, 2706, 2857, 3020, 3144, 3185, 3583, 3617,
3659, 3695, 3926, 4033, 4249, 4426, 4436, 4476, 4742,
4799, 4812, 4813, 4814, 4817
Ruby, Harry *(Librettist)* 1396, 1889, 1935, 1944, 3009,
3659, 3924, 4426
Ruby, Harry *(Lyricist)* 95, 930, 2392, 2638, 4814,
4817
Ruby, Harry *(Producer)* 4426
Ruby, Herman *(Lyricist)* 1643, 2857, 3248, 4806
Rubykate Inc. *(Producer)* 3653
Rudas, Anna *(Choreographer)* 1326
Rudas, Tibor *(Choreographer)* 1326

Rudd, Gertrude *(Cast)* 3026
Rudel, Julius *(Musical Director)* 2839, 4371
Rudel, Julius *(Orchestrations)* 4371
Rudel, Rickie *(Cast)* 821, 2641
Rudetsky, Seth *(Vocal Arranger)* 3004
Rudie, Evelyn *(Choreographer)* 2321
Rudie, Evelyn *(Lyricist)* 2321
Rudie, Evelyn *(Musical Director)* 2321
Rudin, Scott *(Producer)* 3411
Rudisill, Ivan *(Musical Director)* 598, 642, 680, 2276,
2528, 2636, 3508, 3622, 4241, 4360, 4426
Rudlev, Herbert *(Cast)* 4368
Rudnick, Max *(Producer)* 439, 1989
Rudolph, Jerome *(Producer)* 1727
Rudolph, Walter *(Musical Director)* 2089
Rudolph, Walter J. *(Arrangements)* 2090
Rudolph, Walter J. *(Musical Director)* 2090
Ruff, Alton *(Choreographer)* 2969
Ruffelle, Frances *(Cast)* 730, 2442
Ruffin, Clovis *(Costumes)* 2294
Ruffin, Eric *(Cast)* 2197
Ruffini, Giovanni *(Author)* 3197
Ruffo, Titta *(Cast)* 3639
Rugel, Yvette *(Cast)* 1482, 3401
Ruggles, Charles *(Cast)* 628, 2972, 3402, 3622,
3866, 4118, 4464
Ruggles, Charlie *(Cast)* 2479, 3287, 3650
Ruhl, Malcolm *(Cast)* 4740
Ruhl, Malcolm *(Musical Director)* 4740
Ruhl, Pat *(Cast)* 1107
Ruisinger, Thomas *(Cast)* 2689, 2737
Ruivivar, Francis *(Cast)* 2241, 3411, 3944
Ruiz, Randy *(Cast)* 3806
Rule, Arthur *(Musical Director)* 3139
Rule, Bert *(Composer)* 1026, 4393
Rule, Bert *(Lyricist)* 1026
Rule, Bert L. *(Composer)* 1963
Rule, Charles *(Cast)* 98, 273, 1634, 3702
Rule, James *(Composer)* 2662
Rule, Janice *(Cast)* 1745, 4273
Rumble, Andy *(Arrangements)* 846
Rumble, Andy *(Musical Director)* 846
Rumble, Andy *(Orchestrations)* 846
Rumbold, Hugh *(Composer)* 675
Rummler, Tom *(Cast)* 73, 945
Rumshinsky, J.M. *(Composer)* 1208
Rumshinsky, Joseph *(Composer)* 1609, 2356,
3995, 4342
Rumshinsky, Murray *(Composer)* 3559
Rumshinsky, Murray *(Musical Director)* 3559
Rumshisky, J.M. *(Composer)* 1639
Rumshisky, J.M. *(Lyricist)* 1639
Runanin, Boris *(Choreographer)* 1567, 3473, 3505
Rundback *(Composer)* 2341
Rundgren, Todd *(Composer)* 4518
Rundgren, Todd *(Lyricist)* 4518
Rundgren, Todd *(Vocal Arranger)* 4518
Runitch, Emma *(Cast)* 839
Runner, Joseph L. *(Producer)* 1412
Runolfsson, Anne *(Cast)* 949

Ryan, Sue (*Cast*) 2397, 4826
Ryan, T.E. (*Set Design*) 2844
Ryan, Theodore S. (*Cast*) 3325
Ryan, Thomas M. (*Set Design*) 3461
Ryan, Walter (*Cast*) 1582
Ryan, William J. (*Set Design*) 382
Rychtarik, Richard (*Costumes*) 177
Rychtarik, Richard (*Set Design*) 177, 4737
Rydell, Charles (*Cast*) 3863
Ryder, Alfred (*Cast*) 3180
Ryder, Donald (*Set Design*) 279
Ryder, Philip (*Cast*) 3995
Ryder, Ric (*Cast*) 3169, 3873
Ryder, Richard (*Cast*) 1684, 3476, 3661, 4533
Rye, Frank (*Director*) 3361
Ryley, Charles (*Cast*) 1429
Ryley, J.H. (*Cast*) 402
Ryley, Thomas (*Producer*) 1313
Ryley, Thomas W. (*Producer*) 1417, 1579, 2803, 3433, 3626
Ryman, Add (*Cast*) 1913
Ryman, Add (*Librettist*) 1913
Rynharrt, Shryl (*Cast*) 319
Ryskind, Morrie (*Author*) 536
Ryskind, Morrie (*Composer*) 1357
Ryskind, Morrie (*Librettist*) 142, 1357, 1396, 1440, 1446, 2444, 2597, 2827, 3086, 3225, 4179
Ryskind, Morrie (*Lyricist*) 123, 536, 1357, 2827, 3086, 3623

S

Sa Loutos, Connie (*Cast*) 4732
Sabatino, Anthony (*Set Design*) 4402
Sabbar, Demetrius (*Cast*) 214
Sabel, Josephine (*Cast*) 3025, 3030, 3254, 3968
Sabel, Josie (*Cast*) 3609
Sabel, Shelly (*Lighting Designer*) 4016
Sabin, David (*Cast*) 496, 681, 1427, 1441, 2199, 2218, 2898, 3015, 3209
Sabinson, Lee (*Producer*) 1278
Sablon, Jean (*Cast*) 4174
Sac. Air Service Command (*Producer*) 226
Sacha, Ken (*Cast*) 1298
Sachelli, Robert (*Choreographer*) 1004
Sacher, Toby (*Composer*) 3226
Sachs, C. Colby (*Musical Director*) 1757
Sachs, Chuck (*Cast*) 1757
Sachs, Danny (*Composer*) 1873
Sachs, Danny (*Lyricist*) 1873
Sachs, Dorothy (*Lyricist*) 447, 3105
Sachs, Norman (*Composer*) 31, 922, 1089, 1435, 2199, 3059
Sachs, Norman (*Librettist*) 3059
Sachs, Norman (*Lyricist*) 3059
Sackeroff, David (*Lighting Designer*) 508, 2146
Sackeroff, David (*Set Design*) 508, 2146
Sackler, Howard (*Additional Material*) 1857

Sacks, Dorothy (*Lyricist*) 3705
Sacks, Mike (*Cast*) 2749
Sacre Monte Gypsies (*Cast*) 839
Saddler, Donald (*Cast*) 454, 961
Saddler, Donald (*Choreographer*) 1609, 1660, 1762, 1842, 2227, 2578, 2864, 2898, 2958, 3000, 3733, 3743, 3846, 3913, 4090, 4297, 4395, 4399, 4450, 4609, 4734
Saddler, Donald (*Director*) 369, 1382
Saddler, Frank (*Orchestrations*) 126, 256, 378, 559, 805, 965, 968, 1154, 1483, 1598, 1784, 1920, 1922, 2070, 2232, 2430, 2620, 2723, 2858, 2919, 3087, 3146, 3193, 3230, 3237, 3245, 3395, 3488, 3679, 3737, 3923, 4158, 4203, 4555, 4806, 4814, 4860
Sadler, Bill (*Cast*) 2440
Sadler, Frank
    See Frank Saddler.
Sadler, Josie (*Cast*) 559, 1627, 2232, 2938, 3437, 3976, 4222, 4590
Sadusk, Maureen (*Cast*) 3197
Safan, Craig (*Composer*) 595
Safan, Craig (*Librettist*) 595
Saffran, Christina (*Cast*) 146, 3126
Sagall, Solomon (*Producer*) 2075, 2811
Sagan, Leontine (*Director*) 650, 972
Sage, C. Russell (*Cast*) 2996
Sager (*Composer*) 4181
Sager, Carole Bayer
    See also Carole Bayer.
Sager, Carole Bayer (*Composer*) 964
Sager, Carole Bayer (*Lyricist*) 146, 964, 2677, 4334
Sager, Charles (*Cast*) 2721
Sager, Charles S. (*Director*) 2721
Sagittarius Ent. (*Producer*) 546
Sagittarius Productions (*Producer*) 4089
Sahl, Mort (*Cast*) 826
Sahlins, Bernard (*Producer*) 4397
Saidenberg, Ted (*Musical Director*) 3427
Saidenberg, Ted (*Vocal Arranger*) 3427
Saidenberg, Theodore (*Musical Director*) 1864, 2617, 2626, 3274
Saidenberg, Theodore (*Vocal Arranger*) 1864
Saidy, Fred (*Author*) 2234
Saidy, Fred (*Librettist*) 462, 1278, 1300, 1745, 2190, 2234
Saint, David (*Director*) 1236
Saint, Eva Marie (*Cast*) 3324
Saint-Amand (*Author*) 1193
Saint-Saens, Camille (*Music Based On*) 1119
Saint-Subber (*Producer*) 1511, 2000, 2331, 3326, 4329
Sainthill, Loudon (*Costumes*) 634, 1721
Sainthill, Loudon (*Set Design*) 1721
Saitta, Paul (*Lighting Designer*) 2887
Sakash, Evelyn (*Set Design*) 10, 1997, 3181, 4264
Saki, Marion (*Cast*) 4050, 4249
Saks, Gene (*Cast*) 2910
Saks, Gene (*Director*) 1190, 1471, 1721, 1955, 2058, 2713, 2965, 3577, 3644
Salamando, Peter (*Composer*) 4433
Salamando, Peter (*Librettist*) 1648, 4433
Salamando, Peter (*Lyricist*) 4433

Salami, A. *(Composer)* 710
Salami, A. *(Lyricist)* 710
Salata, Gregory *(Cast)* 4172
Sale, Chic *(Cast)* 1460, 1461, 1462, 1836, 2939, 4840
Sale, Chic *(Producer)* 1462
Sale, Virginia *(Librettist)* 2483
Salerno, Mary Jo *(Cast)* 4035
Sales, Soupy *(Cast)* 1841
Salinger, Conrad *(Orchestrations)* 125, 622, 1342, 1493, 1856, 2258, 3365, 3850, 4365, 4374, 4583, 4825
Salisbury, Fran *(Cast)* 1816, 3690
Salisbury, Frances *(Cast)* 3599
Salisbury, Jean *(Cast)* 2518
Sallert, Ulla *(Cast)* 367
Salmon, Scott *(Choreographer)* 1146, 2360, 2953, 3637
Salmon, Scott *(Director)* 1146, 3637
Salonga, Lea *(Cast)* 2905
Salonis, Clarke *(Cast)* 2243
Saloway, Lowell *(Lyricist)* 4273
Salsberg, Gerry *(Cast)* 3066
Salt, Waldo *(Librettist)* 997, 3831
Salt, Waldo *(Lyricist)* 3831
Salt and Pepper *(Cast)* 1460
Salta, Menotti *(Musical Director)* 4777
Salta, Menotti *(Orchestrations)* 4123, 4428
Saltz, Amy *(Director)* 4431
Saltz, Amy *(Librettist)* 4431
Saltzman, Mark *(Lyricist)* 4
Saltzman, Simon L. *(Producer)* 3370
Salvador, Dom *(Dance Arranger)* 3838
Salvatore, John *(Cast)* 3346
Salvio, Robert *(Cast)* 406
Salzer, Eugene *(Composer)* 1174
Salzer, Eugene *(Musical Director)* 465, 1174, 1961, 2448, 2494, 3866
Salzer, Gene *(Musical Director)* 123, 124, 247, 1109, 1272, 1275, 1440, 1453, 1932, 2061, 2105, 2264, 2827, 3005, 3283, 3359, 3623, 3924, 4299, 4374, 4532
Salzer, Gus *(Cast)* 4234
Salzer, Gus *(Musical Director)* 152, 1011, 1088, 1163, 1183, 1297, 1318, 1378, 1455, 1537, 1544, 1598, 1784, 2148, 2214, 2291, 2491, 2527, 2545, 2594, 2638, 2722, 3103, 3220, 3254, 3312, 3431, 3533, 3721, 3753, 3819, 3861, 4212, 4234, 4357, 4545, 4683, 4844
Salzer, Gustave *(Incidental Music)* 4313
Salzer, Gustave *(Musical Director)* 531, 1066, 1110, 1309, 3590, 3613
Sam, Long Tack *(Cast)* 378
Samish, Adrian *(Composer)* 1836
Samish, Adrian *(Lyricist)* 1836
Sammler, B.J. *(Lighting Designer)* 1072
Samoiloff, Adrian *(Costumes)* 1153
Samoiloff, Adrian *(Set Design)* 1153
Sampson, Edgar *(Composer)* 146, 432, 4137
Sampson, Roy *(Cast)* 1619
Sampson, William *(Cast)* 2029
Sams, Jeffrey D. *(Cast)* 1296
Samuel, Harold *(Composer)* 719
Samuel, Peter *(Cast)* 2766
Samuels, Arthur *(Composer)* 1357, 3540

Samuels, Arthur H. *(Composer)* 3783
Samuels, D.S. *(Musical Director)* 2649
Samuels, Lesser *(Librettist)* 1698
Samuels, Lucille *(Costumes)* 2396
Samuels, Maurice V. *(Author)* 4275
Samuels, Rae *(Cast)* 4290, 4806
Samuels, Walter G. *(Composer)* 3086
Samuelson, Rich *(Cast)* 2580
San, Dan *(Lyricist)* 1053
San Francisco Civic Light Opera *(Producer)* 1369, 4798
San Juan, Olga *(Cast)* 847, 3347
Sanacino, Ernest *(Director)* 1940
Sanchez, Dorian *(Choreographer)* 846
Sanchez, Fernando *(Costumes)* 2260
Sanchez, Jaime *(Cast)* 4625
Sanchez, Jaime *(Director)* 4205
Sand, Paul *(Cast)* 1993, 2663, 4397, 4627, 4746
Sand, Paul *(Librettist)* 4627
Sandberg, Steve *(Dance Arranger)* 756
Sandberg, Steve *(Musical Director)* 756
Sande, Margaret *(Cast)* 2068, 4159
Sandeen, Darrell *(Cast)* 4785
Sanders, Alma *(Composer)* 606, 728, 1132, 1174, 2005, 2595, 3069, 3252, 3580, 4283, 4576
Sanders, Alma *(Lyricist)* 606, 728, 2595, 3580
Sanders, Arthur *(Director)* 1562, 4506
Sanders, Dirk *(Cast)* 4363
Sanders, Donna *(Cast)* 3889
Sanders, Fred *(Cast)* 580
Sanders, George *(Cast)* 841
Sanders, Honey *(Cast)* 1158, 3920
Sanders, Jay *(Cast)* 1575
Sanders, Jay O. *(Cast)* 2132
Sanders, Marta *(Cast)* 374
Sanders, Nat *(Lyricist)* 4816
Sanders, Steve *(Cast)* 4764
Sanderson, Julia *(Cast)* 178, 627, 954, 1243, 1544, 1922, 2341, 3153, 3658, 3996, 4219, 4258, 4283, 4434, 4713
Sanderson, Kristen *(Director)* 1291
Sandford, Harold *(Orchestrations)* 4818, 4819
Sandifur, Virginia *(Cast)* 708, 1329, 3444, 3743, 3926, 4029
Sandler, Harold *(Musical Director)* 4567
Sandler, Peretz *(Composer)* 3781
Sandler, Peretz *(Lyricist)* 3781
Sandor, Gluck *(Choreographer)* 1136, 1137, 3501
Sandrich Jr., Mark *(Composer)* 367
Sandrow, Nahma *(Librettist)* 2354
Sands, Billy *(Cast)* 4484
Sands, Christofer *(Cast)* 1940
Sands, Diana *(Cast)* 157, 477, 1389
Sands, Donna *(Cast)* 1093
Sands, Dorothy *(Cast)* 823, 1652, 1655, 1656
Sands, Dorothy *(Lyricist)* 1655
Sandy, Gary *(Cast)* 915, 3925, 4703
Sanford, Bobby *(Director)* 1953
Sanford, Bobby *(Producer)* 1953, 3950
Sanford, Charles *(Musical Director)* 23, 743, 1112, 1815, 1933, 2523, 2707, 2817, 3390, 3813, 3841, 4702, 4782
Sanford, Henry L. *(Composer)* 1866
Sanford, Isabel *(Cast)* 1674

Saver, Jeffrey (*Arrangements*)   198
Saver, Jeffrey (*Dance Arranger*)   198
Saver, Jeffrey (*Musical Director*)   198, 2646
Savile, Edith (*Cast*)   2976
Saville, Nina (*Cast*)   3693
Savin, M. (*Composer*)   2527
Savin, M. (*Orchestrations*)   2527
Savin, Ron Lee (*Cast*)   1509, 4171
Savino, Domenico (*Dance Arranger*)   4086
Savino, Domenico (*Orchestrations*)   297, 612, 1126,
   1135, 1136, 1281, 2379, 4086
Savino, Domenico (*Vocal Arranger*)   2379
Saviola, Camille (*Cast*)   140, 3171
Savo, Jimmy (*Author*)   2551
Savo, Jimmy (*Cast*)   514, 1135, 3005, 3153, 3365,
   4178, 4575, 4640
Savo, Nina (*Author*)   3788
Savoy, Bert
   See also Savoy & Brennan.
Savoy, Bert (*Cast*)   1686
Savoy & Brennan
   See also Bert Savoy and Jay Brennan.
Savoy & Brennan (*Cast*)   1688, 2855, 2900
Savoy Lindy Hoppers (*Cast*)   435
Savoy Producing Cooperative (*Producer*)   3434
Sawyer, Charles Carroll (*Lyricist*)   3259
Sawyer, Connie (*Cast*)   817
Sawyer, Donald (*Cast*)   1847
Sawyer, Ivy (*Cast*)   379, 1723, 2277, 2789, 3006, 3008,
   3250, 3923
Sawyer, Mary Pat (*Choreographer*)   255
Sawyer, Michael (*Librettist*)   1002
Sawyer, Mike (*Librettist*)   766, 3427
Saxe, Phil (*Cast*)   3617
Saxe, Phil (*Musical Director*)   822
Saxe, Templar (*Cast*)   470, 904, 1123, 1188, 2374, 4201
Saxon, David (*Composer*)   520
Saxon, Don (*Producer*)   2925
Saxon, Luther (*Cast*)   653
Saxon, Marie (*Cast*)   2833, 2972, 3659, 4532
Sayag, Edmond (*Producer*)   1411, 2366
Sayer (*Composer*)   3073
Sayers, Henry J. (*Composer*)   1627, 4390
Sayers, Henry J. (*Lyricist*)   4390
Saylor, Peter (*Set Design*)   4774
Sayre, Theodore Burt (*Author*)   1157, 1163, 3220, 4407
Scaasi, Arnold (*Costumes*)   1622
Scaife, Marvin (*Cast*)   4039
Scalici, Jack (*Cast*)   793
Scanga, Richard (*Producer*)   4449
Scanlan, Dick (*Cast*)   3346
Scanlan, James (*Director*)   526
Scanlan, Robert (*Director*)   4147
Scanlon, Walter (*Cast*)   97, 452, 1162, 4056
Scarborough, George (*Author*)   4066
Scarbrough, Jan (*Composer*)   2704
Scarbrough, Jan (*Lyricist*)   2704
Scardino, Don (*Cast*)   135, 1082, 1581, 1737, 2074,
   3389
Scardino, Don (*Director*)   1915

Scardino, Don (*Orchestrations*)   2074
Scardino, Donald (*Cast*)   2318
Scarpelli, Glenn (*Cast*)   4171
Scarritt, Leigh (*Cast*)   2969
Scarsborough, George (*Lyricist*)   4066
Scatamacchia, Charlie (*Cast*)   2968
Scatuorchio, Tee (*Choreographer*)   4309
Schaaf, George (*Lighting Designer*)   2666
Schacher, Richard A. (*Musical Director*)   2007
Schacher, Richard A. (*Vocal Arranger*)   2007
Schaefer, David (*Composer*)   1873
Schaefer, David (*Lyricist*)   1873
Schaefer, George (*Director*)   483, 1507, 4798
Schaefer, George (*Producer*)   1507, 4395
Schaefer, Hal (*Dance Arranger*)   1373, 1422, 3788, 4827
Schaefer, Hal (*Orchestrations*)   1373
Schaefer, Will (*Orchestrations*)   4114
Schaeffer, Carl (*Producer*)   1383
Schaetzlein, Larry (*Composer*)   3405
Schaetzlein, Larry (*Lyricist*)   3405
Schafer, Jerry (*Lyricist*)   362
Schafer, Milton (*Composer*)   519, 1094
Schafer, Natalie (*Cast*)   635, 715, 2386, 2396, 3761
Schafer, Scott (*Cast*)   3643
Schaffer, Lawrence (*Set Design*)   3066
Schaffer, Mary (*Composer*)   3605
Schaffer, Mary (*Lyricist*)   3605
Schaffner, Walter (*Set Design*)   3252
Schak, John (*Director*)   491
Schak, John (*Producer*)   491, 3542
Schall, David (*Cast*)   3697
Schalow, Betty (*Cast*)   2089
Schanzer, Rudolf (*Author*)   1538, 1561, 2384, 2495,
   2666, 2794, 3084, 4121
Schanzer, Rudolf (*Librettist*)   1044
Schanzer, Rudolf (*Lyricist*)   1044
Schapiro, Herb (*Librettist*)   535
Schapiro, Herb (*Lyricist*)   535
Scharer, Jonathan (*Producer*)   1349, 1350, 1371, 3346
Scharf, Walter (*Arrangements*)   974
Scharf, Walter (*Musical Director*)   974
Scharfman, Nitra (*Composer*)   2472
Scharfman, Nitra (*Librettist*)   2472
Scharfman, Nitra (*Lyricist*)   2472
Scharnberg, Kim (*Orchestrations*)   2198
Schary, Dore (*Director*)   4516, 4863
Schary, Dore (*Librettist*)   159, 4863
Schary, Dore (*Producer*)   4516
Schary Productions, Dore (*Producer*)   159
Schasny, John (*Composer*)   2039
Schechter, David (*Author*)   1740
Schechter, David (*Cast*)   1715, 1740, 3162, 3806
Schechter, David (*Composer*)   1740
Schechter, David (*Director*)   1740
Schechter, David (*Lyricist*)   1740
Schechter, Philip (*Cast*)   4371
Schechtman, Richie (*Cast*)   3075
Schechtman, Saul (*Dance Arranger*)   1233
Schechtman, Saul (*Musical Director*)   98, 656, 1233
Schechtman, Saul (*Vocal Arranger*)   656, 1233

Scheck, Max *(Choreographer)* 709, 1014, 1992, 2293, 2622, 3157, 3407, 3472, 3586, 3770, 3849, 4188, 4209, 4372, 4528
Scheck, Max *(Director)* 364, 4484
Schecter, David *(Cast)* 1053
Schecter, Lee *(Librettist)* 3075
Scheeder, Louis W. *(Director)* 699
Scheeder, Louis W. *(Producer)* 1038
Scheerer, Bob *(Cast)* 507, 961, 2439, 4423
Scheff, Fritzi *(Cast)* 252, 1111, 2623, 2915, 3562, 3567, 4465, 4497
Scheidt, Scott *(Lighting Designer)* 3080
Schenck, Eliot *(Musical Director)* 377
Schenck, Joe *(Cast)* 683, 959, 2900, 3144, 4813, 4814, 4815
Schenck, Joe *(Composer)* 4813, 4814, 4842
Schenck, Joe *(Lyricist)* 3144, 4813, 4814, 4842
Schenck, Leopold *(Composer)* 976
Schenck, Mary *(Costumes)* 4117
Schenck, Mary Percy *(Costumes)* 1948
Schenker, Joel *(Producer)* 989
Schenker, Joel W. *(Producer)* 2618
Scherer, John *(Cast)* 2372
Scherman, Thomas *(Musical Director)* 4363
Schermasser, Dick *(Vocal Arranger)* 74
Schertler, Nancy *(Lighting Designer)* 1234
Schertzinger, Victor *(Composer)* 3444, 4381
Schertzinger, Victor *(Lyricist)* 1309, 4381
Schertzinger, Victor *(Musical Director)* 4381
Scheuer, Charles *(Librettist)* 943
Scheuer, Steven H. *(Producer)* 3210
Schick, George *(Musical Director)* 4792
Schickele, Peter
    See The Open Window.
Schielke, Joanna *(Lighting Designer)* 2784, 3297
Schiera, Thom *(Librettist)* 1164
Schierhorn, Paul *(Composer)* 3136
Schierhorn, Paul *(Dance Arranger)* 3136
Schierhorn, Paul *(Librettist)* 3136
Schierhorn, Paul *(Lyricist)* 3136
Schierhorn, Paul *(Vocal Arranger)* 3136, 3175
Schiff, Charlotte *(Producer)* 4678
Schiff, Dan *(Cast)* 2654
Schiff, Larry *(Composer)* 3539
Schiff, Larry *(Librettist)* 3539
Schiff, Larry *(Lyricist)* 3539
Schifter, Peter Mark *(Director)* 4619
Schildkraut, Joseph *(Cast)* 55, 1283, 2487
Schiller, George *(Cast)* 102, 2493
Schiller, Joel *(Set Design)* 1341
Schiller, Miriam *(Choreographer)* 1773, 4253
Schilling, Carl *(Composer)* 4704, 4705
Schilling, Carl *(Musical Director)* 800
Schilling, Gus *(Cast)* 1323, 4545
Schimmel, John *(Cast)* 3608
Schindler, Paul *(Composer)* 830, 1469, 2159, 2286, 3129
Schindler, Paul *(Musical Director)* 830, 1308, 1469, 1738, 2159, 2286, 2347, 3047
Schirmer, Gus *(Cast)* 3103
Schirmer Jr., Gus *(Director)* 1734
Schirmer Jr., Gus *(Lyricist)* 924

Schisgal, Murray *(Author)* 2218, 2598
Schisgal, Murray *(Librettist)* 2925
Schissler, Jeffrey *(Lighting Designer)* 451, 1092, 1785, 2100, 2294, 3864
Schissler, Jeffrey *(Set Design)* 2294, 3261
Schlamme, Martha *(Cast)* 2777, 2941
Schlegel, Jeanne *(Cast)* 1347
Schlein, Hap *(Librettist)* 1436, 2785
Schlesinger, John *(Director)* 2047
Schlesinger, Sarah *(Lyricist)* 3277
Schlinker *(Composer)* 4723
Schlissel, Jack *(Producer)* 1660
Schlitt, Robert *(Librettist)* 3788
Schloss, Irving *(Musical Director)* 2293, 2808, 4673
Schloss, Irving *(Orchestrations)* 4328
Schloss, Sybille *(Cast)* 3441
Schlossberg, Jerry *(Producer)* 1441, 4468
Schmeed Trio *(Cast)* 1815
Schmid *(Composer)* 938
Schmid *(Lyricist)* 938
Schmidt, Douglas W. *(Set Design)* 52, 695, 1015, 1161, 1664, 3309, 3330, 3733, 3806, 4019, 4020, 4334, 4370, 4459
Schmidt, Harvey *(Cast)* 1701, 3542
Schmidt, Harvey *(Composer)* 491, 681, 807, 808, 809, 1023, 1245, 1362, 1364, 1701, 2050, 2244, 3294, 3469, 3479, 3484, 3542, 3940
Schmidt, Harvey *(Director)* 3469
Schmidt, Harvey *(Lyricist)* 1023, 3940
Schmidt, Harvey *(Musical Director)* 807
Schmidt, Harvey *(Pianist)* 3542
Schmidt, Jack *(Cast)* 4062
Schmied, Wally *(Composer)* 3178
Schmied, Wally *(Lyricist)* 3178
Schmitt, Virginia *(Cast)* 1750
Schnabel, Stefan *(Cast)* 2257, 3509
Schneider, Alan *(Director)* 461, 2368
Schneider, C.N. *(Composer)* 248
Schneider, Charles *(Dance Arranger)* 4789
Schneider, Charles *(Musical Director)* 3196, 4789
Schneider, Charles *(Vocal Arranger)* 3196
Schneider, Frank *(Lighting Designer)* 3009
Schneider, Jana *(Cast)* 3070
Schneider, Jeffrey *(Set Design)* 4769, 4799
Schneider & Anderson *(Costumes)* 1026, 1251, 2698, 2830, 4807
Schneider-Anderson *(Costumes)* 685, 4812
Schnitzer, Ignaz *(Author)* 3776
Schnitzler, Arthur *(Author)* 1439, 1456, 1822, 3760, 3763
Schochen, Seyril *(Librettist)* 4380
Schochen, Seyril *(Lyricist)* 4380
Schocket, Steve *(Cast)* 2970
Schoeffel *(Producer)* 4500
Schoeffler, Paul *(Cast)* 949
Schoenfeld, Mae *(Cast)* 2352
Schoenfield, A. *(Author)* 2922
Scholl, Danny *(Cast)* 620, 4314, 4415
Scholl, Jack *(Composer)* 1481
Scholl, Jack *(Librettist)* 2300

Scholl, Jack *(Lyricist)*   714, 1328, 1481, 1989, 2300, 3683

Scholl, John Jay *(Producer)*   1174

Scholtz, Christa *(Costumes)*   2539

Schon, Bonnie *(Cast)*   3644

Schon, Kenneth *(Cast)*   3035, 3151

Schonberg, Claude-Michel *(Composer)*   2442, 2905

Schonberg, Claude-Michel *(Librettist)*   2442, 2905

Schonberger, John *(Composer)*   1120

Schonberger, John *(Lyricist)*   1120

Schonfeld, Alfred *(Author)*   2923, 3529

Schooler, Dave *(Musical Director)*   1843

Schooley, Edgar I. *(Choreographer)*   2455

Schoonmaker, Charles *(Costumes)*   3544

Schoonover, Meredith *(Cast)*   2641

Schoop, Trudi *(Choreographer)*   3046

Schorr, Anschel *(Lyricist)*   1609

Schorr, Eric *(Composer)*   2022

Schorr, Moshe *(Librettist)*   3781

Schorr, William *(Director)*   462

Schottenfeld, Barbara *(Composer)*   674, 2049

Schottenfeld, Barbara *(Librettist)*   674, 2049

Schottenfeld, Barbara *(Lyricist)*   674, 2049

Schottenfeld, Barbara *(Orchestrations)*   2049

Schrader, Frederick E. *(Librettist)*   222

Schrader, Frederick F. *(Lyricist)*   307

Schrager, Rudolph *(Musical Director)*   2032

Schramm Twins *(Cast)*   2090

Schrank, Joseph *(Librettist)*   2504, 3893

Schrapps, E.R. *(Costumes)*   2622, 2628, 2843

Schrapps, Ernest *(Costumes)*   110, 199, 200, 202, 203, 718, 948, 1219, 1462, 1693, 1799, 1831, 2540, 2637, 2747, 2947, 3011, 3148, 3149, 3150, 3152, 3407, 3409, 3523, 3680, 4025, 4104, 4352, 4524, 4670, 4733

Schrapps, Ernest R. *(Costumes)*   324

Schreiber, Avery *(Cast)*   4619

Schreiber, Avery *(Director)*   2016

Schreiber, Edward *(Producer)*   4514

Schreibman, Myrl A. *(Director)*   4402

Schreibman, Myrl A. *(Producer)*   4402

Schreibman, Paul P. *(Producer)*   1884, 4199

Schrode, William C. *(Cast)*   4802

Schroder, William *(Costumes)*   593, 2565, 4645, 4788

Schroder, William *(Set Design)*   593, 4645, 4788

Schroeder, Aaron *(Producer)*   249

Schroeder, Charles *(Composer)*   4030

Schroeder, Charles *(Lyricist)*   4030

Schroeder, William *(Composer)*   387, 640, 1911, 2282, 2390, 2537, 4647, 4716

Schroeder, William *(Musical Director)*   1175

Schuba, Trixi *(Cast)*   2084

Schubert, Franz *(Music Based On)*   463

Schue, Peter A. *(Set Design)*   3202

Schulberg, B.P. *(Producer)*   2751

Schulberg, Budd *(Author)*   3875, 4633

Schulberg, Budd *(Librettist)*   3875, 4633

Schulberg, Stuart *(Librettist)*   4633

Schuller, Gunther *(Musical Director)*   4447

Schuller, Gunther *(Orchestrations)*   4447

Schulman, Arnold *(Librettist)*   2201

Schulman, Howard *(Librettist)*   4627

Schulman, Susan H. *(Director)*   451, 1258, 1873, 2185, 3862

Schultz, Dwight *(Cast)*   1418

Schultz, Michael *(Director)*   3001, 4343

Schultz, Michael A. *(Director)*   1592, 3309

Schultze, Charles *(Author)*   1374

Schulz, Charles M. *(Author)*   4034, 4783

Schulz, Franz *(Author)*   4486

Schuman, Edward L. *(Producer)*   209

Schuman, Howard *(Librettist)*   682, 4522

Schuman, Howard *(Lyricist)*   4522

Schumann, Robert *(Music Based On)*   1815, 2358

Schumann, Walter *(Composer)*   4346

Schumann-Heink, Madame *(Cast)*   2632

Schumer, Leo *(Composer)*   59, 1892, 3664

Schupf, John *(Composer)*   4093

Schurkamp, Richard *(Costumes)*   4731

Schussel, Sandy *(Librettist)*   4679

Schuster, Alan J. *(Producer)*   140, 478, 747

Schutt, Arthur *(Orchestrations)*   1322

Schutz, Herb *(Dance Arranger)*   673

Schutz, Herbert *(Vocal Arranger)*   3664

Schwab, Buddy *(Cast)*   1706

Schwab, Buddy *(Choreographer)*   1233, 1841, 4537

Schwab, Buddy *(Director)*   3484

Schwab, Charles *(Composer)*   3103

Schwab, Charles M. *(Composer)*   303, 1448, 3130, 4367

Schwab, Laurence *(Director)*   3117

Schwab, Laurence *(Librettist)*   642, 1339, 1387, 1628, 2348, 3117, 3138, 3622, 4241, 4267, 4367, 4550

Schwab, Laurence *(Lyricist)*   3117

Schwab, Laurence *(Producer)*   111, 642, 1027, 1145, 1283, 1339, 1387, 1516, 1628, 2786, 3117, 3138, 4241, 4267, 4550

Schwab, Sophie *(Cast)*   305, 2320

Schwantes, Leland *(Cast)*   2785, 3000, 3020

Schwartz, Abe *(Composer)*   1279, 1609

Schwartz, Abe *(Lyricist)*   1279, 1609

Schwartz, Arthur *(Cast)*   3153

Schwartz, Arthur *(Composer)*   117, 213, 216, 294, 347, 383, 536, 603, 663, 844, 1322, 1338, 1456, 1617, 1654, 1657, 1763, 1855, 1893, 2004, 2137, 2201, 2545, 2547, 2743, 2989, 3020, 3086, 3130, 3139, 3143, 3178, 3390, 3444, 3584, 3680, 3699, 3709, 3861, 3919, 3955, 4142, 4159, 4367, 4446, 4569, 4581, 4621, 4824

Schwartz, Arthur *(Lyricist)*   603, 3139, 3143

Schwartz, Arthur *(Producer)*   2137

Schwartz, Ben *(Composer)*   4275

Schwartz, Ben *(Lyricist)*   4275

Schwartz, Bob *(Director)*   1590

Schwartz, Bonnie Nelson *(Producer)*   2204

Schwartz, Bruce *(Composer)*   485

Schwartz, Fred *(Composer)*   3350

Schwartz, Fred *(Musical Director)*   2351

Schwartz, Frederick *(Musical Director)*   77

Schwartz, Gwen Gibson *(Lyricist)*   3530

Schwartz, Jean *(Author)*   4642

Schwartz, Jean *(Cast)*   3153

Schwartz, Jean *(Composer)*   47, 115, 152, 199, 228, 274,

Scott, Thomas *(Cast)*   803
Scott, Timothy *(Cast)*   678
Scott, Vincent *(Lyricist)*   2467
Scott, Winfield *(Composer)*   4264
Scott, Winfield *(Lyricist)*   4264
Scott, Zanzele *(Cast)*   2272
Scott & Raynor *(Producer)*   2771
Scott III, Henry E. *(Set Design)*   2188
Scott Sisters, The *(Cast)*   1491
Scotti, Vito *(Cast)*   3495
Scotto, Vincent *(Composer)*   3387, 3617, 4390
Scotto, Vincent *(Lyricist)*   3617
Scoullar, John *(Cast)*   922, 4488
Scourby, Alexander *(Cast)*   4435
Scribner Choir, Norman *(Cast)*   2775
Scriven, George *(Composer)*   2046
Scriven, George *(Lyricist)*   2046
Scruggs, Sharon *(Cast)*   778, 1172
Scudder, Eugene *(Cast)*   4672
Scudder, Rose *(Cast)*   556
Scudder, William M. *(Lyricist)*   1862
Scurlock, Jerry *(Cast)*   3908
Seabolt, Frank *(Cast)*   283
Seabrooke, Christopher *(Producer)*   2805
Seabrooke, Thomas Q. *(Cast)*   354, 737, 1661, 2156, 2848, 3673, 3784, 4222
Seabury, William *(Choreographer)*   2818, 3007
Seader, Richard *(Producer)*   4272
Seagram, Wilfred *(Cast)*   1460
Seal, Elizabeth *(Cast)*   2150
Sealby, Mabel *(Cast)*   30
Seale, Douglas *(Cast)*   2375
Seale, Douglas *(Director)*   2375
Seale, Douglas *(Librettist)*   2375
Sealey, Carol B. *(Lighting Designer)*   1171
Seamon, Edward *(Cast)*   1669
Sears, Lucille *(Cast)*   2639
Sears, Sally *(Producer)*   3522, 4272
Sears, Ted *(Author)*   4035
Sears, Zelda *(Author)*   2639, 3655
Sears, Zelda *(Cast)*   2569, 3085, 4464
Sears, Zelda *(Librettist)*   780, 2377, 2569, 2686
Sears, Zelda *(Lyricist)*   780, 2377, 2569, 2686, 3184, 3249, 3655
Seary, Kim *(Cast)*   3901
Seary, Kim *(Composer)*   3901
Seary, Kim *(Librettist)*   3901
Seary, Kim *(Lyricist)*   3901
Seastrom, Guje *(Cast)*   4536
Seaton, George *(Author)*   1860
Seaton, Violet *(Cast)*   1707
Seawell, Brockman *(Producer)*   3631
Sebastian, John *(Composer)*   2218, 3739
Sebastian, John *(Lyricist)*   2218, 3739
Sebastian, Mark *(Composer)*   3739
Sebastian, Mark *(Lyricist)*   3739
Sebesky, Don *(Composer)*   3576
Sebesky, Don *(Orchestrations)*   3428
Sebree, Charles *(Author)*   2994
Sebree, Charles *(Lyricist)*   2994

Secombe, Harry *(Cast)*   3482
Second Stage, The *(Producer)*   2132
Secter, David *(Librettist)*   1500
Secter, David *(Lyricist)*   1500
Secter, David *(Producer)*   1500
Secunda, Sholom *(Composer)*   268, 343, 1609, 2352, 2356, 4342
Secunda, Sholom *(Lyricist)*   1609, 2352, 2356, 4342
Secunda, Sholom *(Musical Director)*   343
Sedaka, Neil *(Composer)*   4193, 4264
Sedaka, Neil *(Lyricist)*   4193, 4264
Sedley, Harry *(Director)*   2455
Sedley, Harry *(Librettist)*   2455
Sedley, Roy *(Cast)*   1979
Seegar, Sara *(Cast)*   1194
Seelen, Jerry *(Composer)*   2379, 3121
Seelen, Jerry *(Lyricist)*   2379, 3121, 4131, 4264, 4602
Seeley, Blossom *(Cast)*   697, 1042, 1693, 1845, 2696, 3087, 4158, 4195, 4655
Seeley, Inez *(Cast)*   1989
Seff, Richard *(Librettist)*   4114
Segal, Al *(Cast)*   4730
Segal, Al *(Composer)*   376
Segal, Alex *(Director)*   4609
Segal, David F. *(Lighting Designer)*   415, 693, 1010, 1161, 2001, 2418, 2737, 3233, 3370, 3733, 3838, 4272, 4474, 4659
Segal, David F. *(Set Design)*   2001, 3370, 4659
Segal, Erich *(Librettist)*   3988
Segal, Erich *(Lyricist)*   2075, 3988
Segal, George *(Cast)*   2357
Segal, Kathrin King *(Cast)*   3469, 3542
Segal, Morton *(Producer)*   4541
Segal, Vivienne *(Cast)*   17, 21, 473, 670, 1027, 1312, 1679, 2061, 2549, 2653, 2855, 2900, 3013, 3051, 3153, 3245, 3353, 4350, 4357, 4716, 4760, 4818
Segall, Bernardo *(Composer)*   1770
Segall, Bernardo *(Lyricist)*   1770
Segall, Lee *(Producer)*   4582
Segalla, Irene *(Costumes)*   2392
Segasture, Jack *(Producer)*   3524
Seger, Richard *(Set Design)*   594, 4062
Segovia, Claudio *(Costumes)*   432
Segovia, Claudio *(Director)*   432
Segovia, Claudio *(Set Design)*   432
Segovia, Daisy
   See Daisy de Segouzac.
Segovia, Yolanda *(Musical Director)*   1103, 3444
Segue Productions *(Producer)*   708
Seguin, Tillie *(Cast)*   2127
Seibert, T. Lawrence *(Lyricist)*   3989
Seidel, Virginia *(Cast)*   1597
Seidelman, Arthur A. *(Director)*   406
Seidenman Jr., Sidney *(Musical Director)*   821
Seidle, C.F./Caroline/Mme.
   See also under Siedle.
Seidle, C.F. *(Costumes)*   3585
Seidle, Caroline *(Costumes)*   2101, 2324, 3052, 3387, 3488, 3790, 3805, 4646
Seidle, Mme. *(Costumes)*   2885, 3129, 4497, 4500, 4724

Seidman, Amy *(Lyricist)* 2320
Seidman, John *(Cast)* 4330
Seigal, Maxwell *(Lyricist)* 3889
Seiger, Marvin *(Author)* 339
Seitz, Dran *(Cast)* 1242, 1745
Seitz, George B. *(Producer)* 2363
Seitz, Tani *(Cast)* 1242, 3094
Seitz, W. Thomas *(Costumes)* 4173
Selbert, Marianne *(Choreographer)* 3637
Selden, Albert *(Composer)* 98, 2940, 4018, 4585
Selden, Albert *(Lyricist)* 98, 4018
Selden, Albert *(Producer)* 98, 483, 1567, 2550
Selden, Albert W. *(Composer)* 4585
Selden, Albert W. *(Producer)* 31, 823, 828, 1729, 1730, 2727, 3612, 4537
Selden, Edgar *(Composer)* 697
Selden, Edgar *(Lyricist)* 697, 1526, 3061, 4801, 4802
Seldes, Gilbert *(Librettist)* 4256
Seldes, Marian *(Cast)* 154
Self, Bonnie *(Composer)* 4264
Self, Bonnie *(Lyricist)* 4264
Sell, Janie *(Cast)* 599, 1591, 2026, 2913, 3330, 3666
Sell, Janie *(Choreographer)* 262, 3277
Sells, Edward *(Cast)* 1796
Selten, Morton *(Cast)* 2329
Seltzer, David *(Producer)* 2659
Seltzer, Dov *(Composer)* 2811, 4396
Seltzer, Dov *(Musical Director)* 2811
Seltzer, Dov *(Orchestrations)* 2811
Seltzer, Gary *(Lighting Designer)* 3034
Seltzer, Jerry *(Producer)* 3752
Seltzer, Marjorie *(Cast)* 4673
Seltzer, Milton *(Musical Director)* 73, 461, 4380
Selwyn, Arch *(Producer)* 133, 429, 579, 702, 715, 839, 841, 3699, 3740, 4033
Selwyn, Edgar *(Director)* 468, 1157
Selwyn, Edgar *(Librettist)* 1011, 4589
Selwyn, Edgar *(Producer)* 133, 579, 3740, 4033, 4178, 4179
Selwyn, Ruth *(Producer)* 3172, 4586
Selwyn and Co. *(Producer)* 126
Selwyns, The *(Producer)* 4085
Semans, William H. *(Producer)* 2001
Semos, Murray *(Librettist)* 2584
Senaille, J.B. *(Composer)* 1865
Sendak, Maurice *(Author)* 3668
Sendak, Maurice *(Costumes)* 3668
Sendak, Maurice *(Librettist)* 3668
Sendak, Maurice *(Lyricist)* 3668
Sendak, Maurice *(Set Design)* 3668
Sendholm, Ruth *(Cast)* 225
Sendry, Albert *(Orchestrations)* 223, 3108, 3453, 3493, 4827
Senesh, Hannah *(Author)* 1740
Senesh, Hannah *(Lyricist)* 1740
Senior, Raimond D. *(Costumes)* 18
Senior, Raimond D. *(Director)* 18
Senior, Raimond D. *(Librettist)* 18
Senior, Raimond D. *(Set Design)* 18
Senior, Susanna *(Cast)* 2228
Senn, Herbert *(Lighting Designer)* 2235, 3215, 4633

Senn, Herbert *(Set Design)* 369, 1676, 2235, 3020, 3196, 3215, 3235, 3920, 4028, 4633
Senna, Charles *(Cast)* 2020
Sennes, Frank *(Producer)* 2742
Sennett, Dorothy *(Composer)* 932
Sennett, Dorothy *(Lyricist)* 932
Sennett, Mack *(Cast)* 515, 737, 2915, 3488
Senske, Rebecca *(Costumes)* 3987
Sepia Guild Players *(Producer)* 444
Seplow, Evan *(Cast)* 534
Seppe, Christopher *(Cast)* 705, 3080
Seppe, Christopher *(Composer)* 3080
Seppe, Christopher *(Lyricist)* 3080
Septee, Moe *(Producer)* 576, 4342
Serabian, Lorraine *(Cast)* 3863, 4862
Serban, Andrei *(Director)* 4505
Sereda, John *(Composer)* 3901
Sereda, John *(Lyricist)* 3901
Sereda, John *(Musical Director)* 3901
Sergava, Katherine *(Cast)* 3263
Sergides, Miguel *(Cast)* 2153
Serina, Marie *(Cast)* 4492
Serko, David *(Cast)* 139
Serlin, Oscar *(Producer)* 4600
Serova, Madame *(Choreographer)* 3009
Serpette, Gaston *(Author)* 4298
Serra, Hal *(Musical Director)* 692
Serra, Raymond *(Cast)* 2437, 2759, 4347
Serrano, Charlie *(Cast)* 2242
Serrano, Nestor *(Cast)* 1038
Serrano, Vincent *(Cast)* 3719
Serrecchia, Michael *(Cast)* 746
Servais, Yvan *(Cast)* 2937
Sesma, Thom *(Cast)* 3142
Sessa, Jay *(Producer)* 4220
Seton, Bruce *(Cast)* 325
Setterberg, Carl *(Set Design)* 4047
Seuss, Dr. *(Librettist)* 2015
Seuss, Dr. *(Lyricist)* 2015
Seuss, Dr. *(Producer)* 2015
Sevec, Christine *(Cast)* 4193
Seven Arts Productions, Inc *(Producer)* 4749
764 Californians *(Producer)* 3046
Sevier, Jack *(Cast)* 564, 4288
Sevra, Robert *(Cast)* 2630, 4244
Sevran, Pascal *(Lyricist)* 1638
Sewell, Cissie *(Cast)* 2761
Sewell, Danny *(Cast)* 2375, 3271
Sexton, Al *(Cast)* 764, 1839, 1965, 4050, 4249, 4374, 4741
Seyler, Clifford *(Lyricist)* 702, 3310
Seymour, Anne *(Cast)* 97, 1874, 3150
Seymour, Caroline *(Cast)* 1787
Seymour, Dan *(Cast)* 3255
Seymour, Dan *(Producer)* 4163
Seymour, James *(Author)* 1359
Seymour, Jane *(Cast)* 1187, 2060
Seymour, John *(Cast)* 1013, 1235
Seymour, John D. *(Cast)* 4234
Seymour, Madeline *(Cast)* 1561

Seymour, Paul (Cast)   3501
Seymour, Tot (Lyricist)   2135, 4204, 4427, 4825
Seymour, W.H. (Cast)   402
Seymour, William (Director)   191, 2624, 4103
Seymoure, Norma (Cast)   574
Shactman, Murray (Cast)   1978
Shade, Lillian (Cast)   1137
Shadow (Costumes)   4707
Shafer, George (Producer)   1415
Shafer, Hal (Set Design)   4153
Shafer, Jerry (Producer)   362
Shafer, June (Cast)   2032
Shafer, Robert (Cast)   957, 1973, 3955, 4075
Shaffer, Henry (Costumes)   3997
Shaffer, Paul (Cast)   1512
Shaffer, Paul (Composer)   1512
Shaffer, Paul (Librettist)   1512
Shaffer, Victoria (Costumes)   1073
Shaffer, Wilhelm (Choreographer)   3298
Shaffer, William (Orchestrations)   2800
Shaffner, Walter (Set Design)   606
Shafman, Arthur (Producer)   3909
Shaiman, Marc (Cast)   1713
Shaiman, Marc (Composer)   1638, 1713, 2555
Shaiman, Marc (Librettist)   2555
Shaiman, Marc (Lyricist)   1638, 1713, 2555
Shaiman, Marc (Musical Director)   1713, 2555
Shaiman, Marc (Orchestrations)   1713
Shaiman, Marc (Vocal Arranger)   1713, 2427, 2555
Shakespeare, William (Author)   249, 514, 1104, 2244,
   2257, 2599, 2841, 2859, 3000, 3015, 3231, 3539, 3741,
   3876, 4256, 4485, 4715, 4789
Shakespeare, William (Lyricist)   1616, 1897, 2257, 2859,
   3280, 4129, 4246, 4485, 4715
Shakespeare, William (Lyrics Based On)   3909
Shale, Betty (Cast)   841
Shale, Dorothy (Cast)   292
Shalek, Bertha (Cast)   4761
Shaler, Eleanor (Cast)   2366, 2739, 3005, 3379
Shalhoub, Tony (Cast)   2945
Shalom Yiddish Musical Comedy Theatre (Producer)
   2866, 3670
Shane, Diana (Cast)   821
Shange, Ntozake (Author)   1344
Shange, Ntozake (Lyricist)   1344
Shanina, Yelena (Cast)   2269
Shank, Richard C. (Director)   348
Shanks, Alec (Director)   2364
Shanley, Robert (Cast)   1670, 4142, 4340
Shannon (Producer)   3222
Shannon, Effie (Cast)   1617, 2202
Shannon, Frank (Cast)   2528
Shannon, Harry T. (Cast)   2238, 3379
Shannon, James Royce (Composer)   3910
Shannon, James Royce (Lyricist)   3910
Shannon, Kitty (Costumes)   3291
Shannon, Peggy (Cast)   2476
Shannon, Walter (Cast)   2917
Shanstrom, David (Director)   3571
Shapero, Lillian (Choreographer)   4773

Shapiro, Dan (Composer)   1397
Shapiro, Dan (Lyricist)   145, 204, 673, 1336, 1397,
   2246, 2850, 3178
Shapiro, Danny (Composer)   2379
Shapiro, Danny (Lyricist)   1892, 2379
Shapiro, Debbie (Cast)   478, 2205, 3444, 4114, 4252
Shapiro, Irwin (Producer)   467
Shapiro, Mel (Director)   1999, 2290, 3846, 4485
Shapiro, Mel (Librettist)   4485
Shapiro, Nat (Producer)   4558
Shapiro, Richard (Producer)   2001
Shapiro, Ted (Cast)   1333
Shapiro, Ted (Composer)   1333, 1825
Shapiro, Ted (Lyricist)   1825
Shapiro, Ted (Pianist)   1889
Sharaff, Irene (Costumes)   70, 121, 207, 297, 404, 512, 514,
   601, 603, 630, 901, 961, 1061, 1315, 1413, 1420, 1564,
   1680, 1729, 1760, 2068, 2201, 2252, 2268, 2312, 2386,
   2475, 2679, 2777, 2797, 2850, 3283, 3365, 3913, 4131,
   4174, 4214, 4238, 4446, 4569, 4667
Sharaff, Irene (Set Design)   55
Sharkey, Jack (Cast)   4686
Sharkey, Jack (Librettist)   3112
Sharkey the Seal (Cast)   1894
Sharma, Barbara (Cast)   450, 823, 1729, 1848, 3526,
   4238, 4319
Sharman, Jim (Director)   3742, 4449
Sharon, Ula (Cast)   4077
Sharp, Adelaide (Cast)   2966
Sharp, Bobby (Lyricist)   477
Sharp, Jeffrey Day (Producer)   1073
Sharp, John Marshall (Cast)   3682
Sharp, Michael (Costumes)   1108
Sharp, Michael (Set Design)   1108, 1813
Sharpe, Albert (Cast)   1278
Sharpe, Ernest (Cast)   1874
Sharpe, John (Cast)   2523, 4409
Sharples, Richard (Costumes)   730
Sharrock, Ian (Cast)   3454
Shatner, William (Cast)   4749
Shattuck, Truly (Cast)   1188, 1480, 2254, 2383,
   2517, 3387
Shaughnessy, Michael (Cast)   854
Shaughnessy, Mickey (Cast)   2304
Shavel, L.W. (Set Design)   1401
Shavelson, Melville (Librettist)   2217
Shaver, Bob (Cast)   3108
Shaw, Al (Cast)   1297, 3523
Shaw, Bernard (Author)   134
Shaw, Bill (Composer)   1415
Shaw, Bob (Set Design)   2033, 2359, 2646, 3070
Shaw, Carr (Choreographer)   3912
Shaw, David (Librettist)   3324, 3687, 3800, 4435
Shaw, Deborah (Costumes)   2440
Shaw, George Bernard (Author)   451, 742, 1848,
   3038
Shaw, Hollace (Cast)   4557
Shaw, Howard (Author)   519
Shaw, Jack (Cast)   4683
Shaw, Kendall (Set Design)   1498

Shepard, Joan *(Composer)*   3802
Shepard, Joan *(Librettist)*   3802
Shepard, Karen *(Cast)*   2750
Shepard, Kiki *(Cast)*   166
Shepard, Sam *(Author)*   2468, 3309
Shepard, Sam *(Composer)*   3309
Shepard, Sam *(Director)*   2468
Shepard, Sam *(Librettist)*   3233
Shepard, Sam *(Lyricist)*   3309
Shephard, F. Firth *(Producer)*   3139, 4519
Shepherd, Jean *(Librettist)*   3110
Shepherd, Leonard *(Cast)*   3220
Shepley, Michael *(Producer)*   1418
Sheppard, Drey *(Lyricist)*   2279, 2913
Sheppard, Madelyn *(Composer)*   1972, 2276
Sheppard Jr., John R. *(Producer)*   341
Sher, Gloria *(Producer)*   3928
Sher, Gloria Hope *(Producer)*   2133
Sher, Louis K. *(Producer)*   3928
Shere, Michael *(Lighting Designer)*   2443
Sheridan, Edith *(Cast)*   3103
Sheridan, Eileen *(Cast)*   263
Sheridan, Kenneth *(Composer)*   2222
Sheridan, Liz *(Cast)*   278, 1364, 1590, 1755, 2043,
   3479, 4062
Sheridan, Maura *(Lighting Designer)*   261
Sheridan, Richard Brinsley *(Author)*   71, 2057, 2399
Sheridan, Richard Brinsley *(Lyricist)*   2633
Sheridan, Wayne *(Librettist)*   1412
Sheridan, Wayne *(Lyricist)*   1412
Sherin, Edwin *(Director)*   3702
Sherman, Al *(Composer)*   393, 1127, 1491, 3406, 4821
Sherman, Al *(Lyricist)*   393, 1127, 1460, 1491
Sherman, Allan *(Lyricist)*   1832
Sherman, Allen *(Librettist)*   1273
Sherman, Allen *(Lyricist)*   1273
Sherman, Arthur *(Director)*   2172
Sherman, Arthur *(Librettist)*   3204
Sherman, Arthur *(Lyricist)*   3204
Sherman, Charles *(Director)*   490
Sherman, Charles *(Librettist)*   70, 95, 1322, 1415, 3893,
   4174, 4374, 4498, 4499
Sherman, Garry *(Composer)*   105, 828
Sherman, Garry *(Orchestrations)*   105, 828, 1427, 3610
Sherman, Garry *(Vocal Arranger)*   105, 828, 3610
Sherman, George *(Lyricist)*   4396
Sherman, Hal *(Cast)*   1840, 4795
Sherman, Hiram *(Cast)*   194, 919, 1205, 2014, 2257,
   2859, 3990, 4273, 4346, 4498, 4499, 4557, 4715
Sherman, Jimmy *(Composer)*   478
Sherman, Jimmy *(Lyricist)*   478
Sherman, Joe *(Composer)*   2275, 4829
Sherman, Joe *(Lyricist)*   4829
Sherman, Joe *(Orchestrations)*   4829
Sherman, Kim D. *(Composer)*   2441
Sherman, Kim D. *(Lyricist)*   2441
Sherman, Kim D. *(Orchestrations)*   2441
Sherman, Lee *(Choreographer)*   673, 2707, 3091
Sherman, Lee *(Lyricist)*   4260
Sherman, Loren *(Costumes)*   2852

Sherman, Loren *(Set Design)*   212, 572, 1149, 2852,
   3448, 3598, 3944
Sherman, Milt *(Dance Arranger)*   2750, 3371
Sherman, Noel *(Composer)*   4264, 4829
Sherman, Noel *(Lyricist)*   4264, 4829
Sherman, Richard M. *(Composer)*   589, 1615, 3330, 4561
Sherman, Richard M. *(Lyricist)*   589, 1615, 3330
Sherman, Robert B. *(Composer)*   589, 1615, 3330
Sherman, Robert B. *(Lyricist)*   589, 1615, 3330, 4561
Sherman-Fowler, B. *(Composer)*   934
Sherri, Andre *(Costumes)*   231
Sherri, Andre *(Librettist)*   231
Sherrin, Ned *(Cast)*   3967
Sherrin, Ned *(Director)*   3967
Sherrin, Ned *(Librettist)*   3967
Sherwin, Jeannette *(Cast)*   2526
Sherwin, Julie *(Cast)*   4331
Sherwin, Manning *(Composer)*   266, 418, 1207, 2827,
   3172, 4027, 4510
Sherwood, Blanche *(Cast)*   3154
Sherwood, Gail *(Cast)*   3683
Sherwood, Madeleine *(Cast)*   933, 1060, 2144
Sherwood, Ray *(Lyricist)*   1963
Sherwood, Robert E. *(Author)*   958, 4435
Sherwood, Robert E. *(Librettist)*   2894
Sherwood, Robert E. *(Lyricist)*   1357
Sherwood, Robert E. *(Producer)*   2894
Sherwood, Roberta *(Cast)*   2975
Sherwood, Toba *(Cast)*   2372
Sherwood, Walter *(Set Design)*   458
Shevelove, Bert *(Producer)*   193
Shevelove, Burt *(Director)*   635, 1406, 1729, 1762,
   2940, 3743, 4018, 4038, 4469
Shevelove, Burt *(Librettist)*   635, 1406, 1422, 1762, 2940
Shevelove, Burt *(Lyricist)*   1762, 2940, 4018, 4585
Shevelove, Burt *(Producer)*   192
Shiebler, Howard *(Librettist)*   1493
Shield, Harvey *(Composer)*   1732
Shield, Harvey *(Librettist)*   1732
Shield, Harvey *(Lyricist)*   1732
Shields, Arthur *(Cast)*   4576
Shields, Ella *(Cast)*   4859
Shields, Maud *(Lyricist)*   470
Shields, Ren *(Composer)*   8, 1910, 2885, 4390, 4691
Shields, Ren *(Lyricist)*   8, 662, 1021, 2978, 2996, 4691
Shields, Robert *(Cast)*   547
Shields, Roy *(Musical Director)*   1244
Shields, Thomas *(Cast)*   2730
Shiffman, Jan Frederick *(Cast)*   528, 1155, 3165, 3329, 3997
Shiles, Michael *(Cast)*   4799
Shilkret, Nathaniel *(Musical Director)*   3386
Shimberg, Hinks *(Producer)*   4139, 4297, 4412
Shimerman, Armin *(Cast)*   2064
Shimkin, Arthur *(Producer)*   4785
Shimoda, Yuki *(Cast)*   3340
Shimono, Sab *(Cast)*   302, 2713, 3340, 3711
Shine, John L. *(Librettist)*   3776
Shipley, John *(Set Design)*   3629
Shipman, Helen *(Cast)*   1794, 2351, 2476, 2564, 2960,
   3342, 3369, 3406, 3737

Shubert, Mrs. J.J. *(Costumes)* 3399, 4747
Shubert, Sam S. *(Librettist)* 1243
Shubert, Sam S. *(Producer)* 8, 276, 353, 737, 1041, 1111, 1123, 1178, 1243, 1464, 1522, 1523, 1526, 1535, 1570, 1613, 1768, 1783, 1793, 2282, 2317, 2334, 2745, 2848, 2869, 2914, 2978, 3052, 3085, 3265, 3313, 3486, 3560, 3730, 3805, 4044, 4434, 4493, 4521, 4616, 4666, 4713
Shubert Brothers
   See also J.J. Shubert and Lee Shubert.
Shubert Brothers *(Producer)* 4355
Shubert Jr., J.J. *(Composer)* 3148
Shubert Organization *(Producer)* 16, 39, 393, 678, 1103, 1776, 2033, 2474, 2544, 2558, 3159, 3577, 4068, 4210, 4459, 4861
Shubert Organization, The *(Producer)* 721, 775, 2205, 3285, 3411, 3792, 4129
Shuck, John *(Cast)* 3164
Shull, Richard B. *(Cast)* 36, 1402, 1634, 2874, 3080, 3231, 4560, 4582
Shulman, A. *(Librettist)* 2421
Shulman, Arnold *(Author)* 1611
Shulman, Max *(Author)* 304
Shulman, Max *(Librettist)* 67, 304, 2014
Shulman, Michael *(Cast)* 212
Shuman, Earl *(Lyricist)* 3863
Shuman, Francis K. *(Composer)* 3442
Shuman, Mort *(Cast)* 2188
Shuman, Mort *(Composer)* 2017, 3695
Shuman, Mort *(Lyricist)* 2188, 3695
Shuman, Mort *(Musical Director)* 2188
Shumlin, Herman *(Director)* 2510, 4278
Shumlin, Herman *(Producer)* 2510
Shurley, George *(Choreographer)* 3827, 4302
Shuster, Joe *(Author)* 2163
Shuster, Rosie *(Librettist)* 1512
Shutta, Ethel *(Cast)* 1329, 2201, 2594, 2757, 3036, 3405, 4427, 4683, 4819
Shwarze, Henry *(Choreographer)* 4792
Shy, Gus *(Cast)* 111, 1176, 1628, 2569, 3117, 4050, 4240, 4692
Shyre, Paul *(Director)* 33
Shyre, Paul *(Librettist)* 33, 2055
Sibanda, Seth *(Cast)* 1719
Sibley, Harper *(Producer)* 2754
Sica, Joy Lynne *(Cast)* 1233
Sicangco, Eduardo *(Costumes)* 992, 1146, 1702, 3628
Sicangco, Eduardo *(Set Design)* 992, 1146, 1638, 1702
Sicari, Joseph R. *(Cast)* 825, 956
Sicari, Sal *(Musical Director)* 2055
Sidman, Sam *(Cast)* 2271, 4630
Sidney, Carl *(Costumes)* 2105
Sidney, David *(Lyricist)* 4545
Sidney, George *(Cast)* 592, 3153, 3246, 4686
Sidney, George *(Lyricist)* 3129
Sidney, Robert *(Choreographer)* 95, 961, 4362, 4428
Sidney, Susanne *(Cast)* 2267
Sidney, Sylvia *(Cast)* 1190
Sidon, Herbert *(Costumes)* 1644
Sieber, Christopher *(Cast)* 3227
Siebert, Charles *(Cast)* 807

Sieczynski *(Composer)* 3020
Sieczynski, Rudolf *(Composer)* 3540
Siedel, Mme. *(Costumes)* 618
Siedle *(Costumes)* 2507
Siedle, C.F. *(Costumes)* 1165, 3820
Siedle, Caroline *(Costumes)* 8, 250, 559, 639, 666, 737, 1071, 4181, 4293
Siedle, Edward *(Librettist)* 1458
Siedle, Mme./C.F./Caroline/Mme.
   See also under Seidle.
Siedle, Mme. *(Costumes)* 113, 350, 357, 976, 1543, 1896, 2116, 2345, 2398, 2733, 2824, 3176, 3570, 4098, 4614, 4691
Siedle, Mrs. Edward *(Costumes)* 4723
Siegal, Al *(Producer)* 851
Siegal, Don *(Composer)* 3557
Siegal, Don *(Lyricist)* 3557
Siegal, Michael *(Composer)* 2578
Siegel, Arthur *(Cast)* 2294, 2629
Siegel, Arthur *(Composer)* 679, 817, 871, 943, 2168, 2294, 2416, 2629, 2772, 2998, 3107, 3108, 3110, 3111, 3112, 3178, 3186, 3204, 3320, 3619, 3880, 3890, 3941, 4108, 4279, 4433
Siegel, Arthur *(Lyricist)* 3112
Siegel, Arthur *(Musical Director)* 679, 3890
Siegel, Arthur *(Pianist)* 1873
Siegel, Arthur *(Producer)* 3890
Siegel, Arthur *(Vocal Arranger)* 3890
Siegel, David *(Arrangements)* 4799
Siegel, David *(Orchestrations)* 1701, 3461, 4703, 4799
Siegel, Jerry *(Author)* 2163
Siegel, Joel *(Librettist)* 1289
Siegel, June *(Lyricist)* 4, 2007
Siegel, Larry *(Librettist)* 2663
Siegel, Larry *(Lyricist)* 2663
Siegel, Larry *(Set Design)* 1958
Siegel, M. *(Composer)* 376
Siegel, Mark *(Cast)* 518
Siegel, Maxwell Edward *(Lyricist)* 1049
Siegel, William *(Librettist)* 3670
Sieger, Charles *(Musical Director)* 1831
Siegle, Gloria *(Cast)* 2483
Siegle, Gloria *(Composer)* 2483
Siegler, Robert *(Director)* 1612
Siegmeister, Elie *(Composer)* 3989
Siegmeister, Elie *(Dance Arranger)* 657, 2295
Siegmeister, Elie *(Musical Director)* 3989
Siegmeister, Elie *(Orchestrations)* 3989
Siegmeister, Elie *(Vocal Arranger)* 657, 4015
Siegrist, Topsy *(Cast)* 1526
Siems, Bobby *(Composer)* 2555
Siepi, Cesare *(Cast)* 519, 652
Sievier, Bruce *(Lyricist)* 3020
Siff, Andrew *(Producer)* 1237
Siff, Ira *(Cast)* 755, 1229, 1426, 1715, 2220, 2243, 2579
Siff, Ira *(Costumes)* 2220, 2243, 2478
Siggins, Jeff *(Cast)* 3551
Sigler, Maurice *(Lyricist)* 3822
Sigman, Carl *(Composer)* 137, 857
Sigman, Carl *(Lyricist)* 4264
Sigman, H.E. *(Musical Director)* 917

Sloan, W.H. *(Cast)* 2157
Sloan, W.H. *(Composer)* 2343
Sloan, Will H. *(Cast)* 1640, 2316
Sloan, William *(Cast)* 357
Sloane, A. Baldwin *(Author)* 3436
Sloane, A. Baldwin *(Composer)* 29, 76, 77, 235, 336, 354, 559, 735, 737, 830, 938, 939, 1005, 1031, 1213, 1244, 1246, 1505, 1515, 1535, 1573, 1685, 1686, 1728, 1738, 1752, 1835, 1845, 1927, 2181, 2324, 2373, 2399, 2465, 2485, 2559, 2675, 2711, 2865, 2868, 2917, 3090, 3096, 3575, 3673, 3753, 3755, 3867, 3883, 3989, 4165, 4203, 4206, 4382, 4552, 4608, 4648, 4721, 4723
Sloane, A. Baldwin *(Lyricist)* 1927, 4206
Sloane, Everett *(Cast)* 1893
Sloane, Everett *(Composer)* 1408
Sloane, Everett *(Lyricist)* 1408
Sloane, Frank *(Lyricist)* 559
Sloane, Mae Anwerda *(Composer)* 1728, 2324, 2465
Sloane, Mae Anwerda *(Lyricist)* 2324
Sloane, Mike *(Producer)* 657, 2496, 3801, 4423
Sloat, John *(Lighting Designer)* 4408
Sloate, Maynard *(Librettist)* 1326
Sloate, Maynard *(Producer)* 1326
Slocum, John P. *(Director)* 2722
Sloman, John *(Cast)* 2305, 4517
Sloman, Larry *(Composer)* 3076
Sloman, Larry *(Librettist)* 3076
Sloman, Larry *(Lyricist)* 3076
Slosberg, Bertha *(Choreographer)* 4207
Slovick, Sam *(Cast)* 119
Slutsker, Peter *(Cast)* 595, 2241, 3992
Slyde, Jimmy *(Cast)* 432
Small, Allan *(Orchestrations)* 2705, 4123, 4428
Small, Jack *(Director)* 84
Small, Larry *(Cast)* 1068, 4689
Small, Mary *(Cast)* 861, 3902
Small, Marya *(Cast)* 1664
Small, Neva *(Cast)* 278, 1222, 1380, 1609, 1739, 1846, 2477, 2775, 3577, 3956, 4060, 4062
Small, Ralph *(Cast)* 1120
Smalle, Ed *(Lyricist)* 3973
Smallens, Alexander *(Musical Director)* 1366, 3541
Smalley, Victor H. *(Librettist)* 2840
Smalley, Victor H. *(Lyricist)* 2840
Smalls, Charlie *(Composer)* 4722
Smalls, Charlie *(Lyricist)* 4722
Smalls Jr., Arthur *(Cast)* 4003
Smalls Jr., Arthur *(Composer)* 4003
Smallwood, Mildred *(Cast)* 739
Smallwood, Richard *(Composer)* 3987, 3991
Smallwood, Richard *(Lyricist)* 3987, 3991
Smallwood Singers, The, Richard *(Cast)* 3991
Smart, Dick *(Cast)* 817
Smart, Jack *(Cast)* 3104
Smartt, Suzanne *(Cast)* 2784
Smedberg, John *(Cast)* 1973
Smicoeve Prod. *(Producer)* 563
Smidt, Burr *(Producer)* 2553
Smiley, Joseph *(Cast)* 2233
Smit, Edward J. *(Cast)* 4732

Smith *(Composer)* 1925
Smith *(Librettist)* 950
Smith *(Lyricist)* 1246, 1925, 4697
Smith, Ada *(Cast)* 2044
Smith, Adrian *(Composer)* 3901
Smith, Adrian *(Lyricist)* 3901
Smith, Alexis *(Cast)* 1329, 3515
Smith, Alma *(Cast)* 567, 725, 877, 3707
Smith, Art *(Cast)* 2228, 3947, 4625
Smith, Baker S. *(Costumes)* 4740
Smith, Bert *(Cast)* 1593
Smith, Bessie *(Cast)* 3361
Smith, Bessie *(Composer)* 478, 3297
Smith, Bessie *(Lyricist)* 478, 3297
Smith, Betty *(Author)* 4446
Smith, Betty *(Librettist)* 4446
Smith, Betty Jane *(Cast)* 849, 4702
Smith, Bruce *(Cast)* 4014
Smith, Bruce *(Set Design)* 2964, 2974
Smith, Buddy *(Cast)* 4676
Smith, C. Aubrey *(Cast)* 2952
Smith, Carl *(Composer)* 146, 1638, 3739
Smith, Carl *(Lyricist)* 146, 1638, 3739
Smith, Carolyn *(Costumes)* 580
Smith, Carrie *(Cast)* 432
Smith, Chris *(Composer)* 146, 295, 434, 545, 1544, 2254, 2765, 3297, 3308, 4390, 4833
Smith, Chris *(Lyricist)* 146, 500, 545, 1909, 2254, 3297, 3308, 4804, 4833
Smith, Christopher *(Cast)* 2661
Smith, Clay *(Cast)* 1531
Smith, Cyrena *(Cast)* 1342
Smith, Cyril *(Cast)* 3605
Smith, Darrel H. *(Lyricist)* 750
Smith, Darrell H. *(Lyricist)* 18
Smith, David Rae *(Cast)* 2839
Smith, Dick *(Composer)* 4824
Smith, Dick *(Lyricist)* 4824
Smith, Don *(Musical Director)* 4035
Smith, Don *(Orchestrations)* 3638
Smith, Don *(Vocal Arranger)* 3638
Smith, Doug *(Librettist)* 4786
Smith, Duncan *(Cast)* 846
Smith, Edgar *(Author)* 3436
Smith, Edgar *(Librettist)* 93, 182, 301, 473, 551, 677, 687, 833, 940, 950, 1095, 1188, 1217, 1240, 1264, 1526, 1530, 1607, 1661, 1735, 1738, 1799, 1823, 1836, 1844, 1881, 1900, 1926, 1927, 1994, 2041, 2262, 2334, 2358, 2469, 2471, 2515, 2816, 2826, 2842, 2869, 2963, 2978, 3051, 3258, 3265, 3303, 3424, 3525, 3550, 3573, 3632, 3701, 3737, 3755, 3962, 4148, 4170, 4206, 4382, 4473, 4478, 4521, 4654, 4658, 4681, 4721, 4797
Smith, Edgar *(Lyricist)* 77, 182, 301, 687, 940, 1095, 1188, 1217, 1264, 1881, 1900, 1926, 2469, 2938, 3258, 3303, 3632, 3976, 3989, 4236, 4382, 4473, 4478, 4654, 4681, 4723, 4797, 4804
Smith, Edgar A. *(Lyricist)* 1188, 2471
Smith, Edith *(Cast)* 1157
Smith, Ella *(Cast)* 4113
Smith, Emily *(Composer)* 2871

Smith, Emily *(Lyricist)* 2871
Smith, Ernest Allen *(Set Design)* 729, 3019, 3858
Smith, Ethel *(Cast)* 1157
Smith, Eugene *(Cast)* 159
Smith, F.E. *(Librettist)* 4047
Smith, F.E. *(Lyricist)* 4047
Smith, Felton *(Choreographer)* 1785, 3211
Smith, Frank *(Choreographer)* 2489
Smith, Fred T. *(Composer)* 92
Smith, Fred T. *(Librettist)* 92
Smith, Fred T. *(Lyricist)* 92
Smith, Gary *(Producer)* 3454
Smith, Gary *(Set Design)* 3366
Smith, George Malcolm *(Author)* 180
Smith, George T. *(Lyricist)* 688
Smith, George Totten *(Librettist)* 591, 1003, 1547,
    2107, 2343, 2485
Smith, George Totten *(Lyricist)* 939, 1003, 2341, 2343,
    2485, 2964, 3129, 3820
Smith, Gerald Oliver *(Cast)* 3243, 3379
Smith, Gladys
    See also Miss Pickford.
Smith, Gladys *(Cast)* 1157
Smith, Gordon *(Cast)* 125, 4179
Smith, Grace *(Cast)* 14
Smith, Greg *(Orchestrations)* 2674
Smith, Greg *(Producer)* 580
Smith, H. Jess *(Cast)* 2340
Smith, Harry *(Cast)* 340
Smith, Harry B. *(Composer)* 4258
Smith, Harry B. *(Librettist)* 41, 49, 136, 184, 252, 256,
    350, 361, 380, 405, 457, 613, 618, 659, 666, 718, 734,
    771, 905, 1016, 1066, 1260, 1355, 1375, 1388, 1444,
    1465, 1535, 1538, 1555, 1602, 1712, 1720, 1722, 1896,
    2041, 2101, 2213, 2345, 2373, 2465, 2486, 2502, 2506,
    2528, 2534, 2574, 2622, 2671, 2697, 2716, 2733, 2747,
    2774, 2885, 2892, 2923, 2931, 3053, 3078, 3084, 3085,
    3087, 3229, 3352, 3362, 3363, 3372, 3387, 3566, 3586,
    3658, 3680, 3681, 3710, 3732, 3736, 3771, 3784, 3881,
    3977, 3996, 4094, 4119, 4158, 4181, 4249, 4250, 4258,
    4293, 4348, 4500, 4559, 4603, 4662, 4669, 4691, 4724,
    4801, 4802, 4803, 4804, 4806
Smith, Harry B. *(Lyricist)* 41, 49, 75, 126, 184, 252, 256,
    350, 361, 380, 405, 457, 613, 618, 627, 659, 666, 677, 687,
    718, 734, 771, 905, 934, 947, 1027, 1066, 1111, 1183,
    1228, 1250, 1260, 1313, 1327, 1355, 1375, 1388, 1444,
    1465, 1535, 1538, 1544, 1555, 1711, 1712, 1720, 1722,
    1774, 1844, 1896, 2101, 2149, 2213, 2345, 2373, 2385,
    2424, 2465, 2502, 2506, 2534, 2602, 2620, 2622, 2671,
    2697, 2706, 2716, 2747, 2761, 2885, 2892, 2922, 2923,
    2931, 3020, 3053, 3078, 3084, 3177, 3193, 3229, 3237,
    3304, 3362, 3363, 3372, 3387, 3398, 3420, 3566, 3573,
    3586, 3591, 3627, 3658, 3680, 3681, 3710, 3732, 3736,
    3751, 3784, 3881, 3977, 3994, 3996, 4094, 4119, 4121,
    4181, 4249, 4250, 4258, 4293, 4348, 4352, 4390, 4418,
    4430, 4500, 4555, 4559, 4616, 4644, 4658, 4662, 4691,
    4724, 4799, 4802, 4803, 4804, 4806
Smith, Helen *(Librettist)* 4786
Smith, Henry Clapp *(Librettist)* 2475
Smith, Howard *(Director)* 1251

Smith, Howard *(Lyricist)* 208
Smith, Howlett *(Musical Director)* 2796
Smith, Jabbo *(Cast)* 2302
Smith, Jabbo *(Composer)* 3297
Smith, Jabbo *(Lyricist)* 3297
Smith, James *(Cast)* 4735
Smith, Jay *(Choreographer)* 3318
Smith, Jennifer *(Cast)* 690
Smith, Jo Jo *(Choreographer)* 1637
Smith, Joe
    See Smith & Dale
Smith, Joe *(Cast)* 17, 532, 1132, 3264, 3968, 4204,
    4654, 4686
Smith, Joe C. *(Choreographer)* 2826
Smith, John *(Cast)* 434
Smith, Joseph *(Choreographer)* 4650
Smith, Joseph C. *(Choreographer)* 68, 687, 1026, 1295,
    1578, 2209, 3053, 3205, 3304, 3626, 3951, 4098
Smith, Joseph C. *(Director)* 1307, 4269
Smith, Joseph H. *(Cast)* 4119
Smith, Joy *(Cast)* 4406
Smith, Kate *(Cast)* 1323, 1965, 3153, 3287
Smith, Kenneth *(Cast)* 1085
Smith, Kenneth *(Composer)* 3172
Smith, Kent *(Cast)* 2202
Smith, Kirby *(Cast)* 4486
Smith, Lee Orean *(Composer)* 185, 4201
Smith, Lee Orean *(Musical Director)* 4687
Smith, Lew *(Costumes)* 4750
Smith, Loring *(Cast)* 536, 1456, 4314, 4323, 4702
Smith, Lotte *(Cast)* 1157
Smith, Madame *(Costumes)* 331
Smith, Maggie *(Cast)* 3108
Smith, Mamie *(Cast)* 1288, 2672
Smith, Mark *(Cast)* 2344, 2569
Smith, Martin *(Cast)* 730, 3429
Smith, Maybelle *(Composer)* 432
Smith, Maybelle *(Lyricist)* 432
Smith, Michael C. *(Set Design)* 1171
Smith, Michael R. *(Set Design)* 3306
Smith, Milburn *(Librettist)* 1306
Smith, Mildred *(Cast)* 341
Smith, Muriel *(Cast)* 653, 1887, 3321
Smith, Norwood *(Cast)* 1884, 3151, 3752
Smith, Oliver *(Costumes)* 3815
Smith, Oliver *(Lighting Designer)* 2894
Smith, Oliver *(Producer)* 404, 454, 490, 1064, 1475,
    2268, 3278, 3954
Smith, Oliver *(Set Design)* 95, 98, 269, 270, 341, 367, 404,
    454, 521, 530, 623, 630, 649, 652, 657, 820, 823, 989,
    1012, 1029, 1119, 1315, 1369, 1456, 1475, 1511, 1564,
    1828, 1886, 1990, 2014, 2050, 2106, 2190, 2217, 2268,
    2304, 2582, 2626, 2775, 2894, 2987, 3038, 3164, 3274,
    3278, 3294, 3347, 3564, 3703, 3767, 3787, 3815, 3845,
    3954, 4095, 4270, 4323, 4386, 4450, 4516, 4625
Smith, Paul Gerard *(Director)* 2032, 3966
Smith, Paul Gerard *(Librettist)* 1134, 1419, 1800, 1859,
    2032, 2298, 2700, 3007, 3172, 3342, 3966, 4668
Smith, Paul Gerard *(Lyricist)* 2032, 2298
Smith, Paul Gerard *(Producer)* 2032

Smith, Pete Kite *(Lyricist)* 924

Smith, Polly P. *(Costumes)* 729

Smith, Queenie *(Cast)* 317, 765, 1551, 1819, 2253, 2276, 2540, 2855, 3312, 3754, 4001, 4170, 4392

Smith, Rebecca *(Cast)* 3507

Smith, Reginald *(Cast)* 703

Smith, Rex *(Cast)* 572, 2033

Smith, Robert *(Cast)* 3292

Smith, Robert B. *(Librettist)* 136, 522, 734, 1016, 1243, 1525, 1538, 1552, 1712, 2347, 2774, 2848, 2923, 2931, 3053, 3087, 3372, 3681, 4119, 4209, 4650

Smith, Robert B. *(Lyricist)* 136, 246, 350, 522, 734, 737, 1016, 1243, 1327, 1334, 1523, 1525, 1538, 1547, 1552, 1712, 2347, 2486, 2493, 2574, 2848, 2923, 2931, 3020, 3053, 3087, 3319, 3352, 3420, 3681, 3771, 4119, 4209, 4250, 4478, 4650, 4712

Smith, Rollin *(Cast)* 897

Smith, Rufus *(Cast)* 3279, 3347

Smith, Russell *(Cast)* 2791

Smith, Russell *(Composer)* 4751

Smith, Sally *(Cast)* 3731

Smith, Sammy *(Cast)* 2014, 2019, 3509, 3526, 3577, 4718

Smith, Sheila *(Cast)* 1329, 4196, 4243, 4272, 4388

Smith, Sid *(Director)* 974, 3497, 3499

Smith, Speedy *(Cast)* 444, 691, 981, 2034

Smith, Speedy *(Choreographer)* 691, 981

Smith, Speedy *(Composer)* 981

Smith, Speedy *(Librettist)* 981

Smith, Speedy *(Lyricist)* 981

Smith, Stanley *(Cast)* 1932, 4778

Smith, Steven *(Dance Arranger)* 2969

Smith, Steven *(Musical Director)* 3641

Smith, Steven Scott *(Director)* 784

Smith, Suzanne *(Cast)* 1304

Smith, Sydney *(Choreographer)* 1201

Smith, Sydney *(Librettist)* 2620

Smith, Thorne *(Author)* 2584

Smith, Tom *(Lighting Designer)* 1900

Smith, Toni *(Cast)* 945

Smith, Trixie *(Cast)* 553, 2720

Smith, Tucker *(Cast)* 162, 658, 2742

Smith, Vincent D. *(Librettist)* 4697

Smith, Virginia *(Cast)* 1971, 2569

Smith, Vivian *(Choreographer)* 4273

Smith, W.H. *(Author)* 4606

Smith, W.H. *(Composer)* 3028

Smith, W.H. *(Lyricist)* 1824

Smith, Wallace *(Author)* 2786

Smith, Walt *(Composer)* 181

Smith, Walter *(Cast)* 3658

Smith, Ward *(Cast)* 159

Smith, Webb *(Author)* 4035

Smith, Will H. *(Choreographer)* 2056

Smith, Will H. *(Director)* 3754

Smith, Will H. *(Lyricist)* 1407

Smith, William C. *(Cast)* 2817

Smith, Winchell *(Author)* 577, 773, 4860

Smith, Winchell *(Cast)* 1537

Smith, Winchell *(Director)* 1009, 3535

Smith, Wonderful *(Cast)* 2259

Smith & Dale
  See Joe Smith and Charles Dale.

Smith & Dale *(Cast)* 1395, 1397

Smith and DeForrest *(Cast)* 3512

Smithies, Richard *(Librettist)* 922

Smithies, Richard *(Lyricist)* 922

Smithson, Frank *(Cast)* 1540, 2938

Smithson, Frank *(Director)* 69, 203, 274, 336, 353, 470, 934, 1021, 1031, 1088, 1505, 1518, 1540, 1558, 1560, 1588, 1888, 1972, 2112, 2292, 2324, 2373, 2385, 2419, 2495, 2596, 2601, 2669, 2745, 2865, 2919, 2938, 2966, 3032, 3073, 3134, 3313, 3519, 3581, 3626, 3677, 3776, 3786, 3821, 4064, 4425, 4575, 4644

Smithson, Frank *(Librettist)* 2291

Smithson, Frank *(Producer)* 2373

Smits, Jimmy *(Cast)* 282

Smothers, Tom *(Cast)* 1389

Smothers Brothers *(Cast)* 58

Smuin, Michael *(Cast)* 2523

Smuin, Michael *(Choreographer)* 695, 3944, 4091

Smuin, Michael *(Director)* 695, 3944, 4091

Smyrl, David Langston *(Cast)* 3276, 4744

Smyrl, David Langston *(Composer)* 3276

Smyrl, David Langston *(Librettist)* 166, 3276

Smyrl, David Langston *(Lyricist)* 166, 3276

Smyth, Al *(Musical Director)* 3519

Sneed, Gary *(Cast)* 2630, 2913

Sneed Jr., Ray *(Cast)* 3528

Sneider, Vern J. *(Author)* 2626

Snell, Bruce *(Orchestrations)* 3818

Snider-Stein, Teresa *(Costumes)* 647

Snow, Clarence *(Cast)* 3987

Snow, Harry *(Cast)* 3288

Snow, Norman *(Cast)* 4796

Snow, Ross *(Cast)* 1515, 3750

Snow, Tom *(Composer)* 1804

Snow, Valaida *(Cast)* 445, 740

Snowden, Carolyn *(Cast)* 877

Snowden, Carolynne *(Cast)* 876

Snowden, Monica *(Cast)* 4601

Snowden, William *(Cast)* 4095

Snyder, Bozo *(Cast)* 2850

Snyder, Carrie *(Cast)* 1337

Snyder, Drew *(Cast)* 4151

Snyder, Gene *(Choreographer)* 216, 2161, 2162, 2458, 4772

Snyder, Gene *(Director)* 2161, 2162, 2458

Snyder, Jack *(Composer)* 3974

Snyder, Jack *(Lyricist)* 3974

Snyder, Nancy *(Cast)* 1268

Snyder, Ted *(Cast)* 4521

Snyder, Ted *(Composer)* 149, 179, 511, 830, 1126, 1250, 1327, 1343, 1501, 1523, 1550, 1793, 2149, 2232, 2706, 2978, 2996, 3293, 3401, 3827, 3917, 3985, 4257, 4493, 4521, 4603, 4604, 4655, 4813

Snyder, Ted *(Lyricist)* 149, 1327, 1417, 1519, 1793, 2261, 3665, 3695, 3737, 3917, 4714

Sobol, Edward *(Director)* 1889

Sobol, Louis *(Cast)* 3153

Soboloff, Arnold *(Cast)* 16, 162, 946, 1596, 3018, 3956, 4238

Society of Illustrators *(Producer)*   2105, 4047
Sodero, Domenic *(Orchestrations)*   1266
Soeder, Fran *(Director)*   809, 1496
Sogata *(Costumes)*   2032
Soglow, Otto *(Cast)*   2105
Soglow, Otto *(Librettist)*   2105, 3810
Sohlke, Augustus *(Choreographer)*   284
Sohlke, Gus *(Choreographer)*   506, 639, 2155, 2159, 2334, 3488, 3701, 4589, 4805
Sohlke, Gus *(Director)*   561, 822, 1738, 1927, 2155, 2159, 2347, 3755, 4333, 4364, 4506
Sohlke, Gus *(Musical Director)*   3033
Sohlke, Gustave *(Director)*   2262
Sokol, Lawrence E. *(Producer)*   3902
Sokol, Marilyn *(Cast)*   3937, 4454, 4619
Sokoloff, Vladimir *(Cast)*   223, 979
Sokolov, Lydia *(Choreographer)*   4207
Sokolow, Anna *(Choreographer)*   868, 1748, 2940, 3691, 4015, 4169
Sokolow, Peter *(Orchestrations)*   1609
Solar, Willie *(Cast)*   4465
Solen, Paul *(Cast)*   723
Solis, Bernabe Roxas *(Orchestrations)*   364
Sollar, Fabien *(Author)*   3466
Solley, Marvin *(Cast)*   1770
Solley, Marvin *(Librettist)*   1770
Solly, Bill *(Composer)*   508, 1665
Solly, Bill *(Librettist)*   508, 1665
Solly, Bill *(Lyricist)*   508, 1665
Solman, Alfred *(Composer)*   246, 675, 1504, 2387, 2415, 2671, 3384, 3857, 4054, 4801
Solman, Alfred *(Producer)*   1504
Solms, Kenny *(Composer)*   3112
Solms, Kenny *(Librettist)*   2590, 3111, 3112, 3444
Solms, Kenny *(Lyricist)*   3112
Solomon, Edward *(Composer)*   402
Solomon, Frederic *(Cast)*   1594, 2507, 3652, 4500
Solomon, Frederic *(Composer)*   2029, 2035, 2493, 2964, 2974, 4014, 4662
Solomon, Frederic *(Lyricist)*   2493
Solomon, Frederic *(Musical Director)*   1356, 2481, 3251, 4662, 4802, 4803
Solomon, Renee *(Musical Director)*   1269, 2866, 3670, 4773
Solomon, Renee *(Orchestrations)*   3781
Solomons Jr., Gus *(Choreographer)*   2220
Solotaroff, Mischa *(Set Design)*   3130
Solov, Zachary *(Choreographer)*   2322, 2838
Soloway, Leonard *(Producer)*   1762, 4279, 4396
Solt, Andrew *(Author)*   1506
Solt, Andrew *(Director)*   1506
Somerville, Phyllis *(Cast)*   2243
Sommer, J.W. *(Set Design)*   571
Sommer, Josef *(Cast)*   3175, 4109
Sommer, Kathy *(Dance Arranger)*   3760
Sommer, Kathy *(Musical Director)*   3760
Sommer, Kathy *(Vocal Arranger)*   3760
Sommers, Avery *(Cast)*   3515
Sommers, Bryon *(Composer)*   2171, 4799
Sommers, Joanie *(Cast)*   3275

Somner, Pearl *(Costumes)*   135, 259, 415, 2074, 3928
Sondergaard, Hester *(Cast)*   3180
Sonderskov, Robert *(Narrator)*   2977
Sonderson, Lora *(Cast)*   2602
Sondheim, Stephen *(Composer)*   80, 162, 212, 779, 832, 1060, 1200, 1329, 1406, 1422, 1571, 2143, 2205, 2417, 2536, 2764, 2769, 2822, 2860, 3340, 3411, 3471, 3843, 3967, 4067, 4210, 4233, 4268, 4399, 4474, 4700, 4746
Sondheim, Stephen *(Incidental Music)*   1184, 2144
Sondheim, Stephen *(Librettist)*   80, 3471
Sondheim, Stephen *(Lyricist)*   80, 162, 212, 599, 630, 779, 832, 1060, 1200, 1214, 1329, 1406, 1422, 1571, 1709, 1991, 2076, 2143, 2205, 2417, 2536, 2663, 2677, 2764, 2769, 2822, 2860, 3018, 3340, 3411, 3471, 3843, 3967, 4067, 4210, 4233, 4268, 4399, 4625, 4700, 4746
Song Spinners, The *(Cast)*   4409
Soo, Jack *(Cast)*   1315
Sophocles *(Author)*   1636
Soreanu, Mary *(Cast)*   3670, 3781
Sorel, Dian *(Cast)*   3167
Sorel, Felicia *(Cast)*   3822
Sorel, Felicia *(Choreographer)*   2115, 2202, 2595, 3036, 4479
Sorg, John C. *(Musical Director)*   2996
Soriero, Patrice *(Choreographer)*   595, 4137
Sorin, Louis *(Cast)*   1343, 3767, 4365, 4620
Sorin, Louis *(Librettist)*   1446
Sorkin, Herbert *(Composer)*   226
Soroka, Heather Lee *(Cast)*   2229
Sorvino, Paul *(Cast)*   273
Sosa, Astrid *(Costumes)*   4729
Sosnik, Harry *(Musical Director)*   2313
Sosnowski, Janusz *(Set Design)*   2846
Sotager, Mme. *(Costumes)*   1712
Sothern, Ann *(Cast)*   1207, 1674
Sothern, Jean *(Lyricist)*   3104
Sottile, Michael *(Arrangements)*   1700
Sottile, Michael *(Musical Director)*   1700
Sottile, Michael S. *(Musical Director)*   2237
Soudeikine, Sergei *(Costumes)*   3103
Soudeikine, Sergei *(Set Design)*   710, 1352, 3103, 3541
Soul Stirrers, The *(Cast)*   1636
Soule, Frank *(Cast)*   2156
Soule, Robert *(Costumes)*   1319, 3725
Soule, Robert *(Set Design)*   722, 1319, 1697, 3725, 4292, 4380
Soules, Dale *(Cast)*   3666
Sour, Robert *(Composer)*   3104
Sour, Robert *(Lyricist)*   432, 2985, 3103, 3905, 3986, 4367, 4534
Sour, Robert B. *(Lyricist)*   2751
Sousa, John Philip *(Additional Music)*   1208
Sousa, John Philip *(Cast)*   1396, 1901, 2403
Sousa, John Philip *(Composer)*   118, 527, 698, 749, 964, 1165, 1388, 1901, 3261, 4100, 4297, 4390
Sousa, John Philip *(Incidental Music)*   1208
Sousa, John Philip *(Librettist)*   527
Sousa, John Philip *(Music Based On)*   4297
Sousa, Leone *(Cast)*   4677
Sousa, Pamela *(Cast)*   723, 4196

Spier, Larry *(Lyricist)* 4828
Spiering Jr., Frank *(Lyricist)* 3527
Spigelgass, Leonard *(Librettist)* 2583
Spillane, Sherri *(Cast)* 2584
Spiller, Marshal S. *(Lighting Designer)* 2007
Spina, Harold *(Composer)* 1937, 2165, 4163, 4255, 4825
Spina, Harold *(Director)* 4163
Spina, Harold *(Librettist)* 4163
Spina, Harold *(Lyricist)* 4163
Spinelli, Larry *(Cast)* 4089
Spiner, Brent *(Cast)* 2429
Spinetti, Victor *(Cast)* 2362, 3259
Spink, George *(Composer)* 2383, 3642
Spink, George *(Lyricist)* 2383, 3642, 4723
Spink, George A. *(Composer)* 470, 2982, 4044, 4642
Spink, George A. *(Lyricist)* 470, 4044, 4642
Spink, George F. *(Composer)* 688
Spink, George F. *(Lyricist)* 688
Spink, William *(Composer)* 2906, 4311
Spinola, Marina *(Producer)* 562
Spiroff, Tom *(Cast)* 3178
Spisak, Neil *(Costumes)* 655
Spitalny, H. Leopold *(Composer)* 1414
Spitz, Arthur *(Producer)* 4792
Spivak, Allen *(Producer)* 4534
Spivakowsky, Michael *(Musical Director)* 4863
Spohn, Leslie *(Lighting Designer)* 564
Spoliansky, Mischa *(Composer)* 4235
Spolidoro, A. *(Puppeteer)* 55
Spong, Hilda *(Cast)* 1894
Spooner, Cecil *(Cast)* 3050
Spooner, Cecil *(Producer)* 3050
Spottswood, James C. *(Cast)* 929
Sprague, George R. *(Cast)* 1537
Sprague, Sidney *(Choreographer)* 439
Sprecher, Ben *(Producer)* 155
Spreckels, Geraldine *(Cast)* 1109
Spring, Helen *(Cast)* 1013
Springer, Ashton *(Producer)* 74, 166, 576, 952, 1198
Springer, Phil *(Composer)* 3940, 4435
Springer, Phil *(Lyricist)* 4435
Springer, Philip *(Composer)* 747, 1993, 2294, 3940, 4268, 4828
Sproat, Ron *(Librettist)* 260
Spross, Charles Gilbert *(Composer)* 4590
Sprosty, Paul *(Orchestrations)* 3314
Spyri, Johanna *(Author)* 1815
Squadron, Anne Strickland *(Producer)* 2654
Squibb, June *(Cast)* 669, 1418, 3186
Squire, Jack
    See also Jack Squires.
Squire, Jack *(Cast)* 1033, 1923, 2780, 2972, 3655
Squire, Katherine *(Cast)* 3984
Squires, Gil *(Cast)* 1603, 4118
Squires, Harry D. *(Composer)* 4137
Squires, Jack
    See also Jack Squire.
Squires, Jack *(Cast)* 202, 1756, 2757, 3508, 3980, 4741, 4793
Sroka, Jerry *(Cast)* 843, 4707

St. Albin, Bisson *(Author)* 1663
St. Clair, Stewart *(Librettist)* 2371
St. Claire, Dorothy *(Cast)* 4836
St. Claire, Minnie *(Cast)* 3068
St. Cyr, Lily *(Cast)* 4260
St. Cyr, Val *(Costumes)* 4661
St. Germain, Mark *(Composer)* 2241
St. Germain, Mark *(Librettist)* 1509, 2185, 2229, 2283
St. Germain, Mark *(Lyricist)* 1509, 2185, 2229, 2241
St. John, Betta *(Cast)* 4096
St. John, Howard *(Cast)* 458, 1507, 2484, 3584
St. John, Jai Oscar *(Cast)* 166, 593
St. John, Jill *(Cast)* 2267
St. John, Orford *(Librettist)* 2168
St. Leo, Leonard *(Cast)* 4077
St. Louis, Louis *(Arrangements)* 4031
St. Louis, Louis *(Cast)* 2775, 4459
St. Louis, Louis *(Composer)* 4459
St. Louis, Louis *(Dance Arranger)* 535, 1164, 1664, 3330, 3643, 3792
St. Louis, Louis *(Musical Director)* 535, 1664, 2658, 3792, 4031, 4089
St. Louis, Louis *(Vocal Arranger)* 535, 1164, 1664, 3330, 3792, 4089
St. Matthew *(Author)* 1595
Staats, Phil *(Composer)* 3205
Staats, Phil *(Lyricist)* 3205
Stabile, Bill *(Set Design)* 2877, 2970, 2992, 3169, 3873
Stacklin, Andy *(Set Design)* 2468
Stadlen, Lewis J. *(Cast)* 2874, 2945, 3272
Staff, Frank *(Choreographer)* 4579
Stafford, Adam *(Cast)* 3454
Stafford, Bill *(Composer)* 2080
Stafford, Bill *(Lyricist)* 2080
Stafford, Bill *(Orchestrations)* 2080, 4796
Stafford, Jim *(Composer)* 914
Stafford, Jim *(Lyricist)* 914
Stafford, Joseph *(Cast)* 3453
Stafford-Clark, Max *(Director)* 3884
Stage Managers Club *(Producer)* 4273
Stage Promotions Ltd. & Co. *(Producer)* 2798
Stages Theatrical Prod. *(Producer)* 2177
Stahl, Cordell *(Cast)* 4136
Stahl, Mary Leigh *(Cast)* 695
Stahl, Richard *(Composer)* 436, 998, 4165
Stahl, Richard *(Lyricist)* 436
Stahl, Rose *(Cast)* 3341
Stahlberg, Frederic *(Musical Director)* 4547
Stahlberg, Fritz *(Musical Director)* 1851
Staiger, Libi *(Cast)* 603, 1029, 4090
Stainbrook, Richard D. *(Producer)* 2288
Stair, E.D. *(Producer)* 1641, 1798, 2642
Stall, Karl *(Cast)* 3372
Stallings, Laurence *(Librettist)* 3650, 4569
Stallings, Laurence *(Lyricist)* 1020, 4569
Stamer, Fred *(Composer)* 596
Stamford, Wybert *(Director)* 1626
Stammers, Frank *(Choreographer)* 628
Stammers, Frank *(Director)* 1911, 2056, 2174, 3045, 3207, 3531, 4381

Starr, Lita *(Producer)* 4176
Starr, Wayne *(Producer)* 2633
Starrett, Ken *(Costumes)* 1924
Stauch, Bonnie *(Costumes)* 450
Stauder, Al *(Cast)* 2791
Staudt, Chris *(Composer)* 1282, 4168
Staudt, Christian *(Composer)* 1282
Stauffer, Aubrey *(Composer)* 2358, 3877
Stauffer, Aubrey *(Lyricist)* 2358
Stauffer, Blaine *(Cast)* 1354
Staunton, Virginia *(Cast)* 2765
Steadman, Hugh *(Librettist)* 1887
Steadman, Hugh *(Lyricist)* 1887
Stearns, Roger *(Cast)* 1342, 1448, 3103, 4142, 4777
Stearns, Roger V. *(Cast)* 3325
Stearns, Theodore *(Musical Director)* 1308, 1794
Steck, Hazel Weber *(Cast)* 2925
Steck, Olga *(Cast)* 735, 1378, 2780, 4121, 4194
Steck, Ray *(Musical Director)* 420
Stecko, Bob *(Dance Arranger)* 251
Stecko, Joe *(Musical Director)* 3863
Stecko, Joseph *(Musical Director)* 302, 825, 1878, 2339, 3725
Steel, John *(Cast)* 2698, 3007, 3008, 4813, 4814
Steele, Bernard *(Director)* 966
Steele, Bill *(Cast)* 3802, 4444
Steele, Brian *(Cast)* 643
Steele, Brooks *(Musical Director)* 2458
Steele, David *(Cast)* 2626
Steele, Jevetta *(Cast)* 1636
Steele, Porter *(Composer)* 1235
Steele, Robert L. *(Lighting Designer)* 3439
Steele, Robert L. *(Producer)* 3196, 4124
Steele, Tommy *(Cast)* 1721, 1741
Steele, Vernon *(Cast)* 4730
Steeley, Guy F. *(Librettist)* 1351, 1646, 4161
Steeley, Guy F. *(Lyricist)* 1351, 4161
Steen, Jan *(Director)* 1500
Steen, Jan *(Librettist)* 1500
Steere, Clifton *(Cast)* 1347
Stefanni, Prima
   See also Prima Stephen.
Stefanni, Prima *(Cast)* 4157
Steffan, Ernest *(Composer)* 379
Steffe, Edwin *(Cast)* 347, 1766, 2928
Steffe, William *(Composer)* 3020
Steffen, Paul *(Choreographer)* 943
Steger, Julius *(Cast)* 405, 1375, 1905, 2160, 3834
Steger, Julius *(Composer)* 3753
Stegman, Richard *(Cast)* 2022
Stegmeyer, Bill *(Orchestrations)* 3696, 4828
Stegmeyer, William *(Dance Arranger)* 31
Stegmeyer, William *(Orchestrations)* 2248, 3280
Stegmeyer, William *(Vocal Arranger)* 31
Stehli, Edgar *(Cast)* 4548
Steig, William *(Author)* 99
Steiger, Jimmie *(Composer)* 4668
Stein, Ben *(Producer)* 225
Stein, Debra *(Costumes)* 1353, 2704
Stein, Douglas *(Set Design)* 1234, 2746

Stein, Gertrude *(Librettist)* 1498, 2110
Stein, Gertrude *(Lyricist)* 1366, 1498, 2110
Stein, Harry *(Librettist)* 1038
Stein, Joseph *(Author)* 951, 1190, 4038
Stein, Joseph *(Librettist)* 59, 273, 483, 652, 951, 1265, 1892, 2267, 2268, 2318, 2439, 2987, 3509, 3644, 4038, 4270, 4862
Stein, Julian *(Composer)* 722, 1436
Stein, Julian *(Dance Arranger)* 1369, 1727, 3835
Stein, Julian *(Musical Director)* 1158, 1245, 1369, 1727, 2016, 3920, 4028, 4541, 4764
Stein, Julian *(Orchestrations)* 461, 1245, 1354, 1727, 2016, 3491, 3835, 4541
Stein, Julian *(Vocal Arranger)* 1158, 1369, 1727, 3835, 4028, 4764
Stein, Leo *(Author)* 132, 473, 1066, 1121, 2262, 2509, 2603, 2701, 2836, 2837, 2838, 3053, 3727, 3996, 4553, 4563, 4726
Stein, Meridee *(Director)* 3164
Stein, Walter *(Author)* 475
Steinbeck, John *(Author)* 1864, 3224, 3505
Steinberg, Ben *(Musical Director)* 3452, 3831
Steinberg, Harry A. *(Lyricist)* 2628
Steinberg, Maurice *(Composer)* 4723
Steinberg, Maurice *(Lyricist)* 4723
Steinberg, Neil *(Lyricist)* 2356
Steinberg, Samuel *(Composer)* 4342
Steinbrenner III, George M. *(Producer)* 2437, 3869
Steindorff, Paul *(Musical Director)* 698, 1594, 2156, 2507, 3994, 4500
Steiner, Howard *(Composer)* 898
Steiner, Irwin *(Producer)* 3167
Steiner, Max *(Composer)* 1631, 3420
Steiner, Max *(Musical Director)* 21, 1485, 1643, 1827, 1935, 2336, 2602, 3319, 3472, 3650, 3652, 3770, 3868, 4001, 4283, 4300, 4476
Steiner, Max *(Orchestrations)* 3650
Steiner, Oscar *(Composer)* 710
Steiner, Oscar *(Lyricist)* 710
Steiner, Rick *(Producer)* 394, 2143, 3862, 4031
Steiner, Steve *(Arrangements)* 1969
Steiner, Steve *(Cast)* 3695
Steiner, Steve *(Musical Director)* 1969
Steiner, Steve *(Orchestrations)* 1969
Steininger, Franz *(Composer)* 1415, 3013
Steininger, Franz *(Musical Director)* 3013
Steinman, Harold *(Producer)* 4006
Steinman, Jim *(Composer)* 2953
Steinman, Jim *(Lyricist)* 2953
Stell, John *(Cast)* 3297
Stell, Joseph *(Lighting Designer)* 1370
Stell, Joseph *(Set Design)* 1370
Stempfel, Theo. *(Cast)* 96
Stempfel, Theo. *(Librettist)* 96
Stempfel, Theo. *(Lyricist)* 96
Stempfel Jr., Theodore *(Librettist)* 1405, 2740
Stempfel Jr., Theodore *(Lyricist)* 1405
Stenborg, Helen *(Cast)* 1268
Stenborg, James *(Musical Director)* 3306
Stenborg, James *(Orchestrations)* 4790

Stenhammer *(Composer)* 2803
Stenhammer *(Lyricist)* 2803
Stenod Prods. Inc. *(Producer)* 157
Stephen, Joe *(Costumes)* 4035
Stephen, Prima
   See also Prima Stefanni.
Stephen, Prima *(Cast)* 2776
Stephens, Claudia *(Costumes)* 2229
Stephens, Dick *(Choreographer)* 1581
Stephens, Garn *(Cast)* 1664
Stephens, Greg *(Composer)* 1736
Stephens, Greg *(Lyricist)* 1736
Stephens, Hal *(Author)* 3068
Stephens, Hal *(Librettist)* 561
Stephens, Henry Pottinger *(Librettist)* 402
Stephens, Henry Pottinger *(Lyricist)* 402
Stephens, Kelley *(Cast)* 2928
Stephens, Lannyl *(Cast)* 1161, 3039, 3227
Stephens, Lillian *(Cast)* 939
Stephens, Linda *(Cast)* 4708
Stephens, Norman *(Producer)* 4379
Stephens, Ray *(Cast)* 3279, 3724
Stephens, Stephanie *(Cast)* 3649
Stephens, Ty *(Cast)* 3905
Stephens, Ty *(Choreographer)* 3905
Stephens, Ty *(Composer)* 3905
Stephens, Ty *(Lyricist)* 3905
Stephens, William *(Cast)* 311, 4581
Stephens, William *(Composer)* 700
Stephens, William *(Lyricist)* 700
Stephens, Willie *(Cast)* 30
Stephenson, Albert *(Cast)* 1000
Stephenson, Albert *(Choreographer)* 826
Stephenson, B.C. *(Librettist)* 1080
Stephenson, Laurie *(Cast)* 2737
Steppe, Harry *(Cast)* 806
Steppe, Harry *(Librettist)* 806
Steppenwolf Theatre Co. *(Producer)* 4074
Steppers, Whitey *(Cast)* 1840
Stept, Sam *(Composer)* 850, 1481
Stept, Sam H. *(Composer)* 321, 1481, 1689, 2141, 2587,
   3373, 3907, 4772, 4842
Stept, Sammy *(Composer)* 2850
Sterck, Wilhelm *(Author)* 1219
Steriopoulos, Alkiviades "Alki" *(Musical Director)* 3667
Sterk, Wilhelm *(Author)* 12, 2914
Sterling, Andrew B. *(Composer)* 1404, 2805, 4842
Sterling, Andrew B. *(Lyricist)* 662, 1404, 1526, 1685,
   1897, 1963, 2254, 2299, 2349, 2415, 2805, 3396, 3962,
   4390, 4842
Sterling, Clarence A. *(Cast)* 4756
Sterling, Ford *(Cast)* 522, 2314
Sterling, Lee *(Composer)* 3079
Sterling, Lee *(Lyricist)* 3079
Sterling, Oliver *(Cast)* 1523
Sterling, Richard *(Cast)* 715, 1221
Sterling, Robert *(Composer)* 1036
Sterling, Robert *(Lyricist)* 1036
Sterling, Warren *(Cast)* 4275
Stern, Alan *(Composer)* 4660

Stern, Alan *(Librettist)* 4660
Stern, Alan *(Lyricist)* 4660
Stern, Eric *(Composer)* 3221
Stern, Eric *(Librettist)* 3221
Stern, Eric *(Musical Director)* 171, 747, 809, 2437,
   3221, 3299, 3485, 3644, 4412, 4695
Stern, Eric *(Vocal Arranger)* 2437
Stern, Ernest *(Costumes)* 429
Stern, Ernest *(Set Design)* 1202, 1763, 4667
Stern, Harold *(Composer)* 203, 4352
Stern, Harold *(Lyricist)* 203
Stern, Harold *(Musical Director)* 1840, 3310, 3523,
   4086, 4621
Stern, J.W. *(Composer)* 2892
Stern, J.W. *(Lyricist)* 2892
Stern, Jack *(Lyricist)* 2601
Stern, James D. *(Producer)* 4690
Stern, Reva *(Producer)* 1079
Sternbach, Gerald *(Composer)* 1804
Sternbach, Gerald *(Vocal Arranger)* 1804
Sternberg, Ann *(Composer)* 1498
Sternberg, Ann *(Dance Arranger)* 71
Sternberg, Ann *(Music Adaptation)* 1498
Sternberg, Ann *(Musical Director)* 1498
Sterner, Steve *(Cast)* 2354, 4769
Sterner, Steve *(Composer)* 2630
Sternhagen, Frances *(Cast)* 135, 1620
Sternroyd, Eva *(Cast)* 1534
Stetson, Dale *(Set Design)* 1856, 3131
Stetson, Evie *(Cast)* 4681
Stettheimer, Florine *(Set Design)* 1366
Stettler, Steve *(Director)* 143
Stevens *(Composer)* 4823
Stevens *(Lyricist)* 4823
Stevens, Allan *(Cast)* 2177
Stevens, Augusta *(Cast)* 3979
Stevens, B.D. *(Director)* 3828
Stevens, B.D. *(Producer)* 527, 749
Stevens, Cat *(Composer)* 964
Stevens, Cat *(Lyricist)* 964
Stevens, Connie *(Cast)* 1898, 2553
Stevens, Craig *(Cast)* 1860, 2496
Stevens, D.K. *(Additional Music)* 761
Stevens, D.K. *(Composer)* 306, 3047, 3882
Stevens, D.K. *(Lyricist)* 306, 761, 2934, 3882, 3951
Stevens, David *(Librettist)* 2670
Stevens, David *(Lyricist)* 2670
Stevens, Donna *(Cast)* 914
Stevens, Donna *(Composer)* 914
Stevens, Donna *(Librettist)* 914
Stevens, Donna *(Lyricist)* 914
Stevens, Edward *(Cast)* 3073
Stevens, Edwin *(Cast)* 2179, 2824, 4103
Stevens, Ellis *(Cast)* 4339
Stevens, Fisher *(Cast)* 3852
Stevens, Fran *(Cast)* 2014
Stevens, Gary Keith *(Cast)* 1380
Stevens, Geoffe *(Cast)* 1782
Stevens, Gilbert C. *(Musical Director)* 2080
Stevens, Gilbert C. *(Orchestrations)* 2080

Stevens, James *(Cast)* 1210
Stevens, Jodi *(Cast)* 484
Stevens, Josephine *(Cast)* 1587
Stevens, June K. *(Costumes)* 3217
Stevens, Kenneth *(Cast)* 4316
Stevens, Leonard *(Composer)* 4683
Stevens, Leonard *(Lyricist)* 4683
Stevens, Leslie *(Cast)* 2360
Stevens, Leslie *(Librettist)* 912, 3493, 3914
Stevens, Leslie *(Lyricist)* 912
Stevens, Marti *(Cast)* 808, 4153
Stevens, Morton *(Musical Director)* 2987
Stevens, Morton *(Orchestrations)* 2987
Stevens, Morton L. *(Cast)* 2061
Stevens, Rise *(Cast)* 743, 2550
Stevens, Roger L. *(Producer)* 652, 837, 1294, 1600,
    1897, 2260, 3452, 3577, 3787, 3984, 4004
Stevens, Ronald "Smokey" *(Cast)* 166, 2133
Stevens, Tony *(Choreographer)* 251, 484, 3018, 3444,
    3636, 4114
Stevens, Tony *(Director)* 4701
Stevens, Will H. *(Cast)* 1185
Stevens Productions *(Producer)* 1721
Stevens Studio *(Set Design)* 1984
Stevensen, Scott *(Cast)* 319, 4480
Stevenson *(Set Design)* 1880
Stevenson, Bob *(Cast)* 3259
Stevenson, Bob *(Choreographer)* 3259
Stevenson, Charles *(Cast)* 1434
Stevenson, Charles A. *(Cast)* 2778
Stevenson, Douglas *(Cast)* 736, 4208
Stevenson, Katherine *(Cast)* 4453
Stevenson, Katheryn *(Cast)* 2495
Stevenson, McLean *(Cast)* 1648
Stevenson, Robert *(Costumes)* 2300, 3342, 3379,
    3965, 3968, 4545
Stevenson, Robert *(Set Design)* 2330
Stevenson, Robert Louis *(Author)* 31, 1089, 2197,
    2198, 2199, 3485, 4444
Stevenson, Robert Louis *(Lyricist)* 3450, 3999
Stevenson, Robert T. *(Costumes)* 1880
Stevenson, William *(Composer)* 4534
Stevenson, William *(Lyricist)* 4534
Steward, Johnny *(Cast)* 2615
Steward, Ron *(Cast)* 344, 3825
Steward, Ron *(Composer)* 3825
Steward, Ron *(Librettist)* 3825
Steward, Ron *(Lyricist)* 3825
Stewardson, Jerome *(Musical Director)* 4429
Stewart, Anita *(Author)* 575
Stewart, Anita *(Cast)* 575
Stewart, Anita *(Set Design)* 3853
Stewart, Athole *(Cast)* 841
Stewart, D.A. *(Lyricist)* 1713
Stewart, Daniel *(Choreographer)* 1510
Stewart, Dink *(Cast)* 254, 984, 2690, 4339
Stewart, Don *(Cast)* 249, 2219, 4186
Stewart, Donald *(Cast)* 289, 1448
Stewart, Donald Ogden *(Librettist)* 1275
Stewart, Fred *(Cast)* 837, 933

Stewart, Grant *(Author)* 531, 3508
Stewart, Grant *(Cast)* 1806
Stewart, Grant *(Librettist)* 2886
Stewart, Grant *(Lyricist)* 219, 377, 617, 1455, 2117,
    2126, 2404, 2495, 2855, 2886, 2982, 3753, 3790
Stewart, Gwen *(Cast)* 4460
Stewart, Harrison *(Cast)* 645, 2044, 3358
Stewart, James H. *(Cast)* 4439
Stewart, Jim *(Set Design)* 4488
Stewart, John *(Cast)* 937, 1990, 4292
Stewart, Johnny *(Cast)* 2312
Stewart, Joseph *(Cast)* 4095
Stewart, Katherine *(Cast)* 2614, 3481
Stewart, Larry *(Cast)* 2173
Stewart, Leon *(Cast)* 1262
Stewart, Melville *(Cast)* 618, 767, 906, 1305, 2826,
    2885, 3828
Stewart, Michael *(Librettist)* 534, 607, 656, 1171, 1359,
    1478, 1660, 1776, 1828, 2011, 2058, 2288, 2554, 2660,
    3485, 3664, 3941
Stewart, Michael *(Lyricist)* 305, 1892, 2058, 2246,
    2804, 3664, 3940, 3941, 3942
Stewart, Nellie *(Cast)* 205
Stewart, Paul *(Director)* 524
Stewart, Paul Anthony *(Cast)* 949
Stewart, Paula *(Cast)* 1408, 2449, 4693
Stewart, Ray *(Cast)* 491
Stewart, Red *(Composer)* 4264
Stewart, Red *(Lyricist)* 4264
Stewart, Ronni *(Choreographer)* 3661
Stewart, Rosalie *(Producer)* 2
Stewart, Scot *(Cast)* 4197
Stewart, Sylvester *(Composer)* 3739
Stewart, Sylvester *(Lyricist)* 3739
Stewart, W.G. *(Cast)* 1375
Stewart, William G. *(Cast)* 4646
Stewart & Morrison *(Producer)* 380
Stiasny, Walter *(Musical Director)* 346
Sticco, Dan *(Composer)* 690
Sticco, Dan *(Librettist)* 690
Stickney, Dorothy *(Cast)* 759, 1200
Stiebel, Victor *(Costumes)* 3139
Stieger, Charles *(Musical Director)* 3323
Stiers, David Ogden *(Cast)* 2687
Stiers, David Ogden *(Narrator)* 330
Stigwood, Robert *(Producer)* 1211, 2212, 3636, 3903
Stiles, Leslie *(Lyricist)* 356
Stilgoe, Richard *(Cast)* 2240
Stilgoe, Richard *(Librettist)* 3464
Stilgoe, Richard *(Lyricist)* 678, 3464, 4138
Still, Frank *(Composer)* 2388
Still, Frank *(Dance Arranger)* 2388
Still, Frank *(Musical Director)* 2388
Still, Frank *(Orchestrations)* 2388
Still, Frank *(Vocal Arranger)* 2388
Still, William *(Orchestrations)* 26
Stiller, Jerry *(Cast)* 1600, 2804
Stillman, Al *(Composer)* 3287
Stillman, Al *(Lyricist)* 1138, 1941, 2099, 2161, 3287,
    3640, 4131, 4143, 4569, 4677

Stillman, Albert (*Lyricist*) 2023, 2024
Stillman, Bob (*Cast*) 3181
Stillman, Henry (*Director*) 1235
Stillman, Robert (*Cast*) 2565
Stilwell, Frank (*Composer*) 1963
Stilwell, Gene (*Cast*) 3202
Stimac, Anthony (*Director*) 840, 1249
Stimac, Anthony (*Librettist*) 669, 840, 1249, 3875
Stine, Chas. J. (*Cast*) 1513
Sting
 See also Sting Sumner.
Sting (*Cast*) 4371
Stirling, J.R. (*Producer*) 3998
Stites, Kevin (*Arrangements*) 4703
Stites, Kevin (*Incidental Music*) 1236
Stites, Kevin (*Musical Director*) 1701
Stites, Kevin (*Vocal Arranger*) 1701
Stitt, Milan (*Producer*) 2332
Stix, John (*Director*) 3389
Stobitzer, Heinrich (*Author*) 2619, 2914
Stock, Larry (*Composer*) 4534
Stock, Larry (*Lyricist*) 3739, 4534
Stockdale, Joseph (*Librettist*) 2992
Stockdale, Muriel (*Costumes*) 1589
Stocken, Jasmine (*Cast*) 4016
Stockler, Michael Lee (*Musical Director*) 1082, 2746
Stockton, Frank (*Author*) 170
Stockwell, Harry (*Cast*) 207, 1135, 1494, 2755
Stockwell, Jeremy (*Cast*) 3654
Stockwell, Jock (*Lighting Designer*) 2977
Stockwell, Jock (*Set Design*) 2977
Stockwell, Rick (*Cast*) 1159
Stoddard, Brandon (*Cast*) 4041
Stoddard, George E. (*Librettist*) 735, 1173, 1587, 2214, 2270, 2446, 2491, 2564, 2888, 2944, 3252, 3915, 4437
Stoddard, George E. (*Lyricist*) 735, 1971, 2159, 2214, 2270, 2491, 2888, 2944, 3786, 4437
Stoddard, Haila (*Producer*) 2375, 2418, 2598
Stokkermans, Joop (*Composer*) 1865
Stoklosa, Janusz (*Arrangements*) 2846
Stoklosa, Janusz (*Musical Director*) 2846
Stoklosa, Janusz (*Vocal Arranger*) 2846
Stokowski, Leopold (*Cast*) 3153
Stolber, Dean (*Cast*) 1585, 3714
Stolberg, Ferdinand (*Librettist*) 517
Stolberg, Ferdinand (*Lyricist*) 517
Stoll, Bambi (*Costumes*) 1435
Stoll, Louis (*Musical Director*) 2623
Stoll, Sylvia (*Cast*) 2896
Stoller, Mike (*Composer*) 964, 3428, 3739, 4031
Stoller, Mike (*Lyricist*) 964, 3428, 3739, 4031
Stolz, Robert (*Author*) 475, 967, 4010
Stolz, Robert (*Composer*) 95, 475, 967, 1603, 2985, 3152, 3680, 3946, 4010, 4486, 4550, 4667
Stolz, Robert (*Musical Director*) 340, 2985
Stolz, Robert (*Orchestrations*) 4550
Stone, Agnes (*Cast*) 1080
Stone, Allene (*Cast*) 4150
Stone, Amelia (*Cast*) 132, 830, 1458, 1469, 1900, 2262, 2335, 3313, 3786, 4080, 4165, 4563

Stone, Carol (*Cast*) 4667
Stone, Danton (*Cast*) 1268
Stone, Dorothy (*Cast*) 930, 2479, 3415, 3721, 3860, 4025, 4150, 4345
Stone, Ed (*Lighting Designer*) 3004
Stone, Edward (*Director*) 705, 2993
Stone, Elly (*Cast*) 793, 2188, 3215, 4541
Stone, Ezra (*Cast*) 3365, 4340
Stone, Ezra (*Director*) 2910, 3698, 4340, 4582
Stone, Florence (*Cast*) 3133
Stone, Fred (*Cast*) 17, 736, 930, 1543, 2184, 2394, 3268, 3675, 3721, 4025, 4150, 4393, 4723
Stone, Gene (*Composer*) 1337
Stone, Gene (*Director*) 1337
Stone, Gene (*Librettist*) 1337
Stone, Gene (*Lyricist*) 1337, 4128
Stone, George (*Cast*) 513
Stone, Harold (*Director*) 1194
Stone, Harry (*Cast*) 1433, 3883
Stone, Harry (*Composer*) 708
Stone, Harry (*Librettist*) 708
Stone, Harry (*Lyricist*) 708
Stone, Jerald B. (*Musical Director*) 1500
Stone, Jeremy (*Musical Director*) 314
Stone, Jeremy (*Orchestrations*) 2242
Stone, Jeremy (*Vocal Arranger*) 305
Stone, Jon (*Cast*) 2935
Stone, June (*Cast*) 1465
Stone, Leonard (*Cast*) 3687
Stone, Mark (*Cast*) 766
Stone, Mimi (*Composer*) 3491
Stone, Mrs. Fred (*Cast*) 3721
Stone, Paddy (*Choreographer*) 2682, 3302, 4469
Stone, Paula (*Cast*) 3721, 3916
Stone, Paula (*Producer*) 657, 2496, 3801, 4423
Stone, Peter (*Librettist*) 134, 3060, 3897, 4013, 4167, 4196, 4481, 4695, 4727
Stone, Sid (*Cast*) 84, 1898, 4197
Stone, William (*Author*) 21
Stone, Wilson (*Composer*) 1837
Stone, Wilson (*Lyricist*) 1837
Stone Jr., Melville E. (*Composer*) 2508
Stonebeck, Ric (*Cast*) 695
Stoneburner, Sam (*Cast*) 2945
Stonehill, Maurice (*Lyricist*) 2317
Stonehill, Maurice J. (*Composer*) 1537
Stonehill, Maurice J. (*Lyricist*) 1537, 4544
Stoner, Joyce (*Choreographer*) 2069
Stoner, Joyce (*Composer*) 2069
Stoner, Joyce (*Director*) 2069
Stoner, Joyce (*Lyricist*) 2069
Stoner Arts, Inc. (*Producer*) 2069
Stoppard, Tom (*Author*) 2260
Stoppard, Tom (*Lyricist*) 2260
Storage, Jo (*Cast*) 202
Storch, Arthur (*Cast*) 1571
Storch, Arthur (*Director*) 1611
Storch, Larry (*Cast*) 943, 2554, 3683
Stordahl, Axel (*Composer*) 4743
Storey, Belle (*Cast*) 1901

Styx, Carl *(Musical Director)* 4735
Suarez, Ilka *(Costumes)* 2188
Suarez, Olga *(Cast)* 3013
Subin, Eli *(Cast)* 4543
Sucke, Greer *(Librettist)* 2703
Sucke, Greer *(Lyricist)* 2703
Sues, Alan *(Cast)* 4703
Suesse, Dana *(Cast)* 3153
Suesse, Dana *(Composer)* 173, 397, 417, 420, 662, 924, 1813, 2413, 2460, 3894, 3975, 4235, 4777, 4824
Suesse, Dana *(Lyricist)* 924, 3894, 4777
Suffin, Herb *(Director)* 679
Suffin, Jordan *(Cast)* 2969, 3928
Sugarman, Dave *(Cast)* 4141
Sukman, Harry *(Composer)* 3381
Sukman, Harry *(Musical Director)* 3, 3381
Sullavan, Margaret *(Cast)* 1831
Sullivan, Alex *(Librettist)* 4562
Sullivan, Alex *(Lyricist)* 1065, 1154, 2662, 3614, 4393
Sullivan, Arthur *(Author)* 1948, 2817, 2861
Sullivan, Arthur *(Composer)* 727, 1178, 1913, 1948, 1987, 2348, 2977, 3259, 3280, 3777, 4254
Sullivan, Arthur *(Librettist)* 1446
Sullivan, Arthur *(Music Based On)* 2861
Sullivan, Barry *(Cast)* 347, 1476
Sullivan, Brad *(Cast)* 4124
Sullivan, Brian *(Cast)* 2837, 4169
Sullivan, Charles *(Cast)* 516
Sullivan, Charles *(Composer)* 516
Sullivan, Charles *(Lyricist)* 516
Sullivan, D.J. *(Additional Music)* 761
Sullivan, Dan *(Composer)* 2902, 2934
Sullivan, Dan *(Lyricist)* 2902, 2934
Sullivan, Dan J. *(Composer)* 2662
Sullivan, Dan J. *(Lyricist)* 2662
Sullivan, Daniel J. *(Composer)* 3220, 3642
Sullivan, Daniel J. *(Lyricist)* 3220, 3642
Sullivan, Ed *(Cast)* 3153
Sullivan, Frank *(Director)* 4660
Sullivan, Frank *(Librettist)* 1874
Sullivan, Frank *(Lyricist)* 3409
Sullivan, Frank *(Puppeteer)* 997, 2726, 4710
Sullivan, Henry *(Cast)* 750
Sullivan, Henry *(Composer)* 2227, 2300, 2540, 2545, 3005, 4335, 4374, 4583
Sullivan, Ian *(Cast)* 1959
Sullivan, J.P. *(Cast)* 2310
Sullivan, James E. *(Cast)* 2929
Sullivan, Jerry *(Cast)* 3024
Sullivan, Jo *(Cast)* 2961, 3224, 3444, 4369, 4399
Sullivan, Joe J. *(Cast)* 1758
Sullivan, John Carver *(Costumes)* 1997
Sullivan, Joseph *(Cast)* 2085
Sullivan, Joseph L. *(Cast)* 1759
Sullivan, K.T. *(Cast)* 112, 4371
Sullivan, Lee *(Cast)* 530, 2447
Sullivan, Maxine *(Cast)* 889, 3059, 4256
Sullivan, Niel *(Composer)* 1964
Sullivan, Niel *(Lyricist)* 1964

Sullivan, Patrick *(Cast)* 1612
Sullivan, Paul *(Lighting Designer)* 1412, 1809, 1816, 2630, 2962, 3112, 4192
Sullivan, Sheila *(Cast)* 842, 3516
Sullivan, Terry *(Lyricist)* 336
Sully, William *(Cast)* 3185
Sumac, Yma *(Cast)* 1300
Sumbay, Dormeshia *(Cast)* 432
Summer, Donna *(Composer)* 3636, 3739
Summer, Donna *(Lyricist)* 3636, 3739
Summerhays, Jane *(Cast)* 2798
Summers, Beatrice *(Cast)* 4063
Summers, Bryon *(Composer)* 2171
Summers, Caley *(Costumes)* 2418
Summers, Cecil *(Cast)* 1562
Summers, Sam *(Librettist)* 4741
Summerville, Ada *(Cast)* 3677
Summerville, Amelia *(Cast)* 354, 523, 1123, 1505, 1728, 1793, 2324, 4644
Sumner, George *(Lyricist)* 297
Sumner, Sting
    See also Sting.
Sumner, Sting *(Composer)* 3739
Sumner, Sting *(Lyricist)* 3739
Sumter, Gwen *(Cast)* 1282
Sunbar Productions *(Producer)* 2245
Sundberg, Clinton *(Cast)* 4142
Sunderland, Nan *(Cast)* 1368
Sundgaard, Arnold *(Librettist)* 1085, 2339, 3195, 3703
Sundgaard, Arnold *(Lyricist)* 1085, 2339, 4785
Sundquist, Edward *(Set Design)* 567, 1852
Sunshine, Marion *(Cast)* 335, 468, 558, 642, 953, 1536, 1598, 3207, 4158, 4801
Suntory International Corp. *(Producer)* 775, 2205, 3285
Suppon, Charles *(Librettist)* 2437
Suratt, Valeska *(Cast)* 356, 433, 501, 1900, 3681, 4104
Suratt, Valeska *(Costumes)* 3681
Suratt, Valeska *(Set Design)* 3681
Surovy, Nicolas *(Cast)* 785
Surtees, R.S. *(Author)* 2240
Susann, Jackie *(Cast)* 1546
Susann, Jacqueline *(Author)* 2629
Susann, Jacqueline *(Cast)* 297, 2187, 2397
Susskind, David *(Producer)* 695, 2304, 4279
Susskind, Milton *(Composer)* 1312
Sussman, Bruce *(Composer)* 2022, 2677
Sussman, Bruce *(Librettist)* 846
Sussman, Bruce *(Lyricist)* 829, 845, 846, 2022, 2677
Sussman, Don *(Lighting Designer)* 4401
Suszon *(Orchestrations)* 1134
Sutcliffe, Berkeley *(Costumes)* 1467
Sutcliffe, Berkeley *(Lighting Designer)* 2608
Sutcliffe, Berkeley *(Set Design)* 2608
Suter, William P. *(Producer)* 3724
Sutherland, Claudette *(Cast)* 2019
Sutherland, Evelyn Greenleaf *(Author)* 3730
Sutherland, Lillie *(Choreographer)* 509
Sutherland, Marie *(Composer)* 4098
Sutherland, Marie *(Lyricist)* 4098
Suttell, Jane *(Costumes)* 4229

Sutton, Harry O. (Composer)   246, 1148, 1246, 4762, 4803
Sutton, Harry O. (Lyricist)   4390
Sutton, Julia (Cast)   3429
Sutton, Kay (Cast)   1109
Suzette Producing Company (Producer)   4227
Suzuki, Pat (Cast)   1315
Svar, John (Cast)   3479
Svigals, Phil (Composer)   551, 3012
Svoboda, Josef (Set Design)   2260
Swados, Elizabeth (Additional Lyrics)   3661
Swados, Elizabeth (Cast)   3162
Swados, Elizabeth (Composer)   54, 1053, 1077, 1700,
    1715, 1740, 2237, 2648, 3162, 3661, 3806, 4736
Swados, Elizabeth (Director)   1053, 1700, 1715, 2237,
    2648, 3162, 3806, 4736
Swados, Elizabeth (Librettist)   1053, 1700, 1715, 2237,
    2648, 3806, 4736
Swados, Elizabeth (Lyricist)   54, 1053, 1700, 1715,
    2237, 2648, 3162, 3806, 4736
Swados, Elizabeth (Musical Director)   54
Swados, Elizabeth (Orchestrations)   1077
Swados, Kim (Set Design)   298, 4155
Swaebe, Philip (Producer)   74
Swain, Lillian (Cast)   195, 2116
Swan, Boots (Cast)   1514
Swan, E.A. (Composer)   4534
Swan, E.A. (Lyricist)   4534
Swan, Mark (Author)   2253, 2378
Swan, Mark (Librettist)   60, 1793, 2253, 2519, 2642, 2893,
    3560, 3574, 4425
Swan, Mark (Lyricist)   2893
Swan, Rima (Cast)   3130
Swan & Lee (Cast)   876, 877, 896, 3709
Swanlee (Producer)   615
Swann, Donald (Cast)   220, 221
Swann, Donald (Composer)   220, 221
Swann, Donald (Lyricist)   221
Swann, Francis (Director)   3371
Swann, Francis (Librettist)   3371
Swanset Productions (Producer)   4232
Swanson, Britt (Cast)   3927
Swanstrom, Arthur (Composer)   1063, 1176, 3973,
    4374, 4393, 4824
Swanstrom, Arthur (Librettist)   1687, 3860
Swanstrom, Arthur (Lyricist)   667, 1063, 1685, 1686,
    1687, 1932, 2700, 3584, 3860, 3973, 4087, 4374, 4824
Swanstrom, Arthur (Producer)   3584, 4087
Swarbrick, Carol (Cast)   1093, 1581
Sward, Anne (Cast)   337
Swarthart, G. (Lyricist)   4387
Swartz, Frederick (Librettist)   4679
Sweatnam, Willis (Cast)   1259, 1480
Sweatnam, Willis P. (Cast)   4203
Sweeney, Bob (Cast)   752
Sweeney, Chuck (Lyricist)   2313, 4827
Sweet, Blanche (Cast)   3267
Sweet, Dolph (Cast)   406
Sweet, E. Tracy (Lyricist)   938
Sweet, Jeffrey (Author)   114
Sweet, Jeffrey (Composer)   114, 3557

Sweet, Jeffrey (Librettist)   2065, 2598, 3557
Sweet, Jeffrey (Lyricist)   114, 2065, 3557
Sweet, Marjorie (Cast)   3030
Sweet Olive, Inc. (Producer)   908
Sweetser, Norman (Cast)   1513
Sweningston, P. (Composer)   1562
Swenson, Dean (Orchestrations)   2074
Swenson, Inga (Cast)   134, 270, 817, 3108, 3294, 4715
Swenson, Karl (Cast)   1342, 3104
Swenson, Linda (Composer)   459
Swenson, Rod (Composer)   3739
Swenson, Rod (Lyricist)   3739
Swenson, Swen (Cast)   454, 496, 2248, 2523, 2925,
    4273, 4693
Swerd, Lester (Choreographer)   77
Swerdlow, Elizabeth (Choreographer)   2618
Swerdlow, Robert (Composer)   2618
Swerdlow, Robert (Librettist)   2618
Swerdlow, Robert (Lyricist)   2618
Swerling, Jo (Librettist)   1706, 3130
Swete, E. Lyall (Director)   165, 758, 2802
Swete, E. Lyall (Lyricist)   165
Swibard (Lyricist)   1550
Swift, Allen (Cast)   3059, 4186
Swift, Judith (Director)   2132
Swift, Kay (Composer)   1275, 1448, 2545, 3172,
    3386, 3849
Swift, Kay (Lyricist)   3386
Swift, Thomas (Librettist)   537, 538
Swift, Thomas (Lyricist)   538
Swift, Thos F. (Cast)   1513
Swinburne, Ann (Cast)   902, 2670
Swor, Irene (Cast)   2238
Sydenham, George (Cast)   310
Sydney, Basil (Cast)   715, 2211
Sydney, Robert (Choreographer)   4340
Sydow, Jack (Director)   127, 4090
Syers, Mark (Cast)   1211
Syers, Mark Hsu (Cast)   3340
Sykes, Dick (Cast)   4432
Sykes, Jerome (Cast)   113, 405, 749, 1260, 1375, 1896
Sykes, Jerome (Director)   3570
Sylber, Charley (Cast)   2669
Sylva, Marguerita (Cast)   1355, 1392, 1603, 1712,
    2636, 2714, 2938, 4365
Sylvester, Joyce (Cast)   2133
Sylvon, Jerry (Director)   4110
Sylvon, Jerry (Librettist)   4110
Sylvon, Jerry (Producer)   4110
Symes, Marty (Lyricist)   1951
Symon, Burk (Director)   3002
Syms, Sylvia (Cast)   4337, 4682
Synge, John Millington (Author)   259
Syrjala, Sointu (Set Design)   1734, 3501, 4548
Szabo-Cohen, Laura (Lyricist)   4107
Szarabajka, Keith (Cast)   1077
Sze, Julia (Costumes)   137, 1930
Szell, Lajos (Author)   3537
Szilasi, A.F. (Librettist)   340
Szirmay, Albert (Author)   3583

Szirmay, Albert *(Composer)* 3583
Szony, Francois *(Cast)* 1326

T

TV Asahi *(Producer)* 589, 3862
Tabbert, William *(Cast)* 404, 1242, 3893, 4096
Tabor, Desiree *(Cast)* 771, 1130, 2747
Tabor, Eithne *(Lyricist)* 932
Tabor, Richard *(Cast)* 75
Tabori, George *(Lyricist)* 369
Taffner, Don *(Producer)* 3695
Tagliarino, Salvatore *(Set Design)* 1418
Tahse, Martin *(Producer)* 2958
Taintor, Melinda *(Choreographer)* 4536
Taiz, Lillian *(Cast)* 1113, 4118
Taj Mahal *(Composer)* 3001
Takazauckas, Albert *(Director)* 3476
Take, Marilyn Ruth *(Cast)* 2090
Talbert, George *(Cast)* 689
Talbert, Wen *(Composer)* 2720
Talbot, Arthur *(Cast)* 1087, 3945
Talbot, Howard *(Author)* 1526
Talbot, Howard *(Composer)* 178, 353, 470, 737,
    1526, 1537, 1538, 1626, 2341, 2714, 2938, 3856,
    3857, 3996, 4354, 4663
Talbot, Howard *(Musical Director)* 2524, 4663
Talbot, Sharon *(Cast)* 2007
Talbot Productions *(Producer)* 584
Talbott Choir, Wen *(Cast)* 435
Taliaferro, Edith *(Cast)* 1250
Taliaferro, Hugh *(Composer)* 4433
Taliaferro, Hugh *(Librettist)* 4433
Taliaferro, Hugh *(Lyricist)* 4433
Taliaferro, John *(Cast)* 72
Taliaferro, Mabel *(Cast)* 462, 2336
Tallchief, Maria *(Cast)* 4075
Tallman, Bill *(Cast)* 1858
Tallon, Ninon *(Producer)* 1062
Tally, May *(Lyricist)* 1780
Tally, Ted *(Author)* 829
Tally, Ted *(Librettist)* 4535
Talman, Ann *(Cast)* 4790
Talman, George *(Cast)* 1388
Talsky, Ron *(Costumes)* 2058
Talva, Galina *(Cast)* 619
Tamaino, Anita *(Cast)* 4168
Tamanya, Hesla *(Cast)* 27
Tamara *(Cast)* 418, 1387, 2432, 3009, 3130, 3153, 3713
Tamara, Florenz *(Cast)* 2569
Tamaris, Helen *(Choreographer)* 153
Tamber, Selma *(Producer)* 1017
Tambin, David *(Orchestrations)* 1415
Tambornino, Jeff *(Librettist)* 1086, 2142
Tamir, Moshe *(Librettist)* 2866
Tamiris, Helen *(Cast)* 2167, 2175, 2653
Tamiris, Helen *(Choreographer)* 454, 603, 657, 1242,
    1300, 1679, 2137, 2167, 2751, 3390, 3509, 4524

Tamiroff, Akim *(Cast)* 743
Tamm, Peter *(Cast)* 81
Tananis, Robert *(Cast)* 2114
Tandet, A. Joseph *(Producer)* 2539
Tandy *(Cast)* 3451
Tandy, Jessica *(Cast)* 1372
Tandy, Spencer *(Producer)* 1813, 4454
Tanguay, Eva *(Cast)* 694, 3229, 4223, 4803
Tannassy, Cornell *(Orchestrations)* 1336, 3234, 3280
Tannehill, Bessie *(Cast)* 1295, 3154
Tannehill Jr., Frank *(Director)* 537, 1469, 3021, 3024,
    3028, 3437, 3877
Tannehill Jr., Frank *(Librettist)* 3021
Tannen, Julius *(Cast)* 1131, 1132, 1403, 1847, 2481
Tannen, William *(Cast)* 1448
Tanner, Chris *(Cast)* 2488
Tanner, Florence *(Cast)* 3033
Tanner, James T. *(Author)* 3322
Tanner, James T. *(Director)* 284
Tanner, James T. *(Librettist)* 284, 767, 770, 906, 1544,
    1561, 2131, 2844, 3098, 3313, 3322, 3618, 4430
Tanner, James T. *(Lyricist)* 3020
Tanner, Tony *(Choreographer)* 2242, 3555, 3576, 4062
Tanner, Tony *(Director)* 669, 1635, 1761, 2242, 3555,
    3576, 3600, 4062
Tapla, Jose *(Lyricist)* 4343
Tapper, Lester *(Lighting Designer)* 1837, 3427, 4577
Tapping, Simon *(Lighting Designer)* 3429
Tapps, George *(Cast)* 125, 1112, 1898
Tapps, George *(Choreographer)* 1112, 1898
Tapps, Georgie *(Cast)* 2068, 3036, 4631
Tapps, Herman *(Cast)* 715
Tarasoff, I. *(Choreographer)* 3006
Tarbox, Russell *(Composer)* 1836, 3402
Tarbox, Russell *(Musical Director)* 2569
Tarchetti, I.U. *(Author)* 3411
Tarica, Laurence *(Cast)* 4679
Tarica, Laurence *(Composer)* 4679
Tarica, Laurence *(Lyricist)* 4679
Tarkington, Booth *(Author)* 1501, 1831, 2937,
    3768, 3895
Tarkington, Booth *(Lyricist)* 3768
Taros, George *(Musical Director)* 2278
Taros, George *(Orchestrations)* 2278
Tarr, William *(Lyricist)* 1017
Tarr, Yvonne *(Librettist)* 1017
Tarr, Yvonne *(Lyricist)* 1017
Tarrasch, William *(Musical Director)* 1299
Tarrent, Robert T. *(Librettist)* 1134
Tarrytown Music Hall *(Producer)* 2388
Tartaglia, Bob *(Dance Arranger)* 4022
Tartel, Michael *(Cast)* 2674
Tarver, Ben *(Librettist)* 2731
Tarver, Ben *(Lyricist)* 2731
Tarver, Bernard J. *(Cast)* 114
Tashamira *(Cast)* 3861
Tashman, Lilyan *(Cast)* 683, 2900, 4810, 4811
Tatanacho *(Composer)* 1446
Tatch, Eric *(Librettist)* 4565
Tate, Beth *(Cast)* 179

Tate, Charles (*Director*)   1676
Tate, Harry (*Cast*)   2571
Tate, I. (*Composer*)   246
Tate, James W. (*Composer*)   248, 954, 1208, 1588,
  2698, 3827, 3882
Tate, Neal (*Composer*)   3825
Tate, Neal (*Musical Director*)   3599, 3825, 4192
Tate, Neal (*Orchestrations*)   1198, 2173
Tate, Neal (*Vocal Arranger*)   4192
Tate, Robert (*Cast*)   4309
Tatum, Marianne (*Cast*)   305
Taub, Allen (*Lyricist*)   715
Taub, Theodore (*Author*)   3625
Taub, William L. (*Producer*)   1834
Taube, Sven-Bertil (*Cast*)   2047
Tauber, Chaim (*Composer*)   1609
Tauber, Chaim (*Lyricist*)   1609, 2356
Tauber, Doris (*Composer*)   4131
Tauber, Richard (*Cast*)   4792
Taubman, Alfred (*Producer*)   3299
Taupin, Bernie (*Composer*)   3739
Taupin, Bernie (*Lyricist*)   3739
Tavel, Harvey (*Director*)   1304
Taverne, Joost (*Producer*)   1865
Tavor, Edward M. (*Cast*)   1570
Tax, Yan (*Costumes*)   949
Taylor (*Composer*)   432, 830
Taylor (*Lyricist*)   432
Taylor, Alice (*Cast*)   3267
Taylor, Ann (*Cast*)   455
Taylor, Bert Leston (*Librettist*)   1220
Taylor, Bert Leston (*Lyricist*)   1220
Taylor, Billie (*Cast*)   2209, 2232, 2722, 4553, 4655
Taylor, Billie (*Composer*)   246, 830, 2358
Taylor, Billie (*Lyricist*)   830
Taylor, Billy (*Cast*)   1667, 2300
Taylor, Billy (*Composer*)   2300
Taylor, Charles A. (*Librettist*)   3786
Taylor, Charles A. (*Lyricist*)   3786
Taylor, Charles H. (*Lyricist*)   100, 333, 675, 1043,
  2803, 3857, 3976, 4404
Taylor, Charles M. (*Lyricist*)   246
Taylor, Charles W. (*Lyricist*)   2261
Taylor, Charlotte (*Cast*)   4596
Taylor, Chris (*Lyricist*)   4824
Taylor, Clarice (*Cast*)   166, 1592, 2932, 4722
Taylor, Clifton (*Lighting Designer*)   3561
Taylor, Cornelia Osgood (*Librettist*)   4549
Taylor, David (*Librettist*)   3555
Taylor, Deems (*Cast*)   4565
Taylor, Deems (*Composer*)   584, 1151, 2487
Taylor, Deems (*Librettist*)   1151
Taylor, Deems (*Lyricist*)   1151
Taylor, Deems (*Orchestrations*)   2487, 4372
Taylor, Dwight (*Librettist*)   3326
Taylor, Edwin (*Cast*)   1502
Taylor, Elizabeth (*Cast*)   3361, 4625
Taylor, Eva (*Cast*)   500, 3623
Taylor, Evelyn (*Cast*)   85
Taylor, Gina (*Cast*)   338, 2427

Taylor, Henry (*Cast*)   396
Taylor, Henry (*Librettist*)   3683
Taylor, Hiram (*Author*)   2968
Taylor, Hiram (*Composer*)   2968
Taylor, Hiram (*Director*)   2968
Taylor, Hiram (*Lyricist*)   2968
Taylor, Holland (*Cast*)   1249
Taylor, Irving (*Composer*)   1120
Taylor, Irving (*Lyricist*)   447, 524, 839, 1120, 2588,
  3487, 4006
Taylor, James (*Composer*)   4744
Taylor, James (*Lyricist*)   4744
Taylor, James A. (*Set Design*)   679
Taylor, Jane (*Cast*)   2490, 3042, 3069, 4240, 4276
Taylor, Jeannine (*Cast*)   1897, 1955
Taylor, Jeremy (*Composer*)   4579
Taylor, Jeremy (*Lyricist*)   4579
Taylor, Jonathan (*Choreographer*)   1619
Taylor, June (*Cast*)   1799
Taylor, June (*Choreographer*)   190, 2750, 3371
Taylor, June (*Director*)   2750
Taylor, Kenneth (*Composer*)   2239
Taylor, Laura (*Composer*)   4171
Taylor, Laura (*Lyricist*)   4171
Taylor, Laurette (*Cast*)   2855, 3328, 3432
Taylor, Mary K. (*Cast*)   2996
Taylor, Matt (*Librettist*)   971
Taylor, Morris (*Set Design*)   778
Taylor, Nellie (*Cast*)   2788
Taylor, Noel (*Costumes*)   483, 1742, 3188, 4278, 4633
Taylor, Philip (*Director*)   3522
Taylor, Ray (*Composer*)   90
Taylor, Ray (*Lyricist*)   90
Taylor, Raymond (*Composer*)   722
Taylor, Raymond (*Lyricist*)   722
Taylor, Renee (*Cast*)   32
Taylor, Renee (*Librettist*)   2016
Taylor, Robert Lewis (*Author*)   4577
Taylor, Robert U. (*Set Design*)   482, 1249, 1755,
  2579, 3656, 4431
Taylor, Ron (*Cast*)   2544
Taylor, Ronald (*Producer*)   227
Taylor, Rose Mary (*Cast*)   2618
Taylor, Russ (*Composer*)   1412
Taylor, Samuel (*Author*)   1764, 2435
Taylor, Samuel (*Librettist*)   3187
Taylor, Stephen (*Cast*)   2682
Taylor, Telford (*Composer*)   2122
Taylor, Theda (*Lighting Designer*)   1676
Taylor, Todd (*Cast*)   3249
Taylor, Tom (*Cast*)   4410
Taylor, Tom (*Librettist*)   3249, 4410
Taylor, Valerie (*Cast*)   1618
Taylor & Johnson (*Cast*)   26
Taylor-Corbett, Lynne (*Choreographer*)   721, 1149,
  2199, 3306, 3909
Taylor-Corbett, Lynne (*Director*)   3306, 4325
Taymor, Julie (*Choreographer*)   4442
Taymor, Julie (*Costumes*)   1715
Taymor, Julie (*Director*)   4442

Tetley, Glen *(Choreographer)* 1354
Teuber, Max *(Lighting Designer)* 1126
Teuber, Max *(Set Design)* 3002
Tewkesbury, Joan *(Cast)* 3453
Texas, Temple *(Cast)* 1204, 3505
Thacker, Cheryl *(Lighting Designer)* 788, 3162
Thacker, Russ *(Cast)* 1010, 1059, 1662, 1809, 1959, 3018, 4789
Thacker, Russ *(Producer)* 4731
Thaler, Fred *(Dance Arranger)* 3515
Thaler, Fred *(Musical Director)* 3515
Thaler, Fred *(Orchestrations)* 3515
Thaler, Fred *(Vocal Arranger)* 3515
Thalheimer, Norman *(Composer)* 2754
Thalheimer, Norman *(Lyricist)* 2754
Tharp, Twyla *(Choreographer)* 3992
Tharp, Twyla *(Director)* 3992
Tharpe, Sister Rosetta *(Cast)* 888
Thatcher, Heather *(Cast)* 334, 3569
Thatcher, Torin *(Cast)* 1294
Thawl, Evelyn *(Cast)* 3955
Thayer, Bert *(Cast)* 2675
Thayer, Edith *(Cast)* 37
Thayer, Pat *(Composer)* 702, 792, 2789, 2843
Theard, Sam *(Composer)* 1296, 3840
Theard, Sam *(Lyricist)* 1296, 3840
Theater Opera Music Inst. *(Producer)* 871
Theater-in-Limbo *(Producer)* 3606
Theatre 1972 *(Producer)* 1093, 1662
Theatre Atlanta *(Producer)* 3684
Theatre Collective *(Producer)* 99
Theatre Corp. of America *(Producer)* 3234
Theatre Guild, The *(Producer)* 85, 183, 363, 660, 989, 1446, 1447, 1448, 2144, 2487, 3020, 3263, 3365, 3541, 4146, 4516
Theatre Now *(Producer)* 482, 786
Theatre Projects *(Producer)* 2047
Theatre Royal Drury Lane *(Producer)* 972, 4207
Theatre Workshop *(Producer)* 874, 2572
Theatreworks USA *(Producer)* 2197
Theatrical Art Studios *(Set Design)* 3069
Theatrical Operating Co. *(Producer)* 1964
Thebaud, Estelle *(Cast)* 909
Theise, Mortimer M. *(Librettist)* 1409
Theise, Mortimer M. *(Producer)* 2694
Theodore, Donna *(Cast)* 962, 3928
Theodore, Laura *(Cast)* 338
Theodore, Lee *(Cast)* 3286, 4312
Theodore, Lee *(Choreographer)* 170, 270, 974, 989, 1310, 1648, 1769, 3196, 3286, 3389, 3577
Theodore, Lee *(Director)* 997, 3196, 3498, 4660, 4710
Theodore, Ralph *(Cast)* 1749
Thery, Jacques *(Author)* 2669
Thesiger, Ernest *(Cast)* 792, 4154
Thesiger, Ernest *(Director)* 4154
Theyard, Harry *(Cast)* 3612
Thiele, Bob *(Lyricist)* 4091
Thigpen, Lynne *(Cast)* 593, 3159, 4390, 4744
Thimar, David *(Choreographer)* 3108
Thimar, David *(Director)* 817, 3380, 3524

Thomas *(Composer)* 77
Thomas *(Lyricist)* 77, 560
Thomas, A.E. *(Author)* 1391, 2277, 2691
Thomas, A.E. *(Librettist)* 2495, 2532, 3323
Thomas, A.E. *(Lyricist)* 2495, 2532
Thomas, Augustus *(Author)* 2602
Thomas, Augustus *(Librettist)* 688
Thomas, Beverly Jane *(Costumes)* 2027
Thomas, Brandon *(Author)* 4652
Thomas, Danny *(Cast)* 928
Thomas, Dave *(Cast)* 3347
Thomas, Edward *(Arrangements)* 4278
Thomas, Edward *(Composer)* 278, 2777, 3018
Thomas, Edward *(Producer)* 278
Thomas, Freyda-Ann *(Cast)* 164
Thomas, Frozine *(Cast)* 1425
Thomas, George W. *(Composer)* 478, 3297
Thomas, George W. *(Lyricist)* 478, 3297
Thomas, Henry *(Director)* 4299
Thomas, Hilda *(Cast)* 3952
Thomas, Hugh *(Cast)* 1245
Thomas, Hugh *(Librettist)* 2680
Thomas, James *(Cast)* 676
Thomas, John Byron *(Cast)* 1304
Thomas, John Charles *(Cast)* 17, 93, 168, 1681, 1852, 2614, 3396, 3399, 3424, 4133, 4148
Thomas, Joseph *(Costumes)* 4343
Thomas, Joyce Carol *(Author)* 10
Thomas, Lewis T. *(Composer)* 4751
Thomas, Lewis T. *(Lyricist)* 4751
Thomas, Maceo *(Cast)* 4730
Thomas, Margaret Ward *(Cast)* 4183
Thomas, Marie *(Cast)* 1072
Thomas, Marlo *(Cast)* 928, 1389
Thomas, Martha *(Cast)* 444
Thomas, Maude *(Cast)* 4563
Thomas, Millard *(Lyricist)* 567
Thomas, Milton *(Composer)* 243
Thomas, Olive *(Cast)* 4809
Thomas, Paul *(Cast)* 1347
Thomas, Philip Michael *(Cast)* 3690
Thomas, Queenie *(Cast)* 704
Thomas, Rhys *(Cast)* 727, 1030, 4242
Thomas, Richard *(Cast)* 404
Thomas, Ross *(Lyricist)* 3410
Thomas, Rudolph *(Musical Director)* 689
Thomas, Tasha *(Vocal Arranger)* 2173
Thomas, Trina *(Cast)* 4645
Thomas, William *(Lighting Designer)* 2397
Thomas, Wynn P. *(Set Design)* 2239
Thomas II, T. Gaillard *(Cast)* 870
Thomas II, T. Gaillard *(Director)* 130, 870
Thomas II, T. Gaillard *(Librettist)* 130, 870
Thomas Jr., Augustus *(Librettist)* 2620
Thomas Jr., William *(Cast)* 2360
Thomas Sisters *(Cast)* 3388
Thomashefsky, Boris *(Cast)* 3995
Thomashefsky, Boris *(Librettist)* 3995
Thomashefsky, Boris *(Lyricist)* 1609
Thomashefsky, Harry *(Librettist)* 3995

Thomashefsky, Harry *(Producer)* 3995
Thomason, Brian *(Set Design)* 2006
Thome, David *(Cast)* 1103
Thompson, A.M. *(Librettist)* 246, 954, 4404
Thompson, Aaron *(Dance Arranger)* 1876
Thompson, Aaron *(Orchestrations)* 1876
Thompson, Aaron *(Vocal Arranger)* 1876
Thompson, Alexander M. *(Librettist)* 178
Thompson, Alfred *(Costumes)* 3360, 3887
Thompson, Alfred *(Set Design)* 3887
Thompson, Allistair *(Composer)* 4153
Thompson, Allistair *(Lyricist)* 4153
Thompson, Blanche *(Cast)* 554, 987, 1479
Thompson, Charlotte *(Author)* 2264
Thompson, Donald V. *(Producer)* 3724
Thompson, Elsie *(Composer)* 924
Thompson, Evan *(Cast)* 775, 3802, 4444
Thompson, Evan *(Director)* 3802, 4444
Thompson, Evan *(Lyricist)* 3802
Thompson, Frank *(Costumes)* 369, 943, 1017, 1380,
  2595, 2775, 4689, 4863
Thompson, Fred *(Author)* 1539
Thompson, Fred *(Director)* 1336
Thompson, Fred *(Librettist)* 25, 1153, 1297, 1336,
  1419, 1577, 1610, 1859, 2376, 2379, 2757, 3467,
  3719, 4087, 4300, 4392, 4418, 4419, 4575
Thompson, Fred *(Lyricist)* 4443
Thompson, Frederick *(Librettist)* 1626
Thompson, Frederick W. *(Producer)* 1566, 4046, 4753
Thompson, Hal *(Cast)* 4021, 4235
Thompson, Harlan *(Author)* 1814
Thompson, Harlan *(Director)* 2833
Thompson, Harlan *(Librettist)* 1814, 2516, 2833,
  3042, 4476
Thompson, Harlan *(Lyricist)* 1814, 2516, 2833,
  3042, 4476
Thompson, Helen *(Cast)* 3005
Thompson, Hilda *(Cast)* 1499
Thompson, Jack *(Cast)* 834, 1272
Thompson, James *(Lyricist)* 3450
Thompson, Jay *(Composer)* 1023, 1081, 1408, 2482,
  2804, 3615, 3788, 4388
Thompson, Jay *(Dance Arranger)* 2590
Thompson, Jay *(Librettist)* 1081, 3288, 3788
Thompson, Jay *(Lyricist)* 1023, 1081, 1408, 2804,
  3615, 3788
Thompson, Jay *(Musical Director)* 1081
Thompson, Jay *(Orchestrations)* 1081
Thompson, Jeffrey V. *(Cast)* 4534
Thompson, Jeffrey V. *(Librettist)* 4534
Thompson, John *(Set Design)* 2326, 2543
Thompson, John A. *(Set Design)* 1627
Thompson, Julian F. *(Author)* 601
Thompson, Kay *(Composer)* 1760
Thompson, Kay *(Lyricist)* 1760
Thompson, Kay *(Vocal Arranger)* 1973
Thompson, Keith *(Musical Director)* 778, 4731
Thompson, Keith *(Orchestrations)* 778
Thompson, L.S. *(Composer)* 306, 3951
Thompson, Lewis S. *(Composer)* 306, 4103

Thompson, Lottie *(Cast)* 4088
Thompson, Madame *(Costumes)* 4704
Thompson, Mary *(Cast)* 2521
Thompson, Maudie *(Cast)* 571
Thompson, May *(Cast)* 4784
Thompson, Myrtle *(Cast)* 4756
Thompson, Neil *(Cast)* 2521
Thompson, Paul *(Choreographer)* 99
Thompson, Randall *(Composer)* 266, 1654
Thompson, Randall *(Orchestrations)* 1654
Thompson, Rosewell G. *(Cast)* 4507
Thompson, Rosewell G. *(Librettist)* 4507
Thompson, Sada *(Cast)* 2268, 4474
Thompson, Tazewell *(Director)* 10
Thompson, Tommy *(Cast)* 1037
Thompson, Toni Nanette *(Costumes)* 2488
Thompson, U.S. *(Cast)* 3513
Thompson, Virgil *(Composer)* 1366
Thompson, Vivian *(Composer)* 914
Thompson, Vivian *(Lyricist)* 914
Thompson, W. *(Composer)* 4193
Thompson, W. *(Lyricist)* 4193
Thompson, Woodman *(Costumes)* 1283
Thompson, Woodman *(Set Design)* 799, 1020,
  1027, 1283, 4565
Thomson, Brian *(Set Design)* 3742
Thomson, Carolyn *(Cast)* 4539
Thomson, Henry *(Cast)* 4520
Thomson, Herbert *(Lyricist)* 3996
Thorburn, Don *(Composer)* 924
Thorburn, Don *(Lyricist)* 924
Thorne, Eric *(Cast)* 3213
Thorne, Francis *(Composer)* 1354
Thorne, Raymond *(Cast)* 150, 154, 155, 2731, 4297
Thornhill, Alan *(Librettist)* 1887
Thornhill, Alan *(Lyricist)* 1887
Thornhill, Chester *(Cast)* 3802, 4444
Thornton, Arthur *(Cast)* 3982
Thornton, Clarke *(Lighting Designer)* 4172
Thornton, Clarke W. *(Lighting Designer)* 10,
  1638, 3181
Thornton, Evans *(Cast)* 2615
Thornton, James *(Cast)* 3153
Thornton, Jim *(Cast)* 3968
Thornton, Sandra *(Cast)* 1249, 1498
Thrall, Bernie *(Orchestrations)* 1834
Thrasher, Ethelyn R. *(Producer)* 413
Thrasher, H.E. *(Lighting Designer)* 1435
Thrasher, H.E. *(Set Design)* 1435
Three Berry Brothers *(Cast)* 897
Three Eddies, The *(Cast)* 2366
3 Knights, Ltd. *(Producer)* 721
350 Soldiers *(Cast)* 4770
Three Midnight Steppers *(Cast)* 1980
Three Poms, The *(Cast)* 467
Three Sailors *(Cast)* 1126
Three Stooges, The *(Cast)* 1494
3W Productions *(Producer)* 2017, 2188
Thress, Frances *(Cast)* 3314
Thripp, George B. *(Cast)* 1549

Toussaint, Allen (*Lyricist*)   1890, 4127
Toussaint, Allen (*Musical Director*)   1890
Toussaint, Allen (*Orchestrations*)   1890
Tovar, Candice (*Cast*)   3517
Tovatt, Ellen (*Cast*)   2607
Towb, Harry (*Cast*)   299
Towers, Constance (*Cast*)   63, 161, 181, 1119
Towers, Leo (*Composer*)   3820
Towers, Leo (*Lyricist*)   3820
Towle, George P. (*Musical Director*)   1021
Town Hall (*Producer*)   3802
Townly, Barry (*Producer*)   3580
Townsend, "Babe" (*Librettist*)   4183
Townsend, "Babe" (*Lyricist*)   4183
Townsend, E.W. (*Author*)   2795
Townsend, Florence (*Cast*)   1469
Townsend, Margaret (*Cast*)   236, 3093, 4113
Townsend, William "Babe" (*Cast*)   1906
Townshend, Peter (*Author*)   4676
Townshend, Peter (*Composer*)   3739, 4676
Townshend, Peter (*Librettist*)   4676
Townshend, Peter (*Lyricist*)   3739, 4676
Toy, Christine (*Cast*)   275, 3239
Toy, Malcolm (*Cast*)   382
Toye, Wendy (*Choreographer*)   129, 453, 4009
Toye, Wendy (*Director*)   129, 453
Tozere, Frederic (*Cast*)   1871
Trabert, George (*Cast*)   1384, 1710, 2519
Tracey, Andrew (*Cast*)   4579
Tracey, Andrew (*Musical Director*)   4579
Tracey, Paul (*Cast*)   4579
Tracey, William (*Composer*)   3989
Tracey, William (*Lyricist*)   1531, 3958, 3989, 4804, 4840
Tracy, Arthur (*Cast*)   1395, 3153
Tracy, Cora (*Cast*)   3765
Tracy, George Lowell (*Composer*)   1213
Tracy, George Lowell (*Musical Director*)   761, 1274, 2543
Tracy, Teresa (*Cast*)   2420
Tracy, William (*Librettist*)   1987
Traditional (*Composer*)   39, 114, 143, 166, 306, 466, 642, 662, 887, 906, 964, 979, 1073, 1609, 1713, 1736, 1897, 2180, 2200, 2203, 2356, 2388, 2415, 2464, 2805, 3018, 3020, 3261, 3450, 3598, 3631, 3704, 3739, 3793, 3836, 3840, 3949, 3987, 4111, 4342, 4390, 4438, 4460, 4479, 4534
Traditional (*Lyricist*)   39, 114, 143, 166, 466, 642, 662, 887, 906, 964, 1073, 1609, 1713, 1736, 1897, 2180, 2200, 2203, 2356, 2388, 2415, 2464, 2805, 3018, 3020, 3261, 3631, 3793, 3836, 3840, 3949, 3987, 4111, 4342, 4390, 4438, 4460, 4534
Traditional (*Music Based On*)   422
Trahan, Al (*Cast*)   3861
Trainor, William (*Cast*)   3357
Tramp Band, The (*Cast*)   884
Tramutola, Franklin C. (*Librettist*)   1604
Trantman, Edward (*Musical Director*)   222
Trapp, Maria Augusta (*Author*)   4095
Trappert, Harry (*Composer*)   1459

Traube, Shepard (*Director*)   1548
Traube, Shepard (*Producer*)   1548
Traubel, Helen (*Cast*)   3505
Traver, John (*Lyricist*)   3535
Traver, Sharry (*Cast*)   283
Travers, Alma (*Cast*)   2640
Travers, Ben (*Author*)   3216
Travers, Jean (*Cast*)   3365
Travis, J. Michael (*Costumes*)   820, 1766
Travis, Michael (*Costumes*)   2016, 3543
Travizo, Mary (*Cast*)   2968
Travolta, John (*Cast*)   3330
Traxler, Mark (*Cast*)   3601
Traylor, Gene (*Librettist*)   2100
Traylor, Gene (*Lyricist*)   2100
Traynor, Blair (*Lyricist*)   545
Treacher, Arthur (*Cast*)   1113, 2669, 3359, 3371, 3467, 4235, 4730, 4826
Treadwell, Tom (*Cast*)   4136
Treas, Terri (*Cast*)   3299
Trebitsch, Paul M. (*Producer*)   398, 3069
Trednick, H.W. (*Cast*)   3228
Tree, Dolly (*Costumes*)   611, 2140
Tree, Lady (*Cast*)   2788
Trelfall, David (*Cast*)   2474
Tremaine, Bobby (*Cast*)   3168
Trenet, Charles (*Lyricist*)   1834
Trenholme, Helen (*Cast*)   814
Trenk, William (*Director*)   3046
Trenk, William (*Producer*)   3046
Trenkler, Freddie (*Cast*)   1941
Trent, Ivy (*Costumes*)   2650
Trent, Jackie (*Composer*)   4193
Trent, Jackie (*Lyricist*)   4193
Trent, Jo (*Composer*)   1960, 1983
Trent, Jo (*Librettist*)   1983
Trent, Jo (*Lyricist*)   124, 500, 587, 741, 1134, 1281, 1411, 1960, 1983, 3297, 3660, 3808, 4198, 4766
Trentini, Emma (*Cast*)   1285, 3081, 3424
Tresmand, Ivy (*Cast*)   2547, 4795
Tressler, I. (*Lyricist*)   4387
Trevelyan, Arthur (*Composer*)   4130
Trevillion, Florence (*Cast*)   574
Trevor, Austin (*Cast*)   3214
Trevor, Huntley (*Composer*)   605, 3755, 4206
Trevor, Huntley (*Lyricist*)   605, 3755, 4206
Treyz, Russell (*Director*)   900
Treyz, Russell (*Librettist*)   900
Triaco, Joseph (*Producer*)   1695
Tribble, Andrew (*Cast*)   739, 1909, 2721, 3241
Tribble, Bessie (*Cast*)   646
Tribune, Dean (*Cast*)   2571
Trigg, Helen M. (*Composer*)   4735
Trikonis, Gus (*Cast*)   269
Trinder, Marsia (*Costumes*)   2728
Trini (*Cast*)   200, 969, 4271, 4730
Trinity Square Repertory (*Producer*)   35
Trinkaus, George (*Musical Director*)   4269
Triplett, Sally Ann (*Cast*)   661
Tripolino, Joseph (*Cast*)   3654

Turnbull, Laura *(Cast)* 1279
Turnbull Jr., William J. *(Lighting Designer)* 528
Turner *(Composer)* 2754
Turner *(Lyricist)* 2754
Turner, Elma *(Cast)* 3709
Turner, Elmer *(Cast)* 877, 3709
Turner, Glenn *(Cast)* 1296
Turner, Holly *(Cast)* 1471
Turner, Janet *(Cast)* 1757
Turner, Jayne *(Cast)* 649, 1329
Turner, Jim *(Composer)* 459
Turner, John *(Composer)* 4264
Turner, John *(Lyricist)* 4264
Turner, John Hastings *(Librettist)* 1338, 2392, 2788, 4581
Turner, Kay *(Costumes)* 4637
Turner, Lenny *(Cast)* 2521
Turner, Lily *(Producer)* 3215
Turner, Maidel *(Cast)* 831
Turner, Richard *(Librettist)* 2272
Turner, Roland *(Set Design)* 2110
Turner, Susan *(Librettist)* 2272
Turoff, Robert *(Director)* 1474, 2664
Turoff, Robert Ennis *(Librettist)* 1837
Turque, Mimi *(Cast)* 2727, 3612
Turrin, Joseph *(Composer)* 1382
Turturice, Robert *(Costumes)* 556
Tuschl, Karl *(Librettist)* 1043
Tuschl, Karl *(Lyricist)* 1043
Tushar, James *(Cast)* 72
Tuskegee Institute Choir *(Cast)* 3639
Tuthill, Bob *(Composer)* 1282
Tutt, J. Homer *(Cast)* 291, 449, 731, 816, 980, 987, 1019, 1028, 1479, 1514, 2013, 2791, 2792, 3040, 3062, 3200, 3241, 4520, 4751
Tutt, J. Homer *(Composer)* 449, 987, 1479, 1906, 2013, 2791, 2792, 3040, 3241, 4520
Tutt, J. Homer *(Director)* 1514, 2013
Tutt, J. Homer *(Librettist)* 291, 449, 731, 816, 980, 987, 1019, 1479, 1514, 1906, 2013, 2791, 2792, 3040, 3062, 3200, 3241, 4520, 4751
Tutt, J. Homer *(Lyricist)* 449, 816, 980, 987, 1019, 1479, 1906, 2013, 2791, 2792, 3040, 3062, 3241, 3958, 4520, 4751
Tutt, J. Homer *(Producer)* 291, 731, 816, 980, 1479, 1514, 1906, 2013, 3040, 3062, 3200, 4520, 4751
Tuttle, Howard *(Set Design)* 1801
Tuvim, Abe *(Additional Lyrics)* 27
Tuvim, Abe *(Lyricist)* 2736
Twain, Mark *(Author)* 170, 394, 834, 1086, 2027, 2028, 2029, 2030, 2556, 3571, 4409
Twain, Mark *(Librettist)* 2029
Twain, Norman *(Producer)* 269, 1846, 2568
Tweebeke, Reiner *(Lighting Designer)* 949
Twiggy *(Cast)* 3060
Twine, Linda *(Conductor)* 789
Twine, Linda *(Musical Director)* 394, 789, 2200
Twine, Linda *(Vocal Arranger)* 394
Two Arts Playhouse *(Producer)* 4431
Twomey, John *(Cast)* 1769
Twomey, Kay *(Lyricist)* 1539

Twomey, Neil *(Director)* 3434
Ty Bell Sisters, The *(Cast)* 4753
Tyers, John *(Cast)* 72, 2137, 4479
Tyers, William H. *(Composer)* 295
Tygett, Nanon *(Choreographer)* 1940
Tyler, Bernice *(Cast)* 3647
Tyler, Beverly *(Cast)* 1284, 2234
Tyler, Cornelia *(Librettist)* 1518
Tyler, Cornelia *(Lyricist)* 1518
Tyler, Ed *(Composer)* 4243
Tyler, Ed *(Lyricist)* 4243
Tyler, Edward Lee *(Cast)* 653
Tyler, George C. *(Producer)* 3328
Tyler, Jeanne *(Cast)* 4174
Tyler, Jim *(Orchestrations)* 534, 681, 1146, 1441, 1699, 1721, 1955, 1970, 2208, 2360, 2551, 3231, 3330, 3743, 4297
Tyler, Jim *(Vocal Arranger)* 2728
Tyler, Judy *(Cast)* 3505
Tyler, Marie *(Cast)* 4113
Tyler, Royall *(Author)* 840
Tyler, Steve *(Incidental Music)* 2185
Tyler, Steve *(Musical Director)* 2185
Tyler, Steve *(Vocal Arranger)* 2185
Tynan, Kenneth *(Librettist)* 3233
Tynan, Nicholas J. *(Cast)* 4507
Tyne, George *(Cast)* 4369
Tyrell, Pha *(Cast)* 890
Tyrrel, Henry *(Lyricist)* 1675
Tyrrell, Tara *(Cast)* 198
Tyson, Grace *(Cast)* 2710, 2869, 4804
Tzigane Orchestra *(Cast)* 125

U

U.S. 8th Air Force *(Producer)* 4009
U.S. Ambulance Service *(Producer)* 1632
U.S. Army *(Producer)* 4141
U.S. Army Air Forces *(Producer)* 4706
U.S. Coast Guard *(Producer)* 4287
U.S. Dept. of Agriculture *(Producer)* 2175
Uart, Lottie *(Cast)* 4382
Udall, Lyn *(Composer)* 1038
Udell, Chas. W. *(Cast)* 2642
Udell, Peter *(Librettist)* 105, 135, 828, 3610, 3928
Udell, Peter *(Lyricist)* 105, 135, 828, 3610, 3928
Uffer, Charles *(Cast)* 782
Uggams, Eloise *(Cast)* 441, 444, 3704
Uggams, Leslie *(Cast)* 478, 1729, 1848, 2208
Uhl, Constance *(Composer)* 2363
Uhr, Ira *(Cast)* 1357
Uhry, Alfred *(Librettist)* 112, 693, 3733
Uhry, Alfred *(Lyricist)* 112, 693, 1864, 3733, 4252
Uke, Paul *(Cast)* 23
Ukena, Paul *(Cast)* 4523
Ukena, Paul *(Musical Director)* 23
Ukena Jr., Paul *(Cast)* 4695
Ullett, Nick *(Cast)* 2798

V

Valdo, Pat *(Director)* 3715
Vale, Michael *(Cast)* 1406
Valency, Maurice *(Librettist)* 3694
Valency, Maurice *(Lyricist)* 961, 3694
Valente, Richard *(Composer)* 1069
Valente, Richard *(Librettist)* 1069
Valente, Richard *(Lyricist)* 1069
Valenti, Michael *(Cast)* 4789
Valenti, Michael *(Composer)* 461, 1970, 2278, 2633, 2674, 3231
Valenti, Michael *(Librettist)* 2674
Valenti, Michael *(Lyricist)* 2278, 2633
Valenti, Michael *(Orchestrations)* 2633
Valenti, Michael *(Vocal Arranger)* 2633
Valentina *(Costumes)* 818, 1891
Valentine, Arthur *(Lyricist)* 2698
Valentine, C. Walsh *(Set Design)* 1640
Valentine, C.W. *(Set Design)* 1459
Valentine, Eric *(Lyricist)* 1780
Valentine, Grace *(Cast)* 1749
Valentine, James *(Cast)* 2020
Valentine, P.H. *(Lyricist)* 1208
Valentine, Paul *(Cast)* 1918, 3234, 4718
Valentine, S.B. *(Librettist)* 4047
Valentine, William *(Cast)* 1733
Valentini, Vincent *(Composer)* 3388
Valentini, Vincent *(Director)* 3388
Valentini, Vincent *(Librettist)* 3388
Valentini, Vincent *(Lyricist)* 3388
Valentinoff, Valia *(Cast)* 4569
Valerie & Jenna *(Cast)* 2087
Valerio, Frederico *(Composer)* 1918
Valery, Dana *(Cast)* 4579
Vall, Seymour *(Producer)* 13, 461, 2016, 2018, 2278
Valle, Ernie *(Musical Director)* 3069
Vallee, Rudy *(Cast)* 1492, 1493, 1744, 1949, 1950, 2019, 2406, 3153
Vallee and His Orchestra, Rudy *(Cast)* 1396
Vallely, Helen *(Cast)* 1907
Valli Valli *(Cast)* 804, 1067, 2341, 2385, 2897, 3529, 3613, 3627, 4554
Vallon, Una *(Cast)* 3002
Valor, Henrietta *(Cast)* 426, 1249, 3195
Valori, Bice *(Cast)* 3798
Valsy, Lucette *(Cast)* 672
Valverde, Joaquin *(Composer)* 60, 2407
Van, Billy B. *(Cast)* 21, 201, 1460, 1784, 2209, 2534, 3417, 3604, 3652, 4213, 4637
Van, Billy B. *(Composer)* 2644
Van, Billy B. *(Lyricist)* 2644
Van, Bobby *(Cast)* 59, 1063, 3683
Van, Gus *(Cast)* 683, 959, 2900, 3144, 3264, 4428, 4813, 4814
Van, Gus *(Composer)* 3144, 4813, 4814, 4842
Van, Gus *(Lyricist)* 4813, 4814, 4842
Van, Kitty *(Cast)* 3158
Van, Sammy *(Cast)* 691
Van, Willa *(Costumes)* 2077, 2162
Van Aken, Gretchen *(Cast)* 4588
Van Alstyne, Egbert *(Composer)* 349, 561, 954, 1026, 1247,

1566, 1626, 1629, 1806, 2025, 2232, 2274, 2889, 2892, 3073, 3085, 3205, 3268, 3332, 3400, 3675, 3996, 4840
Van Antwerp, John *(Librettist)* 1286, 1546, 3082
Van Antwerp, John *(Producer)* 1286, 1546
Van Antwerp, Ted *(Producer)* 556
Van Biene, Eileen *(Cast)* 2056
Van Bridge, Tony *(Cast)* 3066
Van Buren, A.H. *(Director)* 2351, 4050
Van Cleave, Carroll *(Cast)* 2573
Van Cleve *(Orchestrations)* 1336
Van Cleve, N. Lang *(Orchestrations)* 2597
Van Cleve, Nathan *(Orchestrations)* 612
Van Dame, Corinne *(Costumes)* 4416
Van Den Ende, Joop *(Producer)* 949
van der Horst, Ellen *(Costumes)* 1865
van der Wurff, Erik *(Composer)* 1865
van der Wurff, Erik *(Musical Director)* 1865
Van Dijk, Ad *(Composer)* 949
Van Dijk, Bill *(Cast)* 949
Van Dijk, Koen *(Librettist)* 949
Van Dijk, Koen *(Lyricist)* 949
Van Dresser, Marcia *(Cast)* 4559
van Druten, John *(Author)* 610, 2064
van Druten, John *(Director)* 2312
von Seyffertitz, Gustave *(Cast)* 4187
von Seyffertitz, Gustave *(Director)* 2528
von Tilzer, Albert *(Composer)* 1038, 4026
Van Dyke, Dick *(Cast)* 607, 1040, 1567, 2072
Van Dyke, Leroy *(Composer)* 4197
Van Dyke, Leroy *(Lyricist)* 4197
Van Dyke, Marcia *(Cast)* 4446
van Eeden, Ron *(Producer)* 1865
Van Epps, Fred *(Orchestrations)* 341, 4586
Van Epps, Jack *(Cast)* 1573
Van Every, Dale *(Author)* 647
Van Fleet, Jo *(Cast)* 1815
Van Fossen, Harry *(Cast)* 801
Van Goetz, Eyck *(Composer)* 4498
Van Griethuysen, Ted *(Cast)* 3215
Van Griethuysen, Ted *(Costumes)* 937
Van Grona, Eugene *(Choreographer)* 447, 1275, 2444
Van Grove, Isaac *(Arrangements)* 4149
Van Grove, Isaac *(Musical Director)* 3647
Van Grove, Isaac *(Orchestrations)* 1299
Van Heusen, James *(Composer)* 879, 2183, 3091, 3100, 3324, 3832, 4255, 4743
Van Heusen, James *(Lyricist)* 879
Van Heusen, Jimmy *(Composer)* 657, 820, 1296, 2443, 3178, 4013, 4256, 4588
Van Heusen, Jimmy *(Lyricist)* 4256
Van Horne, Randy *(Vocal Arranger)* 1326
Van Keyser, William *(Choreographer)* 4244
van Laast, Anthony *(Choreographer)* 1159
van Laast, Anthony *(Director)* 1159
Van Loan, Paul *(Dance Arranger)* 2023, 2024, 2098, 2099
Van Loan, Paul *(Musical Director)* 1941
Van Loan, Paul *(Orchestrations)* 2023, 2024, 2098, 2099, 4143
Van Loan, Paul F. *(Musical Director)* 587

Velez, Lupe *(Cast)*   1979, 4177, 4777

Velie, Janet *(Cast)*   606, 799, 1800, 2328, 2363, 2767, 3245, 3344, 3443, 3783

Velie, Jay *(Cast)*   2, 619, 1643, 2516, 3783, 3900

Velie, Jay *(Composer)*   3783

Veljohnson, Reginald *(Cast)*   1099, 1970, 4127

Velona, Tony *(Composer)*   4193, 4828

Velona, Tony *(Lyricist)*   4193, 4828

Venable, Percy *(Lyricist)*   432

Venable, Sara *(Cast)*   449

Venneri, Darwin *(Composer)*   991

Venneri, Darwin *(Lyricist)*   991

Vennum, Tom *(Composer)*   4041

Venora, Lee *(Cast)*   1766, 2295

Ventre, Frank *(Orchestrations)*   2083

Ventriss, Jennie *(Cast)*   2049

Ventry, Frank *(Composer)*   4006

Ventura, Frank *(Choreographer)*   3181

Venuta, Benay *(Cast)*   601, 868, 1791, 2653, 3091, 3314, 3619

Venuti and His Orcheatra, Joe *(Cast)*   662

Venza, Jac *(Costumes)*   4260

Ver Planck, J. "Billy" *(Orchestrations)*   1099, 1662

Vera, Irene *(Cast)*   284

Vera-Ellen *(Cast)*   601, 4557

Verady *(Costumes)*   423

Verdi, Giuseppe *(Author)*   3035

Verdi, Giuseppe *(Composer)*   1897, 2809, 4579

Verdi, Giuseppe *(Music Based On)*   3035

Verdon, Gwen *(Cast)*   59, 490, 629, 723, 957, 3113, 3687, 4238

Vereen, Ben *(Cast)*   1699, 2212, 3506

Verhoeven, Pauline *(Choreographer)*   1743, 3081

Vermer, James *(Producer)*   2153

Vermont, Ted *(Director)*   3490

Verne, Jules *(Author)*   189, 190, 1161

Verneuil, Louis *(Author)*   495, 2808, 3248

Verneuil, Louis *(Librettist)*   627

Vernon, Charles *(Cast)*   3345

Vernon, Doris *(Cast)*   3045

Vernon, Dorothy *(Cast)*   3674

Vernon, Gilbert *(Cast)*   920

Vernon, H.M. *(Librettist)*   292

Vernon, Michael *(Choreographer)*   1256

Vernon, Nina *(Cast)*   185

Vernon, Olga *(Cast)*   1342

Vernon, Paul *(Cast)*   526

Vernon, Walter *(Cast)*   538, 542

Veronica *(Costumes)*   1840, 4777

Veronica, Betty *(Cast)*   1135

Vertes, Marcel *(Costumes)*   2364, 3899

Vertes, Marcel *(Set Design)*   3899

Verwayen, Percy *(Cast)*   2720

Vessella, Oreste *(Composer)*   3729

Vestoff, Floria *(Cast)*   288

Vestoff, Floria *(Lyricist)*   3810

Vestoff, Virginia *(Cast)*   482, 937, 1233, 1408, 2599, 2731, 2877, 3075, 3897, 4109, 4558

Vetkin, S. *(Composer)*   4176

Vetman, Charlotte M. *(Costumes)*   1630

Vicars, Harold *(Composer)*   1626, 4258

Vicars, Harold *(Lyricist)*   1626, 4258

Vicars, Harold *(Musical Director)*   136, 1538, 1723, 2761, 3658, 3996, 4258

Vici, Berni *(Musical Director)*   2271

Vici & His Symphonic Girls, Count Berni *(Cast)*   2271

Vickers *(Composer)*   627

Vickers, Larry *(Cast)*   3936

Vickers, Larry *(Choreographer)*   4460

Vickery, John *(Cast)*   1015

Vicks, Walker *(Choreographer)*   2306

Victor, Eric *(Cast)*   4782

Victor, Eric *(Choreographer)*   67, 4782

Victor, Lucia *(Director)*   415, 1809, 1816, 4192

Victor, Lucia *(Librettist)*   1816

Video Techniques Inc *(Producer)*   159

Vidnovic, Martin *(Cast)*   253, 808, 1597, 1959, 2470, 3272

Vieha, Mark *(Composer)*   107, 3126

Vieha, Mark *(Lyricist)*   107, 3126

Viele, S.K. *(Costumes)*   452

Viele, S.K. *(Set Design)*   452

Viele, Sheldon K. *(Set Design)*   1357, 2569, 4345

Viera, Sandra *(Cast)*   2611

Viertel, Jack *(Producer)*   992

Viertel, Thomas *(Producer)*   992, 4031, 4076

Vieth, Bradley *(Musical Director)*   158, 4708

Vig, Joel *(Cast)*   3811

Vigal, John *(Cast)*   2302

Vigard, Kristen *(Cast)*   2064

Vigel, Al *(Cast)*   1989

Vigialante, Jeanne *(Cast)*   2658

Viglione, Carolyn *(Cast)*   2027

Vigoda, Bob *(Composer)*   3530

Vilan, Demetrios *(Cast)*   3822

Vilanch, Bruce *(Librettist)*   1159, 1298, 3515

Vilanch, Bruce *(Lyricist)*   1262

Villa-Lobos, Heitor *(Composer)*   2395, 2679

Villani, Paul *(Cast)*   114

Villard, Jean *(Composer)*   4264

Villard, Jean *(Lyricist)*   4264

Villars, Jessie *(Lyricist)*   4094

Villella, Edward *(Cast)*   2556

Villon, Francois *(Composer)*   1736

Vimnera, August *(Set Design)*   1132, 1343, 2330, 3157, 4275

Vinal, Edgar A. *(Composer)*   2455

Vinal, Edgar A. *(Lyricist)*   2455

Vinal, Edgar A. *(Musical Director)*   2455

Vinaver, Chemjo *(Composer)*   2202

Vinaver, Chemjo *(Orchestrations)*   2202

Vinaver, Steven *(Director)*   1056, 2663

Vinaver, Steven *(Librettist)*   1056, 4268

Vinaver, Steven *(Lyricist)*   1056, 2663, 4268

Vinay, Ramon *(Cast)*   4174

Vincent, A.J. *(Cast)*   2654

Vincent, Nat *(Composer)*   1065, 2974, 3770, 3958, 4813

Vincent, Nat *(Lyricist)*   2557, 3402, 4813

Vincent, Nathaniel *(Composer)*   1404

Vincent, Ruth *(Cast)*   3777, 4554

Vincent, Stephen *(Librettist)*   2653

Vorhees, Don *(Musical Director)* 117, 383, 1131, 1132, 4256
Vorhees, Donald *(Musical Director)* 2225, 3172
Vornaholt, John *(Librettist)* 4389
Vos, David *(Composer)* 4062
Vos, David *(Librettist)* 4062
Vos, David *(Lyricist)* 4062
Vos, Richard *(Producer)* 4295
Vosburgh, David *(Cast)* 1068, 3722, 4029
Vosburgh, Dick *(Librettist)* 1000, 2204, 4703
Vosburgh, Dick *(Lyricist)* 392, 1000, 4703
Voskovec, George *(Cast)* 1062
Votos, Christopher *(Cast)* 1060
Vousden, Ernest *(Composer)* 737
Vousden, Ernest *(Lyricist)* 737
Voynow, Dick *(Composer)* 4137
Voytek *(Set Design)* 194
Voznesensky, Andrey *(Librettist)* 2269
Voznesensky, Andrey *(Lyricist)* 2269
Vroom, Lodewick *(Producer)* 3767
Vye, Murvyn *(Cast)* 660

W

WPA *(Producer)* 3495
WPA Federal Theatre *(Producer)* 1871
WPA Theatre *(Producer)* 2038, 2544, 3986
WPA Variety Theatre *(Producer)* 4253
Waara, Scott *(Cast)* 775, 2643, 4619, 4701
Waas, Cinthia *(Costumes)* 2171
Waas & Son *(Costumes)* 4093
Waaser, Carol M. *(Lighting Designer)* 1406
Wachtel, Mussina *(Musical Director)* 2981
Waddell, Geoffrey *(Choreographer)* 945
Waddington, Patrick *(Cast)* 703
Wade, Adam *(Cast)* 4127
Wade, Herman Avery *(Composer)* 1526, 3387, 3693
Wade, Uel *(Arrangements)* 1496
Wade, Uel *(Dance Arranger)* 2598
Wade, Uel *(Musical Director)* 626, 1496, 2598, 3544
Wade, Uel *(Vocal Arranger)* 2598, 3544
Wade, Warren *(Cast)* 4028
Wadsworth, F. Wheeler *(Musical Director)* 4651
Waelder, Fred *(Cast)* 1560
Wager, Michael *(Cast)* 1294, 3439
Waggoner, George *(Lyricist)* 2747, 4291
Wagman, Benny *(Composer)* 2580
Wagner, Brent *(Director)* 4732
Wagner, Charles L. *(Producer)* 2967
Wagner, Chuck *(Cast)* 2143, 4229
Wagner, Daryl *(Cast)* 2436
Wagner, F. *(Composer)* 1538
Wagner, Frank *(Cast)* 2737
Wagner, Frank *(Choreographer)* 107, 272, 382, 427, 1107, 2018, 2052, 3112, 3479, 3889, 4035, 4828
Wagner, Frank *(Director)* 107, 272, 427, 1049, 2737, 3112, 4035
Wagner, Jack *(Cast)* 595

Wagner, John H. *(Librettist)* 2986
Wagner, John H. *(Lyricist)* 1188, 2986
Wagner, Nathaniel *(Cast)* 780, 3056, 3168, 3580
Wagner, Richard *(Composer)* 992
Wagner, Robin *(Librettist)* 3903
Wagner, Robin *(Set Design)* 287, 721, 746, 775, 828, 921, 1103, 1359, 1441, 1717, 2134, 2200, 2212, 2307, 2617, 2659, 2660, 2820, 3279, 3299, 3603, 3636, 3869, 3903, 4067, 4068, 4196, 4252, 4297, 4338, 4560
Wagner, Ruth *(Costumes)* 157
Wagner, Thomas *(Composer)* 3890
Wagoner, Dan *(Choreographer)* 755, 2478, 2579
Wagoner, Dan *(Director)* 2124
Wagstaff, Joe *(Cast)* 1275
Wagstaff, Joseph *(Cast)* 403
Wahl, Walter Dare *(Cast)* 662, 2475
Wahler, David *(Dance Arranger)* 4470
Wailes, Benjamin *(Cast)* 3990
Wain, John *(Lighting Designer)* 2147
Wainer, Lee *(Composer)* 2540, 3105, 3986
Wainer, Lee *(Lyricist)* 875
Wainer, Lee *(Musical Director)* 3105
Wainwright, Bert *(Cast)* 2139
Wainwright, Lee *(Producer)* 1971
Wainwright III, Loudon *(Composer)* 908
Wainwright III, Loudon *(Lyricist)* 908
Waissman, Kenneth *(Producer)* 209, 1164, 1664, 3330
Waite, Bruce *(Cast)* 4205
Waite, Eric *(Cast)* 2077, 2097
Waite, Genevieve *(Cast)* 2728
Waite, Ralph *(Cast)* 477
Waites, Thomas G. *(Cast)* 4295
Waiwaiole, Lloyd K. *(Costumes)* 3463
Wakefield, Ann *(Cast)* 507
Wakefield, Frank L. *(Librettist)* 1824
Wakefield, Oliver *(Cast)* 4824
Wakula, Frank *(Set Design)* 4611
Walberg, Betty *(Dance Arranger)* 162, 1265, 1709, 2163, 2304, 3274, 4625
Walberg, Paul *(Musical Director)* 2084, 2095, 2096
Walberg, Paul *(Orchestrations)* 2084, 2096
Walburn, Raymond *(Cast)* 1422, 4299, 4352
Walcott, Derek *(Director)* 4147
Walcott, Derek *(Librettist)* 4147
Walcott, Derek *(Lyricist)* 4147
Walden, Robert *(Composer)* 2250
Walden, Stanley *(Composer)* 259
Walden, Stanley *(Musical Director)* 259, 1977
Walden, Stanley *(Orchestrations)* 1977
Walden, Stanley *(Vocal Arranger)* 259
Walden, Walter *(Set Design)* 4253
Waldman, Robert *(Composer)* 112, 693, 1864, 3733, 4252
Waldman, Robert *(Dance Arranger)* 3733
Waldman, Robert *(Vocal Arranger)* 3733
Waldock, Dennis *(Librettist)* 4153
Waldon, James T. *(Lyricist)* 3673
Waldron, Jack *(Author)* 4629
Waldron, Jack *(Cast)* 3351, 4542
Waldron, James A. *(Librettist)* 938

Waldrop, Mark *(Cast)*   2968

Waldrop, Mark *(Librettist)*   2022

Waldrop, Mark *(Lyricist)*   2022

Waldrop, Uda *(Composer)*   3921

Waldteufel, Emile *(Composer)*   2772

Waliter, William *(Composer)*   4583

Walke, Gillian *(Cast)*   1412

Walken, Christopher *(Cast)*   270

Walker, Aida Overton *(Cast)*   9, 295, 633, 1909, 2111, 4088

Walker, Aida Overton *(Choreographer)*   9, 295

Walker, Anna *(Choreographer)*   2560

Walker, Bert *(Vocal Arranger)*   2150

Walker, Berta *(Producer)*   3711

Walker, Bill *(Costumes)*   951, 3198, 4109, 4175, 4601

Walker, Billy B. *(Lighting Designer)*   1146, 3126

Walker, Charlotte *(Cast)*   2904

Walker, Chinese *(Cast)*   1821

Walker, Chris *(Arrangements)*   4067

Walker, Chris *(Dance Arranger)*   2798

Walker, Chris *(Orchestrations)*   2798

Walker, Cindy *(Composer)*   4030

Walker, Cindy *(Lyricist)*   4030

Walker, Dan *(Cast)*   1654

Walker, Dan *(Composer)*   1653

Walker, Dan *(Lyricist)*   1652, 1653

Walker, David *(Composer)*   1873

Walker, Dianne *(Cast)*   432

Walker, Don *(Composer)*   84, 454, 911, 2817, 2910

Walker, Don *(Dance Arranger)*   454, 563

Walker, Don *(Music Adaptation)*   1548

Walker, Don *(Musical Director)*   3138

Walker, Don *(Orchestrations)*   84, 135, 145, 161, 162, 180, 216, 270, 273, 323, 372, 454, 512, 596, 601, 610, 619, 649, 657, 660, 680, 901, 911, 943, 957, 1112, 1140, 1265, 1278, 1290, 1310, 1352, 1456, 1475, 1494, 1507, 1548, 1679, 1698, 1764, 1791, 1841, 1848, 1860, 1879, 1918, 1931, 1973, 2432, 2453, 2475, 2539, 2550, 2582, 2590, 2680, 2786, 2797, 2817, 2894, 2961, 3016, 3064, 3278, 3351, 3359, 3390, 3536, 3780, 3900, 3918, 3928, 3972, 4058, 4142, 4214, 4365, 4384, 4423, 4483, 4499, 4516, 4524, 4586, 4633, 4702, 4718, 4734, 4777, 4825, 4826, 4862

Walker, Don *(Vocal Arranger)*   84, 145, 911, 1848, 2797, 3138

Walker, Douglas *(Cast)*   2305

Walker, Edward *(Musical Director)*   349

Walker, George *(Cast)*   1599, 4088

Walker, George *(Composer)*   3820

Walker, George *(Librettist)*   4088

Walker, George *(Lyricist)*   2111, 3820, 4390

Walker, George *(Producer)*   4088

Walker, George W. *(Cast)*   9, 295, 2111

Walker, Hughie *(Composer)*   1876

Walker, Hughie *(Lyricist)*   1876

Walker, James J. *(Lyricist)*   1118, 1897, 3849

Walker, Jerry Jeff *(Composer)*   964

Walker, Jerry Jeff *(Lyricist)*   964

Walker, John *(Librettist)*   3169

Walker, Joseph A. *(Cast)*   344

Walker, Joseph A. *(Librettist)*   344

Walker, Joseph A. *(Set Design)*   344

Walker, June *(Cast)*   1546, 1567, 3048

Walker, Kary M. *(Producer)*   1701

Walker, Mabel *(Cast)*   4254

Walker, Margaret *(Cast)*   3003, 3655

Walker, Marshall *(Composer)*   4840

Walker, Mildred *(Cast)*   165

Walker, Nancy *(Cast)*   95, 304, 372, 868, 1061, 1567, 2582, 2940, 3278, 3473

Walker, Natalie *(Costumes)*   2759

Walker, Peter *(Cast)*   3059

Walker, Peter *(Lyricist)*   1776

Walker, Phil *(Musical Director)*   1562

Walker, Polly *(Cast)*   403, 1836, 2829, 3179

Walker, Ray *(Composer)*   3989

Walker, Ray *(Lyricist)*   3989

Walker, Raymond *(Composer)*   965, 1531, 4195

Walker, Sid *(Librettist)*   3933

Walker, Suzanne *(Cast)*   2231

Walker, Sydney *(Cast)*   461

Walker, Tippy *(Cast)*   635

Walker, W. Raymond *(Composer)*   4806

Walker, William *(Composer)*   703

Walker and Thompson *(Cast)*   2271

Wall, Bill *(Cast)*   2092

Wall, Harry *(Librettist)*   4335

Wall, Max *(Cast)*   1137, 3291

Wall, Phil *(Orchestrations)*   4256, 4569

Wall, Phil *(Pianist)*   1494

Wallace, Art *(Cast)*   2248, 3209

Wallace, Ben *(Costumes)*   4265

Wallace, Beryl *(Cast)*   1127, 1136, 1137, 1138, 3002, 4443

Wallace, Chester *(Lyricist)*   4153

Wallace, Edgar *(Author)*   4207

Wallace, Edgar *(Librettist)*   3500, 3649

Wallace, Edna *(Cast)*   1165

Wallace, Emmett "Babe" *(Cast)*   497

Wallace, Frederick *(Librettist)*   2456

Wallace, G.D. *(Cast)*   3505

Wallace, George *(Cast)*   2201, 3113

Wallace, George D. *(Cast)*   3925

Wallace, Helen *(Lyricist)*   3849

Wallace, Lee *(Cast)*   1699, 2422, 2925

Wallace, Lizzie *(Cast)*   646

Wallace, Oliver *(Composer)*   69

Wallace, Oliver G. *(Composer)*   3297, 3973

Wallace, Oliver G. *(Lyricist)*   3297

Wallace, Pat *(Author)*   4207

Wallace, Paul *(Cast)*   1709

Wallace, Ronald *(Lighting Designer)*   951, 4601

Wallace, Royce *(Cast)*   3286

Wallace, Slappy *(Cast)*   444, 1876

Wallace, W.V. *(Composer)*   1897

Wallace, W.V. *(Lyricist)*   1897

Wallach, Ira *(Additional Lyrics)*   4244

Wallach, Ira *(Librettist)*   1047, 1435, 2284, 2910, 3286, 3473, 3524, 4028, 4244, 4829

Wallach, Ira *(Lyricist)*   1047, 2284, 2910, 3286, 4153

Ward, Edward *(Orchestrations)* 4291
Ward, Elsa *(Costumes)* 573
Ward, Hap *(Cast)* 1646, 4817
Ward, Happy *(Cast)* 1641, 1798
Ward, Happy *(Composer)* 1641
Ward, Happy *(Librettist)* 1641
Ward, Harrison *(Lyricist)* 2543
Ward, Herbert
    See also Ward & Harvey.
Ward, Herbert *(Set Design)* 21, 208, 545, 1391, 1484,
    1485, 2927, 3144, 3623, 4104
Ward, Joe Patrick *(Composer)* 2046
Ward, Joe Patrick *(Lyricist)* 2046
Ward, Joe Patrick *(Musical Director)* 2046
Ward, Joe Patrick *(Vocal Arranger)* 2046
Ward, John *(Set Design)* 3273
Ward, Jonathan *(Cast)* 2027
Ward, Joseph P. *(Cast)* 1647
Ward, Kelly *(Cast)* 4459
Ward, Ken *(Cast)* 2285
Ward, MacKenzie *(Cast)* 3481
Ward, Mackenzie *(Cast)* 4207
Ward, Michael *(Musical Director)* 4246
Ward, Paula *(Cast)* 3202
Ward, Penelope Dudley *(Cast)* 3885
Ward, Phylis *(Cast)* 164
Ward, Sam *(Cast)* **4421**
Ward, Sam *(Librettist)* 1397
Ward, Samuel *(Composer)* 4390
Ward, Solly *(Cast)* 184, 1680, 2747, 3008, 3012, 4733
Ward, Ted D. *(Composer)* 913
Ward, Theara J. *(Cast)* 754
Ward, Theodore *(Author)* 3321
Ward, Theodore *(Lyricist)* 3321
Ward, Toni *(Costumes)* 3831
Ward, William J. *(Cast)* 3327
Ward & Harvey
    See also Herbert Ward and Walter H. Harvey.
Ward & Harvey *(Set Design)* 82, 443, 1916, 2382, 3556,
    4372, 4545
Ward-Stephens *(Composer)* 1009
Warde, Willie *(Choreographer)* 719, 2131, 2524, 3828
Warde, Willie *(Musical Director)* 2509
Wardell, Carter *(Cast)* 2366
Wardell, Harry *(Producer)* 3043
Warden, George *(Cast)* 2791
Warden, Jack *(Cast)* 483
Wardewell, Edward R. *(Cast)* 3325
Ware, Eric *(Cast)* 3001
Ware, Helen *(Cast)* 3730
Ware, N. Harris *(Composer)* 1568, 1573
Ware, N. Harris *(Lyricist)* 1573
Ware, N. Harris *(Musical Director)* 1573
Warfield, Charles *(Composer)* 1425
Warfield, Charles *(Lyricist)* 146, 1425
Warfield, David *(Cast)* 357, 1264, 2041, 2116, 2842,
    3750, 4658
Warfield, Joel *(Cast)* 3217
Warfield, Joseph *(Cast)* 3
Warfield, Ruth White *(Composer)* 174

Warfield, William *(Cast)* 3691
Wargo, Dan *(Director)* 2511
Wargo, Richard *(Composer)* 3864
Wargo, Richard *(Librettist)* 3864
Wargo, Richard *(Lyricist)* 3864
Warhol, Andy *(Costumes)* 322
Warhol, Andy *(Producer)* 2728
Waring, Fred
    See also Fred Waring & His Pennsylvanians, Fred
    Waring Glee Club, Orchestra, Pennsylvanians,
    World's Fair Glee Club.
Waring, Fred *(Cast)* 3153
Waring, Fred *(Composer)* 3131
Waring, Fred *(Musical Director)* 2401
Waring, Fred *(Producer)* 3645
Waring, J. *(Set Design)* 932
Waring, J.D. *(Set Design)* 345
Waring, James D. *(Set Design)* 821, 2028, 2641
Waring, Richard *(Cast)* 55, 814, 2859
Waring, Richard *(Lyricist)* 392
Waring, Tom *(Composer)* 3645, 4170
Waring, Tom *(Lyricist)* 3645, 4170
Fred Waring & His Pennsylvanians/Glee Club/
    Orchestra/Pennsylvanians/World's Fair Glee Club
    See also Fred Waring.
Waring & His Pennsylvanians, Fred *(Cast)* 1839, 2402,
    2405, 3131, 3645
Waring Glee Club, Fred *(Cast)* 2400, 3100
Waring's Orchestra, Fred *(Cast)* 2366
Waring's Pennsylvanians, Fred *(Cast)* 2401
Waring's World's Fair Glee Club, Fred *(Cast)* 173
Warneke, Marleta *(Cast)* 1940
Warner, Edyth *(Cast)* 399
Warner, Jack L. *(Producer)* 2217
Warner, Neil *(Musical Director)* 2727, 3612
Warner, Neil *(Vocal Arranger)* 36
Warner, Russell *(Dance Arranger)* 1665, 2578, 3671,
    3928, 4796
Warner, Russell *(Orchestrations)* 1665, 4537
Warner Theatre Productions *(Producer)* 1068, 3608, 4727
Warnick, Clay *(Composer)* 23, 1101, 1815, 1933, 4377
Warnick, Clay *(Dance Arranger)* 3390
Warnick, Clay *(Lyricist)* 2817
Warnick, Clay *(Musical Director)* 67, 1076, 1811, 1930,
    2187, 2850
Warnick, Clay *(Orchestrations)* 4586
Warnick, Clay *(Vocal Arranger)* 180, 204, 297, 601,
    834, 901, 971, 1076, 1112, 1577, 1604, 1815, 1930,
    2523, 2817, 3036, 3390, 4543, 4702
Warnick, Steven *(Producer)* 4139
Warnow, Mark *(Producer)* 4640
Warrack, David *(Composer)* 3066
Warrack, David *(Librettist)* 3066
Warrack, David *(Lyricist)* 3066
Warrack Prods. *(Producer)* 3066
Warren, Bob *(Cast)* 863, 864
Warren, Brett *(Director)* 1416
Warren, C. Dernier *(Cast)* 4302
Warren, Chandler *(Lyricist)* 916
Warren, David *(Director)* 647

Warren, Frances *(Cast)* 1550
Warren, Harry *(Composer)* 173, 397, 418, 964, 1359, 1638, 1813, 2423, 2772, 2808, 3018, 3020, 3175, 3382, 3796, 3840, 3913, 4235, 4730, 4799, 4815, 4817
Warren, Harvey *(Set Design)* 2742
Warren, Jennifer Leigh *(Cast)* 10, 394, 2544
Warren, Julie *(Cast)* 189
Warren, Lesley Ann *(Cast)* 1094, 1616, 3294
Warren, Mary Mease *(Costumes)* 1671
Warren, Richard Henry *(Composer)* 934
Warren, Richard Henry *(Musical Director)* 934
Warren, Rod *(Composer)* 128, 272, 366, 1049, 1107, 1436, 1437, 1438, 1770, 2279, 2913, 3186, 3484, 3889, 4433
Warren, Rod *(Librettist)* 1436, 2279, 4433
Warren, Rod *(Lyricist)* 128, 272, 366, 1049, 1107, 1436, 1437, 1438, 2279, 2913, 3186, 3484, 3889, 4433
Warren, Rod *(Musical Director)* 62
Warren, Rod *(Producer)* 128, 366, 1436, 1438, 2138, 2279, 2913
Warren, Ruth *(Cast)* 4241
Warren, Tom *(Set Design)* 962
Warrender, Scott *(Composer)* 992
Warshavsky, M. *(Composer)* 4342
Warshavsky, M. *(Lyricist)* 4342
Wartski, Sheila *(Choreographer)* 2147
Warwick, Robert *(Cast)* 276, 2903
Washburn, Jack *(Cast)* 3371
Washburne, Elizabeth *(Cast)* 4313
Washington, Fredi *(Cast)* 2712, 3993
Washington, Geneva *(Cast)* 435, 3704
Washington, George Dewey *(Cast)* 875, 878, 885, 1288, 4177
Washington, Isabell *(Cast)* 290
Washington, Lamont *(Cast)* 1717
Washington, Mildred *(Cast)* 2640, 4184
Washington, Ned *(Lyricist)* 444, 878, 1134, 3002, 3373, 4193, 4545
Washington Square Players *(Set Design)* 1919
Wassall, Edward *(Costumes)* 2443
Wassall, Edward *(Set Design)* 2443
Wassau, Hinda *(Cast)* 420
Wasserman, Allan *(Cast)* 829
Wasserman, Dale *(Director)* 1892
Wasserman, Dale *(Librettist)* 2556, 2727, 3908, 3961
Wasserman, Dale *(Lighting Designer)* 1892
Wasserstein, Wendy *(Librettist)* 4535
Wasson, David *(Cast)* 1291
Watanabe, Gedde *(Cast)* 1053
Watanabe, Trich *(Lyricist)* 1053
Waterbury, Laura *(Cast)* 3015, 3305
Waterbury, Marsha *(Cast)* 4020
Waterhouse, Jane *(Librettist)* 2861
Waterman, Willard *(Cast)* 2713
Waterous, Herbert *(Cast)* 4293
Waterous, Jack *(Cast)* 4621
Waters, Daryl *(Vocal Arranger)* 10
Waters, Ethel *(Cast)* 26, 207, 216, 443, 467, 612, 875, 878, 885, 1499, 2712, 2881, 3241, 3704
Waters, Ethel *(Composer)* 3709
Waters, Ethel *(Lyricist)* 3709

Waters, Fred *(Cast)* 2986
Waters, Marianne Brown *(Librettist)* 3713
Waters, Marianne Brown *(Lyricist)* 3713
Waters, Mr. *(Composer)* 998
Waters, Roger *(Composer)* 3739
Waters, Safford *(Composer)* 934, 1226, 1417, 4414
Waters, Safford *(Librettist)* 1226
Waters, Safford *(Lyricist)* 934, 1226, 1417, 4414
Waters, Tom *(Cast)* 1430
Waterston, Sam *(Cast)* 3000
Watkin, Fen *(Musical Director)* 1255
Watkins, Linda *(Cast)* 2265, 3850
Watkins, Maurine Dallas *(Author)* 723
Watkins, Perry *(Producer)* 315, 341
Watkins, Perry *(Set Design)* 315, 467, 2712, 3495, 4782
Watling, Dilys *(Cast)* 1497
Watson, Betty Jane *(Cast)* 206, 4015, 4428
Watson, Billy *(Cast)* 1032, 1457
Watson, Billy *(Director)* 1032
Watson, Billy *(Librettist)* 1032
Watson, Billy W. *(Librettist)* 1457
Watson, Bobby *(Cast)* 86, 152, 931, 1693, 2148, 3310, 3723
Watson, Brian *(Cast)* 3527, 3697
Watson, Douglass *(Cast)* 3000, 3330, 3468
Watson, Edith *(Orchestrations)* 2034
Watson, Edna *(Costumes)* 1072
Watson, Eric *(Composer)* 1638
Watson, Ernie *(Orchestrations)* 1336
Watson, Frank *(Cast)* 3468
Watson, Frederic *(Composer)* 815
Watson, Harry *(Cast)* 2800, 3404, 4392, 4802, 4804, 4805, 4806
Watson, Harry B. *(Cast)* 671, 2868
Watson, Janet *(Choreographer)* 394, 809, 2229
Watson, Jim *(Cast)* 1037
Watson, John *(Cast)* 169
Watson, Lee *(Lighting Designer)* 1062, 1571, 2664, 2772, 3543, 3619, 3938
Watson, Lisa *(Set Design)* 2272
Watson, Lucile *(Cast)* 1904
Watson, M.G. *(Composer)* 1535
Watson, M.G. *(Lyricist)* 1535
Watson, Milton *(Cast)* 1136, 3822, 4177
Watson, Minor *(Cast)* 2691
Watson, Rita *(Costumes)* 708
Watson, Sam *(Cast)* 1845
Watson, Susan *(Cast)* 367, 491, 607, 681, 2248
Watson, Virginia *(Cast)* 1533, 3752
Watson, Walter *(Costumes)* 4062
Watson, Whitford *(Lyricist)* 1900
Watson II, Harry *(Cast)* 3977
Watson Jr., Harry *(Cast)* 3222, 4801
Watt, Robert *(Cast)* 3910
Watters, Bill *(Producer)* 407, 408
Watters, George Manker *(Author)* 587
Watters, Hal *(Cast)* 369, 4002
Watters, Safford *(Composer)* 4348
Watterston, Henry *(Composer)* 2792
Watts, Al *(Cast)* 2013
Watts, Al F. *(Cast)* 980, 2127

Watts, Al F. *(Librettist)*   2127
Watts, Elizabeth *(Cast)*   1029
Watts, George *(Cast)*   2344
Watts, William E. *(Director)*   3180
Waxman, A.P. *(Producer)*   1112, 3813
Waxman, Franz *(Composer)*   2611
Waxman, Jeff *(Musical Director)*   1077, 1985, 2289
Waxman, Jeff *(Orchestrations)*   4740
Waxman, Jeff *(Vocal Arranger)*   1077, 4740
Waxman, Jeffrey *(Arrangements)*   3752
Waxman, Jeffrey *(Musical Director)*   3752
Waxman, Percy *(Librettist)*   584
Waxman, Percy *(Lyricist)*   584, 1309
Wayburn, Ned *(Cast)*   604
Wayburn, Ned *(Choreographer)*   405, 558, 1801, 1826,
    1967, 2519, 2869, 2914, 3146, 3395, 3768, 4023, 4130,
    4203, 4491, 4687, 4813, 4816
Wayburn, Ned *(Composer)*   1835
Wayburn, Ned *(Costumes)*   604
Wayburn, Ned *(Director)*   354, 604, 638, 683, 1154, 1403,
    1523, 1606, 1640, 1728, 1731, 1783, 1801, 1835, 1922,
    1963, 2035, 2123, 2232, 2378, 2481, 2485, 2493, 2519,
    2600, 2700, 2858, 2900, 2906, 2964, 2974, 2978, 3086,
    3087, 3096, 3265, 3395, 3396, 3422, 3433, 3538, 3575,
    3746, 3747, 3749, 3773, 3855, 4203, 4206, 4382, 4387,
    4437, 4491, 4662, 4687, 4757, 4810, 4811, 4812, 4813,
    4816, 4817, 4831, 4833, 4836, 4837, 4838, 4849, 4851
Wayburn, Ned *(Librettist)*   4437
Wayburn, Ned *(Lighting Designer)*   2378, 3538
Wayburn, Ned *(Lyricist)*   638, 1523, 1920, 2978, 4437
Wayburn, Ned *(Producer)*   1593, 2700, 3086, 3087, 4437
Wayburn, Ned *(Set Design)*   2378, 2519
Wayland, Newton *(Musical Director)*   369
Wayland, Newton *(Orchestrations)*   369
Wayne, Bernie *(Composer)*   673, 4484, 4828
Wayne, Bernie *(Lyricist)*   673, 4828
Wayne, Charles *(Cast)*   4223
Wayne, David *(Cast)*   1278, 1730, 1764, 2267, 3390,
    3800, 3845, 3874, 4764
Wayne, Jerry *(Cast)*   2751
Wayne, Paula *(Cast)*   1601
Wayne, Rollo *(Set Design)*   200, 787, 1618, 3405, 3409,
    4121, 4669
Wayne, Shirley *(Cast)*   1840
Wayne, Sid *(Lyricist)*   4337
Wayne, William *(Cast)*   4241
Wearing, Michael *(Director)*   2153
Weatherly, Fred E. *(Lyricist)*   2891
Weatherly, Frederick E. *(Lyricist)*   3259
Weatherly, Joe *(Cast)*   2721
Weatherly, Michael M. *(Producer)*   4619
Weatherly, Tom *(Director)*   2105
Weatherly, Tom *(Producer)*   1453, 2105, 2545, 3861,
    3919, 4335
Weathersbee, Gary *(Lighting Designer)*   1229
Weathersby, Jennie *(Cast)*   1193
Weaver, Carl Earl *(Cast)*   166, 3739, 4722
Weaver, Carl Earl *(Composer)*   2541
Weaver, Carl Earl *(Librettist)*   2541
Weaver, Carl Earl *(Lyricist)*   2541

Weaver, Dennis *(Cast)*   1674
Weaver, Doodles *(Cast)*   2809
Weaver, Fritz *(Cast)*   64, 270
Weaver, William *(Costumes)*   606, 1384, 3573, 3580
Weaver, William *(Set Design)*   728, 3404, 3580, 3770
Webb, Alan *(Cast)*   1238, 3678, 3906, 4610
Webb, Alice *(Cast)*   2071
Webb, Barbara *(Cast)*   2075
Webb, Charles *(Author)*   1645
Webb, Chick *(Composer)*   146, 432, 4534
Webb, Chloe *(Cast)*   1348
Webb, Clifton *(Cast)*   207, 208, 1322, 2180, 2491, 2545,
    2620, 3087, 3467, 3478, 3613, 3865, 3924, 4212, 4367,
    4443, 4777
Webb, Dorothy *(Cast)*   628
Webb, Elida *(Choreographer)*   876
Webb, Elmon *(Set Design)*   2776
Webb, Janet *(Cast)*   2682
Webb, Jimmy *(Composer)*   3852
Webb, Jimmy *(Lyricist)*   3852
Webb, Kenneth *(Director)*   1956, 1957
Webb, Kenneth *(Librettist)*   1453, 2005, 2105, 4673
Webb, Kenneth *(Lyricist)*   423, 1780
Webb, Kenneth S. *(Director)*   3284, 3419
Webb, Kenneth S. *(Librettist)*   3284
Webb, Kenneth S. *(Lyricist)*   3284
Webb, Laura *(Composer)*   4264
Webb, Laura *(Lyricist)*   4264
Webb, Lizbeth *(Cast)*   453, 1467
Webb, Lyda *(Choreographer)*   3808
Webb, M. Tello *(Cast)*   2154
Webb, Marti *(Cast)*   1619, 4301
Webb, Nella *(Cast)*   1910
Webb, Robert *(Dance Arranger)*   3888
Webb, Roy *(Composer)*   17, 1502, 1780, 3148, 3419, 4644
Webb, Roy *(Lyricist)*   17
Webb, Roy *(Musical Director)*   711, 834, 1447, 2382,
    3436, 3556
Webb, Roy *(Orchestrations)*   711, 834, 2382, 3007, 3436,
    4328, 4821
Webb, Roy S. *(Composer)*   3284
Webb, Roy S. *(Musical Director)*   3284, 4308
Webber, Florence *(Cast)*   2569, 3538
Webber, James Plaisted *(Author)*   1235
Weber, Bernard *(Author)*   2657, 2658
Weber, Edwin *(Composer)*   1944
Weber, Edwin J. *(Composer)*   3405
Weber, Florence *(Costumes)*   1126
Weber, Fredricka *(Cast)*   1049, 2418
Weber, Harry *(Cast)*   77
Weber, Joe *(Cast)*   3639, 3755, 4681
Weber, Joe *(Producer)*   2262, 2494
Weber, Joseph *(Cast)*   182, 258, 301, 510, 677, 940, 1095,
    1217, 1264, 1881, 1900, 1926, 1927, 2041, 2835, 3303,
    3632, 4473, 4478, 4511, 4658, 4797
Weber, Joseph *(Director)*   88, 1881
Weber, Joseph *(Producer)*   88, 182, 301, 677, 940, 1095,
    1162, 1188, 1217, 1264, 1851, 1881, 1926, 1927, 1962,
    2835, 3303, 3304, 3632, 4473, 4478, 4658, 4681, 4797
Weber, Joseph A. *(Cast)*   1806

Weber, L. Lawrence *(Producer)* 1911, 2516, 2818, 2950
Weber, Lawrence *(Cast)* 3427, 3920
Weber, Rex *(Cast)* 125, 1932, 3264, 4368
Weber, Shirley *(Cast)* 2098
Weber, Steve *(Composer)* 3309
Weber, Steve *(Lyricist)* 3309
Weber & Fields
    See Joseph Weber and Lew Fields.
Weber & Rush *(Producer)* 3384
Webster, A.S. *(Producer)* 1206
Webster, Byron *(Cast)* 367, 3274, 3931
Webster, H.T. *(Librettist)* 199
Webster, Howard *(Composer)* 1206, 3021
Webster, Howard *(Lyricist)* 1206
Webster, Howard *(Musical Director)* 1206
Webster, J.P. *(Composer)* 3020
Webster, Jack *(Cast)* 1968
Webster, Jean *(Author)* 2608
Webster, Paul Francis *(Author)* 616
Webster, Paul Francis *(Lyricist)* 59, 616, 673, 751,
    1034, 2246, 2259, 2311, 3002, 3046, 3175, 3739,
    3905, 4091, 4702
Webster, Rev. H.D.L. *(Lyricist)* 3020
Wedgeworth, Ann *(Cast)* 477
Wedgworth, Ann *(Cast)* 2468
Weede, Robert *(Cast)* 935, 2864, 2961, 4155
Weeden, Bill *(Composer)* 2043, 2075, 2279, 2913,
    3181, 3479
Weeden, Bill *(Lyricist)* 3181
Weedon, William C. *(Cast)* 2524, 2836
Weedon, Willliam C. *(Cast)* 4187
Weeks, Ada Mae *(Cast)* 824, 2214, 2491, 2569, 3218, 3420
Weeks, Al *(Librettist)* 1847
Weeks, Alan *(Cast)* 393, 406, 415, 550, 1729, 3231, 3276,
    3741, 4286
Weeks, Alan *(Choreographer)* 1890, 3239
Weeks, Alan *(Director)* 1890, 3239
Weeks, Bonnie *(Producer)* 908
Weeks, Harold *(Composer)* 3297
Weeks, Harold *(Lyricist)* 3297
Weeks, Mabel *(Cast)* 2317
Weeks, Sarah *(Cast)* 4533
Weeks, Sarah *(Composer)* 3181, 4533
Weeks, Sarah *(Librettist)* 3181
Weeks, Sarah *(Lyricist)* 3181, 4533
Wehlen, Emmy *(Cast)* 1561
Wehner, George B. *(Lyricist)* 2857
Wehrle, Helen *(Cast)* 1461
Weick, Richard *(Lighting Designer)* 3080
Weidhaus, G.A. *(Set Design)* 1490
Weidhaus, Gustave *(Set Design)* 1489
Weidhaus, Ted *(Set Design)* 1491, 3086, 4374
Weidlin, Jane *(Composer)* 3739
Weidlin, Jane *(Lyricist)* 3739
Weidman, Charles *(Cast)* 1933
Weidman, Charles *(Choreographer)* 125, 207, 309, 2068,
    2103, 2187, 2475, 2554, 2748, 3105, 3543, 3989
Weidman, Jerome *(Author)* 2048
Weidman, Jerome *(Librettist)* 842, 1280, 2048,
    3551, 4312

Weidman, John *(Librettist)* 112, 212, 1038, 3340
Weigall, Arthur *(Lyricist)* 702, 1733
Weigert, Rene *(Dance Arranger)* 4828
Weigert, Rene *(Musical Director)* 678
Weil, Cynthia *(Composer)* 964
Weil, Cynthia *(Lyricist)* 146, 964
Weil, David *(Producer)* 942
Weil, Oscar *(Composer)* 4598
Weil, Oscar *(Librettist)* 4598
Weil, Raymonde *(Producer)* 4689
Weil, Richard *(Librettist)* 2259
Weil, Robert *(Cast)* 3059, 3288
Weil, Tim *(Musical Director)* 838
Weiler, Norman *(Cast)* 2055
Weill, Harry *(Cast)* 1267
Weill, Harry *(Composer)* 1267
Weill, Harry *(Lyricist)* 1267
Weill, Irving *(Lyricist)* 4010
Weill, Kurt *(Author)* 4368, 4369, 4370
Weill, Kurt *(Composer)* 369, 996, 1085, 1120, 1196,
    1284, 1299, 1755, 2030, 2228, 2323, 2344, 2386, 2591,
    2615, 2653, 2753, 3301, 3647, 3840, 4169, 4368, 4369,
    4370, 4371, 4399, 4504
Weill, Kurt *(Dance Arranger)* 1284, 2591, 2615,
    3301, 4169
Weill, Kurt *(Incidental Music)* 1416, 4495
Weill, Kurt *(Orchestrations)* 1284, 2228, 2344, 2386, 2591,
    2615, 3301, 4169, 4368, 4369, 4371
Weill, Kurt *(Producer)* 2653
Weill, Kurt *(Vocal Arranger)* 1284, 2386, 2591, 2615,
    3301, 4169
Weill, Stephen *(Producer)* 4707
Weille, Blair *(Composer)* 1436, 2876, 4433
Weille, Blair *(Librettist)* 4433
Weille, Blair *(Lyricist)* 4433
Weimar, Lorraine *(Cast)* 2540
Weinberg, Arthur *(Lyricist)* 4642
Weinberg, Charles *(Composer)* 123, 4763
Weinberg, Charles *(Lyricist)* 4763
Weinberg, Charles *(Musical Director)* 4218
Weinberg, Charles A. *(Cast)* 3751
Weinberg, Edwin *(Composer)* 4433
Weinberg, Edwin *(Librettist)* 4433
Weinberg, Edwin *(Lyricist)* 4433
Weinberg, Gus *(Cast)* 47, 1351, 1515, 2868, 4161
Weinberg, Gus *(Librettist)* 3086
Weinberg, Gus C. *(Lyricist)* 47
Weinberg, Tom Wilson *(Composer)* 4309
Weinberg, Tom Wilson *(Lyricist)* 4309
Weiner, Ellis *(Librettist)* 251
Weiner, John *(Cast)* 2360
Weiner, Lazar *(Composer)* 1609
Weiner, Lee *(Composer)* 885
Weiner, Lee *(Lyricist)* 885
Weiner, Mark *(Dance Arranger)* 1978
Weiner, Mark *(Musical Director)* 1978
Weiner, Mark *(Vocal Arranger)* 1978
Weiner, Meri *(Cast)* 4168
Weiner, Robert *(Producer)* 2804, 4278
Weiner, Stephen A. *(Composer)* 4107

Wells, Caroline *(Lyricist)* 2495
Wells, Carolyn *(Librettist)* 2701, 3611
Wells, Carolyn *(Lyricist)* 1417, 2701
Wells, Christopher *(Cast)* 198, 1092, 4297
Wells, Craig *(Cast)* 275
Wells, Deanna *(Cast)* 1701
Wells, Dickie *(Cast)* 899
Wells, Eleanor *(Librettist)* 4572
Wells, H.G. *(Author)* 1721
Wells, Jack *(Composer)* 965, 1334, 3189
Wells, Jack *(Lyricist)* 3189
Wells, John *(Librettist)* 1251
Wells, Matthew *(Librettist)* 1732
Wells, Matthew *(Lyricist)* 1732
Wells, Pauline *(Costumes)* 1244
Wells, Rhea *(Costumes)* 720
Wells, Rhea *(Set Design)* 720
Wells, Robert *(Composer)* 520
Wells, Robert *(Lyricist)* 520, 4346
Wells, Stephen *(Producer)* 2702, 4349
Wells, Tico *(Cast)* 2283, 4171
Wells, Tony *(Cast)* 3927
Wells, William K. *(Director)* 1494, 4572
Wells, William K. *(Librettist)* 67, 1481, 1486, 1487,
  1488, 1489, 1490, 1491, 1493, 1549, 1690, 1779,
  2227, 2734, 2850, 4296, 4300, 4572
Wells, William K. *(Lyricist)* 1549, 2912
Welsh, Harry *(Cast)* 203, 2808
Welsh, Jack *(Producer)* 709
Welsh, Jane *(Cast)* 2547
Welsh, Kenneth *(Cast)* 4129
Welsh, Scott *(Cast)* 2730
Welty, Eudora *(Author)* 3733
Welty, Eudora *(Librettist)* 2554, 2560
Welty, Max *(Cast)* 4528
Welzer, Irving *(Producer)* 3600
Wendall, Beth *(Librettist)* 3103
Wendel, Elmarie *(Cast)* 249, 392, 1018, 1924, 2522,
  3217, 4319
Wendling, Pete *(Composer)* 3737
Wendt, George *(Cast)* 4690
Wenger, John *(Set Design)* 1419, 1485, 1617, 1643,
  1859, 3179, 3379, 3489, 4118, 4532, 4818, 4819
Wenger, Wally *(Director)* 4265
Wenrich, Percy *(Cast)* 3153
Wenrich, Percy *(Composer)* 132, 371, 529, 670, 913,
  929, 1208, 1248, 1687, 1920, 2402, 2403, 2405, 3259,
  3425, 3662, 3712, 4054, 4673
Wenrich, Percy *(Lyricist)* 1687, 3662
Wenter, John *(Set Design)* 3243
Wentworth, Edward S. *(Cast)* 1392
Wentworth, Estelle *(Cast)* 1521
Wentworth, Scott *(Cast)* 147, 1702, 2354, 4619
Wentworth, Scott *(Librettist)* 1702
Wenz, Carol *(Costumes)* 2968, 3688
Wenzel, Leopold *(Musical Director)* 205
Wenzelberg, L. *(Costumes)* 1424
Weppner, Christina *(Costumes)* 2049
Weppner, Christina *(Set Design)* 3908
Werau, A. *(Composer)* 2419

Werba, Louis F. *(Producer)* 21, 966, 1003, 2528, 2886,
  4119, 4476
Werber & Luescher
  See also Louis A. Werber and Mark A. Luescher.
Werba & Luescher *(Producer)* 1849, 3771, 4250
Werfel, Franz *(Author)* 1196, 1660
Werkheiser, John *(Choreographer)* 4168
Werner, Fred *(Dance Arranger)* 837, 2523, 3196, 4238
Werner, Fred *(Musical Director)* 1891, 3526, 4238
Werner, Fred *(Orchestrations)* 4013
Werner, Fred *(Vocal Arranger)* 3815
Werner, Howard *(Lighting Designer)* 1832
Werner, Ken *(Musical Director)* 2426
Werner, Ken *(Orchestrations)* 2426
Werner, Mort *(Vocal Arranger)* 4331
Wernher, Hilda *(Author)* 751
Wernick, Richard *(Composer)* 3186
Wertheim Studios *(Set Design)* 1989
Wertimer, Edward *(Cast)* 750
Wertimer, Ned *(Cast)* 3497
Wertimer Jr., Sidney *(Cast)* 1885
Wescott, Marcy *(Cast)* 514, 3916, 4420, 4479
Wesley, James K. *(Cast)* 2303
Wesley, Richard *(Librettist)* 1099, 4535
Wesley, Ward *(Lyricist)* 4809
Weslyn, Louis *(Lyricist)* 2154, 2291, 2662, 3973, 4723
Wessell, Vivian *(Cast)* 94
Wessels, Henri *(Cast)* 877, 883, 892, 3709
West, Alvy *(Composer)* 3440
West, Alvy *(Musical Director)* 3449, 3498, 4660, 4710
West, Alvy *(Orchestrations)* 2726
West, Alvy *(Vocal Arranger)* 3449, 3498, 4710
West, Arthur *(Cast)* 3842
West, Augusta *(Cast)* 938
West, Bernie *(Cast)* 363
West, Blanche *(Cast)* 1707
West, Bob *(Composer)* 3739
West, Bob *(Lyricist)* 3739
West, Buster *(Cast)* 1336, 2366, 4667
West, Clarence *(Musical Director)* 132, 3052, 3679, 3865
West, Clarence *(Orchestrations)* 2931
West, Con *(Composer)* 792
West, Con *(Lyricist)* 792
West, Dennis *(Arrangements)* 4055
West, Dennis *(Musical Director)* 4055
West, Edwin *(Producer)* 3920
West, Eugene *(Lyricist)* 4197
West, Everett *(Cast)* 420, 3767
West, Fay *(Cast)* 1154
West, Harry *(Cast)* 4762
West, Helen Stevenson *(Costumes)* 750, 4303
West, Helen Stevenson *(Set Design)* 750
West, John *(Cast)* 1332, 2366
West, Mae *(Author)* 1036
West, Mae *(Cast)* 638, 1036, 2870, 4063, 4553, 4656, 4712
West, Mae *(Director)* 1036
West, Matt *(Choreographer)* 330
West, Moritz *(Lyricist)* 205
West, Paul *(Librettist)* 2722, 3134, 3422, 4414
West, Paul *(Lyricist)* 591, 719, 737, 1226, 1246, 1417,

1464, 1504, 1526, 2448, 2722, 2826, 2906, 2990, 3052, 3134, 3229, 3313, 3422, 3450, 3451, 3679, 3710, 3753, 3856, 3857, 3882, 4663, 4666, 4723, 4801

West, Will *(Cast)* 3350

West, Will *(Lyricist)* 3350

West, William Herman *(Cast)* 2959

West and McGinty, Willie *(Cast)* 420

Westbrook, Frank *(Choreographer)* 616

Westbrooke, Evelyn *(Cast)* 574

Westby-Gibson, Richard *(Costumes)* 4540

Westenberg, Robert *(Cast)* 754, 1015, 2065, 2143, 3862, 4210

Westendorf, Thomas P. *(Composer)* 4390

Westerfield, James *(Director)* 4486

Westergaard, Louise *(Producer)* 4091, 4137

Westerly, Pauline *(Cast)* 1647

Western Producing Co. *(Producer)* 1560

Westerton, Frank *(Cast)* 2340

Westford, Owen *(Cast)* 3625

Westley, Helen *(Cast)* 3686

Westley, John *(Cast)* 1904, 2059

Westminster Productions *(Producer)* 1887

Westmoreland, Lillian *(Cast)* 3660

Weston, Charles H. *(Cast)* 3450

Weston, Ellen *(Librettist)* 1997

Weston, Ellen *(Lyricist)* 1997

Weston, Jack *(Cast)* 3299

Weston, Jim *(Cast)* 280

Weston, Lucy *(Cast)* 965, 1524, 4802

Weston, Paul *(Composer)* 3449, 4743

Weston, Paul *(Musical Director)* 192, 193

Weston, R.P. *(Composer)* 336, 1208, 3084, 3117, 3259

Weston, R.P. *(Librettist)* 133, 702, 1855, 2547, 4299

Weston, R.P. *(Lyricist)* 133, 336, 1208, 1784, 1916, 1963, 2833, 2858, 3222, 3259, 4299, 4757

Weston, Ruth *(Cast)* 121, 1352

Westport County Playhouse *(Producer)* 689

Westport Productions *(Producer)* 1609

Wetmore, Joan *(Cast)* 4479

Wever, Edward L. *(Lyricist)* 720

Wever, Ned *(Cast)* 3861

Wever, Ned *(Composer)* 3728

Wever, Ned *(Lyricist)* 418, 3728, 3783

Wexler, Connie *(Set Design)* 602

Wexler, George

　　See also George Wexter Presents Inc.

Wexler, Irving *(Librettist)* 3914

Wexler, Jerry *(Producer)* 3297

Wexler, Peter *(Lighting Designer)* 550, 2248

Wexler, Peter *(Set Design)* 550, 602, 1764, 2248, 2874

Weygandt, Gene *(Cast)* 3461

Weyman, Stanley *(Author)* 3680

Whalen, Harold *(Cast)* 1494, 2140

Whalen, Michael *(Cast)* 831

Whaley, Thomas *(Orchestrations)* 1984

Wharton, Carly *(Producer)* 2940

Wharton, Diana *(Composer)* 1344

Wheat, Lawrence *(Cast)* 1271, 1543, 1826, 2714, 2745, 2906, 2923, 3229, 3882

Wheatley, Clifford *(Director)* 4159

Wheatley, Joanne *(Cast)* 863

Wheaton, Anna *(Cast)* 340, 2668, 2884, 3230, 3395, 3478, 3773, 4360, 4521, 4644, 4853

Wheaton, Gladys *(Cast)* 202

Whedon, John *(Librettist)* 4314

Whedon, Tom *(Librettist)* 73, 2935

Whedon, Tom *(Lyricist)* 73, 427, 1049, 2935

Wheelan, Albertine Randall *(Costumes)* 1484, 3443, 3839, 4066

Wheelan, Alfred *(Cast)* 1305

Wheeler, Bert *(Cast)* 67, 568, 1396, 3121, 3138, 3719, 4366, 4817

Wheeler, Betty *(Cast)* 568, 4817

Wheeler, Billy Edd *(Librettist)* 1781

Wheeler, Billy Edd *(Lyricist)* 1781

Wheeler, Francis *(Cast)* 694

Wheeler, Francis *(Lyricist)* 1343, 2706

Wheeler, Harold *(Dance Arranger)* 798, 3603

Wheeler, Harold *(Musical Director)* 40, 1074, 3603, 4485

Wheeler, Harold *(Orchestrations)* 146, 572, 661, 1103, 1236, 1699, 4286, 4722

Wheeler, Harold *(Vocal Arranger)* 4286

Wheeler, Harris *(Composer)* 474

Wheeler, Hugh *(Librettist)* 2536, 2539, 2805, 4233, 4459

Wheeler, Hugh *(Lyricist)* 2607

Wheeler, John *(Cast)* 4238

Wheeler, Josh *(Cast)* 3841

Wheeler, Margaret *(Cast)* 934

Wheeler, Ruth *(Cast)* 1343

Wheeler, Sandra *(Cast)* 705

Wheeler, Van Rensselaer *(Cast)* 356, 737, 1071, 1470, 1912, 2233, 2399, 2668, 2936, 3805, 3839, 4404

Wheeler, Virginia *(Cast)* 731, 980

Whelan, Alf C. *(Cast)* 618, 1543, 2101, 2548

Whelan, Harold

　　See also Jan & Whelan.

Whelan, Harold *(Cast)* 2636

Whelp, William C. *(Cast)* 3981

Whetsol, Arthur *(Composer)* 895

Whidden, Jay *(Composer)* 4806

Whiffen, Thomas *(Cast)* 3422

Whipper, Leigh *(Cast)* 552, 691, 2792, 3807, 4763

Whipper, Leigh *(Director)* 2645

Whipper, Leigh *(Librettist)* 3807, 4763

Whipper, Leigh *(Lyricist)* 552

Whipple, Waldo *(Cast)* 3030

Whistler, Edna *(Cast)* 929, 3184

Whistler, Rex *(Set Design)* 791

Whitaker, Grenna *(Cast)* 3814

Whitaker, Johnnie *(Cast)* 2553

Whitaker, Mical *(Director)* 3905

Whitaker, Rodgers E.M. *(Author)* 1402

Whitcup, Leonard *(Composer)* 3926

Whitcup, Leonard *(Lyricist)* 3926

White, Alexander *(Cast)* 291

White, Alton Fitzgerald *(Cast)* 789

White, B. *(Composer)* 4193

White, B. *(Lyricist)* 4193

White, D. *(Composer)* 4193

White, D. *(Lyricist)* 4193

White, Dan *(Composer)*   4826
White, David A. *(Cast)*   1822
White, Diz *(Cast)*   1166
White, E.B. *(Librettist)*   1874, 3946
White, Elmore *(Composer)*   2942
White, Elmore *(Lyricist)*   2942
White, Elsie *(Composer)*   4815
White, Frances *(Cast)*   1919, 1992, 2216, 2456, 3466, 4810, 4836, 4840
White, George *(Cast)*   645, 1151, 1482, 1483, 1484, 1485, 1491, 1824, 2734, 2900, 4655, 4805, 4809
White, George *(Choreographer)*   1482, 1489, 1494
White, George *(Composer)*   1491, 3685
White, George *(Director)*   1323, 1481, 1483, 1484, 1485, 1486, 1487, 1488, 1489, 1490, 1491, 1492, 1493, 1494, 2734, 2813
White, George *(Librettist)*   1481, 1483, 1484, 1485, 1486, 1487, 1488, 1489, 1490, 1491, 1492, 1493, 1494, 2734
White, George *(Lyricist)*   1481, 1482, 3685
White, George *(Producer)*   1323, 1481, 1482, 1483, 1484, 1485, 1486, 1487, 1488, 1489, 1490, 1491, 1492, 1493, 1494, 2734, 2813, 3808, 3883
White, Georgie *(Cast)*   1640
White, Harry *(Composer)*   4137
White, Harry Sheldon *(Librettist)*   1562
White, Henry
   See Roland Oliver.
White, Herbert *(Choreographer)*   4256
White, Jack *(Cast)*   1491
White, Jane *(Cast)*   33, 52, 2565, 3088, 3288, 3456, 3664
White, Jane *(Composer)*   2876
White, Jane Douglass *(Musical Director)*   2219
White, Jesse *(Cast)*   2304, 3036
White, Josh *(Cast)*   467
White, Josh *(Composer)*   467
White, Joshua *(Cast)*   2225
White, Kenneth *(Librettist)*   2751
White, Lillias *(Cast)*   261, 3628, 3739, 3757
White, Lilyan *(Cast)*   4150
White, Marjorie *(Cast)*   1831, 1979, 2382
White, Michael *(Producer)*   682, 2006
White, Miles *(Costumes)*   84, 145, 172, 372, 454, 462, 607, 649, 660, 692, 999, 1002, 1101, 1140, 1369, 1475, 1548, 1711, 1791, 1886, 2190, 2864, 3234, 3263, 3619, 3954, 4180, 4270, 4323, 4366, 4386, 4402, 4450, 4499, 4516, 4798, 4826
White, Miles *(Set Design)*   3715
White, Olive *(Cast)*   3759
White, Onna *(Cast)*   183, 1706, 3563
White, Onna *(Choreographer)*   1441, 1511, 1634, 1721, 1744, 1955, 2053, 2058, 2106, 2150, 2449, 2713, 2965, 3016, 3897, 3900, 4270, 4682, 4744
White, Onna *(Director)*   1441
White, Paul *(Cast)*   856, 2259
White, Richard *(Cast)*   1155, 1171
White, Rita *(Cast)*   1950
White, Robert *(Cast)*   1657
White, Roxanna *(Cast)*   3688
White, Ruth *(Cast)*   586, 1220, 4150

White, Sam *(Cast)*   3402, 3958
White, Sammy *(Cast)*   1529, 1577, 1689, 1823, 2814, 3949, 4792
White, Stanley *(Producer)*   4286
White, Susan *(Lighting Designer)*   2250
White, Susan A. *(Lighting Designer)*   3211
White, T.H. *(Author)*   623
White, Terri *(Cast)*   305, 788, 2250, 4619
White, Terri *(Choreographer)*   2100
White, Thelma *(Cast)*   1135, 3713, 3822, 4118, 4299
White, Willard *(Cast)*   4447
White, William *(Composer)*   1919
White, William C. *(Librettist)*   4152
White, Willy *(Composer)*   1919, 1920, 4742
White, Willy *(Lyricist)*   1919
White Heather Producing Co. *(Producer)*   2056
White Horse Tavern Prod. *(Producer)*   2300
White Jr., Al *(Choreographer)*   1476, 2817, 3138, 3823, 4131, 4314
White's Jazz Rabbits, Gonzell *(Cast)*   986
Whitechurch, Missy *(Choreographer)*   564
Whitehead *(Composer)*   2133
Whitehead *(Lyricist)*   2133
Whitehead, Allen *(Producer)*   3526
Whitehead, Fannie *(Cast)*   2285
Whitehead, Joe *(Cast)*   3255
Whitehead, Joseph *(Cast)*   4381
Whitehead, Mary *(Costumes)*   1769
Whitehead, O.Z. *(Cast)*   1342, 2105, 3103
Whitehead, Ralph *(Cast)*   376, 391, 1580
Whitehead, Robert *(Producer)*   837, 3577, 4004
Whitehead, Ron *(Costumes)*   3167
Whitehill, B.T. *(Set Design)*   4462, 4518
Whitehouse, Fred *(Composer)*   3926
Whitehouse, Fred *(Lyricist)*   3926
Whitelaw, Arthur *(Director)*   456, 4034
Whitelaw, Arthur *(Librettist)*   456, 4034
Whitelaw, Arthur *(Producer)*   594, 2874, 3900, 4176, 4264, 4343, 4537, 4783
Whiteman, Paul *(Cast)*   2406, 2638, 3153, 4847
Whiteman, Paul *(Composer)*   1643
Whiteman and His Orchestra, Paul *(Cast)*   662, 1485, 2258, 4817, 4845, 4846
Whitey's Jitterbugs *(Cast)*   497
Whitfield, Alice *(Cast)*   2188
Whitfield, Hugh *(Costumes)*   4629
Whitfield, June *(Cast)*   2608
Whitfield, Norman *(Composer)*   166, 3695, 4534
Whitfield, Norman *(Lyricist)*   166, 3695, 4534
Whitford, Annabelle *(Cast)*   4803
Whitham, Charles W. *(Set Design)*   4103
Whiting, Byron *(Puppeteer)*   997, 4660, 4710
Whiting, Byron *(Voice)*   3498
Whiting, George *(Cast)*   3396
Whiting, George *(Lyricist)*   879, 1134, 2978, 3989, 4808, 4821
Whiting, Jack *(Cast)*   111, 152, 323, 622, 1600, 1791, 1800, 1929, 1931, 1973, 2402, 3312, 3335, 3655, 3659, 3924, 4150, 4180, 4267, 4557, 4651, 4766
Whiting, Mack *(Director)*   2619

Wilder, Jim *(Cast)* 1155
Wilder, Laura Ingalls *(Author)* 3553
Wilder, Thornton *(Author)* 1701, 1828, 2703, 3324, 4008
Wilderman, Steve *(Puppeteer)* 3449
Wilderman, William *(Cast)* 3035, 3691
Wildhack, Robert *(Cast)* 2475
Wildhorn, Frank *(Composer)* 2198, 4229, 4560
Wildhorn, Frank *(Lyricist)* 4229
Wildhorn, Frank *(Vocal Arranger)* 2198
Wile, Everett *(Director)* 2259
Wile, Joan *(Lyricist)* 1023
Wiles, Anthony *(Director)* 732
Wiley, Dennis *(Composer)* 2483
Wiley, Dennis *(Musical Director)* 2483
Wilhelm *(Costumes)* 178, 256, 333, 719, 736, 1454, 1555, 2394, 2666, 3098, 3228, 3268, 3675, 3948, 4393, 4760
Wilhelm, Carl *(Composer)* 3450
Wilhelm, Carl *(Lyricist)* 3450
Wilhelm, Julius *(Author)* 2249, 2594, 3839, 4119, 4490
Wilk, Max *(Librettist)* 63, 943, 3020, 4018
Wilke, Hubert *(Cast)* 1260, 2963, 4500
Wilke, James *(Costumes)* 1940
Wilke, Ray *(Set Design)* 1769
Wilkerson, Arnold *(Cast)* 1072
Wilkerson, Guy *(Cast)* 831
Wilkes, Anna *(Cast)* 1707, 2291
Wilkes, Patricia *(Cast)* 3286
Wilkes, Thomas *(Producer)* 69, 3072
Wilkes, Tom *(Producer)* 4429
Wilkins, Anita *(Cast)* 43
Wilkins, Jeffrey *(Cast)* 4020
Wilkinson, Colm *(Cast)* 2442
Wilkinson, Dudley *(Cast)* 3623
Wilkinson, Dudley *(Composer)* 3623
Wilkinson, Kate *(Cast)* 2965
Wilkinson, Marc *(Composer)* 2260
Wilkinson, Michael *(Cast)* 4830
Wilkinson, Ralph Norman *(Musical Director)* 4409
Wilkof, Lee *(Cast)* 140, 212, 2544, 3557
Wilkof, Lee S. *(Composer)* 3557
Wilkof, Lee S. *(Lyricist)* 3557
Will, Ethyl *(Dance Arranger)* 1146
Will You Remember Prods. *(Producer)* 4251
Willard, Dorothy *(Producer)* 2464
Willard, Harold *(Cast)* 1493
Willard, John *(Cast)* 3147
Willcock, Dave *(Cast)* 4316
Wille, Frank *(Composer)* 2580
Willemetz, Albert *(Author)* 3466
Willemetz, Albert *(Lyricist)* 1176, 3769, 3905
Willeminsky, Ignaz M. *(Author)* 1110
Willemote, Albert *(Lyricist)* 2356
Willens, Doris *(Librettist)* 3476
Willens, Doris *(Lyricist)* 3476
Willenz, Maria *(Costumes)* 2
Willes, Christine *(Cast)* 3901
Willes, Christine *(Librettist)* 3901
Willett, John *(English Lyrics)* 4370
Willett, John *(Librettist)* 4370
Willey, Robert A. *(Producer)* 1698

William, W.R. *(Composer)* 631
William, Warren *(Cast)* 1221
William Patterson College *(Producer)* 1435
Williams *(Lyricist)* 736
Williams, Alexander *(Composer)* 3946
Williams, Alexander *(Lyricist)* 3946
Williams, Alfred *(Set Design)* 284
Williams, Ann *(Cast)* 167
Williams, Barbara *(Cast)* 4173
Williams, Ben *(Cast)* 3022
Williams, Bert *(Cast)* 9, 295, 545, 1599, 2111, 2979, 4088, 4804, 4805, 4806, 4808, 4809, 4810, 4811, 4813, 4838, 4851
Williams, Bert *(Composer)* 9, 295, 2111, 2979, 3820, 4390, 4697, 4804, 4805, 4806, 4808
Williams, Bert *(Librettist)* 4088
Williams, Bert *(Lyricist)* 295, 3820, 4806
Williams, Bert *(Producer)* 4088
Williams, Betty *(Cast)* 3819
Williams, Bob *(Cast)* 1326, 1842
Williams, Charles *(Cast)* 2888
Williams, Charles LaVont *(Cast)* 2908
Williams, Clarence *(Cast)* 500
Williams, Clarence *(Composer)* 146, 432, 443, 500, 1425, 3297, 3709, 3840, 4282
Williams, Clarence *(Librettist)* 500
Williams, Clarence *(Lyricist)* 39, 432, 443, 500, 1425, 3297, 3709, 3840
Williams, Clarence *(Producer)* 500
Williams, Debbie *(Cast)* 2092
Williams, Derek *(Cast)* 2252
Williams, Diane *(Lighting Designer)* 1701
Williams, Diane *(Set Design)* 1701
Williams, Diane Ferry *(Lighting Designer)* 3461
Williams, Dick *(Cast)* 868
Williams, Dick Anthony *(Cast)* 40
Williams, Dorian *(Cast)* 3814
Williams, Edgerton B. *(Cast)* 1867
Williams, Edna *(Composer)* 1212
Williams, Elizabeth *(Cast)* 3676
Williams, Elizabeth *(Producer)* 921, 3862
Williams, Ellis E. *(Cast)* 3285
Williams, Emlyn *(Author)* 2898
Williams, Emlyn *(Librettist)* 2898
Williams, Emlyn *(Lyricist)* 2898
Williams, F.H. *(Composer)* 295, 2111
Williams, F.H. *(Lyricist)* 295
Williams, Florence *(Cast)* 2394
Williams, Frances *(Cast)* 201, 532, 799, 1207, 1489, 1490, 1491, 2135, 2453, 2475, 3131, 4586, 4702
Williams, Frank *(Lyricist)* 3797
Williams, Fred *(Choreographer)* 762
Williams, Freida *(Cast)* 1713
Williams, Fritz *(Cast)* 824, 1926, 2858, 4203, 4359
Williams, George H. *(Set Design)* 4434
Williams, Grace *(Costumes)* 3276
Williams, Grafton *(Cast)* 1561
Williams, Gus *(Cast)* 644
Williams, Gus *(Composer)* 644
Williams, Gus *(Lyricist)* 644

Williams, Hannah *(Cast)* 4235

Williams, Harry *(Composer)* 3020

Williams, Harry *(Lyricist)* 349, 561, 685, 736, 822, 954, 965, 1247, 1566, 2025, 2232, 2889, 2892, 2960, 2990, 3020, 3085, 3205, 3268, 3332, 3675, 3996, 4570, 4753, 4787

Williams, Harry H. *(Composer)* 3259

Williams, Harry H. *(Lyricist)* 3073, 3259

Williams, Hattie *(Cast)* 1066, 1537, 1538, 2498, 2548, 3745, 3751, 3753

Williams, Henry *(Lyricist)* 3525

Williams, Henry "Rubber Legs" *(Cast)* 878

Williams, Herb *(Cast)* 216, 1135, 4637

Williams, Hope *(Cast)* 1972, 3131, 4177

Williams, Hugh *(Composer)* 3605

Williams, Irene *(Cast)* 1385

Williams, Ivan *(Composer)* 1736

Williams, Ivan *(Lyricist)* 1736

Williams, Jack *(Cast)* 1494, 2103, 2453, 2809, 3713

Williams, Jack Eric *(Cast)* 4233

Williams, Jack Eric *(Composer)* 2992

Williams, Jack Eric *(Librettist)* 2992

Williams, Jack Eric *(Lyricist)* 2992

Williams, Jack Eric *(Musical Director)* 2992

Williams, Jesse *(Composer)* 45, 175

Williams, Jesse *(Musical Director)* 1193

Williams, Jill *(Composer)* 2650, 3653

Williams, Jill *(Librettist)* 3653

Williams, Jill *(Lyricist)* 2650, 3653

Williams, Jill *(Musical Director)* 2650

Williams, Jodi *(Cast)* 3788

Williams, John *(Composer)* 4399

Williams, John *(Lighting Designer)* 1701

Williams, John *(Set Design)* 1701

Williams, John H. *(Producer)* 4127

Williams, John R. *(Musical Director)* 1229

Williams, Lotte *(Cast)* 9

Williams, Lottie *(Cast)* 295, 2111

Williams, Malcolm *(Composer)* 2819

Williams, Malcolm *(Lyricist)* 2819

Williams, Marian *(Cast)* 1013

Williams, Marie *(Cast)* 3887

Williams, Marshall *(Lighting Designer)* 1592

Williams, Mary Lou *(Cast)* 467

Williams, Mathew J. *(Lighting Designer)* 2197, 4107

Williams, Maud K. *(Producer)* 2062

Williams, Maude *(Cast)* 904

Williams, Maurice *(Composer)* 4264

Williams, Maurice *(Lyricist)* 4264

Williams, Midge *(Cast)* 889

Williams, Mr. *(Costumes)* 2935

Williams, Musa *(Cast)* 1749, 3541

Williams, Olena *(Cast)* 4253

Williams, Pat *(Orchestrations)* 1611

Williams, PeeWee *(Cast)* 739

Williams, Percy G. *(Director)* 522

Williams, Queenie *(Cast)* 2762

Williams, Ralph *(Cast)* 3918

Williams, Richard *(Set Design)* 2692

Williams, Robert *(Cast)* 4495

Williams, Robert T. *(Lighting Designer)* 227

Williams, Robert T. *(Set Design)* 227, 766, 2941, 3527

Williams, Sammy *(Cast)* 746

Williams, Sarah McCord *(Cast)* 3853

Williams, Spencer *(Composer)* 393, 432, 443, 739, 740, 1813, 1986, 3018, 3297, 3614, 3709, 3840

Williams, Spencer *(Lyricist)* 393, 432, 443, 500, 739, 740, 1813, 2266, 3297, 3614, 3709, 3840, 4282

Williams, Sylvia "Kuumba" *(Cast)* 3297

Williams, Taylor *(Cast)* 1088

Williams, Tennessee *(Author)* 3878, 3879

Williams, Timothy *(Cast)* 4309

Williams, Tom *(Cast)* 1766

Williams, Treat *(Cast)* 2787, 3330, 3852

Williams, Vanessa *(Cast)* 3001

Williams, W.R. *(Composer)* 917

Williams, Wade *(Cast)* 4055

Williams, Walter *(Cast)* 3467

Williams, William *(Cast)* 711, 1145, 1391

Williams Sisters, The *(Cast)* 1487

Williamson, Bruce *(Composer)* 1363, 4433

Williamson, Bruce *(Librettist)* 1049, 4433

Williamson, Bruce *(Lyricist)* 1049, 1363, 1436, 3484, 4433

Williamson, Nicol *(Cast)* 3702

Williamson, Ruth *(Cast)* 3708, 4020

Williamstown Th. Festival *(Producer)* 3195

Williford, Steven *(Cast)* 2737

Willis, Herbert Florence *(Cast)* 1594

Willis, Michael *(Cast)* 1004

Willis, Sally *(Cast)* 1166

Willis, Tom *(Composer)* 459

Willis, Walter *(Choreographer)* 2944

Willison, Walter *(Cast)* 556, 1649, 3311, 4481, 4689

Willison, Walter *(Director)* 556

Willison, Walter *(Librettist)* 556, 3311

Willison, Walter *(Lyricist)* 556, 3311

Willison, Walter *(Producer)* 556

Willman, Noel *(Director)* 989, 2568

Willmetz, Alfred *(Author)* 3295

Willner, A.M. *(Author)* 93, 307, 463, 902, 1066, 1067, 1199, 1680, 1712, 2947, 4119, 4490

Willoughby, Hugh *(Costumes)* 670, 740, 2253, 3489, 4296

Willoughby, Hugh *(Set Design)* 670, 1134, 1135, 1136, 3822, 4296

Willoughby, Joe *(Composer)* 1296

Willoughby, Joe *(Lyricist)* 1296

Willoughby & Jones *(Set Design)* 1529

Wills, Lee *(Composer)* 4264

Wills, Lee *(Lyricist)* 4264

Wills, Lou *(Cast)* 2626

Wills, Mary *(Costumes)* 2092, 3629

Wills, Nat *(Cast)* 712, 1543, 1901, 2865, 4807

Wills, Nat M. *(Cast)* 1118, 2642

Wills, Walter S. *(Cast)* 1975

Wills Jr., Lou *(Cast)* 372, 616, 4629

Willson, Meredith *(Author)* 3016

Willson, Meredith *(Composer)* 1369, 1860, 2510, 3016, 4516

Willson, Meredith *(Librettist)* 1369, 1860, 3016
Willson, Meredith *(Lyricist)* 1369, 1860, 2510, 3016, 4516
Willson, Michael *(Cast)* 2346
Willson, Millicent *(Cast)* 4298
Wilma *(Costumes)* 4777
Wilmer & Vincent *(Producer)* 317
Wilmink, W. Gebe *(Lyricist)* 1865
Wilmink, Willem *(Lyricist)* 1865
Wilmore, Carl *(Composer)* 2902
Wilmot, Gary *(Cast)* 846
Wilner, A.M. *(Author)* 3053, 3996
Wilner, Lori *(Cast)* 1739, 1740, 4342
Wilner, Max *(Producer)* 2601, 2684
Wilner, Sis *(Lyricist)* 4131
Wilshire, George *(Cast)* 1057
Wilson *(Composer)* 3297
Wilson *(Lyricist)* 3297
Wilson, Al *(Composer)* 487, 4763
Wilson, Al *(Lyricist)* 123, 487, 1065, 3443, 4763
Wilson, Andrea *(Lighting Designer)* 2006
Wilson, Art *(Dance Arranger)* 2809
Wilson, Billy *(Choreographer)* 576, 958, 1198, 2539, 2820
Wilson, Billy *(Director)* 3714
Wilson, Brian *(Composer)* 3695, 3739
Wilson, Brian *(Lyricist)* 3695, 3739
Wilson, Clarence *(Composer)* 3958
Wilson, Clarence G. *(Composer)* 2013
Wilson, Clarence G. *(Musical Director)* 4751
Wilson, Dolores *(Cast)* 935, 2064, 4764
Wilson, Don *(Librettist)* 340
Wilson, Dooley *(Cast)* 462, 612
Wilson, Edith *(Cast)* 444, 445, 892, 925, 926, 1980, 1984, 1989, 2034, 2462, 2817, 3513, 3705, 3965
Wilson, Edwin *(Cast)* 2919
Wilson, Edwin *(Producer)* 32
Wilson, Eileen *(Cast)* 587
Wilson, Elizabeth *(Cast)* 3479, 4151, 4370
Wilson, Ethel *(Cast)* 77, 1836
Wilson, Flip *(Cast)* 3264, 3499
Wilson, Frances *(Cast)* 947, 3951
Wilson, Francis *(Cast)* 727, 1030, 1193, 1720, 2502, 2936, 4181, 4430
Wilson, Frank *(Cast)* 2817, 3993
Wilson, Frank *(Librettist)* 2977
Wilson, Gerald *(Composer)* 4091
Wilson, Gerald *(Lyricist)* 4091
Wilson, Hansford *(Cast)* 1182, 3986
Wilson, Harry Leon *(Author)* 1501, 3800
Wilson, Imogene *(Cast)* 4817
Wilson, Jack *(Cast)* 1343
Wilson, Jack *(Composer)* 4566, 4828
Wilson, Jack *(Librettist)* 4566
Wilson, Jack *(Lyricist)* 4566, 4747, 4828
Wilson, Jay *(Cast)* 294, 1322
Wilson, Joe *(Lighting Designer)* 4738
Wilson, John C. *(Director)* 454, 999, 1475, 2331, 2705, 3899
Wilson, John C. *(Producer)* 462, 999, 1238, 3678, 3885, 3906, 4610
Wilson, John P. *(Cast)* 4599

Wilson, John P. *(Librettist)* 106, 1014, 1274, 3560, 4599
Wilson, John P. *(Lyricist)* 1014, 1274, 3560
Wilson, Joseph *(Lighting Designer)* 1455, 2603, 2686, 4064, 4404, 4422
Wilson, Joseph P. *(Lighting Designer)* 3868
Wilson, Julie *(Cast)* 1739, 2217, 2437, 3389
Wilson, K.C. *(Cast)* 1377, 4020, 4288, 4370
Wilson, Knox *(Cast)* 586, 1220, 2408
Wilson, Knox G. *(Cast)* 509
Wilson, Lanford *(Author)* 1268
Wilson, Leola *(Composer)* 478
Wilson, Leola *(Lyricist)* 478
Wilson, Lester *(Cast)* 162, 2796, 4003
Wilson, Lester *(Choreographer)* 1699, 2796, 4003
Wilson, Lester *(Director)* 4003
Wilson, Lester *(Librettist)* 4003
Wilson, Lester *(Lyricist)* 4003
Wilson, Lloyd *(Cast)* 4165
Wilson, Lohr *(Costumes)* 2284
Wilson, Lucille *(Cast)* 876
Wilson, Margaret *(Cast)* 1460
Wilson, Marie *(Cast)* 242
Wilson, Mary Louise *(Cast)* 1049, 1107, 1310, 1364, 1585, 1991, 2072, 3468, 3787, 3889, 4659
Wilson, Nina *(Cast)* 4278
Wilson, Pasean *(Cast)* 484
Wilson, Patricia *(Cast)* 1280
Wilson, Randal *(Cast)* 3741
Wilson, Robert *(Cast)* 2559
Wilson, Robert *(Choreographer)* 4774
Wilson, Robert *(Composer)* 3695
Wilson, Robert *(Lyricist)* 3695, 4774
Wilson, Robert H. *(Cast)* 1532, 3028
Wilson, Robin *(Cast)* 1846
Wilson, Rowland *(Composer)* 418
Wilson, Ruth *(Choreographer)* 55
Wilson, Sandy *(Composer)* 507, 4541
Wilson, Sandy *(Librettist)* 507, 4541
Wilson, Sandy *(Lyricist)* 507, 4541
Wilson, Scat *(Musical Director)* 3814
Wilson, Scott *(Costumes)* 1670
Wilson, Snoo *(Librettist)* 1161
Wilson, Speedy *(Cast)* 435
Wilson, Stuart *(Cast)* 2446
Wilson, Teddy *(Cast)* 3893
Wilson, Thomas *(Composer)* 4679
Wilson, Thomas *(Lyricist)* 4679
Wilson, Trey *(Cast)* 1289, 1372, 3448, 4390
Wilson, Walter *(Cast)* 1098, 4360
Wilson, Walter *(Director)* 2927, 3179, 3655, 3712, 4296, 4648
Wilson, Walter C. *(Cast)* 2836
Wilson, Wesley *(Composer)* 478
Wilson, Wesley *(Lyricist)* 478
Wilson, William E. *(Cast)* 3856
Wilson, William J. *(Choreographer)* 60, 188, 1613, 2334, 2358, 3701, 4509, 4655
Wilson, William J. *(Director)* 60, 106, 276, 340, 2358, 2732, 2789, 3096, 3236, 3342, 3525, 3663, 3729, 4490, 4493, 4521, 4599, 4616, 4657, 4692

Wise, Thomas *(Director)*   2383
Wise, Tom *(Cast)*   2498, 2889, 3163
Wiseman, George *(Musical Director)*   4671
Wiseman, George *(Vocal Arranger)*   3154
Wiseman, Joseph *(Cast)*   2411
Wishy, Joe *(Producer)*   635
Wisinski, Ron *(Cast)*   4288
Wisner, James J. *(Musical Director)*   729
Wisner, James J. *(Producer)*   729, 793
Wisner, James J. *(Vocal Arranger)*   729
Wisner, Jimmy *(Arrangements)*   793
Wisner, Jimmy *(Musical Director)*   3858
Wisner, Jimmy *(Orchestrations)*   2235, 3858
Wisner, Jimmy *(Producer)*   3858
Wisner, Jimmy *(Vocal Arranger)*   3858
Wisner, John *(Set Design)*   63
Wissman, Gary *(Set Design)*   3641
Wiswell, L.C. *(Producer)*   2919
Witchie, Katherine *(Cast)*   3137
Witcover, Walt *(Director)*   3970
Witham, John *(Cast)*   2568
Withee, Mabel *(Cast)*   200, 1033, 2270, 2546, 2888,
    3770, 4085
Withers, Charles *(Cast)*   543
Withers, Jane *(Cast)*   1577
Witherspoon, Cora *(Cast)*   3850
Witherspoon, Marc *(Composer)*   1713
Witherspoon, Marc *(Lyricist)*   1713
Witke, Robert *(Cast)*   3625
Witkin, Stephen *(Librettist)*   3601
Witler, Ben Zion *(Composer)*   2356
Witler, Ben Zion *(Lyricist)*   2356
Witmark, Isadore *(Composer)*   694
Witmark, Julius P. *(Cast)*   1627
Wits' End *(Producer)*   597
Witt, Max *(Composer)*   1535, 2518
Witt, Max *(Director)*   1118
Witt, Max *(Lyricist)*   2518
Witt, Max *(Musical Director)*   1118
Witt, Max S. *(Composer)*   909, 1118, 2879, 3073
Witt, Max S. *(Producer)*   909
Wittlinger, Karl *(Librettist)*   1062
Wittman, Scott *(Choreographer)*   2555
Wittman, Scott *(Composer)*   2555
Wittman, Scott *(Librettist)*   2555
Wittman, Scott *(Lyricist)*   2555
Wittop, Freddy *(Costumes)*   269, 323, 521, 656, 1012,
    1119, 1478, 1764, 1828, 2050, 2078, 2304, 2626, 3274,
    3526, 3731, 4190, 4395, 4482, 4701
Wittstein, Ed *(Costumes)*   519, 681, 1190, 1245,
    2295, 4764
Wittstein, Ed *(Lighting Designer)*   681, 1190, 2357
Wittstein, Ed *(Set Design)*   461, 681, 1049, 1091, 1190,
    1245, 2051, 2295, 2357, 2418, 4288, 4764
Wizoreck, Barry *(Cast)*   2735
Wodehouse, P.G. *(Author)*   3819, 4678
Wodehouse, P.G. *(Librettist)*   163, 334, 611, 1527, 1610,
    1784, 1805, 2340, 2430, 2900, 3163, 3213, 3230, 3243,
    3245, 3250, 3727, 3866
Wodehouse, P.G. *(Lyricist)*   333, 334, 611, 627, 773, 1454,

1527, 1610, 1784, 2204, 2340, 2372, 2430, 2900, 2907,
3018, 3163, 3177, 3213, 3230, 3243, 3245, 3250, 3727,
3766, 3775, 3819, 3866, 3949, 4001, 4357
Woess, Carl *(Composer)*   2931
Wohl *(Composer)*   907
Wohl, David *(Cast)*   3544
Wohl, Herman *(Composer)*   1609
Wohl, Herman *(Lyricist)*   1609
Wohl, Jack *(Lyricist)*   757
Wohl, Jack *(Producer)*   3499
Wohlman, Al *(Cast)*   3842
Wojak, Regina *(Librettist)*   2178
Woldin, Judd *(Cast)*   322
Woldin, Judd *(Composer)*   2320, 2513, 3656, 4288
Woldin, Judd *(Dance Arranger)*   3656
Woldin, Judd *(Librettist)*   2320, 4288
Woldin, Judd *(Lyricist)*   2320, 2513, 4288
Woldin, Judd *(Orchestrations)*   4288
Wolever, Harry *(Choreographer)*   4401
Wolf, Don *(Composer)*   1296
Wolf, Don *(Lyricist)*   1296
Wolf, Edward E. *(Costumes)*   1880
Wolf, Edward E. *(Set Design)*   1880
Wolf, Leo *(Vocal Arranger)*   4331
Wolf, Peter *(Set Design)*   4395
Wolf, Rennold *(Composer)*   4799
Wolf, Rennold *(Librettist)*   1327, 1663, 1849, 3652, 3685,
    4809, 4812, 4813
Wolf, Rennold *(Lyricist)*   335, 1663, 1849, 3031, 3652,
    3685, 4799, 4805, 4809, 4811, 4813, 4831
Wolf, Richard R. *(Composer)*   3527
Wolf, Tommy *(Composer)*   2928, 3094
Wolf, Tommy *(Musical Director)*   3094
Wolf, Tommy *(Vocal Arranger)*   3094
Wolf, Walter *(Cast)*   201
Wolfe, Burton *(Director)*   2177
Wolfe, Burton *(Librettist)*   2177
Wolfe, Burton *(Lyricist)*   2177
Wolfe, Carol *(Cast)*   1597
Wolfe, Edwin R. *(Director)*   1632
Wolfe, George C. *(Director)*   2200
Wolfe, George C. *(Librettist)*   2200, 3368, 3628, 4535
Wolfe, George C. *(Lyricist)*   3368
Wolfe, Jacques *(Composer)*   2225
Wolfe, John Leslie *(Cast)*   564, 1804, 3411
Wolfe, Karin *(Cast)*   239, 1511, 2219
Wolfe, Mindy *(Costumes)*   4740
Wolfe, Sharon *(Lyricist)*   2039
Wolfe, Thomas *(Author)*   135
Wolfe, Tom *(Librettist)*   4690
Wolfe, Wendy *(Cast)*   793
Wolff, Alexander *(Cast)*   99
Wolff, Art *(Director)*   474
Wolff, David M. *(Librettist)*   1556
Wolff, David M. *(Lyricist)*   1556
Wolff, Reuben *(Musical Director)*   3842, 4211
Wolfington, Iggie *(Cast)*   759, 3016
Wolfson, D.S. *(Producer)*   4204
Wolfson, David *(Conductor)*   4251
Wolfson, David *(Musical Director)*   696, 3568

Wooley, Monty *(Director)* 3861
Wooley, Reginald *(Costumes)* 507
Woolf, Edgar Allen *(Director)* 3446, 3717, 3911, 4422
Woolf, Edgar Allen *(Librettist)* 529, 994, 1796, 2601, 2717, 3446, 3740, 3754, 3796, 3911, 4422, 4687
Woolf, Edgar Allen *(Lyricist)* 529, 1796, 2601, 2717, 3446, 3717, 3754, 4080, 4422
Woolf, Walter *(Cast)* 684, 787, 905, 1113, 1219, 2419, 2813, 2856, 3403, 3406, 3680
Woolf, Walter *(Composer)* 2506
Woolf, Walter *(Incidental Music)* 1218
Woolfolk, Boyle *(Composer)* 4215
Woolfolk, Boyle *(Lyricist)* 4215
Woolfolk, Boyle *(Producer)* 1966
Woolford, Hughie *(Composer)* 2223
Woolley, Monty *(Cast)* 130, 2348, 2729, 3283, 4622
Woolley, Monty *(Director)* 111, 423, 689, 1272, 2252, 3131, 3325, 3378, 4583
Woolley, Scot *(Dance Arranger)* 36, 4146
Woolsey, Robert *(Cast)* 78, 468, 1026, 2789, 3207, 3466, 3540, 3712, 3719
Woolverton, Linda *(Librettist)* 330
Wopat, Tom *(Cast)* 426
Worde, Phil *(Composer)* 3022
Worde, Phil *(Lyricist)* 3022
Worde, Phil *(Musical Director)* 3022
Work, Henry Clay *(Composer)* 1897
Work, Henry Clay *(Lyricist)* 1897, 3923
Work, Julian *(Orchestrations)* 620, 1336, 3813
Workman, Jason *(Cast)* 2805
Workmen's Circle, The *(Producer)* 4172
Worley, Jo Anne *(Cast)* 410, 1993, 2663, 3576
Worrall, Tom *(Composer)* 2082, 2482
Worrall, Tom *(Lyricist)* 2082, 2482
Worrall, Tom *(Orchestrations)* 2482
Worsley, Pat *(Cast)* 841
Worth, Adelaide *(Cast)* 1473
Worth, Billie *(Cast)* 649, 911, 1894, 3893, 4374, 4557
Worth, Bobby *(Composer)* 2085, 2086, 2087
Worth, Bobby *(Lyricist)* 2085, 2086, 2087, 2162
Worth, Caroline *(Cast)* 2339
Worth, Gracie *(Cast)* 2444, 3011
Wortheim, Louis *(Set Design)* 2845
Worthley, Abbott *(Cast)* 2448
Worthley, Minthorne *(Cast)* 2448
Worthy & Thompson *(Cast)* 444
Wouk, Herman *(Librettist)* 1957
Wray, Fay *(Cast)* 3168
Wray, John *(Choreographer)* 620, 3105
Wray, John *(Director)* 1858
Wray, Josephine *(Cast)* 1467
Wreford, Reynell *(Composer)* 1187
Wren, Jane *(Cast)* 3450, 3451
Wright *(Composer)* 1460
Wright, Amy *(Cast)* 1268
Wright, Andrea *(Cast)* 2285
Wright, Ann-Marie *(Costumes)* 2197
Wright, Ben *(Cast)* 2143, 3368, 4146
Wright, Bob *(Cast)* 2838
Wright, Charles Randolph *(Cast)* 2784

Wright, Daniel *(Cast)* 3682
Wright, David *(Composer)* 1736
Wright, David *(Librettist)* 1736
Wright, David *(Lyricist)* 1736
Wright, David C. *(Choreographer)* 2676
Wright, David C. *(Director)* 2676
Wright, E.H. *(Cast)* 4343
Wright, Ellen *(Lyricist)* 2506
Wright, Fred E. *(Producer)* 331
Wright, Frederic Colt *(Composer)* 4549
Wright, G.G. *(Cast)* 3270
Wright, G.M. *(Librettist)* 3319
Wright, Garland *(Director)* 3010
Wright, George *(Cast)* 489
Wright, Helena-Joyce *(Cast)* 105
Wright, Hugh *(Composer)* 1391
Wright, Hugh *(Lyricist)* 1391
Wright, Hugh E. *(Lyricist)* 702
Wright, Margaret *(Cast)* 23, 755, 2243, 3418, 4684
Wright, Margaret *(Librettist)* 4209
Wright, Margaret *(Lyricist)* 4209
Wright, Mark *(Producer)* 2418
Wright, Martha *(Cast)* 3013
Wright, Mary Catherine *(Cast)* 1914, 4252, 4390
Wright, Mason *(Cast)* 1882
Wright, Mason *(Lyricist)* 1882
Wright, Michael *(Cast)* 1797
Wright, Michael *(Choreographer)* 2580
Wright, Michael *(Director)* 2580
Wright, Ned *(Cast)* 2415
Wright, Peter *(Choreographer)* 455
Wright, Ray *(Orchestrations)* 3126
Wright, Rebecca *(Cast)* 2820
Wright, Richard *(Author)* 952
Wright, Rick *(Composer)* 3739
Wright, Robert *(Author)* 4383
Wright, Robert *(Cast)* 1918, 4155, 4278
Wright, Robert *(Composer)* 161, 223, 649, 848, 849, 1119, 1415, 1649, 2295, 2327, 3683, 4073, 4075, 4117, 4316, 4383
Wright, Robert *(Director)* 1711
Wright, Robert *(Librettist)* 649
Wright, Robert *(Lyricist)* 161, 223, 649, 848, 849, 1119, 1415, 1649, 1680, 1681, 1711, 2295, 2327, 2679, 3683, 4073, 4075, 4117, 4316, 4383
Wright, Russell *(Costumes)* 1653
Wright, Russell *(Lighting Designer)* 1653
Wright, Russell *(Set Design)* 1653
Wright, Samuel E. *(Cast)* 1086, 3001, 3330, 3548, 4286, 4619
Wright Jr., Fred *(Cast)* 675
Wrightson, Ann *(Lighting Designer)* 4
Wrightson, Ann G. *(Lighting Designer)* 2658
Wrightson, Earl *(Cast)* 1284
Wrigley, Ben *(Cast)* 302
Wroderick Productions *(Producer)* 3235
Wromley, Dan *(Cast)* 645
Wrubel, Allie *(Composer)* 1251
Wuerz, Charles N. *(Director)* 421
Wulff, Derick *(Librettist)* 2330

X

Y

Yuen, Lily *(Cast)* 4763
Yulin, Harris *(Cast)* 4601
Yunker, Ken *(Lighting Designer)* 4732
Yurka, Blanche *(Cast)* 17
Yurman, Lawrence *(Arrangements)* 2945, 4515
Yurman, Lawrence *(Incidental Music)* 2945
Yurman, Lawrence *(Musical Director)* 1589, 2945
Yuskis, Antoinette *(Cast)* 3936
Yvain, Maurice *(Author)* 2637
Yvain, Maurice *(Composer)* 25, 1176, 1425, 2637, 3148, 3295, 3500, 3905, 4815, 4816, 4817, 4831, 4847, 4852
Yvain, Maurice *(Lyricist)* 2637
Yves *(Costumes)* 2599
Yvette *(Cast)* 2696

Z

Zabelle, Flora *(Cast)* 17, 1536, 2730, 2844, 3423, 3828, 4422, 4754, 4762
Zacharias, Emily *(Cast)* 757, 3272
Zagaeski, Mark *(Cast)* 3162
Zagnit, Stuart *(Cast)* 2354, 2646, 2704, 4288
Zakharov, Mark *(Director)* 2269
Zakrzewski, Paul *(Librettist)* 3876
Zakrzewski, Paul *(Lyricist)* 3876
Zaks, Jerry *(Cast)* 4390
Zaks, Jerry *(Director)* 212, 4031
Zakutansky, Peter J. *(Costumes)* 1004, 1155
Zalon, Paul *(Set Design)* 4595
Zalotoff, Max *(Librettist)* 4463
Zaltzberg, Charlotte *(Librettist)* 3656
Zalud, S. *(Costumes)* 764, 1626, 2546, 2939, 3985, 4269
Zalud, Samuel *(Costumes)* 2665
Zamecnik, John S. *(Composer)* 1866, 1868
Zangwill, Israel *(Author)* 2319, 2320, 2321, 2819, 4288
Zanini, Ester *(Cast)* 4113
Zany, King *(Composer)* 4814
Zany, King *(Lyricist)* 487, 4814
Zaremba, Kathryn *(Cast)* 155
Zaret, Hy *(Lyricist)* 7, 146, 1880, 2175, 2447
Zarro, Ron *(Cast)* 1978
Zarrow, Happy *(Cast)* 4859
Zaslow, Michael *(Cast)* 482, 3305
Zavin, Benjamin Bernard *(Librettist)* 1158
Zazarus, Emma *(Lyricist)* 1609
Zbornak, Kent *(Cast)* 544
Zeb, Jolly *(Cast)* 4859
Zehavi, D. *(Composer)* 1740
Zeibarth, Frances *(Costumes)* 396, 1901
Zeitz, Johnny *(Cast)* 562
Zelby, Lottie *(Costumes)* 2321
Zelenko, Michael *(Composer)* 3426
Zelenko, Michael *(Lyricist)* 3426
Zelinka, Sidney *(Librettist)* 924, 1898
Zell, F. *(Author)* 3150, 3151
Zell, Gladys *(Cast)* 2394, 2566, 2835, 2892, 3791
Zell, Violet *(Cast)* 2184, 2902, 4393
Zeller, Gary *(Lighting Designer)* 4536

Zeller, Gary *(Set Design)* 4536
Zeller, Kathy *(Cast)* 1781
Zeller, Mark *(Cast)* 181, 757, 2354
Zeller, Robert *(Musical Director)* 911
Zeller-Alexis, Dana *(Cast)* 1169, 4790
Zemach, Benjamin *(Choreographer)* 1196, 3501
Zender, Marguerite *(Cast)* 136, 1174, 3192, 3420, 3533, 4378
Zeno, Norman *(Librettist)* 1342
Zeno, Norman *(Lyricist)* 532, 1127, 1191, 1342, 3955, 4667
Zentner, Morris *(Musical Director)* 1215
Zentner & His Orchestra, Si *(Cast)* 1326
Zera, Lanie *(Cast)* 81
Zhurbin, Alexander *(Author)* 2012
Zhurbin, Alexander *(Composer)* 2012
Ziebarth, Frances *(Costumes)* 3093
Ziebarth, Frances M. *(Costumes)* 4599
Ziebarth, Mme. *(Costumes)* 2139
Ziegfeld, Florenz *(Librettist)* 4817
Ziegfeld, Florenz *(Producer)* 152, 376, 429, 683, 827, 1175, 1881, 1979, 2308, 2506, 2594, 2715, 2872, 2892, 2900, 3179, 3332, 3387, 3392, 3673, 3719, 3766, 3768, 3819, 3949, 3953, 3980, 4023, 4094, 4357, 4453, 4683, 4712, 4801, 4802, 4803, 4804, 4805, 4806, 4807, 4808, 4809, 4810, 4811, 4812, 4813, 4814, 4815, 4816, 4818, 4819, 4821, 4823, 4831, 4832, 4833, 4834, 4835, 4836, 4837, 4838, 4839, 4840, 4841, 4842, 4843, 4844, 4845, 4846, 4847, 4848, 4849, 4851, 4852, 4853
Ziegfeld, Mignon *(Composer)* 3085
Ziegfeld, Mignon *(Lyricist)* 3085
Ziegfeld, William *(Producer)* 1550
Ziehrer, Carl M. *(Author)* 2334, 2914
Ziehrer, Carl M. *(Composer)* 2334, 2914
Zielinski, Scott *(Lighting Designer)* 1702, 2945
Ziemba, Karen *(Cast)* 131, 4297
Zien, Chip *(Cast)* 1038, 1234, 2143, 2746, 3666, 3711, 4022, 4540
Ziering, Ian *(Cast)* 2064
Ziff, Stuart *(Composer)* 3076
Zimbalist Sr., Efrem *(Composer)* 1962
Zimmer, Bernard *(Author)* 657
Zimmerman, Charles *(Cast)* 998
Zimmerman, Charles *(Composer)* 998
Zimmerman, Charles *(Musical Director)* 3268, 4723
Zimmerman, Charles *(Orchestrations)* 3626
Zimmerman, Harry *(Orchestrations)* 1891
Zimmerman, Mme. *(Costumes)* 2836
Zinberg, Arthur D. *(Producer)* 4595
Zink, Adolph *(Cast)* 1375
Zinkeisen, Doris *(Cast)* 4341
Zinkeisen, Doris *(Costumes)* 791, 792, 1680, 1763, 3214, 3291, 3756, 4154
Zinkeisen, Doris *(Set Design)* 791, 3214, 3756, 4154
Zinn, Randolyn *(Choreographer)* 3010
Zippel, David *(Librettist)* 1597
Zippel, David *(Lyricist)* 4, 146, 775, 1038, 1298, 1597, 1633, 2171, 2283, 2754, 4799
Zippel, Joanne L. *(Producer)* 2283
Zipper, Herbert *(Musical Director)* 309

Zipprodt, Patricia *(Costumes)*   161, 393, 610, 723, 975, 1265, 1497, 2318, 2660, 2664, 2958, 3039, 3299, 3506, 3551, 3897, 3918, 3944, 4019, 4210, 4216, 4252, 4338, 4862

Zipser, Arthur *(Lyricist)*   3226

Ziskin, Victor *(Composer)*   4785

Ziskin, Victor *(Musical Director)*   4785

Zito, Ron *(Arrangements)*   944

Zito, Ron *(Orchestrations)*   944

Zito, Torrie *(Orchestrations)*   1633, 3428, 4020

Zittel, C.F. *(Composer)*   4757

Zittel, C.F. *(Lyricist)*   4757

Zmed, Adrian *(Cast)*   1149

Zodrow, John *(Librettist)*   1637

Zoellner, Peter Lee *(Producer)*   92

Zogott, Seymour *(Lyricist)*   1049, 2611

Zoob, Dave *(Composer)*   4283

Zook, Elizabeth *(Costumes)*   4291

Zoran *(Costumes)*   4533

Zorich, Louis *(Cast)*   1634

Zorina, Vera *(Cast)*   1101, 2061, 2597

Zoritch, George *(Cast)*   3, 1140

Zuber, Catherine *(Costumes)*   158, 2185, 3682, 3937, 4147

Zucca, Mana *(Cast)*   1888

Zucker, Stan *(Producer)*   1898

Zuckerberg, Regina *(Cast)*   3995

Zulu, Mamthandi *(Cast)*   4438

Zur, Menachem *(Composer)*   4514

Zur, Menachem *(Musical Director)*   4514

Zuro, Josiah *(Musical Director)*   1743, 3308

Zwar, Charles *(Composer)*   1408, 2168, 2227, 4153

Zweibel, Alan *(Librettist)*   1038, 1512

Zwerling, Ruby *(Musical Director)*   1898

Zwick, Joel *(Cast)*   963

Zwick, Joel *(Choreographer)*   963

Zwick, Joel *(Director)*   963

Zwroh, Stefan *(Librettist)*   2202

Song Index

A

A + B = C 3490
A-B-C 2014
A.B.C. 3828
A.B.C. Song, The 4160
A.B.C.'s 3110
A-B-C's of the U.S.A., The 4759
A Caroling We Go 4391
A-Choo 1962
I'm a Cuban Girl 1783
A-Hunting We Will Go 4443
A Is For 2069
A.J. 1191
A Kis Grof 4228
A Kisassonyi Ferje 2526
A-L-E 2119
A-L-E-X-A-N-D-R-I-A 2671
A la Gastronome 2691
A La Girl, The 737
A la Hockey 3403
A La Lenox Avenue 876
A La Minute 1962
A la Mode Girl, The 2715
A La Parisienne 68
A La Pimpernel 3491
A la Viennese 3978
A...My Name Is Ellie 2427
A Nier Tzeit 4463
A-1 March 162
A.P.I.S. Parade, The 98
A Razz a Ma Tazz 1120
A-Stage 1116
A-Tangle, A-Dangle 1698
A-Tisket A-Tasket 4534, 887
A-Weaving 705
Aba Daba Honeymoon 3589
Ababu (dance) 2327
Abadaba Club, The 3532
Abandon 1182
Abandoned 2565
Abbe's Appearance 3456
Abbondanza 2961
Abby's Lament 10
ABC of Traffic Sketch, The (inst.) 1657
ABC to XYZ 2784
ABC's of Success, The 4028
Abdication 3766
Abduction 1700

Abduction, The 2727
Abduction Ballet 1245
Abductions, (and so forth) 1245
Abdullah 1079
Abdullah's Farewell 2686
Abe and Me and the Baby 3926
Abe Lincoln 1840
Abe Lincoln Has Just One Country 1476
Aber Nit 2800
Abi Tsu Zein Mit Dir
    (As Long As I'm with You) 1279
Abide with Me 1073
Abiding with You 1037
Abie Baby 1717
Abie's Irish Rose 1250
Abou Ben Adhem 59
About a Quarter to Nine 1359
About Face 1930
About the Ompire 654
About Time 1234
Above! Above! 2551
Above the Law 155
Abracadabra 2847, 4517
Abraham, Martin and John 3018
Absent-Minded Maid 2101
Absent Minded Me 1420
Absinthe 1834, 2287
Absinthe Drip 2287
Absinthe Frappe 2160, 4818
Absolute Don of a Juan 2336
Absolutely Certain 2336
Absolutely Nothing Tonight 3203
Absolution 3944
Absurd As a Chuck-a-Walla Bird 863
Abundance and Charity 754
Abuse 4447
Abyssinia 10
AC/DC 4138
Academic Fugue 1846
Academy Award 338
Academy Award Highlights 407
Academy Awards Theme 3636
Academy Rag, The 1531
Acapulco Polka 865
Accent Makes No Difference in the
    Language of Love, The 1088
Accident!, An 3675
Accidents Will Happen 3068
Accompaniment 1450

Ah, Maien Zeit!   1822
Ah, May the Red Rose Live Alway   4149
Ah Men   3666
Ah, Miss   4233
Ah Oui   1175
Ah, Oui!   3618
Ah, Our Germans   1739
Ah, Paris!   1329, 3967
Ah! Sweet Mystery of Life (Dream Melody)   3081
Ah, Sweet Revenge   3197
Ah, Sweet Youth!   4106
Ah, There   3392
Ah, There You Are   919
Ah, To Be Home Again   3526
Ah, Well, We'll Try to Be Precise   4554
Ah! Wilderness   34
Ah, Wilderness!   4270
Ah! Woe Is Me   104
Ah, Yes, I Am in Love   2701
Ah! Yon Is No Song of Triumph   3732
Ah, Men   33
Ahoy for a Sailor   4357
Ai Yi Yi   4510
Aida   3035
Aida McCluskie   1318
Aimee Is No Angel   35
Ain't Broadway Grand   36
Ain't Cha Coming Back, Mary Ann to Maryland   3963
Ain't Everything Grand!   1387
Ain't Got No   1717
Ain't Got No Tears Left   599, 3278
Ain't Got No Worry Long As Your're My Baby   740
Ain't Gwine to Work No More   352
Ain't Had No Lovin' in a Long Time   3676
Ain't He a Joy?   4764
Ain't I Something?   2437
Ain't It a Grand and Glorious Feeling   3230
Ain't It a Joy   3210
Ain't It a Shame   2556
Ain't It Awful   1271
Ain't It Awful the Heat   4169
Ain't It Awful the Heat?   369
Ain't It de Truth   2190
Ain't It Funny   2067
Ain't It Funny What a Difference a
   Few Drinks Make   4810
Ain't It Funny What a Difference
   Just a Few Hours Make   4754
Ain't It Good   730
Ain't It Romantic   3243
Ain't It Sad   4693
Ain't Love Easy   4398
Ain't Love Grand   487, 942, 1074, 2277
Ain't Love Grand?   1690
Ain't Love Wonderful   642
Ain't Marryin' Nobody   3599
Ain't Misbehavin'   39, 1980, 3020
Ain't Nature Grand   4718
Ain't Nature Grand?   4815
Ain't Never Gonna Find Another Love Song   916

Ain't No Party   1103
Ain't No Place Like Home   1201
Ain't No Women There   564
Ain't Nobody Got a Bed of Roses   4398
Ain't Nobody Here but Us Chickens   1296
Ain't Puttin' Out Nothin'   691
Ain't She Sweet   393, 3175
Ain't She Sweet?   3754
Ain't That Always the Way   2696
Ain't That Delicious   1707
Ain't That Langwidge Though   3908
Ain't That Something   4343
Ain't Too Proud to Beg   4534
Ain't We Got Fun   393, 3842
Ain't We Got Love   4253
Ain't Worth a Dime   562
Ain't You Ashamed?   3210
Ain't You Heard?   2028
Ain't You Never Been Afraid?   2726
Ain'tcha Glad You Got Music?   2034
Aintcha Got Music   1772
Air   1717
Air Conditioning   924
Air Guitar   119
Air Male   1116
Air Minded   1323
Air Strip   1841
Airy Mary   4497
Ajade Papa   4579
Akiwawa   3814
Al Fleagle Arrangement, An   3955
Al Fresco   3837
Al Smith for President   1837
Al the Chemist   42
Alabam   822
Alabam'   561
Alabam' Banjo Man   1223
Alabama   4762
Alabama Barbecue   883
Alabama Bound Blues   43
Alabama Cadets, The   2721
Alabama Coon   45
Alabama Family   3364
Alabama Sam   4801
Alabama Song   369
Alabama Stomp   1128, 1132
Alabamy   1989
Alabamy Bound   1425
Aladdin   44, 2547, 3712, 3958
Aladdin's Daughter   3091
Alaiyo   3656
Alamo Widows' Lament   2573
Alarm   255
Alas for a Man without Brains   4723
Alas for You   1595
Alas, Lorraine   3931
Alas, the Time Is Past   429
Alaura's Theme   775
Alba   533
Albany   2481

All Fall Down   109, 3757
All for a Green Ribbon   4404
All for Charity   2768
All for Him   3347
All for Love   67, 1955
All for One and One for All   4357
All for the Best   1595
All for the Sake of a Girl   1016
All for You   69, 2642, 2723, 2262, 3590, 3843, 4435
All for You, Louis   3840
All Full of Ginger   3087
All Full of Talk   2907
All Fwoo   112
All Gall   221
All Girl Band   4
All Girl Band, The   4483
All Girls Are Like a Rainbow   560
All Glory to the Young   1770, 3280
All God's Chillun Got Movie Shows   1000
All Goes Badly   996
All Goin' Out an' Nothin' Comin' In   2111
All Good Gifts   1595
All Good Things   1770
All Greece   4615
All Hail, Great Judge   2977
All Hail the Bride   4032
All Hail the Empress   161
All Hail the King   3337, 4615
All Hail the Political Honeymoon   2344
All Hail the Queen   3628
All Hail to the General   1027
All Hallowe'en   2394
All Hearts with a Keen Curiosity Burn (Opening
   Chorus)   4258
All I Ask Is to Forget You   4751
All I Ask of You   3464
All I Can Do Is Cry   4533
All I Care About   723
All I Crave Is More of Life   3081
All I Do Is Dream of You   544
All I Got Is You   314
All I Need   1072, 1637
All I Need Is Me (I Need Me Babe)   2172
All I Need Is One Good Break   1310
All I Need Is Someone Like You   2296
All I Need Is the Girl   1709
All I Owe Ioway   4146
All I Remember Is You   1171
All I Want   1308
All I Want from You Is You   3057
All I Want in the Wide, Wide World Is You   1525
All I Want in the Wide, Wide, World Is You,
   Just You   1900
All I Want Is a Home   277
All I Want Is a Little Bit of Fun   3828
All I Want Is a Lullaby   4271
All I Want Is Love   2263
All I Want Is My Black Baby Back   1063
All I Want Is Not to Want   3355
All I Want Is Plenty of Loving   2013

All I Want Is You   3052
All I Want to Do   528
All I Wanted Was a Cup of Tea   1015
All I Wanted Was the Dream   2437
All I've Got Is Me   3576, 154
All I've Got to Get Now Is My Man   3359
All in a Little Dance   2732
All in a Short Half Hour   2214
All in Fun   1611, 4557
All in Love   71
All in the Cause of Economy   1721
All in the Line of Duty   3882
All in the Name of Love   3167
All in the Point of View   2513
All in the Wearing   1478, 2533
All Is Fair   1682
All Is Fair in Love and War   3736
All Is Vanity   1128, 1132
All Is Well   1351
All Is Well in Larchmont   1273
All Is Well in the City   3602
All Kinds of Giants   73
All Kinds of People   3505
All Lanes Much Reach a Turning   1011
All Life Is Full of Pleasure   4687
All Long Island Gossips   2352
All Love, All Love   4523
All Men   3558
All Men Are the Same   4795
All Men Have Their Troubles   4559
All Mucked Up   1619
(They're) All My Boys   2533
All My Days Till End of Life   758
All My Girls   470, 4364
All My Good Mornings   4558
All My Heart's Desire   1636
All My Life   1215, 1345, 2248, 2373, 1750, 3741
All My Life I Lost It for Him   4108
All My Worldly Belongings   2368
All My Yesterdays   3697
All Nature Is at Peace and Rest
   (Forest Song)   3736
All Night Long   3723
All of 'Em Say   2556
All Of a Sudden It's Spring   692
All of It All   3080
All of My Dreams   3517
All of My Laughter   1273
All of My Life   101, 1061, 789
All of Them Was Friends of Mine   317
All of These and More   483
All of Us Are Brothers   109
All of Us Are Niggers   109
All of You   3972
All on Account of Eliza   402
All Our Friends   1478
All Our Tomorrows   4027
All Out Bugle Call   901
All Over My Mind   1216
All Over Town   3649

All Paris   4073
All Pepped Up   4818
All Pleasures in Life   4032
All Pull Together   2571, 3500
All Right   1232
All Roads Lead to Church   353
All Roads Lead to Hollywood   2754
All She Can Do Is Say No   1634
All She Could Say Was 'Oui'   2951
All She Did Was This   2569
All She'd Say Was 'Um Hum'   4814
All-Talking, All-Singing, All-Dancing   2968
All That and Heaven Too   4498
All That Glitters   3909
All That Has Happened   2626
All That He'd Want Me to Be   652
All That I Know   564
All That I Need Is A Hallway   1685
All That I Want   2216
All That Jazz   723, 131
All the Boys Love Mary   4842
All the Children in a Row   3718
All the Comforts of Home   135, 1270, 2494, 4037
All the Dark Is Changed to Sunshine   3418
All the Dearly Beloved   2050
All the Elks and Masons   2475
All the Flowers Turn to Snow   2177
All the Girls Are Lovely at the Seaside   537
All the Girls Have Got a Friend in Me   1663
All the Girls Look Wonderful to Me   1961
All the Girls Love Me   4115
All the Girls Were Pretty   4541
All the Ifs and Maybes   4330
All the King's Horses   4367
All the King's Horses and Men   3774
All the Little Birds in Nests Agree   792
All the Little Glooms Start Dancing   764
All the Little Things in the World Are Waiting   3389
All the Livelong Day (I Hear America Singing)   4744
All the Lovely   778
All the Luck in the World   3493
All the Magic Ladies   1873
All the Men in My Life   259
All the People on the Levee   2225
All the Pretty Little Horses   2958
All the Same for Me   593
All the Stars and Stripes Belong to Me   2869
All the Things You Are   2204, 2372, 3175, 4557
All the Time   1506, 3234, 4142
All the Time in Dixie   1421
All the Time in the World   1377
All the Time Is Loving Time   4276
All the Way   4743
All the Way Down   2918
All the Way Home   2072
All the Way to Here   166
All the While   2363
All the World Is Dancing Mad   1731, 4001
All the World Is Madly Prancing   3395
All the World Is Swaying   1796

All the World Is Wonderful   1176
All the World Loves a Lover   1693, 2293, 2923, 2966, 2771
All the World Loves a Winner   3770
All the World Wants Ragtime   2349
All the World's a Clock Shop   782
All the World's a Hold   669
All the World's in Love   917
All the Wrongs You Done to Me   740
All the Years   708
All the Young Men   1081
All These People I Have Wronged   4212
All These Things   1890
All Things Bright and Beautiful   1329, 2764
All Things to One Man   1699
All This Time   1804
All Those Years   615
All Through the Day   2372
All Through the Love of You   3786
All Through the Night   163
All to Myself   1345
All Together   281
All Together Now   83
All Washed Up   3754
All We Need to Know   227
All WIse Chickens Follow Me   1995
All Woman   607, 614
All Work and No Play   4651
(I'm) All Wrapped Up in You   1207
All Ya Have to Do Is Wait   775
All Year 'Round   1096
All Year Long   779
All You Can Do Is Tell Me You Love Me   2568
All You Gotta Do Is Tell Me   4196
All You Have to Do Is Stand There   4782
All You Need Is a Fife and Drum   3351
All You Need Is a Girl   4001
All You Need Is a Little Love   4536
All You Need Is a Quarter   1061
All You Need Is a Song   4346
All You Need to Be a Star   3538
All You Want Is Always   2185
All Your Own Am I   1183
Allaballa Goo-Goo   3251
Allah Be Praised   84
Allah Guard Thee   2802
Allah Jazz   3404
Allah! Strike for Thee   4201
Allah's Holiday   2292
Allay Up   4815
Allegheny Moon   4264
Allegorical Blues, The   1357
Allegro   85
Alleh Villn   2356
Alleluia   630, 2775, 1258, 755
Allez Oop   1764
Allez-Up   1447
Allez-Vous-En (Go Away)   629
Allied High Command, The   2228
Allies   3590

Another Lovely April Day   3823
Another Mad Scene   2193
Another Melody in F   1321, 2193
Another Memorable Meal   1077
Another Mile   662, 2413
Another Miracle of Judaism   1234
Another Morning   455
Another Mr. Right   146, 2171, 1597
Another National Anthem   212
Another New Day   117
Another New York Day   262
Another Night   261
Another One Gone Wrong   3163
Another Op'nin, Another Show   2331
Another Openin' Another Show   4399
Another Princely Scheme (Tarantella)   3453
Another Road, Another Destiny   2970
Another Sad Penny   4172
Another Sentimental Song   1921
Another Shout   104
Another Sleepless Night   2132
Another Soiree   2565
Another Suitcase in Another Hall   1211
Another Summer   2542
Another Time, Another Place   2355
Another Wedding Song   784
Answer   800, 43
Answer Is No, The   439
Answer Me   1327
Answer My Heart   2034
Answer Song, The   2283
Answer That   3025
Answering Machine   3858
Answers That You Don't Expect to Get   9
Ante-Bellum Days   3425
Anthem   721, 1216, 533
Anthem for Presentation   619
Anthem Song of the Common Wheel, The   4109
Anti-Cigarette Society, The   357
Anticipation   119
An-ti-ci-pa-tion   3051
Anticipation Is Much More Fun, The   3320
Antidote   579
Antidotes   1801
Antigone   1636
Antioch Prison   3469
Antique Man, The   3366
Antiques   25, 159, 600, 2180
Antiquity   2173
Antoinette   3304
Antonio   4662
Antonio's Telegram   3461
Anuska   710
Anvil Chorus   1492
Anxious   1518
Any Afternoon about Five   2680
Any Day Now   239
Any Day-Now Day   273
Any Dream Will Do   2242
Any Fool Can Fall in Love   1577

Any Girl   1796, 2614
Any How, I'm Pleased to Meet You   1308
Any Kind of Man   4063
Any Little Fish   4335
Any Little Girl Will Fall   969
Any Little Melody   764
Any Little Thing   1297
Any Little Tune   3649, 3659
Any Man but Thomas T   453
Any Man Is Easy (If You Just Know How)   3611
Any Moment   2143
Any Moment Now   4019
Any Night on Broadway   3400
Any Night on Old Broadway   2870, 4656
Any Old Alley Is Paradise Alley   3369
Any Old Girl   2318
Any Old Nag   2869
Any Old Night   2107, 4419
Any Old Night (Is a Wonderful Night)   4418
Any Old Night Is a Wonderful Night   3193
Any Old Place I Can Hang My Hat Is
    Home, Sweet Home for Me   3298
Any Old Place in the World with You   4094
Any Old Place in Yankee Land Is
    Good Enough for Me   295
Any Old Place with You   2574
Any Old Port in a Storm   801
Any Old Thing   457
Any Old Time at All   1587, 1902, 3710, 4812
Any Old Time of the Day   261
Any Old Time with You   3399
Any Old Tree   2160
Any Old Where   4327
Any Other Day Will Do   675
Any Other Way   2731
Any Place I Hang My Hat Is Home   4123
Any Place Is Home Sweet Home with You   2387
Any Place the Old Flag Flies   2525
Any Place Will Do with You   487
Any Place Would Be Paradise   4779
Any Place Would Be Wonderful with You   4814
Any Pretty Little Thing   2174
Any Sort of Girl   2803
Any Spare Change?   2051
Any Step   1678
Any Time   500
Any Time, Any Place, Any Way   830
Any Time Is Dancing Time   3866
Any Time Is Love Time   2605
Any Time New York Goes Dry   4547
Any Time's Kissing Time   758
Any Way the Wind Blows   3907
Any Wednesday   160
Any Woman Who Is Willing Will Do   3813
Anya   161
Anybody Round Here Looking for a Scrap   4453
Anybody Wanna Buy a Little Love   2776
Anybody Want a Baby   2749
Anybody's Man Will Be My Man   2645
Anyone   869

B

Baby's Baby   868
Baby's Baby Grand   1460
Baby's Best Friend, A   3521, 3924
Baby's Blue   2
Baby's Born, A   1385
Baby's Eyes   166
Baby's Gone   3134
Baccanale Dance   4283
Bacchanal Rag, The   3395
Bacchanale   322, 1342, 2802
Bacchanale (Ballet)   3301
Bacchanale   3543
Bacchus   3573
Bachanol   1461
Bachelor, The   521, 3230
Bachelor Bear   1560
Bachelor Belles, The   256
Bachelor Days   1558
Bachelor Gal   4633
Bachelor Gay, A   2698
Bachelor Girl and Boy, A   1530
Bachelor Girls   3981
Bachelor Hoedown   673
Bachelor Song, The   2344
Bachelorhood   1048
Bachelors   4619
Bachelor's Button, A   4133
Bachelor's Dance   2188
Bachelor's Dream, The   4849, 4832
Bachelor's Lament   4093
Back Again   258
Back Again, Back Again   402
Back at the Palace   4377
Back Back Back to Akron   1357
Back, Back, Back to the Land!   3092
Back Bay Beat   532
Back from Hollywood   1492
Back from the Great Beyond   3564
Back from Thirty-Six to Twenty-Nine   2710
Back Home   1026, 3841, 4296
Back Home Again in Indiana   3840
Back in Business   4067
Back in Circulation   435, 3329
Back in Circulation Again   3946
Back in My Hometown   1532
Back in My Tumble Down Shack   728
Back in Old Dubuque   538
Back in Show Biz Again   534
Back in the Days of Long Ago   2005
Back in the Dear Old Days   4453
Back in the Kitchen   1729
Back in the Kitchen Again   3410
Back in the Quaint Little School in Caroline   3246
Back in the Street   3548
Back in the World Now   1053
Back in Town   2905
Back o' Town   4162
Back of Life, The   1865
Back on Base   784
Back Out While the Backing Is Good   2665

Back Seat of a Taxi   364
Back So Soon?   3272
Back to American Furniture   520
Back to Broadway   3031
Back to Bundling   3105
Back to Genesis   3824
Back to Him   1842
Back to Killarney   2180
Back to London   3828
Back to My Heart   2293
Back to My Shack   70
Back to Nature   2145, 3763, 3958
Back to Nature with You   3214
Back to New York   4758
Back to Normal   3558
Back to Old Broadway   3417, 3562
Back to Old Montana   2286
Back to Paris   3729
Back to School Again   64
Back to School Ballet   148
Back to Sioux Sioux City   228
Back to the Boulevards   3578
Back to the Dear Old Trenches   1527
Back to the Farm   4826
Back to the Heather   466
Back to the Palace   2143
Back to the Play   3272
Back to the U.S.A.   632, 646
Back to Work   3501
Back to You   4147
Back Together Again   1999
Back with a Beat   3515
Back Your Fancy   178
Backbiting Me   4520
Backlot Blues, The   1048
Backstage   595
Backstage at the Vic   1757
Backstage Babble   167
Backstage Girls   119
Backwards   4468
Backwards Alphabet, The   58
Bacon and the Egg, The   4765
Bad, Bad Men, The   2376
Bad-Bad-Bad   4416
Bad Bill Jones   4199
Bad Boy   1713
Bad Boy and a Good Girl, A   3618
Bad Breath   3653
Bad But Good   4168
Bad Chinaman from Shanghai, A   805
Bad Companions   1614
Bad Girl   1612, 2637
Bad Girl in Paree   3382
Bad Girl of West Seattle, The   2992
Bad Glad Good and Had   1637
Bad Habits   1298
Bad If He Does, Worse If He Don't   4623
Bad Karma   3309
Bad Little Apple and the Wise Old Tree,
   The   2909

Bathing Girls, The   586, 4803
Bathing Lesson, The   1374
Bathroom   3651
Bathtub, the Lodge, and the Rafter, The   1435
Bats About You   2386
Battalion of France   613
Battersea Butterfly, The   1540
Battle, The   1092, 949
Battle   1769
Battle, The (inst.)   2228
Battle, The   2318, 330
Battle at Eagle Rock (inst.)   3059
Battle Ballet (inst.)   3536
Battle Cry   1809
Battle Cry of Freedom, The   1314
Battle for the Western Name   4405
Battle Hymn of Groundhog   1700
Battle Hymn of the Republic   4460, 2203, 3020
Battle Hymn of the Rialto   1049
Battle of Armageddon   655
Battle of B Flat, The   3122
Battle of Chicago, The   2616
Battle of Old Jim Crow, The   2203
Battle of Roses, The   96
Battle of San Juan Hill, The   2228
Battle of the Alamo (inst.)   996
Battle of the Genie   1101
Battle on the Tiles, The   4497
Battle Song   657
Battle Was Over, It Was Quiet Now, The   4163
Battleground Bummer   3159
Battlelines   4297
Battling Butler   2972
Baubles, Bangles and Beads   2327, 4383
Baxter & Company   496
Baxter Avenue   2428
Baxter's Party   1831
Bay of Botany   971
Bayakhala (They Mourn)   1719
Bayakhala (Zulu-The Child)   2147
Bazaar Hymn   1616
Bazaar of the Caravans   2327
Bazaar Opening Chorus   2915
Bazoom   1596
Bazoom!   1730
BBIWY Blues   932
Be a Jolly Molly   938
Be a Lady All the Time   3433
Be a Lion   4722
Be a Little Lackadaisical   1874
Be a Little Sunbeam   3230
Be a Lover   3215
Be a Man   3551
Be a Mess   4432
Be a Mother   2523
Be a Mountain Man   3908
Be a Party at the Party Tonight   1753
Be a Performer!   2523
Be a Phony   2053
Be a Pussycat   3934

Be a Santa   4190
Be a Spy for Love's Sake   2722
Be a Vamp   4543
Be Aesthetic   2387
Be-Angeled   649
Be Anything But a Girl   2805
Be Back Soon   3271
Be Be Beatrice   2490
Be-Bee   4382
Be Black   3825
Be Bop Lullaby   4829
Be Calm   2447
Be Careful   2264
Be Careful, It's My Heart   789
Be Careful What You Do   702, 4808
Be Careful Whom You Kiss   4788
Be Clever   350
Be Courageous   4062
Be Demure   3710
Be-Deviled   649
Be Flexible   3722
Be Fruitful and Multiply   2354
Be Gentle   4789
Be Glad   3846
Be Glad You're Alive   1101
Be Good   4802
Be Good, Be Good, Be Good   2994
Be Good or Be Gone   3608
Be Good to Her   4643
Be Good to Me   4023
Be Grateful for What You've Got   941
Be Happy   1121, 2462, 2874
Be Happy Boys Tonight   3304
Be Happy, Too   3949
Be Italian   3171
Be Joyful   4588
Be Joyful To-day   3024
Be Joyful Today   3028
Be Kind to People Week   314
Be Kind to Poor Pierrot   252
Be Kind to the Young   3764
Be Kind to Your Parents   1242
Be Like a Basketball and
   Bounce Right Back   550
Be Like the Bluebird   163
Be More Aggressive   4488
Be My Baby   2427, 4534, 4193
Be My Guest   1837, 4423
Be My Guiding Star of Love   822
Be My Host   3187
Be My Lady   808, 809
Be My Little Apple Dumplin' Do   3951
Be My Little Baby Bumble Bee   4712
Be My Love   4743
Be My Only Love   757
Be My War Bride   525
Be Naughty   4240
Be Not Afraid   3651
Be Oh So Careful Ann   4620
Be On Your Own   3171

Billy Joe Ju   3684
Billy Noname   415
Billy Phibbs Is Married   1866
Billy Shakespeare
    (The Shakespearian Rag)   3399
Billy Sol Estes   3186
Billy the Bubbler   186
Billy the Kid   4679
Billy's Blues   1107
Billy's Melody   4655
Billy's Very Good to Me   694
Biminy   4818
Bingo Blast   3165
Binnie   624
Birch Bark Boat   823
Bird, a Bottle and a Cigarette, A   998
Bird Americana   2992
Bird and the Bottle, The   4738
Bird Ballet, The   1131
Bird Chorus   3162
Bird Dance   4429
Bird in a Cage, A   143
Bird in a Gilded Cage, A   4390
Bird Lament   3162
Bird of a Chicken, The (dance)   4809
Bird of Gay Bohemia, The   1334
Bird of Love, The   2100
Bird of Paradise   558
Bird of Paradise, The   2636
Bird of Passage, A   2591
Bird on the Wing   3249
Bird Song, The   54
Bird Song   3673
Bird Talk   1975
Bird That Never Learned to Fly, A   4798
Bird Upon the Tree   2268
Bird Watcher's Song
    (We're the Ladies' Walking Society)   1886
Birdcage Walk   792
Birdie   959
Birdie, A   2308
Birdie and Ferdie   4719
Birdie Follies   4011
Birdies   1958, 2669
Birdies in the Trees, The   1557
Birds   1300
Birds, The   4707
Birds and the Bees, The   4524
Birds Are Winging   4188
Birds in the Sky, The   2033
Birds in the Spring   2808
Birds in the Trees, The   1569, 2033
Birds' Nests   325
Birds of a Feather   1481, 3258
Birds of Paradise   424
Birds of Plumage   3406
Birds on High (Birds Up High)   376
Birmingham   2787
Birth of a Beatnik   1697
Birth of a New Revue, The   1129

Birth of American Fantasy Dance   4528
Birth of Dixie   1514
Birth of Passion, The   2667
Birth of the Blues   1489
Birth of the Butterfly (inst.)   250
Birth of the Century Girl, The   683
Birthday...   1369
Birthday, A   2278, 2633
Birthday Ensemble   2390
Birthday Girl   1701
Birthday of the Dauphin, The (scene)   4815
Birthday of the Infantata, The   1689
Birthday Party   4193, 1419
Birthday Party (Rich Kids Rag)   2523
Birthday Party of the King   4155
Birthday Serenade   3151
Birthday Song   337
Birthday Song, The   3496
Birthday Song   1242
Birthday Toast   3339
Birthdays   1497
Birthdays Are Fun   4710
Bis Bolo   3958
Bish Ne Ara   4325
Bismark Is a Herring, Napoleon
    Is a Cake   1667
Bist Mein Krein, Mein Welt   907
Bistro   1358
Bit o' Breeze   1536
Bit O' Dancin', A   994
Bit o' Pink and White, A   452
Bit o' the Brogue, A   4120
Bit of a Ballad, A   4073
Bit of Character, A   3482
Bit of Earth, A   3862
Bit of Foolishness, A   3384
Bit of Gingham, A   1799
Bit of Harmony, A   3877
Bit of Home, A   3485
Bit of Nonsense, A   1340
Bit of Nonsense   2122
Bit of Opera, A   3404, 3958
Bit of Ribbon, a Bit of Love, A   4148
Bit of the Band, A   30
Bit of Villainy, A   2687
Bit Player Polka   3046
Bit Too Far, A   1392
Bitch, Bitch, Bitch   2198
Bite Your Tongue   1816
Bits and Pieces   1634
Bits & Pieces XIV Finale   427
Bits & Pieces XIV Opening   427
Bitten By Love   3966
Bitter Harvest   2655
Bitter Tears   4696
Bitter Twitter   96
Bittersuite, The   430
Bittersweet   3722
Bivouac Song   4616
Bivouac, The   118

Brainwash   194
(Got a) Bran' New Daddy   971
Brand New Day, A   2318
Brand New Dress, A   798
Brand New Friends   1616
Brand New Hammer, A   3181
Brand New Soldier Tune, A   1531
Brand New Start   373
Brand New World   3644
Brandy in Your Champagne   1676
Brava! Brava!   2715
Brave and the Free, The   2072
Brave Deserve the Fair, The   3978
Brave Gendarmes   1392
Brave Girl   1092
Brave Hussar, The   3744, 4228
Brave Old City of New York, The   2134
Brave Soldier Boy, The   2715
Brave You   1508
Brave's Lament, The   412
Bravo!   2150
Bravo, Antonio!   3222
Bravo Bravo   3792
Bravo, Bravo   3464, 771
Bravo! Bravo!   340
Bravo, Bravo, Novelisto   4060
Bravo, Giovanni   519
Brazil   1662, 2897
Brazilian Boogie Woogie   847
Brazilian Can-Can   4571
Brazilian Interlude   4303
Brazilian Max-Cheese   3397
Brazilian Nut   3087
Brazilian Nuts   4131
Brazilian Samba   1414
Brazilian Suite   2540
Breachy's Law   519
Bread   273
Bread and Butter   930
Bread and Butter and Sugar   1831
Bread and Freedom   3644
Bread and Jam   2816
Bread and Kisses   4025
Bread and Love   2106
Bread and Roses   1609
Breadline Dance   1729
Break Into Your Heart   2071
Break It Now, Buck Private   213
Break It Up   323
Break It Up Cinderella   4586
Break Me Out   1985
Break-Me-Down, The   2271
Break-Neck Quadrille, The (inst.)   3613
Break That Party   1074
Break-up Rag   169
Breakfast   322
Breakfast at Thebes   3088
Breakfast at Tiffany's   521, 521
Breakfast Ball   880
Breakfast Ball, The   1014

Breakfast Dance   3172, 3709
Breakfast for Two   4798
Breakfast in Bed   2628, 3163, 4237
Breakfast Over Sugar   2132
Breakfast with Hazel   3036
Breakfast with You   3648
Breakin' 'Em Down   740
Breakin' 'Em In   3965
Breakin' a Leg   4182
Breakin' th' Rhythm   3361
Breakin' the Ice   1941, 2099
Breakin' the Spell   825, 4022
Breaking Camp   4046
Breaking Into the Movies   3842, 4211
Breaking Up a Rhythm   4291
Breath from Bohemia, A   1565
Breath of a Rose   2387
Breath of Spring   2193, 3900
Breath of Spring, A   4780
Breathing In   1053
Breathing the Air   3711
Breeze in the Trees   3258
Breeze Kissed Your Hair, The   672
Breezin' Along   577
Breezy   137
Bremen Town Musician, The   3844
Brendan's Dream   1412
Brent's Credo   3429
Breton Boat Song   49
Brewing the Love Potion   4623
Brewster the Millionaire   1464
Brewster's Millions   577, 4860, 4860
Brian   3493
Brickerty-Brackety—Tootsies   4742
Bridal Bevy, The   351
Bridal Chorus   3028, 526
Bridal Fete   177
Bridal Finale (Bridal Procession)   3772
Bridal Hour, The   1121, 2509
Bridal March   3051
Bridal Song   2793
Bridal Song, The   2673
Bride, The   1250, 2292
Bride and Groom   3243
Bride Bells   4345
Bride of Sirocco   528
Bride Shop   3045
Bride Was Dressed in White, The   3650
Bride Wore Something Old, The   4446
Bride's Song   1537
Bridegroom Trio   2947
Briderlekh Tayere
   (Dear Brothers, Help)   1609
Brides and Grooms   1071
Brides in Love   729
Brides' Lullaby   1911
Bridesmaids   1537, 2816
Bridesmaids Ballet   3850
Bridesmaids' Sextette
   (Chorus of Bridesmaids)   3322

Broadway I Love You   3636
Broadway in Dahomey   2111
Broadway in Paree, A   4657
Broadway in Sahara   3404
Broadway Indians   4817
Broadway Jones   403
Broadway Lady   2141
Broadway Lament   4012
Broadway Lights   4226
Broadway Love   2912
Broadway Love Song   4432
Broadway Mammy   2296
Broadway Mammy Blues   1653
Broadway Means Home to Me   4762
Broadway Melody   544
Broadway Musical, A   550, 602
Broadway, My Street   3900
Broadway My Street   3953
Broadway, My Street   4480
Broadway New York   4011
Broadway of My Heart, The   1380
Broadway Pirates   2870
Broadway Reverie   4823
Broadway Rhythm   3992, 1298, 3636
Broadway Rose   3915
Broadway Sam   3399
Broadway School Days   3400
Broadway Show, The   1464
Broadway Strut   208
Broadway Strut, The   481
Broadway Swell and Bowery Bum   4378
Broadway Tipperary   1826
Broadway to Madrid   1132
Broadway Walk, The   545
Broadway Wedding   556
Broadway Whirl, The   560
Broken   2947
Broken & Bent   562
Broken Blossoms   542, 3775
Broken Bus, The   2679
Broken Doll, A   3827
Broken Guitar, A   4152
Broken Heart, or the Wages of Sin, The   935
Broken Hearted Romeo   4572
Broken Hearts   2686
Broken Idol, A   561
Broken Kimono, The   3108
Broken Pianolita, The   2679
Broken Rhythm   1461
Broken Romance   796
Broken String Blues   3983
Brom and Katrina   239
Brom Bones   2100
Brom's Compaint   2344
Bronco Busters   1528
Bronx Express   563
Bronxville Darby and Joan   3815
Brook, The   2055
Brooklyn   564
Brooklyn Belle   1303

Brooklyn Cantata   3226, 4394
Brooklyn Dodger Strike, The   1289
Brooklyn Heights   1693
Brooklyn U.S.A.   2397
Broth of a Boy, A   1803
Brother   4003
Brother and Sister   4795
Brother Against Brother   3558
Brother Can You Spare a Dime?   125
Brother, Can You Spare a Dime?   1609
Brother Can You Spare a Dime?   3018
Brother Dear   689
Brother Department, The   4481
Brother, Give Yourself a Shove   1755
Brother Masons   4650
Brother Men   1736
Brother of Mine   3084
Brother to Brother   1684
Brother Trucker   4744
Brother, Where Are You?   2245
Brotherhood of Man   2019, 3444
Brothers   168, 2302, 3088
Brothers and Sisters   115
Brothers Came to Egypt, The   2242
Brothers Vendetto, The   1970
Brown   3660
Brown Baby   2245
Brown Buddies   567
Brown-Eyed Girl   905
Brown Eyes   4692
Brown October Ale   3736
Brown Paper Bag   2051
Brown Penny   341, 1977
Brown Skin Baby Mine   2111
Brown-Skin Gal in the
   Calico Gown, The   2259
Brown Sugar   439
Brownies   2155
Brownie's Picnic, The   528
Brownstone   1697
Bruderlein Fein   2249
Brunhilde's   1714
Brunnhilde Rides Again   4467
Brunnhilde Steps Out   70
Brush Off, The   4048
Brush Up Your Shakespeare   2331
Brushing Stone, The   4292
Brussels   2188
Bub Oder Madel?   3771
Bubbe Meises Bubbe Stories   573
Bubbie   3910
Bubble, The   1888
Bubble and the Butterfly, The   3134
Bubble, Bubble   1638
Bubble Bubble   4405
Bubble-Land   719
Bubbles   575, 1096, 1535
(I'll Make) Bubbles   2587
Bubbles   3921, 4547
Bubbles in Me Bonnet   705

C

Carolin'   108
Carolina   2631, 4328, 4421
Carolina in the Morning   3405
Carolina Lou   1963
Carolina Mammy   487
Carolina Rolling Stone   4137
Carolina Sue   3022
Carolina Sunshine   1032
Carolina's Lament   2354
Caroline   2373, 2787, 813, 3904
Carousel   1878, 2188
Carousel in the Park   4524
Carousel Waltz (inst.)   660
Carriage for Alida, A   298
Carrie   702, 661, 661
Carrie Barry   4723
Carried Away   991, 3278, 198
Carried Off   2917
Carrier Pigeon, The   1388
Carrion Train   1216
Carry On   190, 567, 3643, 3674
Carry On, Chums   4062
Carry On Keep Smiling   4023
Carry That Weight   3903
Carryin' On   2682
Carter Song, The   3557
Cartoon Town   4858
Carve Up!   1277
Cary: Who?   407
Caryl Ann   2580
Casablanca   663
Casamagordo   2583
Casanova   3214, 3955
Casanova, Romeo, and Don Juan   3953
Case of Rape, A   1373
Case of the Hum-drum Killer, The   3615
Casey   2682, 1173
Casey Is a Wonderful Name   4317
Casey Jones   3989, 4687
Cash for Your Trash   39
Cash Politics   564
Casino Girl, The   666
Casino Music Hall, The   4327
Cassie   1637
Cassie's Not a Bit Like Mother   2760
Cast Call   4268
Cast of Thousands   4358
Casting Call, A   275
Castle in India, A   3763
Castle of Dreams   2148
Castle on a Cloud   2442
Castle on the Nile   982
Castle Walk, The (dance)   1886
Castles in Spain   3774, 4037, 49
Castles in the Air   2219, 2696, 1392
Castles in the Sand   1797
Castles of the Loire, The (ballet)   1634
Castro Tango!, The   1363
Cat and Fox Song   3495
Cat and Mice   1309

Cat and Mouse   139
Cat and the Custard Pot, The   2240
Cat Came Back, The   3860
Cat Can Look at a Queen, A   111
Cat Duet   541
Catalina   3860
Catalog Woman   4467
Catamaran   3031
Catamarang   2317
Catch   129
Catch a Butterfly   2384
Catch a Star!   673
Catch As Catch Can   4437
Catch 'em Young, Treat 'em Rough,
   Tell 'em Nothing   1552
Catch Hatch   3301
Catch Me   3309
Catch Me If I Fall   674
Catch Me If You Can   3664, 4169
Catch My Garter   1764
Catch of the Season, The   675, 1043
Catch Our Act at the Met
   (Vaudeville Ain't Dead)   4496
Catch That on the Corner   40
Catchy Coo   3828
Caterpillar's Advice   54
Catfish   1985, 3608
Catfish Song   2030
Cathedral of Clemenza, The   4541
Catherine the Great   4374, 4772
Catland   4662
Cat's Away, The   614
Cat's in the Cradle   2470, 3159
Cat's Quartet, The   2315
Catskills, Hello   3146
Caught   4102, 4199
Caught in the Rain   2545, 3508
Caught Ole Blue   2225
Cause I'm Happy   784
Cause of Civilization, The   762
Cause of the Situation, The   403
Cause Uncle Mord'che Is So Smart   2811
'Cause We Got Cake   4420
'Cause You Won't Play House   3103
Caution: Men Cooking   3608
Cautionary Tale, A   533
Cautiously Optimistic   3557
Cavachok   680
Cavalcade of Curtain Calls   2477
Cavalier, The   2836
Cavalier Cat, The   4143
Cavalier Song   2671
Cavaliers   3011
Cavalier's Lament, The   4244
Cavalier's Waltz   2910
Cavalry Captain, A   2659
Cave Girl   4226
Cave Man, The   4553
Cave of the Patriachs   2421
Caveat Emptor   3788

Chiquita 3783, 3022
Chiquita Banana 3175
Chiquita Bonita 1164
Chiquitin Trio 3152
Chiribim 2811
Chiribin 2356
Chiromancy 920
Chiropractic Papa 123
Chirp Along 3258
Chirp, Chirp 3946
Chirp-Chirp 4320
Chivalry 1470
Chivalry Reel 4323
Chivaree 4199
Chivor Dance (dance) 2679
Chloe 2506, 3985
Choc'late Bar 2302
Chocolate Brown 3614
Chocolate Covered Cherries 573
Chocolate Covered Future 4830
Chocolate Dandies 740
Chocolate Drop (inst.) 4697
Chocolate Drops 2111
Chocolate Pas de Trois 4075
Chocolate Shake 2259
Chocolate Soldier 395
Chocolate Soldier, The 742
Chocolate Soldier 4521
Chocolate Soldier, The 743
Chocolate Soldier 743
Chocolate Turkey 1958
Chocolates and Chiclets 639
Choice Is Yours, The 278, 2777
Choices 337, 2289
Choir Boy, The 4165
Choir Practice 2451
Cholesterol Love Song 1049
Chon Kina 1470
Choo Choo Cars 1759
Choo, Choo, Ch'boogie 1296
Choo-Choo Honeymoon 956
Choo Choo Love 2342
Choo Choo Rap 562
Choose! Choose! Choose! 2551
Choose Her in the Morning 336
Choose Your Flowers 1756
Choose Your Partner 911
Choosing a Husband's a Delicate Thing
    2928, 1970
Chop Stick Rag, The 3332
Chop Sticks 1777, 2276
Chop Sticks and Room 202 1032
Chop Stix 2096
Chop Suey 1315
Chopin 4669
Chopin Ad-Lib (Opening Chorus) 611
Choral Prelude 3673
Choral Russe 3091
Chorale 3277
Chords Like These 1521

Chorus and Entrance of Marquis 353
Chorus and Entrance of Regent 1183
Chorus Girl, The 3401
Chorus Girl Blues 266, 3847, 3848, 4781
Chorus Girl's Longing 331
Chorus Girl's Song, A 1643
Chorus of Assistants 1114
Chorus of Citizens 341
Chorus of Constant Lunchers, Constant Diners,
    Constant Dancers and Constant Kissers 186
Chorus of Courtiers 1114
Chorus of Footmen (Servants' Chorus)
    (Charge of the Footmen) 2915
Chorus of Guests 1537
Chorus of Lamentation 1470
Chorus of Laundresses 1114
Chorus of Models 3466
Chorus of Nurses 186
Chorus of Perambulator Girls 3887
Chorus of Poets 947
Chorus of Snobs 2964
Chorus of Soldiers 3586
Chorus of Villagers 2035, 1896
Chorus of Villagers and Policemen 2964
Chorus of Welcome 4121, 4219
Chorus of Welcome to Gilfain 1313
Chorus Picking Time on Broadway 1965
Chosen, The 747, 747
Chosen Doime le Meilech & Rikodle 4773
Chow-Chow's Honeymoon 737
Chow Mein Girls 1131
Chowder Ball 4408
Chris Crosses 750
Christ Is Alive 1716
Christening, The 2979
Christening of the Boat, The 1525
Christian Cowboy 4030
Christianity 1809
Christina Swanson 1316
Christina's Room 3463
Christine 751
Christine Swanson 399
Christmas 4676, 2224
Christmas at Hampton Court 3702
Christmas — Baby Please Come Home 2427
Christmas Buche, A 705
Christmas Carol, A 753, 828, 752, 4155,
    4155, 754
Christmas Carol 2474, 4173
Christmas Carol, A 2980
Christmas Child 2150
Christmas Chimes 4471
Christmas Dances (inst.) 3977
Christmas Day 3603
Christmas Day in the Cookhouse 3259
Christmas Eve 3066, 753, 750, 3918, 3931
Christmas Fair Waltz 250
Christmas Gifts 4732
Christmas in July 3793
Christmas in Laurel Canyon 2992

Come A-Wandering with Me   1456
Come Across   1552, 4378
Come Along (It's a Trifling Affair)   1458
Come Along   3543, 4814, 4816, 4834
Come-Along-a-Me, Babe   4678
Come Along and Tell Me   1849
Come Along, Boys   1600
Come Along Down   2750
Come Along, Honey!   1524
Come Along, Let's Gamble (Finale Act I)   1419
Come Along, Little Girl, Come Along   335
Come Along Little Girls   1588
Come Along, Ma Cherie   3681
Come Along Mandy   437
Come Along, Mandy   2232
Come Along Mandy   4804
Come Along My Boys   2724
Come Along, Pretty Girl   1519, 2317
Come Along, Sunshine   931
Come Along to the Carnival   1154
Come Along to the Movies   4644
Come Along to the Show   213
Come Along to Toy Town
   (Come Along to Toyland)   1208
Come Along to Toy Town   1598
Come Along with Me   387, 629, 1123, 3313
Come and Be Married   3831
Come and Be My Butterfly   1828
Come and Bring Your Instruments   2103
Come and Cuddle Me   3537
Come and Dance   4553
Come and Dance with Me   2684
Come and Float Me Freddie Dear   4801
Come and Get Cozy with Me   90
Come and Go with Me   2203
Come and Have a Smile with Me   4762
Come and Have a Swing with Me   2184
Come and Play with Me   3392
Come and See Our Island   1313
Come and Spend Your Life with Me   181
Come and Take a Walk with Me   2481
Come and Take Me Out of Lonely Land   909
Come and Tell Me   376, 3436
Come and Watch the Moon with Me   1975
Come, Answer to Our Call   4188
Come Around on Our Veranda   3313
Come As a Carrier Dove   1712
Come As You Are   817
Come Avec!   4379
Come Away   4690, 1456, 4789
Come Away Death   3909
Come Away with Me   3429
Come Back, Baby   2173
Come Back Home Baby   2426
Come Back Little Genie   1300, 2234
Come Back Little Girl   1544
Come Back, Little Sheba   3925
Come Back My Honey Boy to Me   1264
Come Back, Sweet Dream!   1530
Come Back to Bohemia   1793

Come Back to Erin   77, 2853
Come Back to God (Me)   989
Come Back to Me   2939
Come Back to Me (2)   3274
Come Back to Me (1)   3274
Come Back to Me   4553, 4655
Come Back to Me Daddy   43
Come Back to Our Alley Sally   4815
Come Back to the Island   3339
Come Back to the Old Cabaret   2854
Come Back with the Same Look in Your Eyes
   4068, 4301
Come Be My True Love   1564
Come Be My Wife   4547
Come Birdie Come   3998
Come Blow Your Horn   2543
Come Boys   4188
Come Buy a Trinket   1439
Come Buy Our Luscious Fruit   2974
Come Buy, Come Boy   1589
Come By Sunday   4153
Come Closer (Come a Little Closer)   2291
Come! Come!   697
Come, Come   4032
Come, Come, Come   3065
Come, Come, Come/Convent Maids   3081
Come, Dance, My Dear   453
Come Dance with Me   1920
Come Dancing, John (inst.)   499
Come Down   3831
Come Down from the Tree   3285
Come Down Ma Evening Star   4478
Come Down Mister Man in the Moon   3951
Come Down, Mr. Man in the Moon   331
Come Down Salomy Jane   4801
Come Down Susie   591
Come Down to Argentine   3369
Come Down to Devonshire   906
Come Down to Earth, My Dearie   4521
Come Down to Me Love   2519
Come Dream, So Bright   3736
Come Drink a Toast to Man and Wife   4554
Come Elijah, Come   3167
Come Farballe   3064
Come Fly with Me   2454, 4743
Come Follow the Band   305
Come from the Dyin'   3612
Come Gather 'Round   4769
Come, Gentle Stanger   613
Come Help Yourself to America, or
   Frank in the Melting Pot   1256
Come Hit Your Baby   551
Come Hither Eyes   1888
Come Home   85, 3682
Come Home and Get Cozy with Me   3914
Come Home My Little Honeycomb   457
Come Home, Runaway   1086
Come In and Browse   1107
Come in from the Rain   2677
Come In My Mouth   2451

Court of Louis XIV, The   4291
Court Office Song   3887
Court Song   2859, 2411
Courting (dance), The   1076
Courting   2029
Courting in the Moonlight   762
Courting Time   2364
Courtly Etiquette   2102
Courtly Lovers   2611
Courtship Ballet (inst.)   1120
Courtship Dance   3177
Cousin Kevin   4676
Cousins   693
Cousins of the Czar   902
Covenant, The   4481
Cover a Clover with Kisses   4235
Cover Girls   4533
Cover Me with Kisses   69
Covered Wagon Days   3133
Covina   408
Cow and a Plough and a Frau, A   183
Cow Boy   1185
Cow Jumped Over the Moon, The   2134
Cow Patty   914
Cow's Divertissement   4620
Cowboy   915, 916
Cowboy Girl, The   917
Cowboy Girl   1182
Cowboy Hoedown   2961
Cowboy Song   4109
Cowboy Songs   381
Cowboy's Burning Desire   3239
Cowshed Rhapsody   4667
Coy Young Maid, A   3981
Cozy Corner   1565
Crabbed Age and Youth   3909
Cracked Her Shell   264
Cradle of Jazz   2023
Cradle of Rhythm   4503
Cradle of the Deep   376
Cradle Song   303
Cradle Song and Aria   2623
Cradle Will Rock, The   919
Cradled in Thy Arms   1522
Craftsmen   426
Cranberry Pickin'   637
Cranes   1865
Crap Game Dance, The (inst.)   1706
Crap Game Fugue   3541
Crashing the Golden Gate   1126
Crashing Through   4166
Cravin' for the Avon   1644
Crazy   280, 1053, 2993
Crazy About Some Boy   2113
Crazy 'Appy Tears   589
Crazy As a Loon   2301
Crazy Downtown   1832
Crazy Elbows   3556
Crazy House Suite   1337
Crazy Idea of Love   4763

Crazy Jane on the Day of Judgment   1977
Crazy New Words   3178
Crazy Night Ballet   2014
Crazy Now   922
Crazy Over You   2518
Crazy People   1813
Crazy Place, The   1699
Crazy Pops   4041
Crazy Quilt   418
Crazy Quilt Sextette, The   418
Crazy Rhythm   1859
Crazy Street   3993
Crazy Walk   1514
Crazy with the Heat (1)   924
Crazy with the Heat (2)   924
Crazy World   2702, 4560
Crazyisms   1912
Cream in My Coffee   4627
Cream of English Youth, The   461
Cream of Mississippi   4388
Cream of Mush   3931
Cream of Mush Song   3501
Cream of the Sky   2889
Creation of Eve, The   4523
Creation of the World and Other Business,
   The   4523
Creation Scene (inst.)   4814
Creative Block   871
Creatures Go to Sleep in Peace   2243
Credit Card   1575
Credit Face   3722
Credit's Due to Me, The   1313
Credo (Rich Is Better)   2014
Creep, Creep, the World's Asleep   1309
Creme de la Creme   95
Creole Blues   2200
Creole Crawl   2371
Creole Crooning Song   1529
Creole Days   336
Creole Gal   3614
Creole Girls from the Follies   489
Creole Love Call   3628
Creole Love Call (inst.)   3709
Creole Love Song, The   3949
Creole Way, The   2200
Creoles   2595
Creon   2918
Crepe Suzette   2751
Crescendo   223
Crescent Moon   3086
Cretonne   3740
Cretonne Girl   1129
Cricket on the Hearth   928, 4250
Crickets Are Calling, The   2430
Cries in the Common Marketplace   272
Crime   4476
Crime des Femmes   68
Crime Doesn't Pay   112
Crime in the Streets   4635
Crime of Giovanni Venturi, The   519

Crinoline Days   3007
Crinoline Girl   2527
Crinoline Girl, The   3397
Crispus Attucks   2748
Crispy and Crunchy   4237
Crispy, Crunch Crackers   1931
Criss Cross   930
Cristobel   779
Critic, The   3235, 4002
Critical List   3667
Critics   2618
Critics' Blues, The   1685
Critters   2027
Cro-Ack   3463
Crockfield   3931
(Oh, Be Careful of the) Crocodile   470
Crocodile, The   767
Crocodile, a Crocodile, A   2658
Crocodile Wife   4863
Crocodiles Cry   2657
Crooked Path, The   1649
Croon-Spoon   919
Crooning   4182
Croquet   3970
Croquet Game, The   2040
Croquet, Croquet   453
Cross On Over   4558
Cross Word Puzzles   3523
Cross Your Fingers   932, 4087
Cross Your Heart   3622, 4506
Crossbridge Dance   1903
Crossing   3001
Crossing Boundaries   4515
Crossing Over   394
Crossing the Red Sea   1715
Crossover   2998
Crosstown   4286
Crossword Puzzle   1648, 2594, 4145
Crossword Puzzle Song   1725
Croupier   4677
Crow   434
Crow, The   4579, 4862
Crowd of Girls   2373
Crown Me   3602
Crown Us with the Truth   4615
Crucifixion, The   2212
Cruel and Brutal   545
Cruel Chief   2293
Cruel One   1119
Cruel Youth, The   4579
Cruelty Man, The   935
Cruelty Stomp, The   4139
Cruikshank March   490
Cruise of the Boozemobile, The   3423
Crumbs in My Bed   1665
Crunch Granola Suite   964
Crusaders March, The   2697
Crush on You   3654
Cry   4264, 10
Cry Baby   1819, 3739

Cry, Baby   4323
Cry, Baby, Cry   59, 3563
Cry for Us All   935
Cry from the Dungeon   4368
Cry Like a Baby   432
Cry Like the Wind   1061
Cry Loud (Lift Your Voice Like a Trumpet)   1073
Cry of the Peacock   4541
Cry the Beloved Country   369
Cry, the Beloved Country   2591, 2591
Crying Jane   804
Crystal Ball   2342
Crystal Ball, The   2495
Crystal Candelabra   672
Crystal Lute, The   118
Crystal Temple, The   2460
Crystal Wedding Day   1780
Csardas   689, 2615
Csibeszkiraly   3537
Cuba Si, Yanqui No   3530
Cuban Glide, The   4804
Cuban Love Song   4251, 4197
Cuban Song   2101
Cubana   2162
Cubes and Abstracts   1878
Cubist Opera, The   1016
Cubs   143
Cuckold's Delight   1017
Cuckoo   2354, 815, 1852
Cuckoo-Cheena, The   2595
Cuckoo Clock, The   1777
Cuckoo Clock   1173
Cuckoo Song   4433
Cuckoo Town   2494
Cuckoo Trio   1518
Cuddle   3951
Cuddle Me As We Dance   969
Cuddle Me Up   728
Cuddle-Uddle, The   1404
Cuddle Up   584, 969, 2098, 3665, 4661
Cuddle Up a Little Closer, Lovey Mine   4364
Cuddle Up Together (My Old Brown Coat)   2756
Cuh-Razy for Love   667
Cuisine!   4139
Cultural Pursuits   2754
Cultural Sunday   2483
Culture Drill   331
Culture Twist, The   3530
Cumbia/Wedding Party   4459
Cunnilingus Champion of Co. C, The   2451
Cup of China Tea, A   4792
Cup of Coffee, A   941
Cup of Coffee, a Sandwich and You, A   702
Cup of Tea, A   1458, 1748, 1962
Cup of Tea, A (Lido Lady, Opening)   2467
Cup of Tea, A   3573, 3882
Cup of Tea, The   4258
Cupid   780, 1532, 1726
Cupid and You and I   4425
Cupid at the Plaza   3193

D

Die Vogelein Singen In Dem Wald   188
Die Zirkusprinzessin   771
Die Zusammenfugung   3112
Died & Died & Died   871
Diet   4645
Diet of Wein   194
Diet Song   2590
Diff'rence of Drink, The   1550
Difference Is Me, The   1985
Different   4558, 4107
Different Days   480
Different Days-Different Ways   1551
Different Drummer, A   415
Different Girls   4434
Different Girls on Broadway   3867
Different Kind of World, A   4689
Different Kinds of Weather   2534
Different Stage, A   1770
Different Times   1045
Different Ways of Making Love, The   4723
Different Ways of Proposing   1573
Difficult Transition, A   3211
Dig, Dig, Dig   3602
Dig, Sister, Dig   2216
Dig Ye Dagos Dig   559
Diga Diga Doo   441, 3905, 4534
Diggin' Up Dirt   4543
Diggywig Two-Step   1561
Dilly   1048
Dime a Dozen   1049, 4034
Dime Ain't Worth a Nickle, A   135
Diminuendo in Blue (inst.)   4091
Dimple on My Knee, The   3225
Dimples   2523, 3180
Din't Cha Mother Tell You Nothin'?   1889
Dinah   26, 295, 4534, 1813, 2009, 3709, 3120
Dinah Lee   116
Dinah Lou   882
Dinah's in a Jam (inst.)   886
Ding-a-ling, Ding-a-ling   974
Ding a Long Dong   3068
Ding Dong   627, 2538
Ding, Dong   2665
Ding-Dong   1540
Ding Dong   4770
Ding Dong Bell   2134, 2457
Ding, Dong Dell (Spells I Love You)   3489
Ding Dong Ding   3623
Ding, Dong It's Kissing Time   1922
Ding Dong School   412
Ding Dong Song, The   4749
Dingere Dingale   4579
Dinghy   4062
Dingle Dangle   4064
Dingle, Dingle, Dingle   4806
Dining Out   1318
Dinky Doodle Dicky   1626
Dinner   3865
Dinner at the Mirklines   3476
Dinner at Thebes   3088

Dinner Bells   2990
Dinner Gong Jazz, The   1972
Dinner Is Served   2201, 2579
Dinner Minuet (dance)   2731
Dinner Pail, The   118
Dinner Party, The   2041
Dinner Song   3390
Dinner Time   8
Dinner with W.R.   695
Dinny Maginnity   2232
Dinny's Serenade   1162
Dino Repetti   1878
Dino's in Love   1878
Dionne Quintuplets   1337
Dior, Dior   2052
Dip, Dip, Dip   4806
Dip in the Ocean, A   2506
Dip Me in the Golden Sea   1776
Diplomacee   639
Diplomacy   1816, 2155, 3613, 947, 3751
Diplomats   1417
Dippermouth Blues   3840
Dipping in the Moonlight   2112
Dipsey's Coming Over   4286
Dipsey's Vaudeville (inst.)   4286
Direct from Vienna   656
Dirge   920, 2243, 3986
Dirge for a Soldier   2344
Dirge for Two Veterans   2433
Dirge Song   2655
Dirt Between My Fingers   3873
Dirty   3752, 4403
Dirty Dig   1693
Dirty Dish Rag   2007
Dirty Dog, The   1748
Dirty Face   2535
Dirty Hands, Dirty Face   487
Dirty Is the Funniest Thing I Know   4449
Dirty Mind   922
Dirty No Gooder Blues   478
Dirty Old Town   4579
Dirty Pitchers, Dirty Books   2705
Dirty, Rotten, Vicious, Nasty Guys   362
Dirty Up the Alley   568
Dirty Words   2451, 2998
Dirty Work   2698
Dis-donc, Dis-donc   2150
Dis Flower   653
Dis Is de Day   1020, 1385
Dis Little While   1385
Disappear   3862
Disappointed in Love   725
Disappointed Suitors   1617
Discarded Blues   280
Disco   52, 2426, 2908
Disco Baby   2426
Disco Destiny   3515
Disco for Margo   167
Disco Rag   843
Disco Shuffle   1637

Don Medigua, All for Thy Coming Wait   1165
Don Medigua, Here's Your Wife   1165
Don Pasquale   3197
Don Pasquale De Mesquita   1521
Don Quixote   2727, 3829
Don's Chorus (The Things That Are
    Done By a Don), The   3818
Don't Advertise Your Man   1425, 3705
Don't Ask!   3243
Don't Ask a Lady   2523
Don't Ask Her Mother   1655
Don't Ask Me   71, 3718
Don't Ask Me Not to Sing   672, 2204, 3735
Don't Ask the Lady What the Lady
    Did Before   2294
Don't Ask Too Much of Love   3385
Don't Bait for Fish You Can't Find   90
Don't Be a Geografoof   1477
Don't Be a Miracle   2618
Don't Be a Sailor   3737
Don't Be a Woman If You Can   3390
Don't Be Afraid   1755, 4196, 4446
Don't Be Afraid of an Animal   134
Don't Be Afraid of Romance   2983
Don't Be Afraid of the Dark   3908
Don't Be Afraid to Love   181
Don't Be Anybody's Moon but Mine   4185
Don't Be Anything Less Than Everything
    You Can Be   4034
Don't Be Ashamed of a Teardrop   1061
Don't Be Blue   2557
Don't Be Cross with Me   1833, 4185
Don't Be Like an Eskimo   1342
Don't Be Like That   1617
Don't Be Like Your Old Man   821
Don't Be Rash   2538, 2668
Don't Be So Cruel, Ducky Dear!   1090
Don't Be Subtle, Don't Be Coy   1577
Don't Be That Way   4137
Don't Be What You Ain't   2951
Don't Believe   376
Don't Believe a Tale Like That   2714
Don't Bet Your Money on de Shanghai   4149
Don't Betray His Love   2630
Don't Bite the Hand That Feeds You   843
Don't Blame It All on Broadway   357, 3525
Don't Blame Me   787, 4197
Don't Blow That Horn, Gabriel   2161
Don't Bother   410
Don't Bother Me, I Can't Cope   1072
Don't Break the Spell   2115
Don't Breathe a Word   68
Don't Bring Her Flowers   3272
Don't Call Me   255
Don't Call Them Dearie   2264
Don't Call Us   459
Don't Change the Way You Love Me   3671
Don't Cheat on the Meat   1917
Don't Choose a Gibson Girl   1593
Don't Come Near Me   2304

Don't Come to Court   3702
Don't Count on It   2702
Don't Count Your Chickens   187
Don't Cry   2961
Don't Cry Anymore   3227
Don't Cry Bo-Peep   251
Don't Cry for Me   2477
Don't Cry for Me Argentina   1211
Don't Cry Swanee   487
Don't Cry When He's Gone   2462
Don't Destroy the World   4396
Don't Dilly Dally on the Way   4027
Don't Do Anything Till You Hear from Me   2574
Don't Do It   1657
Don't Do It Mr. Hermes   3418
Don't Do the Charleston   3179
Don't Don't Stop Loving Me Now   2706
Don't-Don't-Don't   2756
Don't Drop the Bomb   3076
Don't Eat It   3602
Don't Even Start   1630
Don't Even Think About It   2333
Don't Ever Be a Poor Relation   3295
Don't Ever Book a Trip on the IRT   4279
Don't Ever Leave Me   2372, 4234
Don't Ever Run Away from Love   4702
Don't Fall Asleep   3107
Don't Fall for the Lights   4535
Don't Fall in Love with Me   2843
Don't Fall Until You've Seen Them All   2767
Don't Feed the Animals   1426
Don't Forget   1513
Don't Forget (Your Auntie)   3622
Don't Forget   3863
Don't Forget 127th Street   602, 1601
Don't Forget Bandanna Days   2645, 14
Don't Forget Me   1602, 2299, 3024, 3028
Don't Forget the Beau You Left at Home   1845
Don't Forget the Girl from Punxsutawney   532
Don't Forget the Girl You Left Behind   1606
Don't Forget the Lilac Bush   4169
Don't Forget the Number   1593, 4247
Don't Forget the Waiter   4795
Don't Forget to Dream   1811
Don't Forget You're Talking to a Lady   2906, 4311
Don't Forget Your Etiquette   138
Don't Forget Your Old Pal, Al   3982
Don't Get Around Much Anymore   4091
Don't Get Your Hopes Up   3165
Don't Give Up the Hunt, Dr. Puffin   2339
Don't Give Up the Ship   2772
Don't Give Your Love Away   928
Don't Go Away   3051
Don't Go Away Monsieur   383
Don't Go for to Leave Us, Richard Carr   402
Don't Go in the Water   1248
Don't Go in the Water Daughter   1247
Don't Go Into the Lion's Cage Tonight   470
Don't Go Sally   610
Don't Go To Dangerously Nigh   2123

Dubarry, The   1110
Dubbing (Knight of the Woeful Countenance),
    The   2727
Dublin Night Ballet   2268
Dublin Rag, The   2667
Dublin Town   4566
Dublinola   3407
Ducal Cousin, Give You Greeting   1388
Duchess of Central Park, The   3744
Duchess of Devonshire, The   3402
Duchess of Dreams, The   379
Duchess of Killarney, The   1464
Duchess of Table D'Hote   4802
Duchess of the Long Ago, The   3402
Duchess Song, The   3197
Duchess's Entrance   1284
Duck, The   3444
Ducks and Geese   2756
Ducks Call It Luck, The   1343
Ducky   453, 4550
Ducky Daddies   371
Dude All Dude   1116
Dudin' Up   3224
Duel   73
Duel, The   949, 1281, 2358, 3015, 3494
Duel! A Duel!, A   1000
Duello, The   4214
Duet   8, 690, 1624, 3171, 3976, 3549, 4252,
    4537, 526
Duet and Dance   473
Duet for 5 People   1047
Duet for One (The First Lady of the Land)   4004
Duet of the Robin and the Nightingale   526
Duke of Berkshire   1080
Duke's Place   4091
Duke, the Dauphin, The   2028
Dulcinea   2727
Dull and Gay (The Gay and the Dull)   3980
Dullest Couple in Scarsdale   2231
Dumb Bell, The   228
Dumb Girl   1440
Dumb Luck   740
Dumb-Dumb-Dumb-Dumbbell   993
Dumbbells May Be Foolish   3580
Dumber They Come the Better I
    Like 'Em, The   2308
Dummy Juggler   4577
Dumplings   669
D'Une Coquette   1458
Dunerwetter   2667
Dungeons and Dragons   430
Duo Thoughts   3201
Duodecimalogue   2287
During Life   3887
Dus Yiddishe Leid   2356
Dusky Debutante   4677
Dusky Dream   934
Dusky Love   2302
Dusky Salome, The   2978
Dusky Shadows   1064

Dust Bowl Refugee   4740
Dust Chasers   728
Dust in Your Eyes   3002
Dust Storm Disaster   4740
Dustbane: The Ballad of Minka   3601
Dusters, Goggles and Hats   4292
Dusting Around   3965
Dusty Roads   3167
Dutch Cadets, The   586
Dutch Comedians   998
Dutch Country Table   239
Dutch's Song   576
Dutchman's Pants, The   915
Dutiful Wife, A   2836
Duty Calls!   455
Dvoyreh   3781
Dvoyreh Fan Rumeynie   3781
Dwarf's Song   941
Dwarf's Yodel Song (The Silly Song)   4035
Dwight D. Eisenhower   3558
D'Ye Folly Me   1544
D'Ye Love Me?   4212
Dying Business, A   1770
Dying Child   2290
Dying Cowboy, The   1546
Dying Flamingo, The   4730
Dying Is   1450
Dying Schwann, The   128
Dying Swan, The   3314, 4810
Dying to Meet You   924
Dynamic   1918

E

E Didn't Know Just W'at to Say   1925
E-Gypsy-Ann   2009
Each Little Jack   4208
Each Night Is a New Day   2580
Each of Us   4288, 2320
Each Pearl a Thought   3237
Each Tomorrow Morning   1012
Eadie Was a Lady   4267
Eager Beaver   3187
Eagle and Me, The   462
Eagle Rock, The   3397
Eagle Soliloquy   4863
Earl Is Crazy   1139
Earl of Stole   1123
Earl Was Ahead   1139
Early Bird Eddy   1093
Early Hours of the Morn   4657
Early in the Morning   1296, 2342
Early Monday Morning   2748
Early Morning Rain   2007
Early One Morning Blues   344
Early Sunday   1770
Early to Bed   1140
Earth, The   1116

Eglamour 4485
Egon Edgon Band, The 962
Egypt 737, 1537, 4148
Egypt Is Egypt Again 3088
Egypt Land 694
Egypt's No Place for a Lady 69
Egyptian 4811, 4838
Egyptian Ballet 612
Egyptian Dance 1154
Egyptian Dance, The 2264
Egyptian Dance 1867
Egyptian Eyes 3409
Egyptian Melange 4104
Egyptian Night 978
Egyptian Rag 1065
Egyptianna (inst.) 662
Eibig Dein 4463
8 1/2 3171
Eight Bells 3799
8 Days a Week 1074
8:14 to Nooma City, The 3318
Eight Little Daughters 3434
Eight Little Debutantes Are We 356
Eight Little Girls 3322
Eight Little Gringitos 3719
Eight Little Nobodies 3137
Eight Weight Lifters 837
Eight Years 533
Eight-horse Parlay 1590
18 Days Ago 1491
1845 496
1898 3064
1861 4521
Eighteen-Wheelin' Baby 3517
Eighteen Years Ago 1258
18th Century Garden (inst.) 2088
Eighth Avenue 1842
8th Avenue 4684
Eighth Day 1809
Eighth Wonder, The 2250
80 Days 1161
88 Rag, The 4395
Eileen 515
Eileen, Allana Asthore 1162
Eileen Asthore 1163
Eileen Avourneen 4374
Eily Riley 2858
Ein Herbstmanoever 1455
Ein Koloheinu 4773
Ein Nacht in Venedig 3150
Ein Tag Im Paradies 473
Ein Tolles Madel 2914
Ein Walzerlraum 4590
Eine Kleine Nachtmusic Cha Cha Cha 220
Eine Nacht in Venedig 3151
Einstein 2478
Eisenhower-Grandfather Hero
   to the World 2579
Either You Do or You Don't 587
Ekufikeni 4438

El Bravo 1164, 845
El Bravo! 846
El Bruta 2108
El Capitan (inst.) 4390
El Choclo Tango 822
'El Cuando' 1046
El Gaucho 3356
El Matador Terrifico 4572
El Presidente 1536
El Rancho 2479
El Sombrero 4693
Elaine (Girl of My Heart) 3581
Elbow Room 2941
Elderly Actress, The 3235
Eldorado 630, 4575
Eleanor 1169, 3405
Eleanor, I Adore You 3100
Eleanor Roosevelt (A Discussion of Soup) 109
Eleanor Roosevelt: A Discussion of Soap 3757
Elect Me President 242
Election 1971
Election Day 3531, 3963
Election Ensemble 4187
Election Eve 4297
Election Returns 1409
Election Spectacular 3484
Election Time 434
Election, The 3291
Electric Blues 1717
Electric Light Cadets, The 3751
Electric Prophet 1116
Electric Signs 3268
Electric Windows 1497
Electricity 3821, 4390
Elegance 1828, 3113
Elegant Lovers 2611
Elegy (inst.) 1385
Eleleu! 227
Element of Doubt 2246
(That) Element of Doubt 4828
Elements, The 2820, 4412
Elena 2295
Elephant Joke 128
Elephant Skid 231
Elephant Song, The 3900
Elephant Walk 143
Elevation (What I Seen I Done) 2334
Elevator Papa—Switchboard Mama 2337
Eleven Commandments, The 1769
Eleven Levee Street 4214
Eleven O'Clock Number 426
Eleven O'Clock Song 145
Eleventh Commandment, The 3551
Elf King, The 1602
Eli, Eli 1740
Eli Eli 3704
Elijah 1715
Elijah Rock 4645
Eliot Rosewater 1591
Eliot, Sylvia 1591

F

Factory Ballet (dance)   4237
Facts, The   148
Facts   1702, 3661
Facts and Figures   1648
Facts of Life   2637
Facts of Life Backstage, The   1711
Fade Away   1903
Fade Out-Fade In   1227
Faded Flowers   1692
Faded Rose, A   3650
Faded Rose   1209
Fading Girl   965
Fads   1264
Failure   3763
Faint Heart Ne'er Won Fair Lady   4687
Fainting Ensemble   3921
Fair and Warmer Cocktail, The   804
Fair Colonus   1636
Fair Dissenter Lass, The   2633
Fair Enough   953
Fair Flower of Japan   4452
Fair Honeymoon Shine On   4547
Fair India   2571
Fair Is Fair   3128
Fair Lady   466
Fair Land of Dreaming   2622
Fair Men, Square Men   451
Fair Moon   1948
Fair One   870, 1426
Fair Plymouth Maiden   912
Fair Rosita   3117
Fair Senorita of the Argentine   792
Fair Sex, The   4323
Fair Trade   2064
Fair Warning   483, 1029
Fair Weather   4741
Fair Weather Friends   1112, 2950
Fair Women of England   333
Fairest Maiden   762
Fairest of Roses   4497
Fairest of the Fair   470
Fairfield Country   167
Fairies Chorus   1912
Fairies, Fairies, Come Forth   3588
Fairies in My Mother's Flower Garden   3641
Fairies Rule the World   3765
Fairies We   4014
Fairies' Lullaby   350
Fairies' Meeting, The   3422
Fairies' Revel   4649
Fairlight Glen   1262
Fairly Fresh   413
Fairy Beauty's Queen   355
Fairy Bells   4285
Fairy Boat, A   1095
Fairy Dance   764
Fairy Music   2394
Fairy Prince   1610
Fairy Song   1852
Fairy Tale, A   690

Fairy Tale   1935
Fairy Tale, A   2453
Fairy Tales   263
Fairy Tales (Cinderella Tale)   579
Fairy Tales   1164, 2101, 2298, 3555
Fairy Tales Are All Untrue   2504
Fairy Whispers   2412
Fairyland   656, 2035, 3163, 4646, 158
Fairylands (scene)   4816
Faith   1878, 2053
Faith, Hope and Charity   3923, 4467
Faith in Myself   1103
Faith Is Such a Simple Thing   2220
Faithful Crew, The   402
Faithless   404
Fake It   2026
Fake Your Way to the Top   1103
Fakir Man, The   1469
Falcon, The   3774
Falena   2235
Fall In!   3578
Fall of Babylon, The   1611
Fall of Man, The   3727
Fall of the Leaves, The   2843
Fall of Valor, The   4696
Fall River Folly   943
Fallen Angel   1232
Fallen Angels   4689
Fallin'   4334
Fallin'-Out-of-Love Rag, The   1380
Falling   211, 4031, 3966
Falling for You   2275
Falling in Love   742, 796, 1232, 3965, 4335
Falling in Love with Love   514, 4519
Falling Leaves Ballet (inst.)   2900
Falling Off the Wagon   289
Falling Out of Love   4025
Falling Out of Love Can Be Fun   2894
Falling Rain-Dream of You   2850
Falling Star   1450, 3648, 1337
Falling Stars   4803
Falling Through Life   2305
Falling Too Far   181
Fallout Shelter   4433
Falsettoland   1234
Fam'ly We Will Be, A   2064
Fame   3764
Fame!   3988
Fame, Fame, Fame   4634
Fame Is a Phony   82
Family   4399, 690, 1103, 198, 3835
Family Affair, A   871, 1237, 3124
Family Brawl, The   1088
Family Council, The   4616
Family Cycle Car   2454
Family Faces   2385
Family Fallout Shelter   1363
Family Fan, The   717
Family Farewell   1358
Family Fugue   4160

Farmer's Daughter   462, 858
Farmer's Daughters   2897
Farmer's Life, A   1095, 2622
Farmers Market Hoe Down   3046
Farmer's Wife, The   911
Farming   1018, 2453, 4517
Farming Life-Country Life   3996
Farrell Girl, The   67
Fas' Fas' World   295
Fascinating Females   3865
Fascinating Girl   4712
Fascinating Lady   3148
Fascinating Rhythm   2376, 3020
Fascinating Venus   4311
Fascinating Widow, The   1247
Fascinating You   1126
Fascination   1177, 4747
Fascination Waltz   1835
Fashion   1900
Fashion Girl, A   1973
Fashion Parade, The   765
Fashion Parade   2813
Fashion Plates, The   108
Fashion Show, The   1065, 2477, 4555
Fashion Waltz   3958
Fashions   3215
Fashion's Slave, A   965
Fast and Furious   1251
Fast Cars and Fightin' Women   4090
Fast Colors (inst.)   2161
Fast Food   3548
Fast Step Creation, A   1962
Fast Steppers   2939, 3737
Fasten Your Seat Belts   167
Faster and Faster   4325, 3401
Faster Than Sound   1891, 4827
Fastest Man in New York   4704
Fastrigossa's Lament   2811
Fat and Forte   4091
Fat and Greasy   39
Fat City   2618
Fat-Fat-Fatima   2601
Fat, Fat, the Water Rat   4169
Fat Luigi   1108
Fat Song, The   2913
Fat Tuesday Parade   4162
Fatal Blonde   4373
Fatal Curse of Beauty   4544
Fatal Fascination   1322
Fatal Step   1557
Fatality Hop, The   583
Fate   1016, 1453
Fate (It Was Fate when I First Met You)   1687
Fate   2327
Fate, The   3951
Fate   4383
Fate Is Such a Mystic Puzzle   3592
Fate of the Sailor, The   2711
Fate of the Veiled Mugs   2979
Father   3088, 4064

Father and Son   1418, 2923, 4337
Father, Dear Father, Stop Testing   3530
Father Divine   447
Father, Father   459
Father Is a Business Man   1743
Father Keeps on Doing It   3134
Father Knickerbocker Fox Trot   3401
Father Never Raised Any Foolish Children   1565
Father Nile, Keep Us in Thy Care   4724
Father Now, A   4349
Father of Claudine, The   808, 809
Father of Fathers   784
Father of the Bride, The   2050
Father Penn   185
Father Said   3507
Father Speaks, A   4401
Father Thames   1467
Father to Son   2746
Father Wants the Cradle Back   3068
Father Will Be with Us Soon   231
Father William   52
Father, Won't You Speak to Sister Mary?   4165
Father's Always Talking in His Sleep   2159
Father's Argument/Aucassin's Reply   1262
Father's Daughter   298
Father's Day   206, 2289
Father's Pride and Joy, A   1080
Father's Song   2478
Father's Waltz   169
Father's Whiskers   3729
Fatherhood Blues   253
Fatherland Is Free, The   742
Fatherland, Mother of the Band
   (Drink, Drink, Drink)   3379
Fathers and Mothers (And You and Me)   2033
Fathers and Sons   430, 4744
Fathers of the World   1490
Fathers that Wear Rags   3909
Fatima the Fair   3348
Fattening Frogs for Snakes   3657
Fatty   116, 135
Faucett Falls Fancy   823
Faust Finale   3463
Faust Up to Date   3525
Favorite at Maxim's, A   116
Favorite Son   4695, 2783
Favorite Song   595
Favorite Sons   1038
Fear   1227
Fear!   2591
Fear in My Heart   3365
Fear No More   1406
Fear No More the Heat of the Sun   3909
Fearfully, Frightful Love   4793
Fearless Frank   1256
Fearless Waltz, The   3395
Feast of the Lanterns   718
Feast on Me   1074
Feather in a Breeze   1207
Feather in My Shoe   823

Feather Your Nest   2491, 2721
Feathered Friends   427
Feathers   4830
Feathertop   1257, 1258
Feats of Piper   3487
February   2379
Fede, Fede   2142
Fee Fi Fo Fum   2182
Fee, Fi, Fo, Fum   1975
Fee Fi Fo Fum   2134
Fee-Fie-Fo-Fum   4569
Feed Me with Love   3613
Feeding the Chickens   2888
Feeding Time   223
Feel at Home   3619
Feel Free   2483
Feel Like Waltzing   1435
Feel That Jazz   4162
Feel the Beat   1732
Feel the Love   2074
Feelin' Good   3648
Feelin' Loved   135
Feeling Good   3731
Feeling I'm Falling   4443
Feeling in My Chest, A   1169
Feeling in the Air   108
Feeling in Your Heart, A   2829
Feeling Rich   3757
Feeling Sentimental   3953
Feeling We Once Had, The   4722
Feeling Wonderful   3236
Feelings   170
Fees and Dues   3344
Feet   3439
Feet, The   4533
Feet Do Yo' Stuff   1729
Feet Don't Fail Me Now   1890
Feet, Get Movin'   42
Feet on the Sidewalk (Head in the Sky)   3036
Feign a Faint, Ladies   3920
Felicita   139
Feline Wisdom   1871
Fellas Kiss Their Dads   2965
Fellatio 101   2451
Feller from Indiana   2137
(It Seems There Was a) Fellow and a Girl, A   2809
Fellow and a Girl, A   2809
Fellow Like Me Likes a Girl Like You, A   3042
Fellow Needs a Girl, A   85
Fellow Who Might Be Galloping, The   1313
Fellowship   1047
Female Chorus of Muleteers   4032
Female Drummer, A   1259
Feminine Companionship   273
Feminine-inity   4678
Femininity   3234
Femme du Monde   807
Femme Du Monde   3542
Femme Fatale   2201, 2318
Femmes Fatales   2364

Fence, The   1865
Fencing   4817
Fencing Girl, The   2506, 2893
Fencing Girls, The   4801
Fender Mender   3275
Fenwick   1261
Ferban Waltz   1544
Fergus' Dilemma   2820
Ferhuddled and Ferhexed   600
Fernando's Suicide   3456
Fertility Dance   4623
Festa (dance)   3543
Festina Lente   4404
Festival of Mourning   2793
Festival of Roses, The   2673
Festivals   392
Festive Continong, The   1540
Festive March (inst.)   4798
Festive Nights   2939
Festudo   1386
Fetch Yo' Baby Home   1264
Fetish (dance)   2355
Feudin' and Fightin'   2400
Fever   3428
Few Fast Steppers, A   2135
Few Get Through, A   2285
Few Small Tasks, A   3549
Fiasco   798
Fickle Finger of Fate, The   2053
Fickle Fortune   178
Fickle Weather Vane, The   2848
Fiction Writer   572
Fiction Writer Duet   572
Fiddle About   4676
Fiddle and I   3154, 604
Fiddle Dee Dee   1871
Fiddle-Dee-Dee March   1264
Fiddler and the Fighter, The   1227
Fiddler Must Be Paid, The   1746
Fiddler on the Roof   1265
"Fiddler on the Roof medley"   3018
Fiddler on the Roof selections   2205
Fiddler's Tune, The   259
Fiddlers Three   1266
Fiddlers' Green, The   406
Fidelity   2837
Fidgety Feet   69, 3243
Fie, Fie, Fie   632
Fie On Goodness   623
Field and Forest, The   3578
Field By Field   4055
Field Hollers and Work Songs   344
Fiesta   1065, 1979, 2602, 3716, 4796
Fiesta in Madrid, The   4021
Fiesta in Spain   190
Fifi   2083
Fifteen Glorious Years   3445
Fifteen Minutes   3348
Fifteen Minutes a Day   2034, 3042
Fifth Army's Where My Heart Is, The   4340

Freedom Charter   4438
Freedom Choo-Choo, The   597
Freedom Choo Choo Is Leaving Today, The   3217
Freedom Diet   2908
Freedom Is Coming Tomorrow   3836
Freedom Land   2203
Freedom March (dance)   1729
Freedom of the C's   3962
Freedom of the Press, The   919
Freedom of the Seas, The   2150
Freedom Road   3226
Freedom Train, The   1474
Freedomland   3110
Freer Love   337
Freeway Song, The   407
Freeze and Melt   895
Freeze Music   3233
Freezing and Burning   1053
Freight   4138
Freight Train   1496
French   1955
French Auction, The   3780
French Colonial Exposition Scene   3214
French Fling   4000
French Flip Flop   2299
French Flirt   1647
French Have a Word for It, The   4174
French Lesson, The   2691
French Maids, The   591
French Marine Ashore, A   1220
French Militaire   115
French Military Marching Song   1027
French Pastry Walk, The   1345
French Soldiers on Leave Dance   4421
French Song, The   4
French Thing Tango   2332
French Wench   367
French with Tears   59, 3178, 3563
French You Hear on Broadway   3475
Frenchman's Paree, The   3234
Frenetica   4117
Frere Jacques   2364
Fresh Air and Exercise   3301
Fresh and Young   3941
Fresh As a Daisy   3359
Fresh, Bloomin' Health   2240
Freshie, O Freshie   2232
Freshman Song, A   3542
Fresno Beauties   2961
Freud   2478
Freud and Jung and Adler   3379
Freud Is a Fraud   314
Friar's Life, A   1213
Friars' Parade   1399
Friar's Song, The   1394
Friar's Song   1397
Friar's Tune   3876
Frickered Fling   1497
Friday Dancing Class   2439
Friday, Friday   1093

Friday Night   1269
Frieda   1569
Friederike   1384
Friend   4034
Friend Is a Friend, A   825
Friend Like You, A   2731
Friend of a Friend of Mine   1707
Friend of Mine, A   2504
Friend of Mine Gave This to Me, A   2966
Friend of the Family   4586, 2044
Friendliest Thing, The   4633
Friendly Bar, A   971
Friendly Country   3947
Friendly Enemy   1930
Friendly Ghosts   702
Friendly Liberal Neighborhood   2913
Friendly Neighborhood Dump   1750
Friendly Polka   2219
Friends   73, 170, 403, 3539, 1206, 2233, 4022,
   4168, 4528
Friends Ain't S'posed to Die   414
Friends and Lovers   2637
Friends, Dear Friends   698
Friends for Life   2702
Friends Have to Part   2698
Friends That Are Good and True   1926, 3753
Friends, the Best Of   1059
Friends to the End   999
Friends Who Understand   4694
Friendship   1109, 2808, 2951, 1867, 1549, 4517
Friendship Ain't No One Way Street   4750
Friendship and Love   2698
Friendship Leads Us to Love   3369
Friendship's Sacred Touch   1388
Friggin New Orleans Interlude (inst.)   3564
Frightened Fawn, The   2722
Frightened of the Dark   1093
Frills Upon Their Petticoats   2803
Frimbo Special   1402
Fringe of Society, The   4508
Frisa Linda   1374
Frisco, The   4712
Frisco Fanny   4583
Frisco Flo   883
Frisco Frizz, The   1835
Frisco Frizz   2600
Fritzie   278
Frivolette   3769
Frivolity   1526
Frivolity Frolics   3664
Frocks and Frills   1580, 3333
Frog, The   2717
Frog and the Owl, The   361
Frog He Lived in a Pond, A   1682
Frogs, The   1406, 1406
Frolic of a Breeze, The   333
Frolic of a Breeze   675
Frolic of the Bears   4447
Frolic of the Fairies   4649
Frolics of Pierrot, The   1900

G

Girl of the Mystic Star   1776
Girl of the Pi Beta Phi, A   1628
Girl of To-Day, The   3397
Girl of Tomorrow, The   1488
Girl on the Magazine Cover, The   4158, 4799
Girl on the Persian Rug, The   3446
Girl on the Police Gazette, The   4131
Girl on the Prow, The   3117
Girl on the Square   3958
Girl Power   3346
Girl Really Needs a Woman, A   2243
Girl She Can't Remain, A   651
Girl That I Adore, The   2371
Girl That I Court in My Mind, The   4366
Girl That I Marry, The   153
Girl That I'd Call Mine, The   2505
Girl That I'll Adore, The   4170
Girl That Leads the Band, The   187
Girl That You Leave Behind, The   639
Girl That's Most Chased After, The   2020
Girl to Remember, A   1227
Girl Wanted   2209
Girl Who Can Love, A   3319
Girl who Comes from the West, The   3437
Girl Who Doesn't Ripple When She Bends   1140
Girl Who Drinks Champagne, The   3401
Girl Who Gets Her Man, The   1986
Girl Who Is Up-To-Date   350
Girl Who Keeps Me Guessing   4393
Girl Who Keeps You Waiting, The   3319
Girl Who Lives in Montparnasse, The   3954
Girl Who Works in the Laundry, The   3916
Girl Who Wouldn't Spoon, The   1558
Girl with a Brogue, The   178
Girl with a Flame, A   183
Girl with a Ribbon, A   937
Girl with Talent, A   3165
Girl with the Baby-Blue Tights, The   8
Girl with the Banjo Eyes, The   4859
Girl with the Changeable Eyes, The   3384
Girl with the Clocking on Her Stocking, The   353
Girl with the Come Hither Eyes   1285
Girl with the Curls, The   1695
Girl with the Green Eye, The   2187
Girl with the Major General, The   1885
Girl with the Naughty Wink, The   509
Girl with the Orange Hair, The   1496
Girl with the Paint on Her Face, The   4677
Girl with the Prettiest Legs in Town, The   664
Girl with the Yellow Roses, The   1783
Girl without a Name, The   3894
Girl Worth the While   4007
Girl You Dream About, The   1563, 2408
Girl You Left Behind   4636
Girl You Love, The   1071, 3976, 4354
Girl You Never Have Kissed, The   3770
Girl You Take Out to Supper, The   2498
Girl You're a Woman   374
Girl's Song   1977
Girlie   4422

Girlie from the Cabaret, The   2696
Girlie Girl   694
Girlie-Land, A   1111
Girlie of All the Year   2879
Girlie with a Bustle   293
Girlie with the Baby Stare, The   2906, 3820
Girlie with the Winsome Smile, The   248
Girlies   88
Girlies Are Out of My Life   4747
Girlies You've Kissed in Dreams, The   1247
Girlish Laughter   3395
Girls   326
Girls, The   1889
Girls   2835, 2555, 2728, 2847
Girls!   3024
Girls   4798
Girls Against the Boys, The   1567
Girls Ahoy!   36
Girls All Around Me   3712
Girls Along Fifth Avenue, The   1723
Girls and Boys   1567, 4662
Girls and Dogs   2188
Girls and French Chauffeurs   3701
Girls and Rassendyl   4798
Girls and the Gimmies   670
Girls Are Getting Wiser (Every Day), The   1334
Girls Are Like a Rainbow   3146
Girls Are Like the Weather to Me   1482
Girls at Maxim's (Girls, Girls, Girls), The   2836
Girls at Maxims   2838
Girls at Maxims, The   2835
Girls Can't Lie   4409
Girls Do Not Tempt Me   1013
Girls Dream of One Thing   2263
Girls from the Folies Bergeres, The   1868
Girls from the Follies   806
Girls from Yankee Land   3771
Girls! Girls!   837
Girls, Girls   1707
Girls! Girls! Girls!   511
Girls, Girls, Girls   513, 1584
Girls, Girls, Girls (What's a Maiden?)   1768
Girls, Girls, Girls   2869, 4375, 2837
Girls, Girls, Keep Your Figure   4687
Girls Grow More Wonderful Day by Day   2180
Girls I Am Leaving in England Today, The   702
Girls, I Am True to You All
   (I'm True to Everyone)   771
Girls I Have Met   2378
Girls I Left Behind, The   4802
Girls, If I Ever Get Married   543
Girls If You Ever Get Married   1588
Girls in the Band   4196
(There Are Plenty of) Girls in the Sea   1922
Girls in the Sea   3146
Girls in Their Summer Dresses   3110
Girls I've Met, The   2184
Girls Just Girls   2724
Girls Like Me   4190
Girls 'n' Girls 'n' Girls   3108

Girls of DeVere's   2533
Girls of Every Land, The   1417
Girls of Gottenburg, The   1569
Girls of Long Ago   3721
Girls of My Dreams   4814
Girls of New York, The   539
Girls of Summer   1571
Girls of Summer, The   2764
Girls of the Midnight Matinee   4704
Girls of the Night, The   2198
Girls of the Old Brigade, The   3254
Girls of the U.S.A.   2517
Girls Prepare   3958
Girls Pretty Girls   3443
Girls Quartette   2013
Girls Run Along   3627
Girls That Boys Dream About, The   3734
Girls That Can Never Be Mine, The   3579
Girls Want a Hero   341
Girls Were Made for Dancing   1129
Girls Who Go Upon the Stage   3134
Girls Who Sell Orangeade, The   3490
Girls Who Sit and Wait, The   2664
Girls Will Be Girls and Boys Will Be Boys   2964
Girls Would Have Me Blushing, The   1240
Girls You Are Such Wonderful Things   4258
Girly Girly   1926
Girofle-Girofla   2843, 1576
Git on de Boat, Chillun   4479
Gitka's Song, The   4481
Give a Cheer   197, 2935
Give a Girl a Break!   556
Give a Girl a Chance   2768
Give a Little, Get a Little   4496
Give a Little, Get a Little Kiss   2594
Give a Little Thought to Me   4860
Give a Little Whistle (and I'll Be There)   4693
Give a Man Enough Rope   4695
Give a Viva!   2447
Give All Your Love Away   519
Give and Take   3763
Give, Baby, Give   4586
Give 'Em a Kiss   3615
Give 'Em a Lollipop   1727
Give 'Em Hell   1201, 4679
Give 'Em What They Want   1597
Give England Strength   3780
Give, Give   3218
Give Him a Great Big Kiss   338
Give Him a Welcome Quite Spanish   3774
Give Him Back His Job   4421
Give Him the Oo-La-La   1109
Give Him Your Sympathy   381
Give It   1836
Give It All You Got   3234
Give It All You've Got   2057
Give It Back to the Indians   4420
Give It Love   3966
Give It to Me   2451
Give Me   2433

Give Me a Cause   1273, 3159
Give Me a Cozy Corner   2587
Give Me a Good Cigar   515
Give Me a Good Havana   2261
Give Me a Good Old Mammy Song   2235
Give Me a Man Like That   567
Give Me a Martial Air   3442
Give Me a Night   3849
Give Me a Pinch   4319
Give Me a Pink Coat   2240
Give Me a Road   3159
Give Me a Roll on a Drum   2813
Give Me a Share in America   3564
Give Me a Ship   4408
Give Me a Sock with Your Shoes   4041
Give Me a Song I Can Whistle   3104
Give Me a Star   4396
Give Me a Thought Now and Then   1610
Give Me a Thrill   2071
Give Me a Wall   3159
Give Me a Word   2864
Give Me All of You   1309, 2762
Give Me All the Flowers (Flower Song)   2254
Give Me All the Money   2033
Give Me an And   778
Give Me an Old-Fashioned Girlie   3222
Give Me Back My Liza   2675, 4130
Give Me Excess of It   4449
Give Me Four Beats   943
Give Me Love   3697
Give Me Love, Love, Love   2903
Give Me More   2195
Give Me My Mammy   487, 3649
Give Me Old Broadway and I'll Be Satisfied   1332
Give Me One Good Reason   181
Give Me One Hour   4664
Give Me Someone   3236
Give Me Something in a Uniform   1561
Give Me Something in a Uniform of Blue   3525
Give Me That Key   4537
Give Me That Letter   4393
Give Me That Rose   3768
Give Me the Girls   994
Give Me the Land   3972, 4517
Give Me the Love   3830
Give Me the Moonlight   1240
Give Me the Open Air   1214
Give Me the Rain   1460
Give Me the Simple Life   2953
Give Me the South All the Time   1823
Give Me the Sunshine   2302
Give Me Thy Heart Love   1768
Give Me Thy Heart, Love   4187
Give Me Your Heart and Give Me Your Hand   4429
Give Me Your Love   4283, 4763
Give Me Your Tired, Your Poor
   (The New Colossus)   1609
Give Me Your Tired, Your Poor   2894
Give My Regards to Broadway   1478, 2517, 2975
Give Shalom and Sabbath to Jerusalem   4396

Googy-oo 2986
Googy-Oogy-Oo 830
Goona-Goona 364, 1600
Goona Goona 4021
Goose Girl, The 1388
Goose Never Be a Peacock 3837
Goozy Woozy 1568
Gordie 1736
Gordita Es Bonita 2478
Gorgeous 170, 2896
Gorgeous Alexander 3117
Gorgeous Lily 3636
Gorgeous to Gaze At 1414
Gospel 612
Gospel According to King, The 3039
Gospel According to Lillian 2992
Gospel According to St. Matthew, The 1595, 4788
Gospel According to the Leopard 2283
Gospel News 4147
Gospel of Gabriel Finn 4558
Gossip 101, 102, 1171, 2532, 2754, 3013,
    4303, 4169, 4210, 4292
Gossip Song, The 249
Gossip Song 3129
Gossip's Chorus 3675
Gossiping 4010
Gossiping Grapevine 4268
Gossips 4357
Gossips, The 4652
Gossips' Chorus 4754
Got a Bran' New Suit 216
Got a Head Like a Rock 2225
Got a Match 2388
Got a Need for You 879
Got a New Boy Friend 1414
Got a Notion 1985
Got a Rainbow 4443
Got It Again 1448
Got Myself a New Love 3605
Got Myself Another Jockey Now 2302
Got No Time 888
Got That Good Time Feelin' 2400
Got the Lady Dressed 3792
Got the World in the Palm of My Hand 766
Got to Be a Woman Now 1002
Got to Be Bad to Be Good 3278
Got to Be Good Times 1103
Got to Find My Way 4292
Got to Get Away from Here 2551
Got to Go to Town 2423
Got to Have More 2308
Got to Sing Me a Song 3697
Got Tu Go Disco 1637
Got Un Zayn Mishpet Iz Gerekht (God and His
    Judgment Are Right) 1609
Got what It Takes 2850
Got You Right Where I Want You 18
Gott Is Gut 2583
Gotta Be a Dream 2664
Gotta Dance 2582

Gotta Do My Duty 2238
Gotta Find a Way to Do It 3172
Gotta Get a Partner 2196
Gotta Get Back to You 2426
Gotta Get de Boat Loaded 4763
Gotta Get Joy 2400
Gotta Get Out 1164
Gotta Getaway 1638
Gotta Go West 1597
Gotta Hang My Wash Out to Dry 825
Gotta Have a Man Around the House 2516
Gotta Have a Man, Sometime 4180
Gotta Have Hips Now 1836
Gotta Hurry 2307
Gotta Live Free 3035
Gotta Move 2084
Gotta New Song 3173
Gotta Pay 2661
Gotta Pretend 2784
Gotta Take a Chance 3690
Gottet Got 613
Gout, The (The Spasms) (dance) 3274
Governor of the State 2698
Governor of the State, The 1640
Governor of Villaya, The 4430
Governor's Entrance 3081
Governor's Lady 2112
Governor's Son, The 1640
Governor's Song, The 2917
Gown for Each Hour of the Day, A 3387
Gown Is Mightier Than the Sword, The 3538
Gowns 1629
Gowns By Roberta 3735
Gowns Soft and Clingy 4464
Gozinto 4837
Gra Ma Chree 1445
Grab a Girl 1011, 4001
Grab Bag, The 1485, 1643
Grab Me a Gondola 1644
Grab Them While You Can 2048
Grace 3908
Graceful and Fair 3978
Graceful Exit, A 2231
Grade 'A' Treatment 521
Graduate, The 1645
Graduates of Mrs. Grimm's Learning 2001
Graduation 1077, 2224
Grafin Mariza 905
Grafitti 4468
Graft 2848, 4662
Grain of Sand 2539, 3167
Grand and Glorious Fourth, The 2985
Grand Army of Crooks 3537
Grand Banks Sequence 647
Grand Cafe, The 1068
Grand Canal 965
Grand Canal, The 3171
Grand Central Station 3279
Grand Coulee Dam 4740
Grand Diversion, The 2617

H

H.G. Wells' Laboratory   1159
H.M.S. Goldilocks or the Lass That
   Loved a Mailman   4679
H.M.S. Pinafore   1948, 2817
H.N.I.C.   578
Ha! Cha! Cha!   672
Ha Ha Family, The   45
Ha, Ha, Ha   2696
Ha! Ha! Ha!   4649
Ha, Ha, Ha   4777
Ha-Ha-Ha (Gang Song)   4778
Ha, Ha, Ha! Millionaires!   2880
Ha, Ha, They Must Sail for Siberia   3547
Ha-Za-Za   3839
Ha'am Haze   4396
Habanera   2830
Habit As We Go Along, The   1562
Hacienda Garden   1182
Hack 'em   1985
Had to Give Up Gym   1425
Had You But Wit   945
Hagar the Horrible   1714
Haggadah, The   1715
Haggle, The   269
Hah   2153
Hail and Reign   3591
Hail Angele, Our Nightingale   902
Hail! Antonia, Hail!   1682
Hail Bibinski   3972
Hail Bompopka   2159
Hail Britannia   279
Hail Celestial Potentate   1243
Hail David   1769
Hail, Franz of Zilania   4250
Hail Gentle Eros   1768
Hail, Gracious Owner of This Spot   2722
Hail, Hail   4168
Hail, Hail, Hail   3326
Hail Hio   3539
Hail Majesty (1)   3526
Hail Mary!   755
Hail Mary   1716
Hail! Mr. Beverly   333
Hail Number One   2504
Hail Poetry   2977
Hail Sphinx   1848
Hail Stonewall Jackson   3056
Hail the Bridegroom   735
Hail the Conquering Hero   837
Hail, the Conquering Hero!   837
Hail, the Falcon   4550
Hail the Grand Wazir   758
Hail the Groom and Hail the Bride   2936
Hail, the Happy Couple   3379
Hail, the Hero of the Day   1540
Hail the Hero of Today   2139
Hail the King   4620

Hail, the Mythic Smew   2339
Hail the Rajah   3786
Hail the Son of David   2075
Hail the Wedding Pair   4616
Hail to Aurora   4425
Hail to Christmas   250
Hail to Cyril   3378
Hail to MacCracken's   4423
Hail to Monty   4860
Hail to Our General   2419
Hail to Our Noble Guest   3578
Hail to Our Queen   3422
Hail to the Baronet   1021
Hail to the Bey   2500
Hail to the Blood   459
Hail to the Bride   1121
Hail to the Caliph   175
Hail to the Golden Calf   1309
Hail to the Judge   3887
Hail to the King   2317, 2320
Hail to the Magistrate   3882
Hail to the Piccadilly Hero   3882
Hail to the Precarious Isles!   1887
Hail to the Queen of Beauty   331
Hail! To the Queen of Beauty   1458
Hail to the School   4169
Hail to the Sultan   177
Hail U.S.A.   969
Hail, We Hope It's a Male   4590
Hail, Ye Indian Maidens   3865
Hair   1388, 1717
Hair of the Dog that Bit You, The   2335
Hair of the Heir, The   82
Hair Pulling Ballet   1108
Hairdo Hop, The   3628
Hairdresser Sequence   2992
Hairpin Harmony   1718
Hairpin Turn   2032
Halala Song, The   1719
Halevay Volt Ikh Singl Geven
   (I Wish I Were Single Again)   4342
Half a Dozen Little Bits of Lace   3882
Half a Dream to Go   4602
Half a Kiss   4765
Half a Married Man   3727
Half a Moon Is Better Than No Moon   1965
Half a Sixpence   1721
Half Alive   2134
Half and Half   417
Half As Big As Life   3603
Half Caste Woman   4823
Half Moon!   1723
Half of a Couple   534
Half of It, Dearie, Blues, The   2376
Half of Life   602
Half of Me   1497, 3
Half of the World Laughs   1518
Half Past April, and a Quarter to May   2183
Half Past Eight   1726
Half-Past Kissing Time   2209

He's a Cousin of Mine   2765
He's a Dear Old Pet   4642
He's a Fallen Angel   4289
He's a Fan, Fan, Fan!   531
He's a Guy   1189
He's a Jolly Good Fellow   3348
He's a Ladies Man   1628
He's a Man   3871
He's a Man's Man   1339
He's a Peculiar Guy   2478
He's a Right Guy   4058
He's a Winner (Sporting Life)
    (Reporters' Opening)   1529
He's a Wonder   4788
He's All That We Need   2133
He's an American   3158
He's Back   1764
He's Back in Town   1048
He's Beginning to Look a Lot Like Me   1002
He's Coming   3469
He's Coming Home   1852
He's Crazy   4359
He's Dead   3066
He's Goin' Home   4142
He's Going to Call on Baby Grand   4327
He's Going to Die   3937
He's Gone   2974, 143, 4434
He's Gone Away   4111
He's Gonna Keep His Eye on Us   1289
He's Good for Me   3869
He's Good for Nothing but Me   2187
He's Got a Bungalow   2853
He's Got Larceny in His Heart   1420
He's Got the Whole World in
    His Hands   344, 4460
He's Got to Go   4297
He's Here!   2014
He's in Love!   2327
He's Just My Ideal   495
He's Ma Romeo   2631
He's Mah Dancing Man   548
He's Mine   124, 607
He's My B-B-B-Baby   2541
He's My Guy   36
He's My Kiddo   806
He's My Pal   3952
He's Never Too Busy   1441
He's Not for Me   1676
He's Not Himself   3379
He's Not the Prince   1868
He's Not Worth Your Tears   4235
He's on the Police Force Now   476
He's Only Wonderful   1300
He's Our Boy   483
He's Out of His Mind   1864
He's Oversexed!   3379
He's Ravin', Let Him Rave   2964
He's Reliable   702
He's So Good   4807
He's the Hottest Man in Town   2308

He's the Man   2680
He's the Wizard   4722
He's the Wonder of Them All   1845
He's with My Johnny   1748
He's Wonderful   3956
Head Down the Road   280
Head in the Stars   298
Head on Her Shoulders, A   1698
Head Over Heels   792, 1796, 1714
Head Over Heels in Love   1965
Head Song, The   1985
Headache and a Heartache, A   3895
Headin' for a Weddin'   1679
Headin' for a Weddin' in the Sky   2806
Headin' for Harlem   3968
Headin' for Heaven (Down South)   885
Headin' for the Bottom   145
Headin' South   3054
Headin' West   1782
Headless Horseman Ballet   4015
Headlines   3938
Heads I Win   3918
Heads or Tails   1713
Heads Up   3683
Headsman and I, The   3798
Healer Am I of All Sorrow, The   4719
Healing   624
Healing Chant, The (1)   2565
Healing Chant, The (2)   2565
Health Food Man, The   250
Health to Dear Mama, A   4479
Health to Noah   2340
Health, Wealth and the Girl You Love   3028
Healthy Relationship   871
Heap Big Suffragette   3087
Heap Love (An Indian Serenade)   2155
Hear Me, Amelia (Finale Act I)   4430
Hear My Prayer   4438
Hear My Song of Love (Serenade)   4293
Hear O Israel   3995
Hear the Bell   2184
Hear the Coachman Crack His Whip   252
Hear the Guns   459
Hear the Gypsies Playing   1352
Hear the Hunter's Horn   1646
Hear the Trumpet Call   2602
Hear Ye! Hear Ye!   1284
Hear Your Voice   1903
Heard It Through the Grapevine   166
Hearing Voices   1700
Hearings, The   3873
Heart   4399
Heart, The   3703
Heart Ache   2303
Heart and Soul   3444
Heart Beats   3915
Heart Bow'd Down, The   1710
Heart Breaker, The   4801
Heart-Breakers   3962
Heart Breakin' Joe   3808

Help the Drive   3063
Help the Seamen   3822
Help Us Tonight   1667
Help Yourself   434, 1650
Help Yourself to Happiness   4823
Helping   1389
Helping Hand and a Willing Heart, A   2580
Helplessness at Midnight   2702
Hemlines   4679
Hen and the Cow, The   541
Hen and the Weather Vane, The   2534
Hence It Don't Make Sense   3893
Hennie Soup   3757
Henny   3437
Henny Klein   4662
Henrietta   2231
Henry   466, 4099
Henry Dinkenspiel   2800
Henry Is Where It's At   4089
Henry Leek   989
Henry Street   1420
Henry, Sweet Henry   1846
Hep Cat, The   4281
Hep Cats Done Gone High Hat   1917
Hep, Hep, Hep   2108
Hep, Hot and Solid Sweet   4826
Her Anxiety   1977
Her Baggage Was Checked for Troy   1417
Her Bright Shawl   3431
Her Career   944
Her Dream Man   2098
Her Eyes Are Blue for Dear Old Yale   3579
Her Eyes, Her Eyes   2106
Her Eyes Kept Saying
   'Kiss Me!' All the Time   1524
Her Face   656
Her Father's Daughter   4297
Her Faults   2733
Her First Can Can   2986
Her First Kiss   2519
Her First Roman   1848
Her Gentleman Friend   1988
Her Glove   902
Her Heart Was in Her Work   629
Her Is   3351
Her Jazz Drummer   1882
Her Laughter in My Life   2011
Her Lilywhite Hand   4479
Her Love Is Always the Same   468
Her Majesty   3903
Her Mummy Doesn't Like Me
   Any More   1386
Her Name Is Aurora   2333
Her Name Is Leona   3653
Her or Me   2905
Her Pop's a Cop   3986
Her Portrait   2716
Her Song   3539
Her's a Fool   3927
Herb Song, The   3764

Herbert   2168
Here!   1161
Here 'Tis   435, 3966, 3965
Here Am I   1132, 4234
Here Am I-Broken Hearted   202
Here and Now   3576, 1564, 4015, 2250
Here and There   4021, 4798
Here and There and Everywhere   2605
Here Are Your Children   786
Here at Baiae on the Bay   1682
Here at Monte Carlo   2938
Here Be Oysters Stewed in Honey
   (Opening Chorus)   758
Here Beside Me   3286
Here Busted a Captive Heart   2028
Here Come the Blues   90
Here Come the Dreamers   2535
Here Come the Married Men   4037
Here Come the Rah Rah Boys   2490
Here Come the Soldiers   3791
Here Come the Yanks   4838
Here Come the Yanks with Their Tanks   1920
Here Come Your Men   4384
Here Comes Another Song About Texas (Pass the
   Cotton, Pass the Cotton)   3832
Here Comes My Blackbird   441
Here Comes My Show Boat   26
Here Comes Never   3299
Here Comes the Ballad   1056
Here Comes the Big Brass Band   3173
Here Comes the Bride   1626, 2373, 2888, 4655
Here Comes the Groom   379
Here Comes the Hot Tamale Man   1425
Here Comes the Kid   1250
Here Comes the Prince of Wales   3130
Here Comes the Rabbi   1590
Here Comes the Showboat!   2204
Here Comes the Spring   1792
Here Comes the Sun   599, 4008
Here Comes Tootsi   186
Here for the Hearing   373
Here Goes   880
Here Goes Nothing   3837
Here He Is   2068
Here I Am   519, 690, 1489, 1846, 2001,
   3210, 1258, 3342, 1940
Here I Am Again   426
Here I Come   3543, 4629
Here I Go Again   180, 932
Here I Go Bananas!   3539
Here I'll Stay   2615
Here in Cadiz   2500
Here in Eden   170
Here in Minipoora   1638
Here in My Arms   1013
Here In My Arms   2467
Here in My Hands   4055
Here in My Heart   2238
Here in the Dark   1603
Here in the Inn   4244

Hot Foot Dance   981
Hot-Foot'n   3120
Hot Gavotte   2479
Hot Grog   1985
Hot Harlem   4198
Hot Heels   3342
Hot Hindoo   1689
Hot, Hot Honey   3149
Hot, Hot Mama   1251
Hot Jello   3782
Hot Lover   4485
Hot Monkey Love   1149
Hot Moonlight   3946
Hot Music   1938
Hot Number   4825
Hot Off the Oven   1131
Hot Pants   124
Hot Pants Dance   3599
Hot Patata, The   3131
Hot Patootie Land   2700
Hot Patootie Wedding Night   290
Hot Rhythm   1989, 4198
Hot Rod   932
Hot Sands   931
Hot September Dance   1990
Hot Shot   3568
Hot Spell   1125
Hot Spot   3735
Hot Stuff   2513
Hot Tamale Alley   509
Hot Tamale Sam   2792
Hot Time in the Old Town   662
Hot Time in the Old Town, A   3297
Hot Time in the Old Town Tonight   1425, 2796
Hot Time in the Old Town Tonight, A   4390
Hot Voo-Doo   1638
Hot Water   194, 4240
Hot Water Bottles   1993
Hotcha Ma Chotch   4023
Hotel Clerk's Song   934
Hotel Life   2363
Hotel Lobby Scene   919
Hotel Never Tell   3157
Hotel Paradiso   1993
Hotel Passionato   1993
Hotel Stadt-Lemberg   184, 2747
Hotsy Totsy Hats   551
Hotsy Totsy Nazi   1739
Hotten Trot, The   2462
Hottentot Love Song, A   2765
Hottentot Potentate   216
Hottest Knishe   4172
Hound Dog   4031, 3739
Hounds of John Jorrock's, The   2240
Houp-La   1021, 1796
Hour Ago, An   2187
Hour for Lunch   924
Hour for Thee and Me, The   1897, 4149
Hour Is Ripe, The   3527
Hours Creep on Apace, The   2977

Hours I Spent with You, The   1215
House, The   4297, 1750
House and Garden   2961
House Full of People, A   840
House I Live In, The   467, 2447
House in Algiers   3792
House in the Country   4415
House in the Woods, A   1997
House in Town, A   1290
House Is Haunted, The (By the Echo of Your Last
    Goodbye)   4824
House Is Not a Home, A   261
House Is Not the Same Without a Woman, A
    (E Bello Ave 'Na Donna Dentro Casa)   3798
House of Blue Lights   2772
House of Don Pasquale, The   3197
House of Flowers   2000
House of Flowers Waltz (inst.)   2000
House of Grass   1809
House of Leather Theme   2001
House of Marcus Lycus, The (1)   1422
House of Marcus Lycus, The (2)   1422
House on a Cloud   2115
House on East 88th Street   2657
House on East 88th Street, The   2658
House on Rittenhouse Square, A   1475
House on the Hill   4337
House that Hook Built, The   2889
House That Jack Built, The   764, 2123
House that Jazz Built, The   1533
House that Monty's 'Jack' Built, The   577
House Upon the Hill, The   3862
House We'd Build, The   2004
House Where I Was Born, The   3386
House with a Little Red Barn, A   4483
Houseboat on the Styx   2005
Houseboat on the Styx, The   2005
Household Brigade, The   4725
Housekeeping   69
How a Monocle Helps the Mind   2123
How About a Ball?   2681
How About a Boy?   4179
How About a Cheer for the Navy?   4340
How About a Date?   3091
How About a Little Date for Breakfast?   289
How About a Man?   4178
How About It?   111, 3849
How About Me   1146
How About Me?   789, 981
How About Us Last Nite   1697
How About You   3175
How About You and Me   1222
How Actresses Are Made   666
How Am I Doin', Dad?   1770
How America Got Its Name   2132
How Are Things in Glocca Morra?   1278
How Are You Feeling?   2578
How Are You Going to Start the
    American Revolution?   4488
How Are You, Lady Love?   1756

I

I Love Her Oh! Oh! Oh!   1963
I Love Her-She Loves Me   2706
I Love Him   3875, 751, 1743, 2961, 3772
I Love Him for He Loved the
   Love That I Loved   2619
I Love Him, the Rat   1387
I Love His Face   3469
I Love, I Adore Her   2500
I Love It   1063
I Love It Rag   4804
I Love Louisa   294
I Love Love   3584, 4669
I Love Love (I Love You Dear)   3685
I Love Love in New York   95
I Love Lydia   2057
I Love MacIntosh   3322
I Love Me   1785
I Love Me (I'm Wild About Myself)   3405
I Love My Art   1551, 3031
I Love My Boo Boo   1116
I Love My Father   4485
I Love My Little Susie (Camel Song)   930
I Love My Love   2936
I Love My Love with an "A"
   (J'Aime Mon Amour)   1569
I Love My Movie Picture Man   75
I Love My Wife   2050, 2058, 4004
I Love Myself in Two   2243
I Love Nashville   2248
I Love New York   4068
I Love Not but You   3392
I Love Not One but All   3304
I Love Only One Girl in the Wide,
   Wide World   4723
I Love Only You   1453
I Love Order   3469
I Love Paris   629
I Love Petite Belle   2719
I Love Power   1092
I Love Rosie Casey   4317
I Love Someone   945
I Love That Boy   1539
I Love the Boys   2135
I Love the Charleston   4795
I Love the Girls   379
I Love the Ground You Walk On   1552
I Love the Heart of Dixie   3985
I Love the Ladies   367, 2091
I Love the Land of Old Black Joe   1154
I Love the Lassies (I Love Them All)   3146
I Love the Last One Best of All   2765
I Love the Love That's New   3770
I Love the Misses   1972
I Love the Moon   3079
I Love the Name of Mary   310
I Love the Rain   2988
I Love the River and You   4840
I Love the Sun   1282
I Love the Way We Fell in Love   3713
I Love Them All   1759, 2950, 3026, 3586

I Love Them Just a Little Bit   1175
I Love This Child   4764
I Love This Land   4004
I Love, Thou Lovest   2180
I Love to Be in Love   1439
I Love to Be Loved   4809, 4834
I Love to Be Unhappy   1512
I Love to Cry at Weddings   4238
I Love to Dance   287, 545, 1298, 2342, 2446,
   2461, 4158
I Love to Dance When I Hear a March   200
I Love to Flirt with the Ladies   3920
I Love to Flutter   4021
I Love to Follow a Band   1776
I Love to Fox Trot   1961
I Love to Go Shopping   511
I Love to Go Swimmin' with Wimmin'   2601
I Love to Have the Boys Around Me   4603
I Love to Hear a Yankee Doodle Tune   2493
I Love to Linger with You   4851
I Love to Look Again   3921
I Love to Love a Mason   1550
I Love to Quarrel with You   1964, 4440
I Love to Raise the Dickens   4849, 4832
I Love to Ramble   1815
I Love to Read the Papers in the Morning   4649
I Love to Say Hello to the Girls
   (I Hate to Say Goodbye)   3538
I Love to Sing-A   4399
I Love to Sing the Words (While We're Dancing)   3036
I Love to Sit and Look at You   1318
I Love to Two Step with My Man   2990
I Love What I'm Doing   1475, 2590
I Love What the Girls Have   2801
I Love Ya, Love Ya, Love Ya   1120
I Love You   1321, 1484, 1847, 2059, 2481, 2516
I Love You (As Much As I Am Able)   2523
I Love You   2847, 3021, 3117, 3544, 4075, 4143,
   4403, 4719, 4764
I Love You All the Time   3856, 3902
I Love You and I Adore You   4669
I Love You and I Like You (Love You but I Like You
   Even More) 1855
I Love You As You Are   1707
I Love You Babe, and You Love Me   1925
I Love You Because You Are You   830
I Love You Best of All   2126
I Love You but Good   4602
I Love You but I Like You Even More
   (I Love You and I Like You) 1657
I Love You Dear   195
I Love You Dear and Only You   586
I Love You, Dear, I Love but You   2884
I Love You, 'Deed I Do'   3998
I Love You Dolly   2213
I Love You Etcetera   80
I Love You, Evaline   1213
I Love You for That   3210
I Love You, Honey   4198
I Love You, I Adore You   1711, 3978

I Love You, I Love You, I Love You   943
I Love You in Velvet   3052
I Love You Just the Same   335
I Love You Lady Deed I Do   3384
I Love You Ma Cherie   3387
I Love You Madly   4091
I Love You, Mommy   2307
I Love You, Mon Cherie   1188
I Love You More   2877
I Love You More Than Yesterday   3556
I Love You More Today Than Yesterday   2382
I Love You, My Darling   1487, 2747
I Love You No More Than...   4073
I Love You Oh! Oh! Oh!   3134
I Love You Only   4713
I Love You So   758, 2384, 2637, 2673
I Love You So (The Merry Widow Waltz)   2836, 2838
I Love You So   4765, 3547
I Love You So I Keep Dreaming   1999
I Love You So Much Jesus   4788
I Love You Sweetheart   1248
I Love You This Morning   999
I Love You to Distraction   3765
I Love You Today   4090
I Love You Whoever You Are   51
I Love You, You Love Me   4792
I Love Your Brains   3666
I Love Your Laughing Face   3725
I Love Your Sunny Teeth   363
I Love Your Vibrato   4289
I Love Ze American Ragtime   457
I Love Ze Parisienne   3265
I Loved   2188
I Loved a Man   4541
I Loved Her Best of All   2135
I Loved Her Too   4169
I Loved Him But He Didn't Love Me   1018
I Loved Him but He Didn't Love Me   4581
I Loved You Once in Silence   623
I Loved You Wednesday   2060
I Loves You Porgy   3018
I Loves You, Porgy   3541
I-M-4-U   4264
I Made a Deal   3844
I Made a Fist!   2961
I Made It   1073
I Made the Day Shorter   3227
I Made Them Jump   4115
I Made Them Step   3310
I Make Hay While the Moon Shines   3569
I Make Up for That in Other Ways   1979
I Makes Mine Myself   545
I Married an Angel   2061
I Married Seven Brothers   3888
I Marry You   4609
I May   3084
I May Be Crazy but I Ain't No Fool   4697
I May Be Crazy But I Ain't No Fool   2111
I May Be Gone for a Long, Long Time   1919
I May Be Small, But I Have Big Ideas   1065

I May Be Wrong (But I Think You're Wonderful)   3005
I May Be Wrong   4170
I May Believe Half-That's All   1530
I May Blush from Anger   4173
I May Look Strong but I'm Far from Healthy   2619
I May Never Fall in Love with You   4516
I May Never Get Well Again   1035
I May Say Maybe   664
I May Stay Away a Little Longer   4742
I May Want to Remember Today   2617
I Mean No-One-Else-but-You   2567
I Mean to Be a Good Girl Now   3049
I Mean to Be Married as Soon as I Can   3051
I Mean to Introduce It into China   3828
I Mean to Marry a Man   1526
I Mean to Say   4179
I Mean What I Say   4741
I Meant You No Harm   1103
I Met a Girl   363
I Met a Girl on Monday   1176
I Met a Man   3564
I Met My Love   2114, 3280, 4262
I Met My Love in a Restaurant   2383, 2952
I Might   133
I Might Be Your Once-in-a-While   136
I Might Be Your Once-In-a-While   4250
I Might Fall Back on You   3949
I Might Grow Fond of You   4212
I Might Say 'Yes' To You   3658
I, Miles Gloriosus   1422
I Miss a Place Called Home   1536
I Miss Him (Her)   3576
I Miss Him   1045
I Miss My Home in Harlem   4076
I Miss My Mammy's Kissin'   542
I Miss My Swiss, My Swiss Miss Misses Me   710
I Miss the Mississippi Miss   676
I Miss You   808, 809
I Miss You Old Friend   1103
I Miss You So   2532
I Murdered Them in Chicago   1577
I Must Away   45
I Must Be Dreaming   80
I Must Be Going   2467
I Must Be Home By Twelve O'Clock   3953
I Must Be in Love   1059
I Must Be Loved By Someone
   (and That Someone Must Be You)   4079
I Must Be Missing Something   1884
I Must Be One of Those Roses   3584
I Must Devise a Plan   1249
I Must Find Out About Love   2439
I Must Go Now   729
I Must Go to Moscow   4817
I Must Have a Dinner Coat   4677
I Must Have a Lot of Little Girls
   All Around Me   954
I Must Have Been Mistaken   1515
I Must Have Her   652
I Must Have That Man   441

If I Knew   3847, 4516
If I Knew Now   3551
If I Knew Then   2196
If I Knock the 'L' Out of Kelly
   (It Would Still Be Kelly to Me)   4148
If I Lost You   1610
If I Love Again   124, 1932
If I Loved You   660
If I Marry the King of France   2671
If I May   4173
If I Met a Nice Little Girl   1868
If I Never See You Again   1819
If I Never Waltz Again   2755
If I Only a Laugh Could Hear   3592
If I Only Had   2245
If I Only Had a Mustache Like the Kaiser   3673
If I Only Had a Theatre on Broadway   734
If I Only Knew the Way   2938
If I Only Said My Name Was Flannigan   3855
If I Only Were a Boy   1321
If I Possessed Aladdin's Lamp   2880
If I Ruled the World   3482
If I Saw Much of You   3319
If I Should Dream of You
   (When Out on the Desert)   1111
If I Should Lose My Only Girl   2665
If I Should Say Goodbye   3129
If I Sing   784
If I Thought I Could Live
   without You I'd Die   1492
If I Told You   4694
If I Was a Boy   2994
If I Was a Different Man   3888
If I Was a Dove   4004
If I Was a Man   716
If I Wasn't Around   154
If I Were   4309
If I Were a Bandit   4550
If I Were a Bell   1706, 3444
If I Were a Bright Little Star   3805
If I Were a Football Man   3547
If I Were a Girl Instead   3976
If I Were a Hypnotist   586
If I Were a King   4724
If I Were a Man   4560, 3339
If I Were a Man Like That   250
If I Were a Rich Man   1265
If I Were a Sailor   671
If I Were a Woman   1265
If I Were an Actress   4681
If I Were Anybody Else but Me   3081
If I Were 80 Years Younger   3880
If I Were King   265, 466, 978, 2102, 4539, 4709
If I Were King of Babylon   675
If I Were of the Hoi Polloi   2950
If I Were on the Stage (Kiss Me Again)
   2915, 4390, 4818
If I Were Only a Man   68, 1578
If I Were Only Mr. Morgan   3809
If I Were Only Someone   73

If I Were Only Taller   2518
If I Were Really a King   1720
If I Were Sure of You   888
If I Were the Bride of a Soldier   3229
If I Were the Governor of Guam   2160
If I Were the Man   519
If I Were the Man in the Moon   2155
If I Were You   64, 288, 376, 2389, 3924, 3928, 4200
If I Were You, Love   4023
If I Weren't King   759
If I Weren't Me   2898
If I'd Known You   2563
If I'm Going to Die I'm Goin' to
   Have Some Fun   1968
If-If-If-If   1727
If in Spite of Our Attempts   3865
If It Ain't Fun   2568
If It Comes from Dixieland   3158
If It Feels Good, Let It Ride   964
If It Hadn't Been for Me   148
If It Hadn't Been for You   1456
If It Isn't Everything   1076
If It Makes You Happy
   (The Syndicate Song)   410
If It Pleases You   1917
If It Should Be You   1911
If It Was Up to Me   2650
If It Wasn't for My Wife and Family   1308
If It Wasn't for People   410
If It Wasn't for the Fairies   1051
If It Wasn't for the Irish and the Jews   1927
If It Wasn't for the Wife   1270
If It Wasn't for You   273, 2235
If It Wasn't for Your Father   197
If It Were Easy to Do   137
If It Were Mine   717
If It Were True   379
If It's a Dream   3899
If It's Any News to You   3965
If It's Good Enough for Gentlemen   277
If It's Good Enough for Lady Astor   2626
If It's Good Enough for Rector It's
   Good Enough for Me   1123
If It's Love   622, 766, 4362
If Jesus Don't Love You   4270
If Jesus Walked   1282
If Jesus Walked the Earth Today   4168
If Jesus Was a Cowboy   914
If Life Were All Peaches and Cream   2259
If Love Ever Comes My Way   2483
If Love in a Cottage Be All that They Tell   3588
If Love Is Love   2861
If Love Is Madness   2596
If Love Is There   2698
If Love Never Comes   2542
If Love Should Come to Me   2827
If Love Were All   429, 146, 3196, 3235
If Love's Content   4404
If Love's Like a Lark   2339
If Ma Says No   3856, 3857

I'm Gay   2451
I'm Getting Myself Ready for You   3131, 4517
I'm Getting Quite American You Know   3745
I'm Getting Such a Big Girl Now   4327
I'm Getting Tired So I Can Sleep   4340
I'm Glad He's Irish   4626
I'm Glad I Met You   2446
I'm Glad I Waited   4023
I'm Glad I'm from Dixie   1823
I'm Glad I'm Here   2049
I'm Glad I'm Leaving   1791
I'm Glad I'm not a Man   2554
I'm Glad I'm Not Methusalem   3073
I'm Glad I'm Not Young Anymore   1511
I'm Glad I'm Single   1456, 3134
I'm Glad I'm Spanish   487
I'm Glad My Wife's in Europe   965
I'm Glad that I Came Home   326
I'm Glad to Be Back Again   3973
I'm Glad to Get Back to New York   4094
I'm Glad to See You've Got What You Want   681
I'm Glad You Didn't Know Me   2152
I'm Goin' Places   664
I'm Goin' South   487
I'm Goin' to Live Anyhow, 'Til I Die   4390
I'm Goin' to Sea   4452
I'm Going Arla   2307
I'm Going Away   1066
I'm Going Back   363, 1487
I'm Going Back to Dixie   3917, 4655
I'm Going Back to Mobile, Alabam'   4776
I'm Going Crazy with Strauss   3698
I'm Going Down the River and Have Myself
    a Darn Good Cry   4611
I'm Going Home   2472, 801, 3742
I'm Going Home to Dixie Land   3805
I'm Going in for Love   4777
I'm Going Moroccan for Jimmy   849
I'm Going on a Long Vacation   179
I'm Going Through a Change   4645
I'm Going to Be a Boy   2097
I'm Going to Be a Marquis   2803
I'm Going to Be Lonesome   2270
I'm Going to Be Married Today   1360
I'm Going to Dance at Your Wedding   381
I'm Going to Exit   2984
I'm Going to Find a Girl Someday   2430
I'm Going to Follow the Boys   632, 4037
I'm Going to Leave You   1908
I'm Going to Let the Whole World Know
    I Love You   2781
I'm Going to Live Forever   430
I'm Going to Marry a Nobleman   4759
I'm Going to Meet Minnie Tonight   4209
I'm Going to Settle Down   3866
I'm Going to Steal the Moon   1967
I'm Gonna   2043
I'm Gonna Be a Movie Star   1940
I'm Gonna Be a Pop   596
I'm Gonna Be a Star   4684

I'm Gonna Be John Henry   3983
I'm Gonna Change the World   3695
I'm Gonna Cry   1813
I'm Gonna Do It If I Like It   4843, 4853
I'm Gonna Do My Things   344
I'm Gonna Fall in Love   1293
I'm Gonna Get Him   2983
I'm Gonna Get Lit Up   4027
I'm Gonna Git Down on My Knees   2225
I'm Gonna Hang My Hat   1336
I'm Gonna Have a Baby   1676
I'm Gonna Hit the Numbers Today   3528
I'm Gonna Make a Fool Out of April   3, 3381
I'm Gonna Make It   2284, 3697
I'm Gonna Miss Him So   4117
I'm Gonna Miss Those Tennessee Nights   474
I'm Gonna Move   615
I'm Gonna Pin My Medal on the Girl I
    Left Behind   4812
I'm Gonna See My Mother   1485
I'm Gonna Sit Right Down and Write Myself
    a Letter   39
I'm Gonna Take Her Home to Momma   2949
I'm Gonna Walk Right Up to Her   2304
I'm Gonna Wash That Man Right
    Outa My Hair   4096
I'm Good for Nothing but Love   4823
I'm Great   4543
I'm Grover   1448
I'm Growing   2518
I'm Growing Fond of You   2025
I'm Growing Wary   4761
I'm Gwine Lie Down   1958
I'm Gwine to Marry Angeline   2675
I'm Gwine to Talk   2557
I'm Hans Christian Andersen   1741
I'm Happy   348
I'm Happy (Tira e Campa)   3798
I'm Happy Darling, Dancing with You   3726
I'm Harold, I'm Harold   2594
I'm Harvey Ellesworth Cheyne   647
I'm Head and Heels in Love   773
I'm Head and Heels in Love with You   2952, 3065
I'm Headed for Big Things   3837
I'm Here   2200, 1200, 2388
I'm Here Again   75
I'm Here and You're Here   2243
I'm Here Little Girls, I'm Here   1784
I'm Here with Bells On   1999
I'm Hi, I'm Lo   735
I'm His Loving Wife   2869
I'm Home   57, 2033, 260, 647
I'm Honest   691
I'm Hook   3453
I'm Hung   1717
I'm Hungry for Beautiful Girls   2706
I'm in a Highly Emotional State   3869
I'm in a Position to Know   506
I'm in a Tree   3564
I'm in Favor of Friendship   861

I'm to Be a Blushing Bride   1247
I'm to Be Married Today   3245
I'm to Blame   3988
I'm Toein' the Line   4281
I'm Too Young to Die   2163
I'm Trying   1961
I'm Twirling   2046
I'm Unlucky   3537
I'm Unlucky at Gambling   1272
I'm Up Early   1386
I'm Up in the Air Over You   1687
I'm Using My Bible for a Roadmap   4030
I'm Very Fond of Jokes   295
I'm Very Glad to Meet You   2623
I'm Very You, You're Very Me   4068, 4301
I'm Waiting for a Wonderful Girl   3254
I'm Waiting for You   3184
I'm Walkin' the Chalk Line   444
I'm Way Ahead   3869, 4238
I'm Way Ahead of the Game   1373, 4267
Im Weissen Rossl   4667
I'm Well Known   3313
I'm Wide Awake When I Dream   3995
I'm Wild About Wild Men   2706
I'm Wise   3205
I'm Wishing   4035
I'm with You   1227, 4823
I'm Wonderful   4765
I'm Wonderin' Who   587
I'm Wondering   1911
I'm Worried to Death About That   2990
I'm Worse than Anybody   1237
I'm You   2105
I'm Your Girl   2797
I'm Your Guy   1955
I'm Your Man   2615
I'm Your Space Angel   2172
I'm Your Valentine   2887
I'm Yours   3980, 4777
Image of His Papa, The   1306
Image of Me, The   652
Image of Our Retina Has Gone, The   2243
Image of You, The   3726
Imaginary Coney Island Ballet (dance)   3278
Imaginary Invalid, The   3956
Imaginary Man, The   4801
Imagination   1859, 3578, 3729
Imaginative Opera   2686
Imagine   247, 3739, 3936
Imagine Me   1786
Imagine Me without My You (and You
   without Your Me)   4424
Imagine My Finding You Here   3986
Imagine My Frustration   4091
Imagine My Surprise   3448
Imagine That   3931
Imagine You're Alive   2001
Imagining You   424
Imitation   1520
Imitation of Life   1496

Imitation Rag, The   4805
Immigration Rose   4197
Immolation   4139
Immortal Gods   3909
Immortality   973
Imp of Montmartre, The   1199
Impatient Years, The   3324, 3324
Impeachment Waltz, The   3684
Imperial Conference, An   3536
Imperial Guards' March   4201
Imperial March   2655
Importance of Being Earnest, The   1194
Importance of Being Ernest, The   3195, 3236
Important Man, The   2986
Important Things   1809
Imported Yes We Are   3437
Impossibility   4470
Impossible   4067, 759, 1422
Impossible Dream (The Quest), The   2727
Impossible Eyes   3944
Impossible Men   1855
Impossible She, The   4542
Impresario   3682
Impression of the Derby, An   4361
Impressions   3397
Imprisoned   4704
Impromptu Review   3158
Improvements   1095
Improvisation, The   2069
In   661
In a Backyard in Belmont   4147
In a Beauty Shop   335
In a Brownstone Mansion   298
In a Bungalo   1731
In a Bungalow   2950, 2635
In a Bungalow for Two   2448
In a Cape Cod Garden   637
In a Cozy Kitchenette Apartment   3006
In a Curio Shop   487
In a Doll's House   545
In a Dory   2902
In a Far Off Corner of My Mind   31
In a Gadda de Vida (inst.)   3261
In a Garden   1498
In a Garden One Day   1518
In a General Sort of Way   3805
In a Gondola with You   3388
In a Great Big Way   711, 1827
In a Hammock (Hammock Love Song)
   (Swinging the Summer Night Long)   336
In a Hundred Years   1770
In a Hundred Years from Now   2115
In a Hurry   2292
In a Jewelled Grotto   2902
In a Kingdom of Our Own   3791
In a Little Canoe   2490
In a Little Canoe with You   1998
In a Little French Cafe   710
In a Little Stucco in the Sticks   4025
In a Little Swiss Chalet   4667

In His Eyes   2198
In His Own Good Time   1764
In Hitchy's Bouquet   1923
In Holy Divorce   83
In Honeysuckle Time   1198
In Honeysuckle Time (When Emmaline
    Said She'd Be Mine)   3963
In Housekeeping I Am a Martinet   2623
In Italy   3405
In Izzenschnooken on the Lovely
    Essenzook Zee   2522
In Jail   48, 1966, 2293, 3773
In January You May Love Mary   736
In Khorossan   4815
In-Laws   400
In Little Old New York   3404
In Louisiana   4197
In Love   466
In Love Again   152
In Love Am I   2944
In Love in Vain   2372
In Love with a Fool   2075
In Love with All the Girls   1833
In Love with Love   2121, 4150
In Love with Romance   3064
In Love with You   2947
In Lovers Lane   982
In Loving Memory   1373
In Loving Time   1
In Madrid   2777
In Marsovia   2836
In May and June   3466
In Merry, Merry May   307
In Michigan   4723
In Missouria   567
In Monkey Land   3480
In Monte Carlo Town   2869
In Montezuma   356
In Monticello's Kingdom Grand   3591
In My Birch Bark Canoe
    (With Emmy Lou)   3755
In My Birch Bark Canoe   4206
In My Canoe   830
In My Castle in Sorrento   2380
In My Country Oriental   3573
In My Curriculum   2803
In My Day   2200, 1664, 3295
In My Dixie Dreamland Jazz   2009
In My Dream of You   929
In My Dreams   971
In My Dreams of You   1555
In My Garden   2813
In My Garden of Eden for Two   60
In My Hat   1354
In My Heart   3042
In My Heart of Hearts I've
    Always Known   3777
In My Heart, on My Mind   184
In My Home Town   2363
In My Life   2442

In My Little Blue Bonnet   69
In My Little Red Book   4104
In My Little Runabout   1525
In My Love Boat   3849
In My Merry Oldsmobile   4390
In My Museum Now   613
In My Official Capacity   694
In My Old Home   295
In My Own Irresistible Way   1097
In My Own Lifetime   3780
In My Own Little Corner   759
In My Riksha of Bamboo   1243
In My Silent Universe   2220
In My Submarine   2951
In My Tippy Canoe   4815
In New York the Only Sin Is
    Being Timid   3305
In 1999   4757
In No Man's Land (inst.)   2228
In No Time at All   4060
In Nomine Dei   3876
In Nomine Patris   2775
In Old Granada   487
In Old Havana Town   203
In Old Japan   1154, 1417
In Old Kentucky   391, 2034
In Old Mexico   4412
In Old New York   1403, 4754
In Old Versailles   4812
In Old Villanelle   49
In Old Wall Street   4589
In One Cell   253
In Orcania   3626
In Other Words, Seventeen   4557
In Our Chateau in Brooklyn   1048
In Our Childhood's Bright Endeavor   1755
In Our Cozy Little Cottage of Tomorrow   180
In Our Hands   4020
In Our Hide-Away   2983
In Our Little Castle in the Air   2174
In Our Little Home Sweet Home   2794
In Our Little Paradise   3866
In Our Little Salon   3988
In Our Little School   4201
In Our Mountain Bower   4283
In Our Orange Grove   196
In Our Own Orange Grove   1777
In Our Parlor on the Third Floor Back   376
In Our Set   2951
In Our Teeny Little Weeny Little Nest
    for Two   3954
In Our Teeny Little Weeny Nest   2439
In Panama   1524, 3748
In Paradise   1570
In Paree   3877, 4382
In Paris   1246, 1602
In Paris and in Love   1548
In Peacock Alley   1404
In Philadelphia   1900, 2966
In Pity Spare Them   2724

J

K

L

Little More Mascara, A   2360
Little Mother   1992
Little Music, A   3643
Little Music in Your Life, A   1435
Little Musketeer   948, 4670
Little Naked Boy, The   1284
Little Nell   3842
Little Nemo in Slumberland   2534
Little Nest for Two, A   3043
Little Neutral Dog   1852
Little Night Music, A   2535
Little of Everything, A   4801
Little Ol' Boy   4117
Little Old America for Me   3710
Little Old Cabin Door   183
Little Old Dream Waltz   2261
Little Old Dreamy New York
    (Any Side Street of New York)   3150
Little Old Gehenna   1745
Little Old Lady   3955
Little Old Lady in Black   2565
Little Old Main Street for Mine   2559
Little Old New Hampshire   1965
Little Old New York   1390, 1979, 2545, 3626,
    4312, 4817
Little Old New York Is Good Enough for Me   2041
Little One   2649, 4226
Little One's ABC, The   3815
Little Orchestra, The   4363
Little Orphan Annie   150, 154, 155
Little Part of Me That's Mine, The   2617
Little Partner of Mine   4079
Little Peach   2594
Little People   339
Little Persian Rug, The   3446
Little Pie, The   476
Little Pip, A   3923
Little Pitchers Have Big Ears   1886
Little Place of Your Own, A   3042
Little Plastic Man   4398
Little Plate of Soup, A   2216
Little Pony of Mine   381
Little Poppa Satan   612
Little Poster Maid, The   104
Little Pot of Tea, A   2723, 4017
Little Priest, A   4233
Little Prince   2539
Little Princess   4275
Little Privacy, A   1448
Little Quonset in Neponset, A   1892
Little Rag Doll   2731
Little Raindrop   69
Little Rascals, The   2542, 2541
Little Red Book   4853
Little Red Book and a Five Cent Bag, A   2903
Little Red Hat   3294
Little Red Lacquer Cage, The   3007
(Everybody Calls Me)
    Little Red Riding Hood   4150
Little Red Riding Hood   974, 3593

Little Red Roof Tops   1880
Little Red School   1532
Little Revolutionary, The   3441
Little Rhumba Numba, A   2453
Little Rock   2590
Little Rock Roll   3841
Little Rover (Don't Forget to
    Come Back Home)   2706
Little Sambo   4416
Little Sammy   2235
Little Scandal Dolls   1486
Little Ships   732
Little Shop of Horrors   2544
Little Side Street in Paree, A   4104
Little Sir Hugh   4579
Little Sister Kissie   357
Little Skipper from Heaven Above, A   3674
Little Slut of Six, A   702
Little Smile, a Little Sigh, A   1965
Little Smith Minor   3092
Little Snowflake   3855
Little Song in My Heart, The   4249
Little Soubrette, The   586
Little Souvenir, A   1447, 2446
Little Sparrow   2584
Little Sparrows   280
Little Starch Left, A   3059
Little Stick of Candy and a
    Jumping Jack, A   2771
Little Street in Heaven They
    Call Broadway, A   737
Little Streptococcus, The   2187
Little Sunbeam   1726
Little Swing for Swinging, A   4169
Little Tango Maid, A   351
Little Taste of Heaven, A   273
Little Tea, A   4136
Little Tear   249
Little Theatre   2376
Little Thing, The   3819
(Just) a Little Thing Called Rhythm   792
Little Thing Like a Kiss, A   1066
Little Things   2232
Little Things About You   621
Little Things Meant So Much to Me   454
Little Things We Like, The   2447
Little Things We Used to Do, The   3598
Little Things You Do Together, The   832, 3967
Little Tin Box   1280
Little Tin God, The   2591, 4504
Little Tin Pail   2062
Little Tin Soldier   2723
Little Tin Soldier and the Little Rag Doll, The   3500
Little Tittle Tattle Tale   3855
Little Town Gal   879
Little Travelin' Music Please, A   3299
Little Traveling Music, A   673
Little Travelling Music, A   1619
Little Trouble, A   1991
Little Tune Go Away   3740

Log Cabin Days 3808
Log of the Ship, The 4378
Loggers' Song, The 823
Logic! 73
Logic 3921, 4547
Loidy Wot Is Studyin' for the Stoige, A 2041
Loie and Chlodo 3547
Loki and Baldur 1068
Lola 106
Lola (White Witch of Jamaica) 817
Lola 845, 2567
Lola Cornero from the Trocadero 2567
Lola Delaney 3925
Lola in Bavaria 2565
Lola Montez 1363
Lola Waltz (Close in Your Arms) 2564
Lola's Ceremony 3792
Lola's Saucepan 4467
Lola's Theme (Lola Pretty Lola) 3925
Lola-Marie (She Isn't Lola) 3925
Lolaland 2565
Lolita 434, 1567, 2135, 2568, 2568
Lolita, My Love 3953
Lollipop 4264, 4388
Lollipop Lane 3186
Lollipops and Roses 4193
Lolly-Papa 1587
Lollypop Polka, The 2089
Lombardy Hunting Breakfast 621
Lomir Loybn (Let Us Praise) 4342
Lomir Trachtn Nor Fin Haynt 2356
Lona, Partner, Lona 1530
London Bank Clerk Blues, The 605
London Cries 324
London, Dear Old London 611
London Empire Girls 4818
London Is a Little Bit of All Right 1564
London Johnnies 4010
London Pastoral 3235
London Pride 3235
London Talking Blues 4579
London Taps (The Broken Doll) 1588
London Town 3295, 3310
London Underworld (Baker Street Mystery)
    (dance) 270
Lone Star Girl, The 4808
Lonegan 2710
(Manhattan's the) Loneliest Isle 4583
Loneliest Man in Town 167
Loneliness 2551
Loneliness of Evening 759, 4096
Loneliness Song, The 4523
Loneliness Trio 4684
Lonely 1564, 1593
Lonely at the Bottom 3077
Lonely at the Top 2852
Lonely Boy 3541
Lonely Boy Blues 2200
Lonely Canary 705
Lonely Children 3876

Lonely Clearing 4764
Lonely Feet 4361
Lonely for My New York 943
Lonely Girl, A 4276
Lonely Girl 4584
Lonely Goatherd, The 4095
Lonely Heart 207, 789, 4159
Lonely Heartache 1370
Lonely Hearts 463
Lonely House 369, 4169
Lonely in a Crowd 1644
Lonely in Paris 3383
Lonely in Town 3177
Lonely Is the Life 280
Lonely Lady 1737, 2074
Lonely Lamp, The 2162
Lonely Little Extras 2808, 4025
Lonely Little Melody 4818
Lonely M.P. 3460
Lonely Man 1370
Lonely Man, Lonely Woman 430
Lonely Me 599, 3278
Lonely Men (inst.) 3347
Lonely Nest, The 3312
Lonely Nights 2201
Lonely Ones 3863
Lonely Princess, The
    (The Sleeping Princess) 1852
Lonely Road, The 3978
Lonely Room 3263
Lonely Soldier 1610
Lonely Sparrows of Essex, The 962
Lonely Star 3674
Lonely Straggler 2115
Lonely Stranger (Passing Through)
    (Sabishii Tabibito) 1616
Lonely Stranger 4099
Lonely Times 337
Lonely Town 3278
Lonely Voice 2661
Lonely Woman 1857
Lonely Women 2511
Loner, The 916
Lonesome 1131, 2914, 4648, 3856, 3857
Lonesome Alimony Blues 4840
Lonesome Boy 2605
Lonesome Cinderella 4817
Lonesome Cowboy, The 1528
Lonesome Dove, The 1085
Lonesome for You 2155
Lonesome in New York 2052
Lonesome Is As Lonesome Does 4829
Lonesome Little Maid 2671
Lonesome Longing Blues 4182
Lonesome Man 3965
Lonesome of the Road 3806
Lonesome Polecat 3888
Lonesome Romeos 1297
Lonesome Valley 61, 4740
Lonesome Walls 2712

Love Me Best of All   1911
Love Me By Parcel Post   4477, 4530
Love Me Dear   1523
Love Me, Don't You?   4692
Love Me Enough to Remember   4762
Love Me for What I Am   2132
Love Me Forever   2423
Love Me in the Candlelight   684
Love Me in the Morning Early   3045
Love Me in the Spring   627
Love Me in the Winter   2779
Love Me Just a Little Bit   1588
Love Me Just Because   4185
Love Me Just Like Romeo Loved His Juliet   2119
Love Me Lightly   337
Love Me Like a Real, Real Man   2394
Love Me Little, Love Me Long   2906, 129
Love Me Lize   3154
Love Me, Love Me Not   2276
Love Me, Love Me, Dorothy Lamour,
   La Sarong   3651
Love Me, Love Me, Won't You?   1975
Love Me, Love My Children   2618
Love Me, Love My Dog   2915, 4314
Love Me More-Love Me Less   439
Love Me or Leave Me   3020, 3557, 3980, 4683
Love Me or Leave Me Alone   806
Love Me Some Mo   293
Love Me Sweetheart in Sweet Song   2906
Love Me, Sweetheart Mine   4360
Love Me Tender   3739
Love Me to a Viennese Melody   3525
Love Me to That Beautiful Tune   3996
Love Me Tomorrow (But Leave Me
   Alone To-Day)   612
Love Me Tonight   3508, 4539
Love Me Too   2661
Love Me While the Loving Is Good   3396
Love Me While the Snowflakes Fall   545
Love Me While You're Gone   2645
Love Me/Don't   4031
Love Means   564
Love Mill, The   2619
Love Monopoly, The   2907
Love Moon   736
Love Must Be Delicate   3197
Love Ne'er Came Night   3570
Love Needs No Single Words   780
Love Nest   4462
Love Nest, The   2767
Love Nests in France   4853
Love Never Changes   2587
Love Never Dies   2495
Love Never Goes Away   3888
Love Never Went to College   4420
Love, Nuts and Noodles
   (Bring 'Em Back Alive)   289
Love-O-Love   1343
Love-O-Meter   140
Love of a Day   1266

Love of a Maid of a Man, The   4663
Love of a Wife, The   2363
Love of Long Ago   3405, 3491, 3951
Love of Mine   3791, 4719
Love of My Life, The   530
Love of My Life   1846
Love of the Lorelei, The   1016
Love of Your Life, The   3835
Love on a Summer's Day   1570
Love on Our Side   4016
Love on the American Plan   1228
Love on the Street   4388
Love or Money   2542, 4450
Love Pirates   3137
Love Please Stay   2177
Love Potion, The   4328
Love Potion #9   4031
Love Power   1072, 2658
Love, Put on Your Bridal Veil   2428
Love Put on Your Orange Blossoms   1776
Love Racketeer   1836
Love Ranger Rides Again, The   1940
Love Remains the Same   620, 2875
Love Revolution   2058
Love Rules the World   670
Love Runs Deeper Than Pride   3724
Love Scene   169
Love Set, The   1533
Love Ship, The   4194
Love Sick   3042
Love Sign   3575
Love Sneaks Up on You   3899
Love Sometimes Has to Wait   4141
Love Song   369, 392, 400, 550, 681, 1108
Love Song, A   1648
Love Song   2615
Love Song, The   2686
Love Song   2804, 3013, 3506, 4002, 4369
Love Song (Sara Lee)   4480
Love Song   4586, 4371
Love Song of a Thief, The   4539
Love Song of Renaldo   3789
Love Song to Order, A   2519
Love Songs   16
Love Songs Are Made in the Night   4826
Love Spans the World   2571, 3500
Love Spats   902
Love Spell, The   3613
Love Stolen   3733
Love Story   2787, 4635
Love Swept Like a Storm   596
Love Tales, The   1017
Love Test, The   3778
Love That Came Before, The   674
Love That Cannot Be   4539
Love That Game   4099
Love That Is True   1392
Love That Lasts, A   3117
Love that Man   454
Love That's Gone   1266

M

Maid of My Dreams   2485, 2159
Maid of Pekin, The   737
Maid of Santiago   2287
Maid of Sevilla   4757
Maid of the Milky Way   201
Maid of Timbuctoo   4681
Maid to Order Maid   2489
Maid with a Wink in Her Eye, The   2131
Maid's Sextette   3146
Maiden and the Jay, The   3805
Maiden and the Kissing Bug, The   3786
Maiden Fair   735, 2944, 3326
Maiden Let Me In   1096
Maiden of Caprice, The   3613
Maiden of the Wild and Woolly West   4650
Maiden Often Seen, A   1948
Maiden with the Dreamy Eyes   2506
Maiden with the Dreamy Eyes, The   4390
Maiden's Heart, A   3229
Maiden's Prayer (Anorexia)   871
Maiden's Thought, A   3736
Maiden's Voyage   2876
Maidens Aquatic   4704
Maidens Typical of France   629
Maids of Forest   1518
Maids of Killarney   3746
Mail Man, The   2261
Mail Order Annie   2470
Mailman Bring Me No More Blues   580
Mailman Must Be Mad at Me, The   1587
Mailu   4823
Main Event, The   1450
Main Floor, The   1412
Main Street Ballet (inst.)   3683
Maine   3187
Maine Will Remember the Maine   911
Maisie   2844
Maison des Lunes   330
Maja de Goya   2407
Maja Moderna   2407
Majestic Sails at Midnight   207
Major Domo, The   2594
Major General Pumpernickel   2335
Major Margery   2848
Major's Song   470
Majority, The   3661
Make a Date with a Great
   Psychoanalyst   2453
Make a Friend   4435
Make a Fuss of Me   767
Make a Joyful Noise   4398
Make a Little Sunshine   135
Make a Lot of Noise   1968
Make a Miracle   3444
Make a Quiet Day   3691
Make a Wish   2705
Make Allowance for Love   2506
Make an Honest Woman of Me   4469
Make Believe   25, 2204, 3643, 2722, 2230, 3949
Make Believe World   2580

Make Believe You're Happy   2628
Make Believe You're Mine   3084
Make-Believing   2091
Make 'Em Laugh   3992, 1944, 544
Make Every Day a Holiday   1690
Make Friends (inst.)   2772
Make Hay, Hay, Hay   208
Make Hay Little Girl   1626
Make Hey! Hey! Hey!
   (While the Moon Shines)   3291
Make Him Guess   3590
Make Him Think I'm Still Pretty   1508
Make It   2630
Make It Another   871
Make It Another Old Fashioned   1018
Make It Another Old-Fashioned, Please   3359
Make It Happen Now   1497
Make It Hot   203
Make It New   942
Make It Nice   143
Make It Night   2012
Make It Snappy   3828
Make It Up   1537
Make Love in the Morning   1096
Make Love to Me   3562
Make Me   4828
Make Me a Star   2171
Make Me Over   4611
Make Mine Latin   867
Make Mine the Same   1884
Make My Bed Down in Dixieland   4673
Make Our Garden Grow   630
Make Someone Happy   1061
Make the Best of It   4491
Make the Heart Be Stone   3180
Make the Man Love Me   4446
Make the Most of Carnival!   902
Make the Most of Spring   615
Make the Most of Your Music   1329
Make the People Cry   1791
Make Them Hate   1282, 4168
Make Them Pay   2012
Make Up   3873, 1240
Make Up My Heart   4138
Make Up Your Mind   787, 905, 2140, 2610, 4748
Make Way   170, 612, 44, 1985, 3595
Make Way for My Lady   2731
Make Way for the Law   2452
Make Way for Their Excellencies   3339
Make Way for Tomorrow   2204, 1298, 4316
Make with the Feet   297
Make Your Mate Miserable   345
Make Your Own Kind of Music   338
Make Your Own Sunshine   1054
Make Yourself at Home   2708
Make Yourselves at Home   1424
Makes No Difference Now   2897
Makin' Believe   2051
Makin' Guacamole   992
Makin' It (Seeing a Chance and Taking It)   486

May and January   2344
May and September   3770
May Day March (inst.)   2534
May I?   2518
May I Dance with You?   2968
May I Have My Gloves?   1493
May I Present   4363
May I Return to the Beginning   2242
May I Say I Love You?   4087
May I Suggest Romance   1670
May in Manhattan   3810
May It Bring Him Pleasure   2553
May Moon   3163
May 7th, 1901   2703
May Tells All   4557
May the Best Man Win   3142, 3091
May We Come A'Wooing   2880
May We Entertain You   1709
May Wine Polka   3703
May Your Heart Stay Young (L'Chayim)   4863
Maybe   150, 250, 3243, 1701
Maybe Baby   580
Maybe for Instance   2285
Maybe He's Some Kinda of Crazy   2961
Maybe I Could If I Tried   1911
Maybe I Know   2427, 2427
Maybe I Ought to Stay   2925
Maybe I Should Change My Ways   341
Maybe I Will   4226, 4276
Maybe I'll Baby You   1215, 4271
Maybe I'm Better Off   4518
Maybe I'm Doing It Wrong   2852, 2787
Maybe Is a Woman's Word   4366
May-be It's a Bear   3855
Maybe It's Because   95
Maybe It's Love   720
Maybe It's Me   1267, 3436
Maybe It's Not Too Late   484
Maybe It's Time for Me   3931
Maybe Land   965
Maybe Leola Call Today   1496
Maybe, Maybe, Maybe   2064
Maybe, Maybe Not   36
Maybe Means Yes   1827
Maybe Monday I'll Conquer   3165
Maybe My Baby Loves Me   1649
Maybe Now a Little House   2992
Maybe So   138
Maybe the World Has a Chance   2998
Maybe There's a Place   1581
Maybe There's an Angle   4232
Maybe There's More   327
Maybe They're Magic   2143
Maybe This Is Love   4345
Maybe This Time   131, 4480
Maybe Tomorrow   1216
Maybe Yes or No   728
Maybe You Can See Yourself   729
Maybe You Think I Did   4704
Maybe You'll Look Good to Me   2546

Maybe You're My Man   1754
Maybells   2135
Maydee (Pretty Little South Sea
   Island Lady)   1295
Mayer's Fine Coins   3780
Mayfair   4583, 4793
Mayfair Affair   2295
Mayflower I Love You   2789
Mayflower Will Sail, The   912
Mayn Alte Heym   4342
Mayn Rochele   3781
Mayn Ruchele   2356
Mayn Yidishe Meydele   1609
Mayonnaise Marines, The   1220
Mayor   2790
Mayor Doesn't Care, The   1732
Mayor of Harlem, The
   (Meet the Mayor)   888
Mayor of Kankakee, The
   (Entrance of Todd)   1910
Mayor of Tango Town!   1971
Mayor of Tokio, The   2793
Mayor's Chair, The   935
Mayor's Invocation   1092
Maypole Dance (inst.)   4524
Maze, The   699
Mazel Tov   2866
Mazeltov   1660
Mazie   556, 1515
Mazourka   4620
Mazuma (The Plaint of the
   Prima Donna)   4070
Mazuma   3122, 3778
Mazurka (inst.)   630
Mazurka   147, 2623, 3536, 3994
Mazurka, The (inst.)   4798
Mazzini and Mankind   4244
McCoy   1041
McDougal's Cave   4409
McInerney's Farm   4428
McNabb (Who Drives the Cab)   3749
McNally's Row of Flats   1776
McNamara's Band   3479
McSorley's Trip to Paris   1264
Me   508, 1796, 330, 3084, 4004, 4678
Me, a Big Heap Indian   2522
Me Alone   2719
Me an' My Bundle   2894
Me and Bobby McGee   338
Me and Columbus   1658
Me and de Minstrel Band   2111
Me and Delilah   1496
Me and Dorothea   4028
Me and Him   3844
Me and Jesus   2173
Me and Juliet   2797
Me and Lee   3035
Me and Love   868
Me and Marie   2252
Me and My Baby   723, 131, 4480

Mexican Blues   1019
Mexican Hat Dance   1832
Mexican Magic   3444
Mexican Rose   1867
Mexico (To Hell with Mexico)   1447
Mexico   2035, 2387, 2642, 3056, 3332, 1185, 3796
Mexico City   3875, 4796
Mexico Querido   2573
Mexiconga, The   1494
Meyer Chickerman   4619
Mfoka Ngema   4438
Mgeniso WaMgodo WaShambini   4579
MGM   2969
Mi Amigo   4796
Mi Chiquita   2277
Mi-Komash Melon (What Is the Meaning?)   1279
Mi! Mi!   3822
Mi Mi, Tu Li   3573
Mia Cara   728
Mia Luna   3079
(Lead 'Em On) Miami   391
Miami   2987, 4243
Miami Beach   4619
Michael   3448
Michael McGinnity   3220
Michele   3960
Michelemma   2464
Michigan Bound   4252
Michigan Water   2200
Mickey   4204
Mickey O'Toole   2902
Micritza Violetta Doanne   4684
Micro-Chip Jingle   2861
Microbes   1226
Microbes in a Kiss, The   3820
Microfilm   3873
Micromaniac   4826
Midas Touch, The   363
Middle Age Blues   534
Middle Aged   2007
Middle C   4004
Middle-Class-Liberal-Blues   2616
Middle Class Revolution   3876
Middle Class, The   2188
Middle Ground, The   595
Middle of the Night, The   4363
Middle of the Sea   4243
Middle Years, The   4789
Middy, The   2761
Midnight at the Onyx   4137
Midnight Ballet (dance)   3703
Midnight Bells   4077
Midnight Blue   4825
Midnight Blues   3649
Midnight Cabaret   1626, 2645
Midnight Cabaret, The   2854
Midnight Cabaret   14
Midnight Daddy   3533
Midnight Deadline Blastoff   2728
Midnight Flirtation   3011

Midnight Frolic Glide   4809
Midnight Frolic Rag, The   4810
Midnight Girl, The   2854
Midnight Girl, The (One Midnight
   Supper at Home)   3538
Midnight Girl at the Midnight Cabaret,
   The   3397
Midnight-Hot Blood   3741
Midnight Lullabye   2953
Midnight Masquerade   822
Midnight Mass   3741
Midnight Matinee   3885
Midnight Mooch   2800
Midnight Riding   699
Midnight Rounders   2870
Midnight Serenade, The   3999
Midnight Show Trio, A   1652
Midnight Swim Ballet, The   98
Midnight Waltz   2985
Midnight Waltz, The   1347
Midnight Zeppo, The   4836
Midsummer Fox   2240
Midsummer Maiden   3973
Midsummer Night   249, 2064, 3326
Midsummer Night's Dream, A   249,
   1780, 4256
Midsummer Night's Dream   4748
Midsummer Waltz   3087
Midsummer's Eve   4075
Midtown   2300
Midwestern Summer   4659
Mighty Big Dream   3947
Mighty Dollar Greets You, The   3771
Mighty Fortress, A   1592
Mighty Like a Rosenbloom   2870
Mighty Race, A   1092
Mighty Svengali Legree, The   4507
Mighty Whitey   578
Mignonette   250, 3675
Migration   143
Migration Song   2573
Mikado, The   2861
Mikado Anthem   2861
Mike   1267, 3180
Milady   4139, 3384
Milady's Perfume   685
Milady's Toilette Set   1334
Mile After Mile   3647
Mileage Millionaire, The   1402
Miles Gloriosus   1422
Miliaria Rubra   4252
Milindy   981
Milindy Blues   981
Militant Suffragette, The   96
Military, The   4761
Military Ball, The (inst.)   250
Military Band, The   3073
Military Charleston   2843
Military Charley   1374
Military Dance (inst.)   3193

Military Dancing Drill   4178, 4179
Military Decoration Dance   3962
Military Fox Trot Tune, A   2546
Military Glide, The   2939, 4521
Military Irresistibles, The   639
Military Life   620
Military Maid, The   185
Military Maid   3799
Military Maids   2366, 2986
Military Man, The   830, 1188, 1650, 2323
Military Man   4480
Military March   822
Military Marches   1404
Military Mary Ann   1523
Military Model   604
Military Review   1602
Military Song   3887
Military Stamp   1852
Military Touch, The   3092
Military Wedding March   639
Military Wedding of the Nations   1404
Military Willie   1910
Milk and Crackers   203
Milk and Honey   2208, 2864
Milk Bottle Parade, The   2090
Milk, Milk, Milk   2453
Milkmaid   4485
Milkmaid Known As Joan   2026
Milkmaids' Chorus   2880, 4753
Milkmaids from Broadway   3069
Milkmaid's Song   3736
Milky Way, The   584
Millefleurs   3064
Millennium, The   2135, 3092
Miller's Daughter, The   4354
Miller's Son, The   4067, 2536
Millinery Mannequin, The   1922
Millinery Mary   694
Million, A   2716
Million, The   4806
Million Dollar Ball, The   1738
Million Dollar Ball   2834
Million Dollar Pier   1886
Million Dollar Smile   404
Million Dollars, A   3314
Million Eyes, A   3149
(There's a) Million Girls Around Me   685
Million Goes to Million   1354
Million Good Reasons, A   2238
Million Miles from You, A   589
Million Songs   2195
Million Windows and I, A   3941
Millionaire, The   1313
Millionaire's Daughters   1532
Millionaires Don't Whistle   1415
Millions   1073
Millions of Tunes   684
Millwork   4744
Milo (You're Just My Style-O)   246
Milo   984

Milonga   1046
Milord Sir Smith   2131
Milwaukee   1237
Mimette   1768
Mimette Doll, The   3867
Mimi   293, 2336, 2336
Mimi Jazz   2336
Mina   3337
Mind of My Own   1734
Mind Over Matter   3835
Mind Reader, The   2232
Mind the Paint   2871
Mind Where You Are Going   1726
Mind Your Business   2017
Mind Your Own Business   2601
Mind Your Own Heart   2319
Mind Your P's and Q's   1800
Mindin' the Baby   2101
Mine   4399, 2444, 2617, 3279
Mine Celebration (dance)   4862
Mine for Aye   3680
Mine Forever More   1522
Mine 'til Monday   4446
Mine Was a Marriage of
   Convenience   4812
Mineola   4060
Ming Poo   2216
Ming Ting Hai   4110
Miniature Girl, The   3098
Miniatures   764
Mink, Mink, Mink   2804, 3941, 4047
Minnesota   157, 3268
Minnesota Strip   3806
Minnie   1145
Minnie, Ha Ha   4644
Minnie the Moocher   896, 883
Minnie the Moocher's Wedding Day   876, 1813
Minnie's Boys   2874
Minnowillen   4218
Minnows and the Sharks, The   1049
Minny Belle's Song   2228
Minor Prophets, The   1750
Minorities Is No Damn Good   3530
Minsky   3314
Minsky's Metropolitan Grand Opera   1874
Minstrel Band, The   3701
Minstrel Days   799, 3737, 4054
Minstrel Man   444
Minstrel Parade, The   1731
Minstrel Parade   1926
Minstrel Parade, The   1927
Minstrel Parade   2615
Minstrel Parade, The   4603
Minstrel Serenade   3754
Minstrel Show   1604, 3953
Minstrel Show, The   1926
Minstrel Song   1914
Minstrel Tune   1531
Minstrel's Advice   1262
Minstrel's Prayer, The   452

Miss Yankee Doodle   1417
'Miss You' Kiss, A   3899
Missa Solemnis   3066
Missed America   3112
Missed the Toilet Last Night   2945
Missing Person   535
Mission, The   3239
Mission Bells   1777, 2576
Mission Control   2728
Missionary Maids   3031
Missis and the Guv'nor   30
Mississippi   3024, 3530, 4836
Mississippi Cabaret   332
Mississippi Cradle   3677
Mississippi Day   3953
Mississippi Honeymoon   2151
Mississippi Joys   4763
Mississippi Miss   61
Mississippi Moan   2845
Mississippi Mud   1425
Mississippi Steamboat   363
Missouri   567
Missouri Meadowlark   4409
Missouri Mule   2958
Missouri Polka   18
Missus Aouda   189
Mistah Jim   2942
Mistaken in Love   4235
Mistakes Are Apt to Happen   734
Mistakes Will Happen   531
Mister and Mrs. Fitch   4132
Mister Bonaparte   2951
Mister Boy   1319
Mister Brown, Miss Dupree   4432
Mister Cellophane   723
Mister Destiny   2949
Mister Drummer Man   3652
Mister Earth and His Comet Love (The
   Comet and the Earth)   4804
Mister Harvey Pruitt   664
Mister Izzy Always Busy Rosenstein   2119
Mister Jones   2563
Mister Love   3537
Mister Madero and Friend   4609
Mister Man   1476
Mister Mississippi   1799
Mister Moon Man, Turn Off Your Light   2528
Mister Off-Broadway   1023, 3542
Mister Othello   632
Mister Producer   1770
Mister Rag and I   1065
Mister Snow   660
Mister Soldier Man   106
Mister Spaceman   3695
Mister Sun   1866
Mister Washington!   183
Misterioso   97
Mistletoe Bough, The   2697
Mistreated Gypsy   2379
Mistress Mullen and Master Alden   912

Mistress of the Inn   4244, 2910
Misty Mornin' (inst.)   895
Misty Mountain   2168
Misunderstood   490
Mit Zaltz un Fefer   3781
Mittel-Europa   2447, 4331
Mitzi   1763
Mix, The   1053
Mix!   4625
Mix and Mingle   4718
Mix-up Rag, The   2891
Mixed Doubles   2913
Mixed Marriages   2913
Mixed-Up Media   164
Mixing of the Ads, The   639
Mlle. DeLeon   2858
Mlle. Loose Heels   1687
Mlle. Ma Mere   495
Mme. Mangdolin   2770
Mngani Wamina   4438
Mo Ticht-tit!   3673
Mo'lasses   1587
Moan You Moaners   2796
Moana, I Love You So   141
Moana Loa (dance)   3827
Moanin' and Groanin'   1983
Moanin' in the Mornin'   1973
Moanin' Low   2545
Mob Song, The   330
Mobile Squad   2364
Mocambo Mambo   1048
Mock Battle   2556
Mock Turtle Lament   54
Mockin' Bird Hill   4264
Mocking Bird   1474
Mocking Bird, The   3056
Mockowitz, Gogeloch, Babblekroit
   and Svonk (The Lawyer Song)   2827
Mod Man of Manhattan   4611
Model, The   2665
Model Girl, A   2919
Model Happy Fair, A   3591
Model Hasn't Changed, The   2850
Model Maid, A   2454
Model Married Pair   2923
Model of Decorum & Tranquility, A   721
Model of Fashion Am I, A   2834
Model Toddle   200
Model's Complaint   1459
Models, The   200
Models   1493
Moderation   3913
Modern Banditti, The   4616
Modern Bride   765
Modern Butterfly   3057
Modern Century Girls, The   509
Modern Crusaders   3404
Modern Diplomat, A   4227
Modern Duel, The   75
Modern Eve, The   2457

Moon Song   3245
Moon, the Coon, and the Octoroon, The   1188
Moon Was Good Enough for Dad and Mother,
   The   1582
Moon Will Help You Out Maybe, The   250
Moon Will Ride Away, The   277
Moon, Wind, and Sun   1440
Moonbeams   632, 2387
Moonbeams, The   2934
Moonbeams   3024, 3207, 3675
Mooney Time   1520, 187
Moonfall   3070
Moonglade   823
Moonglow   445
Mooning   1664
Moonland   4256
Moonlight   539, 1075, 1758, 2062, 3021,
   4033, 4359
Moonlight and Lace   3078
Moonlight and Love and All   4189
Moonlight and Violins   1352
Moonlight and You   2193
Moonlight Ballet   3719
Moonlight Ballet (inst.)   4817
Moonlight Buggy Ride, A   2481
Moonlight Fancies (inst.)   2500
Moonlight Gavotte   3729
Moonlight in Versailles   3649
Moonlight Kisses   1689
Moonlight Legion   1518
Moonlight Mama   2814
Moonlight on Notre Dame   3386
Moonlight on the Ganges   4153
Moonlight on the Waters   765
Moonlight Passing Through a Window   3760
Moonlight Serenade   4137
Moonlight Soliloquy   3536
Moonlight Waltz   1033
Moonlight, You and I   2717
Moon's Shining Cool, The   4620
Moonshine   2996
Moonshine (inst.)   3312
Moonshine   3719, 4764
Moonshine Lullaby   153
Moonshine of Kentucky (Give Me the
   Moonshine of My Old Kentucky Home)   1270
Moonsong   949, 949
Moonstruck   3020, 3322
Moontime   2174
Moosh, Moosh   3651
Mophams, The   3569
Mopperty Mo   129
Moral Rearmament   3110
Morality   3215, 4303
Morality's a Matter of Geography   405
Morals of a Sailor-Man, The   1962
More and More   596, 3901, 4328
More and More/Less and Less   1660
More Better Go Easy   1809
More Fish   90

More I Cannot Wish You   1706, 3444
More I See of Men the More I Love My Dog, The   628
More I See of Other Girls, The (Elephant Song)   2258
More I See of Others the Better I Love You, The   3304
More I See People, The   593
More Incredible Happenings   4581
More Love than Your Love   603
More Mittel-Europa   4331
More of Everything   3482
More of Me to Love   2049
More of the Same   287, 2018
More Precious Far   2874
More Racquetball   1234
More than Earth   2153
More Than Enough   1132
More Than Ever   1440, 4023
More Than Ever Now   4028
More Than Friends   2219
More Than Just a Pretty Flower   2539
More Than Love   1282, 3858
More Than Music   2319
More Than One Man in Her Life   2674
More Than One More Day   298
More Than One Way   4013
More Than Ordinary Glorious Vocabulary, A   71
More Than These   3989
More Than You Deserve   2953
More Than You Know   1667, 3249, 1232
More the Merrier, The (The More We Are
   the Merrier We Be)   1742
More We Dance, The   1461
More You Get, The   1064
More You See of It, The   4048
Morgan Le Fay   834
Morgana's Entrance   1159
Morgiana's Dagger Dance (inst.)   50
Moriva   2147
Morlock Exterior   1159
Mormon Life, A   1011
Morning   1680, 3277, 4169, 4537
Morning After, The   2056, 2070, 2918
Morning Anthem   369, 4369
Morning Breaking   1213
Morning Cy   2642
Morning Exercises   1556
Morning Glory   582, 1962
Morning Glory Mountain   474
Morning Glow   3506
Morning in Madrid   1112
Morning in Manhattan   1539
Morning in the Gypsy Camp   4046
Morning Is Midnight   2467, 3924
Morning Lark   668
Morning Light   2426
Morning Mist Spread O'er the Mead, The   762
Morning, Morning, Morning   4147
Morning Music of Montmartre, The   3234
Morning of the Dragon, The   2905
Morning Prayer   3543
Morning Song (inst.)   3487

Morning Song   1744
Morning Star   916, 2535
Morning Sun   2958, 3876
Morning Will Break   496
Morning Will Come   487
Morning You Were Born, The   4798
Mornings at Seven   1761
Morning's at Seven   1894
Morocco Dance of Marriage (inst.)   1027
Morphine Tango   2333
Morris Brodkin Loves Me   2422
Morris Dance and Sword Dance   3702
Morris Kaplan of Hampstead Gardens   299
Mort's Telegram   3461
Mos Scoscious   1890
Moscow Belles   3431
Moscow Blues, The   722
Moses Andrew Jackson, Goodbye   2996
Moses Supposes   3992
Moses' Song   1769
Moshi, Moshi   595
Mosquito   1840
Mosquito and the Midge, The   4754
Mosquito Ballet (inst.)   3312
Mosquito Queen   1155
Mosquito Song, The (inst.)   2900
Mosquito Song   4802
Most Beautiful Girl in the World, The   2258
Most Beautiful Girls in the World, The   1137
Most Confused Prince   3654
Most Disagreeable Man (1), A   2064
Most Disagreeable Man (2), A   2064
Most Every Town Has a Broadway   4215
Most Expensive Statue in the World, The   2894
Most Folks Are Dopes   2306
Most Gentlemen Don't Like Love   1018, 2432, 4799
Most Girls   4588
Most Happy Fella, The   2961
Most Important Job, The   1880
Most Important Thing, The   3195
Most Likely   3601
Most Omniscient Maid   118
Most People   2580
Most Popular and Most Likely to Succeed   4454
Most Unpopular Potentate, A   2974
Most Unusual Pair   1695
Most Unusual Weather (For This
   Time of Year)   1577
Most Wonderful Day of the Year, The   3794
Mostes' to Say the Least, The   4543
Motele   4342
Moth and the Bumble Bee, The   47
Moth and the Flame   1286
Moth and the Flame, The   2648
Moth and the Flame   2870
Moth and the Moon, The   2885
Moth For My Flame, The   1485
Moth for My Flame, The   1643
Moth Song, The   3934
Mother's March   169

Mother   249, 1732, 1077
Mother (1)   1852
Mother (2)   1852
Mother   2056, 3056
Mother Africa's Day   2245
Mother and Father   2317
Mother Angel Darling   2148
Mother Come and Fight with Me   483
Mother Darling   2284
Mother Dear   815
Mother Did   47
Mother, Dixie and You   1824
Mother, Dixie, the Flag and You   4033
Mother Doesn't Know   4806
Mother Earth   415, 2962
Mother Eve   1484
Mother Goose   2315, 2964, 4250
Mother Goose and Baby Dolls   671
Mother Goose's School   4382
Mother Grows Younger   1800
Mother Hare's Seance   1600
Mother in Ireland   452
Mother-in-Law   4619, 1890
Mother Isn't Getting Any Younger   1286, 3082
Mother, Look, I'm an Acrobat   2909
Mother Love   1581
Mother Machree   310, 2154
Mother, May I Be Forgiven?   2046
Mother, Me and the Flag   3133
Mother Mississippi   2400
Mother Nature   4623
Mother Needs a Boyfriend   2568
Mother of Exiles   3667
Mother of Mankind, The   4523
Mother of Spring   259
Mother of the Bridegroom   3696
Mother of the Regiment, The   2340
Mother Peep   2146
Mother Phi   870
Mother Pin a Rose on Me   830
Mother Shouldn't Have Daughters   4013
Mother Son   2866
Mother Told Me So   1322
Mother Who's Really a Mother, A   2201
Mother Will Be Pleased   1544
Motherhood   1828
Motherload   3901
Motherlove   2992
Motherly Love   3215
Mothers   3454
Mothers and Sons   841
Mother's Blues   3564
Mother's Complaint   4341
Mother's Day   90, 2616, 4034, 4153
Mother's Getting Nervous   2615
Mother's Heart, A   615
Mother's Kisses, A   2965
Mother's Lament   3487, 3339
Mother's Love, A   3602
Mothers O' Men   3086

My Carolina Hide-Away   667
My Castilian Girl   2706
My Castle in Spain   250, 605
My Castle in the Air   2907
My Castle on the Nile   2111, 4088
My Catamaran   2160
My Cavalier   1689
My Cave Man   4437
My Caveman-My Venus   3915
My Celia   3976
My Charcoal Charmer   1925
My Cherokee Rose   2180
My Chicago   3262
My Chiffon Girl   728
My Child   460
My Children Searching   3814
My Chin Toy   733
My China Rose   3775
My Choc'late Soldier Sammy Boy   1823
My Cigarette   3045, 3748
My Cigarette Maid   2576
My Cinderella   2408
My Cinnamon Tree   767
My City   2790, 2294, 3544, 3869
My Clementine   1374
My Cleopatra   978
My Cleopatra Girl   4657
My Coal Black Mammy   3405
My Coca-Cola Belle   1963
My Coloring Book   131
My Combination Girl   3422
My Conviction   1717
My Cornfield Queen   3877
My Cosey Corner Girl   3857
My Cosy Corner Girl   3856
My Cottage in Sunshine Lane   2378
My Country 'Tis of Thee   3830
My Cousin Beauregard   2072
My Cousin Carus   4803
My Cousin Caruso   2892
My Cousin Christian   3780
My Cousin in Milwaukee   3379
My Cozy Little Corner in the Ritz   1921
My Crazy Sister Rose   2246
My Creole Girl   2557
My Crinoline   906
My Crinoline Girl   1174
My Crooning Melody   2912
My Cubist Girl   60
My Cup Runneth Over   2050, 3542
My Cupie Doll   1173
My Curley Headed Baby   1823
My Daddy   154
My Daddy Always Taught Me to Share   1699
My Daddy Is a Dandy   2994
My Daddy Was Right   2067
My Dahomian Queen   2111
My Dainty Dresden Shepherdess   1118
My Dainty Mermaid   4382
My Darlin' Aida   3035

My Darling   1137
My Darling I Love You March   1116
My Darling Wife   4492
My Darling, My Darling   3444, 4652
My Daughter   3702
My Daughter Fanny the Star   1420
My Daughter Is Wed to a Friend of Mine   2730
My Daughter the Countess   1249
My Daughter, My Angel   3490
My Day   3966
My Day Has Come   109, 3319
My Dear Benvenuto   1284
My Dear Old Chum   4085
My Dear Old Daddie   4716
My Dear Old New Jersey Home   2209
My Dear Public   3036
My Dear Young Ladies   762
My Dearest Dear   972
My Dearest Pal Is Albert, Prince of Wales   3998
My Death   2188
My DeeTees   3916
My Defenses Are Down   153
My Desert Flower   758
My Diabalo Beau   4094
My Diamond Girls   3405
My Diamond Horseshoe of Girls   3007
My Dickey Say Nodings at All   284
My Dixie   4104
My Dixie Girl   2314
My Doctor   3184
My Dog   108
My Dolls   4425
My Dream Book of Memories   4706
My Dream for Tomorrow   3330
My Dream Girl (I Loved You Long Ago)   1096
My Dream Is Through   1786
My Dream of Dreams   3562, 4620
My Dream of Love   1067
My Dream of Love Is You   2363, 2605
My Dream of You   1473
My Dream, Dream Man   2254
My Dreamland   2127
My Dreams   3670, 4357
My Drug Store   3918
My Dusky Baby   632
My Dusky Dago Boy   2485
My Dutch Lady   3406
My Dynamo   1657
My Easy Ridin' Man   1014
My Edelweiss   96
My Egyptian Queen   2695
My Emmaleen   3437
My Empty Arms   709
My Eternal Devotion   1194
My Evaline   2324
My Eyes Speak Love   2880
My Faces of 1958   4153
My Fair Lady (Lady Fair)   4300
"My Fair Lady medley"   3018
My Fair Unknown   2885

My Fairy Prince   1849
My Fairy Tale   2846
My Faithful Stradivari   3839
My Family Tree   1564
My Fannie   2363
My Fatal Charm   1918
My Fate Is in Your Hands   2561
My Father Said   3699
My Father Took Me Dancing   4540
My Father Was a Peculiar Man   4380
My Father's a Homo   2746
My Father's Island   3628
My Father's Wooden Leg   2025
My Favorite Person   787
My Favorite Things   4095
My Favorite Year   3039, 3039
My Feet Are Firmly Planted on
   the Ground   3365
My Feet Took T'Walkin'   1372
My Filipino Belle   2711
My Filipino Pet   2465
My Fire-Fly Lady   2858
My First Girl   2941
My First Long Pants   1703
My First Love   2551, 3810
My First Love Letter   2594
My First Love Song   3731
My First Love, My Last Love   3170
My First Mistake   2283
My First Moment   4689
My First Promise   372
My First Real Christmas   2689
My First Smoke   2481
My First Solo Flight   414
My First True Love   2632
My First Woman   2333
My Flag   1826
My Flower of the South   331
My Fortune Is My Face   1227
My Fox Trot Wedding Day   1901
My Friend   164, 460, 2452
My Friend from India   2291
My Friend Huckleberry Finn   4409
My Friend John   4327
My Friend Lebel   1455
My Friend Yama   371
My Friend, My Father   4690
My Friends   4233
My Friends, the Celebrities   3124
My Frivolity Girl   1404
My Funny Valentine   247, 3175
My Furry Castle in the Air   758
My G.I. Joey   597, 3217
My Gaby Doll   3406
My Gal   1885
My Gal and I   1880
My Gal Is Mine Once More   2137
My Gal! My Gal!   2465
My Galilee   181
My Gang   3723

My Garden   681
My Garden of Perfumes   3443
My Garden That Blooms for You   115
My Gasoline Automobile   2695
My Gasoline Maid   2724
My Generation   3739
My Gentle Young Johnny   4312
My Georgia Gal   2287
My Georgiana   2122
My Geranium   1093
My Gink   797
My Girl   1610, 3949
My Girl and I   4214
My Girl Back Home   4096
My Girl Is Just Enough Woman for Me   3687
My Girl of Chance   2723
My Girl of Dreams   2262
My Girl Takes Another Beau   2334
My Girl's Gone Screwy Over Huey   4374
My God When I Think   2153
My God, Why Hast Thou Forsaken Me?   2236
My Golden Dream Ship   378
My Golden Girl   3043
My Gondolier Queen Good Night   141
My Goo-Goo Queen   4681
My Good Friends of Erin's Isle   1162
My Grammar Book   4687
My Grandfather's Girl   543
My Greatest Day!   4625
My Guiding Star   363
My Gypsy Maid   1908
My Gypsy Sweetheart   3265
My Hairt Is in the Highlands   3732
My Handsome   3813
My Handy Man Ain't Handy Any More   1198
My Handy Man Ain't Handy No More   443
My Hannah   3780
My Hannah Lady   4130
My Harlem Wench   1272
My Havana Maid   4687
My Hawaii   4337
My Haytian Queen   2119
My Head Is Like a Whirring Top   1518
My Head, My Head   758
My Headache   1772
My Heart   3592
My Heart Beats to You   2614
My Heart Begins to Thump! Thump!   3861
My Heart Belongs to Daddy   2432
My Heart Belongs to the U.S.A.   4776
My Heart Belongs to You   1281
My Heart Controls My Head   4365
My Heart Decided   3074
My Heart Flies Blind   2087
My Heart Flies Homing   178
My Heart for You Pines Away   4751
My Heart Goes Out to Dixieland   1332
My Heart Has Come a Tumbling Down   4798
My Heart I Cannot Give You   3996
My Heart Is a Drum   1415

My Kind of Batid   2027
My Kind of Guy   4041
My Kind of Love   3954
My Kind of Night   2615
My Kind of People   3683
My Kind of Person   1846
My Kind of Town   4743
My Kinda Love   124
My King Can Do No Wrong   1849, 3595
My King of Love   2802
My Kingdom for a Queen Like You   2020
My Knees Are Weak   2290
My Lady   1483, 3622, 4766
My Lady 'Tis for Thee   252
My Lady Bug   4130
My Lady Busy   3882
My Lady Fair   335, 356, 4048
My Lady Friends   3184
My Lady Frog   2111
My Lady Hottentot   3298
My Lady Molly Waltz   3049
My Lady Moon   307
My Lady Nicotine   3579
My Lady of Japan   4662
My Lady of the Cameo   684, 2856
My Lady of the Fan   3662
My Lady of the Lake   4720
My Lady of the Lamp   3404
My Lady of the Manor   252
My Lady of the Nile (1)   4810
My Lady of the Nile (2)   4810
My Lady of the Telephone   965
My Lady Silhouette   4104
My Lady Wine   2869
My Lady's Clothes   3222
My Lady's Coach Has Been Attacked   4404
My Lady's Dress   1625, 2939, 3177
My Lady's Fan   539
My Lady's Hand   3314
My Lady's Maid   3052
My Ladye Faire   1570
My Land   310, 1075, 1378, 2662, 3167
My Land of Nod   4185
My Land, My Flag   1901
My Landlady   4806
My Last Affair   3103
My Last Farewell   20
My Last Love   4640
My Last Strike   3485
My Late, Late Lady   4828
My Life Is Love   2698
My Life's a Musical Comedy   2069
My Lips Are Sealed   2196
My Lips, My Love, My Soul   670
My Little Address Book   1482
My Little Baby   357
My Little Belgian Maid   4836, 4839
My Little Blarney Stone   2869
My Little Book of Poetry   3880, 3006
My Little Buckaroo   714

My Little Bugaboo   1919
My Little Buttercup   675
My Little Canoe   3218, 3856, 3857
My Little Castagnette   1027
My Little China Doll   734
My Little Dancing Heart   3345
My Little Deutcher Girl   1783
My Little Dog Has Ego   961
(You're Mighty Lucky) My Little Ducky   4241
My Little Dudeen   3910
My Little Friend   3053
My Little Full-Blown Rose   4194
My Little Girl   2661, 4487
My Little Girl Is a Shy Little Girl   356
My Little Girlie   906, 4354
My Little Grass Shack   4264
My Little Gypsy Maid   4691
My Little Highland Highball   2489
My Little Hong Kong Baby   737
My Little Irish Girl   2763
My Little Irish Rose   1051, 1162
My Little Jail-Bird   4208
My Little Javanese   1685
My Little Kodak Girl   1562
My Little Lady Bug   4806
My Little Lamb   2745
My Little Laplander   246, 248
My Little Lassoo   361
My Little Lost Girl   751
My Little Lotus Flower   3406
My Little Love Bird   1537
My Little Loving Baby Mine   4776
My Little Madamoiselle   115
My Little Mimi San   331
My Little Pansy   405
My Little Pet Chicken   4808
My Little Piano Man   4170
My Little Prayer   12
My Little Queen Bee   2884
My Little Red Book   261
My Little Redskin   953
My Little Room   593
My Little Sea Shell   2446
My Little Sea Shell Told Me So   2564
My Little Submarine   4809
My Little Sunbeam Sue   3753
My Little Sunday Girl   1213
My Little Tailor Maid   2826
My Little Yellow Dress   3845
My Log Fire Girl   1154
My Log-Cabin Home   3443
My Lola   2565
My Lolo Maid   1316
My Long Ago Girl   1690
My Long Lost Love Lenore   20
My Lord and Ladies   1284
My Lord and Master   2312
My Lotus Flower   2254
My Lotus Lady   4324
My Lou   4553

My Louisa   3131, 3214, 4581
My Loulou   2252
My Love   630, 669
My Love Awaits   4724
My Love Belongs to You   4591
My Love Bouquet   969
My Love Carries On   4204
My Love Does No Know   4073
My Love for Her   3760
My Love Goes Down   2055
My Love Has Gone Away   4409
My Love I Dare Not Tell Thee   2803
My Love Is a Blower   118
My Love Is a Flower   2623
My Love Is a Married Man   999
My Love Is a Secret   1911
My Love Is a Wanderer   2227
My Love Is Fair   1213
My Love Is for Thee   3652
My Love Is Greater than the World   3545
My Love Is Like a Butterfly   945
My Love Is Like the River   4207
My Love Is on the Way   1600
My Love Is Young   3103, 3104
My Love Is Yours   4186
My Love of Long Ago   4407
My Love Song   1418
My Love Will Come By   279
My Love Works in a Greenhouse   123
My Love, My Love   3285, 2661
My Loved One   3152
My Lovely Lad   3939
My Lover   3249, 4267
My Lover Is a Scoundrel   3526
My Luck Has Changed   98
My Luck Is Changing   4286
My Lucky Fly   42
My Lucky Lover   4015
My Lucky Star   734, 1339, 3291, 3924
My Lulu   2546
My Lungs   3651
My Madagascar Maid   2770
My Magic Lamp   2327, 4383
My Magnolia   3054
My Maid from Hindoostan   2959
My Maid in the Moon   671
My Mammy   986, 3985
My Man   3905, 1425, 3619, 4815, 4831, 4847, 4852
My Man Blues   3297
My Man Godfrey   3055
My Man Is Good for Nothing but Love   1980
My Man Is on the Make   1800
My Man Must Dance   570
My Man's Gone Now   3541
My Manicure Maids   4375
My Maori Maid   2062
My Marionette   1685
My Master Plan   279
My Matilda   3820
My Matrimonial Bon Bon   1417

My Meadow   708
My Melody   4816
My Melody Man   3523
My Memories Started with You   70
My Merry Go Round   4248
My Merry Oldsmobile   3350
My Mexican Rose   434
My Middy   1726
My Midnight Frolic Girl   4814
My Midnight Girl   4833
My Midnight Sweetheart   3057
My Might-Have-Been   1270
My Military Man   876
My Mimosa   3063
My Mind on Freedom   2203
My Mind Says No   1745
My Mind's on You   2680
My Mindanao Chocolate Soldier   3177
My Miracle Man   1826
My Miss Mary   4312
My Mississippi Miss   4092
My Mississippi Missus Misses Me   2879
My Missus   376
My Mobile Gal   350
My Mocking Bird   3350
My Model Girl   473
My Moment Supreme   890
My Money   81
My Moonlight Lou   1798
My Morning Glory   1798
My Most Embarrasing Moment   3916
My Most Important Moments Go By   2418
My Most Intimate Friend   2252
My Mother Bore Me   3465
My Mother Said   2134
My Mother Told Me Not to Trust a Soldier   3650
My Mother Was a Fortune Teller   2677
My Mother Would Love You   3359
My Mother's Wedding Day   530
My Motter   178
My Moustache Is Twitchin'   4102
My Movie Is Going to Trial   1700
My Movie of the Week   1700
My Moving Picture Man   75
My Musical Comedy Maiden   804
My Name   3271
My Name Is Can   2728
My Name Is Leda Pearl   1139
My Name Is Man   1072
My Name Is Rumpelstiltskin   3844
My Name Is Samuel Cooper   2615
My Name's Abundance   3418
My Name's Marie, Who Wants to Be
    My Peanut Vendor   1492
My New Friends   2677
My New Kentucky Home   1014
My New York   666, 4821
My New York Slip   4467
My Nice Ways   521, 4196
My Night in Venice   2587

My Ninette   4148
My Nose   948, 4073, 4670
My Number Is Eleven   1958
My Object All Sublime   1987
My Official Wife   3685
My Old Banjo   2302
My Old Boy   2631
My Old Brass Band   3423
My Old Brass Bed   4516
My Old Fashioned Garden Flower   531
My Old Flame   4799
My Old Friend   2643
My Old Friends   3059
My Old Girl Is My New Girl Now   4821
My Old Hoss   622
My Old Kentucky Home   2415, 2787, 4149, 1995
My Old Kentucky Rock and Roll Home   3261
My Old Lady   3855
My Old Love Is My New Love   1483
My Old Man   2557, 2979
My Old New Jersey Home   1551, 3770
My Old Times   4055
My Old Town   188, 1316
My Old Virginia Home (On the River Nile)   612
My One and Only   3060
My One and Only (What Am I Gonna Do)   1419
My One and Only Shlemiel   3937
My One Girl   3849
My Only One   545, 1759
My Only Romance   1112
My Operatic Samson   4521
My Orchard of Girls   4813
My Oriental Symphony   69
My Otaheitee Lady   100
My Own   1912, 2833
My Own Best Friend   723, 4480
My Own Best Love   1259
My Own California   2385
My Own Dear Irish Queen   4313
My Own Dear Sue   516
My Own Individual Star   51
My Own Light Infantry
   (Nursery Fanfare)   3740
My Own Little Girl   906
My Own Morning   1729
My Own Paree   2745
My Own Place   3925
My Own Space   16
My Own United States   4251, 4646
My Own Vienna   2914
My Own Way   1104
My Own Willow Tree   718
My Own, or True Love at Last   1256
My Pa   4764
My Palace of Dreams   3011
My Papa from Panama   4180
My Paradise   2292
My Paramount-Publix-Roxy Rose   2475
My Part of Somewhere   3485
My Partners   906

My Party   3422
My Passion Flower   3063
My Peaches and Cream   3679
My Personal Rainbow   4374
My Picture in the Papers   1600
My Picture of You   1646
My Pin-Up Girl   4009, 4141
My Pipe of Peace   3238
My Pirate Lady   3737
My Place or Yours?   2069
My Pleasure   4337
My Plume (My Life)   4073
My Polly Is a Peach   509
My Pony Boy   2892
My Pony Pony Girl   1798
My Poor Wee Lassie-A Scottish Lament   1256
My Post Card Girl   2892
My Potential   3577
My Pousse-Cafe   97
My Prayers Have Come True   4764
My Pretty Little Family   2497
My Prince   73
My Prince (What a Prince!)   4420
My Prince Came Riding   2755
My Prince o' Dreams   2232
My Prince of Wales   2193
My Princess Zulu Lulu   4014
My Private Life   695
My Propensities Are All the Other Way   2131
My Queen of Ping Pong   3820
My Radiant Fire Fly   3805
My Radium Girl   4809
My Rag Doll Girl   250
My Raggedy Doll   1524
My Raggydore   1963
My Rainbow   1779, 3406
My Rainbow Beau   965
My Rainbow Girl   3333, 3652
My Rambler Rose   4816
My Real Ideal   203
My Red Riding Hood   974
My Red-Letter Day   4825
My Regular Man   691
My Religion   2908
My Reuben Girlie   3395
My Reunion Prayer   3181
My Rhapsody   3703
My Riviera Rose   200
My Road   317
My Roly Poly Oly Tulip Maid   2485
My Romance   2031, 2258
My Room and Me   4540
My Rosary of Melodies   4831, 4852
My Rose   274, 2135, 3998
My Rose of Memory   3973
My Rose of Spain   3149
My Rosemarie   1113
My Royal Majesty   4798
My Rules   1633
My Runaway Girl   3400

N

Naval Manoeuvres   2761
Navy, The   1071
Navy Foxtrot Man, The   3923
Nay, Nay Pauline   968
Nazi Party Pooper   2949
Ndinosara Nani?
    (With Whom Shall I Stay?)   4579
Nduna Ngibolekinduku
    (The Zulu Warriors)   4438
Neapoli   1374
Neapolitan Jazz   3403
Neapolitan Love Song
    (Sweet One How My Heart Is Yearning)
    (T'Amo)   3590
Neapolitan Nostalgia   194
Near but Never Too Near   1369
Near Future, The   4813
Near to You   957
Nearing the Day   4529
Nearly True to You   1992
Nearsighted Gambler   1757
Neat Cafe, A   2286
Neat Little Cat, A   1972
Neat Ned Nuff Sed   2792
Neat/Not Neat   2142
Neat to Be a Newsboy   4744
'Neath a New Moon   3117
'Neath Egyptian Skies   208
'Neath Italian Skies   487
'Neath My Lattice   3777
'Neath the Blue Neapolitan Sky   4559
'Neath the Cherry Blossom Moon   718
'Neath the Greenwood Tree   3736
'Neath the Old Cherry Tree   2314
'Neath the Pale Cuban Moon   3709
'Neath the South Sea Moon   4816
'Neath the Southern Moon   3081
'Neath Thy Casement   25
'Neath Thy Window   947
'Neath Thy Window, Senorita   2209
Neauville-Sur-Mer   3214
Nebraska   1991
Necessarily Evil   3568
Necessity   1278
Neckin' Time in Great Neck   1533
Necrology   4076
Nectar for the Gods   1746
Nectar, Sweet Nectar   2650
Needle in a Haystack   2643, 3856
Needle's Eye, The   3631
Needles   2342
Negotiation   2692
Neighbor, Neighbor   4147
Neighborhood   4031
Neighborhood Song, The   2053
Neighbors   4659
Neighbors Above, Neighbors Below   572
Neighbors Song, The   2925
Neither the Time Nor the Place   3526
Nel Blue di Pinto di Blue (Volare)   4137, 4264

Nell Brinkley Girl, The   4802
Nell Gwynne   3730
Nellie Bly   3091
Nellie Kellie   3951
Nellie Kelly   2298
Nellie Kelly I Love You   1478, 2533
Nellie the Manicure   2543
Nellie's Entrance   2533
Nelly Bly   4149
Nelson   2208, 1000
Nemo's Dream of Fourth of July (inst.)   2534
Nenette and Rin-Tin-Tin (Rintintin)   1580
Neptune's Daughter   4808
Neptune's Son   3173
Nero, Caesar, Napoleon   298
Nerves   611, 4020, 1270, 1851, 3866
Nervous   407, 3902
Nervous Set, The   3094
Nervous Wreck, The   4683
Nervous Wrecks   3819
Nesting in a New York Tree
    (Nesting Time in New York Town)   2517
Nesting Time in Flatbush   3230
Nestle By My Side   1650
Network   3548
Neurotic You and Psychopathic Me   2439
Nevada Hoe Down   1918
Nevada Moonlight   1387
Never   3802
Never a Dull Moment   1879, 4142
Never Again   2, 98, 350, 1228, 2617,
    2717, 3308, 3885
Never Any Time to Play   3371
Never Been the Petted Party   2490
Never Borrow Trouble   2770
Never Breathe a Word of This to Mother   1640
Never Can Tell   3456
Never Choose a Girl from Her Photograph   1307
Never Count Your Chicks before They're Hatched   2761
Never Do A Bad Thing   3224
Never Ever Land   1216
Never Feel Sorry for Anybody   957
Never Feel Too Weary to Pray   2510
Never Felt Better in My Life   2229
Never for You   3117
Never Forget Your Parents   2559
Never Get Lost   3696
Never Give a Sucker an Even Break   4577
Never Give Anything Away   629
(I'll) Never Go There Anymore   2304
Never Go Walking without Your Hat Pin   4467
Never Had a Dream   2640
Never Had an Education   2813
Never Had It So Good   898
Never Had This Feeling Before   362
Never in Paris   610
Never in the Wide, Wide World   2697
Never Is Now   494
Never Land   3452, 3453
Never Let Her Go   4015

Nice   2646
Nice As Any Man Can Be   2219
Nice Baby   3926
Nice Baby! (Come to Papa!)   4392
Nice Fella   3224
Nice Girl   303
Nice Girl Like You, A   1786
Nice Girls   4796
Nice Goin'   3138
Nice Goings On   3139
Nice House We Got Here   3224
Nice Little Day   4415
Nice Little Girl on the Side, A   3770, 3791
Nice Little Girls and Boys   1246
Nice Little Home Is What I Sigh For, A   233
Nice Little Plot for a Play   2730
Nice Running in to You   3161
Nice Running Into You   3366
Nice She Ain't   1709
Nice Small Town Girls   2888
Nice to Know   2422
Nice to See You   3140
Nice Town   779
(My) Nice Ways   4196
Nice Work If You Can Get It   921, 3060
Nice Young Man, A   357
Nicer Girl than You, A   2892
Nicest Girl I Know, The   1863
Nicest Man I Ever Saw, The   830
Nicest Sort of Feeling   2112
Nicest Thing, The   2449
Nicest Time of the Year   3278
Nicest Time to Say Goodnight, The   2583
'Nichevo' Means Yes   464
Nicholas Nickleby   3143
Nicholini   2155
Nick   3180
Nickel for a Dime, A   4281
Nickel to My Name, A   297
Nickel Under the Foot   919
Nickel Worth of Dreams   1665
Nicodemus   1118, 3254
Nicol in the Picolo   498
Nicole You Is My Woman Now   2452
Nicolini   1123
Nicotina   1338
Nigger Heaven Blues   2739
Night   1680, 3822
Night After Night   2103, 4367, 3255
Night Alone, A   3448
Night and Day   1453, 1762
Night and the Sea, The   406
Night at Luna, A   632
Night Before Christmas Song, The   3794
Night Before the Morning After, The   383
Night Bird Is Calling, The   3348
Night Birds   2293
Night Boat to Albany   1833
Night Brigade, The   4206
Night Club Nights   2490, 2540

Night Club Opening   4581
Night Flies By   3014
Night Gondolfi Got Married, The   2322
Night Has a Thousand Eyes, The   126
Night! Healing Darkness!   2243
Night, Hold Back the Dawn   4267
Night Idyll   710
Night in June, A   4818
Night in Paris, A   787
Night in the Orient, A   3985
Night in the Ukraine, A   1000
Night Is a Weapon   3817
Night Is Filled with Wonderful Sounds, The   4798
Night Is Young, The   277
Night Is Young and You're So Beautiful, The   662
Night It Had to End, The   3760
Night It Happened, The   2238
Night Lady   2426
Night Letter   4485
Night Life   4621
Night Life in Old Manhattan   4808
Night Life in Santa Rosa   4019
Night May Be Dark, The   2201
Night May Have Its Sadness   133
Night Music   2357
Night of Love   2684
Night of Masquerade, A   2829
Night of My Nights   2327, 4383
Night of Nights   4110
Night of Screams   3944
Night of Shooting Stars   3306
Night of St. Leandre   1119
Night of Stars   3153
Night of Terror   3461
Night of the Ball, The   1203
Night on the Town   846, 3277
Night Out, A   2707, 3157
Night People   4127, 3094
Night Pulse   3576
Night Remembers   3094
Night School for Revue, The   703
Night Song   602, 1601
Night That Made America Famous, The   3159
Night the Hurricane Hit, The   3942
Night the Hurricane Struck, The   3484
Night the Lion Broke Loose, The   4827
Night the Old Cow Died, The   4206
Night They Drove Old Dixie Down, The   3739
Night They Invented Champagne, The   1511
Night Time   1340
Night Time, The   1552
Night Time   1640, 2291
Night Time, The   3319
(It's) The Night Time   3819
Night Time in Araby   1487
Night Time's the Right Time to Spoon with
   the Girl You Love   2448
Night Waltz (1)   2536
Night Waltz (2)   2536
Night Waltzes   4067

O

Oh, The Paying Guests   4713
Oh, the Picnic at Manassas   1474
Oh, the Regatta   4479
Oh, the Rio Grande (Cowboy Song)   2228
Oh, the Shame   2887
Oh, the Things They Put in the Papers
   Now-a-Days   4649
Oh, the Women   3020
Oh! the World Is All Wrong   3256
Oh, the World of Peace   1083
Oh, Theobold, Oh, Elmer   4170
Oh, This Is a Happy Day   1496
Oh, This Is Such a Lovely War   4178
Oh, This Love!   3362
Oh, Those Americans   3800
Oh, Those Boys!   4649
Oh, Those Days   2696
Oh, Those Eyes   1469
Oh Those Thirties   1227
Oh! Thou Art Fair, My Love   2213
Oh, to Be a Movie Star   170
Oh to Be Home Again   4340
Oh, Uncle   3258
Oh, Up! It's Up!   2670
Oh, Waiter   4227
Oh Wasn't It Lovely?   2833
Oh! We Know   4012
Oh! What a Ball!   2357
Oh, What a Beautiful Mornin'   3263
Oh, What a Beautiful Morning   1746
Oh, What a Bump!   4201
Oh What a Circus   1211
Oh What a Delight to Be Dancing   2906
Oh, What a Dream   2465
Oh, What a Filthy Night Court   919
Oh What a Fund of Joy   1905
Oh, What a Girl!   3258
Oh, What a Girl   4651
Oh, What a Happy Day   1378
Oh What a Happy Fisherman Am I   1155
Oh, What a Knight! (The Best Knight of My Life)   3587
Oh! What a Little Whopper   2549
Oh, What a Lovely Day   3622
Oh, What a Lovely Dream   671
Oh, What a Lovely Princess   3378
Oh What a Lovely War
   (Oh It's a Lovely War)   3259
Oh, What a Man   1617
Oh What a Man   4621
Oh, What a Moanin' Man   638
Oh, What a Night for a Party   1423
Oh, What a Night to Spoon   2795
Oh, What a Performance!   3760
Oh! What a Pity!   30
Oh, What a Playmate You Could Make   458
Oh, What a Pretty Pair of Lovers   2287
Oh! What a Siege That Was   2659
Oh, What a Time We Had   159
Oh, What a Wedding   3197
Oh, What a Wonderful Plan   2785

Oh What an Island   3788
Oh, What Bridal Song   4615
Oh What Fools We Mortals Be   2534
Oh, What Is a Woman's Duty?   3588
Oh! What Is the Matter?   104
Oh, What She Hangs Out She Hangs
   Out in Our Alley   1485
Oh, What Will Be the End of It?   1682
Oh, What Will Mother Say?   453
Oh, What You Can Do to Me   2976
Oh What's the Use?   2145
Oh, What's the Use?   2213
Oh, What's the Use   4508
Oh, Why Am I So Happy?   4149
Oh Why, Oh Why, Oh Why   277
Oh, William Morris   2477
Oh Woe Is Me-oh   2293
Oh Woman in Days of Romance   3857
Oh, Won't You Shed a Little Tear for Me?   3774
Oh, World   2785
Oh, Yes! Oh, Yes!   2500
Oh You!   1312
Oh! You   3877
Oh You Bear Cut Rag   3545
Oh! You Beautiful Doll   662, 2231
Oh, You Beautiful Doll   3681, 4799
Oh, You Beautiful Person!   3923
Oh, You Beautiful Spring   3679
Oh! You Bold Bad Men   1455
Oh You Chicago, Oh You New York   2261
Oh, You Circus Days   1738
Oh! You Coon   800
Oh! You Dream   3395
Oh, You Girls!   1911
Oh! You Girls!   2334
Oh, You John   965
Oh You John   2854
Oh! You Kewpie Kandy Doll   2492
Oh, You Lady!   3323
Oh You Lovely Ladies   1530
Oh, You Major Scales   2549
Oh, You Men   3738
Oh, You Silv'ry Bells (Jingle Bells)   1531
Oh, You Summertime Romeo!   4203
Oh! You Sweet Sweet Day   822
Oh, You Sweeties   1065
Oh You Vampire Girls   3402
Oh, You Wonderful Boy   1478
Oh, You Wonderful Girl   2525
Oh You, You Darling!   2886
Oh You're a Wonderful Person   4362
O'Hara   1616
O'Hara See Saw   1051
Ohh! That Kiss   2423
Ohhh! Ahhh!   1856
Ohio   4734
Ohio Afternoon   3261
O'Houlihan   1588
Ohrbach's, Bloomingdale's, Best and Saks   798
Oisgetzaychnet (Out of This World)   4863

Our Day   4117
Our Day of Independence   619
Our Day Will Come   4193
Our Doctor Comes   1570
Our Dollies   2276
Our Emblem Is the Lily   2135
Our Emporium   3882
Our Family Tree   4314
Our Farm   3322
Our Father...   2775
Our Favorite Restaurant   430
Our First Kiss   1494
Our Gang   2541
Our Girls   2282
Our Glorious Stripes and Stars   2701
Our Goose Has a Mint in Her
   Little Insides   2964
Our Goose Is Cooked   4707
Our Health Farm   3426
Our Hearts Were Young and
   Gay   3320, 3320
Our Hero   3332
Our Home   1546
Our Home, Sweet Home   3821
Our Home Town   4815
Our Honeymoon   2871, 1774
Our Hotel   455, 3156
Our Household, a Dream   654
Our Jimmy   2217
Our Just Portion   3653
Our Kind of War   757
Our Land of Dreams   2714
Our Language of Love   2150
Our Last Dance   1476
Our Last Dance Together   1082
Our Last Waltz Together   4365
Our Lips Are Sealed   3739
Our Little Captain   4392
Our Little Desert Island   3866
Our Little Family   3527
Our Little Gray Home (in the Red)   3046
Our Little Kitchenette   2363
Our Little Lady Upstairs   2813
Our Little Nest   3245
Our Little Secret   3603
Our Little World   2143
Our Lives Have Just Begun   732
Our Love Has Flown Away   4186
Our Love Is Here to Stay   3175
Our Lovely Rose   4150
Our Marriage Lines   3313
Our Master Is Free Again   1284
Our Memoirs   3916
Our Miss Gibbs   3322
Our Morals Are Most Refined   3423
Our Native Land   1852, 3994
Our Navy's the Best in the World   4452
Our New Best Friends   128
Our New Jerusalem   747
Our Own Broadway   676

Our Own Way of Going Along   2829
Our Presidents   1536
Our Private Love Song   3036
Our Private World   3279
Our Red Knight   1015
Our Rendezvous   324
Our Secret   324
Our Song   1262, 4572
Our Special Love   2177
Our State Fair   4146
Our Tale Is Told   3777
Our Time   2822
Our Time Together   31, 3059
Our Town   451, 3324, 3324, 1701, 2703, 4166
Our Usual Place   4798
Our Wedding Day   207, 1911
Our Wives   3304
Ours   4288, 1762, 3674, 4517
Ours Is a Happy Little Home   1301
Ourselves Alone (Tiocfaedh Ar La)   533
'Ousing Cha-Cha, The   1319
Out-a-Town   550
Out Comes Oom-Pa-Pa   1815
Out for Blood   661
Out for No Good   1336
Out in Frisco Town   3397
Out in the Barnyard   2966
Out in the Breezy Morning Air   4554
Out in the Cold   3498
Out in the Open Air   3946, 4367
Out in the Sun   1384
Out of a Clear Blue Sky   1135, 1778
Out of a Dream   2458
Out of a Job   4477, 4530
Out of Breath   1448, 3818
Out of Focus   4579
Out of Here   3757
Out of His Heart He Builds a Home   763
Out of Love   708
Out of Luck with Luck   4629
Out of My Dreams   3263
Out of My Mind   4602
Out of My Sight   2224
Out of Sight, Out of Mind   2464, 3210
Out of the Blue   2547, 4234
Out of the Clear Blue Sky   4499
Out of the Dark   2751
Out of the Way   1548
Out of Town   1002
Out of Town Buyers   608
Out on a Limb   3576, 4702
Out on the Loose   3719
Out on the Street   2173, 3806
Out There   305
Out There in an Orchard   3949
Out to Launch   3988
Out to Lunch   3329
Out to Set the World on Fire   3752
Out Town   1701
Out Where the Blues Begin   1827

P

Patchwork Quilt, A   1992
Patent Leather City (dance)   2032
Path to Honeymoon Land, The   2854
Pathway of Love, The   3676
Pathway to Paradise, The   780
Patience   239
Patience and Gentleness   1046
Patience of a Saint   4270
Patient's Lament   3600
Patiently Smiling   4792
Patisserie, The   2705
Patrick J. O'Hara   3545
Patrick Would Be Proud of Me Now   3880
Patriotic Coon   1988
Patriotic Fantasy (inst.)   3261
Patriotic Rally   4178
Patriotic Song   2474
Patrol Mysterioso   712
Patron Saints   1059
Patroness of Art   4798
Patrons of the Play   3685
Patsy   4090
Patsy Bolivar   1632, 2209
Patter Song — Through the Years   576
Patterns   253, 784, 2970
Patti-Cake Waltz, The   2093
Pattison Valse Song   4165
Patty Cake, Baker Man   4725
Patty Dear, Oh, Stop Your Teasin'   3472
'Paul Jones', The (dance)   2148
Paul Poirot Number   2461
Paul Revere   4488
Paula (An Improvised Love Song)   1633
Pauline   3396
Pause for Prayer   2477
Pause Oriental   2919
Pavanne   252, 948
Pavanne (inst.)   2161
Pavanne   4670
Pavilion of Love, The   613
Pavlova Gavotte, The   4657
Pawn for Wernher Von Braun, A   3186
Pay As You Go   3113
Pay Attention to the Girls   867
Pay Day   3054, 3170
Pay Day on Levee   3808
Pay Day Pauline   3184
Pay Heed   612
Pay, Pay, Pay   3067
Pay Phone   1700
Pay the Lawyer   4619
Pay Them No Mind   4
Payador   3170
Payday   4446
Paying Off   3314
Payola   1363
Pazzo   3197
PE   4016
Peace   635, 3366, 3418, 4403
Peace and the Diplomat Ballet   3990

Peace Anthem   3418
Peace, Brother!   4256
Peace Celebration   3764
Peace Come to Every Heart   4384
Peace Love and Good Damn   3825
Peace of Mind   4619
Peace! Peace!   906
Peace, Sister, Peace   4198, 4199
Peace Teachers   3159
Peace to My Lonely Heart   463
Peace Will Come   3276
Peaceful Place, A   2357
Peaceful Warriors   4061
Peach Blossom Time   378
Peach Girl   582
Peach King, The   2722
Peach of a Life, A   2430
Peach on the Beach   3184
(Papa Would Persist in Picking) Peaches   2900
Peaches   4648, 4085
Peachie   1404, 3962
Peachum's Morning Hymn   4370
Peachy Teacher, The   4201
Peacock Alley   1617, 3821
Peacock and I, The   3880
Peacock Dance (inst.)   149
Peacock Parade, The   1482
Peacock Strut   2135
Peanut Butter Affair, The   427
Peanut Butter Affair   3112
Peanut Butter Sandwiches and Hard
    Boiled Eggs   1886
Peanut Song   1958
Peanuts   4034, 4783
Peanuts and Kisses   1932
Pear Tree Quintet   634
Pearl   597, 3217, 4684
Pearl Maiden, The   3423
Pearl of Broadway   2638
Pearl of Ceylon Ballet, The (inst.)   2638
Pearl of Ceylon, The (1)   2638
Pearl of Sweet Ceylon   767
Pearl of the East (scene)   4818, 4819
Pearl We Called Prague, The   1739
Pearls   1012, 4485
Pearl's a Singer   4031
Pearl's Walking Song   99
Pears and Peaches   1116
Pears of Anjou, The   3702
Peasant Girl, The   3399
Peasant Girl   3424
Peasant Wedding Party, The   93
Peasants' Idyll   147
Peasants' Song, The   1785
Pebble Waltz   2958
Peckin'   875
Peckin' (inst.)   885
Peculiar Julia   2695
Peculiar State of Affairs   3801
Peculiar That Way   2579

Perfect Place, A   4136
Perfect Stranger   4268
Perfect Strangers   3070, 1257
Perfect Timing   2065
Perfect Understanding, The   1010
Perfect Year, The   4217
Perfect Young Ladies   507
Perfection   1194, 1797, 3764
Perfection's Palace   1426
Perfectly Alone   2651
Perfectly Charming Visit, A   1993
Perfectly Lovely Couple   1060
Perfectly Marvelous   610
Perfectly Peaceful Person, A   2844
Perfectly Terrible   4425
Perfectly Terrible, Dear   2892
Performance Art   871
Perfume   1130
Perfume and Passion   2857
Perfume Counter on the Rue de la Paix, A
    (At a Perfume Counter)   2460
Perfume Number   3770
Perfume of Love   3045
Perfume of Love, The   3972
Perfume of Paradise, The   2387
Perfume Waltz   2135
Pergola Patrol, The   611
Perhaps   385, 737, 1060, 2723
Perhaps Love's Dream Will Last Forever   1798
Perhaps You May Not Like It   2041
Perils of Paulette, The   4543
Period Piece, A   944
Perish the Baubles   3215
Permissible   1578
Permission   3197
Pernambuco   4652
Peron's Latest Flame   1211
Perpetual Anticipation   2536
Persevere   1568
Persian Fantasy (Persiana)   2601
Persian Love Song   387
Persian Room-Ba   3493
Persian Skies   2700
Persian Way of Life, The   84
Persian Women   1745
Person of Parts, A   4404
Personal Appearance   1342
Personal Heaven   4484
Personal President   3873
Personal Touch, The   62
Personality   403, 1651, 3466, 3304, 2454, 4255
Personally Yours   1874
Personals   4309, 3476
Perspective   3918
Perspiration   3986
Persuasion, The   623
Perusing in Peru   3170
Pervenche   1305
Pesach Has Come to the Ghetto   1715
Pessimistic Voices   2046

Pet of the Family   2261
Petals of the Plum Tree, The   3828
Peteca!   2679
Peter   3827
Peter Pan   418, 1784, 2494, 2717, 3177, 3286,
    3453, 3980, 3454
Peter, Peter   3452
Peter Piper   1921
Peter's Denial   2212
Peter's Journey Ballet (inst.)   247
Petite Belle Lily   2719
Petite Mama   1834
Pets   2453
Petticoat High   3837
Petticoat Lane   4288
Petticoat Lane (On a Saturday Ain't
    So Nice)   455
Petticoat Lane   2320
Pettin' and Pokin'   1296
Pettin' on the Old Porch Swing   2231
Petting Party Baby   2490
Petty Crime   4689
Pffft!   483
Phantom Loves   764
Phantom of the Musical, The   1349, 1350
Phantom of the Opera, The   3464, 3464
Phantom of the Opera   2114
Phantom of the Opera, The   3465, 3462, 3463
Phantom of Your Smile, The   1065
Phantom Patrol   4723
Phantom Rival, The   2614
Phantom Ship, The   3422
Phantom Waltz, The (dance) (inst.)   3538
Phantoms of the Ballroom   2691
Phantoms of the Night   203
Pharoah's Chant   1715
Pharoah's Daughter   4849, 4832
Pharoah's Dream Explained   2242
Pharoah's Story   2242
Phata Phata (Touch, Touch)   2147
Pheira   1308
Phi Phi   3466
Phil the Fiddler   2707
Phil's Entrance   4226
Phil's Medley   1832
Philadelphia   1060, 4004
Philadelphia Drag   1
Philadelphia Drag, The   3395
Philadelphia 1890   4577
Philadelphia Feeling   4428
Philadelphia Maid, The   3784
Philadelphia Press, The   1849
Philanthropist's Progress, The   2935
Philological Waltz   220
Philomel   2937
Philosophic Tale Is Told, The   698
Philosophy   3112
Phinney's Rainbow   3471
Phoebe Snow   2869, 3250, 1866
Phoebus Apollo   4073

Place Called Alimony Jail, A   4619
Place Called Home, A   754
Place in Space   2728
Place in the Country   4443
Place in the Sun   3139
Place in the World, A   3577
Place in Your Heart, A   1161
Place Like This, A   3160
Place of My Own, A   3764
Place of Your Own, A   451
Place to Hide, A   2970
Place Where You Belong, A   3364
Places I Fainted from Hunger   3757
Places, Everybody   4142
Plagues, The   1715
Plain and Simple   273
Plain Clean Average Americans   1591
Plain Girls   1750
Plain in Love   1644
Plain Jane   2768, 589, 3511
Plain Mamie O'Hooley   3229
Plain Men in Dirty Overalls   2175
Plain Ol' Name of Smith, The   3562
Plain, Old Room   3925
Plain Rustic Ride ('Neath the Silv'ry Moon)   2498
Plain We Live   3509
Plan (Tom and Huck's Argument), The   1086
Plan B   2627
Plan It by the Planets   2679
Planet of No Thigh Bulge   1575
Planet Shmanet Janet   3742
Plank, The   3452
Planning   2557, 554
Planning the Bar Mitzvah   1234
Plans A & B   3760
Plant a Radish   1245
Plant Roses in Memory's Garden   3084
Plant You Now, Dig You Later   3353
Plantation Days   1799
Plantation in Philadelphia   183
Plantation Melodies   4429
Planting Fever   4764
Plastic Alligator, The   1860
Plastic Surgery   1747
Plate Dance   3403
Platinum   4216
Platinum Dreams   3515
Play a Half a Chorus   787
Play Away the Blues   275
Play Ball with the Lord   1441
Play-Fair Man!, A   2308
Play-Ground in the Sky   3968
Play Gypsies, Dance Gypsies   905
Play in Native Fashion   4550
Play Is the Bunk, The   2300
Play It Again   2617
Play It Again, Sam   3516
Play It As It Lays   4591
Play Me a Bagpipe Tune   539
Play Me a Country Song   3517

Play Me a New Tune   2789
Play Me a Tune   969, 1923
Play Me a Ukulele   4037
Play Me an Old Time Two-Step   4204
Play Me Something I Can Dance To   3319
Play Me That Tune   4418
Play Me That Tune (Ya-Da-De-Dum-Dum)   2385
Play, Mr. Bailey   4829
Play My Melody   3400
Play Nice   2357, 1510
Play Orchestra Play   3235
Play, Orchestra, Play!   3906
Play, Play, Play   796, 2834
Play Street   4153
Play That Barbershop Chord   4804
Play That Fandango Rag   4803
Play That Wedding March Backwards   1566
Play the Game   356, 1111, 1667
Play the Game and Smile   2686
Play the Music for Me   2200
Play the Queen   3838
Play the Star-Spangled Banner   2902
Play to Win   747
Play Us a Polka Dot   4234
Play Us a Tune   3291
Play with Fire   2384
Play with Me   562
Play Without a Bedroom, A   3006
Play's the Thing, The   4670
Playboy   1800
Playboy of the Western World   259
Playboy's Work Is Never Done, A   4522
Player, The   496
Players' Plaint   3908
Playground of the Planets   2539
Playground Songs   1601
Playhouse Planned for You, A   3511
Playin' the Halls   456
Playing Croquet   2522
Playing Field, The   1289
Playing for Position   3517
Playing Golf   3998
Playing Second Fiddle   3211
Playing the Game   2004
Playland   185
Plays   1422
Playthings of Love   2371
Plaza 6-9423   3990
Plaza Music   3493
Plaza Song, The   253
Plaza, the Barclay and the
   Old Waldorf, The   4093
Plaza Waltz Waltz, The   1049
Plaza's Going Native, The   3479
Plea for Understanding, A   4388
Plea to the Duchess   325
Pleadle-Eadle   4609
Pleasant Company   1684
Pleasant Day   3357
Pleasant Greeting, A   3185

Poker Polka, The   3
Poker Polka   3294
Poker-Polka, The   3381
Polar Bear in a Zoo   143
Polar Bear Strut, The   1654
Police   1354
Police, The   3157
Police Song   4029
Police Trouble   2992
Policeman's Ball, The   2894
Policeman's Lot Is a Happy One, A   3395
Policeman's Song   2348
Policeman's Whistle, A   4588
Policemen's Chorus, The   2500
Policemen's Hymn   3564
Policeology   3921, 4547
Politenss Pays   4258
Political Lady   4323
Political Science   2852, 2787
Politicians' Song   3548
Politics   996, 1745, 2293, 4314
Politics and Poker   1280
Polka   1962, 3011, 3064
Polka, The (dance)   3837
Polka Contest, The   1828
Polka Dot, The   3005
Polka Dot   3344
Polka Dot, The   4001
Polka Dot Polka   2088
Polka Dots   1277
Polka Duet   132
Polka Is Good Fun, The   3996
Polka Mazurka, The   1203
Polla   1183
Pollution   4412
Polly   1374, 3532
Polly and the Polka   1538
Polly Believed in Prepardness   1784
Polly of Hollywood   3009, 3533
Polly of the Circus   2869, 3534
Polly, Pretty Polly (Polly with a Past)   805
Polly Put the Kettle On   2308
Polly Wants a Cracker   1375
Polly With a Past   3532
Polly Wolly Doodle   2415, 3989
Pollyanna   1971, 3236
(They Call Me) Pollyanna   3842
Polly's Lied   4370
Polly's Song   4369
Polnische Wirtschaft   3529
Polo   2803
Polo Dance   4437
Polo Rag (inst.)   4747
Polo Song   934
Polonaise   3536
Polyandry   1435
Polyarts U.   2598
Polyphonic   919
Polythene Pam   3903
Pom-Pom   3537

Pom Pom on Your Hat, The   2751
Pomander Walk   2756
Pompadour   2700, 2813
Pompanola   4345
Poncho's Thoughts (Little Man)   4609
Ponies on Parade   1131
Pony Ballet   1224
Pony Ballet (inst.)   2974
Pony Trot, The   3663
Poodle & Canary, also Tom & Jerry Menage a
    Culinary Croak, The   1450
Poogie-Woo   1314
Pool of Love   2330
Pool Room Papa   876
Pools, The   1619
Poontang   2451
Poopsie Woopsie   2993
Poor   71, 4468
Poor Are Rich, The   3131
Poor As a Church Mouse   3813
Poor Baby   832
Poor Bosie   1010
Poor Bouchette   3251
Poor Boy   1064
Poor but Honest Working Girl, A   2389
Poor Butterfly   396, 4799
Poor Cinderella   2253, 762
Poor Dear Mabel   2519
Poor Don Pasquale   3197
Poor Everybody Else   3869, 4238
Poor Fellow   4824
Poor Fish   4780
Poor Fool, He Makes Me Laugh   3464
Poor Grandma   3329
Poor Horse   451
Poor Isabel   1046
Poor J'en-Ai-Marie   3405
Poor Jerusalem   2212
Poor Joe   85, 2983
Poor Johnny Brown   485
Poor Kitty Popcorn (The Soldier's Pet)   1897
Poor Little Boy   2322
Poor Little Fluttering Moths   1926
Poor Little Foolish Man   2566
Poor Little Girl Like Me, A   2978
Poor Little Hollywood Star   2523
Poor Little Marie   3179
Poor Little Me   180, 4812, 3022
Poor Little Me, I'm on K.P.   4770
Poor Little Me-I'm on KP   4340
Poor Little Model   3848
Poor Little Model Girl   2919
Poor Little Orphans (Sixteen of 'Em)   1667
Poor Little Person   1846
Poor Little Pierette   507
Poor Little Red Papoose   1881, 4473
Poor Little Rich Girl   702, 3020, 3235
Poor Little Rich Girl's Dog   3658
Poor Little Rich Little Me   2214
Poor Little Ritz Girl (1)   3538

Poor Little Ritz Girl (2)   3538
Poor Little Trigger   4710
Poor Little Wall Flower   2180
Poor Little, Shy Little, Demure Little Me   4025
Poor Man, A   3602
Poor Man   4015
Poor Man at Parting, A   3939
Poor Marat in Your Bathtub Seat   3445
Poor Mary Ann O'Shea   1629
Poor Mary Anne O'Shea   3256
Poor Me, Oh My   3318
Poor Michael! Poor Golo!   3379
Poor Mortals   3418
Poor Mouse   974
Poor Mr. Keeley   1966
Poor Mrs. Peachum   4368
Poor Old Dad in New York for the
    Summer   561
Poor Old Florodora Girl   2214
Poor Old Fluff   1318
Poor Old Man   1118
Poor Old Marat   3445
Poor Old World   3723
Poor Pierrot   672, 2833
Poor, Poor Joseph   2242
Poor, Poor Pharoah   2242
Poor Porgy   3605
Poor Prune   2430
Poor Relations   2686
Poor Rose   3672
Poor Sam   1911
Poor Sweet Baby   4034
Poor Teddy Bear   2177
Poor Thing   4233
Poor Tied Up Darlin'   3733
Poor Uncle Gasazus   335
Poor Unfortunate Sister Anne   2974
Poor Wandering One   2348
Poor Wicked Man, The   402
Poor Winter Garden Girl   598
Poor Working Girl   506
Poor Workingman   2527
Poor Young Millionaire   4517
Pop! Fizz! Happy!   3039
Pop, Pop, Pop   4704
Pop Song   3479
Popcorn and Piss   2776
Pophams, The   3243
Poplar and the Rainbow, The   470
Poppa   1601
Poppa Help Me   1265
Poppa Isn't Poppa Anymore   4481
Poppa Knows Best   4481
Poppa's Blues   4138
Poppa's Popular Boy   3626
Poppin'   3202
Poppy   4154
Poppy and the Pink, The   939
Poppy Chorus   4723
Poppy Dear   3540

Poppy Fields   1282
Poppy Land   560
Poppy the Dream Girl   539
Poppyland   2960
Popsey Wopsey   1538
Popsicles in Paris   4395
Popular Girl, A   256
Popular March   1968
Popular Pauline   4735
Popular Pests, The   4813
Popular Rag   1735
Popular Song, A   3268
Popular Songs   2498
Popular Tune, A   2697
Popularity   1478, 1582, 2730, 2757, 2041
Population   23
Population Explosion   3440
Porcelain Maid   3007
Porcelaine De Saxe   710
Pore Jud Is Daid   3263
Porgy (Blues for Porgy)   441
Porgy   3541
Pork, Pork, Pork   11
Port Authority   2648
Port of Debarkation   2876
Porter! Porter!   1033
Porterhouse Lucy   2175
Porterology   2645
Porter's Love Song to a Chambermaid, A
    2337, 3964
Porters on a Pullman Train   114
Portia's Plan   3600
Portion of Caviar, A   1777
Porto Banos   1536
Porto Rico (inst.)   1909
Portofino   3543, 4060, 4268
Portofino P.T.A.   4060
Portrait, The   4, 2317
Portrait for Posterity   2610
Portrait of Jennie   3544, 3544
Portrait of Marie, A   1119
Portrait Parade, The   930
Posey from Over the Sea, A   3828
Posin' (inst.)   886
Posin'   1658
Posing for Venus   3251
Posing Scene   3681
Positively Love You   787
Positively No (Construction Gang)   1425
Positively Wall Street   3077
Posse Im Himmelshof   1925
Possessed   2198
Possibilities   1086
Possum Pie   3557
Post Card Beau, A   3096
Post Cards   96
Post Office   1582
Postage Stamp Principality   1760
Postcard #1   4020
Postcards   3718

Q

R

Rhythm of Life, The   4238
Rhythm of the Day   1131, 4823
Rhythm of the Line, The   3830
Rhythm of the Waves   1126
Rhythm River   882
Rhythmic Rhapsodies on the Piano   4437
Rhythms of a Summer Night   494
Rib of Adam   2992
Ribbons and Bows   4821
Ribbons Down My Back   1828
Ribbons I Will Give Thee   3939
Riblah's Lament   4157
Ricardo's Lament   4459
Rice and Shoes   4491
Rich, The   656, 919
Rich and Famous   1371
Rich and Happy   4067, 2822
Rich Butterfly   1567
Rich Coon's Babe, A   2111
Rich Enough to Be Rude   2580
Rich Girls   154
Rich Is   2874
Rich Man, Poor Man   649, 3177
Rich Man, Poor Man (Beggar Man, Thief)   3265
Rich Man! Poor Man!   4118
Rich Man's Frug (dance)   4238
Rich or Poor   1275
Rich People of Texas   413
Rich People of Texas, The   412
Rich, Rich, Rich   1991
Rich Woman   943
Richard Crudnut's Charm School   3105
Richard Interred   1633
Riches   3733
Richest Man in the World, The   2678
Rick-Chick-a-Chick   2287
Rickety Crickety   2216
Rickety-Rackety-Shack   1215
Ricochet   4264
Riddle, The   2164, 1679
Riddle Diddle Me This   4058
Riddle-Ma-Ree   4425
Riddle Me This   289
Riddle of Life   593
Riddle of You, The   2322
Riddle Song, The   2096
Riddles   1388
Riddleweed   1698
Ride, The   2100
Ride, Baby, Ride   3515
Ride, Cowboy, Ride   1546
Ride 'Em Cowboy   4314
Ride 'Em Cowboys   3086
Ride in the Puff-Puff, A   4430
Ride Me Around with You, Dearie   558
Ride on a Rainbow, A   3800
Ride on to Highest Destiny   4615
Ride Out the Storm   3869
Ride, Ride, Ride   302
Ride the Winds   3711

Ride Through the Night   4190
Ride to the Castle, The (inst.)   2394
Ride to the Course, The   4544
Rider in the Rain   2787
Rider to the Sea   2364
Ridin' High   1018, 1762, 3674, 881
Ridin' on the Breeze   283
Ridin' on the Moon   4123
Ridin' the Rails   4825
Riding   4437
Riding for a Fall   593
Riding Habit   1322
Riding High   3639
Riding in a Motor Car   236
Riding in the Choo-Choos   3092
Riding Lesson, The   1067
Riding Lesson   1498
Riding on a Carousel   2838
Riding on a High Horse   3080
Riding the Range-A Song of the Old West   1256
Riff-Raff-Rafferty   3087
Rig O' the Day, The (Mink)   1644
Rigadoon, The   2917
Rigauden   129
Right   4334
Right About Here   3112
Right Across from Brooklyn (Oh, Yes,
   New York)   2934
Right As the Rain   462
Right at the Start of It   4367
Right Boy Comes Along   3821
Right Brazilian Girl, The   1530
(You're in) The Right Church but the
   Wrong Pew   295
Right Finger of My Left Hand, The   3687
Right Girl, The   1329, 2931, 3712
Right Girls   1237
Right Hand Man   2626
Right Here   2737
Right Image, The   2477
Right Key but the Wrong Key Hole, The   3297
Right Key, Wrong Keyhole   3905
Right Kind of People, The   3427
Right Man, The   551
Right Now   3987, 1246
Right-O   3431
Right of Way   2682
Right Off the Board   1667
Right Out of Heaven Into My Arms   931
Right Place at the Right Time, The   4635
Right Place, Right Time   4138
Right, Right, Right   3788
Right This Way   3713
Right Time, the Right Place, The   101
Right Up Your Alley   3714
Right Way   1319
Rigoletto   1332
Rigo's Last Lullaby   4275
Rilly Great Shew, A   3530
Rin-Tin-Tin   2135, 2594

Rivkele Dem Rebns   3670
Ro-Ro-Rollin' Along   203
Road, The (inst.)   2368
Road Ends Here, The   2224
Road House Rag   1031
Road I'm Taking, The   573
Road that Leads Back Home   1502
Road that Lies Before, The   1784
Road to Anywhere, The   1240
Road to Destiny, The   3403
Road to Dreams, The   2789
Road to Hampton   823
Road to Happiness, The   1110, 1534
Road to Hell, The   3788
Road to Home, The   4372
Road to Mandelay   3729
Road to Paradise, The   1377, 2794
Road to the Girl You Love, The   2774
Road to Yesterday, The   1096, 3730
Road Tour, The   1601
Road You Didn't Take, The   1329
Roam On, My Little Gypsy Sweetheart   1343
Roaming Around the Town   2123
Roaring Twenties Strike Back, The   454
Robbed   2650
Robber-Baron Minstrel Parade, The   4004
Robber Bridegroom, The   3733
Robbers Everywhere   4492
Robbery, The   3938
Robert, Alvin, Wendall and Jo Jo   2801
Robert E. Lee   3513
Robert E. Lee Cakewalk   2231
Robert the Roue   4131
Robert the Roue (from Reading, Pa.)   4174
Robin and the Rose, The   4559
Robin Hood's Arrest   246
Robin Hood's Entrance   3736
Robinson Crusoe   2339, 3737
Robinson Crusoe's Island   4010
Robinson Crusoe's Isle   2951, 2552
Robinson Hotel, The   2376
Robot Man   3695
Robot Will Never Say No, A   2861
Rocco's Dream   1412
Rochelle Hudson Tango, The   3940
Rock, The   2470
Rock-a-Bye Baby   250
Rock-a-Bye-Baby   1823
Rock-A-Bye Baby   3009
Rock-a-Bye Baby Dear (Lullaby)   3740
Rock a Bye Ma Baby   395
Rock-a-Bye River   3950
Rock-a-Bye Your Baby with a Dixie Melody   3985
Rock & Roll All Night   3739
Rock and Roll Bump   4180
Rock and Roll Critic   1978
Rock and Roll Music   3739
Rock Around the Clock   3739
Rock Back the Clock   843
Rock Garden Rock   2092

Rock Is My Way of Life   3515
Rock Island   3016
Rock, Little Children   1300
Rock Me   887
Rock Me in the Cradle of Love   4808
Rock Me in the Cradle of the Deep   3041
Rock Me in Your Loving Arms   764
Rock 'n Horse   2084
Rock 'N' Roll   1813
Rock 'n' Roll Party Party Queen   1664
Rock 'n' Roll Star   1695
Rock 1975   3814
Rock of Rages   2427
Rock, Rock   3531
Rock, Rock, Rock   206, 591
Rock-Rock-Rock Let Me Rock in My
   Old Rocking Chair   2383
Rock with Rock   1822
Rockabye Hamlet   3741
Rockaway Beach   197
Rockaway Mary   4842
Rocket to the Moon   3716
Rockette's Dance   4629
Rockin'   823
Rockin' and Rollin' in Loch Lomond   1771
Rockin' Around the Christmas Tree   338, 3793, 3794
Rockin' at the Cannon Ball   1644
Rockin' in Rhythm   875, 1137
Rockin' in Rhythm (inst.)   885
Rockin' in Rhythm   4091
Rockin' Pneumonia   1890
Rocking Chair Fleet   3712
Rocking Chair Interlude   367
Rocking the Boat   2759
Rocks in My Bed   2259
Rocky on the Rocks   62, 3124
Rocky Road   3631
Rocky Road to Dublin   1532
Rocky Road to the White House, The   3530
Rococo Rag   1249
Rodeo   2332
Rodeo Dreams   3517
Rodeo Rider   3517
Rodeo Romeo   992
Rodgers and Hammerstein   779
Roebling Plan, The   564
Roger De Coverly   2399
Roger the Ox   1262
Roger the Ugly   4469
Rogue Song, The   4251
Role-Playing   2630
Roll a Little Pill for Me   2127
Roll Along   1208
Roll Along, Covered Wagon   1836
Roll Along, Sadie   4499
Roll Call   3630
Roll Call in the Morning, The   2005
Roll 'Em   1930
Roll Jordan   1198
Roll Me   2270

Rosy Morn, The   3681
Rosy, Posy   480
Rosy Red   2065
Rothschild and Sons   3780
Rothschilds, The   3780
Rotisserie, The   201
Rottenest Job   4063
Rouge   3108
Rough and Ready Man   478
Rough Riders   3558
Rough, Rugged and Robust   4117
Rough Stuff   2439
Rough Times   837
Roulette   415, 1182
Roulette Dance   764
Roulette Game, The   3703
Roumania   780
Roumania, Roumania   2356
Roumeynische Libe   3781
Round, A   1162
'Round About Midnight   2555
Round and Round   1245, 4114
Round by Red Mountain   451
Round Every Corner   4193
Round in Circles   4703
Round on the End and High in the
    Middle   1992
Round-Shouldered Man   3862
Round the Clock   4603
'Round the Corner   2549
Round the Corner   4419
Round the Ray Wain   710
'Round the Town   3745
Round the World   1613
Round Up, The   3661
Round-Up, The   1316
Roundabout   4237, 4499
Roundelay   3736
Rounders' Serenade, The   2232
Roundhouse O'Leary   821
Roust-abouts   2845
Roustabouts   3808
Roustabouts' Song (We Follow the Trail)   3648
Routine Exercise, The   4634
Roving Gambler, The   3989
Row, Row   2387
Row, Row, Boatman   1518
Row Row Row   3259
Row, Row, Row   4655, 4806
Row 10 Aisle 6 Bench 114   3277
Rowing   4113
Rowing, Rowing   2711
Rowing Song, The   1566
Roxana   946
Roxane's Confession   949
Roxie   723
Royal Anthem   3445
Royal Bangkok Academy, The   2312
Royal Barge   1281
Royal Blood   3944

Royal Confession, A   4798
Royal Court Dance   3814
Royal Crocodile, The   3073
Royal Damn Fango, The   1651
Royal Dressing Room Scene   759
Royal Family, A   138
Royal Garden Blues (inst.)   3840, 432
Royal Hessian Auction   3780
Royal Honeymoon, A   737
Royal Hussars Are We   1768
Royal March   1110
Royal March, The   1871
Royal Nonesuch, The   394
Royal Pair Are Off Today, The   4014
Royal Radio   3641
Royal Rounds, The   1605
Royal Wedding   3406
Royalty   3791
Rozinkes Mit Mandlen (Raisins and
    Olives)   1279
Rozita   385
Rub a Dub   2986
Rub-A-Dub-Dub (1)   451
Rub-A-Dub-Dub (2)   451
Rub a Dub Dub   2134
Rub-a-Dub Your Rabbit's Foot   290
Rub the Lamp   3098
Rub Your Lamp   2453
Rubadub Dub   324
Rubaiyats from the Rubaiyat   3404
Rubber Man, The   104
Rubber Plant Song, The   3368
Rube Jazz Dance (inst).   1026
Rube Song   2964
Rube Wedding   3426
Ruben's Holiday   2642
Rubenstein Rag, The   1863
Rubies for a Queen   1857
Ruby   4137, 2231
Ruby Baby   4031
Rudolph the Red-Nosed Reindeer   3793,
    3794, 3795
Rue Broadway   1
Rue de la Paix   4249
Ruffian Ballet, The   1965
Rug, Snug   1557
Rugantino in the Stocks (La Berlina)   3798
Ruggles of Red Gap   3800
Ruined   3427
Ruined Maid, The   4467
Ruins   3214
Ruisenor   1414
Rule Britannia   3450
Ruler of Central Park, The   1466
Ruler of My Heart   4127
Rulers of the Earth   4803
Rules and Regulations   3551
Rules of Asylum   1865
Rum Below   3944
Rum-Dum-Dum-Dum   3072

Rum, Tum, Fidele   3395
Rum-Tum-Tiddle   4528
Rum Tum Tiddle   4553
Rum Tum Tugger   678
Rumania, Rumania   1609, 4342
Rumba, The   203
Rumba Rhythm   1135
Rumbatism   1251
Rumble, The (dance)   4625
Rumble of the Subway, The
   (Subway Chant)   2768
Rumble, Rumble, Rumble   3444, 4692
Rumbola   4198
Rumors   147
Rumors from Rome   456
Rumpelstiltskin   1727
Rumplestiltskin   4106
Rumson   3347
Run Along Mr. Ogre Man   1975
Run and Hide   2224
Run Away   2307, 3866
Run Away, Naughty Man   4044
Run Away with Me   1730
Run Between the Raindrops   2754
Run, Brudder Possum, Run   3744
Run, Brudder Rabbit, Run!   3945
Run for Your Life   3576, 4013
Run, Indian, Run   4785
Run Into Your Arms   3507
Run, Musashi, Run   3711
Run on the Bank   740
Run River Run   3724
Run, Run, Run   2449
Run, Run, Run Cinderella   1373
Run Something   4147
Run to Me, My Love   67
Runaway   4827
Runaway Colts   4422
Runaway Little Girl   2264
Runaway Match, A   3618
Runaways   4635
Runnin'   2645, 14
Runnin' for Jesus   3987
Runnin' to Meet the Man   3656
Runnin' Wild Blues   2557, 554
Running   1764
Running Around with Chorus Girls   804
Running Down the Sun   2618
Running for Office   1968
Running Out of Time   692
Running Wild   2044
Rupert Bear Song   4449
Ruritania   1467
Rushing the Growler   4362
Russia the Fatherland   3129
Russian Art   4817
Russian Barcarolle, A   710
Russian Blues   702, 2570
Russian Dance (Opening Act Two)   1066
Russian Dance   2292, 2358

Russian Dance at the Yabacabana   1993
Russian Duo and Dance   3265
Russian Love   2567
Russian Lullaby   789
Russian Maidens, The   1758
Russian Movie   2333
Russian Song   1387
Russian Toys, The   710
Russian Wedding March   2292
Rustic Ann   4054
Rustic Anna   132
Rustic Country Inn, A   3760
Rustic Patrol   1095
Rustle of Your Bustle, The   1127
Rusty Bell   4460
Rusty's Dream Ballet   2949
Rusty's Up in the Air   1323
Ruth   4732, 1769
Ruth St. Denis   3401
Ruthless!   3811
Ruthless   1435
Rutland Bounce, The (Dance)   1791

S

S & M Polka, The   2426
S.A.D.U.S.E.A.   3598
S-E-X   3124
S Eureka Presents (sketch)   3954
S.I.P.   3960
'S Over but the Shoutin'   1929
S.S. Commodore Ebenezer McAffee
   the Third   1373
S-S-Something Comes Over Me   4701
'S Wonderful   1419, 3020, 3060
S'a Mechaye   2811
Sabbath Blessing   4172
Sabbath Prayer   1265
Sabbath Queen   1609
Sabbath Song   2422
Sabot Dance   1570
Sabot Dance (inst.)   4357
Sabra, The   4514
Sabre Song, The   1027
Sabre Song   1745
Sacred Bodies   327
Sacred Tree, The   4447
Sacrifice, The   4139
Sacrifice   825, 2016, 2918
Sacrifice, The   4396
Sacrifice Your Body   4171
Sad Affair, A   2642
Sad at Heart Am I   4792
Sad Bad Man   1458
Sad Experience   2695
Sad Happy, Peek a Boo   456
Sad Is the Life of the Sailor's Wife   1893
Sad Is the Whippoorwill   4161

Saltpeter in the Rhubarb   1730, 1730
Salute   3526, 4201
Salute to Spring   3823
Salute to the King   1975
Salute to the Toreador   188
Salvation   3423, 3824
Salvation Army Girl   2749
Salvation Glide, The   548
Salvation Hymn   559
Salvation Sal   4421
Salvation Tess   4630
Salve Madonna   2220
Salzburg   363
Sam and Delilah   1528
Sam Hill   1736
Sam Johnson's Colored Cakewalk   1776
Sam, You Made the Pants Too Long   3926
Samandoza-we!   4579
Samaris Dance (dance)   2327
Samba at Daybreak   4117
Sambo   3676
Sambo and Dinah   2035
Sambo Was a Bad Boy   3825
Sambo's Banjo   3660
Sambo's Syncopated Russian Dance   2337
Same, The   139
Same As a Man   664
Same As Love, The   214
Same Girl, The   1509
Same Little Girl   4720
Same Mistakes   521
Same Old Clown, The   1514
Same Old Color Scheme   3656
Same Old Crowd The   2213
Same Old Game!, The   4187
Same Old Game, The   4555
Same Old Girl, The   8
Same Old Love   3493
Same Old Love Songs   771
Same Old Me, The   4785
Same Old Moon   3005
Same Old Moon, The   2408, 2638
Same Old Moon   4811
Same Old Places   97
Same Old Silv'ry Moon Is Shining, The   3676
Same Old Song, The   2568
Same Old Song   3401
Same Old Stars, Same Old Moon
   (but Which Is the Girl?)   380
Same Old Story   1054
Same Old Story, The   1316, 1582, 4241
Same Old Story, Nothing New   3784
Same Old Summer   1081
Same Old Sun, The   1469
Same Old Sweethearts, The   538
Same Old Thing Turned Around, The   4037
Same Old Tune, The   2195
Same Old Two, The   48, 3773
Same Old Way, The   2308
Same Old Way   2546

Same One They Picked for Me, The   1963
Same Silver Moon, The   3056
Same Sort of Girl   1544
Same Sweet Baby, The   3663
Same Thing   2008
Same Thing Over Again, The   509
Same Time, Same Place   3301
Same Way Home   2055
Samee Gamee   3828
Sammy   4723
Sammy and Topsy   3660
Samoa Sam   293
Samoan Song (Ka Tahua)   3339
Samovar the Lawyer   1000
Sampson Beauties, The   1970
Samson and Delilah   4542
Samson's Epiphany   3456
Samson's Gonna Be Born   2164
Samson's Thoughts   3456
Samurai Stomp, The   2861
San Antonio   3205
San Fernando   2935
San Francisco   4251, 4635
San Francisco Bay   3387
San Francisco Fair   4630
San Francisco Fran   1390
San Francisco Sadie   4717
San Francisco Waltz   1604
San Gennaro   3696
San Salvatore   2323
San Pasquale   3798
San Slavatore   2323
San Sebastian's Shores   1920
San Simeon   2969
San Toy   2071
Sancocho   3830
Sanctus   2775, 2411
Sand   2153
Sand Flowers   1174
Sand in My Eyes   3818
Sand in My Shoes   3444
Sand Man, The   830, 3981
Sand Witches   2857
Sanders of the River   4207
Sandhog Song   3831
Sandman, The   2784, 3419
Sandow Girl, The   954
Sandpaper   4540
Sands Hotel Song   3832
Sands of Time   2327, 4383
Sandwich for Two   2362
Sandwich Man, The   1891
Sandwich Men, The   834
Sandy   4398
Sandy Mahatma Gandy   1136
Sandy McDougal   2495
Sandy's Bags   1857
Sans-Gene   1114
Sans Souci   4423
Santa Barbara   1216

1919

Say a Prayer for Me Tonight   1511, 3038
Say, Darling   3845
Say! Have You Seen a Daughter?   30
Say Hello to Harvey   3846
Say Hello to the Folks Back Home   4281
Say Hello to Your Feet   2513
Say Hitchy-Koo, That's All   1920
Say It Again   1713, 2950
Say It Isn't So   2437, 789
Say It Loud I'm Black and Proud   3739
Say It Once Again   2387
Say It with a Red Red Rose   3342
Say It with a Sable   1488
Say It with a Solitaire   1779
Say It with a Uke   577
Say It with a Ukelele   199
Say It with Flowers   2222
Say It with Gin   3131
Say It with Girls   1134
Say It with Music   3006
Say It with Toes   1655
Say It with Your Feet   1980
Say Mama   2318
Say No More   298, 2937
Say Not Love Is a Dream (Valse-Song)   902
Say So!   3766
Say That You Love Me   1839
Say the Word   4335
Say the Word That Will Make You Mine   1989
Say the Words   4038
Say to Him   2830
Say 'Uncle'   2522
Say What You Want to Say   1116
Say When   136, 599, 3278, 3849, 3850, 448
Say When-Stand Up-Drink Down   3980
Say Yes, Look No   3215
Say Yes, Sweetheart, Say Yes   905
Say You'll Be a Friend of Mine   3747
Say You'll Be My Own, Dear   2944
Say You'll Stay   4435
Say Young Man of Manhattan   4023
Sayonara   126, 3851
Scaddle-de-Mooch   4833
Scandal   1556, 2123, 2897, 3547, 3580, 4365, 4547
Scandal, and a Cup of Tea   1780
Scandal Club, The   2399
Scandal in the Synagogue   2012
Scandal Number   3011
Scandal! Scandal!   4453
Scandal Town   2614
Scandal Walk   1483
Scandalizing Fashion   3796
Scandals!   556
Scandals Finale   556
Scandals in the Air   93
Scandinavia (Sing Dose Song and Make
     Dose Music)   2857
Scapin   3853, 3853, 4450
Scare Crow Maidie   2635
Scarecrow Dance, The   3024

Scared   280
Scarlet Coat, A   4404
Scarlet Pimpernel, The   3491
Scarlet Trimmings   3920
Scarlett (Skarettu)   1616
Scarlett O'Hara from Seventh Avenue   887
Scars, The (1)   2344
Scars, The (2)   2344
Scat   240
Scat Song, The   4137
Scena (Tingle Tangle)   3014
Scene   3864
Scene and Aria   3864
Scene and Pas de Seul   3735
Scene Au Dancing (inst.)   2753
Scene Changes, The   3596
Scene Dansant   138
Scene with the Grapes, The   4325
Scenes de la Vie de Boheme   2359
Scenes from Some Marriages   3476
Scheherazade   2234
Scheherazade Interlude   1300
Scheherazade Serenade   931
Scheherzade   1448
Schemes   3943
Scherzo   3703, 3864
Schickelgruber   2653
Schlaf Mein Kind   3844
Schlal   4790
Schneeglockchen   4490
Schnitza Komisski, The   3819
Schoe Plattler Tanz   2594
School Bells Ringin' Out   2090
School Days   1902, 2096, 4756
School Days (When We Were a
     Couple of Kids)   3855
School Days Are Over   4209
School Daze   3889
School Don't Mean a Damn Thing   344
School for Scandal, The   2399
School for Waiters   2137
School for Wives, The   127
School Mates   3855
School of Acting   1464
School of Bop   2168
School of Hard Knocks   779
School of Love, The   1274
School Song, The   2152
School Spirit   1418
Schoolboy Blues   4449
Schoolhouse Blues, The   3006
Schoolma'm's Song   4201
School's Out   3739
Schottische   3056
Schottische Scena   4557
Schrafft's   2707
Schrafft's University   3005
Schroeder   4783
Schuetzen Corps, The   2335
Schwabs   1940

Shooting Show   3701
Shooting Star   2470
Shooting Star, The   3643
Shooting Star   3043, 3294
Shooting Stars   3136, 3252
Shop   1784
Shop Girls and Mannikins   4300
Shopkeepers Trio   1697
Shopper's Fugue   1804
Shoppers' Dance   4393
Shoppin' for Clothes   4031
Shopping   1123, 1412, 1526, 1961, 3399,
    3747, 4382
Shopping Around   4718
Shopping at a Woolworth Store   2988
Shopping Bag Lady   2784
Shopping Chorus   2465
Shopping Glide, The   4382
Shopping in the Orient   736
Shopping Is Torture (Even Off the Rack)   3587
Shore Leave   1916, 1916, 2636
Short and Sweet   4602
Short Farewell Is Best, A   1424
Short People   2852, 2787
Short Piano Roll   2200
Shortest Day of the Year, The   514
Shortnin' Bread   4390
Shorty George   889
Shosholaza (A Work Song)   2147
Shotgun Papa   1986
Shotgun Wedding   4118
Should I? (My Land)   2998
Should I   544
Should I Be Sweet?   3249
Should I Be Sweet   4267
Should I Speak of Loving You   3015
Should I Tell You   189
Shoulder Arms   659
Shoulders   3946
Shoulders to Lean On   4591
Shout   4193
Shout On!   2845
Shout, Sister, Shout   1813
Shoutin' Sinners   290
Shove It   2152
Show a Little Pep   3252
Show a Little Something New   2491
Show Boat   3949
Show Business Is My Life   695
Show Business Nobody Knows, The   2451
Show Girl   3953, 4332
Show Girls   534
Show Him the Way   1441, 3848
Show Is On!, The   1119
Show Is On, The   3955
Show Me   1958, 3038
Show Me a Suitcase   4732
Show Me How to Make Love   376, 3762
Show Me Round and Around   88
Show Me 'Round the Town   3045

Show Me the Key   3862
Show Me the Sun   1959
Show Me the Town   2214, 3243, 3766
Show Me the Way   805
Show Me Where the Good Times Are   1990, 3956
Show Me Your Qualifications   3707
Show Must Go On, The   2204
Show Off   4018
Show That Card   696
Show Train   4496
Show Us How to Do the Fox Trot   4603
Show You Care   1609
Show Your Love   3111
Showbiz   1412
Showbiz Finale   4389
Shower   4360
Shower Chorus   178
Shower of Rice, A   4422
Shower of Sparks   2229
Shower of Stars, A   496
Showgirl Victim   2307
Showing a Little Ankle   2069
Showing Off   3960
Showing the Yankees London Town   4759
Show's the Thing, The   1736
Showstopper   4627
Showtune in 2/4   3161
Shpil Gitar (Play Guitar)   4342
Shrimp and a Crab, A   2286
Shrug Your Shoulders   1557
Shtil Di Nacht   1740
Shuffle   376
Shuffle Along   1198, 3963
Shuffle Off to Buffalo   1359
Shuffle the Cards   2565
Shuffle Yo' Black Feet   2640
Shuffle Your Feet (And Just
    Roll Along)   441
Shuffle Your Troubles Away   2757
Shufflin' Home   2462
Shufflin' Sam   4001
Shuffling Bill   4793
Shuffling Shiveree, The   965
Shunned   600
Shunning, The   3509
Shush Katy   1831
Shut de Do'   3987
Shut Up and Dance   690, 3039
Shut Up Gerald   4727
Shy   3288
Shy Little Irish Smile   3431
Shy Little Violet Blue   3626
Shy Little, My Little Girl   3057
Shy Strephon   1768
Shy Suburban Maid, A   1095
Si Petite   839
Si, Si, Senor   1667
Si, Si, Senorita   4121
Si, Signora   3197
Si Vous Aimez Les Poitrines   3214

1929

Slumber On   4201
Slumber On, My Little Gypsy Sweetheart
    (The Fortune Teller)   1355
Slumber Song (Goodnight)   1387
Slumberland   2534
Slumbertown   2893
Slumming   2776, 2993
Sly Musette   2917
Sly Old Fox   2631
Small Apartment   4401
Small Cartel, A   4435
Small Circle of Friends   1770
Small Craft Warnings   3760
Small Fry   3444
Small House of Uncle Thomas, The   2205
Small House of Uncle Thomas Ballet, The   2312
Small Mama—Big Mama   3782
Small Restaurant, A   1149
Small Talk   3351
Small Talk (Marshall)   3691
Small Talk   1048, 4262
Small Things, The   657
Small-Time Crook, The   821
Small Town   4028
Small Town Girl, A   1271
Small Town Girl   407, 1961, 4433
Small Town Girlie (Every Small Town
    Girlie Has a Big Town Way)   3399
Small World   1709, 1048
Smalltown, U.S.A.   3846
Smart   2051
Smart Bootery Scene, The   545
Smart Girls Day, A   333
Smart Little Girls   1494
Smart People   1770, 3924
Smart People Stay Single   2523
Smart Set, The   2399
Smart Set   3365, 4025
Smart Set, The   3098
Smart Set Carbineers, The   434
(It's) Smart to Be Smart   4824
Smarty   2408
Smash Him   1074
Smash the Mirror   4676
Smashing New York Times   167
Smashing, New York Times   550
Smell of Christmas, The   2874
Smell of Money, The   4518
Smellin' of Vanilla (Bamboo Cage)   2000
Smew Song, The   2339
Smile   26, 4020, 4020, 4264, 4019, 2074, 2285,
    4023, 4403, 4666
Smile, a Kiss, A   3011
Smile a Little Smile for Me   3658
Smile and Be Merry   4497
Smile and Forget   4194
Smile As You Go By   3628
Smile at Me   4021
Smile Awhile   911
Smile, Darn You, Smile   4664

Smile for Me   2680
Smile for the Press   4586
Smile, Girls   1709
Smile Is Up, A   314
Smile of Your Dreams   2224
Smile On   1312
Smile On, Sue   3040
Smile She Means for You, The   2667
Smile, Smile   1729
Smile, Smile, Smile   825
Smile, Smile, Smile!   2760
(I Could Learn to Love You When You)
    Smile! Smile! Smile!   3748
Smile, Smile, Smile   4022
Smile with Me   2749
Smiles   61, 1991, 3402, 4063, 4250, 4390
Smiles Go with Tears   928
Smiles of a Summer Night   2536
Smiles, Smiles, Smiles   2959
Smilin' Joe   2462
Smilin' Through   4372
Smilin' Through My Tears   4199
Smiling at the Sea   1342
Smiling Isle   4201
Smiling Rainbows   1597
Smiling Sam   3404
Smiling Sambo   1537
Smiling Through My Tears   4429
Smoke   4422
Smoke and Fire   550
Smoke Dreams   2174
Smoke Dreams IThe Cigarette Song)   4000
Smoke 'Em Up, Smoke 'Em Up!   4561
Smoke Gets in Your Eyes   2204
Smoke Gets In Your Eyes   2372
(When Your Heart's on Fire) Smoke Gets in
    Your Eyes   3735
Smoke Gets in Your Eyes   497
Smoke on the Mountain   4030
Smoke Rings   468, 3593
Smokey Joe's Cafe   4031
Smokey-Mokey Elf, The   3717
Smokin' Reefers   1322
Smooth Sailin'   2089
Smother Me with Kisses   1457
Smut Song, The   373
Snagtooth Gertie   189
Snake   2785
Snake Charmer's Dance   4293
Snake Charmer's Song   2697
Snake Dance   4623
Snake Eyes   1385
Snake Hip Dance   1980
Snake in the Grass Ballet, The (inst.)   1272
Snake in the Grass, A   725
Snap a Wishbone with Me   2857, 3404
Snap Back   430
Snap Decision   1346
Snap 'Em Blues   3614
Snap in My Heart   568

Some Other Girl   2270
Some Other Time   2205, 3207, 3278
Some Party   3923
Some People   1709, 2677, 3055
Some People Make Me Sick   2216
Some Pretty Day   428
Some Quiet Afternoon   1626
Some Ragtime Opera   632
Some Rain Must Fall   977
Some Said They Were Crazy   3831
Some Sort of Somebody   2891
Some Sort of Somebody (All the Time)   4555
Some Sort of Something   4765
Some Special Place for Me   4408
Some Summer Day   58
Some Sunday   4318
Some Sunday Morning   2762
Some Sunny Day   2363, 4182
Some Sweet Day   4018, 4201, 4816
Some Sweet Someone   1617
Some There Are Who Never Venture   1589
Some Things (1)   4863
Some Things (2)   4863
Some Things a Man Must Have   2504
Some Things Cannot Be Explained   1551
Some Things Don't End   3448
Some Things You Can't Learn in College   1879
Some Time   379, 4063
Some Time Ago   4041
Some Times You Get a Good One   632
Some Wonderful Sort of Someone   2373,
    2385, 2587
Somebody   681, 424, 814, 1313, 2598, 3392,
    1540, 3828, 4813, 1804
Somebody Did All Right By Herself   287
Somebody Died Today   2418
Somebody Else   4272, 4793
Somebody Else, Not Me   545
Somebody Lied   295
Somebody Like You Somebody Like Me   1819
Somebody Likes Me   290
Somebody Loves Me   1487
Somebody Loves You   257, 3507
Somebody New   699
Somebody Ought to Be Told   2786
Somebody Said   1447
Somebody Should Have Told Me   382
Somebody, Somebody Hold Me   2630
Somebody, Someplace   1846
Somebody, Somewhere   2961
Somebody Somewhere   3444
Somebody Stole de Wedding Bell   862
Somebody Stole My Gal   4697
Somebody Stole My Heart Away   3953
Somebody Stole My Kazoo   3299
Somebody Thinks I'm Wonderful   3880
Somebody Told Me   1560, 2133
Somebody Touched Me   1816
Somebody Wants to Go to Sleep   4361
Somebody Write Me a Love Song   426

Somebody Wrote the Wrong Words to
    My Song   3741
Somebody's Been Around Here Since
    I've Been Gone   1464
Somebody's Coming to My House   60
Somebody's Crazy About You   1131
Somebody's Dancing with My Girl   965
Somebody's Doin' Somebody All the Time   4450
Somebody's Eyes   4064
Somebody's Going to Throw a Big Party   1272
Somebody's Got To   4416
Somebody's Gotta Do Somethin'   155
Somebody's Keeping Score   4829
Somebody's Stepping on My Olive Branch   1075
Somebody's Sunday   4491
Somebody's Sweetheart   4056
Somebody's Waiting for Me   3508
Someday   1739, 1258, 4286, 3666
Someday, Baby   3364
Someday I'll Find You   3235, 3597
Someday I'll Walk   3711
Someday, If We Grow Up   4584
Someday, Maybe   3920
Someday My Grandson   2422
Someday My Prince Will Come   4035
Someday Soon   1496
Someday Today Will Be the Good Old Times   3715
Someday We'll All Be Free   4786
Somehow   2479, 3823
Somehow I Never Could Believe   4169
Somehow I'd Rather Be Good   3084
Somehow I'm Taller   2630
Somehow It Made Me Think of Home   694
Somehow It Seldom Comes True   2363
Somehow It's Not the Same   20
Somehow I've Always Known   1918
Somehow, Sometime, Somewhere   4490
Someone   466, 1345, 2556, 3084, 3664
Someone a Lot Like You   3217
Someone Else   4560
Someone Else's Dream   494
Someone Else's Story   721
Someone Has Your Number   1240
Someone I Could Love   2750
Someone I Used to Know   4490
Someone I've Already Found   1441
Someone in a Chair   2065
Someone in a Tree   3340
Someone in April   652
Someone in the Know   901
Someone Is Calling Me Home   3461
Someone Is Coming from Dixie   1738
Someone Is Discovering Something   1700
Someone Is Sending Me Flowers   3941
Someone Is Waiting   832
Someone Just Like You   4794
Someone Like Me   2075
Someone Like You   136, 1060, 2198, 2005, 2264
Someone Must Try   4384
Someone Needs Me   2050

Sound of Money, The   2048
Sound of Music, The   4095
Sound of Muzak, The   784, 1648
Sound of Poets, The   1406
Sound of Schmaltz, The   1408
Sound of the Night   4319
Sound of the Sound, The   1962
Sound the Call   2573
Sounds   2801, 3876
Sounds of a World   1809
Sounds of Silence   1878
Sounds of the Day   4319
Sounds of the Drum, The   4328
Sounds We Love to Hear, The   2632
Sounds While Selling   3918
Soup   1663
Soup's On (The Dying Nun Ballet)   3211
Sour Apple Serenade   857
Sour Grape Theme   2084
Souris d'Hotel   1992
Sousa's Marches, The   3701
South America, Take It Away   620
South American Way   1408, 4011, 4174
South Grape High   1734
South of the Rio Grande   1657
South Sea Blues   4154
South Sea Island Blues   4283
South Sea Island Real Estate Association
    of Mariposa, The   1435
South Sea Island Rhapsody   4561
South Sea Islands According to Broadway,
    The   1652
South Sea Isle   3024
South Sea Isles   1923
South Sea Sweethearts   3500
South Wind   446
Southbound Train   1232
Southend-on-Sea   792
Southern Belles Ballet   2540
Southern Charm   4830
Southern Comfort   4619
Southern Discomfort   4153
Southern Heart of Mine   1963
Southern Hobby   3513
Southern Hospitality   1289
Southern Lady, A   1616
Southern Nightingale, The   4859
Southern Nights   1014, 1985
Southern Queen   352
Southland   295, 3677, 3513, 3945
Southwind Is Calling   2371
Souvenir   3064, 3538
Souvenirs   2168, 2227, 3124, 3500, 3921
Sow the Seed and Reap the Harvest   4123
Sow Your Wild Oats Early   136
Spa Music   3171
Space Oddity   3739
Spacious and Gracious   3551
Spade Ballet   4667
Spades Is Trumps   884

Spaghetti Jamboree   3165
Spaghetti Song   3151
Spain   2140, 3953, 4056, 4780
Spanglish   3869
Spaniard that Blighted My Life, The   1963
Spanish   42, 805, 1248, 2373
Spanish Aria, A   1404
Spanish Ballet   3737
Spanish Basque Carol   250
Spanish Bolero   4723
Spanish Dance   969, 1188, 2135, 2362, 2489,
    2794, 2892
Spanish Fado   3523
Spanish Fandango, The   3399
Spanish Fandango Rag, The
    (Dreamy Fandango Tune)   4521
Spanish Fantasie   3392
Spanish Grandee   1570
Spanish Grandee, A   2632
Spanish Harlem   4031
Spanish Jazz, The   1536
Spanish Juanita   200
Spanish Love   545, 1689, 1722, 2602, 1327
Spanish Maid (Nina Espagnola)   4063
Spanish Mazurka   2565
Spanish Melody   2490
Spanish Mick, The   2833
Spanish Moon   3021, 4651
Spanish Panic (dance)   3288
Spanish Rose   607
Spanish Senorita, The   3770
Spanish Serenade, The   2882
Spanish Shawl, A   3149, 3605
Spanish Shawl, The   3719
Spanish Song   1962, 3681
Spanish Sweetheart   3392
Spanish Villa (inst.)   190
Spanky's Clubhouse Show   2541
Spare a Little Love   3310
Spare Me Your Kindness   1097
Spare Rib from the Butcher Shop
    of Life, A   3877
Spare Some Change   1702
Spare That Building   4013
Spark of Creation, The   730
Spark of Life Dance, The   3395
Spark Plug Blues March   2084
Sparkling Champagne   364
Sparkling Eyes   2977
Sparkling Moselle, The   3362
Sparkling Wine   3298
Sparks   4676
Sparrow and Hippopotamus   2317
Sparrow and the Bullfinch, The   2938
Sparrows Can't Sing   2572
Sparrows in the Rain   46
Spats-s-s Palazzo   4196
Speak-Easy   1440
Speak for Yourself John   1580
Speak for Yourself, John   621

Sposalizio   2961, 3444
Spot, The   3696
Spotlight   4114
Spread a Little Happiness   2976
Spread a Little Sunshine   3506
Spread Joy   952
Spread Some Joy Around   4543
Spread the News   2340
Spread Your Knees   1514
Spreadin' Rhythm Around   39
Sprechen Sie Deutsch, Mein Herr?   1569
Sprig of Rosemarie, A   3588
Sprig of Shamrock, A   1051
Spring   490, 1424
(Today Is) Spring   1796
Spring   1971, 2464, 932, 3754, 292
Spring Ballet (inst.)   3409
Spring Beauties   3602
Spring Can Really Hang You Up
   the Most   3094
Spring Chicken, The   4115
Spring Cleaning   572, 2050, 2338
Spring Dance   545, 3888
Spring Day   1258
Spring Doth Let Her Colours Fly   2554
Spring Drive, The   4838
Spring Fever   780, 2475
Spring Has Me Out on a Limb   4048
Spring Hat   2465
Spring in Autumn   1935, 1944
Spring in Brazil   4117
Spring in the City   1158
Spring in Vienna   2068
Spring Is a New Beginning   4764
Spring Is Blue   2736
Spring Is Here   2061, 2638, 4234, 4694
Spring Is Here in Person   4118
Spring Is In the Air   557
Spring Is in the Air   2827
Spring Is Spring   4710
Spring of Next Year, The   1012
Spring Returns   2483
Spring Song   3103, 2411, 4256
Spring, Spring, Spring   942, 3888
Spring, Sweet Spring   4646
Spring Theme, The (inst.)   96
Spring Time   904
Spring Time of the Year   2248
Spring Tra La   2540
Spring Will Be a Little Late this Year   3444
Spring Will Come Again   599, 4008
Springfield Mountain   3989
Springtide   1711
Springtime   1154, 1515, 1534, 1780, 3622,
   1867, 4817, 4839
Springtime Ballet   3977
Springtime Cometh, The   1300, 2234
Springtime Dance   1552
Springtime in Mayo   4120
Springtime in the Country   3399

Springtime Is in the Air   4365
Springtime Is the Time for Loving   480
Springtime of Long Ago   3968
Springtime on the Avenue   3063
Sprinkle Me with Diamonds   2857, 3404
Sprite Dance, The   1159
Sprites of Earth and Air   2977
Spunk   3902
Spy on Time   830
Squab Farm, The   3402
Squabble Song, The   2217
Square Dance   2958
Square Dance (dance)   4314
Squash the Blues Away   3329
Squaw Man, The   4664
Squaw Man Travesty   830
Squeaky Shoes   4847
Squeeze Me   39
Squeeze Me in the Rain   3601
Squeeze Me Tight   3855
Squeeze, Squeeze, Squeeze   2676
Squidgulums   1404
Ssh! Dumas at Work!   1119
Ssh! Ssh! Ssh!   2489
Ssh! You'll Waken Mr. Doyle   4642
St. Agnes Eve   2992
St. Anthony   3066
St. Bridget   2713
St. Columba and the River   3831
St. Cyr March   4794
St. George for England   1235
St. James Infirmary   445
St. Louis Blues   441
St. Louis Blues, The   662
St. Louis Blues   691, 3840, 432, 4460, 1813,
   3704, 4390
St. Martin's Lane (Sidewalks of London)   589
St. Patrick's Day   3746
St. Patrick's Day Parade   3548
St. Pierre   1764
Stability   3780
Stag Movie   4124
Stage and Fashion Hand in Hand, The   2715
Stage Door John   1619
Stage Door Johnnies   457, 3821
Stage Door Johnny   2093
Stage Door Number   4806
Stage Managers' Chorus
   (Walk Upon Your Toes)   1446
Stage Society   3723
Stage Struck   1619
Stage, Stage   1469
Stagedoor Johnny   2874
Staggerlee   4127
Stain on the Name, A   2318
Stairway Leading Nowhere   2754
Stairway Lullaby   390
Stairway of Dreams   4128
Stairway to Paradise   1638
Stairway to the Stars   4137, 4799

Start All Over Again   1605
Start Dancing   3091
Start Stompin'   2253
Start the Ball Rollin'   2103
Start the Band   202, 1462
Startin' Over   4764
Starting at the Bottom   1275
Starting from Now   456
Starting Here, Starting Now   4145
Starting Out Again   54
Starved   3548
State of the Dance, The   1681
State of the Kingdom   73
Statehood Hula   1023
Stately American Rose, The   1753
Stately Homes of England   3235
Stately Homes of England, The   4093, 3885
Staten Island Barcarole   4684
Station   1865
Station L-O-V-E   266
Station Rush (dance)   4190
Statistics   2134
Statue, The   2188
Statue of Liberty   2717
Statue Song   2559
Statues   4170, 4240
Status   2019
Status Quo   2014
Stay   1060, 2307, 3456
Stay a While   4031
Stay and Rest Awhile in California   496
Stay As We Are   3390
Stay at Home   69
Stay Away from Louisville Lou   3428
Stay Away, Joe   4682
Stay Awhile   4279, 1723
Stay Close   4232
Stay East Young Man   1546
Stay Home Here with Me   4769
Stay in My Arms   1119
Stay in the Field   2203
Stay in Your Own Backyard   1038
Stay on the Path   1581
Stay on the Subject   4828
Stay Out, Sammy   3501
Stay, Stay for I Am No Man   402
Stay Well   2591, 4504
Stay with Me   521, 2143, 775
Stay with Me!   949
Stay with Me   407, 3577, 3654
Stay With Me, Nora   1068
Stay with the Happy People   2850
Stayin' Alive   3739
Staying Alive   3956
Staying In   2565
Staying Young   4270
Steady Eddie   4817
Steady Freddy   1561
Steady Job   2001
Steady, Steady   519

Steal Away   258
Steal with Style   3733
Stealin' Apples   1986
Stealin' My Thunder   3782
Stealing   276
Steam Heat   3351
Steam Is on the Beam, The   323
Steamboat   2556
Steamboat Days   500
Steamboat Whistle, The   216, 1338
Steamers Go By, The   3429
Steel Guitars and Barking Seals   3484
Steeple   762
Steeplejack   844
Stein Song   2122
Steinland   3755
Steins   4177
Stella   1534
Stenka Razin   710
Step Across That Line   578
Step Along with Me   3973
Step by Step   114
Step Inside   2527
Step into My World   2173
Step Into the Light   3568
Step-Mama   4459
Step on a Stone   1319
Step on It   3406, 4249
Step on the Gasoline   1831
Step Out and Dance   2168
Step Out in Front   251
Step, Step Sisters   2833
Step, Step, Step   1722
Step This Way   1482, 1544, 4148
Step to Paris Blues   2669
Step to the Rear   2014, 2010
Step Up and Pep Up the Party   931
Step Up and Shake   664
Step We Grandly   3865
Stephanie   157
Steppe Sisters, The   3063
Steppin'   1421
Steppin' Along   2034
Steppin' Baby   3655
Steppin' on It   1989
Steppin' on the Blues   2342
Steppin' Out with My Baby   789
Steppin' School   4858
Steppin' to the Bad Side   1103
Stepping   1250
Stepping All the Way Home   577
Stepping Around   3540
Stepping on Butterflies (inst.)   2148
Stepping Out of the Picture   622
Stepping Out with Lulu   2
Stepping Some   2927
Stepping Stones, The   353, 1657
Stepping Stones   4150
Stepping to the Stars   2728
Stepping with Baby   3243

Strike, Strike, Strike   4241
Strike Up a Bagpipe Tune   2834
Strike Up the Band   3060, 3175, 4179, 4179, 4390
Strike Up the Band!   4178
String 'Em Along   3580
String a Ring of Roses 'Round Your Rosie   4712
String Along with Texas   3342
String of Girls, A   97
String of Pearls, A   3422
String Quartet   1233
Strings Are Sighing   2839
Strip for Action   4180, 4180
Stroll in the Moonlight   2493
Stroll On   2682
Stroll on the Plaza Sant'ana, A   3359
Stroller in Dreamland, A   2494
Strollers, The   736, 1375
Strollin'   576
Strollin' Along   3683
Strolling   130, 1318, 2645, 3805, 14, 1499, 2721
Strolling and Patrolling   1569
Strolling Down Broadway   4192
Strolling Down the Avenue   685
Strolling Eyes   3737
Strolling in Society   3129
Strolling in the Gloaming   2341
Strolling on the Lido (Lido Shores)   3150
Strolling, or What Have You?   4212
Strolling Quite Fancy Free   3865
Strolling 'Round the Camp with Mary   231
Strolling Thru the Park   1840
Strolling Thru the River   350
Strolling with the One I Love the Best   3056
Strong for Girls   3677
Strong Heart   3396
Strong Woman Number   1737, 2074
Stronger Sex, The   657
Strongest Man in the World, The   2163
Struggles   3782
Strut   1587
Strut Lady with Me   3649
Strut Miss Lizzie   2415
Strut Miss Lizzy   4815
Strut Your Stuff   3677
Strutter's Ball, The   1556
Struttin' Hound   1799
Struttin' School   4296
Struttin' the Blues Away   1587
Struttin' Time   3054
Struttin' to Sutton Place   1952
Struttin' with Some Barbecue (inst.)   3840
Struttinest Strutter, The   1033
Strutting Sam   3040
Stub Me Out I'm a Cigarette   2992
Stuck for an Answer   4013
Stuck Like a Sandwich   919
Stuck on You   2022
Stuck-Up   3209
Stuck with Each Other   4435
Stud Shows Us   4611

Student Arch Duke, The   3688
Student Days   96
Student King, A   4187
Student Ponce, The   1277
Student Robin Hood of Pilsen, The   266
Students Ball (We're Havin' a Ball)   2705
Student's Ball, The   3749
Students' Chorus   2892
Students' Glide (Turkey Wing) (inst.)   3681
Students' Life   4188
Students of Art Are We   2665
Students on a Lark   1459
Students' Serenade   2254
Student's Serenade, The   30
Studio Stamp   4373
Studs   583
Study in Black   3025
Study in Black and White, A   3405, 3958
Study in Color   3352
Study in Legs, A   1460
Study in Pink   3384
Study in Porcelain, A   3407
Stuff to Give the Troops, The   844
Stump Caprice   2259
Stupid Mr. Cupid   3951
Stupidina   2551
Stupidity Talks   3441
Stupidly in Love   3600
Stuttering Song   1958
Stygian Shore, The   345
Style   3628, 2040, 2687, 887
Style Show Ballet (inst.)   462
Style, Style, Style   4012
Su L'Boul'vard   2135
Suannee River   3337
Sub-Babylon   2648
Sub-Debs' First Fling   3314
Subito (Nearer to the Lord)   3197
Submarine   130
Submarine Attack   2762
Submarine Fire Bridgade, The (Fighters
   of Flame Are We)   3422
Substitute   2877
Subtle Slough   2259
Subuhi Sana   4579
Suburban Lullaby   3186
Suburban Retreat   3473
Suburbia   842
Suburbia Square Dance   366, 1770, 1438
Subway   1978
Subway (Funky R.T.D.)   4003
Subway Directions   4190
Subway Dream   2134
Subway Express, The   1246
Subway Incident (dance)   4190
Subway Love   3087
Subway Rag   1056
Subway Rider   2173
Subway Song   2707
Subway Squeeze, The   2448

Subway Sun, The   1693
Subway to Coney   1590
Subways Are for Skiing   128
Subways Are for Sleeping   4190, 4190
Success   1061, 3763, 3369
Success Story   1948
Successame Street   2452
Such a Baby   3258
Such a Beautiful World   298
Such a Bore   2760, 3092
Such a Business   4114
Such a Chauffeur   628
Such a Funny Feeling   3307
Such a Happy Family   3319
Such a Little King   2203
Such a Little Queen   1685, 1849
Such a Little While   3696
Such a Lonesome Place   1206
Such a Merry Party   2522
Such a Night   1890
Such a Noble Lover   743
Such a Sociable Sort   4588
Such a Sudden Spring   4191
Such an Education Has My Mary Ann   1776
Such Good Fun (1)   2064
Such Good Fun (2)   2064
Such Is Fame   931
Such Is Life in a Love Song   2516
Such Is Love (How to Woo)   4187
Such Stuff as Dreams Are Made Of   512
Such Sufferin'   3668
Suck Up   4784
Sucker's Soliloquy, A   2426
Sudden Death Overtime   426
Sudden Lilac   3015
Sudden Thrill, The   657
Suddenly   1092, 2560, 4824
Suddenly I'm Real   3876
Suddenly Last Tuesday   3889
Suddenly Love   3019
Suddenly Now   2626
Suddenly, Seymour   2544
Suddenly Seymour   2038
Suddenly She Was There   3548
Suddenly Stop and Think   73
Suddenly the Music Starts   4192
Suddenly the Sunrise   4048
Suddenly There Was You   4108
Suddenly You   1611
Suddenly You're a Stranger   2657
Sue   3846
Sue Me   1706
Sue Ryan   4826
Sue! Sue!   363
Sue, Sue I Love You   591
Suez Dance   189
Suffer   1809, 484
Sufficiency   1537
Suffragettes   2869
Sugar (Doin' It for Sugar)   4196

Sugar Babe   3965
Sugar Baby   2939
Sugar Baby Bounce, The   4197
Sugar Cane   108, 567, 320
Sugar City   3551
Sugar Daddy Blues   3688
(My) Sugar Plum   1460
Sugarfoot   2187
Suicide Song   3934
Suite for a Growing Corpse   2017
Suite for Five Letters   3233
Suite of Dances (inst.)   2205
Suits Me Fine   2705
Sullivan   115
Sullivan Street Flat   1508
Sullivan's Got a Job   2925
Sultana   4056
Summer   2227, 453
Summer Afternoon   4718
Summer Ain't So Hot   692
Summer Day (Two Old Drybones)   3691
Summer Days   4317
Summer Dresses   454
Summer Girl, The   256, 586
Summer Girl   934
Summer Girl, The   2938
Summer Girls   3520
Summer Has Gone   2080
Summer in New York   1648
Summer in the City   3739
Summer in the Snow   490
Summer Incident   1886
Summer Is   483, 2804
Summer Is A-Comin' In   2379, 2554
Summer Is Over   1237
Summer Is Over, The   139
Summer Love   2941, 863
Summer Morn   2107
Summer Night   4794
Summer Nights   1664, 2134, 3660
Summer of Love   1518
Summer Pastimes   4364
Summer Rain   4381
Summer Romance, A   722
Summer Share   3760
Summer Sports   3399
Summer Stock   3970
Summer, Summer   4485
Summer Time   3979
Summer Was Made for Lovers   1772
Summer Weather   919
Summer's Nice   3418
Summer's Symphony   197
Summertime   378
Summertime, The   1831
Summertime   3342, 3541, 3555, 4357,
   4491, 4843
Summertime Is Summertime   3895
Summertime Love   1698
Summertime Moon   4037

Swapping Sweet Nothings with You   1932
Swattin' the Fly   971
Sway Brittania   3955
Swearing Skipper, The   1375
Sweat Song   3831
Sweatheart of Mine   3580
Sweehearts Waltzes   2670
Sweeney Todd   4233
Sweep   1081
Sweep No More My Lady   4503
Sweepin' Up   888
Sweeping Change   1864
Sweepstakes   2702
Sweet Alice   3144, 4817
Sweet Anastasia Brady   1910
Sweet and Hot   4778
Sweet and Low-Down   3060, 4392
Sweet and Pretty   395, 3400
Sweet Angeline   4182
Sweet Annie Moore   666
Sweet Arabian Dreams   381
Sweet as a Rose   1476
Sweet As Sugar Cane   1667
Sweet As You Can Be   468
Sweet Babette (She Always Did
   the Minuet)   2299
Sweet Beginning   3731
Sweet Belinda   2227, 3940, 3942
Sweet Bells of Spring   1925
Sweet Betsy from Pike   3020
Sweet Bitter Candy   1700
Sweet Blossoms   4479
Sweet By and By   3081
Sweet Bye and Bye   4237
Sweet Cactus Rose   381
Sweet Charity   3810, 4238
Sweet Clarissa (Darky Love Song)   104
Sweet Cookies   1516
Sweet Danger   2295
Sweet Dreams (Are Made of This)   1713
Sweet Dreams   1116, 2549, 4393
Sweet Ecstasy   2906
Sweet Emmaline, My Gal   1824
Sweet Emmy Lou   1667
Sweet Eternity   1015
Sweet Evening Breeze   3660
Sweet Fantasy   3167
Sweet Fool   3011
Sweet Georgia Brown   3905
Sweet Geraldine   111
Sweet Girl Graduate, The   2347, 2716
Sweet Girl of My Dreams   3642
Sweet Heaven   846
Sweet Heaven (I'm in Love Again)   845
Sweet Helen   1817
Sweet Henry Loves You   4089
Sweet Inniscarra   4239
Sweet Is the Perfume of Summer Flowers   236
Sweet Is the Rose   2859
Sweet Italian Love   4521

Sweet Jesus, Blessed Savior   3817
Sweet Kentucky Lady   538
Sweet Kisses   4813
Sweet Kitty   2341
Sweet Kitty Bellairs   2340, 4804
Sweet Kitty Kellairs   4650
Sweet Lady   4240, 4283
Sweet Land of Dreams   3021
Sweet Liar   1481, 3532
Sweet Life   251
Sweet Lips   1514
Sweet Lisette, So People Say   4554
Sweet Little Baby O' Mine   691
Sweet Little Buttercup   1824
Sweet Little Devil   4241
Sweet Little Mary Ann   733
Sweet Little Rosey Posey   509
Sweet Little Stranger   2214, 4025
Sweet Longings   4272
Sweet Lorraine   4137
Sweet Love   580
Sweet Madness   3002
Sweet Magnolia Rose   4281
Sweet Mamie   1995
Sweet Man   1425, 2449
Sweet Man o' Mine   3513
Sweet Marie, Make a Rag-a-Time
   Dance with Me   2232
Sweet Matilda   4725
Sweet Memories   3264
Sweet Memory   1497
Sweet Mistress   4244
Sweet Mistress of My Heart   2910
Sweet Music   294
Sweet Nevada (waltz version)   3390
Sweet Nevada (western version)   3390
Sweet Nothings   2927
Sweet Nudity   3214
Sweet Old Fashioned Waltz   3086
Sweet One   487, 3139, 4532
Sweet Onion in Bermuda   4429
Sweet Penelope   4161
Sweet Peter   1013
Sweet Pickings   1777
Sweet Polly Plunkett   4067
Sweet Popopper   3054
Sweet Popularity   3809
Sweet Rhythm   3103
Sweet River   3294
Sweet Rosa Pompetta   3626
Sweet San-oo   3857
Sweet Sans-oo   3856
Sweet Savannah Sue   1980
Sweet Senorita   188
Sweet Seventeen   246, 3792, 1240, 248
Sweet Shirren   2919
Sweet Simplicatas   178
Sweet Simplicity   1687, 3865
Sweet Sixteen   1667, 3545, 4616, 4813
Sweet Sixty-Five   2068

Swing Waltz, The   2089
Swing Your Bag   935
Swing Your Calico   1931
Swing Your Lady Mister Hemingway   4826
Swing Your Projects   4190
Swing Your Tails   3861
Swingaroo Trio, The   4166
Swingin' a Dream   4256
Swingin' Along   1137
Swingin' the Jinx Away   4517
Swingin' the Nursery Rhymes   1953
Swingin' with the Swing Shift   1311
Swingin' with the Wind   3375
Swinging   1573, 2522
Swinging a Dance   2248
Swinging Along   4838
Swinging on the Gate   1831
Swinging the Bhumba   4782
Swinging Uptown   4003
Swinging with Someone   4687
Swing's Gonna Rock Your Bones   2275
Swingtime in Honolulu   886
Swingtime on the Swanee   883
Swingy Little Thingy   3907
Swiss Miss   2376
Swiss Warble   1264
Switch It Miss Mitchell   3782
Switchblade Bess   3954
Switzerland   3525
Swivel, The   3551
Swoop of the Moopem   1958
Sword Dance   3573
Sword for Mine, The   1606
Sword Is My Sweetheart True, The   4787
Sword of Damocles, The   3742
Sword of My Father, The   2340
Sword, Rose and Cape   656
Swordfight   3741
Swordfight, The   1985
Sydney's Hymn   695
Sylvia   306
Sylvia the Gibson Girl   675
Sympathetic Someone   773
Sympathy   742, 1285, 1924, 2837
Sympathy-Tenderness   2198
Symphonic Pantomime (inst.)   4214
Symphonic Poem (inst.)   1174
Symphonie   2877
Symphony   4485
Symphony for Today (inst.)   3683
Symphony in Dress (inst.)   684
Symphony Rap   1713
Syncojassologists   3580
Syncopate   2927
Syncopated City   2389
Syncopated Clock, The   4137
Syncopated Cocktail, A   4813
Syncopated Frolic, A   4838
Syncopated Heart   97
Syncopated Minuet, The   3500

Syncopated Pipes of Pan   1690
Syncopated Strain   2009
Syncopated Vamp, The   4814
Syncopated Walk, The   4603
Syncopated Whisk Brooms, The   2927
Syncopatia Land   1963
Syncopatin'   4192, 4678
Syncopating Baby (Syncopating Sadie)   4819
Syncopation   4747
Syncopation Stenos   3963
Synergy   3309
Syringa Tree   2756
Syringa Tree, The   4248
System   3623, 4241
System of My Own   1173
Szibill   4258

T

T'Ain't Nobody's Bizness If I Do   432
T.E.A.M. (The Baseball Game)   4783
T.L.C. (Tender Loving Care)   2095
T'morra', T'morra'   462
T.N.D.P.W.A.M.   3608
T-W-I-N-S   3831
Ta, Ta, My Dainty Little Darling   1095
Ta Bouche   3295
Ta, Luv   1619
Ta Ra Ra Boom De Ay   429
Ta-Ra-Ra-Boom-Dee-Ay!   4390
Ta-Ra-Ta   1852
Ta Rah Ta Rah   1774
Ta-Ta, Little Girl   2334
Ta Ta, Ol' Bean   3172
Ta Ta, Old Bean   1207
Ta Voo   3404
Table Bay   4579
Table D'Hote Cabaret, The   3319
Table for Two, A   1551, 3401
Table for Two   3968
Table Manners   1815
Table Talk   4727
Table Tango   1878
Table with a View, A   223
Table with a View   1649
Tableland   4147
Tabloid Papers   123
Taboo   3423
Taboo or Not Taboo   1346
Tackin' 'Em Down   4812, 4838
Tact   468, 1313
Taffy   2134
Taffy Finally   3979
Tag   3453
Tag Day   2557
Tahiti   398, 740, 792, 1244
Tahiti Sweetie   4249
T'ai Chi   944

Take Me (Back Again)   1626
Take Me!   2069
Take Me   2135, 1439, 3552
Take Me a Drink of Whiskey   2225
Take Me Along   1360, 4270
Take Me Along with You Dearie   3096
Take Me As I Am   2198
Take Me Away   3368, 1137
Take Me Away to Jail   3041
Take Me Back   60, 3210, 3565
Take Me Back to Dixie Blues   14
Take Me Back to Herald Square   3129
Take Me Back to Manhattan   3131, 4517
Take Me Back to Old Broadway   4094
Take Me Back to Philadelphia, Pa.   4375
Take Me Back to Samoa Some More   199
Take Me Back to Texas   3217
Take Me Back to Texas with You   2705
Take Me Back to Town   2538
Take Me Dear   4119
Take Me Down to Coney Island   357
Take Me Down to Luna   625
Take Me For—   4219
Take Me for a Buggy Ride   478
Take Me for a Honeymoon Ride   4234
Take Me Home   2159
Take Me Home with You   2451
Take Me in Your Arms   4137, 822
Take Me on a Ride of Joy   186
Take Me on the Merry-Go-Round   675, 248
Take Me 'Round in a Taxicab   4802
Take Me Savage   3636
Take Me There   2014
Take Me to Heaven   465
Take Me to That Swanee Shore   558
Take Me to That Tango Tea   3134
Take Me to the Masquerade   1566
Take Me to the Midnight Cakewalk Ball   3399
Take Me to the World   1200
Take Me Up   3724
Take Me with You, Mary   1541
Take More Out of Life   573
Take My Advice   1817
Take My Hand   935, 3871
Take My Hand in Friendship   3490
Take My Heart with You   2397
Take My Place   614
Take-Off   2364
Take Off a Little Bit   4158
Take Off the Coat   454, 4323
Take Off the Mask   3107
Take Off the Sandal   3088
Take Plenty of Shoes   511
Take That   1458
Take That Look Off Your Face   4068, 4301
Take That Off, Too   3626
Take That Smile Off Your Face   3661
Take the "A" Train   4091
Take the 'A' Train   3905, 2259
Take the Air   4271

Take the Book   3180
Take the Eyes of Mabel   2620
Take the Glamour Out of War   1053
Take the Moment   1060
Take the Money   1048
Take the Picture First!   3204
Take the Road   3092
Take the Steamer to Nantucket   1539
Take the Time to Fall in Love   1227
Take the Wheels Off the Wagon   3347
Take the Word of a Gentleman   657
Take Them All Away   702
Take Them Away They'll Drive Me Crazy   1897
Take Things Easy   4293
Take This Little Rosebud   3133
Take Those Lips Away   4817
Take Thy Way to Earth   4014
Take to the Air   4707
Take Up with an Older Woman   367
Take Us Back King George   4635
Take Us 'Round the Island   3423
Take Us to Our Leader   1047
Take Us to the Forest   3164
Take What Comes   3221
Take What You Can   1015
Take What You Will   693
Take Your Hat Off   4558
Take Your Pretty Partner   906
Take Your Time   1918, 2469
Take Your Time and Take Your Pick   3509
Take Yourself a Trip   4777
Taken at Her Word   392
Taken by Surprise   3236
Taken for a Ride   3946
Takes a Heap of Love   4529
Takin' Miss Mary to the Ball   3992
Takin' My Time   3608
Takin' the Light   1637
Takin' the Long Way Home   1103
Taking a Chance on Love   612, 4799
Taking a Wife   2594
Taking Care of You   1611
Taking Chances   3561, 1867
Taking Inventory   1046
Taking It Slow   3608
Taking No Chances   2615
Taking Off   3168
Taking Off the Robe   3233
Taking Our Turn   4272
Taking the Cure   2219
Taking the Easy Way Out   2962
Taking Ways   2455
Tale of a Bumblebee, The   2315
Tale of a Coat, The   1424
Tale of a Decent Married Hen   4704
Tale of a Fan   378
Tale of a Mermaid, The   335
Tale of a Monkey   2793
Tale of a Music Box Shop
   (Tale of a Song Box Shop)   4735

Teahouse of the August Moon, The   2626
Teahouse of the Sliding Screens, The   2861
Team Spirit   3752
Tear Down the Wall   747
Tear Drops from Her Eyes Are Pearls   2004
Tear It Up   1155
Tear Out Your Heart   526
Tear the Town Apart (dance)   4196
Tears   922, 2433
Tears and Tears Ago   3561
Tears of Ice   300
Tears of Joy   3526
Tears of Love   4378
Tease, Tease, Tease   513
Teasing   2358
Teasing Mama (Teasing Baby)   2302
Technique   2535
Tecla's Mood   3536
Teddy Bear and Dresden Doll   1532
Teddy Bear and the Bee, The   263
Teddy Bird, The   3855
Teddy De Roose   4390
Teddy Girl, The   4762
Teddy the Jungle Boogie Man   3134
Teddy Toddle, The   1625
Tee-Oodle-Um-Bum-Bo   2363
Tee Ta Tee   243
Tee-dle-oo   1499
Teenage Love   722
Teenage Tenderness   1418
Teenie-Eenie-Weenie   4228
Teeny Bopper   4584
Teeny Little Nest   2483
Teeny Tiny   1873
Teeny Weeny Genie   177
Teeter-Totter   3065
Teeter Totter Tessie   3292, 4483
Tel-Aviv   3669
Tel-Aviv Construction Worker   2421
Telegram   1155
Telegram, The   4107
Telegraph Girl   2448
Telegraph Me   3626
Telepathetique, The   1276
Telepathic Eye, The   2830
Telephone, The   3873, 2905, 1511
Telephone Duet   2424
Telephone Girl, The   3401, 4298
Telephone Girls   4860
Telephone Hour, The   607
Telephone Jazz, The   1972
Telephone Me Dearie   3520
Telephone Me, Baby   4717
Telephone Song   610, 2303, 3771
Telephone Switchboard Scene   1300
Telephone Tango   920
Telephone to the Moon   719
Telephone Your Riffky Issey   4804
Tell a Little Lie or Two   2968
Tell Her   101, 3695, 946, 1990, 3108, 4384

Tell Her in the Golden Summer   1307
Tell Her in the Springtime   3009
Tell Her Now   949
Tell Her the Truth   4299
Tell Her While the Waltz Is Playing   1516
Tell Him   4193
Tell Him, Tell Her   1161
Tell Him-Tell Her!   455
Tell It All   2160
Tell It All Over Again   3304
Tell It Like It Is   1890
Tell It to a Turtle   4391, 281
Tell It to Bart   3696
Tell It to Me Dad   1955
Tell It to Sweeney   4757
Tell It to the Marines (A Bunch o' Nuts)   3556
Tell It with a Melody   3006
Tell Me   4288, 1823, 2320, 2373, 3402, 3702, 4754
Tell Me a Bedtime Story   3008
Tell Me About Your Eden   1864
Tell Me Again   263, 1722
Tell Me Again, Sweetheart   2697
Tell Me All Your Troubles, Cutie   2900
Tell Me Am I Shooting at the Moon   2950
Tell Me Cigarette (Cigarette Song)   718
Tell Me, Crystal Ball   1580
Tell Me, Daisy   380
Tell Me Daisy   463
Tell Me, Do You Love Me As of Old?   3998
Tell Me Dusky Maiden   2041, 4014
Tell Me Goodbye   2958
Tell Me How   1918
Tell Me I Look Nice   3918
Tell Me Lies   3094
Tell Me Lilac Domino   2486
Tell Me Little Gypsy   4814
Tell Me More!   4300
Tell Me Not That You Are Forgetting   2622
Tell Me of Love   948
Tell Me on a Sunday   4068, 4301
Tell Me Once Again   1602
Tell Me Pray   104
Tell Me Pretty Maiden   1313
Tell Me Shooting Star (Money!
   Money! Money!)   4201
Tell Me Some More   2107
Tell Me Something About Yourself   1874
Tell Me, Tell Me   2568
Tell Me That You Love Me   3349, 4492
Tell Me That You Miss Me   20
Tell Me the French Word for Squeeze Me   2665
Tell Me the Story   4362
Tell Me the Story of Your Life   1596
Tell Me the Truth   1990
Tell Me Tonight   126
Tell Me Truly   3369
Tell Me What Can This Be   2808
Tell Me, What Is Love?   429
Tell Me What You Want   1804
Tell Me what Your Eyes Were Made For   2666

Tete-A-Tete with You, A 1334
Tetrazzini Family, The 511
Tette-a-Tette at 8 2830
Tevye and His Daughters 1265
Tevye's Dream 1265
Texas 3342
Texas Aristocracy 992
Texas Dan 2481
Texas Guinan's Playground 1837
Texas Has a Whorehouse in It 374
Texas Li'l Darlin' 4314
Texas Lullabye 914
Texas Rangers 4311
Texas Rose 580
Texas Steer, A 4453
Texas Stomp 3533
Texas Tommy Swing 4805
Texas Will Make You a Man 4058
Texas, Brooklyn and Love 4237
Texatina 3356
Textile Troops, The 1657
Thad's Journey 2958
Thank God 1059
Thank God for the Homeland 4719
Thank God for the Volunteer
   Fire Brigade 1591, 2038
Thank God I'm Not Old 3059
Thank God I'm Old 305
Thank Heaven for Christmas 753
Thank Heaven for Little Girls 1511
Thank Heaven for the Heathen 1809
Thank Heaven for You 1072
Thank My Stars 289
Thank the Lord 4405
Thank the Lord the War Is Over 742
Thank Them for Your Love 3542
Thank You 846, 2432, 2775, 3602, 3696
Thank You for Coming 2822
Thank You for the Change in My Life 4460
Thank You in Advance 711
'Thank You, Kind Sir!' Said She 2261
Thank You Kindly Sir 2691
Thank You Lord 3599
Thank You, Ma'am 3551
Thank You, Madam 3918
Thank You, Mr. Chaplin 695
Thank You, Mrs. Butterfield 1679
Thank You, No 101
Thank You So Much 1060
Thank You So Much Mrs. Lowsborough-
   Goodby 4517
Thank You Song, The 2681
Thank You, South America 4086
Thank You, South America (dance) 4086
Thank You, You're Welcome, Don't Mention It 4025
Thank Your Father (Thank Your Mother) 1323
Thank Your Lucky Stars and Stripes 4255
Thanks a Lot 572, 1045
Thanks Awful 123
Thanks! Don't Mention It 2523

Thanks for a Darn Nice Time 931
Thanks for a Lousy Evening 1336
Thanks for Nothing 695
Thanks for the Francs 4174
Thanks in Old Age 2433
Thanks Just the Same 4093
Thanks, Sweet Jesus! 1441
Thanks to Love 4798
Thanks to the Banks 2275
Thanks to You (I'm a Brand New Woman) 1107
Thanks to You 2163, 3409, 2540
Thanks to You Mr. Handy 887
Thanksgiving Day 48, 3773
That Aero-Naughty Girl 4803
That Ain't Right 39
That Airship of Mine 3333
That American Boy of Mine 969
That Awful Bogie Man 1515
That Baboon Baby Dance 1738, 4589
That Barber in Seville 487
That Beautiful Isle of the Sea 2671
That Big-Bellied Bottle 1676
That Black and White Baby of Mine 1921
That Bohemian Rag 3397
That Boy of Mine 4780
That Bran' New Gal O' Mine 3144
That Broadway Chicken Walk 683
That Brother of Mine 3846
That Brownskin Flapper 2557
That Certain Feeling 4392
That Certain Look 4433
That Certain Party 1831
That Certain Something 2527
That Certain Thing 4741
That Champagne Glide 1212
That Charleston Dance 740
That Chop Stick Rag 3134
That Colored Jassboray 3973
That Come "Hither" Look 4327
That Creepy Weepy Feeling 1911
That Creole Flower Garden of Mine 980
That Dance of Mine 3877
That Dancing Big Banshee 2782
That Day Will Come 3264
That Deviling Tune (Rag) 2358
That Dirty Old Man 1422
That Does It 4602
That Does the Trick for Me 2230
That Dream-Waltz Melody 2108
That Extra Bit 4512
That Face! 2705
That Face 4435
That Faraway Look 4060
That Feels Good 2992
That Fellow Manuelo 3699
That Forgotten Melody 704
That Frank 2822
That Frisco Melody 804
That Funny Fellow 1215
That Funny Little Movement 2214

That Spooky Tune   3096
That Strictly Neutral Jag   1560
That Stupid Melody   3342
That Summer — That Fall   139
That Swanee River Melody   1378
That Sweet Oblivion-Drink   2233
That Syncopated Bogie Boo, The   3031
That Syncopated Harp   628
That Tantalizing Nod   4247
That Tempting Tango   929
That Terrible Tune   4483
That Terrific Rainbow   3353
That Tinkling Tango Tune   257
(Try This for) That Tired Feeling   288
That Toledo Tune   1501
That Touch   3711
That Tumble Down Shack in Athlone   4576
That Typical, Topical, Tropical Tune   3423
That was Jerry   260
That Was My Way   2224
That Was the Last That I Remembered   4161
That Was Then   4199
That Was Then, Mr. Rassendyl   4798
That Was Wonderful   1270
That Was Yesterday   928, 2864
That Was Your Life   3264
That Wasn't All   4094
That We're Soldiers   1178
That Will Keep Him True to You   1088
That Will Serve Her Right   147
That Winter Was a Spring   4830
That Woman Can't Play No Piano   105
That Woman in the Mirror   944
That Wonderful Girl   1031
That Wonderful Melody   429
That Wonderful 'One' Girl   4258
That Wonderful Rhythm   2168
That Wonderful Thing Called Love   1516
That Would Be Lovely   742
That Zip Cornwall Cooch   130
That'll Be the Day   580, 1745, 4678
That'll Show Him   1422
That's a Beginning   4862
That's a Clue   306
That's a Crime   2150
That's a Man Everytime   1679
That's a Plenty   2979
That's a Ridiculous Statement!   2230
That's a Thing That's Really Wanted   1318
That's a Very Different Thing   4354
That's a Very Interesting Question   4485
That's a Woman   4619
That's a Woman's Way   2937
That's About the Size of It   1264
That's All   4802
That's All Charming   2907
That's All He Wants   2377
That's All Right   580
That's All Right for McGilligan   2358
That's All There Is   2308

That's Amusement   3997
That's an Egg Cream!   3926
That's Art   1243
That's As Far As I Can Go   2216
That's As Far As It Goes   3179
That's As Far As You Can Go   2978
That's Atmosphere   2717
That's Boys Your Boys   4649
That's Broadway   532
That's Called Walking the Dog   3400
That's Class   3091
That's Easy for a Little Girl to Do   1532
That's Enough for Me   3757
That's Enough for Me Duet   3757
That's Fine   4299
That's for Me   1892, 4146
That's for Sure   4423
That's Good   1566
That's Good Enough for Me   2014
That's Good, That's Bad   1207
That's Good-That's Bad   1991
That's Gratitude   3480
That's Happiness   1971, 2888
That's Harmony   4805
That's Her Life   4292
That's Him   369, 3231, 3301
That's How a Woman Gets Her Man   108
That's How Calisthenics Go   4161
That's How Darkies Keep Warm   877
That's How I Get Treated   1458
That's How I Know that I'm in Love   1539
That's How I Learned to Sing the Blues   3428
That's How I Love the Blues   372
That's How I Love You   939
That's How Imitations Look to Me   4247
That's How It Goes   4446
That's How It Starts   4270
That's How Rhythm Is Born   1813
That's How the Cakewalk's Done   2111
That's How the Shannon Flows   2662
That's How We Met the Girl   4801
That's How You Get Your Kicks   1697
That's How You Jazz   2200
That's How Young I Feel   2208, 2713
That's in My Line   1314
That's Life   4583
That's Love   3914, 3543
That's Love with a Capital L   1066
That's Me   1306, 3770
That's Music   2014
That's My Approach to Love   1718
That's My Daisy   4278
That's My Father   3429
That's My Fella   183
That's My Idea of Love   4559
That's My Idea of Paradise   4045
That's My L.A.   3046
That's My Man   4276
That's My Partner   1776
That's My Pop   2653

There Is No Tune Like a Show Tune   2208, 3366
There Is No You   2777
There Is Nothin' Like a Dame   4399, 4096
There Is Nothing Like a Wedding   4798
There Is Nothing Too Good for You   1486
There Is Nothing Wrong with My Life   1605
There Is Old Vienna Town   463
There Is Only One Paris for That   2150
There Is Only One Thing to Be Sure Of   278
There Is Somebody for Everybody but Me   200
There Is Something that I Like About You   4453
There Is That in Me   2433
There Isn't Anything That Can't Be Cured   2724
There Isn't One Girl   4001
There It Is Again   2430
There Lived a King   2977
There May Bloom a Rose for Me   4121
There Must Be a First Time   324
There Must Be a Girl in the Moon   4521
There Must Be One   2490
There Must Be Someone for Me   2847
There Must Be Something Better than Love   183
There Must Be Something on My Mind   2004
There Never Was a Baby Like My Baby   4496
There Never Was a Girl Like You   1481
There Never Was a Town Like Paris   1461
There Never Was a Woman   1614
There Once Was a Corporal Bold   1905
There Once Was a King   2880
There Once Was a Man   3351
There Once Was a Princess   4649
There Once Was a Small Street Arab   3777
There Once Was a War   1624
There Once Was an Owl   252
There Really Isn't Any More to Tell   2893
There Really Must Be Something Nice
   About Me   4354
There She Goes   572
There She Is   1068
There Was a Funny Man   2055
There Was a Hen   2290
There Was a Little Man   2134
There Was a Maid   2717
There Was a Time   1963, 2696, 3299
There Was a Time They Say   3042
There Was a Time When on Broadway   2041
There Was I   3493
There Was Never Such a Charming War   4179
There Was Something About Her   2854
There Was the Punch   969
There Were a Lot o' People for 'Im   4163
There Were Actors Then   4094
There Were Times   2421
There When I Need Him   16
There Where the Young Men Go   1010
There Will Be a Girl (There Will Be a Boy)
   2808, 4025
There Will Be Love Again   2777
There Won't Be Trumpets   162, 2764
There You Are   3070, 4328

There You Are Again   3074
There You Are Sally   3019
There You Go Again   459, 1508
There You Have New York Town   3395
There'll Always Be a Lady Fair (Sailor's Chanty)   163
There'll Be 29 for Dinner   3320
There'll Be a Beautiful Tomorrow   3683
There'll Be a Hot Time in the Old Town Tonight   2415
There'll Be a Rainbow in the Sky for You   1911
There'll Be a Time   2097
There'll Be England Again   3070
There'll Be Life, Love, and Laughter   1284
There'll Be Trouble   4169
There'll Be Trouble Sure   934
There'll Have to Be Changes Made   3035
There'll Never Be Another Girl Like Daisy   3727
There's a Big Cry Baby in the Moon   2576
There's a Big Job Waiting for You   4029
There's a Blip Where There Should Have
   Been a Bleep   2928
There's a Boat dat's Leavin' Soon for New York   3541
There's a Brand New Beat in Heaven   534
There's a Brand New Hero   1598
There's a Broadway Up in Heaven   4021
There's a Building Going Up   59
There's a Charm of Dear Old Ireland in Your Eyes   2763
There's a Chill in the Air   3822
There's a Circus in Town   2368
There's a Coach Comin' In   3347
There's a Comin' Together   1497
There's a Corner of My Heart That's Empty   1707
There's a Country   1477
There's a Devil in Me   3429
There's a Doctor   4676
There's a Fan   2432
There's a Girl   249, 3862
There's a Girl in Havana   3096
There's a Girl Waiting for Our Wave   2555
There's a Great Day Coming Manana   1931
There's a Happy Land in the Sky   4058
There's a Hill Beyond a Hill   3014
There's a Hole in My Sidewalk   4330
There's a Hollywood That's Good   3972
There's a House in Harlem for Sale   879
There's a Joy that Steals Upon You   4361
There's a King in the Land To-day   2317
There's a Lady-Bug A'Waitin'   4725
There's a Land   2111
There's a Light in Your Eyes   1527
There's a Little Bit of Everything on Broadway   2696
There's a Little Bit of Spain in California   69
There's a Little Boy in Every Man   4577
There's a Little Fighting Blood in Me   349
There's a Little Maid I Know   3049
There's a Little Spark of Love Still Burning   89
There's a Little Street in Heaven They
   Call Broadway   3673
There's a Lonely Girl in Honolulu   4037
There's a Long, Long Trail   3259
There's a Lot of Pretty Little Things in Paris   3525

They're on Their Honeymoon   3525
They're Playing Our Song   4334
They're Yours   3960
They've All Got Tails but Me   4710
They've Courage High   1178
They've Got a Lot to Learn   4090
They've Got Me Doing It Too   683
They've Got Nothing on Us 'Over There'   3296
They've Got to Complain   3067
They've Gotcha on the Hutska   2352
Thief (dance), The   722
Thief in the Night   216
Thieves Carnival   3355
Thimbleful   2680
Thin Man, The   3142
Thine Alone   1162
Thine Eyes Are Like Twin Stars   3882
Thing About Willie, The   4827
Thing I Can't Seem to Forget   1275
Thing Like This, A   4750
Thing that Johnny Did!, The   3186
Thing to Do, The   1916
Thingamajig   786
Things   1763
Things!   2475
Things   3636, 4018
Things a Girl Should Be, The   3879
Things Ain't As Nice   2661
Things Ain't Just Right   3358
Things Are Getting Better Every Day   108
Things Are Going Nicely   4659
Things Are Going Well Today   3941
Things Are Gonna Hum This Summer   3895
Things Are Looking Up   921
Things Are Most Mysterious   2877
Things Are Very, Very Bad   42
Things Are Very, Very Good   42
Things Get Broken   2775
Things Go Bump in the Night   1674
Things Have Changed from Then to Now   4507
Things Have Never Been Better   556
Things I Can't Forget   424
Things I Didn't Know I Loved   3162
Things I Learned in Dear Old Jersey   3712
Things I Learned in High School   2152
Things I Never Had, The   2588
Things I Used to Know   4635
Things I've Heard, The   1868
Things Left Unsaid   1746
Things Starting to Grow Again   3418
Things That Cannot Be Explained   765
Things That Go Bump in the NIght   494
Things That Happen Every Day   3205
Things That I Know I Could Do   2317
Things that Lovers Say, The   4015
Things That They Must Not Do   4784
Things That We Don't Learn at School   4723
Things That Were Made for Love, The   3523
Things They Do in Hollywood, The   3375
Things They Told Us Not to Do, The   817

Things to Remember   3731
Things Unfeminine   697
Things We Are Not Supposed to Know   4293
Things We Did Last Summer, The   4743
Things We Leave Unspoken, The   1169
Things We Pay Money to See   387
Things We Think We Are, The   1848
Things We've Collected   4515
Things Were Much Better in the Past   2657
Things Were Out   4468
Things Which Are Equal to the Same Thing   717
Things You Never Learn at School, The   333
Think   339
Think About That   1146
Think About Tomorrow   1149
Think Beautiful   2053
Think Beautiful Thoughts   2940
Think Big   2420, 2224
Think Big Rich   1662
Think Ginger Rogers   2010
Think How It's Gonna Be   167
Think How Many People Never Find Love   1791
Think, Inc.   1047
Think It Over   246, 580, 1319, 3043, 3699
Think It Over Carefully   4759
Think Mink   766
Think of All the Starving Orphans   1664
Think of It   4244
Think of Me   3464, 2477
Think of Meryl Streep   1236
Think of My Reputation   4025
Think of Something Else   4588
Think of That   2145
Think of the Odds   3760
Think of the Time I Save   3351
Think of Where You Might Be Instead of
   Where You Are   3740
Think Positive   140
Think Spring   823
Think Up!   3788
Thinkability   4693
Thinkin'   3505
Thinkin' of You   2342
Thinkin' Things   4270
Thinking   1060, 3531
Thinking About You   3757
Thinking Always Thinking   2241
Thinking of Home Sweet Home   434
Thinking of Me   740
Thinking of No-One but Me   2798
Thinking of Our Childhood Days   3998
Thinking of You   1131, 1297, 1873, 2478
Thinking Out Loud   622
Thinking the Unthinkable   3661
Thinky Thanky Thunk   2254
3rd Avenue El   1023
Third Avenue El   2554
Third Degree of Love, The   1321
Third Finale   4368
Third from the End, The   303

This Is the Love   412
This Is the Missus   1492
This Is the Moment   2198
This Is the Night   2357, 3339
This Is the One   2182
This Is the Perfect Time to Be in Love   1245
This Is the Place to Be   4462
This Is the Show   2356
This Is the Time   627
This Is the Way We Go to School   2134
This Is War   1997
This Is What I Call Love   1760
This Is What I Do When I'm Angry   3806
This Is What I Give to You   3427
This Is What I Want   327
This Is What You Want   2224
This Is Where I Belong   3752
This Is Where I Came In   2379
This Is Where the Bus Stops   716
This Is Winter   2301
This Is Worth Fighting For   4579
This Is Wrong   158
This Is Your Life!   838
This Is Your Year 1976   2785
This Isn't a Gentlemen's War Anymore   1474
This Isn't How I Imagined a Trial to Be   1700
This Jesus Must Die   2212
This Kind of a Girl   1456
This Lady Isn't Right for Me   2420
This Land Is Your Land   4740
This Land We Now Forsake   335
This Life Is Fantasy   1730
This Life Will Roll Along   4550
This Life's the Right One for Me   562
This Little Doll   1617
This Little Girl   3819
This Little Light   3814
This Little Yankee   1991
This Lovely Night   277
This Lovely Night in June   4719
This Lovely Place   757
This Man Could Never Be a Spy   453
This Means War   4796
This Merry Christmas   4483
This Modern Age   2458
This Moment   2785
This Much I Know   1760
This Must Be the End   3368
This Must Be the Place   1699
This Nearly Was Mine   1040, 4096
This New Land   4615
This Noble Land   2047
This Old Ship   344
This One Day   1662
This Other Eden   2364
This Particular Party   971, 4443
This Place Is Mine   3465
This Plum Is Too Ripe   1245
This Rescue Is a Calamity (Finaletto,
   Act II, Scene 3)   3556

This State of Affairs   249
This Time   2172, 2231, 2626, 4172
This Time (Is the Last Time)   4340
This Time It's Hook or Me   3453
This Time It's Love   3312
This Time It's True Love   1564
This Time Next Year   4217, 2030, 4433
This Time No Bananas   2458
This Time of the Year   1278
This Time Tomorrow   299, 1497
This Too Shall Pass   83
This Town   1741, 1990
This Town I Now Must Shake   1948
This Train Is Bound for Glory   3840
This Turf Is Ours   4625
This Tuxedo Is Mine!   3473
This Utterly Ridiculous Affair   101
This War Gets Old   1053
This Was Just Another Day   3895
This Was Meant to Be   490
This Was the War, What Did It Do for Me and
   You?...Didn't It, Did It?   1474
This Way or No Way at All   781
This Way Out   924, 4388
This Week Americans   1060
This Will Be The First Time for Me   1323
This Woman   651
This World (2)   630
This World (1)   630
This World   2801
This World Is a Toy Shop   3710
This World of Confusion   4319
This Year of Disgrace   3186
Thistledown   2768
Thistledown Girl   3791
Thither, Thother, Thide of the The   946
Tho We've No Authentic Reason (Finale Act I)   1013
Tho' Delight, Dany and Night   3308
Tho' I Had Never Meant to Tell You   2178
Thomas Alva Edison   2092
Thomas Jefferson Witherspoon   1955
Thor   1049, 4310
Thoroughly Modern Millie   4743
Thorsping   942
Those ABC's   2285
Those Awful Tattle-Tales   2390
Those Beautiful Chimes   3369
Those Beautiful Girls   1482
Those Canaan Days   2242
Those Come Hither Eyes   913
Those Days Are Gone Forever   611
Those Days Gone By   236
Those Days of Long Ago   1975
Those Dear Old Wedding Bells   4787
Those Dixie Melodies   1823
Those Eyes   3372
Those Eyes of Mine   1699
Those Fat Monkeys   3445
Those Good Old Days Can Never Come Again
   (They Were the Happy Days)   256

1975

Trampin' Along   3436
Trample Your Troubles   4213
Tramps and Scamps   3777
Tramps of the Desert   3660
Tranquil Boxwood, The   3641
Tranquilizers   3942
Transform-ed   158
Transformation, The   3722
Transformation   2198, 2357, 330
Transformation Lullaby   3579
Transition (Bonds)   3691
Transition 1   3411
Transition 2   3411
Transition 3   3411
Transition 4   3411
Transition 5   3411
Transkei Xha Xha   4579
Transparent Crystal Moment, A   2418
Transplant   2876
Transport of Delight, A   220
Transposed Heads, The   4442
Trapp Family Singers, The   4095
'Trapped'   2364
Trapped   2918
Trash   4
Trashy Effeminate Hoodlum, The   2046
Trastmara Rose, The   1369
Travel   4145
Travel Music (chant)   1406
Travel Now   194
Travel On   1031
Travel the Road of Love   3094
Travel, Travel, Travel   1312, 2679
Travel, Travel, Travel, Little Star   3268
Traveler and the Pie, The   4723
Travelin'   731
Travelin' Light   1706
Travelin' Man   2332, 4387
Travelin' On   1222
Travelin' Show, A   2028
Traveling   521
Traveling Memories   4540
Traveling Together   1955
Traveling Troubador   3802
Travellin'   4645
Travellin' Light   4399
Travellin' Man   108
Travellin'   691
Travelling Englishman   346
Travelling First Class Style   4769
Travelling Song   4380
Travelogue   930
Travesty   1033, 1466
Travesty Opera   3258
Treasure Hunt, The (inst.)   2638
Treasure Island   1922, 3485, 4443, 4444, 4444
Treasure Island Trio Dance (inst.)   4744
Treasure of a Girl, A   3031
Treasure to Burn   1985
Treat a Woman Like a Drum   2755

Treat 'Em Rough   98, 303, 1312, 4218
Treat Me Nice   4031
Treat Me Rough   1528
Treaty, My Sweety with You, A   2068
Treble   1648
Tree, The   203, 2801
Tree and the Sun, The   3571
Tree Grows in Brooklyn, A   4446
Tree in the Park, A   3436
Tree Loves   4075
Tree of Life Ballet, The   1310
Tree of Love, The   1462
Tree of Truth   1992
Tree-Top of Love   3238
Tree Without Sun, A   2319
Treeless Leaflets of Times Square, The   1450
Treemonisha in Peril   4447
Treemonisha's Bringing Up   4447
Treemonisha's Return   4447
Trelawney   2041
Tremont Avenue Cruisewear Fashion Show,
   The   2925
Trench Fantasy, A   1502
Trench Girl   371
Trenck Is My Name   307
Trenck March Song   307
Trenck's Entrance   307
Trepak   3013
Tres Bien, Monsieur   4115
Tres Parisien   2839
Trial, The   169, 1214
Trial, The (Ladies of the Jury)   3117
Trial, The   4312
Trial   4788
Trial Before Pilate   2212
Trial By Jury   3204
Trial in Trinidad   1892
Trial of Minnie the Moocher, The   877
Trial of Shimmy Mae, The   4656
Trial of the Century   4635
Trial Song, The   3978
Trials and Tribulations   3515
Trials of a Simple Maid, The   3229
Triangle   3130
Triangle, The   3177
Triangle (sketch)   4496
Triangle, The (scene)   4555
Triangle Blues   303
Triangle Song   164
Tribes   1769
Tribute   2477
Trickeration   3709
Tricks   3753, 4450
Tricks of the Trade   3511, 4114, 2185
Tried Jumpin' You Once   2304
Trieste   1280
Trilby   4809, 4229, 4230
Trim Little Phoebe   402
Trim Them All but the One You Love   4010
Trim Up the Tree   2015

Trust Me, Love Me   1518
Trust Me Tango   4106
Trust Your Destiny to a Star   44
Trustee's Decision, The   1997
Trustee's Song   1997
Truth   837, 2464
Truth, The   2523
Truth About a Big Fish Story, The   4397
Truth About Cinderella, The   4461
Truth About Ruth   4462
Truth and Lies   2766
Truth Cannot Be Treason   2728
Truth Is So Beautiful   178
Truth Is Spoken with Your Eyes, The   2970
Try (Just a Little Bit Harder)   338
Try a Little   3788
Try a Little Harder   430
Try a Little Kiss   2293
Try a Ring, Dear!   4838
Try a Trio   4124
Try Again   3250
Try Again, Johnny   906
Try Again Tomorrow   2467, 3924
Try Dancing   4426
Try Her Out at Dances   3117
Try It on the Day   591
Try It, You'll Like It   4463
Try Me   2216, 2320, 3918
Try Not to Need Her   944
Try the Sky   2332
Try This on Your Pianna Anna   1845
Try to Forget   672
Try to Forget Me   172
Try to Learn to Love   4341
Try to Love Me Just As I Am   3845
Try to Make the Best of It   2657
Try to Remember   1245, 3542
Try to Remember It All   198
Try to See It My Way   3275
Try, Try Again   1226, 2876, 4102
Try, Try, Try   1536
Trying Hard   4343
Trying It On   256
Trying on Dresses   3387
Trysting Tree, The   353
Tsin   1686
Tsing-la-la   1817
Tsivye's Song   4773
Tu Carrisimo   2216
Tu Sais   364, 1656
Tu Way Pocky Way   1890
Tuamani   2085
Tubal Cain   2286
Tubular Bells (inst.)   3739
Tuck Me in a Taxi Cab   4012
Tuesday's Mail (Mail # 2)   1804
Tulip Print Waltz   1872
Tulip Time   60, 4813
Tulips (Two Lips)   675
Tulips and Pansies   3799

Tulips with Your Color So Bright   4509
Tum On and Tiss Me   1483
Tum-Tiddly-Tum-Tum   2216
Tumble El Toro   2385
Tumble Inn   3403
Tumblin Down   914
Tumbrel Song, The   3445
Tummy-Tummy-Tum   1593
Tune for Humming, A   1706, 1741
Tune In (to Station J.O.Y.)   1487
Tune in My Heart   747
Tune in Tomorrow   838
Tune Like You, A   1177
Tune They Croon in the U.S.A., The   473
Tune They Play, The   2377
Tune to Take Away   3890
Tune You Can't Forget, The   4063
Tup'ny Show, The   3976
Turk Has the Right Idea, The   2587
Turkey and the Turk, The   2675
Turkey Baster Baby   4309
Turkey in the Straw   1529, 2415
Turkey Lurkey Time   3603
Turkey Trot   687
Turkey Trot, The   1531
Turkey Trot (inst.)   2528
Turkey Trotting Boy (Oh! You Turkey
   Trotter), The   351
Turkish Corner   2664
Turkish Delight (dance)   3526
Turkish Drill   2013
Turkish Love Song   2254
Turkish Oomph   4131
Turkish Trotteshness   4807
Turlututu   4798
Turn Around   2318, 3619
Turn Back, O Man   1595
Turn Back the Years   3795
Turn Her Out   2648
Turn It Around   900
Turn Me Loose on Broadway   4499
Turn My Life Is Taking, The   1581
Turn My Little Millwheel   3386
Turn My Tears to Smiles   1972
Turn of the Year   2458
Turn on the Charm   2755
Turn on the Lights   798
Turn on the Popular Moon   2950
Turn on the Radio   3931
Turn Out the Light   4267
Turn Over   2481
Turn the Other Cheek   2306
Turn the Tide   992
Turn Those Eyes Away   3384
Turn to Me   2382
Turn Up the Spotlight   3211
Turn Us Again   1073
Turn Your Thoughts and Faces   2389
Turnabout   4467
Turning (Shaker Hymn)   16

U

V

Vanities 3426
Vanity 1536, 2340
Vanity Box, The 3500
Vanity of Human Wishes 284
Variations on a Theme By Bird 269
Variety 666, 3036, 3043, 2896
Variety Is the Spice of Life 4283
Variety Is the Spice of Life, Life, Life 858
Various Sherlock Holmes stories 270
Varsity Bug, The 3500
Varsity Drag, The 1628
Varsovienne 4479
Vase of Flowers, A 143
Vasectomy 4635
Vashti's Farewell 2811
Vatican Rag, The 4412
Vaudeville 485, 2224
Vaudeville Is Back 3594
Vaudeville King, The 4478
Vaudeville, Kosher Style 1279
Vaudeville Pets from the West, The 688
Ve Don't Like It 4340
I've Got Money in the Bank 2761
Ve Vas Germans 613
Veasy Drew 47
Vedi la Vita 3938
Vee Zenen Meine Zibn Gute Yor
    (Where Are My Seven Good Years) 1279
Vegas Revisited 1341
Vegetable Party, The 2041
Vegetable Reggie 705
Vein of Gold, The 490
Velasquez 4341
Velcome to Shul 4325
Velvet Foot 3134
Velvet Lady 4547
Velvet Paws 134
Velvet's Vest 2284
Velvoota Cheese Jingle 1155
Ven I Valse 3113
Ven Sis Du Lieve 4463
Vendors 1038
Vendors' Calls 530
Vendor's Song 279
Vendor's Song (Lawn as White as
    Driven Snow) 4715
Vendor's Song 2909
Venedig, Fair Venedig 4473
Venetia 965, 3981
Venetian 969
Venetian Carnival, The 965
Venetian Glass 720
Venetian Nights 1131, 1460
Venetian Serenade 188
Venetian Skies 1312
Venetian Wedding Moon 1460
Venezia 2073
Venezia and Her Three Lovers (ballet) 3, 3381
Vengeance 635
Vengeance (Ballet) 2357

Vengeance 2732, 4696, 2654
Vengeance of Valdez 3318
Venice 3131
Venice Sings to One and All 2397
Ventriloquism 1824
Ventriloquist, The 2364
Ventriloquist 3955
Ventriloquist and Dummy 3162
Venulia, The 3601
Venus and Adonis Suite 3909
Venus and I Are Pals 4228
Venus Calls and I'll Obey 4228
Venus de Milo 2222
Venus, Goddess of Love 698
Venus in Ozone Heights (Ballet) 3301
Venus In Seide 4550
Venus Waltz, The 3251
Venus Was a Modest Goddess 3301
Ver Der Ershter Vet Lakhn (Who Will
    Laugh First?) 4342
Vera Violetta 4553, 4553
Veranda, The (inst.) 3691
Veranda's Toe 2551
Verandah Waltz, The 935
Verb to Love, A 2546
Verb to Love (I Love You), The 2934
Verbal Abuse 533
Verdi Duo (inst.) 4798
Verdict, The 451, 2472
Verdict Finale, The 1652
Verily, Merrily 2914
Verily, Verily 1282
Veritable Work of Art, A 270
Vermicelli - Minestrone 2464
Vernon 2776
Vernon Duccini (inst.) 4798
Veronica Takes Over 3217
Veronique 3279, 4554
Verrazano Narrows Bridge 157
Versailles 969, 1923, 2843
Versatile DaVincis, The 490
Vertigo 90
Very 3482
Very Best Week of Our Lives, The 4020
Very Careful, If You Please 2938
Very Charming Spot, A 3823
Very Close to Wonderful 4588
Very Far Away 3668
Very First Girl, The 4659
Very First Time, The 4115
Very Fortunate Man, A 2551
Very Full and Productive Day, A 3439
Very Good Friends of Mine 1556
Very Little Thing, A 30
Very Little Time for Loving Nowadays 2761
Very Lonely King, A 1769
Very Merry Christmas, A 752
Very Much in Love 4186
Very Necessary You, The 657
Very Next Girl I See, The 487

W

Wading   336
Wading We Go   2506
Wages of Sin, The   3070, 3664
Wagon Wheels   4824
Wah-Wah   3796
Wah Wah Wah   1116
Wahoo!   4595
Waika Kiki Blues   2462
Waikiki   3752
Waikiki, I Hear You Calling Me   2706
Wail of a Debutante   4104
Wail of the Reefer Man, The   877
Wail of the Tale of the Long, Long Trail, The   579
Wailing Wall   426
Wait   4089, 4233
Wait a Bit   3084
Wait a Bit, Susie   3569
Wait a Little While   3653
Wait and See   718, 1282, 4168, 2654
Wait, Baby, Wait   2965
Wait for Me   2574, 650, 4689
Wait for Me Marlene   3330
Wait for the Big Gate of Lover's Lane   2457
Wait for the Happy Ending   3005
Wait for the Moon   1690
Wait for the Wagon   4390
Wait for Tomorrow   3536
Wait 'Til It Dawns   3272
Wait 'Til My Bobby Gets Home   2427
Wait 'Til We're Sixty-Five   3274
Wait 'til You See My Baby do the Charleston   3297
Wait Till After the Wedding   2551
Wait Till I Get You on Your Own   4703
Wait Till the Cows Come Home   2184
Wait Till the Silver Moon Rolls By   4742
Wait 'Till the Sun Shines Nellie   1897
Wait Till the Sun Shines Nellie   2415
Wait Till To-morrow   2430
Wait Till You See Her   601, 2677
Wait Till You See Me in the Morning   213, 4586
Wait Till You See New York   664
Wait Until It's Bedtime   4581
Wait Until My Ship Comes In   487
Wait Until You See My Madeline   1686
Waiter Girl, The   185
Waiters   771
Waiters, The   3348, 4777
Waiter's Dance   2870
Waiters V. Waitresses   1453
Waitin'   2000
Waitin' at the Station   2165
Waitin' for Ann   589
Waitin' for My Dearie   530
Waitin' for the Evening Train   2201
Waitin' for the Robert E. Lee   2415
Waitin' on the Women   760
Waitin' Tables   3517
Waiting   142, 583, 2846, 1086, 1427, 2193, 2312,
     2590, 2767, 3162, 755, 3717, 4379, 4405, 4016
Waiting All the Time for You   2780

Waiting and the Wedding   1972
Waiting Around the Corner   3245
Waiting at the Church   3952
Waiting for a Certain Girl   4115
Waiting for Life   3285
Waiting for Me   2938, 4490
Waiting for Something   3157
Waiting for the Bride   4250
Waiting for the Bus of Life   2477
Waiting for the Curtain   3561
Waiting for the Girls Upstairs   1329
Waiting for the Leaves to Fall (She Was Poor)   1202
Waiting for the Light to Shine   394
Waiting for the Men   3831
Waiting for the Moon to Shine   30
Waiting for the Ride   4666
Waiting for the Robert E. Lee   1531
Waiting for the Sun to Come Out   4248
Waiting for the Train (Florida)   4392
Waiting for the Whistle to Blow   3965
Waiting for This   2373
Waiting for Trolley Cars to Pass   1342
Waiting for You   147, 1244
(I Was) Waiting for You   2057
Waiting for You   2491, 2698, 2986
Waiting in a Garden   595
Waiting in a Queue   4341
Waiting in the Garden   882
Waiting in the Wings   36, 1597, 3080
Waiting Is Over, The   2766
Waiting Song   3814
Waiting, Waiting   1061
Wait'll My Ship Comes In   3950
Wake, The   4366
Wake, Love, Wake   3865
Wake Me Up a Star   3860
Wake Me Up with a Rag   4487
Wake Up   158, 732, 1319, 3848, 4795
Wake Up and Dream   1018, 4581
Wake Up! It's Cake-Walk Day   3087
Wake Up Little Dream Girl   2092
Wake Up Little Hepzibah   4064
Wake Up Little Susie   3739
Wake Up Little Theatre   2797
Wake Up Miss Aida   978
Wake Up, Sleepy Moon   2300
Wake Up Song   3937
Wake Up Song, A   3091
Wake-Up Sun   2173
Wake Up Your Feet   3343
Wake Us with Your Song   747
Wakin' Up the Folks Down Stairs   443
Waking This Morning   3162
Waking Up Sun   1864
Wal, I Swan! (Ebenezer Frye)   4762
Waldo's Song   2542
Waldorf Suite   3039
Walk   3154
Walk Away   2014
Walk Down My Street   4584

Waltz of Memory, The   2162
Waltz of My Heart   972
Waltz of My Heart's Desire   2385
Waltz of the Cameleopard, The   1086
Waltz of the Mazy   1627
Waltz of the Season   473
Waltz of the Toreadors, The   4592, 3377
Waltz of the Wild, The   4687
Waltz Refrain, The   2131
Waltz Reve d'Amour   2209
Waltz Scream, The   4381
Waltz Serenade   1213
Waltz Song   186, 3772, 3778
Waltz Specialty   387
Waltz that Brought You Back to Me, The   1481
Waltz That Is Fashioned for Love, A   4550
Waltz Time   2378
Waltz Time Girl, The   3679
Waltz, Waltz, Waltz   3384
Waltz Was Born in Vienna, A   2105, 3823
Waltz Was Made for Lovers, The   4760
Waltz with Me   1271, 4352
Waltz with Me, Lady   1770
Waltz without a Kiss, A   4490
Waltz, You Siren of Melody   2701
Waltzes from Vienna   1680
Waltzing   2335, 3313
Waltzing in the Moonlight   1889
Waltzing in the Shadow   1474
Waltzing in Venice with You   3107
Waltzing Is Passing from Land to Land   3472
Waltzing Lieutenant, The   4804
Waltzing on a Moonbeam   2086
Waltzing Tonight Together   4107
Waltzing Wedding Night   3425
Walzer aus Wien   1680
Wanapoo Bay   2636
Wanda   709, 3424, 3673
Wander Away   4077
Wander Off Nowhere   1900
Wanderer, The   1780, 2784, 3545
Wanderin'   3989
Wanderin' in the Wilderness   3724
Wanderin' Man   992
Wandering Child   3464
Wandering in Dreamland   3796
Wandering Minstrel's Song   1602
Wandering Minstrel, A   1987
Wandering, Walking Every Day   2243
Wanderlust   137, 3714
Wandrin' Child   3542
Wand'rin Star   3347
Wand'ring Heart   3699
Wand'ring Lover   383
Wand'ring Man Am I, A   2861
Wang-Wang Blues   4815
Waning Honeymoon, The   4387
Wanna Buy a Duke?   622
Wanna Get Married   4470
Wanna Lotta Love   642

Wanna Make a Bet?   3110
Wanna Trade   4060
Want a Little More   1532
Want to Be Well   3734
Want to Get Retarded?   4584
Wanta, Hope to Feel at Home   3224
Wanted   4469
Wanted: A Fly (Spider and Fly)   2213
Wanting   3644
Wanting Things   3603
Wanting to Be Wanted   2961
Wanting You   465, 3117, 3533
War   3883
War, The   4537
War Against War   4379
War and Rebellion   2719
War Babies   2801, 3737
War Doll, The   371
War Is a Beautiful Jade   3585
War Is a Science   3506
War Is Bully   1169
War Is Good Business   3876
War Is War   1013
War of 1812   3558
War Ritual   3908
War Song   3455
War Song: So Tell Your Children   1903
War That Ended War, The   4178
War-Time Railroad Ride, A   525
War! War!   919
Warm All Over   2961, 3444
Warm and Willing   4197
Warm Breezes at Twilight   4243
Warm Spot in My Heart, A   4633
Warm Up   842, 2578
Warner Brothers   2969
Warrior's Husband, The   601
Warrior's Song, The   559
Wars' Child   1092
Warsaw!   4769
Wart Song, The   3741
Wartime Wedding   3330
Was Always   269
Was Dog a Doughnut   964
Was Ever a Daintier Infant Seen?   4014
Was I?   4823
Was I Blind   3066
Was I Wazir?   2327
Was Mrs. MacBeth Really Sleeping When
   She Took That Famous Walk?   3973
Was She Prettier Than I?   1891
Was That Me Talking?   4522
Was There Love   3873
Was Tut Man Nicht Alles Aus Liebe   1334
Wash Me in the Water   3259
Wash, Wash, Wash! (In the Wash)   2844
Washboard Ballet (inst.)   2302
Washed Away   3209
Washing My Memories Away   2305
Washing Song   4311

Wee Highland Mon   4723
Wee Toy   1312
Weeds in the Wind, The   2153
Week End   4320
Week-End in July, A   3254
Weekend, The   690
Weekend   3970
Weekend Affair, A   1453
Weekend at Hareford, A   2798
Weekend Cruise, A (Will You Love Me Monday
   Morning as You Did on Friday Night?)   2475
Weekend in the Country, A   2536
Weekend Shopping   1697
Weekly Wedding, The   2292
Weenie and Widgee   1613
Weep and You Dance Alone   1763
Weep No More   95
Weep No More, My Baby   3002
Weep No More, My Mammy   2870
Weeping   1116
Weeping Sky, The   3813
Weeping Widow, The   1640
Weeping Willow Tree   1011
Weight of Love, The   4786
Wein, Wein, You're Calling Me   3020
Weird Fun   562
Welcome   599, 757, 4676, 2114, 2201, 3548,
   3970, 4737
Welcome a Hero   4732
Welcome America   910
Welcome and Au Revoir   2262
Welcome Banana   3651
Welcome, Bienvenue   275
Welcome Chorus   3437
Welcome Christmas   2015
Welcome Dance   1991
Welcome Fatima   2974
Welcome, Happy Groom   4550
Welcome Hinges   462
Welcome Home   391, 3800, 3487, 1242, 2330,
   2355, 533, 1604, 4186, 4623
Welcome Home Again   4785
Welcome Home Miz Adams   4004
Welcome Home with You   3506
Welcome, Honey, to Your Old Plantation
   Home   2853
Welcome, Jellie Canvas   1021
Welcome, Little One   4659
Welcome Mr. Anderson   2173
Welcome, Mr. Brue   3882
Welcome, Mr. Golden!   3559
Welcome, Official Mother-in-Law   737
Welcome Oloto   2793
Welcome, Otto, Welcome Home   2745
Welcome Song   279
Welcome Song (You're Indian Family)   751
Welcome Song   2511
Welcome the Boys Back to
   Meadowbridge, Cal.   255
Welcome the Bridegroom   3887

Welcome the Brides   2209
Welcome to a New World   3927
Welcome to a Small Town   916
Welcome to Broadway   2478
Welcome to Brooklyn   3039
Welcome to Concorde   273
Welcome to Greece   3272
Welcome to Havana!   846
Welcome to Hell   2785
Welcome to His Majesty   2341
Welcome to Holiday Inn   3869
Welcome to India   1161
Welcome to Jerry   3359
Welcome to Kafeteria   3587
Welcome to Kanagawa   3340
Welcome to Kindergarten   4
Welcome to L.A.   3643
Welcome to Looneyland   2094
Welcome to Milan   2933
Welcome to My Heart   1792
Welcome to Our Country   1991
Welcome to Paradise   3368
Welcome to Pootzie Van Doyle   1564
Welcome to Prince   4188
Welcome to Princess   356
Welcome to Sherwood   4469
Welcome to Sludgepool   4160
Welcome to Sunvale   4160
Welcome to the Army
   (Brotherhood of Light)   3088
Welcome to the Bride   4361
Welcome to the Club   4619
Welcome to the Fold   496
Welcome to the Kingdom   4035
Welcome to the Landing Stage   4667
Welcome to the Lovely Bride to Be   1783
Welcome to the Moon   2728
Welcome to the Queen   4357
Welcome to the Theatre   167, 602
Welcome to the World   2224
Welcome to This Window   1702
Welcome to Union City   4180
Welcome to Wonderland   56
Welfare Rag   3159
Well All Right   580
Well Beloved, The   3994
Well-Bred Englishman   1161
Well-Bred Girl, A   2803
Well, Did You Evah!   1109
Well Done, Da Costa   4288
Well Fellows, I Guess We're Here   4064
Well, I Just Wouldn't Know   4058
Well I'm Not!   534
Well It Ain't   2663
Well Known Fact, A   2050, 3542
Well Laid Plans   3900
Well Met (dance)   4153
Well of Romance, The   4620
Well, This Is Jolly   3237
Well-to-Do Waltz, The   1702

What a Whalen of a Difference Just a
   Few Lights Make   4847
What a Woman   1306
What a Wonderful World   3795
What a World This Would Be   1488, 2457, 4815
What a Wretched Way to Run St. Anne's   2318
What-a-Ya-Say   1718
What a Young Girl Ought to Know   3139
What About It?   4490
What About Me   280
What About Me?   2392, 3752, 2578
What About Today   4145
What About Today?   4389
What Abraham Lincoln Once Said   4514
What Am I?   413, 4617
What Am I Bio   4114
What Am I Doing?   784
What Am I Doing Here   198, 3603
What Am I Doing Wrong?   614
What Am I Going to Do   1240
What Am I Going to Do to Make
   You Love Me?   2232
What Am I Going to Say   4648
What Am I Gonna Do   2305
What Am I Hangin' Around For?   4536
What Am I Living For?   4127
What Am I Supposed to Do?   2033
What Am I to Do   2729
What Am I with You   1660
What America Means to Me   3684
What an Awful Hullabaloo   3547
What an Evening   2017
What Are Little Girls Made Of   1744
What Are Little Husbands Made Of?   2453
What Are Names?   2937
What Are the Basic Things?   4396
What Are the Facts   1644
What Are They Doing to Us Now?   2048
What Are They Trying to Tell Us?   260
What Are We Coming To?   3308
What Are We Doing in Egypt?   1848
What Are We Going to Do?   3962, 4218
What Are We Going to Do About It?   2665
What Are We Going to Do with
   All the Jeeps?   4340
What Are We Gonna Do Tonight?   339
What Are We Here For   3060
What Are We Here For?   4443
What Are You Doing in Here?   3546
What Are You Doing New Year's Eve   3444
What Are You Going to Do About It?   958
What Are You Going to Do About Love?   3314
What Are You Gonig to Do with Me?   965
What Are You Proposing   1064
What Are You Running from, Mister?   2584
What Art Thou?   2632
What Beautiful Is   1189
What Became of Me?   1601
What Became of the People We Were?   2953
What Becomes of the Broken Hearted   1713

What Better Time for Love   828
What Better Way to Tell You   3833
What Can a Fellow Do?   2966
What Can a Girl Do   3236
What Can Be Sweeter   3532
What Can I Do?   4479, 2224
What Can I Do for You   3651
What Can I Give You?   1191
What Can I Name Him   4764
What Can I Say   466
What Can I Say?   4023
What Can I Tell Her?   2050
What Can It Be?   71
What Can One Man Do?   1186
What Can They See in Dancing?   605
What Can We Do without a Man   742
What Can You Do with a General   4144
What Can You Do with a Man?   514
What Can You Do with a Nude?   101
What Can You Say in a Love Song?
   (That Hasn't Been Said Before?)   2475
What Care We? (Song of Destiny)   4275
What Causes That?   921, 4443
What Chance Have I with Love   2597
What Color Eyes Do You Love Best?   3786
What Color Is the Sky?   2962
What Could Be Better?   253
What Could Be Fairer Than That   2373
What Could Be Fairer Than That?   2898
What Could Be More Romantic   3371
What Could Be Sweeter   2461, 2516
What Could I Do?   495
What Could I Do, but Fall in Love with You   3069
What Could I Have Done?   1700
What D'Ya Say?   771, 1490
What D'Ya Say   2827
What D'Ya Wanna Be?   1770
What Did Della Wear (When Georgie
   Came Across)?   1657
What Did Dey Do to My Goil?   3428
What Did Eve Give Adam for Christmas   1334
What Did I Do?   1577
What Did I Ever See in Him?   607
What Did I Have That I Don't Have   3274
What Did I Lose   3643
What Did Noah Do (When the Big Wind
   Came?)   2190
What Did the Butler See?   4219
What Did the Woggle Bug Say?   2711
What Did We Do Wrong?   2616
What Did William Tell?   86
What Did You Do?   1842
What Did You Expect?   1276
What Did You Put in That Look?   3204
What Difference Does It Make   2780
What Do I Believe In   2177
What Do I Care?   508
What Do I Care   1778, 3586, 4838
What Do I Do?   1168
What Do I Do Now?   1002, 1371, 1662, 3577, 4016

While My Lady Sleeps   4251
While Strolling Through the Forest   2559
While Strolling Through the Park One Day   3989
While the Big Old World Rolls Round   4649
While the City Sleeps   1601, 2070
While There's a Song to Sing   3013
While They Were Dancing Around   1963, 3737
While They Were Sleeping   2284
While We Go Waltzing Around   1831
While We Tell them About It All
   (Opening Act II)   3949
While We're Waltzing   3787
While You Are Young   4778
While You Were Away   3507
While You're Thinking   4646
Whiling My Time Away   2540
Whimsical Peddler, The   702
Whip, The   4827
Whip Dance, The   2565, 3723
Whip Hand, The   2419
Whip-o-Will   552
Whip-Poor-Will   3819, 4860
Whip-poor-wills   4704
Whippoorwill   669, 2190
Whippoorwill (Never Again for Me)   4805
Whippoorwill in a Willow Tree, A   3726
Whirl of the Opera, The   4657
Whirl of the World, The   4657
Whirled Into Happiness   4010, 4010
Whirligig   1682
Whirling   2571
Whirlwind, The   4381
Whirlwind Circle   825
Whirlwind Dance   3154
Whirlwind Trot   1784
Whirlwind Whirl, The   1663
Whiskers   2, 1689
Whiskers' Dance   406
Whiskey Bug   2556
Whisper in My Ear   2856
Whisper on the Wind   1168
Whisper to Me   152
Whispering   1120
Whispering Hope   1897
Whispering Pines   1152, 3641
Whispering Shade   2902
Whispering Song, The   458
Whispering to You   4595
Whispering Trees   2843
Whispering Whispers   3203
Whispers   3296
Whispers on the Wind   4659
(If You Want a Little Doggie) Whistle and
   I'll Come to You   2696
Whistle   3627, 3659, 4476
Whistle a Song   733
Whistle and I'll Come to Meet You   764
Whistle and I'll Wait for You   3868
Whistle and the Girls Come Round   3433
Whistle Away Your Blues   1691

Whistle If You Want Me Dear   4801
Whistle in the Rain   4424
Whistle It   3675, 1173, 4589
Whistle of a Train   1990
Whistle When You Walk Out   2347, 2716
Whistle When You Want Me   2390
Whistle When You're Lonely   2576
Whistle While You Work   4035
Whistle While You Work, Boys   4352
Whistle While You're Lonely   1151
Whistle Works, A   4186
Whistles   459
Whistling   4654
Whistling Bill   3820
Whistling Cowboy Joe   3396
Whistling Dan   3177
Whistling for a Kiss   125
Whistling Wizard, The   4660
Whistling Yankee Girl, The   3387
White and Brown Girl   767
White and Gold Ballet   3899
White and Gray Cadets, The   1925
White and the Pink, The   4479
White and the Red!, The   3732
White Bum   2055
White Cat, The   4662
White Cavaliers, The   4150
White City, The   3322
White Cliffs of Dover, The   3018, 4027
White Fete, The (inst.)   3685
White Flags   3879
White Folks   4504
White Heat   294, 3709
White Horse Inn   4667
White House Resident   2007
White Is the Dove   1056
White Knight, The   54
White Liberal to the Rescue   838
White Lies   3578
White Lies, Black Lies   2710
White Light Alley   1845
White Light Lane   4382
White Lights   4668
White Lights Were Coming   551
White Like Me   2954
White Lilacs   4669
White Man's Hope, The   2710
White Moon   2766
White Queen, The   54
White Rabbit   3739
White Rhapsody   3410
White Rose, Red Rose   1678, 2843
White Roses Red   54
White Russian New York   1370
White Sails   4667
White Sash, A   949
White Sheeting   2290
White Sister, The   4671, 4672
White Slavery Fandango, The   1081
White Trash Motel   1737

Who Needs It   98
Who Needs It?   1990, 3920
Who Needs Love   2235
Who Needs Love?   4542
Who Needs the Birds and Bees   153
Who Needs the Love of a Woman   3653
Who Needs the Vote?   2928
Who Needs to Dream?   846
Who Needs to Dream   845
Who Paid the Rent for Mrs. Rip Van Winkle
   When Rip Van Winkle Was Away   351
Who Paid the Rent for Mrs. Rip Van Winkle
   (When Rip Van Winkle Went Away)   965
Who Paid the Rent for Mrs. Rip Van Winkle
   When Rip Van Winkle Went Away   4823
Who Played Poker with Pocahontas when
   John Smith Went Away?   2939
Who Put Out the Light That Lit the Candle
   That Started the Flame Deep Down in
   My Heart?   1924
Who Said Blackbirds Are Blue   443
Who Said Gay Paree   629
Who Said He Couldn't Dance?   3068
Who Said There Ain't No Santa Claus? (1)   1300
Who Said There Ain't No Santa Claus? (2)   1300
Who Says a Coon Can't Love   4717
Who Says You Always Have to Be Happy?   550
Who Sent Those Persian Plums   3446
Who Shall Be Bold When Love Arrives?   526
Who Started the Rhumba (
   Who Made the Rhumba)   297
Who Swore to Be Good and True?
   (You Swear to Be Good and True) 1080
Who Taught Her Everything?   1420
Who That Knows How I Love You, Love   3588
Who the Hell Do These Wise Guys Think
   They Are?   3600
Who to Love If Not a Stranger   935
Who Walked Across the Water   4147
Who Walks Like a Scarecrow   239
Who Wants to Love Spanish Ladies?   3650
Who Wants to Settle Down?   455
Who Wants to Work?   2935
Who Was Chasing Paul Revere?   391
Who Was I?   4450
Who Was the Last Girl (You Called By Her
   First Name)?   2491
Who? Where? What?   1727
Who-Who-Who-Hoolahan   1188
Who Will Be the Children   1116
Who Will Be There   3901
Who Will Be with You When I'm Far Away
   1120, 3953
Who Will Buy   3271
Who Will Count the Stitches?   3631
Who Will Dance with the
   Blind Dancing Bear   4398
Who Will I Be?   2051
Who Will It Be?   1700
Who Will Lay Hands?   4615

Who Will the Next Fool Be   3608
Who Will Walk with Me?   732
Who Will You Marry Then?   1903
Who Would a Bachelor Be?   1521
Who Would Have Dreamed?   3359
Who Would Have Dreamed   4727
Who Would Have Thought?   962
Who Would Refuse?   2312
Who Would've Thought?   1633
Who Wouldn't   3388
Who? You!   3622
Who'd Be Seventeen?   4016
Who'd Believe   3956
Who'd Ever Guess It?   721
Who'd Have Guessed It?   3201
Who'll Buy?   2591
Who'll Buy My Flowers   2803
Who'll Buy My Violets?   2526
Who'll Help Me Spend My Money?   2041
Who'll Mend a Broken Heart?   3622
Who'll Prop Me Up in the Rain   774
Who's Been List'ning to My Heart?   142
Who's Been Sitting in My Chair?   1614
Who's Boss in Boston   4303
Who's Doing What to Erwin?   2449
Who's Excited   1048
Who's Going to Teach the Children?   2173
Who's Gonna Be the Winner?   404
Who's Gonna Get You?   3648
Who's Got a Match?   850
Who's Got the Pain?   957
Who's It?   1116
Who's Next   4412
Who's on Our Side?   4595
Who's Perfect?   2322
Who's Perfect for You?   2322
Who's Sorry Now   3695
Who's That?   2097
Who's That Girl?   167
Who's That Woman?   1329
Who's the Boss?   4219
Who's the Boy?   1693
Who's the Boy   3849
Who's the Fool?   1319
Who's the Greatest?   2444
Who's the Little Girl?   4644
Who's the Lucky Fellow?   200
Who's the Thief   2242
Who's the Who (Where Has My Hubby
   Gone Blues)   3184
Who's This Chick?   2243
Who's This Geezer Hitler   455
Who's to Blame   924
Who's to Blame?   2516
Who's Who   920, 3019
Who's Who?   4249
Who's Who   4677, 4678
Who's Who Are You?   3249
Who's Who with You   1942, 1944
Who's Who with You?   3478

Who's Who with You   4491
Who's Whom?   4679
Who's Your Gen'man Frien'?   2779
Who's Your Little Who-zis?   393
Who's Zoo in Girl Land   2900
Whoa!   4648
Whoa, Bill   830
Whoa Bill   3298
Whoa Boy   2477
Whoa, Emma!   2789
Whoa-Haw   3020
Whoa Pagliacci   1129
Whoa San   2851
Whoever You Are (I Love You)   3603
Whoever You Are   4038
Whoever You Are, I Love You   261
Whole Hot or Nothin'   3294
Whole Long Year from Today, A   3453
Whole Lot of Happy, A   4798
Whole Lotta Love   3739
Whole Lotta Real Good Feeling   4192
Whole Lotta Sunlight, A   3656
Whole New Ballgame, A   1099
Whole New Board Game, A   721
Whole Story, The   3828
Whole Town's Talking, The   3349
Whole World Loves, The   2813
Whole World Revolves Around You, The   2283
Whole World's Doing It Now Charleston   2700
Whole World's Waitin' to Sing Your Song   2200
Whole Year Round, The   4113
Wholesome Honeys Here at Home   864
Whoop Daddy Ooden Dooden Day   4757
Whoop De Doo   1581
Whoop-de-oodle-do!   611
Whoop-Dee-Doo   2022
Whoop-Diddy-Ay   3841
Whoop 'er Up (with a Whoop-La-La)   2254
Whoop Her Up with a Whoop-La-La!   511
Whoop-La-La   115
Whoop-Ti-Ay   3347
Whoopee!   2004
Whoopee   4320
Whoopem Up   2302
Whoopin' and a-Hollerin'   4314
Whoops-a-Daisy   4719
Whoops My Dear   797
Whoopsie   3924
Whoopsie Daisy Day   4255
Whoopsy Daisy   30
Whoosh, Bang   2542
Whooshin' Through My Flesh   1662
Whoppers   178
Whores Behind the Doors, The   2565
Whose Baby Are You?   3146
Whose Baby Blues   456
Whose Izzy Is He?   3926
Whose Little Angry Man   3656
Whose Little Bird Are You   4537
Whose Little Girl Are You?   4469, 1967, 3486

Whosis-Whatsis, The   1488
Why   109, 299
Why?   322
Why   773
Why?   969, 2430, 2880, 2958
Why   3064
Why?   3165, 3702
Why   4087
Why?   4497, 3221
Why Adam Sinned   2111
Why Ain't I Home?   4023
Why Ain't We Free?   3035
Why Ain't We Got a Dome?   1474
Why All This Fuss About Spain   1176
Why Am I Afraid to Love   3239
Why Am I Blue   4824
Why Am I in Love   4321
Why Am I Me   3928
Why Am I So Happy?   3164
Why Am I So Sad?   969
Why Am I So Sad Today?   762
Why Am I So Wonderful   1297
Why and Because   4659
Why Are Chickens So High?   1823
Why Are They Following Me?   4010
Why Are We Here?   4536
Why Are We Invited Here?   473
Why Be Afraid to Dance?   1242
Why Be Good?   4320
Why Can't a Girl Be a Soldier   1759
Why Can't He See?   2583
Why Can't I?   4118
Why Can't I   4172
Why Can't I Be Happy Too?   2235
Why Can't I Forget You?   2432
Why Can't I Speak   4480
Why Can't I Speak?   4862
Why Can't I Walk Away?   2681
Why Can't I Walk Through That Door?   808, 809
Why Can't It All Be a Dream?   2619
Why Can't It Be Me?   446
Why Can't It Happen Again?   67
Why Can't It Happen to Me?   1784, 2669
Why Can't Me and You?   2173
Why Can't the English?   3038
Why Can't the World Go and Leave Us Alone?   958
Why Can't They Hand It to Me?   3230
Why Can't They Leave Me Alone   3294
Why Can't They Song   4371
Why Can't This Night Last Forever?   1670
Why Can't We All Be Nice   1634
Why Can't We Be Unhappy?   1697
Why Can't You Behave   2331
Why Did Daddy Tell Me Those Lies?   3165
Why Did He Have to Die?   3741
Why Did He Kiss My Heart Awake?   1384
Why Did I Choose You?   4764
Why Did I Do It?   299
Why Did I Forget?   1700
Why Did It Have to Be You   2674

Woman Haters, The   132
Woman, How Dare You!   1083
Woman I Am, The   1630
Woman I Love, The   2220
Woman I Was Before, The   751
Woman in His Room, A   4652
(You Look Like a) Woman in Love (to Me)   1846
Woman in Me, The   484
Woman in My Bathroom, A   2646
Woman in Search of Happiness, A   3456
Woman in the Case, The   2160
Woman in the Palace, A   3802
Woman Is a Rascal   651
Woman Is a Sometime Thing, A   3541
Woman Is a Woman Is a Woman, A   4186
Woman Is How She Loves, A   798
Woman Is Just a Female, A   1002
Woman Is Only a Woman but a Good Cigar
    Is a Smoke (Puff, Puff, Puff), A   2885
Woman Like Beth, A   3305
Woman Looking for Love, A   2617
Woman, Lovely Woman   2383, 2869
Woman Makes the Man   1596
Woman Must Never Grow Old, A   3725
Woman Must Think of These Things, A   3725
Woman Needs Approval, A   4684
Woman Never Understan'
    (Wife Never Understan')   2000
Woman of Importance, A   830
Woman of the Century, The   275
Woman of the World   808, 809
Woman of the Year, The   901
Woman of the Year (1)   4727
Woman of the Year (2)   4727
Woman of the Year, The   4727
Woman of Valor, A   747
Woman on the Run   3927
Woman Ought to Know Her Place, A   3888
Woman Porters   703
Woman Power   3619
Woman Rarely Ever, A   840
Woman Rules the King   2671
Woman, Source of All Our Bliss   2233
Woman Talk   649
Woman That I Am   3561
Woman to Lady   3541
Woman to Woman   1684
Woman Waits for Me, A   2433
Woman Was Meant to Be Woman   2998
Woman Who Lived Up There, The   4169
Woman Who Rules the Kitchen Is the Woman
    Who Rules the World, The   2039
Woman Who Thinks I'm Wonderful, A   958
Woman-Woman   2756
Woman, Woman   2233
Woman Wouldn't Be a Woman, A   3934
Woman's "No" Means "Yes", A   2213
Woman's a Wonderful Thing   3486
Woman's Career, A   2331
Woman's Day, A   4153

Woman's Dream, A   4804
Woman's Dress   1193
Woman's First Thought Is a Man, A   4735
Woman's Hands, A   2659
Woman's Heart, A   3237
Woman's Much Better Off Alone, A   4292
Woman's No, A   2384
Woman's Place   4737
Woman's Prerogative, A   1385, 4123
Woman's Said to Be the Fickle Sex   3051
Woman's Smile, A   1285
Woman's Touch, A   616, 2527
Woman's Touch, The   3243
Woman's Work   2464, 3888
Woman's Work Is Never Done, A   2723
Womb Chant   2478
Women   466, 823
Women!   1017
Women   1534, 2123, 2258, 2546, 2836, 2838
Women Against the World   1101
Women Always Get Their Way   1121, 2509
Women and Light   2939
Women and Men   346, 3902
Women and Song   3250
Women Are All Perfect Pearls   1388
Women Are Here to Stay   3151, 4289
Women Get the Best of Us, The   1555
Women Haven't Any Mercy on a Man   1527
Women in Love   1371
Women in Room Thirteen   3158
Women in Uniform, The   4141
Women of Equity   2855
Women of Temperament   2732
Women of Vienna   3760
Women on the Move   2676
Women Simple   71
Women Weaving   2679
Women, Wine and Jazz   1335
Women, Wine and Song   45
Women with Women-Men with Men   1229
Women Without Men   2064
Women, Women!   68
Women, Women, Women   341, 3117
Women's Club Blues   2615
Women's Eyes   2576
Women's Liberation   3559
Women's Work Is Never Done   4077
Wompom, The   220
Won't Dat Be de Blessed Day   1385
Won't I Do?   4741
Won't It Be a Lark
    (We're Dear Little Girls)   4430
Won't Someone Find Me a Sweetheart?   2486
Won't Someone Marry Me?   3652
Won't Someone Take Me Home?   2667
Won't They Be Surprised   367
Won't You All Fall in Love with Me   1922
Won't You Be My Daddy   3401
Won't You Be My Girlie?   1054
Won't You Be My Little Kewpie   3344

Won't You Be My Lovey Dovey   3753
Won't You Be My Playmate?   2534
Won't You Be My Teddy Bear   3480
Won't You Be My Valentine?   2534
Won't You Buy?   1526
Won't You Buy a Flower?   2706
Won't You Buy a Little Canoe   4551
Won't You Buy a Little Flag   1726
Won't You Buy a War Stamp (War Stamps)   3402
Won't You Charleston with Me?   507
Won't You Come Across?   4692
Won't You Come and Waltz with Me?   1561
Won't You Come Crusading with Me   3378
Won't You Come Home Judge Crater   427
Won't You Come Into My Boudoir   3628
Won't You Come Over   2919
Won't You Come to Margate   1473
Won't You Come to the Party   3439
Won't You Come Under My Merry
   Widow Hat   2826
Won't You Come Up to the Table?   4133
Won't You Cuddle Up a Little Closer?   1270
Won't You Dance?   2884
Won't You Follow Me There?   712
Won't You Go with Us to Monte Carlo   694
Won't You Harmonize with Me   1318
Won't You Harmonize with Me?   2978
Won't You Have a Little Feather   3451
Won't You Have a Little Feather?   3450
Won't You Help Me Out?   4464
Won't You Keep Me Company   2454
Won't You Kiss Me Once Before I Go?   675
Won't You Let Me Build a Nest for You
   (The Robin and the Wren)   2782
Won't You Let Me Carry Your Parcel   1318
Won't You Let Me Creep Into Your Heart   3033
Won't You Let Me Put My Arms Around
   You   830
Won't You Let Me Put My Arms Around
   You?   2122
Won't You Let Me Take a Picture of You?   545
Won't You Marry Me?   837, 3056
Won't You Play the Game?   4851
Won't You Smile?   2922
Won't You Take Me Home with You   2215
Won't You Take Me There?   3626
Won't You Take Me to Paris   4121
Won't You Tell Me?   303
Won't You Tell Me Why?   4299
Won't You Waltz?   2498
Won't You Write to Me (Won't You Send a
   Letter to Me)   3401
Won't You Write Your Autograph in
   My Album   2782
Won't Your Momma Let You Come Out and
   Play   2879
Wond'ring Night and Day   2788
Wonder, A   2731
Wonder Hat   1797
Wonder of the Age   4041

Wonder of the Kingdom   3939
Wonder Where My Heart Is   3920
Wonder Why   3168, 4743
Wonderful   3272, 2516, 3409, 3618
Wonderful!   4450
Wonderful Bad, Wonderful Good   600
Wonderful Cape Cod Girl   637
Wonderful Copenhagen   4399, 1741, 3444
Wonderful Creature, A   1308
Wonderful Dad   4150
Wonderful Dance   1587
Wonderful Day Like Today, A   3731
Wonderful Days   3177
Wonderful Dream   3192
Wonderful Dreams   4540
Wonderful Eyes   30
Wonderful Game, A   2898
Wonderful Game, The   1099
Wonderful Garden of Love   4808
Wonderful Girl   1460, 2270, 4148, 4831
Wonderful Girl-Wonderful Boy   4393
Wonderful Girls   2455
Wonderful Guy, A   4096
Wonderful Hindoo   3434
Wonderful Kiss   4794
Wonderful Land of Romance   904
Wonderful Life, A   4732
Wonderful Love   1549
Wonderful Machine, The   4028
Wonderful Magician, The (Love, the
   Marvelous Magician)   3994
Wonderful Man, A   2422
Wonderful Man   3207
Wonderful, Marvelous You   837
Wonderful Me   1776
Wonderful Mother   4322
Wonderful Music   3294
Wonderful Night with You   1966
Wonderful Nile, The   2071
Wonderful Party   1237
Wonderful Party, A   2376
Wonderful Plan, The   1369
Wonderful Rhythm   4651
Wonderful Something   4528
Wonderful Sun in the Sky, A   1681
Wonderful Sunday   255
Wonderful Thing, A   744
Wonderful Time Up There   4030
Wonderful Time Was Had By All   2446
Wonderful U.S.A. (Your Wonderful
   U.S.A.)   4491
Wonderful Underworld   3204
Wonderful War, A   97
Wonderful Way of Life, A   3810
Wonderful Wizard of Oz, The   4722, 4723
Wonderful Wonderful   4193
Wonderful, Wonderful Day   3888
Wonderful, Wonderful Tulip Land   2262
Wonderful, Wonderful, Wonderful   427
Wonderful World   276, 3329

X

Y

Yo Ho 2490
Yo-Ho 4444
Yo Ho! For a Jolly Good Sail 586
Yo Ho Ho, The (dance) 2019
Yo Ho, Little Girls, Yo Ho! 906
Yo Ho, My Lads, Heave Ho 2851
Yo! Ho! When You're in the Chorus 4507
Yo, Ho! Yo, Ho! 2500
Yodel 3614
Yodel O 2363
Yodel Song 1213, 4806
Yodeler, The 3441
Yodelin' Dixieland 3178
Yodeling Yan 1041
Yodle Song 43
Yoga and Yoghurt 3548
Yokohama 1758
Yokohama Little Charmer 1759
Yokohama Lullaby 4033
Yoo-Hoo 487
Yoo-Hoo! 4210
Yoo-Hoo Blues, The 3292
Yoo Hoo, Hi There! 779
Yoofry 1662
Yorkshire 3322
Yosef's Tango 4082
Yoshe Kalb 4773
Yoshke Fort Avek (Yoshke's Going Away) 4342
Yosl Ber 4342
Yosl, Yosl 4342
Yossel, Yossel (Joseph, Joseph) 1279
You 1990, 3584
You (Tu) 535
You 4038, 4192, 4481, 3041
You After All These Years 3074
You Ain't Gonna Pick Up Where You
    Left Off 105
You Ain't Gonna Shake Them Feathers
    No More 1729
You Ain't Got No Savoir-Faire 111
You Ain't Got Time for Love 1763
You Ain't Heard Nothin' Yet 3985
You Ain't Hurtin' Your Ole Lady None 3564
You Ain't No Astronaut 40
You Ain't Nothin' Yet 646
You Ain't One, Two, Three 1259
You Ain't Seen Ball 1099
You Ain't Seen Nuthin' Yet 2231
You Ain't Seen the Last of Me 154
You Ain't So Hot 3365
You All Remember Jack 494
You Alone 1134
You Alone Would Do 4001
You Always Love the Same Girl 834
You Always Talk of Friendship 3069
You and I 357, 721, 765, 767, 1047, 1090, 1093
You and I (In Old Versailles) 1486
You and I 2159, 2186, 2723
You & I 2854
You and I 3042, 4219

You and I and Cupid 2158
You And I Are Changing Too 2677
You and I Are Passersby 3680
You and I Atta Baby 4283, 230
You and I Could Be Just Like That 2540
You and I Know 4569
You and I Love 934
You and I, Love 3900
You and I Love You and Me 608
You and Me 146, 1729, 1921, 2366, 2446, 3976
You and Only You 20, 345
You and the Girl You Love 4473
You and the Night and the Music 4159, 3699
You and You and Me 4077
You and Your Broken Heart 2748
You Appeal to Me 1679, 2602, 1883
You Are 3112
You Are All I've Wanted 1352
You Are All That's Beautiful 4798
You Are All the World to Me 1525, 3765
You Are an Orphan 762
You Are Beautiful 1315
You Are Doing Very Well 4361
You Are for Loving 372, 2805, 3630
You Are Free 168, 2614
You Are Love 3020, 3949
You Are Me, I Am Thee 1262
You Are Mine Evermore 771
You Are Music 3465
You Are My Darlin' Bride 3035
You Are My Day Dreams 1491
You Are My Downfall 4428
You Are My Fiancee 3820
You Are My Gold 2177
You Are My Heart's Delight 4792
You Are My Heaven 4083
You Are My Hope, Dear 214
You Are My Ideal 2022
You Are My Little Cupid 1565
You Are My Lucky Star 3992, 544
You Are My Melody 1763
You Are My Rain Beau 1688
You Are My Solace 3670
You Are My Songs 1680, 1681
You Are My Woman 1145
You Are Never Away 85
You Are Not Real 170
You Are Not the One for Me 263
You Are Romance 204
You Are So Beyond 2754
You Are So Fair 247
You Are So Lovely and I Am So Lonely 4059
You Are Something Very Special 2968
You Are Standing on My Bed 1717
You Are Still My Boy 900
You Are the One 4550
You Are the Only One 2307
You Are the Only Song 2470
You Are the Someone 1963
You Are the Tree 4617

You're a Grand Old Flag   1478, 1480, 4390
You're a Great Big, Blue-Eyed Baby Boy   4806
You're a Hero   102
You're a Liar   4693
You're a Little Young for the Job   2033
You're a Long, Long Way from America   3815
You're a Lovable Lunatic   3869
You're a Lucky Guy   889
You're a Magician   4021
You're a Man   4186
You're a Mean One, Mr. Grinch   2015
You're a Perfect Jewel to Me   4841
You're a Perfect Little Lady   1533
You're a Queer One, Julie Jordan   660
You're a Regular Girl   4712
You're a Rock   2583
You're a Standout   3442
You're a Stranger in This Neighborhood   615
You're a Sweet Patootie   1886
You're a Wonderful Girl   1722
You're About to Be Beautiful   2535
You're All That I Need   2070
You're All That Queed   2070
You're All the World to Me   3387, 3655, 4741
You're Altogether Model Girls   1925
You're an Eyeful   398
You're an Indian   830
You're an Old Smoothie   3139, 4267
You're As English As   2355
You're As Young As You Feel   2535
You're Asking Me   82
You're at the Music Hall   2737
You're Awfully Smart   4143
You're Bad for Me   817
You're Beautiful   508
You're Colossal   4542
You're Dancing Inside Me   573
You're Dead!   657
You're Delicious   322
You're Devastating   3735
You're Divine   314
You're Dreaming   2618
You're Dreamlike   3813, 4826
You're Driving Me Crazy   3175, 4023
You're Drunk, By Gosh, You're Drunk   1910
You're Dull Johnny   4635
You're Everything in the World I Love   4764
You're Everywhere   4372
You're Exactly My Style of Girl   4589
You're Falling in Love After All   1911
You're False   3035
You're Far Away from Home   4693
You're Far from Wonderful   2554
You're Far Too Near Me   1284
You're Getting to Be a Habit with Me   1359
You're Getting Younger Every Day   2874
You're Going Somewhere, We're Going Nowhere   426
You're Going to Lose Your Husband If You Do   687
You're Gone   4083
You're Gonna Dance with Me, Willie   1791

You're Gonna Love Tomorrow   1329
You're Good for My Morale   2748
You're Gorgeous, You're Fantastic   1974
You're Gwine to Get Something What You
   Don't Have   4804
You're Here and I'm Here   2424, 2761, 3398, 3627, 4644
You're Home   952
You're in Heidelberg   4188
You're in Kentucky   487
You're in Love   1453, 3988, 4372, 4784
You're in New York Now   4029
You're in Paree   662
You're in Paris   367
You're Invited to Attend a Dream   4006
You're Just a Little Better (Than the One I Thought
   Was Best)   3397
You're Just a No Account   889
You're Just a Perfect Peach Beyond My Reach
   2358, 3996
You're Just in Love   619, 4264, 789
You're Just Like a Rose   1631
You're Just Made to Order for Me   2299
You're Just the Boy for Me   3855
You're Just the Girlie   3738
You're Just the Girlie that I Adore   1151
You're Just the One I've Waited For   1557, 4599
You're Just the Same to Me   2155
You're Just the Sort of Boy for a Girl Like Me   1332
You're Like   4623
You're Like a Red, Red Rose   2856
You're Like a Toy Balloon   662
You're Living Right Next Door to Heaven When You
   Live in Dixieland   1823
You're Lonely and I'm Lonely   2597
You're Looking Very Good, Marie   1440
You're Lovely Love   2705
You're Loving Me   3711
You're Lucky to Me   443
You're Married Under False Pretenses   3591
You're Mine   424, 2614
You're Mine, All Mine   596
You're Momma's   1864
You're More than a Name and Address   2397
You're Musical   2368
You're My Baby   4206
You're My Boy   4642
You're My Everything   2423
You're My Family Now   1099
You're My Favorite Lullabye   2648
You're My Girl   632, 1457
You're My Girl (Boy)   1886
You're My Girl   4743
You're My Happiness   3956
You're My Happy Ending   4818
You're My Honey   1798
You're My Kind of Ugly   3410
You're My Last Chance   843
You're My Man   1233
You're My Relaxation   3103
You're My Rose   2807, 4199

Z

Chronological Index

When looking through the dates in this index note dates such as 00/00/1934. The zeros indicate that the exact opening date is not known; available records indicate only the year a particular show opened.

1877

Old Lavender   09/03/1877

1879

His-Mud-Scow-Pinafore   02/21/1879

1881

Cinderella at School   00/00/1881
Billee Taylor   02/19/1881

1884

1776   02/26/1884
Little Duke,The   08/04/1884

1886

Leather Patch, The   02/15/1886
Erminie   05/10/1886
Bridal Trap, The   05/31/1886

1887

Dorothy   11/05/1887

1889

Bluebeard Jr. or Fatima and   01/13/1889
   the Fairy
Seven Ages, The   10/14/1889

1891

Robin Hood   09/28/1891

1892

Fencing Master, The   11/14/1892
Isle of Champagne, The   12/31/1892

1893

La Vivandiere   00/00/1893
Woman-King, The   00/00/1893
Friend Fritz   04/17/1893
Panjandrum   05/01/1893
Girofle-Girofla   05/08/1893
Up to Date   05/15/1893
Knickerbockers, The   06/03/1893
Algerian, The   10/23/1893

1894

Passing Show, The   05/12/1894
Dr. Syntax   06/23/1894
Little Trooper, The   08/30/1894
Devil's Deputy, The   09/10/1894
Gaiety Girl, A   09/18/1894
Little Christopher Columbus 10/15/1894
Rob Roy   10/21/1894
Queen of Brilliants   11/07/1894
Brownies, The   11/12/1894
Prince Ananias   11/20/1894
Jacinta or the Maid of   11/26/1894
   Manzarillo
Flams, The   11/26/1894

1895

Twentieth Century Girl,   The 00/00/1895
Off the Earth   01/21/1895
Madeleine, or the Magic   02/25/1895
   Kiss
Grand Vizier, The   03/04/1895
Aladdin, Jr.   04/08/1895
Tzigane, The   05/16/1895
Daughter of the Revolution, 05/27/1895
   The
Merry World, The (1895)   06/08/1895
Sphinx, The   07/08/1895
Kismet   08/12/1895
Fleur-De-Lis   08/29/1895

Day and a Night in New   08/30/1895
    York, A
Bathing Girl, The   09/02/1895
Princess Bonnie   09/02/1895
Chieftain, The   09/09/1895
His Excellency   10/14/1895
Shop Girl, The   10/28/1895
Merry Countess, The   11/02/1895
Wizard of the Nile, The   11/21/1895
Excelsior, Jr.   11/25/1895
Stag Party, or a Hero in   12/17/1895
    Spite of Himself, A
Artists' Model, An   12/17/1895
School Girl, The   12/30/1895

1896

At Jolly 'Coon'-ey Island   00/00/1896
Minstrel of Clare   00/00/1896
War-Time Wedding or, In   00/00/1896
    Mexico in 1847, A
Black Sheep and How It Came   01/06/1896
    to Washington, A
Gentleman Joe, the Hansom   01/06/1896
    Cabby
Lady Slavey, The   02/03/1896
Goddess of Truth, The   02/26/1896
El Capitan   04/20/1896
In Gay New York   05/25/1896
Caliph, The   09/03/1896
Geisha, The   09/09/1896
Half a King   09/14/1896
Gold Bug, The   09/14/1896
Lost, Strayed or Stolen   09/16/1896
Parlor Match, A   09/21/1896
Santa Maria   09/24/1896
Brian Boru   10/19/1896
Jack and the Beanstalk   11/02/1896
Mandarin, The   11/02/1896
Girl from Paris, The   12/08/1896
Dorcas   12/21/1896

1897

Shamus O'Brien   01/05/1897
Boy Wanted, A   01/18/1897
At Gay Coney Island   02/01/1897
Under the Red Globe   02/18/1897
La Falote   03/01/1897
Boys of Kilkenny, The   03/15/1897
Serenade, The   03/16/1897
Gayest Manhattan or Around   03/22/1897
    New York in Ninety Minutes
Mrs. Radley Barton's Ball   03/26/1897
    or In Greater New York
Miss Manhattan   03/30/1897
Wedding Day, The   04/08/1897
Circus Girl, The   04/23/1897

Isle of Gold, The   04/26/1897
At the French Ball   04/26/1897
Sweet Inniscarra   04/26/1897
Good Mr. Best, The   08/30/1897
Very Little Faust and Much   08/30/1897
    Marguerite
In Town   09/06/1897
Stranger in New York   09/13/1897
French Maid, The   09/27/1897
Belle of New York, The   09/28/1897
La Poupee   10/21/1897
Idol's Eye, The   10/25/1897
1999   11/15/1897
Pousse-Cafe, or the Worst   12/02/1897
    Born
Highwayman, The   12/13/1897
Ballet Girl, The   12/21/1897
Telephone Girl, The   12/27/1897

1898

Gayest Manhattan   00/00/1898
Hot Old Time   00/00/1898
Hotel Topsy-Turvy   00/00/1898
Governors, The   01/03/1898
Who Is Who   02/07/1898
Normandy Wedding, A   02/21/1898
Monte Carlo   03/21/1898
Trip to Coontown, A   04/04/1898
Bride Elect, The   04/11/1898
Koreans, The   05/03/1898
War Bubbles   05/16/1898
Con-Curers, The   05/17/1898
Clorindy, the Origin of the   07/05/1898
    Cakewalk
Kings of Koondom   08/00/1898
Runaway Girl, A   08/25/1898
Charlatan, The   09/05/1898
Hurly Burly   09/08/1898
Golden Horseshoe, The   09/15/1898
Wine, Women and Song   09/19/1898
Little Corporal, The   09/19/1898
Fortune Teller, The   09/26/1898
Sure Cure, A   09/26/1898
Cyranose de Bricabrac   11/03/1898
Dangerous Maid, A   11/12/1898
Jolly Musketeer, The   11/14/1898
Little Host, The   12/26/1898
American Beauty, An   12/28/1898

1899

Jes' Lak White Fo'ks   00/00/1899
Man in the Moon, The   00/00/1899
Onions   00/00/1899
Smugglers of Badayez, The   00/00/1899
Wise Guy, The   00/00/1899
Zaza   00/00/1899
Catherine   01/19/1899

Female Drummer, A 01/23/1899
In Gay Paree 03/20/1899
Helter Skelter 04/06/1899
Arabian Girl and 40 04/29/1899
   Thieves, An
Mother Goose 05/01/1899
Rounders, The 07/12/1899
Cyrano de Bergerac 09/18/1899
Rogers Brothers in Wall 09/18/1899
   Street, The
Whirl-i-gig 09/21/1899
Singing Girl, The 10/23/1899
Sister Mary 10/27/1899
Papa's Wife 11/13/1899
Greek Slave, A 11/28/1899
Ameer, The 12/04/1899
Barbara Fidgety 12/07/1899
Three Little Lambs 12/25/1899

1900

Sons of Ham 00/00/1900
Chris and the Wonderful 01/01/1900
   Lamp
Little Red Riding Hood 01/08/1900
Broadway to Tokio 01/23/1900
Princess Chic, The 02/17/1900
Hearts Are Trumps 02/21/1900
Aunt Hannah 02/22/1900
Mam'selle 'Awkins 02/26/1900
By the Sad Sea Waves 03/05/1900
Regatta Girl, The 03/14/1900
Casino Girl, The 03/19/1900
Viceroy, The 04/09/1900
Knickerbocker Girl, The 06/15/1900
Cadet Girl, The 07/25/1900
Quo Vass Is! 09/06/1900
Rose of Persia 09/06/1900
Fiddle-Dee-Dee 09/06/1900
Monks of Malabar, The 09/14/1900
Rogers Brothers in Central 09/17/1900
   Park, The
Belle of Bohemia, The 09/24/1900
Million Dollars, A 09/27/1900
San Toy, or the Emperor's 10/01/1900
   Own
Military Maid, The 10/05/1900
Arizona 10/18/1900
Hodge, Podge & Co. 10/23/1900
Belle of Bridgeport, The 10/29/1900
Nell Go In 10/31/1900
Foxy Quiller 11/05/1900
Florodora 11/10/1900
Star and Garter 11/26/1900
Sweet Anne Page 12/03/1900
Madge Smith, Attorney 12/10/1900
After Office Hours 12/24/1900
Giddy Throng, The 12/24/1900
Royal Rogue, A 12/24/1900

Miss Prinnt 12/25/1900
Burgomaster, The 12/31/1900

1901

Cannibal King, The 00/00/1901
Champagne Charlie 00/00/1901
Curl and the Judge, The 00/00/1901
Little Dutch Girl, A 00/00/1901
Little Miss Modesty 00/00/1901
Miss Bob White 00/00/1901
My Antoinette 00/00/1901
Girl from Up There, The 01/07/1901
Garrett O'Magh 01/07/1901
Night of the Fourth, The 01/21/1901
Vienna Life 01/23/1901
Little Joker, The 01/27/1901
My Lady 02/11/1901
Governor's Son, The 02/25/1901
Exhibit II 03/10/1901
Romance of Athlone, A 03/18/1901
Prima Donna, The 04/17/1901
King's Carnival, The 05/13/1901
Strollers, The 06/24/1901
Melodius Menu, The 08/01/1901
Tom Moore 08/31/1901
Rogers Brothers in 09/02/1901
   Washington, The
Hoity Toity 09/05/1901
Messenger Boy, The 09/16/1901
Ladies' Paradise, The 09/16/1901
Circus Day 09/30/1901
Liberty Belles, The 09/30/1901
New Yorkers, The 10/07/1901
Sweet Marie 10/10/1901
Little Duchess, The 10/14/1901
Sleeping Beauty and the 11/04/1901
   Beast, The
Supper Club, The 12/23/1901

1902

Explorers, The 00/00/1902
Huckleberry Finn 00/00/1902
Zig Zag Alley 00/00/1902
Toreador, The 01/06/1902
Dolly Varden 01/27/1902
Maid Marian 01/27/1902
Uncle Tom's Cabin 01/27/1902
Hall of Fame, The 01/30/1902
Miss Simplicity 02/10/1902
Foxy Grandpa 02/17/1902
Belle of Broadway, The 03/17/1902
Show Girl or the Magic Cap, 05/05/1902
   The
Wild Rose, The 05/05/1902
King Dodo 05/12/1902
Storks, The 05/18/1902

Chinese Honeymoon, A   06/02/1902
Chaperons, The   06/05/1902
Defender, The   07/03/1902
Sally in Our Alley   08/29/1902
Emerald Isle, The   09/01/1902
Rogers Brothers in Harvard,   09/01/1902
   The
King Highball   09/06/1902
Twirly Whirly   09/11/1902
Old Limerick Town   09/14/1902
Country Girl, A   09/22/1902
Tommy Rot   10/20/1902
Silver Slipper, The   10/27/1902
Mocking Bird, The   11/10/1902
Fad and Folly   11/27/1902
Hungry Women of 1903   12/05/1902
When Johnny Comes Marching   12/16/1902
   Home
Paraders, The   12/21/1902
Sultan of Sulu, The   12/29/1902
Billionaire, The   12/29/1902

1903

Babes in the Wood   00/00/1903
Baron Humbug   00/00/1903
Darktown Circus Day   00/00/1903
Sis Hopkins   00/00/1903
Tom Tom   00/00/1903
Mr. Pickwick   01/19/1903
Mr. Bluebeard   01/21/1903
Wizard of Oz, The   01/21/1903
Jewel of Asia, The   02/16/1903
Nancy Brown   02/16/1903
In Dahomey   02/18/1903
Prince of Pilsen, The   03/17/1903
Running for Office   04/27/1903
My Lady Peggy Goes to Town   05/04/1903
Runaways, The   05/11/1903
Punch, Judy & Co.   06/01/1903
Auf Japan   06/07/1903
Blonde in Black, The   06/08/1903
Mid Summer Night's Fancies   06/22/1903
Princess of Kensington, A   08/31/1903
Three Little Maids   09/01/1903
Arrah-Na-Pogue   09/07/1903
Rogers Brothers in London,   09/07/1903
   The
Peggy from Paris   09/10/1903
Jersey Lily, The   09/14/1903
Under Cover   09/14/1903
Whoop-de-doo   09/24/1903
Fisher Maiden, The   10/05/1903
Babes in Toyland   10/13/1903
Girl from Kay's, The   11/02/1903
Office Boy, The   11/02/1903
Mrs. Delany of Newport   11/03/1903
Red Feather   11/09/1903

Babette   11/16/1903
Winsome Winnie   12/01/1903
Mother Goose   12/02/1903
Mam'selle Napoleon   12/08/1903
Girl from Dixie, The   12/14/1903
Cherry Girl, The   12/21/1903
Little Hans Andersen   12/23/1903
Merely Mary Ann   12/28/1903

1904

Anheuser Push, The   00/00/1904
Elopers, The   00/00/1904
Filibuster, The   00/00/1904
Lambs Frolic   00/00/1904
My Lady Molly   01/05/1904
Terence   01/05/1904
Medal and the Maid, The   01/11/1904
English Daisy, An   01/18/1904
Sergeant Kitty   01/18/1904
Cinderella and the Prince   02/01/1904
   or Castle of Heart's Desire
Glittering Gloria   02/15/1904
Tenderfoot, The   02/22/1904
Yankee Consul, The   02/22/1904
Piff! Paff!! Pouf!!!   04/02/1904
Man from China, The   05/02/1904
Venetian Romance, A   05/02/1904
Southerners, The   05/23/1904
Little Bit of Everything, A   06/06/1904
Paris by Night   07/02/1904
Maid and the Mummy, The   07/25/1904
Isle of Spice, The   08/23/1904
School Girl, The   09/01/1904
Royal Chef, The   09/01/1904
Madcap Princess, A   09/05/1904
Mr. Wix of Wickham   09/19/1904
West Point Cadet, The   09/30/1904
Love's Lottery   10/03/1904
Burning to Sing or Singing   10/07/1904
   to Burn
Sho-Gun, The   10/10/1904
Easy Angel, An   10/17/1904
Higgledy-Piggledy   10/20/1904
Cingalee, The   10/24/1904
Little Johnny Jones   11/07/1904
Mrs. Black Is Back   11/07/1904
Cupid and Co   11/14/1904
Humpty Dumpty   11/14/1904
China Doll, A   11/19/1904
Baroness Fiddlesticks, The   11/21/1904
His Highness the Bey   11/21/1904
Two Roses, The   11/21/1904
Woodland   11/21/1904
It Happened in Nordland   12/05/1904
Smiling Island, The   12/15/1904
Lady Teazle   12/24/1904
In Newport   12/26/1904

1905

All Around Chicago   00/00/1905
All Round Chicago   00/00/1905
Grafter, The   00/00/1905
Pair of Pinks, A   00/00/1905
Girl and the Bandit, The   01/09/1905
Fantana   01/14/1905
Duchess of Dantzic, The   01/16/1905
Forbidden Land, The   01/16/1905
Buster Brown   01/24/1905
Mama's Papa   02/01/1905
Athletic Girl, The   02/15/1905
Me, Him, and I   03/13/1905
Isle of Bong Bong, The   03/14/1905
Yankee Circus on Mars, A   04/12/1905
Sergeant Brue   04/25/1905
Rollicking Girl, The   05/01/1905
Kafoozelum   05/21/1905
Lifting the Lid   06/05/1905
When We Were Forty-One   06/12/1905
Woggle Bug, The   06/20/1905
Geezer of Geck, The   07/24/1905
Pearl and the Pumpkin, The   08/21/1905
Easy Dawson   08/22/1905
Catch of the Season, The   08/28/1905
Ham Tree, The   08/28/1905
White Chrysanthemum, The   08/31/1905
Rogers Brothers in Ireland,   09/04/1905
   The
Miss Dolly Dollars   09/04/1905
Rogers Brothers in Paris,   09/05/1905
   The
Breaking Into Society   10/02/1905
Edmund Burke   10/02/1905
Happyland or the King of   10/02/1905
   Elysia
Fritz in Tammany Hall   10/16/1905
It's Up to You, John Henry   10/23/1905
Wonderland   10/24/1905
Belle of the West, The   10/29/1905
Moonshine   10/30/1905
Veronique   10/30/1905
White Cat, The   11/02/1905
Earl and the Girl, The   11/04/1905
Peter Pan   11/06/1905
How Baxter Butted In   11/13/1905
Press Agent, The   11/27/1905
Umpire, The   12/02/1905
Mayor of Tokio, The   12/04/1905
Society Circus, A   12/13/1905
Mlle. Modiste   12/25/1905
Gingerbread Man, The   12/25/1905
Babes and the Baron, The   12/25/1905

1906

Garden Matinee   00/00/1906
Rosalie   00/00/1906

Man from 'Bam, The   00/00/1906
Maid and Mule   00/00/1906
Lovers and Lunatics   00/00/1906
I.O.U.   00/00/1906
Hottest Coon in Dixie   00/00/1906
Happy Hooligan's Trip   00/00/1906
   Around the World
Girls Will Be Girls   00/00/1906
Girl from Broadway, The   00/00/1906
Rufus Rastus   00/00/1906
Fool House, The   00/00/1906
Cowboy Girl, The   00/00/1906
College Days   00/00/1906
Captain Careless   00/00/1906
At Yale   00/00/1906
Around the Town   00/00/1906
Thebe   00/00/1906
Forty-Five Minutes from   01/01/1906
   Broadway
Blue Moon, The   01/03/1906
Coming Thro' the Rye   01/09/1906
Twiddle-Twaddle   01/11/1906
Way to Kenmare, The   01/13/1906
Vanderbilt Cup, The   01/16/1906
Galloper, The   01/22/1906
Mexicana   01/29/1906
Gay New York   02/01/1906
Abyssinia   02/20/1906
Belle of Avenue A, The   03/05/1906
Beauty of Bath, The   03/19/1906
His Majesty   03/19/1906
Three Graces, The   04/02/1906
Social Whirl, The   04/09/1906
Free Lance, The   04/16/1906
Venus, 1906   04/17/1906
District Leader, The   04/30/1906
His Honor the Mayor   05/28/1906
Seeing New York   06/05/1906
Mam'zelle Champagne   06/25/1906
Little Cherub, The   08/06/1906
Tourists, The   08/25/1906
Marrying Mary   08/27/1906
About Town   08/30/1906
New Aladdin, The   09/00/1906
Man from Now, The   09/03/1906
My Lady's Maid or Lady   09/20/1906
   Madcap
Red Mill, The   09/24/1906
Around the Clock   10/00/1906
Genius, The   10/03/1906
Spring Chicken, The   10/08/1906
Rich Mr. Hoggenheimer, The   10/22/1906
Eileen Asthore   10/22/1906
Girl and the Gambler, The   11/05/1906
Mrs. Wilson, That's All   11/05/1906
My Wife's Family   11/05/1906
Mam'selle Sallie   11/26/1906
Parisian Model, The   11/27/1906
Neptune's Daughter   11/28/1906
Pioneer Days   11/28/1906

Everybody Works but Father   11/30/1906
Belle of Mayfair, The   12/03/1906
Show Girl, The   12/04/1906
George Washington, Jr.   12/12/1906
Dream City   12/25/1906
Student King, The   12/25/1906
Road to Yesterday, The   12/31/1906
Matilda   12/31/1906

1907

Girls of America   00/00/1907
Not Yet but Soon   00/00/1907
Noah's Ark   00/00/1907
Merry Widower, The   00/00/1907
Lucky Dog, A   00/00/1907
In New York Town   00/00/1907
House Melodious, The   00/00/1907
Happy Hooligan's Trip   00/00/1907
   Around the World
Simple Simon Simple   00/00/1907
Dion O'Dare   00/00/1907
Captain Jasper   00/00/1907
Candy Kid, The   00/00/1907
Across the Continent in the   00/00/1907
   Stationary Express
Painting the Town   01/02/1907
Princess Beggar   01/07/1907
Nelly Neil   01/10/1907
Mimic and the Maid, The   01/11/1907
Belle of London Town,   01/28/1907
   The
Little Michus, The   01/31/1907
Girl and the Governor, The   02/04/1907
Rose of Alhambra, The   02/04/1907
White Hen, The   02/16/1907
Tattooed Man, The   02/18/1907
Beauty Doctor, The   02/21/1907
McFadden's Flats   02/28/1907
Grand Mogul, The   03/25/1907
Land of Nod, The   04/01/1907
Song Birds, The   04/01/1907
Orchid, The   04/08/1907
Boys of Company 'B', The   04/08/1907
Miss Camille   04/14/1907
Fascinating Flora   05/20/1907
Honeymooners, The   06/03/1907
Maid and the Millionaire,   06/22/1907
   The
Ziegfeld Follies of 1907   07/08/1907
Time, the Place and the   08/05/1907
   Girl, The
Shoo-Fly Regiment, The   08/06/1907
Happy Days   08/08/1907
Captain Rufus   08/12/1907
Hired Girl's Millions   08/12/1907
Yankee Tourist, A   08/12/1907
Alaskan, The   08/12/1907
Lady from Lanes, The   08/19/1907

Cupid at Vassar   08/23/1907
Dairymaids, The   08/26/1907
Patsy in Politics   09/02/1907
Rogers Brothers in Panama,   09/02/1907
   The
From Across the Big Pond   09/07/1907
Bubbles   09/09/1907
Gay Gordons, The   09/11/1907
Black Politician   09/14/1907
Boy with the Boodle, The   09/16/1907
Lola from Berlin   09/16/1907
Yankee Regent, The   09/17/1907
Pan Handle Pete   09/19/1907
Hurdy Gurdy Girl, The   09/23/1907
Little Yennie Yensen   09/30/1907
Girl Behind the Counter,   10/01/1907
   The
Girl Over There, The   10/02/1907
Gay White Way, The   10/07/1907
Hip! Hip! Hooray!   10/10/1907
Hoyden, The   10/19/1907
Top o' the World, The   10/19/1907
Ma's New Husband   10/20/1907
Merry Widow, The   10/21/1907
Miss Pocahontas   10/28/1907
Girl from Yama, The   11/04/1907
End of the Trail, The   11/05/1907
Tom Jones   11/11/1907
Rejuvenation of Aunt Mary,   11/12/1907
   The
Girls of Holland, The   11/18/1907
King Casey   11/18/1907
Morals of Marcus, The   11/18/1907
Auto Race, The   11/25/1907
O'Neill of Derry   11/25/1907
Talk of New York, The   12/03/1907
Knight for a Day, A   12/16/1907
Original Cohen, The   12/16/1907
Playing the Ponies   12/23/1907
Bad Boy and His Teddy   12/30/1907
   Bears, The
Miss Hook of Holland   12/31/1907

1908

Simple Molly   00/00/1908
Accidental Discovery of the 00/00/1908
   North Pole, An
Blackville Strollers   00/00/1908
Ephraham Johnson from   00/00/1908
   Norfolk
Happy Youngsters   00/00/1908
Little Dolly Dimples   00/00/1908
My Sweetheart   00/00/1908
Oysterman, The   00/00/1908
Panama   00/00/1908
Playing the Ponies   00/00/1908
Merry Widow and the Devil,   01/02/1908
   The

Funabashi   01/06/1908
Toyland   01/08/1908
Billy the Kid   01/11/1908
Yankee Drummers, The   01/19/1908
Lonesome Town   01/20/1908
Waltz Dream, A   01/27/1908
Soul Kiss, The   01/28/1908
Grafters, The   02/02/1908
Fifty Miles from Boston   02/03/1908
Bandanna Land   02/03/1908
Pickings from Puck   02/09/1908
Nearly a Hero   02/24/1908
Big Stick, The   03/16/1908
Honeymoon Trail   03/23/1908
Busy Izzy's Boodle   04/06/1908
Ole Olson   04/19/1908
Flower of the Ranch, The   04/20/1908
Li'l Mose   04/20/1908
Yankee Prince, The   04/20/1908
Merry-Go-Round, The   04/25/1908
Friar's Festival, The   05/14/1908
Gay Musician, The   05/18/1908
Mary's Lamb   05/25/1908
Naked Truth, The   06/00/1908
Ski-Hi   06/02/1908
Three Twins   06/15/1908
Ziegfeld Follies of 1908   06/15/1908
Mimic World, The   07/09/1908
Cohan and Harris Minstrels   08/03/1908
Girl Question, The   08/03/1908
Love Watches   08/29/1908
Prince Humbug   08/31/1908
Algeria   08/31/1908
Girls of Gottenburg, The   09/02/1908
Girl at the Helm, A   09/05/1908
Sporting Days   09/05/1908
Fluffy Ruffles   09/07/1908
Duke of Duluth, The   09/11/1908
School Days   09/14/1908
Mater   09/23/1908
Mlle. Mischief   09/28/1908
Marcelle   10/01/1908
American Idea, The   10/05/1908
Morning, Noon and Night   10/05/1908
Golden Butterfly, The   10/12/1908
Little Nemo   10/20/1908
Boys and Betty, The   11/02/1908
Winning Miss, A   11/21/1908
Blue Mouse, The   11/30/1908
Miss Innocence   11/30/1908
Prima Donna, The   11/30/1908
Pied Piper, The   12/03/1908
Queen of the Moulin Rouge,   12/07/1908
   The
Mr. Hamlet of Broadway   12/23/1908

1909

My Friend from Kentucky   00/00/1909
Yankee Mandarin, The   00/00/1909

Politicians, The   00/00/1909
Colored Aristocrats, The   00/00/1909
Dick Whittington   00/00/1909
Follies of the Day   00/00/1909
Gaiety Jubilee, The   00/00/1909
Golden Widow, The   00/00/1909
Husband, The   00/00/1909
Mayor of Newtown, The   00/00/1909
Miss Molly May   00/00/1909
Kitty Grey   01/25/1909
Stubborn Cinderella, A   01/25/1909
Fair Co-Ed, The   02/01/1909
Havana   02/11/1909
Prince of Tonight, The   03/09/1909
Golden Girl, The   03/16/1909
Newlyweds and Their Baby,   03/22/1909
   The
Beauty Spot, The   04/10/1909
Candy Shop, The   04/27/1909
Red Moon, The   05/03/1909
Midnight Sons, The   05/22/1909
Boy and the Girl, The   05/31/1909
Ziegfeld Follies of 1909   06/14/1909
Motor Girl, The   06/15/1909
Gay Hussars, The   07/29/1909
Broken Idol, A   08/16/1909
Cohan and Harris Minstrels   08/16/1909
Lo   08/29/1909
In Hayti   08/30/1909
Love Cure, The   09/01/1909
Trip to Japan, A   09/04/1909
Dollar Princess, The   09/06/1909
Chocolate Soldier, The   09/13/1909
Rose of Algeria, The   09/20/1909
Girl and the Wizard, The   09/27/1909
White Sister, The (1909)   09/27/1909
Man Who Owns Broadway, The   10/11/1909
Kissing Girl, The   10/25/1909
They Loved a Lassie   10/31/1909
Flirting Princess, The   11/01/1909
Mr. Lode of Koal   11/01/1909
Silver Star, The   11/01/1909
Belle of Brittany, The   11/08/1909
Old Dutch   11/22/1909
Air King, The   12/00/1909
Goddess of Liberty, The   12/22/1909

1910

Cat and the Fiddle,   00/00/1910
   The
City Chap, The   00/00/1910
Face That Wins, The   00/00/1910
Girl and the Drummer, The   00/00/1910
Gotts Schtroff   00/00/1910
Isle of Love, The   00/00/1910
Photo Shop, The   00/00/1910
Possum Hunt Club Revue,   00/00/1910
   The

Jolly Bachelors, The   01/06/1910
Old Town, The   01/10/1910
King of Cadonia, The   01/10/1910
American in Paris, The   01/10/1910
Prince of Bohemia, The   01/13/1910
Arcadians, The   01/17/1910
Barry of Ballymore   01/30/1910
Miss Nobody from Starland   01/31/1910
Young Turk, The   01/31/1910
Katie Did   02/18/1910
Bright Eyes   02/28/1910
Just One of the Boys   03/07/1910
Skylark, A   04/04/1910
Alpsburg   04/08/1910
Molly May   04/08/1910
Lulu's Husbands   04/14/1910
Matinee Idol, A   04/28/1910
Tillie's Nightmare   05/05/1910
Hermits at Happy Hollow,   05/30/1910
   The
Merry Whirl, The   05/30/1910
Girlies   06/03/1910
Summer Widowers, The   06/04/1910
Ziegfeld Follies of 1910   06/20/1910
Up and Down Broadway   07/18/1910
Wife Tamers, The   08/08/1910
Echo, The   08/17/1910
Our Miss Gibbs   08/29/1910
Sweetest Girl in Paris,   08/29/1910
   The
Madame Sherry   08/30/1910
International Cup, The   09/03/1910
Ballet of Niagara, The   09/03/1910
He Came from Milwaukee   09/10/1910
Hans, the Flute Player   09/20/1910
Alma, Where Do You Live?   09/26/1910
Girl in the Train, The   10/03/1910
Deacon and the Lady, The   10/04/1910
Judy Forgot   10/06/1910
Madame Troubadour   10/10/1910
Lower Birth Thirteen   10/16/1910
Girl in the Taxi (1910)   10/24/1910
Gamblers, The   10/31/1910
Bachelor Belles, The   11/07/1910
Getting a Polish   11/07/1910
Naughty Marietta   11/07/1910
Girl in the Kimono,   11/11/1910
   The
Girl and the Kaiser,   11/22/1910
   The
Yankee Girl, The   12/10/1910
Spring Maid, The   12/26/1910

1911

Spoony Sam   00/00/1911
Winter Garden Vaudeville   00/00/1911
   Show

Country Girl, The   00/00/1911
Friar's Frolic of 1911   00/00/1911
In the Jungles   00/00/1911
Little Kiln Club, The   00/00/1911
My Cinderella Girl   00/00/1911
My Pearl Maiden   00/00/1911
Real Girl   00/00/1911
Runaway Slave   00/00/1911
Slim Princess, The   01/02/1911
Marriage a la Carte   01/02/1911
Paradise of Mahomet, The   01/17/1911
Hen-Pecks, The   02/04/1911
Balkan Princess, The   02/09/1911
Two Men and a Girl   02/13/1911
Happiest Night of His Life,   02/20/1911
   The
Everywoman   02/27/1911
Jumping Jupiter   03/06/1911
Pink Lady, The   03/13/1911
La Belle Paree   03/20/1911
Little Miss Fix-It   04/03/1911
Love and Politics   04/03/1911
Merry Mary   04/16/1911
Dr. Deluxe   04/17/1911
Certain Party, A   04/24/1911
Folies Bergere Company   04/27/1911
His Honor the Barber   05/08/1911
Heart Breakers, The   05/30/1911
Red Rose, The   06/22/1911
Ziegfeld Follies of 1911   06/26/1911
Girl of My Dreams, The   08/07/1911
Hello Paris   08/19/1911
Siren, The   08/21/1911
Around the World   09/02/1911
Louisiana Lou   09/03/1911
Miss Jack   09/04/1911
Widow, The   09/11/1911
When Sweet Sixteen   09/14/1911
Kiss Waltz, The   09/18/1911
A La Broadway   09/22/1911
Little Millionaire, The   09/25/1911
Revue of Revues, The   09/27/1911
Never Homes, The   10/05/1911
Duchess, The   10/16/1911
Miss Dudelsack   10/16/1911
Gypsy Love   10/17/1911
Enchantress, The   10/19/1911
Quaker Girl, The   10/23/1911
Three Lights, The   10/31/1911
Wife Hunters,The   11/02/1911
Red Widow, The   11/05/1911
Three Romeos, The   11/13/1911
California   11/20/1911
Undine   11/20/1911
Vera Violetta   11/20/1911
Little Boy Blue   11/27/1911
Cora   11/28/1911
Peggy   12/07/1911
Betsy   12/11/1911
Wedding Trip, The   12/25/1911

1912

Rock and Fulton Act   00/00/1912
Auction Pinochle   00/00/1912
Cohan and Harris Minstrels   00/00/1912
Dr. Beans from Boston   00/00/1912
First Love   00/00/1912
In the Barracks   00/00/1912
Love Wager, The   00/00/1912
Mayor of Newtown, The   00/00/1912
Peck o' Pickles   00/00/1912
Persian Garden, A   00/00/1912
Modest Suzanne   01/01/1912
Over the River   01/08/1912
Bird of Paradise,   01/08/1912
   The
She Knows Better Now   01/15/1912
Rose of Panama   01/22/1912
Pearl Maiden, The   01/22/1912
Macushla   02/05/1912
Hokey-Pokey   02/08/1912
Opera Ball, The   02/12/1912
Whirl of Society, The   03/05/1912
Baron Trenck, The   03/11/1912
Man from Cook's, The   03/25/1912
Winsome Widow, A   04/11/1912
Wall Street Girl, The   04/15/1912
Rose Maid, The   04/22/1912
Let George Do It   04/22/1912
Two Little Brides   04/23/1912
And the Villain Still   05/10/1912
   Pursued Her
Mama's Baby Boy   05/25/1912
Hermits in Paris, The   05/27/1912
Under Many Flags   05/31/1912
Passing Show of 1912, The   07/22/1912
Girl from Montmartre, The   08/05/1912
Hanky-Panky   08/05/1912
Merry Countess, The   08/20/1912
Girl from Brighton, The   08/31/1912
Polish Wedding, A   08/31/1912
Girl at the Gate, The   09/01/1912
Girl in the Taxi, The   09/05/1912
'Mind the Paint' Girl, The   09/09/1912
My Best Girl   09/12/1912
Count of Luxembourg, The   09/16/1912
June Bride, The   09/23/1912
Oh! Oh! Delphine   09/30/1912
Tantalizing Tommy   10/01/1912
Charity Girl, The   10/02/1912
Woman Haters, The   10/07/1912
At the Barracks   10/09/1912
Ziegfeld Follies of 1912   10/21/1912
Lady of the Slipper, The   10/28/1912
Red Petticoat, The   11/13/1912
Dove of Peace, The   11/14/1912
Gypsy, The   11/14/1912
Broadway to Paris   11/20/1912
Roly Poly   11/21/1912
Without the Law   11/21/1912

Pot of Gold, The   11/26/1912
Sun Dodgers, The   11/30/1912
Firefly, The   12/02/1912
Peg o' My Heart   12/20/1912
Frivolous Geraldine   12/22/1912
Exceeding the Speed Limit   12/23/1912
Miss Princess   12/23/1912
Village Blacksmith, The   12/29/1912
Eva   12/30/1912
All for the Ladies   12/30/1912

1913

Earl and the Girls, The   00/00/1913
Out on Broadway   00/00/1913
My Friend from Kentucky   00/00/1913
Mutt and Jeff   00/00/1913
Merry Martyr   00/00/1913
Little Parisienne, The   00/00/1913
In Ethiopiaville   00/00/1913
Girl of Today, A   00/00/1913
Girl from Shanley's, The   00/00/1913
Eternal Waltz, The   00/00/1913
Wrong Mr. President, The   00/00/1913
Die Ballkonigin   00/00/1913
Darktown Politician, The   00/00/1913
Darktown Follies   00/00/1913
Court By Girls   00/00/1913
Boys from Home, The   00/00/1913
Bachelor's Dinner   00/00/1913
Sorority Days   01/16/1913
Somewhere Else   01/20/1913
Man with Three Wives, The   01/23/1913
Isle o' Dreams   01/27/1913
Sunshine Girl, The   02/03/1913
Honeymoon Express, The   02/06/1913
Countess Coquette   02/28/1913
Traitors, The   03/00/1913
All Star Gambols   03/10/1913
American Maid, The   03/13/1913
Dance Dream   03/17/1913
Beggar Student, The   03/22/1913
Purple Road, The   04/07/1913
When Claudia Smiles   04/13/1913
Come Over Here   04/19/1913
Amazons, The   04/28/1913
Kaleidoscope, The   04/30/1913
My Little Friend   05/19/1913
All Aboard   06/05/1913
Ziegfeld Follies of 1913   06/16/1913
Tik Tok Man of Oz, The   06/23/1913
Passing Show of 1913, The   07/24/1913
Trip to Washington, A   08/18/1913
When Dreams Come True   08/18/1913
Doll Girl, The   08/25/1913
Adele   08/28/1913
America   08/30/1913
Lieber Augustin   09/03/1913
Sweethearts   09/08/1913

Marriage Market, The   09/22/1913
Broadway Honeymoon, A   10/03/1913
Her Little Highness   10/13/1913
Glimpse of the Great White   10/27/1913
   Way, A
When Love Is Young   10/28/1913
Oh, I Say!   10/30/1913
Two Lots in the Bronx   11/00/1913
Pleasure Seekers, The   11/03/1913
Little Cafe, The   11/10/1913
Madcap Duchess, The   11/11/1913
Hop o' My Thumb   11/26/1913
September Morn   12/00/1913
High Jinks   12/10/1913
Iole   12/29/1913
Girl on the Film, The   12/29/1913

1914

Choir Rehearsal, The   00/00/1914
Props   00/00/1914
Princess of Ragtime   00/00/1914
New Song Birds, The   00/00/1914
Mr. Ragtime   00/00/1914
Matinee Girls   00/00/1914
Hermits in Vienna, The   00/00/1914
Heart of Paddy Whack, The   00/00/1914
Gus Edwards's New Song   00/00/1914
   Revue of 1914
Society Buds, The   00/00/1914
Captain Rufus   00/00/1914
Bringing Up Father   00/00/1914
Black Crepe and Diamonds   00/00/1914
Alma's Return   00/00/1914
After the Girl   00/00/1914
Trained Nurses, The   00/00/1914
Nuts and Wine   01/04/1914
Whirl of the World, The   01/10/1914
Queen of the Movies, The   01/12/1914
Sari   01/13/1914
Laughing Husband, The   02/02/1914
Shameen Dhu   02/02/1914
When Claudia Smiles   02/02/1914
Maids of Athens   02/19/1914
Midnight Girl, The   02/23/1914
Along Came Ruth   02/23/1914
Crinoline Girl   03/16/1914
Jerry   03/18/1914
Belle of Bond Street, The   03/30/1914
Forward March (1914)   04/13/1914
Red Canary, The   04/13/1914
Beauty Shop, The   04/13/1914
Gay Modiste, The   04/17/1914
Honeymoon Girls, The   04/17/1914
Passing Show, The   04/20/1914
   (London)
Paranoia   04/24/1914
We're All Dressed Up and We   05/22/1914
Don't Know Huerto Go

Madame Moselle   05/23/1914
Ziegfeld Follies of 1914   06/01/1914
Passing Show of 1914, The   06/10/1914
   (New York)
Manicure Girl, The   06/29/1914
Dancing Duchess   08/19/1914
Girl from Utah, The   08/24/1914
Wars of the World   09/05/1914
One Girl in a Million   09/06/1914
Miss Daisy   09/09/1914
Let's Get Married   09/21/1914
Pretty Mrs. Smith   09/21/1914
Dancing Around   10/10/1914
Chin-Chin   10/20/1914
Experience   10/27/1914
Lilac Domino, The   10/28/1914
Papa's Darling   11/02/1914
Only Girl, The   11/02/1914
Suzi   11/03/1914
Jack's Romance   11/26/1914
Debutante, The   12/07/1914
Watch Your Step   12/08/1914
Tonight's the Night   12/24/1914
Lady Luxury   12/25/1914
Hello, Broadway!   12/25/1914

1915

Did You Ever?   00/00/1915
Samples   00/00/1915
On Your Way   00/00/1915
Mutt and Jeff in College   00/00/1915
Little Half Breed, The   00/00/1915
In and Out   00/00/1915
His Excellency, the   00/00/1915
   President
George Washington Bullion   00/00/1915
   Abroad
Down in Bom-Bom Bay   00/00/1915
What's Going On   00/00/1915
Cohen on the East Side   00/00/1915
Clock Shop, The   00/00/1915
Broadway Rastus   00/00/1915
Bringing Up Father   00/00/1915
Beauty Doctors, The   00/00/1915
Within the Loop   00/00/1915
Lonesome Lasses   01/18/1915
90 in the Shade   01/25/1915
Model Girl, The   01/26/1915
Maid in America   02/18/1915
Ziegfeld Midnight Frolic   03/00/1915
Peasant Girl, The   03/02/1915
Fads and Fancies   03/08/1915
Rosy Rapture, the Pride of   03/22/1915
   the Beauty Chorus
Nobody Home   04/20/1915
All Over Town   05/00/1915
Modern Eve, A   05/03/1915
One of the Boys   05/24/1915

Passing Show of 1915, The   05/29/1915
Ziegfeld Follies of 1915   06/21/1915
Hands Up   07/22/1915
Blue Paradise, The   08/05/1915
Girl Who Smiles, The   08/09/1915
No. 13 Washington Square   08/23/1915
Cousin Lucy   08/27/1915
Molly and I   08/31/1915
Ziegfeld Midnight Frolic   09/00/1915
Two Is Company   09/22/1915
Ned Wayburn's Town Topics   09/23/1915
Princess "Pat," The   09/29/1915
Hip-Hip-Hooray   09/30/1915
Miss Information   10/05/1915
Alone at Last   10/14/1915
World of Pleasure, A   10/14/1915
Girl of Tomorrow, The   10/18/1915
Darkydom   10/23/1915
Around the Map   11/01/1915
Sadie Love   11/29/1915
Katinka   12/23/1915
Very Good Eddie   12/23/1915
Stop! Look! Listen!   12/25/1915
Ruggles of Red Gap   12/25/1915

1916

Darktown Follies   00/00/1916
Dear Dorothy   00/00/1916
Garden of Eden, The   00/00/1916
How Newton Prepared   00/00/1916
Lieutenant Gus   00/00/1916
Peace Pirates, The   00/00/1916
Two Husbands and One Wife   00/00/1916
Ziegfeld Midnight Frolic   00/00/1916
Sybil   01/10/1916
Cinderella Man, The   01/17/1916
Cohan Revue of 1916, The   02/09/1916
Kilkenny   02/14/1916
Robinson Crusoe, Jr.   02/17/1916
Pom-Pom   02/28/1916
Road to Mandalay, The   03/01/1916
See America First   03/28/1916
Tickets Please   04/03/1916
Simplex Marriage Parlors   04/24/1916
Come to Bohemia   04/27/1916
Molly O'   05/17/1916
Friar's Frolic of 1916   05/28/1916
Step This Way   05/29/1916
Bride Tamer, The   06/12/1916
Ziegfeld Follies of 1916   06/12/1916
Razzle Dazzle   06/19/1916
Passing Show of 1916, The   06/22/1916
His Heart's Desire   08/00/1916
Yvette   08/10/1916
Broadway and Buttermilk   08/15/1916
His Bridal Night   08/16/1916
Keep Moving   08/27/1916
Girl from Brazil, The   08/30/1916

Big Show, The   08/31/1916
Flora Bella   09/11/1916
Regular Girl, A   09/18/1916
Amber Empress, The   09/19/1916
Theodore and Co.   09/19/1916
Miss Springtime   09/25/1916
Betty   10/03/1916
So Long, Letty   10/23/1916
Show of Wonders, The   10/26/1916
Good Gracious Annabelle   10/31/1916
Century Girl, The   11/06/1916
Follow Me   11/29/1916
Her Soldier Boy   12/06/1916
Go To It   12/24/1916
Kiss for Cinderella, A   12/25/1916

1917

My People   00/00/1917
Ziegfeld Midnight Frolic   00/00/1917
Wanted—A Wife   00/00/1917
Switzerland Sam   00/00/1917
Boys Will Be Boys   00/00/1917
Bringing Up Father Abroad   00/00/1917
Dance and Grow Thin   00/00/1917
Dew Drop Inn   00/00/1917
Fascinating Widow, The   00/00/1917
Girl of Mine   00/00/1917
Gus Edwards's Bandbox Revue 00/00/1917
Jim-Jam Revue   00/00/1917
Mutt and Jeff Divorced   00/00/1917
Mutt and Jeff's Wedding   00/00/1917
My Aunt from Utah   00/00/1917
My Home Town Girl   00/00/1917
Have a Heart   01/11/1917
Love O' Mike   01/15/1917
Canary Cottage   02/05/1917
You're in Love   02/06/1917
Oh, Boy!   02/20/1917
Up Stage and Down   03/08/1917
Eileen   03/19/1917
Out There   03/27/1917
Home, James   03/28/1917
Masked Model, The   04/17/1917
Little Missus, The   04/23/1917
Passing Show of 1917, The   04/26/1917
His Little Widows   04/30/1917
Captain Cupid   05/15/1917
Hitchy-Koo   06/07/1917
Ziegfeld Follies of 1917   06/12/1917
My Lady's Glove   06/18/1917
What Next?   06/24/1917
What Is Love?   07/02/1917
Oh! So Happy   07/19/1917
Ziegfeld Midnight Frolic   07/27/1917
Maytime   08/16/1917
Cheer Up   08/23/1917
Leave It to Jane   08/28/1917
Good Night, Paul   09/03/1917

Rambler Rose   09/10/1917
Riviera Girl, The   09/24/1917
Naughty Princess, The   09/25/1917
Venus on Broadway   10/01/1917
Furs and Frills   10/09/1917
Make Yourself at Home   10/09/1917
Jack O'Lantern   10/16/1917
Doing Our Bit   10/18/1917
Chu Chin Chow   10/22/1917
We Should Worry   10/26/1917
Land of Joy, The   10/31/1917
Miss 1917   11/05/1917
Kitty Darlin'   11/07/1917
Her Regiment   11/12/1917
Odds and Ends of 1917   11/19/1917
Words and Music   11/24/1917
Star Gazer, The   11/26/1917
Over the Top   11/28/1917
Golden Goose, The   11/29/1917
Grass Widow, The   12/03/1917
Gipsy Trail, The   12/04/1917
Flo-Flo   12/20/1917
Going Up   12/25/1917
One Minute Please   12/29/1917
Cohan Revue of 1918, The   12/31/1917

1918

Darkest Americans   00/00/1918
Ten for Five   00/00/1918
Song Birds   00/00/1918
Pack Up Your Troubles   00/00/1918
Married by Wireless   00/00/1918
House That Jack Built, The   00/00/1918
Hooray for the Girls   00/00/1918
Hello America   00/00/1918
Frolics of the Night   00/00/1918
Ziegfeld 9 O'Clock Frolic   00/00/1918
   of 1918
Century Midnight Whirl   00/00/1918
Catching the Burglar   00/00/1918
Bridal Not, The   00/00/1918
Bessie McCoy Davis' Period   00/00/1918
   Dance Review
Annette Kellerman's Big   00/00/1918
   Show
All Aboard   00/00/1918
Ziegfeld Midnight Frolic of   00/00/1918
   1918
Ziegfeld Midnight Frolic   00/00/1918
In and Out   01/22/1918
Girl o' Mine   01/28/1918
Oh, Lady! Lady!!   02/01/1918
Love Mill, The   02/07/1918
Sinbad   02/14/1918
Follow the Girl   03/02/1918
Let's Go   03/09/1918
Toot-Toot!   03/11/1918

Oh, Look!   03/17/1918
Getting Together   03/18/1918
Rainbow Girl, The   04/01/1918
Fancy Free   04/11/1918
See You Later   04/15/1918
Good-Bye Bill   04/22/1918
Back Again   04/29/1918
Kiss Burglar, The   05/09/1918
Rock-a-Bye Baby   05/22/1918
She Took a Chance   06/00/1918
Made in Harlem   06/00/1918
Hitchy-Koo of 1918   06/06/1918
Ziegfeld Follies of 1918   06/18/1918
Passing Show of 1918, The   07/25/1918
Marry in Haste   08/05/1918
Yip! Yip! Yaphank!   08/19/1918
He Didn't Want to Do It   08/20/1918
Everything   08/22/1918
Why Worry?   08/23/1918
Head Over Heels   08/29/1918
Telling the Tale   08/31/1918
Fiddlers Three   09/03/1918
Maid of the Mountains, The   09/11/1918
Girl Behind the Gun, The   09/16/1918
Some Night   09/23/1918
Miss Blue Eyes   10/03/1918
Redemption (The Living   10/03/1918
   Corpse)
Sometime   10/04/1918
Ladies First   10/24/1918
Glorianna   10/28/1918
Canary, The   11/04/1918
Little Simplicity   11/04/1918
Victory Girl, The   11/16/1918
Oh, My Dear!   11/27/1918
Half Past Eight   12/09/1918
Good Luck, Sam!   12/09/1918
Better 'Ole or the Romance   12/19/1918
   of Old Bill, The
Atta Boy   12/23/1918
Listen Lester   12/23/1918
Somebody's Sweetheart   12/23/1918
Voice of McConnell, The   12/25/1918
East Is West   12/25/1918
Melting of Molly, The   12/30/1918

1919

Diri   00/00/1919
Suite Sixteen   00/00/1919
Song Romance, A   00/00/1919
Night Owls, The   00/00/1919
My Midnight Sweetheart   00/00/1919
Midnight Elopers, The   00/00/1919
Merry Mary Brown   00/00/1919
Knockers of 1919   00/00/1919
Hi and Dri   00/00/1919
Hello Paree   00/00/1919

This and That   00/00/1919
Children of the Sun, The   00/00/1919
Bugland   00/00/1919
Big Sensation, The   00/00/1919
Bessie Clayton Vaudeville   00/00/1919
   Act
Baby Blues   00/00/1919
B-R-A   00/00/1919
Visions of 1969   00/00/1919
Water's Fine, The   00/00/1919
Ziegfeld Midnight Frolic   00/00/1919
Up in Mabel's Room   01/15/1919
Velvet Lady, The   02/03/1919
Good Morning, Judge   02/06/1919
Monte Cristo, Jr.   02/12/1919
Just Around the Corner   02/15/1919
Royal Vagabond, The   02/17/1919
Girl in State Room "B"   02/27/1919
Yesterday   03/10/1919
Tumble Inn   03/24/1919
Take It From Me   03/31/1919
Come Along   04/08/1919
I Love You   04/28/1919
She's a Good Fellow   05/05/1919
Toot Sweet   05/07/1919
Lady in Red, The   05/12/1919
I Love a Lassie   05/15/1919
Twinkling Eyes   05/18/1919
Love Laughs   05/20/1919
La-La-Lucille   05/26/1919
Biff! Bang!   05/30/1919
George White's Scandals   06/02/1919
Daly Dreams   06/08/1919
Lonely Romeo, A   06/10/1919
Ziegfeld Follies of 1919   06/16/1919
Honeymoon Town   06/17/1919
Greenwich Village Follies,   07/15/1919
   The
Shubert Gaieties of 1919   07/17/1919
Oh, What a Girl!   07/28/1919
Cohan and Harris Minstrels   08/16/1919
Happy Days   08/23/1919
See-Saw   09/23/1919
Roly Boly Eyes   09/25/1919
Ziegfeld Midnight Frolic   10/02/1919
Hitchy-Koo of 1919   10/06/1919
Apple Blossoms   10/07/1919
Hello Alexander   10/07/1919
Little Whopper, The   10/13/1919
Nothing but Love   10/14/1919
Dream Song, The   10/23/1919
Passing Show of 1919, The   10/23/1919
Capitol Revue ('Demi-   10/24/1919
   Tasse')
Fifty-Fifty Ltd.   10/27/1919
Buddies   10/27/1919
Just a Minute   10/29/1919
Among the Girls   11/00/1919
Eclipse, The   11/00/1919
Little Blue Devil, The   11/03/1919

Magic Melody, The   11/11/1919
Irene   11/18/1919
Son-Daughter, The   11/19/1919
Linger Longer Letty   11/20/1919
Aphrodite   11/24/1919
Rose of China, The   11/25/1919
Elsie Janis and Her Gang   12/01/1919
My Lady Friends   12/03/1919
Miss Millions   12/09/1919
Monsieur Beaucaire   12/11/1919
Morris Gest's Midnight   12/27/1919
   Whirl
Angel Face   12/29/1919

1920

I'll Say She Does   00/00/1920
Sunshine   00/00/1920
Strut Your Stuff   00/00/1920
Satires of 1920   00/00/1920
Rings of Smoke   00/00/1920
Oh, By Jingo   00/00/1920
Mutt and Jeff in Chinatown   00/00/1920
Love Flower, The   00/00/1920
Little Dutch Girl, A   00/00/1920
Keeping Up with the Joneses 00/00/1920
Tattle Tales (1920)   00/00/1920
Girl in the Private Room,   00/00/1920
   The
Emerald Isle, The (1920)   00/00/1920
Dew Drop Inn (1920)   00/00/1920
Dere Mable   00/00/1920
Chin Toy   00/00/1920
Bits and Pieces   00/00/1920
Wet and Dry   00/00/1920
You'd Be Surprised   00/00/1920
Zip Goes a Million   00/00/1920
Always You   01/05/1920
Frivolities of 1920   01/08/1920
Passion Flower, The   01/13/1920
As You Were   01/27/1920
My Golden Girl   02/02/1920
Night Boat, The   02/02/1920
Rose Girl, The   02/11/1920
Lady Kitty, Inc.   02/16/1920
Tick-Tack-Toe   02/23/1920
Look Who's Here   03/02/1920
Ziegfeld Girls of 1920   03/08/1920
Mimi   03/13/1920
Ziegfeld Midnight Frolic of   03/15/1920
   1920
What's in a Name?   03/19/1920
Oui Madame   03/22/1920
Fly with Me   03/24/1920
Three Showers   04/05/1920
Ed Wynn Carnival   04/05/1920
Lassie   04/06/1920
Girl from Home, The   05/03/1920
Honey Girl   05/03/1920

Betty Be Good   05/04/1920
Actors' Equity Benefit   05/09/1920
Page Mr. Cupid   05/17/1920
George White's Scandals   06/07/1920
Ziegfeld Follies of 1920   06/22/1920
Cinderella on Broadway   06/24/1920
Buzzin' Around   07/06/1920
Century Grove Revue   07/12/1920
Girl in the Spotlight   07/12/1920
Midnight Rounders of 1920,   07/12/1920
   The
Silks and Satins   07/15/1920
Poor Little Ritz Girl   07/27/1920
Ziegfeld 9 O'Clock Frolic   08/02/1920
Good Times   08/09/1920
Tickle Me   08/17/1920
Charm School, The   08/21/1920
Greenwich Village Follies,   08/30/1920
   The
Sweetheart Shop, The   08/31/1920
Little Miss Charity   09/02/1920
Dearie   09/05/1920
Honeydew   09/06/1920
Little Old New York   09/08/1920
Night Out, A   09/18/1920
Piccadilly to Broadway   09/27/1920
Pitter Patter   09/28/1920
Broadway Brevities of 1920   09/29/1920
Jim Jam Jems   10/04/1920
Mecca   10/04/1920
Tip Top   10/05/1920
Kissing Time   10/11/1920
Jimmie   10/17/1920
Mary   10/18/1920
Hitchy-Koo of 1920   10/19/1920
Half Moon, The   11/01/1920
Afgar   11/08/1920
Lady Billy   12/14/1920
Sally   12/21/1920
Her Family Tree   12/27/1920
Passing Show of 1921, The   12/29/1920

1921

Song Revue of 1921   00/00/1921
Whirl of the Town, The   00/00/1921
Troubles of 1920   00/00/1921
Town Gossip   00/00/1921
Alabama Bound   00/00/1921
Bamboula   00/00/1921
Chocolate Brown   00/00/1921
Happy Cavalier, The   00/00/1921
Hello 1921   00/00/1921
Irish Eyes   00/00/1921
Let 'Er Go Letty   00/00/1921
Marcus Show of 1920   00/00/1921
Peacock Alley   00/00/1921
Peggy   00/00/1921
Ragged Robin   00/00/1921

Three Kisses, The   01/00/1921
Springtime in Mayo   01/17/1921
Dear Me   01/17/1921
Midnight Rounders of 1921,   02/07/1921
   The
Ziegfeld 9 O'Clock Frolic   02/08/1921
   of 1921 (3rd Edition)
Ziegfeld Midnight Frolic   02/09/1921
   (11th Edition)
Say Mama   02/12/1921
Blue Eyes   02/21/1921
Love Birds   03/15/1921
Right Girl, The   03/15/1921
Dangerous Maid, A   03/21/1921
It's Up to You   03/28/1921
Liliom   04/20/1921
You'll Never Know   04/20/1921
Bringing Up Father at the   04/21/1921
   Seashore
June Love   04/25/1921
Just Married   04/26/1921
Two Little Girls in Blue   05/03/1921
Princess Virtue   05/04/1921
Biff! Bing! Bang!   05/09/1921
Phoebe of Quality Street   05/09/1921
Last Waltz, The   05/10/1921
Hermits on Main Street, The 05/23/1921
Shuffle Along   05/23/1921
Sunkist   05/23/1921
Say It with Jazz   06/01/1921
Snapshots of 1921   06/02/1921
Broadway Whirl, The   06/08/1921
Whirl of New York, The   06/13/1921
Ziegfeld Follies of 1921   06/21/1921
George White's Scandals   07/11/1921
All Star Jamboree   07/13/1921
All Star Idlers of 1921   07/14/1921
Tangerine   08/09/1921
Mimic World of 1921, The   08/15/1921
Sonny Boy   08/16/1921
Put and Take   08/23/1921
Greenwich Village Follies,   08/31/1921
   The
Silver Fox, The   09/05/1921
Music Box Revue   09/22/1921
Blossom Time   09/28/1921
Phi Phi   10/00/1921
O'Brien Girl, The   10/03/1921
Love Letter, The   10/04/1921
Golden Moth, The   10/05/1921
Bombo   10/06/1921
Love Dreams   10/10/1921
Darktown Frolics of 1921   10/11/1921
Good Morning, Dearie   11/01/1921
Perfect Fool, The   11/07/1921
Ziegfeld Midnight Frolic   11/17/1921
Suzette   11/24/1921
Kiki   11/29/1921
Mountain Man, The   12/12/1921
Ain't It the Truth   12/19/1921

1922

Listen to Me   00/00/1922
Shades of Hades   00/00/1922
Plantation Days   00/00/1922
Oh Joy!   00/00/1922
Mutt and Jeff   00/00/1922
Lola in Love   00/00/1922
Lola   00/00/1922
Little Kangaroo, The   00/00/1922
Up and Down   00/00/1922
Hello, Sue   00/00/1922
Flying Island   00/00/1922
Elusive Lady, The   00/00/1922
Bon Bon Buddy, Jr.   00/00/1922
Boardwark, The   00/00/1922
Winkle Town   00/00/1922
Up in the Clouds   01/02/1922
Blue Kitten, The   01/13/1922
Elsie Janis and Her Gang   01/16/1922
Marjolaine   01/24/1922
Chauve Souris   02/01/1922
Pins and Needles   02/01/1922
Bibi of the Boulevards   02/06/1922
Blushing Bride, The   02/06/1922
Frank Fay's Fables   02/06/1922
For Goodness Sake   02/20/1922
French Doll, The   02/20/1922
London Follies   03/06/1922
Rose of Stamboul, The   03/07/1922
Mayfair and Montmartre   03/09/1922
Hotel Mouse, The   03/13/1922
Just Because   03/22/1922
Chinese Lantern, The   04/07/1922
Letty Pepper   04/10/1922
Make It Snappy   04/13/1922
Some Party   04/15/1922
Go Easy Mabel   05/08/1922
And Very Nice Too   05/09/1922
Red Pepper   05/29/1922
Plantation Revue   06/00/1922
Jazz a la Carte   06/02/1922
Strut Miss Lizzy   06/03/1922
Ziegfeld Follies of 1922   06/05/1922
Raymond Hitchcock's   06/15/1922
   Pinwheel
Sue, Dear   07/02/1922
Spice of 1922   07/06/1922
Phi-Phi   08/16/1922
Daffy Dill   08/22/1922
Gingham Girl, The   08/28/1922
George White's Scandals   08/28/1922
Zig Zag   09/00/1922
Molly Darling   09/01/1922
Better Times   09/02/1922
Sally, Irene and Mary   09/04/1922
Joe Hurtig's Social Maids   09/05/1922
Fantastic Fricassee, A   09/11/1922
Greenwich Village Follies,   09/12/1922
   The

Cabaret Girl, The   09/14/1922
Orange Blossoms   09/19/1922
Passing Show of 1922, The   09/20/1922
East of Suez   09/21/1922
Lady in Ermine, The   10/02/1922
Yankee Princess, The   10/02/1922
Queen o' Hearts   10/10/1922
Hitchy-Koo of 1922   10/10/1922
Music Box Revue   10/23/1922
Springtime of Youth   10/26/1922
Up She Goes   11/06/1922
'49ers, The   11/07/1922
Little Nellie Kelly   11/13/1922
Midnight Jollies, The   11/18/1922
Liza   11/27/1922
Bunch and Judy, The   11/28/1922
Our Nell   12/04/1922
Rose Briar   12/25/1922
Glory   12/25/1922
Clinging Vine, The   12/25/1922

1923

Dinah   00/00/1923
Swanee River Home   00/00/1923
Sunbonnet Sue   00/00/1923
Sign of the Rose, The   00/00/1923
Plantation Revue   00/00/1923
Peaches   00/00/1923
North Ain't South   00/00/1923
Hot Chops   00/00/1923
Hello Everybody   00/00/1923
Get Set   00/00/1923
Ted Lewis Frolic   00/00/1923
Courtesan, The   00/00/1923
Chopin project   00/00/1923
Broadway Rastus of 1923   00/00/1923
Box Party   00/00/1923
Bal-Tabarin, The   00/00/1923
Atta Baby   00/00/1923
Arabian Nights   00/00/1923
Polly Preferred   01/11/1923
Stepping Stones, The   01/16/1923
Lady Butterfly   01/22/1923
Dancing Girl, The   01/24/1923
Caroline   01/31/1923
Sun Showers   02/05/1923
Wildflower   02/07/1923
Just Apples   03/09/1923
Go-Go   03/12/1923
Half Moon Inn   03/19/1923
Jack and Jill   03/22/1923
If I Were King   03/25/1923
Elsie   04/02/1923
Cinders   04/03/1923
Rainbow, The   04/03/1923
How Come?   04/16/1923
Dew Drop Inn   05/17/1923
Adrienne   05/28/1923

Hermits in Mexico, The   05/28/1923
Danish Yankee in King Tut's 05/31/1923
  Court, A
Passing Show of 1923, The   06/14/1923
Grand Street Follies, The   06/16/1923
George White's Scandals   06/18/1923
Helen of Troy, New York   06/19/1923
Earl Carroll's Vanities of   07/05/1923
  1923
Raisin' Cain   07/09/1923
Fashions of 1924   07/18/1923
In Love with Love   08/06/1923
Newcomers, The   08/08/1923
Little Jessie James   08/15/1923
Artists and Models   08/20/1923
Little Miss Bluebeard   08/28/1923
London Calling   09/04/1923
Beauty Prize, The   09/05/1923
Poppy   09/13/1923
Greenwich Village Follies,   09/20/1923
  The
Music Box Revue   09/22/1923
Nifties of 1923   09/25/1923
Magic Ring, The   10/01/1923
Hammerstein's Nine O'Clock   10/04/1923
  Revue
Mr. Battling Buttler   10/08/1923
Ginger   10/16/1923
Ziegfeld Follies of 1923   10/20/1923
That Casey Girl   10/22/1923
Runnin' Wild   10/29/1923
Topics of 1923   11/20/1923
Sharlee   11/22/1923
Sancho Panza   11/26/1923
One Kiss   11/27/1923
Kid Boots   12/13/1923
Rise of Rosie O'Reilly, The   12/25/1923
Mary Jane McKane   12/25/1923

1924

Trial Honeymoon, A   00/00/1924
Willow Plate, The   00/00/1924
Vive la Femme   00/00/1924
Amber Fluid, The   00/00/1924
Come Along Mandy   00/00/1924
Cotton Land   00/00/1924
Creole Follies, The   00/00/1924
Everything Will Be All   00/00/1924
  Right
Gallagher and Shean   00/00/1924
Vaudeville Act
Girl from Child's, The   00/00/1924
Honey   00/00/1924
Joy Shop, The   00/00/1924
Moon Maiden, The   00/00/1924
Negro Nuances   00/00/1924
Sittin' Pretty   00/00/1924

Creole Follies, The   01/00/1924
Town Clown, The   01/06/1924
Andre Charlot Revue of 1924   01/09/1924
Lollipop   01/21/1924
Sweet Little Devil   01/21/1924
Moonlight   01/30/1924
Chiffon Girl, The   02/19/1924
Creole Follies, The   03/00/1924
Paradise Alley   03/03/1924
Temple Belles   03/20/1924
Prisoner of Zenda, The   03/23/1924
Vogues of 1924   03/27/1924
Sitting Pretty   04/08/1924
Peg-o-My-Dreams   05/05/1924
Plain Jane   05/12/1924
Melody Man, The   05/13/1924
I'll Say She Is   05/19/1924
Innocent Eyes   05/20/1924
Grand Street Follies, The   05/20/1924
Round the Town   05/21/1924
Keep Kool   05/22/1924
Flossie   06/23/1924
Ziegfeld Follies of 1924   06/24/1924
George White's Scandals   06/30/1924
Belle of Quaker Town, The   07/00/1924
Marjorie   08/11/1924
No Other Girl   08/13/1924
Dream Girl, The   08/20/1924
Keep Moving   08/23/1924
Bye, Bye, Barbara   08/25/1924
Chocolate Dandies, The   09/01/1924
Top-Hole   09/01/1924
Rose-Marie   09/02/1924
Be Yourself   09/03/1924
Passing Show of 1924, The   09/03/1924
Earl Carroll's Vanities of   09/10/1924
  1924
Primrose   09/11/1924
Greenwich Village Follies,   09/16/1924
  The
Hassard Short's Ritz Revue   09/17/1924
In Dutch   09/22/1924
Charlot's Revue   09/23/1924
Dear Sir   09/23/1924
Grab Bag, The   10/06/1924
Artists and Models   10/15/1924
Firebrand, The   10/15/1924
Expressing Willie   10/16/1924
Polly of the Circus   10/20/1924
Dixie to Broadway   10/29/1924
That's My Boy   11/00/1924
Annie Dear   11/04/1924
Peter Pan   11/06/1924
Madame Pompadour   11/11/1924
My Girl   11/24/1924
Magnolia Lady, The   11/25/1924
Lady, Be Good!   12/01/1924
Music Box Revue   12/01/1924
My Boy Friend   12/01/1924
Princess April   12/01/1924

Student Prince, The 12/02/1924
Topsy and Eva 12/23/1924
Betty Lee 12/25/1924

1925

Dixie Brevities 00/00/1925
Out o' Luck 00/00/1925
New Plantation Revue 00/00/1925
How've You Been? 00/00/1925
How's the King 00/00/1925
Hollywood Music Box Revue 00/00/1925
Frank Silvers Revue 00/00/1925
Flashes of the Gay White 00/00/1925
  Way
Dutch Girl, The 00/00/1925
Romany Love 00/00/1925
Daughter of Rosie O'Grady, 00/00/1925
  The
Chocolate Kiddies 00/00/1925
Chatter Box Revue 00/00/1925
Broadway Rastus 00/00/1925
Aces and Queens 00/00/1925
World of Pleasure 00/00/1925
Big Boy 01/07/1925
Comic Supplement (Of 01/09/1925
American Life), The
Love Song, The 01/13/1925
China Rose 01/19/1925
Harry Carroll's Pickings 02/02/1925
Puzzles of 1925 02/02/1925
Bad Habits of 1925 02/08/1925
When Summer Comes 02/15/1925
Natja 02/16/1925
Tangletoes 02/17/1925
Sky High 03/02/1925
Louie the 14th 03/03/1925
Louisiana Lady 03/03/1925
Half Moon Inn 03/09/1925
Ziegfeld Follies of 1925 03/09/1925
Bamboula, The 03/24/1925
Bringing Up Father 03/30/1925
Mercenary Mary 04/13/1925
Tell Me More 04/13/1925
Fourflusher, The 04/13/1925
Birds of the Evening 04/26/1925
Dashing Belles of Yesterday 04/26/1925
  and the Dumbbelles of
  Today, The
Lambs Annual Public Spring 04/26/1925
  Gambol, The
Night in Old Paris, A 04/26/1925
Garrick Gaieties, The 05/17/1925
Brown Derby, The 05/18/1925
Lucky Sambo 06/06/1925
Kosher Kitty Kelly 06/15/1925
Grand Street Follies, The 06/18/1925
George White's Scandals 06/22/1925
Artists and Models 06/24/1925

Earl Carroll's Vanities of 07/06/1925
  1925
June Days 08/06/1925
Lucky Break, A 08/11/1925
Gay Paree 08/18/1925
Oh! Mama 08/19/1925
Night Out, A 09/07/1925
Captain Jinks 09/08/1925
Still Dancing 09/11/1925
Jazz Singer, The 09/14/1925
No! No! Nanette! 09/16/1925
Dearest Enemy 09/18/1925
Vagabond King, The 09/21/1925
Sunny 09/23/1925
All for You 09/24/1925
Merry, Merry 09/24/1925
Some Day 10/06/1925
Arabesque 10/10/1925
Holka-Polka 10/14/1925
Enemy, The 10/20/1925
When You Smile 10/25/1925
City Chap, The 10/26/1925
Florida Girl 11/02/1925
Princess Flavia 11/02/1925
Naughty Cinderella 11/09/1925
Charlot Revue of 1926 11/10/1925
Mayflowers 11/24/1925
Moochin' Along 12/07/1925
Oh! Oh! Nurse 12/07/1925
Cocoanuts, The 12/08/1925
Greenwich Village Follies, 12/24/1925
  The
Tip-Toes 12/28/1925
By the Way 12/28/1925
Song of the Flame 12/30/1925

1926

Hollywood Music Box Revue 00/00/1926
Tan Town Topics Revue 00/00/1926
Sweet Lady 00/00/1926
Miss Happiness 00/00/1926
Miss Calico 00/00/1926
Maiden Voyage 00/00/1926
Magnolia 00/00/1926
Junior Blackbirds 00/00/1926
Thumbs Up! 00/00/1926
Geechie 00/00/1926
Chicago Loop 00/00/1926
Caravan 00/00/1926
Bubbling Over 00/00/1926
Blue Moon 00/00/1926
Fifth Avenue Follies, The 01/00/1926
Night in Paris, A 01/05/1926
Hello, Lola 01/12/1926
Cherry Blossom 01/18/1926
Sweetheart Time 01/19/1926
Suzanne 01/25/1926
Pair o' Fools 01/25/1926

Matinee Girl, The   02/01/1926
Jest, The   02/04/1926
Bunk of 1926   02/16/1926
Patsy   03/08/1926
Greenwich Village Follies,   03/15/1926
   The
Rainbow Rose   03/16/1926
Girl Friend, The   03/17/1926
Cherry Pie Revue   04/14/1926
Cochran's Revue of 1926   04/29/1926
Bad Habits of 1926   04/30/1926
Kitty's Kisses   05/06/1926
Garrick Gaieties, The   05/10/1926
High and Dry   05/10/1926
Nancy   05/16/1926
Great Temptations, The   05/18/1926
Yvonne   05/22/1926
Hearts and Diamonds   06/01/1926
Merry World, The   06/08/1926
George White's Scandals   06/14/1926
Grand Street Follies, The   06/15/1926
No Foolin'   06/24/1926
My Magnolia   07/12/1926
Blonde Sinner, The   07/14/1926
Bare Facts of 1926   07/16/1926
Americana   07/26/1926
Nic-Nax of 1926   08/02/1926
Miss Manhattan   08/09/1926
Earl Carroll's Vanities of   08/24/1926
Queen High!   09/05/1926
Castles in the Air   09/06/1926
Lew Leslie's Blackbirds   09/11/1926
Naughty Riquette   09/13/1926
Countess Maritza   09/18/1926
Ramblers, The   09/20/1926
Honeymoon Lane   09/20/1926
Happy Go Lucky   09/30/1926
Desires of 1927   10/00/1926
Deep River   10/04/1926
Criss Cross   10/12/1926
Katja   10/18/1926
Wild Rose, The   10/20/1926
Princess Charming   10/21/1926
Oh, Kay!   11/08/1926
R.S.V.P.   11/09/1926
Gay Paree   11/09/1926
Twinkle Twinkle   11/16/1926
Desert Song, The   11/30/1926
Lido Lady   12/10/1926
Oh, Please!   12/17/1926
Peggy-Ann   12/27/1926
Listen Dearie   12/27/1926
Betsy   12/28/1926

1927

Arthur Freed's Orange Grove 00/00/1927
   Theatre Revue
Hayfoot Strawfoot (1927)   00/00/1927

Hollywood Music Box Revue   00/00/1927
I Told You So   00/00/1927
Jake the Plumber   00/00/1927
Let's Go   00/00/1927
On with the Show   00/00/1927
Peg O' Mine   00/00/1927
Struttin' Sam from Alabam'   00/00/1927
Studio Girl, The   00/00/1927
Earl Carroll's Vanities   01/03/1927
   Featuring the New Charlot Revue
Nightingale, The   01/03/1927
Lace Petticoat, The   01/04/1927
Piggy   01/11/1927
Bye Bye, Bonnie   01/13/1927
Yours Truly   01/25/1927
Hollywood Music Box Revue   02/02/1927
Rio Rita   02/02/1927
Judy   02/08/1927
Polly of Hollywood   02/21/1927
New Yorkers, The   03/10/1927
Spider, The   03/22/1927
Lucky   03/23/1927
Cherry Blossoms   03/28/1927
Rufus Lemaire's Affairs   03/28/1927
Lady Do   04/18/1927
Circus Princess, The   04/25/1927
Hit the Deck!   04/25/1927
Hoop-La!   04/25/1927
Seventh Heart, The   05/02/1927
Night in Spain, A   05/03/1927
Oh, Ernest!   05/09/1927
He Loved the Ladies   05/10/1927
White Sister, The   05/17/1927
One Dam Thing After Another 05/19/1927
Grand Street Follies, The   05/19/1927
Tales of Rigo   05/30/1927
Merry-Go-Round (1927)   05/31/1927
White Birds   05/31/1927
Talk about Girls   06/14/1927
Bottomland   06/27/1927
Padlocks of 1927   07/05/1927
Africana   07/11/1927
Rang-Tang   07/12/1927
Kiss Me   07/21/1927
Allez-Oop   08/02/1927
Manhatters, The   08/03/1927
Ziegfeld Follies of 1927   08/16/1927
A La Carte   08/17/1927
Footlights   08/19/1927
Strike Up the Band   08/29/1927
Band Box Follies, The   09/05/1927
Pickwick   09/05/1927
Good News   09/06/1927
Burlesque   09/12/1927
Half a Widow   09/12/1927
My Maryland   09/12/1927
Enchanted Isle   09/19/1927
Manhattan Mary   09/26/1927
Merry Malones, The   09/26/1927
Speak Easy   09/26/1927

Joan of Arkansaw   10/00/1927
Sidewalks of New York   10/03/1927
Yes, Yes, Yvette   10/03/1927
Blue Train, The   10/05/1927
My Princess   10/06/1927
5 O'Clock Girl, The   10/10/1927
Just Fancy   10/11/1927
White Lights   10/11/1927
Bow-Wows   10/12/1927
Love Call, The   10/24/1927
Girl from Cook's, The   11/01/1927
Connecticut Yankee, A   11/03/1927
Artists and Models   11/15/1927
Funny Face   11/22/1927
Take the Air   11/22/1927
Harry Delmar's Revels   11/28/1927
Golden Dawn   11/30/1927
Cotton Club Revue   12/04/1927
Happy   12/05/1927
Morning After, The   12/16/1927
Excess Baggage   12/26/1927
White Eagle, The   12/26/1927
Show Boat   12/27/1927
Lovely Lady   12/29/1927

1928

Bringing Up Father at the   00/00/1928
   Seashore
Charlot 1928   00/00/1928
Cotton Club Revue   00/00/1928
Festivities of 1927   00/00/1928
Headin' South   00/00/1928
Oh Johnny   00/00/1928
She's My Baby   01/03/1928
Rosalie   01/10/1928
Optimists, The   01/30/1928
Madcap, The   01/31/1928
Sunny Days   02/08/1928
Yellow Mask, The   02/08/1928
Rain or Shine   02/09/1928
Parisiana   02/09/1928
Mr. Moneypenny   02/16/1928
Lady Mary   02/23/1928
Keep Shufflin'   02/27/1928
Veils   03/13/1928
Three Musketeers, The   03/13/1928
Diamond Lil   04/09/1928
Greenwich Village Follies,   04/09/1928
Present Arms   04/26/1928
Lady Luck   04/27/1928
Blue Eyes   04/27/1928
Here's Howe!   05/01/1928
Blackbirds of 1928   05/09/1928
La Revue des Ambassadeurs   05/10/1928
Grand Street Follies, The   05/28/1928
That's a Good Girl   06/05/1928
Say When   06/26/1928
George White's Scandals   07/02/1928

Earl Carroll's Vanities of   08/06/1928
   1928
Songwriter, The   08/13/1928
Good Boy   09/05/1928
White Lilacs   09/10/1928
Luckee Girl   09/15/1928
Cross My Heart   09/17/1928
New Moon, The   09/19/1928
Chee-Chee   09/25/1928
Billie   10/01/1928
Just a Minute   10/08/1928
Paris   10/08/1928
Ups-a-Daisy   10/08/1928
Hold Everything!   10/10/1928
Three Cheers   10/15/1928
Animal Crackers   10/23/1928
Hello, Yourself!!!!   10/30/1928
Americana   10/30/1928
This Year of Grace!   11/07/1928
Treasure Girl   11/08/1928
Rainbow   11/21/1928
Well, Well, Well   12/00/1928
Angela   12/03/1928
Whoopee   12/04/1928
Falstaff   12/25/1928
Red Robe, The   12/25/1928
Houseboat on the Styx,   12/25/1928
   The
Hello Daddy!   12/26/1928
Ziegfeld Midnight Frolic   12/28/1928

1929

Ziegfeld Midnight Frolic   00/00/1929
Blackbirds of 1929   00/00/1929
Cotton Club Revue   00/00/1929
Duchess of Chicago, The   00/00/1929
Gay Paree (1929)   00/00/1929
Harry Carroll's Revue   00/00/1929
Load of Coal   00/00/1929
Ming Toy   00/00/1929
Open Your Eyes   00/00/1929
Padlocks of 1929   00/00/1929
Wishing Well, The   00/00/1929
Ziegfeld Midnight Frolic   01/07/1929
Deep Harlem   01/07/1929
Polly   01/08/1929
Follow Thru   01/09/1929
Ned Wayburn's Gambols   01/15/1929
Boom-Boom   01/28/1929
Lady Fingers   01/31/1929
Fioretta   02/05/1929
Ziegfeld Midnight Frolic   02/06/1929
Pleasure Bound   02/18/1929
Spring Is Here   03/11/1929
Music in May   04/01/1929
Darktown Affairs   04/22/1929
Messin' 'Round   04/22/1929
Little Show, The   04/30/1929

Grand Street Follies, The   05/01/1929
Pansy   05/14/1929
Friars Frolic for Mayor J.   05/19/1929
  J. Walker
Night in Venice, A   05/21/1929
Hot Chocolates   06/20/1929
Keep It Clean   06/24/1929
Bamboola   06/26/1929
Earl Carroll's Sketch Book   07/01/1929
Show Girl   07/02/1929
Broadway Nights   07/15/1929
Noble Rogue, A   07/19/1929
Murray Anderson's Almanac   08/04/1929
Jerry for Short   08/12/1929
Sweet Adeline   09/03/1929
Street Singer, The   09/17/1929
Cape Cod Follies   09/18/1929
George White's Scandals   09/23/1929
Moon Madness   09/30/1929
June Moon   10/09/1929
Great Day!   10/17/1929
Wonderful Night, A   10/31/1929
Mr. Cinders   11/02/1929
Bitter Sweet   11/05/1929
House That Jack Built, The   11/08/1929
Heads Up!   11/11/1929
Sons o' Guns   11/26/1929
Fifty Million Frenchmen   11/27/1929
Silver Swan, The   11/27/1929
Top Speed   12/25/1929
Woof, Woof   12/25/1929
Great Day in N' Orleans   12/30/1929
Wake Up and Dream   12/30/1929
Ginger Snaps   12/31/1929

1930

Biff-Boom-Bang   00/00/1930
Blackberries of 1930   00/00/1930
Brown Sugar   00/00/1930
Funny Money   00/00/1930
Kitchen Mechanic's Revue   00/00/1930
Runnin' de Town   00/00/1930
Three Little Maids   00/00/1930
Ziegfeld Follies of 1930   00/00/1930
Strike Up the Band   01/14/1930
Ripples   02/11/1930
Nine-Fifteen Revue   02/11/1930
Simple Simon   02/18/1930
Here Comes the Bride   02/20/1930
International Revue, The   02/25/1930
Flying High   03/03/1930
Cochran's 1930 Revue   03/27/1930
Shuffle Along of 1930   04/00/1930
Co-optimists of 1930, The   04/04/1930
Jonica   04/07/1930
Three Little Girls   04/14/1930
Folies Bergere Review, The   04/15/1930
Garrick Gaieties, The   06/04/1930

Change Your Luck   06/06/1930
Artists and Models (1930)   06/10/1930
Mystery Moon   06/23/1930
Fireworks of 1930   06/26/1930
Earl Carroll's Vanities of   07/01/1930
  1930
Who Cares?   07/08/1930
Hot Rhythm   08/21/1930
Second Little Show, The   09/02/1930
Charlot's Masquerade   09/04/1930
Follow a Star   09/17/1930
Luana   09/17/1930
Nina Rosa   09/20/1930
Fine and Dandy   09/29/1930
Prince Chu Chang   10/06/1930
Pajama Lady, The   10/06/1930
Brown Buddies   10/07/1930
Princess Charming   10/13/1930
Girl Crazy   10/14/1930
Three's a Crowd   10/15/1930
Blackbirds of 1930   10/22/1930
Arms and the Maid   11/00/1930
Vanderbilt Revue, The   11/03/1930
Well of Romance, The   11/07/1930
Hello, Paris   11/15/1930
Sweet and Low   11/17/1930
Smiles   11/18/1930
Little Tommy Tucker   11/19/1930
Ever Green   12/03/1930
New Yorkers, The   12/08/1930
Ballyhoo   12/22/1930
Life Is Like That   12/23/1930
Meet My Sister   12/30/1930

1931

Accidentally Yours   00/00/1931
B.S. Moss Varieties   00/00/1931
Blue Bird Revue, The   00/00/1931
Cotton Club Revue   00/00/1931
Hollywood Nine O'Clock   00/00/1931
  Revue, The
Star Dust   00/00/1931
You Said It   01/19/1931
Private Lives   01/27/1931
Through the Years   01/28/1931
America's Sweetheart 02/10/1931
Gang's All Here, The   02/18/1931
Venetian Glass Nephew, The   02/23/1931
Paris in Spring   02/26/1931
Rhythmania   03/00/1931
Making Mary   03/01/1931
Wonder Bar, The   03/17/1931
Rhapsody in Black   05/04/1931
Billy Rose's Crazy Quilt   05/19/1931
Third Little Show, The   06/01/1931
Band Wagon, The   06/03/1931
Ziegfeld Follies of 1931   07/01/1931
Box of Tricks   07/13/1931

Shoot the Works   07/21/1931
Nine O'Clock Revue, The   07/27/1931
Earl Carroll's Vanities of 1931   08/27/1931
Free for All   09/08/1931
Singing Rabbi, The   09/10/1931
George White's Scandals   09/14/1931
Fast and Furious   09/15/1931
Singin' the Blues   09/16/1931
Cherries Are Ripe   09/21/1931
Nikki   09/29/1931
Good Companions, The   10/01/1931
Everybody's Welcome   10/13/1931
Cat and the Fiddle   10/15/1931
   The
East Wind   10/27/1931
Laugh Parade, The   11/02/1931
Here Goes the Bride   11/03/1931
Social Register, The   11/09/1931
Sugar Hill   12/25/1931
Of Thee I Sing   12/26/1931
Experience Unnecessary   12/30/1931

1932

Alarm Clock, The   00/00/1932
Forward March   00/00/1932
Hot Harlem   00/00/1932
Hushabye Lane   00/00/1932
La Ronde des Heures   00/00/1932
Little Racketeer, A   01/18/1932
Lucky Day   02/01/1932
Face the Music   02/17/1932
Marching By   03/03/1932
Hot-Cha!   03/08/1932
Blackberries of 1932   04/04/1932
Friars Frolic   05/08/1932
There You Are   05/16/1932
Yeah Man   05/26/1932
Hey Nonny Nonny!   06/06/1932
Hullabaloo   06/09/1932
Smiling Faces   08/30/1932
Passing Show of 1932, The   09/05/1932
Ballyhoo of 1932   09/06/1932
Flying Colors   09/15/1932
Belmont Varieties   09/26/1932
Earl Carroll's Vanities of   09/27/1932
   1932
Americana   10/05/1932
I Loved You Wednesday   10/11/1932
Cotton Club Parade   10/23/1932
Cotton Club Parade   10/23/1932
Tell Her the Truth   10/28/1932
Harlem Hotcha   11/00/1932
Cyrano de Bergerac   11/04/1932
Music in the Air   11/08/1932
George White's Music Hall   11/22/1932
   Varieties
Dubarry, The   11/22/1932
Take a Chance   11/26/1932

Gay Divorce   11/29/1932
Great Magoo, The   12/02/1932
Walk a Little Faster   12/07/1932
Alice in Wonderland   12/12/1932
Shuffle Along of 1933   12/26/1932
Radio City Music Hall   12/27/1932
   Opening

1933

Show Boat Revue of 1933   00/00/1933
Birdie   00/00/1933
Clowns in Clover   00/00/1933
Cotton Club Parade   00/00/1933
Ever Yours   00/00/1933
Hollywood Be Thy Name   00/00/1933
Hollywood Revels of 1933   00/00/1933
International Revue, The   00/00/1933
Nine O'Clock Revue, The   00/00/1933
Paradise Revue   00/00/1933
Pardon My English   01/20/1933
Melody   02/14/1933
Strike Me Pink   03/04/1933
Home, James   03/10/1933
Die Lindenwirtin   03/30/1933
Cotton Club Parade   04/06/1933
Hummin' Sam   04/08/1933
Threepenny Opera, The   04/13/1933
Hi-De-Ho   05/06/1933
Tattle Tales   06/01/1933
Shady Lady   07/05/1933
Beau Brummel   08/07/1933
Ball at the Savoy   09/08/1933
Murder at the Vanities   09/12/1933
Nice Goings On   09/13/1933
Hold Your Horses   09/25/1933
As Thousands Cheer   09/30/1933
Hollywood Revels of 1934   10/02/1933
Nymph Errant   10/06/1933
Champagne, Sec   10/14/1933
Let 'Em Eat Cake   10/21/1933
Her Master's Voice   10/23/1933
Rose de France   10/23/1933
Please!   11/16/1933
Roberta   11/18/1933
She Loves Me Not   11/20/1933
Blackbirds of 1934 (First Edition)   12/02/1933
Beau Brummell   12/22/1933

1934

Manhattan Music Hall Revue   00/00/1934
Rhythm for Sale   00/00/1934
Billy Rose's Music Hall   00/00/1934
   Revue
Bizarrities   00/00/1934
Casino Varieties   00/00/1934
Chicago Rhythm   00/00/1934

Cotton Club Parade   00/00/1934
Greenwich Village Follies,   00/00/1934
  The
Harmony Hill   00/00/1934
Hearts on Parade   00/00/1934
Hollywood Music Box Revue   00/00/1934
Ice Follies of 1934   00/00/1934
Julie   00/00/1934
Man from Baltimore, The   00/00/1934
Ziegfeld Follies of 1934   01/04/1934
All the King's Horses   01/30/1934
Four Saints in Three Acts   02/20/1934
New Faces   03/15/1934
Cotton Club Parade   03/23/1934
Three Sisters   04/09/1934
Moon Rises, The   04/23/1934
Caviar   06/07/1934
Gypsy Blonde   06/25/1934
Life Begins at 8:40   08/27/1934
Saluta   08/28/1934
Kill That Story   08/29/1934
Blackbirds of 1934 (Second Edition)   09/00/1934
Night of Stars   09/20/1934
Great Waltz, The   09/22/1934
Merrily We Roll Along   09/29/1934
Continental Varieties   10/03/1934
Hi Diddle Diddle   10/03/1934
America Sings   10/09/1934
Bring on the Girls   10/22/1934
Conversation Piece   10/23/1934
Say When   11/08/1934
Anything Goes   11/21/1934
Africana   11/26/1934
Revenge with Music   11/28/1934
Calling All Stars   12/13/1934
Marie Galante   12/22/1934
Fools Rush In   12/25/1934
Thumbs Up!   12/27/1934
O'Flynn, The   12/27/1934
Music Hath Charms   12/29/1934

1935

Casino de Paris Revue   00/00/1935
Cocktails 5 to 7   00/00/1935
Cotton Club Parade   00/00/1935
First Manhattan Music Hall   00/00/1935
  Revue
Hot Chocolates   00/00/1935
Paradise Parade of 1935   00/00/1935
Princess Slips Away, The   00/00/1935
Riviera Revue   00/00/1935
Ubangi Club Follies   00/00/1935
Come of Age   01/12/1935
Hollywood Holiday   02/15/1935
Stop Press   02/21/1935
Post Depression Gaieties,   02/24/1935
  The
Petticoat Fever   03/04/1935

Something Gay   04/29/1935
Parade   05/20/1935
Earl Carroll's Sketch Book   06/04/1935
Kingdom for a Cow, A   06/28/1935
Common Flesh   08/12/1935
Smile at Me   08/23/1935
Moon Over Mulberry Street   09/04/1935
At Home Abroad   09/19/1935
Venus in Silk   10/01/1935
Porgy and Bess   10/10/1935
Jubilee   10/12/1935
Let's Have Fun   10/22/1935
Provincetown Follies   11/03/1935
Jumbo   11/16/1935
May Wine   12/05/1935
George White's Scandals   12/25/1935
Entre-Nous   12/30/1935

1936

Earl Carroll's Palm Island   00/00/1936
  Revue
Hollywood Revels of 1936   00/00/1936
Hot Chocolates   00/00/1936
Palladium Frolics   00/00/1936
Paradise Parade   00/00/1936
Perfect   00/00/1936
Radio City Music Hall   00/00/1936
  production
Illustrators' Show, The   01/22/1936
Lady Precious Stream   01/27/1936
Ziegfeld Follies of 1936   01/30/1936
Murder in the Old Red Barn   02/01/1936
Follow the Sun   02/04/1936
On Your Toes   04/11/1936
Follow the Parade   04/12/1936
Broadway Sho-Window   04/12/1936
Summer Wives   04/13/1936
Lambs Spring Gambol, The   04/25/1936
Waltz Was Born in Vienna   04/25/1936
Private Affair, A   05/14/1936
New Faces of 1936   05/19/1936
Billy Rose's Show of Shows   06/08/1936
Casa Manana   06/08/1936
Last Frontier, The   06/08/1936
Blackbirds of 1936   07/09/1936
Careless Rapture   09/11/1936
Cotton Club Parade   09/24/1936
White Horse Inn   10/01/1936
Red, Hot and Blue!   10/29/1936
Forbidden Melody   11/02/1936
Johnny Johnson   11/19/1936
Family Album   11/24/1936
Red Peppers   11/24/1936
Shadow Play   11/24/1936
O Mistress Mine   12/03/1936
Lambs Winter Gambol, The   12/05/1936
One April Day   12/05/1936
Oh Say Can You Sing   12/11/1936

Black Rhythm   12/19/1936
We Were Dancing   12/24/1936
Show Is On, The   12/25/1936
Dancing Coed, The   12/29/1936

1937

Calling All Men   00/00/1937
Cotton Club Express   00/00/1937
Cotton Club Parade   00/00/1937
Cotton Club Revue, The   00/00/1937
Grand Terrace Revue, The   00/00/1937
Greek to You   00/00/1937
Hollywood Revels of 1937   00/00/1937
Pan-American Casino Revue   00/00/1937
Riviera Follies of 1937   00/00/1937
Pepper Mill   01/05/1937
Eternal Road, The   01/07/1937
Cocktail Bar   01/13/1937
Naughty-Naught '00   01/23/1937
Frederika   02/04/1937
Babes in Arms   04/14/1937
Orchids Preferred   05/11/1937
Sea Legs   05/18/1937
Salute to Spring   07/12/1937
Swing It   07/22/1937
Harlem Uproar House   09/00/1937
Virginia   09/02/1937
Hero Is Born, A   10/01/1937
Fireman's Flame, The   10/09/1937
Bric-a-Brac   10/20/1937
I'd Rather Be Right   11/02/1937
Julius Caesar   11/11/1937
Pins and Needles   11/27/1937
Hooray for What!   12/01/1937
Between the Devil   12/23/1937
Three Waltzes   12/25/1937

1938

Davy Crockett   00/00/1938
Grand Terrace Revue, The   00/00/1938
Hollywood Revue Production   00/00/1938
Paradise Restaurant and   00/00/1938
   Revue
So Proudly We Hail   00/00/1938
Cradle Will Rock, The   01/03/1938
Right This Way   01/04/1938
Let's Play Fair   01/18/1938
Who's Who   03/01/1938
Cotton Club Parade   03/09/1938
Happy Returns   04/19/1938
I Married an Angel   05/11/1938
Two Bouquets, The   05/31/1938
Gentlemen Unafraid   06/03/1938
Sun Never Sets, The   06/09/1938
Come Across   09/14/1938

You Never Know   09/21/1938
Hellzapoppin   09/22/1938
Sing Out the News   09/24/1938
Cotton Club Parade   09/28/1938
Knights of Song   10/17/1938
Knickerbocker Holiday   10/19/1938
Girl from Wyoming, The   10/29/1938
Danton's Death   11/02/1938
Leave It to Me!   11/09/1938
Boys from Syracuse, The   11/23/1938
Great Lady   12/01/1938
Lambs Annual Gambol, The   12/03/1938
Pinocchio   12/23/1938
Policy Kings, The   12/30/1938

1939

Aquacade Revue   00/00/1939
Big Show   00/00/1939
Fair Enough   00/00/1939
Hello Beautiful   00/00/1939
New York World's Fair   00/00/1939
Peter Penny Under the Dream 00/00/1939
   Tree
Turn of the Century, The   00/00/1939
White Flame, The   00/00/1939
Mamba's Daughters   01/03/1939
Set to Music   01/18/1939
American Way, The   01/21/1939
Jeremiah   02/03/1939
One for the Money   02/04/1939
Stars in Your Eyes   02/09/1939
Blackbirds of 1939   02/11/1939
Little Foxes, The   02/15/1939
Swing Mikado, The   03/01/1939
Dancing Years   03/23/1939
Hot Mikado, The   03/23/1939
Cotton Club Parade   03/24/1939
   (World's Fair Edition)
Big Show, The (1)   04/09/1939
Sing for Your Supper   04/24/1939
Railroads on Parade   04/30/1939
Streets of Paris, The   06/19/1939
From Vienna   06/20/1939
Yokel Boy   07/06/1939
Sticks and Stones   08/14/1939
George White's Scandals   08/28/1939
Nice Goin'   09/00/1939
Straw Hat Revue, The   09/29/1939
Man Who Came to Dinner, The 10/16/1939
Too Many Girls   10/18/1939
Cotton Club Parade   11/01/1939
Very Warm for May   11/17/1939
Swingin' the Dream   11/29/1939
Du Barry Was a Lady   12/06/1939
All Clear   12/20/1939
White Plume, The   12/26/1939
Two for Tonight   12/28/1939

1940

At Your Service   00/00/1940
Billy Rose's Aquacade Revue 00/00/1940
Cotton Club Parade   00/00/1940
Georgia   00/00/1940
Ice Follies of 1941   00/00/1940
Let's Go   00/00/1940
New Aquacade Revue, The   00/00/1940
Nights of Gladness   00/00/1940
Organizer, The   00/00/1940
Royal Palm Revue (Fifth   00/00/1940
   Edition)
John Henry   01/10/1940
Earl Carroll's Vanities of   01/13/1940
   1940
Two on an Island   01/25/1940
Two for the Show   02/08/1940
Reunion in New York   02/21/1940
Higher and Higher   04/04/1940
Up and Doing   04/17/1940
American Jubilee   05/12/1940
Keep Off the Grass   05/23/1940
Louisiana Purchase   05/28/1940
Walk with Music   06/04/1940
Merry Wives Swing It!, The   06/14/1940
Two Weeks with Pay   06/24/1940
Little Dog Laughed, The   08/13/1940
Hold on To Your Hats   09/11/1940
Boys and Girls Together   10/01/1940
Cabin in the Sky   10/25/1940
'Tis of Thee   10/26/1940
Panama Hattie   10/30/1940
Thank You, Columbus!   11/15/1940
High As a Kite   11/25/1940
Hi Ya, Gentlemen   11/29/1940
Pal Joey   12/25/1940
Meet the People   12/25/1940
All in Fun   12/27/1940
She Had to Say Yes   12/30/1940

1941

We Did It Before   00/00/1941
Beachcomber Nites Revue   00/00/1941
Florentine Garden Revue   00/00/1941
Hulbert's Follies   00/00/1941
Ice-Capades of 1941   00/00/1941
Joys of Youth   00/00/1941
Silver Screen, The   00/00/1941
Tan Manhattan   00/00/1941
Ubangi Club Follies   00/00/1941
No for an Answer   01/05/1941
Night of Love, A   01/07/1941
Crazy with the Heat   01/14/1941
Rhapsody in Black (1941)   01/20/1941
Lady in the Dark   01/23/1941
Hot from Harlem   05/13/1941
Turnabout! Revues   07/00/1941

Jump for Joy   07/10/1941
It Happens on Ice   07/15/1941
Marinka   07/18/1941
Fun for the Money   08/00/1941
Best Foot Forward   10/01/1941
Fun to Be Free   10/05/1941
Viva O'Brien   10/09/1941
Let's Face It!   10/29/1941
High Kickers   10/31/1941
It Happens on Ice   11/09/1941
They Can't Get You Down   12/00/1941
Sons o' Fun   12/01/1941
Sunny River   12/04/1941
Lambs Annual Dinner, Gambol 12/06/1941
   and Ball, The
Here We Are Again   12/06/1941
Banjo Eyes   12/25/1941

1942

Blackouts of 1942   00/00/1942
Dreamy Kid, The   00/00/1942
Ice Follies of 1942   00/00/1942
Symphony in Brown   00/00/1942
Lady Comes Across, The   01/09/1942
Of V We Sing   02/11/1942
Priorities of 1942   03/12/1942
It's About Time (1942)   03/28/1942
By Jupiter   06/03/1942
Star and Garter   06/24/1942
Stars on Ice   07/02/1942
This Is the Army   07/04/1942
Heels Together   09/15/1942
New Priorities of 1943   09/15/1942
Let Freedom Sing   10/05/1942
Count Me In   10/08/1942
Life of the Party   10/08/1942
Oy Is Das a Leben!   10/12/1942
Beat the Band   10/14/1942
Copacabana Revue   10/17/1942
Rosalinda   10/28/1942
High and Dry   12/05/1942
At Ease   12/11/1942
New Faces of 1943   12/22/1942
Full Speed Ahead   12/25/1942
You'll See Stars   12/29/1942

1943

At Your Service   00/00/1943
Born Happy   00/00/1943
Dancing in the Streets   00/00/1943
Ice-Capades of 1943   00/00/1943
Lunchtime Follies   00/00/1943
Miss Underground   00/00/1943
Nutcracker Jive   00/00/1943
Something for the Boys   01/07/1943

Marching with Johnny   01/22/1943
Copacabana Revue   03/10/1943
Oklahoma!   03/31/1943
Ziegfeld Follies of 1943   04/01/1943
Copacabana Revue   06/02/1943
Early to Bed   06/17/1943
Stars and Gripes   07/13/1943
My Dear Public   09/09/1943
Bright Lights of 1944   09/16/1943
Hairpin Harmony   10/01/1943
One Touch of Venus   10/07/1943
Artists and Models   11/05/1943
What's Up?   11/11/1943
Winged Victory   11/20/1943
Carmen Jones   12/02/1943

1944

Broadway Rhythm   00/00/1944
Copacabana Revue   00/00/1944
Glad to See You   00/00/1944
Ice Follies of 1944   00/00/1944
PFC Mary Brown   00/00/1944
Stovepipe Hat   00/00/1944
Viva Amigos   00/00/1944
WAC Musical   00/00/1944
Marianne   01/10/1944
Jackpot   01/13/1944
Skirts   01/25/1944
Vincent Youmans' Ballet   01/27/1944
    Revue
Mexican Hayride   01/28/1944
Follow the Girls   04/08/1944
Allah Be Praised!   04/20/1944
Helen Goes to Troy   04/24/1944
Tars and Spars   05/05/1944
Dream with Music   05/18/1944
About Face!   05/26/1944
Take a Bow   06/15/1944
Hats Off to Ice   06/22/1944
Hi, Yank!   08/07/1944
Song of Norway   08/21/1944
Copacabana Revue   09/20/1944
Bloomer Girl   10/05/1944
Sadie Thompson   11/16/1944
Rhapsody   11/22/1944
Seven Lively Arts   12/07/1944
Spook Scandals   12/08/1944
Laffing Room Only   12/23/1944
Sing Out, Sweet Land!   12/27/1944
On the Town   12/28/1944

1945

OK, USA!   00/00/1945
Ulysses Africanus   00/00/1945
Lady Says Yes, A   01/10/1945
Up in Central Park   01/27/1945

Overtons, The   02/06/1945
Firebrand of Florence, The   03/22/1945
It's Up to You   03/31/1945
Watch Out Angel   04/03/1945
Carousel   04/19/1945
Blue Holiday   05/21/1945
Memphis Bound!   05/24/1945
Hollywood Pinafore (Or the   05/31/1945
    Lad Who Loved a Salary)
Mr. Strauss Goes to Boston   09/06/1945
Carib Song   09/27/1945
Spring in Brazil   10/01/1945
Polonaise   10/06/1945
Girl from Nantucket, The   11/08/1945
Passing Show of 1945, The   11/09/1945
Are You With It?   11/10/1945
Day Before Spring, The   11/22/1945
Gift for the Bride, A   12/01/1945
Billion Dollar Baby   12/21/1945
Tonight's the Night   12/24/1945

1946

Beachcomber Club Revue of   00/00/1946
    1946
Copacabana Show in Miami   00/00/1946
Holiday on Ice   00/00/1946
Night at the Copa, A   00/00/1946
Nellie Bly   01/21/1946
Lute Song   02/06/1946
Duchess Misbehaves, The   02/13/1946
Three to Make Ready   03/07/1946
Love in the Snow   03/15/1946
St. Louis Woman   03/30/1946
Shootin' Star   04/04/1946
Windy City   04/18/1946
Call Me Mister   04/18/1946
Annie Get Your Gun   05/16/1946
Around the World in Eighty   05/31/1946
    Days
Icetime   06/20/1946
Two Hearts in Three-Quarter   07/08/1946
    Time
Yours Is My Heart   09/05/1946
Flag Is Born, A   09/05/1946
Gypsy Lady   09/17/1946
Sweet Bye and Bye   10/10/1946
Happy Birthday   10/31/1946
Park Avenue   11/04/1946
Chris Crosses   11/22/1946
If the Shoe Fits   12/05/1946
Friars Frolic in honor of   12/15/1946
    Ted Lewis
Pacific 1860   12/19/1946
In Gay New Orleans   12/25/1946
Lovely Me   12/25/1946
Toplitzky of Notre Dame   12/26/1946
Beggar's Holiday   12/26/1946
Affairs of Vanity Fair   00/00/1947

1947

Kitchen Opera   00/00/1947
Meet Miss April   00/00/1947
Meet Miss Jones   00/00/1947
Lady Passing Fair, A   01/03/1947
Street Scene   01/09/1947
Finian's Rainbow   01/10/1947
Washington Square   01/23/1947
Brigadoon   03/13/1947
Barefoot Boy with Cheek   04/03/1947
Our Lan'   04/18/1947
Bless the Bride   04/26/1947
Icetime of 1947-48   05/28/1947
Reluctant Lady   07/00/1947
Shape of Things, The   07/26/1947
Music in My Heart   10/02/1947
Under the Counter   10/03/1947
High Button Shoes   10/09/1947
Allegro   10/10/1947
Here's the Pitch   12/09/1947
Angel in the Wings   12/11/1947
Bonanza Bound   12/26/1947

1948

Big As Life   00/00/1948
Counter Melody   00/00/1948
New Faces of 1948   00/00/1948
Phinney's Rainbow   00/00/1948
Stars on My Shoulders   00/00/1948
Make Mine Manhattan   01/15/1948
Look Ma, I'm Dancin'!   01/29/1948
Copacabana Revue   04/14/1948
Inside U.S.A.   04/30/1948
Hold It!   05/05/1948
Ballet Ballads   05/09/1948
Sleepy Hollow   06/03/1948
Howdy Mr. Ice!   06/24/1948
Hand in Hand   07/06/1948
Hilarities   09/09/1948
Small Wonder   09/15/1948
Heaven on Earth   09/16/1948
Magdalena   09/20/1948
That's the Ticket   09/27/1948
Love Life   10/07/1948
Where's Charley?   10/11/1948
My Romance   10/29/1948
As the Girls Go   11/13/1948
Lend an Ear   12/16/1948
Kiss Me, Kate   12/30/1948

1949

Patricia   00/00/1949
Tambourita   00/00/1949
Sugar Hill   00/00/1949
Flatbush Follies   00/00/1949
Friars Frolic of 1949   00/00/1949

He and She   00/00/1949
Hellzapoppin of 1949   00/00/1949
Ice Follies of 1949   00/00/1949
Lo and Behold   00/00/1949
Mooncalf   00/00/1949
Mr. Ambassador   00/00/1949
Along Fifth Avenue   01/13/1949
All for Love   01/22/1949
All That Glitters   03/19/1949
Belinda Fair   03/25/1949
Tongue in Cheek   03/28/1949
South Pacific   04/07/1949
Howdy Mr. Ice of 1950   05/26/1949
Pretty Penny   06/20/1949
Miss Liberty   07/15/1949
Touch and Go   10/13/1949
Lost in the Stars   10/30/1949
Regina   10/31/1949
A La Carte   11/16/1949
Adamant Eve   11/17/1949
Texas, Li'l Darlin'   11/25/1949
Gentlemen Prefer Blondes   12/08/1949

1950

Break It Up   00/00/1950
Fresh Airs   00/00/1950
Huckleberry Finn   00/00/1950
Ice Follies of 1950   00/00/1950
It's a Small World   00/00/1950
Nantucket   00/00/1950
Happy As Larry   01/06/1950
Copacabana Revue   01/11/1950
Down in the Valley   01/14/1950
Alive and Kicking   01/17/1950
Dance Me a Song   01/20/1950
Arms and the Girl   02/02/1950
Copacabana Revue   02/12/1950
Copacabana Revue   02/22/1950
Great to Be Alive!   03/23/1950
Peter Pan   04/24/1950
Tickets Please!   04/27/1950
Lucky Day   04/28/1950
Talent 50   04/28/1950
Copacabana Revue   05/10/1950
Liar, The   05/18/1950
Personalities, The   06/00/1950
Michael Todd's Peep Show   06/28/1950
Just Around the Corner   07/31/1950
High & Dry   09/11/1950
Little Boy Blue   09/11/1950
Pardon Our French   10/05/1950
Red, White and Blue   10/07/1950
Call Me Madam   10/12/1950
Barrier, The   11/02/1950
Guys and Dolls   11/24/1950
If You Please   11/28/1950
Bless You All   12/14/1950
I Love Lydia   12/18/1950
Out of This World   12/21/1950

1951

Adamses, The   00/00/1951
Bagel Scandals   00/00/1951
Be Yourself   00/00/1951
Lou Holtz' Merry-Go-Round   00/00/1951
My L.A.   00/00/1951
Gay's the Word   02/16/1951
Razzle Dazzle   02/19/1951
Let Me Hear the Melody   03/09/1951
It's About Time   03/14/1951
King and I, The   03/29/1951
Bagels and Yox of 1951   03/30/1951
   (Bagel Scandals)
Copacabana Revue   04/04/1951
Make a Wish   04/18/1951
Tree Grows in Brooklyn, A   04/19/1951
Come Out Swinging   04/27/1951
Flahooley   05/14/1951
Courtin' Time   06/13/1951
Seventeen   06/21/1951
Two on the Aisle   07/19/1951
All About Love   10/17/1951
And So To Bed   10/17/1951
Top Banana   11/01/1951
Paint Your Wagon   11/12/1951
Month of Sundays, A   12/25/1951

1952

Ringling Brothers-Barnum   00/00/1952
   and Bailey Circus
Syn-cyr-ities of 1952   00/00/1952
Curtain Going Up   02/15/1952
Paris '90   03/04/1952
Three Wishes for Jamie   03/21/1952
Shuffle Along of 1952   05/08/1952
New Faces of 1952   05/16/1952
Night in Venice, A   06/00/1952
Wish You Were Here   06/25/1952
Jollyanna   08/11/1952
Baby Face O'Flynn   08/13/1952
Love from Judy   09/25/1952
Copacabana Revue   10/08/1952
Buttrio Square   10/14/1952
My Darlin' Aida   10/27/1952
Seven Year Itch, The   11/20/1952
Two's Company   12/15/1952

1953

Cockles and Champagne   00/00/1953
Great Waltz, The   00/00/1953
Ice Follies of 1954   00/00/1953
Nice to See You   00/00/1953
Ringling Brothers-Barnum   00/00/1953
   and Bailey Circus
Crucible, The   01/22/1953
Arthur Godfrey's TV   01/28/1953
   Calendar Show
Hazel Flagg   02/11/1953
Maggie   02/18/1953
Wonderful Town   02/25/1953
Copacabana Revue   04/22/1953
Can-Can   05/07/1953
Me and Juliet   05/28/1953
Stock in Trade   07/10/1953
Rip Van Winkle   07/13/1953
Hurly-Burly   08/05/1953
Great Scott   08/11/1953
Thirteen Clocks   08/17/1953
High Time   08/17/1953
Little Green Isle   08/28/1953
Wayward Way, The   09/03/1953
Carnival in Flanders   09/08/1953
Himberana   11/13/1953
Golden Fleece, The   11/18/1953
Kismet   12/03/1953
John Murray Anderson's   12/10/1953
   Almanac

1954

Hollywood Ice Revue, The   00/00/1954
Saturday Night   00/00/1954
That's Life   00/00/1954
What's the Rush   00/00/1954
Come On and Play   02/15/1954
Girl in Pink Tights, The   03/05/1954
Threepenny Opera, The   03/10/1954
Golden Apple, The   03/11/1954
Copacabana Revue   04/07/1954
By the Beautiful Sea   04/08/1954
Dolly   04/20/1954
Between Friends   05/01/1954
Huck Finn   05/07/1954
Happy Dollar, The   05/09/1954
Pajama Game, The   05/13/1954
Copacabana Revue   05/26/1954
Melody of Love   05/27/1954
Copacabana Revue   06/10/1954
Arabian Nights   06/25/1954
Walk Tall   07/12/1954
Up in Lights   08/01/1954
Satins and Spurs   09/12/1954
Boy Friend, The   09/30/1954
Pardon Our Antenna   10/16/1954
I Feel Wonderful   10/18/1954
Peter Pan   10/20/1954
Fanny   11/04/1954
Tempest in a Teapot   11/17/1954
Sailor's Delight   11/22/1954
Hello, Paree   11/24/1954
Sandhog   11/29/1954
Mrs. Patterson   12/01/1954
Hit the Trail   12/02/1954
Christmas Carol, A   12/23/1954
House of Flowers   12/30/1954

1955

Dilly   00/00/1955
In the Pink   00/00/1955
Irvin C. Miller's Brown   00/00/1955
   Skin Models
Meet the People of 1955   00/00/1955
Mighty Man Is He, A   00/00/1955
Once Over Lightly   00/00/1955
Society of Illustrators   00/00/1955
   Show 1955
Plain and Fancy   01/27/1955
Silk Stockings   02/24/1955
Shoestring Revue   02/28/1955
Come As You Are   03/00/1955
3 for Tonight   04/06/1955
Merry Widow, The   04/09/1955
Lighter Side, The   04/14/1955
Ankles Aweigh   04/18/1955
All in One   04/19/1955
Phoenix '55   04/23/1955
So What!   04/28/1955
Damn Yankees   05/05/1955
Seventh Heaven   05/26/1955
Chocolate Soldier, The   06/04/1955
Almost Crazy   06/20/1955
Svengali and the Blonde   07/30/1955
King and Mrs. Candle, The   08/22/1955
Catch a Star!   09/06/1955
Romance in Candlelight   09/15/1955
Our Town   09/19/1955
Heidi   10/01/1955
Reuben, Reuben   10/10/1955
No Time for Sergeants   10/20/1955
Vamp, The   11/10/1955
Lark, The   11/17/1955
Vamp Till Ready   11/22/1955
Pipe Dream   11/30/1955
Ali Baba and the Forty   12/26/1955
   Thieves

1956

Ah! Wilderness   00/00/1956
Last Resorts, The   00/00/1956
Four Below   03/04/1956
High Tor   03/10/1956
My Fair Lady   03/15/1956
Strip for Action   03/17/1956
Mr. Wonderful   03/22/1956
Adventures of Marco Polo,   04/14/1956
   The
Ziegfeld Follies of 1956   04/16/1956
Wake Up, Darling   05/02/1956
Most Happy Fella, The   05/03/1956
Cross Your Fingers   05/04/1956
Littlest Revue, The   05/22/1956
Bell for Adano, A   06/02/1956
Holiday   06/09/1956

Shangri-La   06/13/1956
New Faces of 1956   06/14/1956
By Hex   06/18/1956
World's My Oyster, The   07/31/1956
Sudden Spring, A   09/04/1956
Lord Don't Play Favorites,   09/17/1956
   The
Son of Four Below, The   09/27/1956
Sixth Finger in a Five   10/08/1956
   Finger Glove, The
Shoestring '57   11/05/1956
Everybody Loves Me   11/08/1956
Jack and the Beanstalk   11/12/1956
Li'l Abner   11/15/1956
Girls of Summer   11/19/1956
Tom Sawyer   11/21/1956
   Cranks   11/26/1956
Grab Me a Gondola   11/27/1956
Bells Are Ringing   11/29/1956
Candide   12/01/1956
Happy Hunting   12/06/1956
Pleasure Dome   12/13/1956
Stingiest Man in Town, The   12/23/1956
Amazing Adele, The   12/26/1956

1957

Ali Baba and the Forty   00/00/1957
   Thieves
Courtship of Miles   00/00/1957
   Standish, The
Ice Capades   00/00/1957
Ice Follies   00/00/1957
Mistress of the Inn, The   00/00/1957
New Faces   00/00/1957
Pound in Your Pocket, A   00/00/1957
Foolin' Ourselves   01/16/1957
Something Cool   02/00/1957
Ruggles of Red Gap   02/03/1957
Ziegfeld Follies of 1957   03/01/1957
Sin of Pat Muldoon, The   03/13/1957
Cinderella   03/31/1957
Shinbone Alley   04/13/1957
Livin' the Life   04/27/1957
Belinda!   05/03/1957
Mr. Broadway   05/11/1957
New Girl in Town   05/14/1957
Simply Heavenly   05/21/1957
Be My Guest   06/00/1957
Free As Air   06/06/1957
Kaleidoscope   06/13/1957
Sticks and Stones   06/30/1957
Cotton Club Revue   07/09/1957
Mask and Gown   09/10/1957
West Side Story   09/26/1957
Italian Straw Hat, The   09/30/1957
Ziegfeld Follies   09/30/1957
Carefree Heart, The   09/30/1957
Romanoff and Juliet   10/10/1957

Take Five   10/10/1957
Pinocchio   10/13/1957
Copper and Brass   10/17/1957
Jamaica   10/31/1957
Rumple   11/06/1957
Time Remembered   11/12/1957
Pied Piper of Hamlin, The   11/26/1957
Music Man, The   12/19/1957
Junior Miss   12/20/1957

1958

Geografoof, The   00/00/1958
Happy Times   00/00/1958
Hit the Stride   00/00/1958
Sands Hotel Copa Room Show   00/00/1958
Body Beautiful, The   01/23/1958
Oh Captain!   02/04/1958
Hans Brinker or the Silver   02/09/1958
   Skates
Aladdin   02/21/1958
Portofino   02/21/1958
Say, Darling   04/03/1958
Tongue in Cheek   04/05/1958
Hansel and Gretel   04/27/1958
Firstborn, The   04/30/1958
Joy Ride   05/12/1958
Nightcap   05/18/1958
Midsummer Night's Dream, A   06/20/1958
At the Grand   07/07/1958
Winter's Tale, The   07/20/1958
Shoestring Revue in Fort   09/00/1958
   Worth
Copacabana Revue   09/17/1958
Demi-Dozen   10/11/1958
Goldilocks (1958)   10/11/1958
World of Suzie Wong, The   10/14/1958
Little Women   10/16/1958
Diversions   11/07/1958
Salad Days   11/10/1958
La Plume de Ma Tante   11/11/1958
Whoop-Up   11/22/1958
Flower Drum Song   12/01/1958
Of Mice and Men   12/04/1958
Gift of the Magi, The   12/09/1958
   (1958)

1959

Diamond for Carla, A   00/00/1959
Merry Christmas   00/00/1959
Timothy Gray's Taboo Revue   00/00/1959
She Shall Have Music   01/22/1959
Tall Story   01/29/1959
No Man Can Tame Me   02/01/1959
Redhead   02/05/1959
Juno   03/09/1959

First Impressions   03/19/1959
Three to Make Ready (Magic   03/29/1959
   with Mary Martin)
Art Carney Meets the   04/05/1959
   Sorcerer's Apprentice
Once Upon a Mattress   04/11/1959
Destry Rides Again   04/23/1959
Art Carney Meets Peter and   05/03/1959
   the Wolf
Nervous Set, The   05/12/1959
Chic   05/19/1959
Fallout   05/20/1959
Gypsy   05/21/1959
Dr. Willy Nilly   06/04/1959
Billy Barnes Revue, The   06/09/1959
Dig We Must   07/04/1959
Pieces of Eight   09/17/1959
Happy Town   10/07/1959
At the Drop of a Hat   10/08/1959
Mis-Guided Tour   10/12/1959
Pink Jungle, The   10/14/1959
Take Me Along   10/22/1959
Kosher Widow, The   10/31/1959
Girls Against the Boys, The   11/02/1959
Sound of Music, The   11/16/1959
Little Mary Sunshine   11/18/1959
Fiorello!   11/23/1959
Saratoga   12/07/1959
Once Upon a Christmas Tree   12/09/1959
Free and Easy   12/17/1959

1960

Dream Girl   00/00/1960
Four Below Strikes Back   00/00/1960
Freedomland   00/00/1960
Hail Mary   00/00/1960
Harlem Heatwave   00/00/1960
President, The   00/00/1960
Underworld   00/00/1960
Parade   01/20/1960
Do Re Mi   01/26/1960
Russell Patterson's Sketch   02/06/1960
   Book
Beg, Borrow or Steal   02/10/1960
Fings Ain't Wot They Used   02/11/1960
   t'Be
Crystal Heart, The   02/15/1960
Copacabana Revue (1960)   03/02/1960
Greenwillow   03/08/1960
Dear Liar   03/17/1960
41 in a Sack   03/25/1960
Miss Emily Adam   03/29/1960
Bye Bye Birdie   04/14/1960
From A to Z   04/20/1960
Lock Up Your Daughters   04/27/1960
Fantasticks, The   05/03/1960
Ernest in Love   05/04/1960
Christine   05/07/1960

Medium Rare   07/06/1960
Art of Living, The   07/25/1960
Here Is the News   08/15/1960
Vintage '60   09/12/1960
Dressed to the Nines   09/22/1960
Greenwich Village U.S.A.   09/28/1960
Irma La Douce   09/29/1960
Valmouth   10/06/1960
Kittiwake Island   10/12/1960
Shoemaker and the Peddler,   10/14/1960
   The
Tenderloin   10/17/1960
Darwin's Theories   10/18/1960
Invitation to a March   10/29/1960
Unsinkable Molly Brown, The 11/03/1960
Camelot   12/03/1960
Send Me No Flowers   12/05/1960
Wildcat   12/16/1960

1961

Magic Nutcracker, The   00/00/1961
Quillow and the Giant   00/00/1961
Show Girl   01/12/1961
Conquering Hero, The   01/16/1961
Two for Fun   02/13/1961
Tiger Rag, The   02/16/1961
Double Entry   02/20/1961
13 Daughters   03/02/1961
What a Killing   03/27/1961
Tattooed Countess, The   04/03/1961
Happiest Girl in the World, 04/03/1961
   The
Hobo   04/10/1961
Decameron, The   04/12/1961
Carnival!   04/13/1961
Smiling, the Boy Fell Dead   04/19/1961
Young Abe Lincoln   04/25/1961
Donnybrook!   05/18/1961
Calamity Jane   06/05/1961
Billy Barnes People, The   06/13/1961
Paradise Island   06/22/1961
Billy Barnes Party   09/00/1961
I Want You   09/14/1961
Fourth Avenue North   09/27/1961
Hi, Paisano!   09/30/1961
Sap of Life, The   10/02/1961
Sail Away   10/03/1961
Milk and Honey   10/10/1961
Kicks and Co.   10/11/1961
Seven Come Eleven   10/11/1961
Let It Ride!   10/12/1961
How to Succeed in Business   10/14/1961
   Without Really Trying
Do You Know the Milky Way?   10/16/1961
Feathertop   10/19/1961
Another Evening with Harry   10/21/1961
   Stoones
Bei Mir Bistu Schoen   10/21/1961
Kwamina   10/23/1961

O Marry Me!   10/27/1961
Kean   11/02/1961
All in Love   11/10/1961
Automobile Graveyard, The   11/13/1961
Bella   11/16/1961
Gay Life, The   11/18/1961
'Toinette (1961)   11/20/1961
Sing Muse!   12/06/1961
Signs Along the Cynic Route 12/14/1961
All Kinds of Giants   12/18/1961
Not While I'm Eating   12/19/1961
Subways Are for Sleeping   12/27/1961
Madame Aphrodite   12/29/1961

1962

Dick Van Dyke Show, The   00/00/1962
Molly Darling   00/00/1962
Mr. Magoo's Christmas Carol 00/00/1962
Fortuna   01/03/1962
Banker's Daughter, The   01/22/1962
Family Affair, A   01/27/1962
New Faces of 1962   02/01/1962
Fly Blackbird   02/05/1962
We Take the Town   02/17/1962
All American   02/19/1962
No Strings   03/15/1962
Pilgrim's Progress   03/20/1962
I Can Get It for You   03/22/1962
   Wholesale
Half-Past Wednesday   04/06/1962
Difficult Woman, The   04/25/1962
Blitz!   05/08/1962
Funny Thing Happened on the 05/08/1962
Way to the Forum, A
Bravo Giovanni   05/19/1962
Billy Barnes Summer Revue   05/28/1962
Cat's Pajamas, The   05/31/1962
Look at Us   06/05/1962
World of Jules Feiffer, The   07/02/1962
La Belle   08/13/1962
Sweet Miani   09/25/1962
Stop the World - I Want to   10/03/1962
   Get Off
Come On Strong   10/04/1962
O Say Can You See!   10/08/1962
Billy Barnes' L.A.   10/10/1962
Dime a Dozen   10/18/1962
Lady of Mexico   10/19/1962
Mr. President   10/20/1962
Beyond the Fringe   10/27/1962
Old Bucks and New Wings   11/05/1962
We're Civilized?   11/08/1962
Nowhere to Go but Up   11/10/1962
Little Me   11/17/1962
Coach with the Six Insides, 11/26/1962
   The
Never Too Late   11/27/1962
Big Broadcast of 1963   12/00/1962
Riverwind   12/11/1962

1963

All About Life   00/00/1963
Little Night Music, A   00/00/1963
Oliver!   01/06/1963
Establishment, The   01/23/1963
Graham Crackers   01/23/1963
Enter Laughing   03/13/1963
Tovarich   03/18/1963
To the Water Tower   04/03/1963
Sophie   04/15/1963
Hot Spot   04/19/1963
New York Coloring Book   04/22/1963
She Loves Me   04/23/1963
Utopia!   05/06/1963
Put It in Writing   05/13/1963
Beast in Me, The   05/16/1963
Tour de Four   06/18/1963
Around the World in Eighty   06/22/1963
   Days
Money   07/12/1963
Seven Come Eleven   08/00/1963
Zenda   08/05/1963
No Shoestrings   09/16/1963
Political Party, A   09/26/1963
Spoon River Anthology   09/29/1963
Student Gypsy or the Prince 09/30/1963
   of Liederkrantz, The
Here's Love   10/03/1963
Morning Sun   10/06/1963
Gentlemen Be Seated!   10/10/1963
Prince and the Pauper, The   10/12/1963
Ballad for Bimshire   10/15/1963
Jennie   10/17/1963
110 in the Shade   10/24/1963
Streets of New York, The   10/29/1963
Man in the Moon   11/22/1963
Plot Against the Chase   11/26/1963
   Manhattan Bank, The
Girl Who Came to Supper,   12/08/1963
   The
Stones of Jehoshaphat, The   12/17/1963

1964

...And In This Corner   00/00/1964
Golden Gate   00/00/1964
Ice-Travaganza   00/00/1964
Skin of Our Teeth, The   00/00/1964
Jericho-Jim Crow   01/05/1964
Pimpernel!   01/06/1964
Baker's Dozen   01/09/1964
Will the Milk Train Run   01/09/1964
   Tonight?
Athenian Touch, The   01/14/1964
Hello, Dolly!   01/16/1964
Rugantino   02/06/1964
Jo   02/12/1964
Foxy   02/16/1964
Amorous Flea, The   02/17/1964

Any Wednesday   02/18/1964
Sorry, Charlie, Your Time   02/24/1964
   Is Up
What Makes Sammy Run?   02/27/1964
Dynamite Tonight!   03/15/1964
Cindy   03/19/1964
Funny Girl   03/26/1964
Cool Off!   03/31/1964
Anyone Can Whistle   04/04/1964
High Spirits   04/07/1964
Wonderworld   04/07/1964
King of the Whole Damn   04/12/1964
   World!
Cafe Crown   04/17/1964
To Broadway with Love   04/21/1964
America, Be Seated!   04/22/1964
Les Poupees de Paris   04/22/1964
New York World's Fair   04/22/1964
Blues for Mr. Charlie   04/23/1964
Home Movies   05/11/1964
Billy Barnes' Hollywood   05/26/1964
Fade Out-Fade In   05/26/1964
Merry Widow, The   08/17/1964
Awf'lly Nice   09/07/1964
Maggie May   09/22/1964
Fiddler on the Roof   09/22/1964
That Hat!   09/23/1964
Game Is Up, The   09/29/1964
Bits & Pieces XIV   10/07/1964
Gogo Loves You   10/09/1964
Hang Down Your Head   10/15/1964
   and Die
That 5 A.M. Jazz   10/19/1964
Golden Boy   10/20/1964
Secret Life of Walter   10/26/1964
   Mitty, The
Ben Franklin in Paris   10/27/1964
Something More!   11/10/1964
P.S. I Love You   11/19/1964
Bajour   11/23/1964
Rudolph the Red-Nosed   12/00/1964
   Reindeer
I Had a Ball   12/15/1964
Babes in the Wood   12/28/1964
Oh, What a Lovely War   12/30/1964
Royal Flush   12/31/1964

1965

How Do You Do, I Love You   00/00/1965
Kelly   02/06/1965
Pleasures and Palaces   02/11/1965
Baker Street   02/16/1965
Game Is Up, The   03/11/1965
Do I Hear a Waltz?   03/18/1965
Decline and Fall of the   03/30/1965
   Entire World as Seen
   Through the Eyes of Cole
   Porter, The
Wet Paint   04/12/1965

Half a Sixpence   04/25/1965
Flora, the Red Menace   05/11/1965
Roar of the Greasepaint-the 05/16/1965
Smell of the Crowd, The
Game Is Up, The   06/15/1965
Mr. Woolworth Had a Notion   06/16/1965
Mardi Gras   06/26/1965
Hot September   09/14/1965
Love Is a Ball!   09/27/1965
Pickwick (1965)   10/04/1965
Generation   10/06/1965
Mackey of Appalachia   10/06/1965
Drat! The Cat!   10/10/1965
On a Clear Day You Can See   10/17/1965
   Forever
Hotel Passionato   10/22/1965
Just for Openers   11/03/1965
Great Scot! (1965)   11/10/1965
Zulu and the Zayda, The   11/10/1965
Skyscraper   11/13/1965
Man of La Mancha   11/22/1965
Dangerous Christmas of Red   11/28/1965
Riding Hood, The
Anya   11/29/1965
Yearling, The   12/10/1965
La Grosse Valise   12/14/1965
Twang!   12/20/1965
Persecution and   12/27/1965
   Assassination of Jean-Paul
   Marat as Performed by the
   Inmates of the Asylum of
   Charenton Under the
   Direction of the Marquis de
   Sade, The

1966

Ballad of Smokey the Bear   00/00/1966
Go Fly a Kite   00/00/1966
Little World, Hello!   00/00/1966
New Faces of 1966   00/00/1966
Mad Show, The   01/09/1966
Jacques Brel Is Alive and   01/22/1966
   Well and Living in Paris
Sweet Charity   01/29/1966
Jonah (1966)   02/15/1966
Wait a Minim!   03/07/1966
Hooray! It's a Glorious   03/09/1966
   Day... and All That
Pousse-Cafe (1966)   03/18/1966
It's a Bird... It's a   03/29/1966
   Plane... It's Superman
Alice in Wonderland or   03/30/1966
   What's a Nice Kid Like You
   Doing in a Place Like This?
Time for Singing, A   05/21/1966
Mame   05/24/1966
Below the Belt   06/21/1966

Ice Follies of 1967   09/08/1966
Olympus 7-0000   09/28/1966
My Wife and I   10/10/1966
Apple Tree, The   10/18/1966
How the Grinch Stole   10/18/1966
   Christmas
Mixed Doubles   10/19/1966
Autumn's Here   10/25/1966
Canterville Ghost, The   11/02/1966
Alice Through the Looking   11/06/1966
   Glass
Man with a Load of Mischief 11/06/1966
Evening Primrose   11/16/1966
Cabaret   11/20/1966
Walking Happy   11/26/1966
I Do! I Do!   12/05/1966
On the Flip Side   12/07/1966
Agatha Sue I Love You   12/14/1966
Breakfast at Tiffany's   12/14/1966
Joyful Noise, A   12/15/1966
Jorrocks   12/22/1966
Penny Friend, The   12/26/1966
At the Drop of Another Hat   12/27/1966

1967

Ghost Goes West, The   00/00/1967
   Softly   00/00/1967
Two Much   00/00/1967
Golden Screw, The   01/27/1967
Jack and the Beanstalk   02/26/1967
Shoemaker's Holiday   03/02/1967
You're a Good Man, Charlie   03/07/1967
   Brown
I'm Getting Married   03/16/1967
Sherry!   03/28/1967
Hellza-poppin   04/00/1967
Illya Darling   04/11/1967
Hallelujah, Baby!   04/26/1967
Pippin, Pippin   05/01/1967
Dumas and Son   08/01/1967
Peg   08/01/1967
Ice Follies of 1968   09/07/1967
Now Is the Time for All   09/26/1967
   Good Men
Keep It in the Family   09/27/1967
Hair   10/17/1967
There's a Girl in My Soup   10/18/1967
Henry, Sweet Henry   10/23/1967
Freaking Out of Stephanie   10/30/1967
   Blake, The
How Do You Do, I Love You   10/31/1967
Androcles and the Lion   11/15/1967
Mata Hari   11/18/1967
Curley McDimple   11/22/1967
How Now, Dow Jones   12/07/1967
Cricket on the Hearth   12/18/1967
How to Be a Jewish Mother   12/28/1967

1968

Diamond in the Rough   00/00/1968
Exception and the Rule, The 00/00/1968
Four in Hand   00/00/1968
Instant Replay   00/00/1968
Tattered Tom   00/00/1968
Love and Let Love   01/03/1968
Have I Got One for You   01/07/1968
Your Own Thing   01/13/1968
Happy Time, The   01/19/1968
Darling of the Day   01/27/1968
Who's Who, Baby?   01/29/1968
Golden Rainbow   02/04/1968
Here's Where I Belong   03/03/1968
Photo Finish   03/08/1968
Education of H*Y*M*A*N   04/04/1968
   K*A*P*L*A*N, The
George M!   04/10/1968
I'm Solomon   04/23/1968
New Faces of 1968   05/02/1968
Believers, The   05/09/1968
Walk Down Mah Street!   06/12/1968
After You, Mr. Hyde   06/24/1968
In Circles   06/25/1968
Happy Hypocrite, The   09/05/1968
Month of Sundays, A   09/16/1968
Mother's Kisses, A   09/23/1968
Noel Coward's Sweet Potato   09/29/1968
Megillah of Itzak Manger,   10/09/1968
   The
How to Steal an Election   10/13/1968
Just for Love   10/17/1968
Her First Roman   10/20/1968
Maggie Flynn   10/23/1968
Peace   11/01/1968
Love Match   11/03/1968
Zorba   11/17/1968
Up Eden   11/27/1968
Morning   11/28/1968
Promises, Promises   12/01/1968
Jimmy Shine   12/05/1968
Fenwick   12/08/1968
Pinocchio   12/08/1968
Ballad for a Firing Squad   12/11/1968
God Is a (Guess What?)   12/17/1968
Dames at Sea   12/20/1968

1969

Eleanor   00/00/1969
Folies Bergere   00/00/1969
Goldilocks   00/00/1969
Ice Follies of 1969   00/00/1969
Mona and Lisa   00/00/1969
Senor Discretion   00/00/1969
Southpaw, The   00/00/1969
Fig Leaves Are Falling, The   01/02/1969
Horseman, Pass By   01/15/1969

Many Happy Returns   01/16/1969
Oh! Calcutta!   01/17/1969
Celebration   01/22/1969
Get Thee to Canterbury   01/25/1969
Red, White and Maddox   01/26/1969
Canterbury Tales   02/03/1969
Dear World   02/06/1969
Play It Again, Sam   02/12/1969
Come Summer   02/18/1969
Paradise Gardens East   03/10/1969
1776   03/16/1969
Billy   03/22/1969
Tom Jones   04/00/1969
Man Better Man   04/02/1969
Belle Starr   04/30/1969
We'd Rather Switch   05/02/1969
Promenade   06/04/1969
High Diplomacy   06/06/1969
Hello, Sucker   07/08/1969
Tom Piper   07/14/1969
Salvation   09/24/1969
Butterflies Are Free   10/21/1969
Jimmy   10/23/1969
1491   10/28/1969
Rondelay   11/05/1969
Buck White   12/02/1969
Littlest Angel, The   12/06/1969
Sambo   12/12/1969
La Strada   12/14/1969
Gertrude Stein's First   12/15/1969
   Reader
Coco   12/18/1969

1970

Carol Channing with Ten   00/00/1970
   Stouthearted Men
King of Schnorrers, The   00/00/1970
Lovely Ladies, Kind   00/00/1970
   Gentlemen
Serafina   00/00/1970
Wee Bit o' Scotch, A   00/00/1970
Unfair to Goliath   01/25/1970
Last Sweet Days of Isaac,   01/26/1970
   The
Joy   01/27/1970
Exchange   02/08/1970
I Dreamt I Dwelt in   02/12/1970
   Bloomingdale's
Gantry   02/14/1970
Georgy   02/26/1970
Billy Noname   03/02/1970
Show Me Where the Good   03/05/1970
   Times Are
Operation Sidewinder   03/12/1970
Purlie   03/15/1970
House of Leather, The   03/18/1970
Lyle   03/20/1970
Blood Red Roses   03/22/1970

Minnie's Boys   03/26/1970
Look to the Lilies   03/29/1970
Applause   03/30/1970
Cry for Us All   04/08/1970
It's About Time   04/18/1970
Park   04/22/1970
Mod Donna   04/24/1970
Company   04/26/1970
Colette   05/06/1970
Whispers on the Wind   06/03/1970
Hatfields & McCoys   06/20/1970
Rothschilds, The   10/19/1970
Sensations   10/25/1970
President's Daughter, The   11/03/1970
Touch   11/08/1970
Two by Two   11/10/1970
Santa Claus Is Comin' to   12/13/1970
   Town
Isabel's a Jezebel   12/15/1970
Lovely Ladies, Kind   12/28/1970
   Gentlemen

1971

Ice Follies of 1971   00/00/1971
King of the Schnorrers, The 00/00/1971
Night the Animals Talked,   00/00/1971
   The
Victory Canteen   00/00/1971
W.C.   00/00/1971
When Do the Words Come True   00/00/1971
Stag Movie   01/03/1971
Soon   01/12/1971
Ari   01/15/1971
Prettybelle   02/01/1971
Who's Whom?   02/04/1971
House of Blue Leaves   02/10/1971
Lolita, My Love   02/15/1971
Look Where I'm At!   03/05/1971
Blood   03/07/1971
Day in the Life of Just   03/09/1971
   About Everyone, A
Follies   04/04/1971
Six   04/12/1971
70, Girls, 70   04/15/1971
Kiss Now   04/20/1971
Frank Merriwell, or Honor   04/24/1971
   Challenged
Ballad of Johnny Pot, The   04/26/1971
Children's Crusade, The   04/29/1971
Cyrano   05/02/1971
Earl of Ruston   05/05/1971
Godspell   05/17/1971
Me Nobody Knows, The   05/18/1971
Two If by Sea!?   06/18/1971
Two Gentlemen of Verona   07/27/1971
Leaves of Grass   09/12/1971
Jesus Christ Superstar   10/12/1971
Drat!   10/18/1971

Ain't Supposed to Die a   10/20/1971
   Natural Death
To Live Another Summer/ To   10/21/1971
   Pass Another Winter
F. Jasmine Addams   10/27/1971
Grass Harp, The   11/02/1971
Love Me, Love My Children   11/03/1971
Sticks and Bones   11/07/1971
Twigs   11/14/1971
Wild and Wonderful   12/07/1971
Wedding of Iphigenia, The   12/16/1971
Inner City   12/19/1971
Anne of Green Gables   12/21/1971

1972

Ice Follies of 1972   00/00/1972
Let's Celebrate   00/00/1972
Carmilla   01/16/1972
Wanted   01/19/1972
I'm a Fan   01/25/1972
Grease   02/14/1972
Dandelion Wine   03/10/1972
Selling of the President,   03/22/1972
   The
Londoners, The   03/27/1972
Sugar   04/09/1972
Don't Bother Me, I Can't   04/19/1972
   Cope
Clownaround   04/27/1972
Different Times   05/01/1972
God Bless Coney   05/03/1972
Hard Job Being God   05/15/1972
Don't Play Us Cheap!   05/16/1972
Heathen!   05/21/1972
Hark!   05/22/1972
Buy Bonds, Buster   06/04/1972
They Don't Make 'Em Like   06/06/1972
   That Anymore
Sunshine Train, The   06/15/1972
Joan   06/19/1972
Mass   06/28/1972
Safari 300   07/12/1972
Speed Gets the Poppys   07/25/1972
Much Ado About Nothing   08/19/1972
Song for Cyrano, A   09/04/1972
Crazy Now   09/10/1972
Halloween   09/20/1972
Life of a Man, The   10/00/1972
Berlin to Broadway with   10/01/1972
   Kurt Weill
Lady Audley's Secret   10/03/1972
Oh Coward!   10/04/1972
Costa Packet   10/05/1972
Dude (The Highway Life)   10/09/1972
Rebbitzen from Israel, The   10/10/1972
Hurry, Harry   10/12/1972
Mother Earth   10/19/1972
Yoshe Kalb   10/22/1972

Pippin   10/23/1972
Winnie the Pooh   10/29/1972
Comedy   11/06/1972
I and Albert   11/06/1972
Quarter for the Ladies   11/12/1972
   Room, A
Lysistrata   11/13/1972
Twanger   11/15/1972
Dear Oscar   11/16/1972
Ambassador   11/19/1972
Doctor Selavy's Magic   11/23/1972
   Theatre
Contrast, The   11/27/1972
Via Galactica   11/28/1972
Bar That Never Closes, The   12/03/1972
Please Don't Cry and   12/06/1972
   Say No
Rainbow   12/18/1972
Trials of Oz, The   12/19/1972
Davy Jones' Locker   12/24/1972

1973

Caesar's Wife   00/00/1973
Clippity Clop and   00/00/1973
   Clementine
Ice Capades   00/00/1973
Ice Follies   00/00/1973
Stephen Foster Story, The   00/00/1973
Tricks   01/08/1973
National Lampoon's Lemmings   01/25/1973
Look at the Fifties, A   02/00/1973
Shelter   02/06/1973
Great Man's Whiskus, The   02/13/1973
El Coca-Cola Grande   02/13/1973
Little Night Music, A   02/25/1973
Dr. Jekyll and Mr. Hyde   03/07/1973
Try It, You'll Like It   03/14/1973
Karl Marx Play, The   03/16/1973
Seesaw   03/18/1973
Thoughts   03/19/1973
Smile, Smile, Smile   04/04/1973
What's a Nice Country Like   04/19/1973
   You Doing in a State Like
   This?
Hot and Cold Heros   05/09/1973
Cyrano   05/13/1973
Nash at Nine   05/17/1973
Smith   05/19/1973
Rumplestiltskin   05/23/1973
All Together Now   06/08/1973
Faggot, The   06/18/1973
Antiques   06/19/1973
Treasure Island   08/21/1973
Gone with the Wind   08/28/1973
$600 and a Mule   08/28/1973
Whistling Wizard and the   10/17/1973
   Sultan of Tuffet, The
Raisin   10/18/1973

Molly   11/01/1973
Gigi   11/13/1973
Good Evening   11/14/1973
Enclave, The   11/15/1973
More Than You Deserve   11/21/1973
Rachael Lily Rosenbloom and 11/26/1973
   Don't You Ever Forget It
Good Doctor, The   11/27/1973
Aimee   12/02/1973
Borrowers, The   12/14/1973
Pinocchio (1973)   12/15/1973

1974

Many Happy Returns   00/00/1974
Liza   01/06/1974
Let My People Come   01/08/1974
Lorelei   01/27/1974
Great MacDaddy, The   02/12/1974
Rainbow Jones   02/13/1974
Fashion   02/18/1974
Sextet   03/03/1974
Over Here!   03/06/1974
Free to Be - You and Me   03/11/1974
Future, The   03/22/1974
Brainchild   03/25/1974
Pop   04/03/1974
Music! Music!   04/11/1974
Ride the Winds   04/16/1974
Words and Music   04/16/1974
Jumpers   04/22/1974
Ionescopade   04/25/1974
Kaboom!   05/01/1974
Funeral March for a One Man   05/04/1974
   Band
Frogs, The   05/20/1974
Magic Show, The   05/28/1974
Nobody's Perfect   06/00/1974
Laugh a Little, Cry a   06/06/1974
   Little
Good Companions, The 07/11/1974
Sheba   07/24/1974
Mack and Mabel   10/06/1974
Miss Moffat   10/07/1974
For the Love of Suzanne   10/29/1974
In Gay Company   10/29/1974
I'll Die If I Can't Live   10/31/1974
   Forever
Love for Love   11/11/1974
Street Jesus   11/16/1974
How to Get Rid of It   11/17/1974
Sgt. Pepper's Lonely Hearts 11/17/1974
   Club Band on the Road
Prodigal Sister, The   11/25/1974
Up in the Air, Boys   11/29/1974
Peter and the Wolf   12/06/1974
Portfolio Revue   12/06/1974
'Twas the Night Before   12/08/1974
   Christmas

Pretzels   12/16/1974
Hans Andersen   12/17/1974
Big Winner, The   12/20/1974

1975

Gambler's Paradise   00/00/1975
Happy Birthday   00/00/1975
Truth About Cinderella,   00/00/1975
   The
Gabrielle   01/00/1975
Philemon   01/03/1975
Wiz, The   01/05/1975
Shenandoah   01/07/1975
Downriver   01/10/1975
Diamond Studs   01/14/1975
Dance with Me   01/23/1975
Lovers   01/27/1975
Man on the Moon   01/29/1975
Alice in Wonderland   02/19/1975
Straws in the Wind   02/21/1975
Night That Made America   02/26/1975
   Famous, The
Bone Room, The   02/28/1975
Goodtime Charley   03/03/1975
Lieutenant, The   03/09/1975
Rocky Horror Show, The   03/10/1975
Ape Over Broadway   03/12/1975
Wings   03/16/1975
Doctor Jazz   03/19/1975
Be Kind to People Week   03/23/1975
Rainbow Rape Trick,   04/13/1975
   The
Matter of Time, A   04/27/1975
Glorious Age, The   05/11/1975
Rodgers and Hart   05/13/1975
Flatbush Tosca   05/22/1975
Journey of Snow White,   05/29/1975
   The
Chicago   06/01/1975
Cowboy   08/19/1975
Truckload   09/06/1975
Boy Meets Boy   09/17/1975
Captain Jinks of the Horse   09/20/1975
   Marines
Why I Love New York   10/10/1975
5th Season, The   10/12/1975
Chorus Line, A   10/19/1975
Treemonisha   10/21/1975
Me and Bessie   10/22/1975
Musical Jubilee, A   11/13/1975
Mass Murder in the Balcony   11/14/1975
   of the Old Ritz-Rialto, A
By Bernstein   11/23/1975
Boccaccio   11/24/1975
Christmas Rappings   12/00/1975
Rudolph and Frosty   12/00/1975
Rudolph's Shiny New Year   12/00/1975
Tiny Tree, The   12/00/1975
Gift of the Magi   12/01/1975

Tuscaloosa's Calling Me...   12/01/1975
   But I'm Not Going!
Tom Eyen's Dirtiest Musical   12/09/1975
Royal Family, The   12/30/1975

1976

Bojangles   00/00/1976
It's a Brand New World   00/00/1976
Tom Jones   00/00/1976
Home Sweet Homer   01/04/1976
Pacific Overtures   01/17/1976
Fire of Flowers   01/29/1976
Apple Pie   02/13/1976
Rockabye Hamlet   02/17/1976
Bubbling Brown Sugar   03/02/1976
Pinocchio   03/27/1976
Dreamstuff   04/02/1976
Le Bellybutton   04/02/1976
I Knock at the Door   04/12/1976
Rex   04/25/1976
Tickles by Tucholsky   04/26/1976
So Long, 174th Street   04/27/1976
Can You Smell Gas?   04/29/1976
Camp Meeting 1840   05/00/1976
Threepenny Opera, The   05/01/1976
1600 Pennsylvania Avenue   05/04/1976
Baker's Wife, The   05/11/1976
Legend   05/13/1976
Daarlin' Juno   05/14/1976
Something's Afoot   05/27/1976
Greenwich Village Follies,   06/10/1976
   The
Becoming   06/15/1976
Saints   06/30/1976
Sirocco   08/13/1976
Something to Do — A Salute 09/00/1976
   to the American Worker
Sweet Mistress   09/08/1976
For Colored Girls Who Have   09/15/1976
   Considered Suicide/When the
   Rainbow Is Enuf
Lovesong   10/05/1976
Robber Bridegroom, The   10/09/1976
Club, The   10/14/1976
2 by 5   10/18/1976
Don't Step on My Olive   11/01/1976
   Branch
Hellzapoppin   11/22/1976
Peter Pan   12/12/1976
Music Is   12/20/1976
Your Arms too Short to Box   12/22/1976
   with God
Bride of Sirocco, The   12/31/1976

1977

Enter Juliet   00/00/1977
Saturday Night (1977)   00/00/1977

T*ts D*amond   01/00/1977
Nightclub Cantata   01/09/1977
Ichabod   01/12/1977
Ipi-Tombi   01/12/1977
Cockeyed Tiger, The   01/13/1977
North Atlantic   01/16/1977
Castaways, The   02/07/1977
Happy End   03/08/1977
Movie Buff, The   03/14/1977
For Love or Money   03/29/1977
I Love My Wife   04/17/1977
Side by Side by Sondheim   04/18/1977
Dance on a Country Grave   04/21/1977
Annie   04/21/1977
On the Lock-In   04/27/1977
New World!, A   05/09/1977
Toller Cranston's The Ice   05/19/1977
   Show
Up from Paradise   06/14/1977
Love! Love! Love!   06/15/1977
Starting Here, Starting Now 06/19/1977
Chapeau   07/24/1977
Red Blue-Grass Western   08/16/1977
   Flyer Show, The
Children of Adam   08/17/1977
Unsung Cole   09/04/1977
Nefertiti   09/20/1977
Misanthrope, The   10/04/1977
Hot Grog   10/06/1977
Housewife! Superstar!!   10/29/1977
Act, The   10/29/1977
Nightsong   11/01/1977
Radio City Music Hall   11/03/1977
Christmas 1977
Present Tense, The   11/04/1977
Green Pond   11/22/1977
Streets of Gold, The   11/25/1977
Gates of Paradise, The   11/25/1977
Nightmare!!   12/14/1977

1978

Merry Widow, The   00/00/1978
Spotlight   01/08/1978
By Strouse   02/01/1978
Ain't Misbehavin'   02/08/1978
On the Twentieth Century   02/19/1978
Barbary Coast   02/28/1978
Timbuktu!   03/01/1978
Prince of Grand Street, The 03/07/1978
Runaways   03/09/1978
In Praise of Death   03/11/1978
Last Minstrel Show, The   03/20/1978
Dancin'   03/27/1978
History of the American   03/30/1978
   Film, A
Best Little Whorehouse in   04/17/1978
   Texas, The
Bistro Car on the CNR, A   04/23/1978

5th of July   04/27/1978
Angel   05/10/1978
Rosa   05/10/1978
Reunion   05/12/1978
Working   05/14/1978
Alice   05/31/1978
Mahalia   05/31/1978
My Cup Runneth Over   06/08/1978
Piano Bar   06/08/1978
I'm Getting My Act Together 06/14/1978
   and Taking It on the Road
Coolest Cat in Town, The   06/22/1978
Out to Lunch   07/07/1978
Broadway, Broadway   07/31/1978
Back Country   08/15/1978
Eubie!   09/20/1978
King of Hearts   10/22/1978
Laugh a Lifetime   10/22/1978
Music-Hall Sidelights   10/26/1978
Gorey Stories   10/30/1978
Bar Mitzvah Boy   10/31/1978
Jolson   11/08/1978
Platinum   11/12/1978
Helen   11/22/1978
Lady Lily   11/28/1978
Ballroom   12/14/1978
Broadway Musical, A   12/21/1978
Wonderland in Concert   12/27/1978
Taxi Tales   12/28/1978

1979

City Junket   00/00/1979
Magnificent Christmas   00/00/1979
Spectacular, The
Ms. Pres   00/00/1979
Umbrellas of Cherbourg, The   01/02/1979
Grand Tour, The   01/11/1979
My Old Friends   01/12/1979
You Bet Your Assets   01/25/1979
Storyville   01/27/1979
They're Playing Our Song   02/11/1979
Sarava   02/23/1979
Sweeney Todd, the Demon   03/01/1979
Barber of Fleet Street
Joley   03/08/1979
Home Again, Home Again   03/10/1979
Spokesong, or the Common   03/15/1979
   Wheel
Zoot Suit   03/25/1979
Sancocho   03/28/1979
Leave It to Beaver Is Dead   03/29/1979
Carmelina   04/08/1979
Dispatches   04/19/1979
Eddie's Catchy Tunes   04/25/1979
Suddenly the Music Starts   05/03/1979
Bea's Place   05/09/1979
Utter Glory of Morrissey   05/13/1979
   Hall, The

Festival   05/16/1979
Strider   05/31/1979
I Remember Mama   05/31/1979
New York Summer, A   06/01/1979
Miss Truth   06/05/1979
Not Tonight, Benvenuto!   06/05/1979
Scrambled Feet   06/11/1979
Madwoman of Central Park   06/13/1979
   West, The
Got Tu Go Disco   06/25/1979
Sky High   06/28/1979
But Never Jam Today   07/31/1979
Gilda Radner, Live from New 08/02/1979
   York
Daddy Goodness   08/19/1979
Long Way to Boston, A   09/00/1979
Evita   09/25/1979
Sun Always Shines for the   09/27/1979
   Cool, The
King of Schnorrers   10/04/1979
All Night Strut!, The   10/04/1979
1940's Radio Hour, The   10/07/1979
Potholes   10/09/1979
Sugar Babies   10/09/1979
God Bless You, Mr.   10/14/1979
   Rosewater
Snow White and the Seven   10/18/1979
   Dwarfs
One Mo' Time   10/22/1979
Rebecca, the Rabbi's   11/04/1979
   Daughter
Amazing Bone, The   11/25/1979
Tom Taylor As Woody Guthrie 11/26/1979
Comin' Uptown   12/20/1979
Babes in Toyland   12/21/1979

Barnum   04/30/1980
Day in Hollywood/A Night in   05/01/1980
   the Ukraine, A
Happy New Year   05/10/1980
Musical Chairs   05/18/1980
It's Wilde!   05/25/1980
Billy Bishop Goes to War   05/29/1980
It's So Nice to Be   06/03/1980
   Civilized
Chase a Rainbow   06/12/1980
Fearless Frank   06/15/1980
Jazzbo Brown   06/24/1980
Manhattan Showboat   06/30/1980
What Ever Happened to   08/12/1980
   Georgie Tapps?
42nd Street   08/25/1980
April Song, An   08/25/1980
Charlie and Algernon   09/14/1980
Cowboy and the Legend, The   09/16/1980
Zapata   09/17/1980
Girls, Girls, Girls   09/25/1980
Really Rosie   09/30/1980
Matter of Opinion, A   09/30/1980
Streetsongs   10/14/1980
All That Glitters   10/28/1980
Quick Change   10/30/1980
Frimbo   11/09/1980
Philadelphia Story, The   11/14/1980
Ka-boom   11/20/1980
Perfectly Frank   11/30/1980
Trixie True Teen Detective   12/07/1980
Alice in Concert   12/09/1980
Onward Victoria   12/14/1980
Hijinks!   12/18/1980
Swing   12/25/1980

1980

Bojangles   00/00/1980
One Night Stand   00/00/1980
Tell Me on a Sunday   01/00/1980
Watch on the Rhine   01/03/1980
Millionaire in Trouble, A   01/16/1980
Elizabeth and Essex   01/31/1980
Shakespeare's Cabaret   02/01/1980
Harold and Maude   02/07/1980
Housewives' Cantata, The   02/17/1980
Changes   02/19/1980
Censored Scenes from King   03/06/1980
   Kong
Haggadah, The   03/31/1980
Al Chemist Show, The   04/05/1980
Tintypes   04/17/1980
Coupla White Chicks Sitting 04/20/1980
   Around Talking, A
O. Henry Duet   04/21/1980
Fourtune   04/27/1980
Reggae   04/27/1980

1981

Light Up the Ice   00/00/1981
Keystone   01/13/1981
Oh Me, Oh My, Oh Youmans   01/14/1981
Evening with Joan Crawford, 01/20/1981
   An
Ice-Capades (Light Up the   01/21/1981
   Ice)
Dear Desperate   01/23/1981
Real Life Funnies   02/11/1981
Apollo... It Was Just Like   02/19/1981
   Magic, The
In Trousers   02/22/1981
Sophisticated Ladies   03/01/1981
Bring Back Birdie   03/05/1981
America   03/06/1981
Matinee Kids, The   03/10/1981
Marry Me a Little   03/12/1981
Broadway Follies   03/15/1981
Tinseltown   03/20/1981
Reel American Hero, A   03/25/1981

Woman of the Year   03/29/1981
March of the Falsettos   04/01/1981
It's Me, Sylvia   04/13/1981
Copperfield   04/13/1981
Mooney Shapiro Songbook,   05/03/1981
   The
Inacent Black   05/06/1981
Ah, Men   05/11/1981
I Can't Keep Running in   05/14/1981
   Place
Cloud Nine   05/18/1981
Heebie Jeebies   06/03/1981
El Bravo!   06/16/1981
Cleavage   06/23/1981
Fauntleroy   07/02/1981
Pump Boys and Dinettes   07/10/1981
Turn to the Right   08/08/1981
Say Hello to Harvey!   09/14/1981
Life and Adventures of   10/04/1981
   Nicholas Nickleby, The
Double Feature   10/08/1981
Cotton Patch Gospel   10/10/1981
Marlowe   10/12/1981
Roumanian Wedding, The   10/25/1981
Christmas Carol, A   10/30/1981
Oh, Brother!   11/10/1981
Merrily We Roll Along   11/16/1981
First, The   11/17/1981
Joseph and the Amazing   11/18/1981
Technicolor Dreamcoat
Coming Attractions   11/22/1981
Tomfoolery   12/03/1981
Head Over Heels   12/05/1981
Francis   12/15/1981
Dreamgirls   12/20/1981

1982

Little Prince and the   00/00/1982
   Aviator, The
Movie Star   00/00/1982
Queen of Basin Street   00/00/1982
Waltz of the Stork   01/05/1982
Oh, Johnny   01/10/1982
Curse of an Aching Heart,   01/25/1982
   The
Lullaby and Goodnight   02/07/1982
Colette   02/09/1982
Orphan's Revenge, The   02/20/1982
Livin' Dolls   03/09/1982
Nightingale   03/12/1982
Maybe I'm Doing It Wrong   03/14/1982
Great Grandson of Jedediah   03/22/1982
   Kohler, The
Lola   03/24/1982
Is There Life After High   05/03/1982
   School?
Nine   05/09/1982

Forbidden Broadway   05/15/1982
Do Black Patent Leather   05/27/1982
   Shoes Really Reflect Up?
Blues in the Night   06/02/1982
Life Is Not a Doris Day   06/08/1982
   Movie
Herringbone   06/16/1982
Drifter, the Grifter and   06/17/1982
   Heather McBride, A
Play Me a Country Song   06/27/1982
Broadway Scandals of 1928   07/07/1982
Seven Brides for Seven   07/08/1982
   Brothers
Broken Toys   07/16/1982
Little Shop of Horrors   07/27/1982
Death of Baron Von   07/29/1982
   Richthofen As Witnessed
   from Earth, The
Charlotte Sweet   08/22/1982
Great American Backstage   09/15/1982
   Musical, The
Doll's Life, A   09/23/1982
Lennon   10/05/1982
Corkscrews   10/06/1982
Cats   10/07/1982
Rock and Roll! The First   10/24/1982
   5,000 Years
Upstairs at O'Neal's   10/28/1982
Robert and Elizabeth   11/03/1982
Foxfire   11/11/1982
Herman Van Veen: All of Him   12/12/1982
Snoopy!!!   12/20/1982

1983

America Kicks Up Its Heels   00/00/1983
Flim-Flam   00/00/1983
One Wonderful Night   00/00/1983
Prairie   00/00/1983
Shubert Alley   00/00/1983
Shim Sham   01/03/1983
Merlin   02/13/1983
Bundle of Nerves, A   03/13/1983
It's Better with a Band   03/28/1983
From Brooks with Love   03/30/1983
Colette Collage   03/31/1983
Teaneck Tanzi: The Venus   04/20/1983
   Flytrap
My One and Only   05/01/1983
Dance a Little Closer   05/11/1983
On the Swing Shift   05/20/1983
Shakespeare and the Indians   05/27/1983
Taking My Turn   06/09/1983
Five-Six-Seven-Eight...   06/15/1983
   Dance!
Booth Is Back in Town   07/07/1983
American Passion   07/10/1983
Mrs. Farmer's Daughter   07/20/1983

When Hell Freezes Over I'll 07/22/1983
   Skate
Non Pasquale   08/09/1983
Chaplin   08/12/1983
Brooklyn Bridge, The   08/17/1983
Preppies   08/18/1983
La Cage Aux Folles   08/21/1983
Blue Plate Special   10/18/1983
Weekend   10/24/1983
Tallulah   10/30/1983
Sunset   11/07/1983
Amen Corner   11/10/1983
Huck and Jim on the   11/11/1983
   Mississippi
Jean Seberg   11/15/1983
Doonesbury   11/21/1983
Baby   12/04/1983
Marilyn: An American Fable   12/04/1983
Peg   12/14/1983
Backers' Audition, A   12/20/1983
Tap Dance Kid, The   12/21/1983
Lenny and the Heartbreakers   12/22/1983
Human Comedy, The   12/28/1983

1984

Ace of Diamonds   00/00/1984
Hollywood Hollywood!   00/00/1984
Kicks: The Showgirl Musical 00/00/1984
Phantom of the Opera, The   00/00/1984
Portrait of Jennie   00/00/1984
Scandal   00/00/1984
A...My Name Is Alice   02/24/1984
Hey, Ma...Kaye Ballard   02/27/1984
Rink, The   03/09/1984
Peg   04/12/1984
Love   04/15/1984
Shirley MacLaine on   04/19/1984
   Broadway
Sunday in the Park with   05/02/1984
   George
End of the World   05/06/1984
Seduction of a Lady, The   05/11/1984
Blanco   05/11/1984
Dragons   05/12/1984
Nite Club Confidential   05/14/1984
Gotta Getaway!   06/16/1984
Shades of Harlem   08/21/1984
Quilters   09/25/1984
Rap Master Ronnie   10/03/1984
Kuni-Leml   10/09/1984
Mrs. McThing   10/12/1984
Feathertop   10/17/1984
Blockheads   10/17/1984
Ballad of Soapy Smith, The   11/12/1984
Haarlem Nocturne   11/18/1984
La Boheme   11/29/1984
Broadway Baby, A   12/04/1984
Diamonds   12/16/1984

Ann Reinking...Music Moves   12/23/1984
   Me
Everybody Out the Castle Is 12/26/1984
   Sinking

1985

13 Days to Broadway   00/00/1985
My Man Godfrey   00/00/1985
Princess Jimmy   00/00/1985
Sherlock Holmes and the   00/00/1985
   Case of the Missing Santa Claus
Smile   00/00/1985
Hang on to the Good Times   01/22/1985
Streetheat   01/27/1985
Harrigan 'n Hart   01/31/1985
3 Guys Naked from the Waist 02/05/1985
   Down
America's Sweetheart   03/08/1985
Sing, Mahalia, Sing   03/26/1985
Leader of the Pack   04/08/1985
Hannah Senesh   04/10/1985
Grind   04/16/1985
Normal Heart, The   04/21/1985
Dream Team, The   04/23/1985
Lies and Legends: The   04/24/1985
   Musical Stories of Harry Chapin
Big River: The Adventures   04/25/1985
   of Huckleberry Finn
Mayor   05/13/1985
Ladies and Gentlemen,   06/10/1985
   Jerome Kern
Singin' in the Rain   07/02/1985
Options   07/11/1985
Hit Parade, The   07/12/1985
Georgia Avenue   07/30/1985
Game of Love, The   09/00/1985
Roller Derby! The Musical   09/11/1985
Windy City   09/18/1985
Song & Dance   09/18/1985
Mowgli   09/26/1985
Paradise!   09/28/1985
Yours, Anne   10/13/1985
Dori   10/17/1985
Tatterdemalion   10/27/1985
News, The   11/07/1985
Hamelin: A Musical Tale   11/10/1985
   from Rats to Riches
Golden Land, The   11/11/1985
Magnificent Christmas   11/15/1985
Spectacular, The
Personals   11/24/1985
Pieces of Eight   11/27/1985
My Three Angels   12/02/1985
Mystery of Edwin Drood, The   12/02/1985
Just So   12/03/1985
Copacabana   12/03/1985
Lie of the Mind, A   12/05/1985
Hay Fever   12/12/1985

Nunsense   12/12/1985
To Whom It May Concern   12/16/1985
Jonin'   12/17/1985
Jerry's Girls   12/18/1985
Wind in the Willows   12/19/1985

1986

Little Rascals, The   00/00/1986
Sweet Will   01/05/1986
Jerome Kern Goes to   01/23/1986
   Hollywood
Uptown...It's Hot!   01/29/1986
Halala!   03/09/1986
Williams & Walker   03/09/1986
Beehive   03/30/1986
Big Deal   04/10/1986
Goblin Market   04/13/1986
Phantom of the Opera, The   04/19/1986
National Lampoon's Class of   05/22/1986
   '86
Professionally Speaking   05/22/1986
Tropicana   05/29/1986
Olympus on My Mind   07/15/1986
Honky Tonk Nights   08/07/1986
Me and My Girl   08/10/1986
Eleanor (Don't Frighten the   08/15/1986
   Horses!)
Rags   08/21/1986
Angry Housewives   09/07/1986
Brownstone   10/08/1986
Queenie Pie   10/09/1986
Jokers   10/14/1986
Raggedy Ann   10/16/1986
Into the Light   10/22/1986
Little Like Magic, A   10/26/1986
Have I Got a Girl for You   10/29/1986
Transposed Heads, The   10/31/1986
L'Chaim to Life   11/05/1986
Womb, The   11/22/1986
House in the Woods, A   12/09/1986
Sex Tips for Modern Girls   12/19/1986

1987

Abyssinia   00/00/1987
Foggy Day, A   00/00/1987
Graduate, The   00/00/1987
Hagar the Horrible   00/00/1987
Lone Star, The   00/00/1987
Lyle   00/00/1987
Smile   01/03/1987
Rise of David Levinsky,   01/12/1987
   The
Stardust   02/19/1987
Knife, The   03/10/1987
Les Miserables   03/12/1987

Starlight Express   03/17/1987
Staggerlee   03/18/1987
Standup Shakespeare   04/04/1987
Asinamali! (We Have No   04/23/1987
   Money)
Kaleidoscope   05/12/1987
Three Postcards   05/14/1987
Satchmo: America's Musical   07/14/1987
   Legend
Psycho Beach Party   07/20/1987
Grover's Corners   07/29/1987
Moms   08/04/1987
Little Ham   08/31/1987
Sayonara   09/16/1987
Apprenticeship of Duddy   09/30/1987
   Kravitz
Roza   10/01/1987
Bittersuite   10/05/1987
Little Rascals, The   10/07/1987
Butterfly   10/10/1987
Late Nite Comic   10/15/1987
Birds of Paradise   10/26/1987
Don't Get God Started   10/29/1987
Sing Hallelujah!   11/03/1987
Into the Woods   11/05/1987
Oil City Symphony   11/05/1987
Teddy & Alice   11/12/1987
Fat Pig   11/20/1987
No-Frills Revue, The   11/25/1987
Mademoiselle Colombe   12/09/1987

1988

80 Days   00/00/1988
Elmer Gantry   00/00/1988
Chosen, The   01/06/1988
River, The   01/13/1988
Phantom of the Opera, The   01/26/1988
Sarafina!   01/28/1988
Serious Money   02/09/1988
Last Musical Comedy, The   02/12/1988
Gospel at Colonus, The   03/24/1988
Ten Percent Revue   04/13/1988
Mail   04/14/1988
Lucky Stiff   04/25/1988
Chess   04/28/1988
Romance, Romance   05/01/1988
Carrie   05/12/1988
Kaye Ballard: Working 42nd   05/16/1988
   Street at Last
Wonder Years, The   05/25/1988
Urban Blight   06/19/1988
Suds   09/25/1988
Hired Man, The   11/10/1988
Middle of Nowhere, The   11/20/1988
Majestic Kid, The   12/01/1988
Sweethearts   12/07/1988
Legs Diamond   12/26/1988

1989

Nimrod and the Tower of Babel   00/00/1989
Senator Joe   01/05/1989
Songs of Paradise   01/23/1989
Ziegfeld Girl, The   01/23/1989
Black and Blue   01/26/1989
Moon Over Miami   02/14/1989
Jerome Robbins' Broadway   02/26/1989
Together Again for the   02/27/1989
  First Time
Chu Chem   03/17/1989
Fame   03/25/1989
Taffetas, The   04/09/1989
Welcome to the Club   04/13/1989
Starmites   04/27/1989
Legends in Concert   05/10/1989
Blame It on the Movies!   05/16/1989
Showing Off   05/18/1989
Fine and Private Place, A   08/03/1989
Durante   08/12/1989
Privates on Parade   08/23/1989
Carnage, A Comedy   09/17/1989
Frankie   10/06/1989
Dangerous Games   10/19/1989
Angelina   10/25/1989
Rhythm Ranch   11/01/1989
Meet Me in St. Louis   11/02/1989
3 Penny Opera, The   11/05/1989
Closer Than Ever   1i/06/1989
Real Life Story of Johnny   11/08/1989
  de Facto, The
Prince of Central Park   11/09/1989
Grand Hotel   11/12/1989
Up Against It   12/04/1989
City of Angels   12/11/1989
Romance in Hard Times   12/28/1989

1990

Annie 2: Miss Hannigan's   01/04/1990
  Revenge
Junon and Avos: The Hope   01/07/1990
Forbidden Broadway 1990   01/23/1990
Spinning Tale, A   02/20/1990
Jekyll and Hyde   03/14/1990
Jonah   03/20/1990
Aspects of Love   04/08/1990
Animal Fair   04/18/1990
Truly Blessed   04/22/1990
Change in the Heir, A   04/29/1990
Smoke on the Mountain   05/12/1990
Mikado, Inc.   05/16/1990
Further Mo'   05/17/1990
Forever Plaid   05/20/1990
Jekyll and Hyde   05/25/1990
Hannah...1939   05/31/1990
Jekyll and Hyde   06/25/1990
Falsettoland   06/28/1990
Broadway Jukebox   07/19/1990

Once on This Island   10/18/1990
Pretty Faces   10/21/1990
Yiddle with a Fiddle   10/28/1990
Arthur, the Musical   11/01/1990
Buddy: The Buddy Holly   11/04/1990
  Story
Those Were the Days   11/07/1990
Catch Me If I Fall   11/12/1990
Shogun: The Musical   11/20/1990
Gifts of the Magi, The   12/04/1990
Township Fever   12/19/1990

1991

Phantom of the Opera, The   00/00/1991
Ziegfeld a Night at the   00/00/1991
  Follies
Children of Eden   01/08/1991
Assassins   01/27/1991
Unfinished Song, An   02/10/1991
Juba   02/12/1991
Mule Bone   02/14/1991
And the World Goes 'Round   03/18/1991
Murder on Broadway   03/18/1991
Svengali   04/03/1991
How It Was Done in Odessa   04/10/1991
Miss Saigon   04/11/1991
Steel   04/14/1991
Secret Garden, The   04/25/1991
Will Rogers Follies, The   05/01/1991
Pageant   05/02/1991
Hunchback of Notre Dame   05/16/1991
Charge It, Please!   05/23/1991
Song of Singapore   05/23/1991
Forbidden Broadway 1991 1/2 06/20/1991
Book of the Night   06/24/1991
Notre Dame   06/25/1991
Prom Queens Unchained   06/30/1991
Woody Guthrie's American   07/31/1991
  Song
Return to the Forbidden   10/13/1991
  Planet
Conrack   11/07/1991
Nick & Nora   12/08/1991
Finkel's Follies   12/15/1991
Cinderella   12/19/1991

1992

Just a Night Out   02/16/1992
Crazy for You   02/19/1992
Gunmetal Blues   04/04/1992
Five Guys Named Moe   04/08/1992
Groundhog   04/14/1992
Metro   04/16/1992
High Rollers Social and   04/21/1992
  Pleasure Club, The
Jelly's Last Jam   04/26/1992
Ruthless!   05/06/1992

Eating Raoul   05/13/1992
Anna Karenina   05/26/1992
Balancing Act   06/15/1992
Some Sweet Day   08/06/1992
Cut the Ribbons   09/20/1992
You Could Be Home Now   10/11/1992
Bubbe Meises Bubbe Stories   10/29/1992
Good Sports   11/05/1992
Happy Haunting   11/07/1992
Radio City Christmas   11/13/1992
   Spectacular
3 From Brooklyn   11/19/1992
Sheik of Avenue B, The   11/22/1992
Hello Muddah, Hello Fadduh   12/05/1992
My Favorite Year   12/10/1992
Madison Avenue   12/29/1992

1993

Theda Bara and the Frontier   01/09/1993
   Rabbi
Scapin   01/20/1993
Martin Guerre   01/22/1993
Manhattan Moves   01/24/1993
Goodbye Girl, The   03/04/1993
Wings   03/09/1993
Song of Jacob Zulu, The   03/24/1993
Back to Bacharach and David 03/25/1993
Sondheim—Putting It Together   04/01/1993
Easter Show   04/02/1993
Ain't Broadway Grand   04/18/1993
Who's Tommy, The   04/22/1993
Blood Brothers   04/25/1993
Linda   05/02/1993
Kiss of the Spider Woman   05/03/1993
Wild Men   05/06/1993
Prime Time Prophet   06/10/1993
Howard Crabtree's Whoop-   06/29/1993
   Dee-Doo!
Heartbeats   07/07/1993
Annie Warbucks   08/09/1993
Paper Moon   09/08/1993
Johnny Pye and the   10/31/1993
   Foolkiller
Cyrano the Musical   11/21/1993
First Lady Suite   12/15/1993
Red Shoes, The   12/16/1993

1994

Hello Again   01/30/1994
Smiling Through   02/02/1994
Avenue X   02/21/1994
C'mon & Hear   03/22/1994
New York Rock   03/30/1994
Spittin' Image   04/01/1994

American Enterprise   04/13/1994
Fallen Angel   04/14/1994
Beauty and the Beast   04/18/1994
Bring in the Morning   04/23/1994
Passion   05/09/1994
Best Little Whorehouse Goes 05/10/1994
   Public, The
Captains Courageous   05/12/1994
Shlemiel the First   05/13/1994
Hysterical Blindness   05/19/1994
Phantom of the Country   06/22/1994
   Palace, The
Copacabana   06/23/1994
Lunch   06/28/1994
Brimstone   06/29/1994
Truth About Ruth, The   07/00/1994
Das Barbecu   10/10/1994
Diva Is Dismissed, The   10/30/1994
Starcrossed the Trial of   11/03/1994
   Galileo
Sunset Boulevard   11/17/1994
Christmas Carol, A   12/01/1994
Swanson on Sunset   12/07/1994
Petrified Prince, The   12/18/1994
Comedy Tonight   12/18/1994

1995

Busker Alley   00/00/1995
Young Man, Older Woman   00/00/1995
Body Shop   00/00/1995
Cow Pattys, The   00/00/1995
Joseph and Mary   00/00/1995
Lust   00/00/1995
Paramour   00/00/1995
Radio Gals   00/00/1995
Star Wars   00/00/1995
State Fair   00/00/1995
I Sent a Letter to My Love   02/08/1995
Opal   02/18/1995
Slice of Saturday Night, A   03/00/1995
Smokey Joe's Cafe   03/02/1995
Jack's Holiday   03/05/1995
EFX   03/22/1995
Swingin' on a Star   04/05/1995
Off-Key   04/07/1995
Honky-Tonk Highway   04/27/1995
john & jen   06/01/1995
Bad Girls Upset By the   06/04/1995
   Truth
Hundreds of Hats   06/13/1995
Chronicle of a Death   06/15/1995
   Foretold
Another Midsummer Night   06/26/1995
I've Heard That Song Before   07/14/1995
Gig, The   08/10/1995
Victor/Victoria   10/25/1995